Zuni Origins

Zuni Origins

Toward a New Synthesis of
Southwestern Archaeology

EDITED BY
David A. Gregory
AND
David R. Wilcox

WITH A FOREWORD BY
William H. Doelle

The University of Arizona Press   Tucson

The University of Arizona Press
© 2007 The Arizona Board of Regents
All rights reserved

First paperback printing 2009
ISBN 978-0-8165-2893-6 (pbk. : alk. paper)

Library of Congress Cataloging-in-Publication Data
Zuni origins : toward a new synthesis of Southwestern archaeology /
edited by David A. Gregory and David R. Wilcox ; with a Foreword by
William H. Doelle.
p. cm.
Includes bibliographical references and index.
ISBN 978-0-8165-2486-0 (hardcover : alk. paper)
1. Zuni Indians—Origin. 2. Zuni Indians—Antiquities. 3. Zuni
language. 4. Anthropological linguistics—New Mexico. 5. Excavations
(Archaeology)—New Mexico. 6. New Mexico—Antiquities. I. Gregory,
David A. II. Wilcox, David R., 1944–
E99.Z9Z85 2007
978.9'8301—dc22   2007020513

Publication of this book is made possible in part by financial support
from the Museum of Northern Arizona publications endowment
provided by the Margaret T. Morris Foundation and from
the Center for Desert Archaeology Publications Fund.

14   13   12   11   10   09   7   6   5   4   3   2

Contents

Foreword

Zuni Origins is a bold title for an ambitious scholarly undertaking. The scale of the ambition of these anthropologist authors is best conveyed by the conclusion of linguist Jane Hill: "Zuni speakers can be expected to have been present in the Southwest for a *minimum* of 7,000–8,000 years."

As a linguistic isolate with such an extensive time depth, Zunian might be expected to have experienced historical processes and events that resulted in its geographically restricted modern distribution. So from the outset this study had promise as a "strong analytical case" that could test our theoretical and methodological limits. T. J. Ferguson's chapter in this volume provides insight into the time depths of Zuni oral traditions. Most of those recorded by anthropologists reflect the time after the 1680 Pueblo Revolt; however, there are elements of these oral histories that refer to earlier times. If there is an attenuation in the clarity of the picture that emerges from oral history after four or five centuries have passed, that leaves archaeology, historical linguistics, physical anthropology, environmental science, and other approaches dominated by non-Zuni practitioners to push back another seven millennia or more that the linguist tells us could be possible.

An obvious risk in this endeavor is the potential to be either irrelevant or offensive to members of modern Zuni Pueblo. In my limited role as a facilitator in establishing and maintaining institutional relationships on this project, these risks were central concerns as I first drove north from Tucson to the Pueblo of Zuni. Jonathan Damp arranged and attended a meeting by Dave Gregory and me with Zuni Governor Malcolm B. Bowekaty and several council members in June 2001, prior to the seminar. When the first draft of this book was submitted to the University of Arizona Press, David Wilcox and I presented a copy to Governor Arlen P. Quetawki Sr. and several tribal council members on November 27, 2003. In each of these meetings there was an engaged discussion of the nature of this scholarly undertaking. We found that making a comparison between this volume and the previously published book *A Zuni Atlas* by T. J. Ferguson and E. Richard Hart was helpful. The present volume covers earlier time periods than the *Atlas*, and its spatial coverage extends well beyond the modern reservation. There was a general recognition that heritage issues of concern to the Pueblo of Zuni very often extend well beyond the physical boundaries of the reservation. That led to acknowledg-

ment that a scholarly consideration of Zuni's deep historical roots that was initiated and funded independently of the tribe might well have utility as a resource for tribal use in the future.

Soon after the conference and between the two visits with the Zuni governors and council members, David Wilcox, Laurie Webster, and I traveled to Zuni to meet with members of the Zuni Cultural Resources Advisory Team. Our experience with them reinforced the increasing relevance of places beyond reservation boundaries for modern Zuni residents. Several members of the advisory team had just returned from field trips to southern Arizona to visit sites in the San Pedro Valley as part of a National Endowment for the Humanities grant to the Center for Desert Archaeology. The sites that most affected these Zuni travelers were the ones where Puebloan migrants from the north had left a strong archaeological signature in their architecture and artifacts. They commented that they had heard about these places from their grandfathers, but they found it extremely valuable to actually see them. Thus, collaboration between archaeologists and tribal members was helping reaffirm links to a spatially and temporally distant past that was very relevant to the present. Ensuing conversation broached the issue of whether the residents of those San Pedro Valley sites might have been Hopi rather than Zuni. The consensus of the advisory team members was that either possibility left them comfortable. In fact, an acceptance of broader concepts of a shared past often was expressed by Hopi, Zuni, Tohono O'odham, and Western Apache tribal representatives who participated in the center's San Pedro Ethnohistory Project.

As this book goes to press I feel satisfied that the concept of a shared past was advanced by this scholarly study. The multiple perspectives and broad scales for both time and space have not forged a unified or a unilinear story of Zuni origins. Despite a linguistic homogeneity in the present, pursuing broad historical inquiry will continue to be essential in understanding the questions posed by the seminar organizers and addressed in this volume. The expansive concept that the past is a shared human resource can stimulate further collaboration between Zuni and scholars.

It can also broaden support for preserving the archaeological remains of all ancient groups. There is still much to accomplish, but much has been achieved in the effort to see with greater clarity to the time 7,000–8,000 years ago when Proto-Zunian speakers were somewhere within the ancient southwestern landscape.

William H. Doelle
President and CEO
Center for Desert Archaeology

Preface

Constructing and Refining a Research Design for the Study of Zuni Origins

David A. Gregory and David R. Wilcox

Among the native peoples of the American Southwest and Mexican Northwest are the Zuni Indians, a Pueblo group with a unique language. They live primarily today in and around the Pueblo of Zuni, New Mexico, which they regard as the "Middle Place" long sought by their ancestors (Leighton and Adair 1966). The origins and history of the Zuni have intrigued anthropologists for well over a century. This volume presents fresh approaches to the study of those issues from both the scientific perspectives of anthropology and the oral traditions of the Zuni—as known by anthropologists.

We first began this inquiry with a more modest goal: to redefine what archaeologists have called the "Mogollon cultural tradition." However, we quickly were led to ask larger questions about the relationship of Mogollon populations to Zuni, a problem that had engaged earlier students of Mogollon culture (e.g., Rinaldo 1964). The more specific Mogollon-Zuni problem had been largely abandoned some 30 years ago when the intellectual ferment known as the "New Archaeology" diverted attention to other questions and challenged the methodologies previously used to study the Mogollon-Zuni relationship. With the help of the other contributors we here broaden the

inquiry to an Americanist context by framing the problem in terms of Zuni origins. Indeed, it is the Americas as a whole and the initial peopling of this hemisphere that is the ultimate context within which such problems must be approached (see Bellwood and Renfrew 2003).

Our intellectual journey of more than three decades began in 1969, when Gregory came to the Southwest first as a student and then as a staff member at the Field Museum of Natural History's Vernon Field School, directed by Paul Sidney Martin. Wilcox that same year joined the staff of the neighboring Grasshopper Field School (Thompson and Longacre 1966). Both were hotbeds of the New Archaeology, but Gregory eagerly accepted Martin's offer to train him in the traditional ceramic typologies of the area, which Martin and his colleague, John Rinaldo, did so much to define. With Gregory's recommendation Wilcox joined the staff of the Vernon Field School in 1973 and thus also came under Martin's influence. During the early 1970s both of us were graduate students in the Department of Anthropology at the University of Arizona, where we were intensively immersed in a "four-field" approach to the study of anthropology that involved training in cultural and physical anthropology and linguistics

as well as archaeology. In the late 1970s and early 1980s we collaborated on a series of Hohokam studies while we were both employed by the Arizona State Museum at the University of Arizona.

More than a decade later, in the early 1990s, we met for dinner in Tucson, where Gregory outlined for Wilcox some new insights concerning Mogollon that resulted in part from background research conducted for Desert Archaeology, Inc., in conjunction with the Roosevelt Community Development Project (Gregory 1995a). Distinctive patterning in the morphology of Highland Mogollon ceremonial structures from the earliest forms through the latest examples suggested continuity in this aspect of the Mogollon "tradition" that was spatially coherent and that extended beyond the generally accepted date of AD 1000, when "Anasaziation" of Mogollon populations had been argued to mark the "end" of a distinctive Mogollon cultural tradition and the development of Western Pueblo culture (Reed 1948, 1950). Gregory's observations suggested a way to redefine the Mogollon concept in organizationally and ecologically meaningful terms, not simply cultural-historical ones.

Wilcox (1979; Wilcox and Sternberg 1983) had previously suggested that the traditional Hohokam concept of Haury (1976) could be redefined organizationally as a "regional system," but only the Mimbres branch of the Mogollon appeared to be amenable to comparable treatment (Wilcox 1986a). Gregory's findings suggested another way to think about this problem with respect to the entire Mogollon geographic area. When each of us was invited by Stephen Nash to participate in a 1999 Society for American Archaeology symposium celebrating the one hundredth anniversary of Paul Martin's birth, Wilcox prevailed upon Gregory to collaborate on a paper reevaluating the Mogollon concept. That soon reminded us of Rinaldo's (1964) hypothesis concerning Mogollon-Zuni connections. Riding the wave of more recent intellectual currents, we proposed that new methodologies and theoretical perspectives now made it possible to reopen the question of Mogollon-Zuni relationships. We expanded our inquiry to define seven *problem domains* about a Mogollon "adaptation to the mountains"— a phrase taken from Martin's chapter on the Mogollon in the Martin and Plog volume *The Archaeology of Arizona* (1973)—and include revival of the hypothesis of a Mogollon-Zuni connection and the yet larger question of Zuni origins. This paper was our initial attempt to construct a research design with which to attack the problem, and it is reproduced as chapter 10 of this volume.

While discussing revisions of that paper we realized that it could be used as the basis for organizing an advanced seminar to more deeply investigate this set of problems, bringing together people who could marshal large data sets with the kind of scale and diversity that we thought necessary to adequately address them. It is our contention that multidisciplinary approaches—drawing

on all four subfields of anthropology and relevant studies from related disciplines—as well as analyses of interaction on multiple scales are necessary to any adequate solutions of problems of this kind, a point we elaborate on in chapter 20 of this volume. Next, we invited a group of individuals to participate whom we believed were specially suited to address each of these problems. Thus, we were joined in our journey by an outstanding group of scholars who subsequently dedicated themselves to a further clarification and understanding of the Zuni origins problem.

To guide the seminar participants in preparing their papers we formulated a series of more specific research questions for each of them, thus creating the first revision of our original research design. The scholars were also encouraged to ask other related questions and were invited to ignore any we posited if they felt that those questions imposed unwarranted constraints on their explorations of the general problem. Nevertheless, our questions did provide an intellectual context for each participant, and the chapters herein represent the individual participants' answers to our questions.

What is an advanced seminar? In the American Southwest the idea was first successfully implemented over 30 years ago by Douglas Schwartz at the School of American Research in Santa Fe. We attended one of these seminars that compared the Chaco and Hohokam regional systems (Crown and Judge 1991). Usually about eight scholars are brought together for a week to examine a set of themes. Papers are written beforehand and are discussed at the seminar. Room and board are provided, a field trip is taken to break up the time, informal occasions for interactions are built into the schedule, and one or more nationally or internationally

known scholars who have listened to and participated in the deliberations then have their say. Afterward the papers are revised and an edited book is published. The Amerind Foundation has now begun to host advanced seminars as well and to publish the results (e.g., Dean 2000; Neitzel 1999). The Museum of Northern Arizona also aspired to host such events in the beautiful Colton House, so our idea for one was planned with that venue in mind.

We decided to organize the first Colton House advanced seminar a little differently. Four roles were envisioned: *topical presenters, consultants, Zuni representatives,* and *discussants.* The *topical presenters* were to prepare written papers prior to the seminar, present synopses of them, and conduct discussions of their topics. We encouraged topical presenters to involve coauthors as needed, but only the lead participants attended the conference. The *consultants* brought to the discussions cross-cutting perspectives from adjacent areas or in-depth experience within the main areal focus of the seminar. They were both sounding boards and fonts of knowledge about relevant comparative data and also wrote "white" papers in advance of the seminar. *Zuni representatives* were invited to bring a tribal and oral history perspective to bear on all the topics being discussed. The *discussants* provided a vast knowledge of attempts to solve similar problems in other world areas. Altogether there were 17 participants, and we found that there were no ill effects from having more than the usual number of voices clamoring to be heard. The resulting volume, however, is necessarily longer than the published results from many advanced seminars, contains more data, and is more complex thematically.

Prior to the seminar we began trying to learn how to make it a collaborative effort with the Pueblo of Zuni. Gregory and William Doelle, president of the Center for Desert Archaeology, traveled to Zuni and with the assistance of Jonathan Damp, then the Zuni tribal historic preservation officer (THPO), were able to meet with several members of the Zuni Tribal Council to inform them about the seminar. However, efforts to sponsor the participation of a tribal member in the seminar did not succeed. Following the seminar, Wilcox and Doelle, again with Damp's assistance, made a presentation about the seminar's outcome to the Zuni Tribal Council and the next day, accompanied by Laurie Webster, made another presentation to the Zuni Cultural Resources Advisory Team of respected religious leaders who advise the THPO (see Anyon and Ferguson 1995:922). We shared a meal together with the team and began to get to know one another. Perhaps in future seminars representation in the discussions can be broader.

The seminar was held in October 2001 at the Colton House, Museum of Northern Arizona. The Center for Desert Archaeology was a cosponsor of (and provider of funds for) this weeklong event. While we were unable to fully realize our ideal goals (the perspective of physical anthropology is a notable absence from this volume), everyone learned a lot from that experience. Yet the solution to the problem remains elusive. Even how it should be construed, we now agree, must be recast in an even wider and more inclusive way.

For health reasons Gregory was unable to attend the seminar, but Wilcox e-mailed him daily updates on its progress. Afterward the participants sent him a much-appreciated message of goodwill. They assured him that he had "started a very important thing." Jane Hill then elaborated on this, pointing out that "thing" is

derived from Proto-Germanic: "time > reprieve in time > time for an assembly to convene > a political or legal assembly." We all agreed that our time together at the Colton House had been a wonderful "reprieve in time" and a promise of what future advanced seminars could also be. Fortunately, Gregory has been able to participate fully in the editing and writing tasks needed to bring this volume to fruition.

As noted above, at the end of the seminar we did not feel we had solved the problem of Zuni origins, but we had shed considerable light on it. The general task, then, remains one of continuing research design: to show what we now know *and do not know* and to construct frameworks for asking new questions and methodologies for answering them. To communicate all of this to a general reader involves three steps: (1) showing where we began before the seminar; (2) showing where we got to as a result of the seminar; and (3) showing where we think future research can be most fruitfully directed.

With that in mind we have organized the presentation of the essays into a series of 22 chapters that are structured thematically into five parts. In the remainder of this preface we introduce the authors and their topics, preferring to treat more general themes in the introduction to the volume, chapter 1. In that introductory chapter the larger theme, as in all of part I, is on the large-scale contexts for the study of Zuni origins: language, culture, and environment. We thus place the issue of Zuni origins in the context of a general anthropological problem, the unity and diversity of North American Indians, and how that played out in the North American Southwest.

Chapter 2 is an homage to one of the southwestern scholars who, a generation and more ago, contrib-

uted greatly to the understanding of anthropological problems that we are only now again approaching with new methodologies (see also Ford et al. 1972). The late Cynthia Irwin-Williams was a pioneer in the study of the first 10,000 years of southwestern prehistory as well as a significant contributor to Chacoan studies (Irwin-Williams 1973, 1979; Wormington and Agogino 1994). She initiated the modern study of the Early Agricultural period (Huckell 1995; see also Diehl, chap. 11, this vol.) and employed a multidisciplinary approach in these inquiries. The manuscript for her 1967 Society for American Archaeology (SAA) annual meeting paper we find particularly stimulating for its willingness to address important anthropological problems. We are also struck by the near absence of Zuni in her otherwise excellent discussion! This paper is published for the first time as chapter 2 along with our endnotes; it helps to establish what we argue is the necessary scale for inquiries of this kind and foreshadows issues we return to in the conclusion (Gregory and Wilcox, chap. 20, this vol.).

In chapter 3 Jane Hill shows that Zuni is indeed a linguistic isolate and argues that its differentiation must have occurred at least 7,000–8,000 years ago. This means that populations speaking Zunian have occupied one or more places in the American landscape since that time and that Zuni origins probably began in the Paleoindian period. A highly significant—and unexpected—result of the seminar, this finding makes necessary the Americanist scale of our inquiry, something we asked R. G. Matson to address in the first chapter of part II. First, however, in chapter 4 Jeffery Clark spells out modern methodologies for studying migrations, enculturation, and ethnicity from archaeological data. Clark is a southwestern archaeologist with experience in the Near East (Yoffee and Clark 1993) who has contributed original studies to tracking down the migrations of western Anasazi populations during the thirteenth century AD (J. Clark 1995, 2001). His discussion provides the reader with a theoretical basis for evaluating arguments made in subsequent chapters.

Chapters 5 and 6 set forth the temporal and spatial environmental contexts relevant to our inquiry into Zuni origins. When Gregory was unable to attend the seminar, we invited Fred Nials at the last minute to participate in the hope that he would later contribute a chapter to this volume. Fred L. Nials is a geologist and geomorphologist with wide experience in the Southwest, where he worked on the Anasazi Origins Project with Cynthia Irwin-Williams (Durand and Nials 1991; Nials 1991a, 1991b), studied Chacoan Roads (Nials 1983; Nials et al. 1987), and collaborated with Gregory and others in the study of Hohokam canals and the influence of Salt River streamflow on Hohokam canal systems (Graybill et al. 2006; Nials et al. 1987). He has codirected research for the Sundance Archaeological Project, testing hypotheses about the peopling of the New World from the perspective of the Great Basin (Nials 1999), and he was also one of the first to study the effects of El Niño events on human populations in the New World (Nials et al. 1979a, 1979b). In chapter 5 Gregory joins with Nials to articulate a set of findings that has resulted from their long collaboration. They provide an overview of environmental variation over the last 20,000 years as a context for understanding linguistic differentiation and other cultural developments in the Southwest.

One of the great contributions to world knowledge was achieved in the American Southwest with the development of the tree-ring dating method by A. E. Douglass (1929) and its subsequent applications to both archaeology and climatology (Douglass 1929; Fritts 1976, 1991). Jeffrey S. Dean's (1969, 1970) study of dendrochronology at the Tsegi Canyon sites of Betatakin and Kiet Siel is a classic, and he has been a leading figure in a sustained, collaborative effort to model Anasazi adaptive strategies on the Colorado Plateau (Dean et al. 1985; Euler et al. 1979). In chapter 6 he brings his approach and current knowledge of tree-ring data to bear on the Zuni paleoenvironment and its southwestern context.

Part II seeks to place Zuni in the developmental context of southwestern societies from Paleoindian to Mogollon. Chapter 7, by R. G. Matson, leads off with a review of current data on the peopling of the Americas and, using ecological theory, defines expectations for where Zuni-speaking populations may have been during the Archaic period in the Southwest. Matson has conducted research into the arrival of maize in the Southwest and in particular the nature of the Basketmaker populations of the northern Southwest (Matson 1991). He has also written a synthesis of the archaeology of the Northwest Coast that gave much consideration to the peopling of the New World (Matson and Coupland 1995).

In chapter 8 Jonathan Damp reports new findings on the first appearance of agriculture at Zuni (see also Damp et al. 2002). Damp is the current director of the Zuni Cultural Resource Enterprise, which does contract-driven archaeology on federal projects both on and off Zuni lands. Previously, he has also been the Zuni THPO.

Gregory in chapter 9 shows how Paul Sidney Martin and John B. Rinaldo were led to formulate a Mogollon-Zuni hypothesis on the basis of their studies of Mogollon culture in west-central New Mexico and east-central Arizona. Gregory and Wilcox in chapter 10 present their previously unpublished 1999 Society for American Archaeology paper in which they took up the Martin and Rinaldo Mogollon-Zuni hypothesis and formulated the research design that led to the Mogollon-Zuni advanced seminar in 2001. In that light Michael Diehl in chapter 11 provides a careful consideration of Mogollon trajectories and divergences. Diehl's dissertation examined economy and social differences via comparisons of early Mogollon assemblages (Diehl 1994), and in his chapter here he tests the original Gregory-Wilcox attempt to narrow the Mogollon concept to highland branches (chap. 10, this vol.). He rejects this idea, arguing that the Mimbres branch differentiated from a common cultural base starting in the ninth century AD.

The chapters in part III examine Zuni in the Puebloan world in order to test the Mogollon-Zuni hypothesis. An important goal of these analyses is to look for contrasts that may indicate the differences between Mogollon or Zunian populations and neighboring groups and to trace those contrasts through time. Chapter 12 leads off with a systematic study by Wilcox, Gregory, and J. Brett Hill of Zuni in the Puebloan and southwestern worlds. In a joint project of the Museum of Northern Arizona, Western Mapping, and the Center for Desert Archaeology Wilcox for this Zuni origins volume assembled a database of all known sites of 13 rooms or more for the whole North American Southwest for the period AD 1200–1600, now called the Coalescent Communities Database. The authors analyze the patterns apparent in a series of maps generated from these data in successive 50-year periods. Hill is a preservation archaeologist and GIS specialist at the Center for Desert Archaeology and has made substantial contributions to our understanding of settlement variability in the Southwest (Herhahn and Hill 1998; Hill 2000; see also Varien 1999).

Barbara J. Mills in chapter 13 brings her wide experience in the analysis of ceramics in the Zuni area (Mills 1995, 2002a), the southern Colorado Plateau (Goetze and Mills 1993a), and the Mogollon Rim in east-central Arizona (Mills 1998; Mills and Herr 1999; Mills et al. 1999) to the analysis of ceramics, identity, and the question of Zuni-Mogollon relationships. C. Dean Wilson, a ceramic analyst with wide experience (Wilson and Blinman 1994; Wilson et al. 1996), then draws on recent work in the Mogollon Highlands (Wilson 1994) and analysis of ceramics from the Cliff phase Ormand Village site (Wilson 1998a, 1998b) to review Mogollon pottery production and exchange in chapter 14.

Next we turn to the patterns found in rock art characteristics and distributions, followed by those revealed by a study of perishables and exotic goods. Polly Schaafsma, whose comparative studies of southwestern rock art are unexcelled (Schaafsma 1975, 1980, 1999, 2000), and M. Jane Young (1988), whose excellent study of Zuni rock art opened up new comparative opportunities, in chapter 15 review the rock art of the Zuni region in relation to that of adjacent areas. In chapter 16 Laurie Webster, whose dissertation dealt with the effects of European contact on textile production and exchange in the Puebloan Southwest (Webster 1997), accepted our challenge to compare Mogollon and Zuni perishable traditions on a macroregional scale. For many years

Arthur W. Vokes has analyzed shell assemblages from southwestern sites for numerous contract-archaeology projects and has assembled a large database on marine shell artifact characteristics and distributions (Vokes 1986, 1991, 1995, 1998, 2001a). We asked him to extend his studies to assemble a comprehensive database on all shell known to occur in southwestern sites and all copper bells, macaws, and turquoise. He did so, and Gregory then worked with him to identify the structure of exchange networks apparent in these data and the place of Zuni in it.

In part IV we focus on the Middle Place, presenting the view from Zuni in two chapters (see also Damp, chap. 8, this vol.). In chapter 18 Keith Kintigh presents his latest fine-grained study of late prehistoric and protohistoric settlement systems in the Zuni area. He is cautious about the Mogollon-Zuni hypothesis. T. J. Ferguson in chapter 19 closely and elegantly examines Zuni traditional history and cultural geography. He shows that the places named in oral traditions are real places in the modern landscape that continue to be the focus of pilgrimage and prayer offerings.

Finally, in part V we present our conclusions. In chapter 20 we present a synthesis of the findings made in earlier chapters and devise a revised Mogollon-Zuni hypothesis and a new research design to test its propositions. We also show how the methodology we used to structure the Zuni origins advanced seminar and this volume can be generalized to study similar "big picture" anthropological problems. Then, in the final two chapters Don D. Fowler and Stephen A. Kowalewski, the general discussants for the seminar, weigh in with their commentaries. These two individuals

bring a wealth of comparative experience to bear, but each has also been an interested outside student of southwestern archaeology. Don Fowler has been a key player in modern studies of a region contiguous to the Southwest, the Great Basin, and he has directed an original program of Paleoindian studies in that region (Fowler, comp. 2000). His deep interest in the history of southwestern archaeology has resulted in an excellent book (Fowler 2000) and other collaborative efforts (Cordell and Fowler 2005; Fowler and Wilcox 1999; Wilcox and Fowler 2002). His discussion places the present volume in the larger anthropological, linguistic, and political contexts of archaeology today.

Stephen Kowalewski is one of the principal modern synthesizers of Mesoamerican archaeology (Blanton et al. 1981) and has conducted numerous intensive, macroregional surveys in the Oaxaca area (Blanton et al. 1982; Kowalewski 2006). He also has long been active in the study of the archaeology of the American Southeast. His recent paper on coalescent communities places the late prehistoric and protohistoric Southwest in a broad Americanist comparative perspective (Kowalewski 2003a). His discussion in chapter 22 presents a strong methodological critique of traditional "culture history" approaches and shows how the papers in this volume develop new ways to document and explain variation, laying the foundation for a "new kind of past." These discussants thus provide valuable comparative perspectives on the accomplishments and shortcomings of this volume and help us to see where future research efforts should be focused.

Acknowledgments

The editors are especially grateful to Dr. William H. Doelle, president of the Center for Desert Archaeology, for his encouragement to undertake this project and for his unswerving and always generous and kind support during it. We also gratefully thank an anonymous Center for Desert Archaeology donor for the financial support needed to carry out the project; and Dr. Robert Breunig, director of the Museum of Northern Arizona, for his understanding and support. To all the participants for admirably responding so ably to the challenges we posed to them, we can only say that their responses were *awesome*! Linda and Todd Howell participated in the seminar but were unable to provide a written paper, but we remain grateful to them for their insights.

We also thank the Museum of Northern Arizona for providing housing on its campus and for making available the beautiful Colton House as the site of the advanced seminar, held October 14–19, 2001, and especially to Shirley Groenhout for making the arrangements and to Martha Clark, our gracious host at Colton House. Main Street Catering of Flagstaff provided us with excellent meals. Linda Pierce and Sally Thomas, both of the Center for Desert Archaeology, provided invaluable logistical support. Linda also assumed the onerous and often thankless task of checking the final manuscript and preparing it for submission. We appreciate her always careful efforts more than we can say. Linda was assisted especially by Katherine Cerino and by Patrick Lyons, and we thank them both.

We are also grateful to the Pueblo of Zuni, and, in particular, we thank the Zuni Tribal Council and the Zuni Cultural Resources Advisory Team for meeting with us and discussing the seminar project.

Gregory would like to thank William Doelle, Bruce Donaldson, Gary Funkhouser, Fred Nials, coeditor David Wilcox, Katy, Lovey, and other friends and professionals who saw him through the terrible trials of clinical depression and allowed him to continue to participate in this project. The good wishes sent to him by the participants during the seminar were strongly medicinal and very much appreciated. He would also like to thank his wife and son, Carla and Robert, for their patience, perseverance, and moral support throughout the final editing stages of the volume; and special thanks to Carla, who took the time to read several chapters with a keen layperson's eye and provided important insights and suggestions that brought greater clarity to the text.

Wilcox would like to thank his wife, Susan, for her goodwill in supporting his efforts on this project.

Three anonymous reviewers ably commented on a manuscript much longer than normal and contributed to its becoming a much better book. Bruce Donaldson of the Apache-Sitgreaves National Forest read several chapters and provided comments that improved them. We are also grateful to the University of Arizona Press and its editorial board for their willingness to support this innovative project, and especially to Dr. Christine Szuter, head of the University of Arizona Press, and Dr. Allyson Carter, acquisitions editor, for their guidance and support throughout the review and publication process. We are also deeply grateful to Benjamin Smith for his interest and support.

Part I

Large-Scale Contexts for the Study of Zuni Origins

Language, Culture, and Environment

1 Introduction

The Structure of Anthropological Inquiry into Zuni Origins

David R. Wilcox and David A. Gregory

The Archaeological Search for the Zuni Lost Others

On September 19, 1879, a scientific party sent to the Southwest to make collections for the National Museum on behalf of the newly formed Bureau of Ethnology arrived at Zuni Pueblo. Led by James Stevenson, who may have successfully lobbied Congress for the appropriations that made the trip possible (*National Cyclopaedia* 12:556), the party included two others who would contribute profoundly to anthropological knowledge about Zuni culture. One was the formidable Matilda Coxe Stevenson, James's wife, who would return to Zuni and publish a major monograph about Zuni culture (Stevenson 1904). The other was a brilliant young man from western New York whom Spencer Baird hired at age 19 to help represent the Smithsonian Institution at the 1876 Centennial in Philadelphia. Now, three years later, Frank Hamilton Cushing was attached to John Wesley Powell's nascent Bureau of Ethnology to accompany the Stevenson expedition to the Southwest. According to Cushing, Baird told him, "I want you to find out all you can about some typical tribe of Pueblo Indians. Make your own choice of field, and use your own methods; only, get the information" (1882; cited

in Green 1990:3). Cushing chose the Zuni, and his method was linguistic, what later generations of anthropologists would call "participant observation," something Cushing invented as he learned the Zuni language (Cushing 1882; Green 1979, 1990).[1]

Famously, Cushing (1882) began his participation in Zuni culture by moving into the governor's house. While not all Zuni were amused by such audacity, Palowahtiwa, the governor, quickly saw that Cushing could be useful to the Zuni in their necessary quest to find ways to adapt to the new cultural context that the American conquest of the Southwest had created. A collaboration was thus established. Through Cushing the Zuni successfully sent a delegation of important men back east, where on January 26, 1882, they were introduced to President Chester A. Arthur. On the way, by train, they stayed at the most sumptuous hotel that Chicago then offered, the Palmer House; they toured Washington, D.C.; and they visited Boston, where they met many of America's cultural elite (Baxter 1882; Eggan and Pandey 1979; Hinsley and Wilcox 1996). The cultural intelligence about American civilization they were able to bring back to Zuni was of inestimable value.

Cushing later brought Palowahtiwa and two other Zuni leaders to the

summer house of Mary Hemenway at Manchester-by-the-Sea on the Massachusetts North Shore, where they recounted their oral traditions to Cushing while Mrs. Hemenway and her influential lady friends looked on (Hinsley and Wilcox 2002).[2] One of them wrote that it "was like hearing the Homeric songs at first hand" (Mary Elizabeth Dewey, in Hinsley and Wilcox 1995:564). Charmed by this experience, Hemenway (who was probably the wealthiest woman in Boston) agreed to sponsor an expedition to the Southwest to explore Zuni history through archaeology.[3] Cushing thus set forth in 1886 to invent another anthropological method: ethnological archaeology (Hinsley and Wilcox 2002; Wilcox 2004).

Searching for the "lost others" the Zuni oral histories had taught him about, Cushing first visited Zuni at the winter solstice for consultations and then set out on reconnaissance westward by train and then southward by wagon to the Salt River valley, where he saw a set of relationships in the pattern of settlement distribution that he thought was the evidence for which he had been seeking (Hinsley and Wilcox 2002). After nearly a year and a half digging in those sites (Haury 1945a), in May 1888 he had the expedition redeploy to Zuni, where expansion of his house as an "expedition house" soon revealed remains of the Halona South site.[4] Later they excavated a portion of the Heshotauthla site farther up the Zuni Valley. The larger plan for their work was the construction of a Pueblo museum that Mrs. Hemenway planned to build in Salem, Massachusetts; its programs were to involve the training of young men in the Zuni language so that Cushing's methods of ethnological archaeology could become institutionalized.[5]

However, in October 1888 Cushing was recalled to Boston, and in the following year, after successfully petitioning Congress to have the Casa Grande Ruins in Arizona Territory set aside and protected, he was dismissed as director of the expedition.[6] Jesse Walter Fewkes took his place and recommenced work at Zuni but soon moved the expedition to Hopi (Wade and McChesney 1980).[7] With Mrs. Hemenway's death in 1894 the collections were donated to Harvard's Peabody Museum, ending forever the dream of a Pueblo museum that would carry on Cushing's innovative methods of ethnological archaeology.

Zuni archaeology since Cushing has been done differently. In 1909 Clark Wissler, then curator of ethnology at the American Museum of Natural History in New York, obtained funding from Archer Huntington for a southwestern survey. This soon led to Nels Nelson's (1914) work in the Galisteo Basin and that of Alfred Kroeber (1916, 1917) and Leslie Spier (1917, 1918, 1919) at Zuni. The "New Archaeology" was thus created (Wissler 1917) that revolutionized Americanist archaeology generally (see Fowler 2000; Snead 2001; Wilcox and Fowler 2002). In contrast, when Frederick Webb Hodge gained permission on behalf of the Heye Foundation in New York to excavate the Zuni site of Hawikuh, he largely botched the effort. His patron, George Heye (Force 1999;

Kidwell 1999), was an inveterate collector of objects who had little regard for provenience information, something that Hodge did at least understand. Hodge later recounted what happened to many of his Zuni collections:

> When the pottery [from Hawikku] reached New York, it was unpacked, and put on a long table. An improvised table on the upper floor of [George] Heye's garage. And there Heye had various workers going over it . . . I was . . . utterly amazed, dumbfounded to find that these pottery fragments were put in bags. The sherds themselves carried a certain field number. That number was carried over to the bag so there couldn't be any question about the identifications. They [the bags] were all piled on the back of this table and the fellow who got through first picked up a bag and put his in, with a totally different number from that which appeared on the bag. That was devastating, you know. You can imagine how the whole thing could have been terribly mixed up so that I had no use for my field numbers. They were the vital part of the whole business . . . Heye was acquisitive. He didn't care about any information after the collections were found. Specimens. Specimens were his great object in life. Information respecting them didn't concern him [1955:168–169].

After Hodge's death Watson Smith and Natalie and Richard Woodbury (1966) made a yeoman's effort to salvage what could be recovered from this failure. In a famous photograph we see Alfred Vincent Kidder, who became the leader of the New Archaeology, sitting with Hodge at Hawikku: the old archaeology was being superseded by the new. Frank H. H. Rob-

erts (1931, 1932) soon demonstrated the value of the new approach in the Zuni area (see also Woodbury 1956).

The New Archaeology of the 1960s came to Zuni in the El Morro Valley with the work of Patty Jo Watson and her colleagues Steven LeBlanc and Charles Redman (1980). While a full account of their work has yet to appear (but see LeBlanc 1976, 1978, 1989, 2001), a student who worked with them, Keith Kintigh, undertook a systematic restudy of Leslie Spier's collections and combined those data with other findings to produce a major study of Zuni settlement patterns (Kintigh 1985). As a professor he has continued to lead an active program of field school research in the greater Zuni area, and this work is exceptionally well published (see Kintigh, chap. 18, this vol.). Fine-grained "full coverage" archaeological survey is combined with sophisticated ceramic sourcing in these studies. Other important research in the Zuni region by academics can also be cited (Marquardt 1974; Saitta 1987; Woodbury 1956, 1979).

An enormous increase in public support for archaeology in the United States came about with the passage of the National Historic Preservation Act (NHPA) of 1966, the regulations for which were published in the *Federal Register* in 1972. This law, supplemented by other legislation, put in place the modern historic preservation system. State Historic Preservation Offices (SHPOs) were created, and all federal agencies were required to consult with them about the effect the agencies' proposed actions would have on historic resources, which included historic buildings, archaeological sites, and other properties. To find this out, surveys were initiated, and criteria of significance were established for evaluating properties. To mitigate impacts on significant sites, excavation programs were authorized to recover the data judged significant. All of this has had a profound effect on the way archaeology is conducted in the United States—and thus also in the Southwest.

One of the parties with whom SHPOs were to consult was Indian tribes. To handle such requests, southwestern tribes soon began to establish Cultural Preservation Offices, and some of them also initiated programs that could bid on federal projects to do historic preservation work. At Zuni in 1974 such an office was created, and T. J. Ferguson was soon hired to lead it. Others subsequently followed in his footsteps, including Roger Anyon and, more recently, Jonathan Damp. In this way people trained as professional archaeologists have become paid employees of and collaborators with the Pueblo of Zuni in the conduct of archaeological and anthropological projects both on Zuni lands and on adjacent properties. Benefits of this work include jobs for Zuni at home and education for them into the mysteries of professional archaeology. After over a century, since Cushing, there are once again archaeologists who speak Zuni (Anyon and Zunie 1989).

Hundreds of projects have now been conducted, and the results of many have been published. Among them are a study of Zuni farming villages (Mills and Ferguson 1980), *A Zuni Atlas* (Ferguson and Hart 1985), and a report on the return of the Zuni Ahayu:da (war gods) (Ferguson and Eriacho 1990; Merrill et al. 1993). Changes in the regulations for the NHPA of 1966 have now afforded tribes the opportunity to take over the role of the SHPO in Tribal Historic Preservation Offices, which the Zuni have done.

A significant effect of these institutional mechanisms is that outside parties, including archaeologists like us, have a formal way to consult with the Zuni about their history and archaeological origins. In structuring our advanced seminar and this volume about Zuni origins we wanted to bring together our interest in macroregional scales of analysis with a consideration of the view from Zuni, the "Middle Place" where they live today. We also hoped to engage in a dialogue with the Zuni about the meaning of their oral traditions and the search for common ground between scientific perspectives and their internal histories. While we hope a beginning may have been made in regard to the latter goal, as we discuss in the preface, what we have achieved in this volume falls short of that. What has been achieved is a set of comprehensive scientific analyses of the anthropological problem of Zuni origins that include the perspectives of three archaeologists who have been privileged to collaborate with the Zuni people.

Part I: Large-Scale Contexts for the Study of Zuni Origins: Language, Culture, and Environment

One of the principal findings of this volume, discussed in part I, is that the origins of the populations who first spoke Zuni must be sought amid hunter-gatherer groups who first occupied the Americas over 13,000 years ago. After 150 years of archaeological inquiry we still know remarkably little about the first 10,000 years of human occupation in the North American Southwest (Berry and Berry 1986; Huckell 1984a, 1996, 2001). Lanceolate projectile points characterize the first 4,000 years, called the Paleoindian period. By Late Paleoindian times a boundary is evident, with so-called Plano sites only being found in the eastern Southwest and out onto the Great Plains (Irwin-

Williams, chap. 2, this vol.; Judge 1973). Greater diversity is evident during the Archaic period, but initial efforts to understand its anthropological implications (Irwin-Williams 1973, 1979) have been criticized for confusing what Clarke (1968) called "technocomplexes" with ethnic or linguistic groupings (Berry 1982; Berry and Berry 1986; Huckell 1984a). Huckell (1996) proposes that current data permit a temporal division of the Archaic into early (8500 or 8000–5500 B.P.), middle (5500–3500 B.P.), and late (3500–2000 or 1500 B.P.) periods and recommends caution in evaluating spatial variability in the character of technocomplexes.

By the Late Archaic, called Basketmaker II in the northern Southwest (Lipe et al. 1999), the introduction of maize was variably transforming the subsistence-settlement systems in the Southwest, and the frequency and density of archaeological remains dating to this and subsequent intervals are much greater. Current direct dates suggest that maize was likely present in the Southwest by about 4000 B.P. (Abotech 1999; Gilpin 1994; Gregory 1999:118–120, fig. 8.33; Gregory and Baar 1999; McBroom 1999). Huckell (1995, 1996, 2001) proposes the term *Early Agricultural period* to refer to the interval from the arrival of maize to the appearance of a fully developed ceramic container technology (ca. 1850 B.P.), when ceramics became a highly visible element in southwestern assemblages.

When we organized the Mogollon-Zuni seminar, we suspected that Zunian as a discrete language dated back to the Archaic period. Following an idea modified from Krantz (1977), we thought that during the Altithermal period (ca. 7000–4500 B.P.) some Southwest populations may have resorted to high elevations and that in these "islands in the sky" the conditions may have been present for language differentiation to have taken place. In particular, we envisioned that a Zunian "adaptation to the mountains" may have come about, so that when maize was introduced the timing and process of its adoption by the Zuni may have varied from populations at lower elevations, thus serving as a factor in maintaining their linguistic isolation (see Gregory and Wilcox, chap. 10, this vol.).

We were also well aware of Greenberg's (1987; Greenberg et al. 1986) arguments for the derivation of all American Indian languages south of Alaska from a single Amerind language (see Ruhlen 1991) and the important debate about whether the Clovis Paleoindian assemblages, which are found throughout North America, represent the first appearance of humans in the New World, about 13,500 years ago (Dillehay 1989, 1997; Fiedel 1999, 2002; Krantz 1977; Meltzer 1993; Meltzer et al. 1997). Could the considerable linguistic diversity of the Americas and the diversity of cultural adaptations from hunter-gatherers to urban, state-level polities have come about from a single culture and language in a mere 13,500 years? To us that is the preeminent issue in all of Americanist archaeology. Debate about it began in the nineteenth century, when it was framed in terms of the "unity or diversity" of the American Indian (Fewkes et al. 1912; Gallatin 1836, 1845; Meltzer 1993; Morgan 1877; Putnam 1901; Wilcox 1976; Wilcox and Fowler 2002).

For these reasons, we began our inquiry into the relationship between Mogollon and Zuni in the larger context of debate about the unity and diversity of the North American Southwest. Among Puebloan peoples in the Southwest four language families are present: Uto-Aztecan (Hopi), Zuni, Keresan, and Tanoan. The

Hohokam in southern Arizona are thought to have spoken Tepiman, a Uto-Aztecan language (Miller 1984; Shaul and Hill 1998; Wilcox 1986a), and in Sonora there were other Uto-Aztecan groups (such as Opata, Pima Bajo [a Tepiman language], and Cahitan [Mayo and Yaqui]). How did all of this diversity come about in a culture area unified by the shared practice of agriculture, ceramic production, and permanent village life?

A conjunction of theoretical developments encouraged us to think it was an apt time to renew the anthropological inquiry into Zuni origins; specifically, these developments included a renewed cooperation among archaeologists and linguists and a burgeoning interest among archaeologists in the issues of migration and cultural identity. Definition of systemic boundaries is a key element in most of these arguments. Behavioral or systemic boundaries partition architectural or spatial sets on the basis of behavioral contrasts (Green and Perlman 1985). Analyses of such contrasts have been applied widely in southwestern studies to discriminate households, village segments, and larger-scale social entities, including settlement systems, on multiple scales of interaction (e.g., see J. Clark 1995, 2001; Ford et al. 1972; Matson 1991; Wilcox 1995a, 1999a; Wilcox et al. 1981).

To facilitate illustration of such behavioral or systemic boundaries as derived from analysis and to provide a consistent, large-scale geographic context for comparison and contrast, we provided base maps of the Southwest to be used by seminar participants for plotting various locations and distributions relevant to their discussions. This base map is illustrated as figure 1.1 and is duplicated with additional information in several of the chapters that follow.

Passage of the Native American

Graves Protection and Repatriation Act (NAGPRA) in 1990 challenged archaeologists and Native peoples to engage in a new dialogue about the issue of cultural affiliation, to determine which tribes would decide about the disposition of human remains, funerary objects, sacred items, and other items of cultural patrimony. Cultural affiliation "means a relationship of shared group identity that may be reasonably traced historically or prehistorically between a present-day Indian Tribe and an identifiable earlier group" (*Federal Register* 1990:43 CFR pt. 10.14.c). Oral traditions and language were given equal weight with scientific data: kin or cultural affiliation "shall be established using the following types of evidence: geographical, kinship, biological, archaeological, anthropological, linguistic, folklore, oral tradition, historical, or other relevant information or expert opinion" (*Federal Register* 1990:43 CFR pt. 10.14.d). The standard of proof is a "preponderance of the evidence" (*Federal Register* 1990:43 CFR pt. 10.14.e).

Different federal agencies, however, have interpreted the legal requirement to consult with tribes in very different ways, and they have followed different approaches in assessing the preponderance of the evidence (Anyon 1999). Some have proceeded to make determinations largely on the basis of current archaeological knowledge (e.g., USDA Forest Service 1996), while others have gone to much greater lengths to learn what Native peoples believe. Conflicts have resulted (Whiteley 2002a; Wilcox 2004), partly because tribes often place a high value on the secrecy of what they know and partly because many scientific judgments about such matters are premature, as this volume shows. We suggest that scientific progress in this area has been

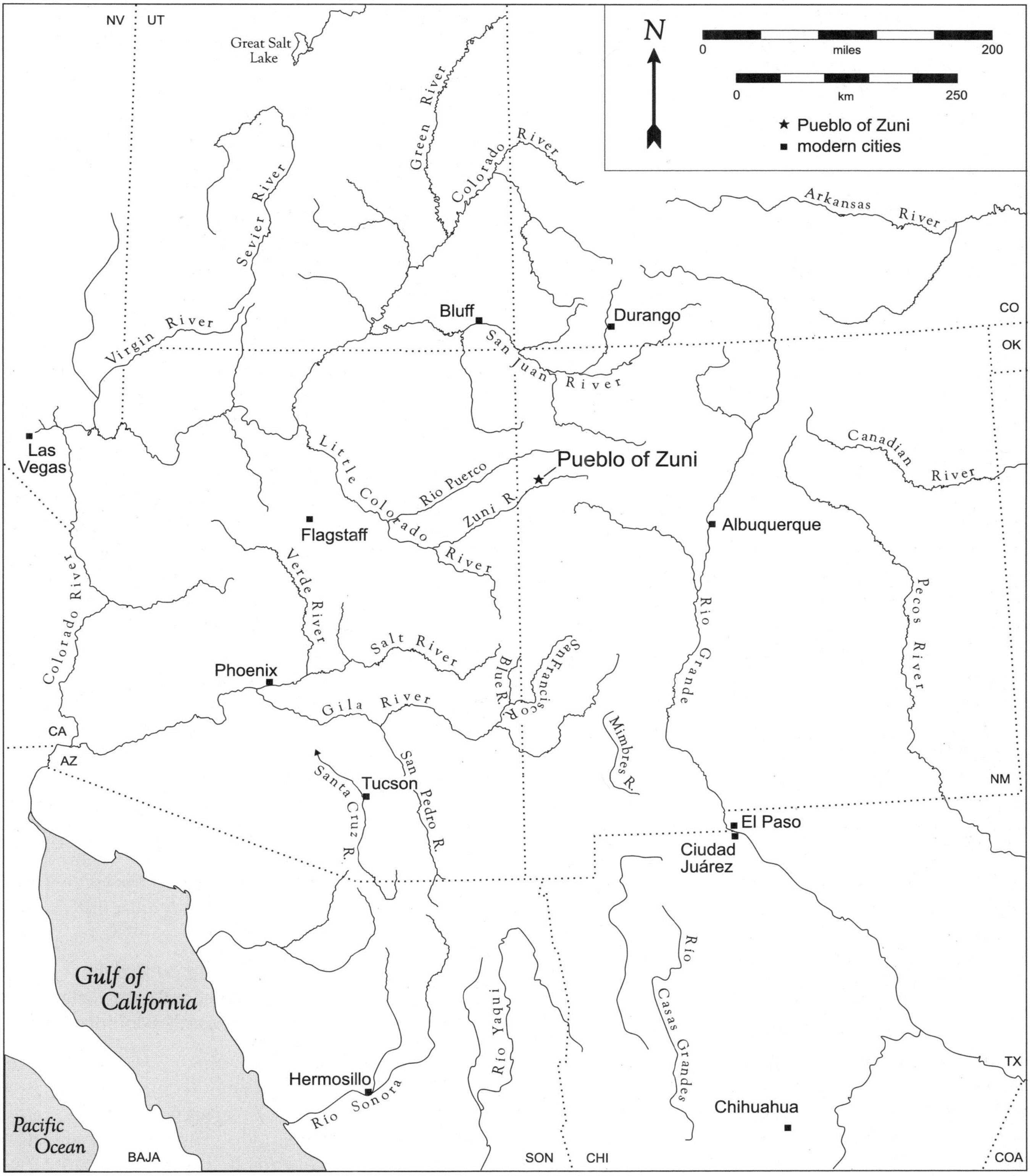

Figure 1.1. Base map of the Southwest, with selected locations and drainages indicated.

retarded by the disavowal of previous efforts by southwestern archaeologists to trace the continuities of modern tribal groups into the past, including rejection of both the culture histories that presented their hypotheses and inferences about migrations that were part of that process (Cordell and Plog 1979; Wilcox and Masse 1981).

Publication of Anthony's (1990) archaeological methodology for studying migration marks the moment when this important social process again became the subject of legitimate inquiry, and southwestern archaeologists eagerly joined in this movement (Cameron 1995; J. Clark 2001; Spielmann 1998; Woodson 1995, 1999). Renfrew's (1987a) lucid study of Indo-European migrations and his subsequent papers dealing with a "new synthesis" of archaeology, linguistics, and molecular biology (Renfrew 1989, 1992a, 1992b, 1996, 1998a), followed by a series of seminars he organized (Renfrew 2000; Renfrew et al. 2000; Bellwood and Renfrew 2003), have created great excitement about multidisciplinary approaches to tracing the history of linguistic groups in archaeology (see Matson, chap. 7, this vol.).

The linguist Jane Hill began to talk to archaeologists and to attend archaeology meetings. An expert in Uto-Aztecan languages, she was stimulated by ideas generated by those in the Renfrew group and now has proposed a radical new theory about the entry of Uto-Aztecan speakers into the Southwest at the beginning of the Early Agricultural period (Hill 2001). In 2001 she, together with two southwestern archaeologists (Steven LeBlanc and R. G. Matson), attended one of the Renfrew seminars (published in Bellwood and Renfrew 2003; see also Matson, chap. 7, this vol.). In her paper for our seminar (chap. 3, this vol.) Hill concluded that the Zuni

language probably became distinct at least 7,000–8,000 years ago. This means that to understand that ethnogenesis at its inception we must examine it in the context of the peopling of the Americas and the linguistic diversification of Paleoindian populations when it is most likely Zuni became a distinct language. Focusing our advanced seminar on the question of Zuni origins and the relationship of Zuni and Mogollon thus has become a means to enter into the world-anthropological debates stimulated by the Renfrew project and to advance new methodological and theoretical approaches to their resolution.

Race, language, and culture have long been known to be independent variables (Boas 1902, 1911, 1940). Even if it is true that Zuni became a distinct language at least 7,000–8,000 years ago, this does not mean we can with certainty expect to discriminate these populations archaeologically from other contemporary hunter-gatherer groups—though that might be possible. We thus asked R. G. Matson to take a hard look at the first 10,000 years of southwestern archaeology to see if it is yet possible to identify any early hunter-gatherer populations as likely Zuni speaking; his findings, detailed in chapter 7, are negative. We also asked him to use ecological theory to construct expectations about where to look for the Archaic antecedents of the modern Zuni (see chap. 7, this vol.); these expectations are consistent with our Mogollon hypothesis that those populations spoke Zunian.

First, however, a look back at earlier efforts by Cynthia Irwin-Williams (chap. 2) to understand "linguistic prehistory" in the Southwest is instructive, partly because the Zuni origins problem was not directly addressed there. Jane Hill's pivotal chapter (chap. 3) then sets the scene

for the remainder of the volume. Jeff Clark's incisive discussion of modern concepts for identifying migrations and past cultural identities using technological style (chap. 4) is complemented by the later discussions by Barbara Mills (chap. 13) and Laurie Webster (chap. 16), which elaborate and apply this approach to ceramics and perishable artifacts, respectively. Not all archaeologists, however, share the same philosophical or methodological notions of how to study such problems, as other chapters in this volume show. We find merit in this diversity of approaches.

To set the scene for all the subsequent discussions two chapters on paleoenvironment are presented next, one emphasizing low-frequency events over the last 20,000 years and the other emphasizing high-frequency events over the last 4,000 years across the whole Southwest. The chapters by Gregory and Nials (chap. 5) and Dean (chap. 6) show how the rich environmental data available for the Southwest can be fruitfully articulated with cultural process to create holistic models of culture and environment. The context of Zunian adaptations is thus clarified. The remainder of the volume is structured chronologically. We encourage readers, however, to read the chapters in any order they choose.

Part II: Placing Zuni in the Development of Southwestern Societies: From Paleoindian to Mogollon

At some point Zunian speakers, whose language probably first became distinct during Paleoindian times (Hill, chap. 3, this vol.), came to occupy a territory in the North American Southwest. That occupation may also date back into Paleoindian times, or it may have come about during the Archaic period, perhaps during the

Late Archaic, when maize was introduced into the Southwest (see Diehl, chap. 11, this vol.). Although, as we will show, this issue currently is moot, it remains an important challenge for future research. Following the appearance of ceramics in the Southwest, however, more data became available, and arguments can be articulated that postulate an equation between Zunian speakers and some of the various populations responsible for what archaeologists have called the Mogollon culture (Haury 1936a; Martin 1979; Wheat 1955). Matson's discussion (chap. 7) of the first 10,000 years of occupation in the Americas and the American Southwest, while showing that Zunians as a distinct group during that period are as yet invisible archaeologically, also shows, on the basis of ecological theory, that the Mogollon populations fit his expectations for where Zunians should be found.

The following four chapters by Damp (chap. 8), Gregory (chap. 9), Gregory and Wilcox (chap. 10), and Diehl (chap. 11) explore several aspects of the Mogollon-Zuni hypothesis. While Gregory (chap. 9) summarizes the cultural-historical approach as exemplified by Paul Sidney Martin and John B. Rinaldo, the other authors elucidate ways to reconceptualize this problem in modern anthropological terms (see also Clark, chap. 4, this vol.).

As a number of chapters in the volume make reference to the traditionally defined "branches" of Mogollon culture, we present here two maps showing the boundaries of these conceptual entities. The first (fig. 1.2a) renders the map originally presented by Wheat (1955:fig. 1), and the second (fig. 1.2b) renders the map published by Martin (1979:fig. 1) in the *Handbook of North American Indians*. Both authors included seven branches: Forestdale, Black River,

Cibola, Mimbres, San Simon, Jornada, and an Eastern Periphery. Danson (1957:99–101) defined and discussed an Alpine branch, but this construction has never been widely used.

While both Wheat and Martin have Mogollon culture extending south of the international boundary to an unspecified distance, comparison of the two maps reveals considerable differences between them. In general, Wheat's map is much less definite, with the boundaries for several branches being incomplete. Martin has all branches completely circumscribed and includes other alterations to Wheat's map, some of which are worth noting. First, the southern boundary of the Cibola branch is moved south at the expense of area included in the Mimbres branch on Wheat's map. Second, the southern boundary of the Black River branch is also moved southward to include all of the Safford Basin. Third, the Forestdale branch is enlarged to include all of the lower half of the upper Little Colorado River valley and is extended north and west to Winslow. Unfortunately, Martin gives no rationale for the changes and includes no discussion of the branches per se. It was, however, his last and presumably most mature formulation of these distributions.

Part III: Zuni in the Puebloan World: Mogollon-Zuni Connections

A recent comparison of the American Southwest with the American Southeast on multiple scales of interaction (Neitzel 1999) showed that the unity of culture in the Southeast (symbolized by the Mississippian concept) contrasts with the diversity expressed in the southwestern concepts of Anasazi, Hohokam, Mogollon, Patayan, and Fremont cultural traditions. The

huge expansion of data in the last 30 years and the decline in the importance of the Pecos Conference as a forum for general discussion (Woodbury 1993) have resulted in a series of Hohokam symposia, Anasazi symposia, and Mogollon conferences. While valuable, such efforts have tended to balkanize knowledge, and the Four Corners state boundaries between Utah, Colorado, New Mexico, and Arizona and, even more, the international boundary with Mexico further partition and restrict what most archaeologists in the Southwest know, or claim to know (Doelle 2003). Temporally, the same kind of divide often exists between those who study the Paleoindian and Archaic periods vs. those who focus on later ceramic periods. If we are to approach a problem like Zuni origins in an anthropologically adequate way, we must construct new approaches that reach beyond such narrow perspectives, approaches that allow us to operate successfully at multiple spatial and temporal scales. There have been attempts to overcome southwestern provincialism (Adler 1996; Mathien and McGuire 1986; Neitzel 1999; Riley 1987; Vierra and Gaultieri 1992; Wilcox and Masse 1981), but they have been uphill struggles. Advanced seminars have been a fruitful source of comparative studies of southwestern settlement systems on a larger spatial scale (Cordell and Gumerman 1989; Crown and Judge 1991; Dean 2000; Gumerman 1988), and the biennial Southwest Symposia have created a new kind of forum for thematic discussions that often are pansouthwestern (and beyond) in their coverage (e.g., Minnis and Redman 1990; Schlanger 2002), although they are heavily biased toward the views of university-based archaeologists. In 2004 the Southwest Symposium was held in Chihuahua City, Chihuahua—a

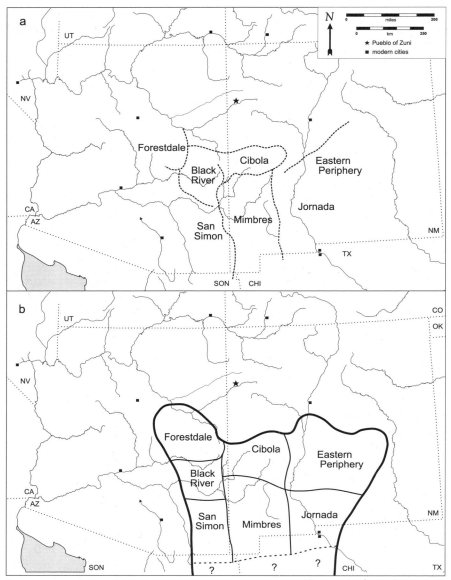

Figure 1.2. (a) Mogollon branches after Wheat (1955); (b) Mogollon branches after Martin (1979).

promising development in the process of overcoming provincialism (Doelle 2003).

Unfortunately, common usage has tended to reify the cultural tradition concepts in more or less their original forms, something some archaeologists applaud (Reid and Whittlesey 1997). Another approach to this situation has been to suggest wholesale abandonment of traditional categories (Speth 1988; Tainter and Plog 1994), and yet another has been to

attempt redefinition of them in organizationally meaningful terms (Wilcox 1979, 1980, 1988a). In this regard it is interesting to note the traditional view of an Anasazi culture split into eastern and western groups on the basis of the distribution of mineral paint vs. carbon paint black-on-white pottery, respectively (Hawley 1936; Roberts 1937). Interestingly, this distinction also marks an organizational difference in Pueblo I times between the Kayenta

(western) Anasazi, who lived in farmsteads and hamlets without great kivas, and the Dolores Valley (eastern) Anasazi, who lived in small villages and at times had circular great kivas (Lipe et al. 1999). During Chacoan times the Chacoan world of great houses and great kivas encompassed most of the eastern Anasazi (exclusive of the Rio Grande), while the western Anasazi, with rare exceptions, were outside of it, having no great houses or great kivas (Gumerman and Dean 1989; Wilcox 1999a; cf. Lekson 1991).[8]

We are convinced that traditional distinctions based on material culture and the terminology devised to refer to them can be rethought in organizationally meaningful ways and that traditional terms can be used (with due caution) to discuss modern concepts. But is that wise (see Kowalewski, chap. 22, this vol.)? In chapter 10 we show that this kind of redefinition can be applied to the traditional Mogollon concept (see also Dean 1988a). Nevertheless, with an eye to identifying Zuni antecedents archaeologically, the fundamental objective of the studies in this volume is to describe patterns of interaction among populations of people on multiple scales, where the social entities that are the context for the interaction are different on each. Such studies are essential in order to identify the *contrasts* that define the boundaries of sociocultural groups, in particular, those of the Zuni (but see Mills, chap. 13, this vol.). Within settlements, the discrimination of household domains (Dean 1969; Rohn 1965; Wilcox 1975; Wilcox et al. 1981) opens the way to analysis of household variability in transactions within and among communities (e.g., Abbott 1994, 2000). Patterns in the distribution of ritual, public architecture (Doelle et al. 1995; Gregory 1987; Gregory and Nials 1985; Wilcox 1999a; Wilcox and

Sternberg 1983) provide an empirical basis for studying interaction on local, regional, and macroregional scales (Wilcox 2005a). The concept of settlement systems then becomes central to the description of these patterns, and it is often unnecessary or even misleading to use the terminology of the traditional cultural categories (see also Ferguson and Anyon 2001; Wilcox 2005b).

The seven chapters in part III show that scale matters, both spatially and temporally. If we consider for a moment the idea of a settlement as a miniature social system, we can ask questions about the matter, energy, and information transfers between it and other settlements. The more such transfers are critical to the survival of a settlement from period A (time x) to period B (time x + 1), the less self-sufficient, or autonomous, it is. Using modern computer technology and mathematical techniques, it is possible in geographic information system (GIS) analyses to model and simulate the matrix of such relationships (e.g., see Gumerman and Gell-Mann 1994; Varien 1999). Sets of settlements that cluster, such as those found close together in a microenvironmental niche like a river valley or on a canal system, also form systems whose relative self-sufficiency we should be able to model.

It is clear that during some periods networks of such systems were open, with considerable exchange going back and forth among neighbors (Plog 1983; Mills, chap. 13, and Wilson, chap. 14, this vol.; see also Abbott 2000). During other periods systems at a certain level were probably attempting to survive as much more closed, autonomous systems, for example, in the face of raiding by external populations that resulted in circumscription of what was previously a more open network (Wilcox et al. 2001a). Even if the magnitude

of natural environmental variation remained within the range wherein an adaptation developed, such shifts in response to changes in the cultural environment may have reduced both the flexibility and potentials of an adaptation (see Gregory and Nials, chap. 5, and Gregory and Wilcox, chap. 20, this vol.). Thus, famine could result, precipitating escalated warfare, migration, or overtures to more open exchanges. The pooling of resources that cooperation engendered within settlement clusters or larger groupings on regional scales could have increased the flexibility and resilience of these systems and supported relatively higher population levels than village autonomy would have allowed—so long as internal or political tensions did not fragment the system. Boundary maintenance strategies probably were important to the achievement of coherence within those settlement systems at several scales. Endogamy, for example, or other controls on acceptable marriage partners are means for achieving such cohesion and might also have been factors in linguistic diversification or isolation.

Concepts of regional and macroregional systems can be used to advantage to describe the nature of the networks within or among settlement systems. Hohokam ball courts, for example, were constructed public places where we infer rituals (perhaps involving ball games) were conducted to mark the social identities of households or suprahousehold village segments within settlements and those of neighboring villages located on the same canal system or in adjacent ones (Wilcox 1987, 1991a; Wilcox and Sternberg 1983). The first appearance of this public architecture is coincident with the emergence of a Hohokam religious ideology expressed in the Gila rock art style, a

cremation death ritual employing a distinctive set of ritual paraphernalia, and the earliest well-defined suprahousehold village segments, which buried their dead in separate cemeteries (Wallace et al. 1995; Wilcox 1991a, 1991b). Most of these elements are expressed in settlements whose ball courts define a distribution that indicates the operation of a regional system centered on the Phoenix Basin, where the greatest density of ball courts is present (Wilcox and Sternberg 1983; see also Marshall 2001).

Some settlements have both large and small courts, while others have only a large or a small court, and still others have two or more small courts (Gregory and Huckleberry 1994), but none of these stand out as preeminent, nor do there appear to be higher-level nodes defined by clusters of settlements integrated in a special way (although the sets of settlements on the same canal system might be viewed in this way; see Wilcox 1991a). The linear distribution of ball court sites that extend outward from the Phoenix Basin to adjacent basins appears to indicate a "down-the-line" exchange connection that overall served to regulate the exchange of valuables that were probably used to maintain marriage networks (Wilcox and Sternberg 1983).[9]

After AD 1000 the ball court network was reorganized into a macroregional system in which some regions (like the Phoenix Basin) retained the cultural identity marked by the Hohokam religion, while in others (such as the Flagstaff area) the cultural identity marked by the Hohokam religion was absent or much attenuated (Wilcox 1999a, 2002). In this stage of the evolving system, supra–canal systems in the Phoenix Basin appear to constitute a new kind of multisettlement node in the system (Wilcox 1999a; see also Abbott

2000; Gregory and Huckleberry 1994; Gregory and Nials 1985).

Wilcox's (1999a) analysis of the so-called Chacoan regional system (Neitzel 1999) argues for an even greater complexity in the sets of social groupings and the ways they were articulated on a *macroregional* scale. Yet another structural pattern is apparent in the case of currently available evidence from the Casas Grandes *region* (Whalen and Minnis 2001, 2003), *macroregional system* (Wilcox 1991b, 1995a), and *world* (Schaafsma and Riley, eds. 1999).[10] Many new questions for future research can be formulated on the basis of such models of regional and macroregional systems or of worlds.

The Coalescent Communities Database introduced in chapter 12 by Wilcox, Gregory, and Hill has made possible, for the first time in southwestern archaeology, a comprehensive study of the relationships among neighboring groups across the entire North American Southwest (see also Wilcox 2005b, 2005c, 2005d). Interestingly, such a study had already been envisioned by A. V. Kidder (1924) 80 years ago![11] Using a method of enumeration of all known sites of 13 rooms or more, much more realistic demographic estimates of population trends and the relative distribution and abundance of human population on the southwestern landscape through time can be determined.

New macroregional patterns of interaction are thus revealed and provide a context for comparing the patterns discussed in chapters 13–17. Ceramic patterns are delimited by Barbara Mills (chap. 13), more specifically, Mogollon ceramic patterns by Dean Wilson (chap. 14), rock art patterns by Polly Schaafsma and Jane Young (chap. 15), perishable traditions and their patterns by Laurie Webster (chap. 16), and the structure

of exchange networks for exotic goods by Arthur Vokes and Gregory (chap. 17). In each case attempts are made to reveal the role of Zuni speakers and to test the Mogollon-Zuni hypothesis. A synthesis of what we have learned about Zuni origins by examining our original Mogollon-Zuni hypothesis (chap. 10) in these multifaceted macroregional analyses is presented in chapter 20.

Part IV: Zuni from the Late Prehistoric to the Middle Place

In part IV we consider the importance of the local level as well as the view from Zuni, where the modern descendants of the populations we are seeking to track archaeologically now live. Compared to the macroregional scale emphasized in earlier chapters, the fine-grained settlement pattern studies reported by Keith Kintigh in chapter 18 are on a micro scale (see also Kintigh et al. 2004). In chapter 19 T. J. Ferguson examines what anthropologists know about Zuni oral traditions, finding that a widespread cultural geography is defined in them in which to this day pilgrimages are made to shrines where songs are sung, prayers are made, and offerings are left. The Zuni do not need archaeologists to tell them their history.

Part V: Zuni Origins: Future Directions and Critical Commentary

In our conclusions to the volume (chap. 20) we draw out of the participant chapters in parts I through IV the data to construct a new research design for future studies of Zuni origins and suggest how our methodology can be generalized to study similar problems. Our general discussants then critically review the whole volume and seek to situate this effort in the general history of American

anthropology. Don Fowler (chap. 21) and Stephen Kowalewski (chap. 22) agree with all of the participants that the scientific question of Zuni origins may not have been solved, but in our "stocktaking" of what is currently known about it much new insight has been achieved. Directions for future research have also been defined, and new methodologies for the future conduct of southwestern archaeology are articulated.

Notes

1. In "My Adventures in Zuni" Cushing (1882) made it seem that he was abandoned at Zuni by the Stevensons, an allegation for which they never forgave him (see note in Cushing vertical file, National Anthropological Archives [NAA]). The Stevensons were intent on their own anthropological project and saw the precocious Cushing as an opportunistic interloper. They all soon hated one another, and that bitterness stayed with them all of their days, something we today need to be cautious in evaluating (see Parezo 1993).

2. One of the Zuni was Wayhusius (Waihusiwa), who served Zuni as governor in 1923 (Ladd 1979a:489).

3. Mary Hemenway (1820–1894) was principally responsible for saving the Old South Church in Boston, thus contributing to the beginnings of historic preservation in America (Holleran 1998). For more about her see Eustis (1955), Hinsley and McChesney (1984), Hinsley and Wilcox (2002), and Wilcox (2002).

4. Hinsley and Wilcox's project to publish a documentary history of the Hemenway expedition while Cushing was director will bring together archival data from the letter books of the expedition that reside at the Huntington Free Library (HFL) in the Bronx, New York, and from other institutions, principally the Southwest Museum (SWM), Los Angeles. In volume 6 in this series the work done at the Zuni sites will be presented, together with an essay being prepared by Keith Kintigh.

5. In a long and remarkable letter to Sylvester Baxter, the secretary-treasurer of the Expedition Board, dated August 2,

1887 (Cushing Letter Book 2:169–212, HFL), Cushing sets forth his detailed plans for this institution, which Hinsley and Wilcox plan to publish in volume 4 of their Hemenway series.

6. The reasons are complex, but ill health due to tapeworm, a deformed stomach that caused diverticulitis, and false accusations by his field secretary, Frederick Webb Hodge, were significant factors. His vision of what the expedition should be also diverged from that of Mrs. Hemenway and the board she had appointed to advise her. Hinsley and Wilcox plan to detail this fascinating story in volume 6 of their Hemenway series.

7. Unlike Cushing, Fewkes (1891) promptly began to publish the results of his work for the Hemenways in the *Journal of American Ethnology*. In the first volume of these results Cushing saw his own turf being invaded and claimed there were many errors of fact, a story that Hinsley

and Wilcox plan to publish in volume 7 of their Hemenway series. It was in part because of Cushing's objections that Fewkes abandoned the Zuni field for Hopi.

8. The exception is in the Low Mountain area just east of Black Mesa, where Chacoan great houses have 60–100 percent Kayenta Anasazi pottery on them (Tusayan White Ware and Gray Ware; see Gilpin 1989; Wilcox 1999a).

9. With the exception of marine shell, the raw materials for most Hohokam valuables come from relatively nearby sources. What makes them distinctive is the knowledge needed to transform them into icons of animals or other forms.

10. The argument by Whalen and Minnis (2001, 2003) that the role of Paquimé was confined to the settlement system within one day's travel of it is to claim autonomy for that system on a regional scale. The fact that sites through-

out the five-day radius of the Chihuahuan Polychrome distribution (Brand 1943; see Wilcox 1991b, 1995a) share the same ceramic assemblage of Chihuahuan pottery types (Amerind Foundation site files) is evidence for an intensity of interaction not accounted for by the autonomy hypothesis. Neither is the fact that over 10,000 sherds of El Paso Polychrome were recovered at Paquimé (Di Peso et al. 1974a).

11. Kidder (1924) anticipated the possibility of the present study: "If we knew the relative date of the founding and abandonment of every ruin in the Southwest, it would be a comparatively simple matter by estimating the approximate population of each, and plotting the results on a series of maps, to visualize the entire history of the Pueblo peoples." We thank Dennis Gilpin for bringing this passage about such a simple matter to our attention.

2 Prehistoric Cultural and Linguistic Patterns in the Southwest since 5000 BC

Cynthia Irwin-Williams

The American southwestern United States is one of the richest and best-known archaeological areas in North America, but research has generally focused on the remains belonging for the most part to the periods after the birth of Christ. Ethnographic research in the American Southwest has likewise been intensive, but linguistic studies have been variable in orientation and coverage.[1]

Recently, the expanding and convergent interests of linguists and archaeologists have focused on the reconstruction of prehistoric languages and linguistic-ethnographic areas. Too often, however, with some notable exceptions dealing with the relatively recent past, insufficient archaeological data have been employed as a basis for or as a control on geographic-linguistic hypotheses. In addition, when archaeological information has been used, too little distinction has been made between cultural-historical evidence that may legitimately be considered in historical-genetic reconstruction and culture-typical evidence that may not. Now a growing body of information is becoming available on very early southwestern culture history and is relevant to the problem. This information, together with the hypotheses derived from linguistic theory, has

been used in the current discussion to construct a suggested outline of certain major linguistic-ethnographic archaeological developments in the American Southwest since about 5000 BC.

It is perhaps necessary to state at the outset that it is realized that a pot speaks no language and that any simple out-of-context equation between an archaeological assemblage and a linguistic group is doomed to failure. However, it is equally misleading and methodologically unacceptable to think solely in terms of disembodied assemblages of artifacts with no relation to once-living human groups. In the same way, linguistic-geographic reconstructions cannot be isolated from these prehistoric groups.

The most accurate reconstructions are variations on what has been called the direct historic approach and deal with the relatively recent past. However, since the solutions are applicable to only a small part of the problem, it is necessary to employ other evidence. Of primary importance is that offered by glottochronology or lexicostatistical dating. It is realized that there is chronologic variability due to differences in interpretation, that the validity of this technique is not universally accepted by linguistics, and that some prefer to express

linguistic distinctions in terms of degrees of divergence rather than in terms of minimum centuries. However, the fact remains that in several well-researched situations archaeological and glottochronological data have produced surprisingly parallel reconstructions and that their combined strength has yielded results of considerable solidity and merit.

The approach employed here seeks to examine the parallels suggested by archaeology and historic linguistics rather than to depend in detail on specific lexicostatistical dates. It is believed that the broad reconstructive hypotheses sought should be based on the totality of linguistic and archaeological evidence for prehistoric population unity, fission, and movement, set against an absolute unidirectional time scale. It must be recognized that these reconstructive models should be considered simply as working hypotheses, guidelines for further research, rather than fixed schemata based on comprehensive data.

In addition, for practical reasons this discussion leaves many areas of inquiry untouched. Thus, the numerous California groups, except the Yumans, are not considered; nor are the Uto-Aztecans of Mexico, the *enigmatic Zuni* [emphasis added], or the fascinating Kiowa, although the latter do present some interesting possibilities. Attention is focused, then, on the principal languages of the American Southwest proper: Keresan, Tanoan, Hopic, Piman, Yuman, and, peripherally, the Numic group. With this in mind it is useful to review certain aspects of the linguistic background and to note some of the more successful attempts at establishing continuity between ethnohistoric groups and recent archaeological materials.

Linguistic evidence relevant to the problem has been derived principally from the researches of Lamb (1958, 1964), Hale (1958, 1962, 1964), Goss (1965), and Romney (1957) on the Northern Uto-Aztecan language group; Davis (1959) and Hale (1962) on the Tanoans and Kiowas; and Davis (1959) on the Keresans. There is some difference of opinion on the details of Northern Uto-Aztecan dispersal, but on the whole the patterns represented are remarkably similar. I will recapitulate using Goss's present model: the initial breaking up of Uto-Aztecans occurred about 4,000–5,000 years ago, with the main Mexican branches (such as Nahuatl, Taracahitic, etc.) separating from the ancestors of the northern group. Between 3,000 and 4,000 years ago Piman split off from the Hopic-Numic and so on; about 3,000 years ago Hopic, Luisenic, and Tubatatulabalic split from the Numic group. Yutish and Shoshoni-Mono split around 1,300 years ago, and subsequently the latter divided into its two main components about 1,000 years ago. Still later divisions are indicated but are beyond the scope of this discussion. Tanoan is generally considered to be a Uto-Aztecan language, but the time depth for unity is very great. In studies on later Tanoan development Davis (1959) believes that Towa and Tiwa/Tewa split about 2,000 years ago; subsequently, Tiwa broke off from Tewa about 1,000 years

ago, and Tiwa divided into its two regional components about 400–500 years ago.[2]

Theories concerning the ultimate geographic origin of Uto-Aztecan tend to fall into two main groups. The first is represented most fully by Taylor (1961) and Hopkins (1965), who place Uto-Aztecan origins in the north, variously, in the northern or southern Great Basin, and consider them to be bearers of the "Desert Culture." The second is represented by Romney (1957), Lamb (1958, 1964), and others and makes the best fit with the linguistic evidence as well as the evidence of early archaeology. This suggests a southern origin for Uto-Aztecan, in the southern Arizona–Sonora–Chihuahua area.

The other dominant Pueblo language, Keresan, has received relatively little recent study and has not to my knowledge been considered in terms of glottochronology. However, on the basis of the internal phonologic-morphologic comparisons of Davis (1959), it seems that the Keresan Pueblos fall into three main groups.[3] Sapir (1929) once suggested a relation between Keresan and the Yuman languages of the Colorado River region, but no recent detailed comparisons have been made. This suggestion, however, is of great interest in view of the archaeological evidence. The Yuman languages themselves have likewise not been studied in terms of relevant detailed external comparisons.

The direct historic and similar approaches have been employed to produce several interesting, reasonable, and in some instances well-documented connections between ethnohistory and the relatively recent archaeological record. Di Peso (1953, 1956) and others have suggested and gathered evidence for continuity between elements of the Hohokam culture and the Piman-speaking

groups. Ellis (1964), with evidence derived from Indian land-claim researches, has presented a good case for the derivation of the Tiwa and Tewa from certain archaeological cultures of the northern Rio Grande; Dittert (1968 [citing Ellis 1964]) likewise shows convincing relations between the Largo-Gallina material and historic Towa groups. Finally, Schroeder (1957, 1960) outlines and supports an unbroken development from certain members of his general Hakataya culture to certain of the Yuman peoples such as the Yavapai and Havasupai. Gunnerson (1962) believes in but lacks evidence for derivation of members of the Numic division from the Virgin/Sevier/Fremont cultures, but Goss (1965) disputes Gunnerson's conclusions on linguistic grounds.

With this background it is possible to review the archaeological evidence for the formulation of a long-range hypothesis on the development of the current ethnographic-linguistic situation. The scene opens at about 6000 BC (see fig. 2.1). I have demonstrated in an earlier paper ("Natural Ecology and Population Dynamics in the Preceramic Southwest" [see Irwin-Williams 1968, ed. 1968]) that on seriational grounds it is possible to document certain demographic patterns in the American Southwest at this early period. Characteristic is a long-term trend toward continued withdrawal of the bison-hunting-oriented Plano cultures from the eastern Southwest and their replacement by economically eclectic groups from the west and south. The boundary in the figure is roughly that indicated by the distribution of Eden-Scottsbluff material. The western group may be identified as the San Dieguito/Lake Mohave culture, which has now been dated as early as 6900 BC. The Southern Unit comprises materials of the earliest Sulphur Springs Cochise, which may date as early as 7300 BC.

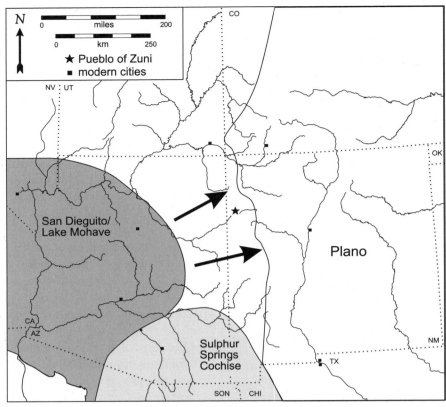

Figure 2.1. Distribution of southwestern technocomplexes, ca. 6000 BC.

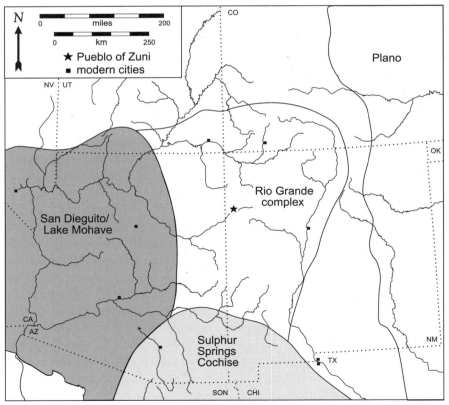

Figure 2.2. Distribution of southwestern technocomplexes, ca. 5000 BC.

By 5000 BC (see fig. 2.2) eastern Lake Mohave–related complexes are already present in the Four Corners region and as far east as the Rio Grande, where they are known as the Rio Grande complex, or La Bajada or "J Point" complex. The detailed similarity of materials from the eastern and western extremities of this spread cannot be overemphasized. In addition, although evidence is necessary, the assemblages seem to be distinct from the contemporary Cochise to the south and from adjacent cultures to the north in their almost complete lack of grinding tools. It is evident that any linguistic unity postulated from ethnohistoric groups that ultimately derived from the eastern and western extremities of this expanse will probably predate ca. 7,000 years ago.

By 3000 BC we are on considerably firmer ground (see fig. 2.3). The American Southwest at this period presents a continuum of cultures in what for the first time can be considered a distinctive and unified culture area. I have employed the term Picosa (Irwin-Williams 1967a) to refer to this unity and have described it in terms of numerous shared characteristics generalized as well as specifically southwestern. One of the most distinctive of the latter is the widespread though not universal use of primitive horticulture by at least 2000 BC. At the same time the continued existence of historically distinct groups is easily seen and well documented. As indicated in this rough outline, the unity between the northwestern and northeastern members seen in the preceding period is still strong and detailed in the Pinto Basin/San Jose relationship. It will also be noted that a well-documented extension of the latter reaches into parts of central Colorado by a well-defined zone centering in the Rocky Mountains.

The southern Chiricahua Cochise

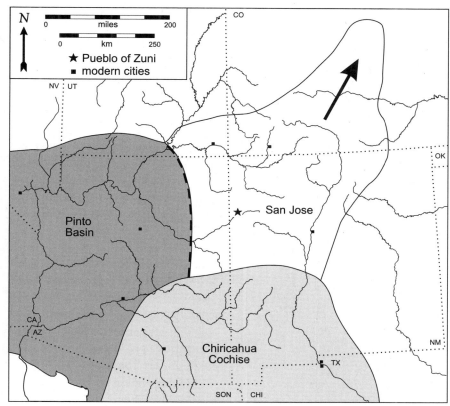

Figure 2.3. Distribution of southwestern technocomplexes, ca. 3000 BC.

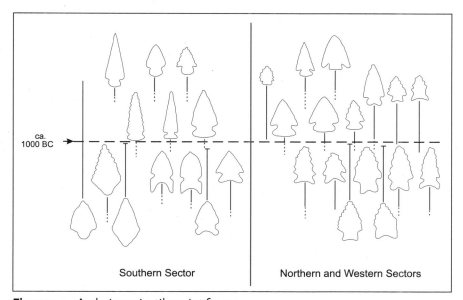

Figure 2.4. Archaic projectile point forms.

can be correlated with Tanoan divergence from Uto-Aztecan.

The next glimpse of the American Southwest dates about 1000 BC (see fig. 2.5). In the northeastern region in northern New Mexico concrete evidence is available for an unbroken development from late San Jose at about 2000 BC into a period tentatively termed Proto-Basketmaker at about 1000 BC and ultimately into Basketmaker II and III. In southern Arizona there are indications of expansion of the Cochise slightly farther west than before, and west-central New Mexico suggests minor northward expansion of Cochise. However, the most significant development is obviously the northward expansion of the Cochise in northeastern Arizona into regions previously characterized by early San Jose materials.

Surface collections suggest that in some but not all areas of northeastern Arizona late Chiricahua / San Pedro Cochise materials entirely replace the San Jose / Proto-Basketmaker assemblages by ca. 1500–1000 BC. It is here suggested that later in-place development in northeastern Arizona resulted in many of the distinctive characteristics of the Western Basketmaker, the Kayenta Anasazi, and ultimately the historic Hopi. The arrival in this area of these southern groups about 1500–1000 BC (3,000–3,500 years ago) agrees well with linguistic estimations of a Pima-Shoshonean split about 3,500 years ago. Further diversification may have occurred shortly thereafter, as suggested by the linguistic evidence of Hopi divergence from the Numic group and from Luisenic and Tubatulabalic. It is possible, though not yet proved, that this is involved in the origin and development of the Kayenta-related Puebloid cultures of Utah and southern Nevada. Alternatively, Cochise-like intrusions from the south may

materials represent in contradistinction to the northern and western groups a distinct and easily definable entity. These cultural-historical differences are reflected in this comparative presentation of projectile point forms (see fig. 2.4). In terms of linguistic relations there is very little to work with. However, it is not impossible that with vastly more data eastern and western divisions of the expanding Cochise will be recognized and

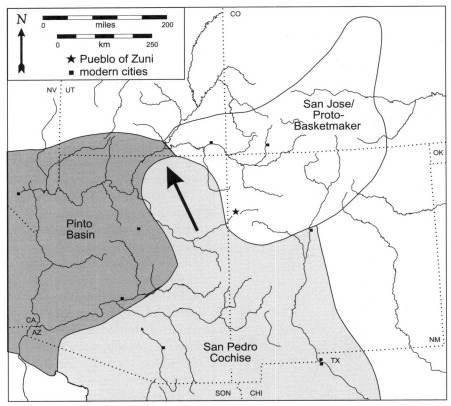

Figure 2.5. Distribution of southwestern technocomplexes, ca. 1000 BC.

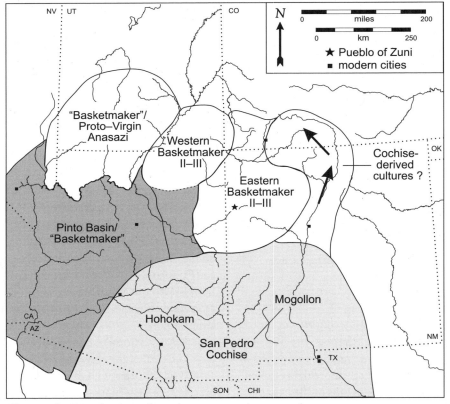

Figure 2.6. Distribution of southwestern technocomplexes, AD 1–400.

have occurred elsewhere in the Southern California–Nevada region more or less independently of developments in northeastern Arizona. At the present time there is no archaeological evidence for or against this latter proposition. In any case, there seems to be good reason to suggest that by at least 1000 BC in northern Arizona and possibly the southern Great Basin Cochise-related groups were present that can ultimately be correlated with the northern division of Uto-Aztecans.

By the period AD 1–400, represented in figure 2.6, it is evident that several significant events have taken place or are taking place. The central Colorado province was evidently abandoned as an area of permanent occupation by southwestern groups about 500 BC. There is increasingly impressive evidence of the intrusion into northern New Mexico and southern Colorado of groups who seem very closely related to the Cochise-derived Mogollon culture. It is perhaps significant that Davis's (1959) suggested date for the earliest division of Tanoan is about 2,000 years ago, or AD 1. As noted above, there is concrete evidence for the development of the early Anasazi (Basketmaker II–III) of northwestern New Mexico directly from a San Jose / Pinto Basketmaker continuum. This, plus evidence from the Durango and Chaco areas, suggests a continued unity for this Eastern Basketmaker II material. Although poorly known, the contemporary Basketmaker remains of northeastern Arizona and southern Utah are easily distinguishable in detailed typology and have many features reminiscent of San Pedro Cochise. There is scant evidence from the southern Utah–northwestern Arizona area, but it seems quite possible that, as Gunnerson (1962) suggests, the scattered "Basketmaker" materials represent the beginnings of

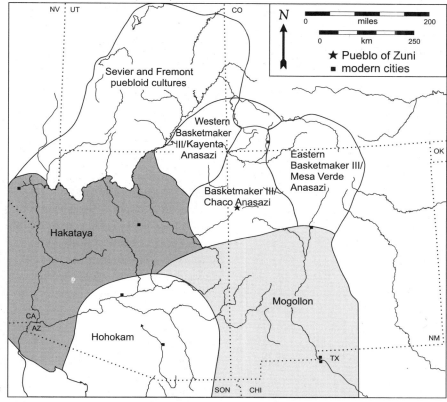

Figure 2.7. Distribution of southwestern technocomplexes, AD 500–900.

the development of the Virgin Anasazi. Whether this is confined to the Virgin area, as suggested by Gunnerson, or whether some dispersal had begun to take place is not known. In the west assemblages earlier labeled "Basketmaker II" such as that at Willow Beach (Schroeder 1961) may now be understood in the light of new evidence such as that from Rose Springs. They evidently represent developments out of the long Pinto Basin continuum in much the same fashion that the early Anasazi of New Mexico evolved from San Jose origins. The similarity of this material to Anasazi/Basketmaker II is of the same order as the similarity between Pinto Basin and San Jose. In the south the pioneer Hohokam in the west and the early phases of Mogollon in the east evidently developed out of San Pedro Cochise origins.

In the succeeding period, AD 500–900 (see fig. 2.7), significant changes

continue to be made. In the northern Rio Grande proper strong Mesa Verde influence is evidently exerted on the brown pottery Mogollon-related peoples, so that in the same way as it occurred later in the south they are essentially absorbed by Mesa Verde Anasazi culture. The Piedra district became a local version of Mesa Verde, and it is even possible, as Ellis (1964) suggests, that some mixing of population occurred. In the Largo-Gallina zone, however, a distinctive regional culture evolved directly from the brownware-using Sambrito phase.

In the old San Jose/Anasazi core area, beginning in Basketmaker III, there are indications of evolving regional styles such as later distinguish the Mesa Verde and the Chaco. Contemporary cultures of northeastern Arizona and southeastern Utah, the nascent Kayenta, exhibit marked differences even during Bas-

ketmaker III in ways frequently reminiscent of Mogollon and Hohokam. By AD 900–950 the Sevier and Fremont Puebloid cultures had developed from the Kayenta-derived Virgin branch and spread rapidly north and east (Gunnerson 1962). In the Hakataya area in-place local developments exhibit differential influence of the Anasazi and Hohokam cultures (Schroeder 1957, 1960). Finally, in the south the characteristic features of the Hohokam are by now well established. Whether this reflects Mexican influence or intrusions is beyond the scope of this chapter. To the east the Mogollon evolved less dramatically; in some areas they seem to reflect an overlap of Mogollon and southern Anasazi influences.

By the period AD 900–1200 (see fig. 2.8) we are entering the realm of the relatively well known in southwestern prehistory, and the period can be dealt with swiftly. Groups from the northern Rio Grande had moved into the Taos area during Pueblo II, while others continued to develop in place. These are believed by Ellis (1964) to represent the Tiwa and Tewa, respectively, and the glottochronological estimate of Tiwa/Tewa divergence fits well. Other Tanoan groups were evidently present in the Rio Grande valley but are not well known. To the west and south regional variants of the core Anasazi culture are now visible, as at Mesa Verde and Chaco. The Kayenta branch abandoned certain of its northern regions or was submerged by Mesa Verde influence. To the north the maximum extent of the northern Puebloid culture was reached. In the Hakataya area in-place development continued, with local and temporary intrusions from the Kayenta and Hohokam. In the Hohokam area proper during the Classic period certain basic pre-Colonial lifeways were reestablished, with possible influence

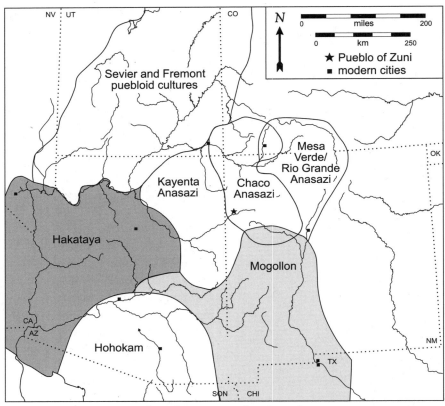

Figure 2.8. Distribution of southwestern technocomplexes, AD 900–1200.

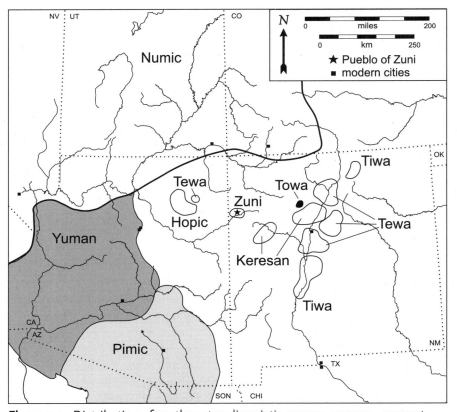

Figure 2.9. Distribution of southwestern linguistic groups, AD 1200–present.

or incursions from the north. To the east the old Mogollon traditions were overwhelmed by massive Anasazi influence, perhaps significantly of the Chacoan variety.

From a point near the end of the preceding period until the ethnographic present (see fig. 2.9) the American Southwest again witnessed considerable demographic change. Most important was the abandonment of the northern Anasazi area and the movement of peoples into the Rio Grande valley. In the northern Rio Grande both archaeological and linguistic evidence indicate that the Tiwa, derived from earlier movements from the Piedra district, split into their northern and southern divisions during the fourteenth and fifteenth centuries AD. The Towa evidently moved south from the Largo-Gallina region to their present position at Jemez and Pecos. Near the end of Pueblo III the Tewa moved south along the Chama into the already populated Galisteo Basin and into the Santa Fe region.

A large group from the Chaco area evidently settled in the Cochiti area. In the Acoma area Dittert (1959; Dittert and Ruppé 1951) found evidence of a local population with continuity well into the San Jose–related preceramic who were joined by increments from the Mesa Verde during the fourteenth century to produce the historic Acoma. Just north of Albuquerque there may be indications that a similar local development from late San Jose onward, with increments from the Chaco area, leads into the historic Zia / Santa Ana. In brief, the total complexion of the evidence on Keres origins thus strongly indicates continuity with the core of the old San Jose / Anasazi tradition. To the west there seems little doubt that the Kayenta Anasazi, with increments from several adjacent groups, is ancestral to the historic Hopi. In southern Utah and Nevada Gunnerson (1962) has suggested that the Fremont culture, stripped of its more sedentary habits, evolved into the Ute / Southern Paiute (Yutish) people, the Sevier into the Shoshone / Comanche, and the Virgin into the Northern Paiute. Goss (1965), however, disputes this on linguistic evidence and places the position of Numic dispersal in Southern California. At present, definitive evidence is simply not available. On the whole, however, it seems eminently possible that the northern Puebloid cultures are intimately involved in the ancestry of the Numic-speaking peoples, but it is doubtful whether specific ties will be practical for some time. Schroeder (1957) has shown convincing evidence for the derivation of several Yuman groups from Hakataya antecedents. Di Peso (1956) has demonstrated the derivation of Piman speakers from the Classic period Hohokam. For the Mogollon the period after AD 1300 is one of progressive shrinkage, abandonment, and absorption by other groups. Some may have moved south into Mexico, and it is just possible that the now-extinct Piro represent a group derived from the Jornada branch of the Mogollon.

To recapitulate, then, the following developmental structure for the American Southwest is suggested by a consideration of the archaeological and linguistic evidence of the last 7,000 years. First, in terms of geographic origins it is believed that the data overwhelmingly support the hypothesized origin of Uto-Aztecan in the northern Mexico–southern Arizona region. There is not one shred of genuine cultural-historical evidence to indicate any major southward movement out of the Great Basin until very recent times. There is scanty but growing and internally consistent archaeological evidence of movements from the south into the northern Southwest and the southern Great Basin areas and during time periods that agree remarkably well with relevant data from historic linguistics. The gathering weight of linguistic data supports these views, and they do not conflict in significant ways with other archaeological evidence farther south. There is increasing evidence for the identification of Yuman with the Lake Mohave / Pinto Basin / Hakataya development and the Keresan with the Rio Grande complex / San Jose / core Anasazi. The strong possibility of the derivation of the latter from the former lends weight to Sapir's (1929) original correlation between Keresan and Yuman and underlines the need for additional comparative linguistic studies.

Finally, the following specific developmental correlations are suggested:

Cochise > Hohokam (Ootam) > Piman

Cochise > early Mogollon and mixed eastern Anasazi > Tanoan

Cochise (?) > Jornada Mogollon > Piro Tanoan

late Chiricahua and San Pedro Cochise > Western Basketmaker > Kayenta Anasazi > Hopi

San Pedro Cochise > Virgin Anasazi > Numic (Plateau Shoshonean)

Lake Mohave > Pinto Basin > Hakataya > Yuman
La Bajada or Rio Grande complex > San Jose > core eastern Anasazi (Mesa Verde, Chaco) > Keresan

Notes

1. This previously unpublished paper was presented at the 32nd Annual Meeting of the Society for American Archaeology, held in Ann Arbor, Michigan, May 4–6, 1967. It has been incorrectly cited elsewhere (è.g., in Hale and Harris 1979; Riley 1995) in that the location of the meetings has been given as Portales, New Mexico; clearly, this is where the paper was written, not where it was read.

We have not altered the text in any major way except as follows. First, we have made editorial changes to correct grammatical and spelling errors and to ensure continuity in style. Second, while the names of various scholars were cited in the original, there were no dates given for the citations, and there was no bibliography included. With the help of Jane Hill we have attempted to include the appropriate dates to go with the names and thus to construct at least a basic bibliography for the paper. Finally, we have added this and other endnotes as we have deemed appropriate or necessary in order to clarify and expand upon points made in the text.

2. For alternative views see Reed (1946, 1949), Trager (1967), Wendorf and Reed (1955), and Whorf and Trager (1937).

3. Davis (1959) actually proposed four, not three, Keresan groups: Cochiti; Santo Domingo and San Felipe; Santa Ana and Zia; and Acoma and Laguna. For a discussion of the various glottochronological findings concerning archaeological-linguistic connections as they existed at the time when Irwin-Williams wrote this paper see Fox (1967:23–30). As Irwin-Williams notes, Sapir (1929) suggested a relationship between Yuman and Keresan, one she makes use of in her reconstructions. However, more recent work (Rood 1973) suggests a remote relationship between Caddoan and Keresan (see Hill 2002). Could it be, then, that Proto-Keresan speakers were a remnant segment of a Paleoindian population represented by the Plano / Eden-Scottsbluff complex, a population that remained in the American Southwest after the plainsward retraction of Eden-Scottsbluff (Proto-Caddoan speakers?) that Irwin-Williams shows in figure 2.3?

3 The Zuni Language in Southwestern Areal Context

Jane H. Hill

The Zuni language is spoken only in the Pueblo of Zuni and its dependent communities by ca. 8,000 people. There is very little dialectal variation reported for the language, although Cushing believed that speech in some ritual contexts was in an "archaic" register (Green 1990:101, 155). The language is a "linguistic isolate"; that is, it has no known relatives. In the first section of this chapter I discuss the concept of linguistic isolate and its implications for using linguistic methods to reconstruct Zuni history. I then evaluate the major claims against the hypothesis of the linguistic isolation of Zuni.[1]

While Zuni is a linguistic isolate, the language is not "isolated." For at least the last 1,000 years speakers of Zuni have been part of a Puebloan regional system, in contact with speakers of several other languages, including at least Hopi, Keresan, and Piman. In the second section of the chapter I discuss this language contact, its impact on the Zuni language, and its significance for the reconstruction of Zuni prehistory.

Zuni as a Linguistic Isolate

Historical linguists recognize four major reasons why two or more languages might resemble one another. Only the first two types, "genetic" and "areal" relationships, provide evidence for the historian. In genetic relationship the languages share a common ancestor. In areal relationship the languages have exchanged linguistic material through the activity of bilingual or multilingual speakers. The third type is "typological" relationship. For instance, in both Zuni and Japanese the verb is always the last element of the sentence. Since many languages around the world, most of them unrelated to one another genetically or areally, share this common typological property, we can draw no historical conclusions from it.

The last reason languages might resemble one another is "chance" relationship, where words resemble one another by accident. Such accidental resemblance in the lexicon is surprisingly common, especially in the words that occur at highest frequency. The reason for this, according to "Zipf's Law," is that common words are short, often consisting of single syllables. Since syllable structure is relatively restricted and since the repertoire of sounds in human languages is not enormous, it is inevitable that in any pair of randomly chosen languages one will encounter words of similar meaning that also have similar sounds.

The likelihood of chance resem-

blance is elevated when we turn to areas of the lexicon that are likely to be "nursery words," reflecting the even more restricted syllable and sound repertoire of small children. These include primary kin terms, words for basic body parts and body fluids, and words for basic bodily processes. Chance resemblance is also likely in sound-imitative words. Words that are likely to be sound-imitative include names for birds, insects, and small animals such as frogs and salamanders and words for "hit," "slap," "blow," "suck," "bubble," and other noise-making activities. The likelihood of chance resemblance is also elevated when we look at very high frequency affixal morphemes such as markers of person and number, plurals, negatives, and so on, since these tend to be very short. I elaborate at this length because the possibility of chance resemblance is grossly underestimated by most nonlinguists (and, unfortunately, by some linguists). A good sense of the likelihood of chance resemblance is especially important as we try to determine the status of isolates. Especially when dealing with deep time depths, it is often difficult to distinguish chance resemblance from resemblances that are the result of common ancestry or contact. Indeed, much of the methodology in historical linguistics is dedicated to helping us accomplish this differentiation.

When we linguists call Zuni a linguistic isolate, we mean that it has no known genetic relatives, that is, languages that resemble it because they descend from a common ancestor shared with Zuni. What, exactly, does this position in regard to Zuni imply? Most historical linguists believe that there were probably no more than a very few episodes of entry into the Americas. It is unlikely that Zuni is the unique descendant of one such entry. Thus, we assume that Zuni has some distant relatives among the languages of the hemisphere, but we have not identified them. While all possible pairs of languages have not been tested, many likely possibilities have been explored by linguists, since finding relatives for an isolate would constitute a major discovery.

Several processes can give rise to a linguistic isolate. An isolate might be the only surviving daughter of a language family that once had other members. Evidence for profound disturbance of populations in the U.S. Southwest and, as pointed out by Diehl (chap. 11, this vol.), in northwestern Mexico from the thirteenth to the eighteenth centuries makes this "sole survivor" scenario a possibility that cannot be ruled out. Or an isolate might be the trace of a very old single-language family that maintained dynamic homogeneity over a very long period of time. Nichols (1992) points out that this situation may be fairly common. Thus, the Zuni protocommunity may have gone its own way 7,000 or 8,000 years ago, maintaining its integrity as a single language community (of the type that Golla calls "compact" [2000:60]) over a very long period of time without undergoing any radiation. If Zuni had diverged from surviving related languages only 4,000 or 5,000 years ago

I am fairly sure that linguists would have found them. Thus, it is likely that any genetic links between Zuni and other surviving languages of North America date back at least 7,000 or 8,000 years, or near the beginning of the Archaic.[2]

Proposals to Deisolate Zuni

Newman (1964) reviewed efforts to find genetic relatives for Zuni up to the time of his own proposal, that Zuni is a sister of "California Penutian." Sapir proposed "a remote linkage between Zuni, Uto-Aztecan, Tanoan and Kiowa" (1929:139). Greenberg (1987), following Newman, placed Zuni within the Penutian subfamily of Amerind. So the first approach to the question, Is Zuni really a linguistic isolate? posed by the organizers of this volume must critique these proposals.

Sapir's (1929) proposal was published without supporting evidence (and with a question mark next to "Zuni" in the list of "Aztec-Tanoan" languages) in an article in the *Encyclopaedia Britannica*. At this period Sapir was very taken with typological evidence of the type that is no longer thought to be probative in establishing genetic relations, and in the article he used typological summaries to characterize the six North American linguistic groups proposed there. Only one part of Sapir's proposal linking Zuni, Uto-Aztecan, Kiowa, and Tanoan has turned out to be right: the relationship between Kiowa and Tanoan is considered to have been demonstrated by Hale (1962, 1967). Whorf and Trager's (1937) famous paper on Uto-Aztecan and Tanoan is deeply problematic (see Campbell 1997; Hill 2002), in spite of Greenberg's (1987:40) endorsement.[3] Most of their etymologies fall apart on methodological grounds, and the remainder do not convince

the specialist looking for strong arguments that the resemblances are due to shared common ancestry rather than language contact or chance resemblance.[4]

Zuni and California Penutian. Newman's (1964) proposal, that the California Penutian languages (Miwokan, Costanoan, Yokutsan, Maiduan, and Wintuan) and Zuni shared a common ancestor, is by far the best-known argument against Zuni linguistic isolation. Lynn Nichols (1999, personal communication 2001) states that a rumor has circulated for years that the paper was intended as a hoax on Carl Voegelin, the longtime editor of the *International Journal of American Linguistics*, in which Newman (1964) appeared. In investigating this further Nichols and I have identified two people who state that Mary Haas told them that Newman told her that he wrote it as a joke. Haas is cited in the acknowledgments for the paper, as is George Trager. Two younger scholars cited in the acknowledgments, William Shipley and Catherine Callaghan, were well known even at the time as strong opponents of long-range comparison of the type that Newman seemed to be attempting.

If the paper is indeed a hoax (and I think it is), it is a very elaborate one. Newman was a major expert on Yokuts, an important group of languages located by some within California Penutian; indeed, his grammar of Yawelmani Yokuts (Newman 1944) is an order of magnitude deeper and more detailed than his minor grammatical sketches of Zuni. At the time of its publication the paper was widely discussed by serious scholars.[5] However, inside Americanist linguistics it was never widely accepted. Indeed, we might see the paper as one of the turning points that led to the reaction against long-distance comparison in the Americas and the "splitting" tendencies that reached their apogee in the famous volume edited by Campbell and Mithun in 1979. Greenberg's uncritical acceptance of Newman's conclusions was one of the points singled out for criticism by several reviewers of Greenberg (1987).

The basic criticism of Newman (1964) is that his sets of proposed cognates do not pass the test of distinguishing resemblances due to contact and chance from resemblances that are due to a common ancestry. If the paper is indeed a hoax, this is of course understandable. However, I think it is worth reviewing the paper carefully so that a nonspecialist can see what specialists find objectionable in it.

First, Newman does not have a reconstruction of California Penutian. Thus, he is comparing Zuni to four Costanoan languages, three Maiduan languages, six Miwokan languages and reconstructed Proto-Miwok, three Wintuan languages, and 10 dialects of Yokuts. This gives him ample opportunity for "cherry picking," that is, finding a resemblant form in only one of the 26 languages (usually it is Yawelmani Yokuts, the language Newman knew best), greatly increasing the likelihood of chance resemblance. Furthermore, since Newman knew that Yawelmani Yokuts has very complex systems of vowel harmony and vowel deletion, he simply ignored the vowels, increasing still further the likelihood of chance resemblance, since he only had to look for resemblant consonants.

The reason Newman has no reconstruction of California Penutian is that no convincing one exists, although Newman does cite Pitkin and Shipley (1958). California Penutian was originally proposed by Dixon and Kroeber (1913) and was accepted by

Sapir but has not fared well in the last 40 years (see DeLancey and Golla 1997 for a very fair-minded overview). Linguists now generally accept that Yokuts and the Utian languages (Costanoan and Miwok) have been shown to be genetically related as "Yok-Utian" (by Callaghan 1997). However, the consensus is that Maiduan and Wintuan cannot be shown to be more closely related genetically to Yok-Utian than to any of a dozen other small language families of Oregon and California. There has been intense contact among the languages of central California for a very long time, and specialists in the field are not convinced that areal resemblances due to this contact can yet be separated from similarities that are due to common ancestry.

We can dismiss the "structural similarities" proposed by Newman. The first of these is that Zuni and California Penutian share an underlying Consonant-Vowel-(Consonant) (CV[C]) syllable structure. This is the world's most common syllable structure and has no historical utility at all. The second is that the order of suffixes in verbs, from left to right, in both Zuni and California Penutian is (1) thematic/derivational and (2) inflectional (Tense/Aspect/ Modality). This is the universal order of affixes in verb-final languages. The fact that derivational affixes are closer to the verb root than the inflectional ones are is one of the defining features that distinguishes derivation from inflection. So, like CV(C) syllable structure, this fact has no historical utility. The few "likenesses" in the affix forms that Newman suggests are not linked to his sound correspondences, so they have little evidentiary value.

Newman's major evidence takes the form of 187 "cognate sets" (his terminology), developed by the method of picking through the available lexi-

con of 26 California languages and dialects in California Penutian to find words that look like Zuni words. Based on these sets he proposes 27 sound correspondences for consonants and reconstructs Proto–California Penutian/Zuni consonants. Of these 27 reconstructions 14 have unexplained exceptions. Furthermore, Nichols (1999) states that the sets include "obvious Keresan loan vocabulary" among the Zuni items.

Among his 187 cognate sets Newman considers sets (124) through (187) to be "problematic." Among the 123 "nonproblematic" sets he assays reconstructions of Proto–California Penutian/Zuni for only 53. It is unclear, then, why the 70 sets for which he proposes no reconstruction are not as "problematic" as sets (124) through (187).

Let us consider the problems with cognate sets in more detail. Here I attend only to the 123 sets in the first part of Newman's list. Among these we find sets manifesting the following methodological problems:

1. Twenty-six sets are words that are clearly sound symbolic, including words for "blow," "suck," "slap," with shapes that are widely found in the languages of the Americas and elsewhere.[6]
2. Twenty-one sets resemble each other in only one consonant (i.e., in a single sound in words of varying length).[7] For instance, set (83) compares Zuni *ʔaʔku* "purple sage" with Coast Miwok *hukúʔme* "sage"; note also that Newman provides no correspondences for vowels, so the shared *u* doesn't count.
3. Fourteen sets involve problematic semantic relationships.[8] For instance, in set (72) Newman includes Yokuts words meaning

both "white oak" and "poison oak" to compare to a Zuni word for "oak." In spite of their English names, "poison oak" (*Rhus* spp.) and "oak" (*Quercus* spp.) are totally unrelated and in no way resemble each other in form or function. Newman must have known this after a decade wandering around the Tehachapis talking to Yokuts elders, so why he included "poison oak" is a real mystery unless the paper is indeed a hoax.

4. Eleven sets are merely resemblant and do not satisfy Newman's own sound correspondences (which have many exceptions in any case).[9]

5. Seven sets are names for birds or small animals of no economic importance that tend to have sound-imitative or expressive "varmint," "critter" words.[10] The bird names are almost all members of widely known areal sets that are scattered all over western North America and are found in many other languages besides those included in Newman's sample. Callaghan (1997) notes this problem and does not include bird names in her resemblant sets for Yok-Utian.[11]

6. Five sets are for primary kin terms.[12]

7. Four sets have closely resemblant forms in Uto-Aztecan languages so are almost certainly areal.[13]

8. Sets (70) and (123) are the words for "yes" and "no," which are all over North America in very similar forms. (The stereotype that Native Americans say "How!" for "Yes!" actually has some basis in fact.)

9. Other sets share a variety of different problems. Many sets share several of the above problems.

Sound-imitative forms, bird names, and primary kin terms are identified in the early chapters of any standard textbook in historical linguistics as problematic and to be invoked only with caution. Thus, it does not inspire confidence to find a high proportion of such words invoked in a daring long-distance comparison.

This leaves a residue of 27 sets that are, to a permissive mind, of potential interest.[14] Among these Newman gives reconstructions for 15; that is, he considers that he has enough evidence for regular sound correspondence, the sine qua non for demonstrating common ancestry, to attempt a reconstruction. Looking carefully at these sets for which he gives a reconstruction, we can identify some worrying questions. For instance, Newman reconstructs set (27) *kʔaš* "fish." The cognate forms are Zuni *kʔaššita*, Lake Miwok *káṣ·i* "salmon," *ká·c* "fish," Yawelmani Yokuts *kʔaṭʔa·natʔ* "salamander," *ka·ṭʔnaʔ* "mythical fish." However, in Miller and Davis's (1963) reconstruction of Keresan, published only a year before Newman's paper in the same journal, we find set (287) *skʔà·šʔ* "fish." Shaul (1982) points out that Zuni *kʔaššita* "fish" is obviously a Keresan loanword, and he is supported by Nichols (1993).

A second problem is very minimal representation in daughter languages. Thus, among the 26 remaining possibly interesting resemblant sets in Newman (1964), sets (30) "to follow," (34) "glutton," (62) "lamp," (66) "mahogany," (73) "to take out," (76) "to play," (97) "to spend," (103) "to swell," and (107) "to tear" have cognates only between Zuni and Yawelmani Yokuts. It seems very risky to take a single form in Yawelmani and reconstruct directly to Proto–California Penutian / Zuni.

Turning to another problem, for set (48) "head" Newman reconstructs *ʔošokʷ*, based on Zuni *ʔošokʷkʷi*, Rumsen (Costanoan) *uṭ*, and Yawelmani *ʔoṭʔow*. (He also gives a Mountain Maidu form *ʔonó* in parentheses.) Newman selects the medial sibilant as the reconstruction because in his sample several of the Yokuts varieties and Coast Miwok show sibilants. However, Callaghan (1997:29) reconstructs with glottalized retroflex stops Proto-Yokuts *ʔoṭʔaw* "head, hair" and Proto-Miwok *úṭu* "whiskers" and considers these to be likely cognates. A cognacy between Proto-Yokuts *ṭʔ* and Zuni *š* is of course possible, but Callaghan's reconstruction is not favorable to Newman's case.

For set (112) "tobacco" the cognates to Zuni *ponne* "cigarette" are both Maiduan: Mountain Maidu *pân* "tobacco" and Nisenan *pan* "pipe." Maiduan is not today considered to be part of a California Penutian genetic entity. Furthermore, Newman suggests that all of these words for "tobacco" are related to his set (7) "to blow." If that is the case, the set must be discarded in any case as probably sound-imitative.

In summary, the number of interesting resemblances that remain after careful critique of Newman's (1964) cognate sets is so small that it is entirely possible that these resemblances are simply due to chance.

I do not want to imply that I consider Newman's hypothesis completely irredeemable. What I do want to suggest is that, even if it is not a hoax, it is emphatically not a final resolution of the long-standing conundrum of Zuni isolation. Yet Newman's proposal is often accepted more or less uncritically. To the best of my knowledge, the few paragraphs above now constitute the most detailed critique (in writing) of Newman's paper anywhere in the Americanist literature![15]

Zuni, Greenberg's "Penutian," and "Amerind." Finally, let us turn to Greenberg's (1987) notion of "Penutian." For Greenberg this is a very large entity, including everything that anybody has ever proposed to be linked to the original California Penutian (Chinookan, Oregon, Plateau, Tsimshian). In addition, Greenberg adds Yukian and the Gulf languages and Zuni, yielding a superfamily that stretches from Queen Charlotte Island to Yucatán and from Cape Mendocino to the Gulf Coast of Florida.

Zuni items appear as cognates in Greenberg's Penutian sets (6) "angry," (7) "arm," (19) "blood," (60) "eat," (75) "feather," (87) "full," (90) "give," (92) "grandmother" (Greenberg uses a word different from Newman's: Greenberg uses *hotta*; Newman uses *kawu* "older sister"), (93) "grass," (98) "hair" (Greenberg uses a word different from Newman's: Greenberg uses *ci* "hair of body"; Newman uses *taya* "hair of head"), (102) "hard," (107) "heart," (150) "look 1" (Zuni "eye"), (153) "make 2," (213) "shoot" (Greenberg gives a form, *towo* "make a thundering sound," different from Newman's *lhak-u* "shoot, stab"), (226) "snow 1," (234) "steal," (236) "stone," and (246) "tell 2." Of these 19 Zuni items, only seven—(19), (75), (90), (93), (107), (150), and (226)—are in Newman's (1964) list.

Why is it that Greenberg does not restrict himself to Newman's list, based on Newman's firsthand control of both Zuni and the California languages? The reason is that Greenberg has cast his net much wider, searching for resemblances not just in the 26 languages and dialects in California that Newman used but in literally hundreds of languages all over North America. This permits Greenberg to open up Newman's (1958) Zuni dictionary and

mine it for any number of new possibilities. Thus, the likelihood that Greenberg will encounter chance resemblances has enormously increased, and we can be fairly sure that he has found many. Many of the Penutian etymologies include only two or three languages separated by thousands of kilometers. For instance, set (6) "angry" includes only Zuni and a word from a Mixe-Zoquean language, Tetontepec.

The result in the opposite direction—that Greenberg uses only seven of Newman's 187 items—is not surprising. As the net of comparison grows larger, relatively solid results (here I give Newman more credit than most would, but compared to Greenberg [1987], Newman [1964] is a model of propriety) drop off geometrically.[16] By now the identification of howlers in Greenberg's lists is old news, but I cannot resist noting just one. While Newman (1964) chooses for comparison the term *lhak-u* "shoot, stab," Greenberg uses a different word, *towo*, for Zuni "shoot" in his set (213). When we turn to Newman's dictionary, we indeed find this form, glossed as "make a thundering sound, shoot." To the best of my knowledge, shooting atlatl darts—the only way to shoot anything in North America at the time of the breakup of "Amerind" or "Penutian"—does not "make a thundering sound." This is an egregious anachronism; Zuni *towo*, a sound-imitative word, cannot have meant "shoot" until the introduction of firearms.

A Snapshot of Lexical Data: How an "Isolate" Looks on the Surface

Let us now turn from the published proposals on long-distance relationships for Zuni and look at the question of Zuni "isolation" using the "method of mass comparison" (although necessarily on a very

small scale). The purpose of this exercise—a classic one that gives the neophyte a feel for what related vs. unrelated languages look like at a casual glance—is to give the reader a sense of exactly how genetically isolated Zuni really is.

In table 3.1 I have listed 22 items of "basic vocabulary" for which I happen to have lexical items at hand. Since "basic vocabulary" is relatively resistant to borrowing, items like these are preferred for preliminary exploration of possible resemblances due to descent from a common ancestor. I chart the lexical items that best translate these in nine languages / dialects: Hopi (Hopi Dictionary Project 1998) and Tohono O'odham (Uto-Aztecan) (Saxton et al. 1983); Towa and Kiowa (Kiowa-Tanoan) (Hale 1962); Acoma and Santa Ana (Keresan) (Miller and Davis 1963); Zuni (Newman 1958); and Lake Miwok (Callaghan 1965). The languages are chosen to represent the major southwestern groups (although Yuman is absent) and Yok-Utian, one element of Newman's California Penutian. I happen to have a dictionary of Lake Miwok in my office, and it is no more absurd to depend completely on Lake Miwok for Yok-Utian than it is to lean as heavily on Yawelmani Yokuts as does Newman (although it could be argued that Yawelmani, spoken in the southern Tehachapis, is geographically closer to Zuni than Lake Miwok, spoken in Lake County north of San Francisco Bay). However, at this level Yok-Utian is Yok-Utian—if Zuni is its sister, we should be just as likely to find cognates in Lake Miwok as in Yawelmani Yokuts. Note that the transcriptions in the table are not identical to those in the sources; they are an approximation using fonts available to me. But they will serve for the present exercise.

The reader will immediately be able to see the relationship between

Table 3.1 What Isolation Looks Like in Basic Vocabulary Lists.

Gloss	Hopi	Tohono O'odham	Towa	Kiowa	Acoma	Santa Ana	Zuni	Lake Miwok
arrow	hoohɨ	hapot	kyã́a	sɔɔ-biⁿ "quiver"	ʔísdûwa	ʔísdúwa	sho	kíwwa
ashes	qötsvi	matai	kʸàhʷǽⁿʔ	sɔɔpʰa̜n	mʔiîş̌ʔai	mʔísç̌ʔai	lu	wiílok
blood	ingwa	ii̧ʔid	ʔ̧ɨⁿ	ʔóⁿ-m	mʔaáçʔi	mʔáʔaçʔí	ʔate	kíccaw
drink	hiiko	ʔii̧ʔi	šíîⁿ	tʰóⁿ-m	-skʔa	-skʔă	tutu	ʔúṣṣu
eye	poosi	wuhi	sɛ̃	ta	-ná	-na	tuna	ṣút
fat, lard	wihɨ	giigɨ̆	sɨ̧ⁿʔ	toⁿ-n	ʔíṣáţʔḷ	ʔiṣaţʔi	ʔisha	ṣétta
feces	kʷita	biit	kʸæ̀ǽ-	sɔɔ-gʸa	ʔiisa	ʔiisa	mahe	keé
give	maqa	maak	mǽ	maaⁿ-gɔ	-dí	-di	ʔuçʔḷ, lhejaa	hiína, tóla, wáya
hair (head)	höömi	kuṣpo	ɬóoʔla	pʰɔɔ-	háazá̧nʔɨ̆	háazá̧nɨ̆	taya	ṣaápa
hand	maa	nowɨ̆	màⁿté	mɔ́ɔⁿ-dɔ	hamʔás-diini	hamʔǎs-díʔini	ʔasi	ʔúkku
hear	navota	kaa	ţʔæ̀-kʸe	ţʔɔ	-ká	-kaá	hatiyaaw	ʔálu
house	kiihɨ	kii	tɨ̃̀-	tóo	-mʔa	-mʔă	heshota, kʔaqe	weéyi
I	nɨʔ	ʔaanʸi	níîⁿ	nɔ́ɔⁿ	hínu-mʔé	hínŭ	hoʔ	kánni
moon	mɨ̈yaw	maaṣad	pʔaɛ̃̆œ	pʔɔ-	dâawʔáaʔçi̧	dáwáaçă̧	yachu	komé-
mouth	moʔa	činʸ	kʸɛ̆ekʷa	so-ʔɔ-l	-kʔa	-kʔă	ʔawati	lúppe
night/black	tookila	čuhug	hɨ̃	kʰoⁿ	-pišu	-pǎš̆ɨ̆	tehlhi "become night," kwʔi "black"	káwul, ʔúme
see	postala	nʸɨid	mɨ̂ⁿ	bôⁿ	-kača	-kǎčǎ	an-kʔoha-kʔa	ʔúṭe-G
smoke	kʷiitsingʷ	kuubs	ʔè	ʔaa-gʸa	gurʔárʔaka	kʔúrarʔǎkǎ	poklhi	kaál
sun	taawa	taṣ	pɛ̃	pa-e	ʔuṣaâça	uṣaâça	yato-kkʸa	hií
tooth	tama	taatamɨ̆	kʷőoⁿ	zóⁿ	-ti	-tɨ̆	ʔoʔna	kút
two	lööyöʔ	gook	wɨ̀-š	yí	dyuûwʔée	dyuûmií	kʷili(n)	ʔóṭṭa
water	paahɨ	ṣuudagɨ̆	pʔœ̀	pʔɔ	cʔíci	cʔícɨ̆	kʔa	kik

Acoma and Santa Ana, which are in fact two dialects of the same language, Keresan. The relationship between Towa and Kiowa is also obvious, with a couple of dramatic and nonobvious yet very regular sound correspondences (e.g., Towa /kʸ/ = Kiowa /s/—this is the sort of evidence that is even more convincing than obvious similarity). The relationship between Hopi and Tohono O'odham is a bit harder to see for the nonspecialist. Hopi and Tohono O'odham are in two different main branches of Uto-Aztecan and are probably separated at a time depth of at least 4,000 years. In fact, there are 13 cognates—words related by regular sound correspondence—in the 22 items, but the average reader will probably be able to spot only three or four.[17] The reader will even be able to notice some of the items that tempted Whorf and Trager (1937), as with "blood," "give," "hand," and "water," where there are Uto-Aztecan and Kiowa-Tanoan resemblances. But Zuni clearly has nothing to do with any of these languages or with Lake Miwok! If Newman's hypothesis were correct, we would expect to see one or two tempting candidates among the Zuni/Lake Miwok pairs. Of course, this is a very small sample, but the situation would not change if we expanded the list to 100 or 200 words. The related languages would look even more related, and still nothing would come up for Zuni.

The famous Amerind /n/ in the word for "I" is obvious in the table; note that Zuni and Lake Miwok stand out as *not* exhibiting /n/, which is quite interesting. However, they are not the only languages in North America that have this property.

The same effect that we see in the table above, with no convincing resemblances between Zuni and any neighboring language, persists when we look at grammatical structure. There we see no pattern of resemblances between Zuni and any other language or languages beyond extremely common structural types that occur in thousands of languages all over the world, such as CV(C) syllable structure or derivational affixes being internal to inflectional affixes, or structural phenomena that are well established as areal in scope, such as switch reference.[18] In summary, linguists have been unable to find convincing evidence against the claim that Zuni is a linguistic isolate without living genetic relatives.

Zuni and Language Contact

In the case of a linguistic isolate, most methods for "linguistic paleontology" —the use of historical-linguistic methods to reconstruct prehistory— are inapplicable. We cannot use the comparative method to reconstruct lexicon for a protolanguage because there is nothing to compare. So-called internal reconstruction is possible with an isolate and can slightly push back the time horizon for phonological, morphological, syntactic, and semantic phenomena. However, such work must be done by experts on the language, and it has not been undertaken.

The major method available to linguistic paleontology when dealing with an isolate is the study of language contact: the identification of borrowed vocabulary as well as syntactic, morphological, and phonological elements either from other languages into the isolate or from the

isolate into other languages. The study of loan vocabulary is often of special interest for what it reveals about the nature of the language contact. However, with Zuni we encounter a rather frustrating situation: Zuni has borrowed (and loaned) surprisingly little vis-à-vis neighboring languages. It is typologically rather different from its neighbors and has relatively few loanwords. Nonetheless, a fortiori, we must turn to what evidence there is.

Could Zuni Be a Creole Language?

Before turning to the details of what is known about Zuni language contact I deal with one question posed by the organizers of this volume: is Zuni a creole? This is not a silly question, since the circumstances of the formation of big pueblos like Zuni and the Hopi towns involved the sort of history that might have given rise to a creole. During a fairly short time period dozens of small communities collapsed and a few large ones formed, almost certainly through ingatherings of refugees, some of whom must have come to these refugia under circumstances of the most extreme disadvantage. It is quite likely that these refugee populations were linguistically diverse. The best ethnographic model for such an event is the Hopi incorporation at the beginning of the eighteenth century of Tewa-speaking people from east of the Rio Grande. Kroskrity (1993) found that Arizona Tewa speakers are bilingual in Hopi (and know other languages as well, such as English and Navajo). However, during the 300 years that the Arizona Tewa have been on First Mesa, their language has borrowed only two words from Hopi (Kroskrity 1993:73). Kroskrity (1998) argues that this is the result of a linguistic ideology of "indigenous purism." Quite similar ideologies

have been identified in the other Rio Grande pueblos (cf. Dozier 1956), and versions of indigenous purism have been reported from throughout the Puebloan area. Indigenous purism seems to be a southwestern areal feature of considerable antiquity, one that has blocked exchange of loan vocabulary.

A second very likely possibility is that, while dialect differentiation is not obvious in Zuni at the present time, in earlier periods there may have been dialect differentiation, just as is found today among the Hopi pueblos. It is possible that the language of Zuni Pueblo today is the product of a certain amount of dialect synthesis, with components originating in different historical dialects of a "compact" language community (Golla 2000:60–61; see also Gregory and Wilcox, chap. 20, this vol.).

Creole formation, however, is more than just the exchange of loans, whether between languages or between dialects of the same language in contact. There is today considerable controversy about whether creole languages should be distinguished as a "type" and, if there is such a linguistic type, what circumstances might give rise to it (Thomason 2001). Creoles can form when pidgin languages —generally formed in multilingual contexts when extreme social distance or mutual antipathy yields a minimalist trade jargon as a means of communication—acquire native speakers (as with the emergence of Tok Pisin in New Guinea), or they can form when successive generations of speakers have less and less opportunity for good input from a target language (as in the plantation stage of the formation of some Caribbean creoles). However, languages that have been called "creoles" have certain typological tendencies that Zuni does not share. Creoles generally do not have much inflection. Word order tends strongly to Subject-Verb-Object order, the most common type. Creole phonology tends to be very simple, with five vowels, about 15 consonants, and a simple syllable structure that avoids consonant clusters.

Zuni does not look like a creole. Creoles tend to be isolating, but Zuni, at least in its system of verbs, is highly agglutinative verging on the polysynthetic. For instance, it has noun incorporation, as shown in the example below (from Nichols 1997):

(1) *no-weʔ wo=kʔosho-kya*
BEAN-PLURAL
PLURAL.OBJECT.=WASH-PAST
"he washed the beans"
(2) *no-kʔosho-kya*
BEAN-WASH-PAST
"he washed the beans"

While Zuni has very limited person and number agreement in the verb (the only person-number prefix is the plural object prefix *ʔaː-~ ʔaːw-*, showing up as *wo=* in [1]), it has complex inflections for tense and aspect and intricate patterns of derivation of complex words from relatively simple roots. The examples below give the flavor of the kinds of constructions that occur (from Nichols 2001).

(3) *ʔaːw-am-peye-kkowaʔ*
PLURAL.OBJECT-PARTICLE-SAY-
PAST.NOMINALIZATION
"the things he said"
(4) *y-ayyuʔya:-n-ʔamme-ʔonaʔ*
REFLEXIVE-KNOW-STATIVE-
NEGATIVE-NOMINALIZED NONPAST
RELATIVE
"that he is foolish"
(5) *tel-ankʔohakʔe-kkya*
OBJECT.EXPLETIVE-DISCOVER-PAST
"(he) discovered that"
(6) *ʔaː-tutu-kʔya-nap-kya*
PLURAL.OBJECT-DRINK-CAUSATIVE-
PLURAL.SUBJECT-PAST
"they watered them"

Creoles nearly always have the order Subject-Verb-Object. In contrast,

Zuni is strongly verb-final. The canonical order is Subject-Object-Verb, for example:

(7) *hoʔ ʔaːwan ču-weʔ ʔaːw=ito-kʔye-kkya*
I TO.THEM CORN-PLURAL
PLURAL.OBJECT=EAT-CAUS.-PAST
"I fed them some corn" (Nichols 1997)

In addition to its very uncreole Subject-Object-Verb order, Zuni has some exotic and interesting syntactic patterns, such as a caselike distinction for plural subjects that some scholars have considered to be ergative-absolutive, contrasting with a nominative-accusative case distinction for singular subjects (otherwise unattested in southwestern languages).

Zuni has a relatively limited phonological repertoire compared to some Native American languages, but, as seen in the examples above, it has glottalized and geminate (doubled) consonants, which would be most unexpected in a creole. It has some fairly elaborate morphophonology (changes in sounds due to mutual interaction when morphemes are combined into words). An example is seen in comparing examples (6) and (7) above. In (6) the past-tense suffix is *-kya*, since the stem ends in a consonant. In (7) the past-tense suffix is *-kkya*, since the stem ends in a vowel. We would not expect to see such alternations in a creole.

Zuni certainly exhibits traces of having participated in an areal linguistic system in which many people must have been multilingual. But the way that the Zuni community incorporated new members seems to have been that they simply learned Zuni, perhaps after a generation or so of bilingualism (or perhaps many generations of bilingualism, like the Arizona Tewa). We do not encounter the characteristic traces that linguists

expect as a signal of an episode of creolization.

Zuni in the Puebloan Areal System

Shaul (1980a) distinguishes two major contact areas among the Puebloan languages. These are a western area, including Hopi and Zuni, and an eastern area, including Tanoan and Keresan. These correspond with culture areas that have long been recognized. Some linguistic features associate Keresan with the western group. Shaul concludes that we must reconstruct an era, probably in the Chaco period (AD 800–1050), when Hopi, Zuni, and Proto-Keresan were in contact.

Grammatical and Phonological Features. In table 3.2 I adapt tables in Shaul (1980a) to illustrate the eastern and western contact areas. I do not use all of Shaul's features, so the table should not be read as "statistical." It is simply intended to show the kind of pattern that we encounter of a substantial set of features shared in the east and another substantial set shared in the west but with a few features that cross the east–west boundary.

I illustrate briefly here the results in Zuni of the adoption of one of the "western" features, switch reference (13), and one of the "eastern" features, a series of glottalized consonants. These are both rather unusual features that would be unlikely to develop independently. If they are present in a language and also in its neighbors, the suspicion is strong that the sharing results from contact.

Switch reference, an areal feature in western North America and in the Southwest, is found also in Hopi, Yuman, and Piman. It is also found marginally in Southern California Uto-Aztecan ("Takic"). Yuman, which has a well-developed system of switch reference in all the languages in the

Table 3.2 Linguistic Features in Shaul's (1980a) Puebloan Contact Areas

A. Features shared in the eastern area only

1. Full series of glottalized consonants: Keresan, Tanoan

2. Full series of aspirated consonants: Keresan, Tanoan

3. Tonal accents: Keresan, Tanoan

4. Subject marking by verbal prefix: Keresan, Tanoan

5. Passive triggered by animacy: (Keresan), Tanoan

B. Features shared across the east–west boundary

6. Glottalized stops: Zuni, Keresan, Tanoan

7. Verb ergativity based on number: Zuni, Keresan

8. Conjunction postposed to verb: Hopi, Zuni, Keresan

C. Features shared in the western area only

9. Internal verb reduplication for iterative aspect: Hopi, Zuni

10. Subject marking by independent nominal: Hopi, Zuni

11. Productive noun plural suffix: Hopi, Zuni

12. -*ti* transitional: Hopi, Zuni

13. Switch reference: Hopi, Zuni

14. Accusative-like direct object marker -*ya* and (?) possessive marker -*aiya*: Hopi, Zuni

Table 3.3 Proto-Keresan and Proto-Kiowa-Tanoan Stops.

Proto-Keresan	p	t	c	ty	ç	k		ʔ
	pʰ	tʰ	cʰ	čʰ	çʰ	kʰ		
	pʔ	tʔ	cʔ	čʔ	çʔ	kʔ		
Proto-Kiowa-Tanoan	p	t	c			k	kʷ	ʔ
	pʰ	tʰ	cʰ			kʰ	kʷʰ	
	pʔ	tʔ	cʔ			kʔ	kʔʷ	
	b	d	z			g	gʷ	
Zuni	p	t	c	č		k	kʷ	ʔ
			cʔ	čʔ		kʔ	kʔʷ	

Source: From Shaul (1982:84).

family, may be the ultimate source of this feature. In switch reference a grammatical element differentiates whether two linked clauses have the same subject or a different subject. This is illustrated in the two Zuni examples below, from Nichols (2000). Note that in example (1) the subject of "I will go out" and of "I will throw up" are the same person. This fact is marked with -*nan*. In example (2) the subjects of the two parts of the sentence are different, and this is marked with -*p*.

(1) *hoʔ kwayi-**nan** hoʔ yakʔo-nna*
I EXIT-**SAME.SUBJECT** I VOMIT-FUT
"I will go out and throw up"

(2) *hoʔ kwayi-**p** Nemmeʔ yakʔo-nna*
I EXIT-**DIFFERENT.SUBJECT** NEMME
VOMIT-FUT
"I will go out and Nemme will throw up"

A feature of Zuni that probably came from the east is feature (6) in table 3.2, a series of glottalized stops. Shaul (1982) observes that Tanoan and Keresan both have a full series of such stops, as shown in table 3.3, which shows Miller and Davis's (1963) reconstruction of Proto-Keresan and Hale's (1967) reconstruction of Proto-Kiowa-Tanoan. However, Zuni has a much more limited system of consonants and does not have a full series of glottalized stops.

Not only does Zuni have far fewer stops and fewer glottalized stops than the eastern languages, but the Zuni glottalized stops have a very low functional load. Shaul (1982) is able to identify only four minimal pairs for plain vs. glottalized stops (e.g., *ca* "stomach" vs. *cʔa* "spiral shell"). He also states that /čʔ/ appears word-initially only as an expressive "phonestheme for liquid perturbation" in six stems with meanings like "splash," "plop" (Shaul 1982:83). The languages to the west do not have glottalized consonants at all. Thus, it seems most likely that Zuni borrowed its series of glottalized consonants from Tanoan and/or Keresan.

Loanwords. Thus, far, scholarship on Zuni has identified loanwords in the language from Keresan, Hopi, and Piman (and of course from Spanish and English). I discuss below these cases as well as cases where Zuni has contributed loans to these languages and loans between Hopi and Keresan. It is important not to draw any statistical conclusions from these lists about the "balance of power" between the speech communities at any particular

Table 3.4 Piman Loans in Zuni.

1. *ho?i* "shallow, tightly woven basket" < Piman *hoa* "basket" (Shaul 1980c)

2. *hoo-c?ana* "Yucca battata," *hoo-k?apa* "Y. whipplei" < Piman *ho-wi* "Y. batata" (Shaul and Hill 1998), + Zuni *k?apa* "flat, broad" (*c?ana* < *c?a-na* "small-stative" [Lynn Nichols, personal communication 2001])

3. *ka* "grain of wheat, small seed" ("corn" [Shaul 1982:83] < Piman *kai* "seed" [Shaul 1982])

4. *kihe* "ceremonial brother" < Piman *kihe/kiha* "some kind of brother" (incorporating *ki-* "house") (Shaul and Hill 1998)

5. *kiwihci* "kiva" < Piman *ki:* "house" or perhaps Hopi *kiva* (Shaul and Hill 1998)

6. *k?ola* "chile" < Piman *ko?okol* "chile" (ultimately from a Uto-Aztecan verb "to hurt, sting") (Shaul 1980c)

7. *kokko* "good kachina" < Tepiman *kok?oi* "spirit of the dead" from PUA **koi* "die" (Shaul and Hill 1998)

8. *Kolowisi* "Horned Serpent" < Tepiman **ko?o-wi* "rattlesnake" from PUA **kowa* "rattlesnake" (but cf. Zuni *kolho* "make a rattling sound")

9. *oka* "woman" < Piman *oks* "old woman" (Shaul 1980c)

10. *shuma?kwe* "Shuma?kwe Society" < Piman *sima-* "bold, mean" + Zuni *-?kwe* "collective suffix" (Shaul and Hill 1998)

Table 3.5 Keresan Loanwords in Zuni.

1. *cha* "child, young of animals" < cf. Santa Ana *tyaá*

2. *isha* "grease, fat, tallow, shortening" < Acoma *?íṣát?i*, Santa Ana *?iṣat?i* "grease, lard"

3. *k?yashshita* "fish" < Acoma *sk?a?šŭ*, Santa Ana *sk?àšĭ*, Santo Domingo *sk?aâšĭ* (Shaul 1982) (with final *-ta* possibly from Santa Ana *-ta* "plural subject" [Nichols 1993])

4. *makk?i* "woman with children" < Santa Ana *màk?ɨ* "daughter" (Shaul 1982; Shaul 1980c suggests that this is ultimately Hopi *ma:na* "girl"; I don't think this is demonstrable)

5. *puula, puulakya* "butterfly" < Acoma *buúr?ai?kǎ*, Santa Ana *buúr?àikǎ*, Santo Domingo *buúr?aga* (originally from Hopi; see Table 3.7)

6. *Shipapolima* "Eastern Kachina Home" < Santa Ana *sip?aap^hɨ* (Bunzel 1992:482, 517)

7. *shiwani* "rain priests" < Keresan **šíĭwanna* "rain deity, priest" (see discussion in Shaul and Hill 1998)

8. *taapuupu* "governor" < Santa Ana *tápuúp^ŭ* "governor" (Shaul 1980a)

9. *te?ci* "arrive, reach" < possibly Santa Ana *-č?ĭ* "arrive"

10. *uwakya* "ceremonial relationship" (Newman 1958), "great-grandson" (religious term) (Bunzel 1992) < Acoma *?úwaákA*, Santa Ana *?úwàakǎ*, Santo Domingo *?uúwakǎ* "baby"

11. *Wenima* "Western Kachina Home" (word in songs for *kolhuwalaawa*) < Keresan *wenimace* (Bunzel 1992:482)

12. *wiha* "baby" < Santa Ana *w?ĭ* "child" (Shaul 1982)

13. *suski* "coyote" < Keresan *cúski* "fox" (Lynn Nichols, personal communication 2001; direction of loan uncertain)

historical period. We have decent dictionaries only for Hopi and Tohono O'odham (a variety of Piman). Newman's (1958) dictionary of Zuni has almost no ceremonial vocabulary and is in any case not a very large dictionary. We have minimal lexical resources for Keresan; Keresan speakers are in general not interested in sharing material on their language, and the pueblo governments prohibit writing in the language except under extremely restricted circumstances.[19] I am sure that if Zuni and Keresan were better documented, we would increase the number of words in the lists below. Basically, what the lists show is that, especially given the Puebloan ideologies of "indigenous purism" and "strict compartmentalization" (between languages) (Kroskrity 1998) discussed above, there is evidence for a fair amount of exchange. The second major conclusion is that the vast majority of loanwords that have been documented are relatively recent—which is why they can be identified at all! (Older loans, which have undergone more phonological change, are harder to spot.) Most of them have to do with kachina ceremonialism and so must have been exchanged within the last 800 years at the most.

The likely candidates for loanwords in Zuni from Piman (probably from an early stage of this language, during the Classic Hohokam) are listed in table 3.4. Zuni gave to Piman *šiwani* "priest" (itself a loan from Keresan; see example [7] in table 3.5), which appears as Piman *siwañi* "lord of a Hohokam great house." Shaul and Hill (1998) suggest that all of this exchange probably happened at a fairly late period, certainly no earlier than the thirteenth century AD and the Classic Hohokam, when speakers of Zuni, Piman, and Yuman were all involved in a multiethnic Hohokam formation.

Table 3.6 Zuni Loanwords in Hopi.

1. Hakto "one of the warrior kachinas in the Shalako kachina line as performed at Hopi" < Zuni -hakto of unknown meaning, e.g., Zuni yamuhakto (Bunzel 1992:522) "paired kachinas"

2. Heheyʔa "a kachina" < Zuni heheʔa

3. Hotooto "the two kachinas that accompany heeʔeʔe in the procession during the Powamuy ceremony" < Zuni Huututu

4. Kookopölö "a kachina with a hunchback" < Zuni kokko "kachina" plus Hopi -pölö "having a round shape"

5. Kooyemsi "Mudhead kachina" < Zuni Koyemshi[a]

6. Korowista "a kachina," said to be a Zuni word

7. Pawtiwa "a kachina" < Zuni Pawtiwa[b]

8. Payatamu "a kachina" < Zuni Payatamu

9. Saʔlako "Shalako, a kind of kachina" < Zuni Shaʔlako

10. Sájartasa "a kachina" < Zuni Saja Tasha "Long Horn"

11. Siitulili "a kachina" < Zuni chittola "rattlesnake"

12. Sólàawici "a kachina"; the plural refers to the entire kachina group of "Zuni-type kachinas" that accompany the Shalako < Zuni Shuʔla:wici

13. Talmopiyaʔkya "a kachina from Zuni"[c]

14. Talmopiyàakya "same as 13" ([13] is probably the Second Mesa pronunciation, [14] is Third Mesa)

[a]Keresan has a word rendered in English as koshare—Keresan *kʔiṣáirí "clown"—that may contain the ko- element, originally from Piman. If this is the case, the word probably reached Keresan by way of Zuni, since, unlike Zuni, Keresan does not incorporate noun roots as CV. The word appears in Hopi as kosari. Lynn Nichols (personal communication 2001) speculates that koyemshi might be the result of a playful metathesis; undoing this would give us ko-sh(ʔ)..., a form even closer to Keresan. However, she notes that -shi may also be a noun class marker; it appears in several names for animals and in the word for arrowhead.

[b]Lynn Nichols (personal communication 2001) comments that the diphthong /aw/ is "decidedly un-Zuni," so this name may originate in yet a third language.

[c]Lynn Nichols (personal communication 2001) states that the second element of these kachina names is from Zuni piya-kʔya "hang-past."

The items in table 3.4 require some discussion. Item (1) may have the same root as item (2), from the word for "yucca." Item (2) is probably associated with the Shumaʔkwe Society curing ritual, which uses a plaque woven of yucca leaves. Items (4) and (5) are the only words in Newman's (1958) dictionary of Zuni that begin with ki-. Items (7) and (8) may contain the same ko- element, about which more below. However, I advance here the speculation that item (8) is related to a widespread Uto-Aztecan word for "rattlesnake." It does not resemble any recorded Zuni word for any kind of snake, nor does it resemble recorded Keresan words for "snake." It does, however, resemble the first Consonant-Vowel (CV) sequence of Piman koʔowi "rattlesnake." The etymology would be the incorporation of the first syllable, ko-, of Piman koʔo-wi into a Zuni compound with -lo-wihci(ʔ), the regular Zuni compounding strategy.

Item (8), Kolowisi "Horned Serpent," is not in Newman's dictionary. I use Bunzel's spelling (1992:515). It is possible that Bunzel's -wisi element is the same as the -wihci, otherwise unidentified, that appears in item (5) and also in the kachina name Shula:wici that appears in the list of Zuni loans in Hopi in table 3.6. Zuni kolho "make a rattling sound" may also be derived from this formative element, which would make it even

more likely that the Uto-Aztecan (probably Piman) word for "rattlesnake" is involved.

The Hopi word for "Horned Serpent" contrasts with the Zuni word in a very interesting way. Hopi Paalölö-qangw "Horned Serpent" is probably composed of paa- "water" plus an element -lölö- that is a reduplicated resemblant of Zuni -lo- in Kolowisi.[20] Hopi löʔö- means "pour out (of liquid)." Water Serpents / Horned Serpents are associated with flooding. Bunzel (1992:516) reports that the image of the Horned Serpent in the Zuni kiva astonishes initiates by vomiting water and seed. Hopi lölö-qangw is the word for "bull snake, gopher snake." Given the general relationship between snakes and water in Hopi, I suspect that the two forms, for "pour out (of liquid)" and "snake spp.," are related. The second part of the Zuni word, -lo, may be related to this etymon. It would have to come from an early stage of Hopi, when Proto-Uto-Aztecan (PUA) **w had already become Hopi /l/ before /o/ but before Uto-Aztecan (UA) **o had become Hopi /ö/.

The Hopi, who use the word cɨʔa "rattlesnake" (probably sound-imitative), have no reflex of the Uto-Aztecan word for "rattlesnake," PUA **kowa. Yet this etymon is present everywhere else in Northern Uto-Aztecan, including in Southern Numic, the immediate neighbor of Hopi (cf. Chemehuevi kogo "snake sp." and Southern Paiute and Ute tokoa-pi "rattlesnake"). This situation suggests a deliberate replacement (and of course rattlesnake, along with bear and coyote, is one of the most commonly "euphemized" animals in western North America). Thus, the Hopi ceremonial terms (or at least the terms that can be spoken in public and put in the dictionary) for the Water Serpent and related snakes perhaps should be thought of as propitiating, mentioning the most positive qualities of the animals, their associations with water, wet places, and the coming of spring. This is in contrast to the Zuni *ko-* words with their association in Uto-Aztecan with pain (PUA **ko-) and death (PUA **koi). PUA **kowa "rattlesnake," **koi "to die," and **ko "hurt, be sick" (the root that shows up in Piman *koʔokol* "chile") may all be related within Uto-Aztecan. Of course, we do not know that these associations with death, so clear in the Uto-Aztecan words, persist in Zuni. They do, however, suggest something of the ideology surrounding the Horned Serpent among the Pimans, who seem to have been the source of the Zuni words. The Hopi tendency to focus on water and life may also be developed in *katsina* "kachina," to which I return below.

Of special interest among the *ko-* words is *kokko* "kachina," almost certainly from Piman *kokʔoi* "spirit of the dead" (Shaul and Hill 1998). As mentioned above, Zuni forms noun compounds and noun-incorporation by taking only the first CV of the noun. Using this process, Zuni has formed many words with *ko-*. Since Newman (1958) includes very few words in the ceremonial vocabulary, these examples are taken from Bunzel (1992): *komosona* "kachina chief" (p. 518), *kopʔekwin* "*pʔekwin* of the kachina chief" (p. 518), *kolhuwalaawa* "kachina village, kachina home (the Western Kachina Home)" (pp. 482, 521), *Koyemshi* "Mudhead kachina, clown" (this word does appear in Newman 1958).[21] The *ko-* in *Kolowisi*, the word for "Horned Serpent," may be part of this set.

Kokko "kachina" was borrowed into Hopi from Zuni but not as the general term for "kachina." It appears in some kachina names, for instance, in Hopi *Kookopölö* "Kokopelli," presumably from Zuni *kokko* plus Hopi *pölö* "hav-ing a round shape, hunchbacked kachina," where *pölö* refers to the curved shape of Kokopelli's back. This is an extremely interesting form. Had Hopi inherited the *kooko-* directly from Uto-Aztecan, it would appear as *köökö*, because in Hopi Uto-Aztecan **o everywhere becomes /ö/. This is part of a "chain shift": Uto-Aztecan *u becomes Hopi /o/, and Uto-Aztecan *o (perhaps to avoid massive homophony) becomes Hopi /ö/. The "Kokopelli" word thus may permit us to date the Hopi sound change PUA *u > Hopi /o/, PUA *o > Hopi /ö/ as prior to the arrival of the kachina cult. A second Zuni loanword in Hopi also shows this: Hopi *hotooto* "the two kachinas that accompany Hee'e'e in the procession during the Powamuy ceremony," from Zuni *huututu*. Hopi doesn't have the vowel /u/, so the Zuni word is pronounced with the nearest vowel, Hopi /o/. This word must have been borrowed after the Hopi shift of PUA *u to Hopi /o/ and also after the shift of /o/ to /ö/, or it would be *hötöötö*. The same point can be made using Hopi *Kooyemsi* "Mudheads" from Zuni *Koyemshi*. (The only Zuni loanwords in Hopi as far as we can tell are 14 names for kachinas; these are shown in table 3.6.)[22] The second element of *kookopölö*, the word for "to be round, ball" as well as for "hunchbacked kachina," is a sound-symbolic word that is very widespread in the western United States; for instance, Newman (1964) noted it in California in both Maidu and Miwok. The Hopi word shows the change from UA *o to /ö/. Thus, the word *kookopölö* has an obvious borrowed word with /o/ in the first part of the compound and a word with the regular Hopi sound change in the second. This is a bilingual compound comprised of the Zuni loanword *kokko* and the indigenous Hopi *pölö*.

It is very interesting that the great majority of the older Uto-Aztecan loanwords in Zuni seem to come not from Hopi but from Piman. However, one Zuni word with possible Uto-Aztecan ancestry would have had to come from Hopi. This is recorded in Bunzel (1992:526) as *paʔetone* "the great shell." The first syllable is Uto-Aztecan *paa- "water" or Uto-Aztecan *paa- "great" (see n. 20), compounded with Zuni *ʔetoo-* "material effigy of a sacred being" (Bunzel 1992:490).[23] This word cannot come from Piman. First, in Tepiman PUA *p in word-initial position appears as /w/. The source cannot be a Tepiman word for "water" for a second reason: during Proto-Tepiman times the Tepimans abandoned PUA *pa "water" in favor of *suudagi "water" (Shaul and Hill 1998). Hopi retained the PUA water word as *paahɨ*.

Zuni has also borrowed a number of words from Keresan (table 3.5). The sources often give Keresan words from a single dialect, since most of these have not been reconstructed to Proto-Keresan. Thus, the table should not be read as saying that a loanword in Zuni is "from Santa Ana" or "from Acoma." Instead, the Santa Ana or Acoma or Santo Domingo word stands in for Keresan in general. Keresan dialect differentiation is so shallow that we can be fairly confident that the source for these loans is Proto-Keresan (or Pre-Keresan).

As with the Piman loans, the words discussed above are a mix of obviously ritual terms and other words that are less obviously linked to the ritual complex. Borrowed kin terms may come from the special kin terms that are used in the kiva. Two of the animals listed in table 3.5, the fish and the butterfly, are both associated with the flowery, watery ritual world that is evoked in ceremonialism. Since Keresan etymology is so shallow (and Zuni has no etymology at all), it is impossible to say much about the historical significance of these loans. They do testify to contact between the two languages, especially around matters of ceremonialism, and the existence of a population of bilinguals.

Finally, as a matter of comparative interest, let us examine the other language in the language-contact system, Hopi (table 3.6). As noted above, the only Zuni loanwords in Hopi are 14 kachina names.

These words are all obviously very recent loans, and many Hopi are aware of their Zuni origin. There have been very few changes except accommodations to the Hopi sound system. For instance, Hopi does not have the Zuni sounds /ch (č)/ and /sh (š)/, so these become Hopi /s/.[24] The small number of these loans is rather striking, since several hundred kachina names have been documented for Hopi (some are almost certainly Keresan in origin). Shaul (1980a) observes that Zuni and Hopi also share a pair of expressive words, ʔali "delicious!" and ʔana "ouch!"

Hopi and Zuni share a pair of words that are extremely interesting and suggestive of contact that may precede the arrival of the kachina cult. The forms are Zuni teshkwi "shrine placed in the house" and Hopi tïïtiskya "shrine." Both languages have related verbs, again with almost identical meanings: Zuni teshla-na "be afraid" and Hopi tïïtïs- "have misgivings about one's safety," Hopi tïïsi "careful, cautious" and Hopi tïïsö "cave, rockshelter, cliff overhang," this last having an etymology in Hopi and PUA, from *tïn "rock" + *so "burrow." So it seems likely that the loan is from Hopi into Zuni, with the Hopi word originally having to do with caves, niches, and rockshelters. Ethnographically and archaeologically, such places are known to be used to store ritual paraphernalia in the Puebloan area. In Uto-Aztecan

thought caves are sacred as the prototypical water sources.

Finally, I list loanwords between Keresan and Hopi in table 3.7. These are based on Shaul (1980c), with a few changes based on recent updates to our knowledge. The words in the first set are originally Hopi, with good Uto-Aztecan etymologies, while the words in the second set are originally from Keresan.[25]

Again, we find a mixed group of forms but dominated by relatively recent ceremonial vocabulary. In the first group of forms discussion is required for item (3), Hopi kacina "kachina." Malotki has carefully reviewed the debate over this form, quite properly concluding that many of the contributions have utterly neglected basic principles of historical linguistics and constitute "folk etymology at its finest" (1991:51). Malotki, along with most other modern authorities, argues that kacina must be a loanword into Hopi from some other language. The reason for this is that in the Northern Uto-Aztecan languages, including Hopi, Proto-Uto-Aztecan *k went everywhere to /q/ before /a/. Thus, Hopi words like kacina, katoya, kawestima in table 3.7 must be loanwords that have come into the language since this sound change. There is no question about the pronunciation of kacina; almost all authorities have recorded it with the /ka/ pronunciation, with the exception being the Voegelins (1957:44). Fewkes (1897:174, cited in Malotki 1991) concluded that this pronunciation showed that the "katcina cultus is extra Tusayan in origin." Miller (letter to Ekkehart Malotki, March 16, 1993, in the files of the Hopi Dictionary Project) believed that the source of the loan was Keresan kʔ-áazíná "third person-ʔ-plural subject," "Kachinas."[26] However, Miller was unable to identify the meaning of the root, áazí, so his argument basi-

cally rests on the claim of being able to identify the Keresan affixes.

I believe that this matter requires more research. Kenneth C. Hill (personal communication 2002) was told by a Hopi consultant that the word is probably not a loan, because, said this source, it is common for the Hopi to modify the pronunciation of ritually important words in order to obscure their origins. That is, this consultant believed that the word was "really" qatsina, with the /qa/ we would predict for a Uto-Aztecan root. The Voegelins may have encountered similar claims, explaining their use of /q/ in their recording of the word.

If the word is indeed "really" qatsina, it may have an etymology internal to Hopi and to Uto-Aztecan more generally, coming from words meaning "to be, to live." Fewkes's assumption of the "extra Tusayan" origin of the kachina cult could then not be sustained, and there would be strong arguments for an origin within Uto-Aztecan, given the probable Hopi origin of the Keresan form and the probable Tepiman origin of the Zuni word. In Hopi a verb qati "to sit, to live" forms a derived noun qatsi "life" by regular processes. However, the more likely derivation for qatsina is qati-ina "to live-cause," with the causative suffix -ina, regular loss of /ï/, and regular change of /t/ to /ts/ before /i/. There are many examples of verbs used as names in Hopi.[27] Thus, qatsina would mean "(the one who) causes things to live." This is an appropriate label for the kachinas, who, as Malotki points out, are especially associated with water and bring rain when they appear.

The problem with this line of derivation is that if qatsina is a verb being used as a name, its plural should be qatsina-ya. Instead, the attested plural is kacina-m, with the regular noun plural. The possible Keresan source word is plural. (The additional plural

Table 3.7 Loans between Hopi and Keresan.

A. Hopi to Keresan

1. *honani* "badger" > Keresan *honani* "badger fetish"

2. *tɨ* "hot" > Keresan *ɨrɨ̈* "hot"

3. *kacina* > Acoma *kʔáazíná* "kachina" (?)

4. *Maasawɨ* "Masawu (connected with words for "ashes" and "skeleton" [Miller 1967:No. 261], with a southern distribution in Uto-Aztecan) > Keresan *Masewi* "one of the twin war gods"

5. *poli-* "butterfly" (combining form of *povoli-hoya* "any of the smaller species of butterflies"; source might be a form like *polɨ-kacina* "butterfly kachina") > Acoma *buúrʔaiʔkă*, Santo Domingo *buúrʔàikă*, Santa Ana *buúrʔaga*

6. *sɨ̈wɨ* "eyebrow" < Keresan *sípă* "eyelash" (Shaul [1980c] gives this one, I don't like it much)

7. *ciro* "small bird" > Keresan *sírʔuú* (Shaul [1980c] mentions that this word has resemblants in Tübatulabal, Tarahumara, and Nahuatl; I suspect it has resemblants in non-Uto-Aztecan languages as well; generally, it is impossible to determine the direction of borrowing of bird names)

8. *yaawi* "ceremonial baton," cf. Uto-Aztecan *yaawi* "carry" > Keresan *yaápí* "staff of office"

B. Keresan to Hopi

1. *Katoya* "two-headed snake patron of the Antelope Society" < Keresan *kʔaáḍɔwi* "mythical two-headed snake" (Parsons 1936)

2. *Kawéstima* "Betatakin Ruin, Northwestern Kachina Home" < Acoma *k-áwʔes-tiima*ᵃ "Mount Taylor" (Keresan *áwʔes* "snowy")

3. *mosarɨ* "buffalo" < Keresan *músêiză* "buffalo"

4. *sipapɨ* "Sipapu" < Santa Ana *sipʔaaphɨ* "Sipapu"

5. *Weenima* "Southeastern Kachina Home" < Keresan *wenimace* (Bunzel 1992:482) (used also in Zuni as a ritual term for the Western Kachina Home)

ᵃThis transcription is from Miller's text "Around Acoma" (Miller 1965:206).

marker *-m* in Hopi is the kind of "doubling up" phenomenon that is common in loan vocabulary—famous examples known to English speakers include "the La Brea tar pits" with both English and Spanish definite articles, and "Rio Grande River," with two words for "river"—and so does not rule out the Keresan source.) If a derivation from Uto-Aztecan origins can be sustained, then *katsina* constitutes a second case, along with the word for "Water Serpent" discussed above, where Hopi usage emphasizes water and life, in contrast to the Zuni use of words associated with death—recall that in Zuni, the generic word for "kachina" is *kokko*, from Tepiman *kokʔoi* "spirits of the dead." Like the

Zuni, the Hopi believe that the kachinas are the perfected spirits of the dead. However, Hopi apparently prefer to emphasize the life-giving force of these beings over their association with death.

I must emphasize that the above proposal is speculative. Further discussion of this point with knowledgeable speakers of Hopi is required. In addition, Miller's Acoma Keres form should also be revisited with speakers of Keres, although I am not optimistic that any will be willing to discuss it.

In the case of the word for "butterfly," a ritually important animal, an ultimately Hopi source for this word, attested as a loan in Zuni as well as in Keresan, must be asserted. The rea-

son is that the combining form *poli* has an etymology within Hopi, from *povoli-hoya*, a reduplicated word from underlying *po-poli-hoya* (*-hoya* is the diminutive suffix).

There is one "snake" word in Keresan that may be an old Uto-Aztecan loan; this is Santa Ana *sûwi·* "snake," possibly related to Takic (California Uto-Aztecan) *sɨwi-t* "rattlesnake," Piman *sòʔowa* "bull snake."

Uto-Aztecan, Tanoan, Keresan, Zuni: The Lesson from Loanwords

To a linguist, all of the loan vocabulary documented in the previous section looks like it is from relatively recent times, certainly within the last millennium and perhaps even postcontact. Most of the Puebloan loanword complex involves ceremonialism dating no earlier than Late Pueblo III. While it is possible that the connection to ceremonialism, along with Puebloan linguistic purism (Kroskrity 1998), would retard change in this vocabulary, this retardation should not mislead us by more than a century or two. Indeed, this purism is by no means absolute; for instance, Hopi certainly reshaped Keresan loans, abandoning their tones and glottalizations and neutralizing Keresan and Zuni sibilants /ch (č)/ and /sh (š)/ to Hopi /s/. Similarly, Zuni simplified the phonology of Keresan loans. There does not seem to be a more ancient loan vocabulary shared among these languages. For this reason we must question Shaul's (1980a, 1980b, 1980c) claim that this loan vocabulary dates to Chacoan times. It seems more likely that it is post-Chacoan, developed in ritual exchanges around kachina ceremonialism. Pueblo people travel long distances today to visit one another's ceremonies. We know that in the seventeenth century, at the time of the Pueblo Rebellion in 1680, the western and eastern pueblos were in contact with one another. It seems likely that this contact has been under way for quite a long time. Thus, we do not have to posit a period when all the Keresans were all together at Chaco in order to explain loans between Keresan and the western pueblos.

In contrast to this very recent suite of loanwords, we may be able to identify a very old layer of loanwords between Uto-Aztecan and Tanoan dating to the time of the arrival of maize cultivation in the U.S. Southwest. Whorf and Trager (1937) found enough resemblances between Uto-Aztecan and Tanoan to develop a hypothesis that they were genetic relatives. However, their argument for genetic relationship is deeply flawed; Campbell (1997) critiques it in detail. Following Shaul (1985), I believe that the array of spurious resemblances identified by Whorf and Trager includes an ancient layer of loan vocabulary between speakers of Proto–Northern Uto-Aztecan, newly intrusive in the Southwest and bringing maize agriculture, and Proto-Tanoan. Some details of the evidence are presented in Hill (2002, 2008). Northern Uto-Aztecan loans into Proto-Tanoan include a suite of five words for "maize cultivation," along with words for "child" (possibly "initiate") and "to lie." Words for "pine nut," "oak," "wild onion," "antelope," and a few others are probable borrowings from Proto-Tanoan into Proto–Northern Uto-Aztecan. There is no comparable complex of very ancient loan vocabulary between the Uto-Aztecan languages and either Keresan or Zuni. Especially, no loans can be identified in cultivation vocabulary.

In the Southwest, Yuman, Tanoan (in which I include Kiowa), and Uto-Aztecan all exhibit relatively large geographical spread and extensive radiation into subgroups. These radiations all seem to date to approximately the same period, at around

3,000 years ago, and are very likely to be associated with the adoption of cultivation. (I have argued elsewhere [Hill 2001] that the Uto-Aztecans in the Southwest were probably migrants who brought maize cultivation from Mesoamerica, probably from its northwest quadrant.) Keresan and Zuni contrast with these families in being very small language families with very shallow radiation (indeed, Zuni, for all practical purposes, has no radiation at all; estimated time depths for Keresan are about 500 years). This suggests that the ancestors of these groups were not involved in the cultivation-driven radiations of the earlier period, which yielded the many branches of Yuman, Kiowa-Tanoan, and Uto-Aztecan in the Southwest. The linguistic evidence indirectly supports the idea that the Zuni and the Keresans may have been part of relic hunter-gatherer groups who were relative latecomers to cultivation.

Conclusion

The organizers of the present volume urged participants to engage in sweeping speculation. In the spirit of this suggestion I present the following speculative history, based on methods of linguistic paleontology and the results reviewed above.

At about 4000–3500 BP Uto-Aztecans, bringing maize agriculture, arrive in the Southwest, establishing themselves as communities of cultivators in the river basins south of the Mogollon Rim. By 3500–3000 BP the ancestors of the Northern Uto-Aztecans are established north of the rim, pushing as far as the Four Corners region of the Colorado Plateau. The leading edge of Northern Uto-Aztecan is in contact with the ancestors of Tanoan, perhaps in the area of southwestern Colorado, where Matson (1991) identifies contact between

the Western Basketmaker II (probable Northern Uto-Aztecans) and the Eastern Basketmaker II (probable Tanoans). Hale and Harris (1979) proposed a glottochronological date for the initial radiation of Tanoan at 3000–2500 BP. These Tanoan ancestors borrow maize cultivation and some cultivation vocabulary from the Northern Uto-Aztecans. Northern Uto-Aztecan borrows several words for important economic plants and animals from Proto-Kiowa-Tanoan. At this early period Zuni and Keresan are not visible to the historical linguist. This is consistent with the possibility that the populations ancestral to these groups continued to practice hunting and gathering until a relatively late date.

By a date that I assume to be Late Pueblo III both Zuni and Keresan are geographically and socially in the picture, or, better put, they are visible to the historical linguist. The cult of the Horned Serpent appears, with the Zuni borrowing the first element of their name for this deity, Kolowisi, from the Tepiman word for "rattlesnake." The Hopi develop their own lexical item, Paalölöqangw, composed of roots involving water. According to Bunzel (1992), the Zuni deemphasize the water component of this sacred being. Is this an early doctrinal split that suggests hostility and conflicting centers of ethnogenesis? Or does it mean that the two groups simply acquire the cult of the Horned Serpent independently of one another, probably from the Tepimans, and provide it with different interpretations? By the time of the arrival of the kachina cult during the thirteenth century, in spite of the evidence for warfare in the archaeological record, the Zuni, Keresans, and Hopi are part of large regional networks of ceremonial exchange, evidenced in the exchange of vocabulary for kachina-related ceremonialism.

In spite of the absence of lexical data I think we can assume that Tanoans were involved in this system, since Shaul has documented grammatical contact between Tanoan and Keresan, and Zuni and Keresan are unquestionably in contact. At the same period Zuni is also in contact with Piman. The Pimans are one source of the kachina cult, contributing their word *kok?oi* "spirits of the dead" to Zuni in the form of *kokko* "kachina." Hopi innovates its own construction, *kacina*, probably derived from a construction referring to life, not to death. Again, these opposing linguistic solutions as to what to call the new sacred beings may represent a doctrinal split. It is interesting to contemplate the possibility that the doctrinal splits manifest in these lexical differences for "Horned Serpent / Water Serpent" and "kachina" may be one component of Hopi-Zuni hostilities, with the Hopi as Rome and the Zuni playing the role of Byzantium. The Hopi succeeded in spreading their word into Keresan, with "spirits of the dead" surviving only in Zuni and in a few isolated kachina names in Hopi, some of which may be late borrowings from Zuni. The kachina cult withered away among the Pimans, who became too impoverished to maintain its elaborate ceremonies (compare the Wi:gida, an O'odham ceremony with masked dancers, and Shalako).

A "Mogollon" system is an excellent candidate, by geographical location, to exhibit this pattern of language contact, with Keresans on their east, Hopi to the north, and Pimans to the west. The Piman contact especially permits us to imagine a group that extended to the south of the Gila headwaters. The linguistic evidence suggests that Zuni ancestors have been living in the Mogollon region at least since the time of their earliest historical linguistic "visibility," per-haps in Late Pueblo III times. This evidence does not, of course, rule out a more ancient Zuni presence in the region.

Notes

1. I am a specialist in Uto-Aztecan, not Zuni. I thank Lynn Nichols and Dave Shaul, who very kindly shared reprints and manuscripts with me, for much-needed help with this chapter. I also thank Kenneth C. Hill for help with Hopi and Ekkehart Malotki for providing materials on the word *katsina*. Finally, I thank Dave Gregory and Dave Wilcox for their editorial suggestions.

Also, a note on transcription conventions used herein: I have slightly normalized transcriptions across the sources, so the originals should be consulted for details. For instance, I have normalized all representations of glottalized consonants to consonant followed by glottal stop, for example, *t?*. Some of Newman's (1958) transcriptions are misleading, so I substituted *?* for his /ʼ/, following the usage in Newman (1964). I have also changed his orthographic /j/ of 1958 to *h* and his orthographic /q/ to *kʷ*. However, I have retained Newman's and Bunzel's use of /sh/ and /ch/ for Zuni *š* and *č*, respectively. For Hopi /ɨ/ I have written the barred-i symbol instead of Hopi orthographic "u" to avoid confusion with /u/ in other languages. The sources differ slightly in usage on a number of points; for instance, some write long vowels with a following colon, some with a following raised dot, and some with double vowels.

2. Note that the same argument may be made for Keresan, exhibiting a dialect continuum within the Southwest but with no known genetic relatives beyond that continuum.

3. Hill (2002) follows Shaul (1985) in suggesting that Sapir's "Aztec-Tanoan" is not a genetic unit but is probably the result of early contact between ancestral Northern Uto-Aztecan speakers and speakers of Proto-Tanoan.

4. A more promising line of attack, looking for a possible common ancestry between Uto-Aztecan and Mixe-Zoquean, has recently been initiated by Wichmann (1999).

5. Nichols reports that one of the sources for the rumor was on the faculty of the University of Chicago. Yet we find Hamp, a distinguished senior linguist of that institution, writing in the *International Journal of American Linguistics*: "With his characteristic acumen and prudence Stanley Newman has offered evidence for a genetic relation between Zuni and California Penutian. . . . He modestly apologizes for the astigmatism perhaps induced by his masterful knowledge of Yokuts and of Zuni. But since I find his whole argument, on reflection, so persuasive, it turns out that the richness of detail, of distinctiveness in phonology, and of quantity in the Yokuts comparisons makes the remarks that follow lean heavily on the Yokuts-Zuni equations" (1975:310). If Hamp's remarks aim to continue the hoax on Voegelin, the florid language becomes utterly delicious. However, my acquaintance with Hamp leads me to believe that, while he is certainly capable of deadpan humor, he has a real soft spot for long-distance comparison (e.g., he was an early defender of the Nostraticists, although not himself a true believer).

6. The sound-symbolic sets are (4), (7), (8), (12), (16), (17), (19), (28), (44), (49), (50), (51), (53), (61), (63), (71), (77), (78), (79), (89), (90), (92), (95), (98), (99), (110). Set (4) is a word that is also in Hopi (e.g., *pölöpɨ* "ball-shaped").

7. The sets that share only a single consonant are (5), (14), (21), (22), (25), (26), (29), (35), (37), (41), (45), (55), (64), (67), (83), (84), (85), (86), (87), (91), (94), and (115).

8. The sets with especially problematic semantics are (10), (24), (33), (43), (54), (57), (68), (69), (72), (75), (88), (93), (94), (114), and (120).

9. The sets that lack correspondences or that Newman himself mentions as "exceptional" are (2), (3), (5), (18), (31), (38), (60), (96), (101), (102), and (117).

10. The bird name / small animal name sets include (9), (24), (46), (47), (81), and (121).

11. On the other hand, Hamp (1975) considers the bird names especially

probative. He bases this evaluation on experience with Algonquian languages.

12. The primary kin term sets are (23), (39), (40), (113), and (118).

13. The sets for which there are close UA resemblants (quite apart from bird names, "yes," "no," etc.) are (15) "chest" (Zuni po?hata, Yawelmani Yokuts pi?is, UA *-pi "breast"); (42) *p'aha "gray" (Cupeño pavepáve'ish "gray" as well as Uto-Aztecan words for "grandfather" with *pa); (52) *piy "to hold" (cf. UA words like Nahuatl piya "guard, keep," Cupeño píqi "touch"); (116) "white" (various words beginning in k'o, ko; Cupeño has the root xwá[ya]).

14. In my view these are sets (1), (6), (13), (27), (30), (34), (48), (56), (62), (65), (66), (73), (76), (80), (82), (84), (97), (100), (103), (105), (106), (107), (109), (111), (112), (115), and (122). Lynn Nichols (personal communication 2001) presents some comments on the sets. In set (6) the final -n in Zuni pona:-n is a subordinating suffix that became frozen as part of certain forms of the root ?a:- "go." For set (56), Zuni ?ulani, Nichols suspects a borrowing from Keresan given the final -ni, a Keresan noun class ending. Nichols is suspicious that set (82), Zuni ?utula, the suppletive plural for "run away," might contain the plural prefix t-, found with other stems, and that u- might be an old third-person marker; this appears also in ?ulate "push." In set (106) the final -n in pen "speak, talk" (Newman's "ask" is wrong) is a frozen subordinating morpheme, as in set (6).

15. Hamp (1975) pays detailed and, on balance, very positive—indeed, unctuously flattering—attention to Newman's proposal. See n. 5.

16. Note that there are 12 more Zuni forms in Greenberg's "Amerind" sets: pali "liver" in set (30) "belly"; Zuni k?o:ppan "belly" in set (50) "breast"; pappa (papa in Newman 1958) "older brother" in set (53) "brother"; Zuni poklhi "smoke" in set (68) "cloud 2" (this form is in Newman 1964); k'a "water" in set (87) "drink 1" (a form in Newman 1964); ?ohhaapa "bee" in set (118) "fly 1"; pachchi "sole" in set (120) "foot 1"; mokchi "elbow" in set (157) "knee

2"; mo?le in set (215) "round" (in Newman [1958] I find only mo "spherical object"); lomo "be or become visible in a flash of light" in set (226) "shine"; yatokka "sun, timepiece" (Newman breaks off -kka as "instrumental") in set (251) "sun 4"; ta "wood" in set (259) "tree 1." For a critique of Greenberg's inclusion of Zuni in Amerind see Manaster Ramer (1996), who develops the argument that Zuni is no closer to Amerind—or to anything else—than it is to Indo-European.

17. These are "blood," "drink," "fat," "feces," "give," "house," "I," "moon," "night," "smoke," "sun," "tooth," and "two."

18. Nichols (personal communication, August 15, 2001) observes that some of the forms in table 3.1 are segmentable, making them even less likely to be related to forms in the other languages. For instance, taya "hair" probably contains -ya "a growing mass of"; yato-kkya "sun" means "cross.the.sky-nominalizer"; and mahe "feces" probably contains a frozen plural suffix -he.

19. Acoma uses "whole language" methods in its bilingual program, which means that words in Keresan are written on colored paper and hung around the classroom; Laguna has permitted Fa. Hilaire Valiquette, Ph.D., to compile a dictionary but prefers that it not be distributed to outsiders.

20. Kenneth C. Hill (personal communication 2001) suggests that this may come from PUA *paa- "large, great" rather than *paa "water." The "great" meaning is found in forms such as Tumpisha Shoshone pa-tɨhɨya "elk, moose" (where tɨhɨya is "deer"); Serrano pa:kiha- "chicken hawk" (where kiha is related to words for "hawk") and pai:havit "supernaturally powerful being"; Huichol pá= Spanish "grande"; and possibly Hopi pas "very" (with -s adverbializer).

21. All modern authorities agree that Zuni has no glottalized /p/, but that is what Bunzel wrote.

22. There is one other word in the Hopi dictionary (Hopi Dictionary Project 1998) that is listed in the database files of the dictionary as "said to be from Zuni." It

is anlo?yta "to have an ineffectual way of doing things." However, a Zuni source for this word has not been confirmed. Kenneth Hill (personal communication 2001) speculates that wi?lɨlɨ "chubby, fatso, overweight person," clearly related to Hopi wi(hɨ) "fat," may also have as a source a Zuni word ?o?lho "become fat." Among the few Navajo loanwords in Hopi, most are mild insults of this type.

23. I am trying to avoid "fetish."

24. Kenneth Hill (personal communication 2001) finds in his notes that for set (10) Sáyartasa "a kachina" < Zuni Saya Tasha "Long Horn" Emory Sekaquaptewa has the pronunciation [sajaʂtasha], a more "Zuni" pronunciation. Sekaquaptewa stated that it is natural that such "foreign" words might have more and less nativized pronunciations.

25. I leave out here two forms that Shaul included originally: Hopi mee "Hark, heed!" and Santa Ana mɨ: "Well," and UA *ha- "indefinite interrogative stem" and Keresan *ha- "interrogative stem." These words are found all over North America.

26. In Miller's *Acoma Grammar and Texts* the form appears in a text, "The Birth of the War Twins," as k?áazíná (1965:248).

27. Kenneth C. Hill (personal communication 2001) points out that Hopi verbal names are all male names. Female names are nouns. The most common suffixes in male verbal names are -iwa "passive" (verbal action has been accomplished), -va "ingressive" (to arrive with, to start doing), -ima "progressive" (to go along doing). Among the verbal suffixes in the 605 male names from Oraibi collected by Titiev, the suffix -(i)na "causative" does not occur as a final element. Only 16 names for supernatural beings are recorded in the Hopi dictionary; many do not have Hopi etymologies. None ends in -(i)na. This may indicate either a special status of the name (q?)/katsina, emphasizing the agentive power of these beings, or it may suggest that the word is indeed borrowed.

4 Archaeological Concepts for Assessing Mogollon-Zuni Connections

Jeffery J. Clark

This monograph examines a possible relationship between the prehistoric "Mogollon" and the historic and contemporary Zuni. The Zuni are a Native American group of ca. 8,000 people who speak a language with no known relative. This group now inhabits a small area in northwestern New Mexico centered on the Pueblo of Zuni and occupied this area before the first arrival of Europeans in the mid–AD 1500s.

The "Mogollon" is an archaeological culture associated with the prehistoric inhabitants of east-central Arizona and west-central New Mexico. The clearest material manifestation of "Mogollon culture" dates to an interval from about AD 200–1000, when the inhabitants of this region resided in distinctive pithouse settlements and produced unique types of pottery and other material culture (Haury 1936a, 1985a; Wheat 1955; see Diehl, chap. 11, this vol.). The Mogollon can probably be traced back to the first millennium BC, if not earlier, but the paucity and unevenness of data preclude all but the most general of comparisons. Potential connections between the pithouse-dwelling Mogollon and Western Pueblo inhabitants of this region during the late prehistoric period are obscured by a number of dramatic events and pro-

cesses (Haury 1986a:453–456), including the pithouse to pueblo transition during the eleventh and twelfth centuries, Kayenta-Tusayan migrations during the late thirteenth and fourteenth centuries, and widespread depopulation of the region during the late fourteenth and early fifteenth centuries.

To identify the most probable candidate for an ancestral Zuni population within the Mogollon culture area, our definition of Mogollon has been restricted to the prehistoric inhabitants of the zone above 1,982 m (see chap. 10, this vol.). Several material culture connections can be traced in archaeological assemblages within this highland region that support cultural continuity throughout much of the known sequence. This "island in the sky" would have also provided an ideal setting for linguistic isolation.

As an isolate, Zuni language must have developed during an extended period of limited contact with other historically documented linguistic groups in the Southwest. Since there is little evidence to suggest that the Zuni are recent migrants to the area, Zuni language probably developed either in a geographically isolated area or prior to the entry of other known groups (see Hill, chap. 3, this vol.). In either case, the Zuni man-

aged to maintain their identity and language for at least two millennia in a "world" that was dominated by speakers of Uto-Aztecan languages (Hill 2001). Ethnographic accounts indicate that, although the Zuni have adopted a number of practices from the outside, its members form a closely integrated and insular society that could have preserved Zuni culture and language in spite of close contact and influence from non-Zuni groups (Fox 1967:7; Roberts 1961:293–294).

Considering the premise of this monograph and our current understanding of the prehistoric Mogollon and the historic Zuni (Roberts 1961:294–296; see Ferguson, chap. 19, this vol.), two basic facts must be demonstrated to firmly establish a Mogollon-Zuni connection. First, it must be shown that an ancestral Zuni population inhabited the Mogollon Highlands for an extended interval during the prehistoric era. Based on earlier work summarized in chapter 10 (see also Gregory and Wilcox, chap. 20, this vol.), this interval should include most of the first millennium AD. Zuni occupation of this area may extend well back into the Archaic period, prior to the arrival of Proto-Uto-Aztecan groups and the spread of maize agriculture into the

Southwest. Alternatively, ancestral Zuni along with other Archaic populations may have been pushed out of southern Arizona, southern New Mexico, or possibly northern Mexico (see Diehl, chap. 11, this vol.) and into high-elevation refugia by Proto-Uto-Aztecan agriculturalists. A second fact that must be established is that either an ancestral Zuni group, representing only a minority of the population in the Mogollon Highlands, immigrated to and ultimately settled at Zuni Pueblo or much of this region was occupied by Zuni speakers, perhaps as a contiguous dialect community, and this population ultimately coalesced into Zuni Pueblo (Roberts 1961:294–295; see also Gregory and Wilcox, chap. 20, this vol.). The most likely interval for either scenario to have occurred was after the end of the Pithouse period (ca. AD 1000) and before the arrival of the first Europeans in the sixteenth century. When the Zuni settled in their present location, the previous inhabitants were either displaced, acculturated, or themselves Zuni speakers (see Ferguson, chap. 19, this vol.).

In order to evaluate a Highland Mogollon–Zuni connection an ancestral Zuni population must be identified and tracked in place and on the move, utilizing linguistic, biological, and archaeological data. This chapter focuses on establishing a reliable method employing the latter with the assumption that Zuni culture was more or less isomorphic with Zuni language. Because this is largely an exercise in culture history, relevant literature from the high-water mark of this paradigm in the 1950s and immediately before the advent of the "New Archaeology" is reviewed. Following this backward glance, more recent literature is discussed and a basic strategy proposed for identifying reliable material tracers for culturally defined groups.

Migration and Diffusion in the 1950s: Traditions and Site-Unit Intrusions

Paul Sidney Martin and John B. Rinaldo's search for connections between Mogollon and the Zuni (see Gregory, chap. 9, this vol.), the theme resurrected in this monograph, occurred during the climax and subsequent decline of the culture-history paradigm within archaeology. Until the renewed interest in migration and cultural identity within the discipline during the 1990s, models and concepts that emerged in the 1950s represented the most sophisticated treatment of these topics (Haury 1958; Rouse 1958; Wauchope 1956). Two cherished concepts of the 1950s are especially relevant to this monograph: tradition and site-unit intrusion.

In 1955 a series of related seminars funded by the Carnegie Institution challenged 25 prominent American archaeologists to move beyond "classification for classification's sake" and discuss "certain matters of cultural dynamics and human relations [that] can be uniquely illuminated through archaeological techniques" (Wauchope 1956:v). Seminars included discussions on both cultural continuity and change.

During this era continuity was perceived as the persistence of archaeological traditions. Haury et al. define an archaeological tradition as "a socially transmitted form unit (or series of systematically related form units) which persist in time" (1956:38). Phillips and Willey offer a similar definition of tradition as "a major large scale space-time cultural continuity, defined with reference to persistent configurations in single technologies or total (archaeological) culture, occupying a relatively long interval of time and a quantitatively variable but environmentally significant space"

(1953:628). Five different types of traditions were recognized: direct (continuous and unitary), converging (fusion of multiple traditions into one), diverging (fission of one tradition into multiples), elaborating (increase in complexity and diversity within one tradition), and reducing (decrease in complexity and diversity within one tradition) (Haury et al. 1956:43–45).

A number of factors were considered responsible for different types of traditions, including biological, environmental, demographic, societal, cultural, contact/diffusion, and inherent. The latter refers to factors intrinsic to the measured trait or attribute, such as raw material or function, that either limit or enhance "play" (variability potential) (Haury et al. 1956:48–49). Low play was associated more with "direct traditions" and high play with "elaborating traditions" (Haury et al. 1956:46). This initial attempt at breaking down material culture variability and correlating it with specific forms of cultural behavior was considered an important direction for future research (Haury et al. 1956:56). Indeed it would be, as will be discussed in the second half of the chapter.

With respect to culture contact/diffusion, two basic archaeological correlates for exogenous change were recognized: site-unit intrusions and trait-unit intrusions. A site-unit intrusion is "a site, or an occupation level in a site, which is sufficiently homogeneous to be regarded as representing the culture of a single place at a single time" (Willey et al. 1956:7). Examples offered for site-unit intrusions include missions, garrisons, and colonies established by carriers of one culture into the territory of another. Notably, the potential for migrant-local coresidence contexts within a site or occupation level was not explored. Hence, only the most conspicuous and segregated migrant enclaves are covered by the term.

A trait-unit intrusion is "an object modified or transported by human agency, a stylistic or technological feature or complex, or a characteristic archaeological association" (Willey et al. 1956:8). Unlike site-unit intrusions, trait-unit intrusions can result from the diffusion of ideas or trade and do not require substantial population movement. From these two definitions it follows that a site-unit intrusion is simply a series of trait-unit intrusions (including architectural elements) found in association within a single site or occupation layer.

Both site-unit and trait-unit intrusions were further differentiated into four subcategories to reflect different outcomes following the introduction of the intrusive element (Willey et al. 1956:9–24). An A1 site-unit intrusion results in the retention of cultural identity and tradition by both migrant and indigenous groups. This is the subtype most often used by Southwest archaeologists to describe Reeve Ruin (Di Peso 1958:13) and other Kayenta-Tusayan enclaves in southern and central Arizona (Haury 1958; Woodson 1999). An A2 site-unit intrusion is the fusion between the two traditions with the dominance of that associated with the local group (e.g., pre-Classic Hohokam–Ootam). An A3 site-unit intrusion is similar to the A2 subtype except that the migrant tradition is dominant (e.g., Spanish-Sobaipuri). Finally, an A4 site-unit intrusion is a complete fusion followed by a revival of the local culture (e.g., Spanish-Incan). Trait-unit intrusion subtypes B1 through B4 were defined along parallel lines. Notably, there is little discussion of how different artifact types and attributes may correlate with either trait-unit or site-unit intrusions and specific subtypes within each category.

In 1958 a symposium was held during the annual Society for American Archaeology meetings in Chicago with the goal of establishing the parameters that constitute sufficient proof for migrations or site-unit intrusions over competing hypotheses such as diffusion or trait-unit intrusions (Thompson 1958). This symposium developed out of the University of Arizona's excavations of a Kayenta-Tusayan enclave at Point of Pines (Haury 1958) and the discovery in 1957 of a cache in a cave 40 km southeast of this site (Wasley 1962) similar to the famous "Sunflower Cache" in the Kayenta region (Kidder and Guernsey 1919:145–147; see also Webster, chap. 16, this vol.). In the introduction Thompson is explicit about the importance of this topic in archaeology: "The concept of migration is one of the most dangerous interpretative tools available to the study of man's past. The archaeologist who is intellectually honest about his [or her] own use of the migration concept can no longer ignore the problem created by the misuse of the concept by others" (1958:v).

The discussant, Irving Rouse (1958:64), proposed five basic criteria, based on the symposium papers, for demonstrating the presence of site-unit intrusions in the archaeological record:

1. Identify the migrating people as an intrusive unit in the region it has penetrated.
2. Trace this unit back to its homeland.
3. Determine that all occurrences of the unit are contemporaneous.
4. Establish the existence of favorable conditions for migration.
5. Demonstrate that some other hypothesis, such as independent invention or diffusion of traits, does not better fit the facts of the situation.

These criteria can be adjusted to generate criteria for culture continuity within a region:

1. Identify the group as the indigenous population in the study region.
2. Trace the temporal depth of the group within the region.
3. Determine that earlier groups with similar assemblages do not exist outside the study region.
4. Establish the existence of favorable conditions for settlement continuity.
5. Demonstrate that some other hypothesis, such as parallel development or emulation, does not better explain observed patterns.

Although Rouse's criteria, the concept of tradition, and the various types of site-unit and trait-unit intrusions remain valid at a fundamental level, they provide more of a logic guiding basic archaeological interpretation than a rigorous methodology. With the exception of the influence of "inherent factors" on traditions, little attempt was made at parsing material culture variability and articulating it with specific cultural behaviors and processes. As the New Archaeology of the 1960s taught us, all artifacts and attributes are not created equal in this regard. Advances in establishing material-behavioral correlates over the past forty years permit considerable honing down of material culture to a discriminating subset that is both resilient within a culturally defined group and unlikely to leave home without its producers.

Migration and Diffusion in the 2000s: The Four *E* Words

As can be inferred from Rouse's first two criteria for site-unit intrusions, establishing the chronological sequence for specific material culture attributes within and outside the study area is essential in following the movements of groups. However, this exercise, while necessary, is not sufficient to establish the physical presence of the target group because diffusionist behaviors, particularly *exchange* and *emulation*, circulate material culture with little or no population movement. These behaviors blur social boundaries and provide competing hypotheses to migration. In the jargon of the 1950s, exchange and emulation are the primary mechanisms by which "trait-unit" intrusions occur.

The theme of this monograph requires a focus on behaviors that are isomorphic with the boundaries of cultural and linguistic groups rather than with those that traverse them. Two behaviors that rarely "diffuse" and as such tend to be associated only with the members of a specific cultural group are *ethnicity* and *enculturation*. The following sections briefly discuss each of these four behaviors with respect to tracking an ancestral Zuni population in the archaeological record. The discussions are by no means exhaustive and serve only to highlight the salient points relevant to this monograph.

Exchange

Exchange is a behavior that is amenable to archaeological study because it involves the circulation of material goods. The most visible exchange systems are those that distribute items that are conspicuous because they are labor-intensive to manufacture or made from exotic raw materials with limited availability. In the American Southwest the presence of long-distance exchange networks that circulated items such as decorated ceramics, marine shell, copper bells, macaws, obsidian, and turquoise has long been established (see Vokes and

Gregory, chap. 17, this vol.). Over the past decade short-distance exchange networks involving less-valued commodities such as utilitarian ceramics have been reconstructed through fine-scale sourcing studies such as petrographic analysis (e.g., Abbott 2000; Miksa and Heidke 1995; Stark and Heidke 1995).

Southwest archaeologists have used potential exchange goods, particularly decorated ceramics, to define social and political boundaries (e.g., Graves and Eckert 1998; Plog 1984; Plog 1990) and to trace population movements (Cordell 1995; Dutton 1963; Gladwin and Gladwin 1935). With respect to the latter, newly arrived migrants may have greater access to these goods than the previous inhabitants of a region if such goods are produced near premigration settlement areas (Adams et al. 1993). In addition, producers of exchangeable commodities may themselves immigrate and continue to manufacture these items in their new settlements (Crown 1994; Duff 2002; Lindsay 1987; Lyons 2003; Triadan 1997). In either case, immigration would result in a dramatic increase in these items within a particular region. In such examples the appearance of new "pots" can be equated with the arrival of new peoples.

However, a long list of cautionary tales warns against the use of items with potential exchange value to define cultural groups and track their movements (Collett 1987; DeCorse 1989; Hodder 1979; Kramer 1977; Plog 1990; Pollock 1983). Exchange can be conducted "down the line" or by itinerant traders with little or no permanent population movement. Trade, as action at a distance (Renfrew 1975), circulates goods across cultural boundaries, hence blurring the material patterns that can be used to identify them. Without other lines of evi-

dence, items that circulate by exchange are not reliable indicators of the physical presence of the producing groups unless on-site production can be confidently demonstrated.

Emulation

Emulation of the practices of one group by another can also throw us off the material trail of the target group. In fact, emulation is a more "insidious" diffusion process than exchange because it involves the production of intrusive forms of material culture by local groups. For the purposes of this brief treatment of the topic, emulation can be broken down into two basic categories: technological and ideological.

Technological Emulation. As discussed at length in cultural selectionist models, technological innovations that provide adaptive advantages increase the probability for survival and propagation of the innovating group (Braun 1995; Dunnell 1978; Leonard and Jones 1987). Considering these benefits, such innovations also have a high probability for emulation by other groups.

The spread of agriculture in both the Old and New Worlds provides ideal examples of this process. Many Old World researchers link the spread of cereal agriculture and cattle herding in Europe (ca. 4500–3000 BC) to that of the Indo-European language family (Anthony 1990:905–908; Bogucki 1987; Renfrew 1987b). The broad extent of the latter is linked to the adaptive advantages provided by the former, including greater carrying capacity and population density. In the currently accepted scenario Indo-European-speaking groups migrated from western Asia along the fertile loess belt in central Europe and into the northern European Plain, where they came into contact with indigenous Mesolithic foragers. The latter groups ultimately adopted the more productive subsistence strategy of the migrants (Bogucki 1987; Sherratt 1990). By the end of this interval cereal agriculture is not a discriminating marker of the boundaries of indigenous and migrant groups, and archaeologists must rely on other material markers such as Linear Pottery and funnel beakers (Bogucki 1987).

A parallel scenario has been presented for the spread of maize agriculture and the Uto-Aztecan language family in the American Southwest (see Hill 2001; Matson 2002; but also see Irwin-Williams, chap. 2, Gregory and Nials, chap. 5, and Gregory and Wilcox, chap. 20, this vol.). In this case Proto-Uto-Aztecan speakers migrated from central Mexico into the American Southwest, occupying river valleys and other optimal zones for cultivation. Indigenous Archaic foragers in the area either were pushed aside, were acculturated, or ultimately adopted agriculture themselves. These indigenous groups included Eastern Basketmaker populations in northern New Mexico and southern Colorado and perhaps an ancestral Zuni population somewhere in the mountains of eastern Arizona, western New Mexico, or northern Mexico. Similar to the adoption of cereal agriculture in the Old World, dependency on maize agriculture in the Southwest by the "late Neolithic" period (post–AD 700) would reveal little concerning the cultural background of the associated group. However, the short growing season in the highland areas insured that hunting and foraging remained important elements in the subsistence strategy throughout the prehistoric interval.

Although the spread of agriculture is an extreme example, it clearly illustrates the problem of using technologies with tangible adaptive advantages to track cultural groups. Innovations that substantially increase carrying capacity, decrease labor expenditure, or improve quality of life are likely to be emulated by groups in close contact with the innovators. Such innovations can be considered probable trait-unit intrusions as defined by Willey and others (1956). However, as discussed later, subtle technological differences that are "neutral" in an adaptive sense and arise between groups isolated from one another can indeed be useful for our purposes.

Ideological Emulation. Artifacts and architecture associated with religion, cosmology, and other high-level ideologies have also been used by archaeologists to demonstrate the presence of specific groups within a region. For example, the construction of Uruk-style temples at Habuba Kabira and Jebel Aruda during the fourth millennium BC is central to the argument that southern Mesopotamian colonists were present along the middle and upper Euphrates during that time (Algaze 1989). Similarly, the penetration of Arab and North African groups into western Africa has been traced by the distribution of early mosques (McIntosh and McIntosh 1984:91–92).

Analogous to technologies that provide adaptive advantages, new religions, rituals, and cosmologies can be powerful ideological tools in organizing and manipulating social groups. As such they are also subject to emulation. In particular, leaders within small-scale societies often selectively borrow the ideologies and associated symbolic material culture of more organizationally complex neighbors to enhance their sociopolitical status (Rathje 1971) and to serve local integrative needs (Doelle et al. 1995:439). Under the label "symbolic entrainment," this type of emulation is central to peer-polity interaction (Renfrew and Cherry 1986), which has been used as an alternative to migration in explaining the widespread distribution of ceremonial architecture, ritual paraphernalia, mortuary practices, and other material expressions of ideology. In the Southwest variants of the peer-polity model have been used to explain the construction of Chacoan great kivas and great houses outside the San Juan Basin (Kintigh 1994; Wilcox 1999a:127–136) and platform mounds outside the Phoenix Basin (Rice 1990). Artifacts and architecture associated with high-level ideology inform on interaction at the broadest of scales (Caldwell 1964) and, as is evident in the modern world religions of Christianity, Islam, and Buddhism, can encompass a wide array of cultures and languages. Similar to technological innovations, symbols and material culture associated with such ideologies have a high probability of occurring as trait-unit intrusions.

Ethnicity

Ethnicity is expressed as group solidarity, usually in opposition to similarly defined groups or larger polities in which these groups are embedded. On a general level, an ethnic group can be defined as a "self-perceived" group of people who hold in common a set of traditions not shared by others with whom they are in contact. Such traditions typically include "folk religious beliefs and practices, language, a sense of historical continuity, and common ancestry or place of origin" (De Vos 1975:9). Kamp and Yoffee (1980:87–89) and Shennan (1989:14) similarly define ethnicity as self-conscious identification with a particular social group based on real or fictitious common ancestries and origins.

At first glance, tracking an ancestral

"Zuni" ethnic group in the archaeological record appears to be a promising approach. Ethnic behavior is often isomorphic with social or cultural boundaries because ethnicity is unlikely to be emulated by other groups unless there is some perceived social advantage. In such cases, language is also likely to be emulated, which would essentially make the borrowing group Zuni from the standpoint of this monograph. Typical criteria for ethnic membership (i.e., shared language, ancestry, and origins that are distinct from other groups) are likely to be associated with an ancestral Zuni group. In addition, the degree of group cohesion required for a linguistic isolate to survive for more than two millennia in a world populated by groups from other language families suggests that the ancestral Zuni may have been a distinctive ethnicity throughout much of this interval (Roberts 1961:293–296).

On the negative side, ethnicity is an emic construct that requires the archaeologist to reconstruct "mind" from material culture, a subjective exercise at best (Watson and Fotiadis 1990). As such, the self-defining symbols of a Zuni ethnic group must be isolated from those of other such groups and the cacophony of social messages consciously expressed on material culture. A precise definition of ethnicity and a concise list of ethnic markers have thus far eluded cultural anthropologists who have the advantage of studying extant societies (Alonso 1993). De Vos and Romanucci-Ross list racial, territorial, economic, religious, cultural, aesthetic, and/or linguistic uniqueness as potential criteria for membership, noting that ethnicity "like any other form of social identity, is essentially subjective; a sense of social belonging and ultimate loyalty" (1975:3).

To complicate matters further for the archaeologist, ethnohistorical case studies suggest that ethnicity is highly situational and that ethnic groups are unstable through time (Geary 1983; Kamp and Yoffee 1980). Contemporary ethnic boundaries rapidly develop and dissolve in response to external political threats or to economic pressures (David et al. 1991; Hill 1989; Wolf 1984:393–396). Group membership can be displayed when socially advantageous, and it can be hidden or suppressed when disadvantageous (Williams 1992), depending on power relations between these groups and larger sociopolitical systems (Wallerstein 1973). Although ethnic behavior has a strong cultural and linguistic component, the instability and context dependency of such behavior limit our ability to establish reliable material correlates for such groups and hence to track them in the archaeological record.

Enculturation

Culturally defined groups can also be defined merely by shared settlement history and close contact over an extended interval. In small-scale and middle-range agricultural societies, such as those inhabiting the Southwest throughout much of the prehistoric era, households are the basic social and corporate units (Hammel 1980:251; Wilk 1991) and constitute "the next biggest thing on the social map after the individual" (Hammel 1984:40). Enculturation (basic cultural training) and social reproduction are included in the range of functions performed by these fundamental units (Wilk and Netting 1984:5–19). During the routine and rhythm of domestic life specific ecological "where-to-dos," utilitarian "how-to-dos," and social "what-to-dos" are passed from old to young through active instruction and passive imitation (Netting 1993:59, 63, 70–72).

Households that have formed stable settlements, communities, and larger social groups develop common frameworks for transmitting such knowledge. This corpus represents a shared enculturative tradition in the behavioral sense whether or not the associated group consciously expresses its identity. Unconscious and deeply embedded elements of enculturation are ideal for our purposes because they define a group merely by contact history. Thus, tracking such groups is an etic approach with minimal subjectivity. Because basic aspects of enculturation infrequently rise to a level of intense scrutiny and self-reflection, these aspects tend to be more stable through time than displayed identities such as ethnicity, more resistant to assimilation in mixed cultural settings, and less likely to be emulated by groups from different cultural backgrounds. As such they have the potential to define groups at considerable time depth.

The persistence of an enculturative tradition within a region constitutes a compelling argument for cultural continuity. Conversely, the appearance of intrusive enculturative traditions would strongly suggest the immigration of new populations from different backgrounds either as classic site-unit intrusions or less conspicuous household-level movements into existing settlements. Artifacts and attributes that are the correlates of these traditions are more likely to remain distinctive in mixed cultural settings and in 1950s terms appear as A1 site-unit intrusions. If the material correlates of enculturation for a particular group can be identified, then it may be possible to track this group through time and space.

Material Correlates of Enculturation

To isolate artifact forms and attributes that correlate with deeply embedded aspects of enculturation a brief digression into the history of style is required, picking up where we left off at the end of the 1950s. The first serious attempt to break down artifact variability and correlate it with specific human behaviors occurred within the New Archaeology. Influenced by the work of Julian Steward (1955), Lewis Binford (1965:206–209) developed a tripartite scheme for partitioning social behavior based on the concepts of cultural tradition, adaptive area, and intersocietal interaction sphere, the latter borrowed from Joseph Caldwell (1964). Material culture variability was partitioned into two broad categories associated with the primary and secondary function of artifacts. Primary function was related to utilitarian use of artifacts within an adaptive area. Secondary function was related to style in the aesthetic sense and cultural tradition. The New Archaeology focused almost exclusively on the former at the expense of the latter.

Binford (1963) can also be credited with borrowing the concept of "cultural drift" from social anthropology and applying it to archaeological assemblages. The term is analogous to "genetic drift" and describes relatively minor variation in functionally equivalent material culture that develops between groups who are not in frequent contact. Binford used the concept to explain variability in Late Archaic lithic assemblages associated with red ocher caches in Michigan. Binford noted that variability "observed in attribute classes suspected as amenable to the operation of the process of cultural drift, should be investigated as hints to population expansions and migrations" (1963:94). Unfortunately, this line of inquiry was not further explored by Binford, and the concept lay dormant within the New Archaeology paradigm.

Style and Message

With the emergence of postprocessual archaeology during the late 1970s and 1980s, topics such as ideology and symbolism, largely ignored in the 1960s approaches, reemerged in explanatory frameworks (e.g., Hodder 1982a). Concomitant with this paradigm shift there was a resurgence of interest in style and intracultural meaning.

In his pivotal article on stylistic behavior Martin Wobst (1977) argued for a functional approach to style consistent with the philosophy of the New Archaeology. To Wobst (1977:330, 335), style was consciously produced on visible media as a means of nonverbal communication. Information exchanged in this manner included important social messages regarding group and individual identity. Polly Wiessner (1983, 1984) took this approach a step farther in explaining variability in artifact assemblages associated with Kalahari San groups of southern Africa. Wiessner partitioned "style with a message" into two dimensions based upon the type of information conveyed. *Emblemic* style conveys messages about group affiliation, and *assertive* style informs on individual identity (Wiessner 1983:257–258).

James Sackett's (1973) conception of style emerged from the famous Binford-Bordes debate on the meaning of artifact variability in lithic assemblages from the French Middle Paleolithic (Binford 1973; Bordes and Sonneville-Bordes 1970). In an attempt to find common ground between "culture as tradition" and "culture as adaptation" Sackett placed style and function within a continuum in which one was the perfect complement of the other and both considered together accounted for all possible artifact variability (Sackett 1977:370). Sackett (1982) introduced the concept of isochrestic variation as a means of articulating his abstract concept of style with tangible cultural behavior. The term *isochrestic* means "equivalent in use" (Sackett 1985:156), and isochrestic variation refers to the fact that there is often more than one feasible technique or tool to accomplish the same task or, simply stated, "more than one way to skin a cat" (Sackett 1990:33). To Sackett, isochrestic variation is style regardless of whether or not this variability is consciously produced or conveys social messages.

Differences in their approaches led to the well-known debate between Sackett and Wiessner during the 1980s (Sackett 1985, 1986, 1990; Wiessner 1984, 1985, 1990). Discussion focused on Wiessner's (1983:253–254) ethnoarchaeological study of style in Kalahari San material culture. In one particularly memorable experiment conducted by Wiessner (1983:269) two infrequently interacting San groups were presented with projectile points produced by each other. This display generated considerable anxiety and discussion within each group, as previously unrecognized differences in point manufacture were abruptly raised to a conscious level. When she asked members of both groups to elaborate on why each group made the same artifact differently, Wiessner elicited frustrated replies from one member, who stated they "made things in a certain way because everything must be made some way and that was the way their parents did it" (1984:95). The San could not have better validated the concept of iso-chrestic variation if Sackett himself had provided the script. In essence, Wiessner's experiment transformed enculturative differences in artifact manufacture that had arisen from dissimilar settlement histories into ethnic symbols.

From the vantage point of hindsight it is obvious that an unconscious and passive dimension of style lay beyond the realm of Wobst's and Wiessner's "style with a message." Sackett's more general model subsumed the conscious dimension and accommodated both. Instead of reaching this conclusion, the debate merely polarized the two positions, with little recognition of common ground. Much of this failure can be attributed to confusion over the meaning and usage of the term *isochrestic*. By the early 1990s there was considerable doubt whether a unified approach to style was possible in archaeology (Hegmon 1992; Wiessner 1990).

Variability in Visibility

Despite the skepticism that followed the Sackett-Wiessner debate, several researchers have attempted synthetic treatments of style. Christopher Carr's (1995) essay "A Unified Middle-Range Theory of Artifact Design" is of particular interest because it provides a basic strategy to differentiate style with and without a message in material culture. Artifact attributes are arranged hierarchically in Carr's (1995:173) model based on three criteria: (1) artifacts and attribute visibility; (2) relative order of attribute in artifact design; and (3) relative order of attributes in the artifact production sequence.

According to Wobst (1977:330), the higher the visibility of the attribute and associated artifact, the greater its message potential. Conversely, low-

visibility attributes have low message potential. The latter are inherently more stable through time because they are less subject to careful scrutiny and self-reflection. They are also less likely to be imitated or emulated. Stylistic similarities in low-visibility attributes largely reflect shared settlement history and a common enculturative background (Carr 1995:195–198, 213).

Carr subdivides visibility into two basic dimensions: physical and contextual. Physical visibility is influenced by size of the attribute and associated artifact, frequency of attribute occurrence on the artifact, degree of contrast with other attributes, complexity, and the relative order of manufacture. Although Carr (1995:185) gives priority to physical visibility in determining message potential, the context of use must also be considered. In order to reduce message potential and maximize the potential for the variability to passively reflect enculturative background, both contextual and physical visibility should be minimized. To reduce contextual visibility, the number of viewers, openness of viewing setting, viewer attentiveness, and average viewing time should be low (Carr 1995:table 7.5). Artifacts and architecture used in public contexts should be avoided because they are likely to be viewed for extended intervals by large audiences. In addition, artifacts and architecture associated with public ceremonies and rituals should be excluded because these conspicuous events are likely to heighten viewer attentiveness. Instead, private domestic settings should be emphasized. The small size and household focus of domestic architecture place restrictions on the number of viewers and openness of setting. Although certain domestic activities may be rich in symbolism and meaning (e.g., Sterner 1989),

most are conducted as part of a daily routine with little attentiveness or self-reflection. The tools, installations, architecture, and refuse associated with domestic life are potentially rich in enculturative markers that can be used to track the physical location of the associated group. Material culture attributes associated with domestic contexts can be further culled by reducing physical visibility (Carr 1995:table 7.5).

Domestic Spatial Organization, Foodways, and Technological Style

Domestic spatial organization is one such attribute that fits both criteria of low-contextual and physical visibility. Patterning in domestic spatial organization is often difficult to comprehend without an abstraction such as a map, especially in settlements comprised of multiroomed buildings. The organization of domestic space reflects the composition of households, the nature of activities these basic units undertake, and the degree to which households are integrated into larger social groups (Ferguson 1996; Flannery 1972; Fritz 1987; Hillier and Hanson 1984; Kent 1990; Lawrence and Low 1990; McGuire and Schiffer 1983). As such, it can vary considerably between groups with different cultural backgrounds (Hillier and Hanson 1984:27; Kent 1990; Rapaport 1969, 1990). In addition, many patterns observed in the layout of domestic architecture have little message content and are the byproducts of multiple construction episodes that reflect the changing needs of the resident household (Agorsah 1986; Goody 1971). Domestic spatial organization is often retrievable from archaeological sites in the form of wall foundations and floor features. Building events can be reconstructed from wall bond-abut patterns, providing the excavator with a temporally compressed sequence that is unavailable to the original inhabitants. Finally, on-site production of domestic architecture can be virtually assumed. Thus, domestic spatial organization represents one data set with a high potential to inform on enculturative background.

At the other end of the size scale are attributes that are so small that they cannot be discerned without close scrutiny or a visual aid. They are also ideal data sets for our purposes. Included in this set are organic refuse, tool use–wear, and manufactured microattributes such as weaving cordage patterns and flaked stone retouch. Organic refuse is particularly useful because these remains reveal domestic foodways and other basic plant and animal uses. Although food staples may not vary appreciably between different cultural groups inhabiting the same environmental zone, differences in flavorings and preparation techniques *are* probable (Baker 1980; Cheek and Friedlander 1990; De-France 1996; Evans 1980). Similar to spatial domestic organization, on-site production can be assumed in most cases for food refuse. These remains have little message content and represent a potential source of variation that can be used to discern different cultural groups.

A third strategy to minimize physical visibility focuses on the relative order an attribute is made within the production sequence of an artifact. All manufactured artifacts reflect the outcome of a series of technical options that compose a production sequence, or *chaîne d'operatoire* (Lemonnier 1986). As first discussed by Binford (1963) in his model of cultural drift, nuances in the design and manufacture of tools with comparable functions can be expected among noninteracting groups simply because of differences in the choices

made by those groups from a range of options. Such nuances constitute technological styles that are shared by tool producers from a common enculturative background (Lechtman 1977; Sackett 1985:158, 1990:33; Stark et al. 1998). The earlier an attribute is produced within the manufacturing sequence, the more likely it is hidden by subsequent steps of additive processes (e.g., ceramic manufacture, weaving, and wall and house construction) or removed by reductive processes (e.g., ground stone and flaked stone manufacture). If measurable traces of these earlier steps survive and on-site production can be demonstrated, associated technological styles represent another class of data from which groups can be tracked.

A final material culture category that may be useful for our purposes includes domestic artifacts and installations with relatively high physical visibility that may still reflect basic enculturation. These include installations related to house construction such as entry boxes (Lindsay et al. 1968) or those that have the potential to inform on culturally distinctive foodways such as hearths and mealing bins. Tools and installations used to manufacture basic household items such as walls, pottery, textiles, and stone artifacts are also potential members of this category. Similar to production steps embedded in manufactured artifact, tools associated with the production of utilitarian artifacts may reveal unique technological styles. Because of the potentially high physical visibility of this category, minimizing contextual visibility is especially important.

Concluding Remarks

This chapter has traced the history of migration, diffusion, and style over the past 50 years with the goal of

establishing a reliable method for tracking culturally defined groups in the archaeological record. We have come a long way from the site-unit and trait-unit intrusions of the 1950s, especially with respect to partitioning material culture variability and correlating it with specific forms of cultural behavior. We can identify and avoid specific classes of material culture that are likely to be exchanged or emulated and hence appear as trait-unit intrusions with little or no population movement.

Material culture associated with ethnicity and enculturation has much greater potential in assessing a Mogollon-Zuni connection. This chapter has argued for an emphasis on enculturation rather than ethnicity and other conscious displays of identity because the former defines a group by shared settlement history, independent of how members of the group actually defined themselves in the past. Hence the subjective exercise of isolating ethnic symbols from other messages conveyed on material is avoided. Shared settlement history is an essential component in the development and maintenance of a language, particularly a linguistic isolate.

Basic enculturation is conservative and as such has the potential to trace insular, culturally defined groups at considerable time depth. The material correlates of enculturation can be retrieved from small, obscure, and complex attributes on utilitarian artifacts from private domestic contexts where contextual visibility is low. Specific data sets include domestic spatial organization, installations and organic refuse related to domestic foodways, and technological styles embedded in the manufacturing processes of utilitarian items such as ceramic containers, textiles, walls, and stone tools. Basic tools and installations associated with the manufacture of household items can also be added to this list.

Ethnoarchaeological case studies drawn from a variety of temporal and geographical contexts (J. Clark 2001:14–22) validate an enculturative approach in tracking the movements of culturally defined groups and in differentiating among them in mixed settings generated by migration. Because material culture variability generated by dissimilar settlement histories is largely a random occurrence, specific artifacts and attributes within these classes that are discerning markers of enculturative background must be empirically demonstrated and will vary from case to case. If unique material tracers can be isolated for an ancestral Zuni population, then it may be possible to track this group back into the pre-Hispanic era and evaluate Martin and Rinaldo's original hypothesis of a Mogollon-Zuni connection with reasonable confidence.

5 The Environmental Context of Linguistic Differentiation and Other Cultural Developments in the Prehistoric Southwest

David A. Gregory and Fred L. Nials

In this chapter we discuss the environmental context of linguistic differentiation and other cultural developments in the Southwest since the arrival of human populations. We implement this discussion in the context of three "nested," large-scale temporal contexts: approximately the last 20,000 years (the Late Pleistocene and the Holocene), the last 5,000 years (the Late Holocene), and an "arbitrary" interval starting in the seventh century AD and extending to the present. The latter is defined to accommodate certain data sets (see below).

We emphasize the potential impacts of low-frequency processes (LFPs), those with a periodicity or amplitude of more than 25 years. Such processes are defined and ably discussed by Dean (1988a; see also chap. 6, this vol.), and, as Dean observes, Southwest tree-ring chronologies are generally of little utility in the study of processes having amplitudes of more than about 200 years (Dean 1988a:134–135; see also Salzer 2000a, 2000b). However, given a focus on larger-scale temporal and spatial contexts of Southwest adaptations, we are much interested in LFPs that have amplitudes greater than 200 years, processes potentially important in the development, per-

sistence, and transformations of southwestern cultural systems. In particular, the time depth of Zuni (and perhaps Keresan) as a linguistic isolate (see Hill, chap. 3, this vol.) and a concern with the differentiation of aboriginal southwestern linguistic groups and adaptations more generally require us to deal with time scales that extend back beyond the range of climatically sensitive southwestern tree-ring chronologies—for most purposes, about AD 500 (but see Salzer 2000a, 2000b).

Thus, we first identify and discuss three global-scale natural phenomena and their possible interrelationships: overall solar activity, triple-event sunspot minima, and the El Niño or El Niño/Southern Oscillation (ENSO) phenomenon. Using the three temporal contexts described above, we then explore potential relationships between low-frequency variation in these phenomena and cultural events and processes in the Southwest.

Solar Activity, Triple-Event Sunspot Minima, and the ENSO Phenomenon

The measure of overall solar activity used here is the well-known curve of atmospheric carbon values (see Damon et al. 1978; Damon and Linick

1986; Stuiver et al. 1991). This curve is based on several data sources, including bristlecone pine tree-ring chronologies for the last 8,000 years of the sequence, and serves as the basis for a number of radiocarbon calibration curves (e.g., Stuiver et al. 1998). Use of this curve as a measure of solar activity and as a proxy for variation in global temperature is accepted among paleoclimatologists (Damon 1988; Eddy 1977; Goudie 1985; Hoyt and Schatten 1997; Stuiver and Brazunias 1988) and has been similarly used by archaeologists (e.g., Bayham and Morris 1986, 1990).

One difference in our representation of the curve illustrated in several figures below must be noted. The carbon isotope ratios that represent the actual measurements used in constructing the curve have both positive and negative values, and the curve is normally represented in the conventional manner, with negative values below and positive values above the x-axis. However, since negative values represent relatively *more* solar activity and positive ones represent relatively *less* solar activity, conventional representations of the curve are somewhat counterintuitive: decreases are up and increases are down. For this reason we have simply reversed the y-axis values so that increasing solar activity is up and decreasing activity is down.[1]

Also considered here are so-called triple-event sunspot minima (Damon et al. 1978; Stuiver and Brazunias 1988), representing a low-frequency process of variation in solar activity. These triple events are defined by the sequential occurrence of Maunder- and Spörer-type sunspot minima, with Maunder events having durations or amplitudes of approximately 180 years and the Spörer amplitudes of approximately 220 years (Damon et al. 1978; Stuiver and Brazunias 1988).[2] Such triple events have an overall periodicity of about 2,200 years, but there has been some variation in the length of intervals separating them (see below).

These events are potentially significant to human populations because each of the constituent events in a triple event represents a relatively rapid high magnitude reduction in solar activity, followed immediately by a relatively rapid increase in activity three to four human generations in length (ca. 90–110 years) in both downward and upward phases. Occurring in series, they constitute radical up-and-down departures from longer-term trends in solar activity at any given time and are likely related to concomitant changes in weather patterns and perhaps climate and thus possibly to geomorphic effects and processes, especially those subject to threshold effects. The total duration for these triple events varies somewhat but is measured in hundreds of years, more than enough to require adjustments by human adaptations in response to any local, regional, or macroregional environmental manifestations they might have produced.

Following an inductive logic, the intervals covered by such events are good places to look for evidence of both environmental and cultural change. That is, they represent inter-vals during which the magnitude of variation in and directionality of existing environmental processes and conditions may have been significantly altered and thus during which the range (magnitude) of environmental variation within which existing adaptations developed had a higher probability of being exceeded.

The third natural process discussed here is the El Niño or ENSO (El Niño / Southern Oscillation) phenomenon. In the last three decades El Niño has been the subject of intensive study by climatologists and scientists in related fields (e.g., Anderson 1992a, 1992b; Caviedes 1988; Enfield and Cid 1991; Michaelsen 1989; NOAA 1999; Quinn and Burt 1970, 1972; Quinn and Neal 1992; Trenberth 1991; Webster and Palmer 1997; Wyrtki 1973, 1975; Wyrtki et al. 1976). The resulting literature is huge, and a number of Internet web sites are dedicated to current tracking of the phenomenon.[3] Briefly, the process involves global variation in sea-surface temperatures that produce "characteristic responses in the atmosphere" (Diaz and Markgraf 1992:1) having global "teleconnections," which, in turn, produce variability in atmospheric conditions and concomitant variability in weather patterns in distant areas, including the North American Southwest (Anderson 1992b; Andrade and Sellers 1988; Caviedes 1988; Diaz and Pulwarty 1992; Douglas and Englehart 1981; Tinsley and Deen 1991; Trenberth and Hoar 1997; van Loon and Madden 1981; L. Wells 1987; Wright 1977; Wyrtki 1975; Yarnal and Kiladis 1985). Next to the cycle of the seasons itself, the El Niño / ENSO phenomenon has been shown to be the single most important source of interannual climatic variability on a global scale (Davis 2000:236; Diaz and Markgraf 1992:1; Kiladis and Diaz 1989) and appears to have been so since at least the end of the Pleistocene (Enfield and Cid 1991; Kerr 1999; Rodbell et al. 1999).[4] The effects of El Niño on recent climate and associated natural processes in the southwestern United States (in particular, precipitation and streamflow) have been documented and studied, thus providing a baseline for interpretations on a larger temporal scale (e.g., Andrade and Sellers 1988; Cayan and Peterson 1989; Cayan and Webb 1992; D'Arrigo and Jacoby 1992; Hirschboeck 1985, 1987; Lough 1992; Meko 1992; Michaelsen 1989; Redmond and Koch 1991; Smith 1986; Swetnam and Betancourt 1992; Webb and Betancourt 1992).

Recently, and with increasing frequency, social scientists and social historians (including archaeologists) have explored historical aspects of the effects of El Niño on human populations (Davis 2000; Fagan 1999; Glantz 1996; Ingram et al. 1981; Kerr 1999; Meggers 1994; Rodbell et al. 1999; see also Nials et al. 1979a, 1979b for an early study of El Niño impacts). We propose to participate in that trend here. This effort is made possible by Quinn's (1992) annual reconstruction of El Niño events, based on Nile River flow data and other historical and quasi-historical sources (Quinn 1992; Quinn et al. 1987; see also Anderson 1992b) and including the interval AD 622–1990. Quinn's reconstruction is the basis for the third temporal context considered here.

The scale of the El Niño phenomenon is such that we expect it to have been an important source of environmental variation within which southwestern adaptations formed and were transformed. Previous studies provide a basis for generating expectations about its effects at various times and in various places in the Southwest, and, since Quinn's (1992) reconstruction is on an annual scale, variability and patterning in El Niño can be compared directly with tree-ring-based climatic reconstructions (see Fritts 1976). The reconstruction also allows us to examine variation El Niño behavior for a lengthy segment of the late prehistoric and all of the protohistoric and historic periods and thus to relate that variation to aboriginal responses in the American Southwest.

The Big Picture

As noted above, the first of our three temporal contexts spans the last 20,000 years. Figure 5.1 represents environmental and cultural events, processes, and identified intervals within this lengthy period. We begin with a synopsis of the cultural side of the equation and then set that discussion against environmental variation.

Cultural Developments

The indicated date for the peopling of the New World south of Alaska (13,500 B.P.) is based on recent re-evaluations of Paleoindian chronology (Fiedel 1999, 2002; see also Matson, chap. 7, this vol.) and assumes the arrival of Clovis Paleoindian populations in the Southwest shortly thereafter.[5] For the remainder of the sequence of cultural periods we employ Huckell's (1996) dates for the Early Archaic and the beginning of the Middle Archaic. A date of 6000 B.P. is used for the domestication of maize in Mesoamerica (but see Fritz 1995; Matson, chap. 7, this vol.), and we place the arrival of maize in the Southwest and thus the start of the Early Agricultural period at 4000 B.P. (see Huckell 1995). Recent research has produced clusters of direct dates on maize that place the arrival of maize just two or three centuries shy of this date (see Gregory 1999:117–119, fig. 8.33), and we antic-

ipate that future research will push the start of this important process to (at least) 4000 B.P. Also based on recent research, we date the first appearance of a full-blown ceramic container technology in the Southwest at ca. 1850 B.P. (AD 150; see Heidke 1999; Heidke and Habicht-Mauche 1999). Several linguistic "events" and processes are shown in figure 5.1. First, the approximate time of arrival of Amerind speakers in the Southwest—after around 13,500 B.P. —establishes the baseline for linguistic differentiation (Fiedel 1999, 2002; Renfrew 1987a; Ruhlen 1994); we assume the validity of Greenberg's (1987; Greenberg et al. 1986) hypothesis concerning Amerind as a once-unified entity. Following Hill's conclusions in chapter 3, we place the minimum date for the differentiation of Zunian at 7,000–8,000 years ago, and this date *may* also serve for Keresan (see below). We also illustrate two theories concerning the relationship between language and the arrival of maize in the Southwest. The first is that of Hill (2001, 2002), which has maize coming to the Southwest as the result of an adaptive radiation of Uto-Aztecan-speaking migrants out of Mesoamerica; the second proposes that maize diffused along an already existing dialect chain of Uto-Aztecan speakers and thus a pre–4000 B.P. date for the presence of Uto-Aztecan speakers in the Southwest (see also Wilcox and Gregory, chap. 1, this vol.). We also illustrate the timing of two theories for the internal differentiation of Tanoan languages, with the split of Tiwa/Tewa from Towa (Davis 1959; Trager 1967).

Renfrew (1987a:120–123) describes three processes of linguistic change within a given area that may be usefully applied to the Southwest: *initial colonization*, *replacement*, and *continuous development*. Initial colonization is the process by which

"human beings enter a previously uninhabited region" (Renfrew 1987a:121), which clearly applies to the peopling of the New World and, scaled down a bit, to the Southwest. Replacement "is the process whereby the language spoken in a particular region is displaced by another, brought in by people from a different, possibly adjacent, region where it is in use" (Renfrew 1987a:121). Continuous development is the most complex of the three processes, involving opposing tendencies of conservatism (replication) and innovation as well as the processes of divergence and convergence (Renfrew 1987a:122). Divergence occurs when "groups of people speaking the same language separate and are no longer in contact" (Renfrew 1987a:122), while convergence is the product of interaction. A final complication in the process of continuous development is that human beings have the ability to speak two or more languages, which is an important factor in the development of creole or hybrid languages (Renfrew 1987a:122–123) and may be important in language substitution or replacement (Renfrew 1998b).

Environmental Processes

At least seven and possibly eight triple-event (TE) sunspot minima have occurred during the last 20,000 years. The seven most recent have occurred since the peopling of the New World and are numbered consecutively in figure 5.1 from oldest to youngest (TE 1–7). Three occurred during the Paleoindian period (TE 1, 2, 3), one during the Early Archaic (TE 4), one at the boundary between the Early and Middle Archaic (TE 5), one during the latter centuries of the Early Agricultural period (TE 6), and one spanning the late prehistoric, protohistoric, and early historic periods (TE 7). Also shown in figure 5.1 is

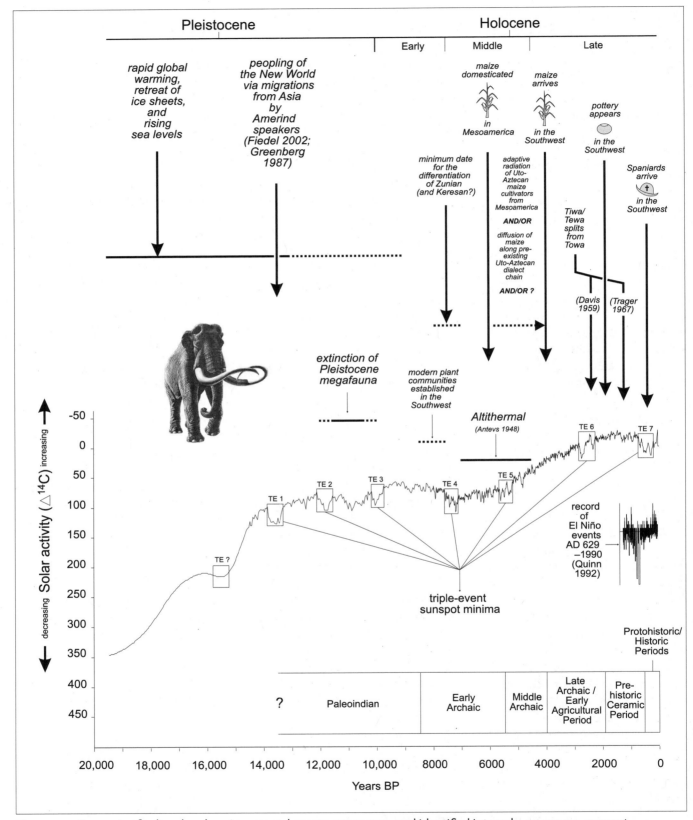

Figure 5.1. Synopsis of cultural and environmental events, processes, and identified intervals, 19,500 BP–present.

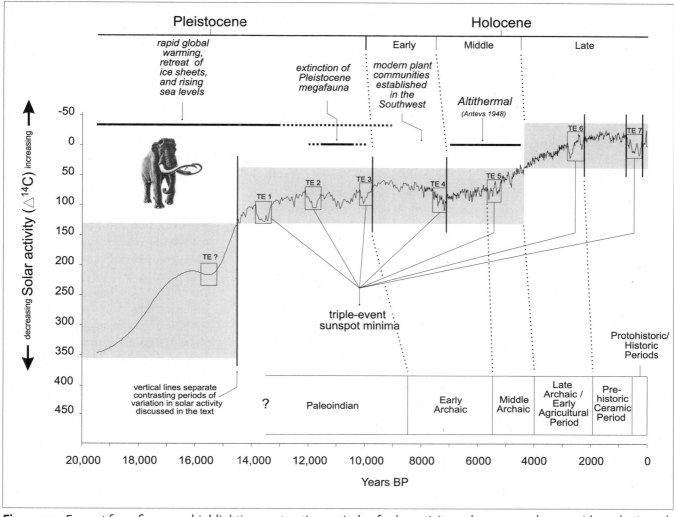

Figure 5.2. Excerpt from figure 5.1, highlighting contrasting periods of solar activity and correspondences with geologic and cultural periods.

the approximately 1,400-year record of El Niño events (Quinn 1992), dealt with in greater detail in subsequent sections; its inclusion here emphasizes the relatively short period of time for which high-resolution data relating to this important process are available.

Figure 5.1 clearly shows that the dominant trend in solar activity over the last 20,000 years has been one of increase. Figure 5.2 duplicates some of the information in figure 5.1 but highlights intervals of differing solar activity at two different scales and identifies correspondences between changes in solar activity and identi-

fied geologic and cultural periods. Three long intervals of differing solar activity are identified (shaded in fig. 5.2), each exhibiting a range of values that is largely mutually exclusive from the other two: 19,500–14,500 B.P., 14,500–4200 B.P., and 4200 B.P.–present. The boundaries between these intervals, at ca. 14,500 and 4200 B.P., define two "thresholds" in solar activity. Also illustrated are periods of differing solar activity *within* and, in one case, *across* these three longer intervals. These shorter periods are based in part on visual observation of the curve, but statistical comparisons of

their means indicate significant differences between them.

As shown in figure 5.2, the magnitude of variation in solar activity in the 5,500 years from 14,500 to 20,000 years ago was about twice that which has occurred in the nearly 15 millennia since. At about 14,500 B.P., or just prior to the peopling of the New World, levels of activity were reached that exceeded anything that had gone before, constituting the first of the two major thresholds.

Considerable variation is apparent from 14,500 to about 9700 B.P., with the end of TE 3 marking the end of this period. It was during the approximately two millennia bracketed by TE 2 and TE 3 that Pleistocene megafauna became extinct and other changes in faunal distributions occurred in the Far West of North America and elsewhere in the hemisphere (Grayson 1993; Martin 1963, 1967; Martin and Klein 1984).

At about 9,500 years ago, approximately coeval with the Pleistocene–Holocene transition, an increase in mean solar activity is detectable, following immediately on the heels of TE 3. For the next 2,500 years there was an overall downward trend in solar activity, gradual at first and then steepening somewhat just before 8000 B.P. The end of this downward trend was punctuated by the end of yet another triple event (TE 4) at 7000 B.P., which corresponds roughly to the boundary between the Early and Middle Holocene (Grayson 1993). Between 8500 and 8000 B.P. the transition from Paleoindian to Early Archaic archaeological manifestations occurred (Huckell 1996) at about the same time that modern distributions of plant communities were established in the Southwest (Betancourt et al. 1990; Dean, chap. 6, this vol.).

Between 7000 and 8000 B.P. Zunian and perhaps Keresan had emerged as distinct languages, and thus the divergence of one or both of these linguistic groups may have occurred prior to or during the transition to modern plant communities in the Southwest. Very low population densities in the Southwest postulated for these intervals (Matson, chap. 7, this vol.) would have provided an ideal context not only for the divergence of Zunian and Keresan (but see Kowalewski, chap. 22, this vol.) but for other linguistic differentiation as well (Renfrew 1987a:122; see also Torroni et al. 1994; Torroni et al. 1993; Wallace and Torroni 1992; Ward 1999).

The possibility that Keresan devel-

oped out of a remnant population representing the Plano/Eden-Scottsbluff tradition (Caddoan speakers?) that remained in the Southwest after the general plainsward retraction of Plano/Eden-Scottsbluff has been suggested (Rood 1973; see Irwin-Williams, n. 3, chap. 2, this vol.). If the relationship between Keresan and Caddoan can be demonstrated, the differentiation of Keresan was likely somewhat later than that of Zunian. Based on current data, the differentiation of either Zunian or Keresan could also have occurred outside the Southwest, with subsequent in-migration of populations that ultimately represent the only groups speaking these languages (see Hill, chap. 3, and Diehl, chap. 11, this vol.). In either case, it is clear that if material differences marking these and other distinct language groups are to be identified, the first place to look for them is in Late Paleoindian and Early Archaic archaeological assemblages and site distributions (see Matson, chap. 7, this vol.).

For the next 4,800 years, from ca. 7000 to 2200 B.P. (200 BC), the solar curve shows its longest period of consistency in slope and the strongest upward trend since the terminal Pleistocene. At about 4200 B.P. a second threshold in solar activity was reached, "straddled" by the nearly five-millennium-long upward trend. This second threshold corresponds approximately to the boundary between the Middle and Late Holocene (see below; Grayson 1993). Prior to this threshold the long-term upward trend was initially more gradual, then steepened with the onset of TE 5. It was during the early centuries of this interval that maize was domesticated in Mesoamerica, and the Altithermal period (ca. 7000–4500 B.P.; Antevs 1948) falls entirely before the threshold.

In his review of paleoenvironmen-

tal evidence relating to the Altithermal in the Great Basin, Grayson (1993) cites numerous studies that demonstrate considerably more variability during this interval than is implied by Antevs's monolithic "Long Drought" characterization (see Bryan and Gruhn 1964; see also Matson, chap. 7, this vol.). Nonetheless, current evidence supports the conclusion that the Altithermal was "an interval that began sometime between 8,000 and 7,000 years ago, and that ended between 5,000 and 4,000 years ago, was warmer or drier, or both, than what came before or after" (Grayson 1993:214; see also Benson and Thompson 1987; LaMarche 1973; LaMarche and Mooney 1967; Lindstrom 1990; Mehringer 1977, 1985; Mehringer and Wigand 1990; Thompson 1984). In the Southwest the Altithermal witnessed a major shift in the regime of alluvial deposition (Haynes 1968), with major erosion occurring between about 7500 and 6000 B.P., followed by deposition between about 6000 and 4000 B.P.

Several aspects of solar variation are worth noting with respect to the Altithermal. Just prior to 7,000 years ago, beginning with the upward phase of the final TE 4 event, the trend in solar activity shifted from decreasing to increasing. A sharp steepening of slope in the curve occurred after 5800 B.P., beginning with TE 5 and continuing well after the end of the Altithermal. The beginning of this upward trend also includes an extended period of high-magnitude variation in solar activity between about 5800 and 4800 B.P., including TE 5 and an isolated Maunder-type minimum beginning at about 5000 B.P. The end of the Altithermal corresponds to the major threshold in solar activity at about 4200 B.P.

Given the fact that Haynes's (1968) alluvial sequence for the Southwest is based on radiocarbon dates, the correspondence between his sequence and solar activity is striking. His period of arroyo cutting (7500–6000 B.P.) was initiated at about the same time that the direction of the curve shifted from downward to upward; further steepening of this upward trend occurred with the onset of TE 5 (6200–5800 B.P.). Haynes's period of deposition (6000–4000 B.P.) corresponds fairly well with the increasing values and high-magnitude solar variation between 5800 and 4800 B.P. Thus, we have the onset of a threshold-controlled alluvial process (arroyo cutting) corresponding with a marked change in the direction of solar activity and a shift to deposition correlating with a marked upward shift in the rate of increase and, subsequently, a period of high-magnitude variation.

Although the timing of the onset of cutting varied somewhat over the Southwest (Haynes 1968; Irwin-Williams and Haynes 1970), most floodplains of the major drainages were rather thoroughly scoured during this interval. This clearly altered the landscapes within which Early Archaic populations were living and likely required at least some adjustments in existing adaptations, possibly including migration. This cutting was also undoubtedly responsible for removing many earlier archaeological deposits within the floodplains (Haynes and Huckell 1985), thus having a major influence on the sample of Paleoindian and Early Archaic remains available for study. Similarly, subsequent rapid and deep alluvial deposition buried Middle Archaic floodplain sites and any remaining Paleoindian and Early Archaic ones, once again altering the landscape and introducing yet another sampling problem in relation to Middle Archaic and earlier remains (e.g., see Gregory 1999; Gregory and Baar 1999).

Northward movement of maize from Mesoamerica may have begun during and continued through the interval of high-magnitude variation that occurred between 5800 and 4800 B.P. Some 500 years after the end of the Altithermal and only a few centuries after the 4200 B.P. threshold in solar activity was reached, maize arrived in the Southwest, marking the beginning of the lengthy Early Agricultural period. The spread of maize across the Southwest was completed during the following interval of steadily increasing solar activity characterized by low interannual variation.

At the end of TE 6 the solar activity curve flattens again for roughly 1,500 years (2200–700 B.P.), an interval characterized by a comparatively narrow range of variability in the magnitude of solar activity. This 1,500-year interval also witnessed the highest mean level of solar activity since at least the beginning of the Pleistocene and the highest levels since the peopling of the New World and the Southwest. Two or three centuries after the end of TE 6 a full-blown ceramic container technology appeared in the Southwest (ca. 1850 B.P.).

With the onset of TE 7 about 700 years ago (ca. AD 1280) the overall trend shifted to one of decreasing solar activity but was accompanied by the high-magnitude variation characteristic of TE minima. It was toward the end of TE 7 that the Spaniards arrived in the Southwest. An apparent upward turn about 200 years ago (AD 1800) is difficult to evaluate because of its short length, its occurrence immediately after TE 7, and more fundamental issues relating to the increase in atmospheric carbon caused by the burning of fossil fuels during and after the Industrial Revolution and the potential effects of nuclear explosions after AD 1945 (see Dean, chap. 6, this vol.).

The Late Holocene

Our second temporal context focuses on the Late Holocene (see fig. 5.3). Cultural and environmental events and processes shown in figure 5.1 are repeated, and we elaborate on some of these and add new ones. First, we have added a line representing the slope of the solar activity curve for the interval between TE 5 and TE 6 and four other lines representing the means of atmospheric carbon values for TE 6 and TE 7 and for two intervals falling between TE 6 and TE 7 (2200–1350 B.P. and 1350–650 B.P.). Second, based on the graph of El Niño events, a dotted line has been added to indicate a major shift in El Niño frequency at 710 B.P. (AD 1290). Third, the full differentiation of Tanoan languages in the Southwest is shown, elaborating on the Tiwa/Tewa split from Towa shown in figure 5.1 and again representing the contrasting theories of Davis (1959) and Trager (1967). Fourth, the interval during which Matson (1991; chap. 7, this vol.) hypothesizes the migration of maize-bearing populations from southern Arizona onto the Colorado Plateau (2900–2300 B.P.) is highlighted. Fifth, intervals defined by two global climate characterizations are added, the Medieval Warm Period (MWP; see Lamb 1995) and the Little Ice Age (LIA; Grove 1990).[6] Finally, we add a composite curve of total Southwest population since the Middle Archaic, combining the estimate for the Middle Archaic given by Matson in chapter 7 and Doelle's (2000) reconstruction spanning the interval from 2000 to 450 B.P. (AD 1–1550).

The last part of the long upward trend in solar activity that occurred between 7000 and 2200 B.P. is readily apparent at this scale, and there was relatively low interannual variation within the overall directional change. Also highlighted at this

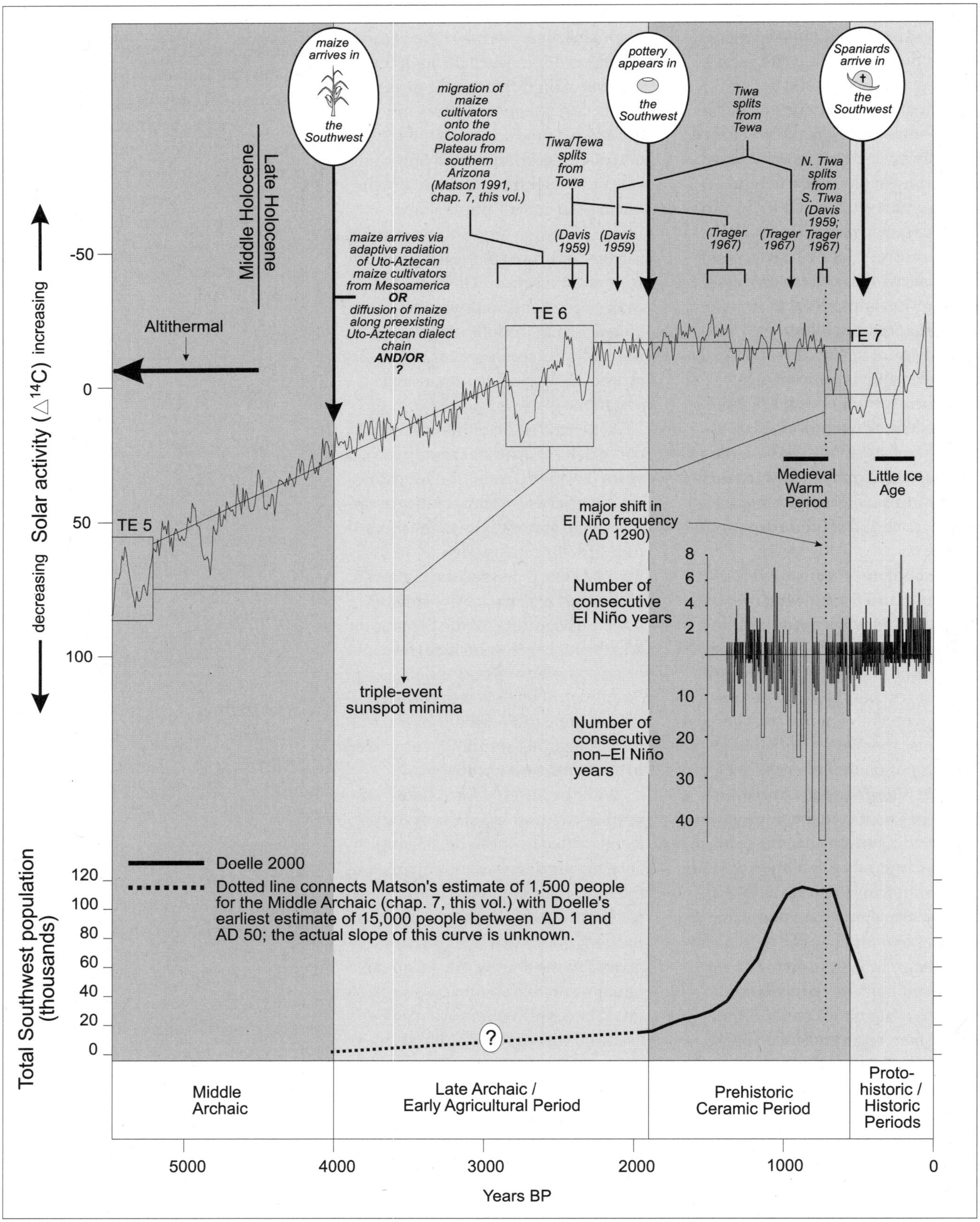

Figure 5.3. Synopsis of cultural and environmental events, processes, and identified intervals, 5500 BP–present.

more refined temporal scale is the high-magnitude variation characteristic of sunspot minima, exemplified here by TE 5 (partial) and by TE 6 and TE 7. As noted above, the curve of solar activity is relatively flat between TE 6 and TE 7, and the overall mean for the 2200–710 B.P. interval represents the highest levels of solar activity in the last 20,000 years. The MWP (1000–700 B.P. [AD 1000–1300]) corresponds to the last three centuries of this interval, and the last decades of the MWP are coincident with the "Great Drought" in the northern Southwest (see below; see also Dean, chap. 6, this vol.). The end of the MWP is coeval with the downward trend in solar activity that occurred at the onset of TE 7 and with the marked increase in El Niño frequencies at 710 B.P. (AD 1290). The LIA (400–120 B.P. [AD 1600–1880]) falls in the latter part of TE 7, coincident with the third minimum in TE 7 and with the lowest levels of solar activity in some 2,500 years.

Population Dynamics and Linguistic Diversity during the Middle Archaic and Before

If we assume Wobst's (1974) estimated figure of 500 people as a necessary condition for the long-term maintenance of a given breeding population, and if we also assume that such minimal breeding populations spoke the same language or dialects thereof, we can evaluate in a preliminary way the relationship between population levels and potential linguistic diversity for the Middle Archaic and earlier intervals in the Southwest. There is a basic problem: either the current population estimates are too low, or the linguistic diversity present at the time of European contact developed later in time.

If Matson's estimate of 1,500 people for the Middle Archaic is approximately correct, a maximum of three linguistic groups may have been present in the Southwest at this time. This would match up on a superficial level with Irwin-Williams's picture of the Southwest at 8000 B.P., where three technocomplexes and their relationships to southwestern language groups are recognized: San Dieguito/Lake Mohave (from which she derives Hokan/Yuman and Keresan), Sulphur Springs Cochise (ancestral to Hopi and Pima as well as Tanoan and Numic), and Plano (not directly represented by later Southwest linguistic groups in her scheme; see Irwin-Williams and Haynes 1970). However, her mapping of this period leaves a large unpopulated area in the central Southwest (see fig. 2.1, this vol.), a gap that is contradicted by archaeological data. And, as she acknowledges, neither Uto-Aztecan per se nor Kiowan nor Zunian is considered anywhere in her scheme, despite the relationships between the first two and other groups she does consider.

If we double Matson's estimate (to 3,000), then the full range of language groups present in later times could have been present during the Middle Archaic: Hokan/Yuman, Uto-Aztecan, Tanoan, Keresan, and Zunian. The sampling problems with Middle Archaic sites and earlier ones discussed above are of fundamental importance to this issue. A relatively large proportion of both Paleoindian and Early Archaic sites removed by scouring (ca. 7000–6000 B.P.) as well as many Middle Archaic sites (and any earlier sites) buried under deep alluvium (ca. 4000 B.P.) are likely to have been floodplain campsites.

Given the arid-lands character of the Southwest, it is hardly a leap of faith to suggest that floodplains were extensively and intensively exploited during these intervals. Thus, the largest sites in their respective subsistence-settlement systems may well have been those most radically affected by geomorphic processes and the kinds of sites most underrepresented in our current sample. If this is the case, and estimated population levels for the Middle Archaic and earlier periods are too low, then the linguistic diversity seen in the ethnographic present may well have been present during the Middle Archaic and perhaps earlier. We think that this is the most likely possibility, but much additional research is necessary to distinguish between these two general alternatives and other more specific ones that may be developed. Any adequate theory must bring into congruence population estimates derived from archaeological data and their implications for linguistic diversification on several geographic and temporal scales.

The Arrival and Spread of Maize

An important question in current research is, By what process did maize cultivation arrive in the North American Southwest? Using Renfrew's (1987a, 1998b) perspective we identify three possible combinations of processes that involve maize, language, and genes (human populations).

In the first instance all three may have moved together as a unit, with populations of maize cultivators moving north and bringing with them not only maize but their language, previously not spoken in the Southwest. Also referred to as "demic" diffusion (Cavalli-Sforza et al. 1988; Cavalli-Sforza et al. 1993; Renfrew 1998a), this is essentially the hypothesis advocated by Hill (2001, 2002, chap. 3, this vol.), who has Uto-Aztecan speakers moving northward out of Mesoamerica (perhaps western Mexico?) and ultimately into the Southwest in a process of adaptive radiation.

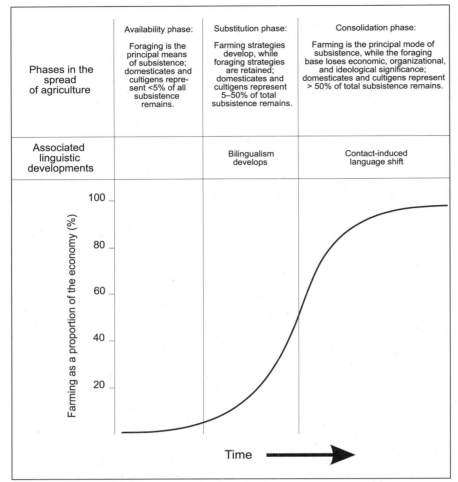

Figure 5.4. Renfrew's (1998a) modification of Zvelebil's (1996) "availability model."

In the second case neither people nor language moves. Rather, the technology of maize cultivation itself diffuses in a down-the-line fashion. The hypothesis that maize cultivation arrived in the Southwest along a pre-existing Uto-Aztecan dialect chain is an example of this kind of process (see Wilcox and Gregory, chap. 1, this vol.); however, such down-the-line movement need not have been between groups speaking related languages. In either case, this is essentially a simple diffusion model, wherein the advantages of maize cultivation were sufficient to facilitate its spread over ecologically diverse landscapes and across culturally and

linguistically diverse groups, absent the wholesale movement of genes and language.

A third possibility (not shown in fig. 5.3) is Renfrew's (1998b) modification of Zvelebil's (1996) "availability model," developed to explain the origin and spread of agriculture in Eurasia (see fig. 5.4). In this case both maize and language would have moved northward without any movement of people (Renfrew 1996:184). In Golla's (2000) terms a new spread language group would thus be formed by Renfrew's replacement process, one that would show considerable internal diversity.

As shown in figure 5.4, Zvelebil's

(1996) original model consists of three phases; Renfrew's (1998b:fig. 7) modification keeps the entire model intact but adds linguistic processes as new elements and renames it the "substitution model" to highlight linguistic elements. During the *availability phase* indigenous hunters and gatherers engage in a foraging lifeway but may be aware of cultigens or even use them in a cursory way. During the *substitution phase* foraging strategies are retained while farming strategies are developed, and, by Renfrew's logic, it is during this phase that bilingualism develops through contact with adjacent farmers and the adoption of linguistic elements associated with farming technology. During the *consolidation phase* farming becomes the dominant subsistence pursuit, while foraging loses economic, organizational, and ideological significance. It is during this last phase that the contact-induced language shift occurs. Thus, this model would predict a time-transgressive spread of maize from Mesoamerica northward, resulting in a series of "frontiers" of domestication (see Zvelebil 1996).

There are a number of problems in applying this model to the Southwest. The figures for farming as a proportion of the economy given by Zvelebil are based on an Old World model and would have to be adjusted for arid-lands environments and for a dearth of domesticated animals in the Southwest. There is also the difficult problem of assessing the relative proportions of cultigens vs. wild plant remains in archaeological assemblages, particularly as regards the issue of maize "dependence" (Diehl 2005a, 2005b, 2005c; Gregory and Diehl 2002; see also Matson, chap. 7, this vol.): application of this model requires some consistent and reliable empirical measure of dependence. Nevertheless, the model is intriguing and may be preliminarily assessed in light of data from recently investigated Early Agricultural period sites in southern Arizona and elsewhere.

In those cases where requisite data are available, even the earliest maize-producing sites have high (> 80 percent) ubiquities of maize in flotation assemblages. However, they also have equally high ubiquities of a wide variety of wild plant remains (Diehl 2005a, 2005b, 2005c; Gregory and Diehl 2002), and associated faunal assemblages show a consistent focus on hunting (Gregory 2001a; Waters 2005). Moreover, this "farming-foraging" pattern was maintained at numerous sites and throughout the two millennia of the Early Agricultural period with remarkable consistency (Gregory 2001a), despite variability in individual site assemblages and even though some (if not all) populations were practicing a rudimentary canal irrigation technology very early on (Damp, chap. 8, this vol.; Mabry 1999; Muro 1998). A radical departure from this pattern occurs during the ensuing Early Ceramic period: maize ubiquities remain high, but the diversity and ubiquities of wild plant remains drop off sharply, as do the density and diversity of faunal remains (Gregory 2001a; Gregory and Diehl 2002).

Given these findings, it is perhaps tempting to interpret the whole of the Early Agricultural period in the Sonoran Desert (and the Chihuahuan Desert?) as falling within the substitution phase of the Zvelebil/Renfrew model, with the Early Ceramic period representing the consolidation phase and the time during which linguistic replacement should have been completed in various areas. From this perspective Middle Archaic and Late Archaic populations would represent

the availability phase, and at least one spread language group that resulted was likely Uto-Aztecan, which does show considerable internal diversity and whose ultimate distribution is consistent with this hypothesis (see Hill 2002).

However, Zvelebil notes that the model cannot "adequately describe societies where the substitution phase extended for a very long time, in other words where a mixed foraging-farming economy became part of an established way of life rather than a phase in a transition" (1996:326). Current data suggest that farming-foraging did indeed become an established and widespread way of life, at least in some parts of the Southwest, and, at present, the data do not seem to fit the model. However, this model remains an interesting one and with appropriate modifications may prove useful in subsequent studies of the arrival and spread of maize in the Southwest.

Given the size of the Southwest region, its ecological diversity, and the cultural and linguistic diversity that undoubtedly existed during Middle Archaic times, it is likely that a variety of processes played a role in the spread of maize, with differing linguistic consequences. Proposed migrations or demic diffusion *within* the Southwest (see below) and ecologically based differentiation of maize cultivation strategies—with maize technology arriving in some areas via down-the-line transmission and without accompanying language and people—could accommodate the linguistic diversity present today, including Zunian and Keresan isolates. For the moment, a simple diffusion model best fits the relatively limited data, but much more research is needed.

By whatever processes, it was shortly after the beginning of the Late

Holocene and roughly coincident with a major threshold in solar activity that maize arrived in the region. The arrival and initial spread of maize occurred during the latter part of the long interval of increasing solar activity and low interannual variability discussed above (ca. 5000–2900 B.P.) and prior to the onset of TE 6. Some have argued that the rapid deposition of alluvium ca. 4,000 years ago created floodplain environments more suitable for cultivation than had previously been the case, thus providing the necessary context for the movement of maize into the Southwest (Mabry 1998). Two critical questions are, Did maize actually arrive *before* this period of deposition (see Gregory 1999:117–119, fig. 8.33; Gregory and Baar 1999)? Were Middle Archaic populations involved in the cultivation or husbandry of cheno-ams and perhaps other species *prior* to the arrival of maize in the Southwest (see Haury 1962)?

Matson (1991; chap. 7, this vol.) suggests that sometime between 2900 and 2300 B.P.—and possibly between 2600 and 2500 B.P.—groups from southern Arizona (Uto-Aztecan speakers?) migrating onto the Colorado Plateau served as the mechanism for the introduction of maize into that area and the basis for the differentiation of Eastern and Western Basketmaker populations. This hypothesized migration occurred during TE 6. This suggests a potentially important environmental context for the proposed migration and perhaps for pan-Southwest population and settlement dynamics during this interval. Could high-magnitude solar variation and its effects on southwestern weather and climate have influenced the population movements hypothesized by Matson?

There is some anecdotal evidence

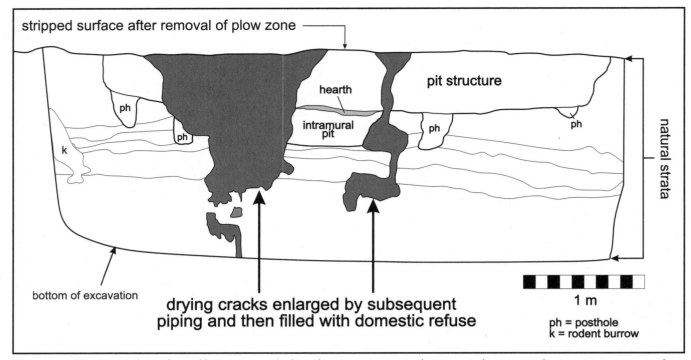

Figure 5.5. Drying cracks, enlarged by piping, intruding the pit structure and associated intramural pit at Los Pozos; cracks are filled with cultural debris. Scale is 1 m long.

for rapid environmental change and floodplain deterioration in southern Arizona toward the end of this interval at the Early Agricultural period site of Los Pozos (Gregory 2001a), located in the Santa Cruz River floodplain in Tucson. The site dates toward the end of TE 6 during a period of rapidly increasing solar activity (2350–1900 B.P.; Gregory 2001b; Schurr and Gregory 2002). Some half-dozen large desiccation cracks were discovered during 1998 investigations at the site, and several were examined in detail. All were quite large (≥ 1 m at the top), all had been enhanced by piping, and all were filled with domestic refuse *during* the occupation. The most spectacular and informative of these features had formed *within* an abandoned, refuse-filled pit structure (see fig. 5.5).

The presence of these natural features indicates that very wet conditions were followed rapidly by very dry conditions within the floodplain, and these changes clearly occurred

during the occupation at Los Pozos. Subsequent piping suggests a falling water table probably caused by incision of the Santa Cruz River channel, located less than 1 km to the west at the time of the occupation. The Los Pozos occupation began during the latter stages of TE 6 and continued through a minor peak in solar activity at the end of that interval; this peak was followed by a short downward trend and then by a relatively rapid increase in activity (see fig. 5.3). It is not possible at this time to definitively attribute local changes in southern Arizona with variation in solar activity, and the role of environmental change in the abandonment of the site at about AD 100 has yet to be fully specified. Drying cracks and piping are, however, proof of rapidly changing conditions, at least on a local scale. Their unquestionable stratigraphic relationship with cultural features at the site provides an excellent example of the kinds of data present in the record that—if duplicated on

a larger geographic scale—may be made to speak to larger issues.

Regional Differentiation of Maize-Based Adaptations in the Southwest

Middle Archaic manifestations in the Southwest clearly indicate that maize arrived in an already differentiated cultural landscape (see Huckell 1996; Irwin-Williams, chap. 2, this vol.; Irwin-Williams and Haynes 1970) that included the full range of Southwest environments. As discussed above, despite estimates of low population densities during the Middle Archaic, the linguistic landscape may have already included Uto-Aztecan (whether newly arrived or already in place), Yuman, and Tanoan; Zunian and Keresan may also have been present. A major research problem for future investigation is how maize cultivation transformed and perhaps reified this already diverse cultural and linguistic landscape.

An extrapolation between Matson's Middle Archaic population estimate and the beginning of Doelle's curve at AD I suggests a roughly tenfold increase in Southwest population during the two millennia of the Early Agricultural period—about six people per year, given the dates used here. Or, if we use the alternative estimate of 3,000 people discussed above, a fivefold increase at a rate of about three people per year is indicated. At present we cannot say whether this was a more or less uniform increase or was punctuated by directional changes, nor do we yet know where Zunian speakers may have been during the Early Agricultural period, but maize cultivators using irrigation technology were in the Zuni area proper by 2300 B.P. (see Damp, chap. 8, this vol.). As noted above, high-magnitude variation in solar activity represented by TE 6 may have been an important factor in at least one hypothesized migration and perhaps in other processes that occurred during this segment of the Early Agricultural period.

In the next section we present additional reconstructions of Southwest population, and there are some differences in maximum population (Doelle and Hill 2003; Wilcox et al., chap. 12, this vol.). However, the general shape of the curve shown in figure 5.3 is duplicated in all cases where they overlap in time: there is an upward trend from about 2000 B.P. onward, gradual at first and then punctuated by a sharp upturn starting at about 1500 B.P. This marked increase culminated in maximum population levels between about AD 1000 and 1300, followed by a sharp decline at AD 1300 or shortly thereafter. We comment further on these curves below. For the moment we note that the overall increase in Southwest population between about 2000 and 1000 B.P. occurred during

a long interval of high solar activity and relatively low interannual variation. It was also during this interval that the greatest levels of sociocultural complexity were achieved in the Southwest in the form of the Chacoan, Mimbres, Hohokam, and Casas Grandes regional and macroregional systems (Wilcox 1979, 1991c, 1996a, 1996b, 1999a). The most important aspect of the natural environment during this interval and in relation to these cultural developments may have been the relative predictability of the environment (see below).

Pottery appeared in the Southwest during this interval, providing a highly visible means for recognition of different populations and settlement systems. By 1500 B.P. or slightly later the major cultural traditions and their identified variations—those that are part and parcel of Southwest archaeology—are recognizable by virtue of ceramic distributions and other aspects of material culture: Hohokam, Mogollon, and Anasazi and, somewhat later, Hakataya, Patayan, Fremont, and Sevier. At a general level these cultural designations represent differing adaptations within differing ecological contexts, and there appears to have been both synchronic and diachronic variation in organizational features of those adaptations and their interrelationships.

These entities and their internal variations represent the latter stages of the long-term differentiation of populations that began with the peopling of the Southwest during Paleoindian times. That longer process was punctuated by the arrival and spread of maize in the Southwest. Subsequent differentiation and development occurred during a lengthy period of high levels of solar activity with low variability between about 700 and 2,000 years ago. It was also during this interval that the

greatest levels of sociocultural complexity were reached in the Southwest (see below).

The Internal Differentiation of Tanoan

At this temporal scale we are able to see the full differentiation of Tanoan languages as hypothesized by Davis (1959) and Trager (1967). Our exclusive focus on the Davis and Trager theories does not imply adherence to either, nor does it represent a criticism of others that advocate alternative orderings of the Tanoan differentiation as well as different timing for the various splits (Eggan 1950; Ford et al. 1972; Wendorf 1954; Wendorf and Reed 1955; Whorf and Trager 1937; see also Fox 1967:23–30 for a discussion of the various theories at that time). Rather, these two theories provide excellent examples of how large-scale perspectives allow the integration of paleoenvironmental data, archaeological data, and linguistic hypotheses to produce new perspectives and hypotheses and ways to test old ones.

Both theories share a common ordering for the differentiation of Tanoan: Tiwa/Tewa first split from Towa, Tiwa then split from Towa, and, finally, Northern Tiwa split from Southern Tiwa. Both place the timing of the Northern/Southern Tiwa split in the late thirteenth or early fourteenth century but differ substantially in the hypothesized timing of earlier divergences. They also vary widely in their hypothesized origins of Tanoan and the geography of subsequent differentiation.

Davis sees the Tanoans as a discrete group coming from the Cochise culture of southeastern Arizona and migrating through the Mogollon area, with all but the Northern/Southern Tiwa split occurring *prior* to their arrival in the Rio Grande. Trager postulates a northeastern (Colorado) origin for the Tanoans, with Kiowa diverging from Tanoan between AD 1 and 500 (see Irwin-Williams, chap. 2, this vol.). He has the Towa split occurring by virtue of a southward migration into the Rio Grande between AD 500 and 750, where they settled among the already-present Keresans. At about AD 900–1000 undifferentiated Tiwa/Tewa speakers who had remained in the north also migrated south, with some of them mingling with the Towa-Keres inhabitants. The result was the differentiation of Tewa as a "pidginized" Tanoan language (Fox 1967:28). Other Tiwa/Tewa speakers bypassed the Keres-Towa populations and went farther south to become the Southern Tiwa.

Several aspects of these alternative theories are of interest. Davis (1959) has both the Tiwa/Tewa split from Towa ca. 2400 B.P. (400 BC) and the subsequent Tiwa split from Tewa ca. 2100 B.P. (100 BC), *prior* to the appearance of a fully developed ceramic container technology in the Southwest. Trager (1967), on the other hand, has these processes occurring much later in time, well *after* the appearance of ceramics, between 1500 and 1250 B.P. (AD 500–750) and at ca. 950 B.P. (AD 1050), respectively. Thus, Trager's Tiwa/Tewa split from Towa occurred during the interval when the major decorated ceramic traditions in the Southwest were developing, while the Tiwa split from Towa happened after the appearance of discrete traditions of decorated whiteware ceramics and just after the White Mountain Red Ware tradition first emerged. If a future research goal is to identify populations and settlement systems that may be associated with different linguistic groups and their histories, then these two theories imply very different expectations about material culture assemblages, especially ceramic assemblages and their geographic distributions.

Davis's (1959) hypothesized migration of Tanoans out of southern Arizona and the subsequent split between Tiwa/Tewa and Towa both occur in the same interval during which Matson (1991; see chap. 7, this vol.) has maize cultivators migrating onto the Colorado Plateau, also from southern Arizona. Thus, both Matson's proposed migrations and the hypothesized divergence of Tiwa/Tewa from Towa occurred during the period of extreme variation in solar activity represented by TE 6. Once again, environmental variation during the interval from 2900 to 2300 B.P. may provide an important context within which to examine population dynamics, linguistic differentiation, and other processes during the Early Agricultural period.

Both Davis and Trager have the separation of Northern and Southern Tiwa occurring at about the same time, 750–700 B.P. (AD 1250–1300) or slightly later. The timing of this hypothesized divergence of languages occurred during the Great Drought on the Colorado Plateau, a radical shift in the curve of solar activity marked by the onset of TE 7, a marked change in the frequency of El Niño events, the start of a rapid decline in total Southwest population, and substantial shifts in the distribution of that population (see Wilcox et al., chap. 12, this vol.).

The Late Prehistoric, Protohistoric, and Historic Periods

Our third temporal context includes the late prehistoric, protohistoric, and historic periods (see fig. 5.6). This interval (AD 622–present) is defined largely to facilitate consideration of Quinn's (1992) reconstruction of El Niño events but also highlights other aspects of environment-culture relationships in the Southwest. As before, cultural and environmental events and processes shown in figure 5.3 are repeated, and we add the following in figure 5.6: five contrasting periods of El Niño activity are identified; sunspot minima are shown in greater detail; a period characterized by climatic "chaos" on the Colorado Plateau is indicated (AD 1250–1450; Dean 1988a, 1996, chap. 6, this vol.; Dean and Funkhouser 1995); the internal differentiation of Keresan as hypothesized by Davis (1959) is shown; three population curves are added to that of Doelle (2000); and a vertical line at AD 1290 as a reference point for discussion of major changes in both environmental and cultural systems in the Southwest has been added.

Long-Term Variation in El Niño and Its Relationship to Other LFPs

The graph of El Niño events shown in figure 5.6 shows the number of consecutive years with and without such events for the period AD 629–1988 (see Quinn 1992). Annual values were assigned on the basis of where a year falls with respect to a series of years *with* (above the x-axis) or *without* (below the x-axis) El Niño events. Thus, for a bounded series of 10 years in which El Niños occurred in the second, third, fourth, ninth, and tenth years, the respective values would be −1, +3, +3, +3, −4, −4, −4, −4, +2, and +2. For the 1,360-year period of record there are 389 years with El Niño events and 971 years without, with the overall frequency of El Niño events being about every three years (.29).[7] This mode of presenting Quinn's data differs considerably from the running averages and similar measures used in other studies of long-term variation in El Niño (Anderson 1992a; Enfield and Cid 1991; Kerr 1999; Lough 1992; Quinn

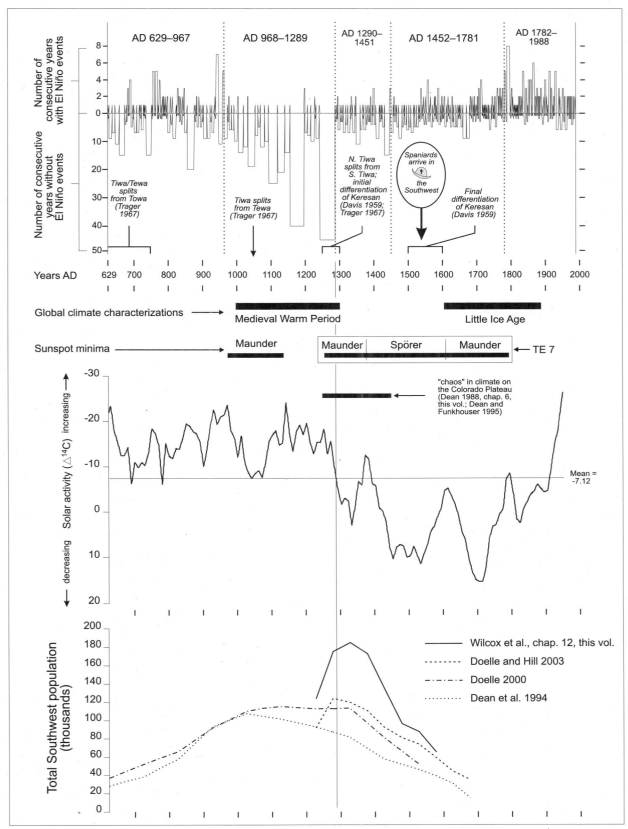

Figure 5.6. Graph of years with and without El Niño events, identified periods of contrasting El Niño frequencies, global climate characterizations, solar activity (to AD 1950), and cultural events and processes, AD 629–present.

Table 5.1 Characteristics of Five Identified Intervals with Contrasting El Niño Frequencies

	All Years	AD 629– 967	AD 968– 1289	AD 1290– 1451	AD 1452– 1781	AD 1782– 1988
N years	1,360	339	322	162	330	207
Mean El Niño frequency	.29	.29	.08	.23	.33	.57
Mean number of consecutive years with El Niño events	.71	.79	.13	.35	.62	1.92
Mean number of consecutive years without El Niño events	7.75	5.96	20.13	5.22	2.97	1.25
Mean Δ^{14}C (solar activity)	−7.12	−15.06	−14.82	−3.01	5.84	−7.18 (to 1950)

et al. 1978) and serves to highlight interannual variation.

Five periods characterized by marked differences in El Niño behavior are identified: AD 629–967, 968–1289, 1290–1451, 1452–1781, and 1782–1988. Descriptive statistics for these periods are summarized in table 5.1. The first and second periods (AD 629–967 and 968–1289) are characterized by relatively high solar activity and relatively low variability, and the second is roughly coeval with the MWP (see below). The second period shows a dramatic decrease in El Niño frequency and thus a marked increase in the mean number of years between El Niño events. The third (AD 1290–1451) witnessed significantly reduced levels of solar activity with much increased variability and a nearly threefold increase in the frequency of El Niño events. The start of this period is coincident with the onset of TE 7 and the beginning of a period of climatic "chaos" on the Colorado Plateau (Dean 1988a, chap. 6, this vol.; Dean and Funkhouser 1995). The fourth (AD 1452–1781) is characterized by the lowest levels of solar activity in more than 2,000 years but high variability (see fig. 5.3), and the LIA begins during the last half of this interval (see below; see

also Grove 1990). As previously discussed, the period between 1782 and 1990 may have been influenced by anthropogenic changes in the atmosphere and is not dealt with further.

The lengths of the remaining four intervals are of interest. As shown in table 5.1, the two earliest and the fourth are of approximately the same length (ca. 320–330 years), while the third is only about half as long (162 years).[8] We tentatively interpret this as a period of transition associated with a "phase change" in the frequency of El Niño events, one that— as noted—coincides almost exactly with the onset of TE 7 and the start of climatic chaos on the Colorado Plateau described by Dean (Dean 1988a, chap. 6, this vol.; Dean and Funkhouser 1995).

As is clear in figure 5.6 and table 5.1, the greatest contrast in El Niño behavior is before and after AD 1290. Table 5.2 highlights these differences, listing those intervals that had four or more El Niño events in sequence and those intervals of 10 or more years without El Niño events. In the nearly six centuries between AD 967 and 1558 there are no intervals having four or more El Niño years in sequence. From AD 1290 to the present there have been only two intervals of 10 or

more years without El Niño events, and both of these occurred before AD 1450. Also highlighted in this table is the extremely low frequency of El Niño events between AD 968 and 1289: in the 127-year period between AD 1073 and 1199 there were only five El Niño years, a frequency of .04, and no El Niño events occurred in the 40 years between AD 1160 and 1199. The longest period without El Niño events (45 years; AD 1245–1289) occurred at the end of this interval and corresponds to the Great Drought on the Colorado Plateau. We also note that the absolute values for solar activity before AD 1290 and those between AD 1290 and 1800 are almost mutually exclusive.

A number of studies suggest connections between the frequency of El Niño events and solar activity (Anderson 1992a, 1992b; Anderson et al. 1992), including sunspot activity (Anderson 1990, 1992a). The general hypothesis is that El Niño frequencies decrease when solar activity is stronger, and the periods between events lengthen. In contrast, El Niño events increase in frequency when solar activity is relatively weaker, and the periods between events shorten. Anderson (1992a:198) notes the correspondence between the long-term minimum in El Niño events and the MWP, a time of greater solar activity. The graph in figure 5.6 and the data in tables 5.1 and 5.2 generally support this interpretation. Various statistical comparisons of these values show significant correlations between the two phenomena but explain only a low proportion of the variance.

Figure 5.7 plots values derived from a 90-year running mean of El Niño frequencies against the absolute Δ^{14}C values for the period AD 674–1800. This atemporal comparison suggests that the El Niño/ solar activity relationship is (not sur-

Table 5.2 Extended Periods of Consecutive Years with and without El Niño Events, AD 629–1988

Intervals Having ≥ 4 Consecutive Years with El Niño Events	Intervals Having ≥ 10 Consecutive Years without El Niño Events
AD 693–696 (4)	AD 651–661 (11)
761–765 (5)	663–677 (15)
769–773 (5)	741–755 (15)
779–782 (4)	861–880 (20)[a]
945–951 (7)	953–962 (11)
963–967 (5)	997–1006 (10)
1558–1561 (4)	1009–1022 (14)
1713–1716 (4)	1024–1035 (12)
1782–1786 (5)	1038–1056 (19)
1790–1797 (8)	1073–1084 (12)
1835–1839 (5)	1086–1095 (10)
1852–1855 (4)	1097–1121 (25)
1864–1869 (6)	1123–1143 (21)
1899–1902 (4)	1145–1158 (14)
1911–1915 (5)	1160–1199 (40)
1928–1932 (5)	1221–1229 (10)
	1245–1289 (45)
	1352–1362 (11)
	1434–1448 (15)

[a]Underlined intervals indicate periods ≥ 20 years.

prisingly) a complex one. Visual inspection reveals that El Niño frequencies generally decrease with increasing solar activity; also apparent are several intervals that differ from one another in their respective mean values. This graphic suggests that threshold effects may be involved in the El Niño/solar activity relationship and that perhaps the direction and rates of change in solar activity over shorter intervals may also be factors. While requiring much further study, the El Niño/solar activity relationship holds promise for a possible retrodiction of El Niño frequencies, based on solar activity measures, that extends back beyond Quinn's (1992) reconstruction.

How the El Niño Phenomenon Affects Southwest Environments

The El Niño/ENSO phenomenon is complex, and its specific effects on Southwest environments have only begun to be elucidated. The modern period of record for climatic variables is lamentably short, and the period during which El Niño has been studied is even shorter. Nonetheless, basic patterns for the modern period have been described (e.g., Cayan and Webb 1992; Meko 1992; Webb and Betancourt 1992), and relevant aspects of these findings may be summarized.

Three principal types of storm systems bring precipitation into the arid Southwest: Pacific frontal storms, monsoonal storms, and dissipating Pacific tropical cyclones. A less frequently occurring phenomenon that also affects Southwest precipitation—sometimes radically over short periods—involves cutoff low-pressure systems (Cayan and Webb 1992; Hirschboeck 1985, 1987; Webb and Betancourt 1992). The relationships between El Niño events and these storm types produce variation in precipitation and streamflow on a macroregional scale and beyond (Cayan and Webb 1992) and appear to have done so for millennia. In general, precipitation in the Southwest increases during El Niño years and decreases during non–El Niño years, in part because the frequency and strength of winter Pacific frontal storms is usually increased during El Niño years and decreased during non–El Niño years. Studies of the relationship between summer monsoonal storms and the El Niño phenomenon, however, have produced contradictory results (Harrington et al. 1992; Higgins et al. 1998; Sheppard et al. 1999; Webb and Betancourt 1992), and this relationship is not yet fully understood (Adams and Comrie 1997; Andrade and Sellers 1988; Sheppard et al. 1999).

On the scale of the Far West, dissipating tropical cyclones produce wetter conditions in the Southwest during El Niño years and dry conditions in the Pacific Northwest; the converse is true during non–El Niño years (Cayan and Peterson 1989; Cayan and Webb 1992; Douglas and Englehart 1981; Kiladis and Diaz 1989). An increased number of Pacific tropical cyclones dissipate over the Southwest during or within six months of El Niño events, potentially enhancing late summer through spring precipitation in these years. Similarly, there appears to be an increased probability of cutoff low-

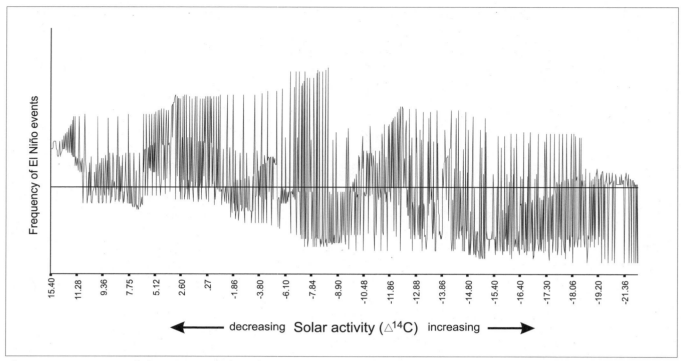

Figure 5.7. Frequency of El Niño events plotted against Δ¹⁴C values for AD 674–1800.

pressure systems during the six months after El Niño events (Cayan and Webb 1992).

Winter storms occur more frequently during El Niño years and generally involve large areas. Most of these track in a southwest–west to northeast–easterly direction and have their greatest direct effects on the northwest "half" of the Southwest (see Cayan and Webb 1992:figs. 3.6–3.8). The total area affected depends upon the strength of individual storms and on the path they take across the Southwest. It appears that the Mogollon Rim—the southern boundary of the Colorado Plateau—may exert a consistent orographic "guiding" effect on such storms, spreading them out and directing them to the east, and this may help to explain the dual pattern of Southwest precipitation described by Dean (1988a, chap. 6, this vol.; see below). In contrast, convectional monsoonal storms affect much smaller areas and influence widespread rainfall pat-

terns principally by virtue of the area over which the general monsoonal pattern occurs and the strength of that pattern in any given year.

During El Niño years winter storms (October–April) result in increased precipitation over large areas of the Southwest and also increased snowpack at elevations above about 2,000 m. As a result, El Niño events influence not only the absolute amount of precipitation but also its spatial and temporal distribution. Consequently, the amount of streamflow and its distribution over the annual period are also affected (Cayan and Webb 1992). This is particularly true in the larger drainages such as the Salt, Gila, and Little Colorado rivers and the Rio Grande, which have significant portions of their catchments at higher elevations. In general, both streamflow and the probability of floods are enhanced during El Niño years, although the latter relationship is more variable, and not all drainages have been stud-

ied in detail (Cayan and Webb 1992; Webb and Betancourt 1992).

In addition to the paths of individual storms a number of other factors not considered here may influence the degree to which El Niño events affect Southwest environments on shorter time scales. These include the relative strength of individual El Niño events and that of the opposite, or La Niña, phase of the ENSO, the rapidity with which the shift from one phase to the other occurs, and whether or not the shift from one phase to the other occurs immediately or is separated by "other" years (see n. 7). Further, individual storms during El Niño years, or the convergence of Pacific-derived storms with cutoff low-pressure conditions (such as was the case with the large floods of 1982–1983 in southern Arizona), may produce "episodic" events (including catastrophic events) that can have significant effects on human populations but are not yet predictable on any meaningful time scale

(Cayan and Webb 1992; Dean 1988a, chap. 6, this vol.; Webb and Betancourt 1992).

It is beyond the scope of this chapter to analyze all possible relationships between paleoenvironmental variation in the Southwest and low-frequency variation in the El Niño phenomenon. However, some areas of apparent correspondence between the periods and processes discussed by Dean in chapter 6 and elsewhere (Dean 1988a, 1994, 1996; Dean and Funkhouser 1995) are worth emphasizing.

Effects on Annual Precipitation. We hypothesize that the long-term pattern in annual precipitation variation across the Southwest described and discussed by Dean (1988a, chap. 6, this vol.; Dean and Funkhouser 1995)—and the breakdown in that pattern between AD 1250 and 1450—may reflect the influence of low-frequency variability in the El Niño phenomenon. Dean (chap. 6, this vol.) describes the long-term precipitation pattern in the Southwest as consisting of a northwestern primary component that occupies the Colorado Plateau and a southeastern secondary component lying primarily in the Rio Grande valley and areas south of the Mogollon Rim. These components are separated by a boundary zone that fluctuates through time (Dean 1996:figs. 4, 8). "This pattern is virtually identical to the documented precipitation distribution of the last 100 years, *in which summer precipitation dominates in the southeast and a bimodal winter–summer regime prevails in the northwest*" (Dean, chap. 6, this vol.; emphasis added; see also Maddox et al. 1995).

It may be argued that the bimodal precipitation pattern for the northwest "half" of the Southwest is strongly influenced by winter storms that have increased frequencies and strengths during El Niño years and that the overall shape of Dean's distribution may be related to the long-term influence of El Niño events, including the orographic guiding effects of the Mogollon Rim proposed above. Thus, the shifting "boundary zone" between the two patterns identified by Dean should move westward and northward during periods of low El Niño frequencies and eastward (and southward?) during periods characterized by high El Niño frequencies. The breakdown of this long-term pattern between AD 1250 and 1450 corresponds to the transitional period marking our proposed phase shift in El Niño behavior. These hypotheses can be tested by comparisons of the data presented here and data discussed by Dean in chapter 6 and elsewhere (1988a, 1996; Dean and Funkhouser 1995).

Effects on Streamflow. Long-term effects of El Niño on Southwest environments are demonstrated with reference to tree-ring-based reconstructions of the streamflow of the Salt and Gila rivers (Graybill et al. 2006); these reconstructions include the period of Quinn's (1992) El Niño reconstruction. Figure 5.8 illustrates the number of years with and without El Niño events, the number of El Niño events per decade, and the respective mean flows for the Salt and Gila rivers for the period AD 629–1988. Despite the fact that there are many more years without El Niño events than years with, the long-term mean discharges for both drainages are clearly increased by larger flows in years having El Niño events, with the Salt being more strongly influenced than the Gila. This is because a significant contribution to Gila flow comes from summer monsoonal storms. As noted above, the relationship between El Niño events and summer monsoonal precipitation in the Southwest is unclear; however, the streamflow data suggest that, over the long term, monsoonal precipitation may be enhanced in non–El Niño years, since the behavior of these two drainages is often diametrically opposite in periods when El Niño frequencies are lowest.

Gila River streamflow is bimodal over the annual period, with peaks in December–April and in August and September; Salt River flow is more nearly unimodal, with peak flows coming in February–May (Graybill et al. 2006). Differences in the timing of the winter–spring peaks in both distributions result from the fact that the average elevation of the Gila River basin is considerably lower than that of the Salt; thus less water is held as snowpack, and increased runoff tends to begin earlier in the year. The significance of these differences for understanding prehistoric irrigation systems along these two drainages has been discussed elsewhere (Graybill et al. 2006).

Van West's (1994, 1996) tree-ring-based reconstruction of middle Little Colorado River streamflow between AD 537 and 1985 (see Dean, chap. 6, this vol.) is based on the same data used for the Salt River reconstruction referred to here (modern Salt River, Verde River, and Tonto Creek flow data). Dean observes that Van West's reconstruction can be viewed as a proxy for Zuni River flow over the same interval. Thus, we may expect a relatively strong correspondence between the behavior of the Salt River and the flow responses of both the Little Colorado and Zuni rivers as regards El Niño events, although these relationships remain to be explored in detail.

Effects on Geomorphic Processes. Based on the work of Karlstrom (1988) and others in adjacent areas (Bryan 1954; Cooley 1962; Dean 1988a; Force and

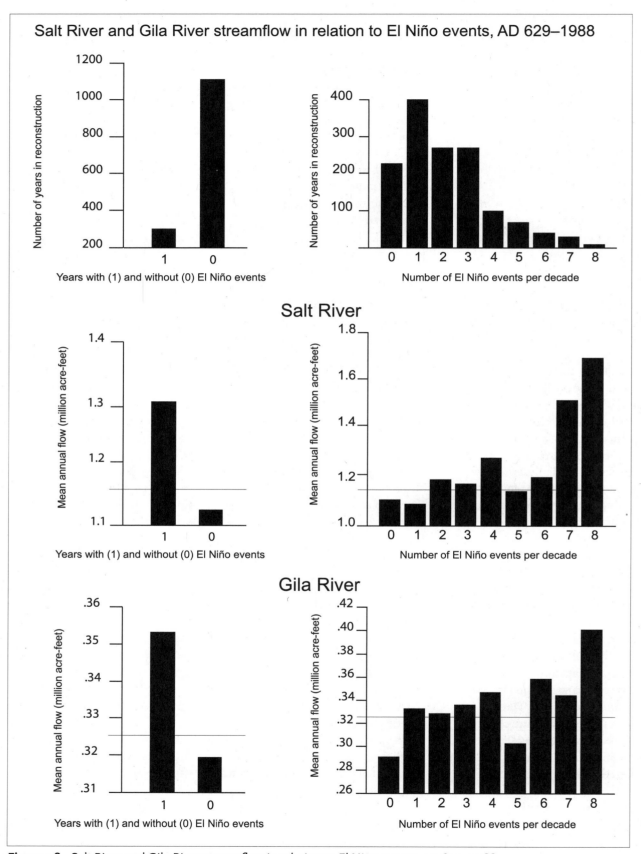

Figure 5.8. Salt River and Gila River streamflow in relation to El Niño events, AD 629–1988.

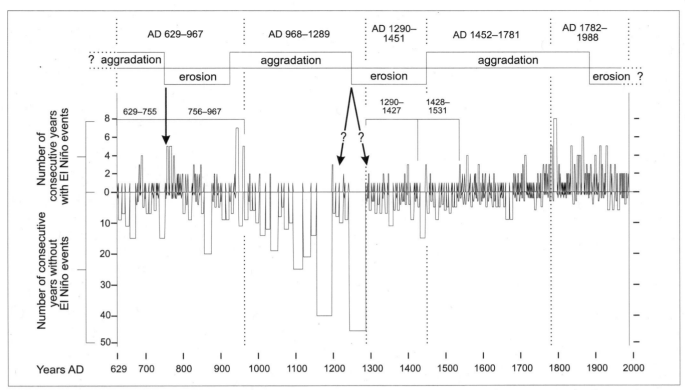

Figure 5.9. Correspondences between identified periods of variation in El Niño events and Dean's periods of contrasting geomorphological processes; arrows indicate the timing of potential triggering events for the onset of erosional processes.

Howell 1997; Force et al. 2002; Hack 1942, 1945; Hall 1977; Love 1980; Schoenwetter and Eddy 1964; Tuan 1966; L. Wells 1987), Dean identifies several periods alternating between aggradation and raised water tables, on the one hand, and erosion or nondeposition and lowered water tables, on the other. Aggradation was the dominant process between AD 350 and 750, 925 and 1250, and 1450 and 1880; erosion or nondeposition characterized the periods between AD 750 and 925 and 1250 and 1450 (Dean 1988a, 1996, chap. 6, this vol.; Dean and Funkhouser 1995).

Dean's geomorphic intervals show a remarkably close correspondence with the periods of variable El Niño frequencies described above (see fig. 5.9). Based on these correspondences, we suggest that low-frequency variation in geomorphic processes on the Colorado Plateau is related to low-frequency variation in the occurrence

of El Niño events. Alluvial systems in arid-lands environments are subject to threshold effects, often triggered by a single storm or a set of storms occurring over a relatively short interval, producing one or more floods and the onset of erosion. Given the geographic spottiness of monsoonal storms, there is a high prior probability that when geomorphic triggering events occur on a regional scale they will be produced by one or more El Niño–related storms—either as a direct result of abnormally high precipitation or because of greater snowpack and consequent spring floods. Further, transitions from erosional intervals to periods of aggradation beginning at about AD 925 and 1450 correspond to decreasing El Niño frequencies and increased average intervals between El Niño events. Thus, over the long term we would predict that aggradation is related in some way to relative decreases in El Niño

frequencies, possibly because the overall energy represented by climatic processes is reduced during such intervals.

Although we have not subdivided the AD 629–967 interval in our scheme, the AD 750 shift from aggradation to erosion corresponds to a marked increase in El Niño frequencies *within* our first period (see fig. 5.6). The onset of erosion follows a 15-year interval without El Niño events (AD 741–755), which was, in turn, followed by two closely spaced intervals during which El Niño events occurred in five consecutive years and then another interval of four consecutive years (AD 761–765, 769–773, and 779–782, respectively; see table 5.2). If we contrast the interval before AD 755 and the interval from AD 756 to 967, there is an increase in the absolute frequency of El Niño events (from .20 to .35), an increase in the mean number of consecutive years with El Niño events (from .34 to 1.1), and a decrease in the mean number of years between El Niño events (from 7.1 to 5).

Similarly, the shift from erosion to aggradation at AD 925 corresponds roughly to the boundary between the first and second periods of contrasting El Niño activity described above (at AD 967; see fig. 5.9). If we compare the AD 756–967 period with our second period of AD 967–1289 instead of using the entire AD 622–967 interval, the contrasts are even greater than those shown in table 5.1: the mean number of El Niño events drops from .35 to .08, the mean number of consecutive years with El Niño events plummets from 1.1 to .13, and the mean number of years between El Niño events increases from 5 to 20.13.

The shift back to erosional processes ca. AD 1250 is only shortly before a shift to much higher El Niño frequencies at AD 1289, which occurred at the end of the longest period without El Niño events in the record (45 years, AD 1245–1289, corresponding to the Great Drought; fig. 5.9) and which forms the boundary between our second and third periods. A closer look at the data suggests that our hypothesis may be supported in one of two ways. First, there was a short interval of somewhat higher El Niño frequencies (AD 1200–1244) between the two longest periods without El Niño events in the entire record (40 and 45 years, respectively). Second, the triggering event(s) for the onset of erosion could have occurred during the minor "flurry" of El Niño events between AD 1200 and 1244 *or* at the shift to higher El Niño frequencies at AD 1290 and following the Great Drought; given Dean's findings, the former is perhaps more likely and would have substantially increased the detrimental regional effects of that decades-long drought.

The next reversal to aggradation at AD 1450 corresponds to the boundary between our third and fourth identified periods (see fig. 5.9 and table 5.2). The change between these periods is characterized by an *increase* in the frequency of El Niño events and in the mean number of years with consecutive El Niño events and a *decrease* in the mean number of years between El Niño events. The shift from erosion to aggradation ca. AD 1450 would appear at first to contradict the hypothesis proposed here. However, we note that this shift is roughly coterminous with a *decrease* in El Niño frequencies beginning in the second quarter of the fifteenth century, including a 15-year interval without El Niño events between AD 1434 and 1448 and continuing through about the middle of the sixteenth century. Ignoring for the moment our common boundary with Dean at AD 1450, we note that the period from AD 1290 to 1427 experienced greater El Niño frequencies (.24), a higher mean number of years with consecutive El Niño events (.34), and a lower mean frequency of years without El Niño events (4.3) than did the period from AD 1428 to 1531 (.18, .26, and 6, respectively; see fig. 5.9). Interpretation of this third interval is complicated by our argument that it represents a period of transition that accompanied a phase change in El Niño frequencies on a larger temporal scale, but the general hypothesis would seem to hold—the shift to aggradation coincides with a period of decreasing El Niño frequencies. A reassessment of our boundaries for this period may thus be in order.

HFPs and Low-Frequency Variation during El Niño. Dean also observes that "especially unfavorable environmental conditions occur when negative LFP and HFP [high-frequency process] variations reinforce one another" (chap. 6, this vol.) to produce environmental stress. For the southern Colorado Plateau, including the Zuni area, he ranks four intervals as representing such particularly difficult times in the following order: (1) AD 1250–1450, including the Great Drought and corresponding to his previously identified period of "chaos" in long-term patterns of annual rainfall; (2) AD 1130–1180 (AD 1120–1160 in the Zuni area), which includes a secondary decline in alluvial conditions and a long drought; (3) AD 1850–1980, with severe arroyo cutting and depressed water tables; and (4) a drought that occupied the entire sixteenth century, in particular, the latter half of that century—albeit mitigated by aggradation and rising water tables.

We reiterate that the first of these intervals begins with the longest period in the record without El Niño events, AD 1245–1289, the Great Drought on the Colorado Plateau. Possible relationships between El Niño events and the chaos on the plateau that began around AD 1250 and continued for 200 years have been noted above, and certainly part of that chaos can be attributed to the marked shift in El Niño frequencies that occurred at AD 1290. If erosion was triggered by one or more El Niño–related storms during the AD 1200–1244 interval, the effects of the Great Drought would have been greatly exacerbated, and this seems the most likely hypothesis at present.

Dean's second-worst environmental period (AD 1130–1180) falls within the previously discussed interval of extremely low El Niño frequencies, AD 1073–1199. In particular, the period from AD 1130 to 1180 witnessed only two El Niño events, and the period from AD 1120 to 1158 experienced only one. Thus, there is a coincidence between the two most severe droughts documented by tree rings and the two longest periods in the record during which El Niño events occurred infrequently or not at all. Once again, future studies hold much promise for enhancing our understanding of the interactions between these LFPs and responses of human adaptations at various scales.

When the World Changed: The Southwest before and after AD 1290

We target the date of AD 1290 to highlight coincident changes in the three LFPs dealt with in this chapter. We say the "world" changed because there are coincident changes in overall solar activity, marked by the onset of TE 7, and the frequency of El Niño events at this time (see fig. 5.6) and because these processes have global effects. The fact that a massive reshaping of southwestern cultural landscapes occurred during the thirteenth and fourteenth centuries (and subsequently) is hardly new, and environmental factors have long been recognized as an important aspect of these changes. Clearly, the important changes in environmental systems began before that date and continued after it, and responses by Southwest populations did not all occur over the span of a single year. However, our goal here is to expand existing notions of how LFPs contributed to the changing contexts to which southwestern adaptations responded in their various ways and, in turn, how these processes shaped subsequent cultural and linguistic landscapes of the Southwest. The date of AD 1290 provides a convenient touchstone for the following discussion.

Changes in Regional and Macroregional Systems and Demographics. We observed above that the differentiation of maize-based adaptations and overall population increase in the Southwest between about AD 900 and 1250 occurred during a long interval

of high solar activity and relatively low variability in that activity and during which no triple-event sunspot minima occurred, that is, during a period of relatively high environmental predictability, regardless of the specific conditions. Predictability would have been conducive to technological and organizational developments in response to relatively stable conditions. For example, did the complex of techniques and strategies documented by Hack (1942) for the Hopi evolve during this interval? Expansion of Phoenix Basin Hohokam canal systems during this interval may also be related (see Graybill et al. 2006).

We have also noted that it was during this interval that the highest levels of sociocultural complexity were achieved in the Southwest, represented first by development of the Chacoan (Keresan speakers [?] and others), Mimbres (Zunian speakers [?]), and Hohokam (Uto-Aztecan/ Tepiman speakers [?]) regional systems (see Wilcox 1979, 1986a, 1991c, 1996a, 1996b, 1999a; see also Wilcox et al., chap. 12, and Gregory and Wilcox, chap. 20, this vol.), and associated developments in the Flagstaff area likely connected the Chacoan and Hohokam systems (Uto-Aztecan speakers [?]; see Wilcox 1986a). The decline of the Mimbres and Chacoan systems has been attributed in part to droughts and other environmental changes (including degradation of the water table and downcutting on the Colorado Plateau) that correspond to the two longest intervals without El Niño events, AD 1160–1199 and 1245–1289 (the Great Drought; see Mathien 1985; Vivian 1990, 1991). A retraction and reorganization of the Hohokam regional system also occurred during the first of these intervals (Wilcox 1979, 1991c).

As shown by Wilcox et al. (chap. 12, this vol.), a geographic division be-

tween populations in the northern and southern Southwest becomes readily apparent between AD 1400 and 1449 and is present, although less well defined, between AD 1350 and 1399 and perhaps even between AD 1300 and 1349 (see figs. 12.17–12.19, this vol.). Changes in exchange systems, ceramic distributions, and distributions of other phenomena are also apparent in association with this emerging division (see Diehl, chap. 11, Mills, chap. 13, Schaafsma and Young, chap. 15, Vokes and Gregory, chap. 17, Webster, chap. 16, and Wilson, chap. 14, this vol.).

This separation resulted in part from the decline of the regional systems discussed above and the shifting population distributions that resulted and in part from an overall decline in population via attrition that began at about AD 1250. That decline in population may have been precipitous, depending upon which estimates of population and out-migration one chooses to employ (see Wilcox et al., chap. 12, this vol.). An important feature of these changes was the rise and subsequent decline of the Casas Grandes regional system (Uto-Aztecan/Opatan speakers [?]; see Wilcox 2002; see also Gregory and Wilcox, chap. 20, Wilcox et al., chap. 12, this vol.).

Changes in the Linguistic Landscape. Depopulation of large areas via redeployment and attrition created contexts for changes in the linguistic landscape of the Southwest in two principal ways. First, there was a substantial physical reduction in the areas occupied by all linguistic groups present in the Southwest prior to AD 1300 (see Wilcox et al., chap. 12, this vol.). This circumstance would have been conducive to maintenance of previously existing linguistic differences and thus to Renfrew's process of divergence, perhaps enhanced by a tendency toward linguistic conservatism or replication within settlements or settlement systems. Second, this process opened up large niches for potential "initial" colonization of depopulated areas by groups speaking other languages, a process that subsequently occurred when Hokan and Athapaskan speakers with largely hunting and gathering lifeways filled these voids.

By the late prehistoric period the geographic extent of both Zunian and Keresan was much reduced—ultimately down to a single village for Zuni and to seven villages for Keresan, each speaking a different dialect (see Gregory and Wilcox, chap. 20, Wilcox and Gregory, chap. 1, this vol.). Davis (1959) argues that Keresan differentiated into four geographically separate dialect groups between about AD 1250 and 1300: Cochiti, Santo Domingo and San Felipe, Zia and Santa Ana, and Acoma and Laguna. He has Keresan subsequently differentiating at the village level, with Santo Domingo splitting from San Felipe, Zia diverging from Santa Ana, and Acoma separating from Laguna, all between 400 and 500 years ago (AD 1500–1600) and just before, during, and/or immediately after the arrival of the Spaniards.

Similarly, Tanoan appears to have been distinct for a long period of time, but, depending upon which theories are correct, much of the internal differentiation of Tanoan may have occurred during the late prehistoric period as well. As previously noted, Trager (1967) has the divergence of Tiwa from Tewa occurring during this interval (ca. AD 1050), and both Davis (1959) and Trager (1967) have Northern and Southern Tiwa diverging between AD 1250 and 1300. Regardless of the specific timing of these splits, the former distribution of Tanoan speakers was much reduced,

ultimately to 11 villages: one Jemez (Towa) village, four Tiwa villages, and six Tewa villages.

The greatest retraction of territory appears to have involved Uto-Aztecan speakers, who may have once occupied much of southern, central, north-central, and northeastern Arizona (see Gregory and Wilcox, chap. 20, and Wilcox and Gregory, chap. 1, this vol.). Ultimately, that distribution was reduced to Hopic speakers occupying several villages on their northern Arizona mesas, Piman speakers occupying a relatively small number of villages along the middle Gila, San Pedro, and Santa Cruz rivers, and the Papaguería in southern Arizona. It is also possible that Uto-Aztecan speakers (Hohokam populations) migrating from southern Arizona in the late AD 1300s or early 1400s contributed to the development of Sonoran "statelets," described by Riley (1987, 1990; see also Sauer 1934; Wilcox et al., chap. 12, this vol.).

By virtue of these changes, the stage was set for a contrasting process, one that was fully realized during the protohistoric period: the geographic spread of other linguistic groups already present in the Southwest and the addition of new linguistic groups, thus constituting "initial colonization" of uninhabited areas in Renfrew's terms and in all cases involving groups whose primary subsistence strategies were—at the time of their movement into the newly abandoned territories—focused on hunting and gathering. Owing to basic differences in subsistence technology and much lower population densities, the adaptations represented by these linguistic groups had substantially different requirements as regards the range of variation in geography and climate within which they could successfully function.

Athapaskan-speaking Proto-

Navajo populations moved into the northern Southwest perhaps as early as the late AD 1400s (see Towner 1996) and possibly on the heels of abandonment of large areas by Tanoan speakers (see Gregory and Wilcox, chap. 20, and Wilcox et al., chap. 12, this vol.); they subsequently expanded into areas previously occupied by Uto-Aztecan, Zunian, and Keresan speakers as well. In this case, contact between Navajo and Puebloan groups produced not only linguistic change (loanwords) but also the adoption of technology (maize cultivation) and ideology (the kachina cult/Yei complex) by the newly arrived Athapaskan speakers. Somewhat later, Apachean groups spread into large areas that had once been the domain of Zunian, Keresan, Tanoan, and Uto-Aztecan speakers, and perhaps their knowledge of these newly abandoned areas resulted from earlier Plains–Pueblo interactions.

Hokan (Yuman) speakers (Pai) expanded into areas of central (Yavapai), west-central (Walapai), and north-central (Havasupai) Arizona formerly occupied primarily by Uto-Aztecans. Ultimately, the Yuman-speaking Yavapai shared a boundary with the Athapaskan Western Apache to the east and with Piman speakers to the south. In this case, increased interaction between Yumans and Athapaskans produced a Yavapai-Apache linguistic mix (a creole?) along that shared territorial boundary.

The MWP and the LIA. Finally, we take the opportunity to comment on the validity of the periods often referred to as the Medieval Warm Period and the Little Ice Age as useful general characterizations of past climate in the Southwest. We have included them in the various graphics above because they are commonly referred to, because there is some correspondence between them and the LFPs considered here, and because some authors have invoked them in the interpretation of archaeological and paleoclimatic data in the Southwest (Jones et al. 1999; LeBlanc 1999; Petersen 1988, 1994; see also Dean 1994).

LeBlanc (1999), for example, recently proposed an environmental explanation for warfare in the prehistoric Southwest using these terms. He argues that the transition between higher temperatures during the MWP and cooler ones during the LIA (with the downward trend beginning in the late 1200s, following Lamb 1995) is "extremely close to those proposed here for evidence of a major cultural change [a shift from a lower to a higher incidence of warfare] in the Southwest. *A priori*, the climatic changes would seem to fit the Southwestern data close enough to merit consideration as a possible causal factor" (LeBlanc 1999:34). LeBlanc subdivides the late prehistoric chronology of the Southwest into three intervals: the early period (AD 1–900), characterized as being "adequate for farming over much of the Southwest, but not optimal"; the middle period (AD 900–1250, i.e., the MWP), characterized as being "very good for agriculture throughout much of the Southwest"; and the late period (post–AD 1250), "a time of much worsened agricultural potential, with some areas rendered unusable and others much more marginal" (1999:36, 37). As LeBlanc's general argument is close enough to some of the perspectives offered here to perhaps be confused with them, some clarification is necessary.

On the scale of the Far West (and including the Southwest), Jones et al. (1999) present alternatives to LeBlanc's positive assessment of the MWP in particular. They cite "serious and abrupt declines in productivity caused by repeated and prolonged droughts" and note such effects as "*increases in interpersonal violence*, declines in health, deterioration of long-distance trade networks, population reductions and/or relocations, site and regional abandonments, and occupational hiatuses" (Jones et al. 1999:138; emphasis added). The particularly unfavorable conditions on the southern Colorado Plateau that prevailed between AD 1130 and 1180 have already been discussed. Dean (1994) finds little evidence in the tree-ring record for either the MWP or the LIA on the Colorado Plateau (but see Petersen 1988, 1994), and Salzer's (2000a, 2000b) recent tree-ring-based studies of long-term variation in temperature do not directly support LeBlanc's general characterizations. And while temperature may have been an important variable for past adaptations, certainly variation in precipitation was equally important. LeBlanc's characterization of AD 900–1200 as "very good for agriculture" on a pansouthwestern scale seems entirely inappropriate.

Thus, there are several fundamental problems associated with use of the terms "Medieval Warm Period" and "Little Ice Age" to characterize past environmental variation in the Southwest and the effects of that variation on human populations. First, an emphasis on temperature to the exclusion of other variables is inappropriate, even if used only as a general characterization; there is simply no evidence that temperature was consistently more important than other variables. Second, all evidence suggests that both *temporal* and *spatial* variations in the natural environment during these intervals were so great as to render Leblanc's characterizations useless as analytic tools. Furthermore, present data support the inference that the effects of climatic variation on Southwest populations during this interval were highly variable, depending on the geographic location of the respective societies and their basic subsistence technologies, including organizational features—that is, on the nature of their adaptations to specific environments.

As has been pointed out elsewhere (Graybill et al. 2006), the period from AD 900 through the late 1300s was indeed salubrious for the irrigation-based societies of southern Arizona, with decreased mean streamflow more than offset by the predictability of flow and a reduced incidence of large-scale floods. On the other hand, the latter half of this period produced at least two severe droughts on the Colorado Plateau, the first of which may have played a role in the decline of the Chacoan system. The second (and possibly the first as well) apparently exceeded the ability of some (but not all) populations to respond and resulted in out-migration, including movement into areas such as the Safford Basin (see Clark, chap. 4, this vol.; Lindsay 1987; Woodson 1999), where irrigation technology was the principal subsistence mode. Appropriate assessment of the effects of climatic variability during these intervals is highly dependent upon which populations one refers to and what subsistence technologies they employed.

We therefore argue that both of these terms represent superficial characterizations of Southwest environmental variation during these intervals and should only be used (if at all) as historical referents to the manner in which past environments have been previously characterized. Their continued use as analytical or pseudoanalytical units can only serve to take attention away from the complexity of relationships that obtained between Southwest adaptations and the changing environments in which they developed and were transformed

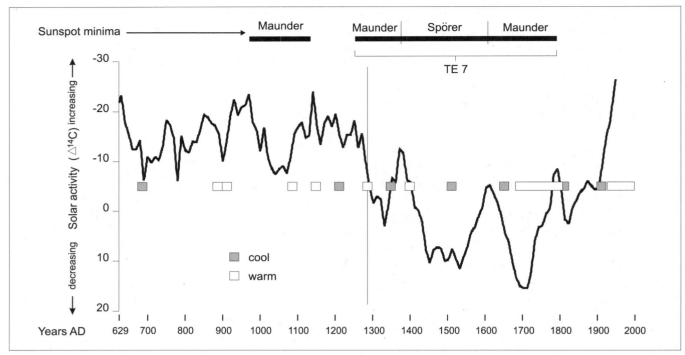

Figure 5.10. Juxtaposition of Salzer's (2000a, 2000b) very warm and very cool intervals for the Colorado Plateau with the curve of solar activity, AD 629–present; a vertical line is shown at AD 1290.

—and, importantly, away from the complexities involved in the study of those relationships. In the meantime we have specified some of the environmental variables involved in that complexity and some of the directions in which fruitful investigation may be directed.

Contexts, Coincidence, Correlation, and Causality

In creating and elaborating upon the three nested temporal contexts presented above (the Late Pleistocene and the Holocene, the Late Holocene, and the seventh century AD to the present) we have necessarily painted with a very broad brush in pointing out some coincidences and correlations between variation in aspects of the natural environment and cultural events and processes. Some observed relationships are highly speculative, while others are more grounded. Our

purpose has been to show how approaches at large temporal and geographic scales may be the source of new hypotheses concerning the complex relationships between culture, language, and the natural environment. In particular, we have emphasized how consideration of LFPs is a necessary component in such hypotheses.

We reiterate Dean's caution voiced in chapter 6: many of the relationships discussed above *are* coincidences and correlations and do not imply causality. Relationships between solar activity, triple-event sunspot minima, and El Niño frequencies and changes in Southwest environments remain to be fully specified. In many cases, new and more refined data and new looks at old data are prerequisites for approaches involving these phenomena and at these temporal and spatial scales. Some phenomena are

more amenable to retrodiction using modern data than others, and new and creative ways are needed to investigate such phenomena and their effects on the environmental contexts in which human populations operated. For the moment, we simply wish to emphasize that scale and context do matter and to highlight the kinds of productive approaches that may be fostered by attention to LFPs at larger geographic and temporal scales.

Several aspects of solar variation represented by triple-event sunspot minima may be important: the direction of change during the events, the magnitude of change, and the relationship of the event to the slope of the overall solar activity curve at the onset of the event and following it. Given these parameters, did variation during TE 1 through TE 7 (and perhaps during other, isolated sunspot episodes) create environmental conditions that played a role in the diversification of adaptations and the process of linguistic differentiation following the peopling of North and South America? More specifically, did variation in solar activity during the interval between TE 4 and TE 5 (or perhaps *during* TE 5?) have some influence on the evolution of maize, perhaps via increased rates of mutation (see Benz and Iltis 1990; Doebley 1990; Iltis 1983, 1987)? And what are the relationships between variation in solar activity and intermediate processes such as the El Niño phenomenon, and how did these relationships influence past climatic variability in the Southwest? In support of the possible importance of solar activity as a relevant variable in understanding past Southwest environments, we offer—without further comment—a graph of solar activity plotted against Salzer's reconstruction of very warm and very cool periods in the Southwest for the interval AD 622–1990 (see fig. 5.10; cf. figs. 5.6, 5.8, and 5.9; see also Dean, chap. 6, this vol.).

With respect to the El Niño phenomenon, modern studies indicate direct effects on climatic variability in the Southwest. What remains is to further specify these relationships and explore their effects on past environments in greater detail. Can relationships between prehistoric El Niño frequencies be correlated with changes in annual precipitation and geomorphic events and processes in the Southwest? Do variable frequencies of El Niño help to explain long-term variation in seasonal rainfall patterns across the Southwest? And can the frequency of El Niño events be retrodicted on the basis of significant correlations between those events and various measures of solar activity?

These questions suggest multiple directions for future research dealing with LFPs in the Southwest. The time scales involved in linguistic differentiation and in the development of variable adaptations to changing environments suggest that such LFPs should be central features of models designed to explain these important aspects of the human career in this region, including the differentiation and maintenance of Zuni as a linguistic isolate.

Notes

1. To create the curve illustrated here we have used a linear interpolation of the decadal and bidecadal values of $\Delta^{14}C$ provided in Stuiver et al. (1998). There are standard deviations associated with each of these, but no attempt has been made here to incorporate that measure of potential variation.

2. Both Maunder- and Spörer-type minima can occur in isolation along with other recognized types of sunspot minima of lesser amplitudes. These could also be considered as LFPs; here we restrict our consideration to triple events. The effects of TE 6 on the distributions of calibrated radiocarbon dates have been discussed elsewhere (Gregory 1996, 2001b); it is predictable that other triple events have similar effects on such dates, a pattern that all archaeologists should be aware of.

3. For an excellent general discussion of the phenomenon and its climatic implications see Davis (2000:214–245); see also Diaz and Markgraf (1992), Philander (1985, 1990), and Quinn et al. (1987).

4. One highly controversial claim is that "ENSO has been punctuated by chaotic flickering or temporary shutdowns" (Davis 2000:235) and in particular that the cycle was "turned off" from about 12,000 to 5000 B.P. As Davis puts it, "Since there is unambiguous evidence of ENSO fluctuations during the glacial maximum (before 12,000 years ago), scientists are baffled by why El Niño would suddenly go *AWOL*" (2000:237; emphasis added; see also Kerr 1999; Rodbell et al. 1999). It is interesting to note, however,

that this period is approximately coincident with the interval between the two thresholds in solar activity discussed here. Potential threshold effects in global climate may be suggested, and this is a worthy area for future research.

5. One need not assume either the "Clovis first" hypothesis or Greenberg's linguistic unity hypothesis for this temporal context to be useful (if not necessary) in evaluating hypotheses concerning both the peopling of the New World and the diversification of language in the Americas.

6. This interval has also been referred to as the Little Climatic Optimum, the Little Optimum, the Secondary Climatic Optimum, and the Medieval Climatic Anomaly (see Ingram et al. 1981; Jones et al. 1999:138; LeBlanc 1999; Petersen 1994; Stine 1990; Sulman 1982).

7. Subsequent research has validated Quinn's reconstruction in terms of the occurrence of El Niño events in particular years, but numerous questions have been raised concerning his estimates of the strength of individual events (Enfield and Cid 1991). See Anderson (1992a), Enfield and Cid (1991), Davis (2000:270–276), and Diaz and Pulwarty (1992) for critical assessments of Quinn's data and in particular of his estimates of the strength of individual El Niño events. Here we consider only absolute frequency, and no attempt has been made to incorporate Quinn's assessments of the magnitude of individual El Niño events. The strength of individual events is nonetheless an important variable in assessing the effects of the phenomenon, especially on shorter time scales.

In addition, years without El Niño events are of two sorts: "La Niña" years, in which the processes opposite those producing El Niño years are regnant (the "cold phase" of the Southern Oscillation; see Philander 1990; Quinn and Burt 1972; Wright 1977), and "other years," in which neither condition is dominant. These "other years" may occur when the process of shifts from El Niño to La Niña conditions is slowed or stagnates or when either phase has occurred in a "weak" form. Quinn's data do not allow consideration of variation in years without El Niño events, and we do not deal with this variation here, despite its obvious importance. What we can say is that some unknown proportion of years without El Niño events were years in which La Niña events occurred; the length of the modern record limits the utility of any estimates of what that proportion might be, but this is another important area for future research.

8. The earliest period is, of course, difficult to assess, because its start is defined by the beginning of the record used by Quinn (1992). Thus, the length of time during which these particular conditions prevailed is unknown. However, the interval is long enough to demonstrate a decided contrast with what comes after.

6 Zuni-Area Paleoenvironment

Jeffrey S. Dean

The focus of the Mogollon-Zuni advanced seminar was on the origin of the Zuni sociocultural pattern and its connections with and derivations from earlier archaeological manifestations in the northern and central Southwest. Within that context I attempt to characterize the environmental stage on which these developments took place. While the modern environment of the study area provides some information on past conditions, a wide range and variety of environmental fluctuations and changes over the last 10,000 years mean that present conditions cannot be taken as accurate analogs of past conditions (see Gregory and Nials, chap. 5, this vol.). Therefore, as broad a range of paleoenvironmental research as possible must be mobilized to adequately explicate the environment of the area.

Different aspects of the total spectrum of environmental diversity are denoted here by specific terms. *Stability* describes conditions that do not vary appreciably over a period of time that must be specified because, in the span of geologic time, everything changes. *Variability* refers to fluctuations that take place within the parameters that define a particular state in one or more components of the environment, including climate, fluvial systems, plant communities,

and animal populations. *Change* occurs when one or more components of the environment pass from one state into another and one set of boundary conditions is supplanted by another.

For methodological reasons it is useful to partition Southwest environmental variability into four overlapping and nonexclusive categories defined by the observed periodicity of the fluctuations in amplitude (Dean 1988a, 1996). In order to relate these environmental phenomena to human behavior roughly one human generation (25 years) has been chosen as the major dividing point.

Stable elements of the environment have not changed appreciably during the time period of interest, in this case the last four millennia or so. Stable factors include climate type, topography, bedrock geology, elevational zonation of plant communities, and the distribution of mineral resources and raw materials. Because these elements have not changed during the study period, their present states are valid indicators of past conditions, and they need not be reconstructed.

Environmental variations due to natural processes with periodicities longer than $\leq$ 25 years are defined as low-frequency process (LFP) factors.

LFP variables include the rise and fall of alluvial groundwater levels, the deposition and erosion of floodplain sediments, low-frequency variations in climate, fluctuations in effective moisture, variations in plant community distributions and composition, and changes in pollen production. Although processes that control such factors vary over periods greater than 25 years, they can produce rapid environmental changes such as the initiation and propagation of arroyo cutting. Environmental variations resulting from natural processes with wavelengths = 25 years are defined as high-frequency process (HFP) variables. HFP variables include various aspects of annual and seasonal precipitation, temperature, streamflow, and low-intensity range and forest fires and spatial and temporal patterning in these variables.

Because HFP and LFP variables exhibit periodicities shorter than the 4,000-year study period, their present states are not valid indicators of past conditions, and their fluctuations must be reconstructed by various paleoenvironmental techniques. The former are revealed primarily by dendroclimatology and dendroecology and by some high-frequency pollen studies. The latter are indicated by alluvial geomorphology, palynology, packrat midden studies, and low-frequency dendroclimatology. It is important to recognize that LFP variables have high-frequency components and HFP variables have low-frequency components that can be invisible to the available paleoenvironmental techniques.

The fourth category includes *episodic events* that have no detectable regularity of occurrence. Episodic events include volcanic eruptions, earthquakes, early and late freezes that may or may not be related to especially cold periods, large-scale wildfires, insect and mammal predation of crops, heavy rainstorms and surface runoff that devastate fields and/or crops, catastrophic hailstorms, and other "random" occurrences. As with HFP and LFP variability, episodic events must be inferred from proxy records such as surficial geology, frost damage to tree rings, fire and flood scars in wood samples, and tree-growth anomalies. Many such events are not visible in the paleoenvironmental record, and their effects on human populations cannot be assessed.

The Modern Environment

Zuni Pueblo and the traditional Zuni use area lie within the much larger region occupied by earlier populations assigned to the Mogollon and Anasazi archaeological traditions that are the focus of this volume. The modern environment of the Zuni use area is thoroughly described by Ferguson and Hart (1985) and need be only summarized here. Zuni Pueblo is located near the southern edge of the Colorado Plateau physiographic province in extreme western New Mexico. The pueblo lies at an elevation of 1,915 m on the middle reach of the Zuni River, a tributary of the Little Colorado River, which flows northwestward into the Colorado River, the master stream of the Colorado

Plateau. To the east and northeast the Zuni River drainage heads in the Continental Divide at 2,743 m along the crest of the Zuni Mountains. To the south and southwest the land rises to more than 3,505 m in the Mogollon Mountains. North and west of Zuni are the open expanses of the Colorado Plateau.

Generally, vegetation reflects elevation modified by topography. The river valley around Zuni Pueblo is characterized by grass and shrub communities flanked by pinyon-juniper woodlands. The mountains support mixed conifer forests dominated by a nearly pure ponderosa pine forest that occupies much of the Mogollon Highlands. The highest peaks of the highlands support spruce-fir and alpine vegetation communities. The plateau is dominated by grass and shrub communities that give way to pinyon-juniper woodlands, ponderosa pine forests, and mixed conifer forests with increasing elevation. Reversals of this zonation occur in situations where Douglas firs grow in sheltered canyon habitats below the pinyon-juniper woodlands of adjacent plateau and mesa tops.

The climate of the Zuni area is semiarid and temperate, warm in the summer and cool in the winter, with temperatures ranging from −17.8 to 38°C (below zero to above 100°F). Extreme and mean temperatures decrease with increasing elevation. One of the most important aspects of temperature for agriculture is the length of the growing season (the "frost-free" period between the last frost of the spring and the first frost of the autumn), which varies inversely with elevation. The length of frost-free interval is a function of cold air drainage from the mountains as well as the ambient temperature. Traditionally, a frost-free period of at least 120 days has been deemed necessary for producing a corn crop on the

plateau (Hack 1942:23). This figure must be modified, however, by the realizations that some varieties of corn mature in fewer than 100 days and that topography and water supply affect the length of the growing season and the rate of plant maturation. Nonetheless, 120 days can be taken as a benchmark for corn production. Ferguson and Hart (1985:14) specify a growing season of nearly 150 days at Zuni Pueblo. The 120-day limit is reached a few kilometers upstream from the pueblo, and corn production becomes increasingly precarious above this point. Downstream from the pueblo decreasing available moisture offsets any advantage that might otherwise accrue from the lengthening growing season. At the elevation where a growing season of 150 days is attained an average of only 20.3 cm of rain falls a year, too little to support dry farming.

Mean annual precipitation in the Zuni area (Ferguson and Hart 1985:12−13) varies directly with elevation, ranging from 20.3 cm near the confluence of the Zuni and Little Colorado rivers to more than 81.3 cm in the White Mountains to the south. The pueblo itself receives approximately 30.5 cm of precipitation a year, right at Hack's (1942:23) minimum for successful crop production. Annual precipitation is bimodally distributed, with the spring drought from April through June separating small winter and large summer precipitation maxima. Although the lesser of the two peaks, winter precipitation from November to March, which falls in prolonged storms and accumulates as snow in the mountains, is vital to providing enough soil moisture to support germination of seeds planted near the end of the spring drought. Summer rainfall, which falls in often powerful convectional storms from July into September, is crucial to plant maturation and seed production. Unlike temperature, which is fairly stable spatially and temporally, precipitation varies considerably from year to year and place to place. Finally, streamflow in the Rio Pescado, Rio Nutria, and Zuni River, which depends on precipitation and temperature, has been an important stabilizing factor on Zuni agriculture. Zuni farming practices (Brandt 1995), which are the culmination of millennia of experimentation by the Zuni and their predecessors, have been refined to take advantage of the nuances of topography, soils, hydrology, and climate of the area.

Paleoenvironmental Reconstruction

In order to understand the environmental variability faced by the Zuni area's inhabitants in developing a subsistence technology attuned to local and regional environmental conditions and variations, it is necessary to reconstruct as fully as possible the nature and range of environmental fluctuations and changes in the region. Ideally, such reconstructions should span the entire elevational range of the region from the river valleys to the mountain peaks and should encompass the open valleys and mesas of the Colorado Plateau and the more confined mountain drainages. This is especially the case if we are to characterize and compare natural and human processes and events in the uplands above 1,982–2,135 m with those in the lower areas that were the focus of post–AD 1200 human occupation of the region.

Unfortunately, limitations of the paleoenvironmental data for the Zuni region render impossible the comprehensive local coverage necessary for this task. Few modern environmental baseline surveys or paleoenvironmental studies have been attempted in the mountains of the

Southwest. Thus, modern analog records and detailed paleoenvironmental reconstructions are not available for a major component of the study area.

Similarly, there have been few paleoenvironmental studies of the lower portions of the Zuni area. The major exception to this statement is a series of analyses undertaken in the 1980s in connection with a Zuni land damage case against the federal government (Hart 1995a). Unfortunately, relevant environmental research done by both the Zuni plaintiffs (Dean 1985, 1989; Geosciences Consultants, Ltd. 1985, 1988; Hall 1985, 1988; Rose 1987, 1989) and the U.S. defendants (Jacoby 1987; S. Wells 1987) is relatively inaccessible. As a result, considerable reliance must be placed on detailed paleoenvironmental reconstructions done elsewhere on the Colorado Plateau, a procedure that rests on the degree of relevance of these studies to the Zuni area. Potentially useful research includes alluvial geomorphic studies, packrat midden analyses, palynological studies, and qualitative and quantitative dendroclimatic and dendroecological studies.

Stable Factors

Several aspects of the modern environment have not changed appreciably in the last 4,000 years and can be used as measures of past conditions in the study area. Bedrock geology and topography provide basically the same resources for human exploitation (raw materials, suitable building sites, arable land, etc.) as they did in the past. Climate type has remained the same since at least the end of the Altithermal (see Gregory and Nials, chap. 5, and Matson, chap. 7, this vol.). Elevational zonation of climatic variables (precipitation, temperature, length of the growing season, etc.)

and plant communities has persisted throughout the study period, although the elevational distribution of climate and the boundaries of plant communities have fluctuated within the limits established by the prevailing system. In the past as well as the present, therefore, river valleys and their margins have been suitable for hunting and gathering and various kinds of agriculture, including dry, floodwater, ak-chin, groundwater, and irrigation farming, while higher forest and alpine zones have been suitable for gathering wild plants and hunting large and small game. In addition, the region provided stone, earth, and wood for construction and raw materials for chipped and ground stone tools, pottery, and other utilitarian and ceremonial items.

LFP Environmental Variability

Packrat midden analyses illuminate low-frequency variability in vegetation and inferred climate over the past 40 millennia. In the absence of Zuni-area packrat midden data the regional pattern must be invoked to characterize the situation in the study area. On a regional scale (Betancourt 1984, 1990; Betancourt et al. 1990) packrat midden records reflect major vegetational changes across the Pleistocene–Holocene boundary at approximately 11,000 years ago. During the Late Pleistocene vegetation zones that characterize the modern environment were depressed in elevation to the extent that typical Sonoran Desert plant communities were restricted to northern Mexico, pinyon-juniper woodlands occupied what are now desert areas, and subalpine woodlands and forest dominated areas now characterized by pinyon-juniper woodlands. This period is notable for the near absence of ponderosa pine, a species that now occupies huge areas of the upland

Southwest. Beginning around 11,000 years ago, plant communities began to shift upward in latitude and elevation as the onset of the Holocene initiated the transition to warmer, drier modern conditions. Ponderosa pine expanded into its current range during the last 10,000 years. Modern plant community distributions on the southern Colorado Plateau were attained by roughly 8,000 years ago. Subsequent local fluctuations in vegetation distributions (Betancourt and Van Devender 1981; Betancourt et al. 1983) did not disturb the overall trend, which established the conditions that allowed the expansion of agriculture into the region (see Gregory and Nials, chap. 5, this vol.).

Alluvial geomorphology is a primary indicator of LFP variability in floodplain processes across the southern Colorado Plateau during the last 2,000 years. Studies of these processes illuminate the deposition and erosion of floodplain sediments and the associated rise and fall of alluvial groundwater levels. Although each alluvial study area differs somewhat from the others and the studies vary widely in spatial scope and chronological control (Force 2004), a pattern has emerged that appears to prevail over much of the southern plateau. This pattern is most evident in the work of Karlstrom (1988) and his associates on and around Black Mesa in northeastern Arizona, primarily because the large number of stratigraphic localities and the refined ceramic and tree-ring dating of buried archaeological sites and tree-ring dating of buried trees (Dean 1988a) provide unequaled spatial extent and temporal resolution. Geomorphic studies in the Kayenta area (Cooley 1962; Hack 1942, 1945), the Hopi Mesas (Hack 1942), Chaco Canyon (Bryan 1954; Force et al. 2002; Hall 1977; Love 1980; Love and Connell 2005), northern New Mexico (Tuan

1966), the Navajo Reservoir District (Schoenwetter and Eddy 1964), and McElmo Creek (Force and Howell 1997) reflect a similar general pattern, with some local departures from the Black Mesa sequence. Stephen Wells's Zuni-area alluvial sequence (1987:fig. 4.29) is similar to several others and to the general pattern, which implies "regional . . . control on erosional and depositional events" (1987:4.57). Given the low resolution of Wells's dating, which depends on sixteen uncalibrated radiocarbon dates spanning nearly 9,000 years, similarities in timing justify a cautious application of the general features of the better-controlled Black Mesa sequence to the Zuni area. The relevance of the Black Mesa sequence to the Zuni area is further supported by the near identity in the stratigraphy and chronometry of post–AD 1850 fluvial events in both areas (Dean 1988a, 1995; Hall 1985; Karlstrom 1988).

These geomorphologic studies reveal a pattern for the last two millennia of deposition and alluvial groundwater accretion alternating with floodplain erosion (channel incision) and groundwater decretion. This cycle appears to exhibit a general periodicity of 550 years, but there is considerable temporal and spatial variation within this pattern. The hydrologic curve (see fig. 6.1b) exhibits primary maxima at ca. AD 150, 600, 1150, and 1700 and primary minima at about AD 350, 800, 1450, and 2000. Because alluvial deposition-erosion bears a threshold relationship with groundwater fluctuations (Dean 1988a), the aggradation-degradation curve exhibits an asymmetrical profile (see fig. 6.1a). Broadly, alluvial aggradation characterized the region from ca. AD 1 to 225, 350 to 750, 925 to 1250, and 1450 to 1880. Conversely, floodplain degradation (or nondeposition) and channel inci-

sion prevailed between AD 225 and 350, 750 and 925, 1250 and 1450, and 1880 and the present. Secondary depositional hiatuses or erosional intervals are centered on AD 600, 1150, and 1700.

Finally, patterning in environmentally sensitive pollen sequences characterizes low-frequency variation in the vegetation and effective moisture of the Zuni area, which lacks local palynological studies. Hevly's (1988) Hay Hollow Valley synthesis reveals low-frequency fluctuations that closely parallel Karlstrom's (1988) hydrologic curve (cf. fig. 6.1b and c).

Recent dendroclimatic research by Grissino-Mayer (1996) illuminates low-frequency aspects of annual precipitation in the area of El Malpais immediately east of the Zuni area. Although El Malpais lies on the eastern side of the Continental Divide, its reconstruction undoubtedly reflects relative trends in low-frequency climatic variability in the Zuni area as well. Grissino-Mayer's (1996:fig. 4) graph of smoothed relative departures in tree growth is remarkably similar to Karlstrom's (1988) hydrologic and aggradation-degradation curves and Hevly's (1988) effective moisture curve (see fig. 6.1a, b, and c), which further supports the idea that the Black Mesa paleoenvironmental research is broadly relevant to the Zuni area. Grissino-Mayer's low-frequency dendroclimatic maxima centered on AD 200, 600, 1050, and 1650 correspond closely to Karlstrom's hydrologic maxima at AD 150, 600, 1150, and 1700, while dendroclimatic minima centered on AD 400, 900, 1500, and 1950 coincide with hydrologic troughs at AD 350, 850, 1450, and 2000. Minor low-frequency dendroclimatic peaks and troughs during hydrologic minima and maxima probably correspond to secondary fluctuations in fluvial processes. The only major discrepancy between

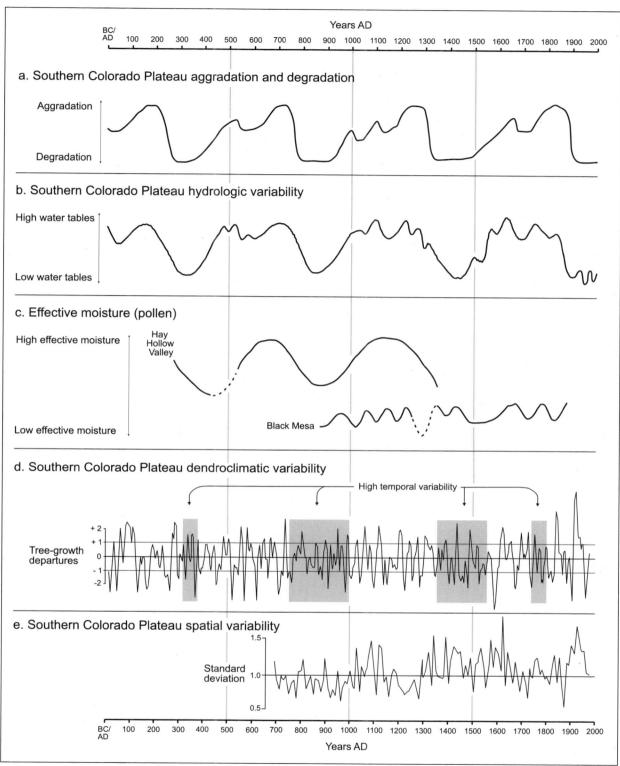

Figure 6.1. Paleoenvironmental variability on the southern Colorado Plateau: (a) floodplain aggradation and degradation; (b) alluvial water table fluctuations; (c) low (Hay Hollow Valley) and high (Black Mesa) frequency variations in effective moisture reconstructed from pollen; (d) relative dendroclimatic variability in decadal standard deviation departure units overlapped by five years with periods of high temporal variability denoted by shading; (e) spatial variability in dendroclimate in standard deviation units. Used with the permission of the Laboratory of Tree-Ring Research, The University of Arizona, Tucson.

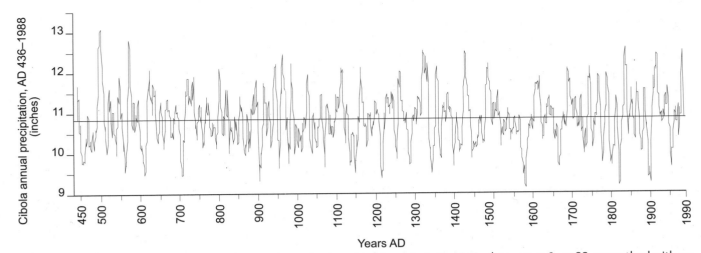

Figure 6.2. Cibola area tree-year (prior August through current July) precipitation in inches, AD 436–1988, smoothed with an eight-year centered moving average. Used with the permission of the Laboratory of Tree-Ring Research, The University of Arizona, Tucson.

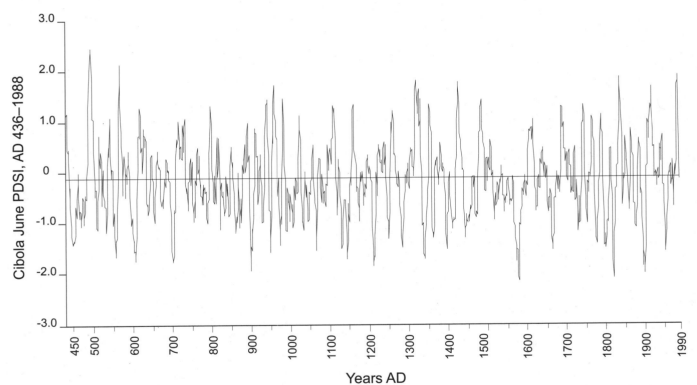

Figure 6.3. Cibola area current June Palmer Drought Severity Indices (PDSI), AD 436–1988, smoothed with an eight-year centered moving average. Used with the permission of the Laboratory of Tree-Ring Research, The University of Arizona, Tucson.

Table 6.1 Extremely Cool and Extremely Warm Intervals, AD 436–1988 (see fig. 6.4)

Extremely Cool Intervals	Extremely Warm Intervals
Middle 500s	Late 500s–early 600s
Late 600s	Early 700s
Early 1200s	Late 800s
Middle 1300s	Early 900s
Early 1500s	Late 1000s
Middle 1600s	Late 1200s (the Great Drought)
Early 1800s	Late 1300s–early 1400s
Early 1900s	1680–1810
	1930–present

the dendroclimatic and geologic records is the steep increase in the former after 1750, which may be due to anthropogenic factors: the Industrial Revolution and global warming. Minor dissimilarities between the two records could be due to the different levels of temporal resolution in the tree-ring (annual) and geomorphic (± 50–100 years) reconstructions.

HFP Environmental Variability

Numerous dendroclimatic reconstructions illuminate HFP environmental variability in and around the study area over the last two millennia. Rose (1987) reconstructed annual precipitation, July Palmer Drought Severity Indices (PDSI), and mean temperature for various parts of the year; D'Arrigo and Jacoby (1991) reconstructed annual winter precipitation; and the Tree-Ring Laboratory's Southwest Paleoclimate Project (SWPP) reconstructed annual "tree-year" (prior August through current July) precipitation and June PDSI for the area around Zuni. These retrodictions are represented here by the SWPP Cibola tree-year precipitation (see fig. 6.2) and June PDSI (see fig. 6.3) reconstructions. These graphs represent annual precipitation and

annual June PDSI values smoothed by the application of an eight-year centered moving average.

Reconstructed Cibola annual tree-year precipitation from AD 436 to 1988 (see fig. 6.2) ranges from less than 15.2 cm to more than 43.2 cm and has a mean slightly less than 27.9 cm. This record exhibits numerous dry and wet intervals that occur in dendroclimatic records from across the northern Southwest. Prominent droughts occur in the late 400s, late 600s, middle 1100s, late 1200s (the Great Drought), early and late 1400s, entire 1500s, early and late 1800s, and middle 1900s. Major wet intervals fall in the late 400s, early 1300s, early 1600s, middle 1800s, and early and late 1900s. The rise at the end of the record marks the beginning of the recent period of extremely high precipitation and temperature that may reflect global warming.

The Cibola PDSI reconstruction (see fig. 6.3) quite naturally resembles the precipitation retrodiction. PDSI (Palmer 1965) measures the effect of meteorological drought on crop production. The statistic has a mean of 0 and generally ranges between −6 and +6. Values greater than +1 represent increasingly good growing conditions, and values below

−1 indicate increasingly poor conditions due to drought. The Cibola sequence has values ranging from −6 to +7.

Historically, temperature has proved more difficult than precipitation to reconstruct with tree rings. This difficulty is due primarily to the fact that temperature and precipitation are so highly negatively correlated (high rainfall is accompanied by low temperature and vice versa) that it is difficult to disentangle one from the other. As a result, all verifiable reconstructions of average annual temperature (Dean and Van West 2002; Rose 1987; Rose et al. 1982) are virtual mirror images of the corresponding precipitation reconstructions (cf. figs. 4.1 and 4.2 in Dean and Van West 2002) and, therefore, are minimally informative.

In a major dendroclimatic breakthrough Salzer (2000a; Salzer and Kipfmueller 2005) used the extended high-elevation bristlecone pine chronology from the San Francisco Peaks, the Southwest's only purely temperature sensitive tree-ring series, to reconstruct annual fluctuations in tree-year mean maximum monthly temperature for the Flagstaff area from 663 BC to AD 1996. Because temperature is far more stable across space and through time than precipitation, the San Francisco Peaks (SFP) reconstruction, at least in relative terms, is broadly applicable to the entire Colorado Plateau in general (Salzer 2000b) and the Zuni area in particular. Salzer (2000a:68–69, table 7) identifies 24 extended (> 10 years) cool periods and 17 extended warm periods since 300 BC. Notable in this record (see table 6.1) are extremely cool intervals in the late AD 600s, the early 1200s, the middle 1300s, the early 1500s, the middle 1600s, the early 1800s, and the early 1900s and extremely warm intervals in the late AD 500s–early 600s, late

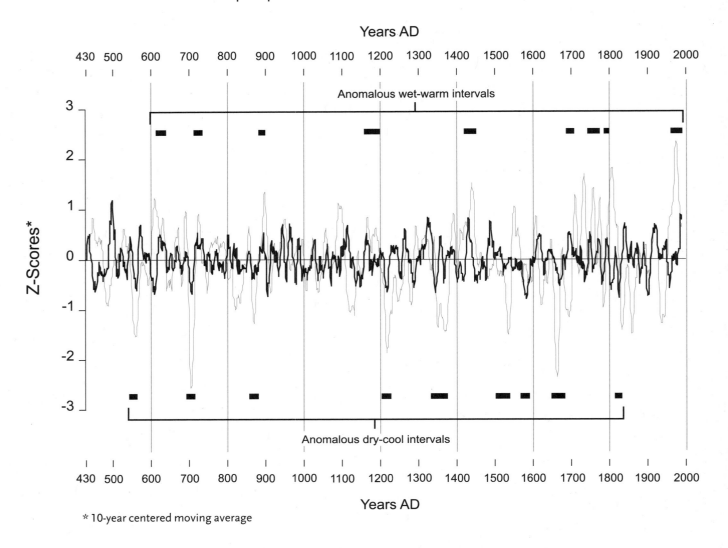

Figure 6.4. Comparison of Cibola annual tree-year precipitation (heavy line) with San Francisco Peaks annual mean maximum monthly temperature (light line), AD 436–1988, precipitation and temperature series normalized (converted to Z-scores) and smoothed with 10-year centered moving average. Used with the permission of the Laboratory of Tree-Ring Research, The University of Arizona, Tucson.

800s, early 900s, late 1000s, middle 1100s, late 1200s (the Great Drought), late 1300s–early 1400s, early 1500s, 1680–1810, and 1930–present. Especially striking are the persistence of warm conditions throughout the AD 1700s and the anomalous surge in temperatures after 1930, which confirms numerous other indicators of global climate change.

In another innovative analysis Sal-

zer (2000a:83, fig. 11; Salzer and Kipfmueller 2005:fig. 6) plotted the SFP high-elevation bristlecone pine temperature record with a Flagstaff-area ponderosa pine precipitation record to compare relative variation in precipitation and temperature for the period common to the two reconstructions, AD 570–1988. Following this procedure, normalized SFP temperature and SWPP Cibola precipitation reconstructions smoothed with a

10-year centered moving average are plotted together (see fig. 6.4) to portray relative temperature and rainfall variability in the Zuni area from AD 436 to 1988. Through most of this period these factors vary as expected, cool periods being accompanied by increased precipitation and warm periods by decreased rainfall. Other periods, however, are characterized by anomalous dry-cool or wet-warm conditions (see table 6.2). Dry-cool

Table 6.2 Anomalous Dry-Cool and Wet-Warm Intervals, AD 436–1988 (see fig. 6.4)

Dry-Cool	Wet-Warm
Middle 500s	Early 600s
Early 700s	Early 700s
Late 800s	Late 800s
	Late 1000s
Early 1200s	Late 1100s
Middle 1300s	Early 1400s
Early 1500s	Late 1600s
Late 1500s	Early 1700s
Late 1600s	Late 1700s
Early 1800s	Late 1900s

weather occurred in the middle AD 1300s, early and late 1500s, late 1600s, and early 1800s, and wet-warm conditions prevailed in the late AD 1000s, late 1100s, early 1400s, late 1600s, middle and late 1700s, and late 1900s. Most notable is the anomalous period 1976–1995, when extremely elevated temperatures and high precipitation coincided.

Applying a statistical relationship between recorded streamflow of the Salt and Verde rivers and Tonto Creek, on the one hand, and that of the middle Little Colorado River, on the other, Van West (1994, 1996) reconstructed streamflow in the middle Little Colorado River for the AD 572–1985 interval. Combining the streamflow data with other measures of past environmental variability, Van West (1996:table 2.1) identified 33 sequent time periods from AD 572 to 1545 whose differing conditions have varying implications for human subsistence in the area. Based on these implications, Van West (1996:29–32) developed a series of hypotheses concerning when settlement on or off the floodplain, surplus production and increased storage, increased or decreased interaction, population aggre-

gation or dispersal, and abandonment should be expected to occur. Although most flow in the middle Little Colorado originates in the stream's headwaters in the White Mountains, Van West's reconstruction probably accurately reflects relative streamflow in the Zuni River, and, to that extent, her hypotheses are relevant to the study area (see also Damp, chap. 8, this vol.).

Often neglected in attempts to relate past human behavior to environmental variability are aspects of HFP climatic variability other than amplitude (high vs. low values). As in the Silver Creek (Kaldahl and Dean 1999:25) and Mesa Verde (Dean and Van West 2002:87; Van West and Dean 2000:26) areas, some extended droughts in the Cibola reconstructions (see figs. 6.2, 6.3) are characterized by sharply reduced variance and a paucity of wet years rather than a high incidence of exceptionally dry years. Two periods were characterized by reduced variance when maxima and minima did not depart greatly from the mean fall at AD 640–720 and 1340–1720. The rainfall pattern of both these intervals departs significantly from the long-term pattern, which exhibits much greater variability around the mean. The AD 1340–1720 period is notable for its 380-year length and may have had important consequences for the human, animal, and plant populations of the study area.

Averaged tree-ring chronologies provide data on decade scale temporal variability in dendroclimate across the southern Colorado Plateau (Dean et al. 1985). High temporal variability occurs when values fluctuate rapidly from one extreme to the opposite. Low temporal variability occurs when the transition from climatic maxima to minima is gradual and spread over several decades. Regional high temporal variability (see fig. 6.1d) prevailed during the periods AD 325–375,

750–1000, 1350–1550, and 1750–1800, while low temporal variability characterized the intervening intervals.

Climate varies across space as well as through time. Standard deviations of decade tree-growth departures for the stations in the SWPP grid (see fig. 6.1e) represent spatial variability in dendroclimate across the northern Southwest. When spatial variability is high, climatic conditions vary considerably from one area to another, and one area may have high rainfall, while nearby areas may be afflicted with low precipitation. In contrast, when spatial variability is low, conditions—good, bad, or indifferent—are similar everywhere across the region. Thus, when it is dry or wet in one area, it likely is dry or wet elsewhere. In general, spatial variability was declining or low from about AD 700 to 1000, 1125 to 1300, and 1625 to 1875 and increasing or high from 1000 to 1125, 1300 to 1625, and 1875 to 1925.

Calculating principal components of 27 climate-sensitive tree-ring chronologies for 100-year periods overlapped by 50 years for the period AD 589–1988 (Dean 1996; Dean and Funkhouser 1995) reveals a persistent pattern in the geographic coherence of the Southwest dendroclimate during the last 1,500 years. The dominant pattern consists of two or three components that distribute consistently in space. The secondary component occupies the southeastern part of the region, principally the Rio Grande valley and the area south of the Mogollon Rim. The primary component occupies the Colorado Plateau northwest of the southeastern component. When present, the tertiary component comprises two Great Basin bristlecone pine chronologies that sometimes form a separate group and sometimes cluster with the northwestern chronologies. The southeastern and northwestern components are separated by an S-shaped boundary zone that fluctuates through time as stations along the boundary zone group with either the primary or secondary cluster (Dean 1996:figs. 4, 8). This pattern is virtually identical to the documented precipitation distribution of the last 100 years, in which summer precipitation dominates in the southeast and a bimodal winter–summer regime prevails in the northwest (Dean 1988a:fig. 5.1, 1996:fig. 5). It is likely that the long-term dendroclimatic configuration represents a seasonal precipitation pattern similar to that of the present, with considerable variation through time in the location and shape of the boundary between the summer-dominant and bimodal regimes.

The strong regional pattern in dendroclimatic coherence breaks down between about AD 1250 and 1450 into a configuration that can only be called chaotic (Dean 1996: fig. 9). As many as six components exist during this period, with stations forming groups that defy climatic logic. Interestingly, the "chaos" is confined to the northwestern part of the Southwest; the southeastern component persists throughout the period, albeit in slightly changing form. Thus, the 200-year interval from AD 1250 to 1450 probably witnessed a breakdown in seasonal precipitation patterns in the northwestern Southwest that had persisted for at least 700 years (see Gregory and Nials, chap. 5, this vol.). The long-term pattern was reestablished after 1450 and persists to the present day. As indicated by the prominence of summer precipitation at Zuni, the study area is situated close to the boundary between the two major components. During the last 1,500 years, however, the Cibola station usually falls into the northwestern (bimodal precipitation) cluster.

Episodic Environmental Events

Episodic events that might have impacted the subsistence activities of the residents of the study area appear in the paleoenvironmental record. Although large alluvial deposition and erosion events are evident in the Zuni-area geological record (S. Wells 1987), they are too poorly dated to be related to specific past human events. Tree-ring-dated scars produced in trees by low-intensity forest fires provide detailed histories of the occurrence, intensity, and extent of past forest fires (Stokes 1980). It is, in fact, possible that some fires were intentionally ignited by humans to replenish certain resources such as grasses or to clear areas for activities such as swidden farming (Sullivan 1982).

The nearest fire history is that constructed by Grissino-Mayer and Swetnam (1997) for El Malpais, across the Continental Divide from the headwaters of the Zuni River. Individual fire scars occur as early as AD 1367 and 1382, but sample depth sufficient to explicate the general fire pattern exists only for AD 1600 to the present. Although individual fires identified in El Malpais may or may not have spread into the Zuni area, the changes in fire frequency noted in the eastern area probably apply to the Zuni area as well. From AD 1600 to about 1880 low-intensity fires occurred about every three years. Major reductions in fire frequency after AD 1880 are attributed to livestock grazing, which removed the fine fuels that support low-intensity ground fires, and to fire suppression by land management agencies. As the frequency of fires decreased, their intensity and extent increased. Similar changes in fire regimes probably characterized the west side of the Zuni Mountains, perhaps modified by extensive logging during the nineteenth century.

Frost-damaged rings in high-elevation tree-ring series identify years in which outbreaks of cold air (LaMarche and Hirschboeck 1984) could have impacted crop production (Brandt 1995). Generally, frost damage to tree rings occurs when temperatures fall below 0°C (32°F) for two consecutive nights and freezing of the moisture in the rings ruptures the cell walls (Salzer 2000a:91). Salzer (2000a:93–96, table 11) tabulates 73 years in which excessive cold damaged rings in San Francisco Peaks bristlecone pine trees. Most of these probably are local phenomena of little relevance to the wider region. It is reasonable, however, to suppose that simultaneous occurrences of frost-damaged rings in two or all three of the published tree-ring records represent conditions sufficiently widespread and severe to have impinged on the Zuni area. Coming from the White Mountains on the California-Nevada border (LaMarche and Hirschboeck 1984), the San Francisco Peaks in central Arizona (Salzer 2000a:93–96, table 11), and Almagre Mountain in the Colorado Front Range (Brunstein 1996), these frost-ring records span the Southwest.

Expectations

Comparing archaeological and historical evidence for past human behavior with the reconstructed records of past environmental fluctuations in the study region is an obvious way to assess human adaptive response to environmental stability, variation, and change. Such a procedure, however, soon devolves into matching patterns between records of the past that are not necessarily comparable and that exhibit different degrees of spatial and temporal resolution. Such a procedure also takes place in an explanatory vacuum in which the fact that correlation (correspondence) does not equal causation undermines inferences drawn from similarities between the different kinds of records. A better approach to this task is to use the paleoenvironmental records to generate expected behavioral responses of human groups to the indicated environmental conditions and fluctuations. This exercise must, of course, be done within the parameters of a general conceptual model (Dean 1988b) of human behavioral adaptation to environmental variability.

Two major sets of interrelated questions are addressed in this way. First, what is the degree to which stable, LFP, HFP, and episodic environmental factors might have affected the subsistence behavior of the agricultural populations of the study area during the last two millennia? Second, what does the paleoenvironmental record suggest about potential subsistence relationships between high (Mogollon Highlands) and low (Colorado Plateau) elevations in the study area?

Agricultural Potential (AD 1–2000)

LFP fluvial processes have important implications for agriculture in the Zuni area (Dean 1988b; Plog et al. 1988). Aggradation and rising water tables create ideal conditions for farming on the floodplains. Except for rare occasions when fields are buried by alluvial deposition, the accretion of sediments periodically renews the soil in which crops are grown. At the same time, alluvial groundwater, which is close to the surface, can be relied on to water the crops either through contact with plant roots or by being tapped for ditch irrigation at points where the water table intersects the surface. In addition, crops are watered by streamflow that spreads out over the valley floors rather than being confined to deep, narrow channels. These conditions

greatly reduce dependence on precipitation, a much less adequate and less reliable source of agricultural water. Thus, aggradation and groundwater accretion create a much more stable, if not more productive, agricultural situation. Conversely, the concurrent erosion of surface deposits and dependence on precipitation to water crops makes upland areas surrounding the valleys less amenable to farming.

Floodplain degradation (surface erosion and channel incision) and groundwater decretion materially reduce the farming potential of the floodplains. Surface erosion and channel incision demolish fields and, more important, destroy large areas of arable land through sediment removal. At the same time, groundwater levels drop far below the level of the terrace surfaces where fields can be planted. Lacking sophisticated water transport technology (pumps, etc.), preindustrial farmers would be unable to raise sufficient water from the flowing streams in the bottoms of the arroyos to the terrace surfaces above. These floodplain conditions dictate far more reliance on precipitation through techniques such as dry, floodwater, and ak-chin farming, irrigation from flowing streams, and other methods that capture atmospheric or surface water. Under these conditions the uplands, where surfaces stabilize and precipitation is greater, become more suitable for farming than they are when aggradation and groundwater accretion prevail in the floodplains.

Considered in isolation, LFP fluvial processes (see fig. 6.1a, b) should promote widespread farming on (and settlement on or near) the valley floors and reduced utilization of uplands during periods of aggradation and groundwater accretion. The broad expanses of arable land and agricultural stability produced by

these conditions might also favor the dispersal of settlements and more permanence in residential behavior. Conversely, upland areas are likely to be more heavily utilized and the floodplains less so during intervals of degradation and falling alluvial water tables. These circumstances might also stimulate changes in settlement locations, logistic subsistence strategies, greater settlement mobility (as groups seek to exploit the more varied conditions), the concentration of settlement (aggregation) in the more restricted localities suitable for farming, increased intergroup competition, or various combinations of these responses. Therefore, we might expect populations in the Zuni area to adopt the first set of adaptive behaviors during periods characterized by floodplain aggradation and groundwater accretion: approximately AD 1–225, 350–750, 925–1250, and 1450–1880. The second set of behaviors likely would be invoked during periods of degradation and groundwater decretion: AD 225–350, 750–925, 1250–1450, and 1880–present. Brief reversions to the second set of responses are likely during secondary downturns in fluvial conditions centered on AD 50, 600, 1150, and 1700.

The effects of HFP and episodic variables on agricultural populations in the study area are more difficult to assess for several reasons. First, the temporal resolution of these reconstructions is so much higher than that of the archaeological record that it commonly is difficult to establish clear chronological links between the events specified by each record. Second, lags in behavioral response made possible by various cultural buffering mechanisms (storage, exchange, spread-the-risk planting practices, etc.) may create temporal offsets between behavioral reactions to their environmental stimuli. Third, short-term behavioral responses to extremes of climate or episodic events are likely to be invisible in the archaeological record except under the most auspicious of circumstances. Fourth, it may be difficult to correctly assign causality to archaeologically visible long-term behavioral changes that are triggered by relatively brief but severe HFP and episodic events. Thus, while some extreme and episodic events that might have impacted the residents of the study area can be identified, it may not always be possible to observe their behavioral effects in the archaeological record.

Short but severe droughts can have disproportionate effects on crop production that ramify through human subsistence systems over a period of years (Burns 1983). The SWPP Cibola precipitation and PDSI reconstructions (see figs. 6.2, 6.3) and Van West's (1994, 1996) streamflow reconstruction specify years of low and high precipitation and stream discharge that might have limited crop production on and off the floodplains or washed out or otherwise damaged floodplain fields.

Prolonged departures from long-term HFP means are likely to have behavioral consequences sufficient to leave traces in the archaeological record. The Cibola precipitation and PDSI reconstructions record numerous droughts between AD 436 and 1988. Extended dry intervals at AD 1120–1160, 1276–1299 (the Great Drought), 1360–1430, and 1520–1600 likely had major agricultural consequences. The low variance characteristic of the late seventh and early eighth centuries and the late fourteenth through seventeenth centuries also would have adversely affected crop production. The rarity of wet years would inhibit recovery from reduced crop yields caused by dry years. In contrast, long wet periods relieved water-supply pressures on

agricultural systems, especially in the uplands, and may have supported agricultural expansion.

Temperature impacts subsistence agriculture through its effect on the location of the upper elevational limit of farming. While it would be inappropriate to assign exact locations to the 120-day limit in the Zuni area on the basis of Salzer's SFP temperature reconstructions, the logic employed by Petersen (1988) can be used to make some inferences about elevational changes in the farmable zone in the Zuni River valley due to the combined effects of temperature and precipitation. His proposition that the upper limit of the farmable zone is controlled by temperature minima and the lower limit by precipitation minima yields four possible outcomes. During dry and warm intervals the entire zone would move up-drainage; during wet and cool intervals the zone would migrate down-valley; during dry and cool intervals the zone would contract as deficient moisture raised the lower limit and cooler temperatures depressed the upper limit; wet and warm conditions would expand the zone by lowering the lower limit and raising the upper limit.

Figure 6.4 pinpoints intervals when such elevational shifts may have required corresponding (or lagged) human settlement relocations or logistic farming operations from established settlements. Settlement or field house locations might drift upstream during long dry-warm periods in the late 500s–early 600s, early 700s, late 800s, middle 1100s, late 1200s, early 1400s, early 1500s, and early 1900s. Conversely, downstream movement may have been triggered by wet-cool conditions in the late 600s, early and middle 800s, early 1100s, early 1200s, middle 1600s, late 1700s, early 1800s, and

early 1900s. Widening of the farmable zone by anomalous wet-warm conditions might have induced expansion in settlement or farming activities both up and down the Zuni River drainage in the early 600s, early 700s, late 800s, late 1100s, early 1400s, late 1600s, early and late 1700s, and late 1900s. Narrowing of the zone during unusual dry-cool conditions may have induced settlement contraction in the middle 500s, late 600s, early 700s, early 1200s, middle 1300s, early 1500s, late 1500s, late 1600s, and early 1800s.

Temporal variability in climate (see fig. 6.1d) has important consequences for human populations in the study area. Surplus production and food storage is a viable response to high temporal variability. Low production in lean years can be offset by stored surpluses from good years when unproductive and productive conditions alternate fairly rapidly. Producing and storing surplus crops is less likely to occur during periods of low temporal variability. During a slow transition from unproductive to productive conditions excess storage is not necessary because production tends to increase through time. Under declining conditions, however, surplus production becomes progressively more difficult to achieve and existing surpluses tend to be rapidly depleted, leaving little to be consigned to long-term storage.

High and low spatial variability in climate (see fig. 6.1e) favor different behavioral responses. High variability promotes the development of inter-area food production differentials. Such differentials favor the exchange of food for nonfood items, with the latter passing from areas of low to high production and food moving in the opposite direction. Groups favored by high production can then "bank" the increased material "wealth" against future times when high spatial variability works against them and in favor of other groups. As a result, periods of high spatial variability should be characterized by archaeological evidence for increased interlocality interaction, what Plog (1983, 1984) and Upham (1982) call "alliances." Raiding of the haves by the have-nots also might increase the archaeological evidence for conflict during periods of increasing to high spatial variability. Production differentials that might allow trade or raiding to offset hard times do not develop during intervals of low spatial variability when everyone is affected more or less equally. In productive periods there is no incentive to trade for food, and in lean periods there are no surpluses to either exchange for other goods or appropriate by force. Therefore, the archaeological evidence for interareal interaction should decrease during periods of low spatial variability.

The evident change in the seasonal distribution of precipitation indicated by the disruption of the long-term coherence pattern between AD 1250 and 1450 would have had major consequences for the occupants of the northwestern part of the Southwest. Agricultural systems that had become adapted to the prevailing bimodal precipitation regime over several centuries likely would have considerable difficulty coping with the more "chaotic" conditions of the period AD 1250–1450. One response to these altered circumstances would be movement out of the afflicted area into the southeastern area, where relatively stable climatic conditions allowed continued pursuit of the prevailing adaptive techniques (Ahlstrom et al. 1995). Accustomed by their location on the boundary between the two patterns to surviving a unimodal rainfall regime, Zuni-area

populations may have been better able to handle the altered situation than more northerly groups. This ability may have attracted northern people to the Zuni area after AD 1250.

Hard freezes in late spring or early fall could have severely damaged crops on the southern Colorado Plateau. Bradfield (1971:6) notes that late spring freezes, though rare, can destroy Hopi crops. Lying in an area of cold air drainage from the Zuni Mountains, crops in the Zuni River valley might have been particularly susceptible to outbreaks of cold air that could impact subsistence for years to come. The co-occurrence of frost-damaged rings in two or more of the three bristlecone pine frost-ring records in the White Mountains of California (LaMarche and Hirschboeck 1984), the San Francisco Peaks (Salzer 2000a:93–96, table 11), and the Colorado Front Range (Brunstein 1996) places potentially damaging frosts in AD 268, 393, 443, 449, 479, 484, 522, 536, 627, 687, 858, 896, 934, 973, 1029, 1057, 1109, 1171, 1200, and 1329. The AD 896 freeze may have been exceptionally damaging because it occurred in the spring. In the Flagstaff area (Salzer 2000a:97) multiple frost years occurred during the especially cool intervals in the late AD 600s, early 800s, middle 800s, early 1100s, early 1200s, middle 1300s, middle 1600s, late 1600s, and early 1800s, and frost damage to crops may have been more prevalent during those times.

Taken together, the diverse measures of past environmental variability in the Zuni area can be used to identify periods of environmental release and stress and to rank these intervals in terms of potential impact on the residents of the area. Other factors impinge on the behavioral-environmental interactions that define these periods and must be fac-

tored into this exercise (Dean 1988b). Among these are the number of people living in the area and the population densities in particular localities. Obviously, low or high population levels favor or inhibit various behavioral adjustments to environmental variations. For example, low populations allow groups to move to more favorable localities when their current location is adversely affected. This type of local mobility is much more limited when large populations already fill every suitable locality, and social adjustments or conflicts are more likely. Pressure from external human groups also may become a factor, as when migrants attempt to settle in or pass through the area, or when other groups attempt to appropriate by force local groups' food or other resources. Such external pressure is, of course, likely to develop during periods of regional environmental stress and high regional populations.

Looking solely at the environmental component of the adaptive relationship, especially favorable conditions occur when positive LFP and HFP variations reinforce one another. By this criterion, the interval from around AD 925 to approximately 1130 was probably the most favorable extended period for agricultural groups throughout the northern Southwest during the last 2,000 years. Floodplain deposition and rising alluvial water tables combined with unusually stable climatic conditions to allow farming to be pursued just about anywhere. High groundwater levels stabilized agriculture on the floodplains, dependable (though not necessarily overabundant) precipitation and equable temperatures supported dry farming in the uplands, high temporal climatic variability favored the accumulation of stored food reserves early in the period, and increasing spatial variability allowed intergroup exchange and "banking" to offset local production shortfalls. The generally good conditions militated against raiding for food because most groups were probably relatively well off, although high spatial variability meant that some groups suffered in particular years. Thus, between AD 925 and the middle 1100s one would expect population growth and expansion, settlement dispersal, limited settlement aggregation except in places where population levels were straining the capacities of local resources, increased reliance on storage early on, and rising intergroup interaction.

Less salubrious but still favorable conditions existed, at least in the valleys, whenever floodplain aggradation and groundwater accretion prevailed. Even if upland farming was negatively impacted during these periods, favorable weather would at times have rewarded agricultural effort in these zones. Lowland populations could have expanded into the uplands during favorable intervals and withdrawn when conditions worsened. Alternatively, less favorable conditions might have stimulated increased interaction, friendly or antagonistic, between upland and valley groups. Secondary downward fluctuations in fluvial conditions, which occurred during periods of primary aggradation and groundwater accretion, could have required temporary adjustments in subsistence behavior and reordered relationships among upland and valley groups. Generally favorable fluvial conditions occurred between approximately AD 350 and 750 and 1450 and 1880, although both these intervals experienced more variability than the period AD 925–1130. Finally, the period between about AD 1180 and 1250 was generally favorable except for a cool interval from about AD 1195 to 1216, which might have driven valley populations downstream and upland populations into lower areas.

Especially unfavorable environmental conditions occur when negative LFP and HFP variations reinforce one another. Without doubt, the period of greatest environmental stress on the agricultural systems of the southern Colorado Plateau came between about AD 1250 and 1450. Falling groundwater levels and rapid channel entrenchment (arroyo cutting) removed a stable source of agricultural water and washed away fields and large swaths of arable land. No longer sustained by a stable supply of groundwater, farming became more dependent on precipitation, a much less adequate and far more variable source of water for crops. To exacerbate matters, the Great Drought (AD 1276–1299) severely reduced the amount of annual precipitation for a quarter century. Low temporal variability in climate reduced the efficacy of storage as a means of adjustment to declining production. Low spatial variability constrained recourse to trade or raiding to offset food production shortfalls. At roughly the same time, the abrupt transformation from high to low spatial coherence in climate upset the seasonal distribution of precipitation to which agricultural practices had become adapted during the preceding seven centuries. These environmental blows came when subsistence systems were especially vulnerable due to high regional and local human populations and population densities.

Given the severe environmental deterioration outlined above, the period beginning around 1250 should have been one of major destabilization for the agricultural populations of the southern Colorado Plateau. The worsening subsistence conditions would have materially enhanced competition for dwindling and increasingly localized resources, particularly arable land on the floodplains. Predictable behavioral responses to the crisis include technological adjustments such as increased dryland, floodwater, ak-chin, and irrigation farming in localities where water could be diverted from perennial or intermittent sources onto fields. Large-scale demographic adjustments would include migration into areas suitable for agriculture under the prevailing conditions, for example, areas characterized by greater precipitation, stable land–water relationships, spatial coherence, or suitability for technological manipulations such as irrigation.

Given the high population levels across the northern Southwest at the time (Dean et al. 1994; see also Wilcox et al., chap. 12, this vol.), such migrations commonly would involve moving into already occupied areas and/or communities, a process that would undoubtedly cause major social problems in integrating newcomers into existing communities and create significant social tensions between host groups and immigrants. Local demographic responses likely would involve aggregation around the best spots for agriculture, primarily valley bottom stream confluence areas, bedrock outcrops, and locations characterized by high alluviation rates. Aggregation would lead to increased size of individual sites or groups of sites. The societal problems attendant on aggregation—greater population densities, controlling and apportioning access to critical resources (especially arable land), group task assignments, dispute resolution, intragroup organization, managing relationships with other groups, and many others— would contribute to social instability engendered by increased environmental uncertainty. Archaeologically visible consequences of these unsettled natural and sociocultural conditions likely would include evidence for hierarchical settlement systems that reflect both increased intragroup cooperation and greater intergroup competition and friction, increased territoriality and control of resources, and, perhaps, intra- and intergroup conflict.

The second most severe combination of negative environmental conditions occurred between AD 1130 and 1180, when a secondary decline in fluvial conditions coincided with an intense dry spell (AD 1120–1160 in the Zuni area) that was longer than the Great Drought and with low temporal and declining spatial variability in climate. These conditions would have required adjustments similar to but less extensive than those of the late thirteenth century.

The third ranked stress period was between roughly AD 1850 and 1980. Arroyo cutting and depressed alluvial water tables, along with major droughts in the late AD 1800s and middle 1900s, would have severely impacted Native American subsistence systems and did, in fact, nearly destroy Anglo agriculture and stock raising in the region.

A severe and lengthy drought that, in the Zuni area, occupied the entire sixteenth century (see fig. 6.2) is ranked fourth on the scale of potential impact on human groups. Especially during the second half of the century, this continental-scale "megadrought" (Stahle et al. 2000) affected the entire Southwest and would have placed all the Puebloans under some degree of stress for half a century before permanent colonization of the region by the Spaniards. The effects of this drought in the Zuni area may have been alleviated by storage strategies allowed by high temporal climate variability during the first half of the century. Production differentials created by increasing spatial variability throughout the century may have promoted exchange or raiding to move food from

areas of high to low production. The primary mitigating factor during this period, however, would have been the favorable conditions for floodplain farming caused by aggradation and groundwater accretion.

In addition to the well-known "droughts" (AD 1130–1180, 1276–1299, 1500–1599) that have been invoked to explain aspects of southwestern prehistory, the SWPP Cibola precipitation reconstruction (see fig. 6.2) reveals other local climatic factors that may have stressed Zuni-area subsistence systems. Deficient precipitation and suppressed variance between AD 630 and 730 likely would have adversely affected any farming that depended primarily on rainfall. Reduced year to year variation would have inhibited a storage strategy that involved using one year's abundance to offset another's deficits. During this interval of aggradation and rising alluvial water tables these effects would have been most pronounced in the uplands. The 380-year period of low precipitation variance from roughly AD 1350 to 1700 was not as dominated by drought as the interval 630–730. Furthermore, the last 250 years of this interval were characterized by favorable fluvial conditions. Nevertheless, the resulting difficulty in producing and storing surpluses could have been particularly serious during the sixteenth-century drought and might have had adverse effects even during wetter periods.

Relationships between High- and Low-Elevation Areas

Relationships between human groups occupying the "lowlands" (below 2,135 m) and "uplands" (above 2,135 m) of the study area may have been important factors in the development of the modern Zuni configuration. Specifically, this issue involves Anasazi populations of the

Colorado Plateau and Mogollon populations of the Mogollon Highlands south of the Zuni area. An important issue, of course, is how the environments of these two zones facilitated or hindered relationships among the people involved and thereby contributed to the development of the Zuni pattern. Although the paucity of paleoenvironmental research in the mountains hampers the effort to compare the two regions, the bountiful paleoenvironmental record of the Colorado Plateau allows some inferences to be made.

Various stable environmental factors define the manifest differences between the two zones. Primary among these are bedrock geology, elevation, and topography, which determine other stable aspects of the zones. The igneous highlands are higher, wetter, cooler, and more rugged than the sedimentary plateau. Flora and fauna reflect these fundamental differences. As a result, the two zones differ considerably in resources needed by humans and offer distinctly different possibilities for exploitation. These differences create the potential for differential responses to LFP, HFP, and episodic environmental fluctuations.

LFP fluvial variations on the Colorado Plateau have some implications for the differential exploitation of the higher and lower environments. For example, when arroyo cutting and depressed alluvial water tables force increased reliance on rainfall, farmers, particularly those living in the plateau uplands and those lacking access to the more restricted floodplain localities suitable for farming, might be attracted to the wetter Mogollon Highlands. Conversely, during periods of aggradation and groundwater accretion highland farmers might be drawn to the productive drainages of the plateau, where crops are less vulnerable to freezing. In general, "hard goods" exchanged for food might be expected to flow from the plateau to the highlands during periods of floodplain degradation and in the opposite direction during intervals of favorable floodplain conditions, but such directional movements might be poorly visible in the archaeological record.

In terms of HFP precipitation and temperature variability the most obvious expected relationship would be increased occupance of the Colorado Plateau during wet and/or cool periods and of the Mogollon Highlands during drier and/or warmer intervals. Predicted responses include population movement into the highlands during dry-warm intervals and onto the plateau during wet-cool intervals. Wet-warm conditions would favor occupation in either area, while dry-cool conditions would be inimical in both the highlands, where lower temperatures would limit farming, and the plateau, where drought would limit farming.

It is hard to imagine how changes in temporal climate variability would affect the relationships between the plateau and the highlands, since both zones are likely to be affected similarly and neither acquires an advantage over the other. Low spatial variability also is unlikely to create production gradients between the plateau and highlands. High spatial variability, however, might very well intensify the differences between the two habitats and reinforce the general pressure to increase the flow of food from areas of high production to low production. As a result, populations in both areas should participate in the heightened interaction activity inferred for such periods. The aberrant weather pattern during AD 1250–1450 might have induced people to move from the plateau into the highlands depending on whether the latter area fell within the zone of relative

climatic stability as opposed to the chaotic zone to the northwest.

Results

Space limitations preclude an exhaustive comparison of the above expectations with the archaeological record of the Zuni area. In any case, the other chapters in this volume offer unlimited grist for this particular mill. In particular, the sequential maps presented by Wilcox et al. (chap. 12, this vol.) provide stunning spatio-temporal data for evaluating the fit between the expectations and human settlement behavior. Therefore, I propose to make only a few observations on both large- and local-scale congruences between human behavior and the expectations developed above.

Regional-scale confirmations of many expectations are presented elsewhere (Dean 1996; Dean et al. 1994) and need be only summarized here. It surely is no coincidence that the period identified as the most stressful for agricultural societies in the last 2,000 years, approximately AD 1250–1450, was characterized by massive population relocations and cultural reorganization. The Four Corners area was abandoned, and Anasazi immigrants moved east and south into areas already occupied by resident populations. Sociocultural upheavals that accompanied these mass movements were compounded by the necessity to integrate immigrants into the societies already established in the target areas. In one of the great metamorphoses in southwestern culture history, the Anasazi Pueblo III pattern was transformed into the altogether different Pueblo IV configuration, a development that adumbrated subsequent sociocultural developments in the Pueblo world.

The second most stressful period, AD 1130–1180, also was accompanied

by major demographic and sociocultural changes. The Chacoan system came to an end, and the core area was depopulated. In many Anasazi areas settlement shifted toward lower elevations, which resulted in the abandonment of upland localities in the Mesa Verde and Kayenta areas. Groups began withdrawing from the far northwestern peripheries of the Anasazi range to congregate in lowland areas where favorable floodplain conditions existed. The eastern Anasazi underwent major sociocultural changes as they adapted to the disappearance of the Chacoan system, while the western Anasazi entered a 50-year transitional period that culminated in the distinctive Tsegi phase pattern.

Demographic, economic, and cultural changes during the third worst interval, AD 1850–1980, are well documented historically. The unsettled conditions of this interval were accompanied by population dislocations and economic transformations attendant on the initiation of arroyo cutting in the late 1800s, the Dust Bowl calamity of the 1930s, and the massive drought of the 1950s. In turn, each of these events caused large-scale migrations, nearly destroyed agriculture and stock raising, and triggered major changes in how these enterprises were managed.

Although epidemiological and demographic effects of the fourth worst episode, the continent-wide, century-long megadrought of the 1500s, have been noted in Mexico (Acuna-Soto et al. 2002), few such consequences are visible in the Southwest archaeological record. This apparent lack of impact may be because this period has not been intensively investigated and, perhaps, because European colonization masked behavioral responses to these conditions. It may be, however, that a century of drought weakened the

Pueblos and made them especially vulnerable to conquest. The concentration of settlements around and downstream from the current location of the Pueblo of Zuni by 1600 (Kintigh 1985:fig. 6.7; see also chap. 18, this vol.) may reflect the necessity to rely on irrigation from flowing streams as a result of this long dry spell.

In local terms the people of the Zuni area participated in many of the regional developments outlined above. The exact nature of this participation and the response of Zuni-area groups to local environmental fluctuations can be assessed by comparing pertinent archaeological data in the other chapters of this book and elsewhere to the paleoenvironmental reconstructions and behavioral expectations described here. Only one example involving local conditions is offered here. Considering the effects of temperature and precipitation (see fig. 6.4) on the extent of the farmable zone led to four expectations about settlement in the Zuni River valley that can be tested with site distributions between AD 1250 and 1625 (Kintigh 1985). The expectation that wet-cool conditions would favor downstream movement during the early thirteenth century is not supported by site distributions at AD 1250 (see Kintigh 1985:fig. 6.1; see also chap. 18, this vol.), but there are no comparable data on earlier site distributions or for lower reaches of the river. The prediction that settlement might move upstream during the dry-warm period in the late thirteenth century (the Great Drought) is supported by the concentration of sites in the upper end of the drainage between AD 1275 and 1325 (Kintigh 1985:figs. 6.2, 6.3, 6.4). The hypothesis that the farmable zone may have expanded during wet-warm conditions in the early fifteenth century receives weak support from the wide elevational range of sites occupied at AD 1400. Finally, archaeological data offer no support for the settlement contraction predicted for the middle fourteenth century. The concentration of sites near and downstream from the present location of Zuni Pueblo at AD 1625 (Kintigh 1985:fig. 6.7), however, may reflect a response to a narrowing of the farmable zone in the early sixteenth century and the prolonged drought that followed. More highly resolved archaeological data on the Zuni area and for downstream reaches of the Zuni River would allow more refined testing of these ideas.

Relationships between the Mogollon Highlands and the Colorado Plateau support some expectations derived from regional-scale environmental variability. In particular, highland and plateau groups were fully involved in the demographic and behavioral transformations associated with the most stressful period, AD 1250–1450. Less is known about highland–plateau human interactions during the second and fourth worst intervals, AD 1130–1180 and the sixteenth century, while European domination precluded major response by Native American groups to the stresses of the third worst period, AD 1850–1980.

Some predicted responses to HFP precipitation and temperature variability are supported by archaeological data. The most obvious of these correspondences is the large-scale movement of northerners into the Mogollon Highlands after AD 1250, a period when the dry-warm Great Drought was part of the large-scale environmental degradation of the period AD 1250–1450. Similar population movements do not seem to characterize other dry-warm intervals, although the highlands were occupied during those predating AD 1350. In contrast, large-scale movements out of the highlands have not been noted for most wet-cool or dry-cool periods. As expected, temporal variability in climate had no detectable effect on plateau–highland relationships. In contrast, highland populations participated in the large-scale interaction systems (alliances) identified by Plog (1983, 1984) for periods characterized by high spatial variability in climate.

Conclusions

The rich paleoenvironmental record of the Colorado Plateau and, to a lesser extent, the Mogollon Highlands provides a solid foundation for assessing the effects of environmental stability, variation, and change on interactions between the human inhabitants of these two regions during the last two millennia and the development of the Zuni sociocultural pattern. Stable, high-frequency, low-frequency, and episodic environmental factors impacted these populations in predictable ways that required demographic and behavioral responses on the part of the affected groups. Demographic responses involved population fluctuations and large-scale population movements. Behavioral responses involved adaptive changes in subsistence systems, changes in settlement locations and sizes, and organizational innovations that coalesced around AD 1350 into the distinctive pattern that still characterizes Puebloan societies.

People of the Zuni area participated fully in behavioral-environmental interactions that ultimately involved the inhabitants of the entire Southwest. Therefore, a typically Zuni mode of response cannot be disentangled from the general pattern that prevailed across the region before the recognizable precursors of the modern Puebloan groups emerged after AD 1300. It seems likely, therefore, that the large-scale human upheavals that began in the late thirteenth century were triggered in part by severe environmental degradation and that the very different archaeological patterns that appeared after AD 1300 are outcomes of the long process of adaptation to changed environmental and sociocultural circumstances.

Acknowledgments

Many institutions and individuals contributed to the work presented here. Analysis of Zuni-area archaeological tree-ring samples has been supported by 10 National Science Foundation grants, the Zuni Archaeology Project, the Zuni Cultural Resource Enterprise, and numerous contract archaeology programs. Living-tree sampling and analysis, climate-sensitive chronology building, and dendroclimatic reconstruction were undertaken by the Laboratory of Tree-Ring Research's Southwest Paleoclimate Project, supported by the National Park Service, the USDD Advanced Research Projects Agency, and the National Science Foundation. Additional dendroclimatic work was funded by the Zuni Tribe in support of its land-damage lawsuit against the United States. Donald Graybill and Gary Funkhouser produced the dendroclimatic precipitation and PDSI reconstructions used here, and Gary created the original versions of figures 6.2, 6.3, and 6.4. David A. Gregory created the versions of all the illustrations that appear in this chapter. Carrie Dean compiled reams of dendroclimatic data that were used to produce figure 6.4. Finally, I would like to thank the Center for Desert Archaeology, the Museum of Northern Arizona, and their representatives for sponsoring and organizing the advanced seminar and providing a unique ambience at the Colton House that fostered congenial and productive intellectual exchange. Special thanks go to David A. Gregory and David R. Wilcox, conveners of the seminar, for the time and effort they devoted to the enterprise that is coming to fruition in this volume.

Part II

Placing Zuni in the Development of Southwestern Societies

From Paleoindian to Mogollon

7 The Archaic Origins of the Zuni

Preliminary Explorations

R. G. Matson

What are the origins of the Zuni? There are many alternative approaches to this question and many different meanings of "origin." In archaeology a successful strategy to answer this sort of question has been to "go from the known to the unknown," the direct historical approach, in which a recent, ethnographically identified assemblage is traced back in time. Here I take the opposite tack and look at the basal hunting and gathering stratum from which the Proto-Zuni must have emerged.

Three aspects of past lifeways are of particular interest in this effort: population size, seasonal round, and group territory. The first gives us an idea of archaeological visibility as well as the parameters of social organization; the second focuses on important resources, site types, and social organization; and the last helps define the environmental limits for the Proto-Zuni homeland. The combination of all these factors places significant limits on possible locations for the Proto-Zuni.

At the request of the editors and in light of Hill's finding (chap. 3, this vol.) about the deep time depth of the Zuni language, we begin with the Paleoindian period and the "peopling of the Americas." I then move on to the Early, Middle, and Late Archaic periods. Embarrassingly, the Early Archaic is much better known than the Middle Archaic, and even the Late Archaic is not much better known than the Early Archaic. This lack of knowledge in itself gives us some hints as to the likely situation of Zuni progenitors in the dramatic setting of the coming of agriculture. After the arrival of maize in the Southwest the "Pre-Pottery Neolithic (PPN)," as William Lipe (Lipe et al. 1999:133) calls it, was the crucible in which the ethnic identity of many southwestern cultures was forged, and some of the new ethnic groups formed during this interval can be traced to the present. This "stage"—hereafter referred to as the Pre-Pottery Formative (PPF) —was a blending situation (Matson 1991, 1999, 2002).[1] There are strong indications of some characteristics being brought into the Southwest by migrants and others continuing from cultures having ancient roots within the region. The location and adaptation of the first PPF populations also influence the assessment of various areas as a likely Proto-Zuni homeland. The complex PPF setting is summarized and the probable environmental setting of the Proto-Zuni is then described, with attention to the identity of Zuni as a linguistic isolate. Actual geographical locations in the Southwest with appropriate characteristics are then reviewed with

Zuni origins in mind, and a number of possibilities are then noted.

The Peopling of the Americas and the Paleoindians

The Zuni, as aboriginal Americans, share with others the settling of the New World. Since they are neither Athapaskan nor Eskimo-Aleut speakers, they are probably descendants of the first migrants, whether or not one believes the Greenberg (1987) tripartite hypothesis. As Hill explains in chapter 3 (this vol.), the Zuni are an isolate, not related to any known language. Given that there were three well-attested migrations (Clovis, Athapaskan, and Eskimo-Aleut), the Zuni can only belong to the Clovis. Theoretically, there remains the possibility that other migrations occurred and that the Zuni were the result of one of these as yet undocumented migrations. Since the Southwest has a well-attested Clovis occupation, this possibility appears to be very unlikely for the Zuni. As Hill also explains, the Zuni must have separated from other linguistic kin at least 7,000 or 8,000 years ago, placing their origin as a separate linguistic group at least into the early Archaic. Thus, they are likely descendants of Paleoindians.

The Clovis Horizon

Empirical support continues to build for the long-accepted idea of an Asian population with Upper Paleolithic technology moving over the Bering Strait land bridge some 11,500–13,000 radiocarbon years ago, after the height of the Wisconsin glaciation and during lower sea-level times toward the end of this interval. This venerable hypothesis has these populations moving down the ice-free corridor between the Laurentide and Cordilleran glaciers along the east side of the Rocky Mountains and being transformed into Clovis along the way (Matson and Coupland 1995:49–66).

Prior to 1985 there was little evidence for a significant ice-free corridor of the appropriate age, nor was there any evidence of Clovis age or earlier material in Alaska. Now there are several potential pre-Clovis cultures known in Alaska, with the Nenana complex (Hoffecker et al. 1993) being the best-described and most likely Clovis progenitor. Briefly, this culture is now known from about a dozen sites, dates to about 11,800 RCYBP, includes a number of Upper Paleolithic technological traits (e.g., prismatic blades, end and side scrapers, and *pièces esquillées*), and overall has a lithic technology very similar to Clovis (Goebel et al. 1991). However, neither Clovis points nor mammoths are known for the Nenana. Mammoths dating less than 15,000 years ago are not clearly present in Beringia, an observation that has been used to explain the lack of Clovis points there. In sum, the Nenana has the Upper Paleolithic character, the dating, and the geographical location to be expected of a Clovis progenitor.

The ice-free corridor hypothesis is not as certain, but there is general agreement that the northern and southern portions have been open

for the last 15,000 years (Mandryk et al. 2001). The central portion, however, may have been closed between 17,000 and 14,000 B.P., but by about 14,000 B.P. the entire corridor appears to have been ice-free. Mandryk (1992; see also Matson and Coupland 1995: 60–61) argues that the environment would not have supported a static population until 12,000 B.P. If this is the case, a migration through the corridor would have been possible ca. 1,000 or 2,000 years before, leaving time for Clovis ancestors to have traveled through and perhaps even to get to Monte Verde in Chile (see Dillahay 1997).[2] Charlie Lake Cave (Fladmark et al. 1988) is located in the central portion of the ice-free corridor and thus should give minimum dates for the viability of this area. All of the dates on the earliest component are on bone collagen, and all are in excess of 10,000 RCYBP.[3] Two (10,450 ± 150 B.P. [SFU 300] and 10,770 ± 120 B.P. [SFU 454]) are on unidentified human-modified bone, and two others are on artiodactyls (10,500 ± 80 B.P. [CAMS 2129]) and bison (10,560 ± 80 B.P. [CAMS 2134]) (Driver et al. 1996), indicating the human viability of the corridor at or shortly after terminal Clovis times.

Recent excavations in Northeast Asia (Goebel et al. 2003) may indicate that the earliest Upper Paleolithic–derived material does not date significantly earlier there than in Beringia. Further, these investigations indicate that the microblade-based cultures found there may date less than 11,000 RCYBP, again similar to earliest secure dates in Alaska for the Denali (Geobel et al. 2003; Mason et al. 2001). These microblade cultures are often associated with ancestors of the Athapaskans. If this association is correct, the relationship between Clovis and Zuni is made stronger, as it is hard to see a later migration pushing through both the Athapas-

kans and Clovis-occupied areas without leaving signs. The later Eskimo-Aleut migration is exactly what would be expected.

Today, faith in the "Clovis first" hypothesis appears to have been justified, although it is amazing that it has taken so long to find a likely Clovis progenitor in Alaska and significant evidence of an ice-free corridor being open at the appropriate time. Still, there are other possible pre-Clovis sites, and the environment along the Northwest Coast included ice-free areas by 15,000 B.P. (Mandryk et al. 2001), raising the possibility of maritime pre-Clovis movement into the New World. The lack of known maritime cultures anywhere in the world in colder climates at these dates makes this unlikely, although it is not impossible.[4] Such remote possibilities notwithstanding, at present the traditional Clovis idea is the one supported by a preponderance of the evidence.

So, people of Asiatic extraction, using an Upper Paleolithic technology, made it south of Canada just before 11,000 RCYBP and spread throughout North America, likely killing naive large mammals who did not realize humans were dangerous. Clovis is now known from the Pacific coast to the Atlantic and from Washington and Nova Scotia to Mexico, and among the populations representing this brief but widespread culture were likely people who contributed biology and culture to what became the Proto-Zuni.

Paleoindians in the Southwest

Clovis. The Clovis or Llano complex is well represented in the Southwest. In addition to the type site at the eastern margin and remains on the Llano Estacado to the east (Wendorf 1961; Wendorf and Hester 1975), numerous Clovis sites are known from the

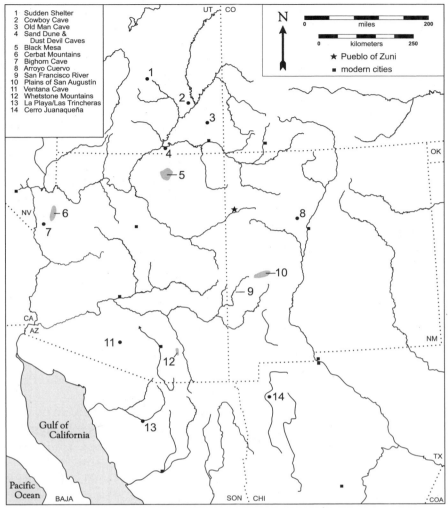

1 Sudden Shelter
2 Cowboy Cave
3 Old Man Cave
4 Sand Dune &
   Dust Devil Caves
5 Black Mesa
6 Cerbat Mountains
7 Bighorn Cave
8 Arroyo Cuervo
9 San Francisco River
10 Plains of San Augustin
11 Ventana Cave
12 Whetstone Mountains
13 La Playa/Las Trincheras
14 Cerro Juanaqueña

★ Pueblo of Zuni
■ modern cities

Figure 7.1. Locations of important Archaic and Pre-Pottery Formative (PPF) sites in the Southwest.

Southwest proper. They are most numerous in the southern Basin and Range Province, represented by the Lehner site (Haury et al. 1959), the Naco site (Haury et al. 1953), Murray Springs (Haynes and Hemmings 1968), and other sites in the same general area (Haynes 1970; Huckell 1984a). These include a probable Clovis point from the lowest level of Ventana Cave (see fig. 7.1; Haury 1975; Haury and Hayden 1975). Clovis sites have also been reported from southeastern Utah, adjacent to Cedar Mesa at Lime Ridge (Davis 1989), and in the upper Rio Grande valley (Judge 1973).

If the traditional population estimate of 20,000–30,000 for the total North American Clovis is used, and if we assume a relatively even population density, then about 1,300–2,000 people lived in what is today Arizona and New Mexico. Since Haynes (1987, 1991, 1993) has given a compelling argument for southwestern Clovis to date in the narrow period of 10,900–11,200 radiocarbon years ago, we have an indication of how visible a relatively small number of people can be, albeit with a very distinctive and much-sought-after material culture.

As noted above, Clovis and later

Paleoindian populations participated in a highly mobile and very widespread cultural tradition. We see somewhat similar situations at contact times with the Northern Athapaskans and Northern Algonkians, spread across the northern interior of the continent. This is usually explained as resulting from high mobility and similarity in the taiga environment over a wide area. In the Paleoindian case I argue that it is the similarity of adaptation, the hunting of the same or very similar species over most of North America. In such a situation we would expect clines in language and culture, as in the northern taiga aboriginally, rather than a series of distinct cultures, particularly when factoring in the high degree of mobility. So the Paleoindians lived in very small groups, were highly mobile, and thus frequently interacted with far-flung neighboring groups. This was the base from which the non-Athapaskan, non-Eskimo-Aleut North American cultures derived.

Post-Clovis. Post-Clovis Paleoindian cultures are also well represented in the eastern portion of the Southwest (Judge 1973). Haynes (1993) dates Folsom to 10,900–10,200 RCYBP, immediately following the Clovis culture. The Folsom is well known for its distinctive projectile point, with large flutes down each side (Ahler and Geib 2000), and for its consistent association with bison kill sites, often involving some sort of drive during which a large number of animals were killed.

A number of Folsom sites do occur close to the center of the Southwest. Judge (1973), in his classic work, located a total of 15 Folsom sites and 14 "localities" (small sites) in the central Rio Grande region, with a total of 117 Folsom points. A total of 217 channel flakes and 128 "preforms" were also found, making projectile point–related classes the dominant part of the assemblage.[5] As Judge notes, his survey resulted in a great increase in known Folsom sites and in the first clear Folsom settlement pattern analysis.

Judge (1973) classed the Folsom sites into three kinds: base camps, armament sites, and processing camps. The three base camps were located near to and northeast of playas near large hunting areas. The seven armament sites contained evidence for both working on projectile points and Judge's famous definition of "overview": the ability to overlook likely hunting areas. The five processing camps did not have the characteristics of armament sites but appeared to be more like small base camps.

On a site visit led by Bruce Huckell in October 1996 to one of the most dense site areas, I was struck by how close the overlook to the Rio Puerco was to the overlook of the Rio Grande and how ravines going into the Rio Grande valley were as close as possible to playas in the Puerco drainage. This gave the impression that settlement factors may have been more complex and flexible than Judge's original presentation and that his emphasis on playas may have been an overstatement; however, this perspective was only arrived at because of his investigations.

Judge (1973) located not only Folsom sites but also sites from two later Paleoindian cultures, the Belen and Cody. The Belen appears to be an early post-Folsom culture, local to New Mexico, often placed in the "Plainview" Paleoindian complex, distinguished by points that look much like unfluted Folsom points. Cody is later, dating about 8500 RCYBP, and is distinguished by Cody knives and Eden-Scottsbluff points. Together these two cultures probably extend from ca. 8,500 to 10,000 years ago. Nine Belen sites

and four localities were found within the survey area.[6]

In settlement patterns the same three categories found in Folsom are also found in Belen but with a greater emphasis on overviews. Two of the nine sites were considered to be base camps, four were armament sites (three at overviews and one within 50 m of a good overview), and three were processing camps, all near playas. In short, a general pattern very similar to that of Folsom (if less intense) is represented.

The final Paleoindian culture Judge (1973) reports on is Cody, represented by five sites and four localities. A total of only 168 artifacts were found, but they showed a pattern very similar to that discerned for Belen (Judge 1973:116). Judge decided that five sites were too few to try to repeat the same settlement-pattern analyses undertaken for the earlier cultures, but he does note that overviews remain important and that playas appear to be less important.

Judge also discussed the population size of the groups represented. He concluded that the Folsom remains could have accrued in "72 band weeks," the result of a single band in the area for a little more than a year! Even if one thinks that only .1 percent of the original Folsom sites were discovered during the survey, this results in an average of two bands being resident in central New Mexico during Folsom times in an area of about 8,000 km² (Judge 1973:309).

Bamforth (1988) reports on some interesting features about Paleoindian hunts in general that should also be applicable to the eastern Southwest. First, recent aboriginal communal hunting locations show repeated use over relatively short times, while Paleoindian hunts typically show gaps of several hundred years (Bamforth 1988:156). Second, more recent

kills show more intensive use of the animals, both by more complete butchering of the animals and the use of bone grease. Unused animals and even a number of caches of meat that were not fully used are reported for Paleoindian kills (Bamforth 1988:156). Most Paleoindian kills were made in the winter, and the animals apparently were simply frozen for future use, rather than in the fall, with the meat being dried and bone grease prepared, as in historic times (Bamforth 1988:156). Another difference appears to be that animals were butchered communally in Paleoindian times, in contrast to a more individualistic manner in later times (Bamforth 1988:180). All these features are consistent with the Paleoindians operating in a less circumscribed environment than later peoples and with an egalitarian, flexible social structure.

Bamforth's (1988:163–183) settlement pattern analysis for Paleoindian sites in the Llano Estacado produced results similar to those reported by Judge (1973). This similarity supports the applicability of Bamforth's generalizations to the Rio Grande area. Another point made by Bamforth (1988:155) is that although small animal and some vegetable processing has been noted on some Paleoindian sites, there is no indication that these resources ever made up more than a small part of the diet.

In the western part of the Southwest the evidence for the 10,000–8000 B.P. period is in accord with an assignment to the San Dieguito culture (Warren 1967, 1984; Warren and True 1961), better known from Southern California. This association with San Dieguito is particularly strong when the remains from Ventana Cave are included as indicative of this culture (Haury 1975). Very little material of this age is from well-dated contexts, and even well-dated material is often not very distinctive, such as the flakes and ground stone tools from southeastern Arizona reported by Waters (1985). Huckell (1984b) reports components from three or four sites in the Santa Rita Mountains south of Tucson that appear to fit this classification, although none are directly dated and all include later material. Huckell (1984b, 1996) has associated these most closely with the San Dieguito/Lake Mohave tradition. This tradition includes crudely flaked cobble tools such as scraper planes that make it very distinctive from the other cultures reported. It is likely that distribution of bison is the reason for the appearance of two archaeological cultures in the Southwest at this time, and these differences in adaptation probably reflect two different "ethnicities" as well.

As this chapter has evolved, I have been struck by how this earliest material in the eastern Southwest is probably the best known of any culture prior to 3,000 years ago. I think this can be attributed to participation in a very widespread culture tradition, so that results from elsewhere can be applied to the Southwest and to Judge's (1973) problem-oriented settlement pattern research. New problem-oriented research in the western Southwest focused on this problem is needed.

The Early Archaic, or up to the Altithermal

Early Archaic cultures that appeared in North America starting about 8000 B.P. shared many characteristics with the Paleoindians, including widespread adaptations and high mobility. It is generally agreed that the Archaic did evolve from the Paleoindian but not necessarily in all places at the same times (see below). Al-though population densities were higher and adaptations were more regionally restricted, these were still highly mobile people that were very sparsely distributed by comparison with later, more sedentary cultures. With regional adaptations involving different seasonal mobility patterns, however, we would expect linguistic differentiation along with the material culture differentiation observed by archaeologists.

In the eastern Southwest the first "Archaic" culture is defined by the stemmed Jay point (Irwin-Williams 1973, 1979). Irwin-Williams (1973) originally had this culture as lasting from 7500 to 6800 B.P. and lacking significant ground stone. As Irwin-Williams pointed out, this point style has similarities with San Dieguito/Lake Mohave points. The latter cultures, though, have earlier beginning dates and do have ground stone. However, as Wiens (1994) and Matson (1991:142–144) have pointed out, contract work on Gallego Mesa resulted in a number of Jay sites being excavated that had abundant ground stone and that date from slightly more than 8000 to 7000 B.P., bringing this culture into line with material farther west; these adjustments to the original Jay culture description were accepted by Irwin-Williams (1994). The faunal remains on these sites are dominated by rabbits, although few projectile points were recovered (Matson 1991; Wiens 1994).

As redefined, then, the Jay tradition begins about 8000 B.P., has stemmed points somewhat similar to San Dieguito/Lake Mohave points, and includes ground stone, as is also documented farther west. I am dubious, though, of considering Jay as being essentially the same as the San Dieguito. I think a detailed comparison reexamining assemblages from both cultures is in order. Further, a comparison between Jay and terminal Paleoindian cultures also is needed (Bamforth 1988; Frison 1991) to determine the relationships in this direction as well, although Irwin-Williams (1994) argued that these were basically different.

For the southeastern portion of the Southwest, Beckett and MacNeish (1994) and MacNeish (1993) have reported on material that appears to be most similar to the western material. The earliest complex, which they term the Gardner Springs phase, is said to have similarities with both Jay and San Dieguito, although with greater similarities to the latter (MacNeish 1993:391–394), with ground stone, scraper planes, and other crude cobble tools present.[7]

Wiens (1994) points out that there are two different views about the beginning of the Archaic in the eastern Southwest, that of devolved Paleoindian, focusing on large mammals (Judge 1982), and that of a very different adaptation, centered around small mammals and small seeds (Irwin-Williams 1973). Substantial ground stone assemblages dating to more than 7,000 years ago are also found on Black Mesa and in the southern Basin and Range (Matson 1991:139; Waters 1985), indicating the presence of this technology over much of the Southwest at this time. I am not certain, however, that this evidence can be taken as indicating a rapid shift to a very different adaptation from the Paleoindian. The temporal link between "Paleoindian" and "Archaic" is not clear, as the period between 8500 and 8000 B.P. is virtually unknown all over the Southwest, thus allowing some time for a gradual shift in adaptation. Further, although the ground stone is present at an early date, it may reflect a minor seasonal aspect of the overall adaptation and is concentrated in the lower elevations, as might be expected if it was only a seasonal variant (Matson 1991:139).

Moving west and north, very different cultural traditions are represented, as indicated by remains from the important northern Colorado Plateau sites of Cowboy Cave and Sudden Shelter (see fig. 7.1; Jennings 1980; Jennings et al. 1980; Matson 1991). Here the basal Archaic culture appears to be one with Pinto points that I found to be widespread across the Southwest (Matson 1991). Huckell (1996) has produced a recent overview of the southwestern Archaic in which he defined Early Archaic as the period from 8500/8000 to 5500 B.P. Huckell finds my suggestion that Pinto points are a reliable marker for the Early Archaic (Matson 1991) "difficult to assess" (1996:336), particularly because projectile points known to date from that time period in the southern Southwest are lacking. My argument was based on the fundamental identity between Bajada and Pinto points and the dating of the latter on the northern Colorado Plateau to that time period. Further, Ventana Cave has a strong Pinto component at the proper place in the stratigraphy, and my evaluation included inspection of some of the points in question. Further, the same sites in the Santa Rita Mountains that Huckell (1984b, 1996) cites as having evidence of San Dieguito/Lake Mohave stemmed-point traditions also have points called "Pinto" by Huckell (1984b), a designation with which I agree. Thus, my view appears still to be valid, although Huckell (1996) points out that there is no good evidence that the stemmed Jay points also are present in the transition between Paleoindian and Archaic, as I suggested (Matson 1991:143), following Judge (1982).

Projectile point styles that follow Pinto vary in different localities. Further, the southern Basin and Range material has lots of "rock knockers"– scraper planes and the like–that are not seen in abundance on the northern Colorado Plateau. These objects are illustrated in the Ventana Cave report (Haury 1975), in Huckell's (1984b) Santa Rita report, and elsewhere.

Huckell also questions (1996:336) whether the Southwest should be considered as a culturally homogeneous unit at this time. I think this is a point well taken, as—unlike the preceding Paleoindian period—there is a lack of evidence from very similar cultures outside the Southwest to fill in the gaps. Further, previously there was a clear division between the "Plains-like" and "San Dieguito–like" cultures that did show distinctions within the Southwest. Nevertheless, there is also insufficient evidence to propose that multiple cultures existed in the Early Archaic. The main point here, I think, is to be aware of this latter possibility, and the current evidence shows a variety of points present together in different components, making it difficult to demonstrate that multiple discrete cultural traditions were present. Which among these populations may have been Zunian speakers remains invisible archaeologically.

New analyses are providing fresh insights about cultural variability during the Early Archaic. Alongside the "Pinto" Early Archaic is the "Desha complex," originally defined on the basis of sandal types (Ambler 1996; Lindsay et al. 1968) and which I think is represented in at least five well-known sites on the northern Colorado Plateau (see fig. 7.1): Sand Dune and Dust Devil caves (Lindsay et al. 1968), Cowboy Cave (Jennings 1980), Sudden Shelter (Jennings et al. 1980), and Old Man Cave (Geib and Davidson 1994; Hansen 1994). Desha-style

"open-twined" sandals date to more than 8000 RCYBP (Geib 2000a), and these deposits do include Pinto/Bajada points as well as other point styles. We also have good subsistence data from three of these sites.

Geib (2000b) has recently defined a "square stem dart point" type from Old Man Cave that is associated with open-twined sandals and thus might be considered to be associated with Desha, although it is unclear that other Desha components have it. Pinto points occur in some assemblages, as do Elko Corner-Notched and Northern Side-Notched points. Geib (personal communication 2002), interestingly enough, does not think that the Desha complex culture unit is useful. As I understand his argument, Geib believes we know too little about the distribution of sandal types and their relationship with other aspects of material culture to make this cultural unit useful and that its use may hinder rather than help communication. Further, there is the issue of the related "plain-weave" form of sandal, discussed below, which further complicates things.

By my continuing to use the Desha complex as a culture unit, we seemingly have at least two different Early Archaic cultural units. They are defined on the basis of very different criteria that overlap at least in part, and their existence south of the Colorado Plateau is in doubt. I previously argued (Matson 1991:137–139) that many of the points from Ventana Cave (Haury 1975) are Pinto, so I believe that a Pinto culture does extend into the southern Basin and Range, but I remain agnostic about the presence of plain-weave and open-twined sandals, as there are no dated sandals known from this environment.

We do have good subsistence information, though, from analyses of coprolites from Cowboy Cave (Jennings 1980), Dust Devil Cave (Matson 1991; Van Ness 1986), and Old Man Cave (Geib and Davidson 1994; Hansen 1994). These three sites are all relatively far north and can be considered to be both Pinto and Desha. They exhibit a hunting and gathering pattern that includes hunting of large and small mammals and gathering of sunflower, drop-seeds, and chenopods. The absence of pinyon pine in most coprolites is likely because of the later spread of this important resource (Matson 1991:165–167). Both common pinyon pines (*Pinus edulis* and *P. monophylla*) are absent from their current range during the Early Holocene and appear to have spread north, being essentially absent north of the Colorado and San Juan rivers during the Early Archaic (Betancourt 1987; Grayson 1993).

At Old Man Cave the coprolites do not contain pinyon, although juniper is found. Considering that this site has pinyon around it today, is located at the lower edge of the present pinyon-juniper zone (1,600 m), and is surrounded by higher-elevation areas, this absence is compelling evidence that pinyon was not present at that time.[8] However, Geib (2000b) reports that pinyon pine did occur in the noncoprolite fill of the Early Archaic layers. I think this difference can best be explained by an invasion of pinyon pine in this area by about 6000 RCYBP (Betancourt 1987), after deposition of the coprolites but still during the Early Archaic; this interpretation is supported by analyses of packrat middens in the same drainages (Betancourt 1984; Matson 1991:65–166).[9]

Some very small "houses" have been identified at Cowboy Cave (Huckell 1996; Schroedl and Coulam 1994). These are less than 3 m in diameter and were probably winter structures within the cave. They show

hearths or "ash pits." In no case, though, is there evidence for long-duration occupation of a site or clear evidence of large numbers of people. The picture, then, is of a broad-spectrum adaptation, involving a range of large and small animal resources, with a very sparse population probably lacking a very regular seasonal round.

Although the Desha complex was first discovered on the northern portions of the Anasazi-occupied Colorado Plateau, technologically similar plain-weave sandals with similar dates have now been found in the southern plateau (Geib 2000a); however, they remain to be identified on the eastern edge or in the southern Basin and Range. Plain-weave sandals also appear on the northern Colorado Plateau beginning about 7000 B.P. and replace open-twined sandals shortly after that time. As Geib (2000a) notes, ties and other details remain different between the northern and southern parts of the plateau, so this should not be taken as population replacement but rather as a replacement in how sandal soles are made. Since definition of this complex is dependent on perishables, which are absent from large areas, the actual extent of these sandal-defined complexes is unclear.

Because of the similarity of the sandals as pointed out by Geib (2000a), I am tempted to see the open-twined and plain-weave sandals together as representing a larger cultural unit lasting from more than 3,000 to ca. 8,000 calendar years ago. This single unit would exist despite a wide range of projectile point styles, which may represent relatively short-term fads generated by out-marrying males, compared to a more conservative, matri-based perishable industry, a pattern similar to that suggested by Ambler (1996). Since the projectile point styles often spread over very

wide distances and change without other shifts in material culture, one cannot see them as reliably indicating "ethnicity" or population movements, although at times they do (Magne and Matson 1982, 1987; Matson and Magne 2007). On the other hand, as Geib (2000b) has pointed out, open-twined sandals are also found at Hidden Cave near Reno, Nevada, which raises questions about the discreteness of such a proposed pattern.

With respect to Wiens's (1994) question about the origins of the Archaic, this evidence is clear: by more than 7,000 years ago the adaptation is not focused on large mammals but on small animals and seeds, at least for substantial parts of the year. As these caves were likely occupied during the winter, it appears that resources such as sunflower, dropseed grass, and chenopods were stored in late summer and early fall for winter subsistence.[10]

Given that Zuni represents a linguistic isolate, as explained by Hill (chap. 3, this vol.) and reviewed above, by sometime in the Early Archaic (ca. 7,000–8,000 years ago) the Proto-Zuni were probably linguistically distinct from their Early Archaic neighbors. The Proto-Zuni almost surely participated in the Pinto culture and also made either open-twined or plain-weave sandals. Given the roughly 3,000-year duration of this period, there were not very many people living in the Southwest at this time. The general picture of very flexible, very mobile, very sparse populations given for Paleoindians is true for this time as well; but here the scale involved is much less, with possibly one archaeological culture incorporating all of the Southwest but allowing for a number of variations, including different languages, perhaps best attested to on the earlier end by two sorts of sandals. How many people were living in the Southwest? I find it difficult to see populations much greater than the Paleoindian peak, perhaps on the order of 2,000–3,000. This adaptation, best known for the period 8000–7000 RCYBP, is that long ago defined by Jennings as the "Desert Archaic" culture.

The Altithermal and the Middle Archaic

On the Colorado Plateau the time period between about 4,000 and 6,000 years ago is clearly one of much reduced population (Matson 1991:150–167). In cave after cave in the northern portions one finds Early Archaic and then a sterile or nearly sterile layer followed by either Late Archaic or Basketmaker II. This gap is illustrated by the absence of dated sandals between about 4,000 and 6,200 calendar years ago (Geib 2000a), and even dated packrat middens are rare during this interval (McVickar 1991; Webb and Betancourt 1990). Because of this reduced occupation very little is known about this period. Huckell (1996) argues that there is greater homogeneity at this time than previously, which would make sense if we are seeing a lowering of population density and therefore an expansion of the scale of annual rounds and contacts. This reduction in population is in accord with the Altithermal, which recent work supports as a real climatic event in both the Basin and Range (Waters 1985) and on the northern Colorado Plateau (Matson 1991:165). Unlike Huckell, however, I find little similarity among the various components known to exist during this time (Matson 1991:167), although we define the Middle Archaic slightly differently (Huckell has it as 5500–3500 RCYBP).

The Altithermal (aka the Hypsi-

thermal, Climatic Optimum, and Middle Holocene) has long been controversial in paleogeographic and archaeological investigations (see also Gregory and Nials, chap. 5, this vol.). According to Grayson (1993:208–210), Antevs's formulation of postglacial climates changed over time from his original formulation in 1948, but the Altithermal was defined consistently as a time of increased temperatures and less-effective moisture somewhere between 4,000 and 8,000 years ago (see Gregory and Nials, chap. 5, this vol.). Grayson's (1993:210–216) review of Great Basin evidence shows that this period includes very good evidence of increased temperatures (increases in the elevation of tree lines) and decreases in effective moisture (drying up of ponds, lakes, and marshes as well as inferences from pollen), albeit very variable and beginning and ending at different dates in different places within the Great Basin. Grayson (1993:214) states that this evidence indicates that the Great Basin Altithermal began after 8,000 years ago and ended before 4,000 years ago.

There is abundant evidence in the Southwest, both on the Colorado Plateau and in the Sonoran Desert, that plant communities moved upslope, indicating warmer temperatures during this time period, yet at the same time some communities moved downslope, indicating greater moisture (Betancourt 1990:286–287)! A proposed solution to a hotter, drier Altithermal in the Great Basin and a hotter, wetter one in the Southwest is that this was a period of decreased Pacific winter moisture (and thus a drier Great Basin) but increased summer monsoon moisture (and thus a wetter Southwest) (Betancourt 1990:287). This solution, though far from being fully accepted, does have some interesting conse-

quences for the spread of pinyon (Neilson 1987). Increased summer moisture and warmer temperatures would have helped the Great Basin *Pinus monophylla* spread, as it is apparently limited by cold winter temperatures and deficient summer moisture today (Betancourt 1987). *P. edulis* requires even more summer moisture than *P. monophylla*, and today the dividing line between the two is basically determined by the amount of summer monsoon precipitation (Neilson 1987). Accordingly, the Altithermal encouraged the rapid spread north of both pinyon species, although not necessarily within their current elevational limits, spreading this important resource over the northern Southwest.

Much remains to be discovered about the environment during this period. The "wetter" Altithermal hypothesis is difficult to reconcile with the absence of archaeological material on the Colorado Plateau, which likely indicates extensive dislocation and likely a much reduced population for the later portions of this period.[11] Grayson (1993:207) reports on the debate about temperature for the Early Holocene and comes down on the side of the Altithermal being warmer. Changes in effective moisture can vary from place to place because of temporal variation in the location of the jet stream, but it is difficult to see how major temperature changes would not be synchronous. More needs to be learned about environmental variation during the Early and Middle Holocene.

Irwin-Williams (1973) has her San Jose phase covering much of the Middle Holocene at Arroyo Cuervo, west of Albuquerque, in the eastern Basin and Range (see fig. 7.1). Just to the west Beckett (1973) reports on the Moquino site, which dates to the end of this period and is dominated by

Northern Side-Notched/Chiricahua points (called Northern Side-Notched, short form, on the Colorado Plateau and Chiricahua in the Basin and Range), which appear to be common in this time period. Huckell (1996) notes that several domestic structures are known from this time, usually small (2–4 m in diameter), shallow pit structures. These, though, do not represent a long duration of occupation or reuse, indicating a mobile foraging subsistence pattern, probably without very regular seasonal rounds. I know of no good subsistence information for the Altithermal.

There was clearly a dramatic shift in settlement pattern and almost certainly a reduced population density during this period, with perhaps only half as many people present as in the Early Archaic. Changes in settlement pattern may be more apparent than real, however, as vegetation zones probably moved higher in elevation, and sites may have shifted in geographic location without the "lived" pattern actually changing. Although projectile points changed, it is not clear that changes in other cultural patterns also occurred, and this time period remains difficult to evaluate in this regard. I still see it as basically heterogeneous, showing a number of different ethnic units, albeit with no single one well represented in the archaeological record.

Lipe et al. (1999:107) cite Binford (1983) in suggesting that the total Archaic population of Arizona, New Mexico, and Utah may have been only 32 bands of approximately 1,000 people in total. A brief evaluation of the figures used (Vierra 1994) indicates that this is at the extreme low end of possible estimates, but the era in which it would be most likely to be true is the Middle Archaic, where my estimate above converts to 1,000–1,500 people. I have no doubt that large parts of the Greater Southwest

did have population densities as low as those suggested by Binford, but, as discussed in the next section, there were probably other areas with higher population densities. Zunian speakers, if located in the northern Southwest, may have experienced a demographic bottleneck during the Middle Archaic; if they were located in the southern Southwest, where it may have been wetter, their population may have been more stable.

The Late Archaic

By about 4,000 years ago cave sites on the Colorado Plateau were reoccupied, and a new projectile point appears all over the Southwest, the Gypsum point, heralding the Late Archaic. At Sudden Shelter Gypsum points become the most common type (Matson 1991:168), although exclusively in Strata 17–21. Faunal remains are dominated by cottontail, deer, and mountain sheep, with the latter being as common as deer for the first time. Flotation samples dating to this period contained abundant chenopods, grasses (*Sporobolus* and *Elymus* spp.), and amaranths, with cactus also present (Coulam and Barnett 1980). At Cowboy Cave (Schroedl and Coulam 1994) Gypsum points also appear in numbers in Late Archaic layers along with Elko Corner-Notched points. Quite a few more milling stones are present than in Early Archaic contexts, and there is evidence of stone boiling for the first time.[12]

Although there are differences in the details of botanical remains between Early and Late Archaic contexts at Cowboy Cave and Sudden Shelter, I am not certain these differences mean anything, given the sample sizes involved. The aspects that appear to be most important are an increase in ground stone, indicating a possible greater emphasis on small

seeds, and the increase in mountain sheep, possibly indicating a corresponding intensified use of lower-elevation areas.

A wide variety of basketry remains was found at Cowboy Cave, although not very many of any single type. Most of the basketry foundation types are also present in earlier periods, but one-rod foundation, intricate stitch and two-rod stacked, and split stitch forms appear for the first time. The most common form, however, is one-rod-and-bundle, stacked, with either noninterlocking or interlocking stitches. The later Western Basketmaker II and Anasazi favorite, two-rod-and-bundle, is not present in any of these layers.

Also present at Cowboy Cave were the slit-twig figurines widely associated with Gypsum points in the southern Basin and Range and extending over the western Colorado Plateau and into California. The site of Bighorn Cave (see fig. 7.1), 30 km west of Kingman, Arizona, confirms a similar Gypsum point, split-twig figurine culture and an "Archaic" subsistence pattern (Geib and Keller 2002; Matson 1991). Analyses of 17 coprolites from this different "Basin and Range" environment show an emphasis on agave, mesquite and cactus (Geib and Keller 2002), although probably all date to time periods when agriculture was well established elsewhere in the Southwest. Split-twig figurines are also found at Walnut Canyon near Flagstaff. They probably represent mountain sheep and were a part of hunting magic. There is a nice correspondence between their presence and the increased use of mountain sheep at this time.

Several sites in the Basin and Range south of the Colorado Plateau have produced abundant Gypsum points—Ventana Cave (Haury 1975), the Lone Hill site (Agenbroad 1970,

1978), and sites in the Santa Rita Mountains (Huckell 1984b, 1996). Fauna from the relevant layers at Ventana Cave indicate a shift from jackrabbits to artiodactyls (Bayham 1982).

The area around Bat Cave and the Plains of San Augustín (see fig. 7.1) in New Mexico was also extensively occupied by makers of Gypsum points.[13] The Bat Cave Archaic occupation probably dates from 4000 to 3000 RCYBP (Matson 1991:176), and the abundant ground stone in this assemblage was probably used to process *Sporobolus* grass, as extrapolated from slightly later remains reported by Wills (1985, 1988a). Bat Cave is relatively small, so the social group using it must have been small.

Irwin-Williams (1973) has the Armijo phase cover this time period and reports that the points appear to be mostly derived from San Jose forms, although Gypsum points are also present (Matson 1991:180). In this phase a new site type appears, the canyon-head, spring-rockshelter base camp, best represented by the Armijo shelter. Sites are much larger than in earlier periods, and the ground stone tool assemblage increases.

Geib (2000a) reports on two directly dated plain-weave sandals from Glen Canyon that fall in this period. Both Geib and I interpret continuity in sandal style as likely indicating population and cultural continuity from the Early Archaic to the Late Archaic on the northwestern Colorado Plateau. My impression is that there is a reasonable degree of homogeneity in the northern and western parts of the Southwest at this time, indicative of either ethnic homogeneity or groups with similar material cultures. The material from Bighorn Cave, particularly the perishables, appears to be significantly different, so that this site seems to be outside this northeastern Colorado Plateau cultural unit. The eastern side

of the Colorado Plateau appears to be quite different as well, given a minimum of two cultural groups on the southern Colorado Plateau. I expect that there were several more, but their locations and makeup remain vague.

Despite a probable multiethnic character, the Late Archaic as defined by the Gypsum point appears to be relatively homogeneous and extends into the southeastern portions of the Southwest (MacNeish 1993:396–398). This homogeneity may be more apparent than real, but there clearly is a much-increased population from that during the Middle Archaic. I estimate the population at about twice that of the Early Archaic, a total of 4,000–6,000 people. The presence of domestic structures indicates a less mobile population, and the abundant ground stone indicates an emphasis on plant resources that agrees with ethnographic accounts for this and surrounding areas derived from the early historic period.

Two Regional Models and Their Implications

Two regional surveys that are dominated by material from this period provide us with an idea of the settlement patterns. One, my dissertation project, took place in the Cerbat Mountains, north of Kingman, just off the Colorado Plateau; the other was conducted in the Whetstones, southeast of Tucson (see fig. 7.1; Whalen 1971, 1973, 1975). The Cerbat project (Matson 1971, 1974, 1991: 223–231) showed a pattern that corresponds closely to that predicted from Walapai ethnography, with winter base camps located near springs at the lower edge of the pinyon-juniper zone, a second locus of activity in pinyon groves (complete with ground stone and house rings), and a third out on the desert flats that included

ground stone. Two unexpected features were the absence of an identifiable agave procurement system and the high visibility of quarrying for both chipped stone and ground stone raw materials. The total range of environments utilized extended from over 2,150 m in the pinyon zone to 850 m along Hualapai Wash.

In the Whetstones (Whalen 1971) low-elevation areas included washes leading to the San Pedro River, and the survey found two locations with base camps, one near springs in the mountains ("montane base camps") and the other along washes leading to the river (Matson 1991:231–240). The former appear very similar to those in the Cerbats. The riverine examples are smaller than the montane base camps but are much larger than the equivalent low-elevation sites in the Cerbats. There are, however, two important resources in the San Pedro valley not present in the Hualapai Valley: *Sporobolus wrightii*, the largest drop-seed grass, and large stands of mesquite. Riverine base camps in the Whetstones were inferred to have been used in the late summer and fall, when mesquite and drop-seed grass seeds would be available. The Whetstone montane base camps, on the other hand, were probably used in the winter. Their locations are close to permanent sources of water and a wide range of resources. Nothing equivalent to the pinyon camps in the Cerbats was located, as pinyon is not found in the Whetstones.

Gregory (ed. 1999) has recently reported on a Late Archaic site in a similar setting in the Santa Cruz River floodplain at Los Pozos in Tucson. Dating to just less than 4000 RCYBP, flotation samples returned very few seeds (Diehl 1999), but drop-seed, mesquite, cheno-ams, and tansy mustard were present. The inferred seasonality of late summer to fall (Gregory, ed. 1999) is the same as that inferred by Whalen for sites in similar settings. Faunal remains are dominated by jackrabbit and unidentified artiodactyls. Few features other than scattered hearths are present, indicative of a diffuse rather than an intensive occupation, but the point style present is the Cortaro point rather than the Gypsum point. Los Pozos, then, supports general inferences made by Whalen (1971) and Matson (1991) for both function and dating.

In both the Cerbat and Whetstone surveys the importance of having different environments in close proximity is obvious: resources that become available in different seasons can be easily accessed. Hassan (1981:53–54) suggests that a hunting and gathering band typically did not have territory with a radius of more than 16–25 km. In both the Whetstones and Cerbats the full range of environments present in surveyed areas can be accessed within territories of similar size, thus making it feasible to incorporate all of these resources in the seasonal round. In both survey situations there were resources that were not available in the other, and the settlement patterns differ accordingly. In the center of the Colorado Plateau a similar adaptation would require a much greater area and a more tenuous existence. It is not an accident that equivalent patterns have yet to be discovered in the central portion of the plateau.

As an example of this, an extensive survey of Black Mesa (see fig. 7.1) revealed only a modest number of Archaic sites. Parry et al. conclude that the Archaic evidence from Black Mesa "indicates sporadic, short-term occupations by small groups. Lithic raw materials from distant sources suggest high mobility and large territories for these peoples" (1994:225). They also state that northern Black Mesa was "only briefly visited on infrequent occasions by highly mo-

bile groups" (Parry et al. 1994:223). I think that this is probably true for most places away from the edges of the Colorado Plateau, with some minor exceptions where sufficient environmental variability was present.

Although the density of occupation was very low, there appears to be long-term continuity in adaptation and, quite possibly, in population and culture. Certainly, analyses of coprolites from Early Archaic Desha period sites fit well with what is found later, with the possible exception of the general lack of pinyon pine during earlier periods. Further, the limited sandal and basketry evidence is certainly more indicative of cultural and population continuities than not. We do not, however, have the kind of Early Archaic settlement pattern analyses to confirm these continuities, and coprolites may be subject to special preservation biases and thus not reflective of the general adaptation. With a relatively large number from three different sites, however, the winter season, at the very least, appears to be well documented for the Late Archaic.

The Pre-Pottery Formative (PPF)

By 3,000 years ago the Southwest no longer was a region of apparently indigenous hunters and gatherers but also included maize agriculturalists, some of whom lived in large settlements and likely migrated from farther south (see also Diehl, chap. 11, and cf. Gregory and Wilcox, chap. 20, this vol.). This cultural stage includes all variants of Basketmaker II (BM II), San Pedro and Cienega phase Cochise and related material, and En Medio material from Arroyo Cuervo. Dates for these materials range from about 3000 to 1500 RCYBP, a very long interval. In contrast to previous inter-

pretations, today it is clear that most PPF cultures were dependent on agriculture, with this best attested for BM II (Chisholm and Matson 1994; Martin 1999; Martin et al. 1991; Matson 1991; Matson and Chisholm 1991; what I mean by "dependence" is detailed below). Many of the San Pedro ("Milagro") and Cienega phase villages in the Tucson Basin were also clearly dependent on maize agriculture, and these date back to at least 2900 RCYBP (Huckell et al. 1995). I have given the name "Milagro" phenomenon, after the first site to demonstrate this pattern, to those San Pedro sites that have clear evidence of the extensive use of maize. The Milagro site revealed a dozen or so pithouses and abundant maize remains in a floodwater farming locality in the northeastern part of present-day Tucson (Huckell and Huckell 1984; Huckell et al. 1995; Matson 1991). There are a number of San Pedro sites that do not show evidence of agriculture, leading Huckell (1996) to judge that the San Pedro culture includes both farming (Milagro) and hunting and gathering variants.

Most surprising to me is the scale of the recently investigated Las Trincheras sites in Chihuahua. These date back to 3000 RCYBP, with the largest, Cerro Juanaqueña (see fig. 7.1), being very large indeed and complete with ground stone, storage pits, and numerous rock rings representing small, round domestic structures (Hard and Roney 1999a, 2005). Although there are very large San Pedro phase and (particularly) Cienega phase sites in the Tucson Basin, these probably represent reuse of good floodwater farming areas, and the actual number of pit structures in use at any given time was likely much less than the total number present (Gregory, ed. 2001; Gregory and Diehl 2002).

Cerro Juanaqueña is about 300 m long, and there is a relatively continuous rock wall around most of it. Such a large, integrated structure only makes sense if a relatively large group of people used it. Similarly, if it was a defensive structure, as other Las Trincheras sites have been interpreted (Wilcox 1978), it would only make sense if a large number of people were present, a group much larger than the expected hunting and gathering band size of ca. 30–40. Over 100 "rings" are present at the site, and test excavations have confirmed that some of them are domestic structures (Hard and Roney 2005). A population estimate of 200 has been given for the settlement. All such estimates have problems associated with them, but the exact figure is not too important. What is significant is that the estimate is several times the expected size of a single hunting and gathering band. It may well be that the settlement was not fully occupied on a regular basis but was instead resorted to in times of stress and that only a smaller group was regularly present.

As noted above, abundant maize remains were recovered from Cerro Juanaqueña, and a possibly domesticated amaranth is present as well. The productivity of this set is unclear, but if we use the figure of 1 ha per adult person often cited for maize dry farming (Matson et al. 1988), between 100 and 200 ha would have been needed to support the maximum estimated Cerro Juanaqueña population. This amount of arable land is readily available along the adjacent Río Casas Grandes.

Unlike the central Colorado Plateau, however, abundant natural resources are available in the southern Basin and Range, so the extreme dependence on maize found on the Colorado Plateau (with an estimated 75 percent or more of total calories

coming from maize) is not necessary for sedentary village life in this area. These natural resources meant that more modest amounts of maize would be enough—when added to resources such as drop-seed grass, agave, and tree legumes—to allow for sedentary villages. "Maize dependency," then, in the Basin and Range did not mean the same percentage of maize in the total diet as was necessary for sedentary life on the plateau (Matson 1991:243). Currently, through a combination of flotation, stable carbon and nitrogen isotope analysis of human bones, and coprolite analysis we have very good estimates for the amount of maize used on the Colorado Plateau, but in the absence of the latter two techniques we are struggling to get direct estimates for the southern Basin and Range. The significance of maize horticulture in both environments, though, is similar: it allowed for sedentary village life and for a dramatic increase in population density, even though the relative proportion of maize in the diet was likely dramatically higher on the Colorado Plateau.

A number of investigators have considered the relative return of domesticates vs. wild crops to determine if domesticates provided greater return per hour of effort (cf. Hard and Roney 2005; see also Diehl 1997). Generally, these studies have discovered that the rate of return for domesticates is not too impressive, a finding supported by worldwide studies (Ellen 1982:123–153). This is, however, not the most significant aspect of agriculture, which is the amount of return (and therefore the number of people) per unit area. It is the resulting potential increase in population density and the feasibility or necessity of sedentary life that are the important contributions of agriculture. Studies of caloric return rates appear to be based on the idea of hunters and

gatherers "accepting" agriculture, but Cerro Juanaqueña points to a very different process, that of an agricultural population moving into a new area. One would expect that "more productive" (in terms of return per calories expended) wild resources would also be heavily used when available.

The La Playa site (see fig. 7.1), adjacent to the Las Trincheras type site in Sonora (Carpenter et al. 2005), appears to represent a very similar phenomenon to that reported from Chihuahua. All these early manifestations are associated with San Pedro points that have no local or northern antecedents.

Over fifty years ago Morris and Burgh (1954) suggested that BM II (and Mogollon) "may" have descended from San Pedro Cochise. Berry and Berry (1986) argued that this hypothesis was true and that the San Pedro and BM II were different aspects of the same culture, which they argued migrated up onto the Colorado Plateau. Irwin-Williams (1967b:5) also saw such a relationship between the Western Basketmaker and San Pedro Cochise. My own work (Matson 1991, 1999) shows that this explanation appears to be valid for the Western BM II but not for the Eastern BM II, supporting a cultural division within BM II (see fig. 7.2) previously recognized by Morris and Burgh (1954) and Irwin-Williams (1967b, 1973). Older dates in the Basin and Range province and later ones on the plateau for PPF support such a source for the Western Basketmaker (Guernsey and Kidder 1921), as does my "evolutionary model" (Matson 1991) of maize agriculture.

Key similarities between Western BM II and San Pedro Cochise include not only projectile points but the occurrence of Z-twist two-ply cordage, two- or four-warp wickerwork sandals, and two-rod-and-bundle basketry, none of which are found on the

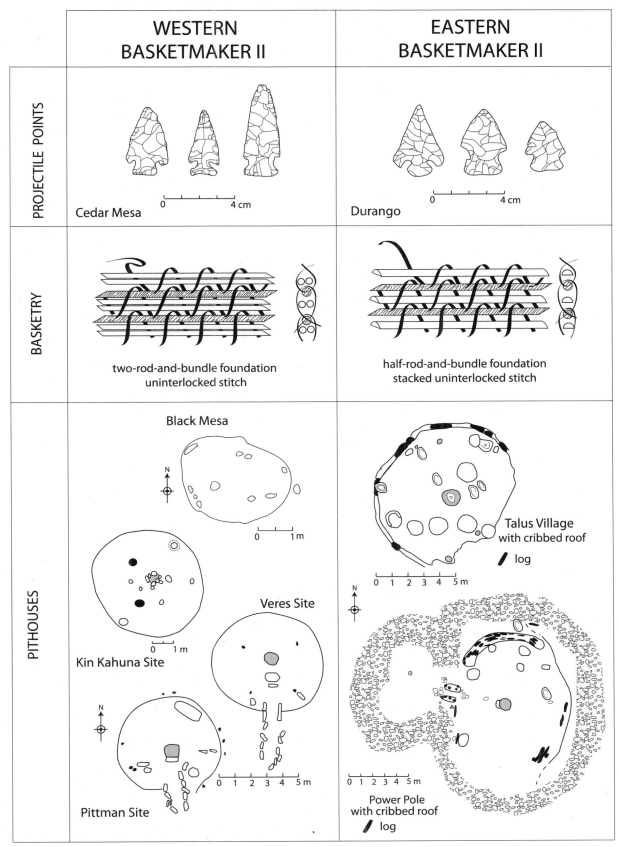

Figure 7.2. Western Basketmaker II vs. Eastern Basketmaker II traits.

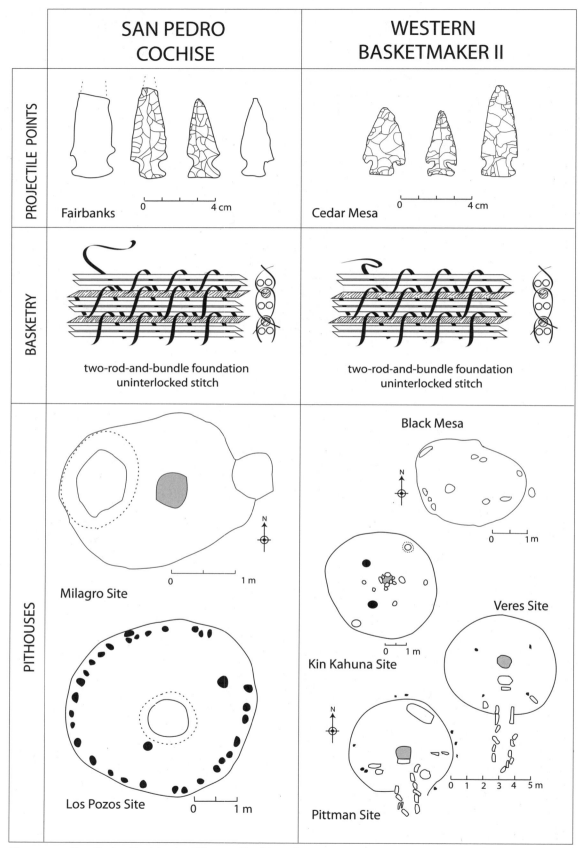

Figure 7.3. San Pedro Cochise vs. Western Basketmaker II traits.

plateau prior to BM II (see fig. 7.3; Matson 1991). The sensitive perishables, then, demonstrate a close link between San Pedro Cochise and the later Western BM II (see Clark's discussion of enculturation, chap. 4, this vol.).

When did this movement onto the Colorado Plateau occur? My understanding is that the Milagro site is still the oldest example of the Milagro phenomenon, at 2900 RCYBP (Huckell and Huckell 1984; Huckell et al. 1995). Western BM II sites are relatively abundant at 2300 RCYBP, and I think these two dates give the outer limits for this event. Although there are dates on domesticates and on pithouses (Gilpin 1994) considerably older than 2300 RCYBP (Matson 1991), I know of no dates significantly older than 2300 RCYBP on an assemblage that can be reliably assigned to BM II. As the western Colorado Plateau had to fill up before 2300 RCYBP (Geib and Spurr 2000), I expect that we will eventually find good BM II assemblages dating to 2600–2500 RCYBP, perhaps on the southern Colorado Plateau, which is at present less well known.

Dates on maize are not the same as dating an agricultural adaptation, and early maize may not have even been grown for the ears. Iltis (2000) and Smalley and Blake (2003) argue that maize was likely first grown for its stalk as a source of sugar. Certainly, there is a long period in Mexico when maize was domesticated and agricultural villages did not exist. The PPF as represented by Cerro Juanaqueña, the Milagro site, and later developments, though, was an agricultural phenomenon.

What is the source of San Pedro Cochise? It apparently entered the Southwest via some sort of migration from the south, although not necessarily too far to the south. Looking at the ethnographic linguistic patterns,

with a long chain of Uto-Aztecan speakers on the west side of the Sierra Madre, this migration probably included Uto-Aztecan speakers (Hill 2001, chap. 3, this vol.).

The scale of Cerro Juanaqueña and similar sites and their dates as the oldest maize-dependent villages in the Southwest are in accord with large-scale migration into hostile territory. As indicated above, this aspect of initial agricultural villages in the Southwest was certainly a surprise to me. It does, however, fit with a model of initial PPF being committed agriculturalists, moving large distances, and having developed a pattern of moving in large groups for protection against the local hunters and gatherers. Once the total agricultural population in the new area reached a certain size, the threat from unacculturated hunters and gatherers would probably not be so important, so one might expect later sites to be smaller and not need to have access to nearby defensive locations. Is this what we see at Milagro and later Tucson-area PPF?

One of the remarkable features about the current evidence is the near simultaneity of agricultural villages in Mexico (now known to extend to 3400 RCYBP) and in the Southwest (at about 3000 RCYBP). As the really good evidence in Mexico only goes back to 3200 RCYBP, this time difference may ultimately turn out to be even less.

The same discontinuity in perishables found on the western Colorado Plateau with the initial BM II has also been reported from the El Paso area at about 3,000 years ago, supporting the idea of a migration of agriculturalists (Hyland and Adovasio 2000). Turner's (1993) analysis of teeth shows Western Basketmaker dentition to be very similar to that of prehistoric central Mexico populations and not at all similar to Eastern Basketmaker, providing evidence that the

ultimate source of San Pedro Cochise is deep within Mexico.

Zuni Origins and Expectations for Identifying Them Archaeologically

Where do the Zuni fit in with this radically restructured understanding of the origins of the Anasazi? The Zuni are a linguistic isolate (Hale and Harris 1979), with previously proposed links to Penutian languages now rejected (Hill, chap. 3, this vol.). I see no reason to think that ancestors speaking Proto-Zuni were deep within Mexico, and although I looked forward to hearing more about such possible links at the seminar, I heard none (but see Diehl, chap. 11, this vol.). Instead, the Proto-Zuni were probably indigenous hunters and gatherers in the Southwest. However, they were likely not located in the northern or eastern parts, as I explain below. Their situation can be clarified by looking at the best-known "indigenous trajectory," Eastern Basketmaker to Eastern Pueblo.

Turner's (1993) dentition analysis also shows a close relationship between Eastern BM II and Eastern Pueblo. The one-rod-and-bundle, stacked foundation is dominant in Eastern BM II and is a form also found in the earlier Archaic and in the Fremont (Matson 1991; Morris and Burgh 1954). They appear not to have the common sandal forms found in the west (see fig. 7.4). The common projectile point is a corner-notched form that may be related to the Elko Corner-Notched point of the earlier Colorado Plateau Archaic, and cribbed roof construction is also found in the earlier Archaic in the Gunnerson Basin. Thus, while belonging to the same cultural stage as the Western BM II, Eastern BM II populations appear to have had a very different ethnicity. A recent burial

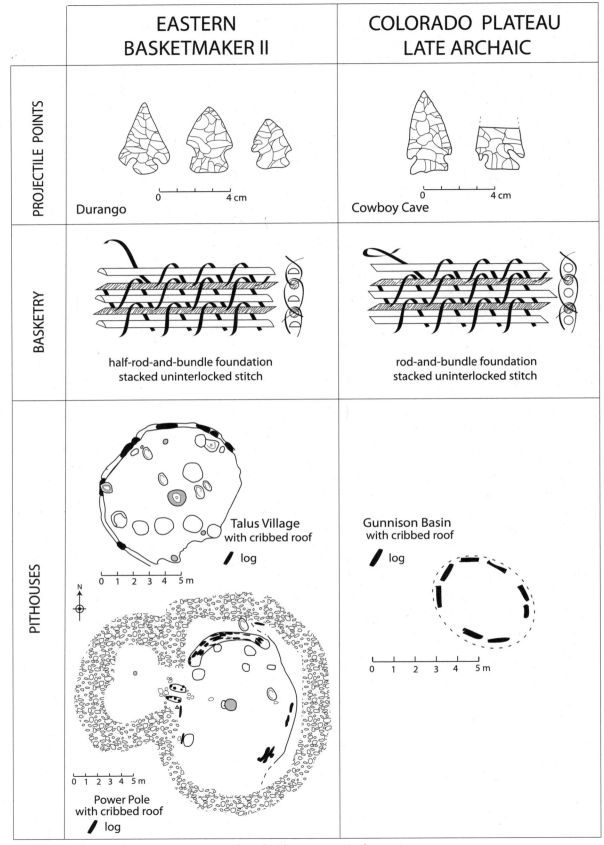

Figure 7.4. Eastern Basketmaker II vs. Colorado Plateau Late Archaic traits.

analysis (Mowrer 2003) supports such a division as well, and I have been told that separate, as yet unpublished skeletal analyses show that Eastern Basketmaker remains are very different from Western Basketmaker and later Pueblo remains.

Current dates indicate that the origin of Eastern BM II is later than in the west, with a transitional form between Archaic and Basketmaker recently identified and dating to just over 2,000 years ago. Then the Durango form developed, and finally the Los Pinos form emerged. Changes between BM II and BM III (Matson 1991:320) can be seen as incorporating aspects first seen in the Los Pinos phase. From this point we have the well-known sequence ending with Mesa Verde Anasazi and the Eastern Pueblos. All these cultures probably spoke a form of Tanoan, with diversification within Tanoan (or Kiowa-Tanoan) coinciding approximately with the earliest sedentary agricultural settlements (Foster 1996; Hale and Harris 1979; see also Ford et al. 1972). The combination of greater sedentism and greater population density would have increased the potentials for linguist diversification, according to the argument presented at the beginning of this chapter. Tanoan speakers likely occupied the northern portions of the plateau (Foster 1996) and possibly extended southeast to Albuquerque. Irwin-Williams's (1967b) scheme is in rough agreement here (see also Irwin-Williams, chap. 2, this vol.).

San Pedro Cochise leads to Western BM II, to the Kayenta Anasazi, and thence to the Hopi (Uto-Aztecan speakers). This sequence was also argued for by Irwin-Williams (1967b) and approaches conventional wisdom today. Thus, we have a situation with a mosaic of ethnicities and languages within the Anasazi culture unit.

I had thought that the history of agriculture in the Southwest differed in fundamental ways from other areas of the world, and I prepared a symposium paper ("Examining the Farming/Language Dispersal Hypothesis," in Bellwood and Renfrew 2003) that argued this conclusion. As a result of participating in this symposium I reached the contrary understanding that the difference was in detail rather than in general process (Matson 2002). This symposium was part of Renfrew's Prehistory of Language Project, which appears to be a development out of his well-known book *Archaeology and Language* (1987a). Although it focuses on Indo-European, the book looks at language dispersals in general and explores the role of farming in such dispersals. The main addition to the 1987 road map in the current project has been the inclusion of mitochondrial and Y-chromosome genetic studies that have developed since that time.[14]

While Renfrew was developing this project, Peter Bellwood (1996, 1997) was coming to similar conclusions about the importance of farming as the primary mechanism behind population dispersals that created large areas occupied by speakers within a single language family. They apparently joined forces to organize the meeting in August 2001 in Cambridge that brought together geneticists, linguists (with Jane Hill representing Uto-Aztecan), and archaeologists (with Steven LeBlanc and myself from the Southwest), a total of about 35 in all, to examine this hypothesis. It was one of those rare occasions where the exchanges that took place (sometimes heated) resulted in learning, and I believe a new consensus developed about this idea not only concerning its importance but also with reference to the relative complexity of this process.[15]

The consensus "model" postulates that the initial spread of agriculture into an area occupied by hunters and gatherers usually resulted in a mosaic: in areas where agriculture was not as feasible or where the resistance of indigenous populations was greater, hunters and gatherers coexisted with the newly arrived agriculturalists. Over time the mosaic became a blend, as clearly seen in the Southwest after BM II times. This blending process occurred several times in the Southwest, and it has been recognized in other areas of the world as well (see Bellwood and Renfrew 2003).

This process is compatible with the Renfrew (2002) "chain model," with individual links in the chain constituted by various temporary stops or the boundaries of different physical and/or social environments. LeBlanc's comments at the symposium pointed to how, over time, a mosaic of, say, 50 percent "new farmer linguistic groups" and 50 percent various different indigenous groups will end up as a 100 percent or nearly 100 percent new linguistic group. In both sets different communities will go to extinction (cultural), but when a unique indigenous group becomes extinct that language is dead, while the new linguistic group will still be present, although some of the languages within it will have died. The Southwest appears to have several examples of this process— Fremont, Cohonina, and Virgin Anasazi are likely cases. In conversations with Hill and LeBlanc at the August 2001 symposium I was struck by our shared opinion that the Southwest linguistic diversity would have decreased through time if developments had not been truncated by Spanish contact.

Apparent southwestern patterns— including migrants and indigenous peoples and with some periods of warfare—are probably more the rule than the exception. However, because of the relative lateness of agriculture and the truncation of indigenous development with the arrival of the Spaniards, this process was stopped at a relatively early point of high diversity. Further, the presence of perishables, allowing for finer distinctions of "ethnicity" and the high-precision dating that is possible, makes the lack of continuity and the reasons for the diversity apparent (Matson et al. 1988; Shennan 2000).

Thus, by 2,000 years ago we have a cultural mosaic in the Southwest. The western Colorado Plateau was occupied by Western BM II populations, likely speaking a Uto-Aztecan language and part of a developmental trajectory ending up with the Hopi. In the northeast we have Eastern BM II, involving populations that probably spoke a Tanoan language, became the Mesa Verde Anasazi, and ultimately ended up as part of the Eastern Pueblo world. Other Tanoan speakers—less well documented but probably living somewhere in northern New Mexico—participated in a similar process. Evidence that the Tanoan community learned maize agriculture from Uto-Aztecan speakers has recently been presented by Hill (2008), who points out that agricultural terms in Tanoan appear to be loanwords from Uto-Aztecan.

Possible Proto-Zuni Homelands

Given the examples, constraints, and general processes, where would the Proto-Zuni be located? When an agricultural population invades areas held by hunters and gatherers without a superior war technology, they will first invade environments that allow a high density of agriculturalists and a low density of foragers. This explains why Western BM II appears to have stopped near Farmington. On the Colorado Plateau areas expected

to have higher numbers of hunters and gatherers would be those with high environmental diversity within a small area, such as around mountains or at the edges of the plateau, or "breaks" within it, as indicated in the discussion of Late Archaic settlement patterns above. Neighboring areas of the Basin and Range are also likely as refugia, as these tend to have more environmental variability and less agricultural potential. I would also think that areas with regular floodwaters and wide floodplains are unlikely settings for the Archaic ancestors of the Zuni, since these would have attracted large agricultural settlements, even 3,000 calendar years ago.

One possibility is that the Zuni have remained where they always have been, at least for the last 4,000 or 5,000 years. I think this is very unlikely. Recent research has shown a great deal of movement in the last 1,500 years or so for most archaeological cultures in the Southwest, making staying in one location, even for this relatively short time, unlikely. Further, the Zuni area does not fit the criteria above for a suitable hunting and gathering location as far as I can see. Finally, as I wrote in the version of this paper precirculated to the members of the seminar, the Zuni area is a good floodwater farming area and thus a likely target for initial colonization of the plateau by agriculturalists, who would probably push the indigenous hunters and gatherers out. At the seminar I heard Damp's presentation (see chap. 8, this vol.), during which he pointed out that this area was indeed settled early by agriculturalists, including a very early canal-using occupation and a more typical, later BM II variant.[16] So we need to look elsewhere for likely places.

In searching for the origins of the

Zuni we are not necessarily looking for the origins of the Mogollon. I assume that the Mogollon, like the Anasazi and the Hohokam, as recently argued by Shaul and Hill (1998), was a multiethnic culture unit. I expect that Morris and Burgh (1954) were correct in suggesting that San Pedro Cochise was one of the Mogollon-originating cultures, given similarities in perishables between the rockshelter Mogollon and the Western BM II, on the one hand, and with the San Pedro Cochise, on the other (Martin et al. 1954; Martin et al. 1952; Matson 1991:281–293). So we are looking for a non–San Pedro Cochise, non-Uto-Aztecan component.

In our search we also need to take into account Tanoan and Keresan speakers and size of the area likely to have been involved. We have already discussed the probable pre-Anasazi positioning of the Tanoans to the north and east of Western BM II. That area can probably be safely eliminated as a probable Zuni homeland. I also find it hard to see how historical processes would reverse the relative positioning of Keresan and Zuni speakers, and thus the likely hunting and gathering refugia around Mount Taylor and along the eastern edge of the Colorado Plateau should be conceded to Keresan speakers. We should also remember that hunters and gatherers need large areas to survive as distinct units. Almost all North American groups had sizes of 1,000 or larger, and Martin (1972) and Birdsell (1957) have shown that there are good demographic reasons to expect a lower limit of about 500. Let us use that as a measure, as a larger group may have had a lot of its area captured by the San Pedro Cochise or its descendants and so may have entered the PPF with a reduced population. This contact was where the Proto-Zuni forged a new adaptation and identity, becoming the Zuni.

Using the Walapai as a hunting and gathering model, a population of about 1,000 would have required an area of about 20,000 km² (McGuire 1983). So a Proto-Zuni minimum population of 500 would need something like 10,000 km² to sustain themselves as hunters and gatherers if they had a similar adaptation and environment. Other figures, of course, can be generated. Vierra (1994) lists a variety of figures for the annual range of hunters and gatherers, some of which are larger than the Hassan (1981) figures cited earlier and others that are at that level or smaller. However, Steward (1955:140) lists a number of other arid-lands examples that are yet smaller. One of the problems in dealing with "territories" is the difference between the range used in a year and the overall area used by a cultural group. The overall area may include large areas that are not exploited in any given year (Vierra 1994) but that may or may not be needed for long-term survival. Because, in this case, we are looking at relatively short-term survival, a relatively limited area is probably appropriate. If one combines the Steward and Vierra data sets, the Walapai example appears to be a fair estimate. If circular in shape, this homeland territory would have a diameter of ca. 160 km.

Given the need for environmental variability, the edge of the Colorado Plateau should be a good bet. Such patterns as I found for the Walapai in the Cerbats (Matson 1971, 1991) and those described by Whalen (1975) for the Whetstones would work well there. One possibility is the edge area west of Zuni and east of Phoenix. This would give access to both plateau resources and Basin and Range resources. Further, some of the ar-

chaeology of the early part of the sequence at Lake Roosevelt suggests a nonmainstream Mogollon development (Elson and Lindeman 1994; Gregory 1995a).

The same environmental arguments can be made for other western edges of the Colorado Plateau, but very distant areas must be considered unlikely. Areas close to Tucson, although representing high-quality hunting and gathering areas, were likely colonized early by San Pedro Cochise, and, given the adjacent early large agricultural populations, I do not expect that these areas were viable refugia. Moreover, as discussed above, it appears that there were San Pedro populations still exclusively engaged in hunting and gathering, suggesting that even adjacent non-farming areas would have been filled. Farther south, toward the Mimbres, though, is another possibility, although the archaeological hints known in the Lake Roosevelt area are not known to exist there. This area is not as good an area for hunters and gatherers (Doleman 2005), so the refugia there would have to have been larger in area than those on the western and southwestern margins of the Colorado Plateau.

Another possibility would include the San Francisco River, directly south of present-day Zuni (see fig. 7.1). The river valley and the White Mountains provide a wide variety of environments for transhumance and a relatively high population density. Two problems exist with this hypothesis: the relatively small area of low-elevation environments available and all the rockshelter information (Martin et al. 1952), including projectile points and perishables, showing this area was colonized by San Pedro Cochise early on (ca. 2500 RCYBP; see Matson 1991:282). Perhaps, though, only a narrow section was colonized.

This area is the heart of the region occupied by the later Mogollon populations.

Discerning the Zuni

How can these possibilities be further investigated? I think BM II archaeology offers the appropriate model: focus on the perishables and human biology. Clark (chap. 4, this vol.) concludes that those material culture items associated with domestic life and having little physical visibility have the highest potential for serving as "enculturative markers." And, pragmatically, perishable technology has demonstrated the validity of this conclusion, as in the BM II case. Given the apparent blended nature of current Pueblo peoples and the multiethnic nature of many of the archaeological culture units, this is an area in which the direct historical approach is not likely to be effective. And we now know what the San Pedro Cochise perishables (Webster, chap. 16, this vol.) and human biology look like, so what we need to find are areas with differences. Once we have these we can look to see if aspects continued into the Zuni. I am sure the Zuni are the result of a complex history, and this particular theme, what local hunters and gatherers contributed and where they were located, is best tackled from the older end, the PPF and Late Archaic. In some cases, going from the unknown to the known does make sense.

Conclusions

From what local indigenous group did the Zuni develop? Where was this group located? These two questions cannot be answered in detail today, nor can any answer about Southwest cultural origins be considered to be very satisfactory without involving Mesoamerican connections. Yet some aspects are becoming clear. The Proto-Zuni shared in the general southwestern Archaic developments outlined in this chapter and 3,000 calendar years ago occupied a territory of 10,000–20,000 km² either on the southern Colorado Plateau or—more likely—along the edge of it.

I have suggested a number of possibilities. Although I do not think we will quickly find where the Proto-Zuni were located, I do think several of these possibilities will be eliminated in the next 10 years or so, resulting in a more intense focus on a very limited set of alternatives.

Acknowledgments

I appreciate the opportunity to participate in this symposium and volume extended by David Gregory and David Wilcox and their encouragement and editing of my contribution. As he has done in the past, Phil Geib shared his knowledge and perspective on southwestern Archaic in ways that increased my understanding as I drafted this paper. Although Bruce Huckell was not directly involved in this chapter, he has also contributed significantly to my understanding of many of the issues involved, as have Steven LeBlanc, Jane Hill, and Bradley Vierra. Susan Matson produced the important graphics and made many suggestions that improved the text. Notwithstanding the above, any flaws and errors that remain are my own.

Notes

1. In order to reduce confusion with readers from the Old World, where the term "Pre-Pottery Neolithic" is used I was asked by the seminar participants to recast this term as the "Pre-Pottery Formative" (PPF), Formative being a New World concept (but see Kowalewski, chap. 22, this vol.).

2. The European evidence makes both the transition to Monte Verde after the last glacial maximum (LGM) and before it unlikely. Strauss (2000) points out that the LGM forced the Western European Upper Paleolithic into a small area in southern France and Spain, the Solutrean. It was not until 12,500 RCYBP that southern England at 50° north was reoccupied, and this was only about 600 km from the nearest Solutrean-occupied territory. So it is unlikely that the Asian Upper Paleolithic would have made it to 60° north and into the Americas and all the way down to southern Chile in the same amount of time. Further, as Goebel et al. (2003) point out, if people were to make it to the Americas before the LGM, that would mean they were present by about 23,000 calendar years ago, some 10,000 years before Clovis, and I believe they would have left many obvious traces.

3. A relevant example: Meltzer et al. (2002) report for the Folsom-type site that an average of collagen dates gave 10,260 ± 110 RCYBP, while six charcoal dates gave 10,890 ± 50 RCYBP.

4. As far as I know, the earliest evidence for regular "long-distance" boat travel is in the Aegean, dating to 11,000 RCYBP, where obsidian was regularly being transported between islands.

5. The most common artifact type recovered during the survey is the end-scraper (n = 308), which Judge calls "transverse scrapers." Eighty sidescrapers, 45 "knives" (bifaces and large retouched flakes), 87 gravers, two drills, 10 spokeshaves, and at least 10 "utility flakes" (i.e., flakes with several different working edges, usually including a graver) were also recovered.

6. The number of artifacts is also much less than for Folsom, with only 247 noted in comparison with 811 for Folsom. Other than projectile point style, Belen appears to differ from Folsom mainly in having fewer preforms and more endscrapers (Judge 1973:116).

7. It has been pointed out to me that, curiously, many of the points illustrated in Beckett and MacNeish (1994) are actually from Irwin-Williams (1973). Thus, for instance, in their figure 3 Beckett and MacNeish label five projectile points in the first row as a–e; a is from Irwin-Williams's figure 3a, b is her 3c, c is 3f,

and e is 2b. There seems to be no overlap between figure 3 of Beckett and MacNeish (1994) and MacNeish (1993) figure VI-2, which also shows the Gardner Springs artifact types.

8. Also present in 15 Old Man coprolites was an *Iva* species (marsh elder). This finding is unique to the Southwest, and its presence here is argued to be dependent on local availability (Hansen 1994); this resource is very abundant in the Midwest.

9. A somewhat similar situation exists at Cowboy Cave, where pinyon pine is absent from the Early Archaic coprolites but where pinyon pine dated to 5960 ± 60 RCYBP (McVickar 1991:48) is reported from a packrat midden. Pinyon pine is found in the area today, although it is sparse, and in later but not earlier packrat middens (the packrat midden is at 1,700 m). In this case, though, the pine was not directly dated, as packrat coprolites were used instead (McVickar 1991). Earlier accounts of Early Holocene pinyon pine in Cowboy Cave deposits (in Jennings 1980) were found to be the result of intrusive recent pine pieces into older deposits (McVickar 1991). I will return to the spread of pinyon pine in the next section when the Altithermal is discussed.

10. According to Van Ness (1986), this is most evident at Dust Devil Cave.

11. Further, for the last 25 years I have been only too aware that in British Columbia the warmest part of the Holocene appears to be 9000–8000 B.P. (Clague and Mathewes 1989; Clague et al. 1992), as indicated by higher timberlines and thus higher summer temperatures. A recent report on the northern limits of various trees in Russia (Kremenetski et al. 1998) also points to 9000–8000 B.P. as the peak period of postglacial warming, suggesting that this is likely a Northern Hemisphere–wide phenomenon. Carrara et al. (1991) report on higher Early and Middle Holocene tree lines in the San Juan Mountains, just north of Durango, Colorado, where peak warming appears to have occurred at 8000 RCYBP. This indicates that this phenomenon probably also occurred at least on the edges of the Southwest.

12. Seven coprolites were analyzed by

Hogan (1980) from Stratum IV. *Sporobolus* and sunflower dominate, followed by cheno-ams, with *Dicoria* and *Corispermum* spp. being less abundant and cactus present only in two coprolites. Although pinyon pine is present in these layers at Cowboy Cave, it is missing from the coprolites. By this time pinyon pine was present over the Southwest (and in the Great Basin; Grayson 1993) and had been incorporated into subsistence patterns.

13. Wills (1985) surface-collected a site on the Plains of San Augustín less than 2 km from Bat Cave that had 47 points—apparently dominated by Gypsum points —and 52 grinding slabs and fragments. Wills (1985) interprets this as a *Sporobolus* collecting and processing site. The Ake site (Beckett 1980), also on the Plains of San Augustín, is dated to about 3500 RCYBP and produced a Gypsum point–dominated assemblage. *Sporobolus* grass is one of the two most common plants at the Ake site today and is also very abundant at Arroyo Cuervo.

14. Volumes in this project include *America Past, America Present: Genes and Languages in the Americas and Beyond* (Renfrew 2000), *Nostratic: Examining a Linguistic Macrofamily* (Renfrew and Nettle 1999), *Time Depth in Historical Linguistics* (Renfrew et al. 2000), and *Archaeogenetics: DNA and the Population Prehistory of Europe* (Renfrew and Boyle 2000).

15. I am proud to say that the three Zuni-Mogollon representatives were significant in this development at this symposium (August 24–27, 2001), entitled "Examining the Farming/Language Dispersal Hypothesis." This appears to be the climactic one (or perhaps one of several climactic ones), part of the Prehistory of Language Project funded by the Alfred P. Sloan Foundation and in many ways specified in chapter 11 of Renfrew's (1987a) *Archaeology and Language: The Puzzle of Indo-European Origins.*

16. After this contribution had been written and revised, information about the Old Corn Site (LA 137258), discovered during the Fence Lake Project (Van West and Huber 2005), became available. The Fence Lake Project area is just south of the Zuni Reservation, and the Old Corn Site contains a number of pit features, including several good-sized bell-shaped pits, with abundant evidence of maize and numerous dates of around 4,000 calendar years ago. Because this project was limited to a road right-of-way, further exploration for domestic structures was not possible. Because of the size of the pit features and the very abundant maize remains, which are not necessarily common even in BM II sites that we know relied on maize, I believe it is currently the oldest good evidence for extensive reliance on maize in the Americas.

The Old Corn Site is located at an elevation of slightly more than 1,830 m next to a broad draw that ought to be good for floodwater farming. Since this location is well up on the Colorado Plateau, we would expect a high dependence on maize, if a sedentary pattern is present, as argued earlier in this chapter. I presume there is a nearby winter "hamlet" of winter structures, as many of the pit features are clearly intended for storage and have maize present, indicating delayed consumption after the growing season. Without coprolites, stable carbon isotopes, or actual evidence of domestic structures, these inferences are not what one could consider well supported, but I believe this is the most likely context.

If this is the case, we have the earliest "Formative" at Fence Lake, and not in Mesoamerica. But it is a "Formative" that didn't survive on the Colorado Plateau, as good BM II is nearly 2,000 years later. It also calls into question whether earlier Formative material is being overlooked in Mexico (Matson 2005:282) or whether the Smalley and Blake (2003) hypothesis that maize was originally domesticated for its sugar content should not be taken very seriously and be the focus of extensive research.

8 Zuni Emergent Agriculture

Economic Strategies and the Origins of Zuni

Jonathan E. Damp

In time their journey eastward led them to plains in the midst of which were great heights with large towns built upon them. The fields were many and the possessions of these people were abundant for they knew how to command and carry the waters, bringing new soil, and this without either hail or rain. And so the ancients, the Áshiwi, hungry from long wandering, gave the battle [Cushing 1988:89].

The prehistory of the Zuni area is the story of maize in the Southwest. The emergence of maize agricultural strategies and subsequent elaborations formed the basis for Zuni ethnic identification during the last 3,000 years. This ethnogenesis had its roots in economic strategies in the prehistory of the Southwest.

One of the questions posed to me by the organizers of the seminar was to discuss recent archaeological work in the Zuni area by the Zuni Cultural Resource Enterprise (ZCRE), previously known as the Zuni Archaeology Program (ZAP). Recent work has focused on the emergence of agriculture, water management, and resulting changes in settlement strategies in the Zuni area. An outcome of this research carried out by scores of projects and as summarized herein posits that Zuni origins are the result of changes in agricultural production that began some 3,000 years ago.

The investigation of Zuni emergent agriculture necessarily has to deal with two competing paradigms that account for early farming practices in the Southwest. The first model, by Irwin-Williams (1973), holds that agriculture went through a lengthy process of acceptance by indigenous populations. Matson's (1991, chap. 7, this vol.; see also Berry 1982) competing model posits a rapid introduction of agriculture coupled with population movements onto the Colorado Plateau. A review of the evidence as it applies to the Zuni area provides support for the Matson model.

Matson noted that the Colorado Plateau "has a dual growing season, with the first relying on stored soil moisture and the second depending on the monsoon" (1991:214). He further suggested three stages in the evolutionary use of maize in the prehistoric Southwest: (1) the early reliance on *chapalote*-like (non-drought-resistant) maize in the Basin and Range province of the southern Southwest, where the growing season is longer and can rely upon rainfall without the risk of early frost; (2) the adoption of maize on the plateau based on floodwater farming; and (3) the development of rainfall dry farming on the plateau with the development of drought-resistant forms of maize. Matson (chap. 7, this vol.) has subsequently refined this model to suggest that immigrant Western Basketmaker populations that are distinct from the indigenous Eastern Basketmaker affected the spread of maize onto the Colorado Plateau. Hill (2001, chap. 3, this vol.) carries this model further by suggesting that the immigrant Western Basketmaker populations were Uto-Aztecan speakers who came into contact with resident populations, including Tanoan speakers.

Wills and Huckell recently characterized the introduction of agriculture in the Southwest by noting: "If Late Archaic populations were organized in small, mobile groups—as the archaeological record seems to indicate—it appears very unlikely that the labor pool existed that could have supported intensive agricultural production. The lack of evidence for water control systems or formal fields is consistent with this view" (1994:50). In the Zuni area implications from preliminary findings of many unreported surveys appeared to indicate that widespread Late Archaic or Early Basketmaker populations existed along the ridgetops at elevations higher than the river valleys in the Zuni area of west-central New Mexico. These populations were viewed as more mobile and less reliant on agriculture than the later Puebloan peoples, who lived primarily in aboveground structures and who were integrated into a formalized regional system.

One focus of the seminar was an examination of the suggestion put forth by Gregory and Wilcox (chap.

10, this vol.) that Zuni origins can be traced to Archaic period high-altitude populations. This scenario of isolated, Archaic, high-altitude roots for the Zuni fit well with the body of data that existed for the Zuni area until the late 1990s. Our current understanding reveals a rapid and dramatic introduction of irrigation agriculture perhaps 3,000 years ago, with subsequent modifications of agricultural production caused by in situ development or expansion of other economic systems that developed within the Greater Southwest. The earlier viewpoints on the origin of Zuni must now yield to a new model that posits sedentary Early Agricultural period households operating within a community structure that managed irrigation systems on the river bottomlands for the production of maize agriculture. These communities apparently appeared in the Zuni area in the last millennium BC and laid the basis for future social and economic development. As such, the present evidence and my interpretation of this evidence support the Matson model—with some modification. The principal modification involves the early role of irrigation in the agroeconomic system.

Within the Zuni River valley the distribution of Early Agricultural period sites indicates a strong preference for bottomland locations. I have not observed aggregation above the household level for the early introduction of irrigation agriculture in the Zuni area (Damp et al. 2001, 2002). Physical aggregation may not have been a factor; rather, individual households that were dispersed along the drainages, including both Y Unit Draw (some 17 km upstream of Zuni Pueblo) and the Zuni River, were probably united through their incorporation into a system of cooperation through irrigation farming. These irrigation communities formed the basis for the emergence of agriculture

in the Zuni area and possibly throughout most of the Colorado Plateau.

The Setting

Modern-day Zuni Pueblo lies within the confines of the fertile Zuni River valley. The surrounding environment is rich in natural resources due in part to the varied topographic and geologic zones in the region and the biotic communities that they support. The area is situated within the Zuni Basin, which sits on the southern edge of the Colorado Plateau. The region surrounding the pueblo is characterized by geological uplifting and erosional downcutting (Ferguson and Mills 1982:19). Exposed buttes and mesas at elevations averaging 2,196 m surround Zuni Pueblo, with average elevations of 1,920 m in the river valley below. Just east of Zuni Pueblo the Zuni River valley reaches its greatest width of 5 km.

The Zuni River drainage system is a major tributary of the Little Colorado River. The headwaters of the Zuni River watershed are located approximately 40.23–48.28 km east of Zuni at 2,225 m above mean sea level, near the northeastern and eastern boundary of the Zuni Indian Reservation. The main tributaries to the Zuni River are the Rio Nutria and the Rio Pescado, which are reliant upon the runoff of the winter snowpack in the Zuni Mountains and also on springs located throughout the watershed. The two rivers converge to form the Zuni River about 12 km east of Zuni Pueblo. The Zuni River, a stream system that trends northeast–southwest, today is deeply incised and runs intermittently. Numerous ephemeral drainages from the surrounding slopes act as tributaries to the Zuni River, which drains a 3,403-km² area at the Arizona border and a 1,810-km² area off the reservation to the north and east (Gellis 1998).

Kintigh's (1985:90–102) review of the Zuni environment and agricultural technology discussed the agricultural potential of Zuni soils. Using the observations of Maker et al. (1974), Kintigh noted that the best agricultural soils are in the lower portion of the Zuni River valley, which includes the project area. Maker et al. assigned this land to "class I" and noted that "class I has few or no limitations for use as cropland under irrigation. It is productive and well adapted to irrigation. High yields of most climatically adapted crops can be obtained on this land with good management" (1974:4).

A U.S. Geological Survey report (Cruz et al. 1994) provides water discharge records for the Zuni River (see fig. 8.1). As is true elsewhere in the Colorado River watershed, flow is generally determined by snowmelt and is greatest during the months of March and April (a mean monthly discharge of 48.9 and 61.7 ft³ per second was recorded at Black Rock just east of Zuni Pueblo between 1970 and 1993) but drops to nearly no flow during the summer months (3.9 ft³ per second mean monthly discharge for the months of May, June, July, August, and September as recorded at Black Rock between 1970 and 1993).

Precipitation in the Zuni region typically is concentrated in the summer months of July, August, and September (see fig. 8.2). Summer precipitation is often characterized by brief but intense afternoon storms that follow monsoonal patterns. Annual average precipitation for 66 years of record at the Zuni station (which is approximately 61 m higher than the village of Zuni) is 301 mm, with a standard deviation of 84 mm (Kintigh 1985:92). Annual precipitation for 41 years of record at nearby El Morro averages 338 mm, with a standard deviation of 79 mm. More recently, Gellis's (1998:6) average

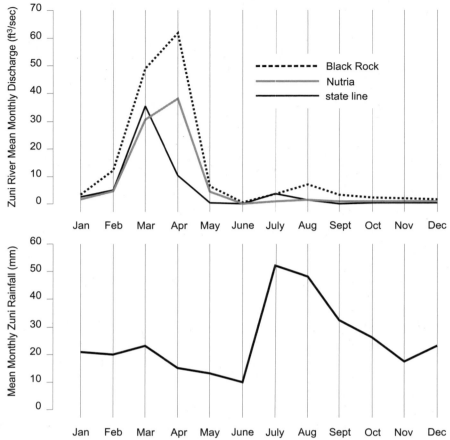

Figure 8.1. Zuni River discharge (after Cruz et al. 1994).

annual precipitation at Zuni between 1950 and 1994 was 315 mm.

Kintigh (1985:95) also provided data regarding mean monthly and annual temperatures at Zuni and El Morro. Mean annual temperature for 64 years of record at the Zuni station is 10°C (50°F). January is the coldest month, with a mean temperature of −2°C (30°F), while July has the warmest mean temperatures at 22°C (71°F). The last spring frost at the Zuni station is typically May 16, and the first fall frost is October 16. At Zuni the average growing season lasts 150 days, with a standard deviation of 21 days (65 years of record). As Bradfield (1971) and Hack (1942) have observed for the Hopi region, maize tends to take 115–130 days to mature. Maize agriculture, then, is inherently risky in the Zuni region.

Grissino-Mayer et al. (1997) carried out a reconstruction of the paleoclimate in the El Malpais area. The El Malpais area is over 70 km to the east and provides the nearest data for the Zuni area. The El Malpais study was based on tree-ring data and extends from 136 BC to AD 1992. The data correlate well with previous studies of regional paleoclimate (Dean et al. 1985; Euler et al. 1979). Seven periods of above-normal and below-normal precipitation comprise the El Malpais record, with short-term intervals of very wet or very dry conditions also observed (Grissino-Mayer et al. 1997:159). Above-normal precipitation was the norm from AD 81 to 257. The longest period of below-normal precipitation began at AD 258 and ended at 520. Grissino-Mayer et al. (1997) noted that tree-ring growth

was reduced beginning around AD 350. Between AD 521 and 660 precipitation was above normal. A period of below-normal precipitation was inferred between AD 661 and 1023. Another period of above-normal precipitation began at AD 1024 and lasted until 1398. Two short-term droughts were identified during this period, with drought from AD 1133 to 1161 and again from AD 1271 to 1296 (the "Great Drought"). From AD 1399 to 1790 another period of below-normal precipitation occurred that was followed by a wetter climate from AD 1791 to 1992.

Van West (1990, 1996) developed a reconstruction of long-term streamflow derived from a model based on data from southwest Colorado. This model employs environmental conditions to predict agricultural productivity in the Southwest. She suggests that "floodplain farming should have been especially attractive during periods of low effective moisture when channel incision, erosion, and low alluvial water tables limited the production of dry-farm plots and runoff-control fields." By contrast, floodplain farming should have been avoided during "high moisture when frequent floods of extreme dimension, channel aggradation, and rising alluvial water tables would have made floodplain fields susceptible to destruction, while similar conditions improved the potential of non-floodplain fields for dry and runoff farming" (Van West and Huber 1995: 3, 13). When charted for our purposes, the distribution of Z-scores—the statistical deviation from the mean expressed in standard deviations—provides an estimate of annual moisture and temperature that affected the mountainous areas and watersheds of the Salt, Tonto, and Little Colorado rivers. Negative Z-scores indicate high floodplain farming potential, and fig. 8.2 shows a long period start-

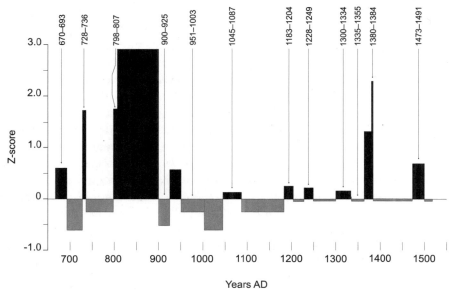

Figure 8.2. Plotted Z-scores for temperature and precipitation in the Salt (including Tonto Creek) and Little Colorado River watersheds.

ing around AD 1000 and ending around AD 1355 in which the potential for floodplain farming was highest.

A Brief Background to the Early Prehistory of the Zuni Area

The Zuni area was extensively and intensively occupied during prehistoric times and continues to maintain a vigorous population. Unlike other areas of the Four Corners region, the Zuni area did not see periods of population abandonment. Rather, the Zuni area repeatedly received influxes of populations from elsewhere in the Southwest (Leonard and Reed 1993). A number of general statements or studies of Zuni settlement through time exist in the literature (e.g., Kintigh 1985, 1996; LeBlanc 1989; Watson et al. 1980). The number and density of sites within the Zuni area attest to the overall past population. Today, Zuni Pueblo has the largest population among all of the pueblos. It is not surprising that archaeologists and historians have recorded many cultural developments for this long occupational sequence. This section,

drawing from the works of Anyon et al. (1983), Ferguson and Hart (1985), Fowler (1980), Kintigh (1996), and Varien (1987, 1990), presents a brief overview of those developments (to the extent they were known) before I began my current investigation of emergent agriculture in the Zuni area.

In the Zuni region evidence of the Paleoindian period is rare (Anyon et al. 1983; Varien 1987). The little evidence there is for occupation during this period tends to occur as isolated projectile points rather than sites. Occasionally, as pointed out in Anyon et al. (1983:48), Paleoindian projectile points are found in much later Puebloan sites such as Village of the Great Kivas (Roberts 1932:plate 58b). Recent cultural resource management projects have discovered Paleoindian projectile points in the Zuni Indian Reservation and in the Rio Puerco of the West drainage just to the north of Zuni. McKenna (1998) located the base of a Paleoindian projectile point on Pia Mesa, south of Zuni Pueblo. Zunie (1996) located a Folsom projectile point in the Salt Water Wash

valley southwest of Gallup, New Mexico. A third Paleoindian (Folsom) point was located in isolation just north of Black Rock Dam during reconstruction activities for the dam (Jerome Zunie, personal communication 2000; Isolated Artifact form on file with the Zuni Heritage and Historic Preservation Office). The Folsom complex of the Paleoindian period ranges from about 8800 to 8300 BC (Judge 1973). Well-recorded Folsom sites are located on the Plains of San Augustín, in the San Juan Basin, and near St. Johns, Arizona (Cordell 1984). These recent discoveries indicate an extensive but not necessarily intensive use of the region during the Paleoindian period.

Following the Paleoindian period is the Archaic, which dates from approximately 5500 BC to the early centuries AD. Traditional interpretations of the Archaic period view a diversified strategy of settlement and subsistence with a trend toward greater sedentism, as reflected by the presence of shallow pit structures (Cordell 1984). Irwin-Williams (1973) developed a classification scheme for the Archaic of northern New Mexico. Six phases were defined in the Arroyo Cuervo area, and these phases may be generally applicable to northwestern New Mexico as well. However, sites representative of these phases have not been located in the Zuni area.

According to the original Pecos classification, the Basketmaker II period may be defined as the "agricultural, atlatl-using, non-pottery stage" (Kidder 1927:490). Vivian (1990:91) added that the Basketmaker II period was proposed as a period characterized by seasonal mobility and simple horticulture but lacking ceramics. Because of the growth in our knowledge of this period and the obvious presence of maize-based agriculture, I have chosen to follow Huckell's terminology and term the early farming phase in the Zuni area the Early Agricultural period. Citing problems with terminology, Huckell (1995) lumps the late developments of the late preceramic together as the Early Agricultural period. Similar problems are involved in the Zuni area using terms such as Archaic (implying a non-agricultural stage) and Basketmaker II.

Sites otherwise considered to be Basketmaker II (AD 100–400) have been recorded in the Zuni area. One such site (LA 129241) was excavated along Zuni Route 4, northeast of Zuni Pueblo. The site contains a shallow pit structure and a roasting pit (Gratz 1977:45). Recent excavations along State Highway 602 in the Y Unit Draw valley, also northeast of Zuni Pueblo, recorded an extensive record of settlement combining pit structure settlement with irrigated farmlands (Damp et al. 2001). A number of radiocarbon dates place the occupation of the habitation features in the first millennium BC. Evidence of irrigation canals in the area at K'yana Chabina (LA 48695) also yielded an extensive radiocarbon-dating record extending to at least 1000 BC. This evidence of settled farmers practicing irrigation techniques to grow their crops is obviously at odds with our traditional view of early farmers throughout the Southwest. This growing body of evidence apparently indicates that early farmers moved into the Zuni area and stayed. If such was the case, this marks the beginning of the ancestral Zuni presence in the area.

The beginning of the Basketmaker III period is marked by the appearance of sand-tempered brownware ceramics in the Zuni area around AD 400, as noted by Varien (1990) and Fowler (1988) at two sites, one in Black Rock and the other on Pia Mesa, south of Zuni Pueblo. In

the Zuni area investigations focused on the Basketmaker III period are few. During the Basketmaker III period more sedentary populations inhabited the region, living in small groups and relying on agriculture as an important part of their subsistence economy (Ferguson and Hart 1985). Habitations were usually semisubterranean, single-room structures with earthen floors and walls and jacal roofing. Several Basketmaker sites have been recorded in the study area. A probable Basketmaker III (AD 400–700) jacal structure is located near Black Rock (Wiseman 1977). Two other Basketmaker III sites that lie along Pia Mesa Road south of Zuni Pueblo contain semisubterranean structures and pits (Varien 1990). A large burned jacal structure, a small slab-lined semisubterranean structure, a pit feature, and a possible pit structure within an Early Basketmaker III site lie on the south side of the airport in Black Rock (Fowler 1988). In addition to the recorded and excavated sites several large and small Basketmaker III sites are generally known to be located along the ridges flanking Galestina Canyon, Peach Orchard Wash, and the Zuni River north of Black Rock.

During Pueblo I (conventionally dated between AD 700 and 950) in the Zuni area habitations generally consisted of deep pit structures with prepared masonry floors, plastered earthen walls, bell-shaped pits, and associated above-ground masonry storage bins. Grinding stones, granaries, and other tools and facilities were used to store and process agricultural produce, indicating the importance of farming to supplement hunting and plant gathering (Ferguson and Hart 1985). Utility ware and decorated pottery production was under way by this time. Numerous Pueblo I archaeological sites exist in

the Zuni area (Gratz 1977; Hunter-Anderson 1978; Spier 1917), and other sites of this period, located west and northwest of the Zuni Reservation, have also been excavated (Roberts 1931, 1939a).

In the Zuni region the number of sites in the Pueblo II period increases markedly, especially during its latter half, and this is considered evidence for an increasing population. Pueblo II sites are the most common type of site in the region (Varien 1987). The period, which dates to between AD 950 and 1150 in Zuni, shows a marked increase in the number of recorded archaeological sites. Many sites have been reported in Cheama Canyon (Fowler 1980), Nutria Canyon (Hunter-Anderson 1978), and Oak Wash (Anyon et al. 1992; Holmes and Fowler 1985). Pueblo II habitations were usually above-ground multi-room structures with full-height masonry walls built around a circular ceremonial chamber, or kiva, typical of Anasazi village layout. While comparatively simple pit structures with few features besides hearths, storage pits, and grinding stones were still used for domestic purposes, more elaborate pit structures with full masonry construction, pilasters, benches, wall niches, and southern recesses were probably used for ritual purposes. During this period great houses, some with great kivas, were constructed as foci of ceremonial centers for communities (Fowler et al. 1987; Kintigh 1996). Roberts (1932) excavated one such center at the Village of the Great Kivas. White Mountain Red Ware ceramics appear at this time. The subsequent prehistory of the Zuni area has been discussed in detail by a number of authors, including Kintigh (1985, 1996; see also other contributions in this volume), and is not germane to the topics discussed in this chapter.

A Review of Prehistoric Agriculture in the Zuni Area

Cushing provided an early description of Zuni agricultural practices and discussed measures taken to control the flow of water during periods of rainfall. Zuni agricultural practices included construction of a network of barriers to water flow so that "with every shower, although the stream go dry three hours afterward, water has been carried to every portion of the field, has deposited a fine loam over it all and moistened from one end to the other, the substratum" (Cushing 1979:255). Ferguson and Hart echo this description in explaining the development of a system of "floodwater irrigation" (1985:37). According to these authors, floodwater irrigation involved the construction of check dams, diversionary dams, and mud walls with the desired effect of diverting runoff from rainfall and snowmelt. These water-management systems were established in order to grow corn in the silted areas behind the check dams by maximizing the utilization of available moisture. Such fields were located in areas with periodic runoff and formed scattered plots of various sizes throughout the Zuni landscape (see also Homburg 2000).

In his comprehensive discussion of Zuni agricultural technology and settlement Kintigh (1985:101) posits three mechanisms for water control in achieving agricultural success. These three mechanisms include (1) the control of surface runoff from slopes or on floodplains in order to divert some of it to the fields, (2) the tapping of sources of groundwater, and (3) the irrigation of fields from permanent springs or streams. The first mechanism, utilizing the control of surface runoff, would have operated more successfully in areas with gradual slopes near the bases of mesas and mountains (Kintigh 1985:102). The second method, the tapping of groundwater sources, was probably restricted to locales in the Zuni area with large springs. And the third method, irrigation, would have been best adapted in the lower Zuni Valley.

Kintigh's review of the evolution of agricultural technology in Zuni led him to suggest that spring-fed irrigation began by AD 1300, when areas near springs witnessed the beginning of site clustering. Similarly, Kintigh (1985:114) dates the association of large pueblo sites in areas with the greatest potential for irrigation to approximately AD 1275–1300 or even earlier. Before AD 1300 floodwater farming was probably the most common mechanism of agricultural production. Coincidentally, the period between AD 1300 and 1500 was probably a time of arroyo cutting in the Southwest (Euler et al. 1979; Kintigh 1985:113) and in Zuni in particular (Gellis 1998; S. Wells 1987).

Leonard (1989) characterized food procurement/production in the Southwest as ranging on a continuum from generalized to specialized. Like Kintigh, Leonard has also linked population distribution to agricultural production. Leonard and Reed saw population "aggregation as the product of changing labor requirements of specialized agricultural systems in the context of a changing environment." In this scenario "fluctuations in available moisture during the late thirteenth century dictated that agriculture could not as easily be practiced in as many settings" (Leonard and Reed 1993:655–656). This change in climate combined with more labor-intensive strategies of production to allow for only certain areas of the Southwest to be effectively farmed. Areas such as Zuni became "labor sinks," with growth in the labor pool required to maintain agricultural production at previous levels. The aggregated pattern of settlement distribution on the Zuni landscape came to be dictated "by the requirements of the organization of corporate labor related to maintaining specialized agricultural production" (Leonard and Reed 1993:655).

Hodge cited the Diego Pérez de Luxán narrative of the 1582–1583 Espejo expedition with regard to the land around Hawikku and Ojo Caliente: "In this pueblo, about one-fourth of a league away, there is a large marsh with many waterholes so that they irrigate some fields of maize with this water. There are two canals with water and ample space to build a city or town, as there are many mountains and good lands" (1937:67). Canal irrigation was not the most common agricultural method, and only a fraction of the Zuni farmland was so irrigated. Traditional Zuni irrigation projects apparently began with canals leading from springs. Before the Spaniards arrived some corn, beans, and squash were irrigated. Within Zuni, as elsewhere, as long as the water flows, irrigation is a productive way of providing water to the crops.

Ford (1995) discussed irrigation technology or farming during historic times. He noted that the Spaniards saw aboriginal canals in the Zuni villages occupied during the sixteenth century. Irrigation also demands certain tasks of the community. Canals need to be cleaned on a regular basis in order to maintain the flow of water, and there is always the potential for social conflict, which might arise through multiple rights to individual feeder canals off the community canal. Local residents maintained water rights under the supervision of *tenientes* and canal bosses. Unlike the pueblos of the Rio Grande, no ceremonies were connected to the opening or the closing of the irrigation canals. Ford noted:

> The essence of Zuni ceremonialism is the bringing of water, rain and snow. The objective of the water control systems is the conservation of runoff moisture, from the sky, from streams, from springs. The traditional irrigation systems in the farming villages conserved water behind dams. No special ceremonies were necessary to open the canals in the spring or close them in the fall. The presence of water was already an answer to their prayers [1995:49].

As recorded on the CD-ROM supporting the Zuni land claim (Zuni Heritage and Historic Preservation Office and Institute of the North American West 1995), the construction of a Bureau of Indian Affairs (BIA) dam at Black Rock (just east of Zuni Pueblo) during the early part of the twentieth century was intended to provide water for the Zuni Irrigation Project. The construction of the dam is an example of governmental largesse, typically not blessed with planning, that led to the diminishment of traditional Zuni agriculture. As one of the largest federal projects during its time, the Black Rock Dam destroyed a Zuni agricultural shrine, blocked water flow that traditionally provided fertile sediments to the floodplain, and resulted in devastating upstream siltation that destroyed the agricultural potential of the Zuni River floodplain. Indigenous agricultural strategies, including prehistoric irrigation technology, were apparently more suited for increasing production, but these strategies were not considered by the BIA in its attempt to privatize land and remove Native Americans from their lands. Apparently, Zuni farmers were also not consulted by a federal government more intent on controlling economic production at whatever cost.

An ongoing focus of ZCRE's research in the Zuni area has been the emergence of agriculture during the first millennium BC and the reconstruction of paleoenvironments related to this time period (Damp et al. 2002). Previous researchers have documented the presence of maize in the Zuni area dating to over 2,000 years ago (Steve Hall and Patricia Ruppé, personal communication 2001). Steve Hall, formerly of the University of Texas, has worked with ZCRE archaeologists in documenting the geomorphological conditions and the changing nature of agricultural productivity. One impetus for some of this study derived from the Zuni land claim referenced above. Results of recent investigations are presented below.

The First Corn: The Early Agricultural Period in the Zuni Area

The beginnings of agriculture in the Zuni area began some 2,000–3,000 years ago. Evidence of this process has been recently investigated by two projects carried out by ZCRE. The first project examined Early Agricultural period sites along Y Unit Draw, a tributary of the Zuni River. This work was carried out as part of the rehabilitation of State Highway 602. The project also examined the evidence of Pueblo II period settlement within Y Unit Draw and compared it to the results from the better-known Village of the Great Kivas excavated by Roberts (1932). The second project (excavations at the location of the new Zuni High School) relied upon the hypothesis and models generated by the State Highway 602 project to focus more closely on early irrigation along the course of the Zuni River. This project was enabled by the discovery of a Pueblo II room block, a Pueblo II pit structure, a Pueblo I pit structure, and numerous well-dated irrigation canals that were located between 1 and 3 m below the modern surface adjacent to the present-day course of the Zuni River just east of Zuni Pueblo. Results of excavations from these two projects have already been presented (Damp et al. 2002; Damp et al. 2001) or are forthcoming.

The State Highway 602 project along Y Unit Draw refocused archaeological inquiry on subsistence strategies in Zuni-area prehistory. Specifically, the project allowed for an examination of the emergence of agricultural production in the Zuni area during the Early Agricultural period and the reorganization of that production during the Pueblo II period. The Early Agricultural period agricultural field sites and their accompanying habitation sites and storage areas provide evidence for a major reinterpretation of the archaeological record as it pertains to the introduction of maize agriculture.

This new knowledge appears to refute the slow, diffusionist scheme for the introduction of agriculture into the Southwest (Irwin-Williams 1973; Wills 1985). We now can explain the emergence of maize agriculture into the Zuni area as representing a movement of people into the relatively well-watered Zuni area. These people brought with them the technological means for growing corn, including irrigation.

Most of the previous archaeological research conducted in the Zuni region focused on events and processes following the wide-scale residential aggregation of the late thirteenth and early fourteenth centuries AD. The large, plaza-oriented pueblos of late Zuni prehistory dominate the region's archaeological landscape and reflect a period of significant social and cultural changes. Yet without a better understanding of settlement and subsistence strategies prior to the large pueblos, our understanding of the processes that contributed to these changes will remain limited. Over 2,000 years of prehistory are represented in the archaeological record of Y Unit Draw, allowing an extensive examination of these processes through time.

Three distinct Early Agricultural period site types were identified within the Y Unit Draw project area (Kendrick 2000). These types included habitations, storage/resource-processing sites, and agricultural fields. Early Agricultural period habitations are represented by components at sites LA 115330 and LA 26306. Storage/resource-processing sites are represented by sites LA 26319, LA 115327, possibly LA 115324 (although it may be earlier), and LA 49838. Agricultural fields were identified at K'yana Chabina and were likely very near each of the sites listed above.

Habitation Sites

Early Agricultural period habitations in Y Unit Draw have a distinct spatial structure. Two types of pit structures were used. One is large (approximately 4 m in diameter) and deep (approximately 1 m or more below the surface), with large internal storage features and a central hearth. The other type is shallow, with fewer internal pits for storage but still with a large floor area (over 15 m²). This pattern has been observed at both sites LA 115330 and LA 26306. The two Early Agricultural period habitations were probably occupied during the entire year. The large, deep pit structures with internal storage features are interpreted as cold-season residences. The shallow pit structures are

believed to represent warm-season residences. In addition to these two types of pit structures, extramural storage pits or thermal features are present. At site LA 115330 these occur to the north of the pit structures. At site LA 26306 the features are on the western side.

Storage/resource-processing sites are typified by clusters of storage pits or thermal features. These sites occur on ridges at the valley margin in Y Unit Draw. Although it is possible that these sites represent habitations (the evidence of which may be located outside the project area boundary), the low artifact density associated with these components suggests they are seasonal or of short duration. Data indicate that agricultural pursuits were a focus of activities at these sites. Smith (2001) identified possible specialization of feature function from analysis of pollen remains. She found that bell-shaped pits might have been used specifically for maize storage, while other pits had more general storage uses. She also identified basin-shaped pits and pits inside structures as maize-processing features. These would have been used in harvest-stockpiling, husking, and drying activities.

The settlement at the habitation sites LA 115330 and LA 26306 occurred within the second and first centuries BC (Damp et al. 2001). Given additional dates at sites LA 48695 and LA 115327 ranging from 75 to 50 BC, the height of Early Agricultural period occupation of Y Unit Draw was during the first century BC. Dating of irrigation features within Y Unit Draw extends to at least 1000 BC and is discussed later.

Maize agriculture was a focus of subsistence during the Early Agricultural period. Maize pollen, cupules, kernels, or cobs were recovered from all of the sites dating to this period. Wild plant resources that were likely

used for subsistence include cheno-ams, sunflower, and probably pinyon. The faunal assemblage recovered from all of the project sites is very small, precluding any detailed discussion regarding its significance in the general diet. The small sample size suggests, though, that hunting was not a focus of subsistence strategies of the early residents of Y Unit Draw. Irrigation features noted nearby at site LA 48695 provide evidence for the intensive cultivation of maize.

Pooling of labor must have taken place during the construction of the irrigation canals. This pooling of labor would not necessarily have entailed the use of a large population. Rather, the cooperation of households located within the confines of Y Unit Draw would have afforded the labor requirements for canal construction. As such, these households, although spatially distinct from one another, would have functioned together as a virtual irrigation community capable of planning and planting annual crops and also carrying out all other roles of socioeconomic success.

During the Early Agricultural period the basic level of organization appears to have been the household, although all households must have been integrated into an overall community. The community in this case was probably predicated upon the socioeconomic demands of irrigation technology. The otherwise dispersed residential pattern, as represented by the habitations during this period in Y Unit Draw, was seemingly organized through participation as members of an irrigation community but also through identity with individual households. Household control over agricultural production may be manifest in the isolated storage/resource-processing sites.

The Y Unit Draw Early Agricultural period pit structures appear to have their counterparts in the region.

The closest similarities to the architecture of sites LA 26306 and LA 115330 are found in the Hardscrabble Wash area, approximately 32 km north of St. Johns, Arizona, in the watershed of the lower Zuni River before its confluence with the Little Colorado River. Berry (1982) summarized the 1977 excavations of the Museum of Northern Arizona at site NA 14,646 in Hardscrabble Wash. Pit Structure I (plan and description in Berry 1982:36–39) at this site was found to be the earliest, and maize macrofossils were recovered from the roof fall. The pit structure itself was roughly circular in shape, with a mean diameter of 4.5 m. An internal fire pit was found just south of the structure's center, and the entrance was a short, southeastward extension of the pit. Four radiocarbon dates from the structure yielded a weighted mean date of 185 BC. The single pit structure from this site is similar in many ways to the deep pit structures at sites LA 26306 and LA 115330. Gumerman (1966) excavated pit structures pertaining to this time period at Black Creek near Houck, Arizona, some 42 km northwest of Zuni. These pit structures formed the basis for his Black Creek phase and consisted of nine pit structures averaging 4.5 m at one site (NA 8937) and four slightly smaller pit structures at the other site (NA 8971). Structures had shallow hearths and no internal pits but were associated with "bell-shaped" extramural pits.

Based on the discussion of research issues above, a general, although preliminary, model of Early Agricultural period settlement and subsistence can be provided. The basic settlement pattern comprises three types of sites distributed throughout the project area with respect to specific environmental locations. These three types of sites are habitations, storage/resource-processing sites, and agricultural fields. Habitations are located on ridges with deep, well-drained sandy soils conducive to pit structure construction. Storage/resource-processing sites are located at the valley margin, adjacent to the base of the western slope in Y Unit Draw. Agricultural fields are situated on the floodplain and include irrigation canals.

Agricultural Sites

Three irrigation canals were identified at K'yana Chabina (LA 48695). The canals were buried by nearly 1 m of gravelly sand with no surface indication of their presence; the distribution of the buried features was determined by archaeomagnetic prospecting. The canals at the time their use was discontinued were about 80 cm wide and 40–60 cm deep, and they were cut into the top of an organic-rich cumulic A-horizon paleosol that formed the surface at that time. The canals were filled with laminar and cross-bedded sand and small gravels deposited by running water. Several large stones that can only have been placed there by humans also occur in the canals. Along the dried muddy bank of one canal a human footprint and a posthole were identified. Charcoal from the sandy fill of one of the canals provided an initial radiocarbon date of 360–280 and 250–90 cal BC (2σ). Pollen from maize and weedy plants, chenopods, and composites indicates that the irrigation canals are a remnant of an early system of maize agriculture. The irrigation canals correlate in time with nearby habitation sites that also contain abundant evidence of macrobotanical maize remains (Damp et al. 2001).

Another irrigation canal was found exposed in the modern arroyo wall of Y Unit Draw at the margin of K'yana Chabina. The geometry of the arroyo canal is similar to the canals nearby, and it too was dug into the same buried surface, defined by the A-horizon paleosol that was present 2,000 years ago throughout the valley. The arroyo canal was filled with cross-bedded sand and thin layers of silty clay that formed as drapes of clay over the bottom of the canal when the flow of water slowed and the fine particles settled out. At least five episodes of filling and clay drapes are preserved in the arroyo canal. One of these episodes was radiocarbon-dated to 1300–1030 cal BC (2σ) (see Damp et al. 2002 for a discussion of the radiocarbon dates from this site).

The valley fill sediments exposed in Y Unit Draw arroyo consist of massive fine sand with lenses of small gravels. An 80-cm-thick, brown cumulic A-horizon paleosol occurs at the top of the massive sand unit, and the paleosol is in turn buried by about 70 cm of sand and small gravels, the top of which forms the surface of the modern valley floor; a 10-cm-thick A-horizon soil occurs at the modern surface. The cumulic A-horizon paleosol was formed by the slow, gradual accumulation of fine sand, silt, and clay on the valley floor by overland flow or water moving over the surface of the valley floor. The thickness of the A-horizon, the absence of a B-horizon, and comparison with similar radiocarbon-dated paleosols elsewhere indicate that the paleosol in Y Unit Draw valley may have required between 500 and 1,500 years to form (Hall 1990).

The paleoenvironmental implications of the paleosol may also apply to the prehistory of the valley. The paleosol represents a geomorphic environment that is not present today in the Zuni area. The slow, steady accumulation of fine sediments that characterizes the development of the paleosol and the absence of evidence of large-scale runoff events such as occur today can be explained by a period of wetter climate and higher density of vegetation, resulting in greater ground cover and reduced flashy runoff. The Y Unit Draw valley apparently did not have an incised channel during the time of paleosol development. The absence of a deep channel during the period of wetter climate may have resulted in a greater amount of groundwater in the alluvial valley with a local water table that was near the valley floor surface, as defined by the topographic position of the paleosol. The irrigation canals are cut into the buried paleosol, indicating that the period of canal construction and use may have been a time of wetter climate in the Zuni area than today.

All of the irrigation canals at Y Unit Draw were cut into the same paleosol, and the top edge of all of the canals coincides with the top of the paleosol. Thus, the paleosol was probably the surface of the agricultural fields to which the water was carried by the canals. Abundant maize pollen was recovered from sediments taken from the top of the paleosol, which supports the interpretation that this surface was farmed.

Another series of prehistoric irrigation canals occurs at K'yawa:n'a Deyatchinanne (LA 129241) on the .85-km-wide floodplain of the Zuni River at the location of the new Zuni High School, 8 km upstream from Zuni Pueblo. Here a succession of four stratigraphic levels of irrigation canals is superimposed, each above the other. The lowest of the four sets of irrigation canals is dated about 1000 BC, and the upper set of the sequence is dated after AD 1000. After this time the use of the floodplain for irrigation at this locality was discontinued. The discontinuation of irrigation is related to the geomorphic history of the Zuni River.

The canals at K'yawa:n'a Deyatchinanne occur in a broad, flat area of the Zuni River floodplain. The floodplain deposits extend to more than 3 m depth and are products of overbank and channel sedimentation during the Late Holocene. The uppermost unit of floodplain alluvium is a 1-m-thick massive red silty sand that completely covers the irrigation canals, leaving no trace of their presence at the modern surface. The K'yawa:n'a Deyatchinanne irrigation canals occur in a sequence of aggrading overbank fine sand, silt, and clay deposits that accumulated on the Holocene floodplain. Adjacent to the series of canals is a paleochannel of the Zuni River characterized by cross-bedded sand that extends to the base of the exposure. Stratigraphic evidence indicates that the Holocene channel and Holocene floodplain were aggrading concurrently. As the floodplain accumulated sediments, burying the older canals, the irrigation farmers had to reestablish their canals on the new floodplain surface.

Pollen analysis of nine field samples from K'yawa:n'a Deyatchinanne produced maize pollen in five samples, although the maize pollen abundance was not as high as at K'yana Chabina. The nine samples were collected from two adjacent profiles that spanned approximately 2.5 m in a trench wall. Radiocarbon dates from the different geomorphic units indicate maize was farmed in this field area from 1000 BC to after AD 1000. Six irrigation channel samples were also analyzed for pollen, and these samples produced unique spectra characterized by no maize, high local tree pollen, and pollen from riparian vegetation.

The features exposed at the excavations into the Zuni River valley fill at K'yawa:n'a Deyatchinanne are not natural gullies or channels; rather, they are canals dug by human activity into the fine-grained sand and silts of the floodplain surface. The geomorphology of the floodplain deposits and the associated archaeology at the canal location both indicate and are consistent with a Late Holocene age for the canals, although radiocarbon dating of the canals and associated stratigraphy is pivotal to establishing a firm chronology.

Twenty-six radiocarbon dates are available for K'yana Chabina and K'yawa:n'a Deyatchinanne. The radiocarbon dates were mainly obtained from small flecks of wood or other plant charcoal embedded in the filled-in irrigation canals or in associated alluvial deposits, and these charcoal flecks were subjected to accelerator mass spectrometry (AMS) dating. The two sets of dates are consistent with one another in showing the use of irrigation canals from 1,000 to 3,000 years ago (Damp et al. 2002).

The chronology obtained from radiocarbon dates is reinforced by the location of several architectural features at K'yawa:n'a Deyatchinanne. A room block dated by ceramic association to ca. AD 1053–1155 lies on top of the brown clayey silt of unit III and is consistent with the dating of that unit; just underneath the unit III soil a pit structure was identified with a ceramic assemblage dating to AD 1031–1083 and a radiocarbon assay of cal AD 1025–1260 (2σ). A second pit structure was encountered within unit IV and was radiocarbon-dated to cal AD 705–910 and 920–955 (2σ). These dates confirm the dating of the buried field layers and the irrigation features in the upper part of the stratigraphy.

At K'yana Chabina the 10 dates obtained from the site are complemented by 22 additional dates from other sites within Y Unit Draw (with several of the dates directly on maize macrobotanical specimens) (Damp et al. 2001). Almost half of these dates pertain to nearby pit structure habitation sites occupied during the last half of the first millennium BC and discussed above. Several other sites contained features dating earlier in the first millennium BC, and these dates are consistent with the dating pattern found at K'yana Chabina. This dating confirms the presence of people within the valley during the construction of the irrigation features.

Post—AD 1050 Settlement in the Zuni Area

Recent work has begun to outline the nature of the early settlement in the Zuni region. Whether due to significant deposition and burial of sites in the river valleys, or a limited population density, or both, there are considerably fewer known sites prior to AD 1050 than later. Anyon and Ferguson (1983) observed that sites prior to AD 1050 are located primarily on ridgetops and benches in the pinyon zone but that their occurrence at lower elevations along major rivers and side washes also has been noted. These latter locations were probably chosen due to their proximity to land that is irrigable.

The majority of sites occupied between AD 1050 and 1150 are small pueblos arranged in a dispersed settlement pattern. Sites commonly contain fewer than 10 masonry rooms and are located along washes and rivers (Anyon 1987; Anyon and Ferguson 1983). Such sites have been documented throughout the Zuni area but specifically along Y Unit Draw, Oak Wash, Cheama Canyon, and other locales that have received greater scrutiny. On occasion, room blocks appear to cluster in a single locale, suggesting the existence of larger, loosely connected communities. Chaco period great houses appear in the area for the first time. The best known of these great houses is Village of the Great Kivas (Roberts 1932), just east of Y Unit Draw.

A distinct settlement pattern is evident after AD 1050 along Y Unit Draw and the general Rio Nutria valley, which drains into the Zuni River. Small households (or habitation sites) along the valley slope and field house structures in the valley bottom typify this settlement pattern along Y Unit Draw. The proximity of these sites to the Village of the Great Kivas suggests some form of interaction. An inspection of the location of other sites of this time period elsewhere on the Zuni Indian Reservation reveals an abrupt extension of settlement into areas away from the floodplains. The expansion of settlement from the floodplain to the higher reaches is documented in the site locational material maintained by the Zuni Heritage and Historic Preservation Office. Specific studies, such as that of Oak Wash near Zuni (Anyon et al. 1992) and Y Unit Draw (Damp et al. 2001), demonstrate that households exploited an extensive range of resources and were not necessarily dependent upon irrigation agriculture. In the Zuni area, sites after AD 1050 were more extensively spread out over the landscape and probably did not rely upon irrigation until approximately AD 1300 (Kintigh 1985). Along Y Unit Draw, for example, these households appear to have demarcated social and economic space that was exploited by larger social groupings.

The development of one such larger social group may have resulted in the formation of great house architecture in the Zuni area. Incorporation of great house architecture may be seen as precocious attempts by households to pull in kin groups (lineage members) to aggregate labor in order to be more competitive vis-à-vis other lineages. The development of Village of the Great Kivas, for example, involved increasing integration of economic production and larger

corporate groups above the household level.

Explaining Settlement and Subsistence in Early Zuni Prehistory

Matson's (1991, chap. 7, this vol.) early agriculture model stressed the early reliance on *chapalote*-like (non-drought-resistant) maize in the Basin and Range province followed by the adoption of maize on the Colorado Plateau based on floodwater farming. Finally, the development of rainfall-fed farming coincided with the development of drought-resistant forms of maize. I assert below that the post—AD 1050 transformation was a result of overall geomorphological process, the adaptation of a new drought-resistant corn, and the resulting increase in rainfall-fed agriculture. This new agricultural pursuit caused the social environment to change.

In the Zuni area the measured streamflow is greatest during the months of March and April. Rainfall peaks during the months of July, August, and September. Without drought-resistant varieties of maize the growing season may not have been sufficiently long. By exploiting the March and April runoff season early agriculturalists would have successfully adapted to the Colorado Plateau by planting the prehistoric equivalent of *chapalote*-type maize in the spring and early summer months. This may not have been possible if early farmers were required to wait until the rainy season for moisture, as the growing season would not have been sufficiently long. Later drought-resistant varieties of maize would have utilized subsurface moisture retained from the spring runoff but would have relied upon the monsoonal rains of the late summer.

Irrigation strategies within the upper Colorado watershed are dependent upon either springs or the melt of the winter snowpack. This is certainly the case for the Zuni River. Benedict (1999) has studied snowpack expansion in the Colorado Rockies and noted that during five periods of unknown duration between 1000 BC and AD 1230 vast areas above timberline remained snow covered for an average of at least 40 weeks per year. Two periods of snowpack expansion, the Late Triple Lakes and the Audubon advances, appear to correlate with the introduction of irrigation systems to the Zuni region during the Late Archaic and to the continued development of this technology up to around AD 1050. If, following this time period, snowmelt in the higher country surrounding Zuni was not sufficient to feed streamflow for irrigation, alternative strategies for the cultivation of maize might have been pursued. One such strategy would have been the fuller acceptance of drought-resistant maize. In addition, Hall (1990) has noted that at around AD 1050 downcutting of stream systems became prevalent. Any downcutting would have seriously reduced the efficacy of irrigation.

The Van West (1990, 1996) model referred to earlier focused on systems of agriculture other than irrigation-based systems. However, when we introduce irrigation into the equation we apparently reverse the expectations of the Van West model. Irrigation-aided farming would be most effective (rather than avoided) during periods of high moisture with frequent floods, channel aggradation, and rising alluvial water table (exactly the conditions identified at K'yawa:n'a Deyatchinanne). We would then expect that the period from around AD 1000 to 1355 would not be attractive for irrigation farming in the Zuni area or in other parts of the Little Colorado River watershed. Indeed, when we plot the use of

the Zuni River watershed for irrigation farming (and exclude the earliest period, since Van West's data do not extend that far back), we find that such practices were prevalent during Van West's periods of positive Z-scores and absent during the periods of negative Z-scores. Thus, during periods of positive Z-scores irrigation farming was favorable, and during periods of negative Z-scores rainfall-fed farming had greater potential.

The acceptance of drought-resistant maize would have allowed farmers to leave the river valleys and practice rainfall-fed farming of previously unutilized environments away from the rivers. In doing so these farmers spread out across the Zuni landscape, and land tenure became marked by the construction of field houses. Any perceived change in population or evidence for in-migration into the Zuni area may well have been a restructuring of economic production and a concomitant change in social relations. The post–AD 1050 settlement pattern in the Zuni area may well map out the network of social relations of extended families dependent upon rainfall-fed agriculture and building their field houses over a large portion of the landscape while centering their social production at great houses such as Village of the Great Kivas (Roberts 1932). This pattern continued until aggregation in larger sites began to occur (Kintigh 1985, 1996). In essence, the adoption of rainfall-fed farming may have caused the territorial expansion of these communities and resulted in the distinct settlement pattern with associated great houses that is found in the Zuni area.

A shift in social organization as witnessed in the widespread distribution of Pueblo II sites throughout the Zuni area and elsewhere may correlate with the increased dependence

upon drought-resistant varieties of maize that did not need irrigation. In the Zuni area, including Y Unit Draw, the pre–AD 1000 maize varieties appear to be the smaller prehistoric equivalent of *chapalote*, with the drought-resistant varieties becoming more accepted after this time period. Toll's (1993) inspection of maize remains from Chaco Canyon found that 12-row cobs were predominant from Basketmaker III / Pueblo I sites and 10-row cobs dominated maize assemblages from the Pueblo II period. Cobs with eight rows were few in number from the earlier sites but occurred in significant numbers from Pueblo II sites. McBride (2001) notes that a similar pattern could be present at Zuni and in other areas outside of Chaco Canyon. Adams's (1990) regional synthesis of maize in the prehistoric record of the Southwest notes that, for both the Mogollon and Anasazi areas, there were sharp changes in the maize records, with lower cob row number varieties becoming more common between AD 700 and 1100.

For whatever reason, the acceptance of drought-resistant maize allowed farmers to leave the river valleys and practice rainfall-fed farming of previously unutilized environments away from the rivers. In doing so, these farmers spread out across the Zuni landscape (thus the presence of Pueblo II period sites everywhere). In spreading out, land tenure became marked by the construction of field houses as seen in Y Unit Draw, Oak Wash, Hardscrabble Wash, and elsewhere. Any perceived change in population or evidence for in-migration into the Zuni area may well have involved a restructuring of economic production and a concomitant change in social relations.

The identification and dating of irrigation features in the Zuni River watershed demonstrates that irrigation technology accompanied the early spread of maize agriculture onto the higher altitudes of the Colorado Plateau in the American Southwest. The immediate source of this agricultural technology was probably the Sonoran Desert of the southern Southwest of the United States and northern Mexico, where similar traits have been identified in the archaeological record. The spread into the American Southwest was accompanied by water-management systems that made it possible to grow early forms of maize in the desert. This strategy was exported from the Sonoran Desert to the Colorado Plateau and adapted there by the new inhabitants of the region. These findings contrast with the view that maize was gradually introduced onto the Colorado Plateau, required no supplemental watering, and was not firmly adopted until the last portion of the first millennium AD. Subsequent transformations in settlement and the archaeological record may also be a reflection in changes in economic production from irrigation to rainfall-fed farming. (Historic Zuni farming is known to have included a number of farming techniques, and components of these techniques may well have been incorporated into past farming practices.)

Social Change: Irrigation and Dry Farming

The implications for early Zuni prehistory of the above statements are considerable. First, rather than requiring a large labor pool to support intensive agricultural production (water-control systems or formal fields), as per Wills and Huckell (1994), early economic strategies in the Zuni area were dependent upon the coordination of individual households in developing irrigation systems for maize production. Such

coordination is within the realm of loosely aggregated households forming irrigation communities.

Wittfogel (1957:23–29) argued that irrigation required high initial capital investment and posited that canal construction would require amassing and central direction of sizable labor crews if the hydraulic technology were of large enough scale. Commenting on the overall organization of water-control systems, Geertz noted:

The construction and maintenance of even the simplest water-control system, as in rainfall farms, requires such ancillary efforts: canals must be dug and kept clean, sluices constructed and repaired, terraces leveled and dyked; and in more developed true irrigation systems dams, reservoirs, aqueducts, tunnels, wells and the like become necessary. Even such larger works can be built up slowly, piece by piece, over extended periods and kept in repair by continuous, routine care. But, small or large, waterworks represent a level and kind of investment in capital equipment foreign not only to shifting cultivation but to virtually all unirrigated forms of premodern agriculture [1963:32].

However, using data from Hawaii, Earle has cogently argued:

The archaeological data from Halelea offer little support for Wittfogel's suggestion that the technology of Hawaiian irrigation resulted in the evolution of centralized management. For construction, the rudimentary technology would not have required special technical knowledge unavailable to the individual farmer. Special features like dams, canals, and pondfield terraces were not massive and show no evidence of preliminary overall design. The

conclusion is that the systems were constructed largely by extension and gradual intensification. Maintenance tasks, especially canal cleaning, are shown by analogy to modern systems to be of minor importance and certainly not to require organized labor crews [1978:108].

Following Pasternak (1972), Earle also argued:

Irrigation results in the weakening of the extended family as the primary production unit and an increased emphasis on the nuclear family. In societies dependent on rainfall agriculture, the extended family recruits the labor necessary to plant a field quickly following the first rains. In contrast, there is no such critical planting time for irrigated crops because water is controlled artificially. As a result, the economic significance of the extended family, for agriculture at least, is negligible and so the extended family breaks apart from internal conflicts [1978:48].

Kirch (1994:160; Kirch and Sahlins 1992) has shown that some irrigation systems require little centralized control or well-developed organization to operate and maintain. Similarly, societies with developed irrigation systems tend to intensify production in the face of stress such as population increase. On the other hand, dryland (or rainfall-fed) farmers tend to face a decrease in fallow and decreased yields.

Kirch's examination of wet and dry agricultural systems in Polynesia demonstrated how different modes of agricultural production (irrigation vs. dryland) articulated in the social relations of production and the development of territorial expansion. Kirch found that the "increased labor demands of intensified short-fallow dryland cultivation could not be satisfied by the male half of the working population alone, requiring a great input of female labor in the agricultural sector" (1994:319). For some Polynesian societies the "impetus to political development and hegemonic expansion arose specifically in those areas where irrigation was absent or a very minor component of the production base" (Kirch 1994:320). In their efforts to increase productivity dryland farmers found an alternative method to the intensification employed by irrigation societies (and generally assumed by anthropologists to contribute to social elaboration). Dryland farmers either reduce the fallow or, through shifting cultivation, *expand their territories.*

Per Earle and Kirch, the pooling of labor would not necessarily have entailed the use of a large population. Cooperation between households located within the confines of the Zuni River watershed could have provided the labor necessary for canal construction. As such, these households, although spatially distinct from one another, would have functioned together as a virtual community, one capable of planning and planting annual crops and also carrying out all other roles for socioeconomic success. A shift in social organization—as witnessed in the widespread distribution of post–AD 1050 sites throughout the Zuni area and elsewhere—may correlate with an increased dependence on drought-resistant varieties of maize that did not need irrigation and thus a shift to dry farming.

Conclusions

The often-ignored and poorly understood early prehistory of the Zuni region has been the focus of a number of recent investigations carried out by ZCRE. These studies have focused on Zuni emergent agriculture, as described above. There are a number of reasons why the early prehistory has been ignored. First, the large, later pueblos that dot the prehistoric landscape are resplendent in the work of Spier (1917) and Kintigh (1985), for example. Second, and perhaps more important, most of the evidence for the emergence of agriculture in the Zuni region is buried under 1–3 m of soil.

Our recent efforts to focus on early agriculture have led us to deduce a series of consequences. For the prehistoric Southwest there are two models that seek to explain the incorporation of agriculture into subsistence systems. The first model, after Irwin-Williams (1973), holds that the incorporation of agriculture was a lengthy process of acceptance. Matson's (1991, chap. 7, this vol.; see also Berry 1982) competing model posits a rapid introduction of agriculture coupled with population movements onto the Colorado Plateau. Archaeologists from the ZCRE have had the opportunity to examine these emergent agricultural systems in the Zuni area during the course of two projects within the last few years.

Ongoing investigations in the Zuni area provide evidence of early agricultural production that dates to the last 3,000 years. This evidence comes from early studies that gathered pollen and macrobotanical data from Bosson Wash, the comprehensive study in Y Unit Draw specifically at K'yana Chabina, and the overwhelming data recently obtained at K'yawa:n'a Deyatchinanne. Recent inquiries have accumulated considerable evidence on early Zuni agricultural fields and early Zuni settlement. Early speculations that Archaic peoples exploited the high country and practiced a generalized economy based on hunting and gathering must now yield to a new model that posits early farming households operating within a community structure that managed irrigation systems on the river bottomlands for the production of maize. These households probably arrived in the Zuni area around 1000 BC, bringing with them an agricultural technology that included water-management systems and crops such as maize. This population transformed the Zuni environment by introducing farming techniques developed farther south.

Apparently, this new agrarian landscape was productive for the next 2,000 years, when the impetus for landscape modification arose around AD 1050. The regional expression of the Chacoan phenomenon in the Zuni area was an expression of this landscape change. In essence, the adoption of rainfall-fed farming may have caused the territorial expansion of post–AD 1050 communities, resulting in the distinct settlement pattern with associated great houses that is found in the Zuni area and elsewhere on the Colorado Plateau.

The question from the onset of this volume has been, Where did the Zuni come from? We can define this question in many ways, as indicated by the perspectives of the volume's authors. Hill (chap. 3, this vol.), for example, discusses the linguistic origins of Zuni and the position of Zuni speakers in the Southwest during the Uto-Aztecan expansion approximately 3,000 years ago; Mills (chap. 13, this vol.) puts emphasis on Zuni ethnic identity as expressed in ceramic traditions; and Ferguson (chap. 19, this vol.) traces the origins of Zuni using Zuni oral tradition. From our perspective in Zuni we have been able to document a cultural presence in the Zuni area for the last 3,000 years. This cultural presence begins with the use of irrigation, a technology probably transferred from the south. Over the following 2,000 years it is probable that additional persons with different ethnic identities made it into the Zuni area. We cannot tell at this time which group, the original or a later group, spoke Zuni, although the Zuni oral tradition itself does imply that Zuni speakers arrived at a later period in time.

Based upon the data presented here I suggest that during the Early Agricultural period migrant farmers moved into the Zuni area carrying irrigation-based maize agricultural technology; they probably also possessed other methods for the cultivation of maize. In the following centuries other peoples likely moved into the Zuni area. Around AD 1050, because of downcutting in fluvial systems and the adoption of new (drought-resistant) maize varieties, new settlement patterns emerged, with preferred settlement no longer focused on river valleys but spread across the landscape in an attempt to benefit from rainfall-fed agriculture. These newly emergent agricultural and social systems may have derived from internal dynamics or from outside pressure, including the presence of newcomers. Conceivably, new arrivals to the area, adept at rainfall-fed farming, may have expanded into the Zuni region, replacing or absorbing the original population.

Others have dealt with Zuni identity in terms of language, ceramics, oral traditions, and other variables. We can also identify the roots of Zuni ethnic identity in economic structures. The establishment of a Zuni ethnic identity, as recognized today, developed through a polyethnic process that was based on land tenure in the definition of political leadership. Barth has shown that within political leadership and the principles of social organization "relations to the land hold the key for the local community [and are] . . . maintained by the joint dependence of all its members on land for its subsistence" (1959:65). Although dress (and symbolism in general), language, and culture history may serve to differentiate ethnic groups and establish boundaries (Barth 1969a), political authority and the basis for Zuni ethnic identity began during the Early Agricultural period with the emergence of an irrigation-based agricultural system and was subsequently repeatedly transformed by the introduction of new forms of agricultural production and new settlement patterns (relations of production).

9 A Mogollon-Zuni Hypothesis

Paul Sidney Martin and John B. Rinaldo's Formulation

David A. Gregory

In modern southwestern archaeology it was Paul Sidney Martin and John B. Rinaldo who developed and pursued a Mogollon-Zuni hypothesis. In the context of an investigation into Zuni origins it is instructive to review in some detail that development and pursuit. While they did not explicitly articulate what we would call today a formal research design, they clearly did work from a problem orientation whose evolution can be easily traced. Had they produced a document summarizing the problems and questions that they pursued together for over two decades they might well have titled it "Chasing the Mogollon through Time and Space," for that is exactly what they did. It was shortly after Haury's (1936a) pioneering work at Harris Village and Mogollon Village and during the time when the nature and validity of the Mogollon concept were being initially debated that Paul Martin moved the Field Museum's research station from southwest Colorado to the Pine Lawn Valley in New Mexico.

It is perhaps not surprising that Martin's (1940:10–11) initial interest in the newly defined Mogollon culture was stimulated by a pottery type: in the argot of southwestern archaeology, he was later often referred to as "Pottery" Paul (Sidney) Martin to distinguish him from the other famous "Pollen"

Paul (Schultz) Martin, and his love of prehistoric ceramics was well known to his students and colleagues. The pottery type was Abajo Red-on-orange, examples of which Martin (1939:487–492) had found during his excavations in southwestern Colorado and which he had interpreted—along with others (e.g., Morris 1939)—as an aberrant but local invention of "Basket Maker" folk. It was as a result of comments from Emil Haury that Martin (1940:11) and Rinaldo became convinced that this type might well be related to Mogollon Red-on-brown pottery. This, as well as other intrusive Mogollon pottery recovered in his Ackmen-Lowry-area investigations, piqued Martin's interest:

> The idea of starting work in a little-known culture (Mogollon) and in a new region fascinated me. I felt I had worked long enough in one area on one set of *problems* and I did not want to become a slave of the Anasazi culture. Further, I wanted to study *new problems* so that I would have a *better understanding of the Southwest as a whole.* Then, too, if the Mogollon culture were merely a peripheral development of the Anasazi, I thought that I would recognize the Anasazi elements very quickly and perhaps be of some help in settling the strug-

gle between those who were in favor of setting up the Mogollon culture as a new and separate cultural root or division and those who were against this idea [1940:11; emphasis added].

In addition to exploring the relatively limited problem of the origins of Abajo Red-on-orange, Martin (1940:11) cited two other problems that concerned him: delimiting the major characteristics of the Mogollon, and the issue of the possible relationships of the Mogollon to a San Juan "nucleus." He also notes a refinement in those problems that occurred during the first season of excavation at the SU site in 1939 as follows:

1. If the Mogollon culture could be given the status of an independent complex, when did Basket Maker–Pueblo traits (which everyone recognized in late Mogollon–Mimbres periods) filter into the Mogollon stronghold?
2. When did the Mogollon culture start? Was it earlier or later than the Hohokam and Anasazi cultures? If earlier, what contributions did Mogollon make to their development?

The importance of our moving into the Mogollon country was

partly gauged by the host of *new problems* which unfolded, and the *new vistas which opened up* [Martin 1940:11; emphasis added].

Thus, Martin took with him to Pine Lawn and to the initial excavations at the SU site not only a problem-oriented approach influenced by emerging data sets but also—if only preliminarily and personally—a mac-roregional view of how best to interpret southwestern prehistory.[1]

Martin also carried an abiding interest in developing means by which the organizational features of prehistoric populations might be inferred. He sponsored Lawrence Roys's (1936) pioneering study of the construction sequence at Lowry Ruin based on wall bonding and abutment relationships and made inferences concerning the growth and population of the settlement on the basis of Roys's analyses (Martin 1936:194–201). He later coauthored (with Rinaldo) an essay entitled "Conjectures Concerning the Social Organization of the Mogollon Indians" (Martin and Rinaldo 1950a:556–569; see also P. Martin 1972).

Excavations at the SU site were conducted in 1939 and 1940 and then, after a hiatus during World War II, again in 1946 (Martin 1943; Martin and Rinaldo 1940, 1947). In the following years they chased the Mogollon both backward (with the help of Ernst Antevs and others) and forward in time and by 1949 had established the sequence of phases from the Chiricahua phase Cochise to the beginnings of the Reserve phase (Martin et al. 1949:207–222). It was following the work at Tularosa and Cordova caves (Martin et al. 1952) and at several other smaller cave sites that, between 1952 and 1954, the chase shifted to later periods in time, resulting in an exploration first of sites representing the Reserve phase (Bluhm

1957; Martin and Rinaldo 1950a, 1950b; Martin et al. 1956) and later of those of the subsequently defined Tularosa phase (Martin et al. 1957; Rinaldo and Bluhm 1956).

It is in the report *Late Mogollon Communities: Four Sites of the Tularosa Phase, Western New Mexico* (Martin et al. 1957) that we find the first reference to possible Mogollon-Zuni relationships, although it is in the context of a suggestion that people from the Zuni area may have moved into the Reserve area ("as early as AD 1000") and not the other way around (Martin et al. 1957:133). However, in a later paragraph the idea that the Tularosa phase Mogollon may have ultimately ended up at Zuni is also expressed: "And then what happened to the people who had worked out an admirable way of life, well suited to their requirements and ecology? We do not know. Our guess is that they moved northward and westward and that some of them eventually wound up in Zuni-land. In fact, they may be responsible for the introduction of rectangular kivas in the Zuni area" (Martin et al. 1957:134).

With the 1955 excavations at Foote Canyon Pueblo (Rinaldo 1959), located along the Blue River and just over the border into Arizona, the possible Zuni connection became more fully articulated. These excavations were conducted entirely by Rinaldo, and he alone authored the subsequent report (Rinaldo 1959). This was because Martin was involved in the administrative efforts necessary to move the Field Museum operation to Vernon, Arizona, as the chase for the Mogollon moved north and west (Martin 1959a:149).

In the preface to Rinaldo's Foote Canyon report Martin reiterated "two main interests [that] have been of primary concern to us and have provided our research goals" (1959a:149). The

first of these clearly expresses a concern with cultural process on a larger theoretical scale:

the search for and recognition of consistent relationships between cultural phenomena in order to establish similarities that might recur within or across cultural boundaries, or indeed even in historically separate areas. If such relationships and similarities could be established and if the particular lines of cultural evolution could be discovered, one might then be able to make systematized statements or formulations that would have possible predictive value.

Such discoveries, by seeking causes and explanations, would throw light on how cultures evolve [Martin 1959a:149–150].

The second concern involved the "historical approach," whereby "the acquisition of historical data permits the description of a particular culture area in time and space in order to make it stand out in unique and bold relief" (Martin 1959a:150). As to the relationship between the two, he had this to say:

Our two main guiding interests are interrelated. It is true that one may do research limited to the historical approach alone; but such research stops short of the major goal described above and therefore possesses a narrow compass of interest for us.

Obversely, our primary interest —that of searching for parallels of limited occurrence in a developmental sequence in order to devise some general formulations as to the ultimate destiny of a culture— cannot be undertaken without the particularizing, detailed, historical analyses of particular areas and culture types [Martin 1959a:150].

At Foote Canyon Rinaldo discovered evidence for an occupation that occurred between AD 1250 and 1350, after the Tularosa phase, and he tentatively defined this as the Foote Canyon phase (1959:286). The characteristics of this phase were never further elaborated, and the designation has never been widely used. As to relationships with Zuni, he was quite explicit with respect to the probable destination of the group that abandoned the site around AD 1350:

> The circumstances surrounding their departure may be important to a knowledge of Southwestern prehistory and culture change, but of perhaps greater importance is the question of where they went. In the final clarification of this question the protohistoric Zuni polychrome pottery types found at Foote Canyon Pueblo seem particularly significant. These contribute additional evidence to a case based heretofore chiefly on more generalized pottery type relationships and on resemblances of some painted animal figures and tablets to historic artifacts used by the Zuni Indians. With the further clarification of this relationship the total culture at the site takes on added meaning, because it forms a link between the earlier Mogollon and Cochise cultures on the one hand, and the historic Western Pueblo cultures, on the other [Rinaldo 1959:284].

After the move to the new location in Vernon the expedition concentrated in 1957 on the excavation of a number of sites of various ages located in the immediate vicinity of that modern hamlet (Martin and Rinaldo 1960). In the first publication on work in this new area Martin articulated five research goals, as follows:

1. to learn more about the nature and chronological position of the various sites in eastern Arizona in the Show Low, St. John's [sic], Springerville district;
2. to ascertain the similarities and differences of this area compared with the Southwest as a whole;
3. *to seek connections, if they exist, between prehistoric and contemporary or historic groups;*
4. to work out in detail the local sequences of culture history and to discover the ways in which the various elements in the cultures evolved, how they worked, and how they were interrelated; and
5. to determine if the peoples of the Reserve area moved into this district when they abandoned the Reserve–Pine Lawn homeland about AD 1350 [1960:3; emphasis added].

Starting in 1958, Martin and Rinaldo focused much of their energy on the upper Little Colorado, first excavating at Table Rock Pueblo and then at Hooper Ranch Pueblo in 1959 (and at the Mineral Creek site near Vernon; see Martin and Rinaldo 1960; Martin et al. 1961). In 1960 they excavated the rectangular great kiva at Hooper Ranch Pueblo and conducted work at Rim Valley Pueblo (near Hooper Ranch) and at the Tumbleweed Canyon site, which overlooks the Little Colorado about halfway between Springerville and St. Johns (Martin et al. 1962).

Excavations at these sites provided evidence of Mogollon connections not only with Zuni but with Hopi as well, but, in the final analysis, Martin and Rinaldo observed that the data gave them confidence that "eventually we can show a clear tie-up with earlier Mogollon traits and later Zuni developments" (Martin and Rinaldo 1960:287; Rinaldo 1962:64–74). In

the preface to the 1961 report on Mineral Creek and Hooper Ranch Martin reiterated the goal of chasing the Mogollon out of New Mexico and west-central Arizona following AD 1350. Specifically, he posed two competing hypotheses: "Had Mogollon influences filtered into the Zuni area or had Mogollon people themselves left their ancient homeland in the mountains of western New Mexico and migrated in to the Zuni region proper?" (Martin 1961:3). In the summary to this same report these questions are tentatively answered with the following extraordinary (and decidedly "Mogollon-centric") hypothesis concerning the influence of Mogollon on both Hopi and Zuni:

> The evidence that is accumulating suggests the strong possibility that the remarkable flowering of the Hopi and Zuni cultures in the fourteenth and fifteenth centuries may have been due, in no small degree, to the influx of the vigorous, distinct, and desirable Mogollon ideas. It may be that the momentum of development of the Zuni and Hopi cultures had, for some reason as yet unknown, slackened, and that unconsciously the people were athirst for some unifying, regenerative, and spiritual influences. It may be that the earlier and original Zuni or Hopi cultures had been diluted by the influx of several uprooted and homeless tribes whose ideas created disharmony. Perhaps the Zuni or Hopi of the day heard good things about their Mogollon neighbors to the south of them, perceived that their way of life functioned smoothly and that their supernatural beings brought them rain, snow, fertility, crops; therefore they may have invited their neighbors to move to Zuni-land where they would not only be able

to continue their much admired way of life but where they might also propagate their customs.

This hypothesis reverses our usual order of thinking. Commonly, we have assumed that the Mogollon peoples were forced, by some as yet unspecified reason or causes, to migrate from the Pine Lawn–Reserve area to the Little Colorado River drainage and later to the Zuni country. Perhaps they were asked by a disturbed community to join with it to create a stable, purposeful society.

Thus, the movement of some or all of the Mogollon peoples in late times might conceivably be explained, at least in part [Martin et al. 1961:168–169].

With the advent of the "New Archaeology" in the early 1960s and Paul Martin's (1971) zealous conversion to the emerging paradigm (see also Wilcox 2003a), the long-term research design that had as a central element the Mogollon-Zuni relationship was abandoned. After the excavation of Carter Ranch in 1961–1962 Rinaldo left the Field Museum and began work with Charles Di Peso at Paquimé. He did, however, have the final word on the issue, with publication of his classic 1964 article "Notes on the Origin of Historic Zuni Culture," in which he made explicit his conception of the connection between late Mogollon manifestations and Zuni, derived from his years of work with Martin:

At the end of the Tularosa Phase and the beginning of the Pinedale Phase construction in the Mogollon area appears to have been of a defensive nature. There is a lack of outside lateral doorways, there is much building of dwellings in caves and remote places in the mountains, on pinnacles or high mesas. . . . Walls were built along the edges of isolated mesas surrounded by cliffs. . . . [T]hey did withdraw from whatever was threatening them and the trail they took seems to have led towards Zuni [Rinaldo 1964:94].

Note

1. Martin later acknowledged that the selection of the Pine Lawn Valley as a locus for long-term investigations resulted from the suggestion of Haury and Sayles, "two of our most valued friends and advisors" (1959a:149).

10 Adaptation of Man to the Mountains

Revising the Mogollon Concept

David A. Gregory and David R. Wilcox

When Paul Martin established the Field Museum research station at Pine Lawn in 1939, culture history was a dominant paradigm in American archaeology.[1] Over approximately the next two decades Paul, John Rinaldo, and numerous other colleagues operated under this general rubric, first in establishing the basic outlines of Mogollon culture (Rinaldo 1941) and subsequently in tracing Mogollon populations through time and space. A principal research emphasis—and in fact a primary reason for the move to Vernon some 15 years later—was on tracing those populations that abandoned the Reserve area in the late 1200s and exploring possible relationships between Mogollon populations and modern Native American groups, in particular the Zuni. Their purposes and questions were clear:

> to seek connections, if they exist, between prehistoric and contemporary or historic groups; . . . to determine if the peoples of the Reserve area moved into this [the upper Little Colorado] district when they abandoned the Reserve–Pine Lawn homeland about AD 1350 [Martin 1960:3].

Had Mogollon influences filtered into the Zuni area or had Mogo-llon people themselves left their ancient homeland in the mountains of western New Mexico and migrated in to the Zuni region proper [Martin 1961:3]?

Excavations at Table Rock, Hooper Ranch, and other sites in the upper Little Colorado area in the late 1950s and early 1960s represented their initial efforts in this direction. With the paradigm shifts of the late 1960s and early 1970s these concerns were relegated to peripheral status and largely abandoned. Rinaldo's classic paper "Notes on the Origin of Historic Zuni Culture" (1964), however, ably summarizes their original ideas and findings.

Today the resurgence of interest in migration, cultural affiliation, and warfare among groups with distinct identities has brought about a renewed interest in explanations of the facts of linguistic diversity in the Southwest, and a new era of dialogue between archaeologists and linguists promises to deepen such inquiry. We propose to take the Martin and Rinaldo hypothesis of a connection between Mogollon and Zuni as a point of departure for a modern methodological inquiry of how archaeological and linguistic facts can be integrated into new anthropologi-cal theories about the evolution of human adaptations and organizations in the American Southwest. Recent critiques of the Mogollon concept highlight the need for just such a reevaluation along adaptationist and organizational lines (Haury 1986b; Speth 1988; Wilcox 1988a). Seven problem domains, ordered in temporal sequence, are identified as the arenas for further research. What follows is but a sketch—the accompanying figures provide a glimpse of data that will be much elaborated in the written version of this chapter.[2]

Unity and Diversity in the Peopling of the Americas

For at least a century and a half (Gallatin 1845) the peopling of the Americas has provoked a debate between unity and diversity proponents (Putnam 1901), and this continues today with greater specificity (e.g., Greenberg et al. 1986). We note, however, that from the Clovis horizon onward the unity hypothesis that the story of New World prehistory is one of differentiation of a common culture has been the principal way in which archaeologists have assessed the data (Griffin 1967; Meltzer 1993; Willey 1966). To explain the multiple linguistic stocks in the American South-

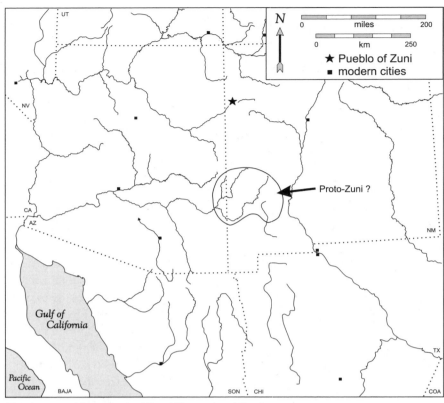

Figure 10.1. Hypothetical Zuni "homeland."

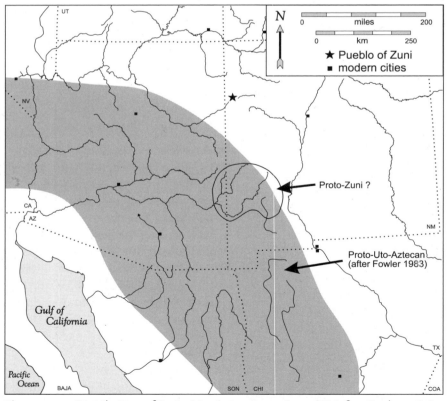

Figure 10.2. Distribution of Proto-Uto-Aztecan, ca. 6000 BP (after Fowler 1983), with hypothesized Zuni homeland inserted.

west, then, we should look for ecological and social conditions that could have produced and maintained such differentiation.

Islands in the Sky

Between about 4,000 and 6,000 years ago the Altithermal created conditions that favored high-altitude adaptations and isolating populations in "islands in the sky" (Krantz 1977). Discoveries of Archaic pithouses in high-altitude settings have been made in several places in the Far West, and we propose that the highland area spreading out from Mount Baldy (see fig. 10.1) is a good candidate for another of these islands, one where Zuni may have become and was maintained as a distinct language group. Some Archaic sites of the appropriate age and at least one site with possible pithouses above 2,743 m have been documented in this region. Our hypothesis is that there was a highland-adapted group in place by the Middle Archaic or perhaps earlier, people who were speakers of a Proto-Zuni language.[3]

Linguistic Distributions and the Spread of Maize

Archaeological evidence now suggests that maize had been rapidly adopted in the Southwest by 3800–3600 B.P., within a millennium of its domestication farther south.[4] One reason for this rapid spread appears to have been the shared linguistic affiliation of many Archaic Southwest populations. The linguistic evidence suggests that a widespread Proto-Uto-Aztecan dialect chain was in place by about 6,000 years ago; we have modified that distribution to accommodate our hypothesis of a highland population of Proto-Zuni speakers (see fig. 10.2).[5] Jane Hill (2001) and others have recently suggested that speakers

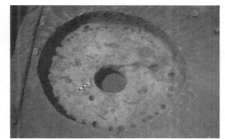
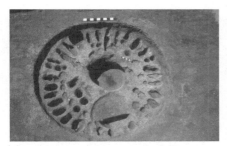

Figure 10.3. Early Agricultural pit structures from Los Pozos in the Tucson Basin. Photo at lower right copyright Adriel Heisey, other photos by D. Gregory.

of Proto-Uto-Aztecan languages were instrumental in the rapid spread of maize and that this process occurred before the split between Northern (including Hopi) and Southern Proto-Uto-Aztecan:

> First, the distribution of early dates for maize . . . is a very good match to the homeland reconstructed for Uto-Aztecan by Fowler (1983). Second, no other language family in North America exhibits a distribution linking Mesoamerican and the Southwest. Third, the Southern Uto-Aztecan languages and Hopi share a complex of lexical items for maize cultivation that are cognate across the languages. Such cognancy could only be present if the lexical items appeared in the languages prior to the breakup of this speech community into the daughter languages [Jane Hill 1996].

The early maize dates from Bat Cave, on the edge of our proposed Zunian population, suggest the early adoption of maize in this highland zone as well. Growing maize in this

environment involves geomorphology, soils, rainfall, and temperature regimes substantially different from those of the lower floodplain environments along which maize appears to have initially and rapidly spread. These differences and, ultimately, a more sedentary lifeway probably served to reify boundaries between mountain-dwelling groups and surrounding populations after the adoption of maize and may have been a factor in the Northern–Southern Proto-Uto-Aztecan split as well.

The Presence of Early Agricultural Period Populations in the Mogollon Area

There is also abundant evidence for the presence of populations in our highland zone during the Early Agricultural period. The Cienega Creek site near Point of Pines (Haury 1957) and data from numerous cave sites (Dick 1965; Martin et al. 1949; Martin et al. 1954; Martin et al. 1952) demonstrate the presence of highland populations during the interval after the adoption of maize and prior to the

appearance of pottery. Startling new data on the Early Agricultural period from the Tucson Basin indicate residence in small pithouses with distinctive morphologies (see fig. 10.3), a tradition that persisted without pottery for more than a millennium (see Gregory 2001b). Review of earlier work in the mountains shows that similar structures were at least occasionally present under later Mogollon sites, including Turkey Creek Pueblo (see fig. 10.4).[6] Other linked traits in a widespread technocomplex include Cienega points, stone pipes, and distinctive notched awls. The latter, while not yet known from sites of this age in the mountains, would later become a defining "Mogollon" trait (Haury 1936a; Nesbitt 1938). Although boundaries between relatively different linguistic groups are well attested archaeologically during this time period in the northern Southwest (Basketmaker II; see Matson 1991), new studies are necessary in our area to determine if boundaries between highland populations and surrounding groups can be similarly demonstrated by contrasts in rock art, technology, or other cultural features.

What Is the Mogollon Tradition?

First defined by Emil Haury (1936a), the Mogollon concept has been stretched geographically and temporally far beyond its original meaning (Gladwin and Gladwin 1929; Lehmer 1948; Sayles 1945). Reexamination of excavated pithouses in the mountainous zone that we have identified above 1,981 m reveals a coherent tradition of ceremonial architecture that persisted in this region for over 1,000 years. Most distinctive are floor grooves, sometimes containing plastered-over logs, that define a "middle place" around the hearth within large, ceremonial pithouses

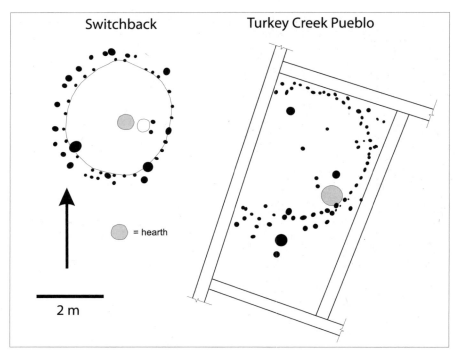

Figure 10.4. Possible Early Agricultural period pit structures at the Switchback Site (after Peckham 1957:fig. 5) and Turkey Creek Pueblo (after Cook 1961:fig. 2).

and later above-ground structures (see figs. 10.5–10.7). This pattern contrasts with a parallel tradition centered in the Mimbres region to the south.[7] Even more striking is the fact that the post–AD 1000 Mimbres regional system with its distinctive religious ideology left the mountainous region untouched.

Thus, we would propose, first, to redefine the Mogollon concept to apply only to populations included in the traditional Forestdale, Black River, and Cibola branches and the northernmost and earlier portion of the Mimbres branch. Second, by narrowing the Mogollon concept in this way we argue for the meaningful extension of it after AD 1000 in this highland area. Instead of overemphasizing broad similarities, as Reed's (1948, 1950) "Western Pueblo" concept does, we argue for the existence of a distinct linguistic group having a recognizable ideological and organizational adaptation to a particular

environment that may be traced for at least several millennia.

Population Movements and Coalescence (AD 1000–1300)

Looking northward, we observe that the spread of Chacoan ideology out of the San Juan Basin penetrated into the Zuni region at least as far south as Quemado, but it left our Mogollon folk untouched.[8] The striking disjunction in the distributions of Chacoan circular and Mogollon rectangular great kivas strongly supports this conclusion (see fig. 10.8). Another fundamental divide is evident in the east–west contrast of great houses with great kivas and great kivas without associated great houses. The great houses of the Zuni/Quemado area, with their Reserve-style pottery, may represent Zunian populations who adopted their own version of Chacoan organization; alternatively, these people may have been Keresan speakers.

To the west the great kivas in the zone from the Hopi Buttes to Forestdale and Flagstaff to Hay Hollow Valley, we argue, were built by western Anasazi populations who were participating on the periphery of the Chacoan economic system.[9] These people were probably Uto-Aztecan speakers, perhaps of a Proto-Hopi language (see fig. 10.9).

In the late AD 1200s these western Anasazi populations migrated south from large pueblos in the Silver Creek region, moving below the Mogollon Rim and extending into areas from the Tonto Basin and the Grasshopper Plateau on the west to (we suspect) Kinishba and to Point of Pines on the east and then southward to the Safford and middle San Pedro valleys. Concurrently, or slightly earlier, we follow Martin and Rinaldo in proposing that the Highland Mogollon population of Zunians moved northward into the upper Little Colorado around Springerville and into the Zuni/Quemado area, coalescing with post-Chacoan populations who may have been their linguistic cousins (see fig. 10.10). The large, oval pueblos in the El Morro area resemble the main ruin at Point of Pines, where some Mogollon lingered in the south for another quarter century. Warfare and the politics of threat and counterthreat appear to have been precipitating factors in these movements (Rinaldo 1964).

Late Prehistoric and Protohistoric Population Distributions

Rinaldo long ago noted the evidence for late prehistoric warfare in the Mogollon area and one of its important implications:

At the end of the Tularosa Phase and the beginning of the Pinedale Phase construction in the

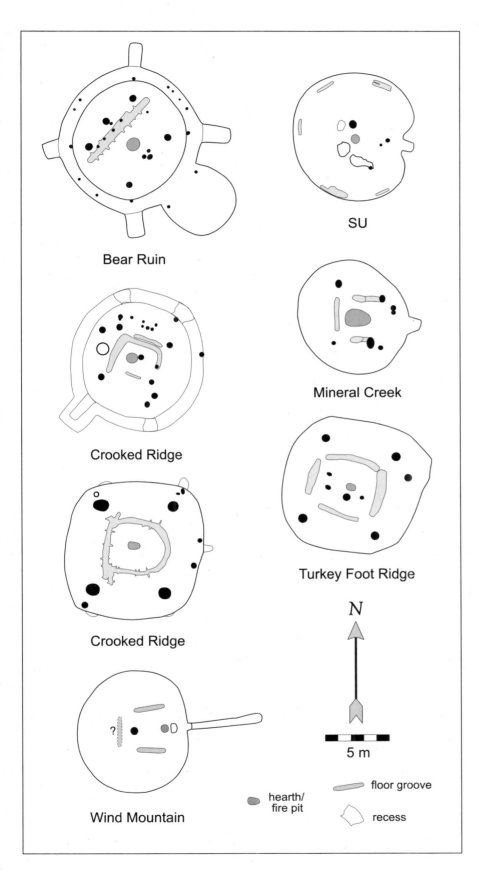

Bear Ruin

SU

Crooked Ridge

Mineral Creek

Crooked Ridge

Turkey Foot Ridge

N

5 m

hearth/
fire pit

floor groove

recess

Wind Mountain

Figure 10.5. Mogollon ceremonial structures (Bear Ruin after Haury 1985a:fig. 19; SU after Martin 1940:map 4; Crooked Ridge after Wheat 1954:fig. 24; Mineral Creek after Martin et al. 1961:fig. 9; Crooked Ridge after Wheat 1954:fig. 25; Turkey Foot Ridge after Martin and Rinaldo 1950b:fig. 101; Wind Mountain after Woosley and McIntyre 1996:fig. 4.16).

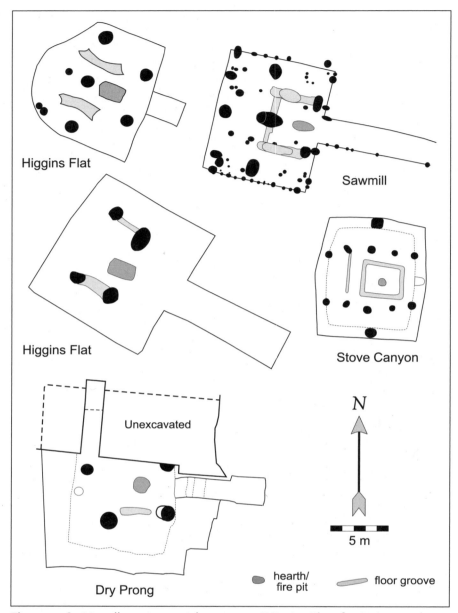

Figure 10.6. Mogollon ceremonial structures (Higgins Flat after Martin et al. 1957:fig. 2; Sawmill after Bluhm 1957:fig. 3; Higgins Flat after Martin et al. 1957:fig. 2; Stove Canyon after Neely 1974:fig. 69; Dry Prong after Olson 1960:fig. 3).

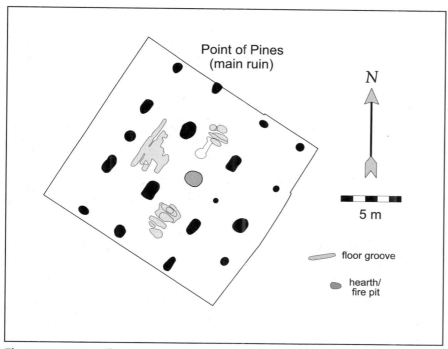

Figure 10.7. Mogollon ceremonial structure (after Gerald 1957:map 8).

Mogollon area appears to have been of a defensive nature. There is a lack of outside lateral doorways, there is much building of dwellings in caves and remote places in the mountains, on pinnacles or high mesas. . . . Walls were built along the edges of isolated mesas surrounded by cliffs. . . . [T]hey did withdraw from whatever was threatening them and the trail they took seems to have led towards Zuni [1964:94].

An escalation of warfare appears to have played a significant role in sharpening social and political boundaries in the late AD 1200s and 1300s as clusters of nucleated, plaza-centered pueblos formed polities of 2,000–3,000 people each. Populations both above and below the Mogollon Rim (LeBlanc 1999; Wilcox et al. 2001b) that dropped below this threshold were soon abandoned, and by AD 1400–1450 only three such clusters were left: a Hopic one in the west, a Zuni one in the middle, and Keresan Acoma in the east, each with its distinctive social and political systems that emerged from unique syntheses of Chacoan and non-Chacoan antecedents (see fig. 10.10).

Conclusion

Obviously, the general model presented here is much in need of refinement and testing. Nonetheless, this conception does include plausible and testable hypotheses about the relationships among archaeological populations and in particular suggests a more restricted and therefore more useful Mogollon concept. The model draws its inspiration and many specific elements from the work of Martin, Rinaldo, and their colleagues. If it serves only to stimulate thought and even controversy, one suspects that Paul Martin would have been pleased.

Notes

1. The text of the chapter presented here is essentially the same as that read at a symposium during the Society for American Archaeology meetings in 1999 held in honor of the anniversary of Paul Martin's one hundredth birthday, with these minor exceptions: we have added a number of endnotes, the slides shown at the meetings have been turned into figures, necessary editorial corrections have been made, and we have added references to more recent work where appropriate. Since many of our colleagues have not made the connection, we note here that the "Adaptation of Man to the Mountains" part of the title is a conceit on the title of Paul Martin's chapter on the Mogollon in Martin and Plog (1973).

2. Plans for an expanded version of this chapter fell through with the collapse of the proposed volume to honor Paul Martin. However, the advanced seminar and the current volume emerged as alternative objectives that, we trust, do honor to the work and memory of both Paul Martin and John Rinaldo.

3. While we think this hypothesis is still worth considering, it has gained little or no support from the participants in the advanced seminar.

4. Ever earlier maize dates suggest that we will soon find that maize arrived in the Southwest by about 4,000 years ago (see Gregory 2001b).

5. The idea for a dialect chain of Uto-

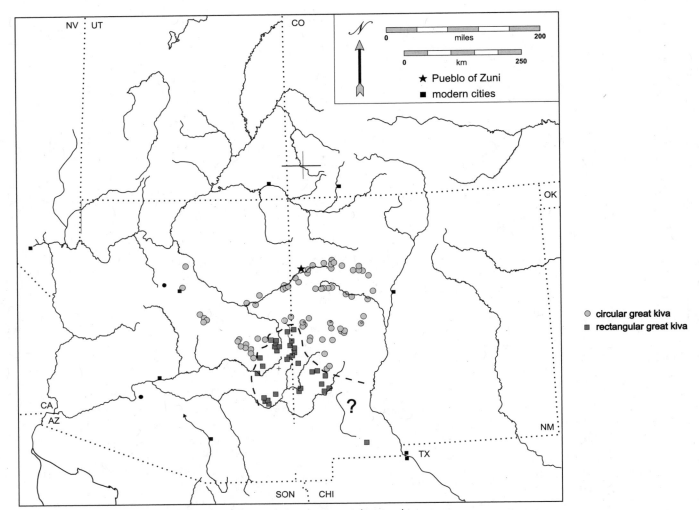

Figure 10.8. The distribution of rectangular and circular (partial) great kivas, AD 1000–1300.

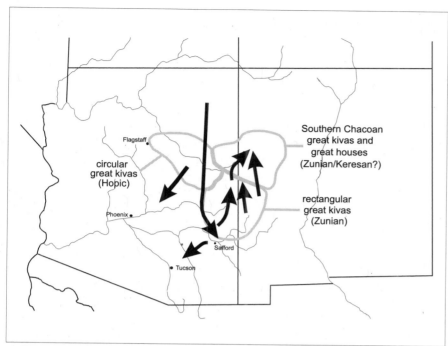

Figure 10.9. Population movements in the northern Southwest, ca. AD 1200–1300.

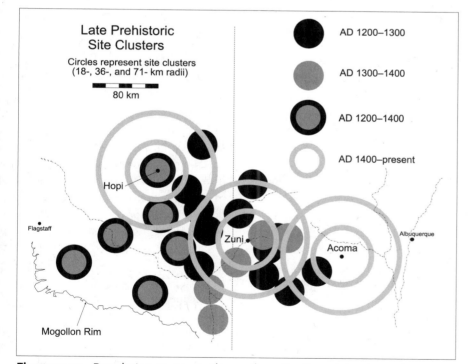

Figure 10.10. Population centers in the northern Southwest, late AD 1200s.

Aztecan speakers rests on the work of Wick Miller (1983; see also Wilcox 1986b); see Hill 2001, 2002 for an alternative view and Wilcox and Gregory, chap. 1, this vol.

6. Additional examples of probable Early Agricultural pit structures in the Mogollon area have been revealed since the writing of this chapter (e.g., see Wallace 1998).

7. See Diehl, chap. 11, this vol.

8. Lekson (1999) has suggested that the Aragon site (LA 3270 and LA 8079; see Hough 1907) may represent a Chacoan great house.

9. See Herr 2001 for an alternative view.

11 Mogollon Trajectories and Divergences

Michael W. Diehl

What is the Mogollon phenomenon? What were its origins, and where did it go? What connections, if there were any, linked the Mogollon area to the ancestral Zuni? The purposes of this chapter are to define the spatial, temporal, and material parameters of the problem of relating the Mogollon or any of its branches to Zuni and to describe my vision—the best "story" that I can concoct—about the trajectory of Mogollon culture change. Toward that end, this chapter explores the genesis of the Mogollon culture from its potential roots during the Early Agricultural period or preceding Desert Archaic culture and traces the developmental sequences within the branches of the greater Mogollon area through the tenth century AD. Evidence of interaction and identity maintenance is discussed, and changes in the organization of subsistence through time are tracked. Specific attention is given to architectural details and material traits that previous scholars have suggested are among the more defining attributes of the Mogollon culture, and attention is also given to the distribution of ceremonial complexes, as suggested by the organizers of this conference (see Gregory and Wilcox, chap. 10, this vol.). It is a daunting task, rife with problems of missing middle-range theory, inconsistent data recovery, and a lamentable dearth of information from fully modern excavations of pithouse villages from the first millennium AD.

This chapter begins by revisiting the concept of "the Mogollon" as it was initially recognized and as it has evolved through time. The second section tracks changes in material culture and communal and residential architecture in four of the Mogollon branches for the first millennium AD. The third section discusses the recent developments from the Early Agricultural period that preceded the Mogollon Pithouse periods in an effort to determine whether population isolates are visible among the first farmers in the Southwest. The fourth section relates explanations for the first use of maize in the Southwest to models of the origins of the Mogollon culture and Zuni. The final section identifies concerns that need to be addressed before archaeologists can confidently identify different ethnic groups in the deep prehistoric past.

The result is that the scope of the problem is outlined and more questions are raised than are answered. There is no evidence that convincingly suggests the presence of an isolated population in the first millennium BC during the Early Agricultural period. Moreover, the Mogollon culture area is quite homogeneous during most of the first millennium AD; there is no basis in ceremonial architecture, residential architecture, material culture, or subsistence practices to differentiate between the Black River, Cibola, Forestdale, and Mimbres branches prior to the ninth century AD (but see Webster, chap. 16, this vol.). There is a modest amount of evidence that suggests that during the ninth century the Mimbres branch began to diverge from the other Mogollon branches, especially with respect to kiva construction and the occurrence of exogenous goods. But despite any patterns that one may observe or fail to observe in the archaeological evidence, there remain unresolved and substantial problems in the basic task of recognizing the boundaries of populations or ethnic groups in the more distant past.

Which Mogollon?

The scope of this chapter encompasses roughly 2,200 years of prehistory (roughly 1200 BC through AD 1000; see fig. 11.1) over a very broad area (see Wilcox and Gregory, chap. 1, and Gregory and Wilcox, chap. 10, this vol.).[1] Since the volume explicitly addresses Mogollon links to Zuni, one reasonable way to proceed is to start with the recognition of things

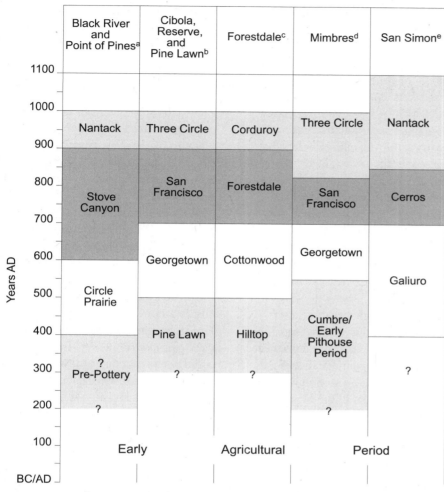

	Black River and Point of Pines[a]	Cibola, Reserve, and Pine Lawn[b]	Forestdale[c]	Mimbres[d]	San Simon[e]
1100					
1000					
900	Nantack	Three Circle	Corduroy	Three Circle	Nantack
800	Stove Canyon	San Francisco	Forestdale	San Francisco	Cerros
700					
600	Circle Prairie	Georgetown	Cottonwood	Georgetown	Galiuro
500					
400		Pine Lawn	Hilltop	Cumbre/ Early Pithouse Period	
300	? Pre-Pottery	?	?		?
200	?			?	
100	Early		Agricultural		Period
BC/AD					

Years AD

[a] after Haury 1989:115, Figure 6.1 [b] after Martin et al. 1949:222 [c] after Haury 1985a: 376, Table 1 [d] after Diehl 1994 [e] after Cordell 1997:203 Table 7.4

Figure 11.1. Mogollon branches and phase sequences at a glance.

Haury's Mogollon

Emil Haury wrote *The Mogollon Culture of Southwestern New Mexico* (1936a) based on the results of his excavations at two archaeological sites: the Mogollon Village near Glenwood, New Mexico, and the Harris Village in the heart of the town of Mimbres, New Mexico. In his introduction Haury specifically included the central Mimbres Valley in his definition of the Mogollon culture. He also included both pithouse occupations and the surface pueblo occupations that are now known as the Classic Mimbres phase. At the outset, then, the definitive Mogollon culture area was not necessarily a montane adaptation, and it specifically included the Classic Mimbres phase.[2] As LeBlanc (1986:299) noted, Haury was unwilling to apply the term Mogollon to surface pueblo occupations in the Forestdale and Point of Pines areas. It therefore seems that for Haury, at least initially, the Mogollon stopped being Mogollon in the eleventh century AD everywhere *except* where the Classic Mimbres phase was manifest. In later studies Haury (1986a) began to refer to the Mogollon as a rustic, mountain folk, although he never withdrew his previous suggestion that the Mogollon endured in the Mimbres area.

Martin and Rinaldo's Mogollon

After his 1941 season at the SU site Paul Martin (1943:113) recognized the Pine Lawn phase as an early expression of the Mogollon culture in the Reserve area.[3] In his effort to synthesize traits of the Mogollon culture Martin produced a list that closely matched Haury's and was probably based on it. In addition, Martin (1943:131) identified a diagnostically Mogollon dart point with diagonal notches and convex expanding bases

Mogollon. The call to confer (see Gregory and Wilcox, chap. 10, this vol.) suggests that the Mogollon are only properly viewed as montane folk who typically lived at elevations above 1,981 m within three specific branches (the Black River, Cibola, and Forestdale) and whose community structures incorporated particular features such as floor grooves. The latter are presumed to be the depressions left by log benches surrounding a central space in the house. Gregory and Wilcox, one must infer, are not especially dogmatic about any of these criteria, since many of the structures mentioned in figures 10.5–10.7 (Gregory and Wilcox, chap. 10, this

vol.) are found at elevations well below 1,981 m, and one of them (Wind Mountain House X) comes from a multicomponent site in the Mimbres branch. As it turns out, structures with floor grooves are more widespread than was previously assumed. There are, moreover, compelling reasons to avoid being too hung up on the montane preference. Rather than limit the scale of this investigation to the three named branches, it seemed more fruitful to go back to the "Mogollon culture area," as it has classically been defined. The question is, What does the original classical Mogollon look like?

(see Rinaldo and Darrow 1943:207 for illustrations). Other diagnostic Mogollon artifacts included "bone pins, side-notched bone awls, multifaced stone pestles, and tubular pipes" (Martin 1943:131). The latter were said to be rare during the Pine Lawn phase. Brown- to red-colored paste also figured prominently in the identification of Mogollon ceramics.

In subsequent years Martin came increasingly to speak of the Mogollon culture as a montane adaptation, possibly because excavations in the Mimbres Mogollon lagged during the decades of the 1950s and 1960s. Martin and Rinaldo's studies of cave sites in the Reserve area also added new dimensions to the lists of Mogollon traits, including "toy" bow fragments, juniper-berry skewers, painted tablets, and certain styles of sandalwork (Bluhm 1952; Grange 1952). Interestingly, Martin seems to have been concerned about the proportional frequencies of artifacts; the section is entitled "Importance of Comparative Frequencies in Evaluating Mogollon Pattern" (Martin 1943:129). At the time, apart from potsherd frequencies, detailed frequency distributions for most artifacts were not typically included in site reports. That dearth of frequency data accounts for the use of "presence-absence" trait lists in the first major synthesis of the Mogollon culture, that of Joe Ben Wheat (1955).

Wheat's Mogollon

In *Mogollon Culture prior to AD 1000* Wheat (1955) attempted the first grand synthesis of Mogollon material traits for all purported branches of the Mogollon culture area. He started with a summary of the geographic variation encompassed by the Mogollon culture and included (1) a chunk of the Colorado Plateau geographic province in the northern and eastern part of the Mogollon area, (2) the

Mogollon Rim and portions of the vast Basin and Range geographic province to the south and west, and (3) a vague and indeterminate boundary to the southeast that he could not trace (Wheat 1955:2; see fig. 1.2, this vol.).[4] Wheat's geographic overview contains a statement that has confused many of the Mogollon scholars that followed. Wheat remarked, "The central portion of this mountainous belt seems to have been the Mogollon homeland" (1955:2). Sometime thereafter the Mogollon culture area seems to have acquired the implication that it was a "montane" culture—an interpretation that ignored the vast stretches of relatively lower elevation hills, desert scrublands, high-elevation desert grasslands, and basins that separate the various ranges and that permeate the various Mogollon branches.

Wheat's second section was entitled "Taxonomy of the Mogollon Culture" and identified six major branches: Black River (Point of Pines), Cibola, Forestdale, Mimbres, San Simon, and Jornada (see Wilcox and Gregory, chap. 1, this vol., fig. 1.2). Of these, the San Simon branch continues to remain enigmatic and has failed to consistently produce sites that conform well to any cultural pattern. In addition, it is now recognized that the Jornada branch is so distinctive in timing of major horizons, organizational changes, and subsistence changes as to be virtually a distinct culture area (LeBlanc and Whalen 1980; Whalen 1994); the Jornada region is the *only* chunk of the Mogollon culture area that unquestionably merits the characterization as a "desert" branch, although the San Simon branch comes close (Diehl and LeBlanc 2001:8–23).

Initially, Wheat (1955:13–21) included the Cibola branch ("Pine Lawn branch" in Wheat's synthesis) in the Mimbres branch. In his chapter 4 discussions of architecture and

village layout for the Mimbres branch exempted the Pine Lawn Valley sites (Wheat 1955:40–41) with the observation that the SU site had more interior storage pits than *other early Mimbres branch sites*, but Pine Lawn only earned the sobriquet "branch" when pottery was discussed in chapter 6. Floor grooves or foot drums were discussed in the architecture chapter (4) but were not accorded any special distinction.

Wheat's discussion of artifact assemblages from Mogollon sites was comprehensive. Not too surprisingly, the San Simon and Jornada branches stood somewhat apart with respect to the presence or absence of many chipped stone and bone artifact types. Unfortunately, Martin's goal of comparing proportional frequencies still could not be met. Instead, Wheat used presence-absence data. Among bifacial projectile points Wheat's (1955:127–129) Types 5a and 5b are common in Mogollon sites in most branches throughout the first millennium. Type 5a is the same style singled out by Martin and Rinaldo. Wheat (1955:139–141) identified two types of notched awls (Types 3a and 3b) as distinctively Mogollon and present in most branches at most times; these are the same kind of notched awl that Martin thought diagnostic. Wheat's (1955:160–163) summary of the Mogollon cultural pattern recognized five major temporal intervals (Mogollon I–V) and was presented in a table that spanned four pages.

Bullard's Mogollon

By 1962 changes in the developmental sequence of intrusive Anasazi ceramics and excavation of a few additional sites had led Bullard to attempt a resynthesis of the Mogollon chronology. The vast critique of Mogollon and Hohokam seriation that forms the central part of his effort is an anachronism best left alone. The Cerro Colorado site report is, however, germane to this volume, since it is broadly within the Cibola branch. Furthermore, his overview of pithouse architecture (the third part of his volume) contains a lot of relevant information. Bullard's conclusion would warm the hearts of the conference organizers, and Bullard's findings still hold up rather well. Bullard wrote:

> The Mogollon may be divided into two parts which will be called "Nuclear" and "Peripheral" Mogollon areas. The Nuclear Area includes the Mimbres and San Simon regions. The Peripheral Area comprises the Pine Lawn, Point of Pines and Forestdale regions. Here the sites are located in high mountain country and in geographically somewhat isolated valleys. It was in the Nuclear Area that the traits most distinctive of the Mogollon culture were developed and where they were most characteristic [1962:184].

Bullard continued, noting that in the peripheral area "no standard house type was evolved" and "local variation was the rule" (1962:185).

In this study I have attempted to replicate the architectural study achieved by Bullard, adding in the few pithouse villages that were excavated in the 1960s through 1980s. Bullard's identification of the Black River ("Point of Pines"), Cibola ("Pine Lawn"), and Forestdale regions as peripheral to the rest of the Mogollon, while debatable for the early going, seems justified for events that transpired after AD 825.

Discussion

Ideally, a comprehensive overview of the traits that comprise a culture area

and its branches would be entered into the world's greatest relational database and GIS system so that one could ask for density plots of the distributions of all manner of objects and architectural details across space and through time. Such a database would include not only the artifact classes mentioned heretofore as distinctly Mogollon but also the styles of basketry, sandals, and wooden artifacts, since Bluhm (1952) and Grange (1952) identified some interesting spatial and temporal trends among these items (see also Webster, chap. 16, this vol.). Likewise, a detailed study of the distribution of human osteological traits throughout the area would go a long way toward establishing whether or not there were population isolates within the Mogollon region. Good information on perishable items comes primarily from cave deposits that were excavated five decades ago (Martin et al. 1952). Perishables are almost never found in Mogollon pithouse villages, Quemado Alegre (site LA 5407; Akins 1998) in the Cibola branch being one notable exception. Whether or not the existence of such a database would resolve the issues raised in this volume remains questionable.

The Mogollon during the First Millennium AD

Quantifying the Mogollon culture is a daunting task. Everyone who has worked in the area is familiar with the problems inherent in the use of old site reports—the differing excavation and recording techniques, the variable use of screens, the lack of quantitative information for most artifact classes other than ceramics, the phase name proliferation, and so forth. Yet, since few Mogollon *pithouse* sites have been excavated in the last 25 years, one must use old

data or give up on the Mogollon Pithouse periods entirely, and that means giving up on the quintessential Mogollon. So the effort is made here to compare regional distributions of Mogollon traits in pithouse sites, recognizing that the data are what they are.

For this study artifact quantities were gleaned from reports. One problem was the task of identifying which, among the myriads of traits, I should examine to explore variation in Mogollon branches in a useful way. This study concentrates on a few commonly accepted Mogollon artifact types—notched awls and oblique or parallel corner-notched convex-stemmed projectile points. I also tracked a few architectural attributes, including the proportion of pithouses with different plans (irregular, round, bean shaped, rounded quadrilateral, and sharp quadrilateral) and the presence and the absence of ramps and antechambers. In addition, I noted the occurrence of structures with floor grooves and the branches and elevations of the sites where they occurred. I notably did not include distributions of textiles and basketry (see Webster, chap. 16, this volume). Juniper berry skewers were also identified as an important artifact by Grange (1952), but these have been recovered only from cave sites; skewers without berries were found in Steamboat Cave (Cosgrove 1947), so there is at least one potential occurrence of this artifact in the Mimbres branch.

For this study I have attempted to capture everything published on Mogollon pithouse villages in the Black River / Point of Pines, Cibola / Reserve / Pine Lawn, Forestdale, and Mimbres branches. The summary is comprehensive, but of course there is always another pithouse village hidden deep in the annals of salvage archaeological reports.[5]

Residential Architecture

Every pithouse is, to a certain degree, unique. Any undertaking of the classification of types of architectural details requires subjective choices. This is made glaringly evident when one attempts to decide whether a given structure is "round" rather than a rounded amorphous blob, a rounded rectangle, or an almost-round asymmetrical ellipse. The results of this study will not surprise many, since it largely replicates Bullard's (1962), and I have elsewhere verified his statistical calculations for average floor surface areas between branches and phases (Diehl 1994). The reinvestigation here substantially confirms Bullard's findings regarding the spatiotemporal distribution of architectural traits, despite the inclusion of sites excavated in the 1960s and 1970s. I primarily discuss the points where I disagree with his empirical findings, because these points of disagreement, ironically, *strengthen* Bullard's claim that the peripheral Mogollon was somewhat different from the nuclear Mogollon.

As is evident in table 11.1, Bullard probably overstated the importance of antechambers as a typical "Anasazi" trait, since they are common in some Mogollon branches. He was, however, apparently accurate in noting that their distribution within the Mogollon culture area is more northward and westward; antechambers have not yet been found in the Mimbres branch. His assessment that "amorphous" pithouses are probably the result of poor preservation (Bullard 1962:115) does not seem warranted. The excavators of these sites otherwise distinguished between original floor plans and intrusive structures, pits, rodent holes, and the like. In addition, many of the amorphous houses are quite deep. There is no reason to suspect that the margins that the excavators delineated were inaccurate. Amorphous or "irregular" pithouses tend to be found almost exclusively outside of the Mimbres branch (see table 11.1) in places that Bullard called "Peripheral."

Ceremonial Architecture

Table 11.2 presents a list of possible ceremonial structures with floor grooves that have been found throughout the various Mogollon branches. By inspection, it should be clear that the log-bench floor groove is found at a range of elevations and in most Mogollon branches. Structures with floor grooves occur *intermittently* from the Georgetown phase onward in the Black River, Cibola, and Mimbres branches. They are present in all branches by the end of the tenth century. Room 73 at Galaz was probably used well into the Classic Mimbres phase (AD 1000–1100/1150). Comparable structures in the Mimbres branch seem restricted to the Three Circle (AD 825/850–1000) and Classic Mimbres phases; Bradfield (1931:see fold-out map at center) may have excavated one at Cameron Creek Village but did not describe it in detail. In the Cibola branch the structure at Sawmill (Bluhm 1957) may have been constructed during the Three Circle phase and used into the Reserve phase. In the Black River branch the Stove Canyon site (Neely 1974) had two structures with floor grooves, "Pit House 3" and the "Great Kiva."

I emphasize the word *intermittently* because I am concerned about the selectivity involved in focusing narrowly on structures with floor grooves. Mogollon pit structures that have been attributed to ceremonial use manifest a wide variety of construction attributes and features, and I would guess that structures with floor grooves comprise about one quarter of the alleged communal structures. The floor groove characteristic has not been very important to most archaeologists. In an overview of Mimbres-Mogollon communal structures (Anyon and LeBlanc 1980), Georgetown phase (AD 550–700) kivas are recognizable primarily by their size and the join between their ramps and main chambers; they tend to be large (but see Diablo Village Structure 5), and they tend to have posts that flank the ramp where it joins the room (but see Wind Mountain House X). The latter attribute gives Georgetown phase structures a "lobed" or bean shape.

By the Three Circle phase ceremonial structures in the Mimbres branch are sharply rectangular and usually have masonry-lined walls. Classic Mimbres phase kivas are small structures that include really small semisubterranean ones, some midsize ones that average about 37 m², and large open-air plazas (most of which were never excavated). Floor grooves do not come into the definition of a kiva; instead, it seems that size is the primary attribute that sets Mimbres-Mogollon ceremonial structures apart from domestic ones.

This discussion raises a thorny problem that has apparently plagued archaeologists since the 1927 Pecos Conference: What makes a kiva a kiva? According to A. V. Kidder, the primal Pecos conferees concluded that "a kiva is a chamber specifically constructed for ceremonial purposes" (1927:490, cited in Lekson 1988:215). That would be an adequate definition if we could interview a few Georgetown and Three Circle phase pithouse dwellers and ask them which ones were built for ceremonial purposes. In their efforts to operationalize the definition archaeologists subsequently relied on contextual comparisons. As Lekson noted, the operational definition of a kiva rather

Table 11.1 Distribution of Selected Architectural and Material Traits in Mogollon Branches

Site	Phase	Architecture								Artifacts	
		Irregular	Round	Bean or D-Shaped	Rounded Quadrilateral	Square Quadrilateral	Ventrance	Antechamber Present	Bench	Type 5 Projectile Points	Type 3 Notched Awl
Cibola / Reserve branch											
LA 6082	Early Pithouse	o	1	o	o	o	o	o	o	—	—
Luna Junction	Early Pithouse	o	1	o	o	o	o	o	o	o	o
Promontory	Early Pithouse	2	3	o	o	o	o	o	o	1	1
Quemado Alegre	Early Pithouse	1	o	o	o	o	o	1	o	o	1
Switchback	Three Circle / Reserve	o	2	o	o	2	—	—	1	2	2
SU	Early Pithouse / Georgetown	7	13	2	o	o	3	5	o	25	9
Turkey Foot Ridge	Georgetown	1	o	o	o	o	o	o	1	—	—
	San Francisco	1	o	1	1	o	2	o	2	—	—
	San Francisco / Three Circle	2	o	o	3	2	5	—	2	—	—
	Three Circle	o	1	o	2	o	3	o	1	—	—
	Georgetown / Three Circle	3	1	1	6	2	10	o	5	2	3
Williams	Early Pithouse / Georgetown	1	2	o	1	o	o	1	1	o	o
Forestdale branch											
Bear Ruin	San Francisco	3	7	o	4	o	10	1	6	>3	o
Bluff	Early Pithouse	3	7	o	o	o	4	2	o	—	o
	Georgetown	o	o	o	3	o	2	o	o	—	o
Mimbres branch											
Cuchillo	Georgetown	1	4	2	o	o	4	o	1	—	—
Galaz	San Francisco	o	o	o	2	o	2	o	1	o	o
	Three Circle	o	o	o	o	9	9	o	2	20	9
Harris Village	Georgetown	o	1	6	o	o	6	o	o	—	—
	San Francisco	o	o	o	6	o	6	o	o	—	—
	Three Circle	o	o	o	3	9	12	o	o	—	—
Mogollon Village	San Francisco	o	3	1	6	o	8	o	o	≥3	6
	Three Circle	o	o	o	o	1	1	o	1	—	—
Wind Mountain	Early Pithouse / Georgetown	1	5	1	o	o	5	o	o	o	—
	San Francisco / Three Circle	o	1	1	11	25	38	o	o	27	—
Winn Canyon	Early Pithouse	o	5	1	o	o	5	o	3	4	o
Black River / Point of Pines											
Crooked Ridge Village	San Francisco	o	o	o	1	o	1	o	o	1	o
	Circle Prairie	3	1	o	12	5	17	8	o	9	10
Nantack Village	Nantack (Circle Prairie)	o	o	o	4	4	5	1	o	4	3

Table 11.2 Mogollon Pithouse Period Great Pithouses or Community Structures with Floor Grooves

Branch	Site	Phase	Elevation	Notes
Forestdale	Bear Ruin	San Francisco	1,999 m	One unique zoomorphic or anthropomorphic "kiva" (Kiva 1) with floor groove.
Mimbres	Diablo	Georgetown	1,676–1,828 m	One bean-shaped "communal structure" (Feature 5) with floor grooves flanking the hearth; area = 31.9 m².
Mimbres	Galaz	Three Circle	1,737 m	One unique rectangular "communal structure" (Structure 73) with three log benches inset into the floor and partially plastered; area = 158.5 m²; two of the log benches more or less enclose the slab-lined box hearth, while the third is offset to the south end of the room; two "greenstones" inset into the floor and an incised arc at the rear of the structure, and a military macaw (*Ara militaris*) wrapped in turquoise beads was interred beneath one of the greenstones; a small sipapu, set forward of the central post between it and the hearth, completed the scene.
Mimbres	Saige-McFarland	Three Circle	1,397 m	One rectangular "great kiva" with typical Mimbres Three Circle phase regularity; area = 56.4 m²; three large floor grooves described as "floor vaults that surrounded the fire pit on three sides."
Mimbres	Wind Mountain	Three Circle	1,731 m	One compressed-circular or almost D-shaped "community structure" with floor grooves (House X); area = 70.5 m².
Black River	Crooked Ridge	Circle Prairie	1,798 m	One rectangular large pithouse (Pithouse 8) with floor groove; area = 25 m²; a wall niche contained a cache that included one stone hoe and 12 pestles or digging tools.
Black River	Crooked Ridge	Circle Prairie	1,798 m	Round "ceremonial" structure with floor grooves around central hearth (Pithouse 9); area = 63.6 m².
Black River	Crooked Ridge	Circle Prairie	1,798 m	Rounded rectangular "ceremonial" structure with weird floor grooves around central hearth (Pithouse 19); area = approximately 105 m².
Black River	Nantack Village	Nantack/Circle Prairie	1,841 m	Rectangular "great kiva" with an irregular east wall; narrow "floor trench" running diagonally in the northwest quadrant of the room, not in alignment with walls or any particular feature; at 140 m² it is large enough to be unusual but otherwise so unlike other "kivas" as to be unique.
Black River	Nantack Village	Nantack/Circle Prairie	1,841 m	Subrectangular "ceremonial" structure (Pithouse 10) with irregular walls and a "subfloor trench"; area = approximately 60 m²; Breternitz (1959) classified it as ceremonial because of the floor trench and its size.
Black River	Stove Canyon	Stove Canyon	1,821 m	Rectangular great pithouse (Pithouse 3) with short entrance and angled floor groove; area = 21.2 m².
Black River	Stove Canyon	Stove Canyon	1,821 m	The "great kiva"; central hearth enclosed by a continuous, rectangular floor groove; second floor groove west of the rectangular one and parallel to the west wall; area = 64.3 m²; no entrance in this house.
Cibola	LA 6083	Three Circle	—	Feature 40, a possible communal structure (greater than 40 m²), had a single "floor trench" parallel to the hearth.
Cibola/Reserve	Quemado Alegre	Early Pithouse	2,224 m	One structure (Feature 39) with a foot drum or floor trench; area = 73 m² not including the attached 18-m² antechamber.
Cibola/Reserve	Sawmill	Three Circle/Reserve	1,981 m	A large rectangular "kiva" with floor-groove "resonators" enclosing a central hearth on three sides; area = 91.4 m²; this kiva was remodeled from an earlier structure of 75.6 m²; the decorated wares are dominated by Mimbres series types (especially Mimbres Boldface Black-on-white), not Cibola White Ware types.
Cibola/Reserve	SU	Early Pithouse	1,962 m	One large bean-shaped structure (Pithouse A) with floor grooves at the perimeter; area = approximately 75 m².
Cibola/Reserve	Turkey Foot Ridge	Three Circle	1,959 m	One rounded rectangular pit structure (Pithouse K) with floor grooves surrounding a central hearth and a partial perimeter bench; area = roughly 47 m² not including the bench.

quickly evolved into "any structure that stands out from the rest" (1988:224).

Lekson made other observations about Anasazi kivas that apply as well to Mogollon kivas: (1) alleged Basketmaker/Pueblo III kivas vary greatly in construction elements through time, and (2) some Basketmaker/Pueblo III kivas may have been large domiciles. Similarly, things that archaeologists have called Mogollon kivas vary greatly in detail, even when the sample is limited to those that have some kind of floor trench. In addition, almost all of the "kivas" listed in table 11.2 had domestic refuse on the floor, and many Georgetown phase kivas are within a standard deviation or two of the mean Georgetown phase pithouse size. Functionally speaking, one could argue that they are just "great pithouses" or at least that they were dual-purpose residence-kivas, as suggested by Anyon and LeBlanc (1980:272). Indeed, of the entire suite of Mogollon kivas discussed in this report, only Galaz Room 73 (Jenks called it the "Kiva of the Parrot") and Bear Ruin Kiva 1 (which might be zoomorphic or anthropomorphic) truly stand out from their immediate or regional surroundings.

Coresident Aliens

Table 11.2 does not mention the "ball court" from the Stove Canyon site in the Black River branch. Neely (1974) attributed the ball court, the existence of several Hohokam-style pithouses, and buffwares to the presence of a small, coresident Hohokam enclave. Stove Canyon joins Lee Village (Bussey 1973, 1975) among later (Three Circle phase and contemporaries) pithouse villages with evidence of guests from different archaeological culture areas. Lee Village included several cremations with buffware ceramics.

Were I forced to attribute the presence of Hohokam in the Cibola or Mimbres branches to something other than good manners, I would suspect that the intensity of interaction between Mogollon and the Hohokam increased as demand for Pacific coast shell items grew (see Vokes and Gregory, chap. 17, this vol.). Anyon and LeBlanc note that there are similarities in size and artwork between Mogollon and Hohokam palettes but described the thin, bordered palettes from Galaz as "Mimbres palettes" (1984:272), specifically contrasting them with the Santa Cruz phase palettes from Snaketown; clearly, they see the similarities as evidence of a parallel development in stone tool technology in the Mimbres Mogollon and Hohokam areas rather than as evidence of diffusion.

The presence of some Hohokam elements in Black River and Mimbres branch sites suggests that Mogollon society was neither closed nor particularly insular during the Pithouse periods. While this observation does not directly address the ancestral connection between Mogollon and Zuni, it does indicate that conditions promoting the linguistic isolation of Zuni (see Hill, chap. 3, this vol.; Upham et al. 1994:187) were not prevalent prior to the twelfth century AD. If that is true, then several possibilities follow. One possibility is that *if* any branch of the Mogollon area is ancestral to Zuni, *then* the Black River and Mimbres branches are ruled out as candidates. An alternative possibility is that the Zuni language is one result of a late (late twelfth century or more recent) "revitalization" movement at Zuni, marked by the erection of linguistic and social barriers to interaction with strangers. For example, Zuni language might be viewed as a contrivance or as a linguistic subset of "whatever the Mogo-

llon spoke" that was expanded after the twelfth century by one Mogollon group (but see Hill, chap. 3, this vol.). It may also be a language artificially redefined to eliminate "foreign" linguistic elements.

Warfare

Any study of ethnic isolation or boundary maintenance demands a discussion of the role of warfare in isolating populations and solidifying boundaries. Steve LeBlanc and I have agreed to disagree on the importance of warfare during the Mogollon Pithouse periods (Diehl and LeBlanc 2001:31–33). LeBlanc views the hilltop locations of most Early Pithouse period (AD 200–550) villages as evidence of the threat of conflict and adds that the cobble alignments present in a few cases are remnant defensive walls. I look at Mogollon hilltops and wonder how the several hundred warriors required to defend the perimeters of these hills would have lived in the 5–20 pithouses that might have been concurrently occupied on most sites. To the Early Pithouse villages we may add Georgetown phase (AD 550–700) sites, since many of these are located on hilltops. By the Three Circle phase (AD 825/850–1000) Mogollon pithouse villages are more commonly found on river terraces than on hilltops, so either the threat of warfare subsided or else hilltops ceased to be valuable to the defense. Direct evidence of warfare, in the form of bodies with embedded arrowheads or healed forearm fractures, has not been observed. The disagreement as to why Early Pithouse villages were located on hilltops may, however, be moot. Two recent surveys have questioned whether or not the temporal association between terraces and hilltops is as strong as the Mimbres Foundation scholars have suggested (Linse 1999; Stokes and Roth 1999).

Subsistence

Mogollon pithouse dwellers were at least partially dependent on cultigens throughout the Pithouse periods. Unfortunately, so few sites have been recently excavated that direct studies of osteofaunal and flotation samples do not yet allow the detailed study of changes in the use of wild and domesticated foods through the first millennium. Enough evidence has been collected to suggest that maize was important and that maize agriculture was augmented by extensive foraging for wild plants and animals. Furthermore, indirect evidence in the form of studies of ground stone tools and chipped stone tools supports the contention that the intensity of agriculture increased during the second half of the millennium.

Whether or not pithouse villagers relied primarily on cultigens is an open question. Ubiquities suggest that maize was at least important. Maize occurred in Early Pithouse period flotation samples from the Duncan site (70 percent), McAnally (50 percent), Quemado Alegre (73 percent), Promontory, and SU (100 percent in samples recovered by Ray Mauldin and Chip Wills in the late 1980s and early 1990s). Munford et al. (1994:171) noted that maize and juniper seeds were found in samples from the Cuchillo site, a multicomponent Early Pithouse period and Georgetown phase site along Cuchillo Negro east of the Black Range.

Turning to later sites, Gilman's excavations at the Mogollon Village, which is primarily a San Francisco phase site, turned up maize in six out of seven tested features (Dean and Powell 1991; McBride 1991). The Mimbres Foundation excavations in Three Circle phase structures at Galaz turned up maize in five of eight (ubiquity 63 percent) features (Minnis 1984). Three Circle phase pithouses at Wind Mountain produced large quantities of maize in 63 percent (24 of 38) of sampled houses (Miksicek and Fall 1996:298–299). Other cultigens include beans and squash. At all sites from which flotation samples were collected, for all time periods, wild taxa include the usual weedy opportunists such as goosefoot, pigweed, and assorted composites. Grass grains are found at sites that are intensively sampled, and juniper and pinyon seeds are often found at sites located in higher elevations; walnuts and acorns are also intermittently found.

Studies of ground stone tools (Diehl 1996a; Hard 1990; Lancaster 1984; Mauldin 1991) show that grain-grinding tools evolved from a generalized tool kit to a combination of specialized and generalized tools. The trend has been attributed to increased dependence on maize beginning during the Georgetown or San Francisco phase and increasing thereafter. Early Pithouse period villages yield shallow basin metates, small round manos, mortars, and pestles. As most of the early investigators like Haury and Martin noticed, these tools do not differ much from Desert Archaic milling tools. During the late Georgetown or early San Francisco phases, however, milling technology evolved into a specialized form involving oblong manos and trough metates and a generalized form that retained the old basin metate and small mano tools. Through time the proportional frequency of trough metates to all metates increased, and the trough metate became the dominant type during the Three Circle phase. Maize-grinding manos increased in surface area—a change that is, by dint of carefully reasoned middle-range theory, design theory, and an overwhelming amount of supporting cross-cultural data, attributed to the need to process maize more efficiently. Basin metates and their manos were retained for general purpose non-maize-grinding tasks.

Animal foraging contributed heavily to pithouse villagers' diets throughout the first millennium. There is evidence for increased consumption of small game through time, with some evidence for statistically significant diachronic changes, at least in the Mimbres Valley (Cannon 2001). Early Pithouse period sites have greater variation in the relative emphasis on large as opposed to small game. In the original excavations at Bear Ruin, the Bluff site, Promontory, the SU site, and Turkey Foot Ridge deer-bone fragments were the most frequently recovered taxon; the deposits were not screened, however, so the faunal inventory is biased toward larger specimens. At Quemado Alegre artiodactyl and large mammals together comprised 22 percent of the assemblage, rabbits and small mammals 38 percent, and other rodents 22 percent (Akins 1998:451). At the Duncan site jackrabbit and cottontail dominated the assemblage, but 43 percent of the identified specimens were from other animals such as antelopes, dogs, and small rodents (Lightfoot 1984:133). In the Early Pithouse and Georgetown phase deposits at the Cuchillo site, analysts reported that rabbits were the majority of specimens, with large mammals following (Munford et al. 1994:146–154). Mimbres Foundation archaeologists simply did not find much at McAnally or Thompson (Diehl and LeBlanc 2001). In Three Circle phase pithouses at Galaz lagomorphs comprised 59 percent of the assemblage and artiodactyls another 14 percent. The rest of the assemblage included a wide variety of small animals, each recovered with low frequencies—small rodents, snakes, undifferentiated birds, dogs or wolves, foxes, skunks, badgers, fish, and the like (Anyon and LeBlanc 1984:216). The same general pattern—an assemblage dominated by cottontails, jackrabbits, and deer but augmented by a wide array of less-frequent taxa—was observed for Three Circle phase contexts at Wind Mountain (McKusick 1996; Olsen and Olsen 1996).

At this juncture it seems appropriate to raise a concern about the notion of the Mogollon as a "montane" culture. The claim is at best inaccurate, and the idea may well be a red herring that has drawn more attention and used up more time and gray matter than it deserves. If any of us were to visit every Mogollon pithouse village, we would observe several things. First, we would note that, in general, people living in the Black River, Cibola, and Forestdale branches more often found themselves in close association with a pinyon or juniper tree than people living in the Mimbres branch. Second, we would note that at many Mimbres branch sites we would often find ourselves breathing the refreshing scents of the gymnosperms, since many Mimbres branch sites are well within the pinyon-juniper zone, even though the archaeological sites may not have pines or junipers growing on them. Third, at almost any pithouse village in the Mogollon area, in any branch, if we care to walk a few kilometers we can move into a fundamentally different biotic province (Brown 1994). I have explored this problem in somewhat greater detail elsewhere (Diehl and LeBlanc 2001:9–17).

The implications are quite simple. The Cibola branch (and only the Cibola branch) stands out as a "montane-adapted branch" if and only if we assume that the subsistence economy of any given hamlet or village only extended to a radius of a few kilometers around each site. In other words, if we embrace the notion of the Mogollon as a mountain-adapted people, then we automatically make assumptions about land-use strategies that portray even the earliest pithouse villagers as either territorially circumscribed or at least quite restricted in their movement. The currently available evidence does not support such a model of prehistoric land use, and most theoretical discussions of Pithouse period land use assume greater amounts of logistical or residential mobility (Gilman 1987; Wills 1988b).

Long-Distance Trade and Exotics and the Mimbres Ceremonial Phenomenon

The movement of goods through trade or exchange is evident from the earliest occupations. Early Pithouse period sites like SU usually produce some Pacific coast shell fragments, most often *Glycymeris* bracelets or fragments thereof (Diehl 1994). They are not common, however, in any of the Mogollon branches prior to the San Francisco phase.[6] At that time, greater quantities of shell begin to occur in mortuary contexts throughout the area.

A surge in regional exchange occurred during the Three Circle phase, primarily in the Mimbres branch. *Glycymeris* bracelets are far more common in Mimbres branch burials than they are anywhere else in the Mogollon region. Lee Village has manufacturing debris from the production of pendants, beads in various stages of manufacture, and plenty of *Glycymeris* bracelets. The occurrence of *Oliva* and *Olivella* beads increased during the Three Circle phase in the Mimbres branch. In addition to the increase in the flow of exotic shell, Mimbres branch pithouse dwellers brought in exotic birds and copper bells. Hargrave's (1970) overview of macaw occurrence indicates an arc-shaped distribution that touches on the Black River area (at Point of Pines Pueblo) but that largely bypasses the Cibola and Forestdale areas. A similar pattern may be observed in the distribution of copper bells: only three are reported from the Cibola branch (two at Kuykendall and one at Apache Creek). In contrast, they have been found throughout the Mimbres branch, and they also occurred at Point of Pines Pueblo and Turkey Creek Pueblo in the Black River branch (Vargas 1995). At Lee Village several cremations with red-on-buff ceramics were identified, suggesting the actual presence of Hohokam groups (perhaps as mercantile middlemen). Red-on-buff potsherds occur in low frequencies in many Mimbres branch Three Circle phase hamlets, but they are rare in the other Mogollon branches.

Two other phenomena occurred during the Three Circle phase and primarily in the Mimbres branch that suggest that a radical change in the alignment of regional networks and social organization may have been initiated during the ninth century AD. Along with increased imports of exotics, one finds the construction of the first really kivalike ceremonial structures at Cameron Creek Village, Galaz (Communal Structure 42A and Communal Structure 73; see Anyon and LeBlanc 1984:121–132), and Wind Mountain. They are several standard deviations larger than the typical 17.5-m² Three Circle phase domestic house. The Galaz community structures are truly remarkable. Feature 42 had six small sand-filled sipapus (two with white sand, one with gray-yellow sand, and four with gray sand) and a large floor box filled with clean sand. Artifacts included several stone bowls with painted exterior surfaces, a carved shell effigy, a green-painted stone frog with beads and crystals, and a vessel containing a *Glycymeris* bracelet, turquoise, and shell and stone beads and pendants. All of these "exotic" artifacts were sealed under the floor with plaster, as were two of the sand-filled sipapus. None of the artifacts occurred with burials. Feature 73 was discussed earlier. House AK is the Three Circle phase entry from Wind Mountain, but I have not discussed it because it lacked floor grooves.

Finally, there is the development of something that seems to me like a sort of mysticism involving animal forms. At Wind Mountain, Cameron Creek Village, and Galaz one finds numerous animal burials, including dogs, bears, thick-billed parrots, various hawks, macaws, turkeys, and, at Wind Mountain, a golden eagle. High frequencies of animal burials do not occur in the peripheral Mogollon branches, although they are more common in the Black River branch than in the Cibola branch. The only remarkable ninth–tenth-century ceremonial structure outside of the Mimbres branch is the zoomorphic or anthropomorphic structure at Bear Ruin. I regard development of the "Mimbres Phenomenon" (the population aggregations, the plazas, the zoomorphic designs on vessels, and the highly ritualistic mortuary treatment) as an event that is first identifiable archaeologically during the Three Circle phase in the Mimbres branch.

Summary of the Mogollon Pithouse Periods

For most of the first millennium AD the Mogollon culture area encompassed the Black River, Cibola, Forestdale, and Mimbres branches with a remarkable homogeneity. The only observable differences prior to the ninth century involved domestic architecture; Mimbres branch pit-houses exhibited a consistency in their attributes and construction that is lacking in the peripheral. Benches and antechambers were more common outside of the Mimbres branch. Ceremonial structures, if there were any, took the form of very large pithouses. In all branches these tended to be round or bean shaped. Floor grooves were not a feature in all ceremonial structures, but ceremonial structures with floor grooves were present in all Mogollon branches. Subsistence economies among all the Mimbres branches followed a general trend of increasing reliance on cultigens and small game. The "montane" character of Mogollon occupations has been greatly exaggerated, since the occupants of most sites in most branches had access to a wide variety of resources from multiple biotic provinces.

Differentiation between the Mogollon branches is apparent during and after the ninth century (including the Three Circle, Circle Prairie, and Nantack phases). In the Mimbres branch the pace of extraregional trade increased, and there is recurring tangible evidence of contact with the Hohokam. In the Mimbres branch a new kind of ceremonialism occurred that involved *obvious* kivas, elaborate mortuary treatment for humans and some animals, and the use of exogenous goods like macaws, shell, and copper bells. In the Mimbres branch the pithouses assumed a formality and conformity of shape that the other branches lacked. While the Classic Mimbres phase (AD 1000–1100/1150) pueblo occupation in the Mimbres branch is described by enthusiasts as something of a "golden age," it represents the final expression of a trend of increasing trade, exchange, interaction, and religious and artistic expression already evident during the preceding Three Circle phase.

Pre-Pottery Occupations in the Mogollon Area

Yet another renaissance in southwestern archaeology is occurring, and the focus of intense research is the Late Archaic or Early Agricultural period from roughly 2000 BC to AD 150. Early Agricultural period sites are interesting because they bear on the argument of in situ cultural evolution vs. migratory incursion concurrent with the introduction of maize in the Southwest. If identifying the relevant markers for ethnicity is difficult for Mogollon sites, it is virtually impossible for early maize sites. In general, early maize sites seem to have little in common apart from being early and having maize.

On the Colorado Plateau recent excavations of Basketmaker II (1000/500 BC–AD 150) settlements in the Chuska Valley have yielded cultigens in addition to wild foods. Domesticates included maize and squash or gourds, and wild foods included pine nuts, grasses, yucca and cactus fruits, and a variety of annuals (Kearns and McVickar 1996:12). Irrigation ditches that are approximately 2,000 years old have been discovered in two locations near Zuni Pueblo (Damp 2001, chap. 8, this vol.), making them coeval with Early Agricultural period or Basketmaker II sites elsewhere.

Late Archaic or Early Agricultural period sites with ancient maize have been found in the Chinle Valley in northeastern Arizona, and these specimens have been radiocarbon-dated to about 3400–3000 B.P. (Gilpin 1994). The Lukuchukai site had three small pithouses, and the Salina Springs site had one small pithouse. These structures are comparable in scale to Cienega phase and San Pedro phase pithouses in Tucson or perhaps slightly larger, but they lack the interior complexity with regard to postholes and bell-shaped pits. Several projectile points were recovered. They are expanding stemmed, corner-notched points, but they are unlike those from late Mogollon sites and no more than casually similar to Cienega and San Pedro points (but see Matson, chap. 7, this vol.).

Work in the Tucson area has resulted in substantial excavations at six large sites, five of which have substantial residential components. They all have maize. Los Pozos, a Late Cienega phase site, yielded Type 3a notched awls (Gregory and Waters 2001:154). Other potentially diagnostic oddities of Early Agricultural period sites include stone balls (Diehl 1996b), chipped and polished stone cruciforms (Ferg 1998:559–565), and clay figurines with big posteriors and braided hair. Pacific coast shell occurs intermittently in Cienega phase sites, and some sites have yielded fragments of *Glycymeris*. Mortuary practices are most commonly flexed inhumations. The ground stone tool technology is indistinguishable from the old Desert Archaic suite—basin metates and small manos. The cruciforms are interesting, since their "home range" encompasses northern Chihuahua and Sonora and southern Arizona and New Mexico (Ferg 1998).

In the greater Mogollon area there is little information from open-air sites that date to the Early Agricultural period. Wills (1996:337–338) tested portions of the SU site and obtained a Cienega phase radiocarbon date from a small structure and associated roasting pit. Bat Cave (Wills 1988a) and Tularosa Cave (Martin et al. 1952:483) had preceramic levels with maize. Reports of Pithouse period sites with enigmatically small, shallow pithouses that lack ramps are rather common; some structures of this kind may have been excavated at Cameron Creek Village

(Bradfield 1931) and at the Cuchillo site (Schutt et al. 1994). "Aceramic pithouse sites" are suspected on the knolls and ridges near Duck Creek in the Gila/Cliff area (Chapman et al. 1985) but have not been excavated. Modest excavations have been undertaken at two sites southwest of Silver City (Turnbow 2000) in the heart of what later became the Mimbres branch.

The Forest Home Site (LA 78089)

This site was situated on a high ridge that straddles the heads of two intermittent drainages. Archaeologists excavated two Cienega phase pithouses and one Mogollon Early Pithouse period structure with good accelerator mass spectrometry (AMS) dates from maize cupules in all three structures. Although the structures were neither substantial nor large, one was occupied long enough to possibly undergo remodeling (Turnbow 2000:67). Apart from early dates and the absence of ceramics, the two Early Agricultural period structures (Features 6 and 33) would not be remarkable in any Mogollon Early Pithouse period site. They are round, have internal posts and central hearths, and lack ramps; however, ramps are not a *required* characteristic of Mogollon pithouses.

The artifact assemblages are unremarkable. There were no awls of any kind, and the projectile points were identified as Cienega and San Pedro points. Most of the animal bones were unidentified, but of the identified bones the proportion of artiodactyls was greater than that of lagomorphs (Turnbow and Smith 2000:504), suggesting that deer were very important in the subsistence economy. Like most Early Agricultural period sites (Diehl 1997; Huckell 2000), the flotation samples yielded a very diverse assemblage.

The Wood Canyon Site (LA 99631)

This Cienega phase site was also located on a ridgetop. Four pithouses were excavated. Of these, one (Feature 80) was protohistoric, with a calibrated AMS date range of AD 1525–1680 from a charred juniper seed (Turnbow and Smith 2000:136). Another structure (Feature 117) was severely bioturbated and undatable. The remaining two were widely separated in time—165 BC–AD 120 (Late Cienega phase or Early Pithouse period) for Feature 28, and 820–540 BC (Early Cienega phase) for Feature 100. Both lacked interior features. As with the Forest Home site, the faunal assemblage was dominated by unidentified mammals, of which 30 percent fell into the medium-large category; recognizable artiodactyls made up 4 percent of the assemblage and lagomorphs 6.8 percent. The plant assemblage was diverse and included maize. Two awls were recovered, one broken and not assignable and the other nondiagnostic. Marine shell (Duncan 2000:500–501) disc beads were recovered from an extramural inhumation (Feature 159) that provided a date of 810–525 BC on a burned juniper seed, making it an Early Cienega phase burial (Turnbow and Smith 2000:151).

Subsistence

It is something of a stretch to speak of the generalized subsistence system that prevailed during the Early Agricultural period. There are not enough cases from different regions to generalize about the Southwest as an entirety or about regions specifically —except for, perhaps, the Tucson Basin. A few facts are, however, readily apparent.

Maize was important in the prehistoric subsistence economy from very early in the sequence. It is typically found in 70 percent or more of sampled features, and some assemblages have also included beans (Karen Adams, personal communication 2001; I tentatively identified a half-cotyledon from a San Pedro phase deposit at Las Capas), and "cucurbit" seeds have been found in some sites. Whether the latter were domesticated or wild remains to be established. The presence of irrigation ditches in Early Agricultural period contexts both in Tucson and near Zuni shows that the knowledge of intensification techniques was widespread, possibly throughout the Greater Southwest. This fact may ultimately provide a clue about ethnic links between early farmers and immigration, since the irrigation canals in Tucson are as old as any yet known in Mexico (Mabry 2002:178).

Although crops were important, it is also clear that wild foods were very important as well. They may even have been more important than crops, since the ubiquities of small starchy seeds are quite high and since the diet breadth of Early Agricultural period forager-farmers is much greater than the diet breadth of Hohokam intensive farmers in the Tucson area (Diehl 1997; Gregory and Diehl 2002). Osteofaunal studies also show that diet breadth was greater in the early maize sites (Diehl and Waters 2005). I attribute the greater diet breadth of Early Agricultural period folks to relatively high losses of grain in storage, low crop yields from early maize, and the need to mitigate these problems by buffering risk through the use of wild foods.

There is much to be said about Early Agricultural period sites in Tucson, but their relevance to the issue at hand is questionable. David Gregory demonstrated convincingly that Early Agricultural period settlements in Tucson, despite their vast size, were hamlets that were occupied by at

most a few families (Gregory and Diehl 2002). Mabry (1998) has argued that a large structure at the Santa Cruz Bend site represents a ceremonial or communal structure. The large Cienega phase house at Santa Cruz Bend does not, however, resemble the "communal structures" at Early Pithouse period Mogollon sites. It may not be safe to extend inferences about Tucson Basin Early Agricultural period social organization to Mogollon-area contemporaries.

Discussion

Materially and ethnically speaking, there is no basis to link the New Mexico Route 90 sites with the sites in the Tucson Basin or to link them with the Basketmaker II/Early Agricultural period sites on the Colorado Plateau. About all that Early Agricultural period sites share in common is that the remnants of their houses are archaeologically detectable, their houses were small in comparison with later sites, and they all contained maize. Houses along the Santa Cruz River floodplain often have large intramural pits, bell shaped in cross section, and these do not occur in the Route 90 duo or in the Colorado Plateau area. Cruciforms, stone balls, and ceramic figurines were absent from the Forest Home and Wood Canyon sites, although stone balls have been recovered from various Mogollon cave sites (Martin et al. 1952); these artifacts were not recovered from the Colorado Plateau sites. About all that the Tucson Basin Cienega phase sites have in common with the NM Route 90 sites are projectile points that fall into a corner-notched group that strongly resembles San Pedro and Cienega points described by Sliva (1999). The NM Route 90 assemblages are otherwise so generic that they would blend in well with any Late Archaic assem-

blage from the various Mogollon cave sites, and the NM Route 90 pithouses are unlike the Cienega phase pithouses in the Tucson Basin.

Early Cultigens in the Southwest: Migration or Diffusion?

It has long been known that the dietary mainstays of prehistoric southwesterners included a variety of crops: maize (*Zea mays*), varieties of beans (*Phaseolus* spp.), and varieties of squash or pumpkin (*Cucurbita* spp.) are the most ancient of these. Cotton (*Gossypium* sp.), chiles (*Capsicum* spp.), and other plants followed somewhat later (Ford 1981). All were developed as crops in Mexico or points farther to the south (Ford 1981; Manglesdorf 1974). In terms of calories, the Upper Sonoran agricultural complex of maize, beans, and squash was the most important and, used together with the greens of wild plants, provided a nutritionally complete diet.

The oldest undisputed dates on cultigens place the entrance of maize into the American Southwest during the second millennium BC, that is, sometime between 3,000 and 4,000 years ago. Las Capas, for example, produced a 3670 ± 40 B.P. AMS date on a maize cupule (Annick Lascaux, personal communication 2000), and the Sweetwater Locus at Los Pozos yielded several maize specimens that were at least three millennia old (Gregory 1999:118–119). One half of a possible bean cotyledon from Las Capas returned an AMS date of 2960 ± 40 B.P. (Beta 140981). It is possible but not yet certain that maize and beans were introduced together to the American Southwest rather than serially, as the evidence once suggested (Ford 1981). There are also intermittent cases of comparably old cucurbit seeds (it has not been ascertained whether these were wild or domesticated taxa) and cotton pollen from other southwestern localities. It is possible that maize, beans, squash, and cotton were introduced together as a "crop complex" (Carter 1945; Linton 1924) prior to 1200 BC.

Obviously, if maize and other crops were domesticated in central Mexico and points farther south, then knowledge of these plants and the techniques used to grow them spread into the American Southwest by diffusion or migration (see also Hill, chap. 3, Gregory and Nials, chap. 5, and Gregory and Wilcox, chap. 20, this vol.). Trade, exchange, intermarriage, or even mere socializing can be a powerful mechanism for the diffusion of knowledge across space and time. Migration, however, requires the physical movement of people from one area into another area. Obviously, the processes are not necessarily mutually exclusive: a small group of émigrés may easily plant the requisite knowledge among an indigenous population.

The most commonly used model for the movement of agriculture in the Southwest was for many years a diffusionist one. Indigenous foragers (the Cochise culture) already living in Arizona and New Mexico came into contact with farmers in northern Chihuahua and Sonora who in turn learned the tricks of the trade from farmers farther south and so on (Haury 1962:114). In contrast, Michael Berry (1982) argued that the Southwest's earliest farmers were emigrants out of Mexico. Matson (1991, chap. 7, this vol.) noted that Berry's model is plausible if the timing of the proposed migration is shifted to approximately the San Pedro phase. Huckell (1990:374) embraced a migration model based on various factors such as the speed of the appearance of maize in the older southwestern contexts and its ubiq-

uity in sites. In a classic understatement he noted, however, that "current archaeological knowledge does not present an easy choice between these two alternative models" (Huckell 1990:380).

Diffusion seems to be a necessary consequence of any discussion that explores the reasons why prehistoric southern Arizonans made the "decision to integrate agriculture into the economy" (Huckell 1995:137). In contrast, to a certain extent, in any migration model the simplest *proximal* explanation for the adoption of agriculture in an area where it was not previously used is that the decision to farm was made *elsewhere* under circumstances that did not necessarily have anything to do with the sociocultural or environmental realities of southern Arizona and that early agriculture in Arizona simply reflected localization and modification of established agricultural methods. In such circumstances the important anthropological questions focus not on why agriculture was practiced but, instead, why people chose to immigrate and how their use of agriculture may have changed as a consequence.

In all cases one must bear in mind that the question of diffusion vs. migration is one that must be answered on a valley-by-valley basis; if San Pedro phase farmers migrated from Sonora into southern Arizona and did not further migrate into the Colorado Plateau or Mogollon Rim, then the diffusion model and corollary questions may still be addressed by studying the archaeology of indigenous foragers in the latter geographic provinces. Wills's (1995) study examining the potential impact of maize in such contact situations represents an important contribution not only because of the theoretical contributions that it makes but also because of the recognition that a single explanation for the introduction of maize does not neces-

sarily work for all localities in the Southwest.

Sky Islands during the Early Agricultural Period: Variations on a Theme

The immigration vs. diffusion argument is a critical one for those who view Zuni as the direct descendants of an isolated population of montane foragers (see Gregory and Wilcox, chap. 10, this vol.). I can imagine scenarios in which the sky island model played out during the Early Agricultural period. In one, most of Arizona and western New Mexico (west of the Rio Grande) were inhabited by a population of Desert Archaic foragers (as defined by Jennings 1964) whose ancestors arrived in the area during the Middle or Early Archaic periods (8500–3000 BC). During the Early Agricultural period Uto-Aztecan farmers arrived and began to drive out the Desert Archaic populations, of which the ancestral Zuni were a part. As Uto-Aztecans expanded northward and upslope along the major drainages they repeatedly pushed groups into higher and more remote locations. In time, the ancestral Zuni began to farm as a response to competition for wild resources and also because maize was a subsistence strategy worthy of pursuit.

If we assume that the Mogollon in some way represent the ancestral Zuni, then sometime between about 300 BC and AD 450 population boundaries stabilized. Perhaps the energy of the Uto-Aztecan wave was spent and diffused in southern Arizona and New Mexico, subsiding to mere ripples lapping against the foothills of the Mogollon Rim. Ultimately, a large area of Desert Archaic territory was occupied by Uto-Aztecan groups and the acculturated indigenes, except where the ancestral Zuni held out as a distinct ethnic group. The Zuni "holdout area" initially encompassed all of the Mogollon region as Uto-Aztecans spilled around both flanks of the Mogollon region, absorbing the Desert Archaic folks of the Colorado Plateau into a cultural blend that rapidly became Basketmaker II–III.

It is also important to consider that the prehistory of the Zuni and most other southwestern groups in New Mexico and Arizona may be very complex geographically, spatially, and temporally. Things may be a lot less linear or local than either the volume editors or the linguistic models assume. For the sake of argument I will offer another scenario. In it I imagine that the ancestral Zuni were themselves one group among a great multiethnic northward migration that occurred around the time that cultigens entered the Southwest. A piece of a population from homelands in the Sierra Madre Occidental (perhaps from the vicinity of the Sierra Huachinera eastward to the area of Paquimé) was driven northward ahead of a wave front of Uto-Aztecan-speaking farmers. These migrating ancestral Zuni already had knowledge of maize cultivation in riskier montane environments. They were hustled along into and out of the low desert areas of Arizona, southern New Mexico, and northern Chihuahua by the Uto-Aztecans pushing up behind them until they finally settled down in the Mogollon Highlands. In this model the ancestral Zuni are not related to the Desert Archaic culture but are themselves immigrants who arrived in the area around the time that maize was introduced (see also Webster, chap. 16, this vol.).

In this scenario related people in the Sierra Madre Occidental were absorbed or destroyed by any of the major upheavals and reorganizations that occurred in Mexico from the thirteenth through the eighteenth centuries, if not before then. Likewise,

extant southwestern Desert Archaic groups were driven out by both the ancestral Zuni and Uto-Aztecans. This scenario has some support in studies of the designs on Classic Mimbres vessels and also in rock art from the northern Chihuahua area and the Mogollon area (Shafer 1995:42–44).

Continuing with the scenario, it is envisioned that a pause in Uto-Aztecan expansion occurred at the boundaries of the traditional Mogollon branches immediately prior to the Early Pithouse period. In these more montane settings the ancestral Zuni's knowledge of upland environments and the ways to integrate maize into upland subsistence systems led to material culture and settlement patterns that archaeologists recognize as the Mogollon culture. A sustainable and strong suite of subsistence and settlement practices allowed the Mogollon to control the low desert and midelevation grasslands in southern New Mexico along the Gila and Mimbres drainages.

Conclusions and Issues for Research

In this overview of Mogollon Pithouse periods and the Early Agricultural period I have suggested that there is little that distinguishes any of the branches of the Mogollon culture area prior to around AD 825/850—the start of the Three Circle phase in the Mimbres branch. Mogollon culture prior to AD 825, like the Early Agricultural period occupations that preceded it, is rather generic. The focus on ceremonial structures with floor grooves is interesting (Gregory and Wilcox, chap. 10, this vol.) but does not allow us to narrow the boundaries or extent of a ceremonial complex to any subset of Mogollon branches. They are found throughout the Mogollon area at high elevations and at low elevations.

If there is any basis to differentiate between Mogollon branches, that differentiation is first recognizable during the Three Circle phase, and it distinguishes the Mimbres branch somewhat from the Black River, Cibola, and Forestdale branches. The Mimbres branch participated in a regional exchange or trade system that directly or indirectly extended to the Gulf of California and involved products from the south (copper bells and macaws) and the southwest (marine shell jewelry) (see Vokes and Gregory, chap. 17, this vol.). Three Circle phase sites in the Mimbres branch can be huge. Eighty or so pithouses were excavated at Lee Village, and these occupied about one third of the site area. Very large Late Pithouse period villages have been identified in surveys of the middle to upper Gila (Chapman et al. 1985). Although large pithouse villages have been found in other Mogollon branches, the really large late sites are in the Mimbres branch.

What do these observations tell us about the origins of Zuni in general or the sky island hypothesis specifically? Frankly, I am not certain that knowledge of these data provides any better resolution on these issues. The problems in resolving questions about the origins of Zuni or anyone else for that matter are problems of middle-range theory and scale. Address these problems, and the investigation will eventually yield more conclusive results as to the origins of Zuni.

One of the major problems that must be addressed is that archaeologists lack a reliable method for identifying ethnic groups in the archaeological record. We are *very* good at it when we have ethnographic or historic documentation that gives us details of worldviews, habits, and identifying characteristics that allow us to identify material hallmarks of ethnic groups. Based on such information we may, through the application of direct analogy, extend our recognition a few hundred years into prehistoric times. For older deposits we rely primarily on the distributions of potsherds and architecture. Potsherds, when properly studied, can tell us much about where pots were made. But are they *always* (or even *usually*) markers of ethnicity? Of language barriers?

In addition, I do not share the conviction that architectural traits are very useful markers of ethnic heterogeneity. Architecture responds to function and use every bit as much as it conforms to ideals. The very rapid transition from pithouses to pueblos in the Mogollon branches is proof that architecture was not particularly conservative in the face of other changes. I am not at all convinced that merely identifying more and more artifacts with more complicated or detailed typological systems will allow us to claim with greater authority that we know anything about ethnicity or languages; however, we will certainly be able to track "differences" better than if we merely study architecture, potsherds, and ceremonial structures.

For the foregoing reasons I likewise doubt the utility of the "phase" concept for any purpose other than chopping up time into manageable intervals when reliable direct-dating techniques may not be applied. For recognizing ethnicity it certainly helps to have as complete a picture of the material record as possible. The "ideal database" that I alluded to at the beginning of this chapter would be a start. It also helps to have the participation of linguists, biological anthropologists, and especially tribal members. There may indeed be artifact classes that are ethnically distinctive, and tribal members may contribute greatly to the discussion. With

this volume we have made a good beginning at recognizing some of the parameters that are pertinent to the question of the Mogollon-Zuni connection.

The second major problem is the selection of an appropriate geographic scale. It is probably a common impression—almost a cliché— that the prehistoric Southwest is very messy. Southwesterners were mobile in space and time. Areas were abandoned or reorganized multiple times. The intensity and orientation of contacts within and between culture areas fluctuated through time. For example, Mimbreños probably started participating in regional trade systems through contact with the Hohokam, but the imagery on Classic Mimbres pots may indicate that the Mimbreños bypassed the Hohokam during the eleventh and twelfth centuries; certainly, the copper bells and macaws originated from somewhere other than southern Arizona.

With such a messy material past we must remain open to the idea that acculturation, isolation, immigration, and diffusion were processes that occurred throughout the Greater Southwest. These processes may not have occurred in a linear fashion, at a constant rate, or in a consistent fashion between different branches. "Sky islands" may ultimately prove to be a powerful concept for understanding changes in the montane regions of the Southwest; however, geographic isolation is likely only one contributing factor that affected culture change in a very complicated set of ethnic and environmental interactions throughout the Southwest.

Notes

1. A word about figure 11.1. These are the names that have been used, not names that I advocate. Simplification and convenience argue for a single sequence

for all Upland Mogollon branches (see Diehl and LeBlanc 2001); but since these names are, of necessity, used in text, the original phase systematics are presented here as a reference tool for the reader.

2. There is no question that Haury envisioned the Mogollon culture as ancestral to the Mimbres culture in the Mimbres Valley and upper San Francisco River areas at least, even if they were later heavily "influenced" or even swamped by contact with other groups. Haury wrote:

> The identification of two villages [Harris Village and Mogollon Village] with the Basket-maker-Pueblo, on the one hand, and the Hohokam, on the other, would have been impossible without unduly stretching the definitions of those cultures. The material at hand is therefore regarded as the manifestation of a third and fundamental group which has been called the Mogollon Culture.... Furthermore, just how the Mimbreños came by their distinctive pottery has always been a moot point. This report on the investigations of these two villages will be found to have a direct bearing on some of these questions [1936a:2–3].

In his sequence of Mogollon culture history Haury specifically included the Georgetown, San Francisco, Three Circle, and *Classic Mimbres* (1936a:3; emphasis added). Thus, Mogollon clearly had a surface pueblo component, the Classic Mimbres phase, at least in these early writings.

3. Martin wrote: "Now that more raw data have been assembled, it will be possible to make a few conjectures concerning the origin, growth, and development of the Mogollon culture and its relation to earlier and later cultures. Certainly we can delineate one earlier aspect of it and can set forth the characteristic or predominating traits of this early period—the Pine Lawn Phase" (1943:113).

4. Note that this is now generally recognized as the direction in which one transitions into the Jornada Mogollon, although relatively recent research by Margaret Nelson, Michelle Hegmon, and the University of New Mexico's Office of Cultural Resource Management tracks

the Mogollon to the west bank of the Rio Grande. Furthermore, Rocek's work at the Dunlap-Salazar site places at least one Mogollon pithouse village in the montane regions east of the Rio Grande.

5. The following Mogollon pithouse sites are considered in this study: Bear Ruin (Haury 1985a), Bluff site (Haury 1985a), Cameron Creek Village (Bradfield 1931), Crooked Ridge Village (Wheat 1954), Cuchillo (LA 50548; Munford et al. 1994), Diablo Village (LA 6538; Dycus 1997; Hammack 1966), Duncan (Lightfoot 1984), Galaz (Anyon and LeBlanc 1984), Gallitas Springs (LA 6082, LA 6083; Kayser 1975), Harris Village (Haury 1936a), Lee Village (Bussey 1973, 1975), Luna Junction (Peckham 1963), McAnally (Diehl and LeBlanc 2001), Mogollon Village (Haury 1936a), Nantack Village (Breternitz 1959), Promontory (Martin et al. 1949), Quemado Alegre (LA 5407; Akins 1998), Saige-McFarland (Lekson 1990a), Sawmill (Bluhm 1957), Stove Canyon (Neely 1974), SU (Martin 1940, 1943; Martin and Rinaldo 1947), Switchback (Peckham 1957), Thompson (Diehl and LeBlanc 2001), Turkey Foot Ridge (Martin et al. 1949; Martin and Rinaldo 1950b), Williams (Smith 1973), Wind Mountain (Woosley and McIntyre 1996), and Winn Canyon (Fitting 1973).

6. Studies of Mogollon burials (the contexts in which such objects most often occur) show that during the Early Pithouse period the most common mortuary treatment was interment with broken vessels or a few stone implements; there is no indication of significant differences in the quantity of artifacts by age, sex, or location, and the only exotics, *Glycymeris* bracelets, are very scarce and rarely occur in multiples. The Georgetown phase duplicates the Early Pithouse period mortuary treatment.

Part III   **Zuni in the Puebloan World**

Mogollon-Zuni Connections

12 Zuni in the Puebloan and Southwestern Worlds

David R. Wilcox, David A. Gregory, and J. Brett Hill

What was the nature of Pueblo polities? At what organizational scale was there economic and political autonomy? At the village level, as Bandelier (1892) famously thought, or on higher levels of sets of pueblos, as others have argued (Jewett 1989; LeBlanc 1999; Mera 1935, 1940; Upham 1982; Wilcox 1981, 1991b, 1992, 2005a; Wilcox et al. 2001a)? A recent survey of pueblo site clusters (Adams and Duff 2004) leans toward small-scale integration. Arguably, however, like the village clusters in the American Southeast at this same time that were also separated from one another by buffer zones (Hally 1993, 2006; Hally and Kelly 1998; but see Schroedl 1998), the pueblo clusters were organized politically into what are called "polities," and some of them were at war with one another (LeBlanc 1999; McKusick and Young 1997; Rice and LeBlanc 2001). Settlement pattern studies are a prelude to constructing models to address such issues.

Both Bandelier (1892) and Spicer (1962) recognized village clustering. The Spaniards specified several characteristics of the pueblos as "nations." They realized that the people of each cluster spoke a distinct language; Ginés de Herrera Horta reported that they had "many local dialects, which correspond to the names of their na-

tions, such as Picuries, Taos, Emes, Queres, Acomas, and various others. Each nation in this province [of New Mexico] has its particular language" (qtd. in Hammond and Rey 1953:647). Politically, they were identified as "provinces" that often were said to have a "principal town" (Hammond and Rey 1940, 1953, 1966). Exchange occurred among the pueblos of each cluster: Marcelo de Espinosa stated that "the people from the same province understand and trade with one another" (qtd. in Hammond and Rey 1953:636). The nature of the political organization was described in seemingly contradictory ways that have been difficult to reconcile (see Wilcox 1981). A new attempt at such a reconciliation is made in this chapter.

When the idea for the advanced seminar that led to the present volume was conceived, it was apparent that the kind of comprehensive settlement pattern maps constructed by Wilcox et al. (2001a) for central Arizona should be extended to include the Zuni area. Those maps went a long way toward clarifying the concept of village clusters and their political geography (Wilcox et al. 2001a). The construction of more comprehensive maps serves to define the economic and political context of Zuni settlements. The time frame was set to include the period from AD 1200 to

1600, and, with Scott Geister's help, the statewide electronic database for all known sites in New Mexico (called NMCRIS) was searched for "structural sites" that fell within the period AD 1200–1599 for an area that stretched from Cliff, New Mexico, to Zuni.

Because NMCRIS does not usually have room counts in the database, in July 2001 Wilcox examined the paper records at the Laboratory of Anthropology, Museum of New Mexico, recording room counts and eliminating sites with fewer than 13 rooms. Keith Kintigh was also particularly helpful in defining site sizes and chronologies for the Zuni area. Geomap, Inc., of Tucson then took all the NMCRIS data as well as those from the Perry Mesa study (see appendices in Wilcox et al. 2001a, 2001b) and entered them into an Access database. From that database eight distribution maps in 50-year intervals were prepared for display at the seminar.

Following the seminar, we decided to keep going, and another NMCRIS search was conducted for the rest of New Mexico. The paper records were once again reviewed, and all appropriate sites were added to the database.[1] Working with other collaborators and incorporating additional data from other repositories and the relevant literature (Adler 1996; Bandelier 1892; Beal 1987; Brand 1943; Danson 1957; Doolittle 1984; Elliott 1982; Fisher 1931; Fowler et al. 1987; Gilpin 1989; Harrington 1916; Hewett 1906; Hough 1907; Kidder et al. 1949; Marshall 1989; Marshall and Walt 1984; Mera 1934, 1935, 1940; Powers and Orcutt 1999; Spier 1917, 1918, 1919), we expanded our coverage into northern Arizona, southern Utah and Colorado, and northern Mexico.[2] William Doelle had previously constructed a database for southern Arizona sites as part of his demographic studies (Dean et al. 1994; Doelle 1995, 2000), and these data, retaining his population estimates, were also added to our database.[3] Drawing on a concept proposed by Stephen Kowalewski (2001), we refer now to the Coalescent Communities Database, which currently contains data on over 3,000 sites broken down into more than 6,000 components.

We are now well on our way toward our goal of having a database that contains all known sites of 13 rooms or larger for the period AD 1200–1599 for the whole Southwest. A new empirical foundation has thus been established that allows us to look at images never before seen—images that portray the structure of pan-Southwest settlement systems for the late prehistoric and early protohistoric periods. This chapter presents the first version of these maps and a series of analyses we have conducted to define that structure. Only the most general structural findings are discussed here, together with a focus on the place of Zuni in the southwestern and Puebloan worlds.

We continue to collect data, and we are finding ways to refine the quality of the data. Thus, the reader should note that it is only the general *trends* in the patterns revealed by this series of maps and not the specifics of the current numbers that we think will

hold up to further study.[4] It is those aspects of the map images that we discuss and on that basis that we suggest empirical generalizations and point out directions for future research. Before presenting the map data and our analyses and interpretations we first discuss the character and limitations of the assembled data. (For a discussion of the theoretical underpinnings of this approach see Wilcox 2005b.)

Mapping Settlement Systems for the Whole Southwest

Maps are a means of expressing relational data. By constructing maps of the distribution of public architecture, whether that be Hohokam-style ball courts and platform mounds (Gregory and Nials 1985; Wilcox 1991d; Wilcox and Sternberg 1983) or Chacoan great houses (Wilcox 1993, 1999a, 2005d), structural patterns can be discerned, particularly when sequential *differences* in these distributions can also be displayed. Such relational patterns become the basis for hypotheses about past social processes of interaction and how those systems of interaction changed through time. Fruitful hypotheses should include implications that lead us to new factual insights relevant to the testing of the hypotheses.[5]

The modern study of anthropological archaeology in the Southwest began about 150 years ago, when conquest converted what had been the northwest of Mexico into the American Southwest (Fowler 2000; Fowler and Wilcox 1999; Wilcox and Fowler 2002). Intellectuals like Albert Gallatin (1845, 1848) and Ephraim Squier (1848) were quick to define the anthropological agenda for studying this region, rejecting the findings of previous Jesuit scholarship (Clavigero 1787) that postulated movement by the Aztecs southward through this

region from an Azatlan supposed to be near the Great Salt Lake. Gallatin (1845) argued for the independent emergence of agriculture and civilization in the New World and their diffusion to the Southwest, a theory subsequently embraced by other Americanist scholars (Adams 1966; Brinton 1891; Kidder 1924, 1936; Wissler 1917; see also Breasted 1935:4–5). Since then a tremendous amount of work has been done to record archaeological sites. Institutions were founded that became repositories of such information (Fowler 2000), and with the coming of the computer age statewide databases have been created to make these data more accessible. We believe the time has come to begin looking at certain classes of these data *as a whole*, across all of the region of the American Southwest and northern Mexico—a region we call the North American Southwest.[6]

There are at least three reasons for such syntheses being timely: (1) it is now possible to do so; (2) meaningful results can be achieved if due caution is exercised in the interpretation of the patterns revealed; and (3) studies of "cultural affiliation" mandated by NAGPRA can then be more adequately undertaken, thus increasing the scientific cogency of evaluations of questions like that of Zuni origins. We believe that after over 150 years of looking we probably now know the locations of all sites larger than 500 rooms. We probably also know where most sites of 100–500 rooms are, although some sites of about 100 rooms are still being found (Larry Hammack, personal communication 2003). We are sure that many more sites in the range of 13–100 rooms remain to be found (see Kintigh, chap. 18, this vol.), but we already know where a great many of those are located as well. Some sites have probably been totally destroyed, perhaps

Kwastiyukwa
LA 482

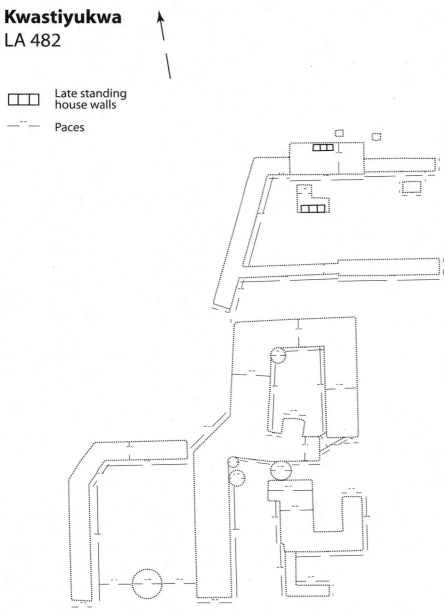

☐☐☐ Late standing
house walls

—˜—˜— Paces

Figure 12.1. Mera's diagram of the Kwastiyukwa Site (redrawn by D. Gregory, based upon an original map in the collections of the Laboratory of Anthropology, Museum of Indian Arts and Culture).

and Whalen and Minnis [2001] for recent contributions).

Data-Quality Issues

Current knowledge about site sizes and temporal intervals is highly variable. Ceramic cross-dating is usually the basis for temporal assessments. Thus, a site can be "bracketed" in time, for example, from AD 1300 to 1600. For some purposes a wide bracketing is desirable, as is done in the NMCRIS database, thus insuring that all sites that *might* be pertinent to a given time period will be included in the sample. For the current study a more refined chronology for individual sites was desired so that trends would not be masked by sites that do not belong in a particular 50-year interval. To accomplish this more refined dating we have relied on chronological models and the dating of particular pottery types provided by other scholars.[7]

Size of a site has also often been a matter of estimation using variable standards. Personal observation by Wilcox or Gregory has helped to refine some of these data.[8] In New Mexico H. P. Mera, in a stunning amount of work, made scale diagrams of numerous sites, giving measurements in paces or feet (see fig. 12.1). For the current study Wilcox produced calculations of areas for these sites by direct measurement of Mera's scaled diagrams and used 12 m² as an average room size to convert area to room counts (see Bandelier 1892; Herhahn and Hill 1998). Survey data often have site size expressed as size-class ranges, and we have also employed size classes in our study. Initially, the size classes devised for the Perry Mesa study were used (see Wilcox et al. 2001a). We then found that three more general size classes were useful: small (13–99 rooms), large (100–499 rooms),

before any record of them was made, and others are likely buried below the modern surface.

In general, however, we now have a huge sample, and it is both desirable and feasible to begin mapping it out so that we can see what patterns are revealed (see also Adams and Duff 2004). These patterns will lead us to ask fresh questions that will more

efficiently guide future research. By looking at where archaeological survey has and has not been done in relation to known settlement distributions we can also begin to evaluate where we may not have adequate data and begin more deliberately to fill the gaps. Quite obviously, northern Mexico is one place where such efforts are badly needed (but see Doolittle [1984]

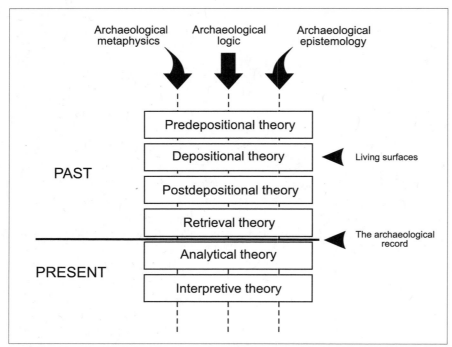

Figure 12.2. A model for an independent archaeological theory (after Clarke 1973).

and very large (500+ rooms). These values are used in the database when room counts are unavailable but when other information indicates which "ballpark" estimate is most appropriate.

Why was 13 rooms selected as a cutoff for inclusion in the database? First, in the Perry Mesa work we wanted to look for site clustering, and we thought it would be interesting to include room blocks with fewer than 50 rooms, the standard that had been applied in earlier studies (e.g., Adler 1996). Second, we found that the number 13 appeared to be a natural break point, with many sites being estimated to be 8–12 rooms or 13–20 rooms. Third, sites with 13 or more rooms were likely the domains of multiple families and thus were hamlets or villages, whereas those sites with fewer than 13 rooms were most likely farmsteads representing the domains of only one or two families (Wilcox 1978). Thus, there is a theoretical reason of some importance

associated with this standard. Finally, as a practical matter, the 13-room cutoff meant that we could restrict the inquiry to manageable proportions. Later it will be possible (and very interesting) to construct databases of field houses and farmsteads and to examine their distributions in relation to those of hamlets and villages.

Similarly, one may ask, Why the period AD 1200–1599? Given that the Spanish colony in New Mexico and northern Arizona was founded in 1598, the latter date is a good marker of a highly significant structural moment in the history of Southwest populations. In our initial study we included Late Pueblo III sites and found that we had a "residual" data set that went back to AD 1200 (and that the map of this first period was very interesting!), so we began to collect data systematically from that date. In the century prior to 1200 ceramic cross-dating is much more uncertain in large portions of the Southwest, and sites of fewer than 13 rooms are

much more important places of habitation on the southwestern landscape.[9] In addition, prior to 1200 pithouse architecture was a common mode, and it is more often problematic to estimate numbers of pithouses from surface data. Thus, for now, AD 1200 seems to be a good place to start. Future studies may seek to extend the database farther back in time.[10]

Once the age range and size of each site were established, the next step was to define size classes that could be assigned a map symbol and then to display the data spatially in a map (Wilcox et al. 2001a). Once we expanded the temporal range to a 400-year period it became desirable to see what could be done to model the "life history" of each site: how many rooms did it have in each 50-year interval? It has long been recognized that southwestern sites had growth and abandonment histories, and methods to discriminate the size of a site on each of its absolutely contemporaneous "living surfaces," or approximations of them, have been devised (Dean 1969; Gregory and Huckleberry 1994; Wilcox 1975; see fig. 12.2). What further complicates this problem is that when a multistoried pueblo falls down, the ruins exposed to surface observation often best facilitate estimation of the number of ground-floor rooms (e.g., Nelson 1914). Estimation of the number of stories that once existed is problematic, though Arthur Rohn's (personal communication 1992) rule of thumb is a reasonable approach: if you are looking down on the ruin, it had one story; if you are looking at the ruin top, the pueblo had two stories; if you are looking up at the ruin, it had three stories or more.

Figure 12.3 presents the series of simple models used to estimate the number of total rooms in large multistoried sites based on ground-floor count and the number of stories

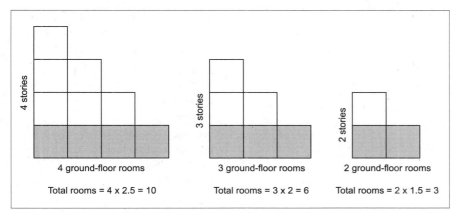

Figure 12.3. A model for estimating the total number of rooms in multistoried pueblos.

Table 12.1 Life-History Model for Kwastiyukwa

Number of Rooms	Date Range (AD)	Component Name
Large	1250–1349	Kwastiyukwa I
Very large	1350–1399	Kwastiyukwa II
1,300–2,600	1400–1499	Kwastiyukwa III[a]
650–1,500	1500–1625	Kwastiyukwa IV

Note: Kwastiyukwa is LA 482; other site numbers include Hewett 47 (Hewett 1906); Harrington 27:21 (Harrington 1916); and Santa Fe National Forest AR-03-10-03-11.

[a] Also known as Giant Footprint Ruin; reservoir and great kiva present.

present. These models assume that multistoried room blocks were terraced—as Spanish accounts (e.g., Hammond and Rey 1966) and other data indicate that they were. Our method for the large multistoried sites has been to give the ground-floor count as a minimum figure and then estimate the total number of rooms as a maximum. Some archaeologists have made estimates of total rooms (Kintigh 1985), and it is important for comparative work to be clear about what kind of estimate is being given. Failure to do this, and the use of only ground-floor counts, have long confused efforts to estimate total pueblo population, whether of rooms or people (see below).

The process of constructing life histories for sites can be illustrated with an example. In August 2002,

guided by Curtis Schaafsma, Wilcox visited the Jemez site of Kwastiyukwa (see fig. 12.1). A model of it is displayed at the Jemez Visitor Center, where it is stated that the site once had a total of 3,000 rooms. Elliott (1982) gives an estimate of 1,300–2,600 rooms. It appeared to Wilcox that the northern room block had been stone robbed and then later a late component had been built on one edge of it. Elliott (personal communication 2003) believes that the southeast wing of the main room block is an earlier component. Combining available room estimates and field observations, we arrive at the model of size over time presented in table 12.1.

All size estimates are now in a systematic database, and we have begun to record the "metadata" on how the

estimates were derived. Thus, all estimates can now be subjected to new testing as more data become available, and new research designs can be constructed to collect the data needed to make better estimates. For now, however, while one should be skeptical about the particulars, general trends in settlement size and distribution revealed by invoking life-history models are likely to represent greater resolution (and accuracy) than they would if we simply used a single size estimate for the entire interval of a site's occupation.

In the database we often show the size estimate as a range of values. From these data we thus constructed variables for minimum size, maximum size, and mean size. For the small, large, and very large estimates we assigned 50, 250, and 750 rooms, respectively, as their mean sizes. Maps and tables presented here were generated on the basis of the mean room estimates for each 50-year interval. We felt that this was a systematic way to correct for the likelihood that not all rooms extant during many intervals were occupied at those times. Kintigh (1985) has suggested a 65 percent correction factor to address this problem, which would yield numbers lower than those presented here.[11] Our view is that all of these numbers are approximations, some of which are better than others, though we cannot know which is which in many cases. Information that does allow us to make better approximations is used in the life-history modeling. Each estimate, therefore, represents our current best guess based on all currently available data. In the aggregate we believe that a "law of large numbers" applies from which we can make warranted inferences about general trends in the data revealed by the maps and their comparison.

In subsequent maps and tables

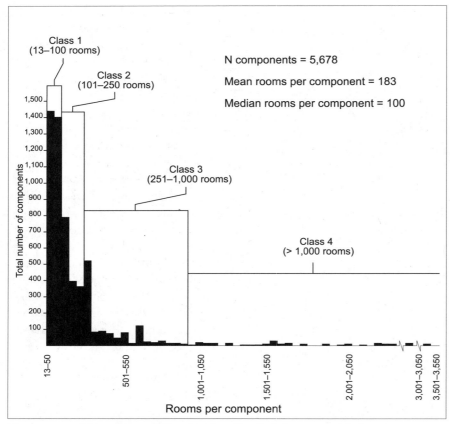

Figure 12.4. A histogram of site-size data for all eight maps and size-class partitions.

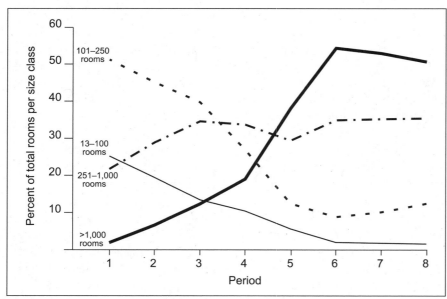

Figure 12.5. A graph of size-class changes, AD 1200–1599, for southwestern communities.

age ranges for defined intervals are expressed as, for example, AD 1250–1299 rather than as the more familiar AD 1250–1300. Thus, sites that end about AD 1300 appear on the AD 1250–1299 map but not on the AD 1300–1349 map, where sites that *begin* at about AD 1300 appear. Another issue is not so easily solved. In some parts of the Southwest, especially north of the Mogollon Rim, advances in ceramic seriation allow discrimination of chronologies in intervals that end or begin ca. AD 1275 or 1325/1330 (Duff 1999; Kintigh 1996; Mills 1998). Thus, room counts for Period 2 (AD 1250–1299) may include occupations that *ended* at AD 1275 as well as those that *began* at 1275. A doubling of room counts for a given area can thus occur, and the densities of site distributions may be misleading. This problem is particularly important in the Zuni region, where small Scribe S sites gave way to large nucleated pueblos ca. AD 1275 (Kintigh 1985; LeBlanc 2001). We return to this problem in the interpretative sections below.

In general, the best way to "read" the maps is to go back and forth between them and the data tables and create a cognitive map that correlates the two. In the Perry Mesa papers (Wilcox et al. 2001a, 2001b) Wilcox was able to publish both the tables and the maps and to associate site numbers with the site symbols on the maps. Because of the sheer number of sites and components involved, that has not been possible here. Eventually, we hope to make the complete database available to the archaeological profession in a geographic information system (GIS) format. Using GIS technology one can zoom in, viewing the sites in a less compressed way, and variables such as drainages, topographic relief, moisture isopleth lines derived from tree-ring studies, biotic communities, and myriad other

Table 12.2 Summary Statistics for the Eight Cost-Surface Maps, AD 1200–1599

	Period 1 1200–1249	Period 2 1250–1299	Period 3 1300–1349	Period 4 1350–1399	Period 5 1400–1449	Period 6 1450–1499	Period 7 1500–1549	Period 8 1550–1600
Number of settlements	1,263	1,433	1,136	906	476	177	163	124
Total rooms	123,339	174,717	184,383	172,418	133,891	95,990	87,108	64,750
Median size	50	63	92	100	137	338	307	300
Mean size	98	122	162	190	281	542	534	522
Percent rooms in settlements of 13–100 rooms	25.2	19.4	13.4	10.4	5.6	2.0	1.8	1.6
Percent rooms in settlements of 101–250 rooms	51.2	45.1	39.7	37.0	26.9	8.8	10.1	12.4
Percent rooms in settlements of 251–1,000 rooms	21.7	28.9	34.6	33.7	29.4	34.9	35.2	35.4
Percent rooms in settlements of 1,000 rooms	1.9	6.6	12.3	19.0	38.1	54.3	52.9	50.6

data can be incorporated into various analyses. The variety of relationships we are now able to study systematically is staggering. In one sense this chapter is merely an introduction to the potentials for future research that are now within our grasp.

Analyses of the Map Data

Locational data were collected for all sites in Universal Transverse Mercator (UTM) coordinates and converted to UTM Zone 12 locations, where the great majority of sites are located. Summary statistics were generated for each period (see table 12.2). Based on a histogram of site-size data for all sites, three size classes were initially defined: 13–250, 251–1,000, and 1,000 rooms. Because we think that hamlets are an important and qualitatively distinct class of sites, we then broke out a fourth size class, 13–100 rooms, to portray them in the maps (see fig. 12.4). The percentage of rooms that fall into each size class can then be calculated for each period (see table 12.2), and the trends can be shown graphically (see fig. 12.5).

Above the hamlet level are three classes of village: small, medium, and large. The latter, especially, might be called "towns," as others have done (e.g., Neitzel 1999), but we think caution is needed here. In medieval studies (Benton 1968) a town is a settlement in which there is considerable differentiation in economic roles—and it is questionable whether that was true in any of these southwestern settlements. Once such a division of labor can be demonstrated it will be time to speak of towns. On the other hand, in the American Southeast the notion of "town" is defined differently: "We define a Mississippian town as a habitation center with a public area, such as a plaza or courtyard, that may be flanked by one or more mounds. . . . The key elements are plazas, mounds, boundaries, and gates" (Lewis and Stout 1998:5, 11). Only in the Hohokam area are there "mounds" in a comparable sense; many southwestern sites have plazas, but many of them are small sites, and thus this is not a good criterion for differentiating villages from towns. Further analysis of this issue is needed.

Several strong patterns are apparent in the map data:

1. Hamlets and small villages dominate Period 1 (AD 1200–1249) but decline rapidly to small percentages in later periods.
2. Medium villages account for 20–35 percent throughout the eight periods.
3. Large villages are rare in Period 1, but in Periods 6–8 (AD 1450–1599) they have in them over 50 percent of all rooms in the sample.
4. The number of sites in Period 8 is a tenfold decrease from the number recorded in Period 1.
5. The median site size goes from 50 in Period 1 to 300 or more in Periods 6–8, peaking in Period 6 (AD 1450–1499). A similar pattern is true for mean site size.

We do not think that these trends will be affected in any major way once data quality is improved or as new sites are discovered and are taken into account (but see n. 4).

The total number of rooms for each period (see table 12.2) also shows some interesting trends, but caution is needed in the interpretation of these numbers. Hamlets and small villages (sites of 13–100 and 101–250 rooms, respectively) account for over 75 percent of all rooms for Period 1 in our sample. This size range is the least likely to be fully accounted for by current archaeological survey coverage. Furthermore, as we show below, Period 1 was also the time when settlements were most widely distributed on the southwestern landscape. Thus, areas not yet surveyed may be expected to yield more small sites dating to the 1200s. Finally, we also know that during Period 1 there were many dispersed communities that produced constituent room blocks with fewer than 13 rooms; thus under-representation of total room counts—and population—is likely greater for Period 1 than for any other interval. We thus infer that the room estimate for Period 1 is too low, and the same may be true for Period 2 but less so. The issue of what these total room counts may mean for studies of prehistoric and protohistoric southwestern demography and the reasons why our findings contrast so greatly with those derived from previous demographic models (Dean et al. 1994; Doelle 2000) are issues taken up in an interpretive section below.

One of our goals is to measure the potentials for interaction among southwestern settlements and to discover structural parameters of that interaction. In earlier studies Wilcox (1993, 1999a; Wilcox et al. 2001a) has suggested the utility of looking at interaction in terms of the concept of the average distance a person on foot can go in a day with a pack. Drennan (1984) has identified 36 km as a statistical measure of this distance parameter. Of equal interest, Wilcox (1993, 1999a) suggests, is the distance one can go *and come back* in a day, which by Drennan's (1984) reckoning would be 18 km. From his reading of Chisholm's (1979) study Wilcox (1988b) has also taken 3 km to be the greatest distance a farmer will go

from his dooryard to farm. To express these ideas on a map Wilcox (1988b, 1999a; Wilcox et al. 2001b) simply drew circles of the appropriate radii.

Varien (1999), in a study of the greater Mesa Verde area, applied similar measures of potential interaction. He argued for an effective radius of 2 km for intensive agriculture and regular interaction, 7 km for more extensive agriculture and resource exploitation (for clay, animals, gathered plants), and 18 km for the distance one could go and come back in a day. Varien (1999) used a cost surface created by Brett Hill that allowed him to take travel time into account in these analyses. Thus, the shorter airline distance one could cover in a given time while crossing a deep canyon can be shown versus the distance covered while crossing flat land.

In our analyses we used Varien's (1999) three measures plus 36 km for a day's travel. First, all sites within 300 m of one another were grouped into "communities."[12] Data from post-Chaco communities such as Hinkson Ranch (Kintigh 1996) were already so grouped, and this procedure assured greater comparability in subsequent comparisons. A terrain cost-adjusted radius around each community was then calculated using half the radius of each interaction measure: 1 km, 3.5 km, 9 km, and 18 km (see Herhahn and Hill [1998] and Hill [2000] for a description of this process). Where these radii intersected a cluster was formed, and a cluster number was assigned to each for each scale of interaction. Using the area of each cluster and its room count, density measures were then calculated. The analysis using 1-km radii did not produce results significantly different from the "community" groupings and is not discussed further. The results of the three other interaction studies are shown below.

When we first examined these

maps, we saw that the clusters at the 3.5-km scale are "islands" or "patches" of population aggregation on the southwestern landscape. We discuss these "population aggregates" in more detail below and show the distribution of their size classes in a second series of maps. First, however, we suggest that readers now examine each of the maps in the first series (see figs. 12.6–12.13), comparing them to one another and looking for what patterning they see in these images before continuing to read our narrative, in which we present what we see in them.

The Basic Structure of Southwestern Settlement Systems (AD 1200–1599)

More than anything else, what these maps do is help us to see which populations were neighbors and how far apart they were. Thus, we may begin to construct studies of interaction between populations in a more systematic manner, and the concept of "pueblo clusters" can be entirely reevaluated and rethought. The new data show clearly that the structure of settlement systems in the Southwest was far more complex and requires us to model economic, social, and political processes and systems on many different spatial scales, all of which were "in motion," becoming restructured into new configurations and relationships through time. No two of what in the past we have called "pueblo clusters" are arranged spatially in the same way.[13] In some periods there are sites that are spatially intermediate between the clusters, and it will be interesting to see if they were linking nodes in larger, intercluster exchange systems. It is going to take some time to digest all of this new information and to begin to construct fresh theoretical approaches to understand it. The more one studies

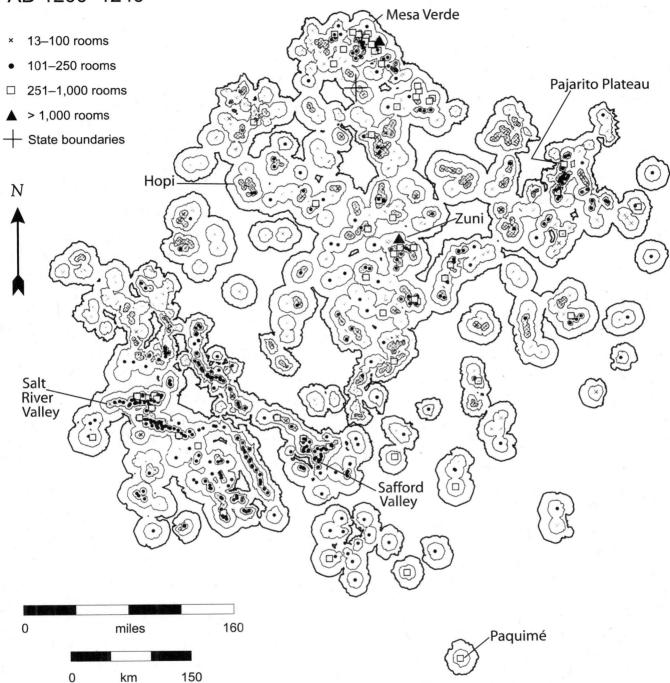

Period 1
AD 1200–1249

× 13–100 rooms

• 101–250 rooms

□ 251–1,000 rooms

▲ > 1,000 rooms

┼ State boundaries

N

Mesa Verde

Pajarito Plateau

Hopi

Zuni

Salt
River
Valley

Safford
Valley

Paquimé

0   miles   160

0   km   150

Figure 12.6. Interaction friction models for all known sites in the Southwest, AD 1200–1249.

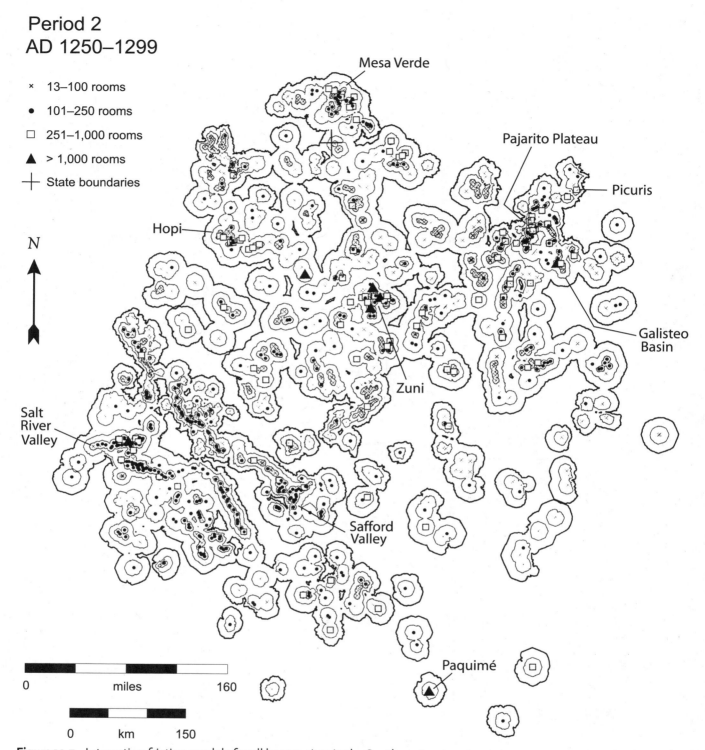

Figure 12.7. Interaction friction models for all known sites in the Southwest, AD 1250–1299.

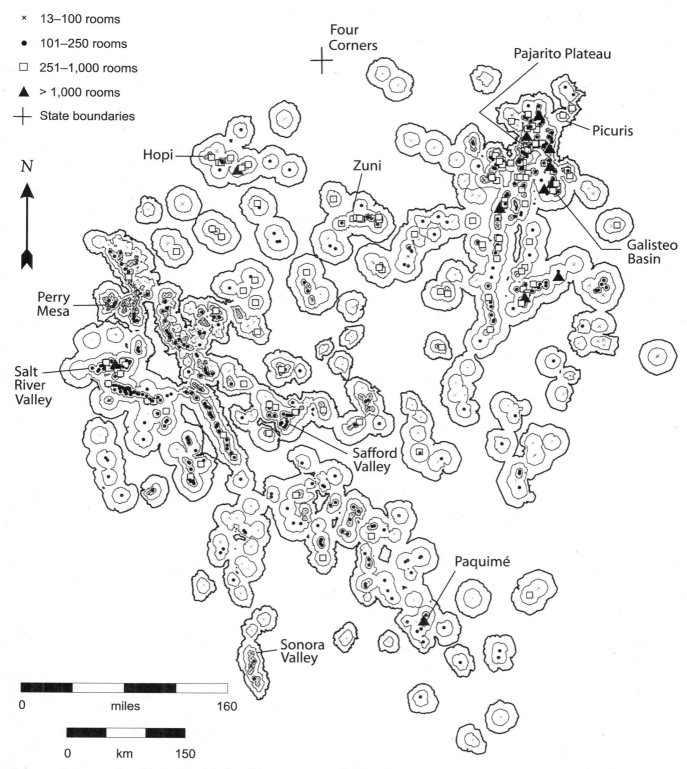

**Period 3
AD 1300–1349**

- × 13–100 rooms
- • 101–250 rooms
- □ 251–1,000 rooms
- ▲ > 1,000 rooms
- ✛ State boundaries

N

Four Corners

Pajarito Plateau

Picuris

Hopi

Zuni

Galisteo Basin

Perry Mesa

Salt River Valley

Safford Valley

Paquimé

Sonora Valley

0   miles   160

0   km   150

Figure 12.8. Interaction friction models for all known sites in the Southwest, AD 1300–1349.

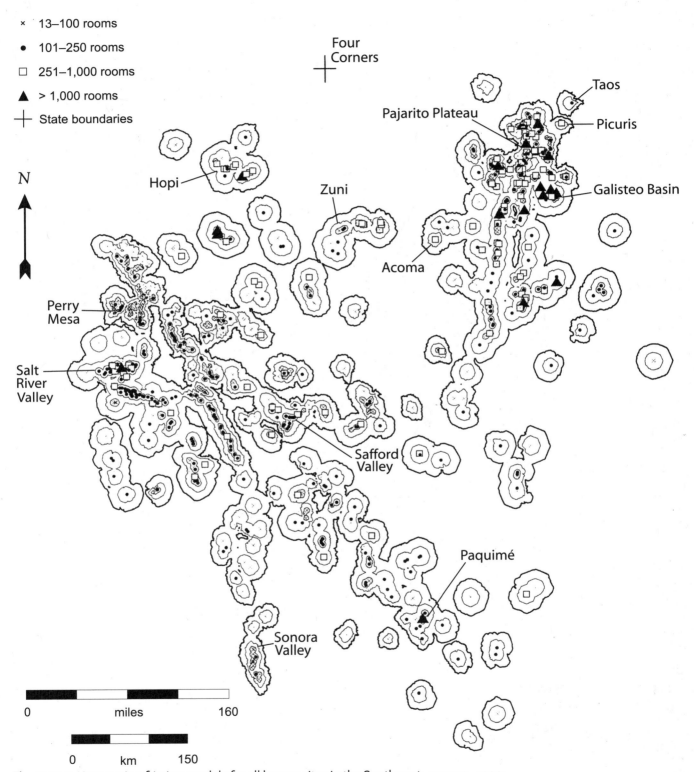

Figure 12.9. Interaction friction models for all known sites in the Southwest, AD 1350–1399.

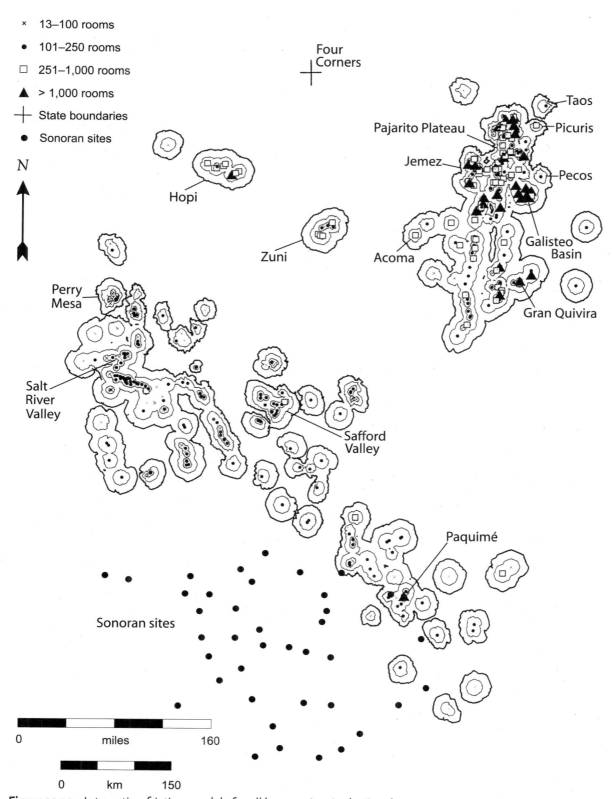

Figure 12.10. Interaction friction models for all known sites in the Southwest, AD 1400–1449.

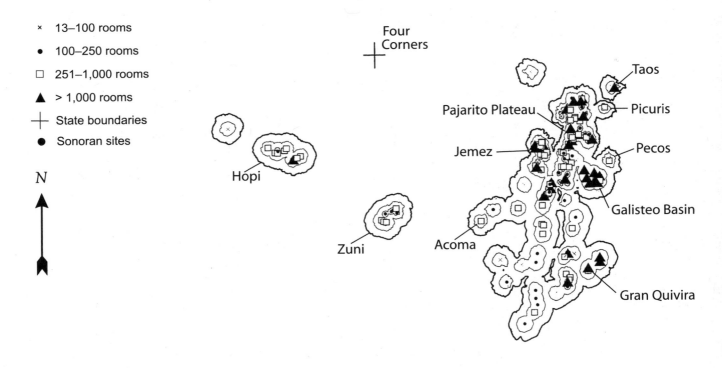

Period 6
AD 1450–1499

× 13–100 rooms

• 100–250 rooms

□ 251–1,000 rooms

▲ > 1,000 rooms

+ State boundaries

● Sonoran sites

N

Four Corners

Taos

Pajarito Plateau

Picuris

Jemez

Pecos

Galisteo Basin

Hopi

Acoma

Gran Quivira

Zuni

0   miles   160

0   km   150

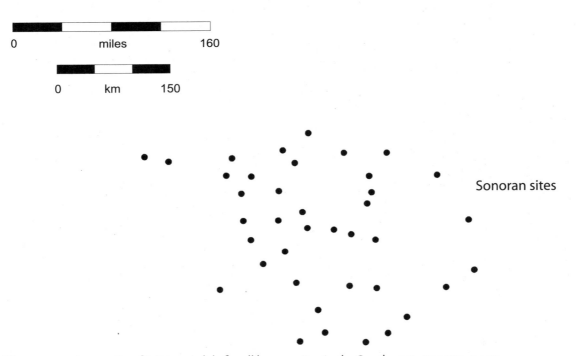

Sonoran sites

Figure 12.11. Interaction friction models for all known sites in the Southwest, AD 1450–1499.

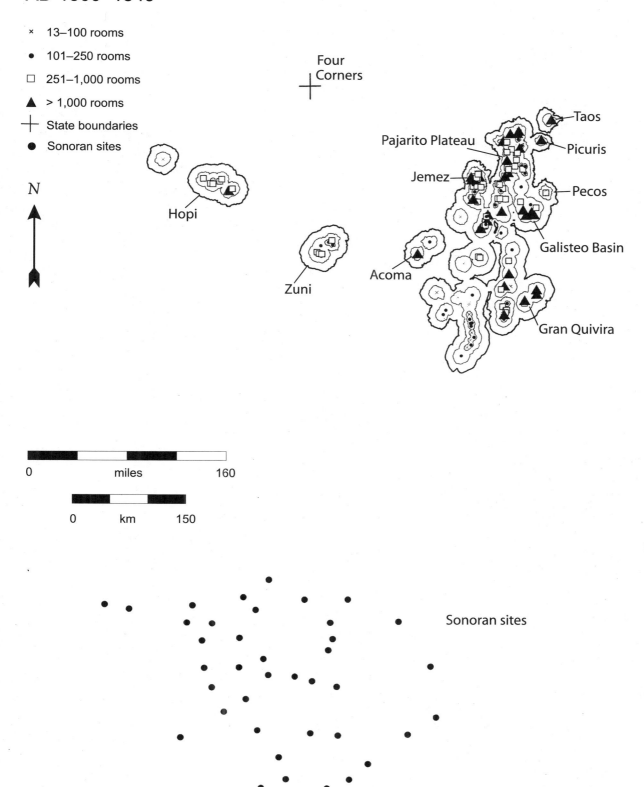

Figure 12.12. Interaction friction models for all known sites in the Southwest, AD 1500–1549.

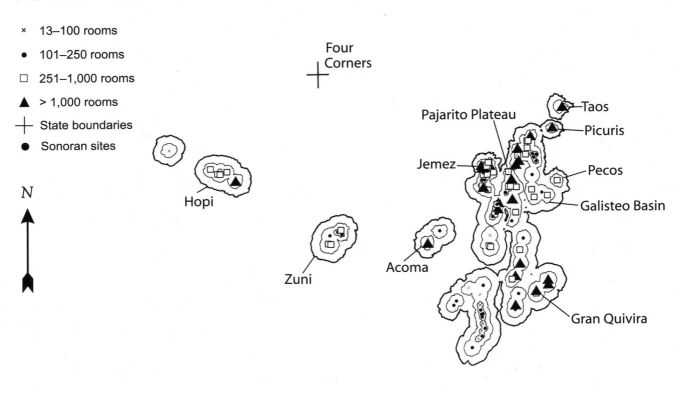

Period 8
AD 1550–1599

× 13–100 rooms

• 101–250 rooms

□ 251–1,000 rooms

▲ > 1,000 rooms

+ State boundaries

● Sonoran sites

N

Four Corners

Hopi

Zuni

Pajarito Plateau

Jemez

Acoma

Taos

Picuris

Pecos

Galisteo Basin

Gran Quivira

0   miles   160

0   km   150

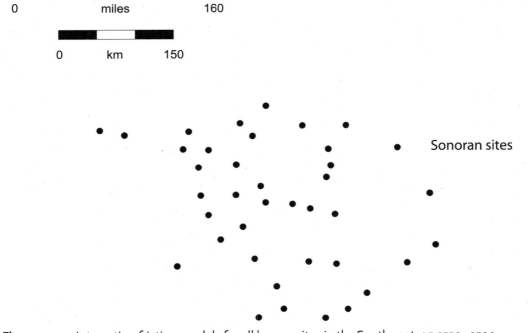

Sonoran sites

Figure 12.13. Interaction friction models for all known sites in the Southwest, AD 1550–1599.

and compares the maps, especially as more detailed understandings about the particulars of each site are brought to bear, the more patterns one sees. Some patterns are more basic, however, and we now describe some of the most obvious or relevant of them.

The most basic structural pattern revealed by these maps is a distinction between what we will henceforth call the "northern Southwest" and the "southern Southwest." The most striking expression of this distinction is seen in the Period 5 (AD 1400–1449) map (where we first noticed it; see fig. 12.10). By AD 1400 the whole Mogollon Rim country was depopulated, opening up a wide "buffer zone" between the Puebloan world (Hopi, Zuni, Acoma, and the Rio Grande Pueblos) and the remnants of the Hohokam world centered in the Phoenix Basin, the Casas Grandes world, and a group of population aggregates in between (San Carlos, Safford Valley, Point of Pines, Red-rock, and Cliff—which arguably were Zunian speakers; see Gregory and Wilcox, chap. 20, this vol.).[14] Looking back at the Period 1 map, however, one can readily see this structure already clearly marked by a narrow buffer zone.

In Period 5, by the reckoning of chronologies used in this preliminary study, there were still about 31,000 rooms in the southern Southwest, all of which we show "going away" in Period 6 (see fig. 12.11). Where did their occupants go? Did they just "go poof in the night" through rapid attrition, or, like the occupants of the northern San Juan two centuries earlier, did they migrate to another part of the Southwest? If migration was involved, it was not as a block to the northern Southwest, which lost population between Periods 5 and 6 (although some in-migration to that area

may have occurred; see Teague 1993). We think it is an important hypothesis that migration did occur and that Carroll Riley's (1982, 1987) hypothesis that Casas Grandes populations redeployed into northern Sonora to become the Opata described by Spanish explorers (Hammond and Rey 1928, 1940) is strengthened by our findings. By a parallel argument, we might suppose that the Hohokam largely redeployed into Pima Bajo settlements whose occupants, like them, spoke Tepiman (Shaul and Hill 1998; Wilcox 1986a).[15] These ideas are discussed in more detail in the interpretative section below; for now, we explain that on the maps for Periods 6–8 (figs. 12.11–12.13) we show Opata/Pima Bajo settlements from Sauer's (1934) map simply to create a visual expression of the *possibility* that the southern Southwest did not simply "go away" but continued to exist into Period 8 and beyond.[16]

With the concepts of the northern (Puebloan) Southwest and the southern Southwest now identified we can examine both the "zones of connection" that existed between them in Periods 1–4 and the gaps inferred to be buffer zones that later separated them. We can then begin to consider what eliminated the earlier connectivity. First, however, it is worth noting that in Period 1 (see fig. 12.6), at the 18-km scale, nearly the whole Southwest is connected together into a single cluster. One could walk a path (Hage and Harary 1983) from one end of the Southwest to the other without spending more than one day walking between settlements along the way. The Flagstaff area is an "island," and there are other islands along the southeastern flank, though in Mexico and perhaps in southeastern New Mexico this may represent an absence of modern surveys more than reality. Comparing the

maps for Periods 1–4, we see that the Mogollon Rim country between the northern and southern Southwest was a zone of dynamic changes before becoming depopulated.

We also note that several gaps in settlement continuity are revealed by the cost-surface maps. In Period 1 (fig. 12.6), for example, an east–west zone 32+ km wide with no settlement separates the Flagstaff area from the middle Verde River. This is a natural buffer zone that corresponds to the dense ponderosa forest that existed north of the Mogollon Rim (Peter Pilles, personal communication). Future GIS investigations should help us to better understand the distribution of such natural gaps, which probably did function to reduce human interaction across them. Of greater theoretical interest are zones that could support habitation but were depopulated due to conflict between populations on either side of them. Creation of such zones served to increase the energy costs of conflict and thus "buffered" groups from danger while at the same time serving as resource zones that could be periodically exploited by many neighboring groups (see DeBoer 1981; Hally 2006; Hickerson 1962, 1965; Hunter-Anderson 1979). Wilcox et al. (2001a, 2001b, 2007; Wilcox 2005c) have inferred that such a buffer zone became established between the Salt River valley Hohokam and their western, northern, and eastern neighbors ca. AD 1100 and that it widened ca. AD 1250. New GIS approaches may be used to test such hypotheses.

From west to east we see five "zones" or axes of connection represented in the cost-surface maps. These patterns are in part spatial and in part based on other kinds of data such as previously documented ceramic distributions.

Between Hopi and the Phoenix Basin

Between the Hopi and the Phoenix Basin Hohokam lay the settlement systems in west-central Arizona that Wood (1987) has called the Central Arizona Tradition and that Wilcox et al. (2001a, 2001b, 2007) have argued were politically confederated. By AD 1100 a buffer zone 48 km wide separated the Phoenix Basin from this confederacy, and that buffer had widened to 80.6 km between the former and Perry Mesa by about AD 1250. North of the Mogollon Rim was the Sinagua area in Flagstaff (Colton 1946), but it became depopulated by about AD 1325. The Homolovi cluster was established ca. AD 1260 from Hopi (Adams 2002; Lyons 2003), while the Chavez Pass village apparently began in the early 1200s but grew large once the Homolovis were founded.

What we may call a "Hopi macro-economy" linked Hopi via the Homolovis and Chavez Pass to the Verde Confederacy, with Winslow Orange Ware (Lyons 2003) and Hopi Yellow Ware moving southward and cotton textiles, salt, copper pigments, obsidian, and other goods moving northward (Wilcox 2005c).[17] The emergence of a 32-km-wide buffer zone south of West Clear Creek Ruin (NA 2806) ca. AD 1330 apparently split the Verde Confederacy (Wilcox et al. 2007; see also North et al. 2003; Wilcox 2005c), and by about AD 1400 the Hopi macroeconomy had disintegrated or was fundamentally reorganized when sites from Bidahochi to the middle Verde River were depopulated.

This is the very moment when a "buffware" tradition like the Hopi Yellow Ware began at Zuni (see Mills, chap. 13, this vol.), while a glazeware tradition continued at Acoma (Dittert and Brunson-Hadley 1999:68), the El Morro Valley was depopulated, and a long-standing ceramic exchange structure that had linked Zuni to Acoma and the middle Rio Grande also disintegrated.[18] The radical shrinkage of the Hopi economy must have resulted in significant economic reorganization, although that is still not obvious archaeologically. However, the beginning of Sikyatki Polychrome production ca. AD 1375 and the fluorescence of kiva mural art and Sikyatki style by the middle AD 1400s may indicate an intensification of social relationships and economic exchanges among the Hopi village population aggregates as well as new external macroeconomic relationships. Similar conclusions about the Zuni region are also indicated. The fact that Sikyatki Polychrome is found in small quantities at Pottery Mound and is present in other Rio Grande sites suggests that new forms of inter-pueblo exchange ties also emerged. Studies that systematically consider the relationships along this east–west axis are needed.[19]

Between Hopi and Central/ South-Central Arizona

From Hopi to Silver Creek, across the Grasshopper Plateau, to Kinishba and Point of Pines, and into the Safford Basin and the San Pedro Valley there was a migration corridor along which western Anasazi populations moved southward during the middle AD 1200s. This movement likely included individuals and small family groups as well as small communities, and such groups were accepted by local populations in "edge" situations, probably serving guard functions (J. Clark 2001; Di Peso 1958; Haury 1958; Lindsay 1987; Lyons 2003; Woodson 1999). Current work in the San Pedro Valley (Jeffery Clark, personal communication 2003) indicates a slightly earlier (initial) migra-tion, marked there by the appearance of northern styles of corrugated pottery. Considerable evidence for warfare exists all along this corridor (Lyons 2003; McKusick and Young 1997; Tuggle and Reid 2001; Wilcox et al. 2001a).

A relatively large movement of northern people into the Grasshopper Plateau started about AD 1290, when many existing hamlets were burned out (Triadan 1997; Zedeño 1994). This circumstance does not support the insistence of Reid and Whittlesey (1997) that the people there were predominantly Mogollon. The absence of rectangular great kivas in Tuggle's (1970) survey data further weakens the case that these were Mogollon (Zuni) people before AD 1290. West of Carrizo Creek the pre–AD 1290 brownware pottery is locally distinctive (Alan Sullivan, personal communication 2003). Given these patterns, we suspect that occupants of the Kinishba settlements included many migrants from the north, a hypothesis that the kiva found by Cummings (1940) in the central plaza at Kinishba may support. The Canyon Creek Cliff Dwelling may also be part of the story of Hopi migration and not just a Mogollon or Zuni site (cf. Webster, chap. 16, this vol.). Continuing study of these issues is needed.

Between Zuni and the Safford Basin

Between Zuni and the Safford Basin were the Highland Mogollon from Mariana Mesa southward through Apache Creek, the Tularosa Valley, and the Blue. Together these culturally affiliated populations formed a north–south axis along which highly valuable exchange items moved during the twelfth and thirteenth centuries (Carlson 1970; Vokes and Gregory, chap. 17, this vol.; Wilcox

1993, 1999b; Wilcox et al. 2000). Gregory and Wilcox (chap. 20, this vol.) postulate that the people of this axis spoke one or more dialects (or languages) of Zuni.

Movement of Mimbres populations eastward across the Black Range (Nelson 1999) was followed by a migration into the Cliff/Redrock area of the upper Gila, where there are close ceramic ties to Point of Pines and Safford (Lyons 2003; Wilson 1998a, 1998b, chap. 14, this vol.). Rinaldo's (1964) hypothesis that the populations of the Blue and Tularosa Valley went northward may be true in part, but quantitatively our data suggest that many more people may have moved *southward* into the Cliff/Redrock/Safford Basin areas. At Foote Canyon (Rinaldo 1959) occupation continued to about AD 1350, and it seems likely that other settlements in this highland zone also persisted, serving as transit nodes in the flow of Zuni Glaze Ware southward from Zuni and the St. Johns/Springerville area to Point of Pines and the Safford Basin.[20] Ceramic assemblages from "establishment contexts" in the Cliff/Redrock sites are needed to test the southward movement hypothesis (see Lyons 2003 for an example of such studies in the Homolovi case).

In the end some of these southern Zuni populations probably moved back to Zuni, joining in the nucleation of Hawikuh and Ketchipawan, where cremation burials in Salado polychrome vessels (Smith et al. 1966) represent a connecting cultural link between these two regions (see also Webster, chap. 16, this vol.). It appears likely that the remaining St. Johns/Springerville populations also participated in that nucleation ca. AD 1400 (Duff 2002; see Mills, chap. 13, this vol.; but also see Kintigh, chap. 18, this vol.).

Between Acoma and the Rio Puerco of the East

From Acoma and the Rio Puerco of the East south to Gallinas Springs and Alamosa Creek is a second migration corridor, this one of putatively "Mesa Verde" populations (Lekson 2000; Pippen 1987; Stuart and Gauthier 1981; Winkler and Davis 1961). Sites in the Rio Puerco of the East have what has been called "late" Chaco-McElmo Black-on-white, which dates to AD 1225–1275 (Bice 1994; Sundt 1972; see also Burns 1978). The latest painted pottery in the great houses of Chaco Canyon is "early" Chaco-McElmo Black-on-white, which Windes (1985) has dated only to AD 1150 but which Wilcox (1999a, 2005d) argues may go later. Confusion between late Chaco-McElmo Black-on-white and what has generally been called "Mesa Verde" pottery (Mera 1940; Winkler and Davis 1961) may be affecting the interpretation of the source area for the intrusive population enclaves at Gallinas Springs and Alamosa Creek (see Pippen 1987:43, 46).

Hawley (1950) was apparently the first to argue that the Chacoans were Keresan speakers and that the populations of the greater Mesa Verde area spoke Tanoan, positions that Ford et al. (1972) also take, with variant details. Emigration out of the *southern half* of the Chacoan world (by Keresan speakers) into the Rio Puerco of the East and then, in some cases, *southward* may account for the sites with Magdalena Black-on-white at Gallinas Springs and Alamosa Creek. Even more interesting is the possibility that populations at the Hummingbird site (LA 578) may have been derived from these putatively Keresan populations of the middle Rio Puerco of the East. Farther south, Pottery Mound (LA 416) was more likely founded by Southern Tiwa or Piro

populations moving up into the lower Rio Puerco.[21] Once again, ceramic assemblages from establishment contexts are needed to test these hypotheses.

The intrusion of the Gallinas Springs/Alamosa Creek enclaves is marked to the east by a set of highly defensive early Piro sites of the Late Elmendorf phase near the mouth of the Salado drainage, which heads in the Gallinas Springs area (Marshall and Walt 1984). To the west the large Mariana Mesa sites are defensively postured, and they and the populations of the Tularosa Valley disappear in the early AD 1300s. We postulate a movement of the latter southward to the Cliff area, one that positioned them in a safer area where irrigation was also possible. More generally, we suggest that these events are related to one another.

From Chupadera Mesa to Casas Grandes

From Chupadera Mesa southward to Casas Grandes the distribution of Chupadero Black-on-white (T. Clark 1999, 2001; Clark and Creel 2002; Creel et al. 2002; Di Peso et al. 1974a; Mera 1943) is evidence of another distinct zone of interaction that linked the northern (Puebloan) Southwest to the southern Southwest. Hewett (1993 [1908]) and Kidder (1916, 1924) regarded the Casas Grandes culture as part of the Puebloan world, but our findings suggest a very different structural relationship. The way architectural space is organized within Paquimé is radically different from the patterns seen in northern pueblo sites generally and in Chaco great houses specifically (Wilcox 1999b).[22]

The Casas Grandes region has long been thought to have been included in the Mimbres interaction sphere of the eleventh and twelfth centuries, and the redeployment of some Mimbres populations may have contributed to the apparent implosion of people into the Casas Grandes world (Carey 1931; Schaafsma and Riley, eds. 1999; Wilcox 1995a; but see Whalen and Minnis 2003). We wonder if the movement of other Mimbres populations east of the Black Range (Nelson 1999) helped to establish new "exchange structures" (see Braudel 1980) that redefined the structural connectivity in the southeastern sector of the Southwest.

The post–AD 1300 buffer zone between the Casas Grandes world and the Pueblo world reported by Wilcox (1991b) is supported by our maps; populations in the boot heel of New Mexico were clearly aligned with the former, as recent studies at the Joyce Well site (Skibo et al. 2002) indicate. Yet the data for Chupadero Black-on-white show that this buffer zone was crossed by economic exchanges (see also Vokes and Gregory, chap. 17, this vol.).[23] Much more research in this critical area is needed. It is from this sector, traditionally classified under the rubric of Jornada Mogollon but deriving in part from both Mimbres and Casas Grandes sources, that the katsina iconography may have sprung, spreading northward up the Rio Grande and then westward to Zuni and Hopi (Schaafsma 1996, 1999, 2000; Schaafsma and Schaafsma 1974; but see Adams 1991; Crotty 1991).

The transformation of Chupadero Black-on-white into Tabira Black-on-white ca. AD 1400 (Toulouse 1960; Wilson et al. 1983) is matched by the emergence of Sikyatki Polychrome ca. AD 1375 and Zuni Buff Ware ca. AD 1400 (see Mills, chap. 13, this vol.).[24] The iconography of Sikyatki style soon appears in all of them (Kelley Hays-Gilpin, personal communication 2003), and, by induction, we suspect that closer examination of Rio Grande Glaze Ware, Jemez Black-on-

white, and biscuitware from the early 1400s may result in the definition of a "horizon style" (Willey and Phillips 1958) or something like it that swept across all of the northern Southwest at that time. Late Kechipawan Polychrome in early-fifteenth-century Zuni sites also exhibits Sikyatki style elements (Andrew Duff, personal communication 2003). Attention to this issue would be a fruitful way to reconceptualize the debate about whether the katsina cult moved from east to west or west to east.

Other Patterns

Within the northern Southwest there are four other structural patterns relevant to a consideration of the role of the Zuni region. First is the sudden, contemporaneous construction of four >1,000-room nucleated pueblos: at Kin Tiel (Wide Ruins), with three stories and a total of 1,300 rooms (Dennis Gilpin, personal communication 2003); at Kluckhohn, with 1,100+ rooms; at Archaeotekopa II, with 1,400+ rooms (Kintigh 1985); and at Box S at Nutria, with 1,000 rooms (Jonathan Damp, personal communication 2003). All four of these sites lie in the southern sector of the old Chacoan world, and Chacoan techniques were used to build the walls of Kin Tiel (Dennis Gilpin, personal communication 2001). A cluster of tree-ring dates from two burned kivas at Kin Tiel (where there were also unburied bodies on the floor) places construction at AD 1276, and it appears likely that the whole pueblo was built all at once (Hargrave 1931a). The point estimate for the construction of the other three is AD 1275 (LeBlanc 2001; Keith Kintigh, personal communication 2002)!

By AD 1299 or a very few years later all three were depopulated, as was the whole Klagetoh Black-on-white region centered on Kin Tiel and the

Jacks Lake area centered on Archaeotekopa II. A wide buffer zone thus opened up between Hopi and Zuni. Warfare probably accounts for these rapid transformations (LeBlanc 2001). Although it has been supposed that the Kin Tiel populations migrated to Zuni (Green 1990; Reagan 1928, 1929; Reed 1941, 1955), we propose that most of them spoke Keresan and that they went primarily to Antelope Mesa, as Hargrave (1935:22–23) postulated; Kawaika'a, for example, is a Keresan word (Harrington 1909).[25] Quantitatively, Antelope Mesa increased in room counts at this time (see also Hargrave 1935:22), while Zuni declined. Ceramic studies of early AD 1300s assemblages from Antelope Mesa sites are needed to test this proposition.[26]

Another striking pattern apparent from a comparison of the 3.5-km clusters on the maps (see figs. 12.6–12.13) is that many regions began as a single cluster and then fragmented into multiple neighboring population aggregates. This happened at Zuni and Hopi and in the Chama Basin, the Phoenix Basin, and the Galisteo Basin, though in the latter case several of the large pueblos were separate from the beginning. The part of the Galisteo Basin that was clustered is the sector that was depopulated by early Glaze E times, ca. AD 1525. All of the Chama Basin was depopulated by AD 1530–1540 (Schaafsma 2002).

The Jemez area, in contrast, began as two clusters (one linked by two hamlets to Zia) and grew into one. By the AD 1620s, however, Fray Benavides says the Jemez country was "almost depopulated by famine and wars which were on the way to finish them off" (qtd. in Ayer 1965 [1916]:346). (Notice that he does not mention disease.) We discuss these patterns in more detail below.

A third pattern is more speculative, but it follows logically from some of our other findings. When the center of the Chacoan world collapsed, what we take to be Tanoan populations in the north (Ford et al. 1972) at first attempted strategies of reorganization or revitalization (B. Bradley 1996; Varien 1999; Varien et al. 1996), only to bail out altogether by the late 1200s, heading for destinations in Rio Grande village clusters (Cameron 1995; Lipe 1995; Lipe et al. 1999). Populations *in the southern half* of the old Chacoan world, which we take to be Keresans, exited earlier, heading out along a broad arc from west to east and (we postulate) ending up in village clusters from Antelope Mesa to the El Morro Valley, Cebolleta Mesa, and the Rio Puerco of the East to the Zia / Santa Ana / San Felipe / Santo Domingo / Cochiti / southern Pajarito Plateau Keresan "wedge" in the midst of a Tanoan world (see also LeBlanc 1999). In the end, by the AD 1300s the enclaves of Keresan populations in the west (Antelope Mesa, Acoma) formed a "Keresan bridge" (to coin a phrase; see Eggan 1950; Fox 1967) that may have facilitated an east–west diffusion of ideas and styles from one end of the Puebloan world to the other—and back.

The sites of Pottery Mound and Hummingbird are well situated to have been important gateways to this "bridge." The position of Pottery Mound, for example, is near the southern end of the Rio Puerco of the East and immediately northwest of the Piro area. Cerro Indio (LA 287), a Glaze A site at the north end of the Piro area (Marshall and Walt 1984), has over 200 katsina-mask petroglyphs and pictographs (Schaafsma 1992). Is it too speculative to suggest that katsina iconography spread from the Piro to Pottery Mound (where there are at least seven kivas with "Sikyatki-style" mural art [Polly Schaafsma, personal communication 2003]) and thence westward via other

Keresan enclaves to Antelope Mesa at Hopi, where the Sikyatki style was first defined (Smith 1952) but where fewer kivas exhibiting it are known (only one)? An implication of this hypothesis is that there should be similar mural art in early-fifteenth-century Acoma and Zuni kivas. Is there?[27]

A fourth pattern of great interest for future studies is the evidence that settlement systems can be defined spatially on multiple scales of interaction. We saw above that during our Period 1 (AD 1200–1249) virtually the entire Southwest is interlinked into a single social and economic network of neighbor to neighbor interactions only a day or less apart. Stepping down, we can identify a series of "worlds" such as the Hohokam world, defined on the basis of platform mound distributions (Doelle et al. 1995; Wilcox 1999a), or a Casas Grandes world (Schaafsma and Riley, eds. 1999) that shares a diverse set of Chihuahuan polychrome ceramics. All of the Rio Grande from the Piro area northward was a single interlinked network, a string of settlements on either side of the Manzano Mountains providing connectivity, though along the Rio Grande this network had been restructured by the 1500s, and a buffer zone appeared between the Piro and Southern Tiwa (Wilcox 1991b).[28]

Stepping down again, the Tompiro area exhibits clusters at the 9-km scale, linking the Chupadera Arroyo villages to the Gran Quivira / Tabira area, Abo / Tenabo, and sites northward to Chilili. However, this pattern fragments in Period 6 (see fig. 12.11), coincident with the onset of the dog-nomad trade that brought bison meat, hides, and tallow into the easternmost pueblos (Baugh 1984; Spielmann 1983; Wilcox 1984; Wilcox et al. 2006). It is then that population apparently shifted out of the Chupa-

dera Arroyo settlements to the plains-edge pueblos of this region and the agrarian settlements farther east were depopulated (Kelley 1984; Stewart et al. 1991), which probably points to a major restructuring of bison procurement and exchange systems.[29] Similarly, at that time population rapidly increased in Taos, Picuris, and Pecos. These patterns point to the fundamental importance of the emergence of a pan-Pueblo macroeconomy. The fact that bison hides were traded as far west as both Zuni and Hopi (Hammond and Rey 1940:299) shows that this macroeconomy integrated the entire northern (Puebloan) Southwest with western plains hunter-gatherers. Competition to control it may be one of the processes that caused fragmentation of some pueblo clusters, especially that of the Galisteo Basin (Wilcox 1991b:151–152, 2005b; Wilcox et al. 2006).[30]

Above the settlement or "community" level our cost-surface analyses reveal the clusters we call "population aggregates." Clearly, there are then also clusters of clusters, which the set of all Hopi or all Zuni population aggregates indicates. These clusters are well defined by the 9-km scale groupings. All of the Chama Basin, however, or all of the Galisteo Basin clusters of clusters are also of considerable interest (cf. Wilcox 1991b). Above that level are the ceramically defined interaction zones of biscuit-ware or glazeware pottery: a cluster of cluster of clusters. It has long been thought that the biscuitware-making populations all spoke Northern Tewa (Mera 1934). Were they also a political confederacy (see Spielmann 1994)? For the glazeware populations, however, the linguistic situation is much more complex; Keres, Southern Tewa (Tano), Southern Tiwa, Piro, and Tompiro all were participants. In contrast, the Jemez cluster of clusters (Towa speakers) is characterized by

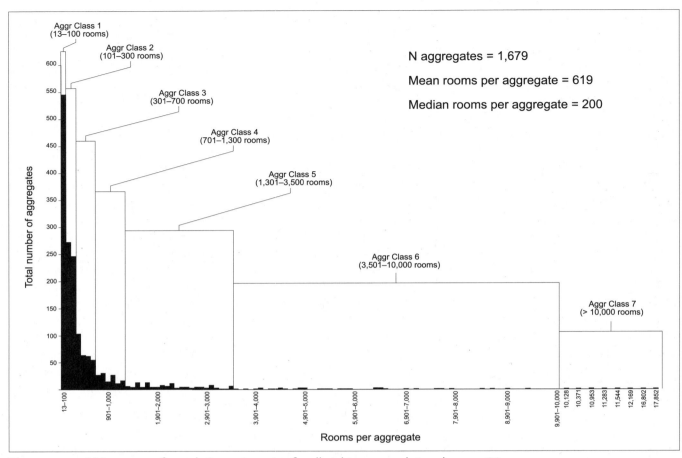

Figure 12.14. A histogram of population aggregates for all eight maps and size-class partitions.

Jemez Black-on-white pottery, but there were ceramic exchange ties to the Keres-speaking Zia cluster (data in ARMS site files), with whom they cluster at the 3.5-km scale.

To the extent that boundaries between these groupings were permeable (with exchange flows transcending them, perhaps more in some periods but less so in others), it might be possible to define a sphere of exchange involving a cluster of clusters of clusters of clusters: a "fourth power" cluster, if you will. The Puebloan macroeconomy resulting from the plains trade would thus be a "fifth power" cluster, and the fact that rare resources continued to cross between the southern Southwest (in central Sonora) and the northern Southwest during the middle sixteenth century (Riley 1982, 1987) sug-

gests that there was still, even then, a Southwest-wide sphere of exchange, a "sixth power" cluster. We have only begun to address this complexity in anything approaching an adequate way, though we believe that, for the Rio Grande, the studies of Anna Shepard (1942), Helene Warren (1970a, 1970b, 1970c, 1973), and Judith Habicht-Mauche (1993), in particular, have taken giant steps in the right direction; Andrew Duff (2002) has similarly set a new standard of this kind for the Colorado Plateau.

A Closer Look at Population Aggregates

A histogram (see fig. 12.14) of the 3.5-km population aggregates suggests seven size classes, as follows: Class 7, >10,000 rooms; Class 6, 3,501–

10,000 rooms; Class 5, 1,301–3,500 rooms; Class 4, 701–1,300 rooms; Class 3, 301–700 rooms; Class 2, 101–300 rooms; and Class 1, 13–100 rooms. Table 12.3 provides summary statistics of room frequencies and densities for each aggregate class for each period. The rank order of each population aggregate in our sample is shown in table 12.4. By assigning a map symbol to each of the population-aggregate size classes, a new map series was generated (see figs. 12.15–12.22). For purposes of comparison, we arbitrarily split the Phoenix Basin aggregate into the Salt and the Gila, and we did this for two other clusters as well (Jemez East from Zia and Nambe from the southern Pajarito Plateau).

These maps allow us to see all those places on the southwestern

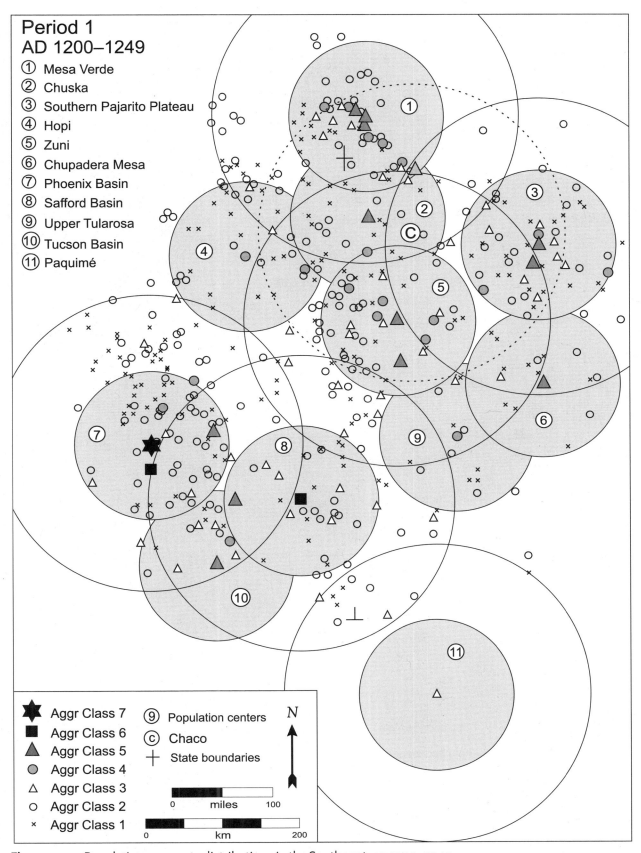

Figure 12.15. Population aggregate distributions in the Southwest, AD 1200–1249.

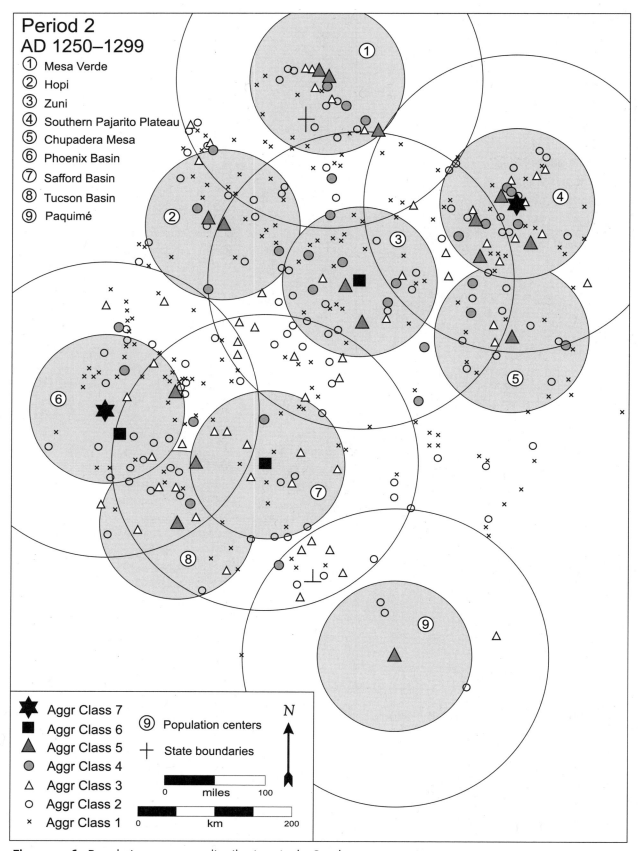

Figure 12.16. Population aggregate distributions in the Southwest, AD 1250–1299.

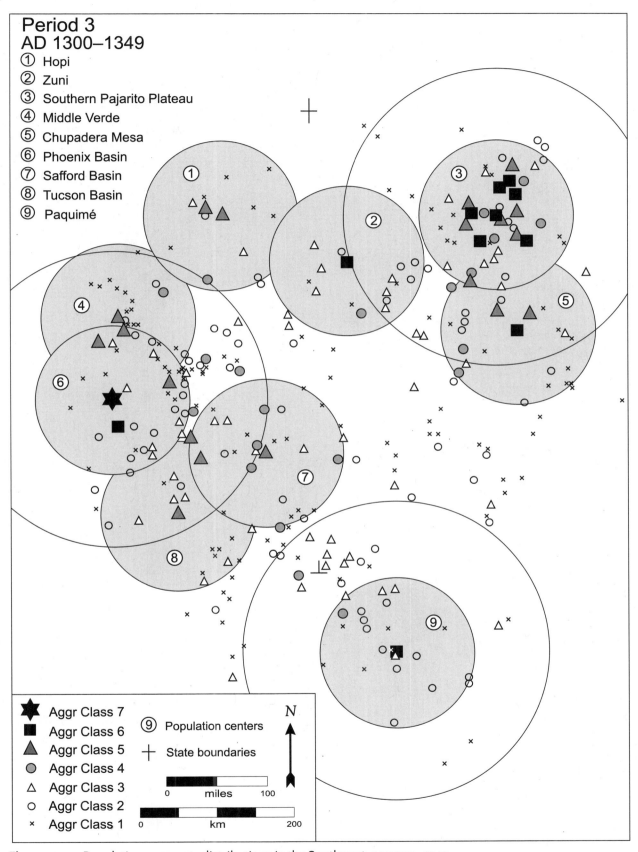

Figure 12.17. Population aggregate distributions in the Southwest, AD 1300–1349.

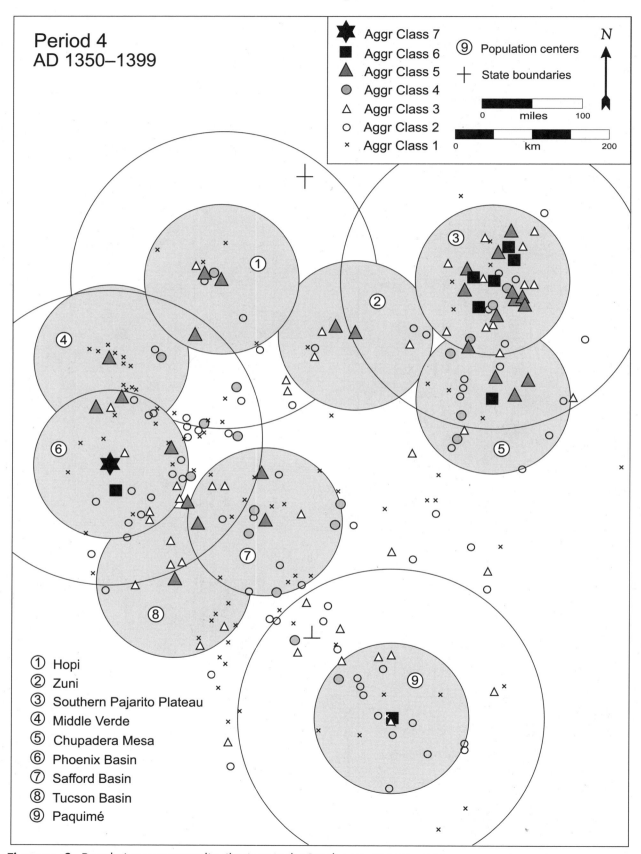

Figure 12.18. Population aggregate distributions in the Southwest, AD 1350–1399.

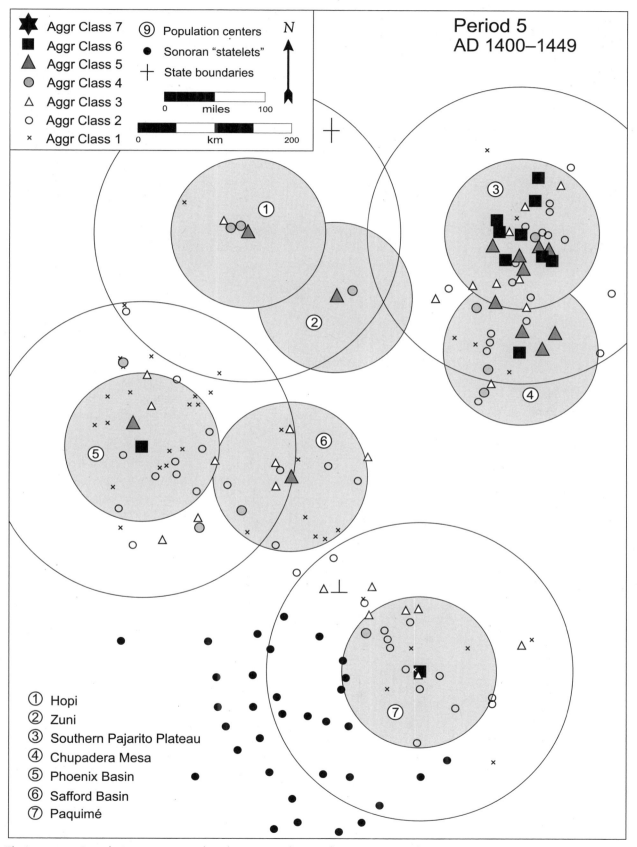

Figure 12.19. Population aggregate distributions in the Southwest, AD 1400–1449.

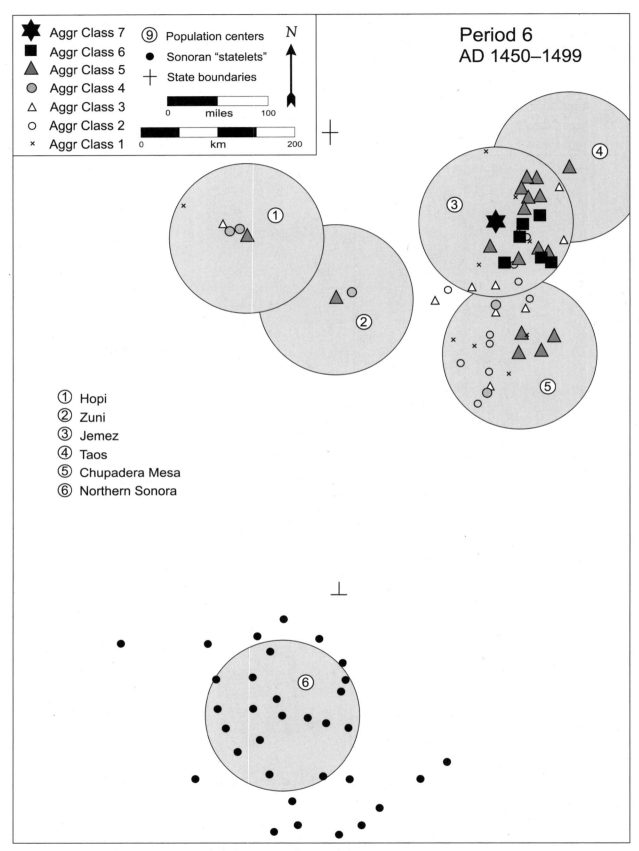

Figure 12.20. Population aggregate distributions in the Southwest, AD 1450–1499.

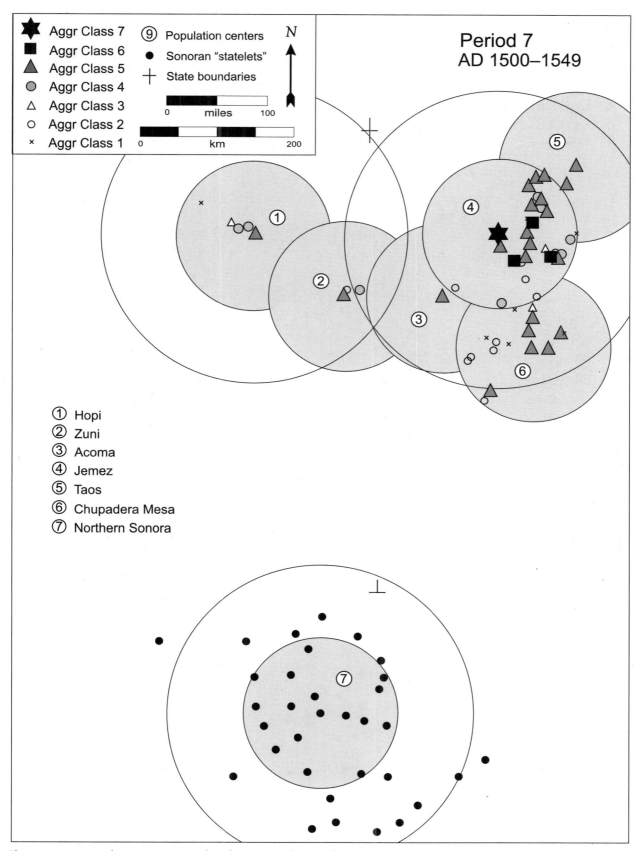

Figure 12.21. Population aggregate distributions in the Southwest, AD 1500–1549.

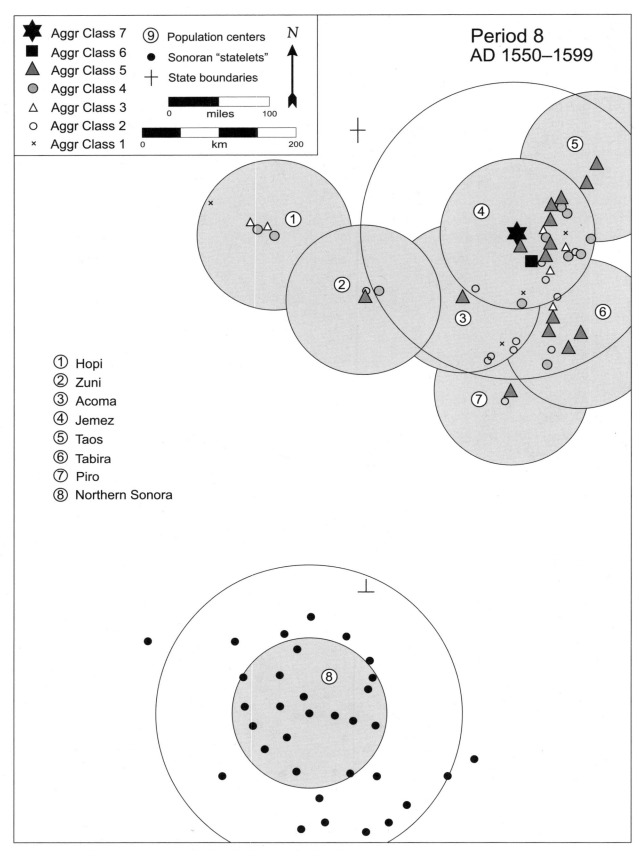

Figure 12.22. Population aggregate distributions in the Southwest, AD 1550–1599.

Table 12.3 Summary Statistics for 3.5-km, 9-km, and 18-km Aggregates for Each Period

Aggregate Data	Period 1 1200–1249	Period 2 1250–1299	Period 3 1300–1349	Period 4 1350–1399	Period 5 1400–1449	Period 6 1450–1499	Period 7 1500–1549	Period 8 1550–1599
3.5 km								
N	378	403	325	256	152	59	56	50
Total area	32,189	35,678	26,154	22,063	12,964	4,870	4,672	3,820
Total rooms	123,339	174,717	184,383	172,418	133,891	95,990	87,108	64,750
Room density	3.83	4.90	7.05	7.81	10.33	19.71	18.64	16.95
Median rooms per aggregate	112	140	200	250	250	650	1032	837
Mean rooms per aggregate	326	432	567	674	880	1627	1556	1295
Proportion of rooms in aggregate Class 1	8.2	5.6	3.8	2.6	2.0	.59	.04	.04
Class 2	16.2	12.8	9.1	8.8	8.0	2.1	2.4	3.5
Class 3	20.1	16.6	15.8	12.8	9.7	4.8	1.6	4.2
Class 4	14.8	16.9	11.2	10.2	7.5	5.5	8.8	17.6
Class 5	23.1	24.0	23.2	33.1	22.1	40.1	54.7	49.8
Class 6	9.2	11.6	30.4	25.8	50.6	35.1	19.4	8.8
Class 7	8.4	12.4	6.6	6.7	0	11.8	12.6	15.6
9 km								
N	102	120	118	95	64	22	19	15
Total area	211,030	124,082	89,682	82,734	49,994	18,600	18,011	15,573
Room density	.58	1.41	2.06	2.08	2.68	5.16	4.84	4.16
18 km								
N	21	23	35	34	32	6	6	6
Total area	242,607	270,169	234,422	195,464	121,212	41,377	41,377	41,377
Room density	.51	.65	.79	.88	1.10	2.34	2.10	2.10

landscape where population was concentrated in the AD 1200–1599 period and how those distributions changed from period to period. Noticing that in Period 1 (AD 1200–1249; see fig. 12.15) there were six overall concentrations of population (and we assume that in the vicinity of Casas Grandes there were more sites than we currently know about; see Whalen and Minnis 2003; Wilcox 2005a), we arbitrarily drew a circle with a radius of 100 km and one of 200 km centered on the largest settlement in each of these six zones. The circles serve heuristically to block out the

spheres of demographic weight or influence that these six zones may have had. We then added a 100-km circle to the other relatively large sites not "captured" by the initial circles. For Periods 5–8 we also show the Opata/Pima Bajo villages from Sauer's (1934) map, our purpose being to reemphasize that the "southern Southwest" may have continued to exist in central Sonora. Once again we encourage readers to study tables 12.3 and 12.4 and the eight population aggregate maps before continuing with our narrative, looking for whatever patterning they may notice.

Many of the patterns apparent in table 12.3 and on the maps reiterate those already discussed above: a sharp decline in the smallest population aggregates, a marked increase in median and mean number of rooms per site, and the greatly increased importance of the larger population aggregates. Densities also increase predictably, given decreases in the total area occupied. Differences between the trajectories of the larger size classes, however, are new: there was a Class 7 aggregate in all but Period 5; Class 5 (1,301–3,500 rooms) rises from about a quarter of all

Table 12.4 Rank Order of 3.5-km Population Aggregates, AD 1200–1599

Rank	Period 1 1200–1249	Period 2 1250–1299	Period 3 1300–1349	Period 4 1350–1399	Period 5 1400–1449	Period 6 1450–1499	Period 7 1500–1549	Period 8 1550–1599
1 N rooms	Salt 10,294	Salt 11,344	Salt 12,169	Salt 11,544	Southern Pajarito Plateau 9,378	Jemez 11,283	Jemez 10,953	Jemez 10,128
2 N rooms	Gila 6,508	Pajarito/Nambe 10,371	Southern Pajarito Plateau 7,643	Southern Pajarito Plateau 8,600	Chama 8,920	Albuquerque 7,560	Albuquerque 7,560	Albuquerque 5,720
3 N rooms	Safford 4,885(+)	Zuni 8,458	Chupadera Mesa 6,596	Gila 6,333	Albuquerque 7,174	Galisteo East 6,480	Tyuoni 4,891	Tonque 3,070
4 N rooms	Mesa Verde 3,340	Gila 6,508	Zuni 6,358	Nambe 5,848	Galisteo East 6,480	Tyuoni 5,491	San Lazaro 4,452	Tyuoni 3,000
5 N rooms	San Pedro 3,100	Safford 5,340	Gila 6,333	Chama 5,677	Nambe 5,200	Nambe 5,000	Pueblo Colorado 3,412	Zia 2,750
6 N rooms	Montezuma Valley 2,573	Casas Grandes 3,500	Albuquerque 4,942	Albuquerque 4,864	Jemez East 4,657	Southern Pajarito Plateau 4,718	Tonque 3,070	Tabira 2,575
7 N rooms	Tonto Basin 2,494	San Pedro 3,488	Nambe 4,903	Chupadera Mesa 4,511	Ojo Caliente 4,575	San Lazaro 4,452	Chupadera Mesa 2,915	Española Valley 2,400
8 N rooms	Southern Pajarito Plateau 2,369	Hopi 3,350	Casas Grandes 4,000	Casas Grandes 4,000	San Lazaro 4,452	Ojo Caliente 3,475	Zia 2,800	Acoma 2,250
9 N rooms	Mariana Mesa 2,340(−)	Tonto Basin 3,293	Jemez East 3,978	Galisteo East 3,423	Chupadera Mesa 4,398	Tonque 3,415	Ojo Caliente 2,800	Santo Domingo 2,218
10 N rooms	Tucson Basin 2,250	Southern Zuni 3,195	Galisteo Basin 3,946	Jemez E 3,107	Jemez W 4,301	San Marcos 3,000	Española Valley 2,675	Abo 2,125
11 N rooms	Zuni 1,930	Puye 3,098	Puye 3,732	Antelope Mesa 3,025	Gila 4,225	Chupadera Mesa 2,740	Tabira 2,575	Taos 2,000
12 N rooms	Cochiti 1794	Galisteo Basin 2,959	Chama 3,567	Los Lentes 2,888	Casas Grandes 4,000	Zia 2,588	Acoma 2,250	Picuris 2,000
13 N rooms	Aztec 1,738	Aztec 2,799	Antelope Mesa 3,175	Safford 2,713	Tonque 3,415	Tabira 2,575	Santo Domingo 2,218	Gran Quivira 1,700~
14 N rooms	Chuska South 1,708	Antelope Mesa 2,735	Los Lentes 2,938	Ojo Caliente 2,650	Zia 3,125	Antelope Mesa 2,400	South Zuni 2,168	South Zuni 1,624
15 N rooms	Chupadera Mesa 1,550	Tucson Basin 2,250	Santo Domingo 2,843	San Lazaro 2,477	San Marcos 3,000	Abo 2,125	Abo 2,125	Puye 1,600
Total rooms	48,873	72,688	77,123	71,660	73,700	67,302	56,864	45,160
Percent	.3962	.4160	.4183	.4156	.5504	.7011	.6528	.6975

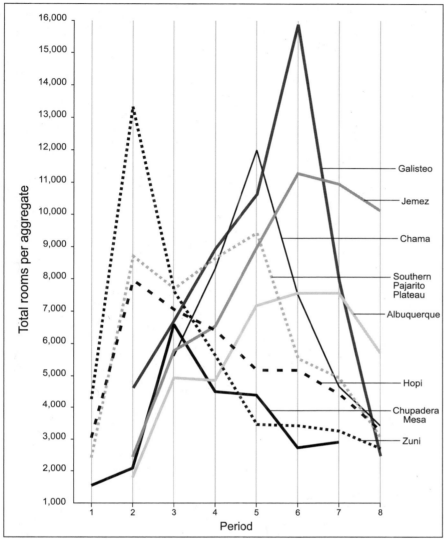

Figure 12.23. Graph of room counts for combined population aggregates in the northern Southwest, AD 1200–1599.

form "clusters of clusters" such as those at Hopi, Zuni, and so on. Tables 12.5 and 12.6 present rank-order data for such combinations, grouping the northern Southwest and the southern Southwest separately. Figure 12.23 presents these data for the northern Southwest in a highly instructive graph. Looking first at table 12.5, we see that overall room counts fell steadily after Period 2, a little faster in Period 6, and more steeply in Period 8, following the initial Spanish *entradas*. In contrast, Period 3 (AD 1300–1349) is the population peak in that part of the southern Southwest represented in our sample (see table 12.6). We suspect that differences between the northern and southern Southwest are produced by an under-representation of sites for the latter area. This results from a relative lack of archaeological survey in northern Mexico and from a too narrow geographic definition of the southern Southwest; arguably, that definition should include the Opata and Pima Bajo areas. For Period 7 Sauer (1935) estimated the Opata at 60,000 people (not rooms) and the Pima Bajo at 25,000 people. He used an estimate of seven persons per household. As researchers today are more inclined to estimate only five persons per household (see also Bandelier 1892:47), we can multiply Sauer's total estimate by five sevenths and thus arrive at a population figure of 60,000 for the southern Southwest in Period 7 (AD 1500–1549). The relationship of room counts to populations of people is discussed further below.

In the northern Southwest, if we were to combine all the population aggregates in the Mesa Verde area within the 9-km cluster, the total room count in Period 1 is about 15,600 rooms. This is only slightly less than the combined Phoenix Basin cluster (at the 3.5-km scale) of

rooms to a third, drops, and then rises in the last two periods to about 50 percent; and Class 6 (3,501–10,000 rooms) rises from about 9 percent to a peak of 50 percent in Period 5 and then falls again at the end to only 9 percent.

Rank-order data (see table 12.4) also provide new insights into just how dynamic, even chaotic, the changing positions were for each population aggregate. The Salt River valley was the largest population aggregate in the Southwest for two centuries (AD 1200–1399), falling

sharply below the middle Gila Valley in Period 5, possibly due to devastating floods that compromised residents' ability to continue irrigation there (Graybill et al. 2006; Nials et al. 1989). From AD 1450 to 1599 total room counts in the Jemez cluster reached levels previously achieved in the Salt, only presumably to crash by the 1620s (see above). The general story here is one of rise and fall, boom and bust.

Another way to look at these data is to combine the room counts for selected population aggregates that

Table 12.5 Rank Order of 3.5-km Population Aggregates in the Northern Southwest, AD 1200–1599

Rank	Period 1 1200–1249	Period 2 1250–1299	Period 3 1300–1349	Period 4 1350–1399	Period 5 1400–1449	Period 6 1450–1499	Period 7 1500–1549	Period 8 1550–1599
1 N rooms	Zuni 4,222	Zuni 13,278	Southern Pajarito Plateau 7,643	Galisteo 8,900	Chama 12,020	Galisteo 15,834	Jemez 10,953	Jemez 10,128
2 N rooms	Mesa Verde 3,340	Southern Pajarito Plateau 8,650	Zuni 7,554	Southern Pajarito Plateau 8,600	Galisteo 10,583	Jemez 11,283	Galisteo 7,864	Albuquerque 5,720
3 N rooms	Hopi 2,995	Hopi 7,905	Hopi 7,000	Chama 8,317	Southern Pajarito Plateau 9,378	Albuquerque 7,560	Albuquerque 7,560	Hopi 3,205
4 N rooms	Montezuma Valley 2,573	Galisteo 4,576	Galisteo 6,673	Jemez 6,532	Jemez 8,958	Chama 7,522	Tyuoni 4,891	Tonque 3,070
5 N rooms	Southern Pajarito Plateau 2,369	Puye 3,098	Chupadera Mesa 6,596	Hopi 635	Albuquerque 7,174	Tyuoni 5,491	Chama 4,678	Tyuoni 3,000
6 N rooms	Mariana Mesa 2,340	Aztec 2,799	Jemez 5,783	Nambe 5,848	Nambe 5,200	Hopi 5,130	Hopi 4,380	Zia 2,750
7 N rooms	Cochiti 1,794	Jemez 2,442	Chama 5,617	Zuni 5,570	Hopi 5,130	Nambe 5,200	Zuni 3,204	Zuni 2,660
8 N rooms	Aztec 1,738	Mariana Mesa 2,212	Albuquerque 4,942	Albuquerque 4,864	Chupadera Mesa 4,398	Cochiti 4,718	Tonque 3,070	Tabira 2,575
9 N rooms	Chuska South 1,708	Chupadera Mesa 2,085	Nambe 4,903	Chupadera Mesa 4,511	Tonque 3,415	Tonque 3,415	Chupadera Mesa 2,915	Galisteo 2,419
10 N rooms	Chupadera Mesa 1,550	Mesa Verde South 1,995	Puye 3,732	Homolovis 3,055	Zuni 3,411	Zuni 3,372	Zia 2,800	Española 2,400
11 N rooms	Mesa Verde South 1,301	Albuquerque 1,797	Los Lunas 2,938	Los Lunas 2,888	Zia 3,125	Chupadera Mesa 2,749	Española Valley 2,675	Acoma 2,250
Total population	71,263	110,760	107,782	103,582	102,323	95,990	87,108	64,750

about 17,000–18,000 rooms. Those considerations aside, in table 12.5 Zuni is shown in the first rank during Periods 1 and 2 and declining after that. However, the room counts for Period 2 are probably a doubling of actual values, given the redeployment from small Scribe S sites to large nucleated pueblos discussed above. The actual count was probably in the same range as the southern Pajarito Plateau and Hopi during Period 2. Nevertheless, population did begin pouring into the El Morro Valley at the upper, eastern end of the Zuni region ca. AD 1225 (Kintigh 1985, chap. 18, this vol.). We see this as being related to the breakup of the Chacoan macroregional system after AD 1200, a kind of "internal migration" within the distribution area of Chacoan great houses (see fig. 12.24). While it has long been assumed that the migrants to the El Morro Valley

Table 12.6 Rank Order of Grouped 3.5-km Population Aggregates in the Southern Southwest, AD 1200–1599

Rank	Period 1 1200–1249	Period 2 1250–1299	Period 3 1300–1349	Period 4 1350–1399	Period 5 1400–1449	Period 6 1450–1499	Period 7 1500–1549
1	Salt	Salt	Salt	Salt	Gila		
N rooms	10,294	11,344	12,169	11,544	4,225		
2	Gila	Gila	Gila	Gila	Casas Grandes		
N rooms	6,508	6,508	6,333	6,333	4,000		
3	Safford	Safford	Casas Grandes	Casas Grandes	Salt		
N rooms	4,885+	5,340+	4,000	4,000	1,850		
4	San Pedro	Casas Grandes	Tonto Basin	Safford	Safford		
N rooms	3,100	3,500	2,804	2,713+	1,450+		
5	Tonto Basin	San Pedro	Safford	Upper San Pedro			
N rooms	2,494	3,488	2,781	2,238			
6	Tucson Basin	Tonto Basin	Southern San Pedro	Lower Verde			
N rooms	2,250	3,293	2,238	1,933			
7		South Tucson	Middle Verde	Perry Mesa			
N rooms		2,250	2,166	1,772			
8			Lower Verde	Northern San Pedro			
N rooms			1,933	1,570			
9			Middle San Pedro	Middle Verde			
N rooms			1,570	1,566			
10			South Tucson	Point of Pines			
N rooms			1,450	1,513			
Total population	52,076	63,957	76,601	73,836	31,568		(85,000 people)

were largely from nearby areas and probably spoke Zunian (see Kintigh, chap. 18, this vol.), it is quite possible that many of them spoke Keresan and came from areas north of the Zuni Mountains. Acoma does claim the upper El Morro Valley as part of its ancestral area (Dittert 1959; Dittert and Brunson-Hadley 1999). New studies are needed to test this possibility.

Occupants of the first rank in the northern Southwest after Period 2 are, successively, the southern Pajarito Plateau, the Galisteo Basin, the Chama Basin, the Galisteo Basin again (at over 15,000 rooms during Period 6), and then Jemez for the last two periods. Except for the Galisteo Basin, which surged into first place a second time (coincident with the onset of the dog-nomad trade), each of these regions then plummeted in

population after peaking, including Jemez in the early 1600s, as discussed above. Thus, the boom-and-bust pattern is reaffirmed at the level of clusters of clusters. The relative position of the Tompiro cluster of clusters would be higher than shown in table 12.5 if we had combined those population aggregates, but it, too, lost population by Period 8, and the whole Tompiro area was totally depopulated by the early 1670s.

Figure 12.23 provides another way to visualize these data. If, in our mind's eye, we correct the Zuni peak, we see that, starting from a range of about 2,200–4,000 rooms in Period 1, the clusters of clusters at Zuni, Hopi, and the southern Pajarito Plateau surged to around 7,000–8,000 rooms in Period 2. In all three cases this is probably due to the movement of people out of the southern part of

the old Chacoan world, the location of which is shown on the Period 1 map (see fig. 12.15). In Period 3 we see a strikingly unique pattern: all of the clusters considered fall within a common range of about 4,500–7,500 rooms. This could indicate that in the final depopulation of the northern San Juan populations went not just to one or two places but spread out more or less equally among many receiving population aggregates. Another striking pattern is in what happens next: many clusters decline while others surge, each with its own trajectory. However, once each of them peaked, all fell to a common level of about 2,500–3,500 rooms. The southern Tiwa of the Albuquerque region, in the second rank in Period 7, were brutally attacked by Coronado's army, 12 or 13 villages were burned, and many people were cruelly burned at the

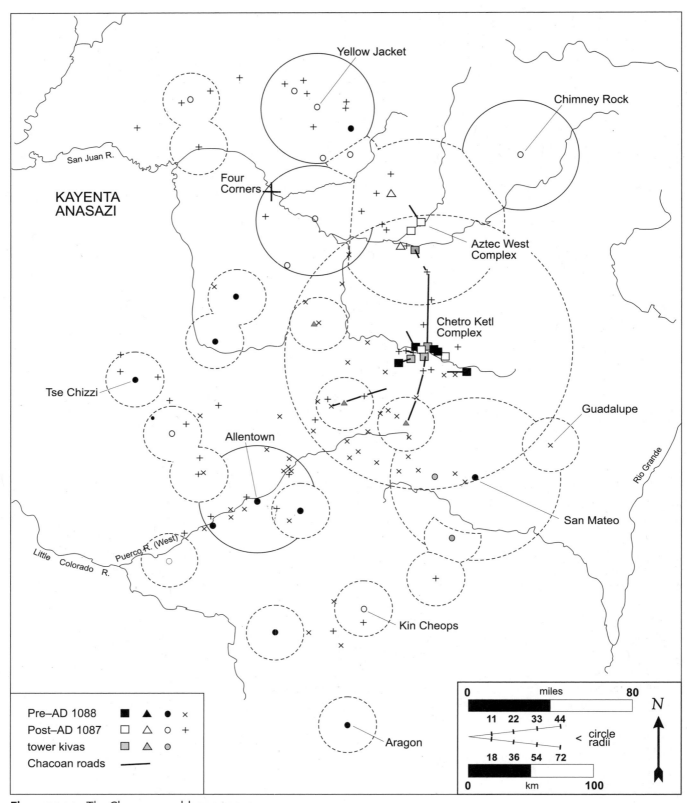

Figure 12.24. The Chacoan world, AD 1050–1149.

stake (Hammond and Rey 1940:338; Riley 1981). The size decrease in Period 8 is probably due, in part, to those events, although the villages retained their relative size rank.

We are led by these data to propose two hypotheses: (1) the range of 2,500–3,500 rooms is an equilibrium level that is characterized by a high degree of village economic autonomy (just as Bandelier [1892] thought), and (2) there was relatively little economic pooling with neighbors. Political authority was weak in that "structural pose" (see Gearing 1962). Fray Benavides in 1630 shrewdly noted that in "all these folk and nations were their gentilism divided into factions, warriors and sorcerers. The warriors tried, in opposition to the sorcerers, to bring all the people under their [own] dominion and authority; and the sorcerers with the same opposition, persuaded all that they made the rain fall and the earth yield up good crops, and other things at which the warriors sneered" (Ayer 1965 [1916]:349).[31] Such factionalism could account for Juan de Oñate's impression, as he reported to the viceroy in 1599, that "their government is one of complete freedom, for although they have some chieftains they obey them badly and in very few matters" (Hammond and Rey 1953:484). Yet elsewhere in the Spanish accounts we can find statements that point to a much more hierarchical organization, and many "provinces" (clusters, or clusters of clusters) are said to have "principal" settlements (Hammond and Rey 1940:72, 185, 215, 1953:635, 1966: 219–220; see also Wilcox 1981). One of the greatest challenges to constructing a "new ethnography" of the Pueblos (Wilcox 1981) has been how we can reconcile these contradictory statements of Spanish eyewitnesses.

The patterns shown in figure 12.23 suggest an answer. In times of external threat or in times of high reli-

gious excitement the power balance described by Benavides would have shifted. At those times one side or the other of the factional forces could have mobilized more support and could also have engaged in greater cooperation with other communities in the same neighborhood. Such occasions seem to be indicated by those times when the population aggregates reached levels of 10,000–18,000 rooms.[32] The Hohokam in the Phoenix Basin appear to have been the most successful in sustaining such levels of integration (Wilcox 1999a, 2005c), while all of the cases in the northern Southwest suggest that such demographic (adaptive) success was maintained for only brief periods before fractionating and plummeting to a lower equilibrium level. Descriptions given to the Spaniards of more hierarchical organization may refer to the *theory* in place during these alternative "structural poses." Edmund Leach's (1954) description of the Highland Burmese social organization might be an analogous kind of alternation between more hierarchical and more equalitarian organization. Alternatively, the ideas about more hierarchical organization may be part of the Pueblos' "cultural memory" of times past that some people thought should be restored. (For other interpretations see Adams and Duff 2004; McGuire and Saitta 1996.)

One other pattern apparent in table 12.4 is worth noting. Comparison of the total rooms, rank by rank, between Periods 7 and 8 shows that in most cases there is a drop from Period 7 to Period 8. This might be evidence of a disease vector *generally* affecting the Puebloan world. The total depopulation of the Chama Basin, AD 1530–1540 (Schaafsma 2002), the partial depopulation of the Galisteo Basin ca. AD 1525, and the somewhat earlier emergence of a gap

in population distribution between the Piro and Tiguex provinces (see above) can all be attributed to warfare and associated famine (Wilcox 1991b). Benavides (Ayer 1965 [1916]), we have seen, attributed the sharp decline he reported of Jemez populations in the early 1600s to similar causes and not to disease. If European diseases were introduced to New Mexico before the Spanish colony was established in 1598, which no one would dispute is *possible*, we would expect it to have affected all Pueblo populations fairly uniformly, not just devastating some groups or affecting only the edges of Pueblo provinces that were at war with one another (Wilcox 1991b). That kind of uniformity seems to be indicated by the data in table 12.4 for Period 8 (AD 1550–1599) compared with Period 7. Alternatively, this pattern may result from the impact of the Coronado *entrada* due to tribute exactions and devastation of the Southern Tiwa villages, which lie in the middle of the Rio Grande macroregion. If the net flow of goods in the Pueblo macroeconomy was reduced by these processes, the general population levels that it sustained may then have been lowered. New studies of these intriguing possibilities are needed.

The Relationship between Room Counts and Human Population

Room counts have often been taken to be a proxy for or a stepping stone to the estimation of population. In the Perry Mesa study (Wilcox et al. 2001a), for example, the average room size in most of central Arizona was estimated to be 16–20 m². Using Naroll's (1962) estimate of 10 m² per person, it was possible to construct a simple equation to estimate population size from number of rooms. Bandelier (1892) long ago showed,

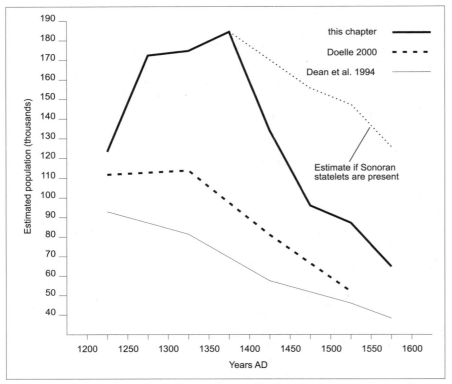

Figure 12.25. Hypothetical population curves for the North American Southwest compared.

however, that average room size in the Rio Grande is smaller, more like 10–12 m². He arrived at those figures by measuring a sample of rooms and taking an average. In light of this we have, as a rule of thumb, been assuming that there were one to two persons per room, and we propose that this is a reasonable way to convert room counts to population counts of humans.[33]

Such an assumption leads to a surprising result. Figure 12.25 shows two previously proposed demographic models of the American Southwest (without inclusion of northern Mexico) and our room-count results, assuming only one person per room. Radically different results are indicated. What explains this? While we believe a full answer to this question will require much more research, several considerations discussed below may be useful in constructing new

research designs about southwestern paleodemography.

Sixteenth-century Spanish accounts speak in terms of "houses" and number of stories (Hammond and Rey 1966). Several statements indicate that occupants of the "houses" were families (Hammond and Rey 1953:644), although one account states that "each house is occupied by a dweller and his family, and in some there are two or three [families]" (Hammond and Rey 1953:658–659). The general fact that historic pueblo room blocks partition well into sets (Adams 1983; Kidder 1958) suggests that what the Spaniards called "houses" are represented by these partition classes (see above). Because tribute was collected on a household basis (Hammond and Rey 1953), the Spaniards had reason to be accurate in such estimates. Given what we now know archaeologically, we may in

future be able to estimate the number of "houses" in the room blocks—from the Mera diagrams, for example. But how many people were there per house?

We often today use an estimate of five persons per family or household. For a Piro two-story house with three to five rooms per house (see Wilcox 1991b:140) this is still more than one person per room. Luxán (Hammond and Rey 1966:171), not necessarily the most careful Spanish observer, claimed that there were 400 Piro in pueblos of 50 houses, or eight persons per house (and about two persons per room). Gallegos, on the other hand, says of Zuni houses that "there is not a house of two or three stories that does not have eight rooms or more" (Hammond and Rey 1966: 108). In that case there may have been less than one person per room, and an average of one person per room appears to be the best general estimate for the northern Southwest.

Let us look further at what room/population estimates the early Spanish accounts give for Zuni compared to our findings (see table 12.5), where we show 3,204 rooms in Period 7 (1500–1549) and 2,660 rooms in Period 8 (1550–1599). The "Relación Postrera de Cíbola" says of the seven Zuni pueblos that "the largest one must have 200 houses; two others have 200, and the rest sixty, fifty, and thirty houses" (Hammond and Rey 1940:309). In contrast, the "Relación del Suceso" says that the Zuni pueblos "consist of three hundred, two hundred, and one hundred and fifty houses each" (Hammond and Rey 1940:285). Pedro de Castañeda (Hammond and Rey 1940:208, 222, 252) makes clear that the largest was Mazaque, with seven stories and 300 houses, while Hawikuh had 200 warriors. So, 300 + 200 + 200 + 150 + 60 + 50 + 30 = 990

Table 12.7 Testimony of Spanish Colonists about Pueblo Populations, AD 1601–1602

Observer	Total Number of Men Who Can Bear Arms	Total Men and Women	Total Men, Women, Children, and Old Men	Smallest Village	Largest Village	Comments
Joseph Brondate			50,000–60,000	30 houses 2 stories	400 houses 4 stories	130 pueblos
Marcelo de Espinosa	14,000–15,000	22,000–24,000	[55,000–60,000]	35 houses 2 stories	400 houses 4 and 5 stories	125–130 pueblos
Gines de Herrera Horta	12,000		[48,000–60,000]			110 pueblos; most pueblos 30–40 houses
C. Juan de Ortega	12,000–13,000		[48,000–>60,000]			
Cristobal Baca			60,000			
C. Bartolomé Romero			>60,000			
C. Alonso Gomez Montesinos			>60,000			
A. Martín Gomez			60,000			
C. Hernán Martín Serrano			>60,000			
Juan Luxán			60,000			
Antonio Correa			>60,000			
Baltasar Martínez		16,000	[>60,000]			
Juan de León		25,000+	[>60,000]	30 houses	400 houses	
Juan Rodriguez		30,000	[>60,000]			
Fray Juan de Escalona		<20,000	[<50,000]			

Source: Hammond and Rey 1953.

houses, each with an average of four to five rooms, yielding an estimate ca. AD 1540 of 3,960–4,950 rooms or people.

By the 1580s there were apparently only six extant Zuni pueblos, Matsaki had fallen to second place behind Hawikuh, and the total room count the Spaniards estimated came to only 448 houses. Multiplying by 4 and 5, we get 1,792–2,240 rooms or people, or only half the number from 40 years earlier inferred from the Coronado documents. Vicente de Zaldívar (Hammond and Rey 1953:921) reported that Cíbola (by which we think he meant Hawikuh) had 170–180 houses ca. AD 1600. Fray Escobar reported that "we came to the province of Quini [Zuni], which has six

pueblos, four of them almost completely in ruins, although all inhabited. The largest and the head town of these was called Scíbola by the Spaniards, and the Indians recognize it by this name, although in their own language it is called Hauico" (Hammond and Rey 1953:1012). We conclude from the comparison of these data that our room estimates are in the right ballpark (± 500–1,000 rooms), and they indicate the right trend of decline in numbers for Periods 7 and 8 (AD 1500–1599).

The Spaniards also gave overall estimates of the total number of Pueblo people. The Oñate documents from 1601 and 1602 are particularly instructive in this regard because the Spanish authorities took detailed and

systematic testimony from many witnesses about Oñate's misconduct, and one of the questions they asked concerns population totals. After taking some of this testimony they constructed a written "interrogatory," the first question of which was, "first, if the witness knows whether there are more than sixty thousand peaceful people . . . in these pueblos" (Hammond and Rey 1953:702). Table 12.7 summarizes the data from these testimonies. Not all of the witnesses interpreted the questions in the same way: some gave estimates of "men, women, children, and old men," while others estimated the number of men at arms, and others still gave numbers of men and women (Hammond and Rey 1953:629, 862, 639).

In the table we have suggested a reconciliation of these estimates to a common statistic, that of total "men, women, children, and old men," as one observer put it. We assume five persons per family/household and give a range derived from "men at arms" by multiplying by both 4 and 5. To convert the "men and women" estimates we divided by .4.

Many of the witnesses commented, as did Cristóbal Baca, that they believed that 60,000 was correct, *"as is well known to everyone"* (Hammond and Rey 1953:706; emphasis added). On the other hand, Capt. Bartolomé Romero declared that there were more than 60,000 and that "he had traveled through the pueblos of the entire land oftener than anyone else" (Hammond and Rey 1953:708). From table 12.7 we conclude that there were at least 48,000 Pueblo people ca. AD 1600, and more likely there were as many as 60,000 or more.[34] There were about 125–130 pueblos. These figures can be compared with our findings that in Period 8 (AD 1550–1599) there were 124 pueblos (still extant today) and about 64,750 rooms (see table 12.2). In round numbers, one person per room fits the facts remarkably well. The downward trajectory of decline during the late AD 1500s would probably reduce the room count by AD 1600 to about 60,000 rooms.

Sixty years before the Oñate observers were in New Mexico Pedro de Castañeda was there with the Coronado expedition (Hammond and Rey 1940). His careful inventory of the pueblos he or his companions saw totaled 66—but they probably did not go farther north than San Ildefonso (Schaafsma 2002:202), and they underestimate the number of Piro settlements. To estimate the total number of Pueblo *men* (which we assume means men capable of bearing arms), he noted that "this can be

easily estimated by the population of the pueblos, for between them there are no villages or houses, but, on the contrary, the land is all uninhabited" (Hammond and Rey 1940:259). That is to say, there were buffer zones on unoccupied lands between the pueblo clusters, something our Period 7 map (see fig. 12.12) and previous studies (Mera 1935; Wilcox 1991b) confirm. Castañeda concluded that "all combined [the pueblos] must contain about 20,000 *men*" (Hammond and Rey 1940:259; emphasis added). Multiplying this figure by 4 and 5, as we did above, this is equivalent to a range of 80,000–100,000 Pueblo people in AD 1540—*and it does not include all of the inhabited pueblos of that time.* We can compare this to our total room count for Period 7 of 87,108 rooms for all inhabited pueblos (see table 12.5). At a minimum, we think these data warrant the conservative conclusion that Castañeda's observations indicate that there were more Pueblo people in AD 1540 than the Oñate settlers reported for AD 1600, just as our room-count totals would predict.

A second point to make about differences between the Dean et al. (1994) and the Doelle (2000) findings and ours is that we can now more adequately sort out differences between the northern and southern Southwest and the demographic components that each contributes to the southwestern totals for each 50-year period. Once we accept that the southern Southwest extended well into northern Mexico (see Wilcox 1986b) and included the Opata/Pima Bajo area, then the demography of those areas (although unknown for most periods) must be considered before we attempt to draw general conclusions. By separating out the northern Southwest for separate evaluation (see table 12.5) we can show that there was a general decline of Puebloan populations after AD 1300 and that

populations still extant at AD 1600 were much larger than Dean et al. (1994) or Doelle (2000) inferred. While admitting that southern Southwest population estimates are underrepresentations, nevertheless, we can see that by including a modified demographic component from Sauer's (1935) study of Opata and Pima Bajo, the radical decline in Southwest populations suggested by Dean et al.'s (1994) and Doelle's (2000) curves considerably flattens out for the Southwest as a whole (see fig. 12.25). Even so, there is still a net decline.

Differences between Dean et al.'s (1994) and Doelle's (2000) findings and those reported here may thus be largely explained by our larger conception of the totality of the southwestern landscape and a greater appreciation for the geographic scale and demographic magnitudes of population redeployments (migrations) on it (but see Hill et al. 2004). Movements on comparable scales (but by smaller populations) have been proposed for earlier periods of southwestern prehistory (Berry 1982; Berry and Berry 1986; Matson 1991, chap. 7, this vol.). They probably indicate what Dean (1988a) might call a "low-frequency process" of adaptation to a climatically fickle arid landscape. How Southwest populations were able to "keep their options open" in this regard is thus shown to be one of the more fundamental problems of southwestern archaeology.

Concluding Thoughts

The idea that it was time, after 150 years of data collection on southwestern site locations and characteristics, to map out some of what is now known for the Southwest as a whole appears to have borne fruit. The two map series presented here have revealed basic structural patterns for the period AD 1200–1599 that have not been previously appreciated. The Coalescent Communities Database organizes these data in a form that can easily be added to or corrected as better data based on superior "local knowledge" are brought forward. A good basis has been established for the comparative study of southwestern settlement systems on multiple scales for the period AD 1200–1599, and a tremendous number of further analyses on many scales of inquiry can also now proceed. For example, complementary data sets should also now be constructed of all known field houses and farmsteads for this period. Comparable data sets for both earlier and later periods may also prove to be more feasible than we first assumed (e.g., see Wilcox 2005b; Wilcox et al. 2006). Many new research designs can be formulated using the Coalescent Communities Database. Finding ways to make these data more accessible to the archaeology profession should also be a top priority.

The Coalescent Communities Database should also greatly facilitate new studies of relationships of culture and environment using the concept of adaptation presented by Gregory and Wilcox in chapter 20, this volume. The distribution of tree-ring stations throughout the Southwest needs to be assessed in relation to the structures apparent in the patterns of settlement system distributions. Would it be advantageous to establish additional stations in certain zones, if that is possible? How do the patterns apparent in paleoenvironmental reconstructions (Dean 1988a, chap. 6, this vol.) correlate with the patterns in settlement systems? Can this intersection be modeled more dynamically than correlation approaches allow? How does the structure of the distribution of low-frequency patterning such as revealed in Gregory and Nials's El Niño study (chap. 5, this vol.) compare with long-term trends in the structure of various scales of settlement systems? A whole new world of investigation is now open before us.

What began as an inquiry into the place of Zuni in the Puebloan and southwestern worlds has thus led to much more general findings. That often happens in the course of problem-oriented research, particularly when it is unconstrained by arbitrary limitations. "Do not block the road to inquiry" is a slogan the American philosopher Charles Peirce had pinned on the door to his office. How pleasing it is to learn what can happen when that adage is followed! The study of Zuni archaeology has thus, once again, been central to the creation of new knowledge of interest to much larger fields of inquiry. We hope this is just the beginning of what now will occur as archaeologists and the Zuni people continue delving into the archaeology of Zuni origins.

Already, however, our findings serve to place the Zuni populations post–AD 1200 into a macroregional context in which demographic changes precipitated by collapse of the Chacoan macroregional system can be better understood. The idea that the Zuni "cluster of clusters" in the AD 1225–1400 time frame consisted of multiethnic communities is an important area for continuing research into questions of cultural affiliation and Zuni ethnogenesis. The findings presented by Mills, Kintigh, and Ferguson (chaps. 13, 18, and 19, this vol., respectively) can be evaluated by the reader in relation to the data of changing settlement systems.

Acknowledgments

We first thank all those archaeologists and others who, over the last 150 years or more, have recorded sites dating to the AD 1200–1599 interval; without their many efforts the present chapter could not have been written. We also thank the keepers of these site records, especially Scott Geister, Tim Seaman, Lou Hacker, and others at ARMS; Sharon Urban and Beth Grindel at the Arizona State Museum; Michael Barton at Arizona State University; John Ware at the Amerind Foundation; and the individuals listed in notes 1 and 2. For substantial financial and moral support we thank especially Dr. William H. Doelle, president of the Center for Desert Archaeology, and Dr. Robert Breunig, director of the Museum of Northern Arizona. Others who have graciously extended us valuable insights or hospitality during the assembling of data reported here include Polly and Curtis Schaafsma, Philip and Mary Ann Essig, and members of the Verde Valley Archaeological Society, especially Marlene and Jack Conklin and Sharon and Norm Olsen. We also thank all the participants in the Zuni origins seminar and especially Martha Clark for her warm hospitality during the proceedings at the Colton House. The cost-surface analyses were conducted by J. Brett Hill, who prepared figures 12.7–12.14. David Gregory prepared the rest with data supplied by Brett Hill, except figure 12.24, which was drafted by Jodi Griffith of the Museum of Northern Arizona. For any errors in fact or faulty interpretations we alone are responsible.

Notes

1. Marlene and Jack Conklin, members of the Verde Valley Archaeological Society, helped Wilcox collect these data. The Center for Desert Archaeology covered expenses for these and previous trips. In August 2002 Geomap produced a new series of eight distribution maps that Wilcox presented in a poster session at the seventy-fifth anniversary Pecos Conference. After the conference database management was transferred to the Center for Desert Archaeology, and J. Brett Hill became the new database manager.

2. The other collaborators include the following: for northern Arizona and southern Utah, Dennis Gilpin, Phil Geib, and Jeffrey S. Dean; for the greater Zuni area,

Keith Kintigh; for the greater Acoma area and the Rio Puerco of the East (and beyond), John Roney and his staff; for many parts of New Mexico, Curtis Schaafsma; for west-central Arizona, J. Scott Wood and Travis Bone; for the Salt River valley, Jerry Howard; for southern Arizona, William Doelle, Jeffery Clark, and Paul and Suzanne Fish. We are deeply grateful to all of these archaeologists and others for their generous contributions to this project.

3. As a result of merging Doelle's data with the rest, where we used his population estimates as though they were room counts, we now know that in the present analysis there is duplication of sites and thus overestimation of some room/population figures. Wilcox has now gone through all of these data and made assessments of room counts and age estimates comparable to other sites in the database; these corrections will inform future iterations of the present analyses (see Wilcox 2005b). Now that Doelle's estimates of population have been replaced by room counts, the total "rooms" in our results are reduced for periods before AD 1450. We are not persuaded that the trends found in the present analyses will be significantly affected, except perhaps as follows: the number of rooms calculated for the AD 1400–1449 period in southern Arizona may be significantly reduced; the total population of the Safford area may be less, although our size estimates here are very rough and may be badly underestimated (in which case the duplication here may have resulted in a more realistic picture!); the patterning in the San Pedro will change. Due to limitations of funding we are unable for the present purpose to redo the analyses with the corrections we now know should be made, and the reader should bear this in mind in evaluating the results discussed.

4. One factor that may affect the magnitude of the trends we display below is the possibility that many of the large New Mexico pueblos exhibit "horizontal stratigraphy"; Jonathan Haas (personal communication 2003) informs us that studies by him and Winifred Creamer in Chama Valley and Galisteo Basin sites support a conclusion that only a part of the huge pueblos in these areas was occupied at any one time, with occupations shifting horizontally over time. We await their demonstration of such a hypothesis.

5. On Perry Mesa, for example, the settlement pattern could be explained by postulating a warfare hypothesis that implied that early warning would be necessary for the system to be effective (Wilcox et al. 1999, 2001a). Discovery that such an early warning system was in place for an approach up the Agua Fria drainage was seen as support for this hypothesis (Wilcox et al. 2001a). A further test came when Wilcox realized that access to Perry Mesa from the south could also have occurred along Cave Creek, and he proceeded to look for a comparable "early warning system" there—and found it. A previously unrecorded 70-room pueblo (Fort Metate, NA 26,007) and a lookout (Six Bar Lookout, NA 26,001) combine to provide the potential for early warning to Squaw Creek Ruin (NA 12,555) and thus to the rest of the Perry Mesa settlement system (Wilcox et al. 2007).

6. The late Robert Euler suggested this term to Wilcox in connection with the protohistoric conference, and he has used it ever since (see Wilcox and Masse 1981).

7. We thus closely examined the ceramic data in the ARMS paper files and applied Curtis Schaafsma's (2002) chronological models to date the types. In our example above, if a site had only Glaze A pottery, we dated it to the AD 1300–1449 interval. For Colorado sites we accept Mark Varien's (1999) chronology. In northern and central Arizona the current evaluations of the chronology of Colton and Hargrave's (1937) typology and subsequent revisions are followed (Downum 1988; Fairley and Geib 1989; Goetze and Mills 1993a; Hays-Gilpin and van Hartesveldt 1998). We accept a beginning date of about AD 1300 for Gila Polychrome, an important marker (Crary et al. 2001), and view Tonto Polychrome as indicating post–AD 1350 occupation. The presence of Sikyatki Polychrome we see as an indicator that occupation may have lasted into the early AD 1400s. For southern Arizona, in the present study we followed Doelle's temporal assessments, which are generous in suggesting that many sites lasted into the early AD 1400s. We are well aware

that nowhere along the Mogollon Rim are there tree-ring dates later than the AD 1387 date from the Perkinsville site (NA 2440). For purposes of this study we follow Haury (Arizona State Museum site cards) and assume that the Point of Pines occupation continued into the early AD 1400s; similarly, following Nelson and LeBlanc (1986), we assume that Cliff phase sites were also occupied into the early fifteenth century. For northern Mexico we accept Doolittle's (1988) dating of Sonoran Valley sites and use Dean and Ravesloot's (1993) redating of the Casas Grandes sequence.

Future iterations of the analyses presented here will take advantage of the recent refinement of the chronology of the San Pedro sites by the Center for Desert Archaeology and Jerry Howard's estimations for the ages of Salt River valley sites (see Wilcox 2005b). We similarly hope to engage other southwestern archaeologists with considerably more local knowledge than we possess to continue to refine the chronological models in our database so that each iteration of the maps is more precise than the last.

8. After over 30 years of experience each, the two senior authors have seen a lot of southwestern sites. They made special trips into the middle Blue drainage to rerecord the Blue Post Office site and others reported by Hough (1907). Wilcox, with the assistance of Curtis and Polly Schaafsma, has been to all of the largest Galisteo Basin sites (except Shé) and to many sites in the Chama Basin. He also has been to Quarai, Gran Quivira, Abo, and Tenabo as well as to Awatovi, Kin Tiel, Box S, and Heshotauthla but not to Kluckhohn or Archaeotekopa II. All of this firsthand experience helps, but more is desirable, as is building greater intersubjective consensus about what the facts are. The Adams and Duff (2004) book was published too late to be used systematically in this chapter.

9. We now are going back to the areas studied in the Perry Mesa work to add AD 1200s sites we initially overlooked. Recent efforts by Travis Bone and Scott Wood to computerize Tonto Forest data have helped in this process. Those data, however, are not reflected in the maps generated for the present study.

10. Further thought about these issues leads us to suggest the following directions for further research. Let us define the "occupancy rate" as the percentage of the total number of rooms (or household domains) that is "in use" at any one time. Let us further define the "domestic rate" as the average number of people occupying each architectural unit (either rooms or household domains). We then may ask, What are the variables and their relationships that affect the occupancy rate and the domestic rate for southwestern pueblos during the period of interest, AD 1200–1599? When a set of pueblo rooms is first constructed, for example, it seems likely that all would, initially, have been put to use, and thus the initial occupancy rate would be 100 percent. As a pueblo ages, some parts of it become ruins, although the room count, at least for a time, may not decline. In this case the occupancy rate would become smaller. The basic point here is that the occupancy rate is dynamic, and our static methods of using the mean of the maximum and minimum number of rooms, or 65 percent of them, are at best crude approximations. Whether the ethnographic cases used by Kintigh (1985) to construct his estimate are suitable analogies for the variables that were operative in the past should be investigated, not assumed.

The "domestic rate" clearly will be affected by the sum of outcomes produced by the developmental cycle of domestic groups (Goody 1958) at a given moment. Domestic groups fluctuate in size as children are born and as marriages add or subtract from the group. In the end one old person may still occupy a house of one or more rooms that once accommodated many more people. In the course of a domestic cycle new rooms may be added or deleted from a household domain. Emigration of households, leaving behind standing rooms, would reduce the occupancy rate, while immigration might increase the domestic rate or, if there is new construction, add to the occupancy rate. Variables such as these must be more adequately modeled if we are to achieve a more realistic understanding of demographic processes in Puebloan sites (see also Wilcox 1975).

11. This issue can be expressed algebraically as follows: let A be the number of ground-floor rooms, and let us say that 2A is the estimate of the total number of rooms. Our method of taking the mean of A + 2A yields the result of 1.5A. Kintigh would multiply A and 2A by .65; if we then divide by 2, we get $(.65A + 1.3A) \div 2 \sim A$.

12. This measure of 300 m was suggested to Wilcox by Phil Weigand, who uses it in his surveys of western Mexico. Further empirical studies of this method are needed (see Kintigh, chap. 18, this vol.).

13. Care is needed to understand difference in usage of the "cluster" concept. Kintigh (chap. 18, this vol.) often uses it to describe clusters of small room blocks that together constitute communities. Wilcox (1981) and Upham (1982) refer to *clusters of communities*, which they infer were politically integrated as "polities" (though their interpretations of the internal structure of these polities are different; see Wilcox 1991b). Others (in Wills and Leonard 1994) apply the term *community* more broadly to refer to the groupings others infer were polities (see critique in Wilcox 1995b). Kintigh (chap. 18, this vol.), like Bandelier (1892), seems unpersuaded that there was political integration above the small community level. New theoretical innovations are needed to help us resolve the debate implicit in this seeming confusion.

14. Common usage by archaeologists has been to say that sites or regions were "abandoned." Pueblo people or their spokesmen have vigorously objected to this, fairly pointing out that the Pueblos still may have strong ties to those sites or regions, places where ancestors may be buried, where resource procurement still continues, or where sacred associations are still remembered (e.g., see Ferguson and Hart 1985). To say that sites were "depopulated" is an effort to describe more exactly the fact that daily occupation ceased without implying that all connection with a site or region was severed (Lipe 1995).

15. Alternatively, the Hohokam may have dispersed and by the 1600s were the people called Pima or Sobaipuri by the

Spaniards (Hill et al. 2004). A hiatus of archaeological data from about AD 1450 to 1600 prevents evaluation of this possibility (see Doelle 1981).

16. Riley's (1982) hypothesis has been criticized by McGuire and Villalpando (1989). Doolittle (1988) looked for Opata settlements in the Río Sonora, but only relatively small sites dating before AD 1400 were found, not the large villages described by sixteenth-century Spanish accounts (Hammond and Rey 1928, 1940). Pailes (1972) suggested the place to look for the latter was under the modern towns, but no adequate effort of this kind has been attempted to date. The fact that many of the houses in the large settlements were made with *petates* (mats) (Hammond and Rey 1928) means that their archaeological signature may be subtle. We suggest it is time to look seriously for those sites using modern methods of stratigraphic and artifact analysis. Dismissal of an hypothesis is no substitute for testing it.

17. The concept of a "Hopi macroeconomy" was proposed by Baugh (1984) as a smaller-scale "world system," but his discussion is compromised by too closely adhering to the sociological distinctions devised to account for modern capitalist societies. Wilcox's (1984) usage looks only to the most basic premise of this sociological insight: an economic system in which there is a division of labor among distinct ethnic groups, none of whom control the system politically (see also Chase-Dunn and Mann 1998).

18. It has long been postulated that the flow of St. Johns Polychrome and Heshotauthla Polychrome into the middle Rio Grande influenced the development of Rio Grande Glaze Ware ca. AD 1315 (Mera 1940; Schaafsma 2002; Snow 1976; Stubbs and Stallings 1953). Dittert and Brunson-Hadley have recently stated that "about AD 1300, excavations at Acoma revealed that active trade began first with the Pueblos near Socorro, New Mexico, and shortly thereafter with the Zia and Santa Ana districts . . . [and] Jemez obsidian now became much more common as trade with Zia increased" (1999:67). Yet the nature of this east–west axis connecting Zuni/Cebolleta Mesa/Acoma/Zia

and the Albuquerque area has never been systematically studied *as a whole* so far as we are aware. Such a study is long overdue! Duff (1999) has shown that already in the 1300s the Zuni region was relatively "self-contained," as Kintigh puts it (chap. 18, this vol.). Thus, increasing autonomy may have begun to break apart the old east–west exchange structure before the depopulation of the Cebolleta Mesa area and the upper El Morro Valley increased the extent of the buffer zone between Zuni and Acoma.

19. The Hopi also at some point established a long-distance exchange structure via the Havasupai to the Mohave and California groups linked by the Mohave Trail (Dobyns and Euler 1970). The presence of Sikyatki Polychrome on sites immediately south of the Grand Canyon in the upper Basin (Alan Sullivan, personal communication 2003), might indicate the initiation of this pattern as early as the fifteenth century. More study of this macroeconomy and its history is needed.

20. Duff (1999, 2002), in an excellent study, has shown that one of the places that Zuni Glaze Ware was being produced was in villages north of Springerville in the Richville Valley.

21. At a conference on Pottery Mound organized by Polly Schaafsma and held at the School of American Research in May 2004 the likelihood of these different derivations for what Hibben (1975) referred to as "sister" settlements along the lower Rio Puerco of the East was discussed. A certain amount of consensus was reached that they may derive from different populations converging from different directions.

22. We find no merit in Lekson's (1999) rather fanciful labeling of a coincidence of alignment the "Chaco Meridian." For a less dismissive but no less critical analysis see Phillips (2000) and Whalen and Minnis (2003).

23. The numerous scarlet macaw images in Pottery Mound murals (Hibben 1975) may indicate another "transworld" connection. Pottery Mound lies on the northwestern edge of the Piro/Tompiro macroregion. The part that is extant is a pure Glaze A/B component, but a Mera diagram (ARMS files, Santa Fe) shows a second room block to the north that has now been destroyed by arroyo cutting. Ceramic samples from it collected in the 1950s before all of it was destroyed suggest it dated to Glaze C and perhaps later, as Mera's earlier ceramic collections from the site suggest.

24. Hayes (1981) believed that Tabira Black-on-white began about AD 1500, but studies at Pueblo Pardo (Toulouse 1960) and Tabira (Wilson et al. 1983) show otherwise.

25. The Antelope Mesa area is at the northwestern edge of the Puerco White Ware tradition, showing that it long was within the Chacoan (Cibola) sphere of interaction centered on the Rio Puerco of the West (Gilpin 1989; Hargrave 1935:22). Between the Rio Puerco of the West and Antelope Mesa lay the Pueblo Colorado drainage, which we postulate was more likely occupied by Keresan speakers. Further study of this matter is needed.

26. Other intriguing issues are "in play" here. The Klagetoh region is a geographic bridge between eastern and western White Mountain Red Ware (Hays-Gilpin and van Hartesveldt 1998; Reed 1941, 1955), and when it collapsed those traditions diverged. Second, Klagetoh Black-on-white is closely similar to Mesa Verde Black-on-white and has sometimes been confused for it (Dennis Gilpin, personal communication 2001). The presumed intrusion of Mesa Verde populations southward along the Chinle, from Poncho House to Canyon de Chelly, was also happening in the late AD 1200s. Was there an alliance between the Klagetoh populations and these Mesa Verde people? Did the latter end up at Hopi too, as Smith (1971) argued?

27. At the Pottery Mound conference (see n. 21) it became clear that Rio Grande style (Schaafsma 1992) and Sikyatki style (Smith 1952) interact in the same mural panels in complex ways; the explanation and meaning of this *blending* (Crotty 1995) remains a topic for continuing research.

28. Mera (1940:18) first postulated such a gap for all of the glazeware period, but the Rio Medio survey by Marshall (1989) showed that there were glazeware settlements throughout the 64.5 km between the Piro and Tiguex provinces.

Wilcox pointed out, however, that while "occupation in that section was dense in early glaze times, by Glaze E nearly all of [the] settlements had apparently been abandoned [depopulated], or only a trace of occupation is indicated" (1991b:133). The data collected for the Coalescent Communities Database confirm this finding. Spanish accounts (Hammond and Rey 1966) also support this conclusion. After leaving the Piro the Espejo expedition detoured through Abo Pass to see Abo and Tenabo before returning to the Rio Grande and continuing northward. From that point on the river, Luxán says, "there were some small pueblos and many deserted ones on this trip of four leagues [ca. 16.1 km] to El Corvillo"; they then went another four leagues to Los Despoblabos, where there were two pueblos close together; within five more leagues (ca. 19.4 km) they had reached the first of the settlements in the Tiguex "league" (Hammond and Rey 1966:176–177). If, when they came back through Abo Pass, they had cut northwestward along a shortcut to the Rio Grande, now marked by a modern road, they would have come out at Belen. The Valencia site (with a Glaze E component) is about 16 km north of Belen and 16 km south of Isleta, seemingly the best candidate to have been Los Despoblabos of Luxán and Piquinaguatengo/Chiquinagua of Gallegos and Pedrosa (Hammond and Rey 1966:103, 116). Another 16 km north is modern Albuquerque, the likely location of Mexicalcingo, the first settlement of the Tiguex league reported by Gallegos and Pedrosa (Hammond and Rey 1966:116). Thus, there are no more than three settlements reported by these observers in the AD 1580s between the Piro and the Tiguex, and two of them are on either side of the river at Isleta (LA 724). Clearly, most of the large Los Lunas population aggregate that once occupied this stretch of the Rio Grande was now gone.

29. During the height of the Casas Grandes macroregional system bison meat and other products may have been moving from the plains edge in the Roswell area to Paquimé (Wilcox 1999a). Recent sourcing studies of Chupadero Black-on-white (Creel et al. 2002) point to

greater distribution of that type from the zone southeast of Tabira to Roswell than the Salinas area proper. Speth's (2004) recent synthesis of his work in the Roswell area fails to reckon with the possibility of an early macroeconomy linking the plains to Casas Grandes (see Vokes and Gregory, chap. 17, this vol.). Many more investigations of the scale of the macroeconomy these data indicate are needed.

30. Although Trager (1967) was skeptical that the Pecos people spoke Towa, the language of Jemez, Fray Benavides reports that, "although these [Pecos] Indians are of the Hemes [Jemez] nation [i.e., of Towa speech], being here alone and strayed out of their territory, they are taken for a separate nation, though it is one same tongue" (Ayer 1965 [1916]:386).

31. Reff, in an interesting discussion, also quotes this passage from Benavides, but he has asserted that "this violence and conflict stemmed in large part from the many dislocations (caused, e.g., by horses, disease, guns, and depopulations) attendant on the European invasion of the Americas" (Reff 1994:60). Alternatively, the initial impact of the Spanish colony was relatively benign or even adaptively positive (Wilcox 1992). The Jemez, for example, may have been on a trajectory governed more by internal factors than external (Spanish) ones. Benavides (Ayer 1965 [1916]) surely would have mentioned disease if that was a factor, but he does not. New approaches to test these alternative hypotheses are needed.

32. Polly Schaafsma (personal communication 2003; see Schaafsma 2000) points out that in the fifteenth century, when many of the Rio Grande Puebloan groups reached their demographic apogees (see fig. 12.23), in the sample of the kiva mural art now available "religion and warfare are woven together into one fabric." Why such coherence was unstable in most southwestern societies is a matter for continued investigation.

33. The estimate of one to two persons per room is a measure of what we above called the "domestic rate," but clearly it is only "reasonable" in the current crude state of our ability to model occupancy rates and domestic rates.

34. It is interesting to notice that alternative approaches to population estimation can achieve fairly good results as well. Let us assume for the sake of argument that our figure of 64,750 rooms is about 50 percent higher than would be derived by using Kintigh's (1985) method of multiplying the maximum and minimum room estimates by 65 percent and dividing by 2 (see n. 11). The latter method would yield ca. 43,167 rooms. However, following Herhahn and Hill (1998), we could multiply this by 1.2 persons per room and arrive at a total population figure of 51,800, which is within the range we have inferred from the Spanish documents, though on the short side.

13 A Regional Perspective on Ceramics and Zuni Identity, AD 200–1630

Barbara J. Mills

For as long as archaeologists have worked in the Zuni area the historical relationship of Zuni to other areas of the Southwest has been an explicit topic of research (Cushing 1888; Hodge 1923; Reed 1941, 1948, 1955; Rinaldo 1964; Roberts 1932; Woodbury 1956). None of these archaeologists saw Zuni as developing in isolation, and they posed various relationships with the San Juan, Mogollon, and even Hohokam areas. Many of these postulated relationships were based on similarities in ceramics between Zuni and its surrounding areas. Most studies, however, were based on traditional, cultural-historical methods that emphasized particular trait distributions.

In this chapter I look at the relationship between Zuni and the Mogollon area through the lens of ceramic variability. At the outset, however, I must point out four major problems with the investigation of Zuni-Mogollon relationships using ceramic data.

First, one major focus of this seminar was on historical relationships that predate the use of ceramics in any area of the Southwest. Ceramic artifacts are not useful indicators of population relationships or interactions before about AD 200–400 in the Zuni and Mogollon areas.[1]

Second, I prefer the phrase "Mogollon area" to "the Mogollon" because I generally ascribe to the idea that whatever was defined by archaeologists as Mogollon applies only to the pre–AD 1000 period. Even before this it is doubtful that there was a single culture in the Mogollon area. In fact, given the variation that archaeologists have identified (often expressed as "branches" of the Mogollon), it seems that we would be on safer ground to say that there were many different cultural groups and let the unitarianists prove their case to the contrary. Population mobility is a given in the Southwest at any time—it is a part of the flexibility in adaptations required for foragers and farmers to survive in this arid-lands environment. I agree with many subsequent researchers, including Haury (1985a), that after AD 1000 there are enough indicators of north–south migration from the Colorado Plateau to the "transition" zone that the Mogollon concept does not apply. Instead, I think we should consider the Mogollon area to be the location of heterogeneous populations. How those heterogeneous population areas were created is a centrally important question.

Third, by limiting ourselves to Zuni and "the Mogollon" I think we limit our fields of investigation. There were social, demographic, linguistic, and technological impacts from many other areas of the Southwest. Exchange does not always occur with the closest groups, and migration patterns often "leapfrog" (Anthony 1990)—the population history of the Southwest is full of circuitous routes. Fortunately, current research has focused on this topic (e.g., J. Clark 2001; Duff 1998; Herr and Clark 1997; Lyons 2003; Mills 1998), and we are now in a better position to talk about some of the particular pathways.

Finally, many archaeologists assume that when we talk about ceramics and identity we are dealing with ceramic *decorative* styles. It is increasingly evident from ethnoarchaeological research, however, that decorative styles are not coeval with social groups (e.g., Dietler and Herbich 1998). In fact, southwestern archaeologists have long noticed that some styles were widely produced on a number of different ceramics (e.g., Sosi style on Sosi Black-on-white of Tusayan White Ware, Holbrook Black-on-white of Little Colorado White Ware, Escavada Black-on-white of Cibola White Ware, and Puerco Black-on-red of White Mountain Red Ware). Colton and Hargrave (1937) called these *analogous styles,* and they were often used to identify ceramics made at about the same time in different areas. Such styles are clearly related and indicate interaction of some kind, but how they were transmitted is a complex question; styles cannot be taken at face value as indicative of similarities in social identity or migration. Some design variability does indicate social identity, but consistent separation of designs with this kind of content is difficult at best. Other methods provide stronger data for addressing how identity can be approached through ceramics. Nonetheless, I *do* think that painted decorations on ceramics have great potential for addressing the relationship between the Zuni and Mogollon areas.

With the above caveats in mind, there are many potentially interesting relationships between those who lived in the Mogollon and Zuni areas that can be approached through the study of ceramics. To characterize these interrelationships I will use the behaviors that Jeff Clark has so cogently outlined (see J. Clark 2001, chap. 4, this vol.): exchange, emulation, enculturation, and migration (or ethnicity). Although I agree with some of the methods that he outlines, I add others that I think may be useful in operationalizing each of these behavioral inferences. I also depart from his discussion in terms of what I see as the independent and dependent variables of interest. I consider each of the above four processes to be separate behaviors that have important effects on material culture variability. Instead of seeing migration as the independent variable, as I think Clark does, I see migration as one of the dependent variables that helps us to get at the independent variable of interest: identity. I use identity rather than ethnicity for reasons discussed below.

Approaches to Ceramics and Identity

Many new methods of interpretation of ceramics have been developed in recent years that allow us to use more than simple trait distributions and decorative styles to address the issue of cultural identity in the archaeological record. These include detailed studies of ceramic provenance, exchange relationships, technological style, and the active use of style. In this chapter I look at how these different lines of evidence can be used to reinterpret the timing, structure, and intensity of relationships between Zuni and surrounding areas posed by earlier scholars, particularly with respect to the Mogollon area to the south and the upper Little Colorado area to the west.

Archaeological studies of identity are relatively few by comparison with those accomplished in the other anthropological subfields and in other disciplines. The literature is vast, but a brief foray is worth making if only to broaden how we might think about "Zuni" and "Mogollon" as entities in the past and, in the case of the former, into the present.

One of the first things to recognize is that there are multiple social scales at which identity can be expressed. By definition, identity implies similarity or sameness. As Jenkins (1996:3) points out, the root comes from the Latin *identitas*, from *idem* "the same," and there are two distinct meanings. One is that of exact sameness or identicalness. The other is that of distinctiveness—one entity is different from another. Thus, identity is defined in relation to something else. The above definition does not imply a specific social scale, yet that is the way most of the anthropological literature in the past has addressed it by considering it as meaning "ethnicity," including the early work of one of the

most important contributors to ideas of identity, Fredrik Barth (1969b). Although calling it ethnicity, he later discussed the intricacies of individuals' diverse identities, including gender, settlement, occupation and class, history/descent, religion, and ethnicity (Barth 1983).

Second, as Barth noted (1969b; see also Jenkins 1996), identities are often situational and expressed in relation to something else. Thus, they are mutable and flexible. This has been one of the aspects of identity that has foiled archaeological approaches to material culture, but only because mutability has been mistakenly interpreted as randomness and thus without pattern. As Jones (1997:125) points out, styles that are associated with identity may be arbitrary across cultures, but they are not randomly distributed within societies.

Third, identities are often best described at social boundaries but are themselves without clear spatial boundaries. Most archaeological work on identity has been explicitly about the search for the convergence of large-scale social boundaries (or ethnicity) and spatial pattern (e.g., Stark 1998; Trinkaus and Ashmore 1987). This, again, has foiled archaeologists because they have been looking for spatial boundaries and clearly defined ones at that. A major problem with this as a program of research is that it ignores other kinds of crosscutting identities. We really don't know when material culture boundaries will conform to one kind or scale of identity versus another. The kinds of identities that ancient southwestern peoples probably shared included those of gender, household or descent group, ritual and other sodalities, community residential groups, regional or multisettlement clusters, and linguistic affiliation.

Another problem is that much of the earlier research was on ethnicity, not identity. This is not just a semantic issue but also a conceptual one. As Clark (chap. 4, this vol.) points out, it is clear that many ethnic groups as we think of them now are the products of interactions with nation-states (Alonso 1993; Gellner 1983; Smith 1987). Southwestern tribal groups are the product of this same process, one that will be relevant when we talk about Zuni identity and ceramics in the Colonial period but not when we talk about the earlier history of Zuni and other groups in the Southwest. Earlier southwestern groups probably did not consider themselves as members of a specific tribe or ethnic group.

If social boundaries are mutable, defined by multiple scales of social interaction, and are without clear boundaries (in both a social and a spatial sense), it is no wonder that archaeologists have had trouble with the concept of identity. In addition, as several archaeologists have noted, not all identity is expressed in material culture. Yet because there are no easy cross-cultural correlates of identity in material culture, it does not follow that identity is absent in material culture. Along with a number of recent researchers (Dietler and Herbich 1998; Dobres 2000; Hegmon 1998; Jones 1997; Stark et al. 1998), I agree that what is needed is more attention to the idea of technological styles and agency-based approaches.

Many archaeologists and especially ethnoarchaeologists have recently argued that identity can be approached through the study of technological choices (Dietler and Herbich 1998; Hegmon 1998; Lemonnier 1986, 1993). These choices are the result of historical contingency and the social setting of potters. The unifying theme in much of this work is Bourdieu's (1977, 1990) concept of habitus, or "systems of durable dispositions" that compel people to act in certain ways but that operate without reference to an explicit set of rules (Dietler and Herbich 1998:246; see also Clark, chap. 4, this vol.). No single attribute can be used to pinpoint identity, but patterning in potters' cumulative choices when they produce a vessel does indicate some degree of social similarity. Again, similarity and difference are expressed, but the result is not ethnic identity. Instead, it is a more flexible concept of an individual's role vis-à-vis other individuals in a group (whatever group that might be), or "personal relations of potters" (Dietler and Herbich 1998:254).

Bourdieu's approach balances two of the most important concepts in the social sciences, structure and agency, because it allows archaeologists to look at material culture that is produced by individuals in relation to their social setting. The mistake that many earlier archaeologists made (e.g., Deetz 1965; Longacre 1970) was in trying to pinpoint the exact social structure (ethnic group, matrilineal residence unit, etc.) when they looked at shared styles. Another mistake was in assuming that cultures were static when they are highly mutable. Bourdieu's concept of habitus allows for this mutability and change because the rules are constantly being reinterpreted by individuals in daily practice.

Identity is frequently based in clothing (e.g., Wobst 1977), and for archaeologists clothing is one of the least likely classes of material culture to survive (but see Webster, chap. 16, this vol.). Another example of the way that identity is expressed is through food. Food choices, recipes, and the social contexts of food consumption are remarkably conservative expressions of identity and difference (see Counihan [1999] and Friedman [1994] for some recent anthropological work on this topic). Food, too, does not preserve well in the archaeological record, but the tools used to prepare and serve food are preserved—especially ground stone and ceramics. Both food and clothing are ways in which identity is embodied, which is one of the strongest ways that individuals express their identity and their distinctiveness.

A number of recent studies suggest ways that material culture patterning can be used to approach the identification of social identity in the archaeological record. These include those that draw on technological style arguments (e.g., papers in Dobres and Hoffman 1999; Stark 1998) as well as those that draw on some of the now classic discussions of active markers of style (e.g., Wiessner 1983). Rather than advocating one side of the active/passive style arguments, archaeologists are selectively using both, depending on the materials and their social contexts. For example, Hegmon (1998:277) lists several ways in which both technological style and more active measures of style may be used to look at identity: (1) complex technologies, (2) very simple designs, (3) production in formal contexts, (4) cross-cutting media, (5) elaboration of objects used in private, (6) highly visible decoration, and (7) everyday domestic items. Many of these can and do apply to ceramics.

In my discussion of Zuni and Mogollon ceramics I draw on several of these lines of evidence to address shared identities in the archaeological record. Those that I think have the most potential for ceramics are sketched below:[2]

1. Technological styles, including similarities in forming and finishing techniques, paste and paint recipes, and brushstroke application. Several of these attributes have been studied by southwestern archaeologists who

look at differences in identity based on ceramics (e.g., Hegmon et al. 1998; Neuzil 2001; Stark et al. 1998; Van Keuren 2001; Whittlesey 1982). Because they are produced, used, and broken frequently, ceramics used in the preparation and consumption of foods provide one of the best opportunities to look at the reproduction of technological knowledge. By concentrating on objects that are used in everyday domestic activities, there is a good fit with the theoretical approach outlined by Bourdieu and identified by Hegmon in her point 7, above. Unfortunately, most of these observations are difficult to make without new detailed studies. There are, however, some observations in the existing literature that I cull out to the extent possible.

2. Active signaling, especially as expressed in highly visible designs on the exteriors of vessels used in corporate or public settings. These are closest to Hegmon's point 6, above. Based on previous research (see summaries in Mills 1999a; Potter 2000; Spielmann 1998), it is highly likely that decorated serving bowls were used in contexts of communal consumption. Thus, I will especially focus on the use of exterior bowl designs. In addition to bowl exteriors, however, there are some cases where anthropomorphic designs are used on the interiors of bowls that are clearly part of some kind of shared ritual participation, if not identity. In particular, I address the depiction of masks on bowl interiors. Both of these examples—highly visible designs on bowl exteriors and anthropomorphic designs on bowl interiors—may overlap with designs that cross-cut media, especially rock art (see Schaafsma and Young, chap. 15, this vol.).

3. The use of ceramics as parts of distinctive southwestern cuisines or foodways (see Clark, chap. 4, this vol.). Following Crown (2000), I distinguish diet from cuisine and consider variation in the latter to include the recipes and tools used in food preparation, flavorings, meal scheduling, meal serving, what foods are appropriate for ritual occasions, and food taboos. Ceramics were traditionally used for meal preparation and consumption in most areas of the Southwest after AD 500. Similar use of ceramics in the preparation and consumption of foods is part of everyday domestic life (see also Clark, chap. 4, this vol.). As vessels that are used to prepare and serve food, they are closely associated with other identity-maintaining activities associated with consumption. In the case of the Zuni and Mogollon areas, are there ceramic vessels that are distinctive choices for doing similar kinds of activities, be they cooking or serving?

4. Use of special forms in ritual contexts. This approach is similar to Hegmon's point 5, or ceramics used in closed contexts. Hegmon's examples include those objects used in private or in relatively restricted social contexts, such as "pots used only in inner rooms." However, this might also apply to all vessels used in ritual contexts, such as those used in initiation ceremonies, as altar furniture, or as repositories of other sacred objects. Knowledge of what is appropriate to produce and use in these contexts is often closely controlled and thus is an excellent way of looking at specialized technological knowledge. Unfortunately, few of these forms have been identified. Specific vessel forms used in burials might also fall into this category, however, if there is a particular vessel class that is minimally present in all burials or only present in burials.

5. Sudden stylistic or technological changes that accompany intentional acts of resistance or other marked social changes that are part of the process of ethnogenesis. This has been discussed for Zuni (Mills 2002b) and the Rio Grande Pueblos (Capone and Preucel 2002) following the Pueblo Revolt. At Zuni and several other Pueblos glaze-painted ceramics ceased to be made sometime during the Pueblo Revolt of AD 1680–1692, and instead matte-paint polychromes were produced. At Zuni the production of these vessels was accompanied by stylistic shifts that included a predominance of feather motifs and the standardization of exterior design layout and content. These technological and stylistic changes correspond exactly with the coalescence of Zuni population into one village for the first time. Thus, they are strong examples of the active manipulation of ceramic manufacture within the process of ethnogenesis.

The above lines of evidence are not the usual ways that southwestern archaeologists think about how shared identities should be approached, which traditionally has been through spatial distributions of specific design styles. But, as Clark notes (chap. 4, this vol.), styles of decoration can be emulated easily. In addition, as Dietler and Herbich (1998) show, simple spatial distributions of decorative styles are likely to cross-cut social boundaries because of exchange. These spatial distributions are the very ones that archaeologists have traditionally observed in the Southwest. In residentially mobile societies exchange is one way of establishing and keeping ties open for future migration pathways. Thus, identifying exchange relationships is an important way of documenting economic ties that are also social ties but that should not be confused with social boundaries. Because stylistic similarities can also be caused by drift, residential moves over short distances, and emulation, if we are really going to tackle identity in the archaeological record, then alternative methods will be needed.

A Chronological Comparison of Ceramics in the Zuni and Mogollon Areas

I divide my discussion of Zuni and Mogollon ceramics into three periods: (1) pre–AD 1000, (2) AD 1000–1300, and (3) AD 1300–1630. Within each of these periods I first summarize ceramic patterns in the Zuni area. I then look at variability by wares, culling as much information as can be used to address shared identities in the archaeological record. Lastly, I summarize patterns that cross-cut wares for each period.

Pre–AD 1000

The first ceramics in the Zuni area date to ca. AD 300s–400s and are plain brownware in simple forms (Varien 1990). This early brownware is now referred to as Obelisk Brown (Reed et al. 2000). By about AD 500 or 550 grayware ceramics had replaced the brownware, and a diversity of forms was produced. The earliest grayware, Lino Gray, was untextured. Like the early brownware, Lino Gray is part of a widespread ceramic technology found in more than just the Zuni area and is virtually indistinguishable from ceramics produced in surrounding areas. Some of these early grayware vessels were coated with a red pigment after firing, producing a Fugitive Red. Surface texturing had been added to the grayware, referred to as Cibola Gray Ware, by the AD 800s. This begins with neck banding followed by the use of finer coils in a style called clapboard corrugations. The sequence of changes in surface texturing is found throughout the Southwest, albeit at slightly different times. No redware has been positively identified as made in the

Zuni area proper between ca. AD 800 and 1000, although some plain polished redwares (and brownwares) occur occasionally in Zuni-area assemblages at this time.

The earliest decorated ceramics in the Zuni area date to the mid–AD 600s. These are decorated in black mineral (predominantly iron oxide) paints on grayish or white surfaces (La Plata and White Mound Black-on-whites). By AD 850 slips had been added to the whiteware, and tempers had changed from sand to crushed sherds. A short-lived type decorated in Kana-a style, called Kiatuthlanna Black-on-white, was produced from about AD 850 to 900. This was followed by one of the most ubiquitous pre–AD 1000 Cibola White Ware types, called Red Mesa Black-on-white. Not only was it produced for about 150 years (beginning ca. AD 900), but it also corresponds with more, and more visible, sites.

Comparison of Zuni and Mogollon Undecorated Wares. One of the traditional distinctions between areas of the Southwest that is still taught in some university curriculums and certainly believed by most of the public is that the Anasazi made grayware, the Mogollon made brownware, and the Hohokam made buffware. Such simplistic and seemingly logical leaps from spatial distributions to culturally meaningful social distinctions permeated archaeology from the late nineteenth through the early twentieth century. It was most actively promoted by the age-area approach of Wissler and archaeologists trained in the Boasian school of material culture distributions up until the last midcentury. Not only do these associations conflate variation within these supposed culturally distinct areas, a major issue for this seminar, but they also ignore other sources of variation in ceramics.

Anna Shepard (1953) was one of the first to correctly note that the color of ceramic vessels is determined by both clay composition (especially the amount of iron) and firing atmosphere (especially the amount of oxygen). Her observations were based on her analyses in the Petrified Forest area, immediately to the west of Zuni, where brownware ceramics were found in what was otherwise considered to be Anasazi territory (i.e., in the general Cibola area of the Colorado Plateau). Other archaeologists also recognized the importance of clay availability for understanding ceramic variation (see Martin 1959b: 84–85 for a statement in a popular volume), but the association of brown pasted ceramics with a Mogollon culture area was so entrenched that it was difficult to pry loose.

Variation in clay composition is now widely recognized as being a factor in the final appearance of finished ceramics. A number of more recent studies, especially those conducting research in a broad swath running parallel to the edge of the Colorado Plateau, note that the available clays south of the plateau were generally limited to brown and red firing clays, while those on the Colorado Plateau had access to a wider range of clays, including those that fire gray and buff (e.g., Crown 1981; Hays-Gilpin and van Hartesveldt 1998; Wilson and Blinman 1994; Zedeño 1994). The Colorado Plateau, with its wide variety of clay sources, does have clays with high iron content, but these were used less often than those that fire to clearer colors.

The earliest ceramics throughout the Southwest were generally brownwares. This common color was not because of a shared cultural background, however, but rather because of shared use of easily accessed alluvial clays (Reed et al. 2000; Wilson and Blinman 1994; see also Olson

1961:2–3). Rather than representing shared cultural background, the earliest brownware horizon represents a more expedient approach to ceramic technology within a residentially mobile population. The technology is based on the use of clays from alluvial contexts that are available throughout the Southwest. Because these clays are readily available, the knowledge of how to use them could be easily transferred from place to place. Even though potters moved frequently, they would have been able to produce vessels in nearly any area of the Southwest. The expedience of the technology also made early southwestern ceramics cheaper to produce than earlier cooking and storage basketry containers, and they represent a labor-saving device over the use of basketry (Crown and Wills 1995a, 1995b). An additional advantage was that foods could be cooked at slightly higher temperatures, increasing their nutritional benefits. Thus, the early brownware found throughout a broad area of the Southwest represents a technological diffusion, through either exchange or mobility, with important evolutionary implications.

Brownware ceramics were first used south of the Colorado Plateau, and most reconstructions suggest that there is a time-transgressive south–north pattern. It is thought that early brownware technology originated in Mexico and then diffused into the Hohokam and Mogollon areas of the Southwest (Heidke 1999; LeBlanc 1982a; Reed et al. 2000). Reed et al. (2000:217) point out that this diffusion could have been through a number of more specific social interactions, including migration and exchange. In either case, it follows a later but similar overall distribution to the diffusion of maize and other domesticates from Mesoamerica.

What is particularly interesting about the overall pattern of early brownware is its great internal diversity. Early brownware is not distributed evenly across the Southwest. This uneven spatial distribution is the reason that it was originally called so many different types in the archaeological literature. Recently, the trend has been to homogenize this variability and recognize it as a widespread pattern, hence the term Obelisk Brown, which now subsumes a variety of former type names (see Reed et al. 2000). Although I agree that it is important to recognize widespread patterns that cross-cut traditional culture areas, much like we now recognize commonalities among preceramic agriculturalists, there is important variation within the expedient technology that we should not ignore. In fact, it is the *variation* in technological styles, which indicate different learning frameworks, that is most important for understanding differences in identity and recognizing migration in the archaeological record.

Two important kinds of variation are present in the distribution of the early brownware ceramics. First, it is evident that there were people living near each other who did not share in the production and use of ceramic technology for at least a few centuries in the early first millennium. I do not think that this is exclusively because of archaeological sampling or visibility. Instead, it appears that at roughly the same time some families used ceramics and some did not. Second, among those potters who *did* produce early brownware ceramics were different technological styles. For example, Adamana Brown from the Flattop site in the Petrified Forest area was formed in a basket and then finished with paddle-and-anvil technology (Wendorf 1953), whereas coil-and-scraping was used on other early brownware ceramics found in the same area (Dykeman 1995; Ferg

1978). These are distinctive ways of forming and finishing a pot that are arguably the best ways of looking at shared learning frameworks. In an interesting twist it now appears that some of the variation in early brownware types does relate to migration, but not because of their brown color. Perhaps we have thrown the baby out with the bathwater (Anthony 1990) in considering the significance of these early brownware types and migration.

The intentional deposition of carbon on the vessel wall, called smudging, also appears earliest in the Mogollon area (Crown 2000). This technological innovation was never widely adopted on the Colorado Plateau.[3] In the Mogollon area smudging appears by AD 400 (Crown 2000:table 7.2). Smudging creates a relatively impermeable surface, and Crown argues that it probably served an important function in keeping harmful bacteria from growing inside food cooking or serving bowls and reducing the amount of time needed to raise the temperature of contents during cooking. Both jars and bowls are smudged, but the overwhelming majority of smudged vessels are bowls. Thus, these were probably used for food serving rather than cooking. An additional variable that argues against the concern for boiling time is the fact that smudging occurs in the one region of the Southwest with the most fuel. Although smudging is known for the Colorado Plateau on vessels after AD 700, smudged vessels are not very common, and when they do occur they tend to occur on brownware ceramics (e.g., Woodruff Smudged from the Petrified Forest area). If smudging was such an adaptive trait, it is surprising that it did not spread more widely. In the case of the smudged Mogollon-area vessels, I think they represent a fundamental difference in cuisine, including the way food was prepared and served, and meal scheduling (perhaps less frequent meals with food kept in vessels for longer periods of time).

The diversity of ceramics produced in the lower Rio Puerco area is not restricted to the earliest brownware. Contemporaneously in this area, some potters produced ceramics from local clays using finishing and firing technologies more commonly found in areas of the Colorado Plateau, while others used technologies more commonly found in areas of the Mogollon Rim and farther southeast.

Sometime after AD 700 unslipped polished brownware is known from sites in an arc that extends from the Rio Puerco of the West to the Mogollon Rim in east-central Arizona (e.g., Ferg 1978; Fowler 1994; Gladwin 1945; Haury 1985a; Hays 1993). Some of these are bright red in places because of their oxidized surfaces, but most of these are heavily fire clouded and range from brown to red on the same surface. Many of these vessels have smudged interiors. These have been called a variety of names, including Forestdale Red and Forestdale Brown, but participants at a recent Museum of Northern Arizona ceramics conference reached a consensus and now call them all Woodruff Brown (with a smudged variety) within Puerco Valley Brown Ware (Hays-Gilpin and van Hartesveldt 1998). Like the earlier brownware ceramics made in this area, these polished red and brown ceramics are the result of the selection of local iron-rich materials but with distinctive surface treatments.

Polished and smudged brownware has not been identified for the Zuni area during this time period. This ware also contrasts with the gray-brown ceramics that occur in the Rio Puerco area contemporaneously with the polished and smudged ware during the AD 700s–900s. The gray-brown ceramics were originally identified as an "intergrade." Intergrades occur when the technology from one area is applied to a different material in another area. In the case of the ceramics from the western or lower Rio Puerco valley, for example, the naturally brown to red firing clays were fired in neutral or reducing atmospheres to make them look like graywares. An entirely new ware has been designated for these "gray-brown" ceramics: Puerco Valley Gray Ware (Hays-Gilpin and van Hartesveldt 1998; Reed et al. 2000). The technology of construction and firing is the same as that shared by a number of other surrounding areas on the plateau, but the raw materials are the iron-rich Chinle Formation clays of the western portion of the Rio Puerco as it approaches the Little Colorado River.

Although the clays in some areas on the Colorado Plateau have high enough iron content to result in brownware, it is evident that potters in the Rio Puerco valley manipulated the firing atmospheres to produce the gray-brown ceramics. Thus, the lower Rio Puerco appears to represent an area in which potters with different backgrounds and identities lived in close proximity to each other, producing ceramics within different technological styles. At least some of this proximity was probably the result of migrants from other areas converging on the lower Rio Puerco valley.

Elaboration of plain wares that occurred prior to AD 1000 in both the Mogollon and Zuni areas includes corrugations, or what Pierce (1999) refers to as "exposed coils." The earliest corrugated pottery dates to the seventh through eleventh centuries, depending on where one is in the Southwest. It appears earliest in the Mimbres Mogollon area (Alma Neck-banded) and latest in the upper Rio Grande area (Pierce 1999:fig. 14; see also Haury 1985a:106). Both neck-banded graywares and brownwares occur in the Quemado area, but the brownware appears to be earlier (Mills 1987a; Wasley 1959). Like the original introduction of pottery, the use of exposed coils follows a time-transgressive pattern from south to north that fits with a model of technological diffusion, possibly through migration (Pierce 1999) and/or small-scale exchanges.

Comparison of Zuni and Mogollon Redwares. Prior to AD 1000 the earliest redwares in the general Zuni and Mogollon areas were fugitive redwares. These are red slipped, but the slip was applied after firing and as a result is less permanent. In the Colorado Plateau area fugitive red slips were applied to grayware (e.g., Lino Fugitive Red) and brownware (Tohatchi Red), and in the Mogollon area these slips were applied to only a brownware (called Fugitive Brown). Fugitive Brown has temporal priority and was made ca. AD 200–650 in the Mimbres area (Anyon et al. 1981; LeBlanc 1982a). Lino Fugitive Red occurs at the later end of this range, or ca. AD 500–850 (Goetze and Mills 1993b), and Tohatchi Red may appear as early as AD 550 (Reed et al. 2000). Accurate counts of these vessels are difficult to come by because the slip is almost completely weathered off in many cases (hence the "Fugitive" appellation). However, the temporal lag in production of red-slipped wares once again fits well with a diffusion-based model of redware production from south to north.

By about AD 500–550 fugitive red-slipped pottery had been replaced in the Mogollon area by a well-polished and slipped pottery called San Francisco Red or one of its varieties (Haury 1936b; Martin 1943; Wheat 1955). Fugitive red-slipped grayware vessels continued to be associated with contexts of this period in the area from Quemado (Bullard 1962:10) to the San Juan Basin (Toll and Mc-Kenna 1997). Besides being polished, the major technological style difference between Fugitive Gray and San Francisco Red vessels is that the latter were slipped and polished prior to firing and thus have a more permanent slip. In addition, the exteriors of these vessels are often intentionally dimpled where the finishing technique did not completely erase the finger marks of the potter. These two redwares are dramatically different from each other in technology and function, which suggests important differences in technological style. It is highly unlikely that the similarity in these two contemporaneous wares is because of migration of potters. Some San Francisco Red has been suggested by Wasley (1959) to be locally produced in the Quemado area, but this redware is almost completely absent from sites in the Cibola area (Carlson 1970:97). Thus, the distribution of these two redwares suggests the presence of a permeable boundary in the Quemado area that does not extend to the Zuni area proper.

Comparison of Zuni and Mogollon Decorated Wares. One of the major similarities between the Zuni and Mogollon areas is that both saw the production and use of white-slipped ceramics with black mineral paint in the latter half of the first millennium. However, the earliest painted ceramics in the Mogollon area were not black-on-white but red-on-brown, while the earliest ceramics in the Zuni area proper were made with black iron oxide paints on grayish to white-slipped surfaces. Mogollon Red-on-brown (Haury 1936b) is often described as a combination of technologies used to produce plain brown and red ceramics. The surface is an unslipped brown, and the paint is the same material that was used to pro-

duce the allover red slip of San Francisco Red (Scott 1983). The designs on this earliest pottery are bold geometrics, largely restricted to the interior of bowls. At a very general level the designs appear to share more similarity to those found on contemporaneous northern Mexico and Hohokam ceramics. Mogollon Red-on-brown vessels have been found as far north as the Quemado area (Bullard 1962; Wasley 1959; see fig. 13.1). Based on the use of local tempering materials, Wasley identified a Cerro Colorado variety of Mogollon Red-on-brown. Although only based on low-power mineralogical identifications, if his identification is correct, the Quemado area appears to have been an area that saw the migration of potters from below the Colorado Plateau and the presence of a permeable boundary between the Quemado area and areas to the south at this time.

A white slip had been added to Mogollon ceramics by about AD 750 to produce what is known as Three Circle Red-on-white (Haury 1936b; Scott 1983; Wheat 1955; see fig. 13.1, upper right). These vessels were painted with designs that begin to share more elements in common with northern ceramics but are more boldly executed (Wasley 1959). Although Haury (1936b) considered Three Circle Red-on-white to be earliest in the Mimbres Valley, Wheat (1955:90–91) points out that it was also commonly found in the Pine Lawn Valley. He also thought that the use of a white coating or slip had precedence in the Anasazi area.

Three Circle Red-on-white also occurs in the Quemado area. Wasley (1959) argued that some of the Three Circle White-on-red from Cerro Colorado was locally produced because of the use of local tempers, like Mogollon Red-on-brown. Potters who originated farther to the south were clearly

implicated. Technologically, these white-on-red ceramics are distinct from other whiteware ceramics made in the area discussed below. If the tempers are indeed from the Cerro Colorado area, then the locally made Three Circle White-on-red ceramics are good candidates for ceramics made by potters who moved there from south of the Colorado Plateau. The Pine Lawn Valley and nearby areas are the closest candidates, but if migration paths leapfrogged, then potentially long distances might have been crossed.

Two additional technological changes had been made by about AD 750 in Mogollon-area ceramics: the use of black paint and a change in firing atmospheres. Rather than firing the ceramics in an oxidizing atmosphere, oxygen was intentionally restricted, and the atmosphere was usually kept neutral. A variety of paint recipes were used, but at least some were iron oxide based. The earliest of these black-on-white types in the Mimbres and upper Gila areas in general has been called Mimbres Boldface, Mangas Black-on-white, or Style I of Mimbres Black-on-white (Anyon et al. 1981; Lekson 1990a; Scott 1983). Excavations at Turkey Foot Pueblo show that there is a relatively smooth stylistic transition between Three Circle Red-on-white and Mimbres Boldface Black-on-white (Martin and Rinaldo 1950b).

Most contemporary researchers now use Styles I, II, and III to describe the sequence of Mimbres Black-on-white ceramics, starting with the bold painted style formerly known as Boldface. Unlike the previous Three Circle Red-on-white and Mogollon Red-on-brown ceramics, however, none of these Mimbres Black-on-white types have ever been identified as made above the Mogollon Rim on the Colorado Plateau.[4] In fact, Wasley (1959) notes a distinct

Figure 13.1. Mogollon Red-on-brown and Three Circle Red-on-white from Cerro Colorado, Quemado Area (after Wasley 1959:fig. 10).

shift from southern to northern technology and design styles in the Cerro Colorado assemblages from Early Pueblo II period contexts.[5] And although Mimbres Black-on-white ceramics have been found as far north as Chaco (Toll and McKenna 1997), they are rare in all plateau assemblages.

The earliest painted ceramics in the Zuni area are La Plata Black-on-white (ca. AD 550–750), White Mound Black-on-white (ca. AD 700–850), and Red Mesa Black-on-white (ca. AD 850–1040).[6] These types were made over a broad area of the Colorado Plateau, including the San Juan Basin, Rio Puerco, Zuni, Acoma, and Quemado areas. A variety of White Mound Black-on-white with volcanic temper (San Marcial variety) was produced as far east as the Rio Grande valley. Local production of White Mound Black-on-white is also likely in the Forestdale Valley. The production and distribution of stylistically similar ceramics over such large areas suggests a high degree of mobility and exchange. In some cases it is possible to distinguish ceramics that

were produced in one area vs. another based on temper variation, although remarkably few compositional studies have been done on these early Cibola White Ware types.

Chaco Canyon, the Rio Puerco, and the Zuni River drainages have continuous sequences of sites with the above types of early Cibola White Ware. Cibola White Ware is the major decorated ware made in these areas prior to AD 1000, and, as the ware designation indicates, it is considered to be the quintessential ware produced in the Zuni area. Variation in styles of decoration, the degree of coverage of the slip, and tempering materials has been recognized (cf. Gladwin 1945; Toll and McKenna 1997), but on the whole the same typological system can be used in all of these areas.

In the Quemado area, however, different decorated wares with contrasting technologies may have been produced and used close in time, if not contemporaneously. Based on the intrusive igneous features of the Quemado area, Wasley (1959) noted that there were both locally made and imported examples of the earliest Cibola White Ware types. La Plata, White Mound, and Red Mesa Black-on-whites were made there as well as being represented by imported vessels from other areas, probably to the north and west. The purported local Cibola White Ware is from the same site as the local Mogollon Red-on-brown and Three Circle Red-on-white, raising some interesting questions about fluctuating social identities in the Quemado area during the long occupation of the Cerro Colorado site (AD 600–1100). Smith (1973) considered all the Cibola White Ware from the Williams site, just south of the Quemado area, to be nonlocally made. Thus, between the Williams site and Cerro Colorado there is an apparent drop-off in the production of Cibola White Ware (see

Wilson, chap. 14, this vol.). This discontinuity can be explained at least partially by access to different kinds of local materials, but the rest of the domestic assemblage at the Williams site, including San Francisco Red and smudged surfaces, suggests further contrasts related to differences in technological styles and cuisine.

In the Forestdale Valley Haury noted that there was little locally produced red-on-brown or white-on-red, despite the widespread use of polished and unpolished brownware. The earliest decorated type is not in the Mimbres sequence, as might be expected if this were indeed a branch of the "Mogollon," but is Cibola White Ware, with black mineral paint and gray paste. Haury called this a "transfer process" and thought that "the most significant attribute in the transfer process . . . was that design styles also were adopted along with the concept of painting the surface of the vessel" (1985a:107).

It is clear that Haury recognized that the black mineral–painted whiteware was not an indigenous development, but his interpretation of this pattern was constrained by at least two factors. The first was his own definition of what migration should look like based on his interpretations of the classic site-unit intrusion at Point of Pines. Here the social scale of migration was above the household level, producing clear contrasts in material culture with the surrounding community. This scale of migration set the bar a bit too high for recognizing smaller-scale migrations in the archaeological record. The second problem that Haury faced was a long but discontinuous occupational sequence in the Forestdale Valley (Mills and Herr 1999). Although he had some very well dated sites, the sequence has gaps that last for centuries.

Haury (1985a) called locally made Cibola White Ware decorated in Red Mesa style "Corduroy Black-on-white." He differentiated locally produced ceramics on the basis of their dark gray paste. What he considered "nonlocal" could have been produced as close as 16 km north because of the proximity of the Forestdale Valley to kaolinitic clay on the Colorado Plateau. Unfortunately, there aren't any good tree-ring dates between AD 800 and 1000 in the Forestdale Valley to better pinpoint when the introduction of Cibola White Ware took place. Based on data just to the north of the valley, however, population increased faster than probable birthrates between AD 900 and 950, suggesting a demographic event or series of events attributable to migration processes (Newcomb 1999). This period coincides with the very time period in which Cibola White Ware makes a regular appearance in the Forestdale assemblages. Thus, at least in this valley, migration of people with new technological styles seems the most likely explanation for the relatively sudden appearance of Cibola White Ware.

Summary of the Pre–AD 1000 Period. The period of ceramic production before AD 1000 is a long one, and there are several important trends that can be identified. First, the earliest ceramics and the dating of early surface texturing (neck banding) indicate that technological innovations were first made in the Mogollon area and then were adopted by potters in the Zuni area along with other areas of the Colorado Plateau. The relative importance of the different processes of small-scale migration, exchange, or emulation cannot be separated in most cases, but they do not appear to be the result of large-scale migrations. The time-transgressive patterns are clear, and although these patterns generally are not produced exclusively by migration, neither should we discount the possibility that some migration events contributed to the pattern. The same debates about small-scale exchange and migration that apply to the early diffusion of maize and other Mesoamerican domesticates apply to the diffusion of ceramic technology into the Mogollon Highlands and the Colorado Plateau.

Second, surface smudging is another technological innovation that appears to have been developed first in the Mogollon area. Unlike the widespread diffusion of brownware or neck banding, however, smudging was not adopted throughout the plateau. It does occur on a variety of wares (white, red, and gray), but only in very small amounts. Exceptions include the Rio Puerco valley. Although the use of smudging appears to have had a strong functional basis (see also Wilson, chap. 14, this vol.), it also can be argued that when smudged vessels became important parts of the domestic cuisine in the Mogollon area they also became important links to social identity. The lower Rio Puerco is a very interesting case because of the diversity of wares in different technological styles made in this area. This appears to be one of the areas where potters from below the Mogollon Rim brought with them the technology of smudging polished red and brown bowls. The geological diversity provided the resources, but the knowledge of how to make these vessels contrasts with many other areas, such as the Zuni area proper, that also had the same geological diversity but no tradition of smudging and polishing brownware ceramics. The Rio Puerco valley appears to have been a magnet for diverse populations at this time, possibly because of its greater irrigation potential in comparison to surrounding areas.

Third, in at least one area of the Colorado Plateau, the Quemado area, there is evidence for migration of potters bringing with them Mogollon painted ceramic technology. Locally produced Mogollon Red-on-brown was identified several decades ago alongside locally produced Cibola White Ware. Like the Rio Puerco valley, this area has the geological variability to produce both wares. If the local identification of ceramics based on compositional variation is correct, then this would be an example of the presence of potters with multiple social identities living in the same area either at the same time or closely sequent in time and making ceramics in different technological styles. Like the smudged and polished brown and red bowls, there is no evidence that potters with the knowledge of how to make Mogollon Red-on-brown ceramics made any significant migrations into the Zuni area.

The last major trend in the period prior to AD 1000 is a north–south one. Many archaeologists have noted that there is an expansion in the distribution of Cibola White Ware south of the Colorado Plateau, beginning with White Mound and Red Mesa Black-on-whites. This corresponds with population increases on the plateau in the Late Pueblo I and Early Pueblo II periods. In the Forestdale Valley it is likely that colonizing families brought Cibola White Ware technology with them, based on the local production of at least a Red Mesa stylistic analog. By contrast, the behavioral processes behind the occurrence of Cibola White Ware below the Colorado Plateau farther to the east appear to involve exchange. Red Mesa Black-on-white more likely occurred at sites in the Pine Lawn Valley and other Mogollon areas through exchange because the clays available for making light pasted whitewares are not available in this area. In fact, this sug-

gestion has been in the literature for a number of years (e.g., Danson 1957:90) but is only now receiving the kind of concentrated attention that it needs (see Wilson, chap. 14, this vol.).

AD 1000–1300

After AD 1000 the technological diversity of ceramics produced in the Zuni area increases, as does the diversity of decorative styles. Cibola White Ware has always been known to be one of the taxonomically problematic wares in the Southwest. Mention Cibola White Ware systematics to just about any archaeologists working on the Colorado Plateau, and they will likely say, "What systematics?" Although some design styles are easy to identify on both whole vessels and sherds, there is extraordinary diversity in the layouts and use of design elements. Some elements are used throughout the series of types (e.g., checkerboards, scrolls, triangles, etc.) and cannot be clearly used as taxonomic identifiers. Most contemporary analysts emphasize design style in Cibola White Ware taxonomy (e.g., Goetze and Mills 1993b; Hays-Gilpin and van Hartesveldt 1998; Sullivan and Hantman 1984).[7]

White Mountain Red Ware was added to the technological repertoire around AD 1030. Although it involves the choice of a different slip (at least in some cases, limonite) and a different firing atmosphere (fully oxidizing), the designs on White Mountain Red Ware generally mirror those on contemporaneous Cibola White Ware. Between AD 1000 and 1100 analogous styles include Sosi, Dogoszhi, and Puerco styles.[8] Interestingly, completely hatched designs are very rare on Puerco Black-on-red, the earliest type in the White Mountain Red Ware, which I think reflects its more restricted production loca-

tions in the lower Rio Puerco valley and Zuni areas.

The use of hachure on Cibola White Ware, called Gallup Black-on-white (see fig. 13.2c, f), was more common in the Chaco and upper Rio Puerco areas at this time (e.g., Toll and McKenna 1997; Windes 1984). Fine-line hachured Chaco Black-on-white is rare at Zuni but does occur at Chaco great houses in the Zuni area (e.g., Village of the Great Kivas; see Roberts 1932) and other contemporaneous sites. In contrast to the Chaco and upper Rio Puerco areas, Puerco Black-on-white dominates Zuni assemblages of the AD 1000s (see fig. 13.3).[9]

By the early AD 1100s a new design style composed of interlocking solid and hatched elements, Wingate Style, is made on both white (Reserve Black-on-white; fig. 13.3f) and red (Wingate Black-on-red and Polychrome) ceramics.[10] The AD 1100s also mark a period in which the first polychromes were made at Zuni (though perhaps closer to 1150). Although the various exterior surface treatments found on Wingate Polychrome were originally distinguished, they are now all considered to be contemporaneous.[11] Snowflake style appears to begin at about this time. It is composed of all solid designs and has more rectilinear step frets than the triangles of Sosi-style Escavada Black-on-white as well as the broad lines that are seen on Sosi and Black Mesa Black-on-whites.[12]

By the beginning of the AD 1200s Zuni assemblages are remarkably homogeneous. Cooking vessels are uniformly indented corrugated grayware, the whiteware is predominantly Tularosa Black-on-white, and the redware is decorated in Tularosa style and is made in both bichrome (St. Johns Black-on-red) and polychrome examples (St. Johns Polychrome). This homogeneity corresponds with

Figure 13.2. Puerco Black-on-white (a, e), Reserve Black-on-white (b), Gallup Black-on-white (c and f?), Chaco Black-on-white (d) from the Whitewater District (after Roberts 1940a:plate 16).

the aggregation of populations into closely spaced room blocks, followed by contiguous room blocks in the mid–AD 1200s. Compositional analyses of St. Johns Polychrome have not been widely conducted, but evidence from the Jaralosa Draw (southwest of Zuni) and the Zuni area itself suggests it was made locally in these areas by multiple villages (Duff 1993, 1994; Stone 1994). Based on its ubiquity (not always safe but in this case I think it is), we can say that it was made in many if not most settlements after AD 1000 and most if not all major settlements on the Zuni Reservation after AD 1200.

During the AD 1200s several important technological changes occurred in Zuni ceramics, though none of these were sudden. First, subglaze paints and then glaze paints were used, with glaze paint predominating on decorated ceramics after AD 1275. Second, the broad white exterior designs of St. Johns Polychrome became the more subtly painted thin white lines of Heshotauthla Polychrome. Third, several new design styles were used. Tularosa style predominates, but vessels also show the use of designs more characteristic of eastern and especially northeastern Arizona, such as those seen in Pinedale, Jeddito, Walnut, Betatakin, and Kayenta styles. Many archaeologists do not use these styles to differentiate types for this period, even if they do in the pre–AD 1250 period. For example, the use of Pinedale Black-on-white is quite rare in published analyses from the Zuni area.[13]

Finally, the use of white slips on White Mountain Red Ware increased, producing vessels with greater contrast in the primary field of decoration —the interior of the vessel. The use of white slips on White Mountain Red Ware combined the technology of Cibola White Ware and White Mountain Red Ware on the same vessel.

Figure 13.3. Cibola White Ware bowls from Village of the Great Kivas. Escavada Black-on-white (a–d), Puerco Black-on-white (e), and Reserve Black-on-white (f) from Village of the Great Kivas (after Roberts 1932:plate 32).

area. Unlike the Silver Creek area to the west, where Roosevelt Red Ware predominates in the painted assemblages of the late thirteenth century (Mills 1999b), Pinto Polychrome is absent from Zuni assemblages of the late 1200s.

Comparison of Zuni and Mogollon Undecorated Wares. An innovation on surface texturing that began around AD 1000 was the production of indented corrugated pottery. Unlike the south–north time transgressive pattern of early pottery and neck corrugations, however, indented corrugated pottery appears to date earliest in the San Juan area and then was adopted throughout most of the Colorado Plateau and the Mogollon area later on (Mills 1987a:112; Pierce 1999:fig. 15). Indented corrugations probably reached the Zuni area by AD 1050, but not the upper Gila or Mimbres areas until AD 1150. Instead, a variety of other surface treatments were employed on brownware in the Mogollon area, including incising (Rinaldo and Bluhm 1956).

The functional significance of indented corrugations was demonstrated by Christopher Pierce (1999), who showed that indented corrugated vessels last longer than plain vessels when subjected to repeated cycles of heating and cooling. This suggests that there is a functional basis for the diffusion of this technological innovation. But Pierce also suggests that because it starts in the Chaco area during the Bonito phase, it might also have had a certain degree of active style associated with it—similar to arguments that have been made about the active style messaging in the use of hachure on Chaco-area ceramics (Toll et al. 1992). Moreover, Pierce (1999:180) suggests that the later adoption of corrugations on Mogollon Brown Ware cannot be explained by the technological advan-

This could not have been done without a concurrent change in paint technology.[14] Most of these slips were on the interiors of bowls, producing what is known as Kwakina Polychrome. Cibola White Ware technology was essentially eclipsed by White Mountain Red Ware during the early AD 1300s in the Zuni area. Of importance to later discussions is the absence of Roosevelt Red Ware as a locally produced ware in the Zuni

tage of greater durability during cooking because many of the indented brownware vessels were not used as cooking pots. Thus, he suggests that there was some kind of meaning associated with indented corrugations to account for the adoption of the technological style to the Mogollon area. What we cannot separate in these discussions is whether this adoption was through migration or emulation. To be able to talk about differences in the technological styles of indented corrugated ceramics we need more of the kind of fine-grained analyses recently conducted by Neuzil (2001), who measured the orientation, depth, and width of indentations on ceramics from the Mogollon Rim area.

Due south of Zuni, at the edge of the Colorado Plateau, it is evident that the frequency of smudged brownware vessels increases through time. Smudging occurs with plain, polished, and corrugated ceramics. In the Quemado area smudged brownware increases between approximately AD 1000 and 1300 (Mills 1987a:fig. 11.6). Based on his identification of local tempering materials, Wasley argued that there is "a progressive increase in the proportion of locally manufactured and imitated Mogollon pottery of the Pine Lawn and Mimbres areas" (1959:192) at the end of the sequence at Cerro Colorado. Although only limited compositional analyses of brownware ceramics from the Quemado area have been conducted, petrographic studies indicate that the brownware in this area is much more homogeneous than the grayware (Mills 1987b:153). Based on its relative homogeneity, the brownware ceramics may come from a small number of production areas.

The increase during the AD 1100s and 1200s in brownware ceramics, especially those with smudged interiors, is correlated with increased import of Cibola White Ware vessels to sites lying south of the Colorado Plateau (see Wilson, chap. 14, this vol.). It is likely that smudged Mogollon Brown Ware vessels made south of the plateau were exchanged for Cibola White Ware vessels made on the plateau during this time period. Nonetheless, because of the accessibility of iron-rich clays, some of the smudged Mogollon Brown Ware could have been made in the Quemado area. Like the Mogollon Rim area to the west (e.g., Zedeño 1994), complex interactions involving both exchange and migration were probably occurring in the Quemado area. More comprehensive ceramic provenance and technological style analyses are clearly needed in this area.

Comparison of Zuni and Mogollon Whitewares. Two major whitewares were made during the post–AD 1000 period in the Mogollon and Zuni areas. Mimbres Black-on-white dominates assemblages between AD 1000 and 1150 in the upper Gila and Mimbres, but Cibola White Ware was more common in the Reserve, Forestdale, Quemado, and Zuni areas. Cibola White Ware was the most popular decorated ware in the upper San Francisco, especially the Pine Lawn Valley area. It is present in assemblages in the Forestdale Valley and is one of the main reasons that Haury (1985a) decided to investigate this area after his excavations at Mogollon Village (Haury 1936a). It is also one of the reasons that the Upper Gila Expedition moved its investigations to the Quemado area—an area that doesn't even lie in the upper Gila drainage.

During the late AD 1000s and 1100s Cibola White Ware styles on the Colorado Plateau show differences from north to south. In recognition of some of this variability the original MNA Cibola White Ware Conference of 1958 designated three spatially distinct series. A Chaco series was identified for Chaco Canyon and some outlying sites in the San Juan Basin. A Puerco series was defined for the middle Rio Puerco, the upper Little Colorado area of eastern Arizona, and the Zuni area. Finally, a Reserve series was identified for Cibola White Ware occurring in west-central New Mexico, although major problems with this series were found. Many of these may be summarized as the style vs. technology problem (Reid 1984). The previous classifications had emphasized both style and technology and did neither consistently.

All hachure designs are most common in the Chaco area, including Gallup Black-on-white and Chaco Black-on-white. Windes (1984) reevaluated the boundaries of the distribution of Chaco series types and defined the southern boundary about where Interstate 40 runs today, or the north side of the Rio Puerco and Red Mesa valleys. In the upper Little Colorado south of the Rio Puerco valley and in the Zuni area proper all hachure designs are less common and solid, and hatched designs predominate. For example, Doyel (1984) notes that Puerco Black-on-white (solid designs separated by vertical panels) are most common in the Springerville area, co-occurring at the same sites with Reserve Black-on-white (interlocked solid and hatched designs). Both of these design styles are also more common in the Zuni area proper and the Quemado areas up until the mid–AD 1100s. Thus, along the Rio Puerco of the West there appears to be a stylistic break in painted designs, possibly coincident with separate clusters of Chacoan great houses in the Rio Puerco of the West (Wilcox 1993, 1999a).

Styles II and III of Mimbres Black-on-white were produced between AD 1000 and 1150. It is now known that these types were not exclusively made in the Mimbres River valley but were also made in the upper Gila and even along the eastern slopes of the Black Range, near the Rio Grande. Geometrically decorated Style III (or Classic Mimbres Black-on-white) appears to have been more widely made than the naturalistically painted designs (Gilman et al. 1994). Although some of these well-known designs are zoomorphic, those with anthropomorphic figures are the geographically most restricted.

Many interpretations of the iconographic content of these vessels have been made (see especially Brody 1977, 1983), including depictions of ceremonial and allegorical figures. These interpretations suggest some kind of shared identity at perhaps multiple social scales. Some of the imagery has been suggested to owe its source to Mesoamerican oral history, such as the Hero Twins and the Popul Vuh (Moulard 1984). Other images have been interpreted as part of the widespread flower cult found throughout the Southwest (Hays-Gilpin and Hill 1999). Still other figures were identified by Fred Kabotie (1982) as those of priests. There is no question that some of the figures depict Pueblo ritual practice, including the planting of prayer sticks and the carrying of staffs of ritual office by some individuals. Caves in the Mimbres and surrounding areas have produced both of these objects, along with other wooden ceremonial objects that were probably parts of altars (e.g., Cosgrove 1947; see also Martin et al. 1954:fig. 101). These artifacts show clear-cut similarities with objects found at Chaco and in other areas of the Pueblo world (cf. Vivian et al. 1978). They represent the ceremonial use and discard of objects used in suprahousehold contexts that link widespread areas of the Southwest well before the kachina cult is

recognizable in the archaeological record.

Between the Mimbres area and the Zuni area the incidence of Mimbres White Ware drops off (Lekson 1990b).[15] Sites to the north, such as those in the Pine Lawn Valley, have Reserve Black-on-white, and sites to the south have Mimbres White Ware. This has raised two interesting problems in the interpretation of Mogollon assemblages for the period AD 1000–1100. One is that most if not all of the whiteware ceramics were imported rather than locally made. The second is that the painted type diagnostic of the Reserve phase in the Pine Lawn Valley, Reserve Black-on-white (ca. AD 1000–1100), is dated by some to the AD 1100s (Mills 1987a; Reid et al. 1995).

If Reserve Black-on-white dates to the AD 1100s rather than the 1000s, it has important implications for continuity of occupation in many areas of the northern Mogollon region and the dating of the transition to aboveground architecture (Wilson 1999a). Wilson argues that there are still too few absolute dates to rule out production of Reserve Black-on-white in the AD 1000s. This type was one of the most common decorated whiteware types in the Quemado area prior to Tularosa Black-on-white (Mills 1987a), and the two are clearly related. If Reserve Black-on-white is pushed back, then either Reserve must have a longer span or Tularosa must have a longer span (or a little of both).

I concur that Reserve may indeed have a longer production span and that it may be earlier in assemblages from the southern Colorado Plateau than the later use of Wingate style in the Gallup area. It is most prevalent not in the Reserve area but in eastern Arizona and western New Mexico in areas lying at the southern edge of the Colorado Plateau.[16] The use of interlocking solid and hatched barbed

designs seems stylistically more closely related to Mimbres Black-on-white, which clearly has temporal precedence. The stylistic similarities aside, however, I do not think that Reserve was made by migrants from the Mimbres area. Some people from the Mimbres area may have moved onto the plateau and into east-central Arizona, but the numbers were probably very small.[17]

The use of hachure has been argued to be a style widely associated with Chacoan sites. Cibola White Ware vessels with this style are predominantly found in the San Juan Basin (Toll et al. 1992). One finely painted type of ceramics with all hachure filled designs, Chaco Black-on-white, occurs on special vessels that have been designated as "votive" offerings (Toll 2001). There is no question that Chaco cylinder jars are overwhelmingly decorated with hachure and are found in only a few special contexts within Pueblo Bonito and a few other great houses. Other forms with hachure occur in Zuni-area assemblages, but not as frequently as they do in the Chaco area. They almost always are present at Chacoan outlier communities and associated sites up until the mid–AD 1100s, when Reserve Black-on-white becomes more common.

During the AD 1200s settlements became more aggregated. In the Zuni area different villages apparently made their own ceramics with their own specific paste and paint recipes (Huntley and Kintigh 2004). The small number of ceramics from outside the Zuni area in these sites suggests that Zuni was relatively inwardly focused, and there is little evidence for migration into the Zuni area. Populations were large and can be accounted for by aggregation of the already large but more disperse population (see Kintigh, chap. 18, this vol.). This pattern was repeated over a

Figure 13.4. Tularosa Black-on-whites (a) from San Cosmos (b–f), from Higgins Flat Pueblo, collections of the Field Museum of Natural History (after Rinaldo and Bluhm 1956:fig. 83).

larger area than the Zuni area proper, and the late sites in the highland areas on both sides of the Continental Divide must be seen as part of this same pattern, including the cluster of sites in the Quemado area. Based on the excavations at Site 616 (McGimsey 1980; Washburn 1977) and private collections from the Quemado area (Barnett 1974), it is clear that styles of decoration from a broad swath of the Southwest were used, including Pinedale, Walnut, Jeddito, Betatakin, and Tularosa styles (see fig. 13.4).[18]

A technological innovation that occurs on both whitewares and redwares is the use of glaze paint. This is most closely associated with ceramics in the late AD 1200s. Glaze paint is earliest in the Mogollon Rim area (Fenn et al. 2006; Haury 1985a), and whiteware collections from the Silver Creek area (such as Roundy Pueblo) indicate that some of these probably date to the AD 1100s. Some AD 1200s vessels in the Jewett Gap site (Barter 1955) and at Mariana Mesa (McGimsey 1980) were painted in a "sub-

glaze." In the Zuni area proper subglaze paints occur on Tularosa Black-on-white and St. Johns bichromes and polychromes.

Comparison of Zuni and Mogollon Redwares. Prior to AD 1000 little redware was produced in the Zuni or other nearby areas. Lino Fugitive Red stopped being produced before the production of White Mountain Red Ware and shows few technological similarities. The fact that San Francisco Red disappears around the time that White Mountain Red Ware began to be produced (Wheat 1955) is not a compelling argument for their historical relationship because they do not geographically overlap during the transition.

The earliest redware type in the Zuni area, Puerco Black-on-red, is closely related to Show Low Black-on-red, except that the former has a mineral paint and the latter carbon paint. Both were produced in the lower Rio Puerco valley in the AD 1000s, with the incidence of Show Low Black-on-red increasing toward the west and south. Although it shares decorative styles with Puerco Black-on-red, Show Low Black-on-red appears to be a distinctive technology that has a more north–south distribution from the Rio Puerco valley to the Mogollon Rim, culminating in Pinto Black-on-red and Polychrome of the late 1200s (Fowler 1994; Hays-Gilpin and van Hartesveldt 1998; Stinson 1996). Neither of the latter types occurs very widely outside of the Mogollon Rim area.[19]

To the east and south of Zuni both Puerco Black-on-red and its successors, Wingate Black-on-red and Wingate Polychrome, are relatively rare. Dittert (1959:408) does not consider these to have been locally made in the Acoma area. Similarly, these early White Mountain Red Ware types are rare at sites that predate AD 1200 in the Quemado area (Mills 1987a).

Figure 13.5. St. Johns Polychrome from the Zuni Route 5 (Nutria Road) Project (after Zier 1976:fig. B-1).

There are several salient facts about White Mountain Red Ware besides its bright red color. First, it increases in frequency between AD 1000 and 1300 until it nearly takes over the painted assemblages of sites in the Zuni, Quemado, Acoma, and St. Johns areas. Second, it occurs most often in bowl form. Third, by the end of the sequence (mid–AD 1100s on) most of the vessels are also decorated with two colors (Wingate and St. Johns polychromes). These polychrome vessels are the beginning of a sequence of production and use of polychrome vessels that is continuous in the Zuni area from this time on. Fourth, the most popular

thirteenth-century White Mountain Red Ware in the Zuni area, St. Johns Polychrome (see fig. 13.5), is one of the most widely distributed ceramics known in the Southwest (Carlson 1970) and perhaps *the* most widely distributed.

The widespread distribution of St. Johns Polychrome is at least partially attributable to exchange. It is also difficult to miss in assemblages, and the ease of recognition of this type may be an important factor. Nonetheless, St. Johns Polychrome was also produced over a wide area. Production outside the immediate Zuni area is harder to pin down because of the lack of compositional analyses. To

the west it is very common on sites in the Springerville and St. Johns areas (Martin and Willis 1940) but perhaps not as common as its name suggests. A fully decorated but unfired St. Johns Polychrome vessel was recovered from Hooper Ranch Pueblo, just north of Springerville (Martin et al. 1961). It is common at Broken K Pueblo in the Hay Hollow Valley (Martin et al. 1967). It is relatively rare in the Mogollon Rim area, however, and researchers working in both the Silver Creek and Grasshopper areas do not believe that it was produced that far west (Mills 1999b). Those few examples that do occur in these two areas are highly heterogeneous in paste and paint recipes, suggesting small-scale exchanges were responsible for their distribution (Fenn et al. 2006).

To the east St. Johns Polychrome was probably made at sites on both sides of the Continental Divide, extending into the Acoma area (Dittert 1959; Ruppé 1990). It has also been suggested to be locally produced in the Quemado area (McGimsey 1980). These areas have black-on-white ceramics with the same design styles.

South of the Colorado Plateau the frequency of St. Johns Polychrome drops off dramatically. At the Jewett Gap site, with occupation in the AD 1100s and early 1200s, the few White Mountain Red Ware whole vessels are Wingate Black-on-red, Wingate Polychrome, and Springerville Polychrome (a late variety of St. Johns with black paint on the exterior) (Barter 1955, 1957a). Sherds of St. Johns are noted to have been present in the Jewett Gap collection (Barter 1955:4), but all the sherds were apparently discarded before full analysis, and relative amounts are unavailable.[20] Other sites attributable to the same period have been designated the Apache Creek phase. One of its attributes is that St. Johns Polychrome is noticeably absent (Berman 1979:56–57; Lekson 1996:170). Later Tularosa phase sites do contain some St. Johns Polychrome (Barter 1957b), though the quantities are much lower than in contemporaneous assemblages in the Quemado and Zuni areas. Barter (1957b:98) thought that some of it was locally made in the Reserve area, though this has never been demonstrated. John Rinaldo (Martin et al. 1952:67) considered St. Johns Polychrome to be a trade ware in the Tularosa Cave assemblage.

St. Johns Polychrome may be one of our best examples of active signaling of identity expressed through highly visible designs on the exteriors of vessels. If these were meant to convey social identity within the household, designs on the interior would suffice. Instead, the designs are placed on the exterior, where they are visible at a distance even if the bowls are full. Except for Wingate Polychrome, exterior designs on bowls are very rare in the Zuni area before AD 1300. Exterior decoration on bowls used to serve food that is carried outside the household provides a way of quickly recognizing ownership. I have argued that the Tusayan-area Tsegi Orange Ware polychromes, which are also bright reddish or orange ceramics with bold exterior designs, were used in contexts of suprahousehold consumption (Mills 1999a). The production and use of these northern polychromes corresponds to a shift to more aggregated settlements. In addition, the Tsegi Orange Ware bowls are larger than contemporaneous Tusayan White Ware bowls, which implies that they were used to feed more people at a time. Although a detailed metric study of White Mountain Red Ware bowls has not been conducted, Carlson's (1970) reported ranges and scaled photographs suggest that St. Johns Polychrome vessels were larger

than earlier Puerco and early Wingate types.[21]

Although archaeologists have recently paid much attention to the role of ceramics in feasting activities in the Southwest (Crown 1994; Potter 2000; Spielmann 1998), these studies largely focus on the late thirteenth and early fourteenth centuries. The use of polychromes in the Southwest, especially the Zuni-area White Mountain Red Ware and the Tusayan-area Tsegi polychromes, is earlier than these other transitions and corresponds to important aggregation trends. In fact, by the mid–AD 1200s aggregated sites in a zone extending from the eastern Zuni to the Quemado areas were probably the largest sites in the Western Pueblo world (Adler 1996). They also share the use of bold yet simple exterior designs that would have been highly visible from a distance when carried or full and that may indicate their use in events taking place above the social scale of the household (Mills 2007).

In the Mogollon area other decorated types were produced that incorporated bold exterior designs. Tularosa White-on-red is a polished redware with smudged interior that has broad white line designs. Like St. Johns Polychrome, these are bowls, and their designs are easily recognized at a distance. Although the temporal priority of Tularosa White-on-red has been a topic of speculation (Rinaldo and Bluhm 1956), the dates are still ambiguous. This type is associated with the Tularosa phase, which started in the late AD 1100s and continued through the 1200s.

The use of vessels with bold exterior designs indicates a distinctive shift in the social contexts of use. I interpret the use of Tularosa White-on-red very similarly to the St. Johns Polychrome vessels—vessels used in suprahousehold consumption events that actively signal some kind of so-

cial identity. If the production and use of these bowls in the northern Mogollon area is an emulation of the St. Johns Polychrome bowls, this may indicate shared participation in similar kinds of suprahousehold activities and shared identities at one social scale. However, by not importing large quantities of St. Johns Polychrome and making their own distinctive bowls instead, potters may have intentionally differentiated themselves from the Zuni area, reinforcing local identities while at the same time participating in increasingly more intensive suprahousehold rituals that characterize the broader region at this time.

Still another ware was produced in the Mogollon area with bold exterior white line designs, Mogollon Brown Ware. McDonald Corrugated is a thirteenth-century indented corrugated brownware with a smudged interior and exterior white line decoration. It occurs throughout the Mogollon area. McDonald Corrugated overlaps St. Johns Polychrome in only a few areas, such as sites in the Hay Hollow Valley (Martin et al. 1967). It was common at sites in the Point of Pines region during the AD 1200s. Examples from the Mogollon Rim area tend to be smaller (see Hough 1903 for illustrations), while those from the Point of Pines area are very large straight-sided vessels (see Haury 1989:fig. 4.12). Two Point of Pines examples were found in a burned room at Point of Pines Pueblo, one of them covering a "Reserve White-on-red" vessel, indicating that they were all stored together.[22]

McDonald Corrugated had been replaced by Cibicue Painted Corrugated and Cibicue Polychrome in the Mogollon Rim area by about AD 1275. These are uniformly small bowls with red slip or paint over the corrugations, outlined with white lines (see

Reid and Whittlesey 1999:146 for an illustration). Recent analysis of these bowls from Grasshopper (Hagenbuckle 2001) indicates that they generally occur in burials and that when they do occur there is usually only one of them.[23] Based on their small size, limited production even in their area of occurrence, and their final placement in burials at Grasshopper, Hagenbuckle argues that these were individual serving bowls with specific ritual associations. Analogously sized vessels are used at Hopi during initiation ceremonies, and Hagenbuckle suggests that Cibicue Polychrome may have been used in such closed contexts. Reid and Whittlesey (1999: 145) note that these bowls are most often found in male burials. Thus, these vessels are excellent examples of ceramics used in specific contexts that indicate membership in some kind of suprahousehold ritual organization. The same usage is not known for any sites in the Zuni area or other Mogollon areas lying to the east.

Summary of the AD 1000–1300 Period. One of the hallmarks of the AD 1000–1300 period is the great diversity in the number of design styles that were used contemporaneously on decorated ceramics of both white and red ceramics. This diversity is probably because of the high degree of population interaction in the area, including migration, exchange, and emulation. If decorative style is any indication of interaction, social boundaries were highly permeable during this time period.

Contributing to our understanding of exchange are recent investigations of the Museum of New Mexico in the northern Mogollon area. Because of the absence of suitable clays it is now apparent that there is no separate area of production of Cibola White Ware south of the Mogollon Rim in the Reserve area.

Southern Colorado Plateau potters provided decorated whiteware ceramics in Reserve and Tularosa styles to the northern Mogollon area. Thus, at least at this time period, the spread of whiteware technology into the northern Mogollon area appears to be fully explained through exchange (see Wilson, chap. 14, this vol.).

Other than shared styles, which could have been the product of exchange and emulation, there are few clear-cut technological style changes that can be attributed to migration during the AD 1000–1300 period. Indented corrugated surface manipulations and hachure have been argued to have a north–south distribution. Both of these can be explained by emulation and, in the case of corrugations, through functional adaptability. Nonetheless, I do think that the argument linking hachure to the cylinder jars is a compelling one for considerations of social identity. The producers of those vessels shared identities of some kind, and they chose to decorate nearly all of the few hundred vessels that have been recovered in an all-hachured design style. The widespread use of hachure on other vessels as indicating some degree of "Chaconess" seems more plausible in this light.

Whitewares had been replaced by redwares in the Zuni area by the AD 1200s. The widespread production and use of St. Johns Polychrome in the Zuni area are striking. Although this type was widely traded, I would argue that it was not widely produced outside the Zuni/upper Little Colorado/Quemado/Cebolleta Mesa areas. By contrast, white–on–smudged red and white-painted brownware corrugated vessels were made and used to the west and to the south during the AD 1200s, partially overlapping with the distribution of St. Johns but also occurring well outside the area in which St. Johns was produced.

Glaze paint is one possible technological innovation that could have been transferred with migrating potters, but it does not take too many potters with this knowledge to introduce glaze paints. The earliest glaze paints appear ca. AD 1275 in the Zuni area, following a brief period of experimentation with subglaze paints in the mid–AD 1200s. Glaze paints were made in the Mogollon Rim area in the late AD 1200s (Fenn et al. 2006). This pattern can be explained through exchange and emulation by some talented potters, perhaps with some small-scale migration.

The strongest indicator of differences and similarities in identity during the AD 1000–1300 period is the use of bowls with bold exterior designs, especially polychromes. The first polychrome vessels at Zuni and surrounding areas correspond to (1) aggregation, (2) increased intensity of suprahousehold ritual, and (3) (probably) increased vessel sizes. I have argued that vessels with these bold exterior designs were important in the construction of social identity, even if we don't know at what social scales these identities were being expressed (Mills 2007). Differences among wares that used these exterior designs may provide the strongest insights into some kind of community or suprahousehold identities. The use of another, smaller size class in the burials at Grasshopper provides a contrasting case study; perhaps this ware was not used in feasting but as personal bowls by members of suprahousehold groups. Based on these cases, the Zuni area appears to be distinct from the Mogollon Rim, Point of Pines, and Pine Lawn Valley areas in how suprahousehold membership is expressed, but all of these areas shared in the importance of these ritual sodalities in community life and used exterior bowl designs in active ways.

AD 1300–1630

Because this period includes the end of occupation in the Mogollon area I summarize the continuities and discontinuities at Zuni and compare them with only those areas that were still occupied in the fourteenth and early fifteenth centuries.

Undecorated Wares. After AD 1300 ceramics in the Zuni area continue to show increasing technological diversity. Undecorated ceramics used as cooking vessels were made in a variety of surface treatments (Indented Corrugated Gray Ware and Buff Ware, Semi-obliterated Corrugated Gray Ware, Obliterated Corrugated Gray Ware, and plain blackware).[24] Although these undecorated surface treatments are generally thought to have been produced in a sequence throughout the Southwest, multiple styles were apparently made and used in the fourteenth and fifteenth centuries at Zuni. Kintigh (1996:table 9.1) does not include obliterated corrugated in his seriation, but he does indicate that blackware is a part of Zuni-area assemblages by about AD 1375.

Ceramics from the Pueblo of Zuni's Middle Village Project indicate that Semi-obliterated Corrugated Gray Ware, Obliterated Corrugated Gray Ware, and blackware all co-occur in excavation units that appear to be relatively unmixed, based on decorated ceramics. These units most likely date to the late fourteenth through fifteenth centuries (Mills 2002a). This diversity in the technological styles of cooking vessels contrasts with the much greater consistency in use of indented corrugated treatments of the thirteenth century. It also contrasts with assemblages of the early sixteenth century, when blackware dominates the culinary assemblage.

The technological styles of cooking vessels with the above surface treatments are not well described in the published literature. In the upper Little Colorado proper, Table Rock Pueblo is described as having both indented corrugated and obliterated corrugated (Martin and Rinaldo 1960). Sites in the Mogollon Rim area and Point of Pines also show the same transition in the late AD 1200s and early 1300s. In the Tusayan area the flattening of coils into a semi-obliterated pattern occurs much earlier, in the AD 1200s on Moenkopi Corrugated (Gifford and Smith 1978). In fact, the temporal precedence of semiobliterated corrugated coils on Tusayan Gray Ware may be an indicator of migration out of the Four Corners area into the Mogollon Rim and even Zuni areas. None of the later transitions, such as from obliterated corrugated to blackware, are well dated, yet they have much potential for explaining the behavioral basis for why new surface treatments were adopted across the Southwest.

Pierce (1999) has suggested that the abandonment of indented corrugations, which made pots more durable over repeated cycles of boiling and cooling, was related to a reduction in the time needed to process corn in cooking vessels. Alternative cooking techniques could have been used, such as soaking and the production of flat breads. Comals were used in the Hohokam area during the Classic period (Beck 2000), but the dates of introduction of flat breads such as *hewe* at Zuni and piki at Hopi are not well known. Jenny Adams has been looking for piki stones in the Homolovi assemblages, but to my knowledge they have not yet been positively identified. Nor have they been recovered from Mogollon Rim assemblages at Bailey Ruin or Grasshopper, even though semiobliterated and obliterated corrugated surface treatments were applied to cooking vessels in both these places by the AD 1280s. Piki is one of the foods associated with the kachina cult, as defined from historic and modern traits by Chuck Adams (1991). Hewe was one of many breads made at Zuni, and hewe stones are present in nineteenth-century assemblages, but the bread's introduction has never been established. The association of these stones with blackware needs further examination and might provide a better explanation for the return to fully smoothed coils on cooking vessels.

Early Zuni Glazes and the Divergence of White Mountain Red Ware Technology. By the late 1200s and into the early 1300s a divergence in White Mountain Red Ware production occurred, resulting in distinctive technological styles in east-central Arizona vs. west-central New Mexico. This divergence has been called the White Mountain and Zuni series of White Mountain Red Ware (Carlson 1970). Both series have antecedents in St. Johns Polychrome, with its white-painted exterior and black-on-red interior, but, as noted earlier, St. Johns probably was not made in the Mogollon Rim area. Thus, this is a new technology for that area but a continuation in the Zuni area. We date this divergence to about AD 1280 (Fenn et al. 2006).

In the Zuni area Heshotauthla Polychrome has a long production span and is decorated in an almost exclusively geometric design style. Heshotauthla Polychrome overlaps with a partially white-slipped type called Kwakina Polychrome. By ca. AD 1350 fully white-slipped glaze-painted types called Kechipawan Polychrome and Pinnawa Glaze-on-white were produced in the Zuni area (Woodbury and Woodbury 1966).[25] I refer to all of these as Early Zuni Glazes or Glaze Wares to distinguish them as a group from the Pinedale/Four Mile types of

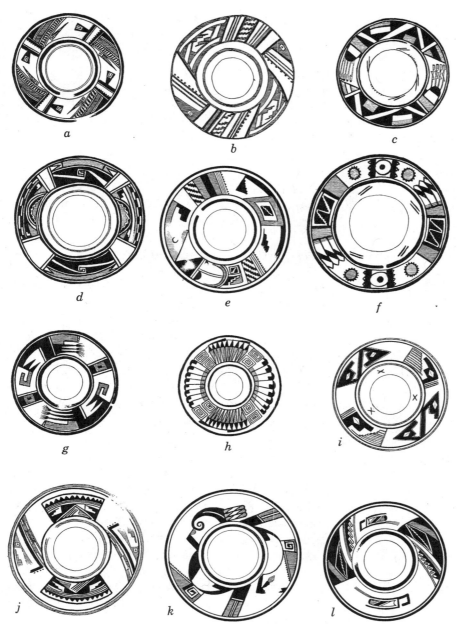

Figure 13.6. Kechipawan Polychrome jar designs from Hawikuh (after Smith et al. 1966:fig. 49).

lections of the National Museum of the American Indian.

Stylistically, there are important contrasts between the White Mountain and Zuni series that fall into what I think can be called active uses of style. In the Zuni area the Early Zuni Glaze Wares are nearly all geometric, occasionally with parrots and other animal forms, but masks are not present. The designs in the Zuni area seem to underplay differentiation and access to esoteric knowledge. Even the bold exterior lines of St. Johns become more subtly painted with the addition of thin white lines. By contrast, the White Mountain series vessels that were produced in the Mogollon Rim area show a diversity of interior designs, including symmetrical geometric and asymmetrical geometric and naturalistic designs. Between AD 1275 and 1325 exterior designs were varied and interior designs highly standardized. After AD 1325 or 1330 some of these interiors are painted with depictions of kachina masks. Van Keuren (2001; Kaldahl et al. 2004) has recently argued that the changes in interior/exterior decoration ca. AD 1325 in the Mogollon Rim area reflect more exclusionary membership in intracommunity groups. Exterior designs become highly standardized, but interior designs are more elaborate on Four Mile Polychrome vessels because of differential access to knowledge within communities. The same degree of differentiation does not appear in the Zuni area, where more homogeneous geometric designs prevail.

The distinction between the White Mountain and Zuni series is not only in the design styles but also based on technological differences in glaze-paint recipes that may have importance for understanding differences in social identity. Compositionally, the glaze paints of both series are copper and lead based, but different

the Silver Creek area and to better indicate that not all of them are redware, yet they share the same basic technology (Mills 1995).

Glaze-painted ceramics dominate the Zuni-area painted assemblages by the early 1300s. The use of hachure decreases noticeably, and Tularosa style is completely replaced by Pinedale style and other styles that are more common in northeastern Ari-

zona. Parrots, eagles, and butterflies are the most common naturalistic designs on these vessels, but most designs are geometric. Some are very simple, but others appear to use designs from textiles that are quite complex (fig. 13.6). I know of only one vessel with a masked figure on these Early Zuni Glaze Ware ceramics, a Pinnawa Glaze-on-white stirrup-spouted jar from Hawikuh in the col-

ratios of these fluxes and other color-ants distinguish the products of potters within regions, sites, and even through time (De Atley 1986; Fenn et al. 2006; Shepard 1942). In general, greener glazes characteristic of higher copper content and purple glazes indicating higher manganese content are more common in the Zuni area. Finer-grained technological styles have been identified by Huntley (Huntley and Kintigh 2004) at the intersite level in the Zuni area, and Fenn et al. (2006) have found differences at the intrasite level in the Silver Creek area. These technological styles allow us to examine learning frameworks at smaller social scales than the original distinction between the Zuni and White Mountain series suggests, but none of these intrasite or intraregional distinctions are discernible without chemical analyses.

Duff (1999, 2002) has observed much greater diversity in the late White Mountain Red Ware / Early Zuni Glazes during the fourteenth century in the area between Zuni and the Mogollon Rim than in their respective areas of concentration. His compositional analyses demonstrate that some of each series were produced in the upper Little Colorado area between Springerville and St. Johns. Differential import of ceramics from the Zuni and Mogollon areas was also evident. Finally, he found that some sites did not have a predominance of either of the White Mountain series but of other wares entirely, especially Roosevelt Red Ware and Jeddito Yellow Ware. He interprets this as evidence for more permeable social boundaries associated with low population density and contrasts these villages with the more homogeneous and densely settled Hopi and Zuni areas.

Glaze-painted White Mountain Red Ware occurs as far south as the Blue River drainage in eastern Ari-zona during the AD 1300s. Foote Canyon Pueblo appears to represent one of the latest sites in that area. Both Heshotauthla and Kwakina Polychromes are present at that site, but there are few examples of the White Mountain series (Rinaldo 1959). No compositional studies have been done on these ceramics, and it is possible that these may not have been locally made.

To the south of Zuni the Quemado area contains both Pinedale and Heshotauthla Polychromes, but most White Mountain Red Ware from Site 616 falls into the technology of the Zuni series (McGimsey 1980). Later, white-slipped Zuni Glaze Ware is not common (e.g., Pinnawa Glaze-on-white and Red-on-white and Kechipawan Polychrome), indicating that the end of the occupational sequence in this area dates to the early AD 1300s.[26] Fully white-slipped Early Zuni Glaze Ware likely begins ca. AD 1350. Most of the intervening Mogollon area was no longer occupied at this time, including the Blue River area, with the exception of Animas phase sites farther to the southeast. Examples of both the White Mountain and Zuni series polychromes are found at these sites, and they are considered to be the product of small-scale exchanges.

To answer one of the questions posed for this seminar, the divergence in White Mountain Red Ware styles appears to be centered around the upper Little Colorado proper. Areas to the west are dominated by Pinedale and Four Mile Polychromes and areas to the east by the Early Zuni Glazes. The latter includes more vessels that are partially or completely slipped white. The boundary extends north to south, just west of the Blue area. This technological boundary has precedence in the distribution of St. Johns Polychrome. St. Johns Polychrome is more closely associated with the pro-duction areas of Early Zuni Glazes, whereas the Pinedale / Four Mile types are made in areas that only had St. Johns in limited amounts through import and were instead dominated by carbon-painted redwares. Recent discussions of design variability on Pinedale Polychrome and migration pathways in the pre–AD 1325 period (Lyons 2003; Van Keuren 2001) all point to a north–south trend from the Four Corners to the Mogollon Rim area. This is paralleled by other hallmarks of migration from the Four Corners, such as perforated plates, which are not found east of the upper Little Colorado River valley proper but are found in a chain of sites from the Kayenta area of northeastern Arizona to the middle San Pedro River and Safford areas of southeastern Arizona.

Overlapping distributions of different wares in the upper Little Colorado show that although distinctive slip colors, decorative styles, and paint types were applied, boundaries were still permeable in the entire area of east-central Arizona during the fourteenth century (Duff 2002). The compositional analyses indicate that there was a high level of exchange occurring along a west–east axis and overlapping in the upper Little Colorado area. If exchange sets up possible future migration pathways, then the conditions were set for a west–east migration from the Silver Creek and other Mogollon Rim communities to the upper Little Colorado area and, soon after, from the upper Little Colorado to the Zuni area. The iconographic content suggests that some elements of the kachina cult may have had temporal priority in the Mogollon Rim area because Zuni-area designs do not include kachinas until at least the mid–AD 1300s.

Buffware. By the early 1400s a new ware was made at Zuni that eventually replaced Early Zuni Glaze Ware. This is a slipped and polished ware called Matsaki Buff Ware that was decorated with various nonglaze mineral paints in red, brownish black, and even white. Early Zuni Glaze Ware overlapped with this buff-ware for a while but was eventually eclipsed. Matsaki Buff Ware became the Zuni Polychrome of its day and was ubiquitous at the latest prehistoric sites and up until the early seventeenth century.

Our best samples of whole vessels of Matsaki Buff Ware come from excavations at the two contact period villages of Hawikuh and Kechipawan (Bushnell 1955; Hodge 1923; Woodbury and Woodbury 1966). Ceramic seriations conducted by Spier (1917) and Kintigh (1982, 1985) provide insight into the replacement of the Early Zuni Glaze Ware. Kintigh's (1996:table 9.1) ceramic complexes indicate that Matsaki Buff Ware became a consistent part of Zuni assemblages around AD 1400. Recent analyses of ceramics from the Middle Village Project indicate that the shift may have been a rapid one, corresponding with an important hinge point in the occupational history of the entire upper Little Colorado area (Schachner 2006). Although there may have been sites below the Mogollon Rim that persisted until AD 1450, there are no tree-ring dates from excavated sites in the Mogollon Rim or upper Little Colorado proper after AD 1390.

There are several interesting features of Matsaki Buff Ware. First, it is decorated in a style that includes asymmetrical designs in Sikyatki style. Second, the designs include the first corpus of recognizable masked figures and shields for the Zuni area (fig. 13.7). Third, the all-important parrots of the Early Zuni Glaze Ware and White Mountain series White Mountain Red Ware no longer appear

(although eagle feathers do). Fourth, the entire focus of bowl decoration has moved to the interior, and exterior designs are either plain slipped buff or have one or two stripes at the shoulder. Fifth, many of the vessels were associated with cremation burials as well as inhumations.

Sikyatki-style decoration and the use of a buff background color have both been suggested to indicate that Matsaki is a Zuni interpretation of Jeddito Yellow Ware. Many of the characteristic element-filling techniques such as stippling are also present. Jeddito does have temporal priority and begins about AD 1325, but the asymmetrical Sikyatki style was not incorporated until the late 1300s —at the same time as Matsaki Buff Ware began to be made. Rather than one inspiring the other, it seems more likely that the style itself is related to close interaction and to a shared ideology. Temporary migrations back and forth are well known between the Hopi and Zuni areas in the historic period. Even closer to Zuni, Table Rock Pueblo has inordinately large amounts of Jeddito Yellow Ware relative to other sites in the same cluster, although it was apparently not made there (Duff 1999, 2002; Martin and Rinaldo 1960).

Kachina masks and shields are not common on Matsaki Buff Ware, but their presence is the first indication of the kachina cult in ceramic iconography on vessels from the Zuni area. Although it is possible that kachinas were present prior to this time and that there was a proscription against their depiction, rock art also suggests that kachinas were not common prior to the fifteenth century in the Zuni area (Schaafsma and Young, chap. 15, this vol.). The late timing is particularly interesting given the imagery on Four Mile Polychrome from the Mogollon Rim region for a few generations before. The imagery on Matsaki

Buff Ware replaces the depiction of parrots with kachinas and with war imagery, especially stars and eagles.

Finally, it has always been of great interest that a large number of cremation burials were present at Hawikuh and Kechipawan, most of which are associated with Matsaki Buff Ware. Approximately one third of the individuals buried at these two sites were cremated (Kintigh 2000:109). Although a large number of these were accompanied with Matsaki Buff Ware, other wares were used, including Salado polychromes (Roosevelt Red Ware), Unnamed White-on-red, and Unnamed Red-on-buff (Smith et al. 1966).

Cremation burials are not generally associated with the Zuni and Hopi areas. They are associated with sites below the Mogollon Rim, including Point of Pines pueblo (Robinson 1958) and Ormand Village (Crown 1994:fig. 6.1). Cremations are associated with the Hohokam area of southern Arizona, the Point of Pines region of southeastern Arizona, and Animas phase sites of southwestern New Mexico. This has raised speculation about migrations from these more distant areas. Because cremations were not uniformly practiced at Hawikuh or Kechipawan, what they seem to indicate is the greater diversity of populations that resided in these sites than in earlier sites in the area (Schachner 2006). This diversity was also reflected in the orientation of individuals in inhumations and in the various wares of ceramics that were associated with any burial (Kintigh 2000). Many of the cremation vessels from Hawikuh and Kechipawan were "killed." Crown (1994:fig. 6.2) illustrates the distribution of Salado polychrome (Roosevelt Red Ware) killed vessels. This distribution ranges from Hawikuh in the Zuni area to the Slaughter Ranch site in the southeastern corner of Arizona and from

shifts at Zuni of the late fourteenth and early fifteenth centuries, strongly suggest that it was produced when or soon after the migrations out of the upper Little Colorado, upper Salt, and upper Gila areas were occurring. As Schachner (2006) argues, the cessation of Zuni Glaze Ware production in favor of Matsaki Buff Ware production was a dramatic change in Zuni ceramics that likely marked the emergence of new identities in the early fifteenth century. Like the later shift to the matte-paint polychromes after the Pueblo Revolt (Mills 2002b), Matsaki Buff Ware appears to be an intentional marker of pan-Zuni identity that coincided with the consolidation of populations into fewer villages. In the case of Matsaki Buff Ware this consolidation took place at villages that remained occupied through the period of initial European contact.

Redware. Both an unidentified white-on-red (see fig. 13.8) and Roosevelt Red Ware occur in Zuni assemblages of the late AD 1300s. The former is not well studied. Several vessels like these were recovered from Table Rock Pueblo (Martin and Rinaldo 1960). Their continued production in the 1300s is suggested by later design styles that are more similar to Four Mile Polychrome but without black paint. White-on-red ceramics occur in the Zuni Middle Village ceramic assemblages dated to the late AD 1300s and early 1400s, possibly as heirloom items brought by migrants to Zuni Pueblo (Mills 2002a). As noted above, some of the Unnamed White-on-red whole vessels from Hawikuh and Kechipawan were recovered from cremation burials.

Roosevelt Red Ware is rare in Zuni assemblages until the late AD 1300s. At this time Gila and Tonto Polychromes occur, but they are never numerous. Samples from Hawikuh were included by Crown (1994) in her

Figure 13.7. Matsaki Polychrome bowl interior designs from Hawikuh (after Smith et al. 1966:fig. 56).

Los Muertos in the Phoenix Basin to Ormand Village on the upper Gila River drainage.

In addition to vessel killing, Smith et al. (1966:205) reports that some Matsaki Polychrome vessels from cremations show a pattern of four rim notches. This very specific practice of notching of cremation vessels has also been reported from AZ W:10:50 (ASM) in the Point of Pines area, one

of the sites that also shows vessel "killing" (Robinson 1958). The complex of cremations, vessel killing, and rim notching is so specific that a direct connection between the Point of Pines area and Zuni seems likely, even though Matsaki Polychrome itself was not produced in the Point of Pines area.

The above attributes of Matsaki Buff Ware, along with the settlement

Figure 13.8. Unnamed White-on-red from Kechipawan, Cambridge University #24.408A. Photograph by Keith Kintigh.

analysis of regional compositional variation. She found that they clustered with a northern group that also included sites in the upper Little Colorado proper. It seems most likely that the Salado polychromes were brought as heirloom vessels by migrants from the upper Little Colorado area when they moved to the Zuni area (Kintigh 2000). In fact, the highest proportions of Roosevelt Red Ware in the Zuni Middle Village Project assemblages are in levels that appear to date after AD 1400 (Mills 2002a), just after the migration from the upper Little Colorado (and perhaps other areas to the south) would have occurred. Like that of the white-on-red ceramics, a slightly later occurrence for the discard of these ceramics in the Zuni Pueblo assemblages than expected suggests that they may have had longer use lives as heirlooms. Also like the white-on-red ceramics, some of the Roosevelt Red Ware whole vessels in the Hawikuh and Kechipawan collections are killed.

Summary of the Post–AD 1300 Period. The distinctive abandonment of glaze-paint technology and the adoption of an entirely new slip background color are major technological transitions in the Zuni sequence. Schachner (2006) explicitly defines this transition as one of an emergent new identity associated with the consolidation of regional populations in the Zuni area. That this occurs at the time that large areas both above and below the Mogollon Rim were no longer occupied must be more than coincidental. The only two buffware traditions in the Southwest prior to this are the Hopi and Hohokam areas. Hopi is, of course, closer, and Jeddito Yellow Ware is well represented in the Table Rock assemblages in the upper Little Colorado. Design styles were also shared, which suggests additional similarities between Matsaki and Hopi vessels. However, red-on-buff pottery is also known for southwestern New Mexico, southeastern Arizona, and even northern Mexico.

The association of the buffware with kachina imagery and with buffware from Hopi also may be important in its widespread adoption. Although buff firing clays are not difficult to find in the Zuni area (they are, in fact, ubiquitous), buffware ceramics were not produced in the area prior to this time. Thus, what seems to be most important about Matsaki Buff Ware is that it was completely different from what was made before in the Zuni area. It was not the Early Zuni Glaze Ware made by the original residents, not the White Mountain Red Ware made by possible migrants from the Rim area, and not the Salado polychromes brought by still others from the upper Little Colorado. It was a break in the technological styles of just about everyone. Heirloom vessels of nonlocal white-on-red, Roosevelt Red Ware, and Early Zuni Glaze Ware continued to be used, but many of these ended up in burials and were apparently not replaced. After AD 1450 most decorated vessels were made in the new technological style.

Matsaki Buff Ware has strong iconographic content not seen in the Zuni area up until this time. Most important among these is the first depiction of kachina masks on ceramics that indicates the importance of ritual in the integration of disparate populations. What is also interesting is that parrots, which were common up to about AD 1450 on Early Zuni Glaze Ware, are not depicted at all on the Matsaki Buff Ware, suggesting a disruption of trade routes for macaws and other feathers and possibly a reorganization of rituals in which they were used. Instead, eagle feathers become redundant parts of the design, including a few that appear to be parts of shield designs. These designs strongly support the interpretation that conflict was an integral part of the fifteenth- and sixteenth-century Pueblo landscape, including the Zuni area.

Around AD 1630 another new ware was made at Zuni, Hawikuh Glaze Ware. This ware was a reintroduction of glaze paint on red-and-white-slipped vessels. Glaze-painted ceramics never ceased being produced in the Rio Grande valley or at Acoma Pueblo. Fray Letrado came from the Salinas district to establish the mission at Zuni in 1629, and he almost certainly brought a few people with him when he moved to Zuni. Within a few decades Hawikuh Glaze Ware almost completely replaced Matsaki Buff Ware. It was produced until the Pueblo Revolt, when another ceramic and social revolution took place. I have interpreted this as an intensive act of resistance, involving potters' intentional break with the past in reforming their identities after the Pueblo Revolt (Mills 2002b).

I bring up these last two examples to underscore the fact that ceramic change can occur quickly. Based on the historic example, these sudden breaks are not random but related to important social changes. Potters actively chose what they wanted to make, and they did so as part of the (re)construction of social identities. Widespread abandonment of old technological styles in favor of new ones was associated with dramatic social changes at Zuni—the introduction of missions in 1630 and the Pueblo Revolt in 1680. The equivalent social event for the adoption of Matsaki Buff Ware in the late 1300s is not as well known because it lies in the period without historic documents. However, it does appear to be correlated with migrations out of the upper Little Colorado and upper Gila areas and the consolidation of populations in the Zuni River valley, and it was almost certainly an intentional break with past technological traditions (Reed 1955; Schachner 2006).

Summary

The long sequence of ceramics at Zuni provides an excellent opportunity to look at the relationship between social identity and ceramics. Unfortunately, many of the kinds of information that are needed to look at identity in the archaeological record have not been widely studied at Zuni or in surrounding areas. This is now changing, and technological style, differences in cuisine, and the active uses of style are being investigated, but many more studies are needed to look at how these might indicate migration. Because of the questions posed in this volume, critical areas in the southern Colorado Plateau and the northern Mogollon area have not been looked at since the mid-twentieth century.

It is clear from my discussion that there was most definitely interaction between the Zuni and Mogollon areas. In some cases this interaction was identified through exchange, in others emulation, and more rarely in others through enculturative behavior (i.e., technological styles) that might indicate migration. There is much more evidence for the latter at the edges of the Zuni area, in the Quemado and lower Rio Puerco areas, than within Zuni itself. This may be a significant finding in and of itself. Zuni did have the same range of clay resources as these two areas, in fact, maybe more so in some parts, but we don't see the same kind of intergrade that we do, for example, in the gray-brown ceramics of the Rio Puerco or the local production of Mogollon Red-on-brown as we see in the Quemado area. This suggests that Zuni was more insulated from some of the population movement that characterized surrounding areas.

There are, however, several examples early in the sequence for technological styles that swept through Zuni from the Mogollon area. This includes the use of ceramics in the first place and the use of neck banding later on. These changes occurred across the Southwest, and there is no reason to favor migration of people over the kind of technological diffusion that results from small-scale movement of people and exchanges. Later, a similar technological style shift occurred with indented corrugated, which appears to have a more north–south pattern. The adoption of indented corrugated vessels has even been suggested to be associated with the adoption of hachure from the Chaco area and thus is closely related to emulation as a behavioral process.

By AD 1000 the influence of Mogollon on Zuni in ceramics is nearly imperceptible, and the opposite seems to be more the case. Cibola White Ware vessels were clearly not produced in the Mogollon area, and most if not all of the whiteware found immediately to the south of the Colorado Plateau in New Mexico was imported from the southern Colorado Plateau, including the Zuni area. This pattern of exchange is very similar to what is seen across the Mogollon Rim in east-central Arizona, with the very same geological constraints: iron-rich clays that are ill suited for making whiteware below the rim and rich beds of sedimentary kaolinitic clays on the plateau.

Because of the contrasts in clay resources we are able to see these interactions on a north–south basis very clearly. What we are not able to see compositionally, however, is the interaction on an east–west basis. Yet stylistic indicators indicate that there were horizontal zones of interaction starting in the AD 1000s, such as the gradation from Gallup to Puerco to Reserve styles on a north–south basis. At first these zones were related to Chaco, at least in the northern portion of the Zuni area. These zones of interaction become even more important in the AD 1200s with the widespread use of Tularosa style on vessels from the western edge of the Silver Creek area to Acoma. This style may have temporal precedence in the Zuni area. Not long afterward a diversity of styles from northeastern Arizona and the middle Little Colorado are added to the decorative repertoire of potters. These, too, occur in an east–west band but originated in the west and then were adopted from west to east. Many of these designs have their basis in textiles, and the association of cotton textiles, ceramics, and diversity in suprahousehold ritual sodalities is a strong one throughout the area.

While it is true that settlement patterns on the plateau had also contracted, there is nothing in the settlement pattern distribution that required style zones to be so extensive. Crown (1994) has discussed this widespread pattern with respect to the distribution of Pinedale style, but I think that Pinedale style is only one of a number of related styles that indicate increased interaction, including migration, during the late thirteenth and early fourteenth centuries. Unfortunately, stylistic interaction is a very amorphous concept, and the use of decorative style alone without other technological attributes is difficult to interpret.

What I think becomes most interesting after AD 1200 is the active use of style and its potential for looking at social identity. Although style is tricky in this regard, there are a number of arguments that have been brought to bear. The earliest polychromes have bold exterior designs, are correlated with periods of aggregation and ritual diversification, and at least in the northern Southwest show distinctively larger sizes than their contemporaneous bichromes. Wingate and St. Johns Polychrome of the Zuni area contrast with the contemporaneous production of white-on-red and white-painted corrugated wares to the west and south. The widespread use of white paint on the exterior of large brownware and redware smudged bowls made in the Mogollon area is clearly related to the use of white paint on White Mountain Red Ware. Because of their large sizes many of these vessels were probably used in ritual feasting at the suprahousehold level (Mills 2007), but this does not mean that all white-painted vessels indicate a shared social identity for their users. Rather, I think that these vessels indicate shared participation in ritual sodalities, the importance of which increased throughout the Southwest during this period.

The divergence in the White Mountain Red Ware into two series is also significant for understanding differences in identity during the Pueblo IV period. Different technological styles in glaze-paint recipes were used, different exterior designs were painted, and, especially after AD 1325, the iconographic content of interior designs was varied. This divergence

is correlated with the St. Johns Polychrome production boundary. Thus, despite the sharing of design elements and styles, I think there are enough indicators to suggest that archaeologists' identification of the two series of White Mountain Red Ware might actually have some association with shared social identities. This makes the sites in the upper Little Colorado area, where production areas of the two series converge, very interesting for looking at ceramics and identity, as Duff (1999, 2002) has recently argued. So, too, are sites in the Petrified Forest area, although these have not been extensively investigated with these questions in mind.

The strongest evidence for migration from the Mogollon area in the late prehistoric area is the large percentage of cremations at Hawikuh and Kechipawan. Every archaeologist who has addressed this interaction (whether he or she believed the Mogollon were a real group or not) has focused on this pattern (e.g., Kintigh 2000; Reed 1955; Rinaldo 1964). In addition, late-fourteenth-century and fifteenth-century white-on-red and Salado polychromes occur in Zuni assemblages from Hawikuh, Kechipawan, and Zuni Pueblo itself (Bushnell 1955; Mills 2002a; Woodbury and Woodbury 1966) that were probably brought by migrants from the upper Little Colorado and upper Gila areas. Interestingly, a diversity of wares is found in both cremations and inhumations, including Early Zuni Glazes, Unnamed White-on-red, and Salado polychrome vessels (Bushnell 1955; Smith et al. 1966:189–192).

Cremations and the diversity of imports are associated with a new technological style of ceramic production that was made at Zuni by the early AD 1400s (Schachner 2006; Woodbury and Woodbury 1966). The new ware, Matsaki Buff Ware, was made and used at all Zuni villages by

the mid–AD 1400s. Some of the Matsaki Polychrome vessels appearing in cremations were killed, with intentionally produced holes placed in the vessels, presumably at the time of the mortuary ritual. Vessel killing was widely practiced in the Mimbres area as well as in later ceramics from the Southwest. Killed and notched vessels are only known from one other area of the Southwest besides the Zuni area, that of Point of Pines (Robinson 1958). This suggests direct continuity of a very specific mortuary ritual.

The practice of cremation burial lasted as late as European contact. The continued use of this mortuary practice indicates that there were still multiple social identities being expressed by some members of the contact period Zuni villages (Kintigh 2000). Thus, the production of a single ceramic, Matsaki Buff Ware, was intentional to indicate shared Zuni identity at one level, but the differential treatment of these ceramics during mortuary ritual was an expression of varying premigration affiliations by village members.

Matsaki Polychrome overlapped with but was then quickly eclipsed by the production of a new ware called Hawikuh Polychrome around AD 1630. The reintroduction of a glaze-painted ware in the Zuni area corresponds with the period of missionization at Zuni. The rapid adoption of a ware associated with Spanish conquest is intriguing, particularly since religious repression was one of the restrictions brought by the Spaniards. Cremation burials also cease about this time (Smith et al. 1966:204).

The association of Hawikuh Polychrome with the Spaniards has been interpreted as the basis for its rejection after the Pueblo Revolt of 1680. When the Zuni consolidated into a single village in the 1690s, a matte-paint polychrome, Ashiwi

Polychrome, was made that is the technological antecedent of the well-known Zuni Polychrome of the nineteenth and twentieth centuries. This dramatic reversal in technological style is related to the reconstruction of Zuni identity in the historic period as settlement consolidated into a single village at Zuni Pueblo.

The Hawikuh to Ashiwi Polychrome transition illustrates how closely ceramics can track important social and demographic changes. These changes are only accessible through the archaeological record at Zuni for earlier time periods. Variation in technological styles and the active use of style are two ways that interpretations about changing identity can be made from the archaeological record. This variation is clearly related to important social changes in the Zuni area, especially those associated with migration, aggregation, and the incorporation of new social institutions. Many of these institutions exist at Zuni today. Although Zuni ceramics have been mostly replaced by other kinds of containers, they still form an important part of Zuni identity and village life. The revival of Zuni pottery making during the late twentieth century is an affirmation of the value placed on ceramics and how these containers provide continuity with the past.

Notes

1. Ceramic vessels are earliest in the southern Southwest, and these dates have now been pushed back to a few centuries BC, especially as a result of intensive investigations in the Tucson Basin (Heidke 1999; Mabry, personal communication 2004). These are primarily figurines and small cups, followed by the production of storage jars. Current dates for the earliest ceramic containers in the Mogollon and Zuni areas are later, in the AD 200–400 range (Haury 1985a; Varien 1990; see also Crown 2000; LeBlanc 1982a; Skibo and

Blinman 1999; Wilson and Blinman 1994 for summaries), but could be pushed back with more research.

2. These really are sketches. Any one of these could form the basis for a major study.

3. One exception is in the Zuni area, though very late in the eighteenth and nineteenth centuries.

4. One could argue that because Mimbres Black-on-white is essentially a brownware with a white slip, one would not expect to see Mimbres Black-on-white made on the Colorado Plateau. But even the distinctive designs are absent from whiteware ceramics produced on the plateau.

5. He also notes that there is little Pueblo I period occupation (AD 800s) in the Quemado area (Wasley 1959:172–173), a pattern that may be generally true for a broad area of the southern Colorado Plateau.

6. I use the most recent dates for these types from Toll and McKenna (1997), who group Kiatuthlanna into an "Early Red Mesa."

7. These types are primarily useful for chronological control, and thus it is important that the design styles be chronologically meaningful.

8. See Colton and Hargrave (1937), Wasley (1959), and Carlson (1970) for discussion of these styles.

9. One cannot ignore that Puerco Black-on-white has been widely defined. Nonetheless, I do not think that it is very easily confused with Gallup Black-on-white.

10. Carlson's (1970) definition of Wingate style may be too restrictive. Alternatively, a separate, earlier Reserve style could be defined that includes more balanced solid and hatched designs but with less massing of the design.

11. William Longacre (personal communication 2001) wonders if Carlson's grouping of Houck and Querino Polychromes into Wingate Polychrome conflated important temporal variability. Carlson apparently did this because of inconsistencies in the definitions of Houck and Querino and the fact that they were originally thought to be later than St. Johns. In Carlson's (1970) figure captions

and discussion he does differentiate early and late styles. Whole vessels from well-dated contexts are rare. Hough (1903) illustrates several from the Petrified Forest area, and some of these do have later interior design styles, more typical of St. Johns Polychrome. Similarly, the interior designs of those from Village of the Great Kivas (Roberts 1932) appear to be Tularosa style. I now think that at least some of these late Wingate Polychromes were made into the AD 1200s, contemporaneously with St. Johns Polychrome.

12. Using this definition prevents the overly broad definitions in use in the Hay Hollow Valley for many years (e.g., Martin et al. 1967).

13. For example, it does not show up on the list of codes in some of the Zuni Archaeology Program reports (e.g., Waterworth 1994), and Duff (2002) notes that Rinaldo did not report Pinedale Black-on-white from Table Rock, even though it is present.

14. On nonglaze Cibola White Ware, including the late type of Tularosa Black-on-white, oxidation would cause the largely iron-oxide paint to turn red. Thus, the shift from Tularosa Black-on-white to the white-slipped Early Zuni Glaze Wares was a shift from neutral to oxidizing atmospheres.

15. However, the stylistic similarities between Cebolleta Black-on-white from the Acoma area (Dittert 1959) and Classic Mimbres Black-on-white geometric style are striking. In addition, Socorro Black-on-white and Chupadero Black-on-white all share the interlocking solid and hatched designs first seen on Mimbres Black-on-white in the AD 1000s.

16. Martin and Rinaldo's (1950a) published definition of Reserve Black-on-white in their monograph on Reserve phase sites in the Pine Lawn Valley was accompanied by illustrations of whole vessels that were mostly obtained from Round Valley and St. Johns in eastern Arizona (see also Martin and Willis 1940). Only a few sherds of this type are illustrated from Wet Leggett Pueblo in the Pine Lawn Valley, and some of these are not even Reserve style.

17. In the Forestdale Valley there is a Cibola White Ware jar with two hum-

mingbirds drinking nectar out of flowers that are rendered in Mimbres-style painting (Haury 1985a:fig. 39a), but this style is anomalous for the rest of the assemblages in that area.

18. The one major difference that I see on the Site 616 vessels are fewer bird forms (the so-called Pinedale bird) and the lack of the "orange-peel" quartered layout more characteristic of Jeddito style. The elements and motifs are western (i.e., more Kayenta-like), but the all-important first brush strokes that define the decorative field are different.

19. When these do occur, they tend to appear in the Tonto Basin and, along with other types made on the Mogollon Rim, are probably evidence of migration and exchange.

20. Tree-ring dates at this site indicate that it is long occupied. There are cutting dates in the AD 1120s but repairs in the 1150s, 1180s, and 1260s (Bannister et al. 1970). Most of the ceramics are early Tularosa Black-on-white, with massed step frets.

21. A metric study of museum collections is much needed to compare White Mountain Red Ware bowl sizes through time, to compare the sizes of contemporaneous whiteware bowls, and to compare early and late Wingate Polychrome.

22. Reserve White-on-red appears to be the same as Tularosa White-on-red except that it lacks indented corrugated fillets just below the exterior rim. It is not necessarily coeval with the Reserve Phase.

23. An important exception is the most elaborate burial from Grasshopper, Burial 140, which had two of these bowls.

24. In our analyses we define semi-obliterated corrugated as coils that have been completely flattened, but one can still follow a coil juncture. Obliterated corrugated are coils that can still be discerned in part, but one cannot follow a continuous coil juncture. Blackware is completely smoothed over. Sometimes the surfaces show clear wiping, which produces a unique texturing almost like a stuccoed surface.

25. In addition, matte red paint was applied to the same white-slipped surfaces and called Pinnawa Red-on-white (Woodbury and Woodbury 1966).

26. Site 616 is the latest excavated site in the Quemado area, and the two rooms that are tree-ring dated both have cutting dates before AD 1300 (McGimsey 1980:Appendix B).

14 Mogollon Pottery Production and Exchange

C. Dean Wilson

Distributions of pottery forms and styles play a critical role in the identification and characterization of possible connections between the prehistoric Mogollon culture and the historic Pueblo of Zuni. Other chapters in this volume present insights and models from a range of southwestern ethnographic and archaeological studies to identify the kinds of pottery and other material culture distributions that may reflect connections between and movements of prehistoric groups and thus interaction and migration. Mills (chap. 13, this vol.), for example, utilizes pottery distributions to examine the movement of traits from the Mogollon Highlands into the Zuni area that may have resulted from migrations and explores the types of connections and relationships that may be indicated.

Such interpretations are part of a long continuum of archaeological studies that have utilized distributions of pottery traits from sites in different areas to define the boundaries of different cultural traditions. Similarities in such distributions and in other material culture classes have been assumed to reflect distinct technologies and decorative conventions associated with long-lived traditions of particular groups of people (Colton 1939; Gladwin and Gladwin 1934; Kidder 1924). For example, sites in

the Mogollon Highlands dominated by Mogollon Brown Ware types have been interpreted as representing a distinct "Mogollon" population. In contrast, assemblages from contemporaneous components in areas just to the north and dominated by Anasazi White and Anasazi Gray Ware types were thought to reflect the "Anasazi" cultural tradition. In addition, the occurrence of significant frequencies of pottery belonging to several different regional traditions has often been interpreted as reflecting the expansion, mixing, or mingling of culturally distinct populations (Danson 1957; Martin 1979; Martin and Rinaldo 1951).

Before the importance of ceramic technologies and distributions can be fully evaluated it is necessary to determine the range of phenomena that may have contributed to spatial and temporal variation in them. This chapter attempts to provide a context for studies concerned with the identification of cultural identity and migration episodes by focusing on other factors that may have influenced ceramic distributions. While patterns reflected in typologically based studies certainly provide a potentially useful tool with which to identify movement and interaction, these phenomena alone do not account for the full range of factors responsible for ceramic variation.

Culturally influenced choices resulting in a particular combination of material types, manufacturing technology, and decorative techniques used by potters in a particular location obviously reflect in part the technologies, styles, and associated meanings embodied in a particular tradition (Hegmon 1995). Still, other factors relating to available pottery resources, settlement patterns, and relationships between groups in different areas also have strong influences on the kinds and ranges of pottery made and utilized (Wilson et al. 1996). Thus, it is necessary to examine pottery from sites in various southwestern provinces in a way that allows us to monitor the effects of a variety of factors, including availability and characteristics of pottery material sources, exchange and interaction between separate groups, and the associated qualities and use of pottery in various activities.

In an attempt to address these issues recent investigations conducted by the Museum of New Mexico in west-central New Mexico have included collection and characterization of the range of clay and temper sources that would have been available to potters at particular locations (Wilson 1994); in all cases, the same analytical conventions and categories were used. These data are employed here to examine various trends in pottery-related production technology and interaction between groups for the long sequence of occupation in the northern Mogollon Highlands and southern Colorado Plateau. The focus is on assemblages dominated by combinations of traits that result in their common assignment to the northern Mogollon culture area, but data from other areas of the Mogollon, southern Anasazi, and Salado culture areas are also discussed as appropriate. Basic trends for periods (Anyon et al. 1981; LeBlanc 1982b; Lekson 1986) and phases (Berman 1979, 1989; Haury 1936b; Martin 1979; Martin and Plog 1973; Nesbitt 1938) are identified and discussed (see Diehl, chap. 11, this vol., table 11.2).

Pithouse Period Trends

An important issue relating to the distribution of ceramic technologies involves the early development and persistence of distinctive "Mogollon" brownware vessels in the Mogollon Highlands. A similar brownware technology appears to have dominated the earliest ceramic-bearing occupations throughout much of the northern Southwest, including not only the Mogollon Highlands but the Colorado Plateau and other regions as well (Stark 1995; Wilson et al. 1996). Thus, the earliest ceramic-bearing sites on the Colorado Plateau are dominated by plain brownware similar to that produced throughout the entire Mogollon sequence. By the seventh century, however, the earlier brownware technology had been replaced by a distinct "Anasazi" gray utility and whiteware decorated pottery that quickly spread over the entire Colorado Plateau (Reed et al. 2000). This shift from brown to gray and white ceramics occurred in the Zuni area as well as other areas of the

southern Colorado Plateau, where early brownware assemblages were replaced by those containing a mixture of Lino Gray and La Plata Black-on-white (Wilson and Blinman 1994).

Consequently, occupations dating after AD 600 in the Mogollon Highlands are dominated by "Mogollon" brownwares, while those on the Colorado Plateau are dominated by "Anasazi" gray and white ceramics, with areas in between displaying varying combinations of pottery representing these two traditions. Observations of these patterns formed the basis for establishment of divisions and boundaries between the brownware-producing "Mogollon" and grayware- and whiteware-producing "Anasazi" peoples. The shift from brownware to grayware on the Colorado Plateau has often been interpreted as reflecting a Mogollon cultural base from which a distinct Anasazi cultural tradition developed.

An alternative explanation is suggested by recent investigations indicating that geographic variation in ceramics may reflect the development of ceramic technologies most suitable to the very different clay and temper resources found in different geological settings (Reed et al. 2000; Wilson and Blinman 1994; Wilson et al. 1996). In some areas of the Colorado Plateau the shift to "Anasazi" grayware and whiteware technology grew out of a period of experimentation with the low-iron clays common in this geological province (Reed et al. 2000). Accompanying the shift to fine, low-iron, shale clays was the addition of a tempering material such as sand, crushed rock, or crushed sherds as well as the development of other conventions such as production of unpolished utility wares and painted whitewares.

By contrast, the distinct geology of the Mogollon Highlands contributed to a long and continuous production

of brownwares (Wilson 1994). Clays similar to those used to produce Anasazi gray and white ceramics were not available in most of the Mogollon Highlands, where the geological strata producing those clays used on the Colorado Plateau are largely covered by later volcanic formations. The only suitable clay sources in the Mogollon Highlands are alluvial or pedogenic clays weathered from the surrounding volcanic outcrops (Wilson 1994). The persistence of Mogollon Brown Ware reflects continued use of a pottery technology suitable to the very plastic, self-tempered, high-iron, homogeneous colluvial and alluvial clays that were earlier utilized over the entire Southwest. Other traits of Mogollon pottery—polished surfaces, intentionally smudged interiors, a rarity of painted decorations, and the fine and elaborate texturing in later forms—all appear to reflect development of technologies and conventions best suited to such clays. Similarities in the dominant brownware associated with almost all Mogollon occupation periods indicate an extremely conservative ceramic technology, one that effectively tailored ceramic production to locally available resources.

There is very little evidence of nonlocal pottery at sites dating to the Early Pithouse period and prior to introduction of decorated pottery during the seventh century, although this may simply reflect difficulties in identifying nonlocal brownwares. The earliest evidence of nonlocal ceramics comes in the form of the first painted pottery in the region, occurring at components dating to the transition between the Early and Late Pithouse periods. The majority of decorated wares at Pithouse period sites in the northern Mogollon Highlands (Reserve area) are represented by types belonging to either the Mogollon Decorated or the Mimbres White Ware tradition, including Mogollon Red-on-brown, Three Circle Red-on-brown, and Mimbres Boldface Black-on-white (Martin 1979; Nesbitt 1938; Wilson 1999b). Assemblages dating to the early part of the Late Pithouse period contain very low frequencies of other nonlocal types as well, including Cibola Gray and Cibola White Ware types from the Colorado Plateau.

The great majority of decorated sherds from Late Pithouse period components in the Reserve area of the northern Mogollon Highlands represent Mimbres White Ware types. It is difficult to determine whether Mimbres White Ware pottery was locally produced, but information concerning paste and slip characteristics provides some important clues. Collections of potential sources of white slip clay from weathered tuff deposits in the Reserve area indicate that local sources contained mica inclusions and fired to a yellowish to buff color (Wilson 1999b). Slips from Three Circle Red-on-white (the earliest Mimbres White Ware type) closely match local slips, while those occurring on Mimbres Boldface Black-on-white and later Classic Mimbres Black-on-white are clearly different in color, texture, and inclusions. Given these differences and strong similarities with Mimbres White Ware types from sites in the Mimbres regions, it is likely that Three-Circle Red-on-white was produced locally in the Reserve area, while later Mimbres White Ware types were not.

While examination of Mimbres White Ware pastes from tenth-century components in the Reserve area show that they contain volcanic rock inclusions similar to those present in brownware types, sherds containing distinctive amounts of larger tuff particles are more common in the Mimbres White Ware sherds and are most similar to inclusions common in the same whiteware types from the Mimbres region. Further evidence of nonlocal production of Mimbres White Ware types is indicated by petrographic analyses, indicating that the inclusions occurring in Mimbres Boldface Black-on-white and Classic Mimbres Black-on-white from the Luna Project area are distinct from those noted in brownware pastes recovered from the same site. Once again, inclusions in Mimbres White Ware sherds appear to be very similar to those noted in samples from the Mimbres region to the south.

These findings indicate that the dominance of nonlocal Mimbres Black-on-white types at tenth-century sites in the Reserve area may reflect the increasing importance of ceramic exchange during the Late Pithouse period. Evidence of the shift to nonlocal Mimbres White Ware pottery may be further indicated by a drop in the frequency of Mimbres White Ware pottery from the San Francisco phase (about 12 percent of the total sherds) to the Three Circle phase (about 6 percent). These trends contrast dramatically with those noted for most surrounding regions, where the total proportion of whiteware sherds increases consistently through time. These trends suggest that Mogollon Black-on-white pottery was produced in the northern Mogollon Highlands for only a very short time and that production was probably limited to Three Circle Red-on-white.

In the tenth century another important shift in ceramic exchange took place in the northernmost parts of the Mogollon Highlands. In the Gallo Mountains north of the Reserve area utility ware assemblages are still dominated by brownware types identical to those from other contemporaneous sites in the Mogollon Highlands, but the dominant decorated pottery is Cibola White Ware, including such types as Red Mesa Black-on-white (Kayser 1972a, 1972b, 1972c, 1975; Kayser and Carroll 1988; Smith 1973). In areas of the Colorado Plateau just north of the Mogollon Highlands (e.g., Mariana Mesa) Red Mesa Black-on-white with identical pastes and styles occurs in assemblages dominated by early plain and neckbanded Cibola Gray Ware types with buff pastes similar to those of the associated Cibola White Ware (McGimsey 1980).

A gradual southward movement of Cibola White Ware types during the tenth century seems to have made the Reserve area the northernmost area where decorated Mimbres White Ware types were dominant. Both architecture and ceramic patterns found in San Francisco and Three Circle phase components in this area appear very similar to those noted at sites in the Mimbres region to the south.

The sequence of changes in Pithouse period pottery assemblages from the Mogollon Highlands may reflect increasing exploitation of the Mogollon Highlands by growing populations. Thus, during the Late Pithouse period interaction between separated communities mainly involved groups in similar environmental settings tied together by economic systems and material culture. Still, differences in elevation within the Mogollon Highlands would have produced some environmental variation that may have been exploited through exchange and interaction between separated groups. Distributions of such boundaries may have been influenced by a combination of population size, environmental conditions, and the nature of subsistence patterns in areas of the Mogollon Highlands. The movement of information and goods reflected in pottery assemblages was mainly between groups residing in similar settings, resulting in unique ceramic distributions roughly corresponding to geographic boundaries within the Mogollon Highlands. The specialized production of well-made early Mimbres Black-on-white pottery types may have facilitated exchange between separated groups residing in pithouse villages.

Pueblo Period Trends

The period beginning during the early eleventh century is characterized by increased differentiation in pottery traits between sites in the northern Mogollon Highlands and the Mimbres area to the south. This shift occurred sometime during the transition between the Late Pithouse period and the early part of the Pueblo period. The great majority of the brownware pottery from Early Pueblo period assemblages is characterized by plain and neckbanded forms similar to those noted in earlier assemblages, although some fully corrugated forms appear at the beginning of the Pueblo period. In the northern Mogollon Highlands locally produced painted pottery was limited to very low frequencies of painted brownwares such as Starkweather Smudged and Tularosa White-on-red (Rinaldo and Bluhm 1956), and Mogollon Brown Ware pottery dominated assemblages in this area throughout the Mogollon occupation of this area. Grayware types are almost completely absent at Pueblo period sites and do not appear ever to have been commonly exchanged into the area.

The most notable change at the beginning of the Pueblo period is the emergence of Cibola White Ware types (Reserve and, later, Tularosa Black-on-white) as the dominant whiteware. The total frequency of whitewares remains very low, about 3–7 percent for Reserve phase sites and 5–7 percent for Tularosa phase

sites. White Mountain Red Wares are also represented in very low frequencies and are most common during the Late Tularosa period. Most of the Cibola White Ware types from Pueblo period components are tempered with sand and crushed sherds, and petrographic analyses indicate considerable variability in paste composition. This may in turn indicate that the Cibola White Wares recovered in this area were produced over an extremely wide area of the Colorado Plateau and may further reflect the long duration of similar ties or networks responsible for the movement of Cibola White Ware pottery into the Mogollon Highlands.

A similar combination of pottery dominated by "Mogollon" brown with lesser frequencies of "Anasazi" whitewares occurs at Pueblo period sites distributed in an east–west band along the edges of the Mogollon Highlands, crossing through much of central New Mexico and the eastern half of central Arizona. Along most of this zone frequencies of Mogollon Brown Ware and Cibola White Ware types are gradational, with frequencies of Cibola White Ware and grayware types increasing as one moves north toward the Colorado Plateau (Wilson 1999b). This results in a series of zones containing different combinations of pottery belonging to various traditions. This variation has sometimes been characterized as reflecting distinct cultural traditions that are neither Anasazi nor Mogollon (Dittert 1959; Ruppé 1966).

Production of Mimbres White Ware types continued in the Mimbres region, but these types are extremely rare to absent at Pueblo period sites in areas of the northern Mogollon Highlands. Mimbres types such as Classic Mimbres Black-on-white continued to dominate assemblages dating to the eleventh and twelfth centuries at sites throughout the Mimbres region

and in areas of the Gila drainage as far north as the town of Glenwood (Peckham 1957). During this time intrusive Mimbres White Wares became more common in the Jornada Mogollon region to the east, possibly reflecting shifts in regional exchange systems.

While the basic distribution of pottery belonging to various traditions was similar during most of the Pueblo period, trends noted at Late Tularosa phase components (late thirteenth and early fourteenth centuries) indicate some important changes. In the Reserve area an increase in the frequency of Cibola White Wares occurred, and there is also evidence of specialized production of elaborately textured and highly smudged brownware during this time (Wilson 1999b).

This interval is also characterized by a significant increase in brownwares in areas of the southern Colorado Plateau. On Mariana Mesa Mogollon Brown Wares become the dominant utility ware for the first time (McGimsey 1980). Another important change is the increase in White Mountain Red Ware types such as St. Johns Polychrome. Such trends are particularly striking in the Mariana Mesa area and the Acoma district, where in some areas White Mountain Red Wares may be the dominant decorated pottery type. The dramatic increase in White Mountain Red Ware pottery appears to reflect important ties with groups to the west. Another trend at sites dating to the Late Tularosa phase is the appearance of glaze-painted types. These are similar to the earliest glazeware types to the west and reflect both eastern migrations into the middle Rio Grande as well as the increased importance in east–west exchange and interaction. Thus, systems that connected the distinct Pueblo of Zuni with groups to the east may have had their origin in earlier systems that linked "Mogollon" and "Cibolan Anasazi" groups together. Evidence of such a shift is seen in the presence of intrusive pottery types at sites in areas of the middle Rio Grande from the Rio Puerco of the East to the Galisteo Basin dating to the late thirteenth and early fourteenth centuries, during which glazewares were introduced and began to dominate decorated ware. Intrusive pottery from areas to the west that appear to have been traded into and influenced ceramic technologies in the middle Rio Grande include Heshotauthla Polychrome, White Mountain Red Wares, Tularosa Black-on-white, and Tularosa Smudged.

The trends discussed above, particularly those relating to the appearance of corrugated decorations in utility wares and the dominance of Cibola White Ware in decorated assemblages, have been previously interpreted as reflecting the movement or intrusion of "Anasazi" groups from the Colorado Plateau into the northern Mogollon Highlands (Danson 1957; Gladwin 1957; Martin 1979). Such an intrusion is sometimes seen as resulting from the mixture and intermingling of peoples, producing a culture that was more Anasazi in character and effectively ending the Mogollon occupation of the northern Mogollon Highlands.

An alternative interpretation emerging from recent studies is one of continuity of occupation of areas such as the northern Mogollon Highlands by the same people but with a gradual shift in the nature of regional exchange ties. Pueblo period shifts in panregional exchange and interaction between groups in the northern Mogollon Highlands and on the southern Colorado Plateau may have been a response to potential weaknesses of earlier networks that were largely confined to areas in the Mogollon Highlands. During times of stress

groups that were spread over wide areas of the Mogollon Highlands may have experienced shortages at the same time, limiting the potential for redistribution of food surpluses between separated groups. Thus, dealing with increased population and environmental uncertainty during the early AD 1000s may have required increasing ties between groups residing in both the Mogollon Highlands and the Colorado Plateau (Tainter 1982; Tainter and Gillio 1980). In areas of the San Juan Basin to the north a response to such conditions is represented by the development of the complex Chacoan network, including a series of outliers established in surrounding regions that may have constituted a panregional redistribution network (Judge 1979; Mathien 1993a; Toll 1985).

One option available to groups residing in smaller and more dispersed settlements along the transition area between the different geographic provinces in west-central New Mexico may have been the establishment of reciprocal ties that facilitated the movement of information and goods between groups in distinct environmental settings (Tainter 1982; Tainter and Gillio 1980). In areas of west-central New Mexico east–west ties between groups in adjacent areas of the Mogollon Highlands and Colorado Plateau may have been particularly suitable for this strategy. North–south ties between adjacent groups in the Mogollon Highlands and on the Colorado Plateau would have also reinforced relations between groups in different environmental zones that may have experienced food shortages and surpluses at different times (Tainter 1982; Tainter and Gillio 1980).

While ties between environmentally distinct areas would have been beneficial during times of shortage in one area, these relationships would

not have been necessary during optimal periods. However, a mechanism for the maintenance of exchange ties between small, undifferentiated, and separated groups during good years also would have been critical and may have been accomplished through the movement of certain desired goods between separated areas. While such exchange ties would have functioned in the movement of foodstuffs critical to the survival of groups during times of shortage, during other years exchange ties may have been maintained to provide access to desired items. The acquisition of such items could have been driven by the relative status of certain nonlocal pottery forms. Thus, the desirability of certain pottery forms, which were produced only in geological provinces where suitable resources were available, may have influenced the development of regional networks over a very wide area.

The production of increasingly elaborate and specialized whiteware pottery in areas of the southern Colorado Plateau and of elaborately decorated and smudged brownware pottery in the northern Mogollon Highlands from about AD 1000 to 1300 may have facilitated the development and maintenance of such networks. Painted whiteware types produced on the Colorado Plateau, for example, may have been in demand among groups in the Mogollon Highlands—groups who lacked clay resources that would allow them to produce their own whiteware vessels. Similarly, elaborately textured and highly smudged utility ware produced in the Mogollon Highlands may have been sought after by groups on the Colorado Plateau. These factors may have influenced the production of functionally superior or elaborately decorated ceramics in different clay resource zones for purposes of exchange. Such exchange would have reinforced potentially beneficial ties between separated groups.

While the widespread exchange of distinctive pottery between groups in the northern Mogollon Highlands and on the southern Colorado Plateau may have ultimately arisen because of aesthetic choices and social interaction rather than the movement of food during times of shortage, the survival or even expansion of such networks may have been influenced by such economic factors. In most societies there is much more to exchange than economic advantage, and associated ties and action involve the common transfer of items that have symbolic and categorical associations (Hodder 1982b). The exchange of appropriate forms of social obligations, status, and power ultimately legitimizes various exchange networks and schedules (Hodder 1982b). Thus, while the development of specialized production and exchange of pottery between groups in separate environmental zones may reflect historic factors (such as the development of specialized technologies relating to social and ideological factors), in times of shortage these relationships may have been critical to the survival of particular groups. Whatever the ultimate cause of conventions and preferences facilitating the production and exchange of various pottery forms, having ties with exchange partners in different environments would have presented an advantage during times of shortage and may have resulted in the persistence and expansion of such networks. These networks and more complex networks to the north would have interacted and ultimately resulted in the extensive panregional patterns and connections noted in the archaeological record.

These factors may have contributed to the gradual expansion of trade of pottery between groups in the northern Mogollon Highlands. Such an expansion is reflected by the appearance of Cibola White Wares as the dominant decorated type at tenth-century components in the Gallo Mountains and at eleventh-century sites in the Reserve area. In areas along the southern Colorado Plateau where Cibola White Ware types occur alongside local grayware pottery produced with the same clays there appears to have been a gradual increase in the frequency of Mogollon Brown Ware types from about AD 1000 to 1100 (Danson 1957; Dittert 1959; Kayser and Carroll 1988; Marshall 1991). Thereafter, during most of the Pueblo period there is a gradual decline in the frequency of brownwares moving north from sites in areas of the southern Colorado Plateau.

Salado Period Trends as Viewed from the Ormand Site

An interesting contrast with previously described ceramic trends is associated with occupations characterized by the presence of Salado polychromes. Components with Salado polychrome types are scattered along the northern and southern margins of the Mogollon area and date after the abandonment of much of the Mogollon Highlands and other areas of the Southwest during the late thirteenth and early fourteenth centuries (see Wilcox et al., chap. 12, this vol.). The current discussion is based on analyses of pottery from the Ormand site, located on the Gila River near Cliff, New Mexico (Wilson 1998a, 1998b). The ceramic assemblage from this site appears to be fairly typical of Cliff phase sites in the immediate area and shows some similarities to post–AD 1300 sites elsewhere in the Mogollon area.

Utility wares from the site exhibit characteristics similar to earlier Mogollon Brown Ware forms and are identical to Cliff Utility Ware types (Nelson and LeBlanc 1986). Three distinctive decorated ware groups are present in significant proportions, including Salado polychromes, Tucson/Maverick Mountain Polychrome, and Gila White-on-red. This combination of pottery is most similar to traditions thought to have first appeared in the Point of Pines region to the west (Lindsay 1987; Zedeño 1994) as well as those in other areas, including the Safford Valley and San Pedro Valley (Franklin and Masse 1976; Lindsay 1987). Fourteenth-century occupations in the Cliff area appear to be part of a series of developments and movements that began in west-central New Mexico and southwestern Arizona.

Evidence for production of these ceramic types recovered from the site indicates that the nature and extent of production and exchange of them was very different from that described for earlier assemblages in the Mogollon Highlands. Comparison of the Ormand material with local clay sources and petrographic analyses indicate that the Cliff utility and redwares, Gila White-on-red Ware, Salado polychromes, and Tucson/Maverick Mountain Polychrome were produced using the same locally available self-tempered clays (Hill 1998). This combination of characteristics supports the hypothesis that the settlement was occupied by immigrant populations who moved into the upper Gila area from areas to the west and who continued to utilize pottery technologies developed elsewhere. Rather than establishing ties with groups in other areas to obtain vessels of various forms and uses, the potters at Ormand employed local clay sources to produce a wide range of pottery types and forms. The very wide and distinctive range of technological and stylistic practices used by the immigrants was readily applied in the Cliff area and elsewhere along the upper Gila, since these practices had developed in areas with a similar geology.

Local production of Cliff Utility, Salado polychromes, Tucson / Maverick Mountain Polychrome, and Cliff White-on-red is surprising, particularly since there is very little overlap in the decorative design motifs and styles represented. The rules utilized to decorate the various types at Ormand were almost identical to those used to produce the same types over an extremely wide area. For example, Gila Polychrome from the site exhibits a range of slipped treatments and painted decorations similar to Gila Polychrome pottery from contemporaneous sites elsewhere where the type was also locally manufactured (Crown 1994). Local production of Salado polychromes and Tucson / Maverick Mountain Polychrome in other areas has been interpreted as representing coresidence of different social groups who participated in different ceramic traditions (Franklin and Masse 1976; Lindsay 1987). Gila White-on-red seems to have developed out of Tularosa White-on-red, and its presence at Ormand may reflect the presence of social groups who were practitioners of the Mogollon Brown Ware technology characteristic of the Tularosa phase.

The only nonlocal pottery types recovered from Ormand were one Chupadero Black-on-white sherd, one Ramos Polychrome sherd, and a small number of El Paso Polychrome sherds. This contrasts with contemporaneous occupations along the Mimbres River, which contain higher frequencies of Chupadero Black-on-white and El Paso Polychrome from the Jornada region to the east and southeast, and with contemporaneous occupations in the Bootheel area, which contain higher frequencies of Casas Grandes pottery (Nelson and LeBlanc 1986). Thus, the occupation

at the Ormand site and other Cliff phase sites in the area may represent a wave of self-sufficient immigrants from the west. The fact that almost all the pottery was produced locally argues for the self-sufficiency of these immigrant groups, and the range of ceramic traditions represented suggests the continuance of a fairly diverse (multiethnic?) and complicated social structure. Such a structure may have allowed such groups to move into areas already occupied and merge with existing groups, including the Zuni. Similar sites in western New Mexico have been subsumed under an eastern Salado label (Lekson 1992).

Summary

The discussion presented above has focused on examination of various phenomena that may have influenced regional pottery trends at prehistoric sites in west-central New Mexico. Observations of both continuity and shifts in pottery distributions have long been described in terms of pottery types assigned to specific traditions and interpreted as reflecting boundaries and movements of specific cultural groups. The studies discussed here indicate that ceramic trends were influenced by a complex combination of factors that includes kinds and qualities of locally available resources, social and economic factors that influenced the desirability of and demand for certain pottery forms, and the nature of interaction and existing ties between groups in different areas.

Examination of ceramic data from sites in west-central New Mexico indicates that the natural resources available in different geological zones dramatically influenced the characteristics of pottery in different areas of west-central New Mexico. The production of Mogollon Brown Ware ves-

sels in areas of the Mogollon Highlands and Anasazi Gray Wares on the Colorado Plateau appears to be directly related to the characteristics and qualities of clays in these different geological provinces. The persistence of these two general ceramic categories in two separate areas may be more a reflection of the development of distinctive technologies best suited to local materials rather than simply distinct traditions or groups of people. The long-term dominance of similar plain brownwares and only gradual changes in textured wares in the Mogollon Highlands reflect a remarkably conservative technology that could reflect the persistence of occupation by a single people.

Other factors reflected in the various ceramic trends identified here are regional shifts in the degree, nature, and direction of exchange ties between groups in different regions. Differences in combinations of pottery traditions noted at components dating to different periods have often been interpreted as reflecting cultural intrusions or mingling of different groups; in fact, such patterns may reflect shifts in regional social and economic networks that developed in response to population pressure and environmental variability over time.

The initial appearance of pottery in the Mogollon Highlands represents the development of a technology well suited to local volcanic clays, a technology that continued to flourish in subsequent periods. Exchange became more common during the Late Pithouse period, and the most common intrusive ceramics are Mimbres White Ware types. This reflects the participation of the northern Mogollon Highlands in a network that linked together much of the Mogollon Highlands and the Mimbres area. The Pueblo period witnessed a dramatic shift in ties linking groups in the northern Mogollon Highlands and the southern Colorado Plateau. In the northern Mogollon Highlands such ties are represented by the presence of Cibola White Wares produced in areas of the Colorado Plateau as the dominant decorated type. Similar ties are reflected by the presence of variable frequencies of Mogollon Brown Wares at sites on the Colorado Plateau. These trends reflect an extremely widespread network that may have developed in response to population growth and environmental uncertainty.

Pottery associated with later reoccupations dominated by Salado polychromes and associated types appears to reflect a wave of migration by groups from other regions. While pottery styles and forms from the Ormand site are similar to those that seem to have developed in the Point of Pines area to the west, pottery belonging to all wares appears to have been manufactured locally. The dominance of new forms that developed elsewhere and the rarity of nonlocal pottery appear to reflect self-sufficient immigrant groups from the west.

15 Rock Art of the Zuni Region

Cultural-Historical Implications

Polly Schaafsma and M. Jane Young

The very term "Zuni origins" raises many questions. To what does the word "Zuni" refer—a cluster of Zuni-speaking historic pueblos, a Pueblo regional culture, the region defined by that culture, or a language merely? How old or recent are things "Zuni"?

Above all, the Zuni Pueblo region is/was linguistically not only distinct but unrelated to other Pueblos (see Hill, chap. 3, this vol.). This has given rise to questions regarding Mogollon-Zuni relationships (see Rinaldo 1964) and the prehistoric ethnicity of the Zuni villages. Or is "Zuni" also understood as a geographic region, centered on Zuni-speaking Pueblo villages, that experienced cultural flux through time as it was influenced differentially by surrounding cultural configurations?

Rock art is one of several archaeological data sets that can be brought to bear on these questions. Rock art is particularly sensitive to details of cultural values, metaphors, and cosmologies. This imagery on stone is the material correlate of ideologies that characterized the Zuni region during various periods of prehistory. These images, in turn, are useful in measuring the extent of networks of communication and information flow beyond Zuni.

While we do not propose to pinpoint "Zuni origins" as such through

rock art, we can suggest how the ancestral Pueblo people of the Zuni region related or did not relate to their neighbors on the ideational level. This chapter examines rock art at Zuni and in the surrounding regions to see how this data set, viewed from a macroregional perspective, may contribute to an understanding of the ideational history of Zuni itself. One of our goals is to determine if there are rock art styles that correlate with an ecological adaptation to the upland forest and grasslands characteristic of the Mogollon and Zuni regions in contrast with other ecological zones. This study addresses continuities and discontinuities between Zuni rock art and that of neighboring regions as a means of determining the geographic extent of the communication of ideas within specific time frames. Discontinuities of style and content indicate communication boundaries. Cultural stability is suggested by the persistence of rock art traditions through time in a given region. Wherever possible, patterns discernible in the rock art will be compared with those available from other kinds of data.

The rock art in the immediate region of the late prehistoric Zuni villages serves as a base reference against which rock art in surrounding regions can be compared. Significant neighboring regions include the middle Lit-

tle Colorado drainage—otherwise known as the Palavayu (McCreery and Malotki 1994:fig. 1.2); the San Juan drainage of the Mesa Verde, Chaco, and Kayenta Anasazi; to the south, Quemado and nearby regions north of the Mogollon Rim; as well as rock art in the high forested mesas and savannahs of the Mogollon Highlands.[1] The Rio Grande region to the east becomes important to this study after AD 1300.

In regard to the ability to determine prehistoric patterns of linguistic affiliations via archaeological data there are numerous cautionary notes. According to Foster, "whether a single artifact category can be meaningfully correlated with language is, to say the least, untested" (1996:95). It is certainly true, for example, that Pueblo pottery types have not adhered to linguistic lines. The Rio Grande valley between ca. AD 1360 and 1475 provides an excellent illustration of such incongruity: while Northern Tewas produced biscuitwares, the Southern Tewas, Keres, Southern Tiwa, and Piro made glazes. More to the point here, of course, is the example of rock art. In regard to style and content, rock art in the Rio Grande valley cross-cuts the lines of linguistic diversity that exist among the modern Pueblos and their immediate ancestors (Schaafsma 2005). Pueblo IV rock art tells us that while certain

Table 15.1 Late Archaic / Early Basketmaker Rock Art, ca. 1000 BC–AD 400 (see figs. 15.1 and 15.4)

Region	Characteristics and Elements
Zuni / Quemado	Figurative–two sites only: Rectangular faces pecked in outline. Small circles for eyes. Mouth occasional. Vertical, usually zigzag lines may fall from eyes. May be associated with sets of vertical lines or rakes. Mask / faces occur in groups.
	Abstracts–Hantlipinkia: long vertical abstracts–herringbone motifs, linked circles, diamond chains, zigzags. Tiny zigzags, wavy lines.
Middle Little Colorado (Palavayu)	Complex shaman figures–large anthropomorphic tradition: Palavayu Linear (PL) and Majestic Basketmaker (MBM) styles (McCreery and Malotki 1994:fig. 2.3). PL figures may have rakelike bodies, faces, two-pronged headgear. MBM figures are broad-shouldered, have horned headgear, hold snakes. Continuity between these styles is indicated.
	Rakes, diamond chains, zigzags, wavy lines, herringbone, dot rows, and others (McCreery and Malotki 1994:fig. 2.12).
Lower San Juan (Western Basketmaker)	Complex shaman figures–Glen Canyon Linear (GCL) and San Juan Basketmaker (SJBM) styles and associated figures (Schaafsma 1980:72–76, 109–119). GCL figures have faces, two-pronged headgear, fending sticks. SJBM figures have rectangular or trapezoidal bodied, broad-shouldered body shape. Tall headdresses, necklaces, sashes. Lobed circles, snakes, lines of dots, atlatls and spears, bags, flayed heads, yucca plants, painted handprints in association.
Upper San Juan (Eastern Basketmaker)	Broad-shouldered shamanic figures rare. Small, plain. Decline in numbers west–east. One reclining figure in Chaco with crescent headdress characteristic of Western Basketmaker region.
Rio Grande	Abstract elements: circles, rakes. Poorly known.

stylistic nuances may conform to areas occupied by discrete linguistic groups, these variations are minimal within the larger picture. While the several Tanoan linguistic groups and the Keres differ to some degree in regard to their mythologies and ritual emphases, overall they share(d) a symbol system and fundamental religious ideology. In other words, as we approach this study we should be aware that patterns of stylistic configurations and content in rock art probably do not accurately reflect linguistic distributions.

The Rock Art

A Zuni rock art database and comparative materials are available from various sources. The Zuni Rock Art Survey (ZRAS) records (Young 1979–1981), while not fully comprehensive, provide an ample representation of the rock art in the Zuni region, and these have been examined in detail. Comparative data from neighboring regional surveys—the New Mexico Rock Art Survey (Schaafsma 1971) and records of the Archaeological Society of New Mexico Rock Art Field School for Chaco and the Reserve / Tularosa regions—were also reviewed. For all other regions published sources were consulted. Substantial data are available for all areas discussed with the exception of Quemado and, especially, Acoma, where fewer sites have been recorded (Frisbie 1986; Schaafsma 1971, 1975). Overall, however, hundreds of sites were available for study. It is impor-

tant to emphasize, nevertheless, that additional data could modify the observations offered here.

The chronological framework into which the rock art is cast is purposefully ambiguous. Dating rock art styles with close accuracy, although sometimes quite possible, is more often difficult. This is especially true when dealing with long-standing traditions involving stylistic continuities and similar subject matter within which changes are gradual, as with Anasazi rock art dating between ca. AD 900 and 1300.

Late Archaic / Basketmaker II (ca. 1000 BC–AD 400)

The near lack of rock art in the Zuni region dating to the Late Archaic / Early Basketmaker time frame is noteworthy, especially since to the immediate west in the middle Little Colorado and north on the San Juan the rock art of this period is both prolific and distinctive. While Archaic and Early Basketmaker remains, although present in the general area of Zuni, have been thought to be limited (Ruppé and Drollinger 1990; Stuart and Gauthier 1981:128), Jonathan Damp's recent findings (chap. 8, this vol.) indicate a widespread Late Archaic / Early Basketmaker population in the Zuni region. There is, nevertheless, a decided paucity of rock art that can be attributed to this stage. The oldest rock art recorded near Zuni is at Hantlipinkia in Hardscrabble Wash, Arizona, about 50 km southwest of Zuni Pueblo (see fig. 15.1). Among the many designs carved above the *tinajas* (natural stone catchment basins) at the head of a small canyon, the earliest images are 13 rectangular faces pecked in outline (see table 15.1; Schaafsma and Young 1983:22–29; Young 1988:66, fig. 25). Similar figures have been recorded near Que-

a   b

c

Figure 15.1. Petroglyphs at Hantlipinkia (ZRAS 17) in Hardscrabble Wash, Arizona, southwest of Zuni Pueblo: (a) petroglyphs above a rock basin picturing a rectangular masklike element with small circular "eyes," a plant motif (left), and wavy lines; (b) various vertical line motifs; (c) panel displaying a variety of vertical linear patterns. Included here are a "rake," a set of wavy lines, lines topped with small circles, and a masklike element. The petroglyphs are believed to be Late Archaic or Basketmaker in origin, and their meaning may have been associated with rain and water, since water collects and is held in the basins at this locality following rains. Photographs by P. Schaafsma.

mado, New Mexico (Schaafsma 1975:fig. 23). In both cases these are the oldest figures at the site, heavily patinated, and superimposed by other petroglyphs. The distinctiveness of these images suggests cultural ties between Zuni and Quemado at an early date.

What "early" signifies in this context is probably Late Archaic. The presence of the masks/faces along with long abstract patterns, the latter also considered to be among the oldest rock art at Hantlipinkia (see table 15.1), is consistent with the dramatic increase of Late Archaic rock

art sites located still farther west in the lower elevations of the middle Little Colorado (McCreery and Malotki 1994). Although these few elements at Hantlipinkia offer possible exceptions to the rather definite cultural boundary hypothesized for this early period (see fig. 15.2), they do not blur the regional cultural distinctions suggested by the figurative rock art.

The faces from Hantlipinkia and Quemado may be tentatively compared with faces of anthropomorphs pictured in the Archaic Linear rock art tradition found elsewhere in the Colorado River drainage. Parallel horizontal lines below the eyes (Schaafsma and Young 1983:fig. 9, left) are found both in the Palavayu art (McCreery and Malotki 1994:vi) and on the faces of Archaic anthropomorphs of the similar Glen Canyon Linear style from the lower San Juan River in southeastern Utah (Pachak 1994:figs. 1, 2, 7). Sets of vertical parallel lines, suggestive of wing feathers and/or rain, are associated with these "faces" in the Zuni/Quemado art and in the Palavayu (compare Schaafsma and Young 1983:figs. 9 and 10 with McCreery and Malotki 1994:fig. 2.3). A peripheral relationship between Hardscrabble Wash and Quemado and a wider domain within the Colorado River drainage might be implied on the basis of these similarities.

Much more difficult to assess are ancient long vertical abstracts, including zigzags and other linear patterns. Present in limited numbers at Hantlipinkia and more frequent in the middle Little Colorado (see fig. 15.3; McCreery and Malotki 1994:fig. 2.12), these could also signify some cultural continuity between these sites (see table 15.1). Much more work is needed on this early material.

To the east of Hantlipinkia and south of Zuni Archaic campsites from the Fence Lake lease area north of Quemado are dated between 5500 BC

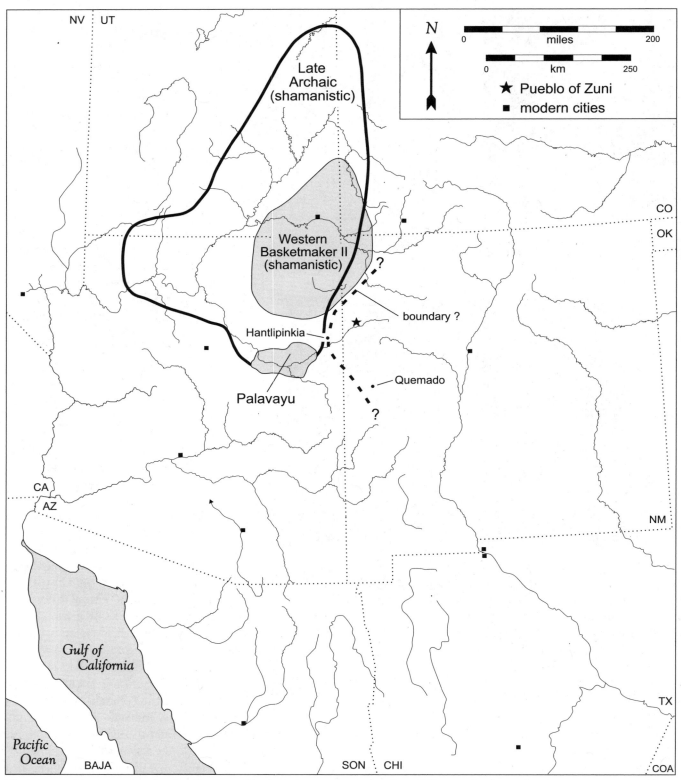

Figure 15.2. Map showing the distribution of Archaic (ca. 4000–400 BC) and Western Basketmaker (ca. 400 BC–AD 400) rock art featuring large anthropomorphic figures.

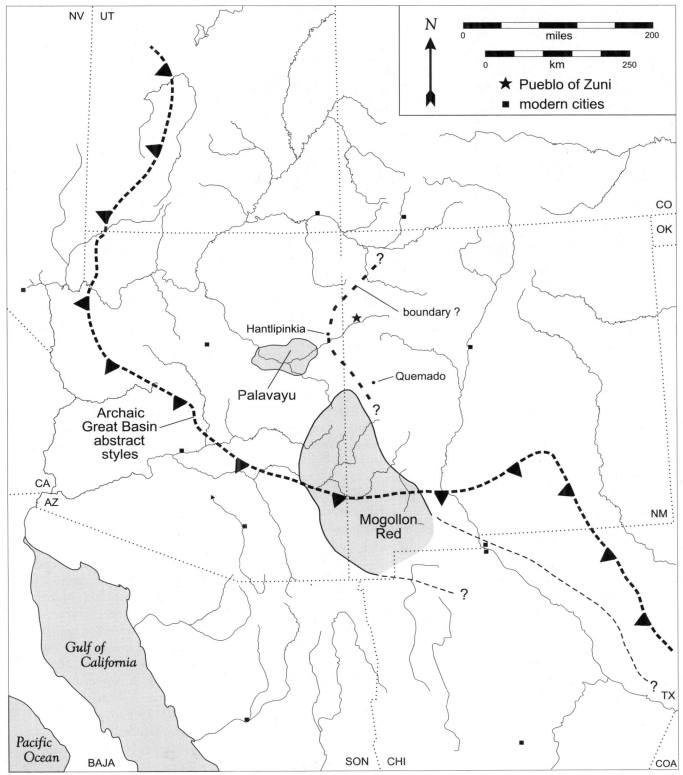

Figure 15.3. The distribution of early rock art styles between ca. 2000 BC and AD 900 that are primarily abstract or nonfigurative in character.

Figure 15.4. Glen Canyon Linear style Archaic figures (left) and Basketmaker anthropomorph (right) near Butler Wash, San Juan River, Utah. The broad-shouldered Basketmaker figure wearing a necklace and fringed garment is superimposed over an earlier Archaic anthropomorph. Photograph by C. Schaafsma, 1995.

and AD 400, with the majority of the point types dating after 3500 BC and representing both the Oshara and Cochise traditions (Hogan 1985:39–41). The Palavayu region, however, falls within the western-based Archaic as defined by Irwin-Williams (1979:32, fig. 2), while southeastern Utah straddles the boundaries between the latter and the Great Basin Archaic. Geographic distributions of point-type traditions, more heavily based on technical considerations that appear to be conservative in the extreme, do not necessarily appear to conform to the distributional patterning of seemingly more fluid ancient ideologies. How imagery relates to particular Archaic traditions as identified on the basis of projectile point types is, however, beyond the parameters of this discussion.

The large corpus of Archaic and Basketmaker II rock art from the middle Little Colorado, including Silver Creek, and the lower San Juan stands in distinct contrast to the Zuni situation (Christensen 1992; Ferg

1974; McCreery and Malotki 1994; Pilles 1975:figs. 6, 8; Schaafsma 1980, 1994). In these adjacent regions to the west and north the Palavayu Linear style and the Majestic Basketmaker of the Palavayu, plus the Glen Canyon Linear followed by the San Juan Basketmaker style in the San Juan drainage (Schaafsma 1980:108–121), are dominated by large, often elaborately decorated anthropomorphic figures (see fig. 15.4, table 15.1). These style complexes suggest the presence of a far-flung powerful shamanic tradition with ideological continuity in the Late Archaic to Basketmaker sequence in these areas. With the possible minor exception of the faces just discussed, this tradition is not evident at Zuni.

In summary, during this early time period the lack of a relationship between the Zuni region and the middle Little Colorado and San Juan is notable. Such a lack of continuity suggests major regional ideological differences at an early date. A major cultural boundary is suggested by the rock art

between the Zuni uplands and the lower elevations of the Little Colorado and the San Juan throughout the Late Archaic / Early Basketmaker period (see fig. 15.2). Ecological factors may have contributed to the cultural differences between hunter-gatherer and early farming populations exploiting these vastly different ecological niches.

Late Basketmaker / Pueblo I (ca. AD 400–900)

In the following centuries (ca. AD 400–900) broad-shouldered and/or bird-headed anthropomorphs in Late Basketmaker through Pueblo I rock art in both the middle Little Colorado and the San Juan drainages indicate a strong continuity with the earlier shamanic tradition (see fig. 15.5 and table 15.2; McCreery and Malotki 1994:150–152, 168–169; Schaafsma 1994). In the lower San Juan atlatls and darts are sometimes depicted with bird-headed figures, elements that suggest a pre–Basketmaker III date. East and southeast of the Four Corners, where large Basketmaker II and later broad-shouldered human figures are increasingly rare west to east, bird-headed figures are even scarcer (Bain 1977–1980; Schaafsma 1963; Yoder and Kolber 2001).

The broad-shouldered human shape, thought to be characteristic of shamans, is uncommon in Chaco petroglyphs as well as in the Zuni region, where it occurs (rarely) at Hantlipinkia. Although triangular-bodied figure types occur on a Basketmaker III La Plata Black-on-white bowl sherd from Chaco Canyon (Brody 1991:31, fig. 16; Roberts 1929a:121–122, fig. 32), these figures are very much exceptions within the spectrum of Chaco iconography.

The rarity of broad-shouldered anthropomorphs and bird-headed figures in the Zuni / Gallup / Quemado

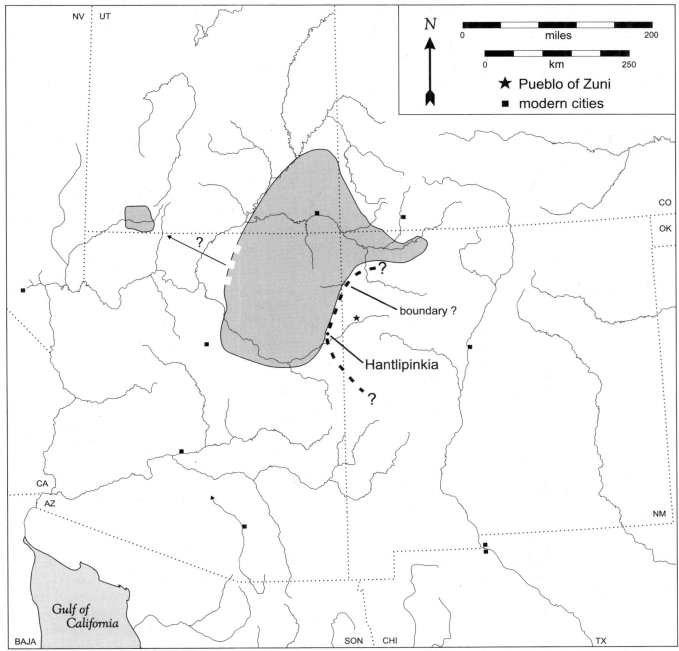

Figure 15.5. Map showing the distribution of broad-shouldered and/or bird-headed anthropomorphs in Anasazi rock art between ca. AD 400 and 900.

region (see Young 1988:fig. 27, left) indicates a continuing ideological boundary between the greater Zuni region and the Little Colorado and San Juan. To date, only a little figurative rock art in the Zuni area has been correlated with the Basketmaker III / Pueblo I period (Young 1988:55, fig. 18, left, 60, fig. 22). Not surprisingly,

some of these figures are found in small numbers at Hantlipinkia (table 15.2). These elements at Hantlipinkia suggest that, following Basketmaker II, the western part of the Zuni region was a little more integrated with the broader Anasazi picture. Hand-holding figures, such as those at Hantlipinkia (see fig. 15.6), are also

pictured on La Plata Black-on-white bowls (AD 575–875) (Cole 1990:fig. 39a; Lister and Lister 1978:figs. 4, 7) and on the exterior of an Early Pueblo I White Mound Black-on-white bowl (MNA 2385, site NA 8939). The left-hand figure in the Hantlipinkia group has a bird on its head, a feature notably rare at Zuni. Females with hair

Table 15.2 Late Basketmaker/Early Pueblo Rock Art, ca. AD 400–900 (see fig. 15.6)

Region	Characteristics and Elements
Zuni	Rock art at Hantlipinkia shows weak links to shamanic traditions of north and west. One bird-headed figure and a few small broad-shouldered anthropomorphs. These links absent elsewhere near Zuni.
	Hand-holding groups and stick-figure fluteplayers from Hantlipinkia. Female with hair whorls.
	Abstract rock art from Hantlipinkia and Pescado. Figures include diamond chains, rake chains, herringbone patterns, linked circles, plain circles, bisected circles, zigzags, parallel zigzags, lines of dots, ticked lines, meandering lines, wavy lines, and two-pole ladders. Small solid animals and animal tracks superimpose these elements and may date from Pueblo I (AD 700–900). This phase of Zuni rock art is best represented at Hantlipinkia.
	Dates for outlined cross-variable.
Middle Little Colorado (Palavayu)	Period poorly defined (see McCreery and Malotki 1994:33). As in the San Juan, Basketmaker III probably a continuation of earlier shamanic tradition. Bird-headed figures are likely to be from this time frame. No rock art style has been identified for Pueblo I.
Lower San Juan	Scale of figures is diminished. Continuation of shamanic rock art with bird-headed figures, both stick and broad-shouldered figures. Some of the latter triangular; ceremonial scenes, processions, hand-holding groups. Twin figures. Crooked staffs common. Stick-figure fluteplayers. Females with hair whorls.
Upper San Juan	Bird heads rare. Small plain broad-shouldered figures, often triangular (Schaafsma 1963), diminishing in numbers west–east. Hand-holding groups. Stick figures, generic animals.
Rio Grande	Abstract figures. Poorly known.

whorls occur on occasion at Hantlipinkia and elsewhere and could date as early as ca. AD 600 (see Hays 1994:fig. 6.3; Young 1979–1981, 1988:69, fig. 26g). Just when the fluteplayer shows up in Zuni rock art is undetermined, although the stick-figure example lacking a hump from Hantlipinkia (Young 1988:70, fig. 27) is characteristic in early Anasazi rock art in the Colorado Plateau to the north and west, beginning with the late Basketmakers.

Other early rock art in the Zuni region consists of abstract elements. At Pescado (ZRAS 5) a sequence of long diamond chains resembles those described at Hantlipinkia but ap-pears less ancient. "Rake chains" together with an outlined cross at ZRAS 25 (Young 1979–1981) are elements found on Basketmaker III ceramics in the La Plata District (Morris 1939:plates 199f, 200e), suggesting that these petroglyph elements may date prior to AD 700 but after 400.[2] At Hantlipinkia most repetitive abstracts (see table 15.2) are believed to postdate those described earlier. Ticked lines, dots, zigzags, and linked circles are found on Basketmaker III ceramics from the Four Corners region of Colorado (Morris 1939:plates 194–209), suggesting that the Zuni elements in question could date as late as ca. AD 500–700.

The importance of the sharing of these rather undiagnostic, widespread, abstract designs on ceramics and in the rock art of the two regions is not clear, other than suggesting some kind of chronological synchroneity.

The several types of tracks occurring with these abstract figures may date from the upper end of the time scale proposed above, and there are a number of small, generic, solidly pecked animals of ambiguous age as well. All of these figurative elements appear to be superimposed on the abstracts. Small generic animals also occur in the Four Corners region on Pueblo I ceramics (Morris 1939:plate 255i).

The abstract elements occur together as a visual field, and some researchers would interpret these as entoptic images seen in the contexts of vision quests. This neuropsychological model for explaining such figures found widely in rock art sites has been highly touted by some rock art researchers (Lewis-Williams and Dowson 1988; Whitley 1994:9–12). If this interpretation has any validity, these abstracts indicate that Hantlipinkia may have functioned as a vision quest site during this early period. Given the possibility that these images were the outcome of shamanic vision quests in Hardscrabble Wash, it is noteworthy that this type of rock art differs significantly from the previously described figurative rock art keyed to Late Archaic and Basketmaker shamanism elsewhere in the Central Little Colorado or in the San Juan drainage to the north.

Finally, with the larger picture in mind, it remains to be pointed out that, as of this date, the so-called Mogollon Red paintings (Schaafsma 1992:48–55), distributed throughout the Mogollon Highlands to the south, have not been found at Zuni (see fig. 15.3). This point of distinction is important to this discussion, as their ap-

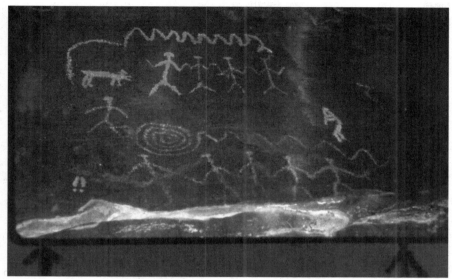

Figure 15.6. Hand-holding human figures and spiral among other petroglyphs, Hantlipinkia, ZRAS 17. The right-hand figure, top row, has a bird on its head. Photograph by M. J. Young, 1980.

parent absence at Zuni differentiates the Anasazi and Mogollon regions prior to AD 900 or 1000. A widespread distribution of red paintings of this type, especially the abstract designs, throughout southern New Mexico and west Texas suggests that some such paintings may be Archaic in origin and that many of these small elements in the caves and overhangs in the Mogollon mountain region were painted by early Mogollon populations (see also Webster, chap. 16, this vol.).

The Pueblo Period (ca. AD 900–1300)

This was a time of population growth in the vicinity of Zuni and eventually population aggregation (Kintigh 1985:1). The two largest pueblos at Zuni date from the 1200s (Kintigh 1985:table 5.3). Beginning with Pueblo I (the Initial Village period: AD 700–900; Kintigh 1985:4–5), Zuni Anasazi culture has been described as being broadly Chacoan or Puerco-Chacoan (see Wilcox 1999a); further, in Rinaldo's (1964:87) opinion High-

land Mogollon culture not only was related to the Chaco-Puerco culture of Zuni but was ancestral to it. In support of these relationships he cites continuities of traits such as full-grooved axes and ceramics after AD 700. The rock art will be reviewed with these relationships in mind.

A clearly identifiable Anasazi rock art configuration dated between ca. AD 900 and 1300 exists from the Colorado Plateau in southwestern Utah to the Rio Grande (see fig. 15.7), indicating a widely shared cosmology. Much, if not most, of the rock art in the Zuni region appears to date from this period (see fig. 15.8). Zuni rock art between ca. AD 900 and 1300+ fits well into the general Anasazi framework, confirming Zuni's participation in a broader Puebloan cosmology and suggesting that communications were fluid between populations at Zuni and the rest of the Anasazi area.

Ceramic data provide further evidence of a high degree of interaction between Anasazi populations by around AD 900 and thereafter (Lang 1982:165; Mera 1935:Map 1; Mills, chap. 13, this vol.). Mills cites Clark's

(chap. 4, this vol.) categories of migration, exchange, and emulation to explain the mechanisms responsible for permeable social boundaries.

The earlier distinct ideological boundaries between Zuni and the middle Little Colorado and the San Juan, if not entirely erased, have been significantly breached. If ecological factors functioned as determinants of cultural differences earlier, they were less operative as time went on. Still, evidence for linguistic affiliations or lack thereof is not suggested by rock art, which, being highly symbolic, largely denotes ideological, ceremonial, and ritual differences.

While a widespread iconography indicates that the prehistoric Pueblos of the Colorado Plateau and the Rio Grande valley held a widely shared cosmology that distinguished them from surrounding cultures on all sides, important regional distinctions are also perceivable. Rock art elements between neighboring Anasazi regions are unevenly shared, suggesting that different emphases prevailed regionally within a generalized ideological framework (see table 15.3). The life forms that the Anasazi chose to represent, for example, are believed to be metaphorical and thus reflect ideological predilections; these, significantly, show an uneven distribution. In this regard the Zuni region has few, if any, distinguishing features of its own (see table 15.4). Long insects, anthropomorphs with decorated rectangular torsos, and two figures holding staffs aloft at Zuni are among the elements that are also found both in the southern Cibola region and in the middle Little Colorado (see fig. 15.9).

Zuni shares its closest rock art affiliations with Chaco. Chaco-Zuni relationships through time have been established on the basis of architecture and pottery types as well (Rinaldo 1964; Woodbury 1979:469). A review

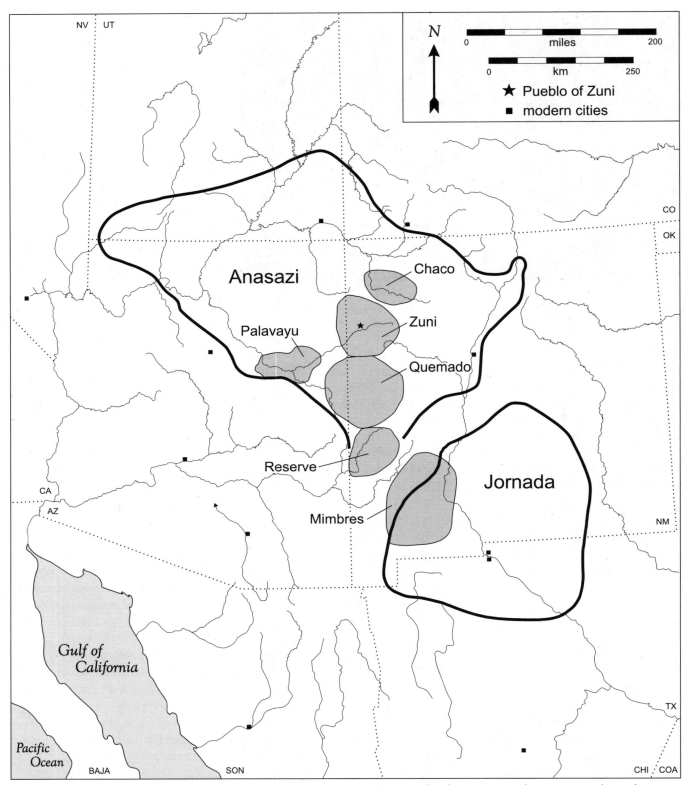

Figure 15.7. Distribution of Anasazi rock art between ca. AD 900 and 1300 with relevant regional variations indicated. Anasazi-style elements appear in the Reserve District around AD 1000.

Zuni is often conceived of as a district together with Acoma, where the rock art is poorly known. Sites west of Acoma and east of the lava flows, known collectively as El Malpais, have been only sporadically photographed. These petroglyph panels are locally distinctive in their mural-like quality: large rock faces are integrated with terraced elements that incorporate stepped cloud designs with birds, curlicues, textile designs, and rectangular-bodied females. These elements as well as a large round-bodied figure suggest dates between AD 1250 and 1400 for these panels, possibly Kowina phase (Dittert 1959). Comparable panels have not been found at Zuni, suggesting significant differences between them.

In general, Anasazi archaeological remains in the Cibola region south of Zuni between AD 500 and 1350, in agreement with the rock art, most closely resemble those found in the Chaco/Cibola regions to the north with the addition of some Mogollon traits (Hogan 1985:10). The Pueblo occupation ends in the early AD 1300s and before 1350 (Kayser and Carroll 1988:3.6; McGimsey 1980). Importantly, fluteplayers are present in Quemado rock art in significant numbers, affirming Anasazi cultural ties (Schaafsma 1992:19, fig. 18; Slifer and Duffield 1994:68, fig. 104). The southern Cibola rock art region near Quemado shares elements with the Springerville vicinity and along with certain elements in Palavayu rock art contains elements that indicate interaction with Mimbres. Nevertheless, the southern Cibola region lacks the complexity of the Palavayu material, and Mimbres elements are much more scarce in Zuni rock art. A similar pattern of interaction between the southern Colorado Plateau Anasazi and the Mogollon areas is also present in ceramics (Mills, chap. 13, this vol.).

Figure 15.8. (a) Water birds and spirals, AD 900–1300, Kyaki:ma, ZRAS-2, photograph by P. Schaafsma; (b) Pueblo II–III petroglyphs, ZRAS 16, photograph by M. J. Young; (c) petroglyphs at the Village of the Great Kivas, ca. AD 1000–1175, photograph by P. Schaafsma.

of over 75 Chaco rock art sites (Bain 1977–1980) shows that Chaco and Zuni closely shared a similar repertoire of what might be regarded as "typical" Anasazi figure types and subjects. Both Chaco and Zuni rock art lack the emphasis on bighorn sheep that is so prevalent among the western Anasazi. Chaco's only distinction within the Anasazi rock art configuration of this period is in the large number of spirals (usually unspectacular) (Schaafsma 1992:figs. 9–12). In sum, what is *absent* is what differentiates—or, more accurately, *unites*—Zuni and Chaco, although there is more variation in Zuni rock art than in that of Chaco.

Table 15.3 Anasazi Rock Art Elements, ca. AD 900–1300
(see figs. 15.8 and 15.9a–d)

Region	Characteristics and Elements
Zuni	Spirals, concentric circles, stick figures, stick figures with legs pointing up, fluteplayers, generic animals, lizard men, lizards. Mountain lion most important animal. Poorly rendered bighorn sheep (rare), handprints, footprints, animal tracks, snakes, wavy lines. Horned lizards, frogs, and long insects (centipedes, scorpions) common. Pottery and textile designs. Vulvas and pits.
	Ritualistic and hunt scenes lacking. Two figures hold staff aloft (see Palavayu).
	Anthropomorphs with rectangular bodies with spiral motifs and interior patterns rare but present. Dates of AD 1250–1400 suggested.
	Outlined cross. Dates variable.
Chaco	Characterized by spirals, wavy lines, stick figures, and poorly defined bighorn sheep. Spirals predominate (found in 60% of sites); concentric circles fewer. Fluteplayers, lizard men, long-tailed animals, handprints, footprints, tracks, snakes. Occasional pottery and textile designs. Occasional hunters with bows (Yoder and Kolber 2001).
Middle Little Colorado (Palavayu)	Quality high. Over 100 life-sized renditions of mountain lions. Variety of human forms, including those with rectangular decorated bodies, faces. Fluteplayers, lizard men, lizards, horned lizards, long-bodied insects, birds, frogs, animal tracks. Fine, elaborate, geometric or textile patterns; outlined cross. Bighorn sheep, antelope, deer, elk. Bears and bear tracks. Interactive scenes: fertility and sexually explicit themes; hunting scenes that include game corrals; ceremonies. Specific ceremonial figures: humans holding aloft variety of pahos, staffs; the one-legged man; "Mother of Game" figure (McCreery and Malotki 1994). Burden baskets.
Southern Cibola region: Quemado/Springerville	Mountain lions common, some large. Stick figures with curved limbs, generic quadrupeds, bighorn sheep, lizards, handprints, footprints, sandal tracks, bear tracks, snakes, tadpole, pottery and textile designs, wavy lines, circle chains, spirals, rakes, outlined cross. Fluteplayers significant (one with curled feather headdress). Anthropomorphs with decorated rectangular torsos and faces. Kachina-like figure with cloud headdress. Long-bodied insects (see Frisbie 1986).
Apache Creek/Reserve	Petroglyphs: spirals, concentric circles (some rayed). Long-tailed quadrupeds of uncertain species plus mountain lions with tails wrapped underneath or with flare on end of tail. Animals portrayed in outline or with head outlined. Stick figures common, many with legs turned up. Spread-eagle fringed birds. Lizards, lizard men, frogs or horned lizards, bear tracks, footprints, other animal tracks, long-bodied insects, outlined cross. Hunt scenes, figures with staffs, bighorn sheep, and fluteplayers rare. Curled feather headdress.
	Mogollon Red style (Schaafsma 1992:48–55).
Acoma	Poorly known. Stick figure lizards. Late (ca. AD 1200–1350): mural-like abstract designs that incorporate cloud terraces; elaborate textile/pottery motifs, rectangular-bodied anthropomorphs with torso decoration.
Rio Grande	Stick figures, fluteplayers, birds, plant motifs with birds, bird "chains." Handprints, footprints. Lizards. Informal abstract elements: circles, linked circles, wavy lines, net patterns, diamond chains, lines of dots.

The Palavayu. The "Palavayu" as defined by McCreery and Malotki (1994:fig. 1.2) includes the middle Little Colorado and lower Rio Puerco regions, from Winslow on the west to just beyond Petrified Forest in the east. They note—and we agree—that "PII–PIII rock art of the Palavayu region is most akin to the widespread rock art tradition of the Plateau Anasazi, although enough differences exist to constitute a regional style of its own" (McCreery and Malotki 1994:40). Although almost all of the figures that occur in Zuni rock art may be found in the vast Palavayu inventory, comparisons show a clear differentiation between these regions (see table 15.3).

Within the area of ceramics a closer middle Little Colorado affinity to the Winslow branch Anasazi to the west (ca. AD 1000–1250) than to Zuni has been proposed (Wells 1989:84). This observation is not contradicted by the rock art.

Pueblo II–III Palavayu rock art is distinguished from that of Zuni by its rich inventory of often very complex individual figures and its incredible diversity of life forms as well as interacting figure groups (McCreery and Malotki 1994:fig. 9.4). The highly elaborated rituals and associated paraphernalia pictured, such as the variety of staffs held by ceremonial participants, are all extremely rare, if present at all, in rock art elsewhere and denote the presence of ritual practices and, in some cases, beliefs peculiar to the Palavayu region. The evidence for these complex rituals and their accoutrements is lacking or extremely rare in the rock art of the Zuni region. In addition, staff bearers and burden baskets in middle Little Colorado rock art before AD 1300 manifest some interaction and idea exchange with the Mimbres, a dynamic generally but perhaps not totally absent at Zuni.[3] The two previously mentioned fig-

Table 15.4 Rough Inventory of Selected Elements Dated between ca. AD 900 and 1350

Element	Palavayu	Zuni	Chaco	Quemado	Reserve
Human: rectangular with face, body decoration	many	very rare	o	many	o
Life form with face	many	rare	very rare	rare	very rare
Fluteplayer	many	many	many	many	rare
Curled feather headdress	very rare	few	o	few	many
Humans in profile with staff held aloft	many: complex	rare	o	o	very rare
Hunters with bows and arrows	many	o	few	rare	very rare
Mountain sheep	many	rare	many	rare	very rare
Mountain lions: tails over backs	many: large	many	few	many	many
Mountain lions: tails underneath	o	o	o	o	few
Mountains lions: flared tails	o	o	o	rare	few
Animals: patterned bodies (often bent legs, large heads)	rare	rare	o	rare	many
Round-bodied horned lizard or frog	many	many	rare	few	many
Long-bodied insects	many	many	o	few	few
Outlined cross	many	rare	very rare	few	many
Spiral	many	many	many: dominant element	few	few

Note: All regions named are united by numerous stick-figure humans, lizards, animal tracks, including bear tracks, miscellaneous long-tailed animals, and spirals. Abstract configurations such as rows of dots, zigzags, wavy lines, meandering lines, linked circles, concentric circles, and so forth are widely distributed throughout these sites, although never forming a cohesive group. Elements in this table were selected for a numerical evaluation on the basis of their usefulness in the consideration of defining cultural boundaries. It should be remembered that these evaluations are tentative, based on the available samples, and are subject to change. The point is to convey a sense of frequency of occurrence.

Sources: Laboratory of Anthropology files, McCreery and Malotki 1994; site files, Laboratory of Anthropology, Museum of New Mexico; Zuni Rock Art Survey files; personal slide collection.

ures holding staffs aloft at Kyaki:ma (see fig. 15.9d, e) suggest either some ritual continuity with the Palavayu or a cultural-historical relationship of both with Mimbres (AD 1000–1150).

The "one-legged man," a seemingly localized motif repeated in Palavayu rock art (McCreery and Malotki 1994:153–155), is essentially absent at Zuni. This distinctive human figure probably had an individual identity in oral history or mythology, and its apparent lack at Zuni denotes another significant break between Zuni and points west. A minor exception to this may be a human figure missing a foot (see fig. 15.9b). This figure occurs rather appropriately at the western Zuni site of Hantlipinkia. Also absent at Zuni is the Tiikuywuuti, or "Mother of Game" figure (McCreery

and Malotki 1994:140, 142, fig. 3.2, fifth and sixth from left), that also appears at Betatakin between AD 1250 and 1280 in the Kayenta region (Schaafsma 2000:25–26, fig. 2.10).

In sum, the rock art indicates that within the spectrum of commonality present within Anasazi rock art of this time frame, a significant distinction existed between Zuni and the Palavayu zones. The Anasazi of the Palavayu had a dynamic rock art tradition that reflected the intricacies of ritual aspects of their culture. The nature of the differences between Zuni and the Palavayu of the middle Little Colorado suggests that these regions participated in different mythological and ceremonial systems, if not exclusively, at least in emphasis. The Palavayu art features

ritual objects and mythological figures not found at Zuni, and from all appearances they had a more complex ceremonial structure. Implications of a disparity between the mythic repertoires of these regions raises the question of whether this is evidence for linguistic discontinuity as well.

In conclusion, during the Pueblo period between ca. AD 900 and 1300 a boundary continues to exist between Zuni and the middle Little Colorado around Hantlipinkia. Finally, it should be mentioned that numerous elements in middle Little Colorado rock art suggest some communication with and receptivity to the ideological world of the Mimbres, whereas this avenue of influence is not in evidence in the Zuni region.

a

b

c

d

e

Figure 15.9. (a) Stinging insects, ZRAS 1, photograph by P. Schaafsma; (b) Pueblo III petroglyphs at Hantlipinkia, ZRAS-17 (note the suggestion of an interior design on the body of the left-hand figure; a human figure lacking its right foot can be seen at upper right, center, a feature that may suggest an ideological tie to the Middle Little Colorado), photograph by M. J. Young; (c) petroglyphs incised on soft sandstone, ZRAS 11 (anthropomorphs such as the one featured here with a rectangular body filled with a geometric pattern and curlicues are characteristic of Late Pueblo III to Early Pueblo IV rock art and pottery designs in the Colorado River region), photograph by M. J. Young; (d) incised figure holding staff aloft with curved element at the top, Kyaki:ma, ZRAS 2 (the apparent "tail" that indicates that this staff bearer is an animal may or may not be an accident of superimposition on this much-worked rock face), drawing by P. Schaafsma; (e) incised and abraded images in this panel at Kyaki:ma include an animal staff bearer; other figures are a kachina mask (note ears) and a bird kachina; barely visible at the far left center are two round masks pecked on the rock angle), photograph by P. Schaafsma.

The Mountain Mogollon: Apache Creek and the Reserve Districts. After a certain date—and this is ambiguous, but probably after AD 1000—there is demonstrable continuity between the iconography of the Mountain Mogollon region and the Anasazi to the north (see table 15.3; Schaafsma 1992:60). The rock art denotes an Anasazi impact on the Mogollon in the vicinities of Apache Creek and Reserve rather than the reverse; ceramic traditions are in agreement with this observation (Mills, chap. 13, and Wilson, chap. 14, this vol.).

While similarities in the rock art of the Anasazi and Mogollon become apparent, there are significant differences, as shown in a tabulation of selected elements in table 15.4. Out of 16 sites documented in the Apache Creek/Reserve region, only two flute-players were recorded, one reclining, the other upright (Schaafsma 1971). A third was recorded by the ASNM Field School (Bain 1977–1980). The scarcity of this popular Anasazi figure, with presumed wider cultural attachments such as oral traditions and myths (see Malotki 2000), is notable, as it appears to have been much less important in the mountain Mogollon region.

On the other hand, absent or rare at Zuni are several stylistic features and elements that occur both in the Mogollon-area rock art and in Mimbres pottery designs. These include mountain lions with tails wrapped around underneath, mountain lions with flared tails, and animals portrayed in outline with large heads and with eyes indicated. In addition, near Reserve and on the Middle Fork of the Gila painted cloud terraces, a stick figure holding a staff aloft, a feline with a flared tail, and a fish (all of which appear on Mimbres Black-on-white) show that red paintings continued to be made by Mogollon populations after AD 1000 (Schaafsma 1992:54,

figs. 63, 64; Snodgrass 1975:138, fig. 237, 177). While these rock art elements indicate Highland Mogollon–Mimbres interaction, they are limited in occurrence.

Characteristic of anthropomorphic figures in the Apache Creek/Reserve rock art is the curved headdress element (see table 15.4). This headgear is not found on figures in Mimbres pottery painting, but it does occur earlier in the San Juan ancestral Pueblo region.[4]

Summary. To conclude, the rock art of Zuni and surrounding regions between ca. AD 900 and 1300 is clearly more closely integrated with that of the rest of the Anasazi world than it is with the Mogollon. Interaction between the Mogollon area and the Anasazi is evident after ca. AD 1000, with Anasazi elements predominating in the Mogollon repertoire in the Apache Creek/Reserve vicinities, suggesting a kind of "Anasaziation" of the Mogollon rather than the reverse. Seemingly, the Mimbres had only a minor impact on the ideologies of the Mogollon Highlands, in striking contrast to the strong continuum that exists between the rock art of the Mimbres and Jornada Mogollon in southern New Mexico (Schaafsma 1980).

Within the Anasazi area itself the rock art indicates that a strong communication network existed between Zuni and Chaco as well as Quemado. Cultural boundaries, though significantly less marked than previously, persisted between Zuni and the middle Little Colorado. This pattern defines a north–south trajectory along the upland corridor that rests essentially above 2,000 m. More research is needed into whether and how ecological factors might have played a part in ideologically uniting these pueblos.

Pueblo IV (ca. AD 1325–1600)

In the fourteenth century large villages and towns define a more geographically constricted Pueblo world that is united by a new iconography and its associated ideologies, marking a discontinuity with the past and reflecting the presence of the kachina and war cults and possibly other societal groups that took precedence over the former cosmology.[5] The Western Pueblo region encompassed Acoma, Zuni, and Hopi as well as ancestral Hopi middle Little Colorado River sites such as the Homolovis (AD 1300–1400) (Cole 1992:66–85). Neighboring villages to the south and east were abandoned during the early part of the Pueblo IV period (see figs. 15.10, 15.11).

Around AD 1300 or 1325 a new border of sorts emerges between the Eastern or Rio Grande Pueblos and Western Pueblos (see table 15.5, figs. 15.10, 15.11). This iconographic boundary appears to mark differing degrees of participation in the kachina and war societies, with the Rio Grande Pueblos showing a strong continuity with the rain cults of the Jornada Mogollon, which was, in turn, the strongest Mimbres heir (see Schaafsma 1980, 1992, 2000 for detailed discussions).

After this date, however, the west was, nevertheless, less impacted by the Jornada than were the Rio Grande Pueblos. Until the late protohistoric and early historic times the emphasis remained on strong localized traditions. In the Rio Grande kachinas, kachina masks, ceremonial participants, warriors, shield bearers, clouds, and horned serpents dominate the rock art inventory, while in the west, although one finds kachina masks after AD 1300, the rock art content is significantly more limited (see fig. 15.9b; see also McCreery and Malotki 1994). Furthermore, McCreery and Malotki (1994:56) note that

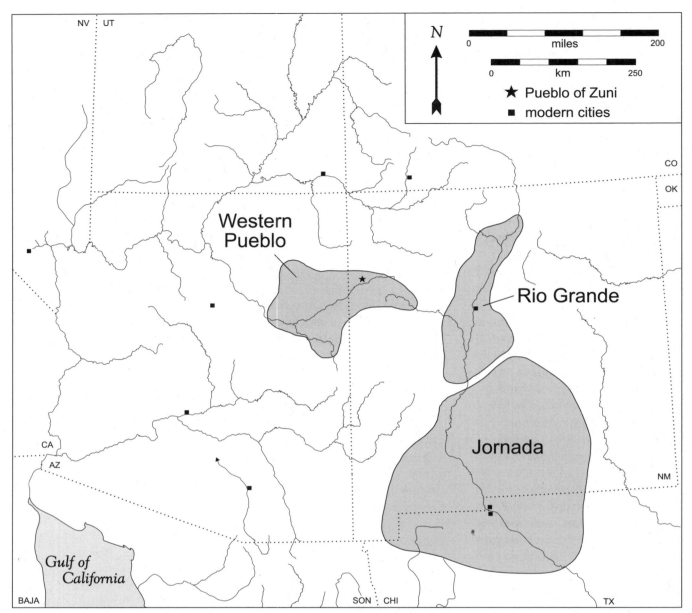

Figure 15.10. Pueblo rock art areas between ca. AD 1350 and ca. 1425, or Early Pueblo IV. The Rio Grande drainage as a distinctive rock art region becomes well defined during this period.

kachina iconography in the Palavayu is "thinly scattered" and deals with a more conservative element inventory. A few kachina masks and other kachina-like figures are present among the rock art images in the Springerville vicinity (Stephenson et al. 1997). Kachinas are also pictured occasionally on pottery in the White Mountain series in the Mogollon Rim area after AD 1325 or 1330 (Mills, chap.

13, this vol.) and on Four Mile Polychrome to the west.[6] However, we are left with the fact that, while present, kachinas are relatively sparsely represented in Western Pueblo media.

Zuni sites with kachina masks include Pescado (ZRAS 5), Kyaki:ma (ZRAS 2), ZRAS 10, 11, 16, 21, 25 (Young 1988:figs. 26B–F, 35B–G), and petroglyph panels near the Hinkson and Ojo Bonito sites (Cole

1992:116, fig. 5.21). At Pescado several masks, large circles possibly representing shields, geometrics, frogs or reptiles with round bodies, a lightning personage, and a corn plant could date from the fourteenth century.[7] Dates from neighboring settlements fall between AD 1300 and 1350 as well as from the historic period as late as the late nineteenth century (Kintigh 1985:53; Mills 1980:table 2).

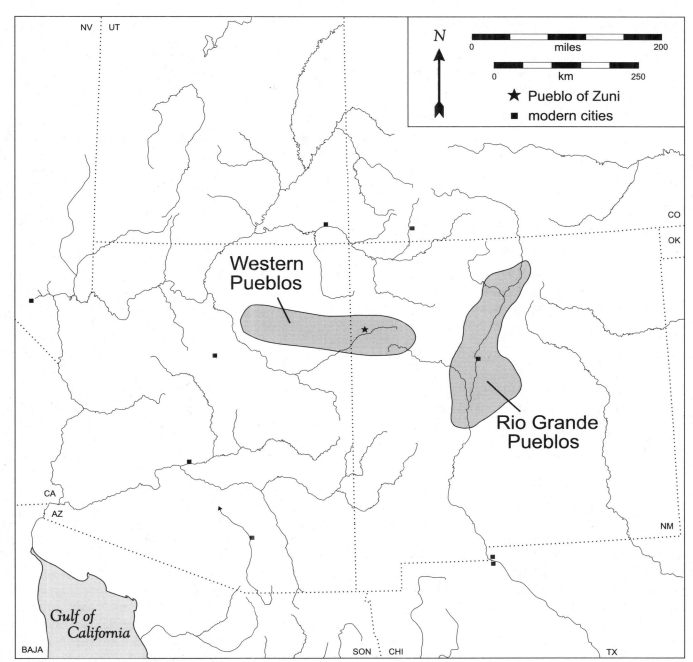

Figure 15.11. Pueblo regions and the distribution of Pueblo rock art dated between AD 1425 and the historic period.

Because of a continuity in rock art content and settlement patterns there are sometimes difficulties in discriminating between Pueblo IV and historic rock art at Zuni (see fig. 15.12a). Nevertheless, the Pueblo IV masks tend to be simpler in concept (see fig. 15.12b, c), while historic masks tend to be incised and manifest characteristics seen in contemporary Zuni kachinas (see fig. 15.12d, e).

Large shields on Dowa Yalanne (ZRAS 2, 3), where the Zuni took refuge from the Spaniards in the AD 1600s (Woodbury 1979:470–471), are likely to be seventeenth century in origin (see fig. 15.12f). Their designs are typical of Rio Grande shields and probably reflect the diverse origins of the Pueblo refugees, who came from the Rio Grande as well as from Zuni. Schaafsma (2000) suggests that shields, even as rock art, served a magical protective function. Thus, the three large shield images abraded, incised, and painted beside the trail to the mesa top at Dowa Yalanne would

Table 15.5 Pueblo IV Rock Art Elements, ca. AD 1300–1700
(see figs. 15.9e, 15.12, and 15.13)

Western Pueblo: Zuni and Hopi Plus greater Little Colorado River region	Kachina masks: present from fourteenth century. Corner masks. Cloud terraces, occasional shields and shield bearers (rare). Small frogs or horned lizards plus "frog men" with faces (see Dorsey and Voth 1901:Plate XXV). Feathered figures with long beaks (Shalako-like)—contrast with historic Shalako figures. Mountain lions, eagles, macaws.
	Note: Elaborate textile designs and human figures with decorated rectangular torsos and faces may date from AD 1250 to 1400, bridging Pueblo III and Pueblo IV. Fluteplayers may end ca. AD 1400.
Eastern Pueblo: Rio Grande	Extensive sites, sometimes with thousands of figures. Numerous kachina masks (key element), various kachinas (including numerous Shalakos, corner masks), cloud terraces, shields, shield bearers, warriors with weapons in hand, war gods, war clubs, four-pointed stars, feather and taloned stars (some with faces); one-horned serpents, two-horned serpents, star-faced serpents, lightning. Large animals in outline with eyes, teeth: mountain lions (some with pointed hats), badgers (rare), bears (rare). Water birds: ducks, cranes; also macaws, turkeys, eagles, swallows. Most fluteplayers probably early within this time frame.

have been appropriately located in regard to the refuge site on top. Images of mountain lions, often perceived as war patrons (Schaafsma 2000:62), are carved close to the shields (Young 1988:fig. 36).

The few Kolowisis (Horned Serpents) in Zuni rock art are usually incised and appear to be historic. This supernatural, although having the same attributes and personality characteristics as the Horned Serpent of the Rio Grande valley, differs in appearance from the protohistoric and historic Rio Grande serpents; instead, it resembles the historic Hopi Paaloloqangw. These appear to be localized Western Pueblo forms of a widespread prehistoric deity present from Casas Grandes through the Mimbres and Jornada Mogollon north to the Rio Grande Pueblos (see fig. 15.13; Brody 1977:plate 11; Schaafsma 1980:257, fig. 199, 1998:37, figs. 11, 12).

The restricted Pueblo IV rock art iconography at Zuni is amplified to a small degree by design elements on Matsaki Polychrome (AD 1375–late 1600s) and Hawikuh Polychrome

(AD 1630–1680) vessels (Kintigh 1996:table 1.9; Mills, chap. 13, this vol.; Smith et al. 1966).[8] Matsaki Polychrome patterns incorporate bits and pieces of an iconographic suite well represented and integrated in northern Rio Grande rock art and kiva murals and in the kiva murals from Antelope Mesa at Hopi. These ceramic design elements include a few masks and one or more shields as well as terraced clouds, four-pointed stars (western style and lacking faces; see Smith 1952:fig. 49a), mountain lion forelegs and paws with claws, various birds, including macaws and eagles, and dragonflies (Smith et al. 1966:figs. 51–72), all of which have symbolic status in Pueblo IV ideology and are featured in Pueblo IV rock art in the Rio Grande valley, butterflies excepted.[9]

It is not clear at what point during the time frame encompassed by Matsaki Polychrome these elements become evident. Pottery designs representing masks, while rare, confirm the presence of the kachina cult at Zuni only sometime after AD 1375 and

before the late 1600s. Mills (chap. 13, this vol.) notes one mask on a Pinnawa Glaze-on-white (AD 1350–1450) jar from Hawikuh.

Discussion

In conclusion, it appears that while selected elements of Pueblo religion and worldview as we know it today appeared early in Pueblo IV among the Western Pueblos, including Zuni, it is clear that we are not dealing with the same comprehensive cosmology related to weather control and warfare that we know was in place in the Rio Grande beginning in the 1300s. Rather, the origin of this religious complex at Zuni is late in time and was imported from the Rio Grande, thus indicating a break with the past in Zuni cultural relationships. This complex, although graphically expressed in the Jeddito murals at Hopi, is not the result of selected borrowing from the Eastern Pueblos. Instead, in a mythologized account these murals are attributed to the Rio Grande, in which it is said that Hopi delegates were sent to acquire this "panoply of ritual knowledge" (Whiteley 2002b:151). The complexity of the knowledge and imagery manifest in these murals, however, also implies the actual presence of Rio Grande immigrants at Hopi. To date, no such iconographic complex is known prehistorically in the Zuni region.

The origins of Zuni's ideological system—as we know it today—appears to be late in derivation and imported from the Rio Grande valley. Migrations are likely to have been involved in this process (see Clark, chap. 4, this vol.), and population movements may have been as late as the seventeenth century, triggered by Pueblo discontent, which was followed by the 1680 revolt against the Spaniards. In Clark's view ethnicity and enculturation are implicated in

a

c

e

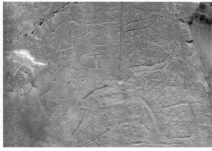
b

d

f

Figure 15.12. (a) Large sun shield or mask carved on top of a pecked stepped cloud, ZRAS 16 (both Pueblo IV [the cloud] and historic [the mask/shield] rock art may be represented here), photograph by P. Schaafsma; (b) eroded kachina mask, Kyaki:ma, ZRAS 2, photograph by M. J. Young; (c) kachina mask on triangular body at Pescado, ZRAS 5 (the square-toothed mouth and round eyes are typical for early kachina depictions throughout the Pueblo realm from Homolovi to the Rio Grande), photograph by M. J. Young; (d) incised historic petroglyphs at Kyaki:ma (pictured are deer with heartlines, pierced with arrows, pursued by bow hunters; a horseman and a dog are visible in the center; at top center the stick headpiece of a Yamuhakto mask seems to serve as the arrow for the hunter to the left, probably made after the mask was carved, an incorporation that is probably intentional, since this kachina is helpful to hunters, among his other attributes), photograph by P. Schaafsma; (e) abraded horned mask, ZRAS 11, photograph by M. J. Young; (f) large incised shield with probable sun symbolism, Kyaki:ma (probably early historic), photograph by M. J. Young.

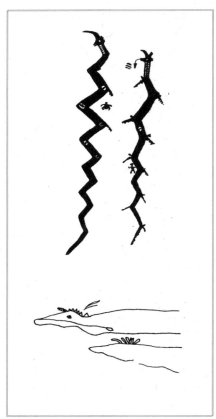

Figure 15.13. Pueblo versions of the Horned Serpent: (*top*) tall paired serpents (about 2 m in height) from south of Abo, east of the Rio Grande valley, AD 1325–1670 (notice the tall, tapered, forward-extending horns and caninelike snouts; feathers project from their bodies); (*bottom*) incised historic horned serpents from Zuni (feathers are indicated behind the horn, at least on the lower figure; the horn is shorter and round, like that on the effigy in current use [see Wright 1985:plate 14]), drawing by P. Schaafsma.

the process of migration rather than simple exchange and emulation, which would have led to a less complete expression of this art form and its content. Possibly, exchange and emulation are implicit in the early indications of the kachina cult at Zuni and elsewhere among the Western Pueblos, unaccompanied by the full iconography.

Conclusions: Boundaries, Traditions, and Networks of Communication

The rock art data set forms one of many lenses through which world-view and ideational values from the past may be viewed. Imagery fixed in the landscape also documents shifting patterns of communication networks and denotes cultural boundaries. The picture drafted in this chapter for Zuni origins and as seen through the medium of rock art over some 4,000 years is at best sketchy but at the same time dynamic and complex. We feel that rock art provides bold outlines of cultural-historical relationships on the ideological front—the changing non-material culture of the Zuni region—and how its relationships with neighboring regions were modified and changed through time.

Through all chronological stages Zuni rock art is regarded as conservative, lacking distinctions of its own.[10] Absences often characterize the prehistoric repertoire of images at Zuni, and no discrete "Zuni rock art style" as such can be identified for any period in Zuni-area prehistory. Unlike the Zuni language, however, the rock art of the Zuni region is not "an isolate."

Initially, Zuni was clearly outside of the distinctive agricultural (Pre-Pottery Formative) cultural configurations forged in the San Juan and middle Little Colorado (see Matson, chap. 7, this vol.). The rock art of these regions documents a shamanic tradition that prevailed through centuries, if not several millennia, apparently derived from a base in the preceding Archaic (Schaafsma 1994). This tradition, being absent in Zuni-region rock art, indicates that important ideological differences separated Zuni from the San Juan and middle Little Colorado Basketmakers. Seen

through the evidence of rock art, this is the clearest cultural boundary between Zuni and its neighbors at any time in Zuni culture history. An ethnic boundary may be implied by these differences.

On the other hand, at no point is Zuni-region rock art closely allied with rock art with Mogollon origins. The absence of Mogollon Red paintings at Zuni is suggestive of a cultural distinction between the populations of the Zuni region and the Mogollon at an early date. Further, the abstract petroglyph styles (Abstract Curvilinear), with estimated dates between ca. 2000 BC and AD 500, distinct from those described at Hantlipinkia, and characteristic of the arid regions of southern New Mexico and Arizona (Schaafsma 1992:46–48), are not present at Zuni.

As previously discussed, from Pueblo I on rock art indicates that agriculturalists in the Zuni region were conversant in an ideology that is widespread throughout the entire Anasazi area, minor regional differences notwithstanding. Nevertheless, we would characterize this period at Zuni as conservative in a thematic sense, with primary affiliations with ancestral Pueblo peoples in the highland corridor between Chaco and Quemado. How closely the rock art of Zuni relates to that around Allentown, a Chaco-Puerco complex (regional polity?), is unknown, since the rock art from that locality is scarcely documented. We would predict, however, that it would be similar to that of Chaco, with the addition of some elements that are found in the Palavayu immediately to the west. Although Chaco Canyon rock art has been reviewed for potential distinguishing and politically significant emblems, it lacks elements or symbols that would distinguish Chacoan sites from other Anasazi sites of the same period (Schaafsma 2006).

Although, during this time, the Zuni region was a participant in the wider ancestral Pueblo cosmology in evidence in rock art throughout the Colorado Plateau, boundaries between Zuni and the middle Little Colorado, evident from the early periods of Anasazi prehistory, persisted through Pueblo III. The rock art content indicates that Zuni was separated from the middle Little Colorado by differences in ceremonial and ritual practices. There is no evidence in the rock art of middle Little Colorado populations eventually being pushed east into the Zuni region.

Mogollon relationships with the Zuni region appear after ca. AD 1000 but with communications moving from the Pueblo area south into the northern Mogollon Highlands. It is interesting to contemplate the possibility that this interaction could have been facilitated by a common language.

At some point after ca. AD 1000 Mimbres elements, distinguishable by style and content, are occasionally present in the southern Cibola and Palavayu regions. Communication networks between the Palavayu and Mimbres between AD 1000 and 1150 are posited on the basis of several shared elements. This pattern of interaction from the Mimbres into east-central Arizona appears for the most part to have bypassed the Zuni region itself.

Population movement at the end of the thirteenth century into the greater Zuni region from both north and south (Hogan 1985:11; Rinaldo 1964:94) resulted in aggregated villages and regional consolidation.[11] Some of the largest villages in the Zuni vicinity came into existence in the late 1200s and consisted of up to 1,200 rooms. Nevertheless, social instability between AD 1250 and 1400 has been pointed out by Kintigh (1985:1, 115), as evidenced by a high

rate of construction, abandonment, and settlement relocation. Such instability may have been caused by strain on the existing social mechanisms for holding together the large pueblos that resulted (Kintigh 1985:1). It has been postulated (Adams 1991; Schaafsma and Schaafsma 1974) that the kachina cult as an institution would have been a new means for intravillage integration. The disjunction between the large villages of the thirteenth century and the lack of direct evidence for the kachina cult at this point remains to be explained. Perhaps it is significant that these villages were short-lived, suggesting that no such social institutions were yet in place (see also Wilcox et al., chap. 12, this vol.).

The widespread changes in Pueblo IV rock art are accompanied by changes in other aspects of Pueblo culture, some of which imply migrations (see Mills, chap. 13, this vol.). Migrations in themselves indicate social and possibly environmental instability. Pervasive cultural changes often involve crises. Hypothetically, social crises, as evidenced by a wholesale Anasazi migration out of the Four Corners region and elsewhere, would have resulted in an increased receptivity to new ideas in the way of a revitalization movement, as postulated by Burger (1988). Receptivity to a new cosmology and participation in the kachina cult, among other things, is indicative of religious-ideological shifts following this population redistribution.

Sporadic kachina-like iconography in rock art of Quemado, New Mexico, and near Springerville, Arizona, before about AD 1400 (Bain 1977–1980; Stephenson et al. 1997) could relate to interaction with the Rio Grande rather than from the earlier Mimbres. The kachina cult is very evident in rock art from the fourteenth century in the Socorro (Piro) region, where

continuities with the Jornada region are strong.[12] This fourteenth-century pattern in regard to kachina iconography occurs on ceramics as well (Mills, chap. 13, this vol.).

While Zuni does not appear to have been a source or even a conduit for the transmission of religious concepts during Pueblo IV, ceramic designs as well as rock art iconography show that the Zuni region with its somewhat limited kachina iconography participated in the changes taking place elsewhere in more dynamic and elaborate forms. Until the very late prehistoric period or early historic period Zuni appears to have been peripheral to Pueblo IV developments on the Rio Grande.

Because of the profound cultural changes, including population movements into Zuni that took place after ca. AD 1200, it is likely that oral traditions regarding Zuni origins (Ferguson, chap. 19, this vol.) may not pertain to the earliest archaeological records but to events of more recent centuries. Certainly, the ancient rock art of the Palavayu has little to do with populations in the Zuni region at all, but rock art indicates that during the Pueblo periods relationships between Zuni and the Palavayu were more fluid.

Finally, the issue has been raised of potential correlations between linguistic relationships in the past and rock art styles. It might be argued that persistent, well-established boundaries, as defined by rock art between Zuni and neighboring regions to the north and west in the early phases of Zuni prehistory, indicate linguistic differences as early as the Late Archaic. While these divisions are easily recognized, their implications in regard to language are not certain at this point. In a reverse scenario, using the protohistoric to historic period in the Rio Grande as an example, it is clear that in a general sense the rich Pueblo symbolic and metaphoric systems, as expressed graphically in rock art and in other media, cross-cut linguistic boundaries (Schaafsma 2005). Therefore, what we are looking for in the rock art is not evidence for linguistic ties but ideological affiliation. Ideology, cosmology, and religion cross-cut linguistic groups. The fact that Zuni participates in a broadly Puebloan idea system for most of its culture history is not confounded by the fact of its being a linguistic isolate. On the other hand, the rock art evidence of only moderate interaction at the most with neighboring regions until recently is perhaps at least consistent with its linguistic status.

Acknowledgments

I want to thank David Gregory and David Wilcox for inviting me to participate in the Mogollon-Zuni advanced seminar. I am much indebted to Jane Young for her willingness to coauthor this chapter and share her extensive knowledge of Zuni rock art and photographs taken during the Zuni Rock Art Survey. Valuable comments offered by Dave Gregory, Steve Kowalewski, and David Wilcox in the course of the seminar and the writing of early drafts are greatly appreciated. Curtis Schaafsma offered technical assistance all along the way. In addition, two anonymous reviewers provided insights that were extremely helpful in finalizing this chapter.

Notes

1. The so-called Palavayu region extends just north of I-40 from east of Petrified Forest National Park, west to Winslow, south along Clear Creek, east to Snowflake, and then northwest to east of Petrified Forest (McCreery and Malotki 1994:3, fig. 1.2).

2. The outlined cross is a design found sporadically in rock art in the Southwest and in neighboring areas sometime after AD 575; its first dated occurrence is on Bas-ketmaker III pottery in the San Juan drainage (Morris 1939:plate 200e). In general, its usefulness in yielding information pertaining to chronology and cultural-historical relationships is questionable. In the Four Corners region it is found most frequently on Pueblo I ceramics (Morris 1939:plates 226j, 240k, 246k, 248g, 253), although it also shows up during Pueblo II (Morris 1939:188, fig. 52). This distinctive motif is frequent in later Palavayu rock art (ca. AD 1000–1300) and on Mimbres Black-on-white pottery (AD 1000–1150). It is also a common design in the rock art of the Reserve region, presumably after AD 1000. The outlined cross is found on rather rare occasions in Zuni rock art. The significance that this very widespread element has for indicating Anasazi/Mogollon interaction is unknown.

3. Brody (1992:97, fig. 13) illustrates a Mimbres bowl painted with a figure holding up a staff that has a curved apparatus on top from which are suspended a fish and a carnivore with its tail curved underneath its body. Figures in profile holding staffs aloft, often topped with moisture-related symbolism, are a recurrent and widespread theme in Mountain Mogollon petroglyphs after ca. AD 1000 as well as in Jornada Mogollon rock art.

The numerous wands or staffs pictured in the hands of Palavayu figures could also denote a similarity between the middle Little Colorado Anasazi and Sinagua ritual practices in the Flagstaff region during Pueblo II–III. The Burial of the Magician, along with 18 staffs, 12 of which were carved, includes a serrated club, perhaps not unlike those carried by figures in the Palavayu petroglyphs (McCreery and Malotki 1994:fig. 3.2; McGregor 1943: plate III, 287–288; Pilles 1996:70).

A small number of "slab pahos" (McCreery and Malotki 1994:142–144) are identical to the burden baskets found in Mimbres petroglyphs (compare McCreery and Malotki 1994:figs. 9.13–9.15 with Schaafsma 1980:206, fig. 160) or as elements in Mimbres pottery designs (Brody 1977:72, plate 16; Davis 1995:171, upper left). The Palavayu figures in question appear to *be* burden baskets and not pahos. Outside of their appearance in the Palavayu rock art these elements are specific to the Mimbres.

4. This headgear is rare in Palavayu art, and at Zuni only two figures were recorded wearing this type of headdress (Young 1988:fig. 24). A detailed rendition of this particular headdress on the previously described fluteplayer in a Quemado petroglyph (Slifer and Duffield 1994:68, fig. 104) shows that it is a curled feather and not a horn, as previously described (Schaafsma 1992:59). Similar headgear is found in its earliest context on presumably male figures in a hand-holding line on a La Plata/Chapin Black-on-white bowl (AD 575 or 600) from near Durango in which male figures alternate with females with hair whorls (Hays 1994:52, fig. 6.3).

5. Nevertheless, the Burial of the Magician in the Elden phase Ridge Ruin site (AD 1150–1250) (McGregor 1943; Pilles 1996; Reid and Whittlesey 1997:216) included, among many unusual ritual items, carved sticks thought to be related to the recent warrior-affiliated sword-swallowing societies (McGregor 1943:296). Sword swallowers are pictured in Pueblo IV rock art in the Rio Grande valley but are curiously absent from iconography anywhere or in any media prior to the fourteenth century. Zuni migration stories state that the Zuni learned the sword-swallowing ritual at Shiba:bulima, the Stone Lions Shrine in Bandelier National Monument (see Ferguson, chap. 19, this vol.).

6. A stone effigy resembling these rock art elements originates from a kiva dated around AD 1230 at Hooper Ranch Pueblo in the upper Little Colorado River valley, Arizona, south–southwest of Zuni (Martin 1979:74, fig. 15; Martin and Plog 1973:137). Following this and other archaeological leads, the Pueblo rock art elements may postdate Mimbres by 80 or even 150 years or more. Martin and Plog suggest that the Hooper Ranch effigy was a cult deity and not a protokachina. Pinedale Polychrome (AD 1300–1350) (Hays 1994:table 8.1) and Four Mile Polychrome bowls (AD 1300–1400) (McCreery and Malotki 1994:fig. 4.4e) have similar figures with kachina-like faces.

7. Typically, "Pueblo II–III" frogs and

lizards are pictured on Pinnawa Red-on-white and Kechipawan Polychrome (Smith et al. 1966:figs. 44k and 47i). Dates for these pottery types fall between AD 1350 and 1450 and 1375 and 1475, respectively (Sundt 1987:table 2). It is, therefore, possible that elements of the earlier style complex, which in most Pueblo regions we suggest ends ca. AD 1300, persisted at Zuni for another one hundred years or more.

8. The extensive sample of pottery provided from the Hodge excavations at Hawikuh provides two or three indisputable examples of kachinas, while there are several more that may be very abstract, iconographically "hidden" depictions (Barbara Mills, personal communication 2001; see also Smith et al. 1966:figs. 51c, 52l, 58d). Among the explicit examples is a Hawikuh Polychrome (AD 1630–1680) effigy vessel of a ducklike bird that may represent a Shalako kachina (Smith et al. 1966:332, plate 26g). Similar broadly triangular figures occur in Rio Grande rock art with beaks, mantas, necklaces, etc. There is a mask with a toothed mouth on Matsaki Polychrome (ca. AD 1475–late 1600s) (Smith et al. 1966:326, fig. 51k); the last, dating from the seventeenth century and looking very contemporary, is the Hopi chief kachina, Ahola, on Hawikuh Polychrome (Smith et al. 1966:fig. 77h).

9. There is at least one painting on a Matsaki Polychrome pot of a typical shield design (Smith et al. 1966:fig. 56h). The circular field is divided vertically (the pot as illustrated should be turned 90 degrees counterclockwise), with bold, curved elements springing from this center line. This design occurs widely as a Rio Grande petroglyph shield design (Schaafsma 2000:39, fig. 3.8c), and the same design is present on one of the Dowa Yalanne shields (Young 1988:81, fig. 36).

10. Yet historically, the finely incised and painted kachina masks, including many that are peculiar to Zuni alone, give Zuni's rock imagery a contemporary identity of its own (Young 1988:figs. 69, 73–76). Most of these figures, with earlier conceptual roots in Pueblo culture history, appear to have originated in the nineteenth or twentieth century.

11. Offerings that include pottery along with beads, animal figurines, and turquoise mosaics at mountaintop shrines in the White Mountains of Arizona indicate that as late as the seventeenth century the Zuni visited shrines that had previously been used by Mogollon people well before AD 1300 (Greenwood and White 1970). In regard to the likelihood that Mogollon populations migrated into the Zuni regions ca. AD 1300, these offerings suggest continued interaction with the Mogollon homeland. Unfortunately, the shrines have been looted. Therefore, it is impossible to calculate the percentages of each of the pottery types that would denote the degree to which these shrines were visited by the Zuni vs. the Mogollon populations.

12. An historic reference (1692) by Governor Vargas to a trail between the Zuni region and Senacu on the Rio Grande below Socorro is of interest: "An Indian from Halona Pueblo on the penol had experience in having traveled the direct route and road from the water hole of El Morro. . . . Paying him well, he will point out the way to go and take me and the camp to the pueblo of Senecu" (Kessell and Hendricks 1992:580). This was a trail unknown to the Spaniards but apparently well known to the Zuni. How long it had been in use is of course unknown, but it does demonstrate that an established Native route existed between the Zuni and the southern Pueblo provinces of the Rio Grande valley. Knowledge of the kachina cult could easily have traveled along similar routes from east to west beginning in the 1300s.

16 Mogollon and Zuni Perishable Traditions and the Question of Zuni Origins

Laurie Webster

Perishables are among the most culturally sensitive of all human creations, long regarded by anthropologists and others as prime markers of social group identity. Their strong analytical value is reflected in the many patterned choices, steps, and manipulations involved in their manufacture. Viewed in concert, these actions convey an artifact signature that is measurable and culturally diagnostic (Adovasio 1970). In the U.S. Southwest and surrounding regions archaeologists have made use of these qualities to explore such issues as technological style, the organization of production, culture change, social interaction, cultural identity, cultural affiliation, and migration (e.g., Adovasio 1970, 1971, 1974, 1980; Adovasio and Andrews 1985; Adovasio and Gunn 1986; Cosgrove 1947; Fowler 1996; Geib 2000a; Hays 1992; Hays-Gilpin et al. 1998; Hyland 1997; Hyland and Adovasio 2000; Kent 1957, 1983; Magers 1986; Matson 1991; McBrinn 2002; Morris and Burgh 1941; Teague 1992a, 1992b, 1996, 1998, 2000; Webster 1997, 1999, 2000, 2003; Webster and Hays-Gilpin 1994; Webster and Loma'omvaya 2004; Weltfish 1932).

My assignment for the seminar was to examine the distribution of perishable artifacts in the U.S. Southwest to see what these patterns might contribute to our understanding of Mogollon-Zuni relationships. For this study I selected 22 classes of fabrics, baskets, sandals, and ritual wooden objects that seemed to me particularly diagnostic for assessing relationships among the Mogollon and surrounding regions. I first examined the distributions of these materials within the various Mogollon branches and then, for comparative purposes, among the neighboring cultures of the Jornada Mogollon, Hohokam, ancestral Pueblo or "Anasazi," the Trans-Pecos region of New Mexico and Texas, the deserts and mountains of northern Mexico, and the eastern Great Basin. Finally, I looked at the distributions of these same material classes at Zuni. Although these 22 artifact classes do not constitute the full range of Mogollon and Zuni perishables, I consider them to represent the most common perishable types used by the people of these societies. With the exception of the Zuni materials, many of which I studied firsthand, most of this information is derived from the literature and not from personal observation.

This chapter is organized into four basic sections. In the first I offer some preliminary interpretations about the origins, trajectories, and regional boundaries of Mogollon perishables vis-à-vis the U.S. Southwest and northern Mexico. Due to space limitations I paint this picture broadly and omit much of the documentation from surrounding regions. After summarizing these patterns, I conclude this section with some thoughts about Mogollon-Basketmaker relationships. In the second section I provide a detailed description of the various classes of Mogollon perishables and their distributions and variability within five Mogollon branches. I follow this with an overview of late prehistoric and early historic Zuni perishables and conclude with some thoughts about what these patterns might mean about Mogollon-Zuni relationships and the question of Zuni origins.

The Mogollon Perishables Database

My literature search for the 22 targeted artifact classes yielded examples from 61 Mogollon and Mogollon-Pueblo sites in the five geographical branches. I use Wheat's (1955) branch designations but incorporate some of Martin's (1979) revisions, such as his extension of the Black River branch south of the Gila River and his inclusion of the Reserve area in the Cibola branch (see figs. 1.1 and 1.2, chap. 1, this vol. for drainage locations and branch boundaries). Figure 16.1 illustrates the geographic distribution of the 61 sites, while table 16.1 lists these sites by branch and summarizes the types of perishables reported from each; site numbers in this table are keyed to those in figure 16.1.

Spatially and temporally, the Mogollon perishables database is an uneven one. Since perishables are most often preserved in dry caves, the Mogollon sample is heavily biased toward seasonally occupied rockshelters and small shrines and against open-air settlements. Because of the frequent and sometimes intensive prehistoric use of caves in the Mimbres, Cibola, Black River, and San Simon branches, quite a bit is known about perishables from these regions. The Mimbres branch produced the greatest number of sites in the sample, largely due to Cosgrove's (1947) intensive survey of caves in the upper Gila. In addition to well-preserved collections from cave shrines such as Mule Creek Cave and Bear Creek Cave, carbonized perishables have also been recovered from the open-air Mimbres sites of Cameron Creek Village, Harris Village, NAN Ranch Ruin, and Swarts Ruin.[1]

The Cibola branch furnished perishables from 14 sites, including the important Reserve-area sites of Tularosa and Cordova caves. Much of our knowledge of Mogollon perishables comes from detailed studies of materials from caves in the Reserve area, some of which saw sporadic use as shrines, others as long-term, albeit seasonal, occupations dating as early as the Early Agricultural period (Martin et al. 1954; Martin et al. 1952). Early perishables were also recovered from Bat Cave, northeast of the Reserve area. (For a discussion of problems related to the dating of deposits from Tularosa Cave and Bat Cave see Bullard 1962:77–79 and Wills 1988a, respectively.) Within the Pine Lawn Valley proper, the Tularosa phase site

of Higgins Flat Pueblo produced a surprising number of burned perishable materials, and two open-air settlements on the northern periphery of the Cibola branch (Quemado Alegre [LA 5407] and Site 616 on Mariana Mesa) also produced charred fabrics and basketry.

Except for some basketry from the pithouse village of Bear Ruin and the large, late assemblage from Canyon Creek Pueblo, practically nothing is known about perishables in the Forestdale branch. However, the adjacent Black River branch produced at least 10 sites and one locale (Mount Baldy) with perishables. McEuen Cave yielded a large and significant (but poorly documented and still essentially unpublished) assemblage of perishables, including an AMS-dated twined bag and atlatl dated to ca. 400–180 cal BC and 721–260 cal BC, respectively (Moreno 2000). This assemblage also contains artifacts probably contemporaneous with the Canyon Creek phase. Early basketry is also known from the Early Agricultural period Cienega Creek site near Point of Pines. A few textiles and wooden artifacts came from the Circle Prairie phase site of Crooked Ridge Village, and an important collection of baskets was recovered from a cave in the Pinaleño Mountains. The post–AD 1250 site of Point of Pines Ruin produced a sizable but poorly preserved and still unpublished collection of charred perishable materials dated to the Maverick Mountain phase. Other late perishables are known from caves near Point of Pines, on Bonita Creek, and along the middle Gila River.

Finally, the San Simon branch yielded perishables from six caves. Winchester Cave, at the western end, has a strong Hohokam feel, whereas sites to the south and east represent a blend of Mimbres, Jornada Mogollon, and northern Chihuahua influences.

This latter region is clearly peripheral to the Mogollon heartland and exhibits strong connections to northern Mexico.

Origins, Trajectories, and Boundaries of Mogollon Perishables

With the preservation biases and uneven spatial distributions of these data in mind I now offer some preliminary interpretations about the origins, trends, and spatial relationships of Mogollon perishables, temporally ordered and based on the results of my literature survey. Readers interested in the technological attributes and distributions of these artifact classes will find a more detailed discussion in the second part of this chapter. I put forth these observations about Mogollon perishables with the caveat that, since direct dates are lacking for nearly all and because I have examined only a handful of them firsthand, I view these ideas as hypotheses to be tested and as a springboard for future research. Except for the radiocarbon-dated twined bag and atlatl from McEuen Cave (see table 16.1), all of the dates and phase distributions discussed here are based on excavation levels, which in cave contexts in particular are notoriously problematic. Some of these interpretations are likely to change when more direct dates become available.

The Early Agricultural Period (ca. 1750 BC–AD 150)

I begin with the idea that the roots of a Mogollon perishable tradition are distinguishable very early on, well before the emergence of the pottery-making, pithouse-dwelling Mogollon. (For a similar conclusion see Adovasio et al. 1996:27; Hyland and Adovasio 2000:148.) This early

Table 16.1 Mogollon and Mogollon-Pueblo Sites with Evidence of Fabrics, Basketry, Sandals, and Wooden Ritual Objects (by Branch)

Site Name	Map Reference[a]	Site Type	Temporal Association	Basketry	Sandals	Fabrics	Ritual Wood	Bibliographic Reference[b]
Black River branch								
Bonita Creek	1	Cave shrine	Tularosa phase	•	•		•	28
Cienega Creek	2	Campsite	Early Agricultural period	•				13
Crooked Ridge Village	3	Pithouse settlement	Circle Prairie phase	•	•		•	30, 31
McEuen Cave	4	Burial cave (early); habitation (later)	Early Agricultural and late prehistoric periods	•	•	•	•	19
Mount Baldy	5	Mountaintop shrine	Late prehistoric and/or historic periods(?)				•	25
Pinaleño cotton cache	6	Cave shrine	Encinas phase and earlier(?)	•				15
Pine Flat Cave	7	Cave habitation	Nantack, Reserve, and Tularosa phases	•	•	•	•	10
Point of Pines	8	Pueblo	Maverick Mountain phase	•	•	•		26, 29
Red Bow Cliff Dwelling	9	Cave habitation with ceremonial room	Canyon Creek phase	•	•	•	•	10
Cave near Solomonville	10	Cave shrine	Undated context			•		18
Tule Tubs Cave	11	Cave habitation	Nantack, Reserve, and Canyon Creek phases	•	•	•		10
Cibola branch								
Bat Cave	12	Cave campsite	Early Agricultural period and Basketmaker III through Pueblo II(?)	•	•		•	8
Cordova Cave	13	Cave campsite (early); habitation (later)	Early Agricultural period through Reserve phase	•	•	•	•	21
Cosper Cliff Dwelling	14	Cave habitation	Tularosa phase		•		•	22
Higgins Flat Pueblo	15	Pueblo	Tularosa phase	•		•		23
Hinkle Park Cliff Dwelling	16	Cave habitation	Transitional Reserve through Tularosa phases	•	•		•	22
Kelly Cave	17	Cave campsite (early); campsite or habitation (later)	Early Agricultural period(?) and Reserve through Tularosa phases and earlier(?)	•	•	•	•	6
Luna Valley caves	18	Cave shrines	Undated context				•	17

Table 16.1 *Continued*

Site Name	Map Reference[a]	Site Type	Temporal Association	Basketry	Sandals	Fabrics	Ritual Wood	Bibliographic Reference[b]
Mariana Mesa Site 616	19	Pueblo	Pueblo III	•		•		24
O Block Cave	20	Cave campsite (early); shrine (late)	Early Agricultural period through Tularosa phase	•	•		•	22
Quemado Alegre	21	Pithouse settlement	Early Pithouse period	•	•	•		2
Saddle Mountain Cliff Ruin	22	Cave habitation and shrine	Reserve through Tularosa phases or earlier(?)				•	6
Spur Ranch region	23	Cave site	Undated context	•		•		18
Tularosa Cave	24	Burial cave and campsite (early); habitation (later)	Early Agricultural period through Tularosa phase	•	•	•	•	18, 21
Y Canyon Cave	25	Cave campsite	Pine Lawn through Reserve phases		•			22
Forestdale branch								
Bear Ruin	26	Pithouse settlement	Forestdale phase	•				14
Canyon Creek	27	Cave habitation with ceremonial room	Canyon Creek phase	•	•	•	•	11
Mimbres branch								
Bear Creek Cave	28	Cave shrine	Reserve through Tularosa phases or earlier(?)	•		•	•	18
Johnson Cave	29	Cave shrine	Reserve through Tularosa phases(?)				•	18
Cameron Creek Village	30	Pueblo	Classic period		•			4
Doolittle Cave	31	Cave campsite (early); shrine (later)	Early Agricultural period(?) and Reserve phase or earlier(?)	•	•	•	•	6
Harris Village	32	Pithouse settlement	Three Circle phase	•		•		12
Lone Mountain Cave	33	Cave shrine	Reserve through Tularosa phases or earlier(?)				•	6
NAN Ranch Ruin	34	Pithouse settlement and pueblo	San Francisco phase through Classic period	•	•	•		1
Swarts Ruin	35	Pueblo	Classic period	•	•			7
Cave 1, Middle Fork	36	Cave campsite	San Francisco through Tularosa phases or earlier(?)		•	•	•	6

Table 16.1 *Continued*

Site Name	Map Reference[a]	Site Type	Temporal Association	Basketry	Sandals	Fabrics	Ritual Wood	Bibliographic Reference[b]
Cave 2, Middle Fork	37	Cave campsite	San Francisco through Reserve phases(?)		•		•	6
Cave 2, West Fork	38	Burial cave (early); campsite (later)	Georgetown phase(?) and Tularosa phase(?)	•	•	•	•	6
Cliff Ruin 2, West Fork	39	Cave habitation	San Francisco through Tularosa phases(?)			•		6
Site 2a, Cave Canyon	40	Cave cache	San Francisco through Tularosa phases(?)	•				6
Site 3, Gila River	41	Cave campsite and shrine	Reserve through Tularosa phases(?)		•		•	6
Site 1, Mogollon Creek	42	Cave shrine	Reserve through Tularosa phases(?)				•	6
Cliff Ruin 1, SA Canyon	43	Cave habitation	San Francisco through Reserve phases(?)			•		6
Cliff Ruin 7, Sapillo Creek	44	Cave habitation	Reserve through Tularosa phases			•	•	6
Gila Cliff Dwellings	45	Cave habitation	Tularosa phase	•	•	•	•	3
Unnamed cave near Gila Cliff Dwellings	46	Cave shrine	Reserve through Tularosa phases(?)				•	16
Greenwood Cave	47	Cave shrine	Reserve through Tularosa phases or earlier(?)			•	•	6, 18
Little Bear Canyon Cave	48	Cave shrine	Reserve through Tularosa phases or later(?)				•	3
Steamboat Cave	49	Cave campsite (early); campsite and shrine (later)	Early Agricultural period(?) and Reserve through Tularosa phases or earlier(?)	•	•	•	•	6
Water Canyon Cave (Cave 6)	50	Cave shrine	Reserve through Tularosa phases or earlier(?)	•	•		•	6
Unnamed cave, Cliff Valley	51	Cave shrine	Tularosa and Cliff phases	•		•	•	27
Cave 1, Goat Basin	52	Cave campsite (early); shrine (later)	Early Agricultural period(?) and Reserve through Tularosa phases or earlier(?)	•	•	•	•	6

Table 16.1 *Continued*

Site Name	Map Reference[a]	Site Type	Temporal Association	Basketry	Sandals	Fabrics	Ritual Wood	Bibliographic Reference[b]
Cave 5, Sipe Canyon	53	Cave campsite	Reserve through Tularosa phases(?)		•	•	•	6
Mule Creek Cave	54	Cave campsite (early); shrine (later)	Early Agricultural period(?) and San Francisco through Reserve phases or earlier(?)	•	•	•	•	6
Cave 9, Table Top Mountain	55	Cave campsite	San Francisco through Tularosa phases(?)	•				6
San Simon branch								
Buffalo Cave	56	Cave campsite	Animas phase(?)	•	•		•	6, 20
Cave 3, Deer Creek	57	Cave campsite	San Francisco through Tularosa phases(?)	•			•	6, 20
Pinnacle Cave	58	Cave campsite	Animas phase(?)	•	•		•	6
Tom Ketchum Cave	59	Cave shrine and rock art site	Encinas phase(?)				•	5
U Bar Cave	60	Cave shrine	Animas phase and earlier(?)	•	•	•	•	20
Winchester Cave	61	Cave shrine	Encinas phase(?)		•		•	9

[a]Numbers correspond to those on the map in figure 16.1.

[b]Primary site references: (1) Adovasio et al. (1996); (2) Akins (1998); (3) Anderson et al. (1986); (4) Bradfield (1931); (5) Burton (1988); (6) Cosgrove (1947); (7) Cosgrove and Cosgrove (1932); (8) Dick (1965); (9) Fulton (1941); (10) Gifford (1980); (11) Haury (1934); (12) Haury (1936a); (13) Haury (1957); (14) Haury (1985a); (15) Haury and Huckell (1993); (16) Hibben (1938); (17) Hough (1907); (18) Hough (1914); (19) Kelly (1937); (20) Lambert and Ambler (1961); (21) Martin et al. (1952); (22) Martin et al. (1954); (23) Martin et al. (1956); (24) McGimsey (1980); (25) Morris (1982); (26) Teague (1999); (27) Walt (1978); (28) Wasley (1962); (29) Webster (2001); (30) Wheat (1954); (31) Wheat (1955).

Mogollon tradition derives from the Cochise culture and has its roots in the Desert Archaic tradition. Early evidence of perishables comes from caves on the margins of the Mimbres, Pinos Altos, and southern Mogollon Mountains and from the Plains of San Augustín (see table 16.1 and fig. 16.1). If the published dates for these early Mogollon cave collections are reasonably accurate (e.g., Dick 1965; Martin et al. 1954; Martin et al. 1952; Moreno 2000; Wills 1988a; but see Bullard 1962:77–79), then by the late Early Agricultural period, if not earlier, a distinctive Mogollon textile and basketry tradition can be identified in the Mimbres, Black River, and Cibola branches, as far west as the Point of

Pines region, and perhaps in other branches where early perishable materials have not yet been discovered or are not preserved. Most of these artifacts probably date to the latter part of the Early Agricultural period, between about 800 BC and AD 150 (see Gregory 2001b). Direct AMS dating of a broad sample of these materials is an important goal for future research.

Hallmarks of this Early Agricultural Mogollon tradition include twined rabbit-fur robes (see fig. 16.2a), twined and looped bags (see fig. 16.2b–d), two- and four-warp wickerwork sandals (see fig. 16.3c, d), and coiled baskets with one-rod, two-rod-and-bundle, and bundle-with-

rod-core foundations (see fig. 16.4a–c). Many of these same technologies continued to play an important role in Mogollon perishable assemblages up through the end of the first millennium AD, demonstrating considerable continuity through time. A rudimentary, cave-focused ritual tradition may also have emerged during the Early Agricultural period, based on the presence of incised twigs and unpeeled simple twig pahos, or prayer sticks, with different forms of attachments in caves of the upper Gila drainage (see fig. 16.5a).

Ancestors of the Mogollon appear to have participated in a widespread Late Archaic hunting and gathering tradition that extended from the

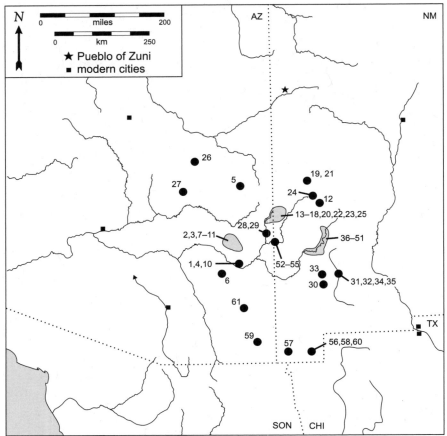

Figure 16.1. The location of 61 Mogollon and Mogollon-Pueblo sites included in the study in the five geographical branches. Site numbers are keyed to table 16.1.

eastern Great Basin to central and northern Arizona and across southern Arizona and New Mexico to the Trans-Pecos region of Texas, western Oklahoma, and inland northern Mexico (e.g., Baker and Kidder 1937; Guernsey and Kidder 1921; Haury 1957; Howard 1932, 1935; Kelly 1937; Kidder and Guernsey 1919; Mera 1938; Moreno 2000; Schroeder 1983). Archaeological correlates of this tradition include the use of caves as burial sites, temporary camps, and storage facilities; the interment of the dead in baskets or twined bags; and a distinctive suite of perishable material culture, including twined rabbit-fur robes, nets, coiled baskets, twined and looped bags, grooved wooden clubs (fending sticks), and atlatls. Adovasio (1970, 1980; see also Hy-

land 1997; Hyland and Adovasio 2000) has argued that this Archaic perishable tradition derives from an early admixture of traits from northern Mexico and the Great Basin. While these assemblages point primarily to a hunting and gathering lifeway, many of these sites also contain evidence of maize agriculture by some of these early groups.

Between 1000 and 500 BC this widespread pattern appears to become more localized across the southern Southwest. Early assemblages from the Mimbres and Reserve areas share important elements of the northern Chihuahuan Desert tradition with sites east of the Rio Grande, whereas the Hueco sites near present-day El Paso show strong connections with the Trans-Pecos region

and Coahuila (Beckes and Adovasio 1982). To the north the perishable traditions of the Jornada Basin show considerable admixture of Cochise- and Trans-Pecos-derived traits (Haury 1950; Hyland 1997; Hyland and Adovasio 2000; McBrinn 2002, 2005).

A decent perishables database exists for early Mogollon, Jornada Mogollon, and Trans-Pecos perishables, but the same cannot be said for areas to the south and west.[2] The only Sonoran Desert site I am aware of that might have produced a sample of Early Agricultural period perishables is Ventana Cave. Although Haury (1950:358, 411, 443) felt that perishable materials were generally not preserved in preceramic levels at the site, some of the Ventana Cave artifacts closely resemble Early Agricultural collections from the Mogollon region and could in fact be early. In the present discussion I follow other researchers (e.g., Matson 1991) in speculating that these materials may represent, to some degree, early technologies in the region, but direct AMS dating is necessary to resolve this question.

One artifact class that appears to have served as an important boundary marker between those Early Agricultural groups utilizing the Mimbres and Reserve areas and people of the surrounding regions is the weft-faced plain-weave sandal, more commonly known as the wickerwork sandal. During the Archaic and Early Agricultural periods most groups in the southern Southwest appear to have used some type of wickerwork sandal, with regional differences found in form and manufacture. For example, people in the Trans-Pecos region, Jornada Basin, northern Coahuila, and probably Chihuahua typically wore a short "scuffer-toe" sandal that covered just the ball and instep of the foot. Most of these sandals were

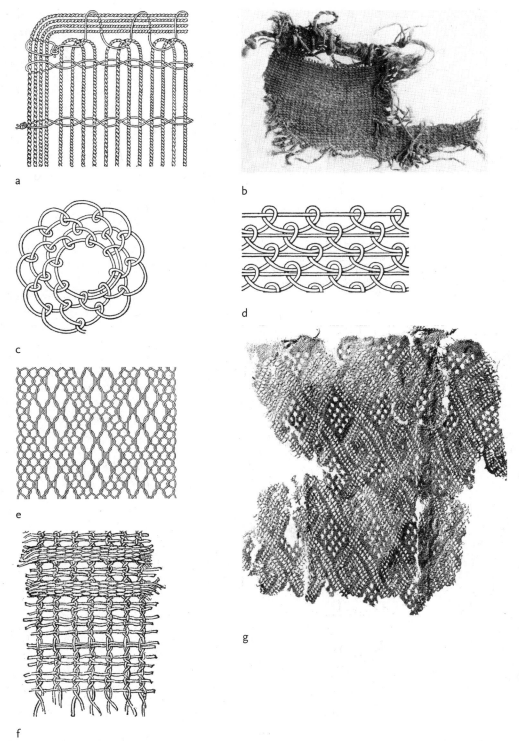

Figure 16.2. Mogollon twined, looped, and openwork fabrics: (a) open-twined fur blanket, Mule Creek Cave, undated, possibly 300 BC–AD 200; (b) close-twined bag fragment, Tularosa Cave, AD 700–825/850; (c) simple looping, showing method of beginning a bag; (d) looping on foundation cords, Steamboat Cave, undated, possibly 300 BC–AD 200; (e) interlinked band, Mule Creek Cave, undated, probably AD 1000–1400; (f) gauze-weave fabric, Bear Creek Cave, undated, probably AD 1000–1400; (g) weft-wrap openwork fragment, Mule Creek Cave, undated, probably AD 1000–1400 (a, c, d, e, and g from Cosgrove 1947:figs. 23a, 26a, 26d, 30b, and 86d, reproduced courtesy of the Peabody Museum of Archaeology and Ethnology, Harvard University; b from Martin et al. 1952:fig. 113, reproduced courtesy of the Field Museum Press; f from Hough 1914:fig. 165).

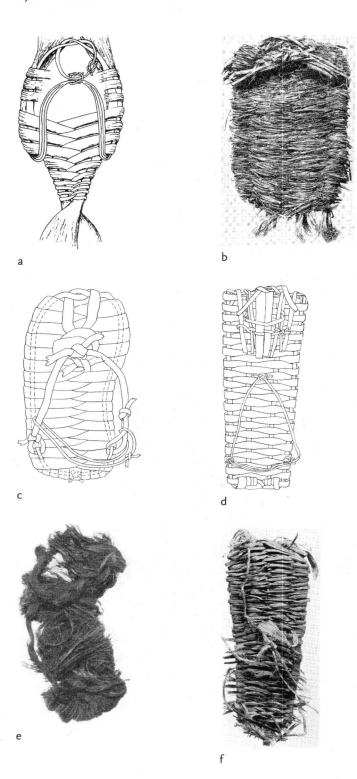

a

b

c

d

e

f

Figure 16.3. Comparison of Late Archaic and Early Agricultural period wickerwork sandals from the Trans-Pecos, Mogollon, Hohokam, and ancestral Pueblo (Kayenta) regions: (a) Trans-Pecos two-warp scuffer-toe sandal with fishtail heel, Hueco area, unidentified site; (b) Trans-Pecos two-warp scuffer-toe sandal, Hueco area, unidentified site; (c) Mogollon full-length two-warp sandal, Tularosa or Cordova cave; (d) Mogollon full-length four-warp sandal with warp elements folded back over toe, Tularosa or Cordova cave; (e) Hohokam two-warp sandal, Ventana Cave; (f) Basketmaker II four-warp sandal, Cave 1, Kinboko Canyon (a, b from Cosgrove 1947:figs. 90, type 4b, 87, type 2b, reproduced courtesy of the Peabody Museum of Archaeology and Ethnology, Harvard University; c, d from Martin et al. 1952:figs. 88c, 90 center, reproduced courtesy of the Field Museum Press; e from Haury 1950:plate 44d, reproduced courtesy of the Arizona State Museum, University of Arizona and The Arizona Board of Regents; f from Kidder and Guernsey 1919:plate 67a).

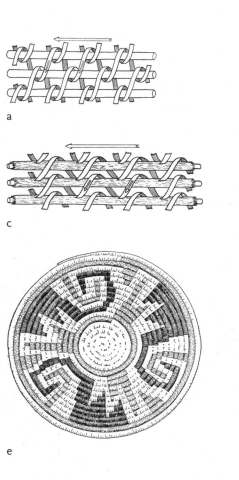

a

c

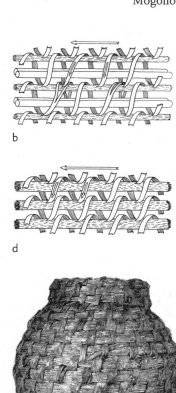

b

d

e

f

g

h

Figure 16.4. Mogollon coiled basketry: (a) one-rod foundation with interlocking stitch; (b) two-rod-and-bundle foundation with noninterlocking stitch; (c) bundle-with-rod-core foundation with noninterlocking stitch; (d) bundle foundation with noninterlocking stitch; (e) decorated basketry bowl with two-rod-and-bundle foundation and interlocking design, Water Canyon Cave, undated, probably AD 1000–1400; (f) coarse-coiled basketry jar with bundle foundation and spaced stitches, Canyon Creek Ruin, AD 1325–1350; (g) coarse-coiled granary basket with bundle foundation, spaced coiling, and lid, McEuen Cave, undated, probably AD 1200–1400; (h) miniature basketry paho with two-rod-and-bundle foundation, Bear Creek Cave, undated, probably AD 1000–1400 (a–d from Morris and Burgh 1941:figs. 3a, 3j, 3g, and 3e; e from Cosgrove 1947:fig. 35a, reproduced courtesy of the Peabody Museum of Archaeology and Ethnology, Harvard University; f from Haury 1934:plate LId, reproduced courtesy of the Arizona State Museum, University of Arizona; g from Kelly 1937:plate VIII, reproduced courtesy of the Arizona State Museum, University of Arizona; h from Hough 1914:fig. 317).

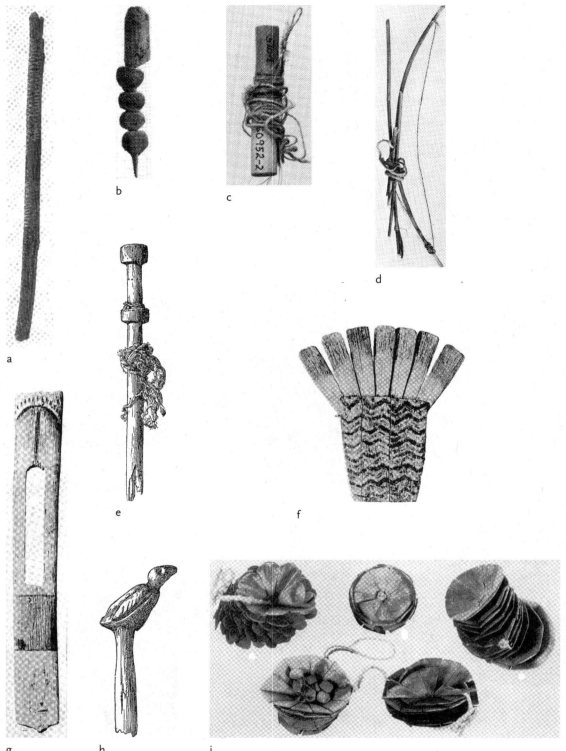

Figure 16.5. Mogollon ritual wooden objects: (a) simple twig paho, Tularosa Cave, 300 BC–AD 200(?); (b) juniper-berry skewer, Tularosa Cave, unidentified context, possibly a trap trigger; (c) reed cigarette, Tularosa Cave, unidentified context; (d) miniature bow and arrows, Tularosa Cave, unidentified context; (e) roundel paho, Bear Creek Cave, undated, probably AD 1000–1400; (f) part of a decorated tablita, Mule Creek Cave, undated, probably AD 1000–1400; (g) decorated split-stick wand, Steamboat Cave, undated, probably AD 1000–1400; (h) carved staff with bird head, Bear Creek Cave, undated, probably AD 1000–1400; (i) carved wooden flowers, Bonita Creek Cache, AD 1280–1300 (a–d from Martin et al. 1952:figs. 148c, 1530, 154d, 152, reproduced courtesy of the Field Museum Press; e and h from Hough 1914:figs. 201, 213; f and g from Cosgrove 1947:figs. 126c, 124e, reproduced courtesy of the Peabody Museum of Archaeology and Ethnology, Harvard University; i from Wasley 1962:fig. 4, reproduced courtesy of the Arizona State Museum, University of Arizona).

finished with a "fishtail" heel, made by allowing the warps to protrude at the rear (see fig. 16.3a, b; see also Cosgrove 1947:figs. 87–90, Types 1–5). In contrast, groups related to the Cochise cultural tradition, including those in the Mimbres and Reserve branches, typically wore full-length wickerwork sandals lacking the fishtail heel. The heels of these sandals were made by tying the warp ends together and trimming them flush with the sandal body to produce a sandal oval to rectangular in outline (see fig. 16.3c–e; see also Cosgrove 1947:figs. 91, 92, Type 8; Martin et al. 1952:figs. 87, 88; McBrinn 2002). The only examples of scuffer-toe or fishtail sandals in my Mogollon sample are a few scuffer-toe sandals from Doolittle Cave on the Mimbres River and Bat Cave on the Plains of San Augustín and some sandals with fishtail heels from a few sites in the San Simon region.[3] Both the scuffer-toe and full-length styles were used by Late Archaic and Early Agricultural groups in the Jornada Basin and areas farther north along the Rio Grande (e.g., McBrinn 2002:tables 21, 22) and by later populations in Chihuahua (King 1974:90; Lister 1958:85).

Overlapping distributions of sandal and atlatl styles in the lower Rio Grande valley of present-day northern Chihuahua, western Texas, and southern New Mexico identify this as a region of considerable population mobility and social interaction during the Late Archaic and Early Agricultural periods (Cosgrove 1947:fig. 32; Ferg and Peachey 1998:189, 191, fig. 8; Hyland and Adovasio 2000:147–148). The presence of four-warp wickerwork sandals, two-rod-and-bundle coiled baskets, looped fabrics, simple twig pahos, and certain mortuary practices at a number of Late Archaic and Early Agricultural sites in this region suggests a close relationship between groups utilizing the Guada-

lupe Mountains and southern Jornada Basin east of the Rio Grande and those of the Mimbres drainage and Mogollon Highlands (Cosgrove 1947; McBrinn 2002; Mera 1938; Schroeder 1983). Early Jornada Mogollon perishable assemblages also incorporate a number of Trans-Pecos- and northern Mexican–derived styles not usually found in contemporaneous Mogollon assemblages, including plaited baskets and mats and wickerwork sandals with fishtail heels, suggesting strong southern connections for these groups.

To the west early people in the Mogollon region, Sonoran Desert, and eastern Great Basin shared the same ovoid style of wickerwork sandal. These sandals, however, exhibit important differences in technological style. Early Agricultural groups in the Cibola, Mimbres, and Black River branches of the Mogollon region evidently used two-, four-, five-, and six-warp varieties of wickerwork sandals (see fig. 16.3c, d), whereas only the two-warp style was found at Ventana Cave and the Nevada site of Etna Cave (see fig. 16.3e; Haury 1950:433–435; Wheeler 1973:18–21, figs. 17, 18, 41). Moreover, the warp construction in the two-warp wickerwork sandals from Ventana Cave differs from that found in the sandals from Tularosa Cave and the upper Gila. The warps of the Ventana Cave sandals are composed of one continuous leaf knotted at the heel, whereas the warps of the Mogollon sandals are typically fabricated from two leaves tied together at the toe and heel (Martin et al. 1952: 234). These differences in low-visibility attributes suggest the presence of different learning or enculturative networks between these groups (J. Clark 2001, chap. 4, this vol.; McBrinn 2002). Together with different constellations of coiled basketry constructions and what appears to be a lesser emphasis on looped fabrics in

the west, these differences suggest the existence of a technological and stylistic boundary in perishable manufacture between people of the western Sonoran Desert and eastern Great Basin, on the one hand, and those of the Mogollon region, on the other, dating as far back as the Early Agricultural period.

The Early Pithouse Period (ca. AD 150–700)

Differences between groups in the Mogollon region and their eastern and western neighbors intensified during the Early and Late Pithouse periods as twined turkey-feather blankets and plain-weave fabrics of yucca and later cotton were added to the Mogollon repertoire. The early appearance of noncotton plain weaves (see fig. 16.6d), a Mexican tradition, at a wide range of Mogollon sites during the Early Pithouse period presages their importance for the remainder of the Mogollon sequence. Although noncotton plain-weave fabrics are found, though not well dated, at Ventana Cave, turkey-feather blankets are not reported from Hohokam sites. Neither tradition is characteristic of the Jornada Basin during this time.

Two new Mogollon sandal types appeared toward the end of this period: plaited sandals (see fig. 16.7g) and multiple-warp cord sandals (see fig. 16.7e). Like noncotton plain weaves, the plaited sandals show strong connections to perishable traditions in Chihuahua and Coahuila. The multiple-warp cord sandals, on the other hand, share their affinities with the Colorado Plateau. Technically a variant of the wickerwork sandal, the multiple-warp cord sandal is rare in the Mimbres branch but relatively common in the Cibola branch at Tularosa Cave and Quemado Alegre. Dates from Quemado Alegre

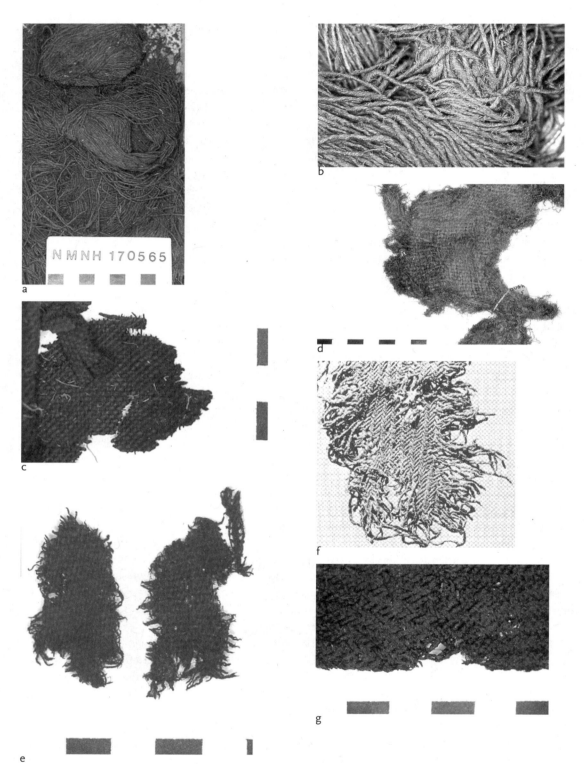

Figure 16.6. Mogollon and Zuni cordage and plain-weave and oblique-interlaced (braided) fabrics: (a) carbonized S-spun yucca yarn, Tularosa Cave, unidentified context, probably AD 1000–1400; (b) carbonized S-spun yucca yarn, Hawikuh Pueblo, ca. AD 1400–1680; (c) carbonized cotton plain-weave cloth, Hawikuh, ca. AD 1400–1680; (d) yucca plain-weave cloth, Spur Ranch, undated, probably AD 1000–1400; (e) carbonized yucca plain-weave cloth, Hawikuh, ca. AD 1400–1680; (f) cotton oblique 3/3 twill interlaced fabric, probably the remains of a sash, Mule Creek Cave, undated context, probably AD 1100–1400; (g) yucca(?) oblique 3/3 twill interlaced fabric, probably the remains of a braided sash, Hawikuh, AD 1400–1680 (a, c, d used courtesy of the National Museum of Natural History, Department of Anthropology, Smithsonian Institution, catalog nos. A-170565, A-305458, and A-232025, photos by the author; b, e, and g used courtesy of the National Museum of the American Indian, Smithsonian Institution, catalog nos. 10/9025, 12/4694, and 12/4696, photos by the author; f from Cosgrove 1947:fig. 84e, reproduced courtesy of the Peabody Museum of Archaeology and Ethnology, Harvard University).

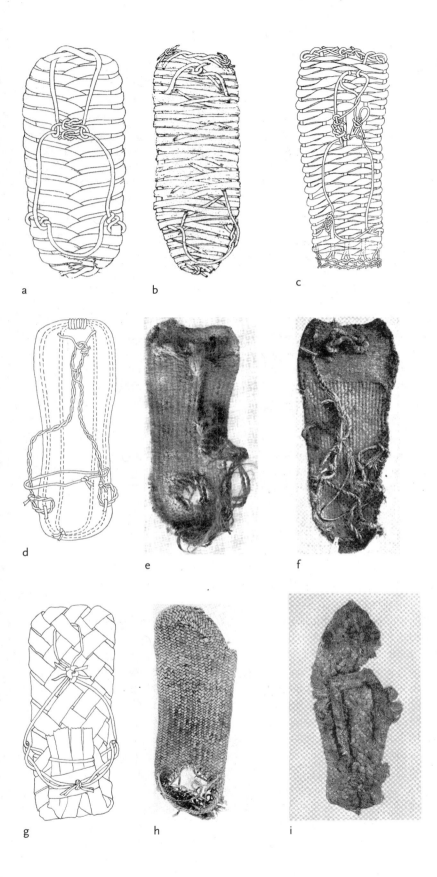

a   b   c

d   e   f

g   h   i

Figure 16.7. Mogollon and ancestral Pueblo plain-weave (wickerwork), twined, and twill-plaited sandals: (a) Mogollon plain-weave two-warp sandal with yucca-leaf warp and shredded fiber weft; (b) Mogollon plain-weave two-warp sandal with yucca-leaf warp and rigid yucca-leaf weft; (c) Mogollon plain-weave five-warp sandal; (d) Mogollon plain-weave four-warp sandal with concentric warp, showing warp arrangement; (e) Mogollon multiple-warp cord sandal with plain-weave center, twined heel, and scalloped toe, Tularosa Cave, AD 600–1000; (f) Basketmaker III twined sandal with scalloped toe, Cave 1, Segi Canyon, AD 600–750; (g) construction of Mogollon plaited sandal with wide agave- or yucca-leaf elements and turned-up heel, Tularosa or Cordova Cave, post–AD 700; (h) ancestral Pueblo plaited sandal, Olla Cave near Kayenta, AD 1100–1300; (i) finely plaited sandal with H-shaped strap, Canyon Creek Ruin, AD 1325–1350 (a, b, c from Cosgrove 1947:fig. 92, Types 11, 8, and 12, reproduced courtesy of the Peabody Museum of Archaeology and Ethnology, Harvard University; d, e, g from Martin et al. 1952:figs. 104 right, 97 center, 94 center, reproduced courtesy of the Field Museum Press; f from Guernsey 1931:plate 9, upper left; h from Kidder and Guernsey 1919:plate 36a; i from Haury 1934:plate XLIId, reproduced courtesy of the Arizona State Museum, University of Arizona).

suggest an appearance for this sandal style sometime after AD 500–550. In general appearance these sandals bear a striking resemblance to Basketmaker III twined sandals from the Four Corners region (see fig. 16.7f; see also Hays-Gilpin et al. 1998). Technologically, however, they are much simpler versions of their Basketmaker counterparts, and their warping methods and weave structures differ. They appear to represent an emulation of the Basketmaker style by people in the Cibola branch and the southernmost extent of a shared stylistic tradition. (A sandal from Bat Cave, discussed in the second section of this chapter, is probably a real Basketmaker III sandal traded into the area rather than an attempt to emulate the style.) The presence of this sandal style as far south as Tularosa Cave suggests a high level of communication and interaction during the late AD 550s and 600s between Highland Mogollon populations of the Cibola branch and Basketmaker III groups on the Colorado Plateau.

Ritual activity also appears to have intensified in the Mimbres and Reserve areas during the Early Pithouse period, as suggested by the earliest documented evidence of reed cigarettes, tablitas (carved wooden objects that serve as wands, headgear, or altar paraphernalia), and ceremonial bows in the U.S. Southwest (see fig. 16.5). Ellis and Hammack (1968:39–40; see also Taube 2001), citing the importance of caves and smoke in pre-Classic Olmec and Maya cosmology, consider that region a likely source for the widespread Mesoamerican religious complex relating caves, clouds, smoke, breath, fertility, and the underworld. An early focus on the ritual use of caves in the Mimbres and Reserve branches appears to link these southwestern groups with this broad complex of beliefs (cf. Hill and

Hays-Gilpin 1999). In fact, the profusion of caves in this region might have served as a draw for populations for whom caves were an essential part of ritual practice. That reed cigarettes and other ritual paraphernalia may occur in caves as early as the Early Pithouse period (again, better dates are needed) suggests the presence of this symbolic complex in the southern Southwest long before its associated imagery appeared on Classic Mimbres pottery (Taube 2001:116).

It is not difficult to imagine Mesoamerican rituals related to rain and fertility being incorporated into early southwestern village life along with other aspects of maize cultivation. I am intrigued by the possible connections between early Mogollon ritual practices and ideas originating on the lower Gulf Coast and in the central valleys of Mexico because this fits my general perception that certain Mexican textile and basketry technologies spread northward along the eastern Sierra Madre Occidental into the northern Chihuahua Desert and the Mogollon region rather than from western Mexico. The apparent lack of reed cigarettes, stick pahos, and other forms of ritual wooden objects from sites in the Hohokam region or the southern Colorado Plateau until considerably later suggests that early societies in the Mogollon region may have been the conduit for the spread of these ritual traditions to neighboring southwestern groups. This may be preservation bias, however, given that so few early perishables are known from Hohokam sites.

The Late Pithouse Period (ca. AD 700–1000)

Encompassing the San Francisco and Three Circle phases, the Late Pithouse period saw the continuation of earlier perishable trends along with some important new additions. Disregard-

ing for a moment the fancier fabrics that appear at Mimbres sites toward the end of this period, the major new fabric to arrive upon the scene was cotton plain weave, yet another perishable tradition that spread north from Mexico. This period also saw increasing use of twill plaiting for mats, ring baskets, and sandals. This incremental addition of southern techniques to the Mogollon repertoire suggests continuing interactions with groups in northern Mexico and possibly the maintenance of ancestral ties between the people of these regions (see Lister 1958:110).

Plaited sandals are reported in small quantities at Mogollon and Basketmaker III sites during the preceding period, but they do not achieve much popularity in either region until after about AD 700. Mogollon and Pueblo plaited sandals tend to be stylistically distinct. Most Mogollon plaited sandals are made with wide yucca-leaf elements that are folded up at the heel and secured with a transverse strip of yucca (see fig. 16.7g). Although a similar style of sandal occurs at some Four Corners sites (e.g., Kidder and Guernsey 1919:plate 35b; Wheat 2003:fig. 5.1), most Pueblo examples incorporate narrow elements and lack the folded heel (see fig. 16.7h). Plaited sandals are rare at Hohokam sites except on the peripheries of the Hohokam region, and twill plaiting seems to be an unimportant Hohokam basketry or matting technique until Pueblo IV.

The carved pahos, painted *and* carved pahos, intricately carved and painted tablitas and split-stick wands, reed cigarettes, and vast quantities of ceremonial bows and arrows (see fig. 16.5) found in caves attributed to the Late Pithouse period suggest an intensification of ritual activities in the Reserve and Mimbres branches during this time. Caves continued to serve as important loci of ceremonial activity, both as shrines and as caches for ritual paraphernalia.

Pueblo II and Pueblo III (AD 1000–1250)

After AD 1000 twill plaiting appears to supersede all other techniques for basketry, matting, and sandals. One new type of object that became popular during this period was the plaited ring basket with braided rim (see fig. 16.8e). This decorative rim feature is also found on Pueblo III plaited baskets from the Four Corners region, where the style likely originated (see fig. 16.8d; see also Morris and Burgh 1941:23). Like the multiple-warp cord sandals of earlier times, these Mogollon ring baskets are more crudely made than their northern counterparts and appear to be local attempts to emulate a northern style.

Several open village sites dating to this period produced small assemblages of carbonized perishables. These include Swarts Ruin, NAN Ranch Ruin, and Cameron Creek Village in the Mimbres Valley, Higgins Flat Pueblo in the Reserve, and Mariana Mesa in the northern Cibola region. All of these yielded characteristic Mogollon perishable assemblages except for Mariana Mesa, which has more of an "Anasazi" or ancestral Pueblo feel (see also Mills, chap. 13, and Schaafsma and Young, chap. 15, this vol.). One textile described in the Mariana Mesa report sounds like twill tapestry, a popular technique on the Colorado Plateau that spread south of the Mogollon Rim in the AD 1200s.

If we had to rely entirely on the perishable remains from these open village sites, we would have little inkling of the fancier fabrics used in Classic Mimbres societies. Fortunately, ceramic depictions offer some clues, and collections from cave shrines provide an even richer pic-

ture, yielding examples of finely woven weft-wrapped openwork, gauze weave, and interlinked fabrics, all labor-intensive techniques (see fig. 16.2e–g). Many of these same fabrics also occur at Hohokam and West Mexican sites during this period, raising the possibility that some of the Mogollon examples could be trade goods. These openwork fabrics also occur at later Sinagua and Salado sites but are rare on the Colorado Plateau. Teague (1998) considers these openwork traditions to represent a major technological boundary between ancestral Pueblo societies on the Colorado Plateau and groups in the southern Southwest.

After about AD 1000 ritual paraphernalia became even more diverse and elaborate in the southern Mogollon region, as reflected by the painted wooden tablitas, split-stick wands, and carved pahos found in the caves of the upper Gila (see fig. 16.5e–g). Painted and carved bird forms appeared (see fig. 16.5h), and reed cigarettes became more highly decorated. Crook and roundel pahos found at these sites bear a strong resemblance to examples from the Colorado Plateau and may represent northern traditions that spread to the Mimbres Mogollon after AD 1000 or Mimbres styles that spread northward to Chaco and other areas (see Vokes and Gregory, chap. 17, this vol.).

Pueblo IV (AD 1250–1450)

The period between AD 1200 or 1250 and the abandonment of the Mogollon region around 1400–1450 is a fascinating time in terms of perishables production. Unfortunately, it is also poorly understood due to the scarcity of perishable collections from large late Mogollon–Pueblo villages. This period saw the continuing production of cotton and noncotton plain weaves, openwork weaves, and

plaited matting, ring baskets, and sandals as well as the appearance of several new techniques and forms, some suggesting influences from the Colorado Plateau or northern Mexico, others local development.

Among the influences believed to be from Mexico are plain-weave fabrics decorated with supplementary weft (brocade) or woven with rag wefts and some new basketry constructions, such as granary containers made by bundle-foundation coiling (see fig. 16.4d, f, g), intricately plaited mats, and round or square twill-plaited baskets, some lacking the wooden hoop at the rim and others double woven or made with doubled selvages (see fig. 16.8f–i). All are common constructions in northern Mexico (Zingg 1940:28–29, 70–89) and appear to represent new and late introductions to the U.S. Southwest. Teague (1996, 1998, 1999, 2000) has attributed the sudden appearance of supplementary-weft and rag-weft weaves to a migration of peoples from inland northern Mexico into the Tonto Basin and perhaps the western Mogollon region as well during the period AD 1320–1400. I agree with her interpretation and suggest that earlier evidence of this migration might be present in the Mimbres and Reserve areas by the AD 1200s and that the new basketry forms mentioned above are also part of this phenomenon. Another late basketry form that appears in the Mogollon region during this time is the wickerwork plaque (see fig. 16.9a). The only examples of these baskets south of the Mogollon Rim occur at the fourteenth-century site of Canyon Creek.

Ritual wooden objects appear to achieve their highest level of elaboration in the upper and middle Gila drainages after AD 1250, as evidenced by the remarkable collections from the Bonita Creek cache (ca. AD 1280–1300; see fig. 16.5i) and the Cliff

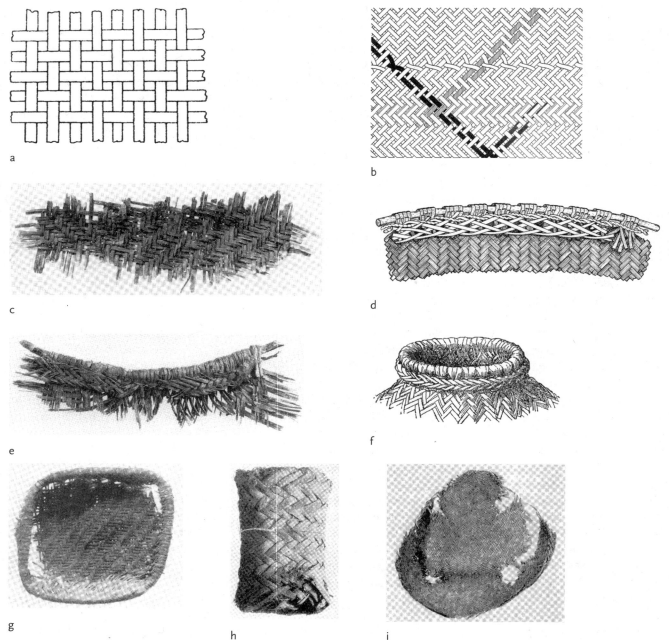

Figure 16.8. Mogollon and ancestral Pueblo plaited basketry and matting: (a) schematic of simple plaiting with 1/1 interval; (b) 2/2 twill-plaited matting, Cave 9, Table Top Mountain, undated, probably AD 1000–1400; (c) 3/3 twill-plaited matting, Tularosa Cave, undated, probably AD 1000–1300; (d) schematic of ornamental rim braid on ancestral Pueblo 3/3 twill-plaited baskets, Mesa Verde, AD 1100–1300; (e) plaited ring basket fragment with reinforcing rod and ornamental rim braid, Tularosa Cave, AD 1000–1300; (f) jar-shaped 3/3 twill-plaited ring basket with reinforcing rod and ornamental rim braid, Bear Creek Cave, undated, probably AD 1000–1400; (g) square plaited ring basket with reinforcing rod and ornamental rim braid, weave undetermined, Bear Creek Cave, undated, probably AD 1000–1400; (h) cylindrical 2/2(?) twill-plaited basket, Spur Ranch, undated, probably AD 1000–1400; (i) square 3/3 twill-plaited tray with double selvage and no reinforcing rod, Canyon Creek, AD 1325–1350 (a drawn by the author; b from Cosgrove 1947:fig. 37, reproduced courtesy of the Peabody Museum of Archaeology and Ethnology, Harvard University; c, e from Martin et al. 1952:figs. 125, upper, and 118, lower, reproduced courtesy of the Field Museum Press; d from Morris and Burgh 1941:fig. 8c; f–h from Hough 1914:fig. 179, plates 17, no. 1, and 16, no. 3; i from Haury 1934:plate XLIXc, reproduced courtesy of the Arizona State Museum, University of Arizona).

Figure 16.9. Mogollon and Zuni wicker basketry and Zuni coiled basketry and plaited matting: (a) wicker plaque, Canyon Creek Ruin, AD 1325–1350; (b) wicker plaque, Hawikuh Pueblo, ca. AD 1400–1680; (c) base of coarse-coiled basket with bundle foundation and spaced stitches, Hawikuh Pueblo, ca. AD 1400–1680; (d) 3/3 twill-plaited matting with diamond design, Hawikuh Pueblo, ca. AD 1400–1680 (a from Haury 1934:plate LIII, reproduced courtesy of the Arizona State Museum, University of Arizona; b–d used courtesy of the National Museum of the American Indian, Smithsonian Institution, catalog nos. NMAI 8/6714, 9/4012, and 9/4009, photos by the author).

effigy cache (ca. AD 1260 +/− 95). At least some of the undated assemblage from Bear Creek Cave probably also dates to this period (see fig. 16.4h). This post–AD 1250 period is also when the earliest documented evidence of ritual wooden objects is found in the western Mogollon Highlands from sites including Canyon Creek and the Point of Pines caves.

Summary of Mogollon Perishable Trajectories and Boundaries

Table 16.2 summarizes the postulated antecedents of various classes of Mogollon perishables, and table 16.3 examines these perishable traditions in relation to surrounding areas. Table 16.4 summarizes the temporal development of these Mogollon perishables and identifies the sites that served as the basis for this chronology.

Based on a database that is poorly dated and heavily biased toward cave collections, nearly all Mogollon textile, basketry, sandal, and ritual traditions seem to find their earliest expression and development among groups utilizing the Mimbres, upper Gila, and San Francisco drainages. Some of these basket and textile technologies and nearly all ritual ideologies appear to have precedence in Mexico and to overlie a Desert Archaic textile and basketry base. The spread of such southern perishable technologies as plaiting (braiding) and loom-woven plain-weave fabrics into the Mogollon region over the course of several centuries suggests continuing interactions between the southern Southwest and northern Mexico through trade, small-scale population movements, and/or return migrations to ancestral homelands.

Groups in the Mogollon and Jornada Mogollon areas shared many of the same perishable traditions until the Early Pithouse period, when increased investment in agriculture and

settled village life by people in the Mogollon region and the persistence of a more mobile horticultural lifeway among groups in the Jornada Mogollon region led to increased differentiation. After AD 1100 textile assemblages remain distinct, but ritual assemblages become more similar, as indicated by the co-occurrence of painted tablitas, split-stick wands, and miniature bows and arrows at sites in both regions.

I have suggested the existence of a technological and stylistic boundary between the Mogollon region and the western Sonoran Desert as far back as the Early Agricultural period, when increasing sedentism and agricultural dependency would have led to growing regionalization in perishable technologies and clothing styles. This is predicated on the assumption that the wickerwork sandals and some other artifact types found at Ventana Cave are representative of Early Agricultural technologies in the region, a presumption yet to be demonstrated by direct dating. Even if the Ventana Cave artifacts do date to the Early Agricultural period, however, they are not necessarily representative of early perishable technologies in the Tucson Basin or the San Pedro drainage. Lacking collections from these areas, nothing can be said about perishable relationships between the Tucson Basin and any of the Mogollon branches. Just east of the San Pedro Valley, the Black River branch assemblage from McEuen Cave shows much stronger affinities to Mimbres, Reserve, and Trans-Pecos assemblages than it does to Ventana Cave.

Whether or not a boundary existed between the Hohokam and Mogollon regions in Early Agricultural times, differences in the perishable technologies of these regions appear to increase through time, especially in regard to more utilitarian kinds of objects. Hohokam and Mimbres Mo-

gollon assemblages share an emphasis on the use of cotton fabrics and openwork weaves, but these items were luxury goods, probably made by highly skilled weavers and limited to ritual use. If we focus instead on the baskets, mats, and clothing of everyday life, we find considerable differences between Hohokam and Mogollon assemblages, such as the general absence of plaited ring baskets, 3/3 matting, and turkey-feather blankets at Hohokam sites. These latter technologies are common, however, in the Mogollon region and in Puebloan assemblages on the southern Colorado Plateau.

Mogollon and ancestral Pueblo sites share many of the same perishable constructions, but there are important differences. Although the idea of plaiting appears to have spread rapidly from northern Mexico into Mogollon and Basketmaker societies, plaited sandals from each region tend to be stylistically distinct. Loom-woven yucca plain weaves and cotton openwork weaves were made south of the Mogollon Rim but are rare on the Colorado Plateau. In the Mogollon Highlands people made highly simplified versions of multiple-warp cord sandals and plaited ring baskets with braided rims, apparently in emulation of ancestral Pueblo styles indigenous to the Four Corners region. After AD 1200 Mogollon-Pueblo assemblages became even more hybridized as a result of Puebloan population movements south of the Mogollon Rim (see, e.g., the discussion of the Bonita Creek Cache in the descriptive section of this chapter). In my view, perishable evidence for strong north–south ties extends back at least as far as the Basketmaker period (see the following discussion on Mogollon-Basketmaker relationships and Mills, chap. 13, this vol.). After AD 1200 new textile and basketry influences characteristic of the Arizona deserts and northern

Table 16.2 Postulated Antecedents of Mogollon Perishables

Perishable Class	Probable Source of Influence to the Mogollon Region	Remarks
Twined rabbit-fur blankets	Great Basin?	Widespread throughout northern Mexico, Trans-Pecos, and Jornada Basin by Late Archaic.
Twined turkey-feather blankets	Mogollon	A local Mogollon development during the Early Pithouse period.
Twined bags	Great Basin	Present in Great Basin by Early Archaic; widespread in Trans-Pecos, Jornada Basin, western Oklahoma (?), northern Arizona, and Mogollon regions by Late Archaic or Early Agricultural period; not found in northern Mexico.
Looped bags and leggings	Mexico	Present in Mexico by Middle Archaic; widespread in central and northern Mexico, Trans-Pecos, Jornada Basin by Late Archaic or Early Agricultural period.
Noncotton plain weaves	Mexico	Widespread in northern Mexico by Late Archaic or Early Agricultural period (?).
Cotton plain weaves	Mexico	Widespread in central and western Mexico by Early Agricultural period; uncommon in inland northern Mexico (Coahuila, Chihuahua); may have spread to the Mogollon region via the Hohokam or western Mexico.
Various complex fabrics	Mexico	Weft-wrap openwork and gauze weaves may have entered the U.S. Southwest from western Mexico; plain weaves with supplementary wefts have an inland Mexican origin.
Coiling, one rod	Great Basin	Present in Great Basin by Early Archaic; widespread in inland northern Mexico, Trans-Pecos, and the western Colorado Plateau by Early to Middle Archaic.
Coiling, two-rod-and-bundle	Great Basin or local development in the northern Chihuahuan Desert?	Widespread among the Mogollon, Jornada Mogollon, Hohokam (?), and Basketmaker II on the Colorado Plateau by Early Agricultural period; not an important technique in northern Mexico or the Trans-Pecos region.
Coiling, bundle-with-rod-core	Great Basin or Mexico	Present among the Mogollon, Jornada Mogollon, and Hohokam and at a few Western Basketmaker II sites by Early Agricultural period; not an important technique in northern Mexico or the Trans-Pecos region.
Coiling, bundle	Mexico	Widespread throughout Mexico and the Trans-Pecos region by Middle to Late Archaic.
Plaited matting	Mexico	1/1 (checkerweave) and 2/2 twill plaiting widespread in northern Mexico, Trans-Pecos region, Jornada Basin by Late Archaic; 3/3 matting is later, spatially restricted to northwestern Mexico, east-central Arizona, west-central New Mexico, and the southern Colorado Plateau.
Plaited baskets	Mexico	Ring baskets may be an ancestral Pueblo innovation during Pueblo II; late forms, including some with double selvages, also occur in northwestern Mexico.
Wickerwork plaques	Mogollon?	A local Mogollon development in Pueblo IV?
Wickerwork sandals	Mexico	Scuffer-toe sandals with fishtail heels widespread in northern Mexico, Trans-Pecos, Jornada Basin by Middle to Late Archaic; sandals without fishtail heels found in eastern Great Basin, Hohokam, Mogollon, and Basketmaker II sites by Early Agricultural period.
Multiple-warp cord sandals	Colorado Plateau	Probably an ancestral Pueblo innovation in Basketmaker II and III.
Plaited sandals	Mexico	Found early in Coahuila and later in Chihuahua but not in the Trans-Pecos region; rare in the Jornada Basin.
Reed cigarettes	Mexico and Mogollon	Present in central and northern Mexico (Tehuacan Valley, Tamaulipas, Chihuahua) by an unknown date (200 BC?), continue into the historic period; influence may derive from the Gulf Coast of Mexico; present but rare in the Trans-Pecos and Jornada Basin; present in the Mogollon region by Early Pithouse period.
Ceremonial bows and arrows	Mogollon	Present in Mexico, but published examples are late; may be a local Mogollon development during the Early Pithouse period.
Painted sticks and pahos	Mogollon and Jornada Mogollon	A local development shared by the Mogollon and Jornada Mogollon during the Early Pithouse period.
Tablitas	Mogollon	Cosgrove's tablita a local Mogollon development during the Early Pithouse period; terraced tablitas may have entered the Mogollon region after A.D. 1250 via Paquimé and the Rio Grande Valley.
Carved birds, flowers, effigy figures	Mexico, Mogollon, ancestral Pueblo	Carved birds and flowers probably related to Mesoamerican Flower World imagery; most southwestern forms postdate AD 1000; wooden effigy figures not present until after AD 1250.

Table 16.3 Relationships and Boundaries of Mogollon Perishables in Comparison with Surrounding Regions

Artifact Class	Tradition Shared with the Mogollon Region	Tradition Absent or Rare
Twined rabbit-fur blankets	Early Agricultural peoples across the southern Basin and Range; Basketmaker II and III peoples on the Colorado Plateau; Great Basin.	None
Twined turkey-feather blankets	Basketmaker III and later peoples on the Colorado Plateau.	Hohokam region
Twined bags	Early Agricultural and later peoples across the southern Basin and Range; Basketmaker II and later on the Colorado Plateau; Great Basin.	Of minor importance in Hohokam region
Looped bags and leggings	Early Agricultural and later peoples across the southern Basin and Range; Basketmaker II and later peoples on the Colorado Plateau. Looping on foundation cords shared with groups in the Guadalupe Mountains but not on the Colorado Plateau.	Of minor importance in Hohokam region
Noncotton plant fiber plain weaves	Inland northern Mexico, especially Coahuila and Chihuahua, also Hohokam, Salado, Sinagua. After AD 1300 present in Upper and Middle Little Colorado, Zuni.	Rare on Colorado Plateau until Pueblo IV, except for a few Western Basketmaker II examples
Cotton plain weaves	Hohokam, Salado, Sinagua, ancestral and historic Pueblos.	Inland northern Mexico, Hueco, and Trans-Pecos regions
Various complex fabrics	Weft-wrap openwork, gauze, and supplementary-weft weaves found at Hohokam, Sinagua, and Salado sites; twill and twill tapestry shared primarily with the ancestral Pueblo, Sinagua, Salado, and, to a lesser extent, the Hohokam.	Jornada Mogollon, Hueco, Trans-Pecos regions. Supplementary-weft and openwork weaves occasionally found at Pueblo III sites on the Colorado Plateau but rare.
Coiling, one rod	Great Basin, northern Mexico (Coahuila and Chihuahua), Hohokam, ancestral Pueblo.	Central and southern Mexico
Coiling, two-rod-and-bundle	Predominant coiling construction among the Mogollon, Jornada Mogollon, and Basketmaker II and III. Continued importance during Pueblo III on the Colorado Plateau.	Of minor importance in the Hohokam, Hueco, and Trans-Pecos regions and northern Mexico
Coiling, bundle-with-rod-core	Jornada Mogollon, Hohokam, a few Basketmaker II sites.	Northern Mexico, Trans-Pecos region
Coiling, bundle	Jornada Mogollon, Hohokam, Salado, Sinagua, historic O'odham. After AD 1300 present in Middle and Upper Little Colorado, Hopi, and Zuni regions.	Rare on the Colorado Plateau prior to AD 1300
Plaited matting	Plaiting widespread throughout Mexico; 2/2 and 3/3 twill plaiting shared with Pueblo II, III, and historic Pueblos on the Colorado Plateau, also the Sinagua and Salado; 2/2 twill plaiting shared with the Hohokam, Trans-Pecos region, and northern Mexico.	1/1 (checkerweave) plaiting common at Hohokam and Jornada Mogollon sites; rare at Mogollon and ancestral Pueblo sites on Colorado Plateau
Plaited baskets	Ring baskets shared with Pueblo II and III on the Colorado Plateau, also Sinagua and Salado. Later, double-weave baskets shared with northwestern Mexico, the Salado, and historic O'odham.	Hohokam region
Wickerwork plaques	After AD 1300 present in Middle Little Colorado, Hopi, and Zuni regions.	Not reported prior to AD 1300 in U.S. Southwest or other regions
Wickerwork sandals	Full-length, two-warp style lacking the fishtail heel also found in the Hohokam and eastern Great Basin regions; full-length, four-warp style lacking the fishtail heel found at Basketmaker II through Pueblo III sites on Colorado Plateau. Two- and four-warp styles shared with the Jornada Mogollon.	Scuffer-toe and fishtail-heel styles predominate in northern Mexico, Trans-Pecos region, Jornada Basin
Multiple-warp cord sandals	Basketmaker III peoples on the Colorado Plateau. Mogollon examples lack the tapestry designs and patterned soles found on Basketmaker examples.	Hohokam, Jornada Basin, northern Mexico
Plaited sandals	Pueblo I through Pueblo III peoples on the Colorado Plateau, also the Salado, Sinagua.	Of minor importance in Hohokam region

Table 16.3 *Continued*

Artifact Class	Tradition Shared with the Mogollon Region	Tradition Absent or Rare
Reed cigarettes	Early tradition may be shared with the Jornada Mogollon. By Pueblo II–III also found at Hohokam and ancestral Pueblo sites. Present in Chihuahua but could be late.	Relatively rare in the Trans-Pecos region
Ceremonial bows and arrows	Hohokam, ancestral Pueblo, Jornada Mogollon, northern Mexico, a few Trans-Pecos sites. Strong tradition in the Mogollon region and among the historic Pueblos.	Relatively rare in the Hueco and Trans-Pecos regions
Painted sticks and pahos	Simpler forms shared with the Jornada Mogollon. More complex and later forms (including crook and roundel pahos) shared with the ancestral Pueblo, Hohokam, Lower Rio Grande, Paquimé regions. Common among the historic Pueblos.	Carved pahos not found in Trans-Pecos region; rare in Hueco area; Hohokam examples are late
Tablitas and split-stick wands	Both traditions shared with the Hueco area but not as prevalent there; wooden tablitas and split-stick wands not reported from Hohokam or ancestral Pueblo sites; other types of flat carved wooden objects found at Chacoan great houses and Pueblo IV Zuni; terraced tablita-like stone objects known from Paquimé; rock art depictions of tablitas common in northern Chihuahua Desert; terraced tablita headdresses common among the historic Pueblos.	Hohokam, ancestral Pueblo regions
Carved birds, flowers, effigy figures	Carved birds found in northern Jornada Mogollon region and at late Hohokam sites. Carved flowers known from Pueblo III sites on Colorado Plateau. Bird and flower imagery depicted on Pueblo IV kiva murals and historic Pueblo altars. Carved effigies found at late Hohokam sites, Paquimé, and among the historic Pueblos.	Hueco and Trans-Pecos regions

Mexico also appear at sites in southern and central Arizona and southwestern New Mexico.

Among the three major southwestern cultural traditions a ritual wooden object tradition appears to be earliest among the Mogollon. Unfortunately, wooden objects have not been recovered from Early Agricultural period sites in the southern Basin and Range (i.e., southern Arizona and northern Sonora), so it is impossible to know what was going on in these areas during this time. As with other kinds of perishables, the Mimbres and Reserve areas produced the earliest evidence for this development. If the dating is correct, the roots of this ritual tradition are present by the end of the Early Agricultural period in the form of simple stick pahos. Most of the ritual wooden forms found at Mogollon sites eventually appear at sites in the Hohokam, ancestral Pueblo, Sinagua, and Salado regions. The exceptions are the tablitas and split-stick wands, which are limited to the southern Mogollon branches and a few Jornada Basin sites until about the AD 1400s. By Pueblo IV virtually all elements of this ritual tradition are present at Zuni, Hopi, and most of the other historic pueblos.

A Few Thoughts about Mogollon-Basketmaker Relationships

Here I backtrack briefly to consider the important and relevant problem of Mogollon-Basketmaker relationships. The origins of the Basketmakers of the Colorado Plateau, the "Hueco Basketmakers" of the upper Gila and Hueco districts, and the "Big Bend Basketmakers" of Texas were the subject of much debate during the middle part of the last century (Cosgrove 1947:175; Morris and Burgh 1954; Roberts 1929b; Setzler 1935). Relationships between early populations in the northern and southern Southwest continue to generate considerable interest (Berry 1982; Berry and Berry 1986; Carpenter et al. 2002; Damp et al. 2001; Huckell et al. 1999; Matson 1991; Webster and Hays-Gilpin 1994).

Cosgrove (1947:169) viewed the Hueco and Big Bend Basketmakers as migrants from northern Arizona, whereas Adovasio and others (Adovasio 1980:352; Adovasio et al. 1996:28; Hyland and Adovasio 2000:158) interpret the early Mogollon and Jornada Mogollon as hybrids of northern and southern populations. Still others (Berry and Berry 1986; Matson 1991: 203, 313, chap. 7, this vol.; Morris and Burgh 1954:80–81, 85) have argued for a southern origin for some northern Basketmaker groups in an effort to explain the early and sudden appearance of maize agriculture on the Colorado Plateau. Given the similarities between Early Agricultural period Mogollon and Basketmaker II perishables, I too am intrigued by these relationships and feel it may be worth revisiting some hypotheses put forth long ago by Samuel Guernsey and

Table 16.4 Chronology of Selected Mogollon Perishable Traditions, Based on Published Dates

Time Period	Types of Object or Construction	Sources
?–AD 200	*Fabrics*: twined fur blankets, twined bags, looped bags(?); possible early evidence of noncotton plain weaves *Basketry*: one-rod, two-rod-and-bundle, and bundle-with-rod-core coiling *Sandals*: wickerwork sandals *Ritual objects*: unpeeled twig pahos with attachments, incised twigs, painted twig pahos, grass-stem pahos(?); possible early evidence of reed cigarettes	Bat Cave, Cienega Creek, Cordova Cave, Doolittle Cave, Kelley Cave, McEuen Cave, Mule Creek Cave, O Block Cave, Steamboat Cave, Tularosa Cave
AD 200–700	*Fabrics*: appearance of twined feather blankets and noncotton plain weaves; continuation of twined fur blankets, twined bags, other twined fabrics, looped bags *Basketry*: appearance of bundle-foundation coiling and twill-plaited matting; continuation of one-rod, two-rod-and-bundle, and bundle-with-rod-core coiling *Sandals*: appearance of multiple-warp cord sandals and plaited sandals; continuation of wickerwork sandals *Ritual objects*: appearance of reed cigarettes, ceremonial bows, and tablita-like objects (black decoration only); increasing popularity of twig pahos with feather attachments, feather pahos	Bear Ruin, Cave 2 on West Fork, Cordova Cave, Crooked Ridge Village, O Block Cave, Quemado Alegre, Tularosa Cave
AD 700–1000	*Fabrics*: appearance of cotton plain weaves; continuation of twined feather blankets, twined bags, looped bags (simple looping and looping on foundation cords), noncotton plain weaves *Basketry*: appearance of twill-plaited ring baskets; increasing popularity of twill-plaited matting; continuation of two-rod-and-bundle, bundle-with-rod-core, and bundle-foundation coiling; decline of one-rod coiling *Sandals*: increasing popularity of plaited sandals; continuation of wickerwork sandals *Ritual objects*: appearance of polychrome designs and carved pahos; increasing popularity of ceremonial bows and arrows and tablita-like objects; continuation of reed cigarettes and painted twigs	Bat Cave, Cordova Cave, Harris Village, NAN Ranch Ruin, O Block Cave, Tularosa Cave, various small caves on the Upper Gila
AD 1000–1250	*Fabrics*: appearance of weft-wrap openwork, gauze, twills, and twill tapestry; continuation of twined feather blankets, looping on foundation cords, cotton and noncotton plain weaves; decline of twined fur blankets *Basketry*: appearance of new forms of plaited basketry; continuation of two-rod-and-bundle, bundle-with-rod-core(?), and bundle-foundation coiling, twill-plaited matting, and twill-plaited ring baskets *Sandals*: predominance of plaited sandals; decline of wickerwork sandals *Ritual objects*: appearance of carved birds; increasing popularity of crook and roundel pahos; elaboration of carved pahos; continuation of reed cigarettes (now decorated), ceremonial bows and arrows, tablitas	Bear Creek Cave(?), Cameron Creek Village, Cordova Cave, Higgins Flat Pueblo, Mariana Mesa Site 616, NAN Ranch Ruin, Pine Flat Cave, Swarts Ruin, Tularosa Cave, Tule Tubs Cave, various small caves of the Mimbres, Reserve, and Upper Gila
AD 1250–1400	*Fabrics*: appearance of plain weave with supplemental weft (brocade); continuation of noncotton and cotton plain weaves and weft-wrap openwork; decline of looping *Basketry*: appearance of wickerwork plaques and new forms of plaiting, some with double selvages; increasing popularity of bundle-foundation coiling (close and coarse coiled, including granary baskets); reappearance of one-rod coiling; continuation of two-rod-and-bundle, bundle-with-rod-core coiling, twill-plaited matting, and twill-plaited ring baskets *Sandals*: appearance of plaited sandals with H-shaped strap; predominance of plaited sandals; wickerwork sandals present only in small quantities *Ritual objects*: appearance of carved flowers, human effigies; probable appearance of basket pahos on sticks; continuation of decorated reed cigarettes, ceremonial bows and arrows, carved pahos, tablitas, and carved birds	Bear Creek Cave(?), Bonita Creek, Buffalo Cave, Canyon Creek Pueblo, Gila Cliff Dwelling, Johnson Cave(?), McEuen Cave, Pinnacle Cave, Point of Pines Pueblo, Red Bow Cliff Dwelling, U Bar Cave, unnamed cave from the Cliff Valley

A. V. Kidder (1921:115), Frank H. H. Roberts Jr. (1929b:14), and Frank M. Setzler (1935:106) suggesting that the deserts of Chihuahua and Coahuila were one important source for certain aspects of Basketmaker culture.

Patterning in the geographic and temporal distributions of perishables suggests that Early Agricultural populations in the Mogollon and Basketmaker II regions are subvariants of a common-antecedent Late Archaic tradition (Morris and Burgh 1954:81). Perishable traditions of the White Dog phase Basketmakers and the Early Agricultural Mogollon both represent a composite of technologies with antecedents in the Great Basin and Mexico. Adovasio's (1980) research on Middle and Late Archaic perishables has traced the spread of Great Basin technologies into northern Mexico millennia before the advent of agriculture, and Hyland and Adovasio (2000:158; see also Adovasio 1980:352; Adovasio et al. 1996; Hyland 1997) have proposed a link between the northward movement of certain Mexican technologies and the diffusion of agriculture from Mesoamerica. These findings provide an excellent springboard for investigating Mogollon-Basketmaker relationships.

Remaining to be explained is how, when, and where these processes of hybridization occurred in various regions of the Southwest. Are similarities in Early Agricultural Mogollon and Basketmaker II perishable traditions due to population migration and direct social interaction, or are they better explained as a consequence of technological diffusion, high mobility, and/or shared social and economic lifeways? Testing these ideas will require a two-prong approach: generating a large body of AMS dates directly from artifacts and analyzing these collections to compare low-visibility attributes of tech-

nological style (see J. Clark 2001, chap. 4, this vol.).

Perishables are especially well suited for testing the hypothesis that early agriculturalists from the southern Southwest spread into northern Arizona, contributing to the White Dog phase of Basketmaker II. Shared attributes of early Mogollon and White Dog phase assemblages include similar styles of atlatls, looped yucca bags, and four-warp wickerwork sandals lacking the fishtail heel as well as the shared mortuary practice of interring the dead (inhumations) in twined bags. Examples of low-visibility attributes that could be compared include sandal warp preparation, directions of cordage and twining twist, basket splices, direction of work, selvage construction, and methods of starting and finishing baskets and bags. Perishable assemblages are available from sites in both regions to test these hypotheses.[4]

Some Basketmaker II perishable traditions exhibit strong affinities to the Great Basin, especially in their emphasis on twining. Other constructions found at White Dog phase sites—looped bags, four-warp wickerwork sandals, and yucca plain-weave cloth with twined selvages—seem to show much stronger affinities to the south. These constructions are of little or no consequence in Late Archaic assemblages from the eastern Great Basin or the Colorado Plateau, nor do they appear to be important at Ventana Cave. They are, however, present in early Mogollon, Chihuahuan, and/or Coahuilan assemblages, suggesting that the cultures of the Chihuahuan Desert and surrounding highlands rather than the Great Basin or the Sonoran Desert might have been the source of these southern influences to the White Dog phase Basketmakers.

Another perishable artifact construction that could be used to trace

the spread of southern influences (or groups of people) into Basketmaker II societies is plaiting (also known as braiding or oblique interlacing; see fig. 16.8). Another new introduction to the Colorado Plateau, plaiting has unambiguous origins to the south (Adovasio 1980). Plaited artifacts do not seem to be a significant component of White Dog phase assemblages but occur in the form of braided sashes, sandals, or tumpbands at several Eastern and Western Basketmaker sites believed to date to late Basketmaker II.[5] The presence of this southern construction may correlate with the appearance of other southern influences, such as early brownware ceramics and new symmetry systems (Reed et al. 2000; Washburn and Webster 2006; see also Amsden 1949:129; Mills, chap. 13, this vol.).

The early distribution of plaiting suggests a closer relationship between Basketmaker II groups on the Colorado Plateau and groups in the Reserve branch and/or Jornada Basin than with those in the Mimbres Valley or southern Arizona (Ventana Cave). Present evidence suggests that plaiting did not achieve much popularity among the Mimbres Mogollon until the Late Pithouse period. Plaited mats and sandals are reported in small quantities from Early Pithouse period levels (AD 200–700) at Tularosa and Cordova caves but appear to be even earlier in the Jornada Basin and the Trans-Pecos regions. A braided animal-hair sash found at Tularosa Cave strongly resembles examples from late Basketmaker II sites on the Colorado Plateau (cf. Hough 1914:72, 75 and Morris and Burgh 1954:66–67, figs. 33, 37, 38). Although this sash is undated, its association with a turkey-feather jacket suggests an Early Pithouse period attribution, which supports the idea that these traditions may be contemporaneous in the Reserve and Basketmaker regions.

In sum, the direct dating and technical analysis of perishable artifacts holds considerable promise for understanding the spread of people or ideas between the Mogollon, Jornada Mogollon, and southern Colorado Plateau regions during the Late Archaic, Early Agricultural, and Basketmaker periods. Unfortunately, a comparable study between the Basketmaker region and northern Sonora or the Tucson Basin is not presently possible, given the lack of early perishable collections from these areas. Although archaeologists have used projectile points to study these relationships (e.g., Berry and Berry 1986; Carpenter et al. 2002; Marmaduke 1978; Matson 1991), I, along with most of my textile and basketry colleagues, would argue that perishables, when available, hold greater promise for tracking the movements of people in the archaeological record. As demonstrated by McBrinn (2002, 2005), similarities among fiber artifacts, with their wide range of low-visibility manufacturing choices, are much more likely to reflect shared social identities among mobile groups than projectile point styles, which are highly visible, widely shared, and probably better measures of participation in broad economic networks than they are of identities (see also Clark, chap. 4, and Matson, chap. 7, this vol.).

A Closer Look at the Mogollon Perishables Database

Although Mogollon perishables have been described by a number of authors (e.g., Adovasio 1970, 1980; Adovasio et al. 1996; Cosgrove 1947; Hyland 1997; Hyland and Adovasio 2000; Kent 1957, 1983; Martin et al. 1954; Martin et al. 1952; Teague 1998), this study represents the first attempt to synthesize data about tex-

tiles, basketry, and ritual wooden objects from sites across the Mogollon region. For perishables specialists and others interested in Mogollon material culture, this section provides a more detailed discussion of the development, technology, and regional variability of the 22 artifact classes considered for the study. Although the original appendix tables prepared for the study could not be included in this volume, they are available online at http://www.cdarc.org/pages/library/zuni_data/.

Mogollon Fabrics

From the many types of fabrics made and used in the Southwest (Kent 1983; Teague 1998) I selected four broad classes for the study: twined fabrics, looped fabrics, cotton and noncotton plain-weave fabrics, and "fancy" textiles made from a variety of weave structures. Figure 16.10 summarizes their temporal development within the Mogollon region, tables 16.5 and 16.6 show their spatial and temporal distribution, and table 16.7 summarizes their source data.

Twined Fabrics. Mogollon twined fabrics appear as two major forms: open-twined blankets of fur or feathers (see fig. 16.2a) and close-twined bands and bags (see fig. 16.2b). All twined fabrics in the sample are weft-faced weaves. Early examples of rabbit-fur cordage and twined blankets, dating at least as early as the late Early Agricultural period, come from McEuen Cave, Bat Cave, and probably several caves in the upper Gila and San Francisco River valleys. Fur cordage is reported from Pre-Pottery (Early Agricultural period) levels at Tularosa and Cordova caves, but turkey-feather cordage does not make its debut until the Early Pithouse period, when both fur and feather blankets (and the remains of

turkeys) are found (Martin et al. 1952:499). At Tularosa Cave twined rabbit-fur blankets continue into the San Francisco phase and feather blankets into Tularosa levels. The remains of twined fur *or* feather blankets are also reported from Tularosa phase (Pueblo III) levels at Higgins Flat Pueblo and Site 616 on Mariana Mesa, but twined fur or feather blankets have not been identified from Point of Pines or Canyon Creek, although some fur or feather cordage was found at both.

Close-twined fabrics are known from seven Mogollon sites. Based on published descriptions, it appears that all wefts in these fabrics twist around each other in a Z-wise fashion (Z-twist twining). A variety of garment types is reported. The earliest known Mogollon example is a twined bag from McEuen Cave with a calibrated radiocarbon date of 400–180 BC (Moreno 2000:353). I consider a second undated bag from McEuen Cave and two undated bags from Kelly and Doolittle Caves to be additional candidates for this early time period (see Cosgrove 1947:70 n. 4). The remains of probable twined bags were also found at Tularosa and Cordova caves, but these are later, postdating AD 700 (see fig. 16.2b).[6]

Twined fabrics are also reported from two Early Pithouse village sites in the Mogollon Highlands and one Classic Mimbres site. Wheat (1954:164) recovered a charred twined fabric, identified as a possible sash fragment, from Crooked Ridge Village (AD 100–400; see Bullard 1962:83 for possible problems with the dating). A charred fragment of a possible twined bag is also reported from Quemado Alegre (ca. AD 500) in the Cibola region. The remains of twined blankets, garments, or shrouds are also known from Classic Mimbres mortuary contexts at NAN Ranch Ruin.

Fabric Type	ca. 1750 BC–AD 200	AD 200–700	AD 700–1000	AD 1000–1250	AD 1250–1400
Twined fur blankets	●	●	●	●↓	
Twined bags	●	●	●		
Looped bags	○?	●	●	●	●↓
Non-cotton plain weaves	○?	●	●	●	●
Twined feather blankets		●	●	●	○?
Cotton plain weaves			●	●	●
Weft-wrap openwork				●	●
Gauze				●	
Twill weaves				●	●
Twill tapestry				●	○?
Plain weave with supplemental weft (brocade)					●

Figure 16.10. Temporal distribution of Mogollon fabric types.

Looped Bags and Leggings. Looping is an important component of the early Mogollon textile tradition (examples are reported from 12 sites in the sample; see table 16.7). The most basic structure is simple looping, also referred to as coiled netting or coiling without foundation (see fig. 16.2c). Examples are known from McEuen Cave, Cordova Cave, Tularosa Cave, and Red Bow Cliff Dwelling. I consider three undated looped objects from McEuen Cave—a human-hair bag or legging, an undecorated bag, and a large bag painted with radiating red and black chevron designs—to be strong contenders for an Early Agricultural period attribution. Another looped bag from McEuen Cave, worked in hair cordage and strips of cotton cloth, is obviously later. The latest looped fabric in the sample is a bag from Red Bow Cliff Dwelling, probably part of a quiver (cf. Dixon 1956:16, 28), dated to the Canyon Creek phase.

Looping on foundation cords (see fig. 16.2d) is another important technique in the Mogollon area, with examples known from McEuen Cave, Steamboat Cave, Tularosa Cave, and possibly U Bar Cave. Although Lambert and Ambler (1961:49, fig. 31) describe the construction of the U Bar Cave bag as "plain coiled netting" (i.e., simple looping), my interpretation of the photographic illustration suggests looping on foundation cords. The only reasonably well dated examples of looping on foundation cords are two fragments from Tularosa Cave, attributed to San Francisco and San Francisco through Tularosa levels (AD 700–1300). However, I suspect that the undated bag from Steamboat Cave could be considerably earlier (see Cosgrove 1947:72). I base this on the fact that the yarns in the bag were colored by the "dry dye" technique (i.e., rubbed with pigment as the weaving progressed), a method described for other Late Archaic and Early Agricultural period looped and twined bags (e.g., Guernsey and Kidder 1921:71, 77). A bag from Pratt Cave in the Guadalupe Mountains, almost identical to the one from Steamboat Cave, produced a radiocarbon date of 250 BC–AD 160 (Schroeder 1983:51, 122). The U Bar Cave bag

may date to an earlier occupation as well (see Matson 1991:291). Finally, fragments of undated coarse nets worked in a loop-and-twist technique were found at McEuen Cave and a number of sites on the upper Gila and San Francisco rivers.

Cotton and Noncotton Plain-Weave Fabrics. Cotton and noncotton plain-weave fabrics, the former usually made with Z-spun elements and the latter with S-spun yarns, are widely distributed at Mogollon sites, occurring in all branches but San Simon (see table 16.6). The greatest proportions of cotton cloth occur at sites in the Mimbres and Black River branches, where conditions were most favorable for its cultivation. Early evidence of cotton fiber is reported from Georgetown phase contexts at Tularosa Cave, but woven cotton fabrics are not present until the San Francisco phase, when cotton and noncotton plain weaves occur in roughly the same proportions. Cotton cloth is also known from undated contexts at McEuen Cave and numerous caves in the upper Gila, Mimbres, and San Francisco drainages.

In the Mimbres area deteriorated fragments of plain-weave cloth made from an as yet unidentified plant fiber (cotton or yucca?) were recovered from Cameron Creek Village and NAN Ranch Ruin. At NAN Ranch Ruin these fabrics are mortuary related and occur as early as the Three Circle phase (AD 750–1000). At Higgins Flat Pueblo plain-weave cloth made of an unidentified fiber was also associated with burials. Both the NAN Ranch and Higgins Flat plain weaves are made from Z-spun yarns, which suggests to me that they might be cotton fabrics.[7]

Cotton cloth is especially common at late Mogollon sites. All of the late plain weaves from Tularosa Cave are cotton, and considerable quantities of

Table 16.5 Distribution of Twined and Looped Fabrics in Site Sample by Time Period and Branch

Fabric Type	Site	750 BC–AD 150	AD 150–700	AD 700–1000	AD 1000–1200	AD 1200–1450	Total
Twined fur blankets	San Simon	—	—	—	—	—	—
	Mimbres	1	1	—	—	—	2
	Cibola	1	~2	>1	—	1	~5
	Black River	3	—	—	—	—	3
	Forestdale	—	—	—	—	—	—
	Subtotal	5	~3	>1	—	1	~10
Twined feather blankets	San Simon	—	—	—	—	—	—
	Mimbres	—	—	—	—	1	1
	Cibola	—	~3	>1	—	~2	~6
	Black River	—	—	—	—	2	2
	Forestdale	—	—	—	—	—	—
	Subtotal	—	~3	>1	—	~5	~9
Other weft-faced fabrics	San Simon	—	—	—	—	—	—
	Mimbres	1	—	—	~3	—	~4
	Cibola	1	1	3	—	—	5
	Black River	2	1	—	—	—	3
	Forestdale	—	—	—	—	—	—
	Subtotal	4	2	3	~3	—	~12
Looped fabrics	San Simon	—	—	—	—	1	1
	Mimbres	1	~1	~5	—	—	~7
	Cibola	—	1	~2	1	—	~4
	Black River	~6	—	—	—	~4	~10
	Forestdale	—	—	—	—	—	—
	Subtotal	~7	~2	~7	1	~5	~22
	Total	~16	~10	~12	~4	~11	~53

Note: Quantities and dates inferred from the literature. Quantities reflect estimated number of original objects, not number of fragments.

cotton cloth were found in Tularosa phase contexts at the Gila Cliff Dwellings. Cotton cloth was also associated with the Cliff phase effigy cache from the Cliff Valley. Charred fragments of cotton cloth also came from the Pueblo III Site 616 on Mariana Mesa. Cotton fabrics from Maverick Mountain contexts at Point of Pines Pueblo comprised roughly 60 percent of the loom-woven assemblage (Teague 1999). Cotton cloth was also plentiful at the Point of Pines caves, including Red Bow Cliff Dwelling, where Gifford (1980:74) found evidence of cotton cultivation in the form of lint, seeds, and bolls. As at Point of Pines Pueblo, cotton cloth made up roughly half the woven assemblage at Canyon Creek. The absence of cotton cloth from sites in the San Simon branch further underscores the peripheral nature of this branch to the core Mogollon and its close affinities with traditions in northern Mexico.

Noncotton plain weaves of yucca, agave, or apocynum (Indian hemp) are another extremely important Mogollon fabric type, especially in the more northern branches. The earliest well-dated example, with a two-ply warp and single-ply weft, comes from a Late Circle Prairie phase (AD 400–

Table 16.6 Distribution of Plain, Openwork, Float, and Twill Weaves in Site Sample by Time Period and Branch

Fabric Type	Site	750 BC–AD 150	AD 150–700	AD 700–1000	AD 1000–1200	AD 1200–1450	Total
Noncotton plain weaves	San Simon	—	—	—	—	—	—
	Mimbres	—	—	2	~2	2	~6
	Cibola	1	—	~7	~7	~22	~37
	Black River	—	1	—	—	~11	~12
	Forestdale	—	—	—	—	~8	~8
	Subtotal	1	1	~9	~9	~43	~63
Cotton plain weaves	San Simon	—	—	—	—	—	—
	Mimbres	—	—	—	~5	~39	~44
	Cibola	—	—	~6	~3	~7	~16
	Black River	—	—	—	~3	~28	~31
	Forestdale	—	—	—	—	3	3
	Subtotal	—	—	~6	~11	~77	~94
Openwork weaves	San Simon	—	—	—	—	—	—
	Mimbres	—	—	—	~5	~3	~8
	Cibola	—	—	—	—	—	—
	Black River	—	—	—	1	1	2
	Forestdale	—	—	—	—	1	1
	Subtotal	—	—	—	~6	~5	~11
Extra-weft float weave (brocade)	San Simon	—	—	—	—	—	—
	Mimbres	—	—	—	—	2	2
	Cibola	—	—	—	—	—	—
	Black River	—	—	—	—	—	—
	Forestdale	—	—	—	—	1	1
	Subtotal	—	—	—	—	3	3
Twill and twill-tapestry weaves	San Simon	—	—	—	—	—	—
	Mimbres	—	—	—	—	1	1
	Cibola	—	—	—	—	~2	~2
	Black River	—	—	—	—	1	1
	Forestdale	—	—	—	—	—	—
	Subtotal	—	—	—	1	~4	~4
	Total	1	1	~15	~26	~132	~175

Note: Quantities and dates inferred from the literature. Quantities reflect estimated number of original objects, not number of fragments.

Table 16.7 Source Data for Mogollon Fabrics

Twined fabrics

MIMBRES BRANCH
Gila Cliff Dwellings (Anderson et al. 1986:22, 217, fig. 11.2a)
NAN Ranch Ruin (Adovasio et al. 1996:5–6)
Various Upper Gila caves (Cosgrove 1947:66, 67, 70n4, figs. 23a, 25, 79g)

CIBOLA BRANCH
Bat Cave (Wills 1988a:105, 122)
Higgins Flat Pueblo (Martin et al. 1956:130)
Mariana Mesa (McGimsey 1980:167)
Quemado Alegre (Akins 1998:54, fig. 24, top right)
Tularosa and Cordova caves (Hough 1914:71–75, 87, 133; Martin et al. 1952:246–248, fig. 113)

BLACK RIVER BRANCH
Crooked Ridge Village (Wheat 1954:164–165)
McEuen Cave (Kelly 1937:31, 39, plate XIV; Moreno 2000:353)

Looped fabrics

SAN SIMON BRANCH
U Bar Cave (Lambert and Ambler 1961:49, fig. 31)

MIMBRES BRANCH
Various Upper Gila caves (Cosgrove 1947:71–72, figs. 26b, d)

CIBOLA BRANCH
Cordova and Tularosa caves (Martin et al. 1952:245, figs. 112a, c)

BLACK RIVER BRANCH
McEuen Cave (Kelly 1937:35–41, fig. 11, plates XII, XIII)
Point of Pines Pueblo (Webster 2001)
Red Bow Cliff Dwelling (Gifford 1980:75, figs. 55, 56)

Plain-weave fabrics

MIMBRES BRANCH
Bear Creek Cave (Hough 1914:76)
Cameron Creek Village (Bradfield 1931:plate IV, fig. 2)
Cliff effigy cache (Walt 1978:13)
Gila Cliff Dwellings (Anderson et al. 1986:219, 220, 310)
Harris Village (Haury 1936a:78)
NAN Ranch Ruin (Adovasio et al. 1996:10–12)
Swarts Ruin (Cosgrove and Cosgrove 1932:67)
Various Upper Gila caves (Cosgrove 1947:23, 69, fig. 79b)

CIBOLA BRANCH
Bat Cave (Dick 1965:81)
Cordova and Tularosa caves (Hough 1914:82; Martin et al. 1952:244)

Higgins Flat Pueblo (Martin et al. 1956:130, fig. 69b)
Mariana Mesa (McGimsey 1980:166)
Spur Ranch and "Head of Tularosa" (unpublished Hough collections)
Table Rock Pueblo (Martin and Rinaldo 1960:282)

BLACK RIVER BRANCH
Bonita Creek (Wasley 1962:381, 391)
Crooked Ridge Village (Wheat 1954:165, 1955:154)
McEuen Cave (Kelly 1937:58)
Pine Flat Cave, Red Bow Cliff Dwelling, and Tule Tubs Cave (Gifford 1980:74, 132, 178, figs. 54, 134)
Point of Pines Pueblo (Teague 1999)

FORESTDALE BRANCH
Canyon Creek Pueblo (Haury 1934:87, 91, 101, 153, plate LXIb)

Openwork fabrics

MIMBRES BRANCH
Bear Creek and Upper Johnson caves (Hough 1914:76–79)
Various Upper Gila caves (Cosgrove 1947:8–10, 29, 75–76, figs. 30a, b, 85, 86a–e; Kent 1983:66–68, fig. 33c)

BLACK RIVER BRANCH
Point of Pines Pueblo (Teague 1999)
Cave near Solomonville (Hough 1914:79)

FORESTDALE BRANCH
Canyon Creek Pueblo (Haury 1934:87–91)

Supplementary weft (brocade) fabrics

MIMBRES BRANCH
Cliff effigy cache (Walt 1978:13, fig. 19)
Gila Cliff Dwellings (Anderson et al. 1986:31–32, 220, fig. 4.8, 11.2b, c; Teague 1998:87)

FORESTDALE BRANCH
Canyon Creek Pueblo (Haury 1934:91, plate LXIa; Teague 1999)

Twill and twill-tapestry weaves

MIMBRES BRANCH
Cliff effigy cache (Walt 1978:13)

CIBOLA BRANCH
Mariana Mesa (McGimsey 1980:166)
Tularosa Cave (Kent 1983:164, fig. 98a; Martin et al. 1952:244–245, 299, fig. 111)

BLACK RIVER BRANCH
Point of Pines Pueblo (Teague 1999)

600) context at Crooked Ridge Village (Wheat 1954, 1955). What might be an even earlier example is a narrow strip of plain-weave cloth of unidentified fiber from Pre-Pottery levels at Cordova Cave; given its early context, I consider it unlikely that this would

be cotton. Noncotton cloth is earlier than cotton cloth at Tularosa Cave (Martin et al. 1952:244), where noncotton cloth resembling modern burlap came from San Francisco and San Francisco through Tularosa levels. Noncotton plain-weave cloth was also

recovered from Level 2 of Bat Cave, tentatively dated between AD 500 and 1000. Hough (1907, 1914) also collected several examples of noncotton plain weaves near the modern towns of Reserve and Luna, New Mexico (see fig. 16.6d). The Mimbres site of

Harris Village yielded another example.

Loom-woven fabrics are almost evenly divided between cotton and noncotton cloth at the post–AD 1200 sites of Gila Cliff Dwellings, Point of Pines, Pine Flat Cave, and Canyon Creek. Some of the effigies from the Cliff Valley cache were wrapped in a large agave blanket and also associated with cotton fabrics. At Canyon Creek noncotton plain weaves were used exclusively as burial wrappings. The use of noncotton plain weaves as shrouds was widespread in northern Mexico and, as will be discussed, also at Zuni.

Other Fabric Structures. A variety of other fabric structures also occur at Mogollon sites (see fig. 16.10). These include gauze and weft-wrap openwork (see fig. 16.2f, g), supplementary-weft weaves (also known as extra-weft float or brocade), a variety of lacelike structures, including interlinking (see fig. 16.2e) and linking on foundation elements, and twill and twill-tapestry weaves. Nearly all of these finer fabrics are worked in cotton. All openwork examples in the sample came from cave shrines in the upper and middle Gila drainages. Although none have been found at Classic Mimbres village sites, this is almost certainly a problem of preservation, as depictions of openwork garments on Mimbres bowls suggest their important ritual role in Mimbres society (e.g., Teague 1998:fig. 3.23). After AD 1200 weft-wrap openwork fabrics are also found at the Gila Cliff Dwellings, Canyon Creek, and Point of Pines Pueblo.

Like weft-wrap openwork, supplementary weft (brocade) is a Mexican technique that appears relatively late in the pre-Hispanic U.S. Southwest. Only three definite examples are known from the Mogollon region, one from the Gila Cliff Dwellings,

another from the Cliff effigy cache, and a third from Canyon Creek, all postdating AD 1250. Teague (1999) suggests that the Canyon Creek textile might have been traded in. She also cites another example from Tularosa Cave (Teague 1998:87), which Kent (1983:164, fig. 98) identified as twill tapestry (see also Martin et al. 1952:fig. 111).

Twill and twill-tapestry weaves occur at Mogollon sites but are generally confined to the more northern regions. This is not surprising, given that twill weaves are more typical of traditions on the Colorado Plateau. McGimsey (1980:166) describes an under-2, over-4 twill weave from Mariana Mesa, and Teague mentions 2/2 twill fabrics from Point of Pines Pueblo. McGimsey also describes what sound like tapestry and twill-tapestry weaves from Site 616 on Mariana Mesa. These latter fragments are not illustrated in the report, so I cannot confirm his identification. As noted above, Kent also identified a decorated fragment from Tularosa Cave as twill tapestry (Martin et al. 1952:fig. 111). Farther south, the Cliff effigy cache contained a small piece of cotton cloth woven in herringbone twill.

Mogollon Basketry

Among the many reported varieties of Mogollon basketry (see Cosgrove 1947; Martin et al. 1952) I selected six of the more common constructions for the study: four coiled basketry constructions (one-rod, two-rod-and-bundle, bundle-with-rod-core, and bundle foundations) and two forms of plaited objects (mats and baskets). Figure 16.11 summarizes the chronological sequence for these constructions, table 16.8 summarizes their spatial and temporal distribution, and table 16.9 provides their source data.

Coiled Baskets with a One-Rod Foundation. One-rod basketry (see fig. 16.4a) is documented as early as the Early Agricultural period in the Mogollon region. The earliest well-dated Mogollon example has interlocking stitches and comes from Cienega Creek near Point of Pines, where it was associated with a cremation dated between ca. 100 BC and AD 100 (another basket associated with the same cremation has a two-rod-and-bundle foundation). Another possible Early Agricultural period (or earlier?) example with interlocking stitches comes from Bat Cave, although Wills (1988a) cites problems with the dating. Two complete, undated baskets from McEuen Cave—one with a woven-in black design, the other with a red-painted decoration applied as the coiling progressed (Kelly 1937:22)—are additional candidates for this early period. The latter coloring process is reminiscent of the aforementioned Late Archaic or Early Agricultural period dry-dyeing technique.

One-rod foundation coiling is present but on the decline during the Early Pithouse period, when examples are known from the Cibola and Black River branches and east of the Reserve but evidently not the caves of the Reserve. From NAN Ranch Ruin Adovasio and others (1996:8) report a Late Pithouse period example with noninterlocking stitches, which they identify as a parching tray. These authors note a high correlation between one-rod foundation coiling and parching trays, which suggests that the decline of one-rod foundation coiling in the Mogollon region may be related to changes in food-processing and food-procurement strategies. The only other example of one-rod foundation coiling from the Mimbres branch is an undated example of sifter coiling (multiple-stitch-and-wrap) from Water Canyon Cave.

Basketry Type	ca. 1750 BC –AD 200	AD 200– 700	AD 700– 1000	AD 1000– 1250	AD 1250– 1400
One rod	●	●	●↓		●
Two-rod-and-bundle	●	●	●	●	●
Bundle-with-rod-core	●	●	●	○ ?	●
Bundle-foundation coiling		●	●	●	●↑
Twill-plaited matting		●	●↑	●	●
Twill-plaited ring baskets			●	●	●
Plaited baskets (new forms)				●	●
Wickerwork plaques					○ (rare)

Figure 16.11. Temporal distribution of Mogollon basketry types.

A late example of one-rod foundation coiling occurs at Bonita Creek in the Black River branch, where a ritual cache yielded 65 miniature baskets made with noninterlocking stitches worked on three different coiling foundations (one-rod, two-rod, and bundle). Other late examples of one-rod foundation coiling are known from the San Simon branch. These baskets suggest a close relationship with northern Chihuahua, where one-rod foundation coiling was a late, dominant coiling technique (King 1974:81, 104–106; Lister 1958:85).

Coiled Baskets with a Two-Rod-and-Bundle Bunched Foundation. Coiling with a two-rod-and-bundle foundation (see fig. 16.4b) and noninterlocking stitches is the most common coiling technique in the Mogollon region (see table 16.8), just as it was on the southern Colorado Plateau. It occurs in significant quantities in late Early Agricultural period levels at Tularosa Cave and was also associated with the previously mentioned Early Agricultural period cremation at Cienega Creek. By the Early Pithouse period evidence of this construction is present at Cordova Cave, O Block Cave, Tularosa Cave, and probably Bat Cave and Quemado Alegre in the Cibola branch. Thereafter it dominates

coiled basketry assemblages throughout the Mogollon sequence.

Bear Creek Cave on the Blue River produced 12 miniature baskets, which Hough (1914:fig. 317) identified as basket pahos. Executed in a stitch-and-wrap technique and painted with simple designs, a few of these baskets were still mounted on sticks when found (see fig. 16.4h). Like the miniature baskets from the Bonita Creek cache, these incorporate a variety of foundation constructions, including two-rod-and-bundle, bundle-with-rod-core, and bundle foundations.

In contrast to most ancestral Pueblo basketry on the Colorado Plateau, most Mogollon two-rod-and-bundle baskets are undecorated. However, the Mogollon sample includes some interesting exceptions. A wedge-shaped carrying basket patterned with simple zigzag designs was recovered from U Bar Cave (Lambert and Ambler 1961:fig. 40) and contained, among other items, an enormous hunting net made of human hair. Although the site's excavators dated this site to the Animas phase (AD 1350–1400), Matson (1991:291) has suggested an earlier attribution for the basket, perhaps as early as the late Early Agricultural period. If depictions of geometrically patterned, wedge-shaped burden baskets on Classic Mimbres bowls are

any indication (e.g., Davis 1995:131, 133, 155, 172, 190, 191), then this specimen would fit quite comfortably within the eleventh- and twelfth-century Mimbres basketry repertoire.

The Pinaleño cotton cache yielded two elaborately decorated two-rod-and-bundle baskets, which produced radiocarbon dates of cal AD 654–873 and 602–770 (2σ). Both have interlocking key designs said to resemble Pueblo III basket designs from Mesa Verde (Haury and Huckell 1993:126, figs. 14–16; cf. Morris and Burgh 1941:39–40, figs. 17d, e, 29a, d). Cosgrove (1947:103, figs. 35a, 97c, 98a, b) recovered three decorated baskets from the upper Gila caves, one with an interlocking hook or key design (see fig. 16.4e) and two with finite designs similar to those used to decorate weft-wrap openwork and gauze-weave fabrics after AD 1000 (see Kent 1983:fig. 135; Teague 1998:145–156). Another elaborately decorated basket from McEuen Cave has an interlocking scroll design reminiscent of Tonto Polychrome (Jeffery J. Clark, personal communication 2003).

Coiled Baskets with a Bundle-with-Rod-Core Foundation. Hyland and Adovasio (2000:147) interpret this structure as a southern (Mexican) technique (see fig. 16.4c). Morris and Burgh (1941:11; see also Nusbaum 1922:96; Weltfish 1932:16), on the other hand, consider it a variant of two-rod-and-bundle. Although this foundation type saw use in the Mogollon region, it has only been found in small quantities and at a limited number of sites (see tables 16.8, 16.9). Early examples are reported from a late Early Agricultural period level at Tularosa Cave (Martin et al. 1952:250–309) and from Bat Cave in levels attributed to this same early horizon (Dick 1965:71). This construction also occurs late in the Mogollon sequence at Red Bow Cliff Dwelling and is one

Table 16.8 Distribution of Baskets and Mats in Site Sample by Time Period and Branch

Basketry Structure or Object Type	Site	750 BC–AD 150	AD 150–700	AD 700–1000	AD 1000–1200	AD 1200–1450	Total
One-rod foundation	San Simon	—	—	—	—	2	2
	Mimbres	—	—	1	—	1	2
	Cibola	>1	1	>1	—	—	>3
	Black River	4	—	~1	—	~20	~25
	Forestdale	—	—	—	—	—	—
	Subtotal	*>5*	*1*	*~3*	*—*	*~23*	*~32*
Two-rod-and-bundle foundation	San Simon	—	—	—	—	>3	>3
	Mimbres	—	~1	1	~10	~13	~25
	Cibola	6	~22	~10	~5	~3	~46
	Black River	3	~1	~2	—	~24	~30
	Forestdale	—	2	—	—	—	2
	Subtotal	*9*	*~26*	*~13*	*~15*	*~43*	*~106*
Bundle-with-rod-core foundation	San Simon	—	—	—	—	—	—
	Mimbres	—	1	—	—	~4	~5
	Cibola	>2	2	2	—	—	>6
	Black River	—	—	—	—	1	1
	Forestdale	—	—	—	—	—	—
	Subtotal	*>2*	*3*	*2*	*—*	*~5*	*~12*
Bundle foundation	San Simon	—	—	—	—	—	—
	Mimbres	—	—	~3	~3	~9	~15
	Cibola	—	1	1	~1	~1	~4
	Black River	—	—	—	—	~29	~29
	Forestdale	—	—	—	—	~4	~4
	Subtotal	*—*	*1*	*~4*	*~4*	*~43*	*~52*
Plaited baskets	San Simon	—	—	—	—	—	—
	Mimbres	—	—	—	—	~6	~6
	Cibola	—	—	~1	~3	~3	~7
	Black River	—	—	—	—	~6	~6
	Forestdale	—	—	—	—	3	3
	Subtotal	*—*	*—*	*~1*	*~3*	*~18*	*~22*
Plaited mats	San Simon	—	—	—	—	—	—
	Mimbres	—	—	~4	~7	~20	~31
	Cibola	—	1	~5	~41	~9	~56
	Black River	—	—	—	~2	~19	~21
	Forestdale	—	—	—	—	~5	~5
	Subtotal	*—*	*1*	*~9*	*~50*	*~53*	*~113*
	Total	*>16*	*~32*	*~32*	*~72*	*~185*	*~337*

Note: Quantities and dates inferred from the literature. Quantities reflect estimated number of original objects, not number of fragments.

Table 16.9 Source Data for Mogollon Basketry

Coiling with one-rod foundation

SAN SIMON BRANCH
Buffalo and Deer Creek caves (Cosgrove 1947:41, 99, fig. 33h, i; Lambert and Ambler 1961:64, fig. 42, right)

MIMBRES BRANCH
NAN Ranch Ruin (Adovasio et al. 1996:8–9)
Water Canyon Cave (Cosgrove 1947:99, 105, figs. 33d, 97a)

CIBOLA BRANCH
Bat Cave (Dick 1965:71–72)
Quemado Alegre (Akins 1998:327, table 22)

BLACK RIVER BRANCH
Bonita Creek (Wasley 1962:385–386, figs. 8, 9)
Cienega Creek (Haury 1957:19; Wills 1988a:138)
Crooked Ridge Village (Wheat 1954:167)
McEuen Cave (Kelly 1937:22, plates VI, VII)

Coiling with two-rod-and-bundle foundation

SAN SIMON BRANCH
Pinnacle and U Bar caves (Lambert and Ambler 1961:62–64, figs. 40, 41, 42, left)

MIMBRES BRANCH
Bear Creek Cave (Hough 1914:89–90, 124–125, plate 24; Morris and Burgh 1941:16)
Gila Cliff Dwellings (Anderson et al. 1986:229, fig. 13.1a)
Harris Village (Haury 1936a:78)
NAN Ranch Ruin (Adovasio et al. 1996:9–10)
Swarts Ruin (Cosgrove and Cosgrove 1932:67, fig. 15)
Various Upper Gila caves (Cosgrove 1947:102–103, figs. 33c, m, 34b, 97c–e, 98a, b)

CIBOLA BRANCH
Bat Cave (Dick 1965:72)
Cordova and Tularosa caves (Martin et al. 1952:250, figs. 85, 117, top)
Higgins Flat Pueblo (Martin et al. 1956:132, fig. 69c)
Mariana Mesa (McGimsey 1980:166)
O Block Cave (Martin et al. 1954:173, fig. 87)
Quemado Alegre (Akins 1998:327, table 22)
Spur Ranch (Hough 1914:90)

BLACK RIVER BRANCH
Cienega Creek (Haury 1957:19; Wills 1988a:138)
McEuen Cave (Kelly 1937:18–20, fig. 6.8, Plate V)
Pinaleño cotton cache (Haury and Huckell 1993:117, 120, 123, figs. 14–16)
Pine Flat Cave and Red Bow Cliff Dwelling (Gifford 1980:86, 180, fig. 71)
Point of Pines Pueblo (Webster 2001)

FORESTDALE BRANCH
Bear Ruin (Haury 1985a:174, 252)

Coiling with bundle-with-rod-core

MIMBRES BRANCH
Bear Creek Cave (Hough 1914:89–90, 124–125, plate 24; Morris and Burgh 1941:16)
Steamboat Cave (Cosgrove 1947:101, figs. 33k, 97b)

CIBOLA BRANCH
Bat Cave (Dick 1965:71)
Cordova and Tularosa caves (Martin et al. 1952:250, 309, fig. 116b, d, f)
Quemado Alegre (Akins 1998:327, table 22)

BLACK RIVER BRANCH
Red Bow Cliff Dwelling (Gifford 1980:86)

Coiling with bundle foundation

MIMBRES BRANCH
Bear Creek Cave (Hough 1914:89–90, 124–125, plate 24; Morris and Burgh 1941:16)
Gila Cliff Dwellings (Anderson et al. 1986:229, fig. 13.1e)
NAN Ranch Ruin (Adovasio et al. 1996:6–8)

CIBOLA BRANCH
Kelly Cave (Cosgrove 1947:26, 104)
Quemado Alegre (Akins 1998:327, table 22)
Table Rock Pueblo (Martin and Rinaldo 1960:282)
Tularosa Cave (Martin et al. 1952:250, 310, fig. 117, bottom)

BLACK RIVER BRANCH
Bonita Creek Cache (Wasley 1962:385–386, figs. 8, 9)
McEuen Cave (Kelly 1937:26, plates VIII, IX, X)
Point of Pines (Webster 2001)
Red Bow Cliff Dwelling (Gifford 1980:86)

FORESTDALE BRANCH
Canyon Creek Pueblo (Haury 1934:73–76, plates LI, LIIa)

Plaited baskets

MIMBRES BRANCH
Bear Creek Cave (Hough 1914:88, 89, figs. 179, 180)
Cliff effigy cache (Walt 1978:12–13, fig. 17)

CIBOLA BRANCH
Bat Cave (Dick 1965:72)
Gila Cliff Dwellings (Anderson et al. 1986:229, 231, fig. 13.1f)
Higgins Flat Pueblo (Martin et al. 1956:132, fig. 69d)
Mule Creek Cave (Cosgrove 1947:111–112, fig. 102b)
Spur Ranch (Hough 1914:89, Figures 3, 4, plate 16)
Tularosa Cave (Hough 1914:89, plate 16, no. 1; Martin et al. 1952:251, 312, fig. 118)

BLACK RIVER BRANCH
McEuen Cave (Kelly 1937:18, plate IV)
Point of Pines Pueblo (Webster 2001)
Red Bow Cliff Dwelling (Gifford 1980:86)

FORESTDALE BRANCH
Canyon Creek (Haury 1934:72–73, plates XLIX, LVIII)

Plaited matting

MIMBRES BRANCH
Bear Creek Cave (Hough 1914:89, plate 16, nos. 2, 6)
Gila Cliff Dwellings (Anderson et al. 1986:231)
NAN Ranch Ruin (Adovasio et al. 1996:12–14)
Various Upper Gila caves (Cosgrove 1947:115–117, figs. 37–39, 107b–f, 108a, 109)

CIBOLA BRANCH
Higgins Flat Pueblo (Martin et al. 1956:133–134, fig. 69e)
Mariana Mesa (McGimsey 1980:166)
O Block Cave and Hinkle Park Cliff Dwelling (Martin et al. 1954:173, figs. 88, 89)
Tularosa Cave (Martin et al. 1952:253, figs. 124, 145)

BLACK RIVER BRANCH
Pine Flat Cave and Red Bow Cliff Dwelling (Gifford 1980:86, 180, figs. 69, 113a, 135b)
Point of Pines Pueblo (Webster 2001)

FORESTDALE BRANCH
Canyon Creek Pueblo (Haury 1934:81–83, plates XLVIc, LIVb, d)

of the foundations used to make the 12 miniature basketry pahos from Bear Creek Cave.

Coiled Baskets with a Bundle Foundation. Two major forms of bundle-foundation baskets occur in the Mogollon region: (1) *close-coiled* baskets with small coils and closely spaced stitches and (2) *coarse-coiled* baskets with thick bundles and widely spaced stitches (see fig. 16.4f, g). The coarse-coiled baskets resemble granary baskets made historically by the Akimel O'odham (Pima) (Haury 1934:74, 76, plate LIIa; Kissell 1916:179–190), whereas the close-coiled ones are similar to historic O'odham and Hopi baskets (Teiwes 1996). Early occurrences of bundle-foundation coiling include one example from the Early Pithouse period site of Quemado Alegre and two crude miniature baskets from Tularosa Cave attributed to Georgetown through San Francisco and San Francisco through Tularosa levels. Baskets with thick coils and spaced stitches, including a collapsed globular storage basket, are reported from San Francisco and Three Circle contexts (AD 650–1000) at NAN Ranch Ruin (Adovasio et al. 1996).

Sometime after AD 1200 large, coarse-coiled, granary-like baskets, some with detachable lids, made a widespread appearance in the Mogollon region. Definite or possible examples come from Point of Pines Pueblo, the Point of Pines caves, Canyon Creek, McEuen Cave, Tularosa Cave, Bear Creek Cave, Kelly Cave, and the Gila Cliff Dwellings (see fig. 16.4f, g). Similar examples are known from Sinagua and Salado sites (e.g., Steen et al. 1962:23, plate 11c; Van Valkenburgh 1954:32). The late appearance of these granary baskets suggests a historic connection with modern Piman speakers.

Bundle foundation is the only shared foundation type among the miniature ritual baskets from Bear Creek Cave and Bonita Creek, with their wide assortment of stitches and foundation types. Two miniature baskets from Tularosa Cave resemble those from Bonita Creek and may be additional examples of this ritual basketry form.

Plaited Matting and Basketry. Twill-plaited mats (see fig. 16.8) are widespread at Mogollon sites (see tables 16.8, 16.9). The earliest plaited mats in the sample come from Tularosa Cave, where small quantities are reported from Georgetown and San Francisco levels (AD 550–825/850). By the Reserve phase (AD 1000) plaited matting was present at virtually all Mogollon sites. People in the Mogollon region wove 2/2 and 3/3 twill matting (the latter predominant) using 90-degree self-selvages and 90-degree pattern shifts (see fig. 16.8b, c). They employed these mats for a variety of purposes, including floor coverings, liners for storage bins, and, after AD 1200, mortuary wrappings.

Plaited baskets are relatively late at Mogollon sites. The earliest well-dated example is a probable ring basket from Higgins Flat Pueblo (AD 1175/1200–1275). Martin and others (1952:497) report one example from San Francisco through Tularosa levels at Tularosa Cave and suggest that plaited basketry displaced coiled basketry in importance during the San Francisco phase. Plaited sandals also gained in popularity during this time.

Two types of twill-plaited baskets occur at Mogollon sites: ring baskets with plaited elements bent over a reinforcing rod and baskets without a rod. Most are woven in 3/3 twill. Ring baskets, or fragments believed to be from ring baskets, are known from Bear Creek Cave, Canyon Creek, Gila Cliff Dwellings, Higgins Flat Pueblo, Mule Creek Cave, Point of Pines Pueblo, and Tularosa Cave. Like those of the

Mesa Verde region, some Mogollon ring baskets have an ornamental braid just below the rim (see fig. 16.8d–f; see also Martin et al. 1952:fig. 118, bottom; Morris and Burgh 1941:23, figs. 8, 35). Ring baskets from Canyon Creek, Higgins Flat Pueblo, Point of Pines Pueblo, Red Bow Cliff Dwelling, and Tularosa Cave bear a stronger resemblance to those from the Colorado Plateau, whereas some from the upper Gila are quite distinct from those found farther north and west. The latter include square or globular (jar-shaped) examples from Bear Creek and Mule Creek caves and the Gila Cliff Dwellings (see fig. 16.8f, g).

The other type of Mogollon plaited basket lacks a reinforcing rod entirely. Some of these also assume forms that are quite distinct from most baskets on the Colorado Plateau. These include cylindrical or bottle-shaped baskets from Bat Cave and Spur Ranch (see fig. 16.8h), an ovoid cradlelike container from the Cliff Valley cache, two square-shaped baskets from Canyon Creek (one with a double selvage) (see fig. 16.8i), and another plaited basket with a double selvage from McEuen Cave, all of which probably postdate AD 1100. Historic analogues for many of these forms and techniques are known from southern Arizona and northern Mexico. The double selvage treatment, in particular, is characteristic of square and round plaited baskets made by the historic O'odham of Arizona, the Yaqui and Pima Bajo of Sonora, and the Rarámuri (Tarahumara) and Tepehuan of Chihuahua (Bennett and Zingg 1935:88; Brugge 1956:8–9; Kissell 1916:fig. 14; Mason 1904:526–527, plate 237; Pennington 1963:200, 1969:195). The historic use of such baskets for straining cheese, nixtamal, and *tesgüino* (corn beer) suggests that their appearance at late Mogollon sites might be related to new culinary practices.

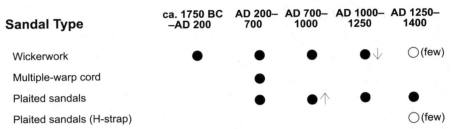

Sandal Type	ca. 1750 BC –AD 200	AD 200– 700	AD 700– 1000	AD 1000– 1250	AD 1250– 1400
Wickerwork	●	●	●	●↓	○ (few)
Multiple-warp cord		●			
Plaited sandals		●	●↑	●	●
Plaited sandals (H-strap)					○ (few)

Figure 16.12. Temporal distribution of Mogollon sandal types.

Wicker Basketry. The only confirmed evidence of wicker baskets (see fig. 16.9a) in the Mogollon region comes from the fourteenth-century site of Canyon Creek, where Haury (1934:78, plate LIII) recovered several wickerwork trays resembling those made historically at Hopi and Zuni (Teiwes 1996; Whiteford 1988; cf. fig. 16.9b). Haury (1934:78) viewed them as a Pueblo IV Mogollon-Pueblo innovation, but their origins remain obscure. I discuss these plaques in greater detail in the section on Zuni basketry.

Mogollon Sandals

Figure 16.12 summarizes the temporal development of sandals within the Mogollon region, table 16.10 shows their spatial and temporal distribution, and table 16.11 summarizes their source data.

Plain-Weave (Wickerwork) Sandals. Weft-faced plain-weave sandals (see figs. 16.3c, d and 16.7a–c), often referred to as wickerwork sandals, are the earliest sandal type in the Mogollon region and the predominant style from the Early Agricultural period through the San Francisco phase (see fig. 16.12 and table 16.10). With few exceptions, Mogollon wickerwork sandals are woven in 1/1 plain weave, are full-length (as opposed to the scuffer-toe type, which typically covers only the ball of the foot), and lack the fishtail heel. To permit comparisons among sites, I utilize Cosgrove's sandal type designations in the following

discussion. Five main variations of plain-weave sandals occur at Mogollon sites: (1) a two-warp sandal with yucca-leaf warp and shredded fiber weft (cf. figs. 16.3c and 16.7a to Cosgrove 1947:90, figs. 91, 92, Type 11); (2) a two-warp sandal with a yucca-leaf warp and rigid yucca-leaf weft (cf. fig. 16.7b to Cosgrove 1947:88, figs. 91, 92, Type 8); (3) a four-, five-, or six-warp sandal with yucca-leaf warp and shredded yucca weft, usually having the warps folded back over the toe (cf. figs. 16.3d and 16.7c to Cosgrove 1947:90, figs. 91, 92, Types 12, 13); (4) a multiple-warp sandal with a concentric warp and usually plied cordage warp and weft (cf. fig. 16.7d to Cosgrove 1947:91, figs. 91, 92, Type 14); and (5) a tightly woven multiple-warp cord sandal made with fine cordage elements (see fig. 16.7e; no Cosgrove equivalent). Evidence from Tularosa and Cordova caves suggests that the two- and four-warp varieties are contemporaneous at these sites (Martin et al. 1952:233–235).

Two-warp wickerwork sandals with yucca-leaf warp and shredded fiber weft (Cosgrove's Type 11; see figs. 16.3c and 16.7a) occur at nearly all Mogollon sites having perishables and are the earliest type in the region. This type is especially prevalent at sites in the Mimbres and Reserve areas. Sandals from Tularosa, Cordova, McEuen, and O Block caves and other caves in the upper Gila reportedly have a warp constructed from two leaves tied together at the toe and the heel. Information is lacking about

the warp construction of sandals from other Mogollon branches. This Type 11 sandal is the oldest type at Bat Cave, Cordova Cave, and Tularosa Cave, where some examples are attributed to the Early Agricultural period. Tularosa Cave produced nine examples from the Pre-Pottery level alone. At Cordova and Tularosa caves this type declined after the San Francisco phase (ca. AD 1000) but is present at later sites in the Point of Pines region.

Cosgrove's Type 8 sandal with rigid wefts (see fig. 16.7b) occurs only on the periphery of the Mogollon region and is not a significant Mogollon type. The only known Mogollon occurrences of this style come from ceramic (?) levels at Bat Cave and Mimbres or Animas phase contexts at Pinnacle Cave in the Alamo Hueco Mountains. Most of these rigid-weft sandals have four warps rather than the two described by Cosgrove.

Cosgrove's Type 13 sandal has four, five, or six yucca-leaf warps, with the warp elements folded over 180 degrees at the toe and a weft of shredded yucca (see fig. 16.3d). Most examples of this style occur at sites in the Reserve area; some from Tularosa and Cordova caves may date as early as the late Early Agricultural period. A variation of this style, in which the warps are not folded over (Cosgrove's Type 12; see fig. 16.7c), is also found in the Reserve area and resembles some Basketmaker III sandals from the Colorado Plateau (cf. fig. 16.3f).

Cosgrove's Type 14 multiple-warp sandal, with a concentric warp and plied cordage warp and weft (see fig. 16.7d), is found at early sites in the Mimbres and Reserve areas as well as late sites in the Point of Pines region. This type appears to be a Mogollon innovation. At Tularosa and Cordova caves it is reported from Pre-Pottery levels and persists into the San Francisco phase. At Quemado Alegre in the Cibola branch it occurs in Early

Table 16.10 Distribution of Sandals in Site Sample by Time Period and Branch

Fabric Type	Site	750 BC–AD 150	AD 150–700	AD 700–1000	AD 1000–1200	AD 1200–1450	Total
Plain weave, two warp	San Simon	~5	—	—	—	~19	~24
	Mimbres	~2	~3	~7	~7	—	~19
	Cibola	~19	~30	~13	~7	—	~69
	Black River	~2	~2	—	—	~1	~5
	Forestdale	—	—	—	—	—	—
	Subtotal	~28	~35	~20	~14	~20	~117
Plain weave, four or more warp	San Simon	—	—	—	—	~2	~2
	Mimbres	—	~5	~4	~3	—	~12
	Cibola	~13	~104	~29	~13	—	~159
	Black River	~1	~1	—	~1	~1	~4
	Forestdale	—	—	—	—	—	—
	Subtotal	~14	~110	~33	~17	~3	~177
Plain weave, multiple cordage warp	San Simon	—	—	—	—	—	—
	Mimbres	—	~1	~1	—	—	~2
	Cibola	—	~10	~6	—	—	~16
	Black River	—	—	—	—	—	—
	Forestdale	—	—	—	—	—	—
	Subtotal	—	~11	~7	—	—	~18
Plaited, wide elements	San Simon	—	—	—	~5	—	~5
	Mimbres	—	—	~4	~52	~6	~62
	Cibola	—	3	~19	~85	~22	~129
	Black River	—	—	—	~6	~68	~74
	Forestdale	—	—	—	—	~5	~5
	Subtotal	—	3	~23	~148	~101	~275
Plaited, narrow elements	San Simon	—	—	—	—	—	—
	Mimbres	—	—	—	—	—	—
	Cibola	—	—	—	~4	~4	~8
	Black River	—	—	—	—	4	4
	Forestdale	—	—	—	—	~8	~8
	Subtotal	—	—	—	~4	~16	~20
	Total	~42	~159	~83	~183	~140	~607

Note: Quantities and dates inferred from the literature. Quantities reflect estimated number of original objects, not number of fragments.

Table 16.11 Source Data for Mogollon Sandals

Wickerwork sandals

SAN SIMON BRANCH
Buffalo, Pinnacle, and U Bar caves (Lambert and Ambler 1961:57–61, Types I, II, III, figs. 38, 39)
Winchester Cave (Fulton 1941:31–32, fig. 7, plate VIIIc)

MIMBRES BRANCH
NAN Ranch Ruin (Adovasio et al. 1996:10–12)
Gila Cliff Dwellings (Anderson et al. 1986:233, figs. 13.2e, 13.2f)
Various Upper Gila caves (Cosgrove 1947:91, 93, 97, table 1, figs. 91, 92)

CIBOLA BRANCH
Bat Cave (Dick 1965:73–77, figs. 48a–c, 49b)
Cordova and Tularosa caves (Hough 1914:83–84, figs. 173–175; Martin et al. 1952:232–235, 239–240, figs. 83, 87–90, 103–106)
O Block and Y Canyon caves (Martin et al. 1954:162, figs. 82, 84, 85)
Quemado Alegre (Akins 1998:54–56, fig. 25)

BLACK RIVER BRANCH
McEuen Cave (Kelly 1937:2–14, plates Ie–j, II)
Pine Flat Cave and Red Bow Cliff Dwelling (Gifford 1980:11, 82, 84, 180, fig. 67c)

Multiple-warp cord sandals

MIMBRES BRANCH
Gila Cliff Dwellings (Anderson et al. 1986:234, fig. 13.2)

CIBOLA BRANCH
Bat Cave (Dick 1965:73–77, fig. 49a)
Quemado Alegre (Akins 1998:54–56, fig. 25)
Tularosa Cave (Martin et al. 1952:237–238, figs. 97–100)

Plaited sandals

SAN SIMON BRANCH
Winchester Cave (Fulton 1941:26, 31, fig. 5, plate VIIId)

MIMBRES BRANCH
Gila Cliff Dwellings (Anderson et al. 1986:231, 233, fig. 13.2a–d)
Swarts Ruin (Cosgrove and Cosgrove 1932:67)
Various Upper Gila caves (Cosgrove 1947:93, table 1, fig. 91, 92)

CIBOLA BRANCH
Bat Cave (Dick 1965:73–77, fig. 49c)
Cordova and Tularosa caves (Hough 1914:83–84, fig. 172; Martin et al. 1952:235–237, figs. 95, 96)
Hinkle Park Cliff Dwelling, Cosper Cliff Dwelling, and O Block Cave (Martin et al. 1954:162, figs. 82, 84, 85)

BLACK RIVER BRANCH
McEuen Cave (Kelly 1937:2–5, figs. 1–3, 7, plate Ia–d)
Pine Flat Cave, Red Bow Cliff Dwelling, and Tule Tubs Cave (Gifford 1980:11, 82–84, 133, figs. 67, 68)

FORESTDALE BRANCH
Canyon Creek (Haury 1934:64–68, plate XLII)

Pithouse period contexts (AD 500–550). As with the Type 13 sandal, a variation of this type also appears at Basketmaker III and Pueblo I sites on the Colorado Plateau.

The multiple-warp cord sandal (see fig. 16.7e) is distinguished from other Mogollon plain-weave sandals by its fine cordage elements and tight weave. These sandals bear a striking resemblance to Basketmaker III twined sandals from the Colorado Plateau (cf. fig. 16.7f). All four sites in the sample that produced evidence of this style are located at the northern reaches of the Mogollon region and are contemporaneous with Basketmaker III. The best-dated examples come from Tularosa Cave (Georgetown and San Francisco levels) and from Quemado Alegre (Early Pithouse period), marking the presence of this style in the Mogollon region by

AD 500–550. At Tularosa Cave the style persisted until AD 700 or later.

Unlike Basketmaker twined sandals, most Mogollon multiple-warp cord sandals are woven primarily in 1/1 plain weave. An exception from Tularosa Cave has a twined heel and toe, but the rest of the sandal is plain woven (see fig. 16.7e). Most examples from Tularosa Cave have scalloped toes, but round and square toes also occur, and all have puckered heels (Martin et al. 1952:237–238). Despite their superficial resemblance to Basketmaker twined sandals, none of the Mogollon examples exhibit the colored decoration, complex fabric structures, or knotted soles characteristic of those made in the north (see Hays-Gilpin et al. 1998). For this reason I view them as local emulations or variations of a northern sandal style rather than as Basketmaker

trade goods. The sole exception is a finely woven sandal with a scalloped toe from Bat Cave (Dick 1965:fig. 49a) that exhibits all the features of a Basketmaker III twined sandal and is probably an import from the north.

Twill-Plaited Sandals. Twill-plaited sandals (see fig. 16.7g, i) are ubiquitous at post–AD 1000 sites in the Mogollon region (table 16.10). Typical Mogollon versions are made with wide yucca elements, turned up at the heel and secured in place by a transverse strip of yucca (cf. fig. 16.7g with Cosgrove's Type 9). Most are woven in 2/1 or 1/1 twill plaiting. Although early examples are reported from plainware levels (AD 200–700) at Cordova Cave, Georgetown levels (AD 550–700) at Tularosa Cave, and Three Circle levels (AD 825/850–1000) at O Block Cave, this style did

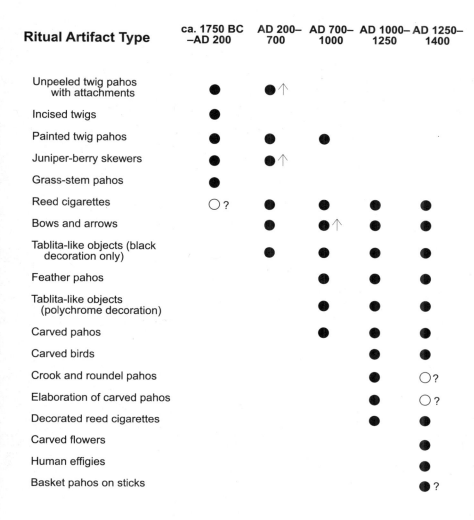

Ritual Artifact Type	ca. 1750 BC –AD 200	AD 200– 700	AD 700– 1000	AD 1000– 1250	AD 1250– 1400
Unpeeled twig pahos with attachments	●	●↑			
Incised twigs	●				
Painted twig pahos	●	●	●		
Juniper-berry skewers	●	●↑			
Grass-stem pahos	●				
Reed cigarettes	○?	●	●	●	●
Bows and arrows		●	●↑	●	●
Tablita-like objects (black decoration only)		●	●	●	●
Feather pahos			●	●	●
Tablita-like objects (polychrome decoration)			●	●	●
Carved pahos			●	●	●
Carved birds				●	●
Crook and roundel pahos				●	○?
Elaboration of carved pahos				●	○?
Decorated reed cigarettes				●	●
Carved flowers					●
Human effigies					●
Basket pahos on sticks					●?

Figure 16.13. Temporal distribution of Mogollon ritual wooden artifact types.

not achieve prominence until later periods. It evidently appeared in the San Francisco drainage around AD 700 or slightly earlier, then grew in popularity, effectively replacing the wickerwork style during the Reserve or Tularosa phase.

In addition to this typical style of Mogollon plaited sandal, a unique style of twill-plaited sandal is also reported from two Pueblo IV sites in the Mogollon-Pueblo region, Canyon Creek (see fig. 16.7i; Haury 1934:64–68, plate XLII), and Red Bow Cliff Dwelling (Gifford 1980:83). This sandal form is characterized by fine plait-

ing, narrow elements, and a distinctive H-shaped woven strap and is even more common in the Tonto and Verde drainages during this time. Not a Mogollon sandal type per se, it seems to be part of a widespread Salado sandal tradition that appeared south of the Mogollon Rim in Pueblo IV, perhaps related to Paquimé (King 1974:90, fig. 87-8; see also Schaafsma and Young, chap. 15, this vol.).

Mogollon Ritual Wooden Objects

Ritual wooden objects are an early and highly significant development

in the Mogollon region. Here I consider five major forms: (1) reed tubes and cigarettes, (2) miniature bows and arrows, (3) pahos and painted sticks, (4) tablitas and painted wands, and (5) carved birds, flowers, and human effigy figures. Although many of these items appear to have antecedents in the Early Pithouse period or earlier, their increased popularity after AD 700 reflects an important shift in ritual activities during the San Francisco period and an elaboration of Mogollon ritual thereafter. Figure 16.13 illustrates the chronological development of these objects in the Mogollon region, table 16.12 summarizes their spatial and temporal distribution, and table 16.13 provides their source data.

Most wooden objects in the sample come from poorly dated caves in the upper Gila and Blue River drainages. Such is the case for Bear Creek Cave, which produced some of the most remarkable ritual offerings from the Mogollon region. Although present evidence suggests a post–AD 1200 date for the ceremonial deposits, it is not yet possible to rule out an earlier component at the site.[8]

Mention should also be made of a functional alternative for the class of Mogollon wooden objects known as juniper-berry skewers (see fig. 16.5b). Grange (1952:366) suggested a ceremonial usage for these artifacts and believed them to be unique to the Mogollon, while Cosgrove (1947:150) interpreted them as bodkins for fastening clothing. More recently, Wylie (1974) has compared them with similar items from the Great Basin and concluded they were triggers for deadfall traps, with the skewered juniper berries serving as bait. For now, this seems the most reasonable interpretation, although this does not preclude a ritual use.

Table 16.12 Distribution of Ritual Wooden Objects in Site Sample by Time Period and Branch

Object	Site	750 BC–AD 150	AD 150–700	AD 700–1000	AD 1000–1200	AD 1200–1450	Total
Reed cigarettes	San Simon	—	—	—	88	~5	~93
	Mimbres	—	—	—	~100	~123	~223
	Cibola	48	19	19	~19	~11	~116
	Black River	—	—	—	~20	~31	~51
	Forestdale	—	—	—	—	~10	~10
	Subtotal	*48*	*19*	*19*	*~227*	*~180*	*~493*
Ceremonial bows and arrows	San Simon	—	—	—	~150	~151	~301
	Mimbres	—	—	—	~1030	~51	~1081
	Cibola	—	~2	~23	~101	~11	~137
	Black River	—	—	—	—	513	513
	Forestdale	—	—	—	—	~5	~5
	Subtotal	*—*	*~2*	*~23*	*~1281*	*~731*	*~2037*
Pahos and painted sticks	San Simon	—	—	—	~30	~56	~86
	Mimbres	—	~38	—	~50	~84	~172
	Cibola	8	27	74	~141	—	~250
	Black River	—	—	—	—	44	44
	Forestdale	—	—	—	—	—	—
	Subtotal	*8*	*~65*	*74*	*~221*	*~184*	*~552*
Tablita-like objects	San Simon	—	—	—	—	12	12
	Mimbres	—	—	—	~34	~13	~47
	Cibola	—	7	~19	~80	—	106
	Black River	—	1	—	—	3	4
	Forestdale	—	—	—	—	—	—
	Subtotal	*—*	*8*	*~19*	*~114*	*~28*	*~169*
Carved birds, flowers, human effigies	San Simon	—	—	—	—	1	1
	Mimbres	—	—	—	3	5	8
	Cibola	—	—	—	—	—	—
	Black River	—	—	—	—	7	7
	Forestdale	—	—	—	—	—	—
	Subtotal	*—*	*—*	*—*	*3*	*13*	*16*
	Total	56	~94	~135	~1846	~1136	~3267

Note: Quantities and dates inferred from the literature. Quantities reflect estimated number of original objects, not number of fragments.

Table 16.13 Source Data for Mogollon Ritual Wooden Objects

Reed cigarettes

SAN SIMON BRANCH
Buffalo Cave and Cave 3, Deer Creek (Cosgrove 1947:41, 121)
Tom Ketchum Cave (Burton 1988:336)
Pinnacle Cave (Lambert and Ambler 1961:20, 73)
Winchester Cave (Fulton 1941:20–23, plate VI)

MIMBRES BRANCH
Bear Creek Cave (Hough 1914:100, 107–110, figs. 222–230, 233–240)
Gila Cliff Dwellings (Anderson et al. 1986:199)
Various Upper Gila caves (Cosgrove 1947:121, figs. 114, 115)

CIBOLA BRANCH
Bat Cave (Dick 1965:84; Wills 1988a)
Cordova and Tularosa caves (Martin et al. 1952:351–354, figs. 132, 154)
Cosper Cliff Dwelling, Hinkle Park Cliff Dwelling, O Block Cave (Martin et al. 1954:203)
Luna Valley caves (Hough 1907:61)

BLACK RIVER BRANCH
McEuen Cave (Kelly 1937:69)
Pine Flat Cave and Red Bow Cliff Dwelling (Gifford 1980:10, 77, 179)

FORESTDALE BRANCH
Canyon Creek Pueblo (Haury 1934:114, plate LXVIIIb–e)

Ceremonial bows and arrows

SAN SIMON BRANCH
Pinnacle and U Bar caves (Lambert and Ambler 1961:12–13, 71, figs. 10, 45c, d)
Winchester Cave (Fulton 1941:15–20, plates V, XIa)

MIMBRES BRANCH
Bear Creek Cave (Hough 1914:97–100)
Gila Cliff Dwellings and Little Bear Canyon Cave (Anderson et al. 1986:19, 185–187, 202, fig. 14.2c)
Unnamed cave south of Gila Cliff Dwellings (Hibben 1938:36–38, plates 3, 4)
Various Upper Gila caves (Cosgrove 1947:130–132, fig. 123a–i)

CIBOLA BRANCH
Hinkle Park Cliff Dwelling and O Block Cave (Martin et al. 1954:180, 210)
Luna Valley caves (Hough 1907:61)
Tularosa Cave (Martin et al. 1952:347–350, 413–414, figs. 147, 152)

BLACK RIVER BRANCH
Bonita Creek cache (Wasley 1962:382, 389)
Mount Baldy summit (Morris 1982:50)
Red Bow Cliff Dwelling (Gifford 1980:93, figs. 73, 74)

FORESTDALE BRANCH
Canyon Creek Pueblo (Haury 1934:106–108, fig. 22)

Painted sticks and pahos

SAN SIMON BRANCH
Adams Cave near Solomonville (unpublished collection, National Museum of Natural History)
U Bar Cave (Lambert and Ambler 1961:75–77, fig. 49a, c, d)

MIMBRES BRANCH
Bear Creek Cave (Hough 1914:93–97, 124–145, 129, figs. 201, 327, 329, 331, 339–348, plates 20, 24)
Gila Cliff Dwellings and Little Bear Canyon cave (Anderson et al. 1986:19, 191–197, 235–236; figs. 10.2, 10.3)
Various Upper Gila caves (Cosgrove 1947:119–130, 132, figs. 117–122)

CIBOLA BRANCH
Cordova and Tularosa caves (Martin et al. 1952:354–359, 371–372, figs. 131, 132)
Mariana Mesa Site 616 (McGimsey 1980:74)
O Block Cave (Martin et al. 1954:200, fig. 100)

BLACK RIVER BRANCH
McEuen Cave (Kelly 1937:69)
Red Bow Cliff Dwelling (Gifford 1980:91, figs. 62b, 72, 74g)

Tablita-like objects and split-stick wands

SAN SIMON BRANCH
U Bar Cave (Lambert and Ambler 1961:76–77, fig. 49b)

MIMBRES BRANCH
Bear Creek Cave (Hough 1914:figs. 217, 339–348, plates 22, 26)
Gila Cliff Dwellings (Anderson et al. 1986:200, figs. 10.4a, 14.2a)
Various Upper Gila caves (Cosgrove 1947:132–134, figs. 41, 125, 126, frontispiece b–j)

CIBOLA BRANCH
Cordova Cave (Martin et al. 1952:354, 421–422, figs. 155–156)
Hinkle Park Cliff Dwelling and O Block Cave (Martin et al. 1954:200–202)

BLACK RIVER BRANCH
Bonita Creek cache (Wasley 1962:387, fig. 10e, f, h)
Crooked Ridge Village (Wheat 1954:164, 166, 1955:153)

Carved flowers, birds, animals, and human effigies

BLACK RIVER BRANCH
Bonita Creek Cache (Wasley 1962:381, 388–389, figs. 6–7, 10g) (flowers, bird)

MIMBRES BRANCH
Bear Creek, Johnson, and Greenwood caves (Hough 1914:103–105, figs. 211, 213, 216–221, plates 21, 22) (birds)
Cliff effigy cache (Walt 1978:9–11, figs. 5–8, 13–15) (animals and human effigies)
Doolittle Cave (Cosgrove 1947:134–135, fig. 126f) (bird)

SAN SIMON BRANCH
U Bar Cave (Lambert and Ambler 1961:77–78, fig. 50) (human effigy)

BLACK RIVER BRANCH
Pine Flat Cave (Gifford 1980:181–182, fig. 135) (human effigy)

Reed Tubes and Cigarettes. The earliest known evidence of reed cigarettes (see fig. 16.5c) in the Southwest comes from sites in the Cibola branch and probably the tributaries of the upper Gila, from where they evidently spread to neighboring regions (Grange in Martin et al. 1952:353). Early examples are reported from Early Pithouse period (AD 200–500) contexts at O Block and Cordova caves. Dick (1965:84) reported even earlier examples from Chiricahua or Early Agricultural period levels at Bat Cave, but Wills (1988a) cites problems with the dating. At Tularosa Cave reed cigarettes appear to be present by the Georgetown phase (ca. AD 550–700) and perhaps as early as Pine Lawn, reaching their peak in Reserve and Tularosa levels.

Mogollon people embellished their reed cigarettes in a variety of ways, adorning them with corn husks, seeds, feathers, cotton yarn, paint, beads, shells, even miniature bows (Cosgrove 1947:121–122; Hough 1914:figs. 222–230, 232–238, 241–245; Martin et al. 1952:351–354, figs. 132, 154). In contrast to some late examples from the Phoenix Basin, Mogollon reed cigarettes were not wrapped in miniature woven cotton sashes. Some of the long reed tubes found at Red Cave, Winchester Cave, and Bear Creek Cave may have been intended for the storage and transport of precious or ritual substances (e.g., pigments or salt) rather than smoking (Ferg and Mead 1993:28).

Ceremonial Bows and Arrows. Ceremonial bows and arrows (see fig. 16.5d) appear to be earlier and more prevalent at Mogollon sites than in other parts of the Southwest. Grange (1952:366) associated their appearance with the introduction of the functional bow and arrow and a ritualized recognition of its new hunting potential. While some examples from

O Block and Tularosa caves are attributed to Pine Lawn levels (Early Pithouse period), most appear to postdate AD 700.

Ceremonial bows and arrows occur in nearly every Classic Mimbres cave shrine in the upper Gila, Mimbres, Blue River, and San Francisco River drainages, often in profuse quantities (see table 16.12; for an example see Hibben 1938). After AD 1200 these items are found at the Bonita Creek Cache, Bear Creek Cave, U Bar Cave, Canyon Creek, and Red Bow Cliff Dwelling. Following Mogollon-Pueblo abandonment of the region, wooden arrows continued to serve as important offerings in mountaintop shrines (see Morris 1982:50).

Pahos and Painted Sticks. Decorated and carved sticks (see fig. 16.5a, e), interpreted by Cosgrove and others as prayer sticks or pahos, also appear to be earliest in the Mimbres and Cibola branches (see table 16.12). If published dates are correct, by the late Early Agricultural and Early Pithouse periods they are present in caves of the upper Gila and the San Francisco River drainages and a few sites farther east. At Tularosa and O Block caves the earliest pahos take the form of bound feathers and incised and painted twigs (see fig. 16.5a).

Carved wooden pahos, some elaborately painted, appear at Mogollon sites after AD 700, reaching their peak in the Reserve and Tularosa phases and continuing until the fourteenth century or later in some areas. Classic Mimbres shrines contain a wide assortment of carved and painted forms, including crook pahos, carved (roundel) pahos (see fig. 16.5e), and reed pahos. The crook and roundel forms are depicted on Mimbres bowls (Cosgrove and Cosgrove 1932:plate 228a–d; Davis 1995:156, 191). Similar paho forms are found on the Colo-

rado Plateau at Chaco Canyon, Canyon de Chelly, and a number of other sites. The late Mogollon–Pueblo sites of Gila Cliff Dwellings, Red Bow Cliff Dwelling, U Bar Cave, and Bear Creek Cave produced especially diverse assemblages of these items.

Tablita-Like Objects and Painted Wands. Objects identified as tablitas (see fig. 16.5f; see Cosgrove 1947:132) make their earliest appearance in the Southwest among the Mimbres Mogollon. Unlike most other ritual wooden objects in the Mogollon region, this type remained a uniquely southern product until relatively late in prehistory. The earliest examples of tablita-like objects are attributed to Pine Lawn (Early Pithouse period, ca. AD 200–550) levels at O Block Cave and possibly also Early Circle Prairie (ca. AD 100–400) contexts at Crooked Ridge Village. They increased in popularity during the San Francisco and Three Circle phases and continued until the end of the Tularosa. These objects were decorated only in black until the end of the Three Circle phase, when polychrome designs appear. Numerous examples are known from cave shrines in the Gila, Mimbres, and San Francisco drainages as well as U Bar Cave farther south. With the possible exception of the object from Crooked Ridge Village, described as a wooden tablet, all Mogollon tablitas are constructed from the bloom stalks of yucca or agave.

Split-stick wands (see fig. 16.5g) are another common offering in Mimbres caves. Like tablitas, they are made from yucca-stalk lath and decorated with cutout and painted designs. Their distribution mirrors that of the tablitas, with most examples recovered from the Mimbres and San Francisco River drainages. Also like tablitas, examples occur at some Hueco sites near modern-day El Paso.

Carved Birds, Flowers, and Effigy Figures. Hill and Hays-Gilpin (1999) have identified Mogollon carved birds and flowers (see fig. 16.5h, i) as localized elements of the Flower World ideological complex that has pervaded Mesoamerican and southwestern cultures for thousands of years. These objects appear to correlate with later occupations of the upper Gila, middle Gila, and San Francisco drainages, with carved birds more common than flowers. Some of the carved birds found by Hough (1914:104) functioned as the heads of staffs (see fig. 16.5h), whereas the Bonita Creek cache produced a cruciform pendant resembling a stylized bird. Most examples of Mogollon carved birds come from undated contexts but probably date to AD 1000–1450.

The best-known Mogollon examples of carved wooden flowers are those from the Bonita Creek cache (Wasley 1962). These extraordinary painted wooden flowers and cones have button centers and are made from pieces of agave wood stitched together (see fig. 16.5i). Based on stylistic similarities between these objects and the cache from Sunflower Cave (Kidder and Guernsey 1919: 145–147, plates 60, 61), Wasley attributed manufacture of the Bonita Creek cache to Kayenta migrants. However, important technological differences exist between the Bonita Creek and Sunflower caches.

The flowers in the Bonita Creek cache are fabricated using the same methods and materials as the Mogollon tablitas, examples of which were also found in the cache. Also, some of the miniature baskets in the Bonita Creek cache are made with bundle foundations, a southern basketry technique. These features suggest to me that the people who made the Bonita Creek cache were well schooled in southern techniques and,

if they were Kayenta migrants, had already incorporated Mogollon perishable traditions into their material culture repertoire through intermarriage or ethnic coresidence.

Finally, carved wooden effigy figures are reported from three late Mogollon sites: U Bar Cave, Pine Flat Cave, and an unidentified cave near Cliff, New Mexico. U Bar Cave produced a kachina-like effigy interpreted as a possible twin war god, and, like Mimbres tablitas, this figure is constructed of agave lath. A cave on the Gila River purported to be near Cliff, New Mexico, yielded a remarkable cache of carved figures, including several cottonwood animal effigies, a stone human figure, and a large carved and painted cottonwood anthropomorph decorated with a mask and kilt, the latter radiocarbon-dated to ca. AD 1260 +/− 95. Pine Flat Cave near Point of Pines produced a humanlike effigy with black-painted midsection. Based on the possible presence of metal cut marks, Gifford (1980:181–182, fig. 135) tentatively identified it as Apache, but a Mogollon-Pueblo, historic Pueblo, or O'odham attribution cannot yet be ruled out.

Late Prehistoric and Early Historic Zuni Perishable Traditions
The Zuni Perishables Database

Little is known about perishables in the Zuni area prior to Pueblo IV. The earliest Zuni site I know of with perishables is the Village of the Great Kivas, where Roberts (1932) found a few charred basket and sandal fragments. Our best information about Zuni perishables comes from the protohistoric sites of Hawikuh (Hawikku) and Kechipawan (Kechiba:wa). Although the Hawikuh collections have yet to be reported in full, Smith and others (1966) describe the ce-

ramics from the site and summarize information from Frederick Webb Hodge's field records for the other artifact classes.

I analyzed the Hawikuh and Kechipawan textiles in the early 1990s and described them in my dissertation (Webster 1997, 2000). While studying the textiles I also made a few brief notes on the Kechipawan basketry in Cambridge, England, and the Hawikuh baskets stored at the National Museum of Natural History. In 2003 I examined the remainder of the Hawikuh basketry at the National Museum of the American Indian. Brenda Shears surveyed the basketry from Hawikuh and Kechipawan in the late 1980s and has kindly allowed me to include some of her information here.

In addition to the collections from Hawikuh and Kechipawan a few fragments of charred textiles and basketry were recovered from Halona (Halona:wa, or modern-day Zuni Pueblo) and Heshotauthla by the Hemenway expedition in the 1880s. All of these collections are deteriorated and fragmentary. I briefly inspected them in 2002 at the Peabody Museum of Harvard. In 2001 I also analyzed the textile and basketry artifacts from recent excavations in the Middle Village at Halona (Webster 2004). Except for one scrap of cotton cloth and a fragment of an imported ecclesiastical fabric, most of these artifacts appear to postdate AD 1850 and are not discussed further here.

Zuni Fabrics

Twined and Looped Fabrics. To my knowledge no examples of twined bags or looped fabrics have been recovered from Zuni sites. However, I suspect that at Zuni, as at Hopi, looping was used for the production of leggings until it was replaced by the European-introduced technique of knitting sometime after contact. The earliest twined textile I know of from the Zuni area is a twined sandal from the Village of the Great Kivas (Roberts 1932). Smith and others (1966) did not report twined rabbit-fur or turkey-feather blankets from Hawikuh, but early Spanish chroniclers documented their use at Zuni during the sixteenth century (Hammond and Rey 1940:308–309; Winship 1896:573).

Cotton and Noncotton Plain-Weave Fabrics. I identified only two fragments of cotton plain-weave cloth in the entire Hawikuh assemblage (see fig. 16.6c) and no cotton examples at all from Kechipawan. One charred and highly deteriorated specimen from Halona could be the remains of cotton plain-weave cloth. I also identified one pre–AD 1850 cotton fragment in the Zuni Middle Village assemblage. The use of cotton at Zuni was far greater than indicated by the archaeological record, given that sixteenth-century Spanish accounts describe the use of cotton blankets and sashes there (Winship 1896:586; see also Spier 1924; Stevenson 1883; Stevenson 1915). As in later times, much of the cotton cloth used at Zuni was probably imported from Hopi, where conditions were more favorable for cotton cultivation. Historically, cotton was grown only in small quantities at Zuni.

Noncotton plain-weave cloth made with final S-twist yarns (see fig. 16.6b), probably of yucca fiber, was the most common fabric type recovered from both Hawikuh and Kechipawan (see fig. 16.6e). Most of these fabrics saw use as burial wrappings. Traces of noncotton cloth were also associated with Burial 5345 from Heshotauthla. At least one and perhaps two of the Kechipawan noncotton plain weaves as well as the cotton fragment from Halona are decorated or mended

with twined double-running-stitch embroidery, a technique commonly associated with Pueblo III assemblages on the Colorado Plateau (Kent 1957:514).

Early Spanish accounts leave little doubt of the importance of noncotton fabrics at Zuni at the time of European contact (Webster 1997:32–34). Members of the Coronado expedition described the wearing of "henequen" (agave or yucca) blankets by the people of Hawikuh (Hammond and Rey 1940:324; Winship 1896:558–559). According to the "Relación del Suceso," the Zuni wore "cloaks of henequen" (yucca or agave) because they did not grow cotton there (Winship 1896:573). Luxán stated that it was the use of this fiber that differentiated Zuni clothing from that worn at the other pueblos, "for even though they wear the same sort of dress as the others, the cloth is of agave fiber," a fiber "so well carded it resembles coarse linen" (Hammond and Rey 1966:185). Eventually, the wool of domesticated sheep replaced yucca and other noncotton vegetal fibers for weaving at Zuni, but both Spier (1924) and Stevenson (1915) discuss the weaving of yucca cloth at Zuni in historic times.

Other Fabric Structures. The only other fabric structures identified for Hawikuh and Kechipawan are 2/2 twill cloth and 3/3 oblique interlacing (braiding), the latter represented by a fragment of a braided sash made with two-ply S-spun, Z-plied yarns (see fig. 16.6g). I believe both of these fabrics to be made of yucca. Hawikuh also produced woolen yarns that I have tentatively identified as the remains of embroidery; alternately, they could be supplementary weft (brocade). Similar examples of woolen embroidery have been identified in seventeenth-century collections from Awatovi, Jemez, Pecos, and San Lazaro pueblos (Fenn 2004; Webster 1997, 2000).

Zuni Basketry

At Hawikuh, baskets were associated with at least 52 inhumations and one cremation (Smith et al. 1966:238–240). Hodge's field notes refer to "a small basket-tray of fine weave," "trays," and woven pot rests or pot rings from the site (Smith et al. 1966:281, 284). The following discussion of Zuni basketry incorporates information from Roberts (1932), personal communication with Shears (2003), and my own notes about the Hawikuh, Kechipawan, and Halona baskets.

Coiled Basketry. Roberts (1932:134) reported a few finely stitched fragments of two-rod-and-bundle coiled basketry from the Village of the Great Kivas. I did not record any examples of this construction in the collections from Hawikuh or Kechipawan, but I did identify one in the Hemenway collection from Halona. Weltfish (1932:33–37) described five examples of two-rod-and-bundle basketry among the nineteenth-century collections made at Zuni by John Wesley Powell. I also identified a historic example of this construction in the Zuni Middle Village assemblage, probably dating to the mid-nineteenth century or earlier.

I am aware of only one coiled basket from Kechipawan (Burial 168). If my brief observations about this basket are correct, it has a one-rod foundation. The Hawikuh collection contains four coiled baskets, one with a three-rod foundation, a type I did not include in my Mogollon sample. (Three-rod foundation coiling is another basketry technique that appears in the Southwest in late pre-Hispanic times.) The other three coiled baskets from Hawikuh employ a bundle foundation. Two of these are coarse coiled with grass-bundle foundations and noninterlocking, spaced stitches (see fig. 16.9c). These baskets appear to be the remains of flat plaques but could also be bases or lids of large baskets. The third bundle-foundation basket from Hawikuh is a miniature, close-coiled basket made with split stitches. This tiny basket is only 4 cm in diameter and has a pronounced 1-cm hole in the center.[9] The hole in the base is reminiscent of some of the basketry pahos recovered by Hough (1914:fig. 317) from Bear Creek Cave (fig. 16.4h). Like those from the Bonita Creek cache and Tularosa Cave, some of Hough's miniature baskets also have bundle foundations.

Plaited Basketry. Roberts (1932:134) reported two fragments of a plaited basket or mat from the Village of the Great Kivas. He described this as diagonal twill basketry with the rim folded over the wall material but did not specify the plaiting interval. Hodge encountered vast quantities of matting at Hawikuh, where large mats were associated with several "ceremonial deposits" and at least 70 inhumations (Smith et al. 1966:240–241). My examination of the Hawikuh basketry collection recorded one example of simple 1/1 plaiting (possibly a sandal), two examples of 2/2 twill plaiting, and eight of 3/3 twill plaiting, including one mat with a diamond design (see fig. 16.9d). Both 2/2 and 3/3 matting were also associated with the Kechipawan burials. Matting was also reported from Heshotauthla.

No examples of plaited ring baskets are known from Kechipawan or Hawikuh. This is surprising because ring baskets were reportedly made historically at Zuni (Morris and Burgh 1941:20) and are still made today at Hopi and Jemez. Plaited pot rests were common at Hawikuh (Smith et al. 1966:281, 284, 329). All nine examples I saw were worked in 2/2 twill plaiting. Archaeological and ethnographic examples of woven pot rests are also known from Halona (Stevenson 1883:369, fig. 488; Webster 2004).

Wicker Basketry. Wickerwork trays or plaques (see fig. 16.9b) were common at protohistoric Zuni. In a probable reference to wicker baskets Hodge's field notes describe "flat baskets, similar to the present-day 'peach baskets' of Zuni," and "a food basket, sufficiently well preserved to prove its identity in style with the typical Osier baskets made at Zuni today" (Smith et al. 1966:240, 281). Smith and others (1966:plates 31d, 33a) illustrate examples of wicker trays from two of the Hawikuh burials, and I observed many others in the Hawikuh and Kechipawan collections. These baskets were common mortuary accompaniments at these sites. Several burials contained multiple examples, and some baskets contained seeds or other foodstuffs when found. Wicker trays and other forms of wickerwork were produced at Zuni well into historic times (Mason 1904:227, 506; Whiteford 1988:158–159).

Zuni Sandals

Roberts reported "a piece of textile probably used as an article of clothing" (1932:104) from the Village of the Great Kivas. He did not describe this textile further, but the site collection at the National Museum of Natural History contains a fragmentary twined sandal (catalog no. 351830) that is probably the textile to which he refers. Finely woven twined sandals have been found at a number of Chacoan great house sites from this period, including Pueblo Bonito, Salmon, and Aztec (Judd 1954:74–80, fig. 10, plate 18; Webster n.d., 2006).

No definite examples of sandals are reported from protohistoric Zuni sites. A few fragments of plaiting in the Hawikuh collections might conceivably be the remains of sandals, but matting is more likely. Smith and others (1966) did not note any examples, nor did I see any in the Kechipawan or Hawikuh collections. This is not particularly surprising, given that Pueblo people largely abandoned the wearing of sandals in favor of hide moccasins during Pueblo IV (Hays-Gilpin et al. 1998:37).

Zuni Ritual Wooden Objects

Carved and painted wooden objects play a prominent role in historic Zuni ritual (Cushing 1920; Parsons 1918a, 1939; Stevenson 1904). Evidence from Hawikuh confirms that this was also the case in the late prehistoric past. Here I provide only a brief overview of ritual wooden objects at Hawikuh and historic Zuni and refer the reader to Vivian and others (1978) for a more detailed discussion of these materials.

Hodge found reed cigarettes in association with several of the Hawikuh burials, and Cushing (1920:162) documented their historic use at Zuni. Hodge also recovered some larger cane tubes, one containing earth and a turquoise bead, another with earth and small pebbles (Smith et al. 1966:79–80, 272–280). Stevenson (1904:163) discussed the use of long cane tubes as fetishes by the Zuni rain priesthood.

Bows, arrows, and sometimes both were associated with several of the Hawikuh burials (Smith et al. 1966:222–223). From Hodge's field notes I infer that all of these were full-sized implements except for one miniature war club and a miniature bow found with an undated burial. A Zuni worker identified one Hawikuh burial as a "priest of the bow," based on the presence of three bows, a woven quiver, and a mass of arrowshafts (Smith et al. 1966:174, 223).

The ethnographic literature contains numerous references to ritual use of bows and arrows at Zuni. Elsie Clews Parsons (1918a:plate III) described the placement of miniature bows in war god shrines, and Stevenson (1904:plate CVIII) noted their use on Zuni altars. Stevenson (1904:439) herself saw a hundred or more full-sized arrows that had been driven into the side of Dowa Yalanne (Corn Mountain) as an offering for a successful hunt. Historically, bows and arrows are among the objects given to small boys at Zuni by masked clowns during the autumn corn dances (Cushing 1920:605).

The Hawikuh field notes record the presence of "prayer sticks," "prayer plumes," or "plume sticks" with 18 of the burials (Smith et al. 1966:272–273). Such items range from small sticks wrapped with corn husks and string bindings, to reeds and wooden sticks painted blue, to unusually long painted prayer sticks with evidence of wrapping. Painted prayer sticks were among the objects in a ceremonial cache found inside a Hawikuh Polychrome jar; another cache contained prayer sticks and reeds with fiber wrapping (Smith et al. 1966:79–80). Hodge also reported a "sacerdotal deposit" from the Hawikuh cemetery that contained a large assortment of prayer sticks in association with food items, medicinal plants, basketry, pottery, and other offerings (Smith et al. 1966:289). Parsons (1918a:381–405, 1939:305, 306, 337, fig. 2) noted an association between carved pahos and Zuni war god shrines and the use of netting rings and miniature bows and arrows as paho attachments.

Several wooden objects found by Hodge at Hawikuh resemble what Cosgrove (1947:132) called "tablitas."

These include "shrine paraphernalia" from Burial 915, consisting of a painted staff and decorated wooden tablet, the latter painted with polychrome designs, including the image of a bear (Smith et al. 1966:214, 217). Terraced wooden objects like those found in the south are used as altar decorations at Zuni (Bunzel 1932a: 1028, plate 40a; Stevenson 1904: plates 38, 58, 104, 108, 122) and worn as headdresses by Zuni women in some dance performances (Roediger 1941:plate 10).

To my knowledge, no archaeological examples of carved wooden birds or flowers have been recovered from Zuni sites. However, carved birds are important components of historic Zuni altars (Stevenson 1904:plates LVIII, LIX, CXVI; Vivian et al. 1978:44). Wasley (1962:393–394) indicates that carved flowers are less common at Zuni than they are at Hopi.

Mogollon-Zuni Relationships and the Question of Zuni Origins

Similarities between Mogollon and Zuni perishables lend support to the hypothesis advanced nearly half a century ago by Paul Martin and John Rinaldo (1960; Rinaldo 1964) of an ancestral relationship between the Mogollon archaeological culture and the modern Zuni people. Although some perishable classes are too widespread to be of much diagnostic value, others, such as noncotton plain-weave cloth, 3/3 oblique interlacing, bundle-foundation coiling, wickerwork plaques, and certain ritual wooden objects, are sufficiently restricted in time and space to suggest a movement of southern ideas, and probably southern peoples, into the Little Colorado River, Zuni, and Hopi regions during Pueblo IV.

If I were to identify one feature of Zuni weaving that shows the strongest connection to Mogollon textile traditions, it would be the intensive use of noncotton plant fiber for the production of loom-woven cloth. An early emphasis on noncotton plain weaves sets the Mogollon tradition apart from that of the Hohokam, Jornada Mogollon, and Basketmaker/ancestral Pueblo and points to an underlying relationship with northern Mexico, where noncotton fabrics commonly served as burial shrouds and articles of everyday dress (Beals 1932:172; Johnson 1971; Johnson in MacNeish et al. 1967:214; Kent 1983:134–136; King 1974:107, 123; Martinez del Río 1953:plate 26B; O'Neale 1948; Teague 1998, 1999; Zingg 1940).

Noncotton plain-weave fabrics persisted throughout the Mogollon sequence and are strongly represented at the late Mogollon–Pueblo sites of Point of Pines, Gila Cliff Dwellings, and Canyon Creek. Noncotton fabrics also occur at late Hohokam, Sinagua, and Salado sites but consistently take a back seat to cotton (Teague 1998, 1999). These fabrics are not characteristic of Pueblo II or Pueblo III loom-woven fabrics on the Colorado Plateau, where only a handful of noncotton examples are known. In northern Mexico and southern Arizona their production is associated with the horizontal staked-down loom (Teague 1998) rather than the upright and backstrap looms used to weave cotton fabrics on the Colorado Plateau.

We presently lack adequate collections from the Zuni area to know what kinds of fibers were being loom-woven there during Pueblo III. The identification of loom holes from three structures at Hawikuh suggests that the upright loom was in use there during Pueblo IV (Webster 1997:237), but this evidence is insufficient to account for all the noncotton plain-weave cloth found there. It is possible that the southern horizontal loom was used at Zuni to produce this non-cotton cloth. At our current level of understanding, loom weaving with noncotton plant fiber seems to be a highland Mexican and Highland Mogollon tradition (and, to a lesser extent, a late Hohokam, Salado, and Sinagua one) that spread northward onto the southern Colorado Plateau during Pueblo IV.

To my mind, the appearance of noncotton plain weaves in the Little Colorado River drainage during the fourteenth century and their strong presence in the Zuni area by AD 1400 provide some of our most compelling evidence in support of a cultural relationship between the Mogollon-Pueblo and Zuni people. One site that may reflect the northward progression of people using these fabrics is Table Rock Pueblo near St. Johns, Arizona, occupied between AD 1300 and 1450 (Martin and Rinaldo 1960:282). Here, plain-weave cloth with S-spun yarns (which I tentatively interpret as noncotton fiber, based on the S-direction of twist of the yarns described in the report) co-occurred with another southern technique, bundle-foundation coiling. If perishable collections from the "catacomb" caves at Casa Malpais near Springerville ever become available for study, these might provide additional evidence of this pattern.

Noncotton plain weaves are the most common fabrics recovered from Hawikuh and Kechipawan, where, as at Canyon Creek and sites in northern Chihuahua, they served an important role as mortuary shrouds. Early Spanish accounts and later work by Stevenson (1915) underscore the importance of yucca cloth in the lives of the Zuni people. The prominence of

yucca cloth at Zuni and its apparent unimportance as a loom-woven fiber among the other historic Pueblos suggest continuation of a Highland Mogollon textile tradition at Zuni, one brought north, perhaps, by people from such sites as Canyon Creek Pueblo, Point of Pines, or some of the Tularosa or Cliff phase sites in the upper Gila.

Another southern construction found at contact period Zuni as well as Hopi is 3/3 oblique interlacing, used for the production of braided sashes. Known prehistorically from the Mogollon site of Mule Creek as well as from the Tonto Cliff Dwellings and Montezuma Castle, 3/3 oblique interlacing is not recorded north of the Mogollon Rim prior to AD 1300 (2/2 is the common ancestral Pueblo braiding technique) but becomes popular at Zuni and Hopi during Pueblo IV (Kent 1983:60; Webster 1997:233, 292–293, 2000).

Yet another probable southern influence in Zuni weaving is the practice of using multiple bobbins for wefts, a technique found prehistorically in northern Mexico and perhaps also in central Arizona (Kent 1983:130–131; King 1974:109; O'Neale 1948:127–129; Teague 1998:89–90; Zingg 1940:23). Zuni is the only historic pueblo in the U.S. Southwest for which the use of multiple bobbins is reported (Spier 1924:71). Interestingly, the use of multiple-bobbin wefts is also common practice among the Rarámuri (Tarahumara) (Zingg 1940), a group with whom the Zuni claim some degree of cultural affiliation.

Not all textiles found at Hawikuh and Kechipawan exhibit a Mogollon-Pueblo flavor. Two plain-weave fragments from Kechipawan and another from Halona are darned or decorated with twined double running-stitch embroidery, a technique not reported

for Mogollon assemblages but common in Pueblo III assemblages on the Colorado Plateau. The twined sandal from the Village of the Great Kivas is another textile of northern derivation, one that may tie this assemblage to the Chaco regional system.

Two basketry forms found at Hawikuh and Kechipawan also provide evidence of southern influences at Zuni. Bundle-foundation coiling is a southern technique that became widespread in central and southern Arizona and New Mexico in the AD 1100s or 1200s. It is not typical of Pueblo II and Pueblo III assemblages on the Colorado Plateau. During Late Pueblo III and Early Pueblo IV the technique appears north of the Mogollon Rim at such sites as Table Rock Pueblo, the ancestral Hopi sites of Homolovi II, Kawaika-a, and Kokopnyama, and the Zuni site of Hawikuh (Hough 1903:339, 341, plates 87, 97; Martin and Rinaldo 1960:282; Mason 1904:509, plates 221, 222; Teiwes 1996:181). The Hawikuh collection contains three examples, including a miniature basket reminiscent of Hough's basketry pahos from Bear Creek Cave.

Finally, the wickerwork plaque is another form that seems to make a sudden appearance on the Colorado Plateau, including at Hawikuh and Kechipawan, in the AD 1300s. Evidence for this basket type is lacking from published Pueblo III basketry collections from the Colorado Plateau, and the technique is also absent from Hohokam, Salado, Sinagua, and most Mogollon assemblages. The only known occurrence of wickerwork plaques south of the Mogollon Rim is at Canyon Creek Pueblo, where a number of examples were found (Haury 1934). Hough (1907:24–25, 50–52) alluded to the presence of wicker basketry at Bear Creek Cave (see also Weltfish 1932:28), but the only wickerwork examples I saw in the collection were identified as snowshoes. North of the Mogollon Rim these items occur at Pueblo IV sites in the middle Little Colorado region (Chevlon and Homolovi I), near the Hopi Mesas (Kawaika-a and Kokopnyama), and at Hawikuh and Kechipawan (E. Charles Adams, personal communication 2002; Fewkes 1904:98; Hough 1903:339, 341, plates 87, 97; Mason 1904:508, plate 219). At this point this basket type appears to be a late and local Pueblo IV innovation in the northern Southwest (Haury 1934:78). If wickerwork baskets originated south of the Mogollon Rim, then their derivation seems to be Mogollon-Pueblo.

Many of the same kinds of ritual wooden objects found at Mogollon sites also play an important role in modern Zuni ritual. By AD 1200 most of these forms were widespread throughout the Southwest. Hence, most are not particularly diagnostic for assessing Mogollon-Zuni relationships. The two types of Mogollon ritual wooden objects that suggest particularly close ties with Zuni are carved birds and the ceremonial bow. Birds are used on Zuni altars, whereas the importance of the bow is reflected in the office of the bow priest, the prevalence of bows as offerings in Zuni shrines, and the historic importance of hunting at Zuni (see also Vokes and Gregory, chap. 17, this vol.).

The origins of modern Zuni society are diverse and complex, with migration an oft-cited element of Zuni traditional history (see Ferguson, chap. 19, this vol.; Ferguson and Hart 1985). The Zuni perishables database, with its many gaps and omissions, suggests that ancestors of the Zuni people participated in a broad Chacoan pattern up through Pueblo III, then witnessed a shift in Pueblo IV to a tradition heavily

weighted with southern influences (see also Schaafsma and Young, chap. 15, this vol.). The lack of well-preserved perishables from late Mogollon–Pueblo villages makes one-to-one site comparisons impossible, but general patterns indicate that Zuni and Hopi (and, if we had any perishable data, probably Acoma and the Rio Grande Pueblos) were strongly influenced after AD 1300 by traditions originating south of the Mogollon Rim (Webster 1999, 2003; Webster and Loma'omvaya 2004). I believe the presence of these southern influences and technologies is best explained by an emigration of people from a number of different regions, including the Mogollon Highlands, into the upper and middle Colorado River and the Zuni and Hopi regions during Pueblo IV. If this was the case, then Mogollon-Pueblo culture was an essential component of the multiethnic mix leading to the formation of modern Zuni society.

Notes

1. Following Wheat's (1955) branch designation system, I have placed Bear Creek Cave and nearby Johnson Cave in the Mimbres branch. Under Martin's (1979) system, Bear Creek Cave is in the Cibola branch (see fig. 1.2, chap. 1, this vol.). Regardless of the system used, both sites are near the boundary that divides the Black River, Cibola, and Mimbres branches, and they exhibit attributes from all of these regions. See note 8 for a discussion of the ceramics from Bear Creek Cave.

2. As much as we would like to know what kinds of textiles, baskets, and other perishable objects were used at such Early Agricultural period sites as Cerro Juanaqueña in the northern Chihuahuan Desert, Las Capas and the Milagro Site in the Tucson Basin, La Playa in northern Sonora, or other important early sites in the southern Basin and Range, no good examples of these artifacts have been

found (see Carpenter et al. 2005; Hard and Roney 1999b; Mabry 2007).

3. AMS dating may prove the scuffer-toe form to predate the full-length style in this region.

4. A potential Early Agricultural period Mogollon site sample would include the sites of Bear Creek Cave, Steamboat Cave, Mule Creek Cave, and Doolittle Cave in the Mimbres branch; Cienega Creek and McEuen Cave in the Black River branch; and Bat Cave, Cordova Cave, Kelly Cave, O Block Cave, and Tularosa Cave in the Cibola branch. All of these sites produced perishables resembling other Early Agricultural period collections. Of particular importance is the assemblage from McEuen Cave (Kelly 1937), which produced a wide range of artifacts, including a twined bag with an AMS date of 400–180 cal BC and an atlatl with a date of 721–260 cal BC (Kelly 1937; Moreno 2000:353). Many of these artifacts strongly resemble collections from White Dog Cave. Several White Dog phase sites in northern Arizona also contain rich perishable assemblages. A comparative sample from this region would include materials from White Dog Cave, Sand Dune Cave, Sagiotsosi–Cave 11, Sayodneechee Burial Cave, and Kinboko–Cave 1. To my knowledge, none of the perishables from these sites have been directly dated.

5. These sites include the Durango Rock Shelters, Obelisk Cave in the Prayer Rock District, and Riggs Canyon near Kanab (Judd 1926:plate 54b; Morris 1980:fig. 52; Morris and Burgh 1954:64, 66–67, figs. 33, 37, 38, 99e).

6. Bluhm (in Martin et al. 1952:248) viewed these items as possible trade pieces from the north, but I see no reason why they could not have been made locally.

7. Single-ply cotton warps and wefts in the Southwest are typically spun in a Z-wise direction. In contrast, yucca and agave warps and wefts most often have a final S-twist.

8. With the assistance of Dr. Kelley Hays-Gilpin I briefly examined the Bear Creek Cave assemblage at the National Museum of Natural History (Smithsonian Institution) in 2003. Our survey of the ceramics produced examples of Tularosa

Black-on-white, Snowflake Black-on-white, St. Johns Polychrome, St. Johns Black-on-red, late Mimbres types, and Kwakina Polychrome. No Classic Mimbres pottery was observed. The pottery assemblage and the presence of 3/3 twill plaited basketry suggest a post–AD 1200 date for these materials. AMS dating is needed to further refine the dating of the perishable assemblage and to rule out an earlier occupation of the site.

9. The catalog card for this object (National Museum of the American Indian 12/4700) identifies it as a carbonized basketry eyepiece from a Koyemshi mask, but I have not found any information to support this identification. Its provenience at Hawikuh is unknown.

17 Exchange Networks for Exotic Goods in the Southwest and Zuni's Place in Them

Arthur W. Vokes and David A. Gregory

Anthropologists have long recognized the importance of trade and exchange in the development and changing nature of cultural traditions (see Adams 1974).[1] Certainly this is true with respect to the development of ethnographically documented Zuni cultural traditions, including material culture items traded out and acquired through trade, formal political structures to insure the protection and safety of trade routes, and even explicitly stated attitudes that encouraged trade and exchange with non-Zuni populations (Ferguson and Hart 1985:52–55). For the historic period the Pueblo of Zuni has been characterized as a "trading center," and it is clear that this identity extended to precontact times:

> When the Spaniards first reached the Zuni villages in the mid-sixteenth century, they found the area, especially Hawikku, to be *the hub of a large regional trade network*, where macaw feathers were traded for turquoise and blue paint; shells for corn; coral for pigment; cotton, cotton thread, and cloth for buffalo hides; and jewelry for blankets. Zunis visited, and were visited by, tribes in what are now California and Mexico, and literally dozens of tribes in between [Ferguson and Hart 1985:53; emphasis added].

In this chapter we describe and discuss macroscale prehistoric exchange networks and the shifting place of Zuni in them. To accomplish this we focus on four classes of "rare" or "exotic" items and materials found in Southwest archaeological assemblages: copper bells, macaws, marine shell, and turquoise. Distributions of these materials reflect the existence of exchange networks that at various times linked areas within the region and beyond. They are generally regarded as prestige goods, and there is evidence that movement and exchange of them were often restricted to and/or controlled by high-status individuals or groups within local settlements and communities. In addition, as indicated by their recovery contexts, the value of these items to Southwest populations was often dependent on the symbolism attached to them in the context of ideological systems and their sociological representations. These aspects of the materials considered here are fundamentally important in understanding and interpreting their archaeological distributions.

"Rare" and "exotic" are obviously relative terms. Three classes of items considered here—marine shell, copper bells, and macaws—were obtained from sources outside of or at the margins of the Southwest and are "rare" in

that spatial context. In the case of copper bells the raw material is relatively rare within the Southwest, and, more important, the metallurgical knowledge necessary to manufacture the bells appears to have been nonexistent or at least extremely limited (see below). Macaws and parrots were generally not native to the Southwest (but see below), and the survival of live specimens required specialized husbandry in environments alien to these species. Marine shell has a relatively restricted spatial distribution and was differentially available to Southwest populations, in part as a function of distance; in addition, items manufactured from shell in one area of the region may have been "value-added" in another. Turquoise is available from a number of sources within the region and on its northwestern and western peripheries, but it is still relatively uncommon. However, in a macrospatial sense it is relatively common in the Southwest but occurs only rarely in areas farther south, where it was a highly valued commodity.

Trade Routes: Physical Connections

Exotic materials arrived in and left the Southwest at various times over numerous well-defined routes. In some cases these routes were still active when Europeans arrived and were later used as wagon trails, and some remain active today as roads and highways that traverse the region. In other instances evidence of former routes remains only in the form of worn pathways, materials discarded along them, and macrospatial patterning in materials recovered from the surface of surveyed sites and in assemblages from excavated sites (Wilcox 1999a; Wilcox et al. 2000).

Early attempts to develop models of prehistoric trade often focused on the physical routes over which materials were transported into the Southwest from more distant areas (Brand 1938; Davis 1961; Tower 1945), and it is appropriate to establish this spatial context for subsequent discussions. Known and inferred routes are shown in figure 17.1 and summarized in table 17.1 and are grouped and enumerated by their regions of origin: coastal and interior Southern California to the west and northwest (PC 1–4); northern Mexico, including the Gulf of California coastline, to the south and southwest (GC 1–5); and the Gulf of Mexico/Plains regions to the east and southeast (GMP 1–5). Relationships between these routes and Zuni trade routes as illustrated by Ferguson and Hart (1985:Map 19) are also shown in figure 17.1.

Pacific Coast Routes (PC 1–4)

Routes linking the coastal regions of Southern California with the Southwest were extensions of a complex of trails used by the populations of coastal and interior Southern California (Davis 1961) and provided both unworked shell and finished shell artifacts to Southwest populations. Distinctive types of shell derived from the cold-water biotic communities of the Californian province include *Haliotis* (abalone), *Dentalium* (tusk shells), and *Olivella biplicata* valves,

from which a number of bead forms were fashioned. The two northernmost routes (PC 1 and PC 2) may have also functioned in the acquisition of turquoise from sources along the eastern perimeter of the California network and in north-central Nevada. Heizer and Treganza (1944:335) suggest that California turquoise sources were exploited by Puebloan groups that traveled into the region for this purpose.

Pacific coast routes appear to have considerable antiquity. Middle Archaic trade between Pacific coast populations and the interior Great Basin has been inferred (Bennyhoff and Hughes 1987), and Pacific coast shell in later Basketmaker II sites likely reflects a southern and eastern extension of the Great Basin trade. Artifacts manufactured from Pacific coast shell have been recovered from Early Agricultural period sites in the Tucson Basin (ca. 3750–1750 B.P.), and similar artifacts were recovered from Late Archaic deposits at the Indian Hill Rock Shelter in the Anza-Borrego Desert (McDonald 1992:332). This suggests that a portion of the Early Agricultural period material in southern Arizona may have been acquired through contacts with populations in the San Diego area via PC 4 and possibly PC 3 (Vokes 1998:465).

Frequency and intensity of use of Pacific coast routes varied through time. PC 4 appears to drop out of general use during the Hohokam era but may have seen a resurgence in the later protohistoric and early historic periods. Other routes appear to have been fairly active throughout the prehistoric and historic eras, and portions of several are largely isomorphic with modern highways.

Gulf of California Routes (GC 1–5)

Five possible routes may have served as conduits for the import of exotic

goods from the Gulf of California, western Mexico, and areas farther south in Mesoamerica and for the southward movement of materials out of the Southwest, notably turquoise (see below). Four of these originate at the mouths of and subsequently proceed upstream along drainages flowing into the Gulf of California: GC 1 (Colorado River), GC 3 (Río Ascension), GC 4 (Río Sonora), and GC 5 (Río Yaqui). The fifth is the more generalized trans-Papaguería route (GC 2), running in a broad band from the coast across the deserts of southwestern Arizona. All five routes probably functioned in the movement of marine shell into the Southwest, and at least three (GC 3, GC 4, and GC 5) also may have been involved in the northward movement of copper bells and macaws. A route along the coastline could have variably connected the starting points of the five numbered routes and is shown in figure 17.1 but not enumerated.

At present, the best documented of these is the trans-Papaguería route (GC 2; see Brand 1938; Ezell 1954; Fontana 1965; Hayden 1972; Kean 1965; Tower 1945; Vivian 1965). Specifics for the other four routes are less certain, and their existence is based largely on inference and documented historic patterns (e.g., Di Peso et al. 1974d). This is particularly true of the two that originate along the southern Sonoran coastline (GC 4 and GC 5, the two most likely involved in the northward movement of copper bells and macaws), where the relative absence of archaeological research in intervening areas limits data-based reconstructions.

Gulf of Mexico/Plains Routes (GMP 1–5)

Five routes connecting the Great Plains and, ultimately, the Gulf of Mexico with the Southwest have been

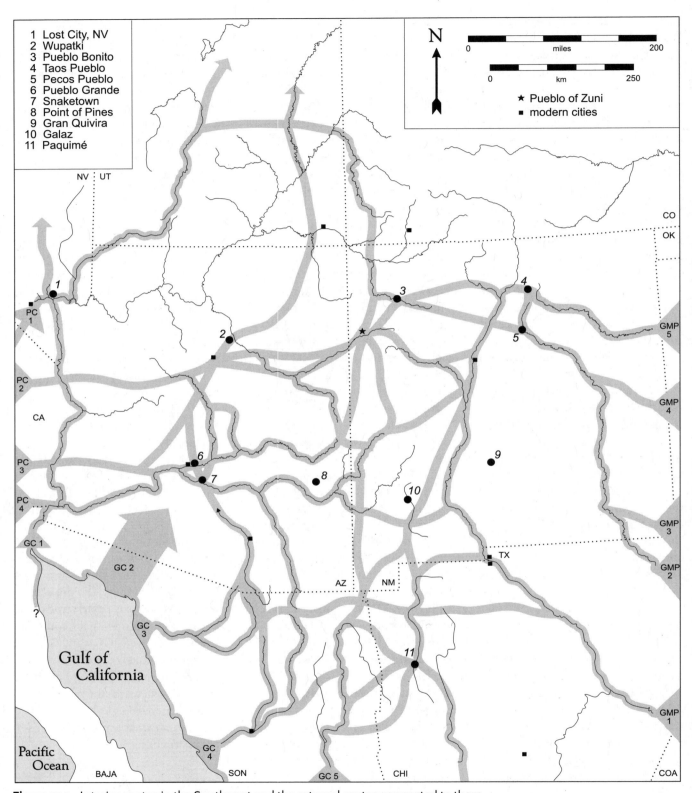

1 Lost City, NV
2 Wupatki
3 Pueblo Bonito
4 Taos Pueblo
5 Pecos Pueblo
6 Pueblo Grande
7 Snaketown
8 Point of Pines
9 Gran Quivira
10 Galaz
11 Paquimé

★ Pueblo of Zuni
■ modern cities

Figure 17.1. Interior routes in the Southwest and the external routes connected to them.

Table 17.1 Routes into the Southwest from External Areas

Map No.	Point of Origin	Materials from Point of Origin	Comments and References
PC 1	Los Angeles area	Pacific coast shell, turquoise(?)	The Old Spanish Trail (Brand 1938; Tower 1945; Wilcox et al. 2000)
PC 2	Los Angeles area	Pacific coast shell, turquoise(?)	The Mohave Trail; the route passed just south of the Halloran Springs turquoise source and may have served as a conduit for the distribution of turquoise (Farmer 1935; Colton 1941; Tower 1945, Route P-3; Wilcox 1999a; Wilcox et al. 2000)
PC 3	Los Angeles area	Pacific coast shell	Known as the Bouse, La Paz Trail, and San Gorgonio/Big Maria Trail; Davis (1961) indicates use back to at least A.D. 900, and the trail was active into the historic era (Davis 1961, Routes 78, 83, 86, 92; Simpson 1950; Wilcox 1999a)
PC 4	San Diego area	Pacific coast shell	San Diego to Yuma to the Gila Bend/Phoenix area (Brand 1938; Davis 1961, Routes 94, 95; Tower 1945, Route P-1)
GC 1	Colorado River mouth	Gulf shell	Largely hypothetical, as little is known of the archaeology along the Colorado River (Brand 1938; Tower 1945, Route G-4)
GC 2	Puerto Peñasco/Bahía Adair (Rocky Point area)	Gulf shell	Earliest use dated to the Early Archaic and continued into the historic era (Brand 1938; Hayden 1972; numerous survey reports from the Barry M. Goldwater Range)
GC 3	Río Ascensión mouth	Gulf shell	Appears to be active in the Late Archaic and throughout the ceramic era, with increased importance during the Hohokam Classic period (Brand 1938; Craig 1982; Tower 1945, Route G-1)
GC 4	Río Sonora mouth	Gulf shell, possibly copper bells and macaws	Specifics of the route within Sonora are largely hypothetical, and dates of use are uncertain (Brand 1938; Tower 1945, Route G-2)
GC 5	Río Yaqui/Río Mátape mouth	Gulf shell, copper bells, macaws	Route is indicated by the presence of shell species in Chaco assemblages with distributions restricted to the Nayarit/Jalisco coastal area; a variant proposed by Di Peso has the route beginning at the mouth of the Río Mátape, across to the Río Yaqui and up the Río Aros and over to the upper Río Casas Grandes and on to Paquimé; possible route for turquoise moving south; specifics within Sonora hypothetical, and dates of use are uncertain (Brand 1938; Di Peso et al. 1974d:166; Tower 1945, Route G-2)
GMP 1	Rio Grande mouth	Gulf of Mexico shell	Largely hypothetical (Brand 1938; Tower 1945, Route A-4)
GMP 2	Rio Grande–Pecos confluence	Gulf of Mexico shell	Largely hypothetical (Brand 1938; Tower 1945, Route A-1)
GMP 3	Rio Colorado (Texas) basin	Gulf of Mexico shell	Route proposed to explain the presence of Gulf of Mexico shell in the Pecos assemblage; largely hypothetical (Brand 1938; Tower 1945, Route A-2)
GMP 4	Brazos River basin	Buffalo hides, Gulf of Mexico shell	Route proposed to explain the presence of Gulf of Mexico shell in the Pecos assemblage; largely hypothetical (Brand 1938; Tower 1945, Route A-3)
GMP 5	Canadian River basin	Buffalo hides, nacreous freshwater shell	Route identified with the Plains-Pueblo fairs among the eastern pueblos and the presence of Gulf of California shell in deposits at Spiro Mound; also represent a source of relatively robust nacreous freshwater shell (Kozuch 2002)

postulated: GMP 1, along the Rio Grande; GMP 2, up the Rio Grande and thence along the Pecos River; GMP 3, up the Rio Grande and thence along the Rio Colorado of Texas; GMP 4, along the Brazos River; and GMP 5, up the Mississippi, the Red River, and thence along the Canadian River. Both GMP 3 and GMP 4 involve tra-

verses from their headwaters that connect to the upper portions of the Pecos River (GMP 2). These routes were never important with respect to the classes of material considered here. Marine shell from the Gulf of Mexico has extremely restricted temporal and spatial distributions in the Southwest, at present including only

a few genera and a very limited range of artifact forms from the Pecos Pueblo assemblage (*Strombus gigus*, *S. pugilis* [possibly misidentified], *Dinocardium robustum*, and *Fascolaria lilium* [formerly *distans*]; Kidder 1932). It was, however, the presence of these materials at Pecos that prompted Brand (1938:7) to propose the routes directly connecting the Gulf of Mexico with the Southwest.

Exchange relations between Puebloan and Plains populations were extremely important from the late prehistoric through the early historic period and included trade fairs at Pecos, Taos, and the Salinas pueblos that brought bison hides and other bison products into the Southwest. GMP 5 clearly functioned in the context of these relationships, and GMP 4 may have played a role as well. The other routes are based largely on directness of access and have little or no archaeological basis. It is likely that the important part of any and all of these routes was that portion that traversed the plains environment and that direct connections to the Gulf of Mexico, if any, were epiphenomena of the Pueblo-Plains network.

Movement of marine shell out of the Southwest and onto the Great Plains during the late AD 1300s is demonstrated by recent identification of nearly 14,000 *Olivella dama* beads in a burial at the Spiro Mound site in eastern Oklahoma, with the most probable route for movement of this material being GMP 5 (Kozuch 2002:703). The time depth and extent of such exports are not well studied, but at present they appear to be restricted to the late prehistoric period and after.

Internal Routes

Extensions of these various routes into the interior of the Southwest also served as conduits for the movement of goods *within* the region. Figure 17.1 shows documented and inferred routes within the Southwest and includes selected archaeological sites to provide orientation. This representation is not intended to be exhaustive, but the principal routes in use at any given time are likely shown. Once again, correspondences be-

tween these routes and Zuni trails as illustrated by Ferguson and Hart (1985:Maps 19 and 20) are highlighted. In subsequent distribution maps the internal routes most likely involved in the movement of materials discussed here are shown.

Copper Bells

Copper bells, or crotals, have been recovered from a relatively few, often large, settlements in the Southwest and have been viewed as a class of material exchanged between elites through restricted networks. The most likely source of Southwest copper bells is western Mexico, including the modern states of Jalisco, Nayarit, Colima, and southern Sinaloa. There is no evidence that the knowledge necessary to manufacture bells ever reached the Southwest. Di Peso and others (1974c) argued for copper metallurgists in residence at Paquimé, but Vargas (1995) persuasively disputes this hypothesis.

Metallurgy is believed to have been introduced into this region through maritime contact with populations in Central and South America (Hosler 1988a:841–843). This transfer of knowledge may have taken place as early as AD 650 (Vargas 1995:17) and was definitely present in western Mexico by AD 800 (Hosler 1988b), predating the earliest reported occurrences of copper bells in the Southwest by at least a century. While a number of artifact forms (open rings, needles, and tweezers) were made by western Mexican metallurgists (Hosler 1988a:839), it is primarily the copper bell that was acquired and valued by inhabitants of the Southwest (Withers 1946).

Development of the western Mexican metallurgical tradition has been divided into two phases based on technological, chemical, and stylistic features (Hosler 1988b). Phase I (AD

800–1200/1300) is characterized by the use of nearly pure native copper, with the addition of small amounts of arsenic in some instances. Phase I bells are relatively simple globular and pear shapes and most often lack surface embellishments (see fig. 17.2a–g). Between AD 1200 and 1300 western Mexican metallurgists began to manufacture products made with copper alloys involving the addition of silver and tin as well as arsenic. The result was a stronger and more colorful product that allowed production of thinner, lighter bells whose surfaces were often embellished with intricate wirework designs (see fig. 17.2h–n).

Temporal and Spatial Patterns

Vargas (1995) has summarized the typological characteristics and spatial and temporal distributions of known southwestern copper bell specimens. We draw heavily on her analyses in our discussion and add some specimens not included by her. Unfortunately, Vargas used the western Mexican typological chronology to structure her temporal analyses. The AD 1200–1300 period of overlap in the two western Mexican phases witnessed substantial changes in the southwestern social landscape, and important patterns are muddied if not totally obscured by use of this chronology. In addition, the various maps provided by Vargas to illustrate her Phase I and Phase II distributions contain a number of inaccuracies in site locations, some misnumbered sites, and some missing numbers for sites listed in tables and discussed in the text.

To overcome these problems and to clarify some important patterns, the dating of sites in Vargas's lists has been reevaluated, based on archaeological data from the sites themselves, independent of bell type. As a result, the sites have been separated

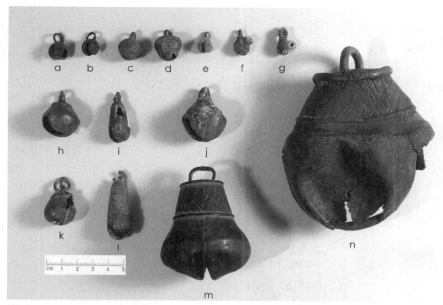

Figure 17.2. Copper bell forms.

into two intervals, AD 800–ca. 1250 and post–AD 1250, and have been plotted in their actual locations. The emphasis here is more on the dating and distribution of bells and less on typological diversity. An even more careful reassessment of temporal data would be useful in the future, as would a more refined look at typological diversity.[2]

AD 800–ca. 1250. Southwestern sites with copper bells and dating between AD 800 and ca. 1250 are summarized in table 17.2; the distribution of bells dating to this interval is shown in figure 17.3, along with the trails most likely involved in the movement of bells. Vargas identified four loose clusters of sites in her analyses, all of which are apparent in figure 17.3: the Hohokam area, the Mimbres area, Chaco Canyon, and the Flagstaff area. Based on our reassessment of dates, we add a fifth minor cluster of three occurrences in the upper reaches of the San Francisco River drainage along the Tularosa River. All but 12 bells assigned to this interval occur within these clusters, with the excep-

tions occurring at four "isolated" sites or attributed to general areas.

Citing the high frequency and diversity of forms represented in the Gatlin site assemblage, Vargas (1995:52–54) concludes that most if not all of the copper bells found in Phase I assemblages were probably obtained through trade networks tied to the Hohokam, who were obtaining the bells directly from populations in western Mexico. She finds support for this proposal in the fact that (with the exception of the "Tlaloc" bell at Wupatki) all styles reported from the Southwest are replicated in the Gatlin area assemblages, including some rare variants. She also notes that the 28 bells from Snaketown were recovered from what appears to have been a storehouse that also contained other exotic goods such as shell (Vargas 1995:52; see Gladwin et al. 1937; Haury 1976) and infers that this deposit may reflect the settlement's role in an exchange system involving prestige goods.

There are a number of potential problems with this interpretation. Phase I bells in the Hohokam area

tend to occur in multiples (see table 17.2), including the bells from Snaketown. This suggests that many of these deposits could represent the remains of special garments or costumes, and the Romo Cache (near Tucson) clearly represents a specialized deposit (Haury and Gifford 1959). This circumstance would considerably reduce the frequency with which bells may have reached the Hohokam area, despite the relatively large numbers of these artifacts present. In addition, the style of bell in the Snaketown deposit (IC14a) and several of those in the Gatlin assemblages are not common in assemblages outside the Hohokam area. In this interpretation the Hohokam bells can be seen as arriving as the result of more ad hoc and small-scale processes rather than within the context of a regularized exchange system.

A plausible alternative explanation is that most bells that entered the region prior to about AD 1250 did so in the context of a macroregional exchange network that evolved as a result of Chacoan demand for these items. Wilcox (1999a, 2002; Wilcox et al. 2000) has proposed this alternative, which, he argues, connected Mimbres, Chaco, and the Flagstaff area (Wupatki). The small cluster of bells in the upper San Francisco River shown in figure 17.3 would tend to support his hypothesis, as this area lies along the most likely route from Mimbres to Chaco. As we shall see, patterning in the dating and distributions of other exotic items also tends to support this interpretation.

Zuni lies between the Tularosa Valley and Chaco and is also on the route between the Mimbres and Chaco, and settlements in the Zuni area during this interval were clearly part of the Chacoan network (Ferguson and Hart 1985:53). Thus, we would expect copper bells to be found in future

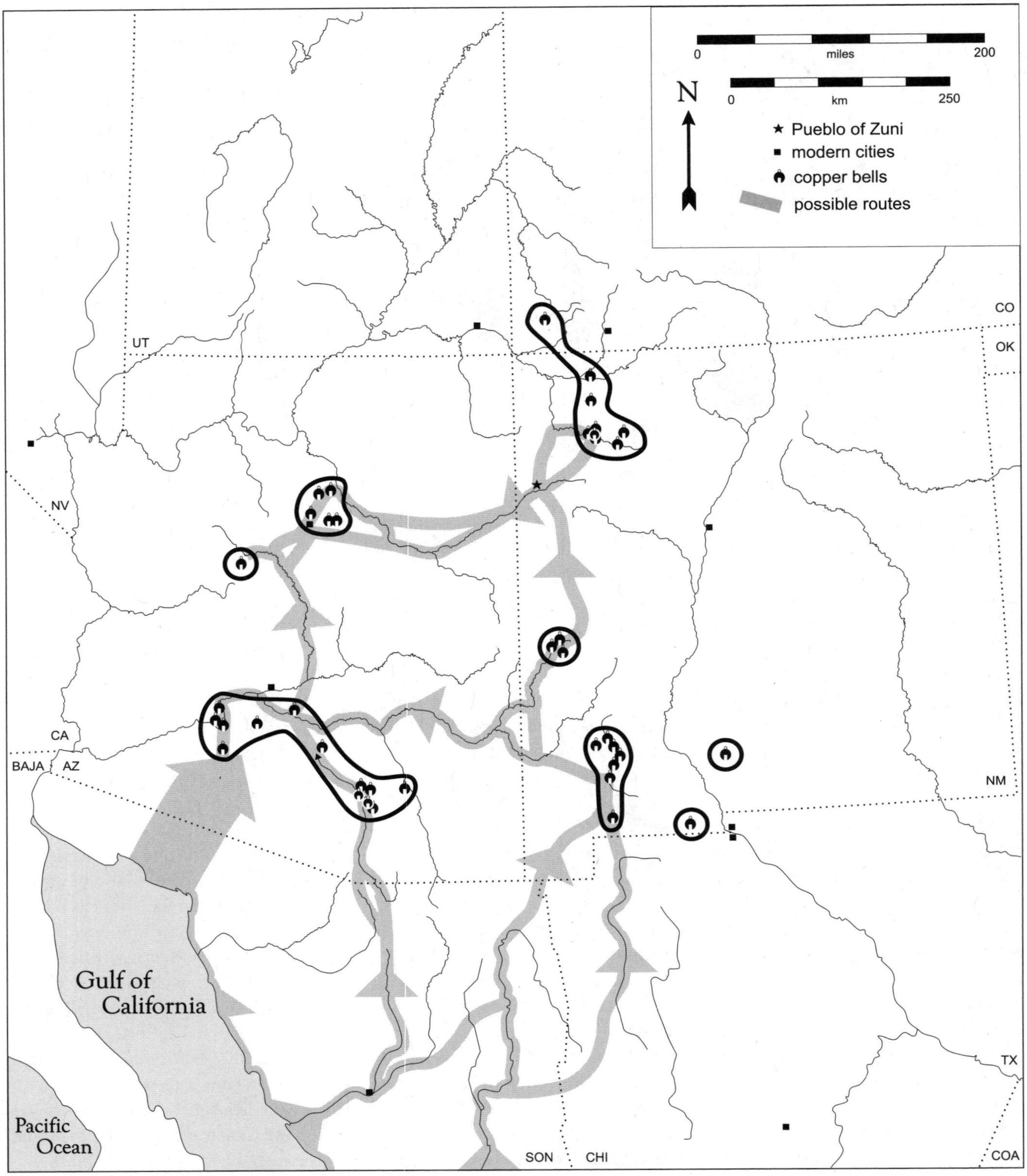

Figure 17.3. Distribution of copper bells, AD 800–ca. 1250.

Table 17.2 Copper Bells, pre–AD 1250

Cluster/Site Name	Number of Typed Bells	Number of Untyped Bells	Number of Types Represented	Total Bells
Chaco Canyon cluster				
Pueblo Bonito	10	8	3[a]	18
Pueblo del Arroyo	—	5	—	5
Casa Rinconada	—	3	—	3
Pueblo Alto	1	—	1	1
Eleventh Hour Site	—	1	—	1
Bis'san'ani	—	1	—	1
Aztec/West Ruin	1	—	1	1
Aztec Ruin area	1	—	1	1
Goodman Point (Colorado)	1	—	1	1
Flagstaff cluster				
Wupatki	6	3	3	9
Tse Tlani Ruin	1	—	1	1
San Francisco Peaks:14:1 (GP)	2	—	1	2
Winona Village	1	—	1	1
Canyon de Flag	2	—	1	2
Copper Bell Ruin	5	—	1	5
NA 627	1	—	1	1
NA 8762	—	1	—	1
Flagstaff area	1	—	1	1
Upper San Francisco cluster				
Delgar Ruin	1	1	1	2
Apache Creek	1	—	1	1
Upper San Francisco River	—	1	—	1
Cox Ranch	2	—	2	2
Mimbres cluster				
Cameron Creek	1	—	1	1
Galaz Ruin	3	1	3[a]	4
Mattocks Ruin	1	—	1	1
NAN Ranch	1	2	1	3
Old Town	1	—	1	1
Osborn Ruin	10	—	2[a]	10
McSherry Ruin	4	—	2	4
Hohokam cluster				
Alder Wash Site	—	1	—	1
Hodges Ruin	1	—	1	1
Los Morteros Ruin	2	—	—	2
Rooney Ranch Site	1	—	1[a]	1
Marana	13	—	1[a]	13
Romo Cache	15	10+	1	25+
Snaketown	28	—	1[a]	28
Maricopa Road Site	1	—	1[a]	1
Pinnacle Peak Site	1	—	1[a]	1
Gatlin Ruin	56	—	6[b]	56
Gatlin area	13	2	4[c]	15
Homestead Site	1	—	1	1
Gillespie Dam Site	9	—	1	9
Isolates				
Mount Riley area	1	—	1	1
Alamogordo	—	2	—	2
Sundown Site	2	—	1	2
Edge of Cedars Ruin	—	3	—	3
Russel Grove Site	1	—	1	1
Robinson Site	2	1	1	3

Sources: Vargas (1995), Mathien (1991).
[a]Type represented is unique to this interval.
[b]Includes two types unique to this interval.
[c]Includes three types unique to this interval.

excavations of the Chacoan great house sites located there.

Post–AD 1250. Southwestern sites with copper bells dating after ca. AD 1250 are summarized in table 17.3; the distribution of bells assigned to this interval is shown in figure 17.4, along with the trails inferred most likely to have been involved in their movement. Substantial differences from the earlier distribution of bells are apparent.

From her Phase II data Vargas (1995) once again identifies four clusters of sites with bells, albeit quite different from those of Phase I. On the basis of these distributions she proposes that during Phase II there were two contemporaneous exchange networks that extended north from the production centers of western Mexico through which copper bells were being exchanged (Vargas 1995). The western system supplied the Hohokam/Salado populations of central and eastern Arizona. The eastern, or Paquimé, system is argued to have provided bells to settlements along the Rio Grande and possibly communities of the central Arizona highlands.

In figure 17.4 we identify only two clusters rather than four. We suggest that most Phase II bells could have originated at Paquimé and that there is only one exchange system operating rather than the two proposed by Vargas. The presence of bells at two Salado sites in the upper San Simon valley (Webb and Kuykendall) suggests connections with Paquimé, and bells in the upland regions of eastern Arizona and in the Flagstaff area could easily represent an extension of the Paquimé system into the Safford Basin, the Globe/Miami area, and beyond. There are no Phase II settlements located *on* the Rio Grande that have produced bells, although Pottery Mound, with one bell, is not far up a

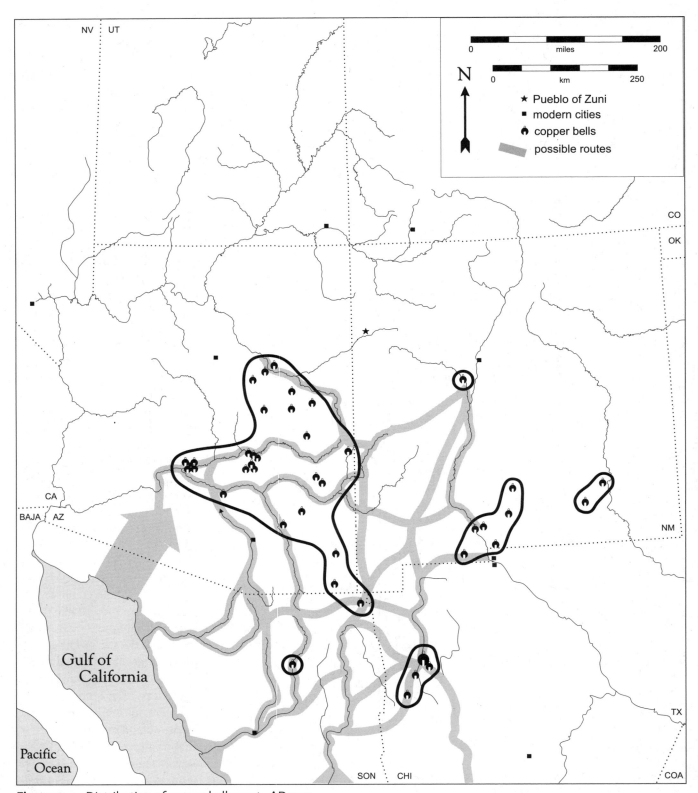

Figure 17.4. Distribution of copper bells post—AD 1250.

Table 17.3 Copper Bells, Post—AD 1250

Area/Site Name	Number of Typed Bells	Number of Untyped Bells	Number of Types Represented	Total Bells
Paquimé area				
Paquimé	117	—	11	117
Rancho San Miguel	2	—	1	2
San Joaquin Canyon	12	—	1	12
Santana Ranch	1	—	1	1
Ojo de Agua	1	—	1	1
Rio Sonora				
San Jose Baviacora	1	—	1	1
Jornada Mogollon				
Bloom Mound	4	3	2	7
White Sands	—	1	1	1
Three Rivers	—	1	1	1
Cox Ranch	2	—	2	2
Russel Grove	1	—	1	1
Doña Ana Target Range	1	—	1	1
Highland Mogollon				
Q Ranch	10	8	7	18
Foote Canyon Pueblo	1	—	1	1
Grasshopper	3	—	1	3
Kinishba	1	—	1	1
Four Mile	1	—	1	1
Chavez Pass	1	—	1	1
Anasazi				
Pottery Mound	1	—	1	1
Pollock Site	2	—	1	2
Homolovi II	1	—	1	1
Hohokam				
Mammoth (Big Bell)	1	—	1	1
Casa Grande	7	1	2	8
Los Hornos	1	—	1	1
Pueblo Grande	1	2	1	3
La Ciudad	—	2	?	2
Las Colinas	—	10	?	10
Pueblo del Monte	—	1	1	1
Salado				
Webb Site	2	—	2	2
Kuykendall Site	2	1	1	3
Gila Pueblo	39	1	6	40
Hilltop House	1	6	?	7
Griffin Wash	1	—	1	1
Armour Ranch	—	1	1	1
Livingston Ruin	2	—	1	2
School House Mesa	1	—	1	1
Togetzoge	1	—	1	1
76 Ranch	3	—	1	3

Sources: Vargas (1995) and Adams and Elson (1995).

major tributary, the Rio Puerco of the East. The other three sites near the Rio Grande are located north and east of El Paso, and Phase II bells in the upper Rio Grande drainage net are rare compared to their distribution farther west and south. Once again, we shall see below that post—AD 1250 distributions of other exotics tend to support this interpretation.

Also of interest are artifacts of clay that clearly represent imitations of copper bells (Withers 1946:51–53, figs. 4, 5). Although an exhaustive search has not been undertaken, such artifacts appear to occur exclusively in late prehistoric, protohistoric, and possibly early historic period assemblages and thus postdate the Paquimé system. Multiple examples are documented from Pecos Pueblo (189 specimens; Glaze V contexts) and from Awatovi and Kawaika-a (a combined 95 specimens; late prehistoric or later contexts), and a single undated (?) example is reported from the Double F Ranch near Dragoon, Arizona (Withers 1946:51). As Withers (1946:53) notes, such imitations appear to occur only in sites where real copper bells have not been found, and we add that most, if not all, of them may have been manufactured after access to copper bells produced in western Mexico ceased (Hosler 1988b) and after the abandonment of Paquimé.

Attempts to duplicate this form in clay—after the real items became unavailable—probably reflect the general importance once attached to them by aboriginal southwestern peoples. The rapid decline in even these later imitations suggests a parallel decline in the ideological and cosmological orientations that emanated from Paquimé along with the bells and other exotic items (see below).

Macaws and Parrots

Use of the brightly colored plumage of macaws and parrots in ritual contexts is well documented among native Southwest populations, for example, as elements in prayer sticks (pahos) and ceremonial dress (Judd 1954:263; Ladd 2001; McKusick 2001). The volume of feathers needed for these purposes can be prodigious. Ladd (2001:12) indicated that each Zuni individual, depending on his or her religious role in the community, must "plant" between 16 and 80 prayer sticks a year, using from 80 to 400 feathers of various kinds. During his excavations at Pueblo Bonito in the 1920s Judd (1954) reported that there were then four macaws alive at Zuni, and macaw feathers were reaching Hawikuh in quantity when the Spaniards first arrived (Ferguson and Hart 1985:53).

Use of macaw and parrot feathers for such purposes has considerable antiquity in the Southwest. Macaws are depicted both naturalistically and in the abstract in painted decorations on Classic period Mimbres bowls and on later Four Mile Polychrome, Sikyatki Polychrome, and several other later types; they are represented in ceramic effigy vessels from a number of areas; and they appear in kiva murals at several sites. The few reported perishable items incorporating feathers (see table 17.4) appear to represent ritual paraphernalia that was exchanged widely in the Puebloan world. These images and artifacts, as well as ethnographic data, reflect the importance of these birds in southwestern ritual and ideological systems.[3]

Three species are relevant to the current discussion: the military macaw (*Ara militaris*), the scarlet macaw (*A. macao*), and the thick-billed parrot (*Rhynchopsitta pachyrhyncha*). Several biological charac-

teristics of these birds and a number of facts about their contexts of recovery are relevant to an understanding of their role in prehistoric exchange and clearly demonstrate that it was their feathers that were in demand.

Neither macaw species is indigenous to the Southwest. The military macaw is native to southern Sonora and Chihuahua. It has been reported as far north as the modern community of Soyopa, Sonora, some 282 km south of the international border (Hargrave 1970:10), and as far west as the Río Yaqui and the Río Bavispe (Russell and Monson 1998:128). It is most common in the foothills and barrancas of the Sierra Madre, where it inhabits arid and semiarid pine and oak forest at altitudes of up to 2,438 m. The scarlet macaw is indigenous to the tropical lowlands of southern Mexico, with the present northern limits of its natural habitat being in the states of Tamaulipas and Oaxaca. Thus, both species would have been exotic to most populations in the American Southwest, although the military macaw might have been familiar to some inhabitants of the extreme southern parts of the region (McKusick 1974:272). Although both species of macaws are definitely represented in Southwest faunal assemblages, there has been considerable debate regarding the accuracy and validity of methods used to discriminate them in skeletal remains (Bullock 1991; Hargrave 1970; McKusick 1974:283–284, 2001; Ruble 1996). Macaws are subsequently treated here as an undifferentiated category.

In contrast, the thick-billed parrot is native to the southern Southwest, formerly ranging as far north as the grasslands and mountains of southeastern Arizona and southwestern New Mexico. The plumage of this parrot is similar in color to that of the military macaw, but the bird is much smaller, 38–40.6 cm in length. Thick-

billed parrots are clearly depicted on Classic Mimbres vessels (Creel and McKusick 1994:512–515) and in the kiva murals at Pottery Mound (Hibben 1975; McKusick 2001:87).

As noted by both Hudson (1978) and Neitzel (1989), macaws were indeed quite rare in the prehistoric Southwest. Of the over 700 examples considered here, only 215 came from sites other than Paquimé (see below). Age analyses of these specimens clearly indicate that it was primarily immature birds (4–11 months) that were obtained by Southwest peoples. Creel and McKusick (1994:518) report that 94 percent of all macaws from archaeological contexts north of the international border were between 10 and 13 months old at time of death, about the age at which they first have fully developed plumage. In Hargrave's (1970) earlier analysis there were no juveniles (seven weeks to four months) in the sample, and in McKusick's (2001:72) more recent summary of macaws of known age only one juvenile is reported. The vast majority of specimens are either newly fledged birds (71 percent in Hargrave's sample and 70 percent in McKusick's) or adolescents one to three years in age. Of the adolescents, most are between 12 and 13 months (McKusick 2001:72) and thus would have just achieved their full plumage. The number of older birds in these samples is relatively few: McKusick reports only seven specimens of breeding age (four or more years) or older. Hargrave (1970:53) suggested that these older birds were likely pets, as some were recovered in association with human burials (see n. 6). There is no evidence that actual breeding of macaws occurred at any sites north of the international border.

It appears, then, that most macaws must have entered the region as young juvenile or immature birds. At this early stage in the development of

Table 17.4 Sites with Nonosteological Remains of Macaws and Thick-Billed Parrots

Site	Nature of Material	Period	References
Mogollon			
Water Canyon Cave	Two scarlet macaw feathers, cordage paho	Late Pithouse/Classic Period	Cosgrove (1947), Creel and McKusick (1994)
Gila Cliff Dwellings	One Scarlet Macaw Feather, four cordage pahos (parrot)	Late AD 1200s	Creel and McKusick (1994), Fenner (1986), McKusick (2001)
U-Bar Cave	Scarlet macaw feather lining of small bag	AD 1150–1400	Creel and McKusick (1994), Lambert and Ambler (1961)
Pinnacle Cave	At least one scarlet macaw feather	AD 1150–1400	Creel and McKusick (1994), Lambert and Ambler (1961)
Tularosa Cave	Bundle of parrot feathers	Unknown	Creel and McKusick (1994), Hough (1914)
Tularosa Cave	One scarlet macaw feather	Unknown	Creel and McKusick (1994), Martin et al. (1952)
Tularosa Cave	One military macaw feather	Unknown	McKusick (2001)
Anasazi			
Pueblo Bonito	A bundle with four feathers believed to be macaw	AD 930–1130+	Judd (1954:266)
Antelope House	"Corn Mother" fetish with scarlet macaw feathers	AD 1140–1270	McKusick (1986, 2001)
Antelope House	Cotton cloth with 47 scarlet macaw feathers interwoven	AD 1140–1270	McKusick (1986, 2001)
Lavender Cave, Utah	Apron made of cords of rabbit fur completely covered with scarlet macaw feathers	AD 1275–1300	McKusick (2001), Time-Life Books (1992), Fields and Zamudio-Taylor (2001:fig. 24)

their basic plumage and musculature they would have been highly susceptible to respiratory illness from being chilled (Shelley 2001:128). Thus, while it probably would have been relatively easy to physically transport the birds, success in maintaining their health was likely to have been very difficult and must have required considerable attention.

Ruble (1996:11) notes that macaws are most often found in formal burials, some with human interments. Many, however, are buried alone in pits that appear to have been excavated specifically for that purpose, often in proximity to human burials. The size of these pits indicates that the bird had been plucked of its longer feathers prior to burial (Ruble 1996).

Numerous researchers have remarked on the relative scarcity of macaws and parrots in Hohokam contexts. To date we know of only 12 reported specimens, with several represented by only one or two elements. Among the earliest occurrences are three macaws and two parrots reported from Snaketown that are thought to date to the Late Pioneer and Early Colonial periods (McKusick 1976:375–376). These are represented by five isolated occurrences recovered from general contexts (McKusick 1976:376) rather than from the mortuary contexts most common in other areas of the Southwest. "Most" Hohokam macaw remains are assigned to the Classic period. The very low number of remains, their recovery contexts, and a geographically dispersed distribution across the area are all factors that invite the hypothesis that the birds were being obtained very infrequently and on an ad hoc basis rather than via a systematized exchange system.

At present, the only sites with definitive evidence of macaw breeding facilities and evidence of hatchlings are Paquimé (McKusick 1974) and settlements in the surrounding region (Minnis et al. 1993:272–274). Nesting boxes were identified in at least six of the excavated areas at Paquimé, and a number of entrance stones and plugs were recovered (Di Peso et al. 1974c:219–230), Minnis et al. 1993:271). In addition, several effigy vessels from the site are thought to represent macaws with their heads extended through openings of breeding pens (see fig. 17.5). McKusick (1974, 2001:73) documents the remains of 504 macaws and seven parrots from the site, and while an overall dominance of newly fledged birds is apparent in the sample (McKusick 1974:276–278), some survived into the breeding stage (four or more years). The latter remains

Figure 17.5. Ceramic effigy vessel showing parrot in breeding pen (ASM catalog no. GP3710).

tended to occur in the area of the breeding pens, and the recovery of eggshell fragments from the floors of nesting boxes supports the idea that these pens were for breeding macaws (McKusick 1974:281). Thus, it appears that the Paquimé region was the most likely (and probably dominant) source of macaws traded into the Southwest during the fourteenth and fifteenth centuries.

Temporal and Spatial Distributions

The following discussion is based on recorded archaeological occurrences of 698 macaw remains, 15 instances of thick-billed parrot remains, and seven specimens that may be either macaws or parrots. We have sorted this sample into two periods roughly equivalent to those discussed above for copper bells: pre– and post–AD 1250.

Pre–AD 1250. Specimens assigned to the pre–AD 1250 interval are listed in table 17.5, and their distribution is shown in figure 17.6. The earliest remains of macaws and parrots may date as early as AD 700 in the Hohokam region and between AD 650 and 750 in the Mimbres. In both cases the sample is not large, and relatively few birds are represented. There are few

other cases in the Southwest dating prior to AD 1000, but there is a marked increase in the number of specimens thereafter. Despite an early presence among the Hohokam, specimens from this area are few and tend to be isolated skeletal elements.

The distribution of macaws and parrots in the pre–AD 1250 interval shows striking similarities to that of copper bells, and our interpretation of this pattern once again involves Mimbres/Chaco/Flagstaff connections. In the Mimbres region most specimens occur in post–AD 1000 contexts. At about this same time there is a sharp increase in demand for these birds, as indicated by the number of specimens reported from other areas in the Southwest. This increased demand appears to have been fueled largely by the needs of two central communities in the northern Southwest: Pueblo Bonito and Wupatki. These two communities account for roughly 75 percent of all specimens dating between AD 1000 and approximately AD 1250. Once again, it has been suggested that these two communities were linked, central components in an economic and political system (Wilcox 2002) that was actively involved in the acquisition of prestige goods, including macaws and parrots.

Taking into account the apparent ad hoc character of Hohokam acquisitions, the principal structure of the pre–AD 1250 exchange system for macaws and parrots is thus defined by three major nodes (Mimbres, Chaco, and Wupatki) and one minor one (the upper San Francisco River) in the overall distribution. Further, it appears that Mimbres populations were the "brokers" directly involved in acquiring the birds from areas farther south and moving them north.

Post–AD 1250. Specimens assigned to the post–AD 1250 interval are listed in

table 17.6, and their distribution is shown in figure 17.7. Once again, the distribution of macaws and parrots for this interval shows strong similarities to that of copper bells and is interpreted as defining the skeleton of the regional exchange system centered at Paquimé.

McKusick (2001:74–76) indicates that there appears to be a hiatus in demand for macaws and parrots after AD 1200 that was followed by a sharp resurgence in demand around 1275. We believe that the resurgence in demand may have begun somewhat earlier but nonetheless interpret this pattern as representing the decline of the earlier Chaco-related exchange system and the subsequent rise in the system emanating from Paquimé. Some of the macaws from Point of Pines share unique genetic cranial abnormalities with birds from Paquimé (McKusick 2001:77), indicating a strong connection between these populations.

Shell

Traditionally, southwestern archaeologists have considered the Hohokam to have been the principal suppliers of shell to other parts of the region, with the center of Paquimé taking over some of this role late in the sequence. The general view has been that, prior to the rise of Paquimé, Anasazi and Mogollon populations acquired finished shell products from the Hohokam (Haury 1937a).

Sources

Aboriginal populations in the Southwest had four distinct sources of shell available to them. Three of these are marine sources, while the other is the freshwater genera endemic to the region. By far, the majority of the shell employed in the manufacture of

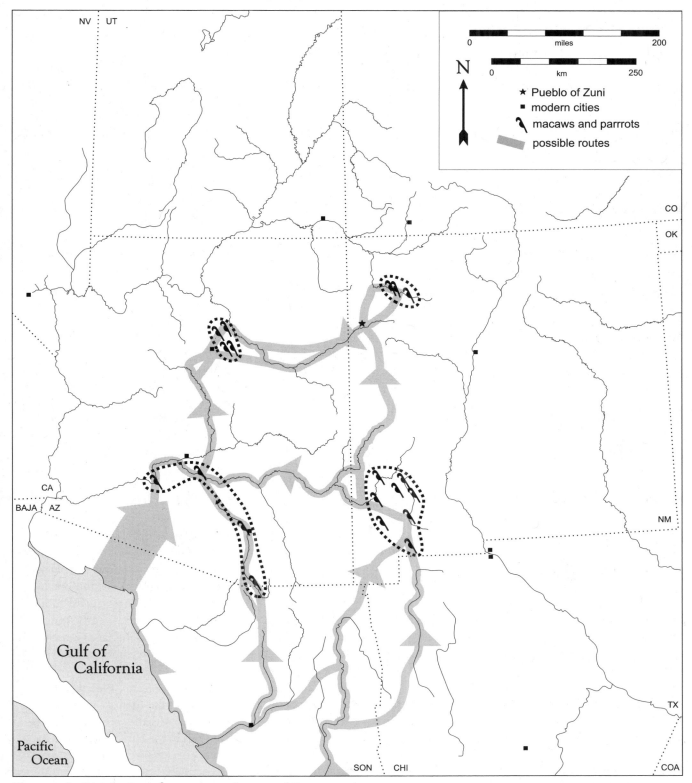

Figure 17.6. Distribution of macaw remains, pre–AD 1250.

Table 17.5 Macaws and Parrots, Pre–AD 1250

Area/Site Name	Macaws	Macaws/ Parrots	Parrots	Total
Southern Arizona—Hohokam				
Gatlin	1	—	—	1
Snaketown	3	—	2	5
Southern Arizona—other				
El Macayo	1	—	—	1
Mimbres area				
Cameron Creek	1	1	1	3
Galaz	4	5	2	11
Old Town	1	—	—	1
Osborn	1	—	—	1
Treasure Hill	—	—	1	1
Wind Mountain	1	—	—	1
Freeman Ranch	1	1	—	2
Mitchell Site	(1)	—	—	(1)
Chaco area				
Pueblo Bonito	31	—	2	33
Pueblo del Arroyo	5	—	—	5
Kin Kletso	1	—	—	1
Northern Arizona—Anasazi				
Wupatki	41	—	4	45
Nalakihu	1	—	—	1
Northern Arizona—Sinagua				
Winona	1	—	—	1
Ridge Ruin	4	—	—	4
Pollock Site	1	—	—	1

Sources: Compiled from Creel and McKusick (1994), Hargrave (1970), McKusick (1974), Powell (1977), Ruble (1996), and Shelley (2001).

ornaments and other objects was from marine sources. The three marine sources are the Pacific Ocean off the California coast, the Gulf of California, and the Gulf of Mexico. Each of these is dominated by distinct oceanic currents and conditions that determine the nature of marine communities within them. While there is some overlap in genera and species, the marine fauna from each of these areas tend to be distinctive, and in some cases particular species are restricted to only one of these potential sources. *Haliotis* (abalone) and *Olivella biplicata*, for example, occur only in the colder waters off the Pacific coast. *Spondylus*, all of the large conch shells (*Strombus*, *Murex*, and *Melongena*), and many of the smaller univalves are restricted to the warm tropical waters of the Gulf of California, although some have related forms native to the Gulf of Mexico. Nonmarine shell resources are restricted to a few species of freshwater nacreous shell belonging to the family Unionidae. Their distribution in the Southwest is separated into two broad zones by the Continental Divide. To the west is found the fragile *Anodonta californiensis*, while to the east the more robust *Uniomerus tetralasmus* is endemic to the Rio Grande and southern Mississippi tributaries (Brandauer and Wu 1978:56–58; Venn 1984:228).

Regional Patterns of Occurrence

The earliest shell assemblages in the Southwest are from Early Agricultural period settlements in the southern Basin and Range. Most identified species originated in the Gulf of California, but a significant amount of material was also obtained from coastal California, primarily *Haliotis* but also including artifacts made from *Olivella biplicata* and other California coastal gastropods. The most common artifacts are whole shell beads, with spire-lopped forms manufactured from various *Olivella* species dominating. Pendants are the second most common artifact, and a distinctive feature of Early Agricultural period assemblages is the virtual absence of *Glycymeris* bracelets.

Hohokam. Perhaps the most striking feature of the shell assemblage associated with the introduction of ceramics in the Hohokam area is the marked increase in the occurrence of *Glycymeris* bracelets. When combined with the reworked fragments, bracelets represent nearly 55 percent of all finished artifacts from recently excavated Early Ceramic period settlements in the Tucson Basin (Vokes

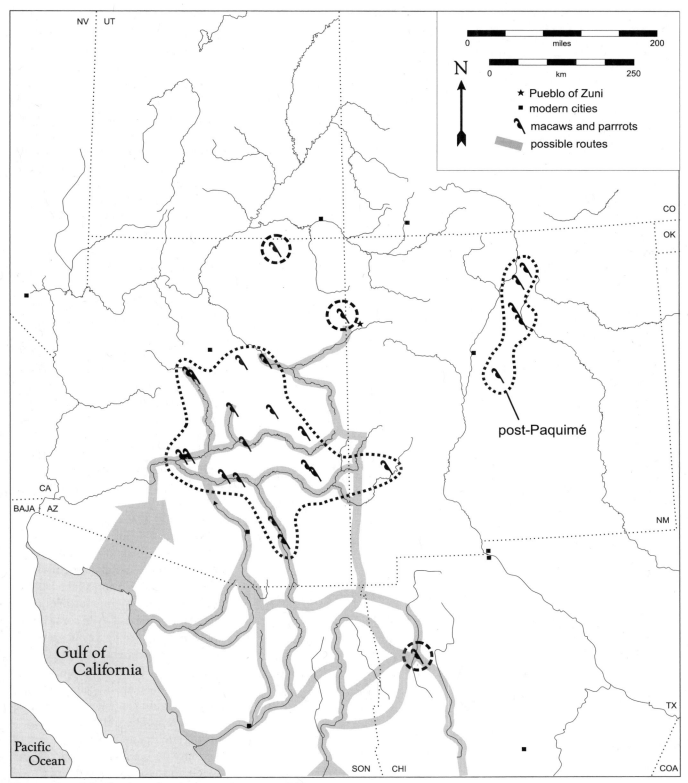

Figure 17.7. Distribution of macaw remains, post–AD 1250.

Table 17.6 Macaws and Parrots, Post—AD 1250

Area/Site Name	Macaws	Macaws/ Parrots	Parrots	Total
Casas Grandes area				
Paquimé	503	—	2	505
Southern Arizona—Hohokam				
Pueblo Grande	2	—	—	2
Las Colinas	1	—	—	1
Las Fosas	1	—	—	1
Los Morteros	2	—	—	2
Southern Arizona—other				
Reeve Ruin	1	—	—	1
111 Ranch Ruin	1	—	—	1
Griffen Wash Site	1	—	—	1
Meredith Ranch Site	1	—	—	1
Pinal Pueblo	2	—	—	2
Mimbres area				
Gila Cliff Dwellings	1	—	1	2
Highland Mogollon				
Grasshopper	23	—	—	23
Kinishba	4	—	—	4
Turkey Creek	12	—	—	12
Point of Pines	27	—	—	27
Northern Arizona—Anasazi				
Kiet Siel	2	—	—	2
Homolovi III	2	—	—	2
Rio Grande pueblos				
Picuris Pueblo	1	—	—	1
Garcia Site	1	—	—	1
Pecos Pueblo	2	—	—	2
Arroyo Hondo	3	—	—	3
Gran Quivira	1	—	—	1
Northern Arizona—Sinagua				
Tuzigoot	3	—	—	3
Montezuma's Castle	1	—	—	1

Sources: Compiled from Clark (personal communication 2003), Creel and McKusick (1994), Gillespie (1995), Hargrave (1970), James (1995), Lang and Harris (1984), McKusick (1974), Mills and Mills (1975), Olsen (1990), Pierce (2001), Rea (1981, 1983), Ruble (1996), and Szuter (1984).

1998). This frequency is comparable to some later Hohokam assemblages and, as noted above, forms a major contrast with Early Agricultural period assemblages. Other types of Early Ceramic period artifacts include whole shell beads and cut geometric pendants. These forms are present in the Early Agricultural period as well, perhaps suggesting some continuity in style and technology. However, the relative proportion of these forms is much reduced by the sudden popularity of bracelets.

All marine genera represented during the Early Ceramic period are also present in earlier assemblages, but because of the increase in bracelets *Glycymeris* becomes the dominant genus. *Olivella* continues to be present, as does *Haliotis*, although the latter in very limited quantities. Even so, the presence of *Haliotis* confirms continued access to materials from the California coast, although the nature of that access is as yet unclear. Indeed, *Haliotis* continues to be present in small quantities throughout the Hohokam sequence and into the historic period (Di Peso 1956:46–47; Vokes 1984:470, 1987:265).

Among the Hohokam shell is a relatively common and widely distributed class of material. Particularly in the Phoenix Basin core of the Hohokam regional system, most Hohokam habitation sites and even some temporarily occupied field house sites have shell ornaments as part of their assemblage. The most ubiquitous artifact is the plain bracelet made of *Glycymeris*. In general, smaller habitation sites produce relatively simple forms and few genera, while larger settlements often have greater diversity in forms and in the genera represented.

The abundance of shell in Hohokam sites has led researchers to distinguish between high-value and low-value forms (McGuire 1993:101–

102). The former occur only in low frequencies, if present at all, and examples include etched shell, trumpets, shell mosaics, and some styles of pendants. Low-value forms include bracelets, beads, most geometric and some effigy pendants, and the like; they are found in relatively large numbers and occur in some combination at virtually all sites (Jernigan 1978; Nelson 1981, 1991).

There is clear evidence for the manufacture of shell artifacts throughout the Hohokam sequence, with larger sites generally having greater amounts of production debris and a greater variety of artifact forms represented.[4]

Mogollon. Prior to about AD 1000 there is relatively little shell in the Mogollon area. Mogollon Village (primary San Francisco phase) produced a shell assemblage of only 26 specimens representing relatively few species (Haury 1936a:46–47, 109); the assemblage from Harris Village is only somewhat larger and included material from the Three Circle phase component (Haury 1936a:78). Martin's (1940, 1943; Martin and Rinaldo 1947) extensive excavations at the SU site also produced very little shell. Virtually all shell objects from pre–AD 1000 Mogollon sites have been recovered from caches or mortuary deposits (Haury 1985b:249).

Mogollon shell during this interval has often been assumed to have reached the area through exchange with Hohokam populations (Jernigan 1978; Tower 1945), and some have argued that this pattern was true after AD 1000 as well (Johnson 1965). Prior to the Classic Mimbres period, many Mimbres shell artifacts are identical to Hohokam Colonial period forms, and the Hohokam-Mimbres connection during this interval seems likely. (Hohokam-style palettes and cremation burials are present as well.)

Tower (1945:43) also noted the possibility of "subsidiary routes" up the Sonora and Yaqui rivers, into Chihuahua, and thence possibly into the Mimbres area and the Rio Grande, thus providing an alternative to the Hohokam source. Whether or not this latter alternative was in place before about AD 1000 remains unclear, but it was probably the primary source of Classic period Mimbres shell.

The quantity and diversity of Mogollon shell increased considerably after AD 1000, particularly in the Mimbres area (Haury 1936a:109). The Galaz Ruin (Anyon and LeBlanc 1984) produced a shell assemblage that dwarfs earlier ones (approximately 225 complete and fragmentary bracelets and thousands of shell beads, along with numerous pendants of various forms), and Swartz Ruin produced a similarly impressive assemblage. At the latter site bracelets were present in 30 of the 1,009 excavated burials, and two individuals were accompanied by large numbers of them (Burial 389 with 26 bracelets and Burial 442 with 39 bracelets; Cosgrove and Cosgrove 1932:66). The total number of beads is not reported, but it is clearly substantial: Burial 308 had a mass of over 5,000 disk beads around the neck and on the chest of the individual.

Clearly, the amount of shell being amassed by some individuals was substantial, and it is just as plain that not all of the population enjoyed equal access to these products. It is quite possible that these individuals represent elites that were intimately involved with the shell trade, brokering both the material coming north along the eastern route and any material entering from the Hohokam.

This pattern of increasing diversity, along with increasing frequencies of shell products over time, is seen in nearly all areas of the Mogo-

llon region. However, one feature remains constant, which is that the great majority of these items are recovered in a relatively few mortuary deposits, suggesting once again that access among the inhabitants of these settlements was not uniform.

With the reorganization of the Mimbres area in the middle of the twelfth century large communities declined in size or were abandoned entirely, with much of the population shifting to the east into the western tributaries of the Rio Grande (Hegmon et al. 1999). This would have occurred at roughly the same time that the Chaco great house system was undergoing its own restructuring and the exchange network that had passed through the Mimbres region was intensified and perhaps restructured into a more formal system. It is possible that the absence of large villages and entrenched elites in the new social order of the Mimbres area allowed the Chacoan elite to extend a firmer control over the transport and dissemination of these materials, thereby limiting the role, and access, of the local elite. Later, the rise of Paquimé and the Casas Grandes system appears to have further isolated the late Mimbres populations from the Hohokam and fully incorporated these groups into the Casas Grandes network (R. Bradley 1996; see also Wilcox 1991b, 1999a).

The location of Paquimé in northwestern Chihuahua would have placed it somewhat east of the route that extends up the Río Bavispe but well placed for material moving up the Río Casas Grandes (Di Peso et al. 1974d:167). The shell material associated with the early Viejo period is unremarkable; beads make up over 98 percent of the items, with the remainder being pendants of various forms and plain bracelets. There is virtually no evidence to indicate local production of the shell artifacts, leading Di Peso and Fenner (Di Peso et al. 1974b:392) to suggest that the inhabitants were obtaining the items as finished ornaments. This contrasts sharply with the following Medio period shell assemblage, which is remarkable for both its size (nearly four million pieces) and its complexity. Again, beads were by far the most numerous artifact forms present, with one form—the *Nassarius* whole shell bead—accounting for over 95 percent of the entire assemblage. Di Peso and Fenner (Di Peso et al. 1974d:170) report that the *Nassarius* probably came from the central part of the Gulf of California coast, near Guaymas.[5]

There is also a wide variety of other artifacts, ranging from plain bracelets to elaborately carved bracelets and pendants, and substantial evidence for local production in the form of unmodified shells, unfinished pieces, and manufacturing debris. For example, in addition to the massive number of beads, over 21,000 unmodified *Nassarius* shells were recovered (Di Peso et al. 1974d:170). That relatively little of the shell material was recovered from mortuary deposits (only .2 percent from mortuary or other ritual contexts such as caches) suggests that much of the shell was not produced for local consumption but was intended for trade or distribution elsewhere.

Anasazi. A few forms dominate Anasazi shell assemblages over time. Whole shell beads and pendants occur throughout the sequence. Some forms are always present, while others rise and decline in popularity over time. Spire-lopped *Olivella* beads occur throughout the sequence and are widely distributed. The vast majority of these are *Olivella dama*, but a few examples of the Pacific coast *O. biplicata* are present. The latter is represented in Basketmaker deposits at the Dead Horse Site (Adams 1973), and *O. dama* is well represented at the Twin Buttes Site (Wendorf 1953) as well as in later contexts (Kidder 1932; Urban 1991). Cut shell pendants, most often in geometric forms, also occur throughout the Anasazi sequence, and even Archaic period examples are known (Lindsay et al. 1968).[6]

The consistent occurrence of whole shell beads contrasts with the temporal distribution of a related artifact form, variously described as barrel, cylindrical (Vokes 1984:478), or truncated beads (Di Peso et al. 1974b:417–418). These were also made from *Olivella* valves, formed by grinding both ends of the valve to form a barrel or cylinder. This bead form is restricted to Pueblo II (when it appears to have enjoyed some popularity) and Pueblo III contexts, but there are no reported occurrences in sites occupied after Pueblo III. The first occurrence and increased popularity of this form is paralleled in the Hohokam area, and this is likely the ultimate source of many Anasazi "barrel" beads. However, in the Hohokam area this style continued to be very popular into the Late Classic period. Its disappearance in the Anasazi area may reflect the decline of the Chaco macroregional system and associated exchange networks that brought this form into the area, and perhaps its initial appearance reflects the earlier development of that same system.

Glycymeris shell bracelets or armlets show a similar pattern. From Basketmaker III through Pueblo II bracelets were very common in Anasazi sites. For example, Roberts (1931:162) reports that most Pueblo I burials at Kiatuthlanna were accompanied by shell bracelets, with as many as 20 occurring in a single interment. In contrast, no bracelets were recovered from the Pueblo III room blocks at the site, and bracelets were absent from all of the Pueblo III assemblages reviewed in the preparation of this chapter. Once again, this form has a different history in the Hohokam area, where it continues throughout the sequence. And, once again, it may be that most of the Anasazi examples came from the Hohokam via exchange networks involving the Chacoan system; once that system declined, the source of these artifacts was essentially eliminated. A single specimen was recovered from the Pueblo IV Homolovi II site (Urban 1991), but this example may recycle from an earlier site, indicate participation in the later Paquimé exchange system, or simply be an isolated acquisition.[7]

Another interesting pattern involves shell tinklers manufactured from *Conus* and *Oliva* valves. This artifact form does not appear in the Anasazi area until the Late Pueblo II to Early Pueblo III times, but, once present, it spreads quickly across the region. During Pueblo IV it is reported from virtually all sites that have shell as part of their assemblage and is the only shell artifact form to exhibit such a pattern. We know from ethnographic sources that these artifacts were worn in clusters about the body and on the clothing of dancers. Strings of them marked the leggings of the early-thirteenth-century Burial of the Magician found at Ridge Ruin near Flagstaff (McGregor 1943). Adams (1991) has suggested that there was an increase in public ceremonialism during the Pueblo IV period associated with the spread of the kachina cult, and the rising popularity of the tinkler may well be related to an increase in public ceremonies and performance rituals. Interestingly, this temporal pattern is paralleled in the Hohokam area.

As with the Mogollon, most Anasazi shell has been recovered from mortuary or ritual deposits. In the Chaco area shell beads and pendants have been found, often with turquoise (see below), as votive offerings in pilasters that supported kiva roofs and in wall niches within kivas (Mathien 2001:110–111), and this pattern may extend back to Basketmaker III times (Mathien 2001). With the later introduction of new construction modes incorporating the use of pilasters as kiva roof supports, there is a substantial increase in both the richness and number of such offerings in Chacoan sites. The other context in which shell is reported is in mortuary deposits (Akins and Schelberg 1984:93). For example, materials accompanying the burials below Room 33 at Pueblo Bonito included many shell beads, numerous bracelets, and a shell trumpet (Akins and Schelberg 1984:91). Not all shell in Chacoan sites has been recovered from mortuary or votive contexts, and a small number of items has been recovered from nonvotive architectural and other contexts. As an example, 19 pieces of shell were recovered from the Spadefoot Toad site, 18 from architectural contexts or extramural pits, and only one from a midden deposit (Mathien 1993b).

At Wupatki "shell ornaments, bone awls, and mosaic pieces (in caches) were rare, but were found with several burials, along with other bits of turquoise" (Stanislawski 1963:60). Instead, the considerable shell assemblage was concentrated in architectural (possibly votive?) contexts. Stanislawski (1963:352) describes multiple occurrences of shell associated with Rooms 7, 35, and 45 and with the ceremonial dance plaza, Room 66. It is interesting that Room 35 had an ornamental architectural element consisting of one to four courses of black basalt boulders placed near the base of one wall along its length, and Room 45 was noted as a possible kiva (Stanislawski 1963:515).

Spatial and Temporal Distributions of Selected Species

Once again using our two-part temporal division, interesting patterns are revealed when we consider the distributions of the genera *Strombus* and *Murex* (see table 17.7). The larger shells were often used as trumpets, while smaller specimens appear to have been employed as handles for sticks or wands (McGregor 1943). Both of these uses appear to have had religious and ideological significance among Southwest populations. Figure 17.8 shows the pre–AD 1250 distribution, and figure 17.9 shows the post–AD 1250 distribution. These distributions closely parallel those identified above for copper bells and macaws. And, once again, the earlier distribution can be explained with reference to the Mimbres / Chaco / Flagstaff exchange system, while the later reveals the structure of the Paquimé system. Although comparable analyses have not yet been completed, it appears that similar patterns occur in the distributions of *Nassarius* beads.[8]

In the post–AD 1250 interval there are really two temporally distinct patterns, Paquimé and post-Paquimé. The latter is represented by Pecos Pueblo and several other late sites in the general area, the only sites in the Southwest where Gulf of Mexico species are definitively represented (including both *Strombus gigas* and *S. pulgis* found there). Interestingly, this pattern parallels to some degree that of the post-Paquimé imitation copper bells discussed above. It also correlates with the new importance of the Plains trade in bison products exchanged for maize and other goods (Spielmann 1982; Wilcox 1984, 1991b, 2005b; see also Wilcox et al., chap. 12, this vol.).

Turquoise

The three previously discussed exotic materials are alike in the fact that they originate outside of the Southwest. An important question is, What was being exchanged for these valued items? The material commonly cited as a probable medium for exchange is the mineral turquoise, which was in great demand among the "high cultures" of Mesoamerica. Turquoise was highly prized in part because nearly all of its natural occurrence is limited to a few areas peripheral to and at considerable distance from central and southern Mexico and Central America.

Throughout Mesoamerica and its northern periphery turquoise had both sacred and social connotations that far exceeded other minerals. Among the complex cultures of central Mexico this blue-green stone was associated with rain, fertility, fire, time, and life itself (Caso 1971:339; Weigand 1994:22). Turquoise also figures prominently in the symbolism of aboriginal southwestern cultures. For example, Wilcox (1999a:137–138, 2003b, 2003c) discusses the occurrence of turquoise-encrusted frog (toad?) and raptorial bird effigies in late prehistoric sites throughout the Southwest, where they appear to have served as emblems of social and ritual office. And turquoise has an important symbolic role in oral traditions of the Zuni, Hopi, O'odham, and other groups.

Sources

All large deposits of chemical turquoise in western North America are found in the northwestern region of Mexico or in the American Southwest (Harbottle and Weigand 1992:78). In Mexico the major sources of turquoise are located in the modern state of Zacatecas and in

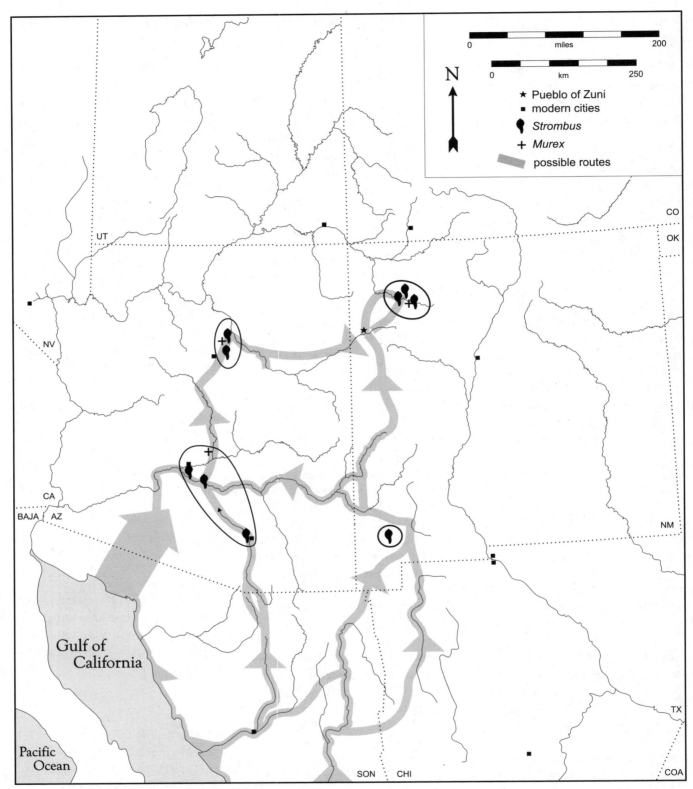

Figure 17.8. Distribution of *Strombus* and *Murex*, pre–AD 1250.

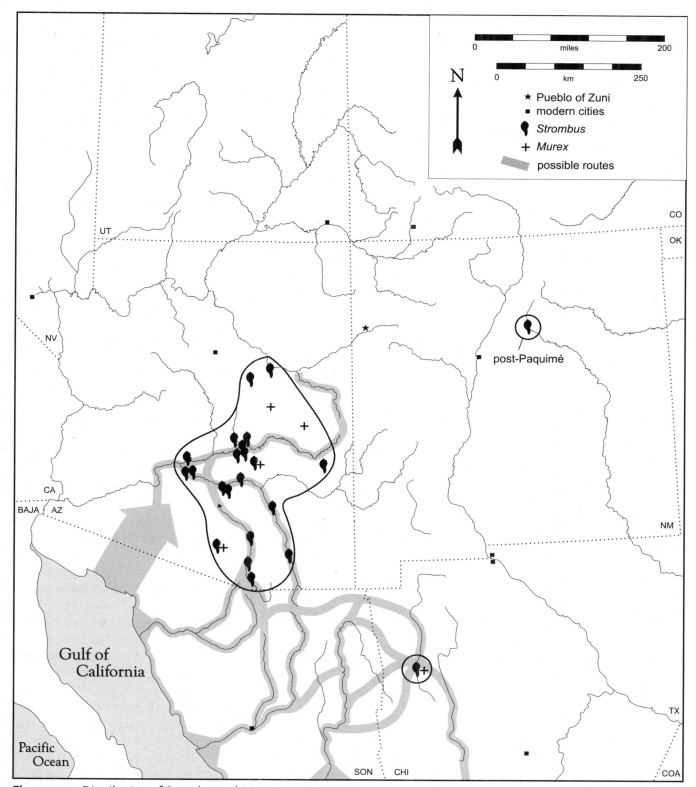

Figure 17.9. Distribution of *Strombus* and *Murex*, post–AD 1250.

Table 17.7 Occurrences of the Genera *Strombus* and *Murex* in the Southwest

Site	Species	Count	Reference
Pre—AD 1250 occurrences			
Snaketown	*S. galeatus*	2	ASM Cat. GP52739/GP53226
Grewe	*Strombus* sp.	42	AWV analysis form
Hodges	*S. galeatus*	1	ASM Cat. A-22488
Wupatki	*S. galeatus*	1	Stanislawski 1963:343
New Caves	*S. gracilior*	1	ASM Cat. GP38978
Wind Mountain	*S. galeatus*	1	Woosley and McIntyre 1996:263
Pueblo Bonito	*Strombus* sp.	12+	Pepper 1920; Judd 1954
BC 50 (Tseh So)	*S. gracilior*	1	Tower 1945
29SJ627	*S. galeatus*	1	Mathien 1997:1160
AR-03-12-01-565	*Muricanthus* sp.	1	Stone 1995:258
Pueblo Bonito	*Murex* sp.	2	Pepper 1920; Tower 1945
Wupatki	*M. nigritus*	1	Stanislawski 1963:343
Post—AD 1250 occurrences			
Las Colinas	*S. galeatus*	1	ASM Cat. A-37074
Los Muertos	*S. galeatus*	2	Haury 1945a:159
Las Acequias	*S. galeatus* (?)	2	Nelson 1981:230
Escalante Ruin	*S. galeatus*	1	ASM Cat. 76-4-53
Casa Grande (B)	*Strombus* sp.	12+	Fewkes 1912:144–145
Casa Grande (F)	*S. galeatus*	9	AWV analysis form
San Xavier Bridge	*S. galeatus*	1	Vokes 1987
AZ DD:8:57(ASM)	*S. galeatus*	2	ASM Cat. A-31211
Paloparado	*S. galeatus*	4	Di Peso 1956:424
Second Canyon	*Strombus* sp.	1	ASM Cat. A-40483
AZ EE:4:4(ASM)	*S. galeatus*	1	ASM Cat. A-24532
Jackrabbit Ruin	*S. galeatus*	1	ASM Cat. A-812
Gila Pueblo	*S. galeatus*	3	ASM Cat. GP38450/GP42022
AZ U:8:450(ASM)	*S. gracilior*	1	Bradley 1997:465
Bass Point Mound	*S. galeatus*	2	McCartney 1995:352
AZ V:5:119/997	*Strombus* sp.	1	Griffith and McCartney 1994:802
AZ V:5:76/700	*S. gracilior*	1	Griffith and McCartney 1994:802
Grapevine Vista	*S. gracilior*	1	Vokes 1994:555
Nuvakwewtaqa	*Strombus* sp.	1	Fewkes 1904:92
Chevlon Ruin	*Strombus* sp.	multiple	Fewkes 1904:92
Pecos Pueblo	*S. gigas*	2+	Kidder 1932
Pecos Pueblo	*S. pugilis*	2	Kidder 1932
Pecos Pueblo	*Strombus*	2	Kidder 1932
Turkey Creek	*Strombus* sp.	1	Johnson 1965
Paquimé	*S. galeatus*	181	Di Peso et al. 1974a:514-524, 551, 1974d:180
Grasshopper	*M. nigritus*	2	AWV analysis form
Kinishba	*M. nigritus*	2	ASM Cat. 24312/25675
Gila Pueblo	*Murex* sp.	1	ASM Cat. GP7283
Paquimé	*M. nigritus*	2	Di Peso et al. 1974b:457, 521
Jackrabbit Ruin	*Murex* sp.	1	ASM Cat. A-811

northern Sonora. In Zacatecas extensive areas of prehistoric mining activity have been identified, including simple adits, pits, mine shafts (including chambered shafts), and open quarries (Weigand 1968). These mining activities appear to have been associated with the Chalchihuites culture of southwestern Zacatecas and western Durango (Harbottle and Weigand 1992; Weigand 1968). In the western United States evidence for prehistoric turquoise mining in the form of excavated deposits and associated stone tools is found across a broad area, including sites in Arizona, western California, Colorado, Nevada, New Mexico, and Utah (Harbottle and Weigand 1992:84; Weigand and Harbottle 1993:162–163). Many of these are within the Greater Southwest.

Sources sampled by Weigand and Harbottle (1993:162–163) are listed in table 17.8, and their distribution is shown in figure 17.10. Of these, 17 have definite evidence of prehistoric mining activities, and an additional 11 locales produced inconclusive evidence of mining (Weigand and Harbottle 1993:162–163). Physically, the largest complex of outcrops occurs in Grass Valley, Nevada (Weigand and Harbottle 1993:162). Other large and more formal mining complexes have been documented at Cerrillos, Azure/Tyrone, and Old Hachita, all New Mexico sources, and Halloron Springs in California; simpler mines are reported from numerous other locations across the Southwest.[9]

The map in figure 17.10 reveals an interesting and potentially important macrospatial pattern in the distribution of Southwest turquoise sources. As is easily seen in this map, the distribution of sources is not at all even over the Southwest. Roughly the west-central and extreme southwestern portions of the Southwest *lack turquoise sources*, including nearly

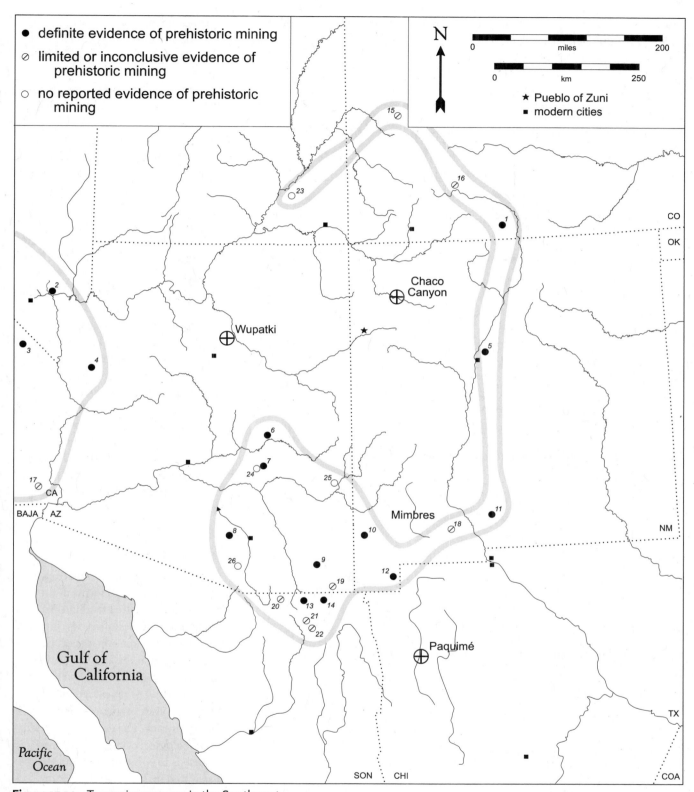

Figure 17.10. Turquoise sources in the Southwest.

Table 17.8 Possible Sources of Turquoise Cited and/or Sampled by Harbottle and Weigand (1992), Weigand and Harbottle (1993), or Weigand (1994) (see fig. 17.10)

Map No.	Site Name	State
Sites with definite evidence of prehistoric mining		
1	La Jara	Colorado
2	Crescent Peak	Nevada
3	Halloran Springs / Himalaya	California
4	Mineral Peak	Arizona
5	Cerrillos Mountains	New Mexico
6	Canyon Creek	Arizona
7	Sleeping Beauty	Arizona
8	Silver Bell / El Tiro	Arizona
9	Courtland / Gleeson	Arizona
10	Azure / Tyrone	New Mexico
11	Jarilla Mountains	New Mexico
12	Old Hacita	New Mexico
13	Los Campitos	Sonora
14	Cananeta	Sonora
Sites with limited or inconclusive evidence of prehistoric mining		
15	Leadville	Colorado
16	Villa Grove	Colorado
17	Quartz Mountain	California
18	White Signal	New Mexico
19	Bisbee	Arizona
20	Campo Frío	Sonora
21	Arroyo Cuitaca	Sonora
22	El Verde	Sonora
Sites with no reported evidence of prehistoric mining		
23	Happy Jack	Utah
24	Inspiration	Arizona
25	Morenci	Arizona
26	Esperanza	Arizona

all of Arizona except the southeast quarter, all of western New Mexico except for the extreme southern portion, much of the southwest corner of Colorado, and most of central and southern Utah. The largest concentration of sources (15) is in an area that includes southeastern Arizona, northern Sonora, and southwestern New Mexico, and the remaining

sources form a sparse linear pattern that follows north along the Rio Grande through New Mexico (three sources), up into Colorado (three sources), and then back down into Utah (one source). A western cluster is also apparent, including one source in extreme western Arizona, one in extreme southeastern California, and one in extreme southern Nevada. Another cluster (not shown) is present in west-central and central Nevada.

Thus, while turquoise sources are relatively common in the Southwest when viewed from outside the region, they are not at all common over large areas within the region. If access is measured simply by distance to the nearest source, then there were substantial differences among Southwest populations with respect to direct access of turquoise. Notable in this regard is the fact that both Chaco Canyon and the Zuni area lie near the center of the large area where turquoise sources are absent. The Mimbres area and Paquimé, by contrast, are both much closer to numerous turquoise sources (see fig. 17.10).

Mesoamerican Demand

In assessing the nature and importance of turquoise in terms of the trade structures that facilitated movement of this material across the prehistoric landscape it is important to remember that the U.S. Southwest and northwestern Mexico were part of the northern edge of a massive exchange system incorporating all of Mesoamerica. The earliest recorded archaeological occurrence of turquoise is in some high-status burials excavated in the modern state of Guerrero that date to around 600 BC (Harbottle and Weigand 1992:80; Weigand 1994:25), and it is present in minor quantities in burials from the Jalisco area that date between 300 BC and AD 400 (Weigand 1994:25). Around AD 350 demand for turquoise increased dramatically with the establishment of complex ceremonial centers in the Chalchihuites region of Zacatecas. Refuse from extensive workshops at the ceremonial center of Alta Vista (ca. AD 700) shows that a tremendous amount of turquoise was obtained from local mines as well as from more distant sources, and chemical analyses indicate that Cerrillos was one of the latter. Weigand (1994:25) suggests that this connection to the Southwest may have been established around AD 500. Around AD 900 the Alta Vista complex ceased to operate, ceremonial centers were depopulated, and the mines were abandoned. The reasons for this are unclear but are thought to lie in events elsewhere in Mesoamerica (Weigand 1968:59, 1994:27).

With the rise of Tula and the Toltec Empire around AD 900 the demand for turquoise continued to increase, resulting in the expanded exploitation of known sources and the development of new ones. About this time settlements in Chaco Canyon undergo a dramatic expansion in size and complexity. It has been suggested that the catalyst for these developments was pressure from Mesoamerican sources for increased production (Weigand et al. 1977:21) or the physical presence of *pochteca*-like groups (long-distance Mesoamerican merchants who often served as political agents) (Kelley and Kelley 1975). Both of these hypotheses are highly controversial (Mathien 1991; Mathien and McGuire 1986), although many would agree that there may have been increased interaction of some kind between these regions.[10] After the decline of the Toltec system in central Mexico (post–AD 1200) demand for turquoise in Mesoamerica continued to grow. At this same time, coincident with the appearance of the Paquimé

settlement system, there was also increasing demand among populations in the Southwest.

Regional Patterns of Use

Anasazi. The earliest exploitation of turquoise resources in the Southwest may have been at Cerrillos (Weigand et al. 1977:19), and substantial quantities of material from this source may have reached the Chalchihuites area as early as AD 500 (Weigand 1994:25; Weigand et al. 1977). However, no physical evidence for intensive exploitation of this source region by local Basketmaker populations or outside populations has been reported (Warren and Mathien 1985:120), although it is possible that more recent activity may have obscured earlier traces. Turquoise appears only in very small quantities in Anasazi assemblages dating before about AD 900 (Mathien 1997:1143–1151; Whalen 1994:128–129).

During Pueblo II demand for turquoise among Anasazi communities greatly expanded, particularly within the San Juan Basin. This increase coincided with development of the Chacoan system and is especially apparent at Pueblo Bonito and other central great house sites. These centers appear to have controlled much of the material originating from sources in the northern portions of the Southwest, including Cerrillos (Harbottle and Weigand 1992:81; Mathien 1997:1130). There have been some attempts to explain the rise of these centers as an effort to control the acquisition and distribution of this mineral: it is at this time that export of unprocessed turquoise to Mesoamerican sites virtually ceased (Harbottle and Weigand 1992:81).

At many sites within the San Juan Basin evidence for workshops appears to reflect the development of part-time, household-based specialists in

the production of turquoise beads and other ornaments (Mathien 1997:1205, 2001; Windes 2001). These activities also took place at virtually all Chaco Canyon great houses, including some of those outside the canyon area proper (Windes 2001: 162). All of these communities seem to have produced beads and pendants, but production of mosaic tesserae was apparently restricted to great house sites (Windes 2001:162). This pattern, though insufficiently understood, may reflect the specialized nature and/or the high social significance of mosaics. However, most of these sites, including the outlying great houses and all of the small settlements around them, appear to be lacking finished turquoise artifacts (Windes 2001:160–163). The concentration of finished turquoise goods in the Chaco Canyon great houses may be an expression of what Renfrew (2001) terms a ritual economy associated with a "Location of High Devotional Expression (LHDE)." In this model the object of devotion—represented by the great houses of Chaco—receives offerings or payment for ritual or ceremonial services (Renfrew 2001:23), and turquoise would be a logical medium of ritual payment.

The virtual absence of finished turquoise ornaments associated with many of the settlements is even more dramatic in light of the vast amounts of finished material at a few central great houses within the canyon, especially Pueblo Bonito. It has been estimated that there are between 200,000 and 500,000 pieces of turquoise in the assemblages from these sites (Harbottle and Weigand 1992:81). This total includes a number of substantial deposits of finished ornaments in ritual contexts at these central communities, including votive deposits within kivas, offerings in shrines, and mortuary accompaniments. For example, in a small room located in the core of the oldest part of Pueblo Bonito (Room 33) were found the remains of at least 14 individuals (Pepper 1909). Two extended inhumations under the floor had an extraordinary amount of turquoise associated with them: together with turquoise scattered in the fill of the room above there were roughly 56,000 pieces of turquoise, mostly beads, pendants, and ornate mosaics (Pepper 1909, 1920:163–177; Windes 2001:159).

With the demise of the Chaco Canyon great house system in the late twelfth century (see Wilcox 2005c) there is an expansion in the use of turquoise among other Puebloan populations, with individuals in most large communities and some of the smaller settlements apparently gaining access to items made of turquoise. During the Late Pueblo II and Pueblo III no single site or settlement system exercised the apparent level of control over this resource that was exercised by the Bonito phase sites of Chaco Canyon. Great house communities like Aztec Ruin, Salmon Ruin, and Guadalupe Ruin all have late assemblages that exhibit greater frequencies and wider ranges of personal ornaments made of turquoise than were found in their earlier Bonito phase components.

An apparently related pattern is seen at Wupatki, which was established around AD 1130 and may have lasted as late as AD 1250 (Adler and Johnson 1996:257; Wilcox 1999a:121, 2002). Its initial construction using Chaco-like core-and-veneer masonry and its unroofed great kiva suggest late Chaco connections. Interestingly, a substantial amount of turquoise was recovered, including beads, tabular and carved pendants, mosaics, and inlay (Stanislawski 1963). The only other settlement in the area that has produced significant amounts of turquoise is Ridge Ruin, and all of this

material came from a single context, the famous Burial of the Magician (McGregor 1943). With over 800 items, this burial includes one of the richest mortuary deposits ever discovered in the Southwest, comparable in many ways to the materials below the floor of Room 33 at Pueblo Bonito discussed above. Several turquoise mosaics were included in both cases.

Mimbres. The Mimbres area of southwestern New Mexico and northwestern Chihuahua, located as it is between the centers of west-central Mexico and the Chaco region and close to many turquoise sources, would have been ideally situated to benefit from the movement of turquoise between these areas. Therefore, it is not surprising that Anyon and LeBlanc observed that "compared to many sites in the Southwest, Galaz had a lot of turquoise" (1984:306). Nesbitt (1931:93) noted that turquoise pendants were the most common type of pendant at the Starkweather Ruin. In contrast, smaller sites may not have had the same level of access (Lekson 1990a:71–72). Indeed, present evidence indicates that turquoise was not commonly acquired by all inhabitants of even the larger settlements. Carrying a bag of turquoise with them, however, Mimbreños on pilgrimages to the Guaymas coast would have been able to trade for bells, macaws, or other exotics moving northward out of Sinaloa (Wilcox 1999a, 2002).

Following Classic Mimbres (ca. AD 1140), smaller settlements at lower elevations in the Mimbres Valley and those in areas to the east do not seem to have had the same access to turquoise. Nelson and LeBlanc (1986:192) report that only four pieces were recovered during their excavations of small Cliff phase (AD 1300s) sites in the Mimbres Valley,

which they noted was substantially less than what might be expected based on the earlier periods. This decline appears to be reflected in other exotic materials, including shell (Nelson and LeBlanc 1986:191), although sites in the eastern Mimbres area saw an increase in ceramic diversity, including nonlocal wares. This suggests that this region was not isolated from the larger regional networks but that it had ceased to participate actively in the exchange network of elite-related exotic materials. This decline may in part be related to the rise of the Casas Grandes regional system to the south and the development of large aggregated settlements in the upland areas of the Mogollon Rim and the White Mountains of eastern Arizona.

Mogollon Highlands. The earliest turquoise recovered in the highlands of eastern Arizona and western New Mexico was a single tabular pendant that was found at the Lunt Site (AZ W:9:83 [ASM]) (Neely 1974). This low incidence seems to continue for the Point of Pines area during the period prior to the Tularosa phase occupation, when there is a subtle increase in the occurrence.

In contrast, Grasshopper Pueblo produced a relatively large assemblage of turquoise artifacts (Agenbroad 1982:45), including beads, pendants, and mosaic tesserae. This material is reported to be distributed in a number of deposits about the site, but unfortunately there is yet to be a quantified analysis of this material. One significant deposit that has been mentioned is Room 113, where there was a work area that contained manufacturing debris and artifacts in various stages of production (Agenbroad 1982).

This apparent abundance at Grasshopper is somewhat misleading in terms of the regional picture, as the community appears to have had access to a local source of turquoise, the Canyon Creek Turquoise quarry (Haury 1934:15–16; Welch and Triadan 1991), which lies approximately 29 km south of Grasshopper. Samples from various outcrops have been matched to specimens recovered from Room 113 at Grasshopper (Reid and Whittlesey 1999:81–82; Welch and Triadan 1991). Thus, Grasshopper seems to have been a local producer of turquoise artifacts that could have been traded to other communities.

Hohokam. Among the Hohokam we find that there were some communities using turquoise to manufacture personal ornaments relatively early in their history. However, these are generally the exceptions, and shell appears to have played the role that turquoise held in other regions. The use of turquoise by Hohokam populations never appears to have attained the levels seen in the Mogollon and Anasazi communities.

Beginning around AD 700, we begin to see use of turquoise by the Hohokam of southern Arizona. The general pattern appears to be that access to turquoise was restricted to the larger communities that had central roles in the ball court system and, later, in the platform mound system. Many pre-Classic sites have a few pieces of turquoise in their assemblages, but few have substantial numbers of items. Wasley and Johnson (1965:32) report the presence of turquoise in only two contexts at the Gatlin site, a pre-Classic central community with dual ball courts and a platform mound.

Snaketown, long recognized as a central settlement in the Hohokam macroregional system (Wilcox 1999a:124–127; Wilcox et al. 1981; Wilcox and Sternberg 1983) had sev-

eral thousand pieces and thus stands apart even among larger settlements. The relative absence of turquoise in surrounding communities suggests that Snaketown may have also exercised some level of control over local distribution of turquoise as well. Haury (1976:299) noted that there were 54 different deposits from the 1964–65 excavations that contained turquoise beads, representing nearly two-thirds of all deposits with stone beads. In addition, eight deposits produced turquoise pendants, and 36 contexts had mosaic tesserae. An additional 98 occurrences of turquoise were reported from the 1934–35 excavations (Haury 1937b:129).

Sourcing studies of Snaketown turquoise (Colberg Sigleo 1975; Haury 1976:277–278) show that a substantial amount came from the Halloran Springs/Himalaya mine complex near Baker in eastern California (see fig. 17.10). This source is roughly 178 km west of the Lost City site (Virgin Anasazi). Lyneis (1992:66) suggests that some shell artifact forms from that site may have been obtained from the Hohokam, and it is possible that Lost City may have served as a conduit for movement of California turquoise into the Salt-Gila Basin. Other sourcing studies of Snaketown turquoise (Harbottle et al. 1994:385) show that Cerrillos was another major source of material. There is little evidence to suggest that local manufacturing of turquoise beads and pendants occurred at Snaketown, so it seems likely that these objects were obtained as finished items, possibly through contacts with the Mimbres.

In the Tucson Basin area to the south the pattern is somewhat different and may reflect a discontinuity between the regions. With two particular exceptions, early settlements in the Santa Cruz Valley generally

have a relatively low incidence of turquoise in their assemblages. Most of the personal ornaments present are made from shell and to a lesser extent argillite, a source of which lies in the Tucson Mountains.

There are, however, some striking exceptions. Redtail Village, which is a medium-size community in the northwestern Tucson Basin that was occupied primarily during the early Colonial period (AD 750–850), produced an assemblage that contained 3,261 pieces of turquoise, including beads, pendants, and mosaic tesserae (Bernard-Shaw and Hohmann 1989). Perhaps the most remarkable feature of this collection is the presence of a substantial amount of debitage and unmodified nodules, which indicate the inhabitants were actively engaged in the acquisition and processing of the raw material. At the time of excavation there were no known mines in the Tucson Basin region; however, more recent work in the Silverbell area—roughly 44 km to the northwest—has revealed the presence of a likely turquoise source along El Tiro Wash (Rowe 1997a:331).[11]

During the Classic Hohokam period the distribution of turquoise appears to be somewhat more diffuse, although there is some tendency for material to continue to be concentrated in certain settlements: those at the head of canal systems and large complex sites like Casa Grande. In the Phoenix Basin excavations of the compounds associated with the Pueblo Grande platform mound by Soil Systems, Inc., recovered a moderately large assemblage of 1,206 pieces, representing 13.8 percent of all stone ornaments (Stone and Foster 1994: 239). Sourcing studies identified six areas that contributed to the assemblage. The largest group of specimens probably originated at the Cerrillos complex. Other source areas include the Jarilla Mountains and the Azure mine complexes in southern New Mexico and mines in the Morenci area of east-central Arizona. Additionally, one (and possibly more) piece was identified as being from the Crescent Peak source in southern Nevada. Thus, while the Cerrillos complex continued to be a major source of turquoise for Southwest populations, other areas were being exploited after AD 1200, probably as a response to increasing demand for this prized material.[12]

Current data indicate that equal access was not available to all social ranks in a given population. The analyses of mortuary assemblages from Pueblo Grande, Casa Buena, and Grand Canal (Mitchell 1991, 1994) indicate that turquoise ornaments are significantly clustered within a few burials and that these burials tend to cluster in a few burial areas central to the settlements (Mitchell 1991:122–123, 1994:91). These studies indicate that within these communities there existed differences in social rank as reflected by access to items such as turquoise that reflect personal wealth. In contrast to the burials at Pueblo Bonito differences between these individuals were not so sharply marked as to indicate the presence of social classes; rather, these differences in grave wealth appear to form a relatively continuous gradation. This would be consistent with ranking within a kin-based organization, where the heads of the household groups formed a group-oriented, or corporate, mode of leadership (Feinman 1995).

Early Classic period sites in the Tucson Basin and to the south along the Santa Cruz River are characterized by the pattern of low turquoise use found at most pre-Classic sites in the region. Bayman (1994) reported that the excavations at the large Marana platform mound complex, which

lies across the Santa Cruz valley from Los Morteros, produced a relatively large shell assemblage but virtually no turquoise. Similarly, the Rabid Ruin, a Classic period settlement that produced a large mortuary assemblage with almost 6,000 pieces of stone and shell jewelry, contained only four turquoise beads and one teardrop-shaped pendant (Huckell 1976). Although there appears to have been some increased interest in turquoise during the Late Classic period, it is still relatively limited. Di Peso's (1956) excavations in the late component at Paloparado (Di Peso's San Cayetano del Tumacacori) reported 258 pieces of turquoise, mostly beads but including some pendants and inlay. These were spread over 23 different contexts, mostly burials.

Tonto Basin and the Salado. Prior to AD 1200 the region formed by the lower Verde River, Tonto Creek, and the uplands around the modern community of Globe do not appear to have been particularly active in the acquisition of turquoise. Sites like Scorpion Point (Towner et al. 1998:116) on the Verde River and Roosevelt 9:6 (Haury 1986c:280) and the Hedge Apple Site (Adams and Elson 1995:138) in the Tonto Basin produced a few ornaments made of turquoise, while other sites lack it entirely.

In Classic period assemblages (post–AD 1200) from the Tonto Basin and Globe region, however, there was a substantial increase in the amount of turquoise present. It is represented by both finished ornaments and raw material/debris (Vokes 2001b:446) and tended to be concentrated in the larger sites such as Griffin Wash (Adams and Elson 1995:120), Las Tortugas, Granary Row, and Los Hermanos (Vokes 2001b) and the platform mound communities that were along the Salt River valley (Adams and

Elson 1995:120; Rice et al. 1998:129; Wilcox 1987). Much of this material is in mortuary contexts. In the Tonto Creek project assemblage (Vokes 2001b) over 99 percent of the turquoise was associated with mortuary contexts.

In post–AD 1300 Gila phase settlements turquoise was recovered from both mortuary and secular contexts, although it seems to be somewhat rare in the former. Six of 102 mortuary features at Schoolhouse Point produced turquoise, but only two had considerable quantities (Loendorf 1997). This pattern led Loendorf (1997:586) to speculate that turquoise may have been too valued a resource to be placed within burials, where it was lost to the local economy. It is difficult to assess this idea at this point, but, if accurate, it may also be reflected in patterns reported from other regions during the late prehistoric era.

One feature characteristic of the turquoise mosaics encountered in the assemblage from the Tonto Basin is the reuse of beads and pendant fragments as mosaic tesserae. The incorporation of these pieces, which were not remodeled, gives the mosaics an unsophisticated and sloppy appearance. This practice of reusing fragmented turquoise ornaments is also relatively common in the material recovered by Hodge (1921:19) from excavations at Hawikuh.

Casas Grandes and Northwestern Mexico. The increasing prominence of the Casas Grandes macroregional system around AD 1200 in northwestern Mexico placed it in a position to exploit or at least to participate in the exchange of exotic materials that passed between the Mesoamerican centers to the south and the Southwest populations that exploited and traded in turquoise. At present there are no known sources within the immediate regions around Casas Grandes, so the mineral would have to have been obtained through exchange, presumably with populations to the north and west.

The crux of the debate over the role of turquoise in the Casas Grandes system lies in the fact that "only" 5,895 pieces of turquoise were found during the excavations by the Joint Casas Grandes Expedition (Di Peso et al. 1974c, 1974d:187). It can be argued that this is a substantial quantity in comparison to other contemporaneous sites in the Southwest, but it is small in comparison to the quantities of turquoise in the earlier centers at Chaco Canyon and in comparison to the volume of shell recovered from the same excavations at Paquimé. However, it can also be argued that the role of turquoise in the Chaco system was substantially different from the one it served in the Casas economy. In contrast to Chaco, the inhabitants do not appear to have had control over sources, so they could not have concentrated the material in the same way that Pueblo Bonito was able to do.

The distributions may also reflect differences in the nature of the socioeconomic structures. Most of the material at Paquimé was recovered from architectural or other nonmortuary, nonritual deposits. In their discussion of Postclassic Mayan exchange Rathje and Sabloff (1975:13) note that the loss of goods through "leaks" such as the diversion of goods to contexts that result in the removal of wealth from the system (e.g., mortuary contexts) is poor management in a market system. Di Peso (Di Peso et al. 1974d:187) suggests that the lack of material in mortuary contexts may reflect on the extreme value of turquoise to the community and/or social attitudes toward mortuary behavior. He proposed that this mineral might have been so valued that to remove it from the economy by placing it in graves was socially unacceptable. However, the fact that nearly a thousand pieces—mostly beads and some pendants—were placed in contexts identified as caches or "troves" argues against Di Peso's hypothesis.

Some archaeologists have argued that Paquimé was an end-of-the-line consumer of turquoise and that its population was not engaged in exchange with populations to the south (Schaafsma and Riley 1999:247). However, we know from the presence of macaws, copper bells, and shell that the inhabitants were actively acquiring material from the south through exchange networks. While the network (or networks) supplying these goods was not necessarily on a massive scale (the copper bells at the site would fit into a single basket), it did exist, and it seems counterintuitive that the participants would not be actively engaged in trading for these products with turquoise, a product that was in extremely high demand in the source regions for these other items.

The presence of debris and unfinished ornaments in some architectural contexts indicates that a portion of the mineral being received by Paquimé was as raw material that was then fashioned into tesserae, beads, and pendants. Mosaic tesserae account for nearly one third of the finished pieces of turquoise recovered from Medio period contexts. Di Peso (Di Peso et al. 1974d:187) notes that this was probably the most desired form for exchange, as most of the turquoise present in markets of Mesoamerica is in the form of mosaics. Furthermore, sites to the east of Paquimé in the Río del Carmen valley, including Loma de Moctezuma, and sites to the north are reported to have large quantities of turquoise-manufacturing debris present (Maxwell and Antillon 2003), suggesting that not all turquoise moving south to Mesoamerican centers was necessarily passing through Paquimé.

Trade networks that were actively acquiring turquoise did not end with the demise of the Casas Grandes system in the late fourteenth or early fifteenth century. Its disappearance would certainly have required a reorganization of exchange networks, but the exchange process clearly continued. The nature of the network(s) that arose to continue the trade is poorly understood. Riley (1985) has suggested that the appearance of a series of small "statelets" (large village clusters) along the middle and upper reaches of the Río Sonora, Río Yaqui, Río Montezuma, and Río Bavispe during the fifteenth and sixteenth centuries marks the principal trade routes at that time. These small statelets could have controlled the trade of exotics coming north from the western coast of Mexico and the center in Mesoamerica while trading with the Pueblos for turquoise, hides, and other products. These communities were in essence trying to take on the mantle of the Casas Grandes system. Riley (1987), indeed, argues that some portion of the Casas Grandes populations shifted into Sonora to become the Opata participants in this putative system (see also Wilcox et al., chap. 12, this vol.).

Discussion

The above review indicates that copper bells, macaws and parrots, unmodified shell and a diversity of shell artifacts, and turquoise were widely traded throughout the American Southwest and northwestern Mexico during prehistoric, protohistoric, and historic times. Exchange appears to have occurred along multiple channels both within and between cultural and regional systems, and the nature of such connections and their rationales changed through time.

Neitzel (1989) argues that different kinds of exchange networks were responsible for the distributional patterns of the very "rare" items (copper bells and macaws) as opposed to those exhibited by the more common shell and turquoise. She concludes that copper bells and macaws were exchanged by relatively few large central communities, with macaws being the most restricted in terms of numbers and associated settlements. In contrast, turquoise and (especially) shell were exchanged in much greater quantities and involved networks that incorporated many more sites of all sizes. Communities acquiring the rarer materials (copper bells and macaws) were also involved in the exchange of turquoise and shell, but the inverse is not necessarily true (Neitzel 1989:169–171).

The patterns described above and further illustrated below generally support Neitzel's interpretation with certain caveats. First, a few shell artifacts and species (*Strombus* and *Murex* trumpets, *Nassarius*, and others?) duplicate spatial and temporal patterns seen for bells and macaws and thus appear to fall into the same category. Second, her distinctions likely do not apply prior to development of the Mimbres/Chaco/Wupatki system or after the decline of Paquimé (see below). We also note that these exotic goods—particularly the two more common materials, shell and turquoise—appear to have functioned differently within the two sequential regional systems. These contrasts in local perception and use as well as the exchange networks that linked communities within the regional systems with each other and with the larger macroregional structure reflect on the nature of the economic and social organization operating at a given time. Now that these exchange structures have been delineated, the role(s) of Mogollon popula-tions and those living in the Zuni area can be assessed.

Before Chaco

It is clear that some exotic materials did reach various portions of the Southwest prior to the emergence of the exchange system(s) involving Mimbres, Chaco, and Wupatki. The distribution of bracelets and some pendant styles indicates that shell items of Hohokam origin were reaching the Mimbres area, the Colorado Plateau, and even some Highland Mogollon sites prior to AD 900. The relative abundance of bracelets, irregular bead pendants, and bilobate beads in Late Basketmaker III burials at the Twin Butte Site (Wendorf 1953) and of bracelets in the Pueblo I deposits at Kiatuthlanna (Roberts 1931) demonstrates some kind of link between the plateau and the Hohokam. Similarly, the presence of numerous bracelets in Mimbres burials and, in particular, remarkable similarities between the shell components of the Citrus Site cache from the Gila Bend area (Wasley and Johnson 1965) and a cache of material in a child's burial at NAN Ranch Ruin (Cosgrove and Cosgrove 1932:67, plate 76) show that these regions were also linked prior to AD 1000.

Copper bells appear in the Southwest within a century or two after the introduction and spread of metallurgical technology into western Mexico about AD 800 (Hosler 1988a, 1988b). Some of these items may predate development of the Mimbres/Chaco/Wupatki system, but the dating of specimens in the Hohokam area is ambiguous. The earliest known Hohokam occurrences may be the 28 bells recovered from 6G House 8 at Snaketown (Gladwin et al. 1937; see Haury 1976) and other Sedentary period deposits, including the 80+ crotals from the Gatlin site and additional specimens from other sites in the Gila Bend area. However, all of them may date to the eleventh century. Furthermore, there is some evidence to suggest that the Hohokam may have been acquiring bells directly, both before and after development of the Chaco-related macroregional exchange system. As noted above, the 28 bells from Snaketown represent a style (Type IC14a) that, although reported in several other Hohokam collections, was never common in the Mimbres (one specimen at Osborn) or at Chaco (three at Pueblo Bonito). While these isolated examples *could* represent items of Hohokam origin, it is perhaps more likely that they reflect a diversity of supply contacts in western and northwestern Mexico. Similar arguments may be applied to possible pre–AD 900 macaws, and, as previously noted, much of the turquoise from Snaketown may have been acquired by direct contact with people near the Halloran source.

Whether these infrequently occurring items moved in an ad hoc, down-the-line manner or in an earlier, more formal, and as yet unrecognized exchange system is not known, and this is an important topic for future research. At present, the former hypothesis seems most plausible, although the presence of a series of pseudocloisonné artifacts in Hohokam sites (Haury 1976), which also derive from western Mexico prior to AD 900, strengthens the view that a more formal structure may have been present in the context of what Wilcox (1986a) has called the "Tepiman Connection."

AD 900–1250 Patterns

By about AD 900 the Chaco and Mimbres regional systems began to crystallize (see Crown and Judge 1991; Diehl, chap. 11, this vol.), and after this the distributions of copper bells, macaws, some shell artifacts, and turquoise are all best explained with reference to formal exchange structures that connected Mimbres with Chaco and, later on, Chaco with Wupatki (Wilcox 1999a, 2002). The Hohokam role in these systems appears to have been peripheral, primarily a function of their late connections to Wupatki—this despite earlier (pre–AD 1000) Hohokam contacts with Mimbres. Copper bells, the very few macaws, and the limited amounts of turquoise recovered from Hohokam sites of this interval are perhaps best explained by ad hoc acquisitions (perhaps in some cases direct, as with the Halloran turquoise source?) that did not occur in the context of formal, large-scale exchange networks. It is also possible, of course, that a few items made their way to Hohokam communities from Mimbres along the Gila River.

Figure 17.11 shows the combined pre–AD 1250 distributions of previously identified clusters of copper bells, macaws, and selected shell species. A dotted line encompasses the Mimbres, Chaco, and Flagstaff clusters but excludes the Hohokam, and it is argued that this line approximates the maximum spatial extent of the Chacoan macroregional exchange system that began to develop after AD 900 and existed in some form until about AD 1250.

Around AD 1100 there was a dramatic reorganization in the Southwest, with traditional trading networks reorganized and restructured. Around AD 1000 the Hohokam ball court system underwent a contraction of its area extension to the east, with the upper Gila, San Pedro, and Tucson Basin ball court sites being abandoned (Wilcox 1999a). LeBlanc (1983; see also Minnis 1985) notes that after AD 1000 Hohokam elements appear to drop out of Mimbres assemblages. A century or so later Mimbres popu-

lations appear to begin an eastward shift in emphasis (Hegmon et al. 1999:148) that culminated in the major reorganization around AD 1140 with the abandonment of much of the region west of the Mimbres river and movement of people from the higher elevations. This signifies the end of the Classic Mimbres period and resulted in the reorganization of the Mimbres populations into communities that were located along the lower Mimbres River and in the drainages to the east that lead to the Rio Grande (Hegmon et al. 1999; Nelson 1999). These restructurings of the ball court system and the Mimbres settlement systems would likely have strained or even interrupted the exchange network that previously linked these regions.

Roughly concurrent with these developments, the Chaco region underwent a period of reorganization and restructuring of its social and economic systems (Wilcox 1999a; see also Wilcox 2005c). In Wilcox's model the period around AD 1100 is one of major change in relationships between the core sites in Chaco Canyon with outlying great house communities. He postulates that there was a shift in governance from a system where the outlying communities in the San Juan Basin were largely autonomous, with lineage and social ties to the elites of the core settlements in Chaco Canyon, to a more highly structured relationship in which these elites centralized political power and organized peripheral communities within the San Juan Basin into defensive entities through construction of tower kivas and road networks. Wilcox (1999a) sees the outlying great houses functioning as "entrepôts" that facilitated the flow of goods into the central community in Chaco Canyon and protected the surrounding populations from raids launched by neighboring polities.

Several communities that were outside the immediate interaction sphere appear to have developed into independent peer polities with their own settlement hierarchy. As a result, there likely would have been an increased demand for elite goods in these communities, for ritual display, for ceremonial flare, and for elite gift presentations or exchanges that functioned to maintain the necessary political networks. Thus, the exchange networks that supplied these exotic and treasured goods would have become increasingly important, and it is quite likely that the structure of these networks would have become more formalized as a result.

Spatially, the Zuni area lies south of the San Juan Basin and is linked ceramically to the Puerco of the West great houses (see Mills, chap. 13, this vol.). It lies between the Rio Puerco of the West and the Tularosa Valley, where the site of Aragon may have been the southernmost great house (Lekson 1999; see also Wilcox et al., chap. 12, this vol.). Any formalization of the long-distance north–south movement of prestige goods into Chaco Canyon likely had important implications for Zuni-area great house communities.

There are good indications that the network linking the Chaco region with the western coastal regions of Mexico was in existence prior to AD 1100. The presence of an unmodified valve of *Episcynia medialis*—a small gastropod indigenous to the southern end of the Gulf of California and south along the coast (Keen 1971:381)—at 29SJ-627 (Mathien 1997:1160) indicates the Mimbres/Río Yaqui trade network was probably in use by the tenth century. Furthermore, images on Mimbres ceramics of young macaws being transported by traders support the idea that the Mimbres were the middlemen transporting these birds north along with copper

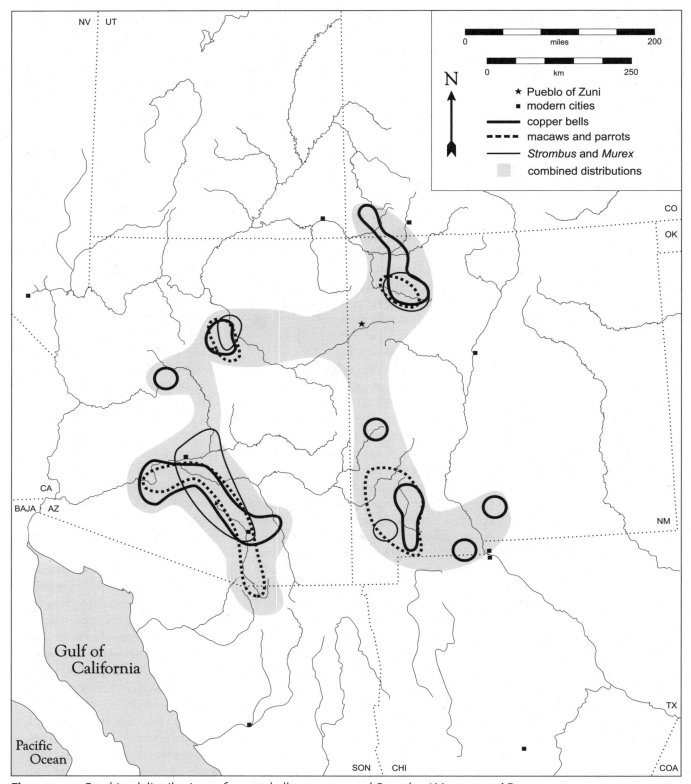

Figure 17.11. Combined distributions of copper bells, macaws, and *Strombus/Murex*, pre–AD 1250.

bells and shell. It is currently uncertain who in the eleventh and twelfth centuries was supplying these goods *to* the Mimbres and others in the Southwest, except that western Mexico generally is the probable source. New research on this issue is needed.

The Hohokam ball court macroregional system underwent an expansion to the north during the late eleventh century, extending into the San Francisco Peaks area. In Wilcox's (1999a, 2002; Wilcox et al. 2000) Wupatki nexus model, establishment of Wupatki as a gateway community linked Chaco trade networks with those of the Hohokam ball court system along with the Mohave trail to the west. It is clear that these sources had been passing goods to the populations on the Colorado Plateau and to Chaco prior to this development, but the establishment of Wupatki can be seen as an attempt to structure and control access to these sources. The masonry ball court at Wupatki, located some distance from the settlement's core, and a great kiva/amphitheater that is intimately part of the core provide evidence of this role.

The site was in a position to acquire exotic materials such as abalone from California via the Mohave trail (PC 2 in fig. 17.1) and the wide variety of marine shell originating in the northern portion of the Gulf of California via the Hohokam. The presence of 42 macaws and nine copper bells at Wupatki indicates the close relationship between the settlement and the Chaco macroregional system. For the local population of the Flagstaff area the presence of Wupatki is seen in the florescence of the Elden phase, when exotic material from both the Hohokam and Chaco systems (shell, textiles, turquoise, copper bells, macaws) was available in some quantity, most dramatically illustrated by the Ridge Ruin Burial of the Magician (McGregor 1943) and in the Bab-

bitt collection of mortuary goods, which contains over 25,000 shell items (David Wilcox, personal communication 2004).

During the same period that the ball court system was expanding to the north, the Hohokam settlements in the Phoenix Basin and the surrounding regions were adopting a new form of public architecture—the platform mound (Doelle et al. 1995; Gregory 1987, 1991; Gregory et al. 1985). Ultimately, by about AD 1250 and roughly coincident with the abandonment of Wupatki the ritual complex that had been associated with the ball court was replaced by a new form of larger and size-differentiated platform mounds with residential structures on top and a surrounding rectangular compound wall (Gregory 1987, 1991; Wilcox et al. 2001b).

With the end of the great house system and the subsequent population shifts (see Wilcox et al., chap. 12, this vol.) exchange networks were thrown into disarray. This coincides with a hiatus in the importation of macaws that occurred in the early and mid–AD 1200s (McKusick 2001:74, 76). This sharp decline in demand illustrates how dominant the Chaco "market" appears to have been in the Puebloan world prior to about AD 1200.

AD 1250–1450 Patterns: Paquimé

Soon after the decline of the Chacoan and Mimbres macroregional systems and the breakup of associated exchange structures, another large-scale exchange system emerged, one deriving its impetus from the regional center of Paquimé. Figure 17.12 shows the combined post–AD 1250 distribution of previously identified clusters of copper bells, macaws and parrots, and shell genera, minus the post–AD 1450 occurrences, and with a dotted line around the clus-

ters. It is argued that this line approximates the maximum northern spatial extent of the Paquimé macroregional exchange system that began to develop about AD 1250 and lasted until about AD 1450.

These distributions indicate a strong exchange structure into the populous Pueblo IV settlements northwest of Paquimé and a weaker one into the less populous areas to the northeast. Interestingly, Wilcox (1991b) portrayed a virtually identical geographic pattern based on the distribution of Salado polychromes to the northwest of Paquimé and El Paso Polychrome to the northeast. Thousands of sherds of both types were found at Paquimé (Di Peso et al. 1974b). Only one copper bell (from Pottery Mound) is known to lie outside this bilobed distribution pattern. These findings support the concept of a "Casas Grandes World" (Schaafsma and Riley 1999) and raise questions about the more "insular" conceptions of a narrowly defined Casas Grandes "region" proposed by Whalen and Minnis (2001; cf. Wilcox 1995a) or the Roswell-centric view recently presented by Speth (2004). What was moving back to Paquimé besides pottery? Perhaps bison hides and other products from the northeast and deer hides and other products from the northwest? New research that also takes account of processes on these macroregional scales is needed.

Zuni was apparently outside the sphere of the Paquimé exchange structure, although Safford Valley populations and those at Point of Pines were enmeshed in it. The emergence of large depopulated areas in the formerly Mogollon Highlands by AD 1350 (see Wilcox et al., chap. 12, this vol.) apparently split the Safford Valley, Point of Pines, and Cliff Valley populations from those concentrated along the Zuni River. By about AD 1400 this had resulted in a major

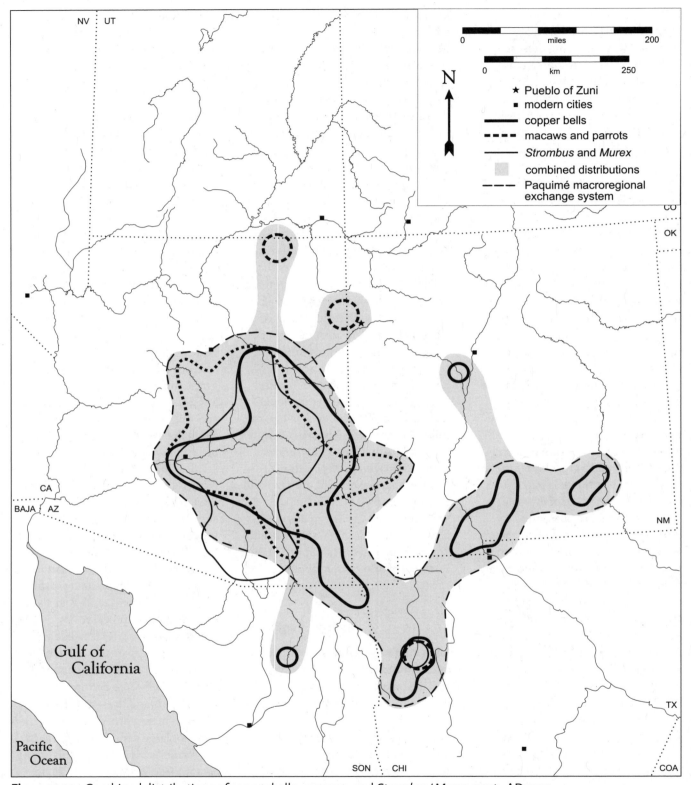

Figure 17.12. Combined distributions of copper bells, macaws, and *Strombus/Murex*, post–AD 1250.

realignment of Zuni exchange relationships along an east–west axis, as indicated by the radical shift to the Sikyatki-like Matsaki Polychrome and more visible acceptance of the kachina cult (Mills, chap. 13, this vol.). Presumably, this means that the Zuni area also became a link in the chain of exchange that moved *Olivella* beads out onto the Great Plains, though new excavation data are needed to test this possibility. In any case, this east–west structure remained a fundamentally important aspect of Zuni trade and exchange well into the historic period (see Ferguson and Hart 1985:53, 55).

Post-Paquimé Patterns

Based on the items reviewed here, the decline of Paquimé in the middle fifteenth century signaled the end of the last reasonably well documented macroregional economic systems involving prestige exchange of the pre-Hispanic era and led to a further reorganization of exchange networks (see Spielmann 1998; Wilcox 1984, 1991b; Wilcox et al., chap. 12, this vol.). Other than the fact that many former connections were broken, the exact nature of these changes is as yet poorly understood (but see Riley 1987; Wilcox et al. 2000; Wilcox et al., chap. 12, this vol.). However, it is clear that exchange in exotic items originating in distant areas to the south continued, although the list of exotic items is reduced by one. Copper bells no longer reached the Southwest after about AD 1450, and manufacture of these items in western Mexico apparently ceased with the arrival of the Spaniards if not somewhat earlier (Hosler 1988a, 1988b). Locally manufactured clay imitations of these artifacts have already been cited as evidence of the still high regard in which they were held (Withers 1946), but

such manufacture apparently ended with the arrival of the Spaniards or perhaps somewhat before. Macaws and shell continued to reach the still-occupied areas of the Southwest, and turquoise was widely traded.

In the southern portion of the Southwest region and immediately on the heels of Paquimé's demise it appears that local elites in some settlements on the western periphery of the Casas Grandes region may have begun to assert themselves. These might have subsequently developed into regional power centers had it not been for the arrival of the Spaniards. Riley (1985, 1987) proposes a model in which a series of small "statelets" developed along the middle and upper reaches of the Río Sonora, Río Yaqui, Río Montezuma, and Río Bavispe during the fifteenth and sixteenth centuries. The so-called statelets were clusters of large villages, not unlike those in the Rio Grande region at this time (Riley 1987; see Wilcox et al., chap. 12, this vol.). These rivers are believed to have been the principal trade routes at that time, and these statelets were situated to control movement of exotics coming down from the north and up from the Gulf of California and western Mexico to the west and south, that is, to take on the mantle of the Paquimé system. Riley (1985:424–427) indicates that they sent northward high-demand items such as parrots and macaws (or their feathers), shell, and other luxury goods in exchange for turquoise, other semiprecious stones, and bison and deer hides.

That this trade continued after contact is demonstrated by early Spanish accounts. Cabeza de Vaca reported that natives in Sonora (possibly the Opata) traded "parrot" feathers for green stones (turquoise?) far in the north (Hargrave 1970, quoting a translation from Bandelier 1890).

He did not elaborate on the characteristics of the parrots, but later accounts are more specific. Kino reported that the local populations in and around San Xavier del Bac raised macaws for feathers, which were then exchanged with other groups. In his memoirs of travels in Pimería Alta Kino recorded on April 10, 1701, that "this day we rested here at San Xavier. . . . We received great consideration from these very fine natives. They gave us many of their foods, many of their good fabrics and mantas of cotton, many coritas, antelope skins, colored feathers of the *many macaws that are raised hereabouts*, etc." (emphasis added).[13]

Use of the word *guacamayas* clearly indicates that the birds being raised were macaws, but the ambiguity of the feather color makes specific identification impossible. However, Father Luis Xavier Velarde, who served in the missions of Pimería Alta during the early 1700s and would have ministered to the Sobaipuri population at San Xavier del Bac, has also left a record of the raising of the macaws that sheds light on the issue of species. He recorded that "there are also birds of almost every kind or species as in the rest of New Spain. At San Xavier del Bac and neighboring rancherías there are many macaws that the Pimas raise for their beautiful red feathers—and other colors, similar to those of the peacock—which they pluck during the spring for their adornment."[14] Thus, it would appear that the birds were scarlet macaws. Given the cryptic reference by Cabeza de Vaca as well as later ethnographic evidence, it would seem that exchange of some exotic materials continued into the historic era and that turquoise (likely the green stone referenced by Cabeza de Vaca) continued to be highly prized by indigenous populations.

The Waning Importance of Prestige Goods at Zuni during the Protohistoric Period

The sources for turquoise are likely the pueblos along the Rio Grande and those in the interior of western New Mexico, including Zuni. Warren and Mathien (1985), in their investigation of the sites in the immediate area of the southern Cerrillos turquoise sources, found that the associated ceramic assemblages indicated that the most intensive mining of these sources was during Pueblo IV or later, with over 71 percent of the identified ceramics being late glazewares (Mathien 2001:104). Thus, it is likely that this could be the source of the "stones" that Cabeza de Vaca reported. Hodge noted the use of a mixture of cornmeal and turquoise in some of the ceremonial deposits at Hawikuh (Smith et al. 1966). Ferguson and Hart (1985) note that the Zuni obtained turquoise from the Cerrillos source for use and for trade, and Mathien quotes Frisbie as observing that modern Zuni craftspeople "have a very high regard for turquoise and attempt to gather up even the finest flakes of it to be saved and used in conjunction with corn meal in ceremonial activities" (1997:1163).

Ferguson observes that Zuni participation in late prehistoric and early contact period trade networks can be observed in the presence of exotic goods in the mortuary assemblage recovered by Hodge during excavations at Hawikuh (Hawikuh). Shell is reported to have been the most common material represented among personal ornaments associated with the burials (Smith et al. 1966:254). Shell beads were recovered from 55 inhumations and from a number of cremations. The inhumations appear to be of all ages and both genders, although Smith et al. (1966:254) suggest that there was a tendency for

shell beads to be associated with males in the adult population. In addition, 34 inhumations, mostly infants and adolescents, had one or more shell pendants associated with them (Smith et al. 1966:256–257), and one of these is noted as being made of iridescent shell (*Haliotis?*). Other shell associated with these mortuary deposits included two bracelets, a shell tinkler, and several unworked valves and fragmentary pieces.

This same burial population produced 32 individuals with turquoise ornaments. Smith et al. (1966:260–263) report that beads were the most common turquoise ornament but that there were also six inhumations with associated mosaics and that four had turquoise pendants. Hodge (1921) reports that the mosaics were mounted on wooden bases and that many incorporated tesserae made from beads and small pendants, thus recycling small fragments of the highly valued turquoise.

Unfortunately, information on the nonmortuary assemblage from Hodge's excavations is quite meager (Smith et al. 1966:45), and nothing is known about the use of these and other exotic materials in the larger community. Clearly, there is some exotic material entering the Zuni system, but this seems to be on a very small scale, as the mortuary deposits discussed above were drawn from a population of approximately 955 individuals: the most common exotic, shell beads, was present in less than 6 percent of the burials.

Howell (1994a) has examined the mortuary data from Hawikuh to determine the structure of leadership at the pueblo during the late prehistoric era and at the time of contact. His analysis indicates that the community leaders did not exercise any degree of economic control (Howell 1994a:89), did not enjoy any advantage in diet or

health (Howell 2001), and do not appear to have controlled the acquisition or distribution of exotic goods. Thus, leadership at Hawikuh at time of contact appears to have been relatively centralized, but the society was, in general, not strongly stratified (Howell 1994a:89). In the dual-processual model (Blanton et al. 1996) the Hawikuh leadership seems to have had some network aspects (leadership restricted to a few kin-based groups) but was predominantly corporate based, with an absence of visual wealth and few advantages to the holders of the offices.[15]

An important aspect of post-Paquimé exchange structures in the Southwest was development of a strong east–west axis in the northern Southwest. As Wilcox et al. (chap. 12, this vol.; see fig. 12.6) have shown, a division of Southwest populations into the "northern" and "southern" Southwest is apparent as early as AD 1200 and is fully developed before the time of contact. Following the decline of Paquimé (and possibly before?), an east–west exchange axis connecting Puebloan populations in the northern Southwest facilitated movement of shell and other goods from the California coast and other areas to the west via the Mohave trail (see Dobyns and Euler 1970) and of bison hides and other plains products from the east (Spielmann 1982; Wilcox 1984). Zuni played an important role in this exchange structure, which was well developed prior to contact and which also articulated with the structures bringing goods from the south.

Conclusions

In the foregoing discussion we identified four intervals during which contrasting exchange systems were responsible for observed archaeological distributions of exotic items in the Southwest. Prior to about AD 900 it appears that such distributions were largely produced by ad hoc, down-the-line forms of exchange and that regional and macroregional exchange structures having some form of centralized or otherwise highly organized supply and demand structure or control were lacking. Between about AD 900 and 1250 and between about AD 1250 and 1450 two sequential and much more formalized systems of exchange connected large areas of the Southwest, first the Mimbres/Chaco/Wupatki system and, later, the system that developed in relation to the Casas Grandes regional system, centered at Paquimé in northwest Chihuahua. Both of these appear to have been predicated in part on the value of exotic items in the context of ideological frameworks that supported in various ways the social and political structures in centers of relative power. The fourth, post-Paquimé system was clearly less centralized, and initiation of exchange does not appear to have been restricted to a very few high-status, powerful individuals or groups. Rather, the organization of exchange was at the village level and perhaps even involved smaller groups within villages (e.g., religious societies or kin groups), and it is likely that many more people were involved in exchange than in the earlier systems.

Further refinements of the current study are possible and desirable, and the distributions documented here suggest several directions for further refinement of our understanding of these systems. Given the patterning in the occurrence of trumpets (and probably *Nassarius*), a more careful look at particular shell artifact forms and species is in order. Examination of the artifacts included in such contexts as the Burial of the Magician (McGregor 1943) might provide clues as to which items to trace. A more refined look at turquoise would also likely produce interesting results,

including quantitative measures of the relative amounts present, particular artifact forms, and recovery contexts. In addition, the temporal and spatial distributions of artifacts that combine exotic materials, such as turquoise mosaics on shells representing toads and raptors, should be carefully examined. For the moment, the distributions described above provide a more refined spatial definition of these four systems and constitute a firm basis from which to proceed.

Notes

1. For practical reasons and with Gregory's assistance, Vokes's original seminar paper has been cut in half by consolidating data into figures and tables and omitting extensive theoretical interpretation using current anthropological models of exchange (e.g., Blanton et al. 1996; Frankenstein and Rowland 1978; Hudson 1978; Jones 1994; Polyani 1968; Renfrew 1975, 1977, 1986) in favor of an emphasis on empirical patterns.

2. Vokes did look at the distribution of bell types in his original seminar paper, but, except as noted, these data do not appear to contribute significantly to the present discussion.

3. McKusick (2001:1–4) developed a classificatory structure based on the perceived use of birds and outlined a set of criteria to distinguish between them. She distinguishes between birds that were kept for social reasons such as house pets, those whose plumage was desired for ritual and ceremonial purposes, and those birds used for sacrifice. Macaws are one of the principal birds that McKusick (2001) identified as "birds of sacrifice" among southwestern groups. In contrast with other avian remains that are often encountered in middens and other trash deposits macaw remains are generally found in discrete burials, sometimes in association with human interments but often as individual deposits. They are generally articulated skeletons and appear to have been interred after having been plucked (Ruble 1996:11).

McKusick states that these birds were part of a Mesoamerican type of ceremonial system, which she characterizes as a "pan Southwestern socio-politico-religious complex" (2001:80) that was imported into the Southwest perhaps as early as the Archaic period but certainly by AD 1000. It is her belief that this complex continued into the historic era in areas where it was not replaced by the development of the Pueblo kachina cult (McKusick 2001:80). Present in this complex are a number of specific Mesoamerican religious deities and ritual associations. McKusick (2001:67–78, 81–89) proposes that the scarlet macaw was associated with the cult of Quetzalcoatl and that the military macaw and the similarly colored thick-billed parrot were associated with the deity Chalchihuilicue, the patron of lakes, streams, and other bodies of water. The latter deity is also associated with green stones such as jade and turquoise. Based on age-at-death patterns she asserts that both types of macaws were ritually sacrificed at the spring equinox after being plucked of their feathers (McKusick 2001:74). While the validity of this hypothesis is not addressed here, few would dispute that the plumage of these birds (and perhaps, at times, the birds themselves) served a role in rituals and possibly in displays of office and personal wealth.

4. One exception to the general pattern is bracelets. While it is not uncommon to find one or two bands in process at larger sites, production of bracelets appears to have been concentrated in a band along the northeastern perimeter of the Papaguería. Prior to the late Sedentary period groups in the Papaguería appear to have acquired *Glycymeris* shells from the coast of the northern Gulf and then transported them to relatively large, permanent settlements closer to the Gila and Santa Cruz rivers. These include sites like Gu Achi (Ferg 1980), Shelltown and the Hind Site (Marmaduke and Martynec 1993), and, later, Gatlin and other sites in the Gila Bend area (Teague 1981; Wasley and Johnson 1965). In the interior of the Papaguería Verbena Village (Ahlstrom and Lyon 2000; Olszewski et al. 1996), Lost City (Fontana 1965; Hayden 1972), sites in the Quijotoa Valley (Rosenthal et

al. 1978), and many small campsites in the Growler and Santa Rosa washes have abundant evidence of shell ornament production. During this transport the manufacturing process was initiated, with the backs of the shell removed and the margins roughly flaked to general shape. The result is the presence of many small campsites that contain quantities of flaked shell debris and broken blanks located along the north–south valleys in the interior Papaguería. At the larger settlements the remaining raw *Glycymeris* shells and bracelet blanks were finished into plain and carved bracelets, which were then exchanged into the Hohokam interior and farther afield.

During the late Sedentary and Classic periods there is a shift in this pattern. Larger, perhaps seasonal settlements are established along the interior valleys (Ahlstrom and Lyon 2000; Olszewski et al. 1996; Rankin 1995; Rosenthal et al. 1978); the quantities of raw material and production debris indicate that these settlements were a focus of shell ornament production, particularly of bracelets. The presence of finished artifacts in these assemblages has led some researchers to suggest that these populations retained much of their production and that the manufacture of bracelets for Hohokam populations in the Phoenix Basin had in fact shifted to these sites (Howard 1983, 1985; McGuire and Howard 1987). However, this model has not been supported by subsequent work at Classic period Phoenix Basin (Gross and Stone 1994:179).

5. It has been proposed that the Mimbres had contacts with populations in the Guaymas area of the Gulf Coast in order to obtain shell. Jett and Moyle (1986:715) argue that many of the images of fish on Classic Mimbres Black-on-white vessels reflect a familiarity with the marine aquatic fauna of the Gulf of California that resulted from repeated visits by Mimbres people to the Guaymas area. They cite the presence of macaws and copper bells in Mimbres site assemblages in support of these contacts (Jett and Moyle 1986:715). However, these identifications have recently been questioned by other archaeologists (Bettison et al. 1999:123–124), who argue that these images are more

likely representations of local freshwater fish. Regardless of the ultimate outcome of this debate, we believe that such a Mimbres–coastal Mexico connection probably existed by at least AD 1000 and possibly earlier. Its existence is generally accepted during the later Phase II period, when the Paquimé system was in place, and it is likely that these connections have considerable antiquity.

6. There are also some zoomorphic forms in the sample, including a stylized lizard from Pueblo Bonito (Judd 1954:96, fig. 15). It should be noted that zoomorphic representations in other media such as argillite and jet are present in Anasazi sites.

7. While present in the Medio period assemblage at Paquimé, bracelets did not occur in great numbers (328) when one considers the total Medio period shell assemblage (Di Peso et al. 1974b:494–510).

8. The fact that pre–AD 1250 *Nassarius* is far more common in Mimbres/Chaco/Flagstaff area sites than in Hohokam sites provides independent evidence of a Mimbres-Guaymas connection.

9. Prehistoric efforts in one area within the Cerrillos complex are reported as having removed the entire north side of a hill (Pogue 1974:52). Although this appears to have been somewhat of an overstatement, the excavations are very impressive.

10. Wilcox has suggested two alternative models for Mesoamerican-Southwest connections: (1) the Tepiman model (Wilcox 1986a), which posits a dialect chain that may have connected the Chalchihuites area of northwestern Mexico with the Hohokam in southern Arizona and along which pyrite-encrusted "mirrors" may have moved ca. AD 800–950; and (2) the Wupatki nexus model (Wilcox 1999a, 2002; Wilcox et al. 2000), which the patterns documented here appear to support.

11. Near that turquoise source is Scorpion Village, a small settlement composed of two pithouses and evidence for some temporary brush structures (Slawson 1997). The assemblage from this site produced a very high incidence of turquoise material, including raw material and partially worked pieces (Rowe 1997a:333),

along with concentrations of manufacturing tools demarcating discrete work areas (Rowe 1997b:371; Slawson 1997:139). A reassessment of ceramics from these excavations (ASM Accession 2001-41) indicates that the principal occupation of this site was contemporaneous with that of Redtail, thus making it a likely source for the Redtail turquoise.

The high frequency of turquoise debitage and raw material at both sites indicates the possible presence of part-time specialists in the manufacturing of turquoise ornaments. That other sites in the area do not appear to have participated in this abundance raises the possibility that it was being exchanged into the Salt-Gila Basin or with traders from farther to the northeast. Alternatively, the inhabitants may have been exchanging it with groups to the south in northwestern Mexico. While this option is advocated by Rowe (1997b), currently there is no analytical information to support any of these hypotheses.

12. Other settlements along the canal system that heads at Pueblo Grande also produced varying amounts of turquoise in their assemblages. If one indexes the frequencies of turquoise to other materials employed to make ornaments, the Pueblo Grande collection has somewhat more turquoise in the sample, but the relative presence is not that striking. The assemblages from Casa Buena—a platform mound community midway down Canal System 2—and those of the Grand Canal Ruin—a nearby nonplatform mound, compound settlement—produced moderate frequencies of turquoise ornaments. In contrast, Las Colinas, located at the end of the canal system, had a relatively low occurrence of turquoise (Euler and Gregory 1988:314). Thus, access to turquoise seems to have been variable but relatively uncontrolled with respect to sites in the region.

13. Transcription of document, AGN, Misiones 27, f. 78; translation by Dale Brenneman, Office of Ethnohistoric Research, Arizona State Museum. An oft-cited previous translation by Bolton (1948:I:291–292) translates the term *coloradas* as "red," but the first definition for the term in *Cassell's Spanish Dictionary* is

"colored," followed by "ruddy, florid." The Real Academia Española's *Diccionario de la lengua española* assigns the same order to these somewhat different meanings. Since Kino's native language was actually Italian, and the Italian word *colorata* also refers first to "having color," the translator chose to use the more ambiguous "colored" over "red" or "reddish."

14. Transcription of document, AGN, Historia 393, f. 86; translation by Dale Brenneman, Office of Ethnohistoric Research, Arizona State Museum.

15. Additional research by Kintigh (2000) indicates that the villages that comprised the Zuni community at time of contact were loosely organized sets of communities in which some villages seemed to have greater access to the leadership roles of the coalition but whose authority over the constituent population was limited. Kintigh (2000) suggests that this loose but hierarchical structure was a reflection of group diversity, which was the result of migrations identified in traditional Zuni oral history.

Part IV   **Zuni from the Late Prehistoric to the Middle Place**

18 Late Prehistoric and Protohistoric Settlement Systems in the Zuni Area

Keith W. Kintigh

The Challenge

This contribution is intended to provide a summary of Zuni-area settlement systems from ca. AD 1000 to 1600 in the context of addressing the emergence and economic and political organization of settlement clusters. Although I readily admit considerable uncertainty about the organizational issues, we are considerably closer to good answers than we were twenty-five years ago. Because considerable work in progress bears quite directly on these questions (including a dissertation by Deborah Huntley [2004] and one in progress by Gregson Schachner), our knowledge relating to some of these questions will be substantially advanced in the next few years.

The Zuni Area

I define the Zuni area as approximately coextensive with the drainage of the Zuni River upstream from the confluence with Jaralosa Draw north and east of St. Johns (see fig. 18.1). The area is bounded by the Zuni Mountains and the Continental Divide on the northwest and west. It conspicuously includes the modern Zuni Indian Reservation and the El Morro Valley as well as a considerable area on the south, about which considerably less is known.

While this restrictive definition serves for present purposes, Steven LeBlanc (1989) observes that we can better view the boundary of the Zuni area as varying through time. For example, less similarity in settlement configurations and ceramic assemblages during Pueblo II times may imply inclusion of less area to the south. On the other hand, in Pueblo III and Early Pueblo IV times we might reasonably extend the boundary farther south to include, for example, the Mariana Mesa sites (McGimsey 1980). During the protohistoric and historic periods the area of intensive Zuni use contracts substantially from the boundaries suggested here. However, Ferguson and Hart (1985) make clear that the Zuni area as I define it constitutes but a small fraction of the area of historic Zuni land use.

Acoma Pueblo lies about 115 km east of Zuni Pueblo. While many would divide the domains of Zuni from Acoma at the Continental Divide, as I have done here, Dittert reports that Acoma has substantial ties to the El Morro Valley sites. To the southwest of the Zuni area is the upper Little Colorado River area (Duff 2000, 2002). The protohistoric Hopi villages lie about 170 km to the north-west. A very large area within which little systematic archaeological work has been done lies north and west of the upper Little Colorado River area and between the core Zuni and Hopi areas.

The Nature of Zuni Settlement Data

The Zuni area is blessed with a remarkably well behaved archaeological record. Most ceramic types are reasonably well dated. For much of the AD 1000–1600 interval stylistic change is complex but blessedly rapid. Surface assemblages typically contain abundant tree-ring-dated slipped ceramics (about 50 percent), about 30 percent of which are identifiable by type. Thus, it is possible to date sites with respectable accuracy, even with modest surface collections.

Indeed, the area has been a veritable proving ground for methods of frequency seriation, starting with Kroeber's (1916) and Spier's (1917) precocious efforts. El Morro Valley ceramics were used by Marquardt (1974, 1978) and LeBlanc (1975) in their pioneering, high-resolution "microseriations" of attribute frequencies backed up with stratigraphic and tree-ring associations. Duff (1996) used these same assemblages

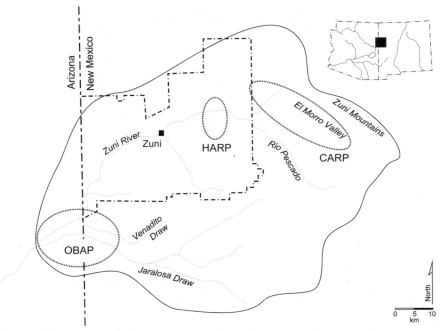

Figure 18.1. The Zuni area.

to demonstrate that comparable temporal resolution can be achieved through judicious use of frequencies of traditional types (as is done here).

Much of this chapter is concerned with the identification of settlement clusters. In the Zuni area surface visibility of masonry structures is generally good (though where it is not we will sometimes not realize it). Pithouses, especially in sand dune areas, tend to be visible only under fortuitous circumstances. Zuni Cultural Resource Enterprise excavations in Oak Wash demonstrate that even substantial pueblos can be pretty thoroughly buried. Despite the generally good surface visibility, I am *not* prepared to assume that we are aware of all of the sites of 100 rooms or more, especially if we consider a tightly packed cluster of room blocks to be a site.[1] We are aware of only a tiny fraction of sites with fewer than 50 rooms. Apart from the huge, nucleated sites that postdate AD 1250, we usually cannot recognize settlement clusters in

the absence of systematic survey. Thus, I briefly discuss the level of survey coverage in the area.

Leslie Spier's remarkable study, *An Outline for a Chronology of Zuni Ruins* (1917), effectively defined the sequence of nucleated Zuni settlements postdating AD 1250 and provided considerable information regarding the settlement patterns of earlier ceramic periods. Although Richard Woodbury (1954) did an extensive survey in the Zuni area during the early 1950s, little or no systematic survey was done until the early 1970s. Since that time there has been a substantial amount of systematic survey, some devoted to large blocks and many others to small or irregularly shaped parcels that are less easily incorporated in settlement pattern studies.

Charles Redman surveyed quadrats in the El Morro Valley as a part of the Cibola Archeological Research Project (CARP), which he codirected with Patty Jo Watson and Steven

LeBlanc (Watson et al. 1980). At the same time, a Wake Forest University project directed by Ned Woodall surveyed in the western portion of the El Morro Valley. Starting in the mid-1970s, the Pueblo of Zuni developed its own archaeology enterprise, the Zuni Archaeology Program (ZAP), now the Zuni Cultural Resource Enterprise (ZCRE). It completed a number of systematic surveys of significant blocks of land, several of them associated with the "chaining" of canyon floors to clear them of trees (Fowler 1980; Holmes and Fowler 1980; Kintigh 1980). Also in the 1970s the University of New Mexico's Office of Contract Archaeology did a substantial survey for the proposed Yellow House Dam (Hunter-Anderson 1978), and the National Park Service completed an intensive survey of El Morro National Monument. More recently, Dean Saitta has added to the Wake Forest survey in the El Morro Valley, and Robert Leonard of the University of New Mexico has surveyed near Badger Springs in the northwestern part of the Zuni Indian Reservation.

Finally, Arizona State University has, under my direction, systematically surveyed 10.4 km² of very densely occupied land on the Zuni Indian Reservation around the Pueblo IV site of Heshot uła (Heshotauthla Archaeological Research Project [HARP]; Kintigh et al. 2004). Our Ojo Bonito Archaeological Project (OBAP; Kintigh et al. 1996) has surveyed 58 km² near Ojo Bonito, adjacent to the southwestern corner of the Zuni Indian Reservation. (Stone [1992, 1994] provides an earlier settlement pattern analysis of some of these data.) Finally, in the last few years we have added to Redman's CARP survey in the El Morro Valley (see fig. 18.1).

Identification of Settlement Systems and Settlement Clusters

Settlement System Transitions

Since Spier's original study it has been clear that there is a dramatic break in the settlement patterns between what we would now call the Late Pueblo IV period (ending between AD 1350 and 1400) and the protohistoric period. However, the apparent sharpness of that transition seems to be the exception. Typically, the data suggest less a sequence of distinct settlement systems than a shifting demographic landscape in which some configurations are more stable than others.[2] I apply a periodization scheme that attempts to respond to these modalities with the caution that the resulting inferences may be sensitive to the particular characteristics of this temporal scheme.

Settlement Patches and Settlement Clusters

From the earliest ceramic periods through the present, occupation of the Zuni landscape has been quite patchy, and the patches of landscape densely occupied during one period are often not the same ones utilized later. Much of this patchiness is undoubtedly due to environmental constraints and the agricultural technologies applied (see Dean, chap. 6, this vol.). However, I believe that social processes are responsible for a substantial part of this patterning. Of course, to speak of patches is to take refuge in the intentional imprecision of the term.

The term "settlement cluster" provides less room in which to hide. At the very least, settlement clustering entails a spatial coherence and separation from neighboring clusters. Use of this term seems to imply approximate contemporaneity and, more important, that the component settlements share a significant social identity that is distinct from those of neighboring clusters. In the absence of a good operational definition of a settlement cluster there is considerable danger that what one takes to be a "cluster" of settlements lies in the eye of the beholder, especially if one draws a circle around it. The relationship of settlement clusters to communities or polities is manifestly unclear (Kintigh 2003) and will require both some explicit definitions and more intensive archaeological investigation.

As we look at the 600-year period of interest here (AD 1000–1600), sites are always spatially clustered but to differing degrees. Some of these site concentrations are settlement clusters by any standard, the one (or two, and therein lies the problem) formed by the protohistoric sites being the most obvious. However, it is not so clear where one draws the line between a settlement cluster and something less distinguished. As a consequence, I will assess the degree of spatial clustering in different periods and later discuss the limited evidence regarding the social significance of the apparent concentrations (see also Wilcox et al., chap. 12, this vol.).

The Necessity of Full-Coverage Survey

As indicated above, in the absence of systematic survey it is impossible to assess settlement clustering prior to the Pueblo IV period nucleation. For the Pueblo II and Pueblo III periods I rely mainly on two of the larger block surveys, our Ojo Bonito (OBAP) and Heshot uła area (HARP) systematic surveys. Both projects used the same field methodology, all the ceramics were typed by three researchers working closely together, and the temporal intervals that were independently derived correspond well.[3] Maps of OBAP and HARP settlement locations are based on ongoing analysis of these data. (Earlier results for the two areas are presented by Kintigh and Duff [1993] and Kintigh et al. [2004], respectively.)

Site Contemporaneity

Wilcox et al. (chap. 12, this vol.) properly remind us that settlement contemporaneity is a critical issue insofar as we want settlement clusters to represent social phenomena, not just sets of closely spaced dots on a piece of paper. The 50-year interval they use represents a reasonable compromise with respect to the larger sites that dominate their regional maps (Wilcox et al., chap. 12, this vol.). Fifty years strains our ability to infer occupation intervals from the available data but nonetheless probably exceeds the occupation spans of most sites. And, for the longer-lived sites, the available data are almost always inadequate to estimate changing site size through time.

Temporal Periods

Despite the attractiveness of shorter intervals I will frame the following discussion in terms of six longer intervals that seem responsive to the changes in patterning. This serves to economize the presentation and responds to what appears to be considerable settlement stability of the protohistoric sites and to the limitations of our data for the smaller sites. For ease of discussion I will call these the Early and Late Pueblo II, Pueblo III, Early and Late Pueblo IV, and protohistoric periods. As they are defined below, these periods do not exactly

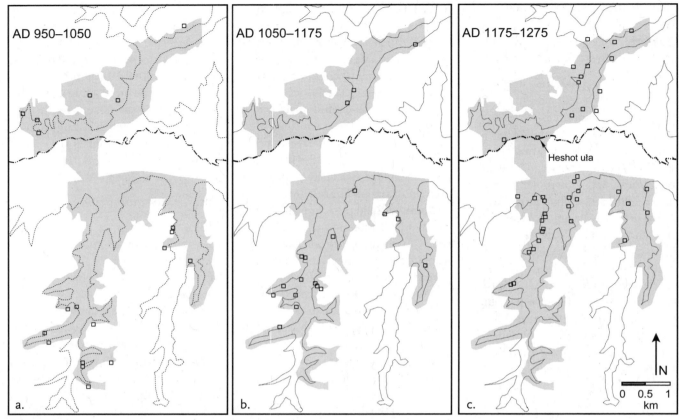

Figure 18.2. Heshot uła survey dated site locations: (a) AD 950–1050; (b) AD 1050–1175; (c) AD 1175–1275. Shaded area indicates extent of survey. Canyon edges are indicated by dotted lines.

coincide with the canonical dates of the Pecos classification (the Pueblo III period is squeezed from both ends) but better reflect the structure of the data than do the traditional dates.

The Emergence and Development of Settlement Clusters
Early Pueblo II (AD 950–1050)

The total population of the Ojo Bonito and Heshot uła survey areas is relatively low, though the sites are spread over a large area in topographically diverse settings. In the Heshot uła area (see fig. 18.2a) settlements exist both along the edges of the main drainage and on the mesa slopes, especially toward the upper ends of side canyons. Pueblos and a rock-

shelter are found, but only one kiva was recorded. The 19 sites located all have 12 or fewer rooms and together total only 105 rooms (mean of six rooms).

In the Ojo Bonito area (see fig. 18.3a) we recorded 25 sites dating to the Early Pueblo II period. While the occupation is concentrated on the floor of Jaralosa Draw, occupation during the preceding century continued in the duned areas on the mesas north of the Zuni River and south of Jaralosa Draw. Our survey located a dense cluster of small pueblos in the southwestern portion of our survey area that also began in the preceding AD 850–950 interval and continued through this period. These sites lie within a 400-x-700-m area, slightly elevated from the floodplain of Jaralosa Draw. We also found a pre-

viously unrecorded Chacoan great house complex, the H-Spear site, which includes a great kiva and earthen berm (Mahoney et al. 1995). It is located on the tip of a low dune ridge in the southeastern part of the surveyed area. It is probably not coincidental that the H-Spear site was found on the northern edge of an enormous pithouse village (with two great kivas) that dates to the preceding interval.

With the single exception noted, there is little evidence of distinct settlement clustering. The Early Pueblo II sites contain indications of masonry architecture that range from well-defined room blocks to ambiguous stone features. Some of the latter probably represent communal storage facilities used by pithouse occupants; others may represent a

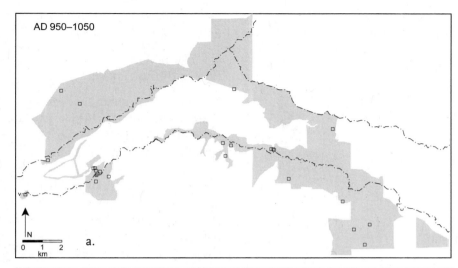

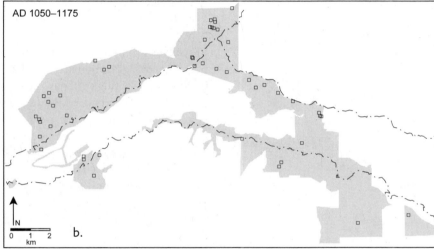

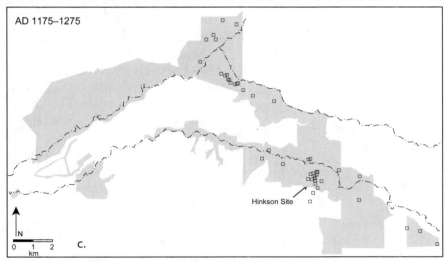

Figure 18.3. Ojo Bonito survey dated site locations: (a) AD 950–1050; (b) AD 1050–1175; (c) AD 1175–1275. Shaded area indicates extent of survey.

combination of basal masonry and jacal superstructure habitations (Roberts 1939b). In the Ojo Bonito area the Chacoan great house complex represents the most striking evidence of public architecture, yet it is also strikingly distant from much contemporaneous habitation. Kivas were recorded at two Ojo Bonito area sites (in addition to the great kiva at the H-Spear site).

Late Pueblo II (AD 1050–1175)

During Late Pueblo II times the picture changed substantially. In the Ojo Bonito survey area (see fig. 18.3b) Late Pueblo II sites are strongly associated with the duned areas and the bottomland along Venadito Draw down to its confluence with the Zuni River. There is a greatly reduced occupation of the central and lower reaches of Jaralosa Draw. Pueblos range in size from two to nearly 30 rooms, but an average size is about 10 rooms. Among the 49 sites several rubble mounds reach 1 m in height; four have distinct kiva depressions, and one has an apparent great kiva. While many room blocks are separated by only a few hundred meters from their nearest neighbors, clustering is not well defined at a scale that we can detect it.

In the Heshot uła survey area (see fig. 18.2b) the concentration of sites increases, with most settlement found along the margins of a 2-km stretch of the middle portion of the southwestern side canyon that we surveyed. In contrast, there is less settlement along the main (Rio Pescado) drainage. Altogether, during the Late Pueblo II period there are 226 rooms in 19 sites, the largest of which has about 35 rooms (mean of 12 rooms). Only a single kiva depression was recorded. The well-known Chacoan great house, Village of the Great Kivas (Eckert et al. 2000; Roberts 1932),

Figure 18.4. The Hinkson site.

Ojo Bonito Archaeological Project
Hinkson Site

0   100   200
m

N

dates to this period and lies about 8 km north of Heshot uła.

Pueblo III (AD 1175–1275)

There are 40 sites with 791 rooms (mean of 20 rooms) in the Heshot uła survey area during the Pueblo III period (see fig. 18.2c). In contrast to the preceding periods kivas were common; at least one kiva was recorded at 17 of these sites. Sites are concentrated along the edges of lower portions of the side canyons, a pattern showing little spatial overlap with that of the preceding periods.

In the center of the densest such concentration (near the mouth of the canyon south of Heshot uła) is a post-Chacoan great house (see site 81 in Spier 1917; Kintigh 1985) with a blocked-in kiva and great kiva depression in front. Including the great house, there are 371 rooms in a cluster of 21 sites along a single 3-km stretch of the canyon. There are 107 more rooms in five sites at the mouth of the adjacent canyon less than a kilometer to the east and another 273 rooms in a cluster of 12 sites at the mouth of the canyon extending north from the Rio Pescado. During this period most sites lie within a couple of hundred meters of their closest neighbors. While one can perhaps see clusters within this overall distribution, the most distant sites are only about 6 km apart, so this could also be seen as one large cluster. Unfortunately, the scale of our survey was not sufficient to observe the larger context of this clustering.

At Ojo Bonito (see fig. 18.3c) the 44 Pueblo III sites are even more densely clustered, and the western portion of the survey area now appears to lack occupation. Early in the period there is a cluster of sites near the confluence of Venadito Draw with the Zuni River and another along Jaralosa Draw in the southeastern part of the survey

**Ojo Bonito Archaeological Project
Jaralosa Site**

0 10 20 30 40 50
m

N

Figure 18.5. The Jaralosa site.

increasingly concentrated at two sites near the southeast corner of our survey area. Settlement in other portions of the area disappeared by AD 1225 (Eckert 1995). The largest of these sites is the Hinkson site (see fig. 18.4; Kintigh et al. 1996), which was founded near the beginning of the Pueblo III period. By the end of that period it had 33 room blocks with 560 rooms spread in a Y-shaped pattern along a low ridge. (At most about 400 of these rooms were occupied at any one time; see Eckert 1995.) The Hinkson site is focused on a post-Chacoan great house complex that includes an earthen berm, roads, and an oversized, unroofed great kiva. About 3.5 km to the east is the crescent-shaped Jaralosa site, with 120 rooms in 10-room blocks (see fig. 18.5), which was established somewhat later. Our 58-km² survey of the Ojo Bonito area may, fortuitously, have captured much of a large-scale settlement cluster focused on the Hinkson site.

> [The] Hinkson site is the center of a large community occupied between about AD 1200 and 1275. This community includes 70 room blocks and nearly 900 rooms within a 9 km radius of the Hinkson site great house. . . . While our survey extended as far as 15 km from the Hinkson site, *all* contemporaneous occupation is within 9 km. . . . Outside our survey area, the nearest known contemporaneous communities are Fort Atarque, 16 km east of the Hinkson site; Ceadro Pueblo (AZ Q:4:159 [ASM]), 16 km west; the Bean Patch site, 18 km southwest; and the Ojo Caliente Community, 15 km north (Kintigh [1996]). If these population concentrations are taken to indicate centers of different social entities, then the radius of a single organizational

area. Throughout the Pueblo III period sites are generally on the slightly elevated margins of the floodplain. Extensive sets of gridded agricultural fields on natural terraces of the basalt mesa separating Jaralosa from Venadito Draw are generally located close to Pueblo III sites and likely date to this period. The shift away from duned areas suggests a more complete reliance on runoff farming.

During the Pueblo III period population not only increased, it became

unit would appear to be on the order of 9km [Kintigh et al. 1996:292].

During the Pueblo III period in both the Heshot uła and Ojo Bonito areas long-term population growth culminated in the development of settlement clusters focused on post-Chacoan great houses. However, if we look farther afield, the patterning appears more complex. Some clusters dating to this period lack great houses and great kivas, and the El Morro Valley, at the eastern end of the Zuni area, lacks the long-term antecedent population seen in the Ojo Bonito and Heshot uła surveys. Indeed, the valley seems to have little occupation prior to about AD 1225 but an explosion of population in the mid-1200s.

On a mesa overlooking the El Morro Valley the 60-room Los Gigantes great house is surrounded by a 20–room block (190-room) residential community (Schachner 1998). Like the Hinkson site, it also has an oversized (31 m) unroofed great kiva. Located less than 4 km to the northwest, also on the southern margin of the valley, the 154-room Pettit site may also be considered to be a great house. It is surrounded by a community with at least 24 additional room blocks with 414 rooms (Schachner 1998). The Scribe S site is on the north side of the El Morro Valley, opposite (6 km northeast of) the Los Gigantes great house. It dates mainly from AD 1240 to 1275 (Watson et al. 1980) and has 410 rooms in 15 room blocks. While it is similar in scale to the Hinkson site, it lacks public architecture. A smaller cluster with 203 rooms, also lacking evident public architecture, is found in the middle of the valley, 6 km east of Los Gigantes, in the vicinity of the later Cienega and Mirabal sites. However, taking a broader view of the known Pueblo III site concentrations in the El Morro Valley, this apparent segregation of the El Morro Valley clusters may be, in part, a consequence of survey boundaries. Considerably more systematic investigation will be required to form a coherent picture.

Finally, the ceramic evidence suggests that many and perhaps most of the large, nucleated pueblos in the Zuni area were constructed late in the Pueblo III period, between AD 1250 and 1275. Indeed, some of the nucleated pueblos may already have been abandoned by about AD 1275 (Kintigh 1985).[4] If the major stylistic changes in the ceramics occur simultaneously across the Zuni area, then the latest clustered room block settlements have significant temporal overlap with the earliest large, nucleated pueblos.[5] Understanding the fine details of these overlaps will be difficult but is essential to our understanding of the process of nucleation at Zuni.

Early Pueblo IV (AD 1275–1325)

From what we can tell, the architectural transition from comparatively small room blocks (with from perhaps four to as many as 80 rooms) and room block clusters to the large nucleated pueblos (180–1,400 rooms) characteristic of the Pueblo IV period was relatively rapid.[6] In the Zuni area it apparently began about AD 1250, and nucleation was essentially universal by AD 1300. After AD 1300 occupation seems to be exclusively in pueblos composed of a single room block with from 180 to more than 1,000 rooms. Several of the Pueblo III room block clusters in the El Morro Valley saw the development of large, planned pueblos nearby. However, some of the Early Pueblo IV nucleated pueblos may not have emerged in areas with high Pueblo III site densities.[7]

The distribution of Early Pueblo IV nucleated pueblos is shown in figure 18.6 (Kintigh 1985). Most or all of the sites depicted were probably established by about AD 1275 and have overlapping occupations on the early end. However, it appears that by AD 1300 quite a number of them were no longer occupied. This figure also includes a few nucleated pueblos whose occupation may have ended by AD 1275 (see n. 4). For the Zuni area as defined here, we are probably aware of all of the large Pueblo IV and protohistoric sites and certainly know about nearly all of them.[8]

These sites are generally composed of a single large block of rooms surrounding a plaza. In many cases the shapes are quite regular and the construction was clearly planned, as indicated by the bonding and abutting patterns and the continuous outside walls (Watson et al. 1980). A number of these pueblos have a regular oval plan, others are clearly rectangular or trapezoidal, and a couple have a composite shape with both square and ovoid architectural constituents.[9] These shape differences *must* mean something. As it seems that everyone wants to have a go at looking for the spatial patterning of these shapes, they are plotted on the map.

These large pueblos are found in a variety of environmental settings, ranging from mesa tops to the floors of broad and narrow canyons. With very few exceptions they are in the higher portions of the Zuni area. Nearly all have elevations above 2,000 m. Some are in wooded areas, and others are in open environments. A few could be said to have defensive locations, but most do not.

While the population is certainly concentrated in a relatively small number of very large sites, meaningful settlement clustering is not obvious. One could view all these sites as forming a loose cluster of sites with a 20-km radius centered on the eastern portion of the Zuni area, accompanied

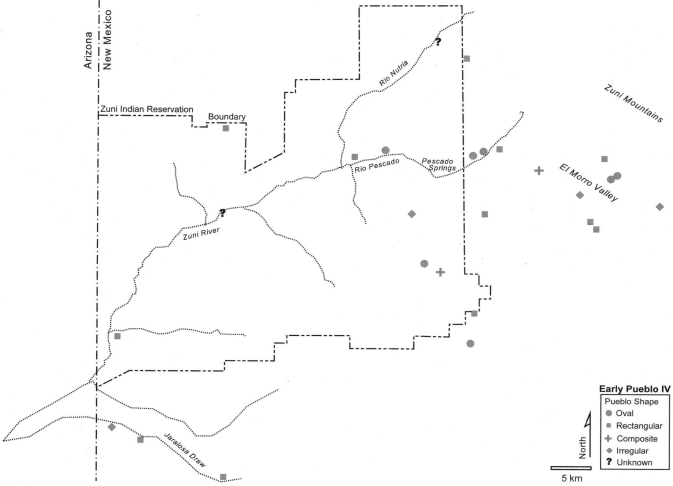

Figure 18.6. Early Pueblo IV site locations.

by a handful of outliers. Within this cluster there is a large range of site sizes and no clearly dominant sites. Alternately, one could identify a number of smaller clusters 10–15 km in diameter. I cannot bring myself to draw any essentially arbitrary circles around them.

Late Pueblo IV
(AD 1325–1350/1400)

As can be seen in figure 18.7, there are many fewer sites dating to the Late Pueblo IV period.[10] Heshot uła and a few of the Early Pueblo IV sites in the El Morro Valley continue their occupation. Four new sites are established near Pescado Springs in the

eastern portion of the Zuni Indian Reservation. These sites seem to have a strong focus on sources of permanent water and lie close to springs or along a major drainage.

During this period there is an obvious separation between the three El Morro Valley sites and the five in the neighborhood of Pescado Springs. The clusters would each have a radius of about 5 km and would be separated by 20km. Again, there are outliers. The sites in the Ojo Bonito area (in the far southwest corner of fig. 18.7) are probably socially as well as spatially separated from the center of the action farther east (Duff 2002; Huntley and Kintigh 2004).

Protohistoric Period
(AD 1350/1400–1600)

During the protohistoric period, of course, we have undisputed settlement clusters at Zuni, Acoma, and Hopi, each of which is relatively compact and separated from its neighbors by a considerable distance. At Zuni the protohistoric transition is characterized by the abandonment of pueblos in the El Morro Valley and the Pescado Springs area and the construction of the protohistoric towns from the neighborhood of modern Zuni Pueblo downstream. Without serious question, Kechiba:wa (Kechipawan), Hawikku (Hawikuh), Kwa'kin'a, Halona:wa North, Mats'a:kya, and

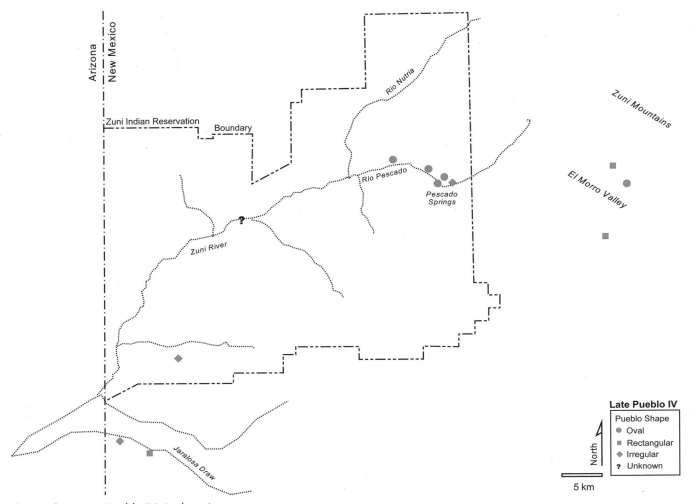

Figure 18.7. Late Pueblo IV site locations.

Kyaki:ma were occupied at the time of the Spanish invasion of the Southwest in 1539 and 1540 (see fig. 18.8; Hodge 1937; Kintigh 1985).[11]

The dates of the *establishment* of the protohistoric sites are less well settled. Despite extensive excavation of Kechiba:wa (Kintigh 2000) and Hawikku (Smith et al. 1966), some of the best data come from Spier's stratigraphic test units (excavated in 6-in levels) at Mats'a:kya, Binna:wa, and Chalo:wa (Kintigh 1985). These data suggest little overlap with the Late Pueblo IV settlement distribution, indicating a relatively rapid transition late in the fourteenth century. Barbara Mills's (2002a) ongoing analysis of samples recently excavated

from the Middle Village at Zuni (Halona:wa North) suggest that it was established slightly earlier, in the mid–AD 1300s. Todd Howell (personal communication 2003) reports that the Middle Village excavations yielded cutting dates of AD 1347, 1439, and 1548. (However, the architectural configuration of the protohistoric component is unknown because of its continuous and dense occupation since the Pueblo Revolt in 1680.)

Settlement Clustering Summary

In preceding sections I have commented on observable spatial clusters during individual time periods. A priori, it seems to me that the likelihood

that spatial clusters are socially significant increases if there is a distinct separation from adjacent clusters and if centrally located settlements within the clusters are larger or otherwise architecturally distinguished. Interpretations of settlement clusters must recognize that the tremendous changes in the settlement patterns between AD 950 and 1500 are accompanied by orders of magnitude change in demographic scale. Single, short-lived Pueblo IV sites have larger populations than we project for vast areas only a few centuries earlier.

The strongest indications of meaningful settlement clustering within the Zuni area are on a scale smaller than the radius of 18–36 km

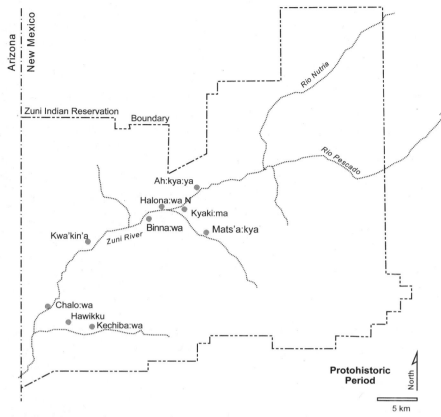

Figure 18.8. Protohistoric site locations.

6,300 rooms. Nonetheless, the spatial patterning is not clearly indicative of settlement clustering, except that the Early Pueblo IV sites as a group are tightly clustered relative to the regional landscape. During the Late Pueblo IV period two distinct groups of sites (8 and 10 km across) appear in the eastern part of the Zuni area, separated by about 20 km (Huntley and Kintigh 2004).

In the frame of the protohistoric landscape of the northern Southwest the protohistoric sites form a compact cluster about 25 km across that is separated from adjacent clusters at Hopi and Acoma by many times this distance. Within the Zuni distribution there are hints of two subclusters, each about 8 km across, with Kwa'kin'a poised in between the upstream and downstream clusters (Mills 1995:201–202). Site sizes do not suggest a strong political hierarchy. Two of the three largest sites (each of which has about 800 rooms) are separated by only 6 km in the southwestern concentration; the other is on the southeastern periphery of the eastern group (Kintigh 2000:102–103).

Finally, it may be useful to look at plots of site size for the last three periods considered plus a selection of Late Pueblo III communities (see fig. 18.9). While the room estimates for individual sites may be problematic, a fairly strong pattern is evident. From the Early Pueblo IV through protohistoric periods there are distinct site size modes at around 200 and 900 rooms, with a less distinct mode in the neighborhood of 400 rooms. While there tend to be fewer sites in the larger modes, there are always multiple sites in the largest size mode. Where there are clusters, there is frequently more than one of these large sites in a single cluster.

suggested by David Wilcox (see Kintigh 2003 for a discussion of spatial clustering, cluster radius, demographic scale, and community).

During the Pueblo III period in the Ojo Bonito area we have evidence for communities that are spatially segregated from one another with centers 15–18 km apart (i.e., having a radius on the order of 7–9 km). Our evidence suggests that the entire Hinkson community would have had more than 900 rooms. Although not all of these rooms were strictly contemporaneous, by the end of the period it appears that more than 500 rooms were clustered in two sites about 3 km apart and surrounded by an empty zone with a radius on the order of 9 km.

During the Pueblo III period our Heshot uła survey located nearly 700 rooms in an irregularly shaped area

that is only 6 km in its maximum dimension. The later half of the Pueblo III period (not separated in fig. 18.3c) has on the order of 450 rooms within 3 km of the Pueblo IV ruin of Heshot uła (with an unknown number of additional rooms buried beneath that large site). Unfortunately, our survey covered too small an area to see how this fits into the larger-scale pattern. At the same time (AD 1225–1275) the El Morro Valley had apparent clusters of pueblos with from 200 to more than 500 rooms. However, gaps in the survey coverage make the patterning difficult to interpret.

During the Early Pueblo IV period the demographic scale is ratcheted up a notch, with several sites or closely spaced pairs of sites having upward of 1,000 rooms. A single 9-km radius circle centered near the Kluckhohn site could take in on the order of

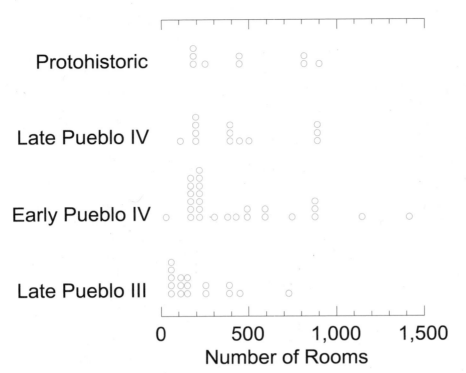

Figure 18.9. Dot plot of site sizes.

The Integration and Organization of Settlement Clusters
Pueblo II (AD 950–1175)

There is a definite patchiness to the distribution of Pueblo II sites on the landscape (also true of the other periods), and while some sites seem to be spatially clustered, many otherwise similar sites do not. It seems reasonable to assume that neighboring sites had more interaction than distant ones, and it is certainly possible that some settlement clusters represented distinct political identities. However, the lack of spatial separation in much of the available survey suggests that the landscape was not neatly partitioned into competing territories at small (2–4 km) or medium (10–20 km) scales.

Pueblo II period kiva depressions are relatively rare in both Ojo Bonito and Heshot uła survey areas, suggesting less need for formal integration than is seen later. Interestingly, the location of the relatively Early Pueblo II Chacoan great house complex in the Ojo Bonito area (the H-Spear site) appears to be much more strongly associated with the large pithouse village that predates it than it is with contemporaneous habitations.[12] In fact, the only clear-cut cluster of Early Pueblo II room blocks in the area is 13 km to the west. Thus, the H-Spear site is *not* the center of a large residential community, as has been hypothesized for other Chacoan great houses (Kantner and Mahoney 2000; Mahoney 2000).

During the Late Pueblo II period the Heshot uła survey has one cluster of 11 sites that is 2 km long and 1 km wide, with 154 rooms. The largest site, centrally located in this cluster, has 35 rooms and a kiva depression. However, it is about 8 km from the nearest known Chacoan great house (Village of the Great Kivas).

Available data from systematic survey suggest that loose communities, on a scale of 2–4 km, may have developed during the Pueblo II period. Data from the Heshot uła survey suggest that these small-scale communities may have been focused on larger sites with kivas. Ceramic data from the Ojo Bonito area suggest that these communities, and perhaps the more dispersed settlements as well, participated in substantial ceramic exchange (Mahoney et al. 1995). The Chacoan great houses were architecturally distinctive, but we are not yet in a position to understand the roles they played in any larger-scale organization.

Pueblo III (AD 1175–1275)

Interpretations of this post-Chacoan settlement system vary. Based on our Ojo Bonito work, I have suggested that there may have been competing polities separated by 15–18 km focused on post-Chacoan great houses (Kintigh 1994). Stein and his colleagues (Fowler et al. 1987; Fowler and Stein 1992; Stein and Lekson 1992) stress a much larger scale unity. In any event, the Ojo Bonito area shows a marked population aggregation focused on an impressive great house complex at the Hinkson site.

Suzanne Eckert (1995) refined the seriation of the Pueblo III sites in the Ojo Bonito area and compared excavated midden deposits from the Hinkson site great house and 13 of the room blocks at the site. Her analysis indicated that when compared with the surrounding room blocks, the great house deposits were enriched in serving bowls and cooking pots but depleted in slipped storage jars, suggesting association of the great house with food preparation and feasting but not with storage. Her comparison of the midden deposits did not suggest substantial differentiation among them or patterning with respect to their proximity to the great house.

Table 18.1 Frequencies of Identifiable Wild Birds at El Morro Valley Pueblo IV Sites

Shape	Site	Waterfowl	Raptors	Perching	Total
Rectangular	Pueblo de los Muertos	5	35	50	90
Rectangular	Atsinna	0	2	2	4
Oval	Cienega	23	6	14	43
Oval	Mirabal	5	6	5	16

Source: Potter (1997:198).

Andrew Duff's (1993, 1994) compositional analyses of the ceramic pastes at Pueblo III sites in the Ojo Bonito area identified three separate ceramic production zones: the dispersed room blocks north of the mesa procuring clay from one of the Dakota formations; the Hinkson site procuring clay from the Mancos formation; and the Jaralosa site procuring clays from the Chinle formation and from another Dakota formation source. Although gray corrugated vessels were made of clays deriving from all three formations (and presumably were produced in all production zones), the Jaralosa site produced between 60 and 70 percent of the grayware found at all room blocks, suggesting more than casual interaction. St. Johns Polychrome was also made in each production zone, but the dispersed room blocks apparently produced the bulk of the local redwares found at the Hinkson and Jaralosa sites. Ceramics produced at the Hinkson site were not exchanged widely. The asymmetric character of the interaction with the Hinkson site may suggest its centrality to this larger community, as we have earlier suggested (Kintigh et al. 1996:271). Eckert's (1995) subsequent seriation indicates that the Hinkson site and Jaralosa Pueblo were occupied longer than the more dispersed room blocks, so we caution that some of this patterning may be due to the movement of people (with their pots) and not exchange.

Early and Late Pueblo IV
(AD 1275–1400)

Most of the Pueblo IV towns appear to have had planned layouts. Kivas are relatively uncommon and are rectangular or D-shaped, in distinction to the circular kivas that we believe characterize earlier periods. Where we have good data (Watson et al. 1980), it appears that the initial construction was carried out on a large scale, probably often accomplished with a ladder-type construction technique (LeBlanc 1999:64–66). This represents a level of organized, collective effort on a scale much greater than is evident at any earlier time. Nonetheless, it appears that the vast majority of these massive sites had short occupations; certainly less than 50 years and perhaps less than 25. To me, this indicates a lack of social stability (Kintigh 1985).

Other than the construction and the spatial patterning of sites, direct evidence on the organization of Pueblo IV sites in the Zuni area comes from Potter's (1997, 2000; Potter and Perry 2000) work on the El Morro Valley sites, focusing on the fauna, and from Deborah Huntley's (2004; Huntley and Kintigh 2004) and Andrew Duff's (2002) analyses of ceramics from Heshot uła and several El Morro Valley sites.

Potter (1997:224–226; Potter and Perry 2000:72–74) suggests that the duality in site layout (oval and rectangular) may indicate a ritual complementarity that would have structured interactions among the Pueblo IV sites. Potter's argument is that different sorts of wild birds (as opposed to turkeys) differ in their ritual significance. Ritual complementarity is supported by a finding that raptors and perching birds are more common at the rectangular sites and that waterfowl are more common at the oval ones. While this is an intriguing hypothesis, sampling considerations suggest that the empirical basis of this interpretation is weak (see table 18.1). The samples of identified wild birds at two of the four sites are extremely small (4 and 16 for Atsinna and Mirabal, respectively).

The argument thus rests primarily on two sites, Pueblo de los Muertos and Cienega, one rectangular and one oval, with sample sizes of 90 and 43, respectively. Aggravating the sampling concerns, wild bird bones are far from evenly distributed across the excavated assemblages, and deposit types sampled vary among the sites (Potter 1997:135–144, 173–174, 199–204). Based on the available evidence, we cannot reject the possibility that the observed patterning could be dramatically altered with the addition of a quite modest amount of new data. Although Potter dismisses the concern (Potter and Perry 2000:72–73), it is notable that Cienega, the site with by far the largest number of waterfowl bones (23), has a large, prehistorically improved spring in the middle and that Mirabal, the other oval site, is less than 300 m away.

Duff's and Huntley's Pueblo IV neutron activation data suggest that most pottery was produced at or near the sites on which it was found. To the extent that pots moved, they moved from west to east. Their data suggest that, within the Zuni area, there was some movement of pots from Heshot uła to the El Morro Valley sites, but not vice versa. However, there is significant overlap in paste composition groups represented at the El Morro sites and Heshot uła, but the likely distances involved are small enough that we cannot be certain whether this indicates use of chemically similar clay sources or is due to exchange.

During the Early Pueblo IV period frequencies of the white-slipped interior, red-slipped exterior Kwakina Polychrome (which may be symbolically charged [Crown 1994]) are lower in all three of the oval pueblos sampled than they are in the two rectangular ones (Huntley and Kintigh 2004; however, we recognize that this, or the opposite pattern, has a 1 in 5 probability of happening by chance). This pattern disappears and the range of values narrows during the Late Pueblo IV period, indicating increased homogeneity of the sites sampled.

Huntley (2004) recently completed a comprehensive technological and stylistic study of the Pueblo IV ceramics oriented to the question of intraregional settlement integration in the Zuni area. Huntley analyzed the chemical compositions of ceramic pastes (using instrumental neutron activation analysis) and glaze paints (using both electron microprobe and stable lead isotope analysis) and examined a number of directly observable technical, formal, and stylistic attributes of a large sample of potsherds from a number of Zuni area sites. This multivariate approach did not point to a clear-cut definition of socially and spatially distinct settlement clusters but indicates a structure of social interaction that is more complex and often crosses boundaries of the spatial clusters.

Protohistoric Period
(AD 1350/1400–1600)

In contrast to the Pueblo IV sites, most of the protohistoric sites seem to have been quite long lived, many

having been occupied from sometime before AD 1400 until the Pueblo Revolt in 1680 (Kintigh 1985). They generally consist of multiple room blocks and plazas. To the limited extent that we know about kivas (from Kechiba:wa and Hawikku), they are exclusively rectangular, as they are today.

As indicated above, the protohistoric distribution of sites suggests that there may have been an upstream (western) and downstream (eastern) cluster. If there were two distinct political units, this structure is not strongly indicated in the ethnohistoric documents. While Hawikku may have been the most important politically, there are indications that the Spanish saw Hawikku (western) and Mats'a:kya (eastern) as the two principal towns, despite the fact that Kechiba:wa was as large as the other two (Hodge 1937; see also Wilcox et al., chap. 12, this vol.). Mills (1995) has pointed out that the clays used in making the Zuni Glaze Ware ceramics would not have been readily available to the western sites. As these types are relatively common in the western sites, a significant level of interaction must have been maintained.

Howell's (1994b, 1995; Howell and Kintigh 1996) analysis of the large mortuary assemblage from Hawikku best fits a model in which power was concentrated in religious offices that are maintained within a small fraction of the lineages at Zuni. Adding to Howell's work, my recent comparison of the two large western sites, Hawikku and Kechiba:wa (Kintigh 2000), shows that Hawikku had significantly more graves with a high diversity of grave goods than did Kechiba:wa. Furthermore, these strictly contemporaneous sites differed dramatically in the proportions of different ceramic types found in graves, in their representation of different

classes of grave goods, and in grave orientation. This suggests to me that social identities that were different or that existed in markedly different proportions were maintained at the two sites *within* the same cluster. This may reflect ethnic differentiation of the population. The differences in grave richness may also indicate the ritual or political prominence of Hawikku.

Concluding Thoughts

Because we are so reliant on systematic survey it is difficult to get a comprehensive big-picture view of the Pueblo II and Pueblo III periods. Throughout these periods utility ceramics were of gray corrugated ware. True brownwares dating to this period are generally rare to absent in the Zuni area, though their representation increases as one moves south out of the area. Similarly, Zuni-area kivas are round in contrast to the square ones a bit farther south. In contrast, the Pueblo II and Pueblo III black-on-white and black-on-red ceramic traditions, including Reserve and Tularosa Black-on-white types and Wingate and St. Johns Red Ware types, transcend this southern boundary. In the central Zuni area northern Puerco Black-on-white traditions persist side by side with the Reserve Black-on-white ceramics (Mills, chap. 13, this vol.).[13] This suggests that we must exercise considerable caution in inferring boundaries from the distributions of even highly visible cultural traits.

As Duff (2000, 2002) has most comprehensively discussed, during the Pueblo IV period the Zuni area seems to have been relatively self-contained. He showed that there is little movement of Zuni-produced ceramics into the upper Little Colorado area (and a surprising degree of local production in the upper Little Colorado of "Zuni" types). Salado poly-chromes and Hopi and Rio Grande types are essentially absent at Zuni (Kintigh 1985) but are relatively common in the upper Little Colorado nearby. Nonetheless, it is notable that the ceramic sequences at Zuni and Acoma to the east are remarkably similar (though the types often have different names) up until the late-fourteenth-century introduction of Zuni Buff Wares (Dittert 1998).

This does not mean that there was no population movement into the area during the Pueblo IV period. Indeed, looking at the regional demographic picture it seems likely that there was migration into Zuni. The indications of internal differentiation within and among Pueblo IV Zuni villages discussed above may be a result of internal post-Chaco political developments, immigration, or both. Nonetheless, the relative homogeneity of the archaeological record (and the near absence of exotic goods) suggests that any long-distance immigrants must have, to a large extent, been quickly assimilated (Cordell 1995).

For the protohistoric period, Zuni becomes less insular, with significant amounts of Salado polychromes appearing with increased amounts of Hopi ceramics and obsidian. However, Rio Grande glazes remained remarkably rare. Cremation joins inhumation as a method of interment; about a third of the graves at both Kechiba:wa and Hawikku were cremated. We can tentatively accept Howell's reconstruction of a lineage-based political organization that is ritually legitimated, similar to that recorded ethnographically at Zuni. Data from Hawikku and Kechiba:wa provide clear indications of differences between and perhaps within villages.

Interestingly, as Suzanne Eckert has pointed out, the two most dra-matic settlement transitions are accompanied by major ceramic changes. Glaze paints were introduced near the end of the Pueblo III period at about the same time as the development of the large nucleated pueblos. While Late Pueblo III sites have abundant subglaze paints, paints that reach a full shiny glaze only appear on the Pueblo IV types. The protohistoric transition is accompanied by the introduction of matte-painted, buff-slipped pottery (with a continuation of the glaze-paint tradition) and a plain (rather than indented corrugated) utility ware.

Zuni-Mogollon Connections

Based on traditional concepts of culture areas and the associated culture-trait distributions, Zuni has long been seen as occupying the southern edge of the Anasazi area or as transitional between Anasazi and Mogollon. I am not aware that anyone is prepared to claim that the Mogollon ever represented a coherent cultural group with a tangible identity, and the few such broad claims about the Anasazi revolve around the Chaco phenomenon and its aftermath. It is my sense that with the possible exception of the Chaco system (and probably only the central parts of that) and notwithstanding the kachina or southwestern cults, the most salient cultural identities operative in the prehistoric northern Southwest were probably of a scale measured in kilometers or a few tens of kilometers, not in hundreds of kilometers.[14] This perspective makes it difficult to get a firm grasp on the question (and thus the answer) of the relationship between Zuni and Mogollon.

At least in part because of its increasing spatial isolation, it becomes easier to think of Zuni as some sort of semicoherent entity during the Early Pueblo IV period, and, of course, this is just when the last of the Mogollon (considered most expansively) are disappearing. The disappearance of *sites* from the Mogollon area, of course, creates some of the spatial segregation. However, does the disappearance of *people* who are recognizably Mogollon (into Zuni?) also contribute to the Pueblo IV coherence of Zuni?

There were a lot of people already on the Zuni landscape in the early AD 1300s, as there were in the early 1200s. I do not doubt that there was some migration into Zuni, probably throughout the 600-year period considered here. Some of that migration may well have come from villages archaeologists identify as Mogollon. I also do not doubt that the effect of those migrants was partly and perhaps importantly constitutive of Zuni—perhaps similar in kind, if not in magnitude, to the contributions of southern migrants to contemporary Hopi documented by Ferguson and Lomaomvaya (1999).

However, it is far from clear that migrants made up a large component of the Zuni population. Our best-analyzed demographic data come from the Heshot ula survey (Kintigh et al. 2004). We see what appears to be an aggregate growth rate of about .6 percent per year from AD 950 to 1275. However, our current analysis suggests a period of low or modest growth ($<$ .5 percent) between AD 950 and 1125, followed by rapid growth—on the order of 1.75 to 2 percent per year—between AD 1125 and 1225 and population stability between 1225 and 1275. The AD 1275 population in the immediate area is probably not too different from the initial population of the Pueblo IV site of Heshot ula. Further, our survey area is small, and much if not all of the growth we observe could easily be due to internal growth and to population movements of only a few kilometers. Certainly, the El Morro Valley experienced a population explosion, but it is also clear that the eastern part of the Zuni Indian Reservation had Pueblo II and Early Pueblo III populations that were quite large. We simply do not have the data to assess the extent of migration from outside the Zuni area.

Furthermore, I do not see evidence that the Zuni area, which was already populous and had a long cultural trajectory behind it, exhibits changes that are indicative of a major cultural transformation late in prehistory. This does not suggest that in some way Mogollon became Zuni. To the extent that any time has the appearance of such a transformation, it is the protohistoric transition that is too late to account for a Mogollon migration and appears to happen in a period of population decline, not expansion.

Acknowledgments

I first acknowledge the many archaeologists who have collected important data for the Zuni area as well as those whose arguments have stimulated those made here. I am especially indebted to Andrew Duff, Suzanne Eckert, Donna Glowacki, Todd Howell, Deborah Huntley, and Gregson Schachner, who have worked with me closely on different components of my own fieldwork and analysis and whose research on the resulting data I have drawn on extensively in this presentation. I am most grateful to Andrew Duff, Suzanne Eckert, Todd Howell, Gregson Schachner, and David Wilcox for their helpful comments and ideas on an earlier draft.

I am also most grateful to the Pueblo of Zuni for permitting the research on and around Heshot uła and to the late Mabel Hinkson-Hanshaw, who allowed us many seasons of productive work on her ranch. T. J. Ferguson and Roger Anyon provided critical advice and assistance during fieldwork at Zuni and much useful counsel in subsequent years. Charles Redman and Patty Jo Watson provided access to the invaluable data from the CARP project.

Notes

1. For example, we view the Hinkson site (Kintigh et al. 1996) as a site, but Beeson (1966) recorded the room blocks as 20-odd distinct sites.

2. The fuzziness of the shifts might also be a consequence of the inadequacy of the data and the imprecision of our inferential procedures.

3. Data for the two projects were analyzed separately, OBAP by Andrew Duff and HARP by Donna Glowacki and me.

4. This is likely for Spier 61, Kay Chee, Pescado Canyon, and Lower Deracho Ruin (Kintigh 1985).

5. The concern is whether the stylistic changes in ceramics that we use as temporal markers (especially use of glaze paint, the Pinedale design style, and use of a white-slipped bowl interior on Kwakina Polychrome) happen at the same time across the area (LeBlanc 1976).

6. Duff (2000) discusses the division of Pueblo IV into two periods.

7. In the El Morro Valley Pueblo de los Muertos is adjacent to the Scribe S site, CS142 is in the neighborhood of the CS56–64 cluster, and the Kluckhohn site is in the midst of a dense concentration of sites with more than 550 rooms, including the impressive Pettit site (Saitta 1991, 1994). Survey around the large Cienega/Mirabal site complex found room blocks with only 203 rooms. Our survey has demonstrated that Heshot uła developed in the midst of a cluster of at least 22 room blocks with 453 rooms that are dated from AD 1225 to 1275. However, informal reconnaissance around the Box S site has not revealed any evidence of a substantial concentration of earlier room blocks.

8. Three large sites have been found in the last 25 years, the Pueblo IV sites of Pescado Canyon and Spier 170 (the latter was not located by Spier, though he had a report of it) and the protohistoric site of Ah:kya:ya (Anyon 1992).

9. Note, however, that Heshot uła, which is nominally classed as oval, has a distinctly square corner, and three of the sites classed as rectangular (Box S, Spier 170, and the Fort Site) have a markedly rounded corner.

10. The latest tree-ring date from the Zuni area is AD 1349, from Atsinna in the El Morro Valley. Above the Mogollon Rim the latest prehistoric tree-ring date other than from clearly protohistoric sites is AD 1384, from the Showlow Ruin (Haury and Hargrave 1931). In the upper Little Colorado, closer to Zuni, there is an AD 1370 date from Raven Ruin and a 1378 date from Table Rock Pueblo (Duff 2002). The end of the Late Pueblo IV period at Zuni is not well dated but is certainly after AD 1350 and probably before 1400.

11. If there truly were *seven* cities of Cibola, as Spanish legend suggests, the last is up for grabs. Based on the documentary evidence, a case could be made for either Binna:wa or Chalo:wa. While collections from both sites look earlier than those from the six mentioned above (Kintigh 1985), we do not understand the precise timing of some major stylistic transitions. In any event, the historical evidence (Hodge 1937) makes clear that those two sites and Ah:kya:ya (Anyon 1992) were no longer occupied early in the historic era.

12. Even if the occupation of the H-Spear site were pushed into the Late Pueblo II interval, it would still have very few contemporaneous neighbors within a 5-km radius.

13. At least in our Heshotauthla survey, the relative proportions of Reserve to Puerco increase from Early to Late Pueblo II times.

14. This does not, of course, imply a lack of awareness or even interaction with quite distant groups. There may well have been multiple levels of more inclusive identities that were activated when circumstances warranted.

19 Zuni Traditional History and Cultural Geography

T. J. Ferguson

The traditions of the Zuni people derive from the occupation of their homeland for more than a millennium. These traditions are tied to named places in a cultural landscape that provides the Zuni people with the means to symbolize and recall the ancient past. The Zuni landscape incorporates an extensive geographical area and considerable time depth, representing the long period during which the Zuni people migrated from their place of emergence to Zuni Pueblo. The area occupied by their ancestors during this migration has continuing historical and religious significance to the Zuni people. It is through the cognition and use of this landscape that the ancient past is projected into the contemporary world and kept alive (Ferguson and Anyon 2001; Young 1987:4–9).

A robust archaeological theory of Zuni origins has to take into account Zuni traditional history and cultural geography. Zuni traditions constitute an independent source of historical information that can and should be used as a gauge in evaluating archaeological data. Inasmuch as Zuni traditions are congruent with archaeological data, we have corroboration for archaeological theories. In instances where archaeology and Zuni traditions diverge we are faced with the challenge to explain this disparity in a manner that makes anthropological sense and that respects both archaeological and traditional sources of knowledge.

The Zuni comprehend the archaeological record in terms of their ancestors, whom they call Ino:de:kwe or A:łashshina:we. These ancestors traveled far and wide on their migrations, and their history is maintained in a multiplicity of oral accounts conveyed by kiva groups, priesthoods, and religious societies. The Zuni view of the past is more dynamic than that of archaeologists, who rely on relatively static archaeological cultures as the framework for historical reconstruction (Dongoske et al. 1997:604). According to the Zuni, their ancestors were sequentially affiliated with many different archaeological cultures as they moved through time and space. At present, our methodological ability to use Zuni traditions in archaeological research is nascent. If we pursue this endeavor, however, one day it will be possible to transform southwestern archaeology into historical archaeology. And, like other forms of historical archaeology, the more sources of information we use in studying the past, the more we will learn.

The goal of this chapter is to summarize what we currently know about Zuni traditional history and cultural geography. The chapter begins with a review of the anthropological use and critique of Pueblo traditions as history. This review provides historical context for the approach taken in the rest of the chapter. The cultural context of Zuni oral traditions is then considered, and the sources of information for Zuni traditional history are identified and evaluated. Zuni traditions of origin and migration are next summarized in a synthetic overview. This is followed by a more detailed geographic analysis that maps the spatial domain inherent in Zuni traditions. The routes of Zuni migration are then compared to Zuni aboriginal land use to illustrate how traditional history relates to the use of montane areas above 2,000 m elevation. The chapter concludes with observations about what Zuni traditional history means in terms of the problem of Mogollon-Zuni relationships. The chapter thus provides a foundation for integrating Zuni traditional history with the archaeological data presented in the other chapters in this volume.

Anthropological Use and Critique of Pueblo Traditions as History

Anthropologists have been using Puebloan traditions as a source of historical information since the late nineteenth century. Over time the popularity of this approach has waxed and waned. At the outset of anthropological research in the Southwest scholars like Fewkes (1900) and Mindeleff (1891:16–40) treated Puebloan accounts of migration more or less as literal history. Other scholars were more cautious, neither accepting nor rejecting the history of migration narratives in their entirety. Curtis (1922:16), for instance, believed that the roots of migration "legends" are embedded in truth and that these traditions, while not historically accurate in all details, nonetheless provide an indication of the spatial directions that various groups traveled in their migrations.

In the early twentieth century, however, Boasian anthropologists vigorously sought to rebut the historicity of Puebloan migration accounts (Benedict 1925:460; Parsons in Stephen 1929:2). Benedict (1935:xlii–xliii, xv) treated Zuni traditions as idealistic "folktales" that entailed various literary combinations of events in different plot sequences but provided no basis for the reconstruction of history. Parsons, in her comprehensive comparative study of Pueblo religion, notes that Pueblo history is largely a tradition of migrations, "not of actual migrations but of migrations according to a traditional pattern" (1939:17) of emergence from the underworld, with accounts of subsequent migrations localized in the ruins that mark the southwestern landscape. Parsons asserts, "These legends have, I think, little or no historic validity; rather they are notable as indicating the ceremonial associations of maternal families and their clans—contemporaneous associations" (1933:25).

Kroeber took a similar approach in writing about Zuni, describing what he called an "unhistorical" conservatism of the present (1917:203–204). Kroeber considered Zuni origin and

migration narratives to be a mythological conceptualization of the past that explained the current situation, and he therefore thought anthropological use of Puebloan migration traditions was "pseudo-historic interpretation" (1917:135). However, Kroeber also acknowledged that the Zuni preserve fragments of a knowledge of the past that approximate what non-Indians consider history, and he thought that direct inquiry would reveal historical traditions, even if these were not the kind of discourse the Zuni would normally engage in. In this regard it is relevant to note that Bunzel (1932c:547) took a somewhat opposite view, noting that the Zuni are as preoccupied with the origins and early history of their people as the ancient Hebrews or Europeans.

Nonetheless, the Boasian perspective was adopted by many anthropologists in subsequent generations. Writing from an ethnological perspective, Eggan (1950:104) concluded that the Pueblo people tended to rationalize "mythology" to account for their present situation and that it was therefore impossible to take legends at face value. Many archaeologists expressed a similar view, although some of them also recognized that Puebloan traditions contained useful information. Kidder, for example, wrote, "Although I am disinclined to allow any great degree of historical accuracy to the Hopi and Zuni clan migration stories, they do seem to indicate that both communities received increments of population from the north and the south" (1962:341).

Other anthropologists, however, came to view "myths" as a form of tribal autobiography, handed down by oral transmission from one generation to the next. According to Wittfogel and Goldfrank (1943:17), the realistic foundation of myths cannot be questioned. However, they

thought the realities described in myths are reshaped by religious and artistic elements such that they include novelistic motifs with symbolic rather than historical meaning. For this reason, they thought scholars should carefully analyze myths with their limitations and possibilities in mind, including due consideration of the cultural context of oral transmission.

In commenting on the usefulness of Native American oral traditions, Goldfrank observed:

Archeology and history are giving us a firm fundament of facts. But even in the Southwest where we already have a very considerable body of such data, many, and to the ethnologist crucial, aspects of culture have not as yet been clarified, and quite possibly may never be clarified by these means. Thus, we have to be willing to use other methods to gain insight, even when we recognize their shortcomings. It would be foolish to refuse to use anecdotes and myths because certain elements included in them can be shown to be fictional. . . . [T]hey should not stop us from continuing to use dynamic concepts as working hypotheses, even when exceptions can be documented [1954:658–659].

After 1946, in large part due to the Indian Claims Commission, archaeologists like Florence Hawley Ellis began to seriously reconsider the historical information in Pueblo traditions. Migration was viewed as a problem in which archaeological and linguistic relationships could be used to substantiate, disprove, or aid in interpretation of tradition. Ellis (1967:35) noted that Pueblo peoples are not history minded in the sense of assigning dates to the various events of migration but that under the "frosting of symbolism" there remains a framework of events that can be checked with archaeological data to provide a history of Pueblo migrations. She cautioned, however, that "in considering the possibility that Pueblo oral history is a more or less specific account of past movements of a people, it is necessary to look past most of the heavy embroidery resulting from native preoccupation with religion, except as explanations after the fact" (Ellis 1979:439).

In commenting on the problem of reconstructing migrations, Ellis concluded that "the very difficulty of complete agreement upon its solution, after some seventy years of considerable anthropological concentration on an area in which even the newcomer is struck by the broad parallels between the prehistoric and modern Pueblo culture suggests the difficulties confronting any serious reconstructionist" (1951:150). Ford et al. amplified this point by observing that Puebloan traditional history, when interpreted literally, has confounded many archaeologists and led to "elaborate, if not impossible, cultural reconstructions" (1972:10–12). However, they also note that close examination of archaeological data and traditional history reveals that "it is obvious that migrations were a diverse complexity of fission and fusion that cannot be wished away" (Ford et al. 1972:21). Archaeologists have to deal with ancient migrations and with the Puebloan traditions about these movements.

Today, implementation of the Native American Graves Protection and Repatriation Act (NAGPRA) mandates that oral traditions be considered along with archaeology and other lines of evidence in determining cultural affiliation between present-day Indian tribes and past identifiable groups. As defined in NAGPRA, oral traditions include

many types of information, including what some non-Indians call "myths." We have thus entered yet another period, when archaeologists and anthropologists are coming to terms with what Puebloan origin and migration traditions mean in the interpretation of the archaeological record.

"Myth" is an intellectually charged term with two fundamental meanings (Lévi-Strauss 1978:29–37). First, a myth can be understood as a traditional story, either partially or wholly fictitious, providing an explanation that embodies popular ideas about natural or social phenomena, religious beliefs, and rituals involving supernatural persons and events. Many tribal accounts of origin and migration contain "mythical" elements in this regard. Second, the term "myth" is also used to denote widely held stories or beliefs that are entirely untrue. In this second sense a myth is a misconception or misrepresentation of the truth based on an exaggerated or idealized conception of the past. Although scholarly analysis of "myths" can provide powerful and useful information for historical research, many people construe the word "myth" to be a derogatory term implying a false story. For this reason, the neutral terms "oral tradition" and "traditional narrative" are substituted for "myth" whenever these terms apply in this chapter.

The perspective pursued in this chapter is that Zuni traditions of origin and migration encapsulate important historical information. These traditions are more than literal history because they include powerful metaphorical and symbolic information of a religious nature. As one Zuni exegetist pointed out after providing a list of the places referenced in his origin account, "These are the places that are discussed as a trail, but it is a religious idea, or religious trail that is recited in the prayer and not an

actual path of people walking on the trail" (Ferguson and Hart 1985:21). Another religious leader in a similar circumstance remarked, "The trail or road is one of . . . symbolic nature. The place names and the symbolic trail are the ones we have been talking about, the actual road is not the same as the symbolic road" (Ferguson and Hart 1985:21).

Fieldwork with Zuni elders, however, indicates that the migration routes described in Zuni traditions are in fact grounded in real places, most of which are still identifiable by virtue of their continuing use or geographical description in cultural landscapes. While Zuni traditions have certain symbolic and metaphorical dimensions, they are also part of a real landscape traversed during pilgrimages and visits to shrines. The named places that help define this landscape gain meaning from their historic context. Zuni geography thus provides a setting for both esoteric meanings and historic knowledge. This geography constitutes an important line of evidence in the archaeological reconstruction of the Zuni past.

Cultural Context of Zuni Oral Traditions

The Zuni people have a rich and well-documented body of oral traditions. These traditions include *chimiky' ana-kona penane*, "from the beginning talk," which describes Zuni emergence and subsequent migration to Zuni Pueblo, the Middle Place (Benedict 1935; Bunzel 1932b, 1932c; Cushing 1896; Parsons 1923; Stevenson 1904), and *telapnawe*, which are folktales or legends (e.g., Boas 1922; Cushing 1901; Handy 1918; Harrington 1929; Nusbaum 1926; Parsons 1917, 1918b; ten Kate 1917). Zuni folktales are generally set in and around the Zuni Valley and are often told for didactic purposes or entertainment. Some historical narratives (e.g., Bunzel 1933; Parsons 1918b; Quam 1972) recount "ancient times" but describe livestock and thus refer to the period after AD 1540. Other traditional narratives do not provide information about origin or migration (Tedlock 1972).

This chapter analyzes the traditional history embedded in chimiky' anakona penane. The narratives in this body of oral literature are referred to as "talks," and many of them are preserved in fixed ritualistic form and recited as chants or prayers during ceremonies. These traditions are known in Zuni as *tewusu pena:we*, "prayer talk" (Bunzel 1932c:548, 1932d:615). These prayers and talks are formally learned using a repetition of fixed formulae and are performed with gestures and oral elements that supplement their verbal content. Fixed traditions in Zuni culture are transferred as esoteric knowledge that sanctions the ceremonial organization of the tribe. There is not a single origin talk but an array of talks, each one explaining how the members of a specific religious group came to live at Zuni Pueblo. The talk of Kyaklo, for instance, recounts the origin of the Zuni people, the basis of the Kyaklo ceremony, and the migrations of the Zuni people in search of the Middle Place (Bunzel 1932c:548; Cushing 1896:373). Curtis describes this talk:

> Páuṭiwa, the Ká-mássânna ("god chief"), directed his Péqinně, Kyáklo to prepare the people for a visit from the Kákkâ ("gods"). So Kyáklo was carried from Káhlualawa to Ittiwanna on the backs of the Kóyĕmǎśhi, and after repeating to the people the story of their emergence from the lower worlds and their wanderings in search of the centre of the earth, he told them to

build six kivas in which to receive the Kákkâ eight days later [1926a:127].

Quadrennially in March on the sixth day after the new moon, Kyaklo is carried into the village on the backs of the Koyemshi, or Mudheads. He is painted with the pink clay obtained at Kołuwala:wa, his home. Kyaklo descends into the kiva and joins other priests. "He then repeats very rapidly (and indistinctly, owing to his mask) an exactly worded synopsis of the origin and migration legend. The sentences are largely suggestive; that is, the recital is not a detailed narrative, but consists of little more than mnemonic captions uttered in chanted tones" (Curtis 1926a:128). Kyaklo repeats his prayer in all of the kivas and is carried away to the west toward the sacred lake.

Additional talks are maintained by other Zuni priesthoods and religious societies (Bunzel 1932d; Parsons 1930:2–5, 1939:966–967). Few of these ritual recitals have been recorded at Zuni (Parsons 1939:215).

In addition to the esoteric versions of the origin talks there are also narratives that recount the main outlines of Zuni origin and migration as known by uninitiated members of the tribe. As Bunzel notes, in these exoteric versions "the history myth is not fixed in form or expression and varies in comprehensiveness according to the special knowledge of the narrator" (1932c:548). These less esoteric and more comprehensive accounts are often told by older men to younger men in informal settings in the kivas during the winter solstice or other ceremonies. The record of these accounts is fragmentary because these narratives are often considered too etiological or explanatory of ceremonial life to be told freely to outsiders (Parsons 1939:216).

Still other versions of origin and

migration accounts are performed for family members, often around the hearth during winter (Benedict 1935:xxxii). These accounts vary because each narrator stresses the organization or ceremony he is associated with or because he has a didactic objective specific to his audience. These public renditions of origin and migration traditions are the narrative form that has most often been shared with anthropologists and made available in publications (e.g., Parsons 1923). This circumstance adds variability to the documented body of historical information, and different versions of origin and migration narratives referring to the same incidents can be quite different (Benedict 1935:257).

The reduction of oral traditions to a written form is essential for their scholarly study. However, it should be noted that this process is accompanied by a certain cultural danger because it reduces a dynamic oral tradition to a more static and narrow view (Mills and Ferguson 1998:40). Zuni tribal members reading this chapter should realize it represents an anthropological view of Zuni traditional knowledge, and, as such, it is secondary to the teachings they receive from tribal elders in their kivas, religious societies, and homes. As a scholarly work this chapter is subject to revision as the Zuni people reveal more about their traditional history or offer corrections for the inevitable mistakes and cultural misunderstandings that may be inadvertently incorporated into the manuscript.

Sources of Information for Zuni Traditional History

Anthropological documentation of Zuni origin and migration narratives includes esoteric and exoteric versions recounted by Zuni tribal members, synthetic and interpretative abstracts of Zuni traditions arranged in a manner coherent to scholars, and depositions of Zuni religious leaders taken during litigation of land claims. Several publications provide accounts or analyses compiled from other sources or general abstracts of Zuni traditions (Bahr 1977; Bartlett 1914; Cushing 1920; Lévi-Strauss 1967: 202–228; Parsons 1930, 1939:218–236; Wiget 1980). Secondary or general accounts offer useful background information to corroborate or amplify other publications but provide little locational data that can be analyzed geographically for the purposes of this chapter. The nine most useful sources of information about Zuni origin and migration are discussed below.

Two sources are based on the initial ethnological research at Zuni sponsored by the Smithsonian Institution between 1879 and 1901. Cushing's (1896) "Outlines of Zuni Creation Myths" is the first extensive treatment of Zuni traditions. In this classic work Cushing provides both a synthesis of "pristine Zuni history" and abstracts of Zuni accounts of origin and migration in a poetic interpretation rather than a verbatim translation. Cushing identifies 24 locations associated with Zuni origin and migration. In "The Zuñi Indians: Their Mythology, Esoteric Fraternities, and Ceremonies," the first comprehensive ethnography of the Zuni, Stevenson (1904:20–62) includes a section on Zuni "mythology" that provides abstracts of traditions about the creation of the universe, the emergence of the Zuni people into the present world, and their subsequent migration to Zuni Pueblo. Stevenson (1904:73–88) also provides a Zuni-language transcription and free translation of the origin talk ritually performed by Kyaklo during the initiation of new kiva members. The performance of the Kyaklo constitutes a reenactment of a visit

made by this religious personage when he traveled from Kołuwala:wa to Itiwana in the ancient past. In the prayer of Kyaklo documented by Stevenson the names of 54 springs and other places at which the Zuni stopped during their migration are identified. Stevenson (1904:407–569) also provides abstracts of the migration traditions maintained by Zuni religious societies.

Five sources provide information published between 1923 and 1935. With one exception these sources represent the work of students sent by Boas to work at Zuni. A secular version of Zuni origin traditions was published by Parsons (1923). This provides an example of Zuni traditions in the form in which they may be known by anyone in the pueblo. Curtis (1926a:113–123), the sole non-Boasian scholar publishing in this period, provides an extensive abstract of the Zuni account of origin and migration in volume 17 of *The North American Indian*. While best known for his photographs, Curtis and his staff of researchers also compiled existing ethnographic information about the tribes featured in his publications. In many respects the account provided by Curtis is similar to those of Cushing and Stevenson, but Curtis includes additional information that demonstrates that he collected some original ethnographic data in his work at Zuni.

Bunzel (1932b, 1932c, 1932d) presents a substantial amount of information about Zuni traditions in a series of three publications. This information includes a Zuni-language version and English translation of the origin talk performed by the *komosona* (kachina chief) during the final initiation of boys in the kachina society (Bunzel 1932c:548–584). This talk is an esoteric ritual form of the origin narrative recited for purposes of instruction during the winter retreat.

In an analysis of traditional narratives as poetry Bunzel provides the Zuni text and English translation for Sayatasha's Night Chant. Sayatasha, a Zuni *kokko* (kachina), plays a leading role in the Shalako Ceremony, and the Night Chant is performed by Shalako priests during the public culmination of the ritual. This chant, 750 lines long, identifies 29 springs associated with the migration from Kołuwala:wa to Zuni Pueblo (Bunzel 1932d:710–756). Benedict (1935:1–6) treats Zuni traditions as a form of folklore and provides a nonesoteric version of emergence and migration. Benedict's account refers to elements recorded by other scholars but not included in her account.

The final source of information about Zuni origin and migration is provided by 12 depositions of Zuni religious leaders taken during litigation of Zuni land claims in 1980 (Ferguson 1995; Hart 1995a). These depositions were conducted by lawyers interrogating Zuni religious leaders testifying under oath about sites used by the Zuni for religious and utilitarian purposes. While Zuni religious leaders declined to reveal esoteric information, they provided information about Zuni sacred sites by identifying their names, locations, historical context, and religious use. Several deponents provided a catalog of place-names mentioned in their prayers. The religious leader serving as Kyaklo, for instance, identified 37 places in the prayer he performs during kiva initiations. Another deponent, prominent in the Newekwe Society, started in the middle of his prayer at Shiba:bulima and enumerated the places mentioned along the migration route to Zuni. After he did this he then proceeded to name shrines from the place of emergence to Shiba:bulima. Edmund J. Ladd, the Zuni anthropologist who served as interpreter during the depositions,

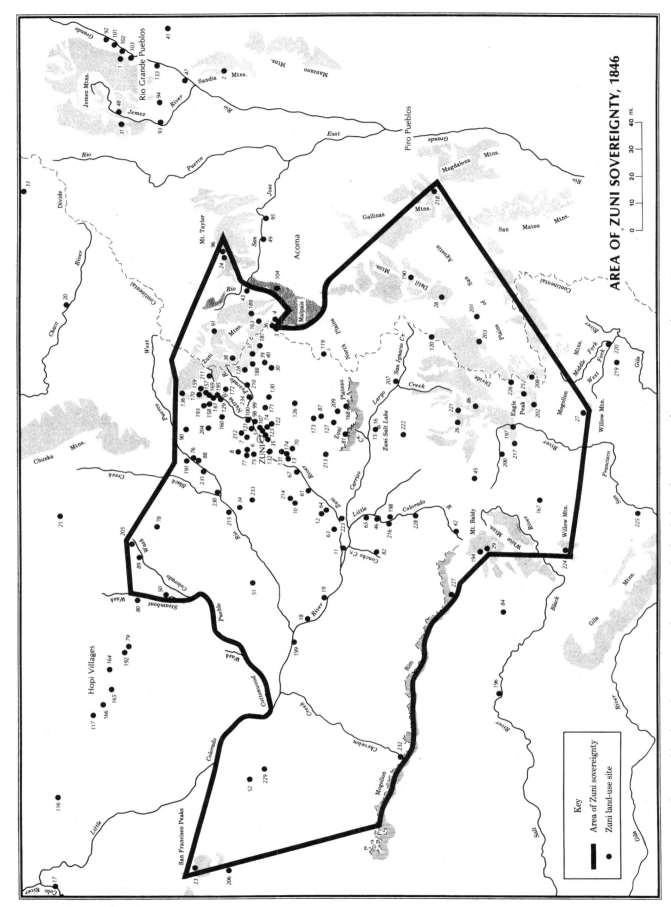

Figure 19.1. Zuni aboriginal land in relation to sites documented in land-claim depositions (from Ferguson and Hart 1985:20).

describes these depositions as "some of the most remarkable ethnological documents that have ever been created for any purpose" (1995:232).

The Zuni land-claim depositions formed the basis for several academic publications (Ferguson 1995; Ladd 1983), including *A Zuni Atlas* (Ferguson and Hart 1985). *A Zuni Atlas* maps 234 land-use sites within and outside the area claimed by the Zuni, an area that the United States Claims Court determined was their aboriginal land in 1846 (see fig. 19.1). *A Zuni Atlas* includes an abstract of Zuni origin and migration that integrates information from the Zuni depositions with previously published sources (Ferguson and Hart 1985: 20–23). It should be noted that reanalysis of the depositions for this chapter yielded additional information about the use of specific sites that was not included in *A Zuni Atlas* (a point that anyone using the atlas for cultural resources management should take into account).

Critical reviews of the published sources summarizing Zuni traditions point out that they contain considerable shortcomings and distortions (Bunzel 1932c:547; Tedlock 1983:34–36). Bunzel, for instance, asserts that Cushing's (1896) account "contains endless poetic and metaphysical glossing of the basic elements, most of which explanatory matter probably originated in Cushing's own mind" (1932c:547). Tedlock (1983:34) echoes this view, adding that Cushing's work incorporates a monotheism that reflects nineteenth-century anthropology rather than Zuni belief. Bunzel (1932c:547) criticizes Stevenson's (1904) work because it seeks to provide a coherent account of mythology in a relatively narrow relation to ritual. Tedlock adds to this criticism by noting that Stevenson provides descriptive summaries of Zuni performances rather than verbatim translations and that she "ignores the possibility of alternate versions and attempts to place each story in a chronological sequence which reflects her own Western preoccupation with history more than actual Zuni practice" (1983:36). Parson's (1923) version of Zuni origin and migration is criticized because it represents folklore that "suffers in vividness and subtlety of expression from having been recorded through an interpreter" (Bunzel 1932c:547). Tedlock (1983:36) criticizes the work of all the Boasian fieldworkers at Zuni, including Parsons, Handy, Bunzel, Benedict, and Boas himself, because they attempted literal translations but failed because of methodological issues relating to transcription and lack of attention to parallelism.

Even with the limitations described by Bunzel and Tedlock, the nine published sources of Zuni traditions contain important information about the early history and migrations of the Zuni people. Analyzed as a set, they can be productively used to check one another and to reveal the geographical patterns inherent in Zuni traditional history.

A Composite Overview of Zuni Origin and Migration

An overview of Zuni origin and migration is presented here as a prelude to the more detailed geographic analysis that follows in the remainder of the chapter. This summary maps the broad geographical patterns of Zuni migrations as they are recounted in the nine primary sources of Zuni traditions (see fig. 19.2). This composite account, or abstract, represents a simplified and generalized synthesis of information and does not depict all of the places mentioned in Zuni traditional history (Ferguson and Hart 1985:21). Generalization is necessary because some events are recounted as occurring at different locations in different narratives, so only the major incidents and main thrust in geographical movement are depicted.

The Zuni people emerged at Chimik'yana'kya dey'a, a place deep within a canyon along the Colorado River. Prior to their emergence, under divine instruction, the Zuni had learned many prayers, rituals, and sacred talks. Thus, they were guided by religious societies, including the Shiwannaqe (Priesthood), Newekwe (Galaxy Society), Saniakyaqe (Hunter Society), Łe'wekwe (Sword Swallower Society), and Make'lhanna:kwe (Big Fire Society). As described in the origin talks, the Zuni migrated up the valley of Kyawanahononnai, or "Red River," the Little Colorado River. As they traveled the Zuni stopped and built villages and stayed in them for "four days and four nights," a ritual phrase that Zuni exegetists explain denotes a longer period of time variously interpreted as four years, four centuries, or four millennia.

At one of the first springs they came to slime was washed off their bodies, their webbed hands and feet were cut, and their genitals, originally placed on their foreheads, were rearranged so that people came to appear as they do today. The migration continued, and the springs, stopping places, and mountains that were encountered became sacred shrines remembered in prayers, with the people returning to them for ritual pilgrimages after they moved on.

As the Zuni moved eastward they traveled to Sunha:k'yabachu Yalanne (the San Francisco Peaks), Kumanch an A'l Akkwe'a (Canyon Diablo), and Denatsali Im'a (Woodruff Butte). At one point in the Little Colorado River valley the Zuni were given a choice of eggs that led to their splitting into several groups. One group chose the plain colored egg, from which

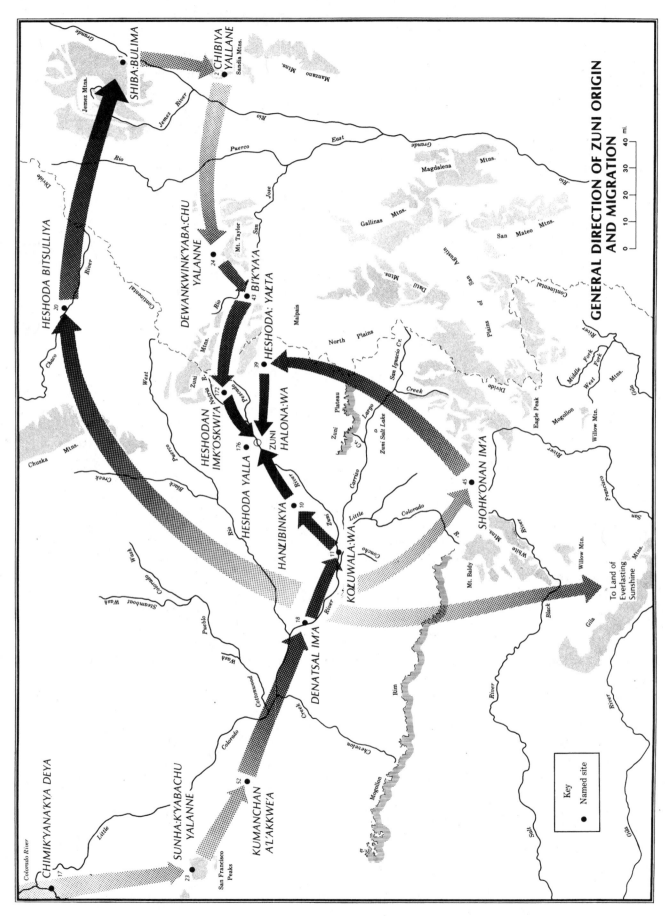

Figure 19.2. General direction of Zuni origin and migration (from Ferguson and Hart 1985:20).

hatched a brightly colored parrot. This group, referred to as *i'nodekwe wshimalde dekyalenankwe ahwakona* (ancient ones who journeyed to the Land of the Everlasting Sun), or the "lost others," migrated far to the south, never to return. A second group chose a brightly colored blue egg, from which hatched a black raven. This group was destined to continue toward the Middle Place.

As the group that chose the brightly colored egg continued its migration, it split again, forming three groups. One group continued eastward, arriving at a spot near the confluence of the Little Colorado and Zuni rivers, a location associated with the creation of the Koyemshi (Mudheads), born as the result of an incestuous act between a brother and sister who had been sent ahead to scout the trail. As the Zuni began to cross the river the children turned into water creatures, biting their mothers, who were carrying them. The mothers then dropped their children into the stream. The remainder of the mothers were instructed not to let their children go, and after they crossed to the other side the water creatures turned back into children. The Koyemshi and the water creatures who had been dropped entered a lake at Kołuwala:wa, where they were transformed into kokko. The kokko continue to reside in Kachina Village, sometimes referred to in English as Zuni Heaven, as this is where Zuni go after death. During their migration the Zuni received instructions about ritual use of Kołuwala:wa.

From Kołuwala:wa the Zuni traveled to the canyon of Hanłibinkya, where the Zuni clans received their names, an event memorialized in the petroglyphs still visible at the location. As they continued east the leaders of the Zuni encountered a group of people at Heshoda Yala:wa, and a

fierce battle ensued. The Zuni retreated back to Hanłibinkya, where the Ahayu:da were created by the Sun Father in the foam of a waterfall. The Ahayu:da led the Zuni into another epic battle, lasting four days, and this time they overcame the people at Heshoda Yala:wa. The people of the Yellow Corn at Heshoda Yala:wa had turned black because of medicine they used to protect themselves during the battle. These people were spared because they possessed a powerful sacred object, and because of their color they became known as the Black Corn people. Heshoda Yala:wa was determined to be close to but not at their final destination, so the Zuni continued their migration to a series of settlements in the Zuni River valley, eventually settling at Halona:Itiwana, the Middle Place, now called Zuni Pueblo.

As the main body of Zuni journeyed directly up the Zuni River valley to arrive at Halona:Itiwana, other groups followed a different trail. A group following the Łe'wekwe (Sword Swallower Society) and the Make'lhanna:kwe (Big Fire Society) traveled north. This group migrated through the Rio Puerco valley and the San Juan Basin, eventually arriving at Shiba:bulima, the origin place of many of the Zuni medicine societies, located in the Jemez Mountains west of the Rio Grande. From Shiba:bulima this group migrated southward to Chi:biya Yalanne (Sandia Peak) and then westward to Dewankwin K'yaba:chu Yalanne (Mount Taylor) and Heshodan Imk'oskwi'a (near Nutria). Here these people discovered the rest of the Zuni living at Halona:Itiwana, and they were reunited with their relatives at Zuni Pueblo.

Another group migrated to the south with the Newekwe (Galaxy Society). This group traveled along the upper Little Colorado River valley to

the round valley beneath Shohk'onan Im'a, "Flute Mountain," today known as Escudilla Peak. From here they migrated to the northeast, to Aqualhenna:yalla:we, the upper drainage of the Zuni River in the Zuni Mountains. This group lived for a time at Heshoda Ts'in'a (Pescado) and other villages. This southern group eventually migrated westward, joining relatives at Halona:Itiwana, where the Zuni people were at long last reunited.

Geographical Analysis of Places Associated with Zuni Origin and Migration

The following geographical analysis of places associated with Zuni origin and migration talks provides a more detailed appreciation of Zuni traditions by mapping individual sites rather than the broad directions of travel. A total of 112 place-names are identified in the nine published sources recounting Zuni traditional history (see table 19.1). The locations of 49 of these places, 44 percent of the total, are known well enough to depict them on figure 19.3. An additional 28 places listed in table 19.1 occur on the Zuni Reservation but are not placed on figure 19.3 because of issues of scale; that is, they are simply too numerous to map at the scale of the map. Although Zuni religious leaders know the locations of the sites on their reservation, the sites are not placed on a larger-scale map in order to maintain their security by not divulging their exact position. Minimally, therefore, the Zuni know the location of 77 sites, or 69 percent of the total number of places mentioned in origin and migration traditions. It is likely that Zuni religious leaders actually know the locations of more sites than they have chosen to reveal to non-Indians.

Table 19.1 divides the places identified in Zuni traditions into five

Table 19.1 Places Associated with Origin and Migration Talks

Map No.	Place-Names	A	B	C	D	E	F	G	H	I
		\<References spanning A–I\>								

Map No.	Place-Names	A	B	C	D	E	F	G	H	I
Emergence and initial migration										
17	Chimik'yana'kya dey'a (Place of Emergence, Grand Canyon)	(1)	1	1	(1)	1	(1)		(1)	1
	Ii'mikĭanakate'a (zone of emergence in Grand Canyon)		3							
	Yamun K'yay'a (zone of emergence in Grand Canyon)		2			5				2
	Ts'ik'on K'yay'a (zone of emergence in Grand Canyon)		3							3
	Danin K'yay'a (zone of emergence in Grand Canyon)		4							4
	Da:melank'yay'a (in drainage of Little Colorado River)	4	5		3	5			4	5
	K'eyadi:wa or K'eyadina:wa (in drainage of Little Colorado River)	2	6					7		X
	A'wisho ᵗkĭai'akwi (Moss Spring, in drainage of Little Colorado River)		2	7		2	2		2	X
	Banelunan K'yay'a (in drainage of Little Colorado River)			8						6
	Ladaw K'yay'a (in drainage of Little Colorado River)			9						7
	ᵗHlän'ihlkoha ᵗkĭai'akwi (Aspen Spring, in drainage of Little Colorado River)			10						
	Tésak'ya Ÿäla (Place of Nude Mountains, in drainage of Little Colorado River)	3								
	A'wełuyan kaiakwi (Massed Cloud Spring, in drainage of Little Colorado River)						3			
	Ci'pololon kaia (Mist Spring / Fog Place, in drainage of Little Colorado River)	5	4			7	4			
	Ubulemi (in drainage of Little Colorado River)			11		4	6			8
	Tśiko-ţíqawĕ (in drainage of Little Colorado River)					6				
	Batsichina:wa (in drainage of Little Colorado River)			12						9
	U'teyan ĭn'kwi (Flower Place, in drainage of Little Colorado River)			13						
	To:papik / a-ya (in drainage of Little Colorado River)			14						10
23	Sunha:K'yabachu Yalanne (San Francisco Peaks)									X
52	Kumanch an A'l Akkwe'a (Canyon Diablo)									X
18	Denatsali Im'a (Woodruff Butte, in drainage of Little Colorado River)				7					11
19	Da:bilayanku (east of Woodruff Butte in drainage of Little Colorado River)									X
	K'yashhida K'yay'a (in drainage of Little Colorado River)			15						12
	Molan K'yay'a (in drainage of Little Colorado River)			16						13
11	Hadin K'yay'a (Listening Spring, near confluence of Zuni and Little Colorado Rivers)		6	17		8				14
11	Kołuwala:wa (Zuni Heaven, near confluence of Zuni and Little Colorado Rivers)	6	5	18	(8)	9	8	1	(5)	14
63	K'ya:dul Łana (along lower Zuni River)			19						15
	Te'wulᵗla i'tiwa pi'ᵗkĭaia kwi (Valley Middle Watercress Place)			20				2		
10	Hanłibinkya (Hardscrabble Wash)	7	7	21	9	10	9	4	6	16
64	He / epat / chi:wa (lower Zuni River)			22				3		17
	Heshoda Yala:wa (House Mountain, on Zuni Reservation)	8	10		10		11			
	Heshatoyalakwi (on Zuni Reservation)				11					
	A' 'kälikwin (Rock-in-the-River)					(11)	10			
127	Kyama:kya (Jalarosa Draw)		8							X

Table 19.1 *Continued*

Map No.	Place-Names	A	B	C	D	E	F	G	H	I
Migration along the middle route										
236	Kyana Baɬta (last series of springs place, Zuni River Valley)			23				5		
235	Kyana Itiwanna (middle series of springs place, Zuni River Valley)			24				6		
66	Idwa K'yan'a (Middle Spring, Zuni River Valley)			25						18
67	Kolo:wisi An K'yakw'a (Zuni River Valley)			26				8		19
	Pi'kĭaia kwi (Watercress Place, Zuni River Valley)			27				7	3	
	K'ya'ts'i' K'yan'a (Zuni Reservation)			28						20
	Patsikänakwi (Zuni Reservation)							9		
	Bo'sho'wa (spring in cavity of a mound, Zuni Reservation)			29				10		X
	Lu'kĭana ʰkĭai'akwi (Ashes Spring, Zuni Reservation)			30				11		
	To'seluna ʰkĭai'a' (High-Grass Spring, Zuni Reservation)			31				12		
	A'mitolan ʰkĭai'akwi (Rainbow Spring, Zuni Reservation)			32				13		
	K'yabe'Kwayin'a (Zuni River Valley)									X
	Wa'tsita'nakwi (Zuni River Valley)							15		
	Sha'lak'ona:wa (Zuni Reservation)			33				16		21
	Ts'oklik Ikna:wa (Zuni River Valley)									22
13	K'ya'na'a or K'yapkwayina'a (Ojo Caliente, Zuni Reservation)		9	34				14		X
	A'ɬabatts'i'a (Zuni Reservation)			36				18		24
	A'ts'ina:wa (Zuni Reservation)			37				19		23
	Bi:shu'k'yay'a (Zuni Reservation)			38				20		25
	K'yan Uɬ'a (Zuni Reservation)			39				21		26
	Doloknana'a (Zuni Reservation)			40				22		X
	K'ya:dechi'a (Zuni Reservation)			41				23		27
	Uhana'a (Zuni Reservation)			35				17		28
	Opbon Biya'a (Zuni Reservation)			42				24		X
	A:yaya'kya (Zuni Reservation)			43				25		29
5	Dowa Yalanne (Zuni Reservation)	25	14	44	16			27		30
	Ideɬakukya dey'a (Zuni Reservation)			45						31
	Häl'on kwa'ton (ants entering, Zuni Reservation)			46				26		
	Ä'sha ʰkĭaia (Vulva Spring, Zuni Reservation)			47						
	Kĭa'nayältokwi (Spring High Place, Zuni Reservation)			48						
	Wilatsu'u:kw An K'yan'a (Zuni Reservation)			49						33
	Sumk'yana'a (Zuni Reservation)			50						32
Migration along the northern route										
	Úk'yawane (Rio Puerco)	9								
	Hékwainankwin (Mud-Issuing Springs, Rio Puerco)	10								
88	/amequelleyawa (Manuelito Canyon)									X

Table 19.1 *Continued*

Map No.	Place-Names	References A	B	C	D	E	F	G	H	I
89	Shoya K'yaba'a (near Ganado)									X
21	Canyon de Chelly									X
116	Bittsemi Deyatchi:wa (on Second Mesa)									X
117	Mokkwi Deyatchi:wa (Hoatvela)									X
118	Kyane:lu Yala:we (near Shiprock)									X
	Rope Hill								7	
20	Heshoda Bitsulliya or Ki:wihtsi Bitsulliya (Chaco Canyon)									X
22	Mesa Verde									X
1	Shiba:bulima (Stone Lions Shrine, Bandelier National Monument)	11		55	14	13				X
133	K'yawa:na Łana'a (Rio Grande)									X
	Tsilhinn/yalh/a (ford at Rio Grande)									X
135	Dopbolliya:K'yan'a (Taos Blue Lake)									X
101	/iyanik/a:waisha (Rio Grande)									X
102	Yash:tik/u:tu (Rio Grande)									X
103	Mi/ashu:k/awa/ka (Rio Grande)									X
31	He:mushina Yala:we (Jemez Mountains)									X
92	Kiwaikukuk/a (Jemez Mountains)									X
2	Chi:biya Yalanne (Sandia Peak)		X							
24	Dewankwin K'yaba:chu Yalanne (Mount Taylor)									X
96	Shak'yay'a (a peak on Mount Taylor)									X
97	Kashi:kuk/a:tu (at eastern end of Zuni Mountains)									X
39	Heshoda Yałta (the village on top of El Morro)									X
128	Habana: A'lakkwe'a (northeast of Ramah)									X
195	Doya (Nutria)		X		15	15			8	

Migration along the southern route

Map No.	Place-Names	References A	B	C	D	E	F	G	H	I
	Shohk'onan Im'a ("Home of the Flute-canes," or Round Valley)	12								X
45	Shohk'ona: Yalanne ("Flute Mountain," or Escudilla Peak)	13								X
	Yála Tétsinapa ("Mountain of Space-speaking Markings")	14								
	Shíwina Téu'hlkwaina (Upper Zuni River valley)	15								
238	Heshoda Ts'in'a ("Town of the Speech Markings," or Pescado, Zuni Reservation)	16								
	Places close to and at the middle									
	Kwakina (Zuni Reservation)	17								
175	Hawikku (Zuni Reservation)	18				12				X
	K'ya'na'a (Ojo Caliente)	19								
	Hampasawan (Zuni Reservation)	21								
58	Kyaki:ma (Zuni Reservation)	22								34
72	Mats'a:kya (Zuni Reservation)	23	11	51	12			28	9	35

Table 19.1 *Continued*

Map No.	Place-Names	A	B	C	D	E	F	G	H	I
						References				
174	Kechiba:wa (Zuni Reservation)									X
	Komkwayikya dey'a or K/lolink/a-ya (Zuni Reservation)			52						36
	Halona:wa (ant place, Zuni Reservation))			53						X
	Komkwayikya dey'a (Zuni Reservation)									36
9	Dwankwin Onan Baniyna'a (Zuni Reservation)									X
83	Halona:Itiwana (Zuni Reservation)	24	12	54	13	14	12	29	10	37
15	Ma'k'yaya'a (Zuni Salt Lake)		13							

Note: Numbers denote the order in which places are discussed in the narrative; numbers in parentheses are places that are discussed but not named. Numbers for Zuni land claims denote the order of the prayer of Kyaklo. *X*s denote migration sites referenced in Stevenson or Zuni claims from contexts other than prayers.
References: (A) Cushing (1896); (B) Stevenson (1904); (C) Stevenson (1904)—Kyaklo; (D) Parsons (1923); (E) Curtis (1926a); (F) Bunzel (1932c); (G) Bunzel (1932d); (H) Benedict (1935); (I) Zuni Land Claims, Ferguson and Hart (1985).

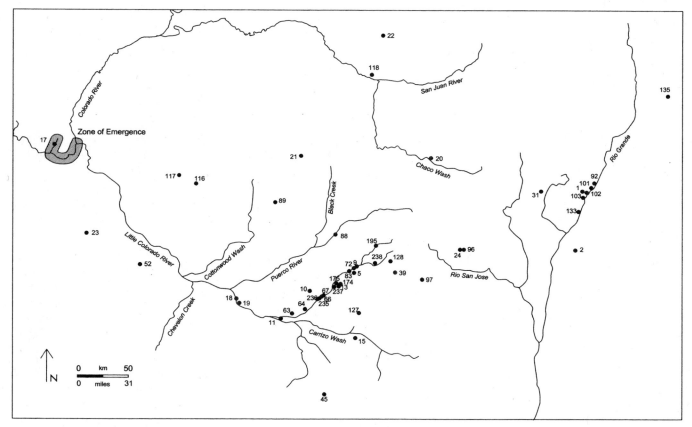

Figure 19.3. Location of 49 places referred to in Zuni origin and migration talks (see table 19.1 for site numbers and names).

sections, including emergence and initial migration, migration along the middle route, migration along the northern route, migration along the southern route, and places close to and at the middle. These divisions are not found in Zuni traditions; they are imposed simply to facilitate the investigation of Zuni cultural geography. As discussed below, many sites occur in more than one Zuni tradition; for example, some sites are referred to in both the traditions of Kyaklo and the traditions of religious societies. Different sources sometimes include the same sites but list them in a different order. The numbers in table 19.1 denote the order in which places are discussed in particular narratives; numbers in parentheses indicate places that are referred to but not identified by name. Two columns are derived from information provided by Stevenson (1904), one for her general abstract of the Zuni origin tradition and a second for the places mentioned in the prayer of Kyaklo. Numbers in the column for information from the Zuni land claim indicate the order of sites in the prayer of Kyaklo; an "X" is used to indicate migration sites referenced in other contexts, for example, information provided about the migration of religious societies.

Emergence and Initial Migration

The place of emergence is Chimik'yana'kya dey'a, which the Zuni locate at Ribbon Falls, located along Bright Angel Creek in the Grand Canyon (Hart 1995b:3). According to traditional history, the Zuni emerged here in a group that included the Havasupai and Hualapai. The Hopi emerged at the same time but in a different location in the Grand Canyon. In describing Chimik'yana'kya dey'a one Zuni leader recently wrote:

The Zunis or A:shiwi as we call ourselves, came into the first light of Sun Father at a beautiful spot near Ribbon Falls. Naturally the first things that happened to us and the first things that we saw became prominent in our prayers, ceremonies, and religion. The point from which the first ray of sunlight reached us over a spot on the canyon rim; the plants that grew along the stream that flows from Ribbon Falls to the Colorado River; the birds and animals that we saw as we traveled out into the world; the brilliantly colored minerals in the rock walls of the canyon; all of these things are recounted sacred in our prayers, and have a central place in our ceremonial religious activities and way of life [Chimoni and Hart 1994:1].

Chimik'yana'kya dey'a has symbolic importance in Zuni culture, but it is also a natural landscape with features that are still used. Pilgrimages to Chimik'yana'kya dey'a continue to be undertaken to collect water, plants, and other resources for religious use at Zuni Pueblo. The place of emergence, sometimes conceptualized as the womb of Mother Earth, is physically connected to Zuni Pueblo through an umbilical cord formed by the Colorado, Little Colorado, and Zuni rivers (Hart 1995b:8). It is along these rivers that the Zuni people were instructed to migrate to find the Middle Place.

As they left Chimik'yana'kya dey'a and started their migration the Zuni are described as wanderers, living on the seeds of grasses and eating slain animals (Cushing 1896:388). They stopped at at least four springs in what is considered a zone of emergence in the Grand Canyon, an area extending from Ribbon Falls up the Colorado River to its confluence with the Little Colorado River (Hart 1995b). These springs include Ii'mikianakate'a, Yamun K'yay'a, Ts'ik'on K'yay'a, and Danin K'yay'a.

The locations of 12 places that figure in the early migration of the Zuni people are not well known in relation to modern cartography. These springs include Da:melank'yay'a, K'eyadi:wa, A'wisho ʾkĭai'akwi (Moss Spring), Banelunan K'yay'a, Ladaw K'yay'a, ʾHlän'ihlkoha ʾkĭai'akwi (Aspen Spring), Tésak'ya Yäla (Place of Nude Mountains), A'wełuyan kaiakwi (Massed Cloud Spring), Ci'pololon kaia (Mist Spring/Fog Place), Ubulemi, Tšiko-ṭíqawĕ, Batsichina:wa, U'teyan ĭn'kwi (Flower Place), and To:papik/a-ya.

According to Benedict, the choice of eggs occurred at "prayer stick place." Although Benedict does not provide a Zuni name for this location, it is presumably Da:melank'yay'a, translated by Stevenson as "prayer plume standing place." Bunzel (1932c), however, identifies K'eyadi:wa (Cornstalk Place) as the place the choice of eggs was offered, with the ones who were to go to the Middle Place taking the raven egg. Cushing (1896:388) notes that it is while the Zuni were at K'eyadi:wa that the prey monsters on the earth's surface were turned to stone by a cataclysmic fire.

A'wisho ʾkĭai'akwi, often translated as "Slime Spring," is identified in many sources as the spring where the slime was washed off the Zuni and where their physiology was changed by creating mouths and anuses, cutting the webbing on their hands and feet, and cutting off their tails and "horns" (Benedict 1935; Ferguson and Hart 1985; Parsons 1923; Stevenson 1904:28). Curtis (1926a), however, says that it is at Ubulemi that the "great shocks of hair" that projected from their foreheads and their hairy tails were cut off. The name "Ubulemi" is said to derive from the hair that was put into the spring.

Benedict (1935) and Stevenson (1904) also name A'wisho ʻkʼaiʼakwi as the location where the Zuni learned how to plant corn, make fire, and cook. Bunzel (1932c), however, implies that it was at Ubulemi where the Zuni planted their seeds, producing the first mature corn, which was made sweet when it was pecked by ravens.

Cushing describes how the Zuni encountered other people during the initial period of migration. For instance, in describing Da:melankʼyayʼa Cushing alludes to warfare and violence, a recurring theme in Zuni traditional history. He writes: "At times they met people who had gone before, thus learning much in the ways of war, for in the fierceness that had entered their hearts with fear, they deemed it not well, neither liked they to look upon strangers peacefully" (Cushing 1896:390). Some of the Zuni perished when they did not heed the call to continue the search for the Middle Place. As the Zuni approached Ci'pololon kaia they saw the smoke of other men's fires and a great assemblage of houses spread over the hills before them (Cushing 1896:390). All of the interaction was not violent, however, as Cushing (1896:391) also describes ritual contests between different groups to create soil and water to grow plants. Some of these ritual contests culminated in the merging of groups. In Cushing's words, "thus, happily were our fathers joined to the People of the Dew, and the many houses on the hills are now builded together in the plain where first grew the corn plants abundantly" (1896:398).

The farther east the Zuni migrated up the Little Colorado River valley, the more identifiable the places referenced in traditional history become with reference to modern cartogra-

phy. These places include Sunha:kʼya-bachu Yalanne (the San Francisco Peaks), Kumanch an Aʼl Akkweʼa (Canyon Diablo), Denatsali Imʼa (Woodruff Butte), and Da:bilayanku (east of Woodruff Butte). East of Woodruff Butte there are two places, Kʼyashhida Kʼyayʼa and Molan Kʼyayʼa, whose exact locations are not known, except for the fact they are in the drainage of the Little Colorado River between Da:bilayanku and Kołuwala:wa.

The next area identified in Zuni traditions is a complex of shrines near the confluence of the Little Colorado and Zuni rivers. This complex includes Hadin Kʼyayʼa (Listening Spring) and Kołuwala:wa as well as associated shrines not documented in the sources used in this chapter. The importance of Kołuwala:wa is evident in the fact that it is mentioned in all published traditions of Zuni origin and migration. Kołuwala:wa is home to the kokko, and it is where the Zuni reside after death. As Cushing documents, during the nineteenth century Kołuwala:wa was part of a large complex of active Zuni shrines in the upper Little Colorado River valley (Ferguson and Hart 1985:66–67).

In several accounts Kołuwala:wa is said to be where the Zuni separated into various groups traveling in different directions. Cushing (1896:405) reports that this is where the "Seed clans" or "Lost Others" turned southward, never to return. Parsons (1923) identifies Kołuwala:wa as the place where the Zuni were given the choice of eggs, with groups subsequently splitting, one heading south, another north, and a third traveling east.

In addition to being an important sacred area for the Zuni, Kołuwala:wa is also a shrine used by Hopi and Keresan pueblos. They know the area as Wenima, a name that also appears in esoteric Zuni songs (Boas 1928:226–

227; Bunzel 1932b:482; Curtis 1926a:172–177; Fewkes 1897:312, 1900:592, 1902:500, 1904:144, 1906:365; Stephen 1936:191, 442, 1168; White 1943:314, 1962:111). The historical relationship that ties Zuni, Hopi, and the Keresan pueblos to Kołuwala:wa is significant but has yet to be explicated by anthropologists.

Kołuwala:wa is the destination of a quadrennial pilgrimage still conducted by Zuni religious leaders (Meshorer 1995; O'Neil 1995). The continuing significance of Kołuwala:wa is apparent in the fact that this sacred area was removed from the Zuni's land claim because the Zuni Tribe refused to accept payment for a shrine they considered they still owned by virtue of unbroken and continuing use. After litigation of the claim the Zuni petitioned the United States Congress, which authorized the land exchanges needed for Kołuwala:wa to be placed in trust as part of the Zuni Reservation (Hart 1995c).

After leaving Kołuwala:wa Zuni traditions recount that the people traveled to Kʼya:dul Łana, located along the Zuni River, and to Teʼwulʻla iʼtiwa piʼʻkʼaia kwi (Valley Middle Watercress Place). Kʼya:dul Łana, known to archaeologists as Kiatuthlanna (Roberts 1931), is a multicomponent ancestral site containing early pit structures and a later Chacoan great house. It is not clear which of these components is referenced in Zuni traditions.

The Zuni are said to have migrated next to Hanłibinkya, along Hardscrabble Wash near what is now the Arizona state line, and He/epat/chi:wa, along the Zuni River. Some traditions recount that the people were led to Hanłibinkya by the Newekwe (Curtis 1926a). Hanłibinkya, referred to in all published Zuni traditions, is well known because it is the birthplace of

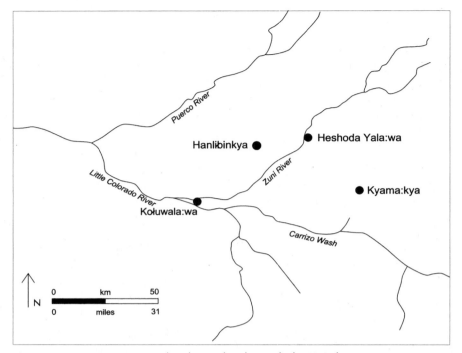

Figure 19.4. Sites associated with epic battles with the Kanakwe.

the Ahayu:da (war gods), created to help the Zuni prevail in a fierce battle with the Kanakwe, the original occupants of the region. It is also the place where Zuni clans received their names, chosen from some object seen at the time (Cushing 1896; Stevenson 1904:40). Hanłibinkya is marked today with many petroglyphs that denote religious icons and clan symbols (see Schaafsma and Young, chap. 15, this vol.). Zuni traditions recount that priests traveled from Hanłibinkya back to Kołuwala:wa to receive instruction in religious matters and rituals (Benedict 1935).

Accounts of the epic battle with the Kanakwe vary in their geographical details (Curtis 1926a; Cushing 1896; Stevenson 1904). Some traditions say it involved the gods at Kołuwala:wa, hunting in the area of Kyama:kya, along Jalarosa Draw (Benedict 1935; Curtis 1926a:173–176; Parsons 1923; Stevenson 1904). Other traditions describe the battle as occurring when the Zuni left Kołuwala:wa on their way to Hanłibinkya or when they left

Hanłibinkya on their way to Heshoda Yala:wa. In these versions the Ne-wekwe are said to have scalped two Kanakwe girls. In all versions the Kanakwe, led by Chakwena, a giant female warrior, engaged the Zuni in battle. At first Chakwena was undefeatable, but through spiritual intervention the Ahayu:da learned that her heart was in the rattle she carried. By shooting at the rattle rather than at her body, the Ahayu:da were ultimately able to defeat the Kanakwe and to free the game animals that had been imprisoned by the Kanakwe.

Cushing provides a vivid description of the Ahayu:da as they were engaged in the epic battle. They were well equipped with armaments

as warriors of old, with long bows and black stone-tipped arrows of cane-wood in quivers of long-tailed skins of catamounts; whizzing slings and death-singing slung-stones in fiber pockets; spears with dart dealing fling-slats, and blood-drinking broad-knives of gray

stone in fore-pouches of fur-skin; short face-pulping war-clubs stuck aslant in their girdles, and on their backs, targets of cotton close plaited with yucca. Yea, and on their trunks, were casings of scorched rawhide, horn-like in hardness, and on their heads wore they helmets of strength like to the thick neck-hide of male elks, whereof they were fashioned [Cushing 1896:422].

The locations of the sites mentioned in the varying traditions of the battle with Chakwena are illustrated in figure 19.4. All four sites are located along the Zuni River or nearby drainages tributary to the Little Colorado River. Two traditions refer to the battle at a place named A"kälikwin (Rock-in-the-River), the location of which is unknown (Bunzel 1932b; Curtis 1926a).

According to Stevenson (1904:43), it was at Hanłibinkya that the Pi'chikwe (Dogwood Clan) was divided by the choice of eggs, with the people choosing the blue egg sent eastward to find the Middle Place and others going to the north. Harrington (1929) documents a petroglyph at Hanłibinkya that was interpreted by the Zuni as depicting the process of migration (see fig. 19.5). Harrington's Zuni guide explained to him that "these little circles are the places where our ancestors stopped when they were coming from the West . . . and the lines between them are the trails from one stopping place to the next" (1929:6). This man also said, "You see that place where the line splits into three, up near the top? Well, that is where the tribe split into three parts, one swinging to the north, one to the south, and the other going straight ahead, eastward. You see the lines all come together again up above? That means the three bands all came together again at the

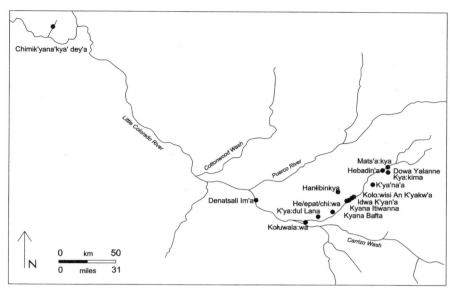

Figure 19.6. Places associated with the middle route of migration.

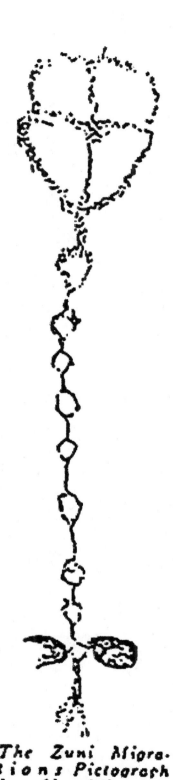

Figure 19.5. Zuni petroglyph at Hanłibinkya depicting migration (from Harrington 1929).

Middle Place, where Zuni stands today" (Harrington 1929:9).

In several accounts it is at Heshoda Yala:wa (House Mountain), located near Ojo Caliente on the Zuni Reservation, where the preexisting population of the Zuni area was assimilated by the A:shiwi, and the two groups became one people (Bunzel 1932c; Parsons 1923, 1939; Stevenson 1904). One account refers to Heshatoyalakwi, a name similar to Heshoda Yala:wa (Bunzel 1932c). However, it is not known if the two names actually refer to one place. As recorded by archaeologists, Heshoda Yala:wa is a large, rectangular, plaza-oriented pueblo occupied ca. AD 1250–1275 or later (Kintigh 1985:32–33; Spier 1917:219–220).

The Middle Route Described in the Traditions of Kyaklo and Sayatasha

The middle route of migration to Zuni Pueblo, after the division of the tribe, is recorded in detail in the ritual prayers associated with kiva initiations and ceremonies associated with the kokko, principally, the prayers of

Kyaklo and Sayatasha's Night Chant (Bunzel 1932c; Ferguson and Hart 1985; Stevenson 1904). The prayer of Kyaklo begins by naming Chimik'yana'kya dey'a, the place of emergence, and proceeds to recount the 12 springs discussed in the preceding section whose locations are not known (see table 19.1). The second place identified in the Kyaklo prayer whose location is known is Denatsali Im'a, Woodruff Butte in the Little Colorado River valley (see fig. 19.6). Two additional springs whose locations are not known are named in the area between Denatsali Im'a and Kołuwala:wa. After Kołuwala:wa an additional 39 springs and villages are mentioned. With the exception of Shiba:bulima in the Jemez Mountains, all of the places east of Kołuwala:wa mentioned in the Kyaklo prayer are in the Zuni River valley.

Eleven of the places east of Kołuwala:wa are depicted on figure 19.6. (The locations of the other places are known to Zuni religious leaders, but their precise positions have not been divulged.) The 11 places mapped in figure 19.6 include villages at K'ya:dul Łana and He/epat/chi:wa, springs at

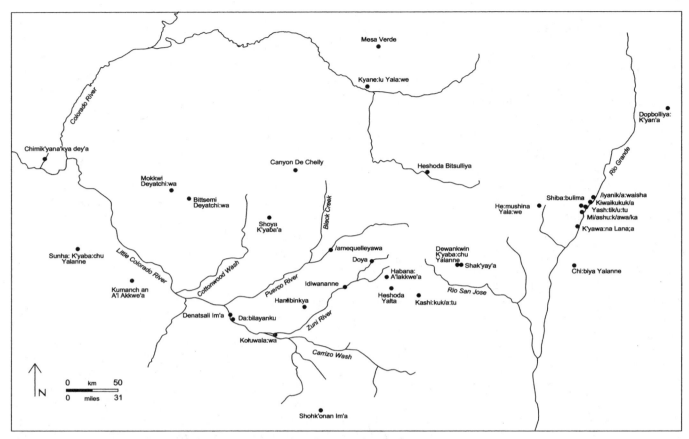

Figure 19.7. Places associated with the northern route of migration of religious societies.

K'yana Baɫta, K'yana Itiwanna, Idwa K'yan'a, Kolo:wisi An K'yakw'a, and K'ya'na'a (Ojo Caliente), the imposing mesa of Dowa Yalanne, and protohistoric villages such as Mats'a:kya and Kyaki:ma. The springs along the Zuni River continue to be visited during the quadrennial pilgrimage along the Barefoot Trail to Koɫuwala:wa. Twenty-eight springs mentioned in the prayer of Kyaklo, located on the Zuni Reservation but not depicted in figure 19.6, also continue to be used as active shrines.

Sayatasha's Night Chant starts at Koɫuwala:wa and then recounts the springs encountered on the middle route to Zuni, closely tracking the same springs that are mentioned in Kyaklo's prayers (Bunzel 1932c). The occupation of the springs and villages recounted in the prayers of Sayatasha and Kyaklo leads in an unbroken sequence to the establishment of Hepadina shrine at the center of the world, located at Halona:Itiwana, or Zuni Pueblo. According to Cushing, the Macaw Clan and other Summer people were led to Halona:Itiwana by the Zuni bow priests, following the middle and most direct route.

The Northern Route Described in the Traditions of the Religious Societies

The traditions of the Ɫe'wekwe (Sword Swallower Society), Newekwe (Galaxy Society), and Make'lhanna:kwe (Big Fire Society) describe the migration routes of the Zuni who traveled northward from the Little Colorado River valley. Forty places are identified in these traditions, 31 of which are depicted on figure 19.7. The traditions of the religious socie-

ties begin at Chimik'yana'kya dey'a, the place of emergence, and recount migration up the Little Colorado River valley, with stops at Sunha:k'yabachu Yalanne (the San Francisco Peaks), Kumanch an A'l Akkwe'a (Canyon Diablo), Denatsali Im'a (Woodruff Butte), Koɫuwala:wa, and Hanɫibinkya.

In various traditions the religious societies are said to have split off from the Zuni at Kumanch an A'l Akkwe'a, Koɫuwala:wa, or Hanɫibinkya. One shrine associated with the religious societies, Shohk'onan Im'a (Escudilla Peak), is located in the headwaters of the Little Colorado River to the south of these places. With this exception, all the other places associated with the migration of the religious societies after they split from the main body of the Zuni are located to the north in a broad area extending from the Hopi

Mesas to Mesa Verde and the Rio Grande. Some of the shrines in the northern area are associated with a single religious society, while others are associated with two or more religious societies. This suggests that the religious societies did not travel together in a single group but split into several groups following different paths of migration.

In addition to the religious societies the traditions of the northern migration are also associated with the Bear, Crane, and Grouse clans (Curtis 1926a; Cushing 1896). The association of clans with this migration may be cultural rather than historical, as these are clans associated with winter, and Cushing (1896:403) remarks that some members of all the clans traveled with each of the groups that split off. Although few details have been recorded about the events said to have transpired during the northward migration of the religious societies, it is clear that Chaco Canyon plays a prominent role in the traditions. Cushing describes how the people who migrated north "fought their way fiercely into the valley of the Snow-water river (*Úk'yawane*—Rio Puerco of the West)" (1896:426). They then continued traveling north, building towns along the cliffs and plains.

Eleven places are located on the Colorado Plateau. These include Úk'yawane (Rio Puerco), Hékwai-nankwin (mud-issuing springs, Rio Puerco), /amequelleyawa (Manuelito Canyon), Shoya K'yaba'a (near Ganado), Canyon de Chelly, Bittsemi Deyatchi:wa (on Second Mesa), Mokkwi Deyatchi:wa (Hotvela), Kyane:lu Yala:we (near Shiprock), Rope Hill, Heshoda Bitsulliya (Chaco Canyon), and Mesa Verde. The place-name of Chaco Canyon, Heshoda Bitsulliya, recalls the "round" buildings or great kivas that are a distinctive part of the settlement in the canyon. An alternate name for Chaco Canyon is Ki:wihtsi Bitsulliya, a direct reference to round kivas.

During the northward migration the members of the Make'lhanna:kwe (Big Fire Society) are said to have traveled far to the northeast, where they met the Ke'pachu ("buckskin Navajos"). The Ke'pachu understood medicine and other rituals, and they taught the Zuni ritual songs (Stevenson 1904:486). Łe'wekwe traditions of the northern migration refer to the Su'ni'a'shiwanni, a group of Zuni who became offensive during a dispute. This group was "tossed" far to the north, where they remained (Stevenson 1904:445).

Ten places associated with the northern migration are located in either the Jemez Mountains or along the Rio Grande. The destination of the northern migration was Shiba:bulima, today known as the Stone Lions Shrine in Bandelier National Monument (Curtis 1926b; Ferguson and Hart 1985; Parsons 1923:159; cf. Hodge 1910). It is at Shiba:bulima that the Łe'wekwe say they learned the ritual of sword swallowing (Stevenson 1904). Shiba:bulima is the origin place of medicine societies and prey animals. The dangerous "beast gods" who live at Shiba:bulima are associated with the medicinal plants that occur there as well as the power that makes these plants effective (Bunzel 1932a:528). Bunzel (1932a: 482) notes that upon their death medicine men who possess the shamanistic powers of "calling the bear" join the beast priests at Shiba:bulima in the east.

Five places are located along the west side of the Rio Grande between the pueblos of Santa Clara and Cochiti. These include K'yawa:na Łana'a, Tsilhinn/yalh/a, /iyanik/a:waisha, Yash:tik/u:tu, and Mi/ashu:k/awa/ka. Dopbolliya:K'yan'a (Taos Blue Lake) is located in the Sangre de Cristo Mountains to the east of the Rio Grande. Two shrines, He:mushina Yala:we and Kiwaikukuk/a, are located in the Jemez Mountains. Several medicine societies were introduced to the Zuni when they were living along the Rio Grande, including the Halokwe (Ant Society) and Shuma:que (Shell Society) (Stevenson 1904:528–548). These medicine societies were subsequently integrated into Zuni religious culture. The number of shrines along the Rio Grande and in the Jemez Mountains associated with medicine societies attests to this history. Some kiva groups and longhorn priests at Zuni also use shrines in the Jemez Mountains, but the historical context of this use has not been divulged to anthropologists (Hart 1995a).

Eventually, the religious societies migrated south to seek their relatives who had journeyed along the middle route. One of the prominent places associated with this leg of the migration is Chi:biya Yalanne (Sandia Peak). The patron gods of the Shuma:que (Shell Society) live at Chi:biya Yalanne, including Kokko Łanna (Great God), the Shumaikoli of the six regions, and the attendant Sai'apa warriors (Stevenson 1904:530). The traditions about these gods recount incidents of warfare with other pueblos (Parsons 1939).

After leaving Chi:biya Yalanne the religious societies migrated west. The places associated with this travel include Dewankwin K'yaba:chu Yalanne (Mount Taylor), Shak'yay'a (a peak on Mount Taylor), Kashi:kuk/a:tu (at the eastern end of the Zuni Mountains), Heshoda Yałta (the village on top of El Morro), and Habana: A'lakkwe'a (northeast of Ramah). Eventually, the people migrating from the Rio Grande came to Doya (Nutria), where they lived for a time (Cushing 1896; Parsons 1923:159). Some traditions say this group lived in the village at Heshodan

Figure 19.8. Map petroglyph showing route followed by Łe'wekwe during migration (from Stevenson 1904:plate CVII).

societies (see figure 19.8). This petroglyph and its interpretation offers a Zuni view of the route followed by the Łe'wekwe (Sword Swallowers). Stevenson writes:

> This etching is believed by the Zunis to have been made by the original director of the 'Hle'wekwe fraternity. The wavy line crossing the stone indicates the course of migration of the 'Hle'wekwe from Hän'ʰlipînkîa in the west to Shi'papolima in the east. After traveling a long distance northward, the 'Hle'wekwe turned south, and then proceeded to Shi'papolima in the east. The line crossing the bend in the road was followed by the fraternity to obtain certain medicinal plants. They returned to the point where they started for the plants and then resumed their journey. The pits north of the line of travel indicate mesas and mountain peaks. The significance of the hand symbol is not clear. The larger pit east of the hand is an extensive basin filled with water from rains and snows. The dots surrounding the pit represent Ursa Minor. The short lines, no longer than a few centimeters in the pictograph, indicate the number of years consumed by the 'Hle'wekwe in going from Hän'ʰlipînkîa to Shi'papolima and thence to I'tiwanna, the site of the present Zuni. The human figure is an ancient Shiwi before the tail and water moss had been removed and the webbed hands and feet cut. The dots about this figure denote hail, for the director of the 'Hle'wekwe fraternity desired much hail. The straight line extending east and west across the slab indicates the road from Hän'ʰlipînkîa to the Salt Mother before she left her home east of I'tiwanna. The cross near the east end of this line and south of it sym-

Imk'oskwi'a, a large plaza-oriented pueblo near Nutria (Ferguson and Hart 1985:23). Heshoda Yałta and Heshodan Imk'oskwi'a (Box S Ruin) are both large, plaza-oriented pueblos occupied during the thirteenth and fourteenth centuries (Kintigh 1985:78–79).

Stevenson (1904:plate 57) illustrates a petroglyph that the Zuni interpret as a map of the northern migration route taken by the religious

bolizes the morning star. The group of seven dots denotes Ursa Major; the group of four the Pleiades. The short heavy line indicates the road followed by the Kia'nakwe on their way to the place where they were found by the A'shiwi [1904:444–445].

The Southern Route

The southern route is only known from the abstract of Zuni migration published by Cushing (1896). According to Cushing, the Keepers of Fire and the Ancient Brotherhood of Paiyatuma (Newekwe) led the Corn, Sun, Badger, and other Summer clans through the southern valleys. These people are said to have traveled peacefully up the Little Colorado River valley, building towns of beauty and greatness and leaving petroglyphs depicting their rituals.

Five places are associated with this southern migration, two of which are depicted on figure 19.9. After splitting from the main body of the Zuni at Kołuwala:wa or Hanłibinkya, the people traveled south to Shohk'onan Im'a (Escudilla Peak). Cushing translates Shohk'onan Im'a as ("Home of the Flute-canes," or Round Valley) and gives Shohk'ona: Yalanne as the name for Escudilla Peak. When they left the villages in this area these Zuni are said to have traveled eastward, where they built "clan-towns" and fought wars with the kokko. Cushing says they finally reached Yála Tétsinapa, the "Mountain of Space-speaking Markings," possibly El Morro, where they turned back westward to join the people living in Shíwina Téu'hlkwaina, the upper Zuni River valley. Here they built Heshoda Ts'in'a ("Town of the Speech Markings") and other towns, which Cushing says were all round and divided into parts. Heshoda Ts'in'a is a large plaza-oriented pueblo occu-

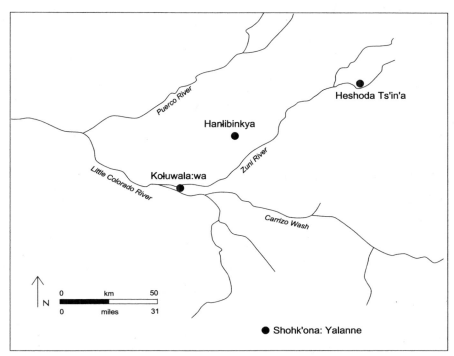

Figure 19.9. Places associated with the southern route of migration.

pied during the fourteenth century, located at Pescado on what is now the Zuni Reservation (Kintigh 1985:54). This village takes its name from the numerous petroglyphs found in this vicinity. From Heshoda Ts'in'a the people migrated west to join their relatives who had already arrived at the Middle Place of Halona:Itiwana.

Places Close to and at the Middle

Ten villages associated with Zuni migration are located on the Zuni Reservation (see fig. 19.10). These villages are of interest because they are the settlements occupied by the Zuni during the very last period of migration. All 10 of these villages are large, plaza-oriented pueblos occupied after the thirteenth and fourteenth centuries (Kintigh 1985). This suggests that the ancestors of the Zuni whose traditions are maintained in oral narratives arrived at the Middle Place relatively late in the occupational sequence of the Zuni River valley. These villages

include Heshoda Ts'in'a (Pescado), Doya (Nutria), Kwakina, Hawikku, K'ya'na'a (Ojo Caliente), Hampasawan, Kyaki:ma, Mats'a:kya, Kechiba:wa, and Halona:wa. In some accounts these villages were occupied sequentially as the people got closer and closer to the Middle Place, finally finding it at Halona:Itiwana. In other accounts Halona:Itiwana was established first, and then other protohistoric villages were founded (Parsons 1923).

Zuni Migration Traditions Compared to Zuni Aboriginal Land Use

Ancestral villages and shrines associated with Zuni origin and migration make up a substantial proportion of the total number of documented Zuni land-use sites. The total area of Zuni land use, however, is much more extensive than the area mapped in origin and migration traditions and incorporates more than 130 additional

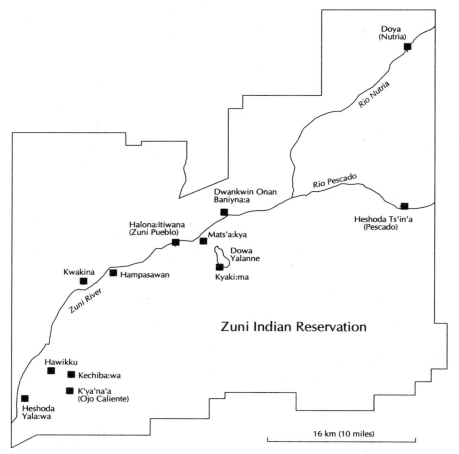

Figure 19.10. Ancestral villages close to and at the Middle Place on the Zuni Reservation.

land-use sites. These land-use sites are components in a nineteenth-century land-use system that included four basic zones (see fig. 19.11). The first zone contains the villages and intensive farming areas used by the Zuni. The second zone includes the extensive area of Zuni agriculture. The third zone is the area the Zuni used for grazing livestock, including cattle and sheep. The fourth zone is the area used for hunting and gathering of natural resources. Religious-use areas extended throughout and beyond the four zones. Schematically, these zones were irregularly shaped nested polygons, with the type of land use in the outer zones also being undertaken in the inner zones (Ferguson 1995). Thus, for instance, hunting and gathering took place throughout

the entire area of land use, including zones 1, 2, and 3, in addition to zone 4.

This traditional land-use system provided the basis for Zuni sovereignty and self-sufficiency (Ladd 1979a, 1979b). As Zuni lands were taken by the United States and transferred to states and private parties, Zuni access was impeded by the construction of roads and fences. It thus became increasingly difficult for the Zuni to continue to use extensive areas for subsistence activities, and Zuni lands eventually were reduced to a relatively small Indian reservation. The religious use of the landscape, however, has proven to be one of the most persistent and conservative elements of Zuni land use. To this day the Zuni continue to travel to and use shrines and sacred sites located

at great distances from their reservation. The religious use of the landscape is undertaken in a quiet and respectful manner that does not attract undue attention and that is therefore not well known by non-Indians.

Many of the shrines still used by the Zuni are located in areas above 2,000 m. In an ethnographic overview of Zuni culture, social organization, and religion Ladd (1983:171) illustrated the high-altitude areas with cultural importance for Zuni (see fig. 19.12). Ladd pointed out that

> nearly every high mountain in the Southwest was at one time or another used for religious and other purposes by the Pueblo people. The general boundaries of the modern *a:shiwi* lands, from the point of religious and other uses, are the high mountains and geographical regions which are held in special reverence and are especially sacred to different classes of ceremonial and religious activities. These include the Sandia Mountains, the Jemez Mountains, Mount Taylor, Blue Mountain in southern Utah, the Grand Canyon, the San Francisco Peaks, and the Mogollon, White, and Tularosa Mountains. . . . Within this geographical area are numerous springs, streams, ponds, caves, mesas, trails, and buttes that are of special religious significance [1983:1700].

One Zuni deposed during the land-claim litigation pointed out that the general name for all high mountains is Aweshoyallawe, translated as Moss Mountains (Hart 1995b). These include all the mountain tops where fog forms and from which rain comes. Prayer sticks are taken to these areas for the ancestors and for the animals. The mountainous areas are also used for hunting game and

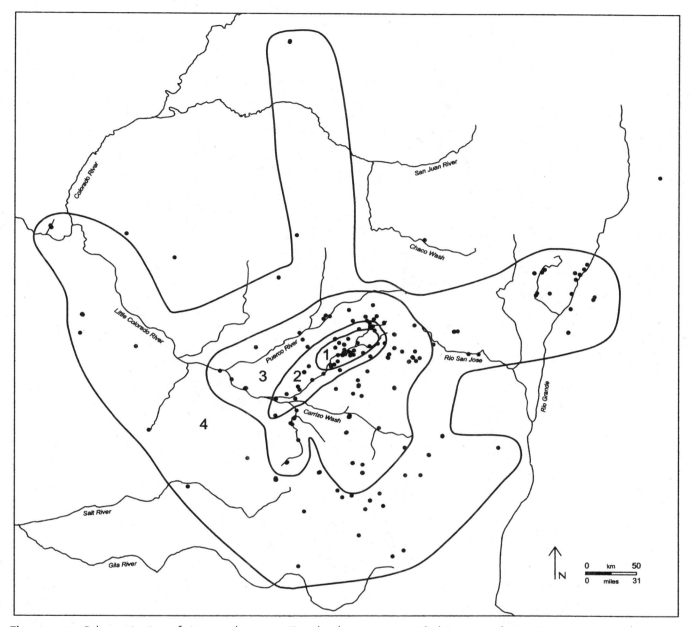

Figure 19.11. Schematic view of nineteenth-century Zuni land-use system with documented sites. Zone 1 contains the villages and intensive farming areas. Zone 2 includes the extensive area of Zuni agriculture. Zone 3 is the area used for grazing livestock. Zone 4 is the area for hunting and gathering of natural resources. Religious use extended throughout and beyond the four zones.

collecting herbs as well as for religious purposes.

Analysis of the information collected during the Zuni land-claim research indicates there are many shrines that are not mentioned in origin and migration traditions (see fig. 19.13). These include shrines in the Abajo, Jemez, Zuni, and Mogollon

mountains. The 13 Zuni shrines in the Mogollon culture area to the south of Zuni are particularly relevant to the topic being explored in this volume. These shrines include K'yak'yali an Yalanne (Eagle Peak), Sa'do:w Yalanne (Hardcastle Peak), Piliayalla:we (Willow Mountain), U'laɬimna: Yalawe (Mount Baldy, White Mountains),

Ɫi'akwa k'yakwe'a (a sacred spring in the White Mountains), Chishe:na / A'lakkwe'e (Apache Creek), Sha:k/aya (Datil Mountains), K/na/tsi/yall/a (Lyman Lake), /awak/on:yellan/a (a sacred spring between Luna and Reserve), K'ya:ts'i K'yan'a (north of Lyman Lake), Dona Yala:we (south of the Datil Mountains), Deshukt Ɫan

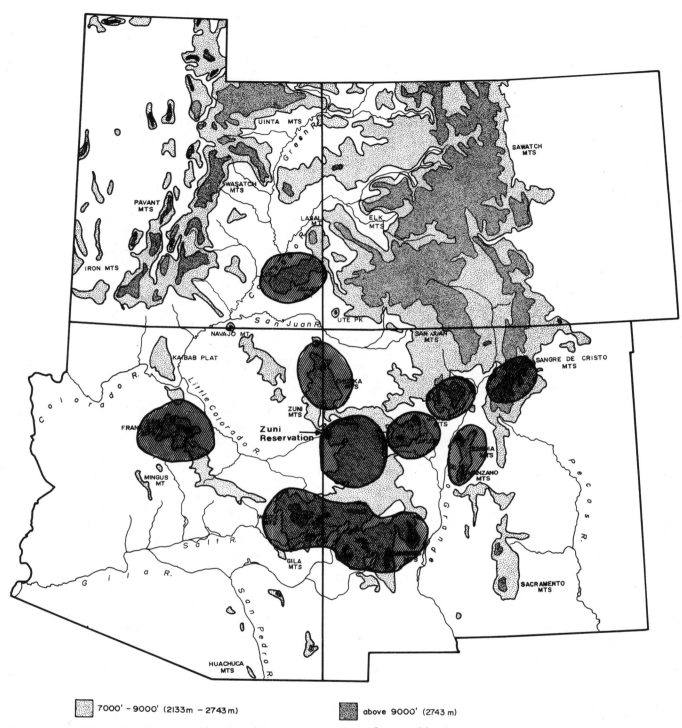

Figure 19.12. High-altitude areas with cultural importance to Zuni (from Ladd 1983).

Im'a (west of El Malpais), and Deshukt
Dina:wa (west of El Malpais).

Many of these shrines are associated with Zuni religious societies,
including the Saniakyaqe (Hunter Society) and Newekwe (Galaxy Society).

The historical context of these shrines,
however, is not well understood by
non-Indians. The Zuni claim they
inherited the knowledge of these
shrines and the spiritual responsibili-
ties to use them from their ancestors

who resided in the area before migrating to Zuni. This seems like a reasonable supposition. The geographical
placement of the 13 shrines in the area
south of Zuni thus implies the Zuni
have ancestors who resided in the

Legend: 7000'–9000' (2133m – 2743m) | above 9000' (2743m)

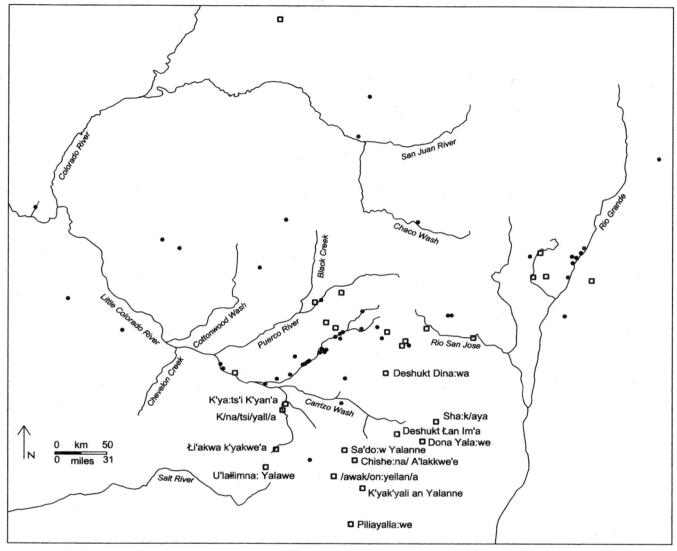

Figure 19.13. Places referenced in origin and migration traditions (circles) in relation to additional Zuni shrines (squares).

Mogollon area, even if the traditions of these ancestors are not part of most of the origin and migration talks recorded by anthropologists.

The geography of Zuni shrines in the Mogollon area has been noticed by archaeologists. Rinaldo, for instance, points out that the general area

> covered by the present-day Zuni Indians when visiting their distant shrines extends into the northern periphery of the Mogollon complex. Thus, today the Zuni make ceremonial trips not only south-

west to Hantlipinkia . . . and to the Red and Green Lakes at Kiatuthlana, but also to the shrines west of there . . . in the area claimed in their myths as the scene of their former migrations in search of the "Middle" [1964:87–88].

Greenwood and White (1970) describe a ceremonial pattern involving ritual activities at high-altitude shrines and springs located far from village settlements. These shrines and springs are located at elevations from 2,590 to 3,532 m, an environment Greenwood and White suggest is of

little direct economic consequence to agriculturalists. Archaeologists have recorded shrines on Mount Baldy, Green's Peak, Mount Ord, Rose Peak, Red Mountain, Sugar Loaf Peak, and Eagle Peak and ritual springs at Escudilla Peak, Little Valley, Point of the Mountain, Coon Creek, and Bead Spring in the Mogollon Mountains (Greenwood and White 1970; Morris n.d.). Two of these shrines, Mount Baldy (U'laɬimna: Yalawe) and Eagle Peak (K'yak'yali an Yalanne), are still used by the Zuni. These high-altitude shrines are associated with ceramics, beads, sherd disks, stone and ceramic effigies, projectile points, and turquoise mosaic fragments (Morris n.d.). Greenwood and White interpret these artifacts as deposits from a "votive ritualism which involved ceremonies at both mountain tops and springs" (1970:298).

Over time there was a concentration of ritual activities at a fewer number of selected shrines (Greenwood and White 1970:301). As people moved out of the mountainous Mogollon area they continued to use shrines in the least accessible locations, that is, ritual areas in the tundra zones far from occupied villages. Greenwood (1983:55) suggests that this ritual pattern had a dual origin. Many aspects of the pattern had well-defined precedents in the Pine Lawn branch of the Mogollon; other elements were related to input from the Chaco branch. The historical implications of Zuni shrines in the Mogollon area need further research, and this research will best be pursued by archaeologists working in collaboration with Zuni traditionalists.

Conclusion

Zuni traditional history and cultural geography are meaningful in the investigation of the relationship between the Zuni people and the Mogollon archaeological culture. This meaning is best summarized in a working hypothesis proposed by Cushing more than a century ago. In Cushing's (1888, 1896) reconstruction of Zuni history he argues that the Zuni are descended from at least two or more peoples and that they are the heirs of at least two cultures. Cushing suggests that one branch was aboriginal in the Zuni area and that the other branch "was intrusive, from the west or southwest, the country of the lower Rio Colorado, their earliest habitat not so clearly defined

and their remoter derivation enigmatical" (1896:342) because of their long period of migration. Cushing argues that the aboriginal branch of the Zuni was the largest but that the smaller western branch is most spoken of in the origin talks, and it is spoken of in the first person as being the original A:shiwi, or Zuni. The western branch was thus culturally dominant as several groups were assimilated into the Zuni tribe.

In Cushing's opinion the "elder nations" of the aboriginal branch "were direct and comparatively unchanged descendants of the famous cliff dwellers of the Mancos, San Juan, and other canyons of Utah, Colorado, and northern New Mexico" (1896:343). The western branch was related to a people resembling the Yumans or Pimans. Cushing thought that part of the western branch split off at a location south and west of the Little Colorado and Puerco rivers and traveled south, far into Mexico. Cushing (1888) claims to have traced the archaeological sites associated with this migration as far as the coast of Mexico. The rest of the Zuni separated into several groups, migrating to Zuni Pueblo by different routes. One of these routes traversed the northern portion of what is now known as the Mogollon culture area. Cushing (1896:342–343) thought that shortly before the arrival of the Spaniards the Zuni conquered some Keres towns south or southeast of Zuni and incorporated these people into the Zuni tribe.

Cushing offers two archaeological correlates of Zuni migration. First is that the dual origin of the Zuni is evident in the twofold nature of their mortuary practices when they were first encountered by the Spaniards, that is, inhumation and cremation (Cushing 1896:365–366). Any archaeological reconstruction of Zuni history has to account for these burial

customs. The second correlate is that the western branch of the Zuni was associated with square architectural structures. Cushing (1896:352–355) also recognized that the Zuni Salt Lake was an important resource in the ancient past. In this regard most southwestern archaeologists have not adequately considered the importance of the Zuni Salt Lake in models of settlement and subsistence systems and ancient migrations.

In the last 50 years archaeologists have recast Cushing's working hypothesis using current classifications of archaeological cultures. Reed (1950), for instance, has written about the development of Western Pueblo culture in the period from AD 300 to 1400. Reed argues that the Western Pueblos, including Zuni, developed from a blend of Hohokam, Mogollon, and Anasazi cultures. Similarly, Rinaldo (1964) argues for a historical relationship between late Mogollon culture and Zuni. While Rinaldo recognizes that Zuni culture during the Pueblo I to Pueblo III periods was broadly Chacoan in nature, he thinks much of the later Zuni culture is Mogollon in derivation. It is commonly thought that Zuni is an amalgamation of Anasazi and Mogollon cultures (Crampton 1977; Woodbury 1979).

Several archaeologists have also suggested that the ancient history of the Zuni region entails a number of Keresan elements (Fewkes 1915:549). Ellis, for instance, suggests that the original inhabitants of the Zuni area were of "Anasazi culture very similar to or duplicating that of what now is known as the Acoma area" (1967:37). She thinks these people were Keresan-speaking people, some of whom retreated toward Acoma during the thirteenth to fifteenth centuries, while the rest were "submerged" by immigrants who came from eastern Arizona, where they were related to groups that also migrated to Hopi. Ellis thinks the Zuni language was brought to Zuni by the most recent immigrants.

It is clear from archaeological reconstructions and Zuni traditional history that investigation of the development of Zuni culture requires a regional perspective encompassing a large portion of the Southwest and several archaeological cultures. Investigation of Zuni history in relation to a single archaeological culture like the Mogollon provides only part of the overall picture. This conclusion is reinforced by Zuni ethnography. For example, the religious societies at Zuni sing songs in six languages, including Zuni, Keres, Tewa, Pima, Navajo, and Hopi (Stevenson 1904: 424). The incorporation of songs in foreign languages into Zuni ceremonialism represents a long process of migration and social interaction with peoples across the entire Southwest.

Zuni traditions are qualitatively different from academic forms of history in that they emphasize space over time. Movements across the land are more important than a chronology of events in terms of a fixed calendar. Much of this movement is in large measure a recounting of the springs at which the ancestors halted during their migration (Hough 1906). It is only after severe environmental deterioration began ca. AD 1250 (Dean, chap. 6, this vol.), accompanied by population shifts across the Colorado Plateau, that the place-names of villages become dominant in Zuni traditional history.

Some important elements of Zuni traditions are set in various locations. For instance, the choice of eggs and the subsequent division of the tribes into separate groups is variously given as having occurred at Da:me-lank'yay'a, K'eyadi:wa, Kumanch an A'l Akkwe'a, Koluwala:wa, and Hanli-binkya. What is important is not that different traditions recount the division of the tribe in different locations but that all of these locations are situated in the valley of the Little Colorado River. While the precise location where the tribe split cannot be known with anthropological certainty, it seems reasonable to hypothesize that while the Zuni were migrating up the Little Colorado they split into several divisions, taking different routes on their quest to find the Middle Place. Taken at face value, this may seem like the pseudohistory that Kroeber (1917) criticized. Taken as a working hypothesis, however, this idea can be used to evaluate archaeological data and reconstructions of culture history.

Other narrative themes that run through Zuni traditions can provide additional sources of hypotheses for scientific research. These include the frequent references to warfare or violent interaction with other groups of people; the assimilation of various groups of people in complex processes of ethnogenesis; and the description of various groups as having different kokko, suggesting a complex and accretional development of kachina religion. The groups implicated in Zuni traditions include the tribe as a whole, clans, and various religious societies. From this it is clear that archaeologists need to develop models of migration that include a wide range of migrating groups.

In closing I note that the Zuni traditional history described in this chapter should not be construed in a manner that is overly literal. As Zuni exegetists have explained, the route defined by the places mentioned in prayers was not the exact route taken by all ancestral groups during their quest to find the Middle Place. There is no doubt that the ancestors of the Zuni traveled through and lived in other areas of the Southwest in addition to the ones mapped in this chapter and that in the process they occupied a considerable number of villages in addition to the ones whose names are commemorated in prayers. Be this as it may, the series of place-names associated with Zuni traditions define a trajectory of migration that holds important clues for the cultural history of Zuni. This information creates opportunities and challenges for archaeologists interested in the cultural and historical relationship between the Zuni people and their ancestors who lived in the Mogollon area.

Acknowledgments

I gratefully acknowledge the help of many Zuni people who have patiently explained the aspects of tribal origin and migration that can be shared with the public. Over many years I also learned a tremendous amount from discussions about Zuni history with Roger Anyon, E. Richard Hart, Edmund J. Ladd, and Barbara J. Mills.

Part V   **Zuni Origins**

Future Directions and Critical Commentary

20 A New Research Design for Studying Zuni Origins and Similar Anthropological Problems

David A. Gregory and David R. Wilcox

The opportunities for generating new anthropological knowledge of southwestern archaeology through the synthesis of existing data using innovative theoretical perspectives and modern computer technology are enormous. This volume is a substantive example of what can now be done by applying a holistic anthropological approach in a cooperative effort. The inquiry into Zuni origins started with some simple observations and suspicions about the nature of those populations traditionally classified as Mogollon and about the nature of the relationships between those populations and their neighbors through time and across space. It then evolved into a general research design with seven broad problem domains: unity and diversity in the peopling of the New World; an ecologically based focus on "islands in the sky" as a possible mechanism in the differentiation of prehistoric populations and Zunian speakers in particular; linguistic distributions and the spread of maize agriculture; the presence and character of Early Agricultural period populations in the traditional Mogollon area; the nature of the Mogollon tradition; population movements and coalescence between AD 1000 and 1300; and late prehistoric and protohistoric population distributions (see Gregory and Wilcox, chap. 10,

this vol.). As the idea for an advanced seminar evolved, Zuni origins became the encompassing rubric for these general problems; specific research questions were constructed, flowing out of and in some cases elaborating the general problem domains and tailored to the expertise of individual participants. The original questions derived from this process are available on the web site of the Center for Desert Archaeology.

Based on this evolving research design the important anthropological problem of Zuni origins has now been assessed. We do not claim to have solved this problem. However, by phrasing the issue in terms of a research design consisting of general problem domains and specific research questions and by bringing together a diverse set of scholars to attack those questions, we have laid bare its complexity and charted many ways that further understanding of it can be achieved. Better informed and with a new synthesis of existing data, we now have new problems and new questions. This volume as a whole is, then, but the latest iteration of a research design for understanding the Zuni origins question. We synthesize the results here, formulating a new research design for the continuing study of Zuni origins, and then generalize the methodology so

that similar anthropological problems can be studied in a comparable way.

The Continuing Study of Zuni Origins

We began this inquiry into Zuni origins with an initial research design (see Gregory and Wilcox, chap. 10, this vol.) and the thoughts of an earlier student of "linguistic prehistory," Cynthia Irwin-Williams (chap. 2, this vol.). Jane Hill's finding (chap. 3, this vol.) that the Zuni language differentiated at least 7,000–8,000 years ago places that process back into Paleoindian times, much earlier than we originally supposed. The same early period of differentiation is likely true for Keresan and Tanoan, which are also relatively small language families (see Hill, chap. 3, this vol.; see also Ruhlen 1991). This means that Irwin-Williams (chap. 2, this vol.) was right to try and identify where the populations that spoke these languages were during the southwestern Archaic. As a matter of sound archaeological theory one may agree with the criticisms mounted by Berry and Berry (1986) and Huckell (1984a, 1996), but it is legitimate to seek ways to identify the cultural boundaries that Hill's findings suggest were present. The concepts discussed by Clark (chap. 4, this vol.) point us in new directions for doing this. However, it does not follow necessarily from Hill's analysis that the differentiation of Zuni, Keresan, or Tanoan occurred in the Southwest proper: it could have occurred elsewhere in the Americas, with the representative groups migrating into the Southwest at some later time. Diehl in chapter 11 suggests such a possibility, and Matson's argument (1991; chap. 7, this vol.) illustrates how models for such a process can be constructed. Webster (chap. 16, this vol.) proposes alternative possibilities. Clearly, from the standpoint of science the question of Zuni origins remains undecided.

Linguistic Differentiation in the Southwest

In light of what we have learned from the experience of the Mogollon-Zuni advanced seminar and the preparation of this volume on Zuni origins we now present a revised research design to define future directions for continuing anthropological investigations of this important issue. We also show that the methodology that informs this design can be generalized to investigate similar anthropological problems, such as the origins of the Hopi, Keresans, and Tanoans. A good place to start is with a dramatic model of the migration of a language family into the Southwest provided by Hill (2001; see also Bellwood 1996, 1997; Diamond and Bellwood 2003). She proposes that Proto-Uto-Aztecan speakers were in proximity to the "heartland" in Mesoamerica where maize was domesticated, thus giving them (and others similarly positioned) an adaptive advantage and allowing the Proto-Uto-Aztecans to migrate rapidly northward so that they arrived in the Southwest and Great Basin about 4,000 years ago. Her argument hinges in part on the reconstruction of cognate forms that

constitute a proposed "maize complex" in Proto-Uto-Aztecan. Against the interpretation of Lamb (1958), Miller (1984), and Cortina-Borja and Valiñas (1989), who see Uto-Aztecan as conforming to Bloomfield's (1933) "mesh principle" (see also Swadesh 1971:285–293), Hill argues for a "tree theory" of "splits defined by shared innovations" (2001:917).

The first question about Hill's (2001) theory, then, is linguistic: whose description of the structure of Uto-Aztecan is more correct? To better understand this issue we turn to Victor Golla's concept of a "spread language," a language community spread widely across a landscape into "chains of intelligibility" or networks in which the constituent dialects "tend to diverge in phonology, grammar, and vocabulary at a steady rate" (2000:60). Such sets are polythetic (Mayr 1942); that is, they are ordered sets "in which speakers of adjacent dialects can fully understand one another's dialects, but speakers from the dialects at the opposite ends of a chain may not" (Golla 2000:60; see also Lamb 1958:99). Uto-Aztecan, therefore, which is distributed from Oregon southward through the Great Basin, the Southwest, western Mexico, and into the Basin of Mexico and beyond (Miller 1984), may have differentiated from a spread language into a "spread family" (Golla 2000:62) *in place*. It was thus, hypothetically, the result of initial family-level differentiations that were taking place during Paleoindian times, with this difference: unlike Zunian or Keresan, whose distributions were apparently more bounded and discrete, the dialect speakers of Uto-Aztecan continued to interact intensively, slowing the process of differentiation into bounded language communities. The ecological reasons why one group would become discrete and others would remain a connected chain are

issues that archaeologists may join in trying to explain.

If archaeologists and linguists could collaborate in studies of such processes using geographic information system (GIS) techniques, the results could be most interesting! Anderson and Gillam (2000), for example, apply GIS to model the spread of Paleoindians into the Americas according to several scenarios about the initial point of entry. Unlike Krantz (1977; see below), they do not consider linguistic data, but we think collaboration with linguists would enrich the kind of findings they present. We know that during the 4,000 years of the Paleoindian sequence in the Americas initial Clovis assemblages, which are nearly identical across all of North America, are replaced (differentiated?) into a plethora of extensive but less widely distributed spatial and temporal cultural units (Meltzer 1993). As Mellars has argued for the Upper Paleolithic of the Old World, this process may well be significantly correlated with linguistic differentiation, given that "linguistic differences, once established, become by far the most powerful and effective means of reinforcing and maintaining social divisions between distinct ethnic groups—as for example all the literature on documented tribal *divisions* in recent hunter-gatherer communities clearly reveals" (1998:101–102; see, e.g., Petersen 1976). Mapping out that process of differentiation (diversification?) in both time and space in the Americas would be most instructive, as it would also bring critical data to bear on the issue of the rate of change in culture and probably language. It would not surprise us if the rate of change is much more rapid than Nichols (1990, 1998), for example, has assumed.[1]

A third alternative was explored in an innovative, iconoclastic, and neglected essay by Grover Krantz

(1977; see also Ruhlen 1991:350). He postulated that linguistic family-level differentiation would have begun in *early* Paleoindian times due to separations resulting from the westward penetrations at four different points along the Rocky Mountains (a barrier) and their fanning out afterward. Interestingly, he also postulates a parallel coastal southward movement by boat of Athapaskans at about that time. Depopulation of vast areas during the Altithermal opened the way for subsequent expansions, giving some groups greater advantages for occupying new territory than others. He suggests that about 5,000 years ago Uto-Aztecans moved southward from the Colorado Plateau into southern Arizona and northern Mexico (Krantz 1977). He sees Zuni and Keresan as differentiating at this time in what later is the Mogollon area (Krantz 1977:49). The scale of his model is impressive (the entire Far West), and its positivist logic deserves more careful consideration than it has apparently received.[2]

The conception of linguistic family-level differentiation among American Indian languages happening in Paleoindian times and, subsequently, the appearance of increasing linguistic distance due to innovations being channeled by those boundaries are consistent with Greenberg's (1987) theory of Amerind, if not in agreement with all its details. So, too, is Krantz's (1977) model (Ruhlen 1991:350). To the extent that we understand her argument, Hill (2001) has not definitively shown that a mesh principle does not best describe the structure of Uto-Aztecan. And there are archaeological considerations she and other linguists have failed to address.

Spatially, between those languages grouped as Northern (including Hopic) and Southern Uto-Aztecan were once the Hohokam in southern Arizona, the proposed Central Arizona Tradition populations north of the Hohokam, and the Sinagua and Cohonina in the greater Flagstaff area. All of them were maize farmers. The Hohokam arguably spoke Tepiman (Shaul and Hill 1998; Wilcox 1986a, 1986b). The Sinagua (Colton 1946) may have spoken a language close to Hopic, and it may be argued that the Cohonina should be grouped as a subset ("branch") of the western Anasazi (Wilcox 1995b, 2002; USDA Forest Service 1996) and thus probably spoke a language close to Hopic. The people of the Central Arizona Tradition may well have spoken a language intermediate in linguistic distance (see Cortina-Borja and Valiñas 1989) between Tepiman and Hopic (Wilcox et al. 2007). These data suggest that a dialect chain may have once existed connecting Hopic to Tepiman, one that was first split apart and then broken altogether when the intermediate territories were depopulated prior to AD 1450 (see Wilcox et al. 2007; Wilcox et al., chap. 12, this vol.). Linguists need to include this possibility in their reasoning. The "gap" between the Northern Uto-Aztecans and Southern Uto-Aztecans noted by Miller (1984:19; see also Cortina-Borja and Valiñas 1989) before AD 1450 was not necessarily filled by Yuman speakers (cf. Miller 1984:19) and may have been occupied by Uto-Aztecans.

Recent studies of the genetics of maize (Benz and Iltis 1990; Doebley 1990; Iltis 1983, 1987) and archaeological findings of early maize distribution (Pearsall 1995) shed light on the northward spread of maize (cf. Diamond and Bellwood 2003). The region in Mexico with the greatest documented diversity in races of teosinte, the progenitor of maize, is western Mexico, and it is there, too, where the teosinte closest to maize (*Teosinte parviglumis*) is prevalent (Doebley 1990). Currently, "a hearth of maize domestication has not been found" (Fritz 1995:308), and "that archaeologists have not yet found the intermediary ears linking teosinte and maize is not surprising, for up to now they have not looked in the right place" (Iltis 1987:213). Should the central Río Balsas or some other part of western Mexico prove to be that place (see Doebley 1990), then many theories about the diffusion of maize and its linguistic correlates will have to be rethought (Fritz 1995). Hill (personal communication 2004) feels that her theory (Hill 2001, 2002) would not be affected by a western Mexico "hearth" for maize, but we suggest that the timing she suggests would be more dubious: why, once maize was initially domesticated, did it take so long for the putative migration to occur? By the mid-sixth millennium B.P., however, it appears that true maize was already present in the Tehuacan Valley (Benz and Iltis 1990; Long et al. 1989) and other parts of Mesoamerica (Pearsall 1995). That means that 1,500 years apparently intervened between domestication and the arrival of maize in the American Southwest; again, why so long? (see Gregory and Nials, chap. 5, and Matson, chap. 7, this vol.).

The "maize complex" identified by Hill (2001) includes cognates that mean such things as "digging stick," "to plant," "turtle, tortoise, rattle," "*Phaseolus vulgaris*," "flooded," "canal," and "to nibble small pieces of food." Clearly, none of these cognates necessarily points directly to a maize complex. Hill further points out that her colleague Lyle Campbell also told her that "the words in the maize complex [probably] are not, in fact, originally words involving maize at all but, rather, words that originated within a foraging adaptation and then underwent semantic shift to refer to maize and maize processing as the original foraging community adopted cultivation" (Hill 2001:926).

Archaeologists have long supposed that there was such a widespread foraging adaptation during the Middle Archaic in which cultivation of small-seeded plants was added to the collecting regimes. Haury (1962) was among the first to suggest such a hypothesis, and it continues to receive broad support today:

> Given both direct and indirect evidence that weedy annuals had an important economic role during the middle Archaic in cool temperate environments, the possibility that these plants were encouraged or cultivated seems good. Chenopodium and other annuals were cultivated historically in the Great Basin, and several researchers [Winter and Hogan 1986:137; see also Bohrer 1991; Keeley 1995] have suggested that pre-maize plant cultivation was likely practiced in the Southwest [Wills 1995:227].

Toll and Cully (1983:386) argued that chenopodium and amaranth "have an adaptive advantage under disturbed conditions and thus might form a loose symbiotic relationship with humans as locations that were repeatedly utilized in successive years" (Wills 1995:227). If so, the likelihood would be increased that maize, a larger seed plant, simply diffused among such foragers as a way for them to intensify and add greater diet breadth (but see Matson, chap. 7, and Damp, chap. 8, this vol.). Maize terminology in an open (dialect chain) linguistic environment may well have spread rapidly by diffusion as well. What this means, we suggest, is that it may prove possible to show that Hill's (2001) theory is wrong, both on the basis of archaeological and linguistic evidence, but this has not yet happened. Nor has the alternative—

that Uto-Aztecan differentiated in place—been shown to be wrong. There may have been no wholesale migration of Uto-Aztecan (or other language families) into the Southwest after all.

Renfrew (1998a; see also Ehret 1988; Zvelebil 1996; Zvelebil and Zvelebil 1988) has also postulated a further model that relates the variables of language, agriculture, and genetics (see fig. 5.4, this vol.), one that should be carefully evaluated by southwestern archaeologists. The idea here is that the dispersal of agriculture, which spreads by diffusion, may also lead to language spread due to acculturation, or "adjacency acceptance," without population migration. What we find most interesting about this model is that, as Renfrew points out, "in such cases, where the new speech is acquired by substitution rather than by demic diffusion, we should expect the newly emerging language family to show more diversity, and to owe more to the language being replaced (which would form a more evident substrate) than in the demic diffusion case" (1998a:184). That is, a polythetic language structure would be expected, but one that might be different from one that emerged from differentiation in place from a common protolanguage. Thus, it seems that both linguistic and archaeological methods could be brought to bear to evaluate the "fit" of the data we have with this model. (For further discussion of this point see Gregory and Nials, chap. 5, this vol.) Exciting new research directions are thus indicated.

A New Mogollon-Zuni Model

It was from the ideas formulated by Martin and Rinaldo (see Gregory, chap. 9, this vol.) that our own ideas about the relationship of Mogollon and Zuni took flight (Gregory and Wil-

cox, chap. 10, this vol.). Indeed, at the time we joked that we probably could have done better by just cribbing more from Rinaldo's (1964) "Notes" article! In light of what we learned from the seminar, however, and the ideas set forth in part I, we now have moved on to a much different conception of how Mogollon-Zuni relationships should be explored.

Our new position begins with the simple insight that 8,000 years is a long time. Although today we only know about one Zuni speech community, it is logically possible that during the millennia between the present and its first appearance Zunian differentiated into several Zuni languages, only one of which survived into the historic period. Frank Hamilton Cushing, who lived at Zuni between 1879 and 1884, and who learned the language, reported that there were several dialects still extant in his time (Green 1990).[3] Zuni oral tradition speaks of those who went to the land of the everlasting sun and did not return (see Ferguson, chap. 19, this vol.). Such a migration and separation could result in linguistic divergence and the emergence of distinct Zunian dialects or languages. Drawing on the findings of the chapters in part II, we now propose a new Mogollon-Zuni model that represents a synthesis that should help to focus future research efforts. As a methodological framework for this model we now introduce two conceptual schemes. The first is a concept of adaptation developed by Gregory as a heuristic device for analysis. The second is a set of ideas about linguistic groupings proposed by Victor Golla (2000).

Adaptation. In the 1960s "adaptation" was a widely used concept in the natural sciences (e.g., Williams 1966) and anthropology (Vayda 1969). Martin and Plog (1973) applied it to the Mogollon, and we took up a phrase from them in our reanalysis (see Gregory and Wilcox, chap. 10, this vol.). We view adaptation as that arrangement of organizational, technological, and ideological systems by which a population perpetuates itself within a natural environment or set of environments perceived to be within the defined territory of said population. By including the element of territory in the definition, we are able to relate adaptation to the important concept of boundaries. An adaptation is also seen as having a cultural environment external to its territory yet with which it variably interacts.

The natural environment within which societies exist and persist will vary both temporally and spatially. Temporal variation in natural environmental variables may be characterized in terms of their *magnitude*—the range of variation within which the adaptation developed and exists to a given point in time—and their *amplitude*—the range of environmental variation over a given period of time. These distinctions may also be expressed in terms of Dean's (1988b; chap. 6, this vol.) contrast between high-frequency (< 25 years) and low-frequency (> 25 years) variation. Spatial variation in the environment(s) encompassed by an adaptation may range from constant or stable (e.g., point resources such as clay or mineral sources) to highly variable (e.g., variation in natural yields of wild plant resources). Closely related is the idea of *predictability*, or the degree to which populations are able to successfully anticipate variation in the natural environment from the interannual period to the generational time scale (see also Gregory and Nials, chap. 5, this vol.).

Adaptations also have a cultural environment, including the "worlds" of interaction between neighbors on multiple scales. The neighboring great houses in Chaco Canyon, for example, form a macrocommunity (Vivian 1991) that is a cluster on the landscape of the San Juan Basin (Wilcox 1999a), which in turn constituted a region of interacting Chacoan communities integrated by redistribution (Judge 1979, 1989), pilgrimage (Toll 1985), tribute (Wilcox 1999a, 2005a), or staple finance (Earle 2001) relations. On a wider landscape or macroregion, Chacoan communities extended throughout most of the eastern Anasazi area and were culturally linked by relations of emulation, peer-polity interaction, or "religiosity" (Fowler and Stein 1992; Lekson 1999; Wilcox 1999a; Yoffee 2001). Adjustments of organization, technology, or ideology—or territory—may result from failure of expectations about how neighbors will behave and the innovations made to deal with new situations. Faced with endemic raiding from neighbors, for example, a population may invoke its potential to reorganize and thus be able to mount military efforts that make the defensive strategies of its aggressive neighbor untenable. What the neighbors do in turn may be transformed and escalate the nature of raiding and conflict relations between these neighbors and thus have ramifying effects on other contiguous populations as well (see Wilcox 1999a, 2005d; Wilcox et al. 2001a, 2001b).

Given this definition, it follows that any adaptation has inherent flexibility and variable potentials. *Flexibility* refers to the combined ability of organizational, technological, and/or ideological systems to respond and adjust to the magnitude of temporal variation that characterizes the environment *within which* the adaptation developed and continues to exist. *Potential* refers to the ability of these various systems to respond to temporal variation that *exceeds* that previously experienced. In general, the narrower the range of magnitude and amplitude in natural environmental variation and the greater the specificity of technological, organizational, and ideological forms relative to that variation, the lesser the potentials of any given adaptation.

Flexibility is obviously a critical aspect of all adaptations. To take advantage of or mitigate the effects of environmental variation across its territory, for example, a population may alter the manner in which people are deployed over their territorial landscape, they may place increased emphasis on storage and redistribution via alliances between internal settlements or kin groups, or they may form new economic relationships with populations outside their territory. The exercise of potentials inherent in any adaptation may take the form of technological innovations—the adoption of new water-control techniques, for example, or a decision to attempt expansion of existing territory. Similarly, some instances of migration may be seen as an extreme organizational response to a magnitude of environmental variation that far exceeded the variation within which the adaptation developed and had been previously maintained—essentially a decision to replace one environment with another, such as happened with some Anasazi populations during the extreme droughts on the Colorado Plateau in the late thirteenth century (Lipe 1995). To accomplish that strategy also required negotiation of new cultural relationships or elaboration and transformation of existing ones with groups that either received them in some cultural role or objected to their presence in some part of their territory.

There are a number of advantages to such a conception. The first is that it views the natural environment as a context for rather than a determinant of human behavior. While extreme environmental events or processes may act as determinants (there are, after all, such things as natural catastrophes; see, e.g., Graybill et al. 2006; Nials et al. 1989), more often human populations exhibit remarkable abilities to change and adapt. Another is that it incorporates the cultural environment as a separate variable, potentially equal in importance to that of the natural environment in any given instance. A third advantage is that it allows us to compare and contrast adaptations or groups of them at any scale. For present purposes, it is particularly useful to be able to operate at the macroregional scale and to move back and forth between that larger geographic context and smaller ones. A fourth advantage is that environmental variation is subject to relatively fine-scale quantification, and in the Southwest, at least, the record of variation in precipitation, resulting streamflow, temperature, and associated geomorphic processes is relatively lengthy (see Gregory and Nials, chap. 5, and Dean, chap. 6, this vol.). Thus, we may reasonably expect that we will be able to reconstruct the range of environmental variation within which various populations existed over a given period of time and within a given geography, set that variation against continuity and change in the archaeological record, and thus generate hypotheses concerning the adaptations represented at various scales. Fifth, when combined with a macroregional approach such a conception facilitates comparison of the effects upon and responses of different adaptations to large-scale, low-frequency environmental variation such as major shifts in climatic regimes. Examples of such large-scale variation and its variable effects on Southwest populations are provided by Gregory and Nials in chapter 5, this volume.

Similarly, the restructuring of cul-

tural worlds, once neighbors with previously unknown adaptations are brought into conjunction by migration, can generate adaptations on a larger scale based on new organizational forms and ideologies that transcend previously separate groups. The emergence of the Pueblo macroeconomy discussed by Wilcox et al. in chapter 12, this volume, is an example of this process (see also Habicht-Mauche 1993; Spielmann 1983, 1994; Wilcox 1984).

Our initial concept (Gregory and Wilcox, chap. 10, this vol.) of a high-elevation adaptation during the Altithermal, when many populations were confined to "islands in the sky" (cf. Krantz 1977), was a first attempt at conceiving a model of long-term adaptation that later took the form of Highland Mogollon culture.

Language Communities and the Zunian Language Community/Family. The anthropological linguist Victor Golla (2000) has suggested a helpful set of concepts for thinking about linguistic distributions and their differentiation or divergence. A *dialect community* is a relatively "small social group all of whose members regularly interact with one another using the same, or nearly the same, patterns of linguistic behavior" (Golla 2000:59). On a more abstract level, a language community "can be loosely defined as the group of individuals whose linguistic patterns are sufficiently similar to allow for the possibility of effective social communication, even when the situations in which this would occur are rare or non-existent" (Golla 2000:59). As we saw above in the introduction (Wilcox and Gregory, chap. 1, this vol.), a language community can be spread widely across a landscape into "chains of intelligibility," which Golla calls a "spread language" (2000:60).

Golla also distinguishes *compact languages,* or "language communities

whose constituent dialect communities are closely adjacent and share a common interaction sphere (connected by trade, intermarriage, ritual, and intergroup alliances and hostilities)" (2000:60). Where the dialects of a compact language community differentiate into distinct languages, a *compact family* is formed, while the differentiation of a spread language forms a *spread family* (Golla 2000:63–64).

Our original gambit (see Gregory and Wilcox, chap. 10, this vol.) was to postulate that there was an "adaptation to the mountains" and to narrow the Mogollon concept to only the Cibola, Forestdale, and Black River branches in a highland zone lying largely above 1,981 m. These populations, in Golla's terms, constituted an interaction sphere with a common ideological system (as seen in the continuity in ceremonial structures) and probably were a compact language community. Rinaldo's (1964) hypothesis—that these populations were ancestral to Zuni—specifies what that language was (see also Ford et al. 1972; Wendorf 1954; Wendorf and Reed 1955). We continue to think that these two ideas are viable, but we now want to argue that the compact language community was larger and may have been differentiated into a compact Zunian language family. This hypothesis represents a synthesis of the findings of the authors in part II (see also Ferguson, chap. 19, this vol.). In addition to the Highland Mogollon dialects we set forth arguments that current data allow a case for including Mimbres, the Safford Basin, and participants in the southwestern portion of the Chacoan world as Zunian speakers.

Mimbres. Our original proposal to, in effect, narrow the Mogollon concept left open the question of what language was spoken by the Mimbres.

(We thought at that time it might have been Uto-Aztecan.) Diehl's persuasive critique (chap. 11, this vol.), however, leads us now to postulate that the Mimbres populations were part of the same language community with the Highland Mogollon. The early Mogollon thus constituted a "common interaction sphere" such as Golla (2000) postulates; that sphere was then partitioned with the emergence of the Mimbres religious ideology, which highland groups did not accept; accordingly, they shifted their sphere of exchange interactions northward (see Wilson, chap. 14, this vol.). The Mogollon/Zunian language community may have then become a compact language family. The migration of late Mimbres populations southward and eastward in the late AD 1100s or early 1200s (Creel 1999; Nelson 1999) left a buffer zone in the upper Gila that was filled not long after by Cliff phase populations. In Golla's (2000:63) terms, the Mogollon/Zunian language community was thus moving toward becoming a "spread family," or language chain.

Safford Basin. The Mogollon/Zunian language community was subject to forces of differentiation on two other fronts as well. Hohokam-style ball courts were built in the Point of Pines and Safford Basin areas in the period between AD 800 and 1000, and expressions of the Hohokam death ritual also appeared in these regions (Neely 1974; Wilcox and Sternberg 1983). The Hohokam religion flowered in the ninth century, growing out of Pioneer period antecedents (Wallace 1994; Wilcox 1991d), and it paralleled the appearance of the Mimbres religion as described by Diehl (chap. 11, this vol.). Although we now still know relatively little about the archaeology of the Safford Basin, it appears that Hohokam elements dropped out

by about AD 1100 (Gregory 1995b, 1995c, 1995d; Wilcox 1999a), and its populations were not particularly receptive to Mimbres overtures.

We postulate that continued research will show that Safford Basin populations were Mogollon culturally and linguistically (as Wheat's [1955] and Martin's [1979] distribution maps imply; see fig. 1.2, this vol.). It may also be that this period of contact with Hohokam peoples (and presumed Uto-Aztecan speakers) accounts for the Piman-Zunian loanwords and hypothesized contact between the two groups outlined by Shaul and Hill (1998; but see Hill, chap. 3, this vol.). The experience by Safford Basin residents of Hohokam ideas and their life in a lowland desert basin with rich desert resources and irrigation technology probably differentiated them from other Mogollon groups to the degree that a distinct language emerged. Their adaptation was different from that in the Mogollon Highlands or in the Mimbres area.

Evidence from the late prehistoric and early protohistoric periods supports this analysis of cultural affiliation of the Safford Basin populations and links them to historic Zuni. Ceramically, the Safford Basin was closely tied to Point of Pines and other population aggregates farther up the Gila in the Redrock and Cliff areas (Lyons 2003; Wilson 1998b; see also Wilcox et al., chap. 12, and Wilson, chap. 14, this vol.). Considerable amounts of White Mountain Red Ware and some Early Zuni Glaze Wares are also found in this ceramic province (Gregory 1995b, 1995c, 1995d). The cremation ritual and burial in Salado polychrome vessels found there is also a prominent feature of burial assemblages in the fifteenth-century Zuni sites of Hawikuh and Ketchipawan (Smith et al. 1966). A migration of remnant populations from the Safford Basin, upper Gila, and Point of

Pines settlements to Zuni seems likely (Duff 1998; see also Mills, chap. 13, this vol.). More detailed ceramic sourcing and other studies are needed to test this hypothesis.

Of special interest is the report of early Spanish observers who directly link populations in the Safford Basin area to Zuni. The *entrada* of Francisco Vásquez de Coronado (Hammond and Rey 1940) passed through this area on their way to Zuni, the province of which they called Cíbola. Somewhere near the Safford Basin, possibly in the Fort Grant area (Duffen and Hartmann 1997), they report seeing the ruins of a site they called Chichiltecalli (from the Nahuatl, "red house"). Pedro de Castañeda states that "Chichilticale received its name because the friars found in this region a house formerly inhabited by *people who broke away from Cibola*. It was built of brown or red earth" (Hammond and Rey 1940:251; emphasis added). We see this report as strong evidence for our postulated Zuni connections with this area.

Puerco of the West. North of the Mogollon Rim, Mogollon populations extended into the Forestdale and Cibola branch areas, and Wilson (chap. 14, this vol.) sees their presence in the Marianna Mesa area. What, then, of the Zuni Valley or the other areas of "gray-brown" pottery such as the Rio Puerco of the West (Hays-Gilpin and van Hartesveldt 1998)? Damp et al. (2002; see also Damp, chap. 8, this vol.) have shown that there were people using ditch irrigation in the Zuni Valley 3,000 years ago. Who were these people linguistically? They may have been Keresan speakers: Zuni oral traditions speak of conquest of this area by the Zuni who came from the west (see Ferguson, chap. 19, this vol.). Logically, it is quite possible to suppose that Zunian speakers occupying the

Mogollon Highlands moved northward into lower-elevation zones in a *transhumance* adaptation such as Fritz (1974) postulated for populations in the Hay Hollow Valley during the Early Agricultural period. Mills (chap. 13, this vol.) sees the Puerco of the West, a well-watered valley that could have supported irrigation, as a place where many people converged during Pueblo I times. It is not unlikely that Zunian speakers were among them.

In an analysis of the distributional structure of Chacoan great houses, Wilcox (1993, 1999a, 2005c; see also fig. 12.24) showed that the linear array of great houses in the Puerco of the West was centered on the Allentown site and that as a set they stood apart from the San Juan Basin distribution of great houses. He argued that the great houses in the Puerco of the West were economically and politically integrated into a common polity and that they were politically independent from the San Juan Basin system, which was centered on the Chaco Canyon core community. He came to similar conclusions regarding the San Mateo great house system (Wilcox 1999a, 2005c).[4] The Zuni Mountains lie east–west between these two systems, and to the south of them was an array of great houses starting from both the San Mateo and the Puerco of the West systems that converges on the Tularosa Valley, where Lekson (1999) proposes that the Aragon site (LA 3270 and LA 8079; Hough 1907) was also a great house, which we believe is a plausible inference.

Long-distance exchange of scarlet macaws, copper bells, and other valuables from western Mexico likely passed through the Tularosa Valley via the Mimbres to Chaco Canyon (Wilcox 1993, 1999a; Wilcox et al. 2000; see also Vokes and Gregory, chap. 17, this vol.). The pattern of great house distribution south of the

Zuni Mountains may have been put in place to control the northward flow of those valuables. If so, it follows that the Puerco of the West and San Mateo systems controlled the access by Chaco Canyon to those valuables. Excavations in great houses of these systems are needed to test this inference.

What we now think is that the predominant populations in the Puerco of the West great houses spoke a Zunian language.[5] We would further postulate that the great houses in the Zuni area proper, such as the Village of the Great Kivas (Roberts 1932; see also Kintigh, chap. 18, this vol.), were placed there by the Puerco of the West polity. The ceramics of this area, as in the Puerco of the West, are dominated by Puerco Black-on-white and then by early White Mountain Red Ware (Mills, chap. 13, this vol.). These settlement systems were highly dynamic, even volatile, and we suspect that to document the processes of change in them will require much more refined chronologies and the kind of fine-grained settlement pattern analyses now being conducted by Keith Kintigh and his students (see chap. 18, this vol.)—but that needs to be done over much larger areas than have yet been studied.

Summary. A heuristic concept of adaptation that acts as an intervening variable between culture and environment has been introduced to aid in the construction of future research designs to investigate Zuni origins and the linguistic prehistory of other southwestern groups. Golla's (2000) concepts of compact and spread language families also add helpful precision to such inquiries. Applying these concepts and the findings of the chapters in part II, we propose a new model of a Zunian compact language community composed of populations with four different adaptations. They include the Highland Mogollon, the

Mimbres, the Safford Basin / Point of Pines / Cliff populations, and Chacoan groups centered on the Puerco of the West that extended into the area south of the Zuni Mountains. New research is needed to test these propositions.

Why Scale Matters

Why does scale matter? It matters because the explanation of what happens in any given spatial and temporal domain cannot be fully or adequately understood without reference to processes that act on both smaller and larger scales whose outcomes impact on the domain of choice. Braudel (1972, 1980) has shown that to understand the history of an event one must also seek understanding of the history of conjunctions and the history of what he called "the longue durée." The same is true in the natural world (Butzer 1971, 1982). It is all about context and about the realization that context is multidimensional. This finding has profound implications for how archaeology should be conducted to maximize what can be learned in the contexts of a given opportunity. Zuni origins cannot be understood without careful consideration of all of these contexts.

Most of the funding available for doing archaeology in the Southwest today is generated by the historic preservation system at the federal and state levels. Using the federal or state procurement systems, agencies issue "requests for proposals" that companies respond to, competing for contracts that specify what archaeology will be undertaken. Research designs often inform both the agencies' request and the company's proposal. Perhaps inevitably, given the volume of work and the repetitive nature of many of its aspects, many of these research designs often repeat "by rote" summaries of background information that reify cultural categories rather than investing them with fresh and innovative perspectives. This kind of boilerplate makes it easier and cheaper to construct research designs, but the public benefit of such practices is questionable. What new knowledge is being gained thereby? What opportunities are overlooked or neglected?

Part of the problem, we think, is a failure to appreciate the multidimensional nature of context—that scale matters. Continuing synthesis is needed not just on one scale but on many. The combined results of such efforts are what is needed to revise the standard boilerplate more frequently than is currently done. How are such syntheses generated?

Advanced seminars, such as the one that led us to the present volume, are one mechanism for new syntheses. We think that the biennial Southwest Symposia, if appropriately organized, could be used to greater advantage in this regard. A closer look at how the modern historic preservation system is structured suggests additional ways both to stimulate new efforts at synthesis and to cultivate consensus about the new findings.

Before agencies can proceed they must consult with the State Historic Preservation Office (SHPO), whose mandate is to make judgments about "significance." Four criteria are well established for doing this, the one most often applied to archaeological cases being that information from a site or set of sites (information that can be recovered through archaeological survey or excavation projects) is likely to be "important in history or prehistory." But is the information important in itself, or is importance to be judged relative to some further standard? The efforts by SHPOs to establish historical "themes" and "contexts" suggest the latter. The reason for them is to assist SHPO staff in making informed determinations of significance. Once established, however, such "themes" and "contexts" can, in fact, inhibit creative construction of new knowledge, becoming straightjackets into which the "problem domains" of the archaeologist must be squeezed or crammed in order to satisfy bureaucratic demands. We believe the profession of archaeology needs to play a much more active role than it typically has in defining and redefining the "themes" and "contexts" to which the SHPOs give such credence.

One of the great advantages of advanced seminars over other formal social gatherings of archaeologists is that they are designed to discuss research findings, whereas most others allow time only to present papers, with little or no discussion. The recent innovation by the Society for American Archaeology at its annual meetings of having "electronic symposia," where the papers are posted online before the meeting and then are discussed at the meeting, is an excellent advance. More mechanisms of this kind are needed.

What we believe the chapters in this volume show is that it is possible today, in spite of a vast literature and huge amounts of data, to think constructively about the North American Southwest *as a whole* and even to put that region in the context of larger domains such as the Far West or the Americas as a whole. Without computer technology and the software that is now available that might not be so. Certainly, decades-long efforts by SHPOs and others to construct statewide databases of archaeological site information, such as NMCRIS in New Mexico and AZSITE in Arizona, have been invaluable. High-level conferences to reevaluate the structure and content of these databases in light of what else is now possible, and on a multistate basis, would be helpful.

We have shown (Wilcox et al., chap. 12, this vol.) that systematically adding room counts to these databases would be a useful undertaking. Another excellent addition would be systematic lists of ceramic types that occur at each site, with counts, if available. Just as Harold Gladwin and his colleagues did manually with "sherd boards" at Gila Pueblo in the 1930s, using the computer with such data would allow us to see what current data show about the overall distribution of the types, allowing us, for example, to reevaluate the findings of Carlson's (1970) classic study of the distribution of White Mountain Red Ware—and many other similar studies. It is also entirely feasible today to scan images of sherds and the designs on them and then to make those data available on the Internet. Ceramic encyclopedias could thus be constructed that would enormously increase the potential for comparative ceramic studies. The same is true for many other classes of artifacts, including projectile points, bone awls, jewelry, and so on.

Reconciling Different Worldviews

Our experience in investigating Zuni origins from a set of scientific perspectives and trying to communicate with the leadership of the modern Pueblo of Zuni about this results in the very anthropological inference that two different worldviews are in play (Geertz 1973), each having a very different conception of what "truth" is and what is "true" about the past. In the Zuni worldview oral traditions about and conceptions of their origins are—a priori—true and relatively immutable, varying perhaps only in the "telling." In the scientific worldview of the archaeologist the "truth" about Zuni origins or those of any other group is—a priori—intrinsically incomplete, subject to continuing rein-

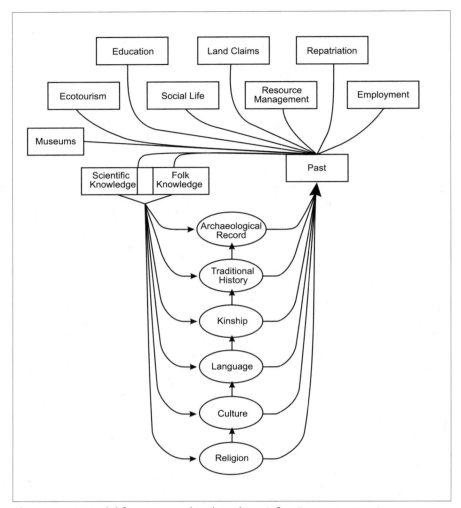

Figure 20.1. Model for reciprocal archaeology (after Ferguson 2003).

terpretation based on new data or new ways of looking at existing data, and so on. An essential difficulty with bureaucratically mandated determinations of cultural affiliation involves the tension between these different notions of "truth" embodied in different worldviews.

Anthropological interest in oral traditions is not new (e.g., Lévi-Strauss 1966; Malinowski 1926; Urton 1990; Vansina 1965, 1978; Wiessner and Tumu 1998). Often called "myths" or "folklore," these accounts have long been the focus of comparative study, not least because the sacred texts of the Western tradition derive from analogous antecedents. At the seminar Stephen Kowa-

lewski urged us to widen our inquiry into Zuni oral tradition by comparing those accounts to parallel ones reported for other American and world cultures. We believe that is a worthy challenge that should be pursued, but that is not something we are prepared to do here. To chart a future direction for continuing research on Zuni origins we want to focus on a more pragmatic issue: how can collaboration between the Zuni people and professional archaeologists be enlarged and deepened?

Cushing's experience may provide us with a clue. He let the Zuni leaders use him, just as they reciprocally let him use them. He declined to marry a Zuni woman and instead chose to

mark his separate identity as an ethnographer (anthropologist) by marrying (in 1882) Emily Magill and bringing her and her sister, Margaret, and a black butler(!) back to Zuni, where they set up housekeeping on the south side of the river across from Zuni (Green 1990; Margaret Magill in Hinsley and Wilcox 1995:535–550). What is it, then, that the Zuni could use that professional archaeologists can provide? We need to ask them this question. T. J. Ferguson (Anyon and Ferguson 1995; Ferguson 2003), who has actively collaborated with a number of southwestern tribes for many years, suggests that there are many areas for fruitful collaboration.

Ferguson (2003) calls this approach "reciprocal archaeology." His conception, by beginning with the categories of information recognized in NAGPRA, identifies six domains that contribute to an understanding of the past: material culture, traditional history, kinship, language, culture, and religion. In figure 20.1 we broaden his "material culture" to the whole archaeological record, believing that material culture is only a part of the data archaeologists can observe in the archaeological record (see Wilcox 2005b; Wilcox et al., chap. 12, this vol.).

Intervening between the study of the past and a series of domains to which such study can contribute Ferguson (2003) places a domain of scientific knowledge. Again, we have enlarged this conception. First, we indicate a domain of folk knowledge whereby the domains of knowledge about the past are interpreted. Second, as in a Venn diagram, we indicate that folk knowledge and scientific knowledge overlap: some folk knowledge is scientific knowledge, and some knowledge regarded as scientific is folk knowledge. Both scientific and folk knowledge are a basis for gaining knowledge from the archaeological record, traditional history, kinship, and the other domains of information about the past. Similarly, scientific knowledge can be used to understand folk knowledge and vice versa: folk knowledge is used to understand scientific knowledge. Complex interchanges on multiple levels can come about as the Zuni and professional archaeologists attempt to communicate with one another, a process well described by Anyon and Ferguson (1995).

Both archaeologists and Indian people bring a combination of folk knowledge and scientific knowledge to the table when they seek to communicate with one another. In this sense we are all equals, though each person knows more about some topics than others, and each may have different interests or questions that intrigue him or her. Assistance with the development of tribal museums and the curation of collections may be other fruitful contexts for collaboration. Collaboration may not be easy, but we think it is possible, as the recent experience of tribal archaeologists shows (Anyon and Ferguson 1995). New contexts for collaboration need to be established that can benefit both Indian tribes *and* the pursuit of scientific knowledge that we call archaeology. We think a fascinating new era is just now beginning. We hope that with hard work the future will bring new knowledge and new cultural understandings that bridge different worldviews and facilitate new forms of communication to the benefit of all.

Generalizing the Methodology

In the process of assessing the issue of Zuni origins we find that a general methodology for addressing such "big picture" questions has also evolved (see also Wilcox 2005a). We now suggest that this methodology is generally applicable to many other fascinating problems and that it provides members of our discipline—if they should decide to accept the challenge—with the possibility of adopting exciting new conceptual frameworks for the conduct of southwestern research. Several general elements of this methodology can be sketched as follows:

Anthropological Holism and Cooperative Efforts

By anthropological holism we mean the incorporation into archaeology of theoretical perspectives, methods, and data from the three other major subfields of anthropology and related disciplines. The key here is to incorporate such perspectives and to involve individuals that represent them at the research design stage. In this way we broaden our problems and questions and insure that all appropriate avenues for research are considered.

It is now standard procedure for archaeologists to engage in what has been called a "multidisciplinary" approach, whereby paleobotanists, palynologists, geomorphologists, and other such specialists are routinely involved in archaeological research. Importantly, this involvement commonly begins at the research design stage of projects, when such specialists contribute to the development of problem domains, specific research questions, and data collection methodologies. We propose that this model may be usefully extended to "higher" levels to include linguists, physical and cultural anthropologists, and others. Obviously, implementation of this perspective requires cooperative efforts among many scholars.

In our efforts to construct a research design for the study of Zuni origins we attempted to implement a holistic approach, one that is fairly well represented in this volume.

However, our advocacy of this perspective highlights a glaring absence here, that of physical anthropology. Especially as regards the history of populations, this subdiscipline has much to offer (e.g., see Torroni et al. 1994; Torroni et al. 1993; Wallace and Torroni 1992); however, our efforts to include such a perspective in the Zuni origins study did not meet with success. There are a number of legal, moral, ethical, and sociological issues associated with, for example, the exploration of cultural affiliation through analyses of human remains and collection of DNA samples from modern populations. Nonetheless, such issues must be taken on and solved if the full range of useful perspectives on anthropological problems is to be exploited.

Relational Data, Depositional Process, and Interaction

The questions we posed in this volume rest on the premise that relations observable in the archaeological record are data and that their study permits archaeologists to make statements about human behavioral interactions that are testable using new observations of the archaeological record. Thus, for example, the domains of social groups can be specified using relational data such as doorway access patterns, and the people who utilized those domains can be conceptualized as the agents responsible for the depositional events and their "traces" (Sullivan 1978) that produced important parts of that record. Once such social domains have been identified, comparisons among them can be initiated that include sourcing studies of the artifacts found in each, adding new data to a growing matrix of "transactional" behaviors that link these domains to one another (Abbott 1994). In many cases existing archaeological data can be reconceptualized in this way, and new insights into interaction patterning can be achieved (Wilcox 2005b).

Operating on Multiple Temporal and Spatial Scales

In the context of answering the general question, How did things come to be as they are? the need to be aware of and to operate at different temporal scales stems from a basic characteristic of cultural processes: different processes that influence human behaviors can and do occur at different rates, and it is important to recognize and study the interrelationships of such processes. For example, linguistic differentiation may develop over longer time spans than population coalescence, and both may, in turn, occur in the context of low-frequency environmental processes having longer amplitudes than either. The latter may strongly influence both of the former by imposing limitations on or creating new opportunities for different adaptations, depending upon existing technologies and organizations, and so on. Successful interpretation of the behaviors represented in a site (or a set of sites, a settlement system, a regional system, etc.) demands recognition and study of not only the processes influencing those behaviors but the differential rates at which those processes may occur.

In parallel fashion we argue for the need to operate at multiple spatial scales. Once again, successful interpretations of past behaviors represented at a site (a set of sites, a settlement system, a regional system, etc.) depend in part upon recognition and study of processes operating differentially and simultaneously on multiple spatial scales. Here again relationships are the key to identifying processes, particularly those relations

derived from the comparison of changing patterns from one period to the next or one area to another. Such relational facts can be accounted for by postulating processes whose implications can be tested using other classes of archaeological data.

Population Thinking and Boundaries

In chapter 22 Kowalewski emphasizes the need for *population thinking* as opposed to typological thinking, that is, the need to deal with variation within and across populations as a key to inferences concerning past behaviors, "instead of submerging it [variation] prematurely into categorical types." *Populations* may be actual human populations or populations of particular site types (e.g., great house sites), artifact types or other material remains (e.g., macaws and copper bells), tree-ring series, and myriad other archaeological phenomena targeted for study by virtue of the behavioral inferences they may allow.

With respect to demographics, such thinking implies the need for *quantification* (estimating past populations) and the related notions of *boundaries* and *neighbors*. The latter also raise the difficult operational issue of identifying boundaries between populations. Several chapters in this volume (Diehl, chap. 11, Mills, chap. 13, Schaafsma and Young, chap. 15, Vokes and Gregory, chap. 17, Webster, chap. 16, Wilcox et al., chap. 12) illustrate various ways in which such quantification and identification may be approached.

Adaptation as an Organizing Principle

Earlier in this chapter we proposed a heuristic concept of adaptation that serves as an organizing principle for the differentiation and study of hu-

man populations. It incorporates human (population)–natural environmental relationships as well as human (population)–human (population) relationships so that the important aspects of each may be given appropriate weight in any given study.

Synthesis as a Continuing Goal

As exemplified in many of the chapters above, huge quantities of data produced over the last several decades as a result of contract research and from other sources provide a basis for new syntheses relating to any number of research problems. Thus, synthesis, what Fowler (chap. 21, this vol.) calls "stock taking," should be a continuing goal in our efforts. At the outset the construction of research designs provides an opportunity for synthesis, and such research designs may be seen as a kind of synthesis—statements of where we are with respect to a given set of problems and what needs to be done to answer them. By pursuing those problems holistically and relationally, on multiple temporal and spatial scales, and in the context of adaptation, subsequent new syntheses will emerge.

Some Suggested Problem Domains

These elements together constitute a methodology for systematically examining archaeological data in a way that permits the formulation of anthropologically meaningful statements about the past. The present volume illustrates the application of this methodology to a significant anthropological problem, that of Zuni origins. We have demonstrated that it is imperative to examine this issue on a nested set of spatial scales, from the household level to macroregional scales over the entire Southwest and even all of the Americas. Temporally, it is necessary to consider processes operating in the present and those operative as long as 20,000 years ago. And it is important to bring to bear a wide range of multidisciplinary expertise and to operate in a holistic manner to develop and employ relational data. We dare say that the same is true for many other anthropological problems.

A few examples drawn from points touched on in the present volume can readily be defined as problem domains amenable to future synthetic research using the general methodology we propose. There are some obvious overlaps in specific research questions implied by these problem domains, highlighting the connectivity and cross-fertilization implicit in research undertaken in a holistic manner and at multiple temporal and spatial scales.

Archaic Period Populations, Boundaries, and Linguistic Distributions. Implementation of research under this problem domain would include a systematic and Southwest- and Great Basin–wide reexamination of Archaic projectile point distributions; expert consensus should be the basis for classification of types and materials, and GIS should be used to explore the parameters of distributions in time and space. Questions of Archaic period boundaries and interaction could then be revisited and issues of linguistic distributions and differentiation further addressed.

A Geomorphic Model of Archaic and Early Agricultural Period Settlement Location. This problem domain could guide a comprehensive, Southwest-wide analysis of geomorphic settings designed to reconstruct the succession of landscapes occupied by Archaic and Early Agricultural period populations. As in the Sundance Archaeological Project in the Great Basin (Nials 1999), locations where buried sites are likely can thus be targeted, tested, and managed. A much better baseline for assessing southwestern demographic structures during these periods could thus be made. The Center for Desert Archaeology is now engaged in similar research on a smaller geographic scale, focusing on the Early Agricultural period in the principal drainages of the Gila River above its confluence with the Salt.

The Nature of Pueblo I Populations, Boundaries, and Linguistic Distributions. This problem domain could provide the context for extension of the Coalescent Communities Database to intervals prior to AD 1200. In particular, a systematic, Southwest-wide synthesis of archaeological data for the Pueblo I period (AD 750–900) could be undertaken to provide a basis for study of demographics, boundaries, and linguistic distributions during this important interval in Southwest prehistory.

The Development and Temporal Distribution of Perishable Technologies. In chapter 16 Webster demonstrates the value of perishable materials in assessments of cultural identities and boundaries. This problem domain would guide a systematic, Southwest-wide program to directly date perishables, classify their technologies, and study the resulting spatial and temporal distributions to further current understandings of cultural identities and boundaries through time.

Keresan and Tanoan Origins. Given what has now been accomplished with respect to Zuni, one obvious direction is to undertake similar studies emphasizing the other Puebloan linguistic groups. Despite the fact that multiple villages are represented, Keresan, too, is a linguistic isolate and a "compact language family" (Golla 2000). The same kinds of problems and questions used in the study of Zuni origins could be directly applied to Keresan. While Tanoan presents a slightly more complex picture, such approaches should also prove fruitful with reference to this language group. Many other similar problem domains can easily be formulated, and the foregoing simply are meant to provide useful examples that may be emulated.

Kowalewski's strictures (chap. 22, this vol.) about the impossibility of recognizing linguistic groupings archaeologically at first sight might deter us from such an effort. However, his enthusiasm for what has been accomplished in the process of searching for Zuni origins suggests that many valuable, if "unintended," consequences (to cite Fowler's observation) encourages us to view such research as highly worthwhile.

A Final Word

In closing we draw on findings included in the present volume to suggest some hypotheses for further anthropological inquiry into how southwestern linguistic distributions came to be as they are. Using data presented in chapter 12 and elsewhere in this volume figs. 20.2–20.4 specify a comprehensive set of hypotheses about southwestern linguistic distributions from AD 1200 to 1600 that are amenable to future anthropological inquiry and testing. Let these maps and the hypotheses they represent be the final word—for now.

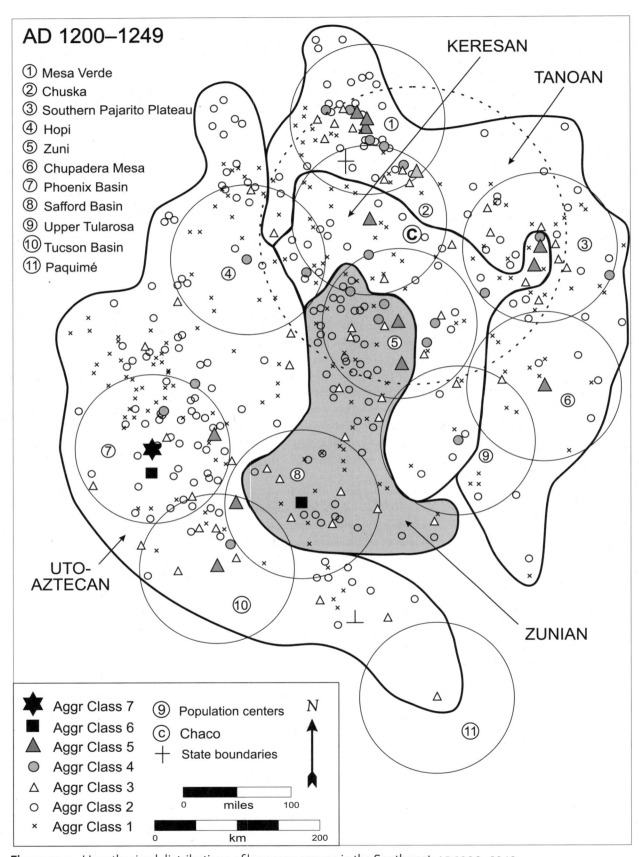

Figure 20.2. Hypothesized distributions of language groups in the Southwest, AD 1200–1249.

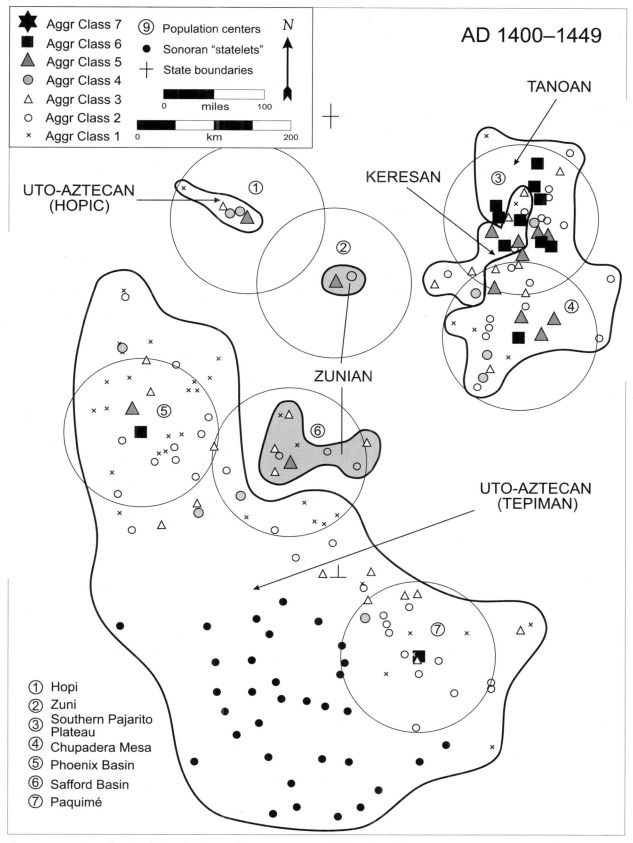

Figure 20.3. Hypothesized distributions of language groups in the Southwest, AD 1400–1449.

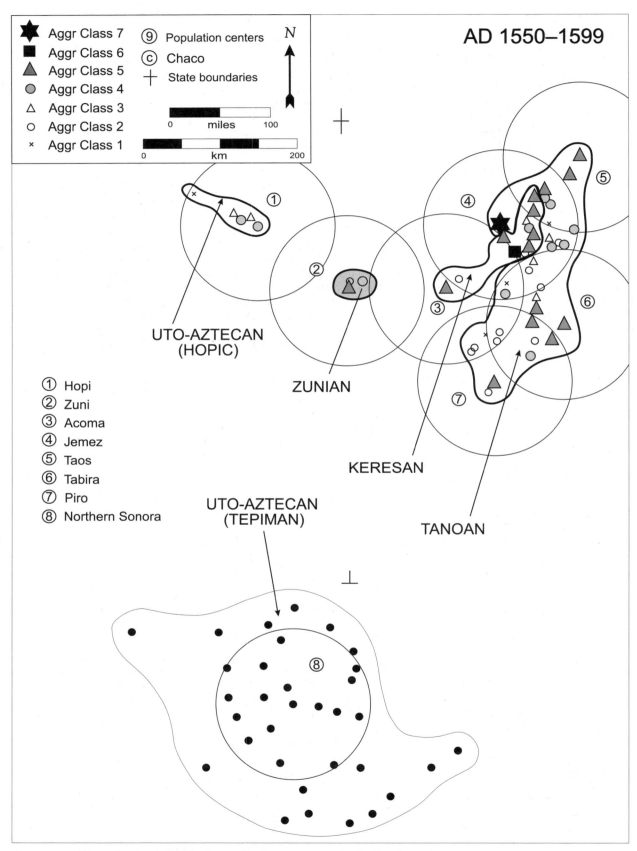

Figure 20.4. Hypothesized distributions of language groups in the Southwest, AD 1550–1599.

Notes

1. Nichols (1990, 1998) applies an average figure for linguistic differentiation, assuming a uniform rate of change, and concludes that the Americas must have been occupied as early as New Guinea or Australia, that is, by 35,000 B.P. or earlier. By her own argument, however, if the rate of differentiation was much greater than she assumes, as it may well have been when *Homo sapiens sapiens* spread into a pristine hemisphere, the sand supporting her conclusions wafts away very rapidly; so, too, if any of the arguments for linguistic superstocks in the Americas are correct.

2. Krantz (recently deceased) was a physical anthropologist and longtime faculty member at Washington State University and, apparently, a well-respected member of the profession. One possible reason for the fact that his ideas concerning the population of western North America have not been widely considered may have had nothing to do with critical evaluation of his anthropological work. In the late 1970s and early 1980s Krantz apparently became fascinated with the Big Foot or Sasquatch phenomenon and devoted considerable time and energy to pursuing that interest (obsession?). This related turn in his life may have unduly influenced others' view of his more conventional anthropological studies (Fred Nials, personal communication 2003).

3. The late Edmund Ladd questioned just how well Cushing succeeded in learning Zuni, but it is difficult to evaluate his critique. Cushing did begin work on a Zuni dictionary, the results of which modern linguists may consult in the archives of the Southwest Museum in Los Angeles.

4. Following Hawley (1950) and Ford et al. (1972) we would presume that the Chacoans of the southern San Juan Basin spoke Keresan. The San Mateo Chacoans may also have done so; if they were in part ancestors of the populations of Cebolleta Mesa and Acoma, it might be that the difference between eastern and western Keresan dates to the eleventh century, when the San Mateo "polity" marked its independence from the San Juan Chacoans. Much more "local knowledge" than we now possess is needed to elucidate the plausibility of these suggestions and then, if warranted, to test them.

5. Possibly the first two stages of the Palavayu rock art style (McCreery and Malotki 1994) were also made by Zunian speakers (cf. Schaafsma and Young, chap. 15, this vol.). The geographic domain of the style is coincident with the way the Forestdale branch has been drawn (Martin 1979; Wheat 1955). During Pueblo II–III that area is occupied by the distribution of circular great kivas that form a periphery of the Puerco of the West Chaco system (Herr 2001). However, what rock art styles may be present in the Puerco of the West is unknown (Ekkehart Malotki and Polly Schaafsma, personal communications 2002). The latest Palavayu style is more clearly produced by Hopi speakers who occupied this domain in Pueblo IV times (Lyons 2003). Much more research on these intriguing possibilities is needed.

21 Comments on Zuni Origins

Toward a New Synthesis of Southwestern Archaeology

Don D. Fowler

The most interesting intellectual excursions are often those that start out with one goal or destination in mind and wind up somewhere else. Such, it seems, has been the fate and good fortune of the Mogollon-Zuni conference. The organizers brought together a band of diverse scholars and gave them the assignment of attempting to make some "valid statements" (see below) about the relationships between two seeming anthropological "anomalies" in the greater North American Southwest (hereafter, the Southwest): "Zuni" and "Mogollon." I place "anomalies," "Zuni," and "Mogollon" in quotes to mark them as intellectual constructs that take on different meanings within different "specific theoretical frameworks" (again, see below). In the end it is uncertain how many valid statements are made herein about the specific relationships in question, although certainly a number may prove to be so. The chapters collectively represent a thorough vetting of what is known, asserted, or suspected about the culture histories of the region and the changing landscapes on which those histories were played out. There is a concomitant vetting of the databases and methods of collecting and interpreting those data on which the knowledge, assertions, or suspicions are based. In the process some atten-

tion is paid to the larger philosophical issues that underlie archaeological inquiry in general (Trigger 2003; Wylie 2002).

It is not my intent to discuss in detail the many new data sets and dozens of interesting and provocative new ideas contained in the chapters in this volume. My intent, rather, is to discuss some of the issues raised in a broader intellectual history context and comment on the uses of archaeology for *heritage* as well as *historical* purposes in the Southwest. I begin with some general considerations relating to archaeological knowledge making.

According to Hardesty and Fowler, "Archaeology is concerned with the things, relations, processes, and meanings of past sociocultural/environmental totalities and their temporal and spatial boundaries, organizations, operations, and changes over time and across the world" (2001:73). Put less verbosely, archaeology is an organized inquiry into the relationships and meanings of the places and objects of the past. The central methodological question in archaeological inquiry is, "How do you get from the distributions of artifacts, ecofacts [plant and animal remains] and geofacts [soils, sediments, minerals], and their relationships on and in the ground, to valid statements about past

patterned human behavior within specific theoretical frameworks?" (Hardesty and Fowler 2001:73).

"Valid statements" about "past patterned human behavior" are agreed-upon archaeological answers to the questions of who, what, where, when, how, and why. *Who* refers to "populations" or "groups" defined genetically, culturally, linguistically, or some combination of the three. *What* refers to material remains: artifacts, ecofacts, and geofacts as well as the sites and land forms on and in which they occur. *Where* refers to specific geographic regions, areas, or locales in which the *who* lived and left material remains. *When* refers to chronologies, or increments of chronologies, strung along some portion of the "absolute" time scale represented by the BCE/CE (BC/AD) continuum. *How* refers to the organization, operation, and changes within and among the things, relations, and processes of past sociocultural/environmental totalities. *Why* refers first to the meanings archaeologists give to their data "within specific theoretical frameworks" and, second, to the inferences they make about how and what things, relations, processes, and places may have meant to past populations or groups.

Attempts to answer the questions, and the methods used to arrive at the answers, collectively comprise the history of archaeological inquiry (Trigger 1989). In the Southwest such inquiry has been under way since about 1845 (Cordell and Fowler 2005; Fowler 1992, 2000; Snead 2001; Wilcox and Fowler 2002). Some of the questions are perennial, addressed and readdressed as new data, methods, and theoretical frameworks provide new and seemingly valid answers. Two intellectual processes seem to be at work here: agenda setting and stock taking, or, "Here's where we should go" and "Where are we, and where do we go from here?"

David Wilcox and I (Fowler and Wilcox 1999; Wilcox and Fowler 2002) have used the concept of "agenda setting" as a way of discussing intellectual shifts in southwestern anthropology. A scholar poses a question or series of questions or hypotheses, thus setting a new research agenda. Various "worker bees" then proceed to generate, sift, and order many new data in support or refutation of the question(s). Grossly oversimplified, there have been about half a dozen agendas set since 1845. The first three were set by Albert Gallatin (1845, 1848), Lewis Henry Morgan (1881), and Frank Hamilton Cushing (1888) (see Fowler 2000:50–70, 148–160).

Part of Cushing's agenda was to develop a culture history, especially migration history, by using archaeology to verify Pueblo (specifically, Zuni) legend and myth. Jesse Walter Fewkes and, to a degree, Walter Hough pursued this part of Cushing's agenda (see Fowler 2005). As noted below, between 1904 and 1914 Edgar Lee Hewett set partial new agendas by defining ethnic-geographic subareas in the Southwest and focusing attention on cultural-environmental relationships. The first "New Archaeology" (Kidder 1924, 1927; Wissler 1917; see also Roberts 1935) set a new agenda focused on time-space relations (the what, when, and where questions), and concerns with cultural-environmental relationships were pushed into the background until the 1930s. The second "New Archaeology," beginning in the 1960s and metamorphosing in various ways since then, set agendas centered on issues of process (the how and why questions).

There have also been periodic stock takings to assess the research agendas and the results of investigations stimulated by them. The 1927 Pecos Conference (Kidder 1927) was certainly the first and most important. There has only ever been one overall stock taking of southwestern anthropology, in 1953 (Haury 1954). Follow-up efforts include Jennings (1956) and Lister (1961). In my discussion of several relevant questions I draw from these various efforts because they have direct salience and current relevance for the data sets, ideas, suppositions, and suspicions set forth in the present effort at stock taking and agenda setting. My discussion is best organized around a series of questions.

Question 1. Peopling of the Western Hemisphere

The first (and oldest) perennial question relates to the "first peopling" of the Western Hemisphere (hereafter, WH), or, as David Meltzer (2003) puts it, the "Who, When, from Where, How and How Often?" question. It is a matter of irony to some scholars that answers to Question 1 were not very different in 2005 than they were in 1780 or 1925. The German anatomist Johann Blumenbach (1865:273–274) in 1780 postulated that the WH was colonized from Northeast Asia by three distinct populations moving across the Bering Strait, the latest being the Eskimos (Inuit). In 1925 the American physical anthropologist Aleš Hrdlička (1925) agreed with Blumenbach about the area of origin and guess-timated that when solid geomorphological and paleontological evidence was found, the peopling of the WH would prove to be as early as ca. 15,000 B.P. Both the area of origin and the timing are still regarded as generally valid by most Quaternary geologists, archaeologists, linguists, and human biologists. Whether the colonists came by land or by sea—or both—has been debated for centuries (Huddleston 1967) and is a matter of great current discussion (Meltzer 2003).

It is ironic that Hrdlička's guess about timing would be published in the same year that the first hard evidence was discovered for a "deep time" colonization of the WH and the coexistence of humans and Pleistocene megafauna in the Southwest (Fowler 2000:319–320). By 1940 the Clovis, Folsom, and other early tool traditions were accepted, as was the idea of "Clovis first" (Roberts 1940b). But from the outset there were those who campaigned, on scant and questionable evidence, for various "pre-Clovis" peoples, most notably, Alex Krieger (1953:238–243) and others much farther out toward fringe science. Five decades later the campaign continues, still hotly contested, still without general acceptance (Gonzalez et al. 2003; Haynes 2002; Huckell 2005; Meltzer 2003), although many pre-Clovis campaigners are regarded as mainstream rather than fringe scientists. More work needs to be done.

The difference between the assertions of Blumenbach, Hrdlička, and Krieger and contemporary theorizing is an enormously larger set of databases, painstakingly compiled and vetted over the past 50 years. While many specifics of timing, routes, and demographics remain frustratingly vague and contentious, extant geological, paleoecological, taphonomic, and archaeological databases (Betancourt 2003; Thompson et al. 2003; Yesner and Slobodin 2003) now allow much more fine-grained statements about the lives, times, and activities of the initial WH colonizers and their early descendants—those populations whose tool kits are variously labeled "Paleoindian," "Paleoarchaic," and "Early Archaic." Drawing on some of these databases, Matson (chap. 7, this vol.) is able to paint a rather detailed, if still speculative, picture of the timing and activities of such peoples in the Southwest.

Question 2. Changing Southwestern Paleoenvironments

From 1850 until about 1910 scant attention was paid to the question of past environments in which early populations lived. Much of this had to do with the prevailing opinion that WH culture history was a matter of shallow, not deep, time (Sapir 1949 [1916]). The geographer Ellsworth Huntington (1914) made the first systematic attempt to relate past climates —and, hence, past environments—to archaeological cultures in the Southwest. At the same time, partly stimulated by Huntington's work, Edgar Lee Hewett (Hewett et al. 1913) called attention to the need to consider environment and climate in relation to Rio Grande Puebloan development. While Huntington's (1915, 1924) environmental deterministic assertions were not palatable to many, his work helped stimulate the systematic study of past climates and environments in the Southwest and elsewhere (Nash and Dean 2005). But it was not until the acceptance of the idea that humans began colonizing the WH in deep time that systematic questions began to be asked, and answered, about the

nature and timing of "paleoclimates" and "paleoenvironments" in Late Pleistocene and Holocene times. By the 1930s the answers made it possible for southwestern archaeologists to begin the development of relatively fine-grained models of sequential human–environment interactions within theoretical frameworks at first called "economic geography," then "human ecology" (Hargrave 1931b, 1934; see also Forde 1934), and later "cultural ecology" (Steward 1936, 1937, 1955).

In 2005 thousands of carefully collected and analyzed ecofact and geofact data sets and their stratigraphic and chronological relationships allowed extremely sophisticated reconstructions of southwestern paleoclimates and environments. There is no comparable database for any other region of the world (Betancourt 2003; Thompson et al. 2003). Chapter 6 by Jeffrey Dean is a tour de force summary of what is currently known and a demonstration of how that knowledge can be used to help create valid statements about human demographics, adaptive behavior, and migrations in the region. Chapter 5 by Gregory and Nials ranks as a complementary tour de force, relating paleoclimates to larger cyclical weather patterns on hemispheric and worldwide scales. Both chapters reflect the practice of science at its best: the patient, painstaking development of methods of data collection; careful, ongoing scrutiny of the methods and the collected data; and continued formulation and testing of new hypotheses to best account for extant data.

Most geographers and archaeologists long ago rejected Huntington's *environmental determinism* in favor of some form of *environmental possibilism*. Possibilism is a vague but very useful concept. It simply means that, in any specified time frame, a given population using extant technology

may "adapt to" or make a living from an extant environment in a *variety of possible ways*. "Adapting to" an environment means learning about it and its edible and useful resources and developing new technologies, social forms, and ideas to better utilize those resources.

Possibilism implies "agency" in the broad sense, that is, the recognition that humans in all times and places are intelligent, proactive, inquisitive, and inventive, acting in their own best interests as they define those interests. The nineteenth-century conundrum that "savage," "tribal," or "peasant" folk were/are "bound by tradition," hence uninventive, resistant to change, and so on, was and is simply colonialist/imperialist propaganda (Wolf 1999). The extreme materialist position that humans are "driven by forces of history" outside their control is specious and essentialist. Current ideas that hunter-gatherers forage "optimally" in accordance with principles of twenty-first-century corporate greed are equally untenable. (Kelly [1995] provides a judicious review of the roles that stereotypical hunter-gatherers and their purported behaviors have played in anthropological theory.) The chapters in this volume demonstrate, it seems to me, both possibilism and agency at work in the pre-European Southwest. The Hohokam and ancestral Puebloan cultures are ongoing case studies over three-plus millennia of proactive and inventive material and ideological adaptations by individuals and groups to changing environments through processes of migration, social fission, and social fusion, coupled with technological and ideological development.

Question 3. Linguistic Relationships

It has been recognized for centuries that language "family" relationships have major implications for sorting out culture histories of regions throughout the world. Systematic classifications of the indigenous languages of North America have been ongoing for two centuries (Goddard 1996). The Zuni language is of particular importance for the present volume. It is an apparent "isolate"; that is, it cannot be demonstrably linked to any other WH (or, indeed, Eastern Hemisphere) language family, as the chapter by Jane Hill in this volume demonstrates. Zuni's status as an isolate makes it particularly intriguing and frustrating for those attempting valid statements about southwestern culture history and indeed is a major impetus for the present volume. I return to the issue of linguistic relationships below.

Question 4. What Were the "Demographics" of Pre-European Populations?

The question of how many people lived in the WH or regions thereof during specific time periods prior to the advent of Europeans has vexed historical demographers, anthropologists, and archaeologists for over a century. The short answer is, no one knows. Estimates vary, often by orders of magnitude; none have a firm foundation (Henige 1998). Questions about historical demography have been asked repeatedly in the Southwest since the 1840s (Fowler 2000:3). Archaeologists and others have looked at all those ruins and wondered how many folk lived in each one and when. The vexing questions are, How many of the rooms in each ruin were "living" rooms or "family units," and how many were occupied during any specific time period? Much depends on the answers, which in turn depend on the assumptions made by the analyst. If 80 percent of the rooms in a 3,000-room pueblo are classified as living

rooms and thought to have been occupied during specific decades, then models of sociopolitical coalescence and complexity emerge (Kintigh, chap. 18, this vol.; Lekson 2005) that are different from, say, a 30 percent figure. Several of the authors herein grapple with this thorny issue and arrive at "best guesses." The value of the guesses is that their underlying assumptions are made explicit; previously, this was not always the case.

Question 5. The Advent of Agriculture

Albert Gallatin (1848) was apparently the first to recognize that the major southwestern cultigens, especially maize, were of tropical origins. Archaeologists, biogeographers, and plant geneticists have devoted enormous amounts of research time to formulating what they hope are valid statements about the origins of agriculture as well as the timing and routes of its spread in the WH. The answers underlie major questions about southwestern culture history and cultural processes that have been posed for over a century: What were the environmental and sociocultural consequences over time of the advent —and subsequent development—of agricultural practices (Cordell 1997: 127–441)? Several chapters in this volume address this issue on archaeological, environmental, and linguistic grounds.

Question 6. Trade Relations: Baubles, Bangles, Birds, and Bells

The sociopolitical implications of internal trade relationships within the Southwest and external trade connections with other regions have long intrigued archaeologists and anthropologists. The exhaustive review by Vokes and Gregory (chap. 17, this vol.)

of the internal and external trade of exotics provides a heretofore unavailable critical summary of the points of origin and movements into and out of the Southwest of shell, turquoise, macaws, copper bells, and other classes of apparently prestational items (Mauss 1954). It will provide a baseline data set for years to come for those concerned with the implications of trade for internal sociopolitical and ideological processes within the Southwest and for the external relationships between the Southwest and adjacent and distant regions.

Issues of external trade and its implications were, in effect, put on hold in southwestern archaeology from about 1917 to 1945. As Carl Sauer noted,

> The notion of *Apartheid* of a southwestern culture would not have arisen . . . if Mexico had been the center from which anthropological studies spread through North America. The notions about southwestern culture originated in the years when it was considered proper to infer endemism as dominant in culture, to maximize development in situ and to minimize the significance of dispersal and diffusion. A familiar example is the postulated succession of stages from Basketmaker I to Pueblo V, construed mainly as autochthonous "evolution" [1954:553].

It is generally accepted that Emil Haury's (1945b) article on contacts between the Southwest and Mexico mortally wounded assertions of endemic autochthonous apartheid and reopened the way for systematic investigations of relationships across an invisible line that did not exist until the 1850s (Jennings 1956; Kirchoff 1954; Wilcox 1986b). Thus, Vokes and Gregory are able to summarize and critique nearly six decades of research on southwestern-Mesoamerican relationships as reflected in the movement of exotics.

Question 7. The Chameleonic Natures of Ethnicity and Ethnogenesis

The bulk of the chapters in the present volume address, from various perspectives, the related issues of ethnicity and ethnogenesis and their relationships to questions of migration. Issues of ethnicity and ethnogenesis have been matters of dominant concern in Americanist and, indeed, world ethnological and anthropological discourse for five centuries (Eriksen and Nielsen 2001; Fowler 2000) and are the central concern of the present volume. The basic anthropological question is, When, where, how, and why did human groups begin differentiating themselves as they moved across and/or settled into various regions of the world (Gamble 1994; Sykes 2001)? Some have argued that self-defined human groups (see the discussion below) have used various markers to set themselves apart from relevant "others" since at least Upper Paleolithic times. Some (e.g., Marshack 1991) speculate that the origins of personal ornament ("assertive styles" on the individual level; see Clark, chap. 4, this vol.) lay in visibly marking the oppositional otherness of "us vs. them" by "emblemic styles" (again, see Clark, chap. 4, this vol.) on the group level: "We wear three-strand dentalia shell necklaces to set us apart from others in our known world," etc. Visible and nonvisible "ethnic" labels/markers have been imposed by dominant groups on subordinate groups of all sorts in imperialist/colonialist contexts ever since there have been imperialism and colonialism in the Eastern and Western Hemispheres over at least five millennia (Scarre and Fagan 1997).

Whether self-defined or imposed, visible ethnic marking trickles down through culture histories in various forms: sumptuary clothing laws, self-defined clothing and ornament styles in general, medieval military heraldry, tattooing, weapons styles, pottery designs and manufacturing techniques, rock art, architecture, ritual paraphernalia, parietal art, textile designs and manufacturing techniques, etc., etc. Nonvisible markers include languages, religious ideologies, and an enormous range of patterned behaviors—the ideational and social-interactional aspects of human cultures. These sometimes can be teased out for those past cultures having decipherable written records. For other past cultures, identifying and interpreting either visible or nonvisible markers become much more problematic. That problem is the key issue the current chapters grapple with in trying to sort out ethnicity, ethnogenesis, and migration.

Ethnogenesis

Jonathan Hill (1996:1) notes that "cultural anthropologists have generally used the term *ethnogenesis* to describe the historical emergence of a people who define themselves in relation to a sociocultural and linguistic heritage." For such a people there is usually some sort of oral or written canonical text defining a place and/or process of emergence or origin and the relevant visible and nonvisible markers of difference that set the people apart from others. Robert Preucel (2005) lists three approaches to ethnicity that have been applied at various times in southwestern archaeology: primordialist, instrumentalist, and practice based. Each attempts to construct valid statements about culture histories but within different theoretical frameworks.

Primordialist models assume that

ethnicity is an "innate aspect of human identity inherited by birth and persisting through all social formations" (Preucel 2005:186). This is, of course, a very old idea in Western discourse, harking all the way back to Sumerian, Egyptian, and biblical times, for example, "Sumerians" vs. "Akkadians," "Egyptians" vs. "Nubians," "Hebrews" (and, later, "Jews") vs. everyone else. In modern anthropological discourse primordialist models are closely identified with the German concept of *Volk* most clearly established by Johann Herder (1966 [1800]) in the early nineteenth century. Each Volk was defined by a specific combination of "race," language, and culture. Each had a unique "Volk psychology" formed by the interaction of the Volk and its environment. Early-twentieth-century German culture historians, such as Gustaf Kossinna and his colleagues, took Herder's ideas to their absurd racialist conclusions (Fowler 1987; Poliakov 1974). Elsewhere in Europe and the Americas primordialist models were particularly favored by those espousing polygenetic theories of human origins (e.g., Nott and Gliddon 1854).

With the advent of processual archaeology, instrumental approaches to ethnicity became common in southwestern studies. Instrumental approaches, according to Preucel,

> regard ethnicity as a means of establishing social relations and negotiating access to economic and political resources. . . . [T]here is a recognition that ethnicity is not a stable quality and that it varies over time and space in accordance with local conditions and characteristics. Specific cultural traits may signal ethnic differences in some cases but not in others [2005:195].

As several of the chapters in this volume demonstrate, "ethnic" markers can be diffused, emulated, adopted, traded, or co-opted and take on other meanings in new contexts. The recognition of this fact is what makes teasing out "real" ethnic markers from the archaeological record so difficult. Instrumental approaches often focus on matters of style (Carr and Neitzel 1995; Conkey and Hastorf 1990). Style is seen as a social variable, a boundary marker, useful in alliance formation and ethnogenesis studies. Patricia Crown's (1994) excellent study illustrates just how useful the concept of style can be in studies of migration, social formation, and ideology. The principles she and others have established are applied in several of the present chapters.

Practice-based approaches to ethnicity, according to Preucel, center on agency. Citing Andrew Duff (2002), he argues that "ethnicity can be viewed as a role that actors consciously adopt depending on their self-interest and specific structural constraints" (Preucel 2005:201). This approach is useful in considering how groups may have assumed new "ethnic" identities as they moved, merged, and melded in the Southwest from AD 1100 on (Wilcox 1991b). Preucel, Traxler, and Wilcox (2002) have also adopted a practice-based approach in their studies of post-Spanish Pueblo archaeology in the Southwest.

Models of Ethnicity and Ethnogenesis in the Southwest
Cushing's Quasi-Primordialist Theory

The German ethnologist Adolf Bastian merged the Cartesian concept of innate ideas with Herder's concept of *Volk* and postulated that each Volk had a unique and specific set of "Elementary Ideas" developed in its localized, "original homeland" (Koepping 1983). These unique ideas were expressed in conceptual plans of sociocultural spaces, social forms, material cultures, and ideologies. Fowler (1992) and Preucel (2005) have argued that Frank Hamilton Cushing (1888) adopted Bastian's Elementary Ideas in his conceptualization of the culture history of the "*Original* Pueblo, Aridian or Shiwian peoples." In this model the original Pueblo homeland was the San Juan Basin. The people were forced to move and settled in the Gila Basin, where their "original ideas" of Middle Place and septenary segmentation were expressed in the ruined "cities" later to be labeled Hohokam sites. Earthquakes forced abandonment and population dispersal ca. 1,500–2,000 years ago. Groups dispersed in various directions, but some finally reached the "Middle Place" to coalesce into the historic Zuni. Some became other southwestern Pueblo groups; still others possibly were ancestral to Mexican groups and even the Inca of Peru (Cushing 1888; Fowler 1992:25–27).

While Cushing's model is primordialist, he does not adhere to the strict German model of Volk as a unique combination of phenotype, language, and culture. He has little to say about physical types, apparently assuming that all Puebloans are basically physically the same. Language is an independent variable: non-Zuni-speaking groups hive off from the Gila River dispersal point. At least one of the groups apparently spoke ancestral Zuni, which became the dominant language after the several groups arrived at the long-sought-for Middle Place from different directions (see Ferguson, chap. 19, this vol.).

Hewett's "Ethnic Districts"

The first apparent use of the concept of ethnicity in southwestern archaeology was by Edgar Lee Hewett in his 1908 doctoral dissertation. For Hewett, a "culture area [is] a region where one predominant type of culture is found" (1993 [1908]:9); in the Southwest this is the "Pueblo Region." The region encompasses portions of four river basins, the Rio Grande, San Juan, Little Colorado, and Gila, and one "closed basin," the Chihuahua Basin. Each basin "represents a sub-area of culture and each has its own individuality." Each sub-area has "numerous districts . . . in which common cultural peculiarities are to be found, while special differences in construction, decoration, industrial techniques, mortuary customs, etc. display *ethnic variations*. *These sub-areas are called ethnic districts*" (Hewett 1993 [1908]:10–11; emphasis added). Examples include Chaco Canyon and Mesa Verde in the San Juan Basin and Pajarito and Pecos in the Rio Grande Basin. Hewett later states that "sub-division by ethnic district should apply to the culture only, for there is no analogy whatever between cultural and linguistic areas" (1993 [1908]:29). He is, in effect, partially rejecting a primordialist model, reserving "ethnic" to refer to sets of material culture markers, such as ceramics, architecture, and settlement organization, that are different enough to warrant their being distinguished from marker sets in adjacent areas.

Cushing and Hewett are cited to indicate that concerns with ethnogenesis and ethnicity are long-standing in southwestern archaeology. The present volume represents the most recent effort to address these concerns.

Demonstrating Ethnicity, Ethnogenesis, and Migration in the Southwest
The Perils and Pleasures of the "Ceramic Bacillus"

Pottery, wherever it occurs, is an archaeological workhorse. Crocks, broken and whole, have many potential uses. They provide databases for hypotheses about migrations, sociocultural aggregation and complexity, family and lineage organization, demographic change, technological change, ideology, and ethnicity and ethnogenesis. One might reasonably ask, How many hypotheses can a pot hold? Walter Taylor asserted that

> not only has the Southwest nurtured ceramic studies, but ceramic studies have dominated southwestern archaeology.... The so-called culture classification has been dominated by ceramic criteria. This is particularly so of the Pecos classification and Colton's [1938, 1953] handling of the Gila Pueblo classification [Gladwin and Gladwin 1934]. In fact, Colton has been so much influenced by pottery that he identifies his ceramic categories with aboriginal sociopolitical groups on a one-to-one basis; in other words, to him, pottery distinctions are indicative of tribal distinctions [1954:568–569].

J. O. Brew and Watson Smith rejected the Gladwin/Colton systems of classification and the culture history models based on those systems. In commenting on the concept of area cotradition they wrote, "We must ... guard against getting into the difficulty with this new terminology, that we have just experienced in the period of wasted time [1934–1953] and fruitless argument over 'types,' 'wares,' 'branches' and 'phases'" (Brew and Smith 1954:587). Cynthia

Irwin-Williams (chap. 2, this vol.) expressed a similar sentiment in 1967: "A pot speaks no language[,] and ... any simple out-of-context equation between an archaeological assemblage and a linguistic group is doomed to failure." Robert Lister would later say, "Pottery has always been of concern to most southwestern archaeologists, and is almost worshiped on the altar by some" (1961: 43). Such overblown emphasis on crockery and the questions it may be made to answer was called by A. V. Kidder (1957, cited by Fowler 2000:285) the southwestern "ceramic bacillus."

Kidder certainly helped let the ceramic bacillus loose by his support of Anna Shepard's studies of ceramic sourcing and technology (Bishop and Lange 1991). Dean Wilson's excellent study (chap. 14, this vol.) is a lineal descendant of Shepard's work. The work of Patricia Crown (1994) and Barbara Mills and her students (Mills, chap. 13, this vol.; Mills et al. 1999) demonstrates just how useful carefully analyzed ceramic data can be in getting from artifactual relationships on and in the ground to valid statements about human behavior, culture history, and culture processes of the sorts listed above.

Multiple Markers of Ethnicity

There are numerous potential ethnicity markers besides ceramics. The problem is knowing them when you see them. Rock art is one of the most enigmatic, and hotly debated, "markers" worldwide. Polly Schaafsma has devoted several decades to carefully studying rock art in the Greater Southwest and sifting and sorting hypotheses about its possible uses and meanings by its makers. Ethnographically, we know that some rock art marks legendary migration trails, emblemic

boundary markers (clan or lineage lands), and shrines of various kinds. Rock art may also reflect ideology, such as Crown's (1994) postulated southwestern cult. There will likely never be consensus on the meaning of specific rock art motifs or styles, but judicious analysis combined with other forms of potential markers make rock art potentially very useful.

Jeffery Clark's chapter on the "four *E* words"—exchange, emulation, ethnicity, and enculturation—provides very useful tools for sorting out spurious from potentially useful data sets to support models of migration and assignment of valid ethnicity markers (chap. 4, this vol.). The chapter provides a useful summary of efforts to get beyond the simplistic pots-equal-people model that Taylor, Brew and Smith, and Irwin-Williams found objectionable. Clark's basic point is that exchange and emulation "circulate material culture with little or no population movement." He notes also that emblemic designs on pottery may well be ethnic markers but are also subject to emulation. Again, Crown's (1994) study of Salado pottery designs provides an excellent example. Clark argues, as have others (e.g., Adovasio and Andrews 1986; Barber 1994; Carr and Maslowski 1995; Cordell and Yannie 1991), that material production technologies that children learn at their kinsperson's knee, that is, by enculturation, are not intended to be publicly emblemic. Yet precisely because they are handed down relatively unchanged over many generations, they may be the most valid and useful markers of ethnicity and migration. Textile-manufacturing techniques, architectural construction details, domestic spatial organization, foodways, ground stone tools, chipped stone tools, and undecorated ceramic utility wares are all candidates for Clark's "enculturative markers."

Close studies of their distributions in space and time provide data sets on which valid statements about migration and ethnicity can be based. Certainly, it is the application of such studies that has led southwesternists to postulate with considerable certainty the Anasazi migrations into the Mogollon Rim country and the coalescence of large groups in the fourteenth and fifteenth centuries. The chapters in this volume by Wilcox et al. (chap. 12), Damp (chap. 8), and Kintigh (chap. 18) all use the kinds of data sets Clark discusses.

Migration and Genetic Models

Among Franz Boas's several contributions to anthropology was his insistence that race, language, and culture are independent variables. The contribution of his early students, especially Clark Wissler, A. L. Kroeber, Edward Sapir, and Robert Lowie, was to refine the culture area/age area hypotheses (Fowler 2000:220–245). The New Archaeologists (Wissler 1917) in the Southwest made it Job One to trace out the temporal and spatial distributions of "traits"— ceramics, textiles, stone tools, architecture, and trait clusters—with no preconceived notions as to their linkages to populations or languages. Once that task was accomplished (although for many it became an end in itself, pursued for half a century), then questions about linkages could be asked; that is, "genetic models" could be proposed, attempts to link agglomerations of "traits"—seen as "cultures" or "traditions"—with phenotypically defined groups and specific languages or language groups. There were some linkages made, especially the spurious ones between "dolichocephalic" Basketmaker and "brachycephalic" Pueblo "races," an error not expunged until 1944

(Seltzer 1944). Colton's simplistic equations of pots equal people, assailed by Taylor, Brew and Smith, are other examples.

In the late 1950s and early 1960s, perhaps in response to the overall reassessments of western North American prehistory (Haury 1945b, 1954; Jennings 1956), there were various attempts to develop "genetic models," to link languages and archaeological assemblages and sometimes human biological data (e.g., Irwin-Williams, chap. 2, this vol.; Romney 1957; Taylor 1961; Wendorf and Reed 1955). There were also various related attempts to link Great Basin languages and cultures, including the southwestern-like Fremont cultures of Kidder's (1924) "Northern Periphery" (Madsen and Rhode 1994). For example, although he recognized it was "risky business," Walter Taylor (1961:71) attempted to account for the distribution of "Hokaltecan" and "Utaztecan + Aztec-Tanoan" languages all across western North America, including Mexico. He had the Hokaltecans entering western North America from the north, developing a basic Desert Culture, and then spreading southward into Mexico. Subsequently, Utaztecans came on the scene also from the north, adopted a basic Desert Culture lifeway, then spread southward, pushing the Hokaltecans aside. Not surprisingly, Taylor's model is at variance with others as well as that proposed by Hill (chap. 3, this vol.). I agree with Taylor that genetic models are indeed "risky business," but that does not mean we should abandon attempts to develop them.

In a similar vein, although the first New Archaeologists rejected Cushing's and Fewkes's attempts to link migration legends to archaeological sites or districts, it is clear from Ferguson's chapter (chap. 19, this vol.)

that such linkages can in fact be productive.

Ethnicity, Ethnogenesis, Heritage, and the Law

The reality of the political contexts of knowledge making and access to certain databases underlies the chapters in this volume. Anthropologists, archaeologists, and linguists share in a tradition of inquiry based on two suppositions. First, all human knowledge should be part of the intellectual commons of humanity, accessible to all; second, the making of new knowledge should be unrestricted. This is basically the view of science first clearly enunciated by Francis Bacon in the seventeenth century (Shapiro 2000). The view has been taken for granted by scholars and researchers in Europe and Euro-America ever since. (I am quite aware that it has often been abrogated by governmental and sacerdotal rules of secrecy and the like.) However, some indigenous peoples in many parts of the world, including the Southwest, disagree. Certain forms of ritual, social or linguistic knowledge, or various material culture objects are not to be shared outside a specified group. Scientific knowledge derivable from studies of human remains is unacceptable to some, and they feel such studies should not be allowed. Others disagree.

Archaeologists and human biologists in the United States and, increasingly, elsewhere recognize these concerns as matters of ethics and respect and refrain from studies of remains known or asserted to be associated with groups who find such studies offensive. Indeed, legal barriers exist or are being erected (Hutt 2004), in many instances to prohibit or restrain such studies. Thus, although some DNA-based studies of Native Americans exist (Crawford 2001), more extensive studies—such as those by Sykes (1999, 2001) specifically focused on Native American / First Nation populations—may not be undertaken anytime soon in the United States or Canada (but see Gonzalez et al. 2003). Again, this is not a matter of lament but rather of respect on the part of archaeologists and human biologists who share interests with indigenous peoples in their cultural and demographic histories. There are other paths toward "valid statements," as the chapters in this volume demonstrate.

The concept of self-defined groups (SDGs) is useful here. (In chapter 4 Clark, citing various sources, uses the synonyms "self-perceived" and "self-conscious" groups.) SDGs has become a key concept in the worldwide discourse of "native peoples" or "indigenous peoples" who see themselves as comprising the Fourth World as they struggle for recognition under national and international laws and covenants (Bowen 2000; Fowler et al. 2006; Rosen 1997; Ziff and Rao 1997). SDGs see themselves in *opposition* to colonialist and / or imperialist nation-states and multinational entities (such as the United Nations and giant corporations) that comprise the First and Second Worlds. SDGs often see themselves as "nations" but not as "nation-states" in the contemporary sense and thus contrast their Fourth World status with that of Third World nation-states. Both "worlds" see themselves as subordinated to the First and Second Worlds in various ways and struggle to rectify problems created by that subordination.

In *Possessed by the Past: The Heritage Crusade and the Spoils of History* David Lowenthal (1996) distinguishes between "history" (including archaeology) and "heritage." History, he says, is an ongoing scholarly enterprise that "explores and explains pasts grown ever more opaque over time; *heritage clarifies pasts so as to infuse them with present purposes*. . . . [H]eritage aims to convert historical residues into witnesses that attest to our own ancestral virtues" (Lowenthal 1996:xi–xii; emphasis added). Heritage, in short, converts the (hopefully, objective) data and hypotheses of history and archaeology into tools for political purposes (Fowler 1987).

Heritage, particularly primordialist claims of ethnogenesis and ethnicity, has become a major tool of SDGs in their ongoing legal and public relations campaigns to acquire various forms of compensation for past takings of land and resources and the imposition of other inequities by entities of the First and Second Worlds. Heritage has also become a major weapon in battles between indigenous SDGs living in the same region over which of them is entitled to that compensation (see Hutt 2004 for a comprehensive review of the legal issues). The battles have expanded to include issues relating to control over and access to "traditional places" claimed to be of sociocultural importance by SDGs (King 2003).

Although many heritage issues have been in contention for decades in the United States, the passage in 1990 of the Native American Graves Protection and Repatriation Act (NAGPRA) provided a major new mechanism for contesting such issues (McLaughlin 2004). The law was intended to create a process by which museums and other research entities would return human remains, associated artifacts, and items of cultural patrimony to their "rightful" owners. "Owners" are defined as federally recognized tribes. The law was crafted by archaeologists, federal solicitors and bureaucrats, and Indian people who basically used a primordialist model (Lovis et al. 2004). It has proven to be a classic case of Adam Ferguson's "law of unintended consequences" (1966 [1767]:201), which may be paraphrased as "People often think they know what they do and why they do it; but what they do has unintended consequences far beyond their intentions, expectations, or wishes." A major heritage example has been the bureaucratic debacle and legal tangles over Kennewick Man (Schneider 2004). Here, the primordialist assumptions underlying NAGPRA are laid bare. Both the scientific definition of the human remains in question as "unaffiliated" and the Indian claims of deep ancestral affiliation are examples of primordial ideas of ethnicity and ethnogenesis.

NAGPRA and concepts of traditional property, both real and intellectual, have provided new tools in heritage battles in the Southwest and elsewhere in the United States (Brown 2003; Nason 2001; Tsosie 1999, 2002; Winslow 1996). Again, the unintended consequences come into play. The ongoing contest over land between the Navajo Nation and the Hopi Tribe is a prime example. Archaeologists interested in ethnogenesis and ethnicity in the context of Lowenthal's concept of history / archaeology find their data and hypotheses utilized in unintended ways for heritage purposes. Archaeologists employed by tribal governments find their data and hypotheses used for explicitly political purposes. A sampling of southwestern tribal Internet sites reflects an interesting mixture of heritage and history / archaeology concepts (Hopi Tribe 2003; Jemez Pueblo 2003; Navajo Nation 2003; Taos Pueblo 2003). Some groups have also brought the issue of proprietary vs. common knowledge into play. The Internet web site for Taos Pueblo (2003) says, "How old is Taos Pueblo? Our people have a detailed oral history which is not divulged due to religious privacy. Archaeologists say that ancestors of the Taos Indians lived in this valley long before Columbus." Most recently, issues of "copyrighting the past" have begun to emerge in which primordialist, instrumentalist, and practice-based ethnogenetic claims are being heard in the contexts of ongoing debates and legal struggles over who "owns" the artifacts, eco-facts, and geofacts of the past and who has the "right(s)" to interpret them.

A detailed study of contemporary uses of ethnicity and ethnogenesis in heritage and history/archaeology contexts in the Southwest is beyond the scope of this discussion. I point to the need for such a study because the multiplicity of data, hypotheses, assertions, and suspicions in the present volume will, when published, enter into the heritage arena. I see this as a good thing. I fully agree with Roger Echo-Hawk (2000), Joe Watkins (2000), and the cooperative endeavor initiated by the participants in the present project: the more "voices" there are, the more we will learn about life and times—past and present—in the Greater Southwest.

22 From Out of the Southwest, a New Kind of Past

Stephen A. Kowalewski

The Mogollon-Zuni project is a significant development in southwestern anthropology. It is also representative of an emerging "new past," another "New Archaeology" made possible by large databases and accompanying visions of biocultural systems or political economies of a much larger spatial scale than heretofore comprehended.

Since each of the preceding chapters presents information from a separate perspective, it is intellectually stimulating to attempt to draw the perspectives together. I try some synthesis, in a small way, around a few topics, especially several themes that transcend the Southwest and have relevance to anthropology as a whole. I credit the authors of ideas or quotations by their last names and their chapter numbers in this volume in parentheses.

The first part of my chapter concerns culture history and its related notion of cultural affiliation. The Mogollon-Zuni project participants struggled to apply cultural-historical concepts to the question of Zuni as a linguistic isolate and modern political entity. What they ended up with are results more sophisticated than anticipated, a more powerful approach to the past.

Perhaps this new comprehension could not have been achieved had the organizers not been committed to a central tenet of American anthropology: holism. Gregory and Wilcox brought together an unusually wide range of expertise and asked each author to do new research directed toward specific objectives. The conclusion that the individual chapters have in common is that separate realms of material culture (and speech) and, often, subcategories such as phonology/morphology and utilitarian/fancy artifacts reflect different spheres of activity and different ways in which people could be alike and unalike. "Identities" are fuzzy, flexible, situational, multiscalar, multiple (Mills, chap. 13, this vol.), and this is apart from the issue of subjectivity, or self-identification, which archaeology does not deal with. The chapters in this volume replace the typological thinking of culture history with a greater respect for variation in different spheres of human activity and a greater respect for the archaeological record. This archaeological appreciation of "independently assorted" variation parallels recent developments in cultural anthropology. Although not everyone will agree with my conclusion, I think that the contributions in this volume effectively demolish prehistoric cultural affiliation (Who were those people?) as a scientific concept, and in the process they replace it with an anthropology more attuned to complex social behavior (What were people doing?).

What happened in the Southwest after AD 1200 has certain parallels to events in some other middle-range societies around the world. I refer to "coalescence" (see Kowalewski 2006), the relatively sudden, widespread abandonment of places and aggregation into new, larger settlements, with major transformation and innovation affecting virtually every aspect of culture. Coalescence does not explain anything, it is only a term for a common (not universal) cultural pattern that, where it occurred, had long-term effects on cultural evolutionary trajectories. Knowing that similar (but not identical) things took place elsewhere may be of comparative interest, so I examine aspects of coalescence in the Southwest, with reference to other places, in the latter part of this chapter.

Cultural Affiliation and Culture History

Culture history has various colloquial and technical meanings. Sometimes we mean a raw ordering and dating of temporally sensitive artifact changes, a sequence. Often the term is shorthand for a boilerplate section in the front of a report. By culture history I refer here to a particular way of conceptualizing the world, the theoretical approach that assumes that humanity is segmented into types (cultures) according to discrete prescriptions for behavior. Culture history in this sense is not an innocent activity, it is a theory, however implicit or confused it may be sometimes. Culture history is a way of proceeding, thinking, making units, and writing. Culture history is particular to studies of people; it is not like ecology, a field that is not limited to our species. Culture history assumes that humanity is divided into types of the same order (cultures, ethnic groups, civilizations) and that such units are the ones of primary importance for participants and observers alike. The types are identifiable on the basis of material culture traits. Culture history favors definitions of culture that emphasize the prescriptions or recipes for behavior. People are governed by culture or tradition. Culture will have an enduring and thus traceable identity assignable to "a people." This is the theory behind cultural affiliation. Tracing cultural affiliation back from the present may also be influenced by contemporary political identities, which may not be quite the same entities that archaeologists had in mind when they used cultural-historical names.

A seemingly straightforward example of culture history and its implicit theory is the statement by Martin cited by Gregory (chap. 9, this vol.): "Had Mogollon influences filtered into the Zuni area or had Mogollon people themselves left their ancient homeland in the mountains of western New Mexico and migrated into the Zuni region proper?" (1961:3). A critical dissection of this question finds ambiguities with (at least) direction, influence, filtering, and "Mogollon." As Gregory and Wilcox (chap. 10, this vol.) say, determining cultural

affiliation from archaeological remains is a deeply problematic challenge. For reasons brought out by the seminar participants and reviewed below I doubt that older concepts such as these will work any better when dressed up in newer "organizational" or "culture-history revival" clothes.

An Intricate History

The following section is a review of the major historical inferences that I gleaned from the chapters by the conference participants. I think that the results reveal ambiguity and the deeply problematical nature of culture history and cultural affiliation.

Outlines of a culture history for Zuni were sketched in the 1960s by Irwin-Williams, Martin and Rinaldo, and Ellis. Several authors in this volume add subplots but tell essentially the same story. Irwin-Williams (chap. 2, this vol.) derived the major later prehistoric and historic ethnolinguistic groups from Archaic taxa in the same geographical areas. She saw an east–west division, Western and Eastern Basketmaker. Western Basketmaker became Hopi; in New Mexico the Archaic San Jose became core eastern Anasazi, which she thought was Keresan. Tanoan she traced through eastern Anasazi back to Mogollon and Cochise.

Matson's (1991; chap. 7, this vol.) more recent work specifies differences in sandals, projectile points, pithouse architecture, and thread twist between Western and Eastern Basketmaker. Eastern Basketmaker in the north spoke Proto-Tanoan, which differentiated about the time of sedentary agricultural villages. Matson's chapter takes up the case for a Uto-Aztecan, Neolithic migration into the Southwest (see Hill 2001 for a recent model). In other world areas, such as Europe, some recent inter-

pretations have an initial spread of agriculture resulting first in a mosaic of hunter-gatherers and agriculturalists, followed by a blend of the peoples or their adaptations. Matson sees this happening in the Southwest after Basketmaker II.

From my Mesoamerican perspective I do not see much that would be central Mexican in the "Pre-Pottery Formative" of northwestern Mexico / southwestern United States. Round pithouses, Cienega and San Pedro points, a desert adaptation, and no pottery do not describe the Mesoamerican Early Formative. In chapter 11 Diehl notes that the Early Agricultural remains across the Southwest are, so far as is known now, anything but uniform. This southwestern Neolithic heterogeneity is unlike the widespread homogeneity of the expanding Neolithic (Linear Pottery Culture) of Central Europe (Gronenborn 1999). We need more sites, especially in Sonora and Chihuahua.

Matson (chap. 7, this vol.) says the Archaic occupation of the high, cold, and dry Colorado Plateau was likely to have been at low population densities. Groups probably did not reside permanently on the Colorado Plateau but used it from its edges. Polly Schaafsma and Jane Young (chap. 15, this vol.) point out that there is considerable Archaic rock art on the Colorado Plateau. Could that be territorial marking on the contested boundaries of joint-use areas? Gregory and Nials (chap. 5, this vol.) argue that the low population density of the Archaic would have been an ideal condition promoting linguistic diversity. The opposite might be argued just as well, that the advantage of fluid social boundaries at low population densities would promote linguistic interintelligibility, as in the widespread Algonkian, Athapaskan, and Inuit languages.

Following Matson's argument, the

location of modern Zuni, about 100 km north of the southern edge of the Colorado Plateau, would have been a less than ideal base for hunter-gatherers. Damp (chap. 8, this vol.) says there are Paleoindian sites in the Zuni area as well as Early Agricultural sites but not Archaic ones, although Archaic sites may be covered by alluvium in the Zuni River valley.

Matson (chap. 7, this vol.), Damp (chap. 8, this vol.), Gregory (chap. 9, this vol.), and Wilcox et al. (chap. 12, this vol.) would not say the Zuni have "always been there"; rather, they bring people into the Zuni area permanently from somewhere else, that being the Mogollon Highlands. When that move is said to occur varies, from 1100 BC, with the earliest agriculturalists (Damp), to as late as the AD 1200s (Gregory and Wilcox, chap. 10, this vol.). This latter idea, an update of Martin and Rinaldo's, would have Zuni moving north from the Mogollon Highlands of eastern Arizona onto the southern Colorado Plateau on the upper Little Colorado River around Springerville and the Quemado area (100 km south of Zuni) and fusing with post-Chacoans of the Puerco of the West/Zuni area.

Zuni stories (as told by Cushing: see Ferguson, chap. 19, this vol.) tell of people living in the Zuni area before the coming of the Zuni from the West and the Little Colorado River. Gregory and Wilcox (chap. 20, this vol.) suggest that the autochthonous people were Keresan speakers (an idea that Ferguson attributes to Ellis) and that northern Chacoans spoke Tanoan and southern Chacoans spoke Keresan (and Zuni?). They propose that people speaking Zuni at one time or another encompassed a much larger area: all branches of the Mogollon, including Mimbres and San Simon (in the Basin and Range in southeastern Arizona), but not Jornada Mogollon of southern New Mex-

ico, plus people on the southwestern edge of the Chacoan system. In this scenario a larger Zunian group of languages equals "Mogollon" or most of its "branches," but only one Zunian language survives today.

There is a long sequence of human occupation at Zuni. Whether it is absolutely unbroken remains to be seen. The upper watersheds of the Little Colorado and Zuni rivers are relatively moist, favorable places for human settlement (see Dean, chap. 6, and Damp, chap. 8, this vol.), but the paucity of Archaic sites lends support to Matson's (chap. 7, this vol.) claim that the Colorado Plateau was sporadically used in Archaic times. The negative Archaic archaeological evidence at Zuni is still not convincing.

Zuni falls on the boundary of the proposed east–west stylistic difference in fiber artifacts and projectile points (Matson, chap. 7, this vol.); in any case, Late Archaic social groups would have been open and mobile such that artifact fashions were widely shared from the Great Basin across the Colorado Plateau through the Mogollon Highlands to the Sonoran and Chihuahuan deserts (Webster, chap. 16, this vol.). Yet if Hill (chap. 3, this vol.) is right, Zuni had already separated from other languages in Early Archaic times.

Around Zuni there are numerous sites from the Early Agricultural and Basketmaker periods (Damp, chap. 8, this vol.). Early ceramics are in the tradition of expedient brownwares found widely across the Southwest (Mills, chap. 13, this vol.). The rock art of the Zuni uplands differs from that of the (shamanic) Little Colorado and the San Juan in the Late Archaic and Early Basketmaker, continuing into Basketmaker III (Schaafsma and Young, chap. 15, this vol.). This is a stylistic boundary that lasted a long time; the boundary line was gone in Pueblo I and II.

During Chacoan times the Zuni region had a proliferation of small, dispersed sites (Damp, chap. 8, and Kintigh, chap. 18, this vol.). This should have been a favorable period for upland dry farming, as it was across much of the Colorado Plateau (Dean, chap. 6, this vol.). Above-ground masonry structures were common, but there was considerable variation in residential and ceremonial architecture. Some communities had great houses, some did not. Cibola whitewares of Pueblo I and II were locally made but quite similar from the Rio Grande to the Rio Puerco of the West (Mills, chap. 13, and Wilson, chap. 14, this vol.). In the period AD 1000–1300 Wilson sees ceramic evidence of considerable exchange linking the southern Colorado Plateau and the northern Mogollon Highlands. Chaco and Zuni shared the same rock art style, and, indeed, between AD 900 and 1300 the Colorado Plateau east to the Rio Grande was all one rock art style zone. Zuni was part of this larger sphere (Schaafsma and Young, chap. 15, this vol.).

The present-day Zuni area during the period AD 1175–1275 saw major population aggregations at the post-Chacoan great house sites of Hinkson and Jaralosa (Kintigh, chap. 18, this vol.; see the maps in chap. 12, this vol.). "The expectation that wet-cool conditions would favor downstream movement during the early thirteenth century is not supported by site distributions at AD 1250" (Dean, chap. 6, this vol.). If there was a downstream movement, it occurred later, between Late Pueblo IV and the protohistoric period, when the Rio Pescado sites upstream from the modern pueblo were abandoned.

Zuni-area pottery assemblages were homogeneous, corresponding with the aggregation into closely spaced room blocks and, a little later, contiguous room blocks. Evidently, each place made its own pots, and there is little ceramic indication of migration bringing other styles to Zuni. This observation holds for other places, too (Mills, chap. 13, this vol.). The popular White Mountain Red Ware in the Zuni area, St. Johns Polychrome, was quite widely distributed across the Southwest. These pots had designs on the exterior of large bowls. At Zuni there was a trend toward increasing bowl size, and the same trend is seen in the Kayenta area. Zuni shared in the ceramic style and in the concordant change in vessel size seen in multiple regions. If there were speakers of the Zuni language in the area at the time, they may have been linguistically isolated, but they were not a ceramic isolate. I do not know how the style sharing worked.

Glaze paints first appeared in the Zuni region in Late Pueblo III. In one sense Zuni was ceramically self-contained, in that foreign-made pottery did not enter and the locally made pottery did not travel. If there were immigrant potters living in Zuni, they were apparently assimilated, because the styles were homogeneous. But the types were widespread, and the ceramic sequences of Zuni and its eastern neighboring region, Acoma, were similar (Kintigh, chap. 18, this vol.).

In the late AD 1200s and into the 1300s a geographical split occurred within White Mountain Red Ware between east-central Arizona and west-central New Mexico, the former becoming somewhat more esoteric in interior designs (Mills, chap. 13, this vol., citing Van Keuren 2001). In the 1300s there are ceramic-style grounds for positing migration from Silver Creek, about 125 km southwest of modern Zuni, east first to the Little Colorado River, and then up the Zuni River, perhaps bringing some ka-

china iconography (Mills, chap. 13, this vol., citing Duff 2002; see the relevant maps in chap. 12).

The Late Pueblo III towns around Zuni were large, planned, and short-lived. Domestic and ceremonial architecture was not homogeneous. Initially, there may have been social distinctions by room blocks, but these appear to have diminished over time (Kintigh, chap. 18, this vol.). By the early AD 1400s Early Zuni Glaze Ware (which sometimes showed parrots) had been replaced by Matsaki Buff Polychrome (with eagles, masked figures, and shields) on interiors (Mills, chap. 13, this vol.). The style was like Hopi, and, like the rock art of the same time, it indicates a shared ideology. Matsaki coincides with further settlement aggregation. Mills (chap. 13, this vol.) writes, "Potters actively chose what they wanted to make, and they did so as part of the (re)construction of social identities."

By this time the Rio Pescado (upstream from Zuni) and El Morro (across the Continental Divide to the east) clusters of pueblos had been abandoned. The Zuni and Acoma pottery styles diverged as this settlement separation occurred. Kintigh (chap. 18, this vol.) describes long-lived, large towns, perhaps separated into an upstream and a downstream cluster, but he is cautious about what the clusters might mean in terms of political organization. Hawikuh may have had more prestige and power than other towns. Several participants repeatedly brought up the fact that there were cremations and inhumations at the protohistoric towns at Zuni and some highly specific burial furnishings seen farther south, in the Arizona Mogollon area. In the AD 1500s, if I read Dean's chapter (chap. 6, this vol.) correctly, the Zuni River should have been aggrading, but there were prominent droughts. Across the Southwest there was high

spatial variability in climate, but the present-day seasonality pattern was established at Zuni after the "chaotic" period of AD 1250–1450.

Kintigh (chap. 18, this vol.) describes continual settlement reorganization in the Zuni region but with demographic continuity. I gather that there is disagreement about whether there are material traits at Zuni attributable to migrants. Is there evidence from room counts of an influx of people from other regions as settlements consolidated into large towns? In the conference discussion Todd Howell, Wilcox, and Ferguson agreed that there was no population surge at any point. It was suggested that migrants into the Zuni area were never the bulk of the population.

We might summarize by letting Dean (chap. 6, this vol.) have the last word: "People of the Zuni area participated fully in behavioral-environmental interactions that ultimately involved the inhabitants of the entire Southwest. Therefore, a typically Zuni mode of response cannot be disentangled from the general pattern that prevailed across the region before the recognizable precursors of the modern Puebloan groups emerged after AD 1300."

Holism and Variation

How can scenarios about Zuni origins and history be evaluated? In his chapter Clark (chap. 4, this vol.) concludes, "If unique material tracers can be isolated for an ancestral Zuni population, then it may be possible to track this group back into the pre-Hispanic era and evaluate Martin and Rinaldo's original hypothesis of a Mogollon-Zuni connection with reasonable confidence." Unique material tracers have not been identified. Great pithouses with floor grooves, suggested as a significant marker (Gregory and Wilcox, chap. 10, this vol.), are a variant form of a broad category of ceremonial architecture, according to Diehl (chap. 11, this vol.), who likewise discounts the significance of a round vs. square kiva distinction, noting that some ceremonial structures in the Mogollon area tended to be round or bean shaped. Webster (chap. 16, this vol.) identifies no fiber or perishable artifacts particular to any tribal group; Schaafsma and Young (chap. 15, this vol.) identify no rock art style particular to any tribal group. The chapters by Wilson (chap. 14, this vol.), Kintigh (chap. 18, this vol.), and Mills (chap. 13, this vol.) identify no unique ceramic style or technology tracers other than the obvious association between historical tribes of the sixteenth century and the pottery they used.

Diehl's Mogollon architecture chapter (chap. 11, this vol.) relies on the culture-history method of the trait list, which makes his results that much more remarkable: "I am not at all convinced that merely identifying more and more artifacts with more complicated or detailed typological systems will allow us to claim with greater authority that we know anything about ethnicity or languages." He finds that all branches of Mogollon are indistinguishable until the ninth century, when Mimbres began to look a little different. (Webster [chap. 16, this vol.] has a parallel observation based on ritual objects.) Mogollon was not especially closed during the Pithouse period, nor was it specifically a mountain adaptation. If cultural distinctiveness and boundedness were preconditions for linguistic isolation, then the conditions for linguistic isolation were not present until the twelfth century. With this logic one could conclude that Zuni was a very late, post-twelfth-century, contrived isolation (but Hill [chap. 3, this vol.] would disagree; see below).

As for earlier periods, Diehl (chap. 11, this vol.) writes, "If identifying the relevant markers for ethnicity is difficult for Mogollon sites, it is virtually impossible for early maize sites, given the current information," and "there remain unresolved and substantial problems in the basic task of recognizing the boundaries of populations or ethnic groups in the more distant past."

Why is it so difficult, if not virtually impossible, to identify "cultures" in the archaeological past? The answer may have less to do with archaeological remains than it does with the essentialist concept of "cultures" vs. the fleeting character of socially constructed human groups. The difficulty is as much theoretical as it is archaeological. Mills in chapter 13 shows why.

Mills's contribution, drawn from cultural theory more recent than the 1960s, provides answers by way of cautionary statements and warnings. She says that, yes, there are indeed identities, things defined in relation to something else: the same internally, different toward the outside. (As several contributors mentioned, emic self-identification may or may not correspond to material or behavioral patterns and is beyond the scope of archaeology anyway.) Social boundaries are not necessarily isomorphic with spatial boundaries. In other words, gaps in settlement forming a boundary between settlement clusters or a spatially complementary distribution of architectural forms may not have an obvious significance in terms of social or territorial behavior. According to Mills, "We really don't know when material culture boundaries will conform to one kind or scale of identity versus another." Identity is not the same thing as ethnicity; decorative styles are not necessarily isomorphic with social groups; tech-

nological styles point to yet another kind of identity.

In sum, Mills says that identities are situational, scalar, mutable, and flexible. To put this another way, at any one time a human landscape is crisscrossed by many boundaries, there are overlaps and nonoverlaps between layers, and significant groups may form not as polygons but interspersed in neuron or spindle fashion. It seems to me that analytical segmentations of these complex social landscapes that were drawn early in the course of archaeological study will most likely be grossly incorrect due to sampling error and inappropriate merging of distinct behavioral spheres. Mills and others note that Mogollon and other similarly drawn types are internally heterogeneous and not sharply defined on the boundaries. Southwestern tribes are in part a creation of the interaction with nation-states, so projecting a twentieth-century tribe model back to pre-Hispanic times would require special argument. Hohokam or Mogollon, taxa dating to the 1930s are aggregates of uncertain definition and behavioral meaning compared to the 1980s concept of "ball court network," which is intentionally of a different order, restricted to behavior associated with one aspect of material culture. Even a restricted concept like ball court network still has uncertain behavioral significance.

Puebloan populations were mobile. Gregory and Wilcox (chap. 10, this vol.) interpret Puebloan mobility as an adaptation to a climatically fickle land. Varien's (1999) study of household, community, and regional sedentism and mobility provides a good feel for the spatial and temporal scale of population movement. Because of its many connotations, one should be careful with the term *migration*. Mobility may vary by the numbers of people involved (amplitude), frequency (timing), permanence, and distance. With small-scale movements of people back and forth between communities it might be very difficult to say what is migration and what is exchange. Is a circulating connubium migration or exchange? (For an example of long-distance marriage networks see Rogers [1962] on the Round Lake Ojibwa.) An interesting example comes from Webster's (chap. 16, this vol.) study of fiber artifacts, in which she concludes that Early Agricultural period textiles are a fusion of Great Basin and northern Mexican technologies. She infers that the fusion was brought about by migration, but an alternative would be in situ development (what does that mean here?) in the context of exchange among fairly mobile populations.

The Mogollon-Zuni project was motivated in part by a classically good question: What accounts for the unity and diversity of the American Indian? One of the axes of unity and diversity is linguistic, and the project asks, How can we account for the fact that Zuni is a language isolate? Hill (chap. 3, this vol.) assures us that it is indeed an isolate, having no demonstrable genetic relationship to any other language or protolanguage. It is structurally and phonologically different from its neighbors. Zuni features intricate derivation of complex words from simple roots, a fairly limited sound system, and elaborate morphophonology. It has exchanged relatively few loanwords with its neighbors, but the pattern of loanwords suggests to Hill that Hopi, Zuni, and Keresan were in contact in Chaco and kachina ceremonialism; many older loanwords in Zuni come from Pima. Given the pattern of contact, she concurs that the Mogollon would be a good historical location for Zuni.

Diehl (chap. 11, this vol.) makes the alternative suggestion that the con-ditions for social and thus linguistic isolation did not obtain until the AD 1200s. Several conference participants referred to Dozier's (1956) observation that Puebloans tended to practice a linguistic purism, the maintenance of high barriers around their languages, even as they shared and exchanged quite a lot with their neighbors in other realms of culture. Linguistic purism would be a historically determined strategy, in force at some times and not others. It is appropriate to consider when those times would have been. Although Diehl's suggestion is attractive, one must pay attention when Hill (chap. 3, this vol.) concludes, "If Zuni had diverged from surviving related languages only 4,000 or 5,000 years ago I am fairly sure that linguists would have found [the genetic links]." I am skeptical of linguistic and genetic clocks that tick at a constant rate, so the difference between the Early Archaic or 4,000–5,000 years ago for a language separation would not necessarily be problematic. But Hill is saying that an 800-year-old split yielding no demonstrable genetic ties to another language is unheard of. Gregory and Wilcox (chap. 20, this vol.) speculate that Zuni had been a much larger language (geographically), and it shrank only in the last 800 years. If that were true, one would not have to explain why it is an isolate—Zuni would be a case not unlike other relatively small southwestern language families (Keresan, Tanoan).

We will never be able to reconstruct linguistic prehistory from archaeology. Perhaps a consensus may develop, but I do not see how hypotheses about past language speaking can be archaeologically tested following the normal canons of science and critical scholarship. However, as Hill's active participation in the Mogollon-Zuni project makes abundantly clear, we have a lot to learn from further linguistic research. We wish there were more trained professionals working on American Indian languages.

If there is no certain one-to-one relationship between language and culture, does that mean an impasse in archaeological and linguistic research? Here the Mogollon-Zuni project participants offer some very optimistic, innovative, and intellectually exciting answers. There are reachable frontiers, but, as Fowler (chap. 21, this vol.) reminds us, there is conceptual baggage that needs to be checked and jettisoned. What I see as innovative and potentially quite productive arises from the Mogollon-Zuni project's commitment to holistic anthropology.

Listen to Webster, whose chapter (chap. 16, this vol.) is far more than a catalog of textiles and perishable artifacts: "Similarities among fiber artifacts, with their wide range of low-visibility manufacturing choices, are much more likely to reflect shared social identities among mobile groups than projectile point styles, which are highly visible, widely shared, and probably better measures of participation in broad economic networks." The implication is that making and using fiber is a separate domain of behavior to be analyzed independently, and only when that behavior is understood on its own terms is it brought back together with the evidence of other kinds of action. Webster is saying that different domains of behavior have their own peculiarities and need their own conceptual development.

Similarly, Vokes and Gregory (chap. 17, this vol.) show how different types of materials (e.g., shell, turquoise, macaws, copper bells) were traded in different networks.

These materials may be further sub-divided so that, for example, shell bracelets, pendants, and beads seem to have distinct modes of production and exchange. A lesson from their study is that exchange networks may cross-cut networks defined on other criteria (platform mound architecture, in this case). And, as Vokes and Gregory show, these networks changed over time.

Wilcox (2005b) has maintained over many years that archaeology is at its best when it develops its own concepts. The corollary is that different domains of material culture have distinct behavioral significance and require independent conceptualization prior to systemic reunification.

An error of culture history was to presume that different domains of culture would be isomorphic and would mean the same thing. Kintigh's (chap. 18, this vol.) regional surveys around Zuni find distributional patterns that are potentially quite informative. During Pueblo II and III there were great house and non–great house communities. Kiva forms, ceramic plainware spheres, and decorated ware spheres did not necessarily coincide. These are respectably complicated patterns of variation. What can they tell us now about what we might assume to be major ethnic or political groups? Kintigh says it's not simple: "We must exercise considerable caution in inferring boundaries from the distributions of even highly visible cultural traits."

Schaafsma and Young (chap. 15, this vol.), coming from their deep expertise in rock art, develop a stance very similar to Webster's. Rock art speaks to shared ideology, not necessarily shared language. Shared ideology was not isomorphic with polity, ceramic exchange sphere, regional settlement cluster, or the communities that shared a common set of origin and migration myths. (As a Mesoamericanist the notion of ideology shared among people speaking different languages is very familiar to me.)

Recall Mills's (chap. 13, this vol.) concepts of identities as "situational, scalar, mutable, and flexible." I think Webster, Vokes and Gregory, Schaafsma and Young, and Kintigh are on the same path. In the same way linguistic studies, such as Hill's (chap. 3, this vol.) observations on Zuni loanwords, give us another important domain of behavior, analyzed first on its own terms and then brought into juxtaposition with other domains. Recognizing that different fields of action have different significance and are not isomorphic helps liberate us from culture history's typological thinking. It is interesting that Wilson (chap. 14, this vol.) and Mills (chap. 13, this vol.) both reiterated that certain major differences in pottery on and off the Colorado Plateau were due to clay geology and the technologies for dealing with available clays, not Mogollon or Anasazi cultures. (Dean's [chap. 6, this vol.] research tradition of dendroclimatology and other indicators of environmental conditions, with its love of variation, has always operated under the rule of "population thinking.")

In distributional studies (Webster, Wilson, Vokes and Gregory, Hill's loanwords) it may be useful to use a geographer's standard rather than culture-history names like Mogollon to compare "expected" against "observed." Things vary; nearby things resemble each other, distant things differ, and when they don't, it's interesting. Vokes's seminar paper cited studies that employ such models. Formal models like these have the advantage of preserving variation in the analytical process.

The holistic breadth and conceptual innovations expressed in the Mogollon-Zuni project undermine culture history but open up new fields of inquiry. "Cultural affiliation" is hardly archaeology's forte, partly because subjective identification is beyond our grasp but mainly because cultural affiliation cannot stand up to theoretical scrutiny. Affiliations are not singular and fixed long enough to be traceable; they are multiple and fleeting, involving different domains, and socially constructed and shaped by power and resistance. I think the Mogollon-Zuni project initially posed some unanswerable questions but quickly transcended these to establish new benchmarks for anthropology. I draw attention to some of these accomplishments in the final section of this chapter.

Coalescence: In Other Places and in the Northern Southwest

After the Chaco phenomenon the Greater Southwest saw three centuries of aggregation into larger villages and towns, demographic stagnation or decline, and creation of new institutions. In many respects what happened in the Southwest in that period was not unique, having parallels in similar events in other parts of the world and at other times. I have written about coalescent societies as a repeated historical pattern that took place in different culture areas (Kowalewski 2006) and pursued one angle, the relationship between warfare, settlement nucleation, and intensification in another paper (Kowalewski 2003b). Here I briefly review the idea as it may be relevant, giving some emphasis to one well-attested feature of coalescence in the Puebloan Southwest, the increased production and exchange of items involved in ceremonial life.

In the southeastern United States during the seventeenth century native groups that were under the pressure of epidemic death, displacement, and warfare came together in new towns, in new places, with new institutions of governance, ideology, and social organization. These were the historical confederacies such as the Choctaw, Creek, and Cherokee. Such confederacies replaced the earlier, pre-Hispanic polity form, the Mississippian chiefdom (Hudson 2002).

Coalescence in the Southeast involved reshaping and creating whole cultural systems. It was a widespread, peer-polity process, affecting multiple regional societies and linguistic groups. The new polities were formed from core and attached remnant or refugee groups, sometimes speaking different languages. They were often multiethnic. Towns were located in new places; sometimes the towns were larger than those of the prior constituent groups. Collective defense was a major reason for organizing at this scale. Towns were palisaded, no small undertaking. Leadership in these coalescent societies was more collective than that of the personalized, apical, hierarchical Mississippian chiefdoms. War chiefs may stand out as an exception, but in civil government tribal councils, council houses, and confederacies were the rule.

Community and polity integration was achieved by means of new institutions or older ones given new emphasis. Corporate descent groups (matriclans) were probably more important during the seventeenth century than they had been in Mississippian chiefdoms. Red and white moieties and older-younger distinctions were used to order inter- and intracommunity relations. Rituals of intensification such as the Green Corn Ceremony played a more significant role in polity integration. Toli, the ball game, was another integrative institution.

Coalescence required its own ideology: collective, corporate, participatory, and universalizing. The mythology of chiefly times was modified to reflect the collective urgencies of the seventeenth and eighteenth centuries. Constituent group rights and obligations were spelled out by mythological constitution. New social orderings were elaborated in cosmovision and in migration stories.

What makes these developments relevant for the Puebloan Southwest is the potential for comparison and the totalizing character of the transformations. People at other times and places underwent similar (not identical) cultural transformations under similar (not identical) conditions. Coalescence occurred on the Great Plains during late pre-Hispanic times, among some but not all societies in Amazonia during the Colonial period and perhaps earlier, in the Mixteca Alta in Mesoamerica during the Late and Terminal Formative periods, perhaps in some places in Europe during the Bronze and Iron Ages, in certain places in highland New Guinea during the twentieth century, and in the northern Southwest after Chacoan times. These are places with quite disparate cultural traditions, yet they went through somewhat similar experiences. In all cases the transformation was totalizing, affecting every part of culture. The creation of new institutions had long-lasting effects that shaped subsequent developments.

Zuni origin and migration stories must be a rich and respectable literature. Ferguson's chapter (chap. 19, this vol.) clearly elucidates what kind of histories these are. I wonder if there is not a relative time order in the structure and movement toward the Middle Place. Springs are the early places, how to plant corn happens early, groups merge and diverge, there are battles, clans get their

names, the kiva societies gain their knowledge and ceremonies and show a "complex and accretional development of kachina religion" (Ferguson, chap. 19, this vol.). As the story moves upstream events are younger in time and there is more local detail. Villages are named.

The migration myths of other coalescent societies establish social segments and organize relationships (often of precedence) among them. The Creek origin tales from the Southeast and those of Bororo in central Brazil and Vaupes in Amazonia are examples of such oral constitutions (Kowalewski 2006). The Zuni oral histories discussed by Ferguson accomplish a similar ordering of society. The Zuni and other Puebloan origin and migration stories also make connections to neighbors near and far and mark a larger landscape. As unwritten constitutions oral histories are useful, simultaneously venerable and flexible.

It is unlikely that there was a single cause for coalescence in different parts of the world at different times. In the agriculturally marginal environments of the Southwest we tend to think first of climate change as a precipitating cause. The upheavals (and coalescence) in the Puebloan Southwest beginning after AD 1250 are an example of events we tend to think of as caused by widespread and serious drought. Yet there is much at the local, regional, and macroregional scales that needs to be understood on the human side of the equation. Similar coalescences have happened without the severe environmental change, and I am not sure that in the Southwest we could predict the specific responses from the state of the environment, settlement, and population in AD 1250. Once set in motion the political forces of coalescence must have been difficult to stop, and overall, as the maps in chapter 12 show, there was no reversal, even, for example, during fairly wet conditions during the early AD 1300s in the Cibola area (see Dean, chap. 6, this vol.).

We need better connection between environmental variability and human action. The model (Dean's) that has been in use for 20 years now goes something like this: environment > farming > population/settlement > exchange. It is a sophisticated model in that it generates fairly specific expectations that may or may not match observed behavior at different scales. I think its environmental refinement has outpaced its anthropological development, which now seems to me a bit mechanical and needs another infusion of economic anthropology and social anthropology. People do things in an institutional and social context; social power is always involved. We need to work on this political-economic context.

Generally, when new, larger villages or towns were formed from prior, dispersed settlement through coalescence or through some other process, people had to intensify production. Dispersed settlement patterns often are optimal for maximizing efficiency in food production. If for other reasons, such as the threat of war, people form larger, nucleated settlements, they typically had to alter the social and technological means of production ("intensification under duress"). New demands are made on labor. Conceivably, cause may flow the other way: a general shift in the mode of production may lead to settlement nucleation at the local level. Studies referred to in this volume show that maize, cotton, and textile production underwent social and technological changes, especially in how labor was organized, during the fourteenth and fifteenth centuries. Gender-specified intensive production during Pueblo

III and IV (Mills 2000) is similar to the increasingly gendered division of labor with intensified production in New Guinea and the Great Plains.

Intensification of trade is another common feature of coalescence. Increased trade is also associated with the cases of "intensification under duress" that I examined (Kowalewski 2003b; see also Vehik 2002 for the Great Plains). Why this should be is not obvious. If people must nucleate to protect themselves from hostile neighbors, and they go to considerable trouble to do so, why does it appear that there is more exchange with their neighbors, the people who would seem to be hostile?

One answer might be that nucleated populations, having lost the production benefits of living dispersed near key resources, must now make up for the increased collective risk of shortfall by exchange with other towns. Perhaps one is not fighting all the neighbors all the time, so exchange partners are always available. Exchange with nonhostile neighbors allows nucleated settlements a buffer against bad years. This might be called hedging exchange.

"Hedging exchange" is problematic. As the process of nucleation and abandonment advances, the distances between towns increases, making transport of bulk goods costlier. The exchange price must have been quite high to move heavy staple goods over distances of several days' walk in sufficient volume and with enough regularity to make up for presumed shortfalls. In the Southwest we do not find archaeological evidence for the regular movement of bulk food over long distances, either because long-distance food exchange was not a regular practice or because it is archaeologically invisible.

But what is archaeologically visible—as the chapters by Webster,

Vokes and Gregory, Wilson, and Mills show—is long-distance exchange of nonfood items. Wilson (chap. 14, this vol.) observes an increase in exchange beginning in the Late Pithouse period. Vehik's (2002) evidence for increasing trade on the Great Plains consists mainly of marine shell, distinctive nonlocal stone, and exotic ceramics. In the Southwest the long-distance exchange items seen by archaeologists are birds, shell, copper, obsidian, turquoise, and perhaps ceremonial mantas and open-weave shirts. Vokes's seminar paper attempted to show how competitive emulation, symbolic entrainment, and increased demand for the currency of displays heightened the volume of exchange, production, and craft specialization, intra- and inter-community. Many of these items are part of ceremonies. The linguistic evidence cited by Hill (chap. 3, this vol.) and the songs in other languages at Zuni referred to by Ferguson (chap. 19, this vol.) also point to ceremonial institutions as key players in long-distance exchange.

Coalescent towns intensify production. Damp's chapter (chap. 8, this vol.) discusses labor organization and canal irrigation at Zuni. Other studies in the Southwest have linked intensive agricultural schemes to late prehistoric major towns. Lightfoot (1993) describes mulched fields in the Galisteo Basin. Whalen and Minnis (2001:72–75) point out the potentials for irrigation and intensification at Casas Grandes. In the Puebloan Southwest during Pueblo III–IV more labor went into preparing maize for food, the most obvious evidence for which may be changes in how maize grinding was carried out and the elaborate preparation of piki. Webster's (chap. 16, this vol.) research documents the increased use of cotton on the Colorado Plateau, and there must have been an intensification of cotton growing. Mills (chap. 13, this vol.) notes the complicated, well-executed designs, often textilelike, on Tularosa Black-on-white pottery of the late AD 1200s. (Are pre–AD 1300 pottery designs related to the symbolism of social segments, as the contemporary rock art might be, i.e., pre–AD 1300 pottery style : post–AD 1300 pottery style :: pre–AD 1300 rock art style : post–AD 1300 rock art style?)

Ceremonial institutions played a key part in intensifying production. Dances, feasts, and rituals motivated people to spend time working on costumes, paraphernalia, insignia, and ritual objects; cleaning and refurbishing facilities; collecting wild and cultivated plants; and cooking and presenting elaborate food. Schaafsma and Young (chap. 15, this vol.) note the ideological importance of war, maize, rain, and fertility in Pueblo IV rock art and kiva murals. Here again, ideological emphasis is placed on the activities most central to existence: intensified food production, war, and the integration of many different groups into large communities and polities.

In theory, the production and exchange of nonstaple items should have been fostered by the economic efficiencies of towns. Compared to the dispersed communities of Pueblo I–II, the large villages and towns of Pueblo IV times had the advantages for exchange found in central place systems: concentration, efficiency in scheduling, regularization, specialization, economies of scale, and so on. Kohler et al. make an interesting case that "the northern Rio Grande economy of the Classic period was increasingly structured around and by market activity" (2000:199). In contrast, they suggest, "the emerging market economy was weaker in the Zuni-Cibola region than in the Rio

Grande and still more so in the Hopi region, and that as a consequence (or, perhaps, as a cause of the poor penetration of markets) these societies retained more elements of the older kin-group organization and more elements of the reciprocal economy" (Kohler et al. 2000:202). Vokes and Gregory's data (chap. 17, this vol.) could suggest that the Rio Grande pueblos were less involved in the macaw and copper bell trade than contemporary centers to the south and west. Although Schaafsma and Young (chap. 15, this vol.) attribute the Eastern Pueblo rock art emphasis on Tlaloc, rain, fertility, and kachinas to influences from Mexico, the ideological emphasis might be explained locally by the Rio Grande's intensified staple production and competitive exchange.

As seen in the Southeast, Amazonia, Oaxaca, and the Great Plains and best documented in the Southwest, during the process of coalescence there were substantial changes in the social and technological means of production and exchange, closely interlocked with new political-ceremonial institutions. The observations by Wilson (chap. 14, this vol.) and Mills (chap. 13, this vol.) on fancy ceramics, Schaafsma and Young (chap. 15, this vol.) on rock art, Vokes and Gregory (chap. 17, this vol.) on the shell, bells, and birds used in ceremonial display, Webster (chap. 16, this vol.) on the fancy shirts and mantas, and Kintigh (chap. 18, this vol.) and others on plazas and kivas provide what appears to be wonderful evidence on the role of integrative and alliance-building ceremonials in production and exchange. However, to tie all of this together and call it coalescence explains nothing; it would be all too neat and overdetermined. I think the Mogollon-Zuni participants would say we need to go

back to the variation, to compare, to see how the macroregional processes were playing out in different regions.

A New Past

As regional archaeology and research design was a product of the original New Archaeology of 35 years ago, macroregional theory and concepts ought to be a research goal for the newest archaeology (Kowalewski 2004). The Mogollon-Zuni project is in the vanguard of this larger, richer, and very challenging "new past."

The Mogollon-Zuni conference participants agreed, I believe, on two fundamental principles for research. One is the commitment to anthropological holism. The project demonstrates the value of comprehending as many components of biocultural systems as we can. The list of kinds of data assembled by the participants is impressive: public architecture, ceramics, funerary treatments, settlements, population, language, traditional history, rainfall and temperature, hydrology, rock art, textiles, other perishables, marine shell, copper, turquoise, animal bone, plant remains, farming practices, early European accounts, ethnography, ceremonial organization, polities, warfare, lithics. Human biology is not represented, unfortunately. More specific attention might be paid as well to social organization (from households up); undoubtedly, other realms of culture might be brought in. The principle is that human biocultural behavior is rich and no realm of behavior stands for all.

The other major principle for research is the importance of scale. As Dean (chap. 6, this vol.) said, processes at different spatial and temporal scales are due to different causes. Everyone agreed that in order to understand something local, one had to understand a much bigger picture. One does not understand the local by studying the local. Puebloan culture is a large-scale phenomenon; pueblos are its local franchises. Ferguson (chap. 19, this vol.) put it well: Zuni traditional history is bound up with that of Hopi and the speakers of Keresan.

This brings me to the settlement data and maps in chapter 12. Wilcox et al. (and their collaborators—every archaeologist who has ever recorded a site in the Southwest) have assembled "stunning spatiotemporal data" (Dean's words, chap. 6, this vol.) on every site greater than 13 rooms, by 50-year intervals, over the 400 years between AD 1200 and 1599, for a large part of the Southwest, an area of some 600,000 km². Up until now no one has been able to see or comprehend, with empirical grounding, phenomena at the scale of a whole culture area. Here we have new population estimates and the ecologist's ideal of distribution and abundance of the species over time and space. This is a major contribution to southwestern archaeology and to archaeology in general.

There are flaws in this data set. From my background doing archaeological surveys I can appreciate Kintigh's (chap. 18, this vol.) doubts about whether all sites greater than 100 rooms, let alone 13 rooms, have been mapped. Many areas are still unsurveyed. There are problems with the chronological assignments. The early periods, with small sites and dispersed settlement, are not as well represented. At the large, late pueblos the occupational histories are difficult to separate into 50-year phases. Sonora and Chihuahua are hardly surveyed.

In spite of the problems in coverage and chronology no other culture area in the world can match the completeness, large scale, and 50-year

chronological control of these southwestern settlement data. And what is just as impressive is that no other area in the world can match the year-by-year climate information, the textile and perishable collections, the ceramic information, the rock art coverage, the architecture, and the other data that are tied to the settlement patterns. What makes this a new past is not only the macroregional scale but the holistic richness of the information.

One might ask some deceptively simple questions: What was the political-economic basis of the regional and macroregional clusters? How was value transferred from one point to another? How did that change from AD 1200 to the 1400s? To what extent were the multiregional clusters *systems*? To what extent were they bounded? What were the flows of people, information, and things that made them interacting and interdependent? In what dimensions of behavior? How do we explain the in-tandem change in multiple, regional ceramic sequences described by Wilson (chap. 14, this vol.) and Mills (chap. 13, this vol.)? What were the key institutions permitting regional and interregional interaction? In other words, if there were multiregional systems, however weak or strong, then what made them systems?

As Wilcox et al. say, "It is going to take some time to digest all of this new information and to begin to construct fresh theoretical approaches to understand it." This indeed is the challenge of the new past. How does one hold in mind the variation, region to region? Then, how does one comprehend how all that variation changes through time? We need visual or graphic tools as well as new theoretical concepts.

To illustrate, I refer back to figures 12.15 (AD 1200–1249) and 12.19 (AD 1400–1449). We know there are data

problems: "only" the northern part of the Northwest / Southwest is represented (Sonora and Chihuahua are largely absent), and over the rest of the area not all the settlements have been found, mapped, and dated. Even so, we can see that at AD 1250 the archaeological landscape is composed of settlements, communities, regional clusters, two greater clusters (the Sonoran / Chihuahuan Desert or Hohokam / Trincheras / Paquimé and the Colorado Plateau or Puebloan), and, at the largest scope, the southwestern culture area. By the 1400s people had coalesced into fewer but larger towns and fewer regional clusters.

The big-picture maps in chapter 12 show concordant change, meaning that regional social systems across the study area were affected by broad-scale processes, so they tended to move in similar ways at roughly the same time, but the broad-scale processes played out differently in each region. On close inspection, the changes over time in local, regional, and macroregional clusters were hardly all alike. The Verde Valley, Perry Mesa, and the Galisteo Basin, for instance, had very different trajectories. Many of the changes from one 50-year interval to the next appear unpredictable, given current knowledge. Movement downstream and to lower elevations is one general trend on the Colorado Plateau, but that does not seem to explain the jostling in the Rio Grande area after AD 1300. Older, smaller clusters (as opposed to larger or new, on-the-rise clusters) tend to be the ones that dropped out, but that does not explain the demise of some very large clusters, like the Salt, Chama, and Galisteo East.

Understanding these processes will require population thinking, not typological thinking. We will have to respect local and regional variation, holding variation for its secrets as long as possible instead of submerging it prematurely into categorical types. One way these issues can be explored with the settlement data is through modeling and simulation using the database and GIS. Dean's (chap. 6, this vol.) ecological framework respects and exploits variation in this way. Similarly, the theoretical and methodological "independent assortment" advocated strongly in the chapters by Mills, Webster, Vokes and Gregory, and Diehl, which in fact is the operational procedure used by many of the participants, thrives on variation and comparison.

Conclusions

The Mogollon-Zuni project has been much more than a quest for Zuni origins. What are the history and origins of Zuni or Zunian (in ancient, archaeological times)? What is the relationship between Mogollon and Zuni? These questions are not answerable given the standards of testing and evidence expected in science and scholarship. Such questions posit an unverifiable and unlikely continuity of subjective identity not reflected or translated into specific material culture. Archaeology is not going to tell us what language(s) people spoke in the past, even in a place as well studied as the Southwest. The notion of "cultural affiliation" does not stand up well to theoretical scrutiny in re-

cent cultural anthropology; for archaeology, with its greater time depth, cultural affiliation studies are even more difficult to justify. Tracing cultural affiliation back into the past is like dividing oatmeal (one way is as good as another) or like trying to trace the history of individual molecules of the amino acids in an owl's eye back to their origins at the beginning of life (impossible, and if you could, why would you?). However, if the question is phrased without the reified culture history or present-day political identities to ask, How did the Pueblos come to be as they are? (Wilcox's [1976] wording), then the research problem is more straightforward. We investigate histories (local) and larger histories (regional, macroregional). During the discussion at the conference Wilcox suggested "history" instead of "culture history." I think this should mean a history freed from the nominalism of fixed cultural identity categories, a history concerned with what people did (not what we call them). And, as is shown in the chapters in this volume, the new southwestern archaeology is holistic and consciously multiscalar. This vision of a "total social history" is one of several major accomplishments of the Mogollon-Zuni seminar.

This project has taken a giant step forward for southwestern studies and for anthropology in general. Its contributions are products of an archae-

ology that has become quite a different field than it was 30 years ago, just after the last New Archaeology revolution. The Mogollon-Zuni project has assembled rich linguistic and archaeological studies, grounded by year-by-year climate information and linked to maps showing the distribution and abundance of people at 50-year intervals at a scale covering some 600,000 km². Some of the major substantive results include new population estimates; a new assessment of Zunian as a linguistic isolate and its limited loanword sharing with other southwestern languages in ceremonies and ordinary activities; demonstration of concordant change and common culture across the Puebloan Southwest in textiles, pottery, rock art, architecture, and exotic items; the recognition of multiple, multiscalar, nonisomorphic spheres of human activity; an update of the Archaic and Early Agricultural periods to take account of the recent recognition of the beginning of maize agriculture in the second millennium BC; and an outline of the processes surrounding the formation of larger villages and towns and concomitant cultural changes (coalescence) after the demise of Chaco. I sincerely thank the organizers and participants for the opportunity to witness their impressive intellectual work. In my opinion the Mogollon-Zuni project is a landmark in anthropological scholarship.

References Cited

Abbott, David R.

1994 *Hohokam Social Structure and Irrigation Management: The Ceramic Evidence from the Central Phoenix Basin.* PhD dissertation, Arizona State University, Tempe. University Microfilms, Ann Arbor.

2000 *Ceramics and Community Organization among the Hohokam.* University of Arizona Press, Tucson.

Abotech

1999 Ancient Kernel Sheds Light on Early Humans. Electronic document, http://www.abotech.com/Articles/Misc01.htm, accessed October 15, 2003.

Acuna-Soto, Rodolfo, David W. Stahle, Malcolm K. Cleaveland, and Matthew D. Therrell

2002 Megadrought and Megadeath in 16th Century Mexico. *Emerging Infectious Diseases* 8:360–362.

Adams, David K., and Andrew C. Comrie

1997 The North American Monsoon. *Bulletin of the American Meteorological Society* 78:2197–2213.

Adams, E. Charles

1983 The Architectural Analogue to Hopi Social Organization and Room Use and Implications for Prehistoric Northern Southwest Culture. *American Antiquity* 48:44–61.

1991 *The Origins and Development of the Pueblo Katsina Cult.* University of Arizona Press, Tucson.

2002 *Homol'ovi: An Ancient Hopi Settlement Cluster.* University of Arizona Press, Tucson.

Adams, E. Charles, and Andrew I. Duff (editors)

2004 *The Protohistoric Pueblo World, AD 1275–1600.* University of Arizona Press, Tucson.

Adams, E. Charles, Miriam T. Stark, and Deborah Dosh

1993 Ceramic Distributions and Ceramic Exchange: The Distribution of Jeddito Yellow Ware and Implications for Social Complexity. *Journal of Field Archaeology* 20:3–21.

Adams, Ethan Charles

1973 The Dead Horse Site. Unpublished Master's thesis, Department of Anthropology, University of Colorado, Boulder.

Adams, Jenny L., and Mark D. Elson

1995 Personal Ornaments, Pigments, Rocks, and Mineral Specimens. In *Stone and Shell Artifacts*, edited by Mark D. Elson and Jeffery J. Clark, pp. 115–149. The Roosevelt Community Development Study, Vol. 1. Anthropological Papers No. 14. Center for Desert Archaeology, Tucson.

Adams, Karen R.

1990 A Regional Synthesis of *Zea mays* in the Prehistoric American Southwest. Paper presented at the Conference on Corn and Culture in the Prehistoric New World, Minneapolis.

Adams, Robert McCormick

1966 *The Evolution of Urban Society: Early Mesopotamia and Prehispanic Mexico.* University of Chicago Press, Chicago.

1974 Anthropological Perspective on Ancient Trade. *Current Anthropology* 15:239–258.

Adler, Michael A. (editor)

1996 *The Prehistoric Pueblo World, AD 1150–1350.* University of Arizona Press, Tucson.

Adler, Michael A., and Amber Johnson

1996 Mapping the Puebloan Southwest. In *The Prehistoric Pueblo World, AD 1150–1350*, edited by Michael A. Adler, pp. 255–272. University of Arizona Press, Tucson.

Adovasio, James M.

1970 The Origin, Development and Distribution of Western Archaic Textiles. *Tebiwa* 13(2):1–40. Idaho State University Museum, Pocatello.

1971 Some Comments on the Relationship of Great Basin Textiles to Textiles from the Southwest. In *Great Basin Anthropological Conference 1970, Selected Papers*, edited by C. Melvin Aikens, pp. 103–108. University of Oregon Anthropological Papers 1. Eugene.

1974 Prehistoric North American Basketry. In *Collected Papers on Aboriginal Basketry*, edited by Donald R. Tuohy and Doris L. Rendall, pp. 133–153. Nevada State Museum Anthropological Papers 16. Carson City.

1980 Prehistoric Basketry of Western North America and Mexico. In *Early Native Americans: Prehistoric Demography, Economy, and Technology*, edited by David L. Browman, pp. 341–362. Mouton Publishers, New York.

Adovasio, James M., and Rhonda L. Andrews

1985 *Basketry and Miscellaneous Perishable Artifacts from Walpi Pueblo, Arizona.* Ethnology Monographs 7. Department of Anthropology, University of Pittsburgh.

1986 Artifacts and Ethnicity: Basketry as in Indicator of Territoriality and Population Movements in the Prehistoric Great Basin. In *Anthropology of the Desert West: Essays in Honor of Jesse D. Jennings*, edited by Carol J. Condie and Don D. Fowler, pp. 43–89. University of Utah Anthropological Papers No.

110. University of Utah Press, Salt Lake City.

Adovasio, James M., and Joel D. Gunn

1986 The Antelope House Basketry Industry. *Archeological Investigations at Antelope House*, edited by Don P. Morris, pp. 306–397. USDI National Park Service, Washington, D.C.

Adovasio, James M., D. C. Hyland, and Rhonda L. Andrews

1996 Perishables Industries from NAN Ranch Ruin, New Mexico: A Unique Window into Mimbreño Fiber Technology. Paper presented at the 61st Annual Meeting of the Society for American Archaeology, New Orleans.

Agenbroad, Larry D.

1970 Cultural Implications from the Statistical Analysis of a Prehistoric Lithic Site in Arizona. Unpublished Master's thesis, Department of Anthropology, University of Arizona, Tucson.

1978 Cultural Implications from the Distributional Analysis of a Lithic Site, San Pedro Valley, Arizona. In *Discovering Past Behavior: Experiments in the Archaeology of the Southwest*, edited by Paul Grebinger, pp. 55–71. Gordon and Breach, New York.

1982 Geology and Lithic Resources of the Grasshopper Region. In *Multidisciplinary Research at Grasshopper Pueblo, Arizona*, edited by William A. Longacre, Sally J. Holbrook, and Michael W. Graves, pp. 42–45. Anthropological Papers of the University of Arizona No. 40. University of Arizona Press, Tucson.

Agorsah, E.

1986 House Forms in Northern Volta Basin, Ghana (Evolution, Internal Spatial Organisation and the Social Relationships Depicted). *West African Journal of Archaeology* 16:25–51.

Ahler, Stanley, and Phil Geib

2000 Why Flute? Folsom Point Design and Adaptation. *Journal of Archaeological Science* 27:799–820.

Ahlstrom, Richard V. N., and Jerry D. Lyon (editors)

2000 *Desert Foragers and Farmers of the Growler Valley: An Archaeological Survey of 8,065 Acres on the South Tactical Range on the Barry M. Goldwater Air Force Range in Southwestern Arizona.* SWCA Cultural Resource Report No. 98-140. SWCA, Tucson.

Ahlstrom, Richard V. N., Carla R. Van West, and Jeffrey S. Dean

1995 Environmental and Chronological Factors in the Mesa Verde–Northern Rio Grande Migration. *Journal of Anthropological Archaeology* 14:125–142.

Akins, Nancy J.

1998 *Excavations at Gallo Mountain Sites, NM 32, Catron County, New Mexico.* Archaeology Notes No. 65. Museum of New Mexico Office of Archaeological Studies, Santa Fe.

Akins, Nancy J., and John D. Schelberg

1984 Evidence for Organizational Complexity as Seen from the Mortuary Practices at Chaco Canyon. In *Recent Research on Chaco Prehistory*, edited by W. James Judge and John D. Schelberg, pp. 89–101. Reports of the Chaco Center No. 8. Division of Cultural Research. USDI National Park Service, Albuquerque.

Algaze, Guillermo

1989 The Uruk Expansion: Cross-Cultural Exchange in Early Mesopotamian Civilization. *Current Anthropology* 30:571–608.

Alonso, Ana María

1993 The Politics of Space, Time, and Substance: State Formation, Nationalism, and Ethnicity. *Annual Review of Anthropology* 23:379–405.

Ambler, J. Richard

1996 Dust Devil Cave and Archaic Complexes of the Glen Canyon Area. In *Glen Canyon Revisited*, edited by Phil Geib, pp. 40–52. University of Utah Anthropological Papers No. 119. University of Utah Press, Salt Lake City.

Amsden, Charles A.

1949 *Prehistoric Southwesterners from Basketmaker to Pueblo.* Southwest Museum, Los Angeles.

Anderson, David G., and J. Christopher Gillam

2000 Paleoindian Colonization of the Americas: Implications from an Examination of Physiography, Demography, and Artifact Distribution. *American Antiquity* 65:43–66.

Anderson, Keith M., Gloria J. Fenner, Don P. Morris, George A. Teague, and Charmion McKusick

1986 *The Archeology of Gila Cliff Dwellings.* Publications in Anthropology 36. Western Archeological and Conservation Center, Tucson.

Anderson, Roger Y.

1990 Solar-Cycle Modulations of ENSO: A Mechanism for Pacific and Global Climate Change. In *Proceedings, Sixth Annual Pacific Climate (PACLIM) Workshop*, edited by Julio L. Betancourt and A. M. McKay, pp. 77–81. California Department of Water Resources, Interagency Ecological Studies Program Technical Report 23.

1992a Long-Term Changes in the Frequency of Occurrence of El Niño Events. In *El Niño: Historical and Paleoclimatic Aspects of the Southern Oscillation*, edited by Henry F. Diaz and Vera Markgraf, pp. 193–200. Cambridge University Press, Cambridge.

1992b Possible Connection between Surface Winds, Solar Activity and the Earth's Magnetic Field. *Nature* 358:51–53.

Anderson, Roger Y., Andy Soutar, and Thomas C. Johnson

1992 Long-Term Changes in El Niño/Southern Oscillation: Evidence from Marine and Lacustrine Sediments. In *El Niño: Historical and Paleoclimatic Aspects of the Southern Oscillation*, edited by Henry F. Diaz and Vera Markgraf, pp. 419–434. Cambridge University Press, Cambridge.

Andrade, E. R., and W. D. Sellers

1988 El Niño and Its Effect on Precipitation in Arizona and Western New Mexico. *Journal of Climate* 8:403–410.

Antevs, Ernst V.

1948 *The Great Basin, with Emphasis on Glacial and Postglacial Times III.* Bulletin 38(20):168–191. University of Utah, Salt Lake City.

Anthony, David W.

1990 Migration in Archeology: The Baby and the Bathwater. *American Anthropologist* 92:895–914.

Anyon, Roger

1987 Prehistoric Cultures. In An Archaeological Reconnaissance of West-Central New Mexico, the Anasazi Monuments Project, edited by Andrew P. Fowler, John R. Stein, and Roger Anyon, pp. 20–28. Manuscript submitted to the Office of Cultural Affairs, Historic Preservation Division, State of New Mexico, Santa Fe.

1992 The Late Prehistoric and Early Historic Periods in the Zuni-Cibola Area, AD 1400–1680. In *Current Research on the Late Prehistory and Early History of New Mexico*, edited by Bradley J. Vierra, pp. 75–83. New Mexico Archaeological Council Special Publication, Vol. 1. Albuquerque.

1999 Implementing NAGPRA: Cultural Affiliation and Repatriation. In *Transcripts and Papers, February 20–21,*

1998, pp. 109–120. Affiliation Conference on Ancestral Peoples of the Four Corners Region Vol. 2. Center for Southwest Studies, Fort Lewis College, Durango, Colorado.

Anyon, Roger, Susan M. Collins, and Kathryn H. Bennett
1983 *Archaeological Investigations between Manuelito Canyon and Whitewater Arroyo, Northwest New Mexico.* Zuni Archaeology Program Report No. 185. Zuni, New Mexico.

Anyon, Roger, and T. J. Ferguson
1983 Settlement Patterns and Changing Adaptations in the Zuni Area after AD 1000. Paper presented at the 2nd Anasazi Symposium, San Juan Museum Research Center, Bloomfield, New Mexico.
1995 Cultural Resources Management at the Pueblo of Zuni, New Mexico, USA. *Antiquity* 69:913–930.

Anyon, Roger, Andrew P. Fowler, Barbara E. Holmes, Robert D. Leonard, Mark D. Varien, and Regan Verycrusse
1992 Prehistoric and Historic Land Use in Oak Wash, Zuni Indian Reservation, McKinley County, New Mexico. Zuni Archaeology Program Report No. 244b, draft manuscript. Zuni, New Mexico.

Anyon, Roger, Patricia A. Gilman, and Steven A. LeBlanc
1981 A Reevaluation of the Mogollon-Mimbres Archaeological Sequence. *Kiva* 46:209–225.

Anyon, Roger, and Steven A. LeBlanc
1980 The Architectural Evolution of Mogollon-Mimbres Communal Structures. *Kiva* 45:253–277.
1984 *The Galaz Ruin: A Prehistoric Mimbres Village in Southwestern New Mexico.* Maxwell Museum of Anthropology and University of New Mexico Press, Albuquerque.

Anyon, Roger, and J. Zunie
1989 Cooperation at the Pueblo of Zuni: Common Ground for Archaeology and Tribal Concerns. *Practicing Anthropology* 11:13–15.

Ayer, Mrs. Edward E. (translator)
1965 [1916] *The Memorial of Fray Alonso de Benavides, 1630,* annotated by Frederick Webb Hodge and Charles Fletcher Lummis. Horn and Wallace, Albuquerque.

Bahr, Donald M.
1977 On the Complexity of Southwest Indian Emergence Myths. *Journal of Anthropological Research* 33(3):317–349.

Bain, James
1977–1980 Archaeological Society of New Mexico Rock Art Survey. Records on file, Laboratory of Anthropology, Museum of New Mexico, Santa Fe.

Baker, Vernon G.
1980 Archaeological Visibility of Afro-American Culture: An Example from Black Lucy's Garden, Andover. In *Archaeological Perspectives on Ethnicity in America: Afro-American and Asian American Culture History,* edited by Robert L. Schuyler, pp. 29–37. Baywood Publishing Company, New York.

Baker, W. E., and A. V. Kidder
1937 A Spear Thrower from Oklahoma. *American Antiquity* 3:51–52.

Bamforth, Douglas
1988 *Ecology and Human Organization on the Great Plains.* Plenum, New York.

Bandelier, Adolph F.
1890 *Contributions to the History of the Southwestern Portion of the United States.* Papers of the Archaeological Institute of America, American Series No. 5. Peabody Museum of American Archaeology and Ethnology, Cambridge.
1892 *Final Report of Investigations among the Indians of the Southwestern United States, Part II.* Papers of the Archaeological Institute of America, American Series No. 4. Peabody Museum of American Archaeology and Ethnology, Cambridge.

Bannister, Bryant, John W. Hannah, and William J. Robinson
1970 *Tree-Ring Dates from New Mexico M–N, S, Z, Southwestern New Mexico.* Laboratory of Tree-Ring Research, University of Arizona, Tucson.

Barber, Elizabeth W.
1994 *Women's Work, the First 20,000 Years: Women, Cloth and Textiles in Early Times.* W. W. Norton, New York.

Barnett, Franklin
1974 *Sandstone Hill Pueblo Ruin: Cibola Culture in Catron County, New Mexico.* Albuquerque Archaeological Society, Albuquerque.

Barter, Eloise R.
1955 An Analysis of the Ceramic Traditions of the Jewett Gap Site, New Mexico. Unpublished Master's thesis, Department of Anthropology, University of Arizona, Tucson.
1957a Pottery of the Reserve Area. In *Late Mogollon Communities: Four Sites of the Tularosa Phase, Western New Mexico,* pp. 89–105. Fieldiana: Anthropology

Vol. 49, No. 1. Chicago Natural History Museum, Chicago.
1957b Pottery of the Jewett Gap Site. In *Late Mogollon Communities: Four Sites of the Tularosa Phase, Western New Mexico,* pp. 106–125. Fieldiana: Anthropology Vol. 49, No. 1. Chicago Natural History Museum, Chicago.

Barth, Fredrik
1959 *Political Leadership among Swat Pathans.* Monographs on Social Anthropology 19. London School of Economics, London.
1969a Pathan Identity and Its Maintenance. In *Ethnic Groups and Boundaries: The Social Organization of Culture Difference,* edited by Fredrik Barth, pp. 117–134. Little, Brown and Company, Boston.
1969b Introduction. In *Ethnic Groups and Boundaries: The Social Organization of Culture Difference,* edited by Fredrik Barth, pp. 9–38. Little, Brown and Company, Boston.
1983 *Sohar: Culture and Society in an Omani Town.* Johns Hopkins University Press, Baltimore, Maryland.

Bartlett, Florence
1914 The Creation of Zuni. *Old Santa Fe* 2:79–80.

Baugh, Timothy G.
1984 Southern Plains Societies Eastern Frontier Pueblo Exchange during the Protohistoric Period. In *Collected Papers in Honor of Harry L. Hadlock,* edited by Nancy L. Fox, pp. 157–168. Papers of the Archaeological Society of New Mexico No. 9. Albuquerque.

Baxter, Sylvester
1882 An Aboriginal Pilgrimage. *Century Magazine* 24(n.s. 2): 526–536.

Bayham, Frank E.
1982 *A Diachronic Analysis of Prehistoric Animal Exploitation at Ventana Cave.* PhD dissertation, Arizona State University. University Microfilms, Ann Arbor.

Bayham, Frank E., and Donald H. Morris
1986 Episodic Use of a Marginal Environment: A Synthesis. In *Prehistoric Hunter-Gatherers of South Central Arizona: The Picacho Reservoir Archaic Project,* by Frank E. Bayham, Donald H. Morris, and M. Steven Shackley, pp. 359–381. Anthropological Field Studies No. 13. Department of Anthropology, Arizona State University, Tempe.
1990 Thermal Maxima and Episodic Occupation of the Picacho Reservoir

Dune Field. In *Perspectives on South-western Prehistory*, edited by Paul E. Minnis and Charles L. Redman, pp. 26–37. Westview Press, Boulder.

Bayman, James M.

1994 *Craft Production and Political Economy at the Marana Platform Mound Community*. PhD dissertation, Department of Anthropology, Arizona State University, Tempe. University Microfilms, Ann Arbor.

Beal, John D.

1987 *Foundations of the Rio Grande Classic: The Lower Chama River AD 1300–1500*. Southwest Archaeological Consultants, Santa Fe.

Beals, Ralph L.

1932 *The Comparative Ethnology of Northern Mexico before 1750*. Ibero-Americana 2. University of California Press, Berkeley.

Beck, Margaret

2000 Tortillas and Women's Labor in the Hohokam Classic Period. Paper presented at the 6th Gender and Archaeology Conference, Flagstaff, Arizona.

Beckes, Michael R., and James M. Adovasio

1982 Perspectives on the Origins and Affinities of Mogollon on the Eastern Periphery. In *Mogollon Archaeology: Proceedings of the 1980 Mogollon Conference*, edited by Patrick H. Beckett, pp. 201–209. Acoma Books, Ramona, California.

Beckett, Patrick H.

1973 Cochise Culture Sites in South Central and North Central New Mexico. Unpublished Master's thesis, Department of Anthropology, Eastern New Mexico University, Portales.

1980 *The Ake Site: Collection and Excavation of LA 13423, Catron County, New Mexico*. New Mexico State University, Department of Sociology and Anthropology, Cultural Resources Management Division, University Park.

Beckett, Patrick, and Richard S. MacNeish

1994 The Archaic Chihuahua Tradition of South-Central New Mexico and Chihuahua, Mexico. In *Archaic Hunter-Gatherer Archaeology in the American Southwest*, edited by Bradley J. Vierra, pp. 335–371. Contributions in Anthropology Vol. 13, No. 1. Eastern New Mexico University, Portales.

Beeson, William J.

1966 *Archaeological Survey near St. Johns, Arizona: A Methodological Study*. PhD dissertation, Department of Anthropology, University of Arizona, Tucson. University Microfilms, Ann Arbor.

Bellwood, Peter

1996 The Origins and Spread of Agriculture in the Indo-Pacific Region: Gradualism and Diffusion or Revolution and Colonization. In *The Origins and Spread of Agriculture and Pastoralism in Eurasia*, edited by David R. Harris, pp. 465–498. UCL Press, London.

1997 Austronesian Prehistory and Uto-Aztecan Prehistory: Similar Trajectories? Manuscript on file, Department of Anthropology, University of Arizona, Tucson.

Bellwood, Peter, and Colin Renfrew (editors)

2003 *Examining the Farming/Language Dispersal Hypothesis*. McDonald Institute for Archaeological Research, Cambridge.

Benedict, James B.

1999 Effects of Changing Climate on Game-Animal and Human Use of the Colorado High Country (U.S.A.) since 1000 BC. *Arctic, Antarctic, and Alpine Research* 31:1–15.

Benedict, Ruth

1925 Review of *The North American Indian* by Edward S. Curtis. *American Anthropologist* 27:458–460.

1935 *Zuni Mythology*. 2 vols. Columbia University Press, New York City.

Bennett, Wendell L., and Robert M. Zingg

1935 *The Tarahumara, an Indian Tribe of Northern Mexico*. University of Chicago Press, Chicago.

Bennyhoff, James A., and Richard E. Hughes

1987 *Shell Bead and Ornament Exchange Networks between California and the Western Great Basin*. Anthropological Papers Vol. 64, Pt. 2. American Museum of Natural History, New York.

Benson, L. V., and R. S. Thompson

1987 Lake-Level Variation in the Lahontan Basin for the Past 50,000 Years. *Quaternary Research* 28:69–85.

Benton, John F.

1968 *Town Origins: The Evidence from Medieval England*. D. C. Heath, Boston.

Benz, B. F., and H. Iltis

1990 Studies in Archaeological Maize, 1. *American Antiquity* 55:500–511.

Berman, Mary Jane

1979 *Cultural Resources Overview of Socorro, New Mexico*. USDA Forest Service, Albuquerque, and Bureau of Land Management, Santa Fe.

1989 *Prehistoric Abandonment of the Upper San Francisco River Valley, West-Central New Mexico: An Economic Case Study*. PhD dissertation, Department of Anthropology, University of New York at Binghamton. University Microfilms, Ann Arbor.

Bernard-Shaw, Mary, and William D. Hohmann

1989 Turquoise Artifacts and Other Minerals. In *Archaeological Investigations at the Redtail Site, AA:12:149 (ASM), in the Northern Tucson Basin*, edited by Mary Bernard-Shaw, pp. 151–157. Technical Report No. 98-8. Center for Desert Archaeology, Tucson, Arizona.

Berry, Claudia F., and Michael S. Berry

1986 Chronological and Conceptual Models of the Southwestern Archaic. In *Anthropology of the Desert West: Essays in Honor of Jesse D. Jennings*, edited by Carol J. Condie and Don D. Fowler, pp. 253–327. University of Utah Anthropological Papers No. 110. University of Utah Press, Salt Lake City.

Berry, Michael S.

1982 *Time, Space and Transition in Anasazi Prehistory*. University of Utah Press, Salt Lake City.

Betancourt, Julio L.

1984 Late Quaternary Plant Zonation and Climate in Southeastern Utah. *Great Basin Naturalist* 44(1):1–35.

1987 Paleoecology of Pinyon-Juniper Woodlands: Summary. In *Proceedings —Pinyon-Juniper Conference*, compiled by R. L. Everett, pp. 129–139. Intermountain Research Station, USDA Forest Service, General Technical Report INT-215, Ogden, Utah.

1990 Late Quaternary Biogeography of the Colorado Plateau. In *Packrat Middens: The Last 40,000 Years of Biotic Change*, edited by Julio L. Betancourt, Thomas R. Van Devender, and Paul S. Martin, pp. 259–292. University of Arizona Press, Tucson.

2003 The Pleistocene–Holocene Transition in Subtropical North and South America. Paper presented at the 16th INQUA Congress, Reno.

Betancourt, Julio L., Paul S. Martin, and Thomas R. Van Devender

1983 Fossil Packrat Middens from Chaco Canyon, New Mexico: Cultural and Ecological Significance. In *Chaco Canyon Country: A Field Guide to the Geo-*

morphology, *Quaternary Geology, Paleo-
ecology, and Environmental Geology of
Northwestern New Mexico*, edited by
Stephen G. Wells, David W. Love, and
Thomas W. Gardner, pp. 207–217.
American Geomorphological Field
Group 1983 Field Trip Guide Book.

Betancourt, Julio L., and Thomas R. Van
Devender

1981 Holocene Vegetation in Chaco Canyon, New Mexico. *Science* 214:656–
658.

Betancourt, Julio L., Thomas R. Van
Devender, and Paul S. Martin (editors)

1990 *Packrat Middens: The Last 40,000
Years of Biotic Change.* University of
Arizona Press, Tucson.

Bettison, Cynthia Ann, Roland Shook,
Randy Jennings, and Dennis Miller

1999 New Identifications of Naturalistic
Motifs on Mimbres Pottery. In *Sixty
Years of Mogollon Archaeology: Papers
from the Ninth Mogollon Conference, Sil-
ver City, New Mexico, 1996*, edited by
Stephanie M. Whittlesey, pp. 119–125.
Statistical Research, Inc., Tucson,
Arizona.

Bice, Richard A.

1994 Some Thoughts on the Naming
and Dating of San Ignacio Black-on-
white Pottery (Late Chaco-McElmo
Black-on-white) in the North-Central
Region of New Mexico. In *Papers in
Honor of Gordon Page*, edited by Meliha
S. Duran and David T. Kirkpatrick,
pp. 27–40. Papers of the Archaeologi-
cal Society of New Mexico No. 20.
Albuquerque.

Binford, Lewis R.

1963 "Red Ocher" Caches from the Michigan Area: A Possible Case of Cultural
Drift. *Southwestern Journal of Anthropology* 19:89–108.

1965 Archaeological Systematics and the
Study of Culture Process. *American
Antiquity* 31:203–210.

1973 Interassemblage Variability—the
Mousterian and the "Functional"
Argument. In *The Explanation of Cul-
ture Change*, edited by Colin Renfrew,
pp. 227–254. University of Pittsburgh
Press, Pittsburgh.

1983 Long Term Land Use Patterns:
Some Implications for Archaeology. In
*Lulu Linear Punctated: Essays in Honor
of George Irving Quimby*, edited by Robert C. Dunnell and Donald K. Grayson,
pp. 27–53. Anthropological Papers No.
72. Museum of Anthropology, University of Michigan, Ann Arbor.

Birdsell, Joseph B.

1957 Some Population Problems Involving Pleistocene Man. *Cold Springs Har-
bor Symposium on Quantitative Biology*
22:47–69.

Bishop, Ronald L., and Frederick W.
Lange (editors)

1991 *The Ceramic Legacy of Anna O.
Shepard.* University Press of Colorado,
Boulder.

Blanton, Richard E., Gary M. Feinman,
Stephen A. Kowalewski, and Peter N.
Peregrine

1996 A Dual-Processual Theory for the
Evolution of Mesoamerican Civilization. *Current Anthropology* 37:1–14.

Blanton, Richard E., Stephen A. Kowalewski, Gary Feinman, and Jill Appel

1981 *Ancient Mesoamerica: A Comparison
of Change in Three Regions.* Cambridge
University Press, Cambridge.

1982 *Monte Alban's Hinterland, Part I:
The Prehispanic Settlement Patterns of
the Central and Southern Parts of the
Valley of Oaxaca, Mexico.* Memoirs of
the Museum of Anthropology, University of Michigan No. 15. Ann Arbor.

Bloomfield, Leonard

1933 *Language.* Holt, Rinehart and
Winston, New York.

Bluhm, Elaine

1952 Clothing and Textiles. In *Mogollon
Cultural Continuity and Change: The
Stratigraphic Analysis of Tularosa and
Cordova Caves*, pp. 231–330. Fieldiana:
Anthropology Vol. 40. Chicago Natu-
ral History Museum, Chicago.

1957 *The Sawmill Site: A Reserve Phase Village, Pine Lawn Valley, Western New
Mexico.* Fieldiana: Anthropology Vol.
47, No. 1. Chicago Natural History
Museum, Chicago.

Blumenbach, Johann F.

1865 *The Anthropological Treatises of
Johann Friederich Blumenbach*, translated by T. Bendyshe. Longman,
Green, London. Originally published
1775–1786.

Boas, Franz

1902 Rudolf Virchow. *Science* 16:441–
445.

1911 *Handbook of American Indian Lan-
guages*, Pt. 1. Bulletin No. 40, Bureau of
American Ethnology, Smithsonian
Institution, Washington, D.C.

1922 Tales of Spanish Provenience from
Zuni. *Journal of American Folk-Lore*
35:62–98.

1928 *Keresan Texts.* 2 pts. American Ethnological Society, New York.

1940 *Race, Language, and Culture.* Mac-
millan, New York.

Bogucki, P.

1987 The Establishment of Agrarian
Communities on the North European
Plain. *Current Anthropology* 28:1–24.

Bohrer, Vorsila

1991 Recently Recognized Cultivated and
Encouraged Plants among the Hohokam. *Kiva* 56:227–236.

Bolton, Herbert E.

1948 *Kino's Historical Memoir of Pimeria
Alta.* 2 vols. University of California
Press, Berkeley and Los Angeles.

Bordes, François, and D. de Sonneville-
Bordes

1970 The Significance of Variability in
Paleolithic Assemblages. *World
Archaeology* 2:61–73.

Bourdieu, Pierre

1977 *Outline of a Theory of Practice.* Cambridge University Press, Cambridge.

1990 *The Logic of Practice*, translated by
R. Nice. Stanford University Press,
Stanford.

Bowen, John R.

2000 Should We Have a Universal Con-
cept of "Indigenous Peoples' Rights"?:
Ethnicity and Essentialism in the
Twenty-first Century. *Anthropology
Today* 16(4):12–16.

Bradfield, Maitland

1971 *The Changing Pattern of Hopi Agri-
culture.* Occasional Paper No. 38. Royal
Anthropological Institute of Great
Britain and Ireland, London.

Bradfield, Wesley

1931 *Cameron Creek Village: A Site in the
Mimbres Area in Grant County, New
Mexico.* Monographs No. 1. School of
American Research, Santa Fe.

Bradley, Bruce A.

1996 Pitchers to Mugs: Chacoan Revival
at Sand Canyon Pueblo. *Kiva* 61:241–
255.

Bradley, Ronna J.

1996 *The Role of Casas Grandes in Prehistoric Shell Exchange Networks within
the Southwest.* PhD dissertation, Department of Anthropology, Arizona
State University, Tempe. University
Microfilms, Ann Arbor.

1997 Shell Artifacts from the Schoolhouse Point Mesa Sites. In *The Archaeology of Schoolhouse Point Mesa, Roosevelt Platform Mound Study: Report on
the Schoolhouse Point Mesa Sites,
Schoolhouse Management Group, Pinto
Creek Complex*, edited by Owen Lindauer, pp. 463–69. Roosevelt Mono-

graph Series 4, Anthropological Field Studies 33. Office of Cultural Resource Management, Department of Anthropology, Arizona State University, Tempe.

Brand, Donald
1938 Aboriginal Trade Routes for Sea Shells in the Southwest. *Yearbook of the Association of Pacific Coast Geographers* 4:3–10.
1943 The Chihuahua Culture. *New Mexico Archaeologist* 5–6:3.

Brandauer, Nancy, and Shi-Kuei Wu
1978 *The Freshwater Mussels (*Family Unionidae*).* Natural History Inventory of Colorado, Pt. 2. University of Colorado Museum, Boulder.

Brandt, Carol B.
1995 Traditional Agriculture on the Zuni Indian Reservation in the Recent Historic Period. In *Soil, Water, Biology, and Belief in Prehistoric and Traditional Southwestern Agriculture*, edited by H. Wolcott Toll, pp. 291–301. Special Publication No. 2. New Mexico Archaeological Council, Albuquerque.

Braudel, Fernand
1972 *The Mediterranean and the Mediterranean World in the Age of Philip II*, translated by Sian Reynolds. Harper and Row, New York. Originally published 1949 in French.
1980 *On History*, translated by Sarah Matthews. University of Chicago Press, Chicago.

Braun, David P.
1995 Style, Selection, and Historicity. In *Style, Society, and Person: Archaeological and Ethnological Perspectives*, edited by Christopher Carr and Jill E. Neitzel, pp. 123–138. Plenum Press, New York.

Breasted, James Henry
1935 *The Oriental Institute*. University of Chicago Survey Vol. 7. University of Chicago Press, Chicago.

Breternitz, David A.
1959 *Excavations at Nantack Village, Point of Pines, Arizona.* Anthropological Papers of the University of Arizona No. 1. University of Arizona Press, Tucson.

Brew, J. O., and Watson Smith
1954 Comments on Joe Ben Wheat, Southwestern Cultural Interrelationships and the Question of Area Co-traditions. *American Anthropologist* 56:586–590.

Brinton, Daniel G.
1891 *The American Race: Linguistic Classification and Ethnographic Description*

of the Native Tribes of North and South America. N. D. C. Hodges, New York.

Brody, J. J.
1977 *Mimbres Painted Pottery*. School of American Research Press, Santa Fe.
1983 Mimbres Painting. In *Mimbres Pottery: Ancient Art of the American Southwest*, edited by J. J. Brody, Catherine J. Scott, and Steven A. LeBlanc, pp. 69–125. Hudson Hills Press, New York.
1991 *Anasazi and Pueblo Painting.* A School of American Research Book. University of New Mexico Press, Albuquerque.
1992 Mimbres Art: Form and Imagery. In *The Ancient Americas: Art from Sacred Landscapes*, edited by Richard F. Townsend, pp. 89–102. Art Institute of Chicago, Chicago.

Brown, David E. (editor)
1994 *Biotic Communities: Southwestern United States and Northwestern Mexico.* University of Utah Press, Salt Lake City.

Brown, Michael F.
2003 *Who Owns Native Culture?* Harvard University Press, Cambridge.

Brugge, David M.
1956 Pima Bajo Basketry. *Kiva* 22(1):7–11.

Brunstein, F. Craig
1996 Climatic Significance of the Bristlecone Pine Latewood Frost-Ring Record at Almagre Mountain, Colorado, U.S.A. *Arctic and Alpine Research* 28(1):65–76.

Bryan, A. L., and R. Gruhn
1964 Problems Relating to the Neothermal Climate Sequence. *American Antiquity* 29:307–315.

Bryan, Kirk
1954 *The Geology of Chaco Canyon New Mexico in Relation to the Life and Remains of the Prehistoric Peoples of Pueblo Bonito.* Smithsonian Miscellaneous Collections Vol. 122, No. 7. Washington, D.C.

Bullard, William Rotch, Jr.
1962 *The Cerro Colorado Site and Pithouse Architecture in the Southwestern United States prior to AD 900.* Papers of the Peabody Museum of Archaeology and Ethnology Vol. 44, No. 2. Harvard University, Cambridge.

Bullock, Peter Y.
1991 Macaws at Casas Grandes and in the American Southwest. Unpublished manuscript on file, Museum of New Mexico Office of Archaeological Studies, Santa Fe.

Bunzel, Ruth
1932a Zuni Katcinas. In *Forty-seventh Annual Report of the Bureau of American Ethnology, 1929–1930*, pp. 837–1086. Smithsonian Institution, Washington, D.C.
1932b Zuni Ceremonialism. In *Forty-seventh Annual Report of the Bureau of American Ethnology, 1929–1930*, pp. 467–544. Smithsonian Institution, Washington, D.C.
1932c Zuni Origin Myths. In *Forty-seventh Annual Report of the Bureau of American Ethnology, 1929–1930*, pp. 545–609. Smithsonian Institution, Washington, D.C.
1932d Zuni Ritual Poetry. In *Forty-seventh Annual Report of the Bureau of American Ethnology, 1929–1930*, pp. 611–835. Smithsonian Institution, Washington, D.C.
1933 *Zuni Texts.* Publications of the American Ethnological Society 15. Stechert, New York.
1992 Introduction to Zuni Ceremonialism. In *Zuni Ceremonialism*, pp. 467–546. Reprinted. University of New Mexico Press, Albuquerque. Originally published 1932, Bureau of American Ethnology, Smithsonian Institution, Washington, D.C.

Burger, Richard L.
1988 Unity and Heterogeneity within the Chavin Horizon. In *Peruvian Prehistory*, edited by Richard W. Keating, pp. 99–144. Cambridge University Press, Cambridge.

Burns, B.
1978 Tentative Ceramic Chronology for the Middle Puerco Valley and Chronometric Analysis. In Archaeological Investigations in the Area of the Middle Puerco River Valley, New Mexico, May 1–December 1, 1978, edited by Cynthia Irwin-Williams. Unpublished progress report to the Bureau of Land Management, Albuquerque.

Burns, Barney Tillman
1983 *Simulated Anasazi Storage Behavior Using Crop Yields Reconstructed from Tree Rings: AD 652–1968.* PhD dissertation, Department of Anthropology, University of Arizona, Tucson. University Microfilms, Ann Arbor.

Burton, Jeffery F.
1988 Hunters and the Hunted: The Prehistoric Art of Tom Ketchum Cave. *Kiva* 53:335–356.

Bushnell, G. H. S.
1955 Some Pueblo IV Pottery Types from

Kechipauan, New Mexico, U.S.A. In *Annais do XXXI Congresso Internacional de Americanistas, São Paulo—1954,* Vol. 2, pp. 657–665. Editora Anhembi, São Paulo.

Bussey, Stanley D.

1973 *Late Mogollon Manifestations in the Mimbres Branch, Southwestern New Mexico.* PhD dissertation, Department of Anthropology, University of Oregon, Eugene. University Microfilms, Ann Arbor.

1975 *The Archaeology of Lee Village.* Monograph No. 2. Center of Archaeological Study, Las Cruces, New Mexico.

Butzer, Karl

1971 *Environment and Archaeology: An Ecological Approach to Prehistory.* Aldine, Chicago.

1982 *Archaeology as Human Ecology.* Cambridge University Press, Cambridge.

Caldwell, Joseph

1964 Interaction Studies in Prehistory. In *Hopewellian Studies,* edited by Joseph R. Caldwell and Robert L. Hall, pp. 133–143. Illinois State Museum Scientific Papers No. 12. Springfield.

Callaghan, Catherine A.

1965 *Lake Miwok Dictionary.* University of California Publications in Linguistics Vol. 39. University of California Press, Berkeley.

1997 Evidence for Yok-Utian. *International Journal of American Linguistics* 63(1):18–64.

Cameron, Catherine M.

1995 Migration and the Movement of Southwestern Peoples. *Journal of Anthropological Archaeology* 14:104–124.

Campbell, Lyle

1997 *American Indian Languages.* Oxford University Press, Oxford.

Campbell, Lyle, and Marianne Mithun (editors)

1979 *The Languages of Native America: A Comparative and Historical Assessment.* University of Texas Press, Austin.

Cannon, Michael D.

2001 *Large Mammal Resource Depletion and Agricultural Intensification: An Empirical Test in the Mimbres Valley, New Mexico.* PhD dissertation, Department of Anthropology, University of Washington, Seattle. University Microfilms, Ann Arbor.

Capone, Patricia, and Robert W. Preucel

2002 Ceramic Semiotics: Women, Pottery, and Social Meanings at Kotyiti

Pueblo. In *Archaeologies of the Pueblo Revolt: Identity, Meaning, and Renewal in the Pueblo World,* edited by Robert W. Preucel, pp. 99–111. University of New Mexico Press, Albuquerque.

Carey, Henry A.

1931 An Analysis of the Northwestern Chihuahua Culture. *American Anthropologist* 33:325–374.

Carlson, Roy L.

1970 *White Mountain Redware, a Pottery Tradition of East-Central Arizona and Western New Mexico.* Anthropological Papers of the University of Arizona No. 19. University of Arizona Press, Tucson.

Carpenter, John P., Jonathan B. Mabry, and Guadalupe Sánchez Miranda

2002 O'odham Origins: Reconstructing Uto-Aztecan Prehistory. Paper presented at the 67th Annual Meeting of the Society for American Archaeology, Denver.

Carpenter, John, Guadalupe Sanchez, and María Elisa Villalpando C.

2005 The Late Archaic/Early Agricultural Period in Sonora, Mexico. In *The Late Archaic across the Borderlands: From Foraging to Farming,* edited by Bradley Vierra, pp. 13–40. University of Texas Press, Austin.

Carr, Christopher

1995 A Unified Middle-Range Theory of Artifact Design. In *Style, Society, and Person: Archaeological and Ethnological Perspectives,* edited by Christopher Carr and Jill E. Neitzel, pp. 171–258. Plenum Press, New York.

Carr, Christopher, and Robert F. Maslowski

1995 Cordage and Fabrics: Relating Form, Technology, and Social Processes. In *Style, Society, and Person: Archaeological and Ethnological Perspectives,* edited by Christopher Carr and Jill E. Neitzel, pp. 297–344. Plenum Press, New York.

Carr, Christopher, and Jill E. Neitzel (editors)

1995 *Style, Society, and Person: Archaeological and Ethnological Perspectives.* Plenum Press, New York.

Carrara, Paul, Deborah Trimble, and Meyer Rubin

1991 Holocene Treeline Fluctuations in the Northern San Juan Mountains, Colorado, U.S.A., as Indicated by Radiocarbon-Dated Conifer Wood. *Arctic and Alpine Research* 23:233–246.

Carter, George F.

1945 *Plant Geography and Culture History*

in the American Southwest. Publications in Anthropology No. 5. Viking Fund, New York.

Caso, Alfonso

1971 Calendrical Systems of Central Mexico. In *Archaeology of Northern Mesoamerica, Part 1,* edited by Gordon F. Ekholm and Ignacio Bernal, pp. 333–348. Handbook of Middle American Indians, Vol. 10, Robert Wauchope, general editor. University of Texas Press, Austin.

Cavalli-Sforza, L. L., A. Menozzi, P. Menozzi, and J. Mountain

1988 Reconstruction of Human Evolution: Bringing Together Genetic, Archaeological and Linguistic Data. *Proceedings of the National Academy of Sciences* 85:6002–6006.

Cavalli-Sforza, L. L., P. Menozzi, and A. Menozzi

1993 Demic Expansions and Human Evolution. *Science* 259:639–646.

Caviedes, C.

1988 The Effects of Enso Events in Some Key Regions of the South American Continent. In *Recent Climate Change,* edited by Stanley Gregory, pp. 252–253, 264. Belhaven Press, London.

Cayan, Daniel R., and D. H. Peterson

1989 The Influence of North Pacific Atmospheric Circulation on Streamflow in the West. In *Aspects of Climate Variability in the Pacific and the Western Americas,* edited by Daniel H. Peterson, pp. 375–397. Geophysical Monograph 55, American Geophysical Union. Washington, D.C.

Cayan, Daniel R., and Robert H. Webb

1992 El Niño/Southern Oscillation and Streamflow in the Western United States. In *El Niño: Historical and Paleoclimatic Aspects of the Southern Oscillation,* edited by Henry F. Diaz and Vera Markgraf, pp. 29–68. Cambridge University Press, Cambridge.

Chapman, Richard C., Cye W. Gossett, and William J. Gossett

1985 *Class II Cultural Resource Survey, Upper Gila Water Supply Study,* Central Arizona Project, Vols. 1 and 2. Deuel and Associates, Inc., Albuquerque.

Chase-Dunn, Christopher, and Helly M. Mann

1998 *The Wintu and Their Neighbors: A Very Small World-System in Northern California.* University of Arizona Press, Tucson.

Cheek, Charles D., and Amy Friedlander

1990 Pottery and Pigs' Feet: Space, Ethnicity, and Neighborhood in Washington, D.C., 1880–1940. *Historical Archaeology* 24(1):34–60.

Chimoni, Harry, and E. Richard Hart

1994   Zuni and the Grand Canyon. Paper delivered at the Annual Meeting of the Western History Association, Albuquerque, New Mexico.

Chisholm, Brian, and R. G. Matson

1994   Carbon and Nitrogen Isopic Evidence on Basketmaker II Diet at Cedar Mesa, Utah. *Kiva* 60:239–256.

Chisholm, Michael

1979   *Rural Settlement and Land Use: An Essay on Location.* 3rd ed. Hutchinson University Library, London.

Christensen, Don D.

1992   Pre-Pueblo Rock Art in the Little Colorado River Drainage. In *American Indian Rock Art*, Vol. 17, edited by Donald E. Weaver Jr., pp. 36–43. American Rock Art Research Association, El Toro, CA.

Clague, John, and R. W. Mathewes

1989   Early Holocene Thermal Maximum in Western North America: New Evidence from Castle Peak, British Columbia. *Geology* 17:277–280.

Clague, John, R. W. Mathewes, W. M. Buhay, and T. W. D. Edwards

1992   Early Holocene Climate at Castle Peak, Southern Coast Mountains, British Columbia, Canada. *Palaeogeography, Palaeoclimatology, Palaeoecology* 95:153–167.

Clark, Jeffery J.

1995   The Role of Migration in Social Change. In *The Roosevelt Community Development Study: New Perspectives on Tonto Basin Prehistory*, edited by Mark D. Elson, Miriam T. Stark, and David A. Gregory, pp. 369–384. Anthropological Papers No. 15. Center for Desert Archaeology, Tucson, Arizona.

2001   *Tracking Prehistoric Migrations: Pueblo Settlers among the Tonto Basin Hohokam.* Anthropological Papers of the University of Arizona No. 65. University of Arizona Press, Tucson.

Clark, Tiffany C.

1999   Understanding Prehistoric Ceramic Commodities: An Analysis of the Spatial and Temporal Distribution of Chupadero Black-on-white. Paper presented at the 64th Annual Meeting of the Society for American Archaeology, Chicago.

2001   Reconstructing Exchange Relations in Southwestern New Mexico: A Petrographic Study of Chupadero Black-on-white. Poster presented at the 66th Annual Meeting of the Society for American Archaeology, New Orleans.

Clark, Tiffany C., and Darrell Creel

2002   Tracking the Production and Long-Distance Exchange of a Ceramic Commodity: A Preliminary Analysis of Chupadero Black-on-white Pottery. Paper presented at the 67th Annual Meeting of the Society for American Archaeology, Denver.

Clarke, David

1968   *Analytical Archaeology.* Methuen, London.

1973   Archaeology: The Loss of Innocence. *Antiquity* 47:6–18.

Clavigero, Francesco Saverio

1787   *The History of Mexico. Collected from Spanish and Mexican Historians, from Manuscripts, and Ancient Paintings of the Indians.* 2 vols. G. G. J. and J. Robinson, London. 1979 facsimile ed. *The History of Mexico*, 2 vols. Garland Publishing, New York.

Colberg Sigleo, Anne

1975   Turquoise Mine and Artifact Correlation for Snaketown Site, Arizona. *Science* 189:459–460.

Cole, Sally J.

1990   *Legacy on Stone.* Johnson Books, Boulder.

1992   *Katsina Iconography in Homol'ovi Rock Art, Central Little Colorado River Valley, Arizona.* Arizona Archaeologist No. 25. Arizona Archaeological Society, Phoenix.

Collett, David

1987   A Contribution to the Study of Migrations in the Archaeological Record: The Ngoni and Kololo as a Case Study. In *Archaeology as Long-Term History*, edited by Ian Hodder, pp. 105–116. Cambridge University Press, Cambridge.

Colton, Harold S.

1938   Names of the Four Culture Roots in the Southwest. *Science* 87:551–552.

1939   *Prehistoric Culture Units and Their Relationship in Northern Arizona.* Museum of Northern Arizona Bulletin No. 17. Flagstaff.

1941   Prehistoric Trade in the Southwest. *Scientific Monthly* 52:308–319.

1946   *The Sinagua: A Summary of the Archaeology of the Region of Flagstaff, Arizona.* Museum of Northern Arizona Bulletin No. 22. Flagstaff.

1953   *Potsherds: An Introduction to the Study of Southwestern Ceramics and Their Uses in Historic Reconstruction.* Museum of Northern Arizona Bulletin No. 25. Flagstaff.

Colton, Harold S., and Lyndon L. Hargrave

1937   *Handbook of Northern Arizona Pottery Wares.* Museum of Northern Arizona Bulletin No. 11. Northern Arizona Society of Science and Art, Flagstaff.

Conkey, Margaret W., and Christine A. Hastorf (editors)

1990   *The Uses of Style in Archaeology.* Cambridge University Press, New York.

Cook, Edwin A.

1961   A New Mogollon Structure. *Kiva* 26(3):24–32.

Cooley, Maurice E.

1962   Late Pleistocene and Recent Erosion and Alluviation in Parts of the Colorado River System, Arizona and Utah. In *Geological Survey Research 1962: Short Papers in Geology, Hydrology, and Topography, Articles 1–59*, pp. 48–50. Professional Paper 450-B. U.S. Geological Survey, Washington, D.C.

Cordell, Linda S.

1984   *Prehistory of the Southwest.* Academic Press, San Diego.

1995   Tracing Migration Pathways from the Receiving End. *Journal of Anthropological Archaeology* 14:203–211.

1997   *Archaeology of the Southwest.* 2nd ed. Academic Press, New York.

Cordell, Linda S., and Don D. Fowler (editors)

2005   *Southwest Archaeology in the Twentieth Century.* University of Utah Press, Salt Lake City.

Cordell, Linda S., and George J. Gumerman (editors)

1989   *Dynamics of Southwest Prehistory.* Smithsonian Institution Press, Washington, D.C.

Cordell, Linda, and Fred Plog

1979   Escaping the Confines of Normative Thought: A Reevaluation of Puebloan Prehistory. *American Antiquity* 44:405–429.

Cordell, Linda S., and V. J. Yannie

1991   Ethnicity, Ethnogenesis and the Individual: A Processual Approach to Dialogue. In *Processual and Postprocessual Archaeologies: Multiple Ways of Knowing the Past*, edited by Robert W. Preucel, pp. 96–107. Southern Illinois Center for Archaeological Investigations, Occasional Paper 10. Carbondale.

Cortina-Borja, Mario, and Leopoldo Valiñas C.
1989 Some Remarks on Uto-Aztecan
Classification. *International Journal of
American Linguistics* 55(2):214–239.

Cosgrove, Cyril B.
1947 *Caves of the Upper Gila and Hueco
Areas in New Mexico and Texas.* Papers
of the Peabody Museum of American
Archaeology and Ethnology Vol. 24,
No. 2. Harvard University, Cambridge.

Cosgrove, Harriet S., and C. Burton
Cosgrove
1932 *The Swarts Ruin: A Typical Mimbres
Site in Southwestern New Mexico.*
Papers of the Peabody Museum of
American Archaeology and Ethnology
Vol. 15, No. 1. Harvard University,
Cambridge.

Coulam, Nancy J., and Peggy R. Barnett
1980 Paleoethnobotanical Analysis. In
Sudden Shelter, edited by Jesse Jen-
nings, A. R. Schroedl, and R. N.
Holmer, pp. 171–195. University of
Utah Anthropological Papers No. 103.
University of Utah Press, Salt Lake
City.

Counihan, Carole M.
1999 *The Anthropology of Food and Body:
Gender, Meaning, and Power.* Routledge, New York.

Craig, Douglas B.
1982 Shell Exchange along the Middle
Santa Cruz Valley during the Hohokam Pre-Classic. Paper presented at
the Tucson Basin Conference, Tucson,
Arizona.

Crampton, C. Gregory
1977 *The Zunis of Cibola.* University of
Utah Press, Salt Lake City.

Crary, Joseph S., Stephen Germick, and
David E. Doyel
2001 Exploring the Gila Horizon. *Kiva*
66:407–446.

Crawford, Michael H.
2001 *The Origins of Native Americans: Evidence from Anthropological Genetics.*
Cambridge University Press, New
York.

Creel, Darrell G.
1999 The Black Mountain Phase in the
Mimbres Area. In *The Casas Grandes
World,* edited by Curtis F. Schaafsma
and Carroll L. Riley, pp. 107–120. University of Utah Press, Salt Lake City.

Creel, Darrell G., Tiffany Clark, and Hec-
tor Neff
2002 Production and Long Distance
Movement of Chupadero Black-on-
white Pottery in New Mexico and

Texas. In *Geochemical Evidence for
Long-Distance Exchange,* edited by
Michael Glasscock, pp. 109–132.
Bergin and Garvey, Westport,
Connecticut.

Creel, Darrell, and Charmion McKusick
1994 Prehistoric Macaws and Parrots in
the Mimbres Area, New Mexico. *American Antiquity* 59:510–524.

Crotty, Helen
1991 A Consideration of the Formal
Qualities of Jornada Style Rock Art
with Implications for the Origins of
Pueblo Ceremonialism. In *Mogollon V,*
edited by Patrick H. Beckett and Regge
N. Wiseman, pp. 133–145. COAS Publishing and Research, Las Cruces, New
Mexico.
1995 *Anasazi Mural Art of the Pueblo IV
Period, AD 1300–1600: Influences, Selec-
tive Adoption, and Cultural Diversity in
the Prehistoric Southwest.* PhD dissertation, Department of Art History, University of California, Los Angeles. University Microfilms, Ann Arbor.

Crown, Patricia L.
1981 Ceramic Assemblage. In *Prehistory
of the St. Johns Area, East-Central Arizona: The TEP St. Johns Project,* edited
by Deborah A. Westfall, pp. 233–290.
Arizona State Museum Archaeological
Series 153, University of Arizona,
Tucson.
1994 *Ceramics and Ideology: Salado Polychrome Pottery.* University of New Mexico Press, Albuquerque.
2000 Women's Role in Changing Cuisine. In *Women and Men in the Pre-
hispanic Southwest: Labor, Power, and
Prestige,* edited by Patricia L. Crown,
pp. 221–266. School of American
Research Press, Santa Fe.

Crown, Patricia L., and W. James Judge
(editors)
1991 *Chaco & Hohokam: Prehistoric
Regional Systems in the American Southwest.* School of American Research,
Santa Fe.

Crown, Patricia L., and W. H. Wills
1995a The Origins of Southwest Con-
tainers: Women's Time Allocation and
Economic Intensification. *Journal of
Anthropological Research* 51:173–186.
1995b Economic Intensification and the
Origins of Ceramics in the Greater
American Southwest. In *The Emer-
gence of Pottery,* edited by William
Barnett and John Hoopes, pp. 241–
256. Smithsonian Institution Press,
Washington, D.C.

Cruz, R. R., R. K. DeWees, D. E. Funder-
burg, R. L. Lepp, D. Ortiz, and D.
Shaull
1994 *Water Resources Data, New Mexico,
Water Year 1993.* U.S. Geological Survey Water-Data Report NM-93-1,
Albuquerque.

Cummings, Byron
1940 *Kinishba, a Prehistoric Pueblo of the
Great Pueblo Period.* Hohokam Museums Association and the University of
Arizona, privately printed, Tucson.

Curtis, Edward S.
1922 *The Hopi.* The North American Indian, Vol. 12, Frederick Webb Hodge,
general editor. Plimpton Press, Norwood, Massachusetts.
1926a *The Tewa, the Zuni.* The North
American Indian, Vol. 17, Frederick
Webb Hodge, general editor. Plimpton
Press, Norwood, Massachusetts.
1926b *The Tiwa, the Keres.* The North
American Indian, Vol. 16, Frederick
Webb Hodge, general editor. Plimpton
Press, Norwood, Massachusetts.

Cushing, Frank Hamilton
1882 My Adventures in Zuni. *Century
Magazine* 25(December):191–207.
1888 Preliminary Notes on the Origin,
Working Hypothesis and Primary
Researches of the Hemenway South-
western Archaeological Expedition.
*Proceedings of the International Congress
of the Americanists* 7:151–194.
1896 Outlines of Zuni Creation Myths.
In *Thirteenth Annual Report of the
Bureau of Ethnology,* pp. 321–447. U.S.
Government Printing Office, Wash-
ington, D.C.
1901 *Zuni Folk Tales.* Putnam's, New
York. Republished 1976, AMS, New
York.
1920 *Zuni Breadstuff.* Indian Notes and
Monographs 8. Museum of the Ameri-
can Indian, Heye Foundation, New
York.
1979 *Zuni: Selected Writings of Frank
Hamilton Cushing,* edited by Jesse
Green. University of Nebraska Press,
Lincoln.
1988 *The Mythic World of the Zuni,* edited
by Barton Wright. University of New
Mexico Press, Albuquerque.

Damon, Paul E.
1988 Production and Decay of Radiocarbon and Its Modulation by Geomagnetic Field–Solar Activity Changes
with Possible Implications for Global
Climate. In *Secular, Solar, and Geomagnetic Variations in the Last 10,000 Years,*

edited by F. R. Stephenson and A. W. Wolfendale, pp. 267–285. Kluwer, Dordrecht, the Netherlands.

Damon, Paul E., J. C. Lerman, and A. Long
1978   Temporal Fluctuations of Atmospheric ¹⁴C: Causal Factors and Implications. *Annual Review of Earth and Planetary Science* 6:457–494.

Damon, Paul E., and T. W. Linick
1986   Geomagnetic-Heliomagnetic Modulation of Atmospheric Radiocarbon Production. *Radiocarbon* 28:266–278.

Damp, Jonathan
2001   Early Irrigation on the Colorado Plateau near Zuni Pueblo, New Mexico. Paper presented at the 66th Annual Meeting of the Society for American Archaeology, New Orleans.

Damp, Jonathan E., Stephen A. Hall, and Susan Smith
2002   Early Irrigation on the Colorado Plateau near Zuni Pueblo. *American Antiquity* 67:665–676.

Damp, Jonathan E., James Kendrick, Donovan Quam, Jeffrey Waseta, and Jerome Zunie
2001   *Households and Farms in Early Zuni Prehistory: Settlement, Subsistence, and the Archaeology of Y Unit Draw—Archaeological Investigations at Eighteen Sites along New Mexico State Highway 602*. New Mexico State Highway and Transportation Department Technical Series 2001-3/ZCRE Research Series No. 11. Zuni, New Mexico.

Danson, Edward B.
1957   *An Archaeological Survey of West Central New Mexico and East Central Arizona*. Papers of the Peabody Museum of American Archaeology and Ethnology No. 44. Harvard University, Cambridge.

D'Arrigo, Roseanne D., and Gordon C. Jacoby
1991   A 1000-Year Record of Winter Precipitation from Northwestern New Mexico, USA: A Reconstruction from Tree-Rings and Its Relation to El Niño and the Southern Oscillation. *Holocene* 1:95–101.

1992   A Tree-Ring Reconstruction of New Mexico Winter Precipitation and Its Relation to El Niño/Southern Oscillation Events. In *El Niño: Historical and Paleoclimatic Aspects of the Southern Oscillation*, edited by Henry F. Diaz and Vera Markgraf, pp. 243–258. Cambridge University Press, Cambridge.

David, Nicholas, Kodzo Gavua, A. Scott MacEachern, and Judy Sterner
1991   Ethnicity and Material Culture in North Cameroon. *Canadian Journal of Archaeology* 15:171–177.

Davis, Carolyn O'Bagy
1995   *Treasured Earth: Hattie Cosgrove's Mimbres Archaeology in the American Southwest*. Sanpete Publications and Old Pueblo Archaeology Center. Tucson.

Davis, Irvine
1959   Linguistic Clues to Northern Rio Grande Prehistory. *El Palacio* 66(3):73–84.

Davis, James T.
1961   *Trade Routes and Economic Exchange among the Indians of California*. Reports of the California Archaeological Survey No. 54. Department of Anthropology, University of California, Berkeley.

Davis, Mike
2000   *Late Victorian Holocausts: El Niño Famines and the Making of the Third World*. Verso, New York.

Davis, W. E.
1989   The Lime Ridge Clovis Site. *Utah Archaeology* 1989 2:66–76.

Dean, Glenna, and Valli S. Powell
1991   Macrobotanical Remains. In The Mogollon Village Archaeological Project, 1989, edited by Patricia A. Gilman, Raymond P. Mauldin, and Valli S. Powell, pp. 65–67. Manuscript on file, USDA Gila National Forest, Silver City, New Mexico.

Dean, Jeffrey S.
1969   *Chronological Analysis of Tsegi Phase Sites in Northeastern Arizona*. Papers of the Laboratory of Tree-Ring Research No. 3. University of Arizona, Tucson.

1970   Aspects of Tsegi Phase Social Organization: A Trial Reconstruction. In *Reconstructing Prehistoric Pueblo Societies*, edited by William A. Longacre, pp. 140–174. University of New Mexico Press, Albuquerque.

1985   Dendrochronological Dating of Floodplain Erosion on Zuni Indian Lands, Northwestern New Mexico. Plaintiff's Exhibit 4,000. Expert testimony submitted to the United States Claims Court as evidence in the case *Zuni Indian Tribe v. United States*, Docket 327-81L.

1988a   Dendrochronology and Paleoenvironmental Reconstruction on the Colorado Plateaus. In *The Anasazi in a Changing Environment*, edited by

George J. Gumerman, pp. 119–167. Cambridge University Press, Cambridge.

1988b   A Model of Anasazi Behavioral Adaptation. In *The Anasazi in a Changing Environment*, edited by George J. Gumerman, pp. 25–44. Cambridge University Press, Cambridge.

1989   Rebuttal Report: Dendrochronological Dating of Floodplain Erosion on Zuni Indian Lands. Plaintiff's Exhibit 4,000. Expert testimony submitted to the United States Claims Court as evidence in the case *Zuni Indian Tribe v. United States*, Dockets 327-81L and 224-81L.

1994   The Medieval Warm Period on the Southern Colorado Plateau. *Climate Change* 26:225–242.

1995   Dendrochronological Dating of Alluvial Deposition and Erosion in the Zuni Area. In *Zuni and the Courts: A Struggle for Sovereign Land Rights*, edited by E. Richard Hart, pp. 149–172. University Press of Kansas, Lawrence.

1996   Demography, Environment, and Subsistence Stress. In *Evolving Complexity and Environmental Risk in the Prehistoric Southwest*, edited by Joseph A. Tainter and Bonnie B. Tainter, pp. 25–56. Santa Fe Institute Studies in the Sciences of Complexity, Proceedings Vol. 24. Addison-Wesley Publishing Company, Reading.

Dean, Jeffrey S. (editor)
2000   *Salado*. University of New Mexico Press, Albuquerque.

Dean, Jeffrey S., William H. Doelle, and Janet D. Orcutt
1994   Adaptive Stress, Environment, and Demography. In *Themes in Southwest Prehistory*, edited by George J. Gumerman, pp. 53–86. School of American Research Press, Santa Fe.

Dean, Jeffrey S., Robert C. Euler, George J. Gumerman, Fred Plog, Richard H. Hevly, and Thor N. V. Karlstrom
1985   Human Behavior, Demography, and Paleoenvironment on the Colorado Plateaus. *American Antiquity* 50:537–554.

Dean, Jeffrey S., and Gary S. Funkhouser
1995   Dendroclimatic Reconstructions for the Southern Colorado Plateau. In *Climate Change in the Four Corners Region: Implications for Environmental Reconstruction and Land-Use Planning*, pp. 85–104. U.S. Department of

Energy, Grand Junction Projects Office.

Dean, Jeffrey S., and John C. Ravesloot
1993 The Chronology of Cultural Interaction in the Gran Chichimeca. In *Culture and Contact: Charles C. Di Peso's Gran Chichimeca,* edited by Anne Woosley and John C. Ravesloot, pp. 83–104. University of New Mexico Press, Albuquerque.

Dean, Jeffrey S., and Carla R. Van West
2002 Environment-Behavior Relationships in Southwestern Colorado. In *Seeking the Center Place: Archaeology and Ancient Communities in the Mesa Verde Region,* edited by Mark D. Varien and Richard H. Wilshusen, pp. 81–99. University of Utah Press, Salt Lake City.

De Atley, Suzanne P.
1986 Mix and Match: Traditions of Glaze Paint Preparation at Four Mile Ruin, Arizona. In *Technology and Style,* edited by W. David Kingery, pp. 297–329. Ceramics and Civilization, Vol. 2. American Ceramic Society, Columbus, Ohio.

DeBoer, Warren R.
1981 Buffer Zones in the Cultural Ecology of Aboriginal Amazonia: An Ethnohistorical Approach. *American Antiquity* 46:364–377.

DeCorse, Christopher R.
1989 Material Aspects of Limba, Yalunka and Kuranko Ethnicity: Archaeological Research in Northeastern Sierra Leone. In *Archaeological Approaches to Cultural Identity,* edited by Stephen J. Shennan. Unwin Hyman, London.

Deetz, James F.
1965 *The Dynamics of Stylistic Change in Arikara Ceramics.* Illinois Studies in Anthropology No. 4. University of Illinois Press, Urbana.

DeFrance, Susan D.
1996 Iberian Foodways in the Moquegua and Torata Valleys of Southern France. *Historical Archaeology* 30(3):20–48.

DeLancey, Scott, and Victor Golla
1997 The Penutian Hypothesis: Retrospect and Prospect. *International Journal of American Linguistics* 63(1):171–201.

De Vos, George
1975 Ethnic Pluralism: Conflict and Accommodation. In *Ethnic Identity,* edited by George De Vos and Lola Romanucci-Ross, pp. 5–41. University of Chicago Press, Chicago.

De Vos, George, and Lola Romanucci-Ross (editors)

1975 *Ethnic Identity.* University of Chicago Press, Chicago.

Diamond, Jared, and Peter Bellwood
2003 Farmers and Their First Languages: The First Expansions. *Science* 300:597–603.

Diaz, Henry F., and Vera Markgraf
1992 *El Niño: Historical and Paleoclimatic Aspects of the Southern Oscillation.* Cambridge University Press, Cambridge.

Diaz, Henry F., and Roger S. Pulwarty
1992 A Comparison of Southern Oscillation and El Niño Signals in the Tropics. In *El Niño: Historical and Paleoclimatic Aspects of the Southern Oscillation,* edited by Henry F. Diaz and Vera Markgraf, pp. 175–192. Cambridge University Press, Cambridge.

Dick, Herbert
1965 *Bat Cave, Catron County, New Mexico.* Monograph No. 27. School of American Research, Santa Fe.

Diehl, Michael W.
1994 *Subsistence Economies and Emergent Social Differences: A Case Study from the Prehistoric North American Southwest.* PhD dissertation, State University of New York at Buffalo. University Microfilms, Ann Arbor.

1996a The Intensity of Maize Processing and Production in Upland Mogollon Pithouse Villages, AD 200–1000. *American Antiquity* 61:102–115.

1996b *Archaeological Investigations of the Early Agricultural Period Settlement at the Base of A-Mountain, Tucson, Arizona.* Technical Report No. 96-21, Center for Desert Archaeology, Tucson, Arizona.

1997 Rational Behavior, the Adoption of Agriculture and the Organization of Subsistence during the Late Archaic Period in the Greater Tucson Basin. In *Rediscovering Darwin: Evolutionary Theory and Archeological Explanation,* edited by C. Michael Barton and Geoffrey A. Clark, pp. 251–265. Archaeological Papers No. 7. American Anthropological Association, Arlington.

1999 Paleobotanical Remains. In *Excavations in the Santa Cruz River Floodplain: The Middle Archaic Component at Los Pozos,* edited by David A. Gregory, pp. 49–59. Anthropological Papers No. 20. Center for Desert Archaeology, Tucson, Arizona.

2005a When Corn Was Not Yet King. In *Subsistence and Resource Use Strategies*

of Early Agricultural Communities in Southern Arizona, edited by Michael W. Diehl, pp. 1–18. Anthropological Papers No. 34. Center for Desert Archaeology, Tucson.

2005b Early Agricultural Period Foraging and Horticulture in Southern Arizona: Implications from Plant Remains. In *Subsistence and Resource Use Strategies of Early Agricultural Communities in Southern Arizona,* edited by Michael W. Diehl, pp. 73–90. Anthropological Papers No. 34. Center for Desert Archaeology, Tucson.

2005c Epilogue: "Farmaging" during the Early Agricultural Period. In *Subsistence and Resource Use Strategies of Early Agricultural Communities in Southern Arizona,* edited by Michael W. Diehl, pp. 181–183. Anthropological Papers No. 34. Center for Desert Archaeology, Tucson.

Diehl, Michael W., and Steven A. LeBlanc
2001 *Early Pithouse Villages of the Mimbres Valley and Beyond: The McAnally and Thompson Sites in the Cultural and Ecological Contexts.* Papers of the Peabody Museum of Archaeology and Ethnology Vol. 83. Harvard University, Cambridge.

Diehl, Michael W., and Jennifer A. Waters
2005 Aspects of Optimization and Risk during the Early Agricultural Period in Southeastern Arizona. In *Forging Theory and the Transition to Agriculture,* edited by Douglas J. Kennett and Bruce Winterhalder, pp. 63–86. University of California Press, Berkeley.

Dietler, Michael, and Ingrid Herbich
1998 Habitus, Techniques, Styles: An Integrated Approach to the Social Understanding of Material Culture and Boundaries. In *The Archaeology of Social Boundaries,* edited by Miriam T. Stark, pp. 232–263. Smithsonian Institution Press, Washington, D.C.

Dillehay, Thomas D.
1989 *Monte Verde: A Late Pleistocene Settlement in Chile: Paleoenvironment and Site Context* Vol. 1. Smithsonian Institution Press, Washington, D.C.

1997 *Monte Verde: A Late Pleistocene Settlement in Chile: The Archaeological Context* Vol. 2. Smithsonian Institution Press, Washington, D.C.

Di Peso, Charles C.
1953 Foodstuffs of the Sobaipuri. In *The Sobaipuri Indians of the Upper San Pedro River Valley, Southeastern Arizona,* by C. C. Di Peso, pp. 236–237.

Amerind Foundation Series No. 6. Dragoon, Arizona.

1956 *The Upper Pima of San Cayetano del Tumacacori: An Archaeohistorical Reconstruction of the Ootam of the Pimería Alta.* Amerind Foundation Series No. 7. Amerind Foundation, Inc., Dragoon, Arizona.

1958 *The Reeve Ruin of Southeastern Arizona: A Study of Prehistoric Western Pueblo Migration into the Middle San Pedro Valley.* Amerind Foundation Series No. 8. Amerind Foundation, Inc., Dragoon, Arizona.

Di Peso, Charles C., John B. Rinaldo, and Gloria J. Fenner

1974a *Dating and Architecture.* Casas Grandes: A Fallen Trading Center of the Gran Chichimeca, Vol. 4. Amerind Foundation Series No. 9. Amerind Foundation, Inc., Dragoon, and Northland Press, Flagstaff.

1974b *Ceramics and Shell.* Casas Grandes: A Fallen Trading Center of the Gran Chichimeca, Vol. 6. Amerind Foundation Series No. 9. Amerind Foundation, Inc., Dragoon, and Northland Press, Flagstaff.

1974c *Stone and Metal.* Casas Grandes: A Fallen Trading Center of the Gran Chichimeca, Vol. 7. Amerind Foundation Series No. 9. Amerind Foundation, Inc., Dragoon, and Northland Press, Flagstaff.

1974d *Bone—Economy—Burials.* Casas Grandes: A Fallen Trading Center of the Gran Chichimeca, Vol. 8. Amerind Foundation Series No. 9. Amerind Foundation, Inc., Dragoon, and Northland Press, Flagstaff.

Dittert, Alfred E., Jr.

1959 *Culture Change in the Cebolleta Mesa Region, Central Western New Mexico.* PhD dissertation, University of Arizona, Tucson. University Microfilms, Ann Arbor.

1968 Some Factors Affecting Southwestern Populations during the Period AD 900–1540. In *INQUA Symposium on Southwestern Prehistory, Eastern New Mexico Contributions in Anthropology* 1(1):14–16.

1998 The Acoma Culture Province during the Period AD 1275–1500: Cultural Disruption and Reorganization. In *Migration and Reorganization: The Pueblo IV Period in the American Southwest,* edited by Katherine A. Spielmann, pp. 81–90. Arizona State University Anthropological Research Papers No. 51. Tempe.

Dittert, Alfred E., Jr., and Judy L. Brunson-Hadley

1999 Identifying Acoma's Past: A Multidisciplinary Approach. In *La Frontera: Papers in Honor of Patrick H. Beckett,* edited by Melilia S. Duran and David T. Kirkpatrick, pp. 59–69. Papers of the New Mexico Archaeological Society No. 25. Albuquerque.

Dittert, Alfred E., Jr., and R. J. Ruppé Jr.

1951 The Archaeology of Cebolleta Mesa: A Preliminary Report. *El Palacio* 58(4):116–129.

Dixon, Keith A.

1956 *Hidden House: A Cliff Ruin in Sycamore Canyon, Central Arizona.* Museum of Northern Arizona Bulletin No. 29. Northern Arizona Society of Science and Art, Flagstaff.

Dixon, Roland B., and A. L. Kroeber

1913 New Linguistic Families of California. *American Anthropologist* 15:645–655.

Dobres, Marcia-Anne

2000 *Technology and Social Agency.* Blackwell Publishers, Oxford.

Dobres, Marcia-Anne, and Christopher R. Hoffman

1999 *The Social Dynamics of Technology: Practice, Politics, and World Views.* Smithsonian Institution Press, Washington, D.C.

Dobyns, Henry F., and Robert C. Euler

1970 *Wauba Yuma's People: The Comparative Socio-political Structure of the Pai Indians.* Prescott College Studies in Anthropology No. 3. Prescott, Arizona.

Doebley, John

1990 Molecular Evidence and the Evolution of Maize. *Economic Botany* 44(3 supplement):6–27.

Doelle, William H.

1981 The Gila Pima in the Late Seventeenth Century. In *The Protohistoric Period in the North American Southwest AD 1450–1700,* edited by David R. Wilcox and W. Bruce Masse, pp. 57–70. Arizona State University Anthropological Research Papers No. 24. Tempe.

1995 Tonto Basin Demography in Regional Perspective. In *The Roosevelt Community Development Study: New Perspectives on Tonto Basin Prehistory,* edited by Mark D. Elson, Miriam T. Stark, and David A. Gregory, pp. 201–226. Anthropological Papers No. 15. Center for Desert Archaeology, Tucson, Arizona.

2000 Tonto Basin Demography in a Regional Perspective. In *Salado,* edited by Jeffrey S. Dean, pp. 81–106. University of New Mexico Press, Albuquerque.

2003 Back Sight. *Archaeology Southwest* 17(2):16.

Doelle, William H., David A. Gregory, and Henry D. Wallace

1995 Classic Period Platform Mound Systems in Southern Arizona. In *The Roosevelt Community Development Study: New Perspectives on Tonto Basin Prehistory,* edited by Mark D. Elson, Miriam T. Stark, and David A. Gregory, pp. 385–440. Anthropological Papers No. 15. Center for Desert Archaeology, Tucson, Arizona.

Doelle, William H., and J. Brett Hill

2003 Large Sites, GIS, and a Regional Perspective: Broadening Our View of Southwestern Archaeology. Paper presented at the 68th Annual Meeting of the Society for American Archaeology, Milwaukee.

Doleman, William H.

2005 Environmental Constraints on Forager Mobility and the Use of Cultigens in Southeastern Arizona and Southern New Mexico. In *The Late Archaic across the Borderlands,* edited by Bradley Vierra, pp. 113–140. University of Texas Press, Austin.

Dongoske, Kurt E., Michael Yeatts, Roger Anyon, and T. J. Ferguson

1997 Archaeological Cultures and Cultural Affiliation: Hopi and Zuni Perspectives in the American Southwest. *American Antiquity* 62:600–608.

Doolittle, William E.

1984 Settlements and the Development of "Statelets" in Sonora, Mexico. *Journal of Field Archaeology* 11:13–24.

1988 *Pre-Hispanic Occupance of the Valley of Sonora, Mexico.* Anthropological Papers of the University of Arizona No. 48. Tucson.

Dorsey, George A., and H. R. Voth

1901 *The Oraibi Soyal Ceremony.* The Stanley McCormick Hopi Expedition. Field Columbian Museum, Publication 55, Anthropological Series Vol. 3, No. 1. Chicago.

Douglas, A. V., and P. J. Englehart

1981 On a Statistical Relationship between Rainfall in the Central Equatorial Pacific and Subsequent Winter

Precipitation in Florida. *Monthly Weather Review* 109:2377–2382.

Douglass, Andrew Endicott
1929 The Secret of the Southwest Solved by Talkative Tree Rings. *National Geographic Magazine* 56(6):736–770.

Downum, Christian Eric
1988 *"One Grand History": A Critical Review of Flagstaff Archaeology, 1851 to 1988.* PhD dissertation, Department of Anthropology, University of Arizona, Tucson. University Microfilms, Ann Arbor.

Doyel, David E.
1984 Stylistic and Petrographic Variability in Pueblo II Period Cibola Whiteware from the Upper Little Colorado. In *Regional Analysis of Prehistoric Ceramic Variation: Contemporary Studies of the Cibola Whitewares*, edited by Alan P. Sullivan and Jeffrey L. Hantman, pp. 4–16. Arizona State University Anthropological Research Papers No. 31. Tempe.

Dozier, Edward
1956 Two Examples of Linguistic Acculturation: The Yaqui of Sonora and Arizona and the Tewa of New Mexico. *Language* 32:146–157.

Drennan, Robert D.
1984 Long-Distance Transport Costs in Pre-Hispanic Mesoamerica. *American Anthropologist* 86:105–112.

Driver, J. C., M. Handly, K. R. Fladmark, D. J. F. Nelson, G. M. Sullivan, and R. Preston
1996 Stratigraphy, Radiocarbon Dating and Culture History of Charlie Lake Cave, British Columbia. *Arctic* 49:265–277.

Duff, Andrew I. L.
1993 An Exploration of Post-Chacoan Community Organization through Ceramic Sourcing. Unpublished Master's thesis, Department of Anthropology, Arizona State University, Tempe.
1994 The Scope of Post-Chacoan Community Organization in the Lower Zuni River Region. In *Exploring Social, Political and Economic Organization in the Zuni Region*, edited by Todd L. Howell and Tammy Stone, pp. 25–45. Arizona State University Anthropological Research Papers No. 46. Tempe.
1996 Ceramic Micro-Seriation: Types or Attributes? *American Antiquity* 61:89–101.
1998 The Process of Migration in the Late Prehistoric Southwest. In *Migration and Community Reorganization: The Pueblo IV Period in the American Southwest*, edited by Katherine A. Spielmann, pp. 31–52. Arizona State University Anthropological Research Papers No. 51. Tempe.
1999 *Regional Interaction and the Transformation of Western Pueblo Identities, AD 1275–1400.* PhD dissertation, Department of Anthropology, Arizona State University, Tempe. University Microfilms, Ann Arbor.
2000 Scale, Interaction, and Regional Analysis in Late Pueblo Prehistory. In *The Archaeology of Regional Interaction: Religion, Warfare and Exchange across the American Southwest and Beyond*, edited by Michelle Hegmon, pp. 71–98. University Press of Colorado, Boulder.
2002 *Western Pueblo Identities: Regional Interaction, Migration, and Transformation.* University of Arizona Press, Tucson.

Duffen, William, and William K. Hartmann
1997 The 76 Ranch Ruin and the Location of Chichilticale. In *The Coronado Expedition to Tierra Nueva: The 1540–1542 Route across the Southwest*, edited by Richard Flint and Shirley Cushing Flint, pp. 190–211. University of Colorado, Niwot.

Duncan, Gwyneth A.
2000 Faunal Remains from Forest Home, Wood Canyon, and Beargrass. In *A Highway through Time: Archaeological Investigations along NM 90*, Vol. 2, edited by Christopher A. Turnbow, pp. 487–507. TRC Inc., Technical Series No. 2000-3. New Mexico Highway and Transportation Department, Albuquerque.

Dunnell, Robert
1978 Style and Function: A Fundamental Dichotomy. *American Antiquity* 43:192–202.

Durand, Stephen R., and Fred L. Nials
1991 Environment of the Middle Rio Puerco Valley. In *Anasazi Puebloan Adaptation in Response to Climatic Stress: Prehistory of the Middle Rio Puerco Valley*, edited by Cynthia Irwin-Williams and Larry L. Baker, pp. 8–32. Eastern New Mexico University, Portales.

Dutton, Bertha
1963 Las Madras in the Light of Anasazi Migrations. *American Antiquity* 29:449–454.

Dycus, Don Lee
1997 The Mangas Phase Is Dead but It Won't Lie Down: An Analysis of LA 6537 and LA 6538, Catron County, New Mexico. Unpublished Master's thesis, Department of Anthropology, University of Oklahoma, Norman.

Dykeman, Douglas
1995 *The Hogan Well Project: Archaeological Excavations at Early Mogollon and Late Anasazi Sites in the Puerco River Valley, Arizona.* Navajo Nation Papers in Anthropology 31. Window Rock, Arizona.

Earle, Timothy K.
1978 *Economic and Social Organization of a Complex Chiefdom: The Halelea District, Kaua'i, Hawaii.* Anthropological Papers No. 63. Museum of Anthropology, University of Michigan, Ann Arbor.
2001 Economic Support of Chaco Canyon Society. *American Antiquity* 66:26–35.

Echo-Hawk, Roger
2000 Ancient History in the New World: Integrating Oral Tradition and the Archaeological Record in Deep Time. *American Antiquity* 65:267–290.

Eckert, Suzanne
1995 The Process of Aggregation in the Post-Chacoan Era: A Case Study from the Lower Zuni River Region. Unpublished Master's thesis, Department of Anthropology, Arizona State University, Tempe.

Eckert, Suzanne L., Janet Hagopian, and James W. Kendrick
2000 The Ceramics from Y Unit Draw. In *Households and Farms in Early Zuni Prehistory: Settlement, Subsistence, and the Archaeology of Y Unit Draw, Archaeological Investigations at Eighteen Sites Along New Mexico State Highway 602—Part 2.* New Mexico State Highway and Transportation Department Cultural Resource Technical Series 2001-3. ZCRE Report No. 593, ZCRE Research Series No. 11, pp. 549–585. Zuni, New Mexico.

Eddy, John A.
1977 Climate and the Changing Sun. *Climate Change* 1:173–190.

Eggan, Fred
1950 *The Social Organization of the Western Pueblos.* University of Chicago Press, Chicago.

Eggan, Fred, and T. N. Pandey
1979 Zuni History, 1850–1970. In *South-

west, edited by Alfonso Ortiz, pp. 474–481. Handbook of North American Indians, Vol. 9, William C. Sturtevant, general editor, Smithsonian Institution, Washington, D.C.

Ehret, Christopher
1988 Language Change and the Material Correlates of Language and Ethnic Shift. *Antiquity* 62:564–573.

Ellen, Roy
1982 *Environment, Subsistence and System: The Ecology of Small-Scale Social Formations*. Cambridge University Press, Cambridge.

Elliott, Michael I.
1982 *Large Pueblo Sites near Jemez Springs, New Mexico*. Santa Fe National Forest Cultural Resources Report No. 3. Santa Fe.

Ellis, Florence Hawley
1951 Pueblo Social Organization and Southwestern Archaeology. *American Antiquity* 12:148–151.
1964 *A Reconstruction of the Basic Jemez Pattern of Social Organization, with Comparisons to Other Tanoan Social Structures*. University of New Mexico Publications in Anthropology 11. Albuquerque.
1967 Where Did the Pueblo People Come From? *El Palacio* (Autumn):35–43.
1979 Laguna Pueblo. In *Southwest*, edited by Alfonso Ortiz, pp. 438–449. Handbook of North American Indians, Vol. 9, William C. Sturtevant, general editor, Smithsonian Institution, Washington, D.C.

Ellis, Florence Hawley, and Laurens Hammack
1968 The Inner Sanctum of Feather Cave, a Mogollon Sun and Earth Shrine Linking Mexico and the Southwest. *American Antiquity* 33:25–44.

Elson, Mark D., and Michael Lindeman
1994 The Eagle Ridge Site, AZ V:5:104/1045 (ASM/TNF). In *Introduction and Small Sites*, edited by Mark D. Elson and Deborah L. Swartz, pp. 23–116. The Roosevelt Community Development Study, Vol. 1. Anthropological Papers No. 14. Center for Desert Archaeology, Tucson, Arizona.

Enfield, D. B., and S. Cid
1991 Low-Frequency Changes in El Niño–Southern Oscillation. *Journal of Climate* 4:1137–1146.

Eriksen, Thomas H., and Finn S. Nielsen
2001 *A History of Anthropology*. Pluto Press, London.

Euler, R. Thomas, and David A. Gregory
1988 Pecked, Ground, and Polished Stone Artifacts. In *Material Culture*, by David R. Abbott, Kim E. Beckwith, Patricia L. Crown, R. Thomas Euler, David A. Gregory, J. Ronald London, Marilyn B. Saul, Larry A. Schwalbe, Mary Bernard-Shaw, Christine R. Szuter, and Arthur W. Vokes, pp. 299–317. The 1982–1984 Excavations at Las Colinas, Vol. 4. Arizona State Museum Archaeological Series No. 162. University of Arizona, Tucson.

Euler, Robert C., George J. Gumerman, Thor N. V. Karlstrom, Jeffrey S. Dean, and Richard H. Hevly
1979 The Colorado Plateaus: Cultural Dynamics and Paleoenvironment. *Science* 205:1089–1101.

Eustis, Frederic A.
1955 *Augustus Hemenway, 1805–1876, Builder of the United States Trade with the West Coast of South America*. Peabody Museum, Salem.

Evans, Williams S., Jr.
1980 Food and Fantasy: Material Culture of the Chinese in California and the West, circa 1850–1900. In *Archaeological Perspectives on Ethnicity in America*, edited by Robert L. Schuyler, pp. 89–96. Baywood Publishing Company, New York.

Ezell, Paul H.
1954 An Archaeological Survey of Northwestern Papaguería. *Kiva* 19(2–4):1–26.

Fagan, Brian
1999 *Floods, Famines, and Emperors: El Niño and the Fate of Civilizations*. Basic Books, New York.

Fairley, Helen C., and Phil R. Geib
1989 Data Gaps and Research Issues in Arizona Strip Prehistory. In *Man, Models and Management: An Overview of the Archaeology of the Arizona Strip and the Management of Its Cultural Resources*, edited by Jeffrey H. Altschul and Helen C. Fairley, pp. 219–244. Statistical Research, Tucson.

Farmer, Malcolm F.
1935 The Mojave Trade Route. *Masterkey* 9:154–157.

Federal Register
1972 National Historic Preservation Act. *Federal Register*, Washington, D.C.
1990 Native American Graves-Protection and Repatriation Act. *Federal Register*, Washington, D.C.

Feinman, Gary M.
1995 The Emergence of Inequality: A Focus on Strategies and Processes. In *Foundations of Social Inequality*, edited by T. Douglas Price and Gary M. Feinman, pp. 255–279. Plenum Press, New York.

Fenn, Forrest
2004 *The Secrets of San Lazaro Pueblo*. One Horse Land and Cattle Company, Santa Fe.

Fenn, Thomas R., Barbara J. Mills, and Maren Hopkins
2006 The Social Contexts of Glaze Paint Ceramic Production and Consumption in the Silver Creek Area. In *The Social Life of Pots: Glaze Wares and Cultural Dynamics in the Southwest, AD 1250–1680*, edited by Judith A. Habicht-Mauche, Suzanne L. Eckert, and Deborah L. Huntley, pp. 60–85. University of Arizona Press, Tucson.

Fenner, Gloria J.
1986 Feather Artifacts. In *The Archeology of Gila Cliff Dwellings*, by Keith M. Anderson, Gloria J. Fenner, Don P. Morris, George A. Teague, and Charmion McKusick, pp. 235–243. Publications in Anthropology No. 36. Western Archeological and Conservation Center, Tucson, Arizona.

Ferg, Alan
1974 Petroglyphs of the Silver Creek/Fivemile Draw Confluence, Snowflake, Arizona. University of Arizona, University Field School.
1978 *The Painted Cliffs Rest Area: Excavations along the Rio Puerco, Northeastern Arizona*. Arizona State Museum Contribution to Highway Salvage Archaeology in Arizona No. 50. Arizona State Museum, Tucson.
1980 Shell from Gu Achi. In *Excavations at Gu Achi: A Reappraisal of Hohokam Settlement and Subsistence in the Arizona Papaguería*, by W. Bruce Masse, pp. 371–394. Publications in Anthropology No. 12. Western Archeological Center, Tucson, Arizona.
1998 Rare Stone, Fired Clay, Bone and Shell Artifacts. In *Archaeological Investigations of Early Village Sites in the Middle Santa Cruz Valley: Analyses and Synthesis*, Pt. 2, edited by Jonathan B. Mabry, pp. 545–654. Anthropological Papers No. 19. Center for Desert Archaeology, Tucson, Arizona.

Ferg, Alan, and Jim I. Mead
1993 *Red Cave, a Prehistoric Cave Shrine in Southeastern Arizona*. Arizona Archaeologist No. 26. Arizona Archaeological Society, Phoenix.

Ferg, Alan, and William D. Peachey
1998 An Atlatl from the Sierra Pinacate. *Kiva* 64:175–200.

Ferguson, Adam
1966 [1767] *An Essay on the History of Civil Society*, edited by D. Forbes. Edinburgh University Press, Edinburgh.

Ferguson, T. J.
1995 An Anthropological Perspective on Zuni Land Use. In *Zuni and the Courts*, edited by E. Richard Hart, pp. 103–120. University Press of Kansas, Lawrence.
1996 *Historic Zuni Architecture and Society: An Archaeological Application of Space Syntax*. Anthropological Papers of the University of Arizona No. 60. University of Arizona Press, Tucson.
2003 Anthropological Archaeology Conducted by Tribes: Traditional Cultural Properties and Cultural Affiliation. In *Archaeology Is Anthropology*, edited by Susan D. Gillespie and Deborah L. Nichols, pp. 137–144. Archaeological Papers of the American Anthropological Association No. 13.

Ferguson, T. J., and Roger Anyon
2001 Hopi and Zuni Cultural Landscapes: Implications of History and Scale for Cultural Resources Management. In *Native Peoples of the Southwest: Negotiating Land, Water, and Ethnicities*, edited by Laurie Weinstein, pp. 99–122. Bergin and Garvey, Westport, Connecticut.

Ferguson, T. J., and Wilfred Eriacho
1990 Ahayu:da Zuni War Gods: Cooperation and Repatriation. *Native Peoples* 4:6–12.

Ferguson, T. J., and E. Richard Hart
1985 *A Zuni Atlas*. University of Oklahoma Press, Norman.

Ferguson, T. J., and Micah Lomaomvaya
1999 *Hoopoq'yaqam niqw Wukoskyavi (Those Who Went to the Northeast and Tonto Basin): Hopi-Salado Cultural Affiliation Study*. Hopi Cultural Preservation Office, Kykotsmovi, Arizona.

Ferguson, T. J., and Barbara Mills
1982 *Archaeological Investigations at Zuni Pueblo, New Mexico, 1977–1980*. Zuni Archaeology Program Report No. 183. Zuni, New Mexico.

Fewkes, Jesse Walter
1891 *A Journal of American Ethnology and Archaeology*. 5 vols. Houghton Mifflin, Boston.
1897 Tusayan Katcinas. In *Fifteenth Annual Report of the Bureau of American Ethnology for the Years 1893–1894*.

U.S. Government Printing Office, Washington, D.C.
1900 Tusayan Migration Traditions. In *Nineteenth Annual Report of the Bureau of American Ethnology for the Years 1897–1898*, Pt. 2, pp. 573–634. U.S. Government Printing Office, Washington, D.C.
1902 Minor Hopi Festivals. *American Anthropologist* 4:482–511.
1904 Two Summers' Work in Pueblo Ruins. In *Twenty-second Annual Report of the Bureau of American Ethnology for the Years 1899–1900*, Pt. 1, pp. 3–195. Smithsonian Institution, Washington, D.C.
1906 Hopi Shrines near the East Mesa, Arizona. *American Anthropologist* 8:346–375.
1912 Casa Grande, Arizona. In *Twenty-eighth Annual Report of the Bureau of American Ethnology to the Secretary of the Smithsonian Institution, 1906–1907*, pp. 25–179. U.S. Government Printing Office, Washington, D.C.
1915 Unit Type Pueblo Architecture. *Journal of the Washington Academy of Sciences* 5(1):543–552.

Fewkes, J. Walter, Aleš Hrdlièka, William H. Dall, James W. Gidley, Austin Hobart Clarke, William H. Holmes, Alice C. Fletcher, Walter Hough, Stansbury Hagar, Paul Bartsch, Alexander F. Chamberlain, and Roland B. Dixon
1912 The Problems of the Unity or Plurality and the Probable Place of Origin of the American Aborigines. *American Anthropologist* n.s. 14:1–59.

Fiedel, Stuart J.
1999 Older Than We Thought: Implications of Corrected Dates for Paleoindians. *American Antiquity* 64:95–116.
2002 Initial Human Colonization of the Americas: An Overview of the Issues and the Evidence. *Radiocarbon* 44:407–436.

Fields, Virginia M., and Victor Zamudio-Taylor
2001 *The Road to Aztlan: Art from a Mythic Homeland*. Museum Associates, Los Angeles County Museum of Art, Los Angeles.

Fisher, Reginald G.
1931 *Santa Fe Sub-quadrangle A: Second Report of the Archaeological Survey of the Pueblo Plateau*. New Mexico University Survey Series, Bulletin 1(1). Albuquerque.

Fitting, James E.
1973 *An Early Mogollon Community: A Preliminary Report on the Winn Canyon Site*. Artifact 11, Nos. 1 and 2. El Paso Archaeological Society, El Paso.

Fladmark, Knut, Jonathan Driver, and Diana Alexander
1988 The Paleo-Indian Component at Charlie Lake Cave (HbRf 39) British Columbia. *American Antiquity* 53:371–384.

Flannery, Kent
1972 The Origins of the Village as a Settlement Type in Mesoamerica and the Near East. In *Man, Settlement, and Urbanism*, edited by Peter Ucko, Ruth Tringham, and G. W. Dimbleby. Duckworth, London.

Fontana, Bernard L.
1965 An Archaeological Survey of the Cabeza Pieta Game Range, Arizona. Manuscript on file, Arizona State Museum Library, University of Arizona, Tucson.

Force, Eric
2004 Late Holocene Behaviour of Chaco and McElmo Canyon Drainages (Southwest U.S.): A Comparison Based on Archaeologic Age Controls. *Geoarchaeology: An International Journal* 19:583–609.

Force, Eric, and Wayne Howell
1997 *Holocene Depositional History and Anasazi Occupation of McElmo Canyon, Southwestern Colorado*. Arizona State Museum Archaeological Series 188. University of Arizona, Tucson.

Force, Eric R., R. Gwinn Vivian, Thomas C. Windes, and Jeffrey S. Dean
2002 *Relation of "Bonito" Paleo-Channels and Base-Level Variations to Anasazi Occupation, Chaco Canyon, New Mexico*. Arizona State Museum Archaeological Series 194. University of Arizona, Tucson.

Force, Roland W.
1999 *Politics and the Museum of the American Indian: The Heye and the Mighty*. Mechas Press, Honolulu.

Ford, Richard I.
1981 Gardening and Farming before AD 1000: Patterns of Prehistoric Cultivation North of Mexico. *Journal of Ethnobiology* 1:6–27.
1995 Testimony. In *CD-ROM of the Zuni Land Claim*, compiled by Zuni Heritage and Historic Preservation Office and Institute of the North American West, distributed by University Press of Kansas, Lawrence.

Ford, Richard I., Albert H. Schroeder, and Stewart L. Peckham
1972   Three Perspectives on Puebloan Prehistory. In *New Perspectives on the Pueblos*, edited by Alfonso Ortiz, pp. 19–39. University of New Mexico Press, Albuquerque.

Forde, C. Daryll
1934   *Habitat, Economy and Society: A Geographical Introduction to Ethnology.* Methuen, London.

Foster, Michael K.
1996   Languages and the Culture History of North America. In *Languages*, edited by Ives Goddard, pp. 64–110. Handbook of North American Indians, Vol. 17, William C. Sturtevant, general editor, Smithsonian Institution, Washington, D.C.

Fowler, Andrew P.
1980   *Archaeological Clearance Investigation: Acque Chaining and Reseeding Project, Zuni Indian Reservation, McKinley County, New Mexico.* Zuni Archaeology Program Report No. 66. Zuni, New Mexico.
1988   *Archaeological Testing of Site NM:12:K3:263 at Blackrock, Zuni Indian Reservation, McKinley County, New Mexico.* Zuni Archaeology Report No. 250. Zuni, New Mexico.
1994   Ceramics. In *Excavation at Early Puebloan Sites in the Puerco River Valley, Arizona: The N-2007 Project*, edited by Mark B. Sant and Marianne Marek, pp. 323–383. Zuni Archaeology Program Report No. 271, Research Series No. 8. Pueblo of Zuni, New Mexico.

Fowler, Andrew P., and John R. Stein
1992   The Anasazi Great House in Space, Time, and Paradigm. In *Anasazi Regional Organization and the Chaco System*, edited by David E. Doyel, pp. 101–122. Maxwell Museum of Anthropology Papers 5. University of New Mexico, Albuquerque.

Fowler, Andrew P., John R. Stein, and Roger Anyon
1987   An Archaeological Reconnaissance of West-Central New Mexico: The Anasazi Monuments Project. Manuscript on file, New Mexico State Historic Preservation Office, Santa Fe.

Fowler, Catherine S.
1983   Some Lexical Clues to Uto-Aztecan Prehistory. *International Journal of American Linguistics* 49:224–257.
1996   Western North America Textile Sequences. Appendix to Eastern North American Textiles: A Western Perspective. In *A Most Indispensable Art: Native Fiber Industries from Eastern North America*, edited by James B. Petersen, pp. 180–199. University of Tennessee Press, Knoxville.

Fowler, Don D.
1987   Uses of the Past: Archaeology in the Service of the State. *American Antiquity* 52:229–248.
1992   Models of Southwestern Prehistory, 1840–1914. In *Reconsidering Our Past: Essays on the History of American Archaeology*, edited by Jonathan E. Reyman, pp. 15–34. Avebury Press, Aldershot.
2000   *A Laboratory for Anthropology: Science and Romanticism in the North American Southwest, 1846–1930.* University of New Mexico Press, Albuquerque.
2005   The Formative Years: Southwestern Archaeology, 1890–1910. In *Southwest Archaeology in the Twentieth Century*, edited by Linda S. Cordell and Don D. Fowler, pp. 16–26. University of Utah Press, Salt Lake City.

Fowler, Don D. (compiler)
2000   Sundance Workshop, 2000. Electronic document, http://www.unr.edu/cla/anthro/sundance/confer.asp, accessed December 23, 2005.

Fowler, Don D., Edward A. Jolie, and Marion W. Salter
2006   Archaeology and Ethics in Context and Practice. In *Handbook of Archaeological Theory*, edited by Herbert D. G. Maschner and R. Alexander Bentley. AltaMira Press, Walnut Creek, California.

Fowler, Don D., and David R. Wilcox
1999   From Thomas Jefferson to the Pecos Conference: Changing Anthropological Agendas in the North American Southwest. In *Surveying the Record: North American Scientific Exploration to 1930*, edited by Edward C. Carter II, pp. 197–224. Memoirs of the American Philosophical Society Vol. 231. Philadelphia.

Fox, Robin
1967   *The Keresan Bridge: A Problem in Pueblo Ethnology.* London School of Economics, Monographs on Social Anthropology 35. Athlone Press, London.

Frankenstein, Susan, and M. J. Rowland
1978   The Internal Structure and Regional Context of Early Iron Age Society in South-Western Germany. *London University Institute of Archaeology Bulletin* 15:241–284.

Franklin, H., and W. Bruce Masse
1976   The San Pedro Salado: A Case for Prehistoric Migrations. *Kiva* 42:47–55.

Friedman, Jonathan
1994   *Consumption and Identity.* Harwood Academic Publishers, Char, Switzerland.

Frisbie, Theodore R.
1986   The Mystery of the Veteado Mountain Anthropomorphs and Related Matters. In *By Hands Unknown: Papers on Rock Art and Archaeology in Honor of James G. Bain*, edited by Anne Poore, pp. 61–78. Archaeological Society of New Mexico No. 12. Ancient City Press, Inc., Santa Fe.

Frison, George C.
1991   *Prehistoric Hunters of the High Plains.* 2nd ed. Academic Press, San Diego.

Fritts, Harold C.
1976   *Tree Rings and Climate.* Academic Press, New York.
1991   *Reconstructing Large-Scale Climatic Patterns from Tree-Ring Data: A Diagnostic Analysis.* University of Arizona Press, Tucson.

Fritz, Gayle
1995   New Dates and Data on Early Agriculture: The Legacy of Complex Hunter-Gatherers. *Annals of the Missouri Botanical Garden* 83:3–15.

Fritz, John M.
1974   *The Hay Hollow Site Subsistence System: East Central Arizona.* PhD dissertation, Department of Anthropology, University of Chicago. University Microfilms, Ann Arbor.
1987   Chaco Canyon and Vijayanagara: Proposing Spatial Meaning in Two Societies. In *Mirror and Metaphor: Material and Social Constructions of Reality*, edited by Daniel W. Ingersoll Jr. and Gordon Bronitsky, pp. 313–349. University of America Press, Lanham, Maryland.

Fulton, William S.
1941   *A Ceremonial Cave in the Winchester Mountains, Arizona.* Amerind Foundation 2. Dragoon.

Gallatin, Albert H.
1836   A Synopsis of the Indian Tribes of North America. Archaeologica Americana. *Transactions and Collections of the American Antiquarian Society* 2:1–422.
1845   Note on the Semi-civilized Nations of Mexico, Yucatan, and Central-

America. *American Ethnological Society Transactions* 1:1–352.

1848   Ancient Semi-civilization New Mexico. *American Ethnological Society Transactions* 2:liii–xcvii.

Gamble, Clive
1994   *Timewalkers: The Prehistory of Global Colonization.* Harvard University Press, Cambridge.

Gearing, Fred
1962   *Priests and Warriors: Social Structures for Cherokee Politics in the 18th Century.* American Anthropological Association Memoir No. 93. Menasha, Wisconsin.

Geary, P. J.
1983   Ethnic Identity as a Situational Construct in the Early Middle Ages. *Mitteilungen der Anthropologischen Gesellschaft in Wien* 113:15–26.

Geertz, Clifford
1963   *Agricultural Involution: The Process of Ecological Change in Indonesia.* University of California Press, Berkeley.

1973   Ethos, World View, and the Analysis of Sacred Symbols. In *The Interpretation of Cultures*, pp. 126–141. Basic Books, New York.

Geib, Phil R.
2000a   Sandal Types and Archaic Prehistory on the Colorado Plateau. *American Antiquity* 65:509–524.

2000b   Early Archaic Square-Stem Dart Points from Southeastern Utah. *Utah Archaeology 2000* 13:51–61.

Geib, Phil, and Dale Davidson
1994   Anasazi Origins: A Perspective from Preliminary Work at Old Man Cave. *Kiva* 60:191–202.

Geib, Phil, and Donald Keller
2002   *Bighorn Cave: Test Excavation of a Stratified Dry Shelter, Mohave County, Arizona.* Bilby Research Center Occasional Papers No. 1. Northern Arizona University, Flagstaff.

Geib, Phil, and Kimberly Spurr
2000   The Basketmaker II–III Transition on the Rainbow Plateau. In *Foundations of Anasazi Culture*, edited by Paul Reed, pp. 175–200. University of Utah Press, Salt Lake City.

Gellis, A. C.
1998   *Characterization and Evaluation of Channel and Hillslope Erosion on the Zuni Indian Reservation, New Mexico, 1992–95.* U.S. Geological Survey Water Investigations Report 97-4281.

Gellner, Ernest
1983   *Nations and Nationalism.* Basil Blackwell, Oxford.

Geosciences Consultants, Ltd.
1985   Changes in Geomorphology, Hydrology, and Land Use on the Zuni Indian Reservation, McKinley and Cibola Counties, New Mexico, 1846–1946. Plaintiff's Exhibit 2,000. Expert testimony submitted to the United States Claims Court as evidence in the case *Zuni Indian Tribe v. United States*, Docket 327-81L.

1988   Rebuttal Report: Changes in Geomorphology, Hydrology, and Land Use on the Zuni Indian Reservation, McKinley and Cibola Counties, New Mexico, 1846–1946. Plaintiff's Exhibit 2,000. Expert testimony submitted to the United States Claims Court as evidence in the case *Zuni Indian Tribe v. United States*, Dockets 327-81L and 224-81L.

Gerald, M. Virginia
1957   Two Great Kivas at Point of Pines Ruin. Unpublished Master's thesis, Department of Anthropology, University of Arizona, Tucson.

Gifford, James C.
1980   *Caves of the Point of Pines Region.* Anthropological Papers of the University of Arizona No. 36. University of Arizona Press, Tucson.

Gifford, James C., and Watson Smith
1978   *Gray Corrugated Pottery from Awatovi and Other Jeddito Sites in Northeastern Arizona.* Papers of the Peabody Museum of Archaeology and Ethnology Vol. 69. Harvard University, Cambridge.

Gillespie, William B.
1995   Vertebrate Remains from Los Morteros. In *Archaeological Investigations at Los Morteros, a Prehistoric Settlement in the Northern Tucson Basin*, by Henry D. Wallace, pp. 673–719. Anthropological Papers No. 17. Center for Desert Archaeology, Tucson, Arizona.

Gilman, Patricia A.
1987   Architecture as Artifact: Pit Structures and Pueblo in the American Southwest. *American Antiquity* 52:538–564.

Gilman, Patricia A., Veletta Canouts, and Ronald L. Bishop
1994   Production and Distribution of Classic Mimbres Black-on-white Pottery. *American Antiquity* 59:695–709.

Gilpin, Dennis
1989   Great Houses and Pueblos in Northeastern Arizona. Paper presented at the 1986 Pecos Conference, Payson, Arizona. Manuscript on file,

Museum of Northern Arizona Library, Flagstaff.

1994   Lukachukai and Salina Springs: Late Archaic/Early Basketmaker Habitation Sites in the Chinle Valley, Northeastern Arizona. *Kiva* 60:203–218.

Gladwin, Harold Sterling
1945   *The Chaco Branch: Excavations at White Mound and in the Red Mesa Valley.* Medallion Papers No. 31. Gila Pueblo, Globe, Arizona.

1957   *A History of the Ancient Southwest.* Bond Wheelwright Company, Portland, Maine.

Gladwin, Harold S., Emil W. Haury, E. B. Sayles, and Nora Gladwin
1937   *Excavations at Snaketown: Material Culture.* Medallion Papers No. 25. Gila Pueblo, Globe, Arizona.

Gladwin, Winifred J., and Harold S. Gladwin
1929   *The Red-on-buff Culture of the Gila Basin.* Medallion Papers No. 3. Gila Pueblo, Globe, Arizona.

1934   *A Method for Designation of Cultures and Their Variations.* Medallion Papers No. 15. Gila Pueblo, Globe, Arizona.

1935   *The Eastern Range of the Red-on-buff Culture.* Medallion Papers No. 16. Gila Pueblo, Globe, Arizona.

Glantz, Michael
1996   *Currents of Change: El Niño's Impact on Climate and Society.* Cambridge University Press, Cambridge.

Goddard, Ives
1996   The Classification of the Native Languages of North America. In *Languages*, edited by Ives Goddard, pp. 290–323. Handbook of North American Indians, Vol. 17, William C. Sturtevant, general editor, Smithsonian Institution, Washington, D.C.

Goebel, Ted, Roger Powers, and Nancy Bigelow
1991   The Nenana Complex of Alaska and Clovis Origins. In *Clovis: Origins and Adaptations*, edited by Robson Bonnichsen and Karen L. Turnmire, pp. 49–79. Center for the Study of the First Americans, Corvallis, Oregon.

Goebel, Ted, Michael Waters, and Margarita Dikova
2003   The Archaeology of Ushki Lake, Kamchatka, and the Pleistocene Peopling of the Americas. *Science* 301:501–505.

Goetze, Christine E., and Barbara J. Mills
1993a   Ceramic Chronometry. In *Across*

the Colorado Plateau: Anthropological Studies for the Transwestern Pipeline Expansion Project, Interpretation of Ceramic Artifacts, Vol. 16, edited by Barbara J. Mills, Christine E. Goetze, and María Nieves Zedeño, pp. 87–146. Office of Contract Archeology and Maxwell Museum of Anthropology, University of New Mexico, Albuquerque.

1993b Classification Criteria for Wares and Types. In Across the Colorado Plateau: Anthropological Studies for the Transwestern Pipeline Expansion Project, Interpretation of Ceramic Artifacts, Vol. 16, edited by Barbara J. Mills, Christine E. Goetze, and Maria Neives Zedeño, pp. 21–85. Office of Contract Archeology and Maxwell Museum of Anthropology, University of New Mexico, Albuquerque.

Goldfrank, Esther S.
1954 Intercultural Relations in the Greater Southwest. American Anthropologist 56:658–662.

Golla, Victor
2000 Language Families of North America. In America Past, America Present: Genes and Languages in the Americas and Beyond, edited by Colin Renfrew, pp. 59–72. McDonald Institute for Archaeological Research. Cambridge, England.

Gonzalez, Silvia, José Concepción Jiménez-Lopez, Robert Hedges, David Huddart, James C. Ohman, Alan Turner, and José Antonio Pompa y Padilla
2003 Earliest Humans in the Americas: New Evidence from Mexico. Journal of Human Evolution 44:379–387.

Goody, Jack (editor)
1958 The Developmental Cycle in Domestic Groups. Cambridge Papers in Social Anthropology 1.
1971 The Developmental Cycle in Domestic Groups. Cambridge University Press, Cambridge.

Goss, James A.
1965 Ute Linguistics and Anasazi Abandonment of the Four Corners Area. In Contributions of the Wetherill Mesa Archaeological Project, compiled by H. Douglas Osborne, pp. 73–81. Memoirs of the Society for American Archaeology 19. Salt Lake City.

Goudie, Andrew
1985 The Nature of the Environment: An Advanced Physical Geography. Basil Blackwell, London.

Grange Jr., Roger
1952 Wooden Artifacts. In Mogollon Cultural Continuity and Change: The Stratigraphic Analysis of Tularosa and Cordova Caves, pp. 331–451. Fieldiana: Anthropology Vol. 40. Chicago Natural History Museum, Chicago.

Gratz, Kathleen E.
1977 Archaeological Excavations along Route Z4, near Zuni, New Mexico. Research Paper 7. Museum of Northern Arizona, Flagstaff.

Graves, William, and Suzanne L. Eckert
1998 Decorated Ceramic Distributions and Ideological Developments in the Northern and Central Rio Grande Valley, New Mexico. In Migration and Reorganization: The Pueblo IV Period in the American Southwest, edited by Katherine A. Spielmann, pp. 263–279. Anthropological Research Papers No. 51. Arizona State University, Tempe.

Graybill, Donald A., David A. Gregory, Gary S. Funkhouser, and Fred L. Nials
2006 Long-Term Streamflow Reconstructions, River Channel Morphology, and Aboriginal Irrigation Systems along the Salt and Gila Rivers. In Environmental Change and Human Adaptation in the Ancient American Southwest, edited by David E. Doyel and Jeffrey S. Dean. University of Utah Press, Salt Lake City.

Grayson, Donald K.
1993 The Desert's Past: A Natural Prehistory of the Great Basin. Smithsonian Institution Press, Washington, D.C.

Green, Jesse (editor)
1979 Zuni: Selected Writings of Frank Hamilton Cushing. University of Nebraska Press, Lincoln.
1990 Cushing at Zuni: The Correspondence and Journals of Frank Hamilton Cushing, 1879–1884. University of New Mexico Press, Albuquerque.

Green, Stanton W., and Stephen M. Perlman
1985 The Archaeology of Frontiers and Boundaries. Academic Press, Inc., Orlando.

Greenberg, Joseph H.
1987 Language in the Americas. Stanford University Press, Stanford.

Greenberg, Joseph H., Christy H. Turner II, and Stephen Zegura
1986 The Settlement of the Americas. Current Anthropology 27:477–497.

Greenwood, Ned H.
1983 High-Altitude and Non-village Cer-

emonialism of the Cibola Branch of the Anasazi. Manuscript on file at Apache-Sitgreaves National Forest.

Greenwood, N. H., and C. W. White
1970 Mogollon Ritual: A Spatial Configuration of a Non-village Pattern. Archaeology 23(4):298–301.

Gregory, David A.
1987 The Morphology of Platform Mounds and the Structure of Classic Period Hohokam Sites. In The Hohokam Village: Site Structure and Organization, edited by David E. Doyel, pp. 183–210. American Association for the Advancement of Science, Glenwood Springs, Colorado.
1991 Form and Variation in Hohokam Settlement Patterns. In Chaco & Hohokam: Prehistoric Regional Systems in the American Southwest, edited by Patricia L. Crown and W. James Judge, pp. 159–193. School of American Research Advanced Seminar Series, School of American Research Press, Santa Fe.
1995a Prehistoric Settlement Patterns in the Eastern Tonto Basin. In The Roosevelt Community Development Study: New Perspectives on Tonto Basin Prehistory, edited by Mark D. Elson, Miriam T. Stark, and David A. Gregory, pp. 127–184. Anthropological Papers No. 15. Center for Desert Archaeology, Tucson, Arizona.
1995b Prehistoric Ceramic Variability. In The San Carlos Reservoir Cultural Resources Survey, edited by Andrew T. Black and Margerie Green, pp. 43–50. Archaeological Consulting Services, Ltd. Cultural Resources Report No. 87. Tempe.
1995c Prehistoric Site Variability: Morphology, Chronology and Location. In The San Carlos Reservoir Cultural Resources Survey, edited by Andrew T. Black and Margerie Green, pp. 51–121. Archaeological Consulting Services, Ltd. Cultural Resources Report No. 87. Tempe.
1995d A Chronological Framework for the Prehistory of the Safford Basin. In The San Carlos Reservoir Cultural Resources Survey, edited by Andrew T. Black and Margerie Green, pp. 123–148. Archaeological Consulting Services, Ltd. Cultural Resources Report No. 87. Tempe.
1996 New Issues in the Interpretation of Archaic Period Radiocarbon Dates. Paper presented at the Conference on

the Archaic Prehistory of the North American Southwest, Maxwell Museum, University of New Mexico, Albuquerque.

1999 Data Integration and Synthesis. In *Excavations in the Santa Cruz River Floodplain: The Middle Archaic Component at Los Pozos*, edited by David A. Gregory, pp. 85–124. Anthropological Papers No. 20. Center for Desert Archaeology, Tucson, Arizona.

2001a Variation and Trend during the Early Agricultural Period. In *Excavations in the Santa Cruz River Floodplain: The Early Agricultural Period Component at Los Pozos*, edited by David A. Gregory, pp. 255–280. Anthropological Papers No. 21. Center for Desert Archaeology, Tucson, Arizona.

2001b An Evaluation of Early Agricultural Period Chronology in the Tucson Basin. In *Excavations in the Santa Cruz River Floodplain: The Early Agricultural Period Component at Los Pozos*, edited by David A. Gregory, pp. 237–254. Anthropological Papers No. 21. Center for Desert Archaeology, Tucson, Arizona.

Gregory, David A. (editor)
1999 *Excavations in the Santa Cruz River Floodplain: The Middle Archaic Component at Los Pozos*. Anthropological Papers No. 20. Center for Desert Archaeology, Tucson, Arizona.

2001 *Excavations in the Santa Cruz River Floodplain: The Early Agricultural Period Component at Los Pozos*. Anthropological Papers No. 21. Center for Desert Archaeology, Tucson, Arizona.

Gregory, David A., and Sam W. Baar IV
1999 Stratigraphy, Chronology, and Characteristics of the Natural and Cultural Deposits. In *Excavations in the Santa Cruz River Floodplain: The Middle Archaic Component at Los Pozos*, edited by David A. Gregory, pp. 13–32. Anthropological Papers No. 20. Center for Desert Archaeology, Tucson, Arizona.

Gregory, David A., and Michael W. Diehl
2002 Duration, Continuity, and Intensity of Occupation at a Late Cienega Phase Settlement in the Santa Cruz River Floodplain. In *Traditions, Transitions, and Technologies: Themes in Southwestern Archaeology*, edited by Sarah H. Schlanger, pp. 200–223. University Press of Colorado, Boulder.

Gregory, David A., and Gary Huckleberry
1994 *An Archaeological Survey of the Blackwater Area, Volume 1: The History of Human Settlement in the Blackwater Area*. Archaeological Consulting Services Cultural Resources Report No. 86. Tempe.

Gregory, David A., and Fred L. Nials
1985 Observations Concerning the Distribution of Classic Period Platform Mounds. In *Proceedings of the 1983 Hohokam Symposium*, edited by Alfred E. Dittert Jr. and Donald E. Dove, pp. 373–388. Occasional Paper No. 2. Phoenix Chapter, Arizona Archaeological Society, Phoenix.

Gregory, David A., Fred L. Nials, Patricia L. Crown, Lynn S. Teague, and David A. Phillips Jr.
1985 *The 1982–1984 Excavations at Las Colinas: Research Design*. Archaeological Series 162, Vol. 1, edited by Carol Ann Heathington and David A. Gregory. Cultural Resource Management Division, Arizona State Museum, University of Arizona, Tucson.

Gregory, David A., and Jennifer A. Waters
2001 Bone Artifacts. In *Excavations in the Santa Cruz River Floodplain: The Early Agricultural Period Component at Los Pozos*, edited by David A. Gregory, pp. 153–161. Anthropological Papers No. 21. Center for Desert Archaeology, Tucson, Arizona.

Griffin, James B.
1967 Eastern North American Archaeology: A Summary. *Science* 156:175–191.

Griffith, Carol A., and Peter H. McCartney
1994 Shell Artifacts from the Livingston Area. In *Archaeology of the Salado in the Livingston Area of Tonto Basin, Roosevelt Platform Mound Study: Report on the Livingston Management Group, Pinto Creek Complex*, edited by David Jacobs, pp. 799–808. Roosevelt Monograph Series 3, Anthropological Field Studies 32. Office of Cultural Resource Management, Department of Anthropology, Arizona State University, Tempe.

Grissino-Mayer, Henri D.
1996 A 2129-Year Reconstruction of Precipitation for Northwestern New Mexico. In *Tree Rings, Environment and Humanity: Proceedings of the International Conference, Tucson, Arizona, 17–21 May 1994*, edited by Jeffrey S. Dean, David M. Meko, and Thomas W. Swetnam, pp. 191–204. Radiocarbon, Tucson.

Grissino-Mayer, Henri D., and Thomas W. Swetnam
1997 Multi-century History of Wildfire in the Ponderosa Pine Forests of El Malpais National Monument. In *Natural History of El Malpais National Monument*, compiled by K. Mabrey, pp. 163–171. New Mexico Bureau of Mines and Mineral Resources Bulletin 156. Socorro.

Grissino-Mayer, Henri D., Thomas W. Swetnam, and Rex K. Adams
1997 *The Rare, Old-Aged Conifers of El Malpais: Their Role in Understanding Climatic Change in the American Southwest*. New Mexico Bureau of Mines and Mineral Resources Bulletin 156. Laboratory of Tree-Ring Research, University of Arizona, Tucson.

Gronenborn, Detlef
1999 Variation on a Basic Theme: The Transition to Farming in Southern Central Europe. *Journal of World Prehistory* 13(2):123–210.

Gross, G. Timothy, and Tammy Stone
1994 Marine Shell. In *Material Culture*, edited by Michael S. Foster, pp. 167–202. The Pueblo Grande Project, Vol. 4. Soil Systems Publications in Archaeology No. 20. Soil Systems, Inc., Phoenix.

Grove, Jean
1990 *The Little Ice Age*. Routledge, London.

Guernsey, Samuel J.
1931 *Explorations in Northeastern Arizona*. Papers of the Peabody Museum of American Archaeology and Ethnology Vol. 12, No. 1. Harvard University, Cambridge.

Guernsey, Samuel J., and Alfred V. Kidder
1921 *Basket-Maker Caves of Northeastern Arizona*. Papers of the Peabody Museum of American Archaeology and Ethnology Vol. 8, No. 1. Harvard University, Cambridge.

Gumerman, George J.
1966 Two Basketmaker II Pithouse Villages in Eastern Arizona: A Preliminary Report. *Plateau* 39(2):80–87.

Gumerman, George J. (editor)
1988 *The Anasazi in a Changing Environment*. School of American Research, Santa Fe.

Gumerman, George J., and Jeffrey S. Dean
1989 Prehistoric Cooperation and Competition in the western Anasazi Area. In *Dynamics of Southwest Prehistory*, edited by Linda S. Cordell and George J. Gumerman, pp. 99–148. Smithsonian Institution Press, Washington, D.C.

Gumerman, George J., and Murray Gell-Mann
1994　*Understanding Complexity in the Prehistoric Southwest*. Santa Fe Institute Studies in the Sciences of Complexity Proceedings Vol. 16. Addison-Wesley, Reading, Massachusetts.

Gunnerson, James H.
1962　Plateau Shoshonean Prehistory: A Suggested Reconstruction. *American Antiquity* 28:41–45.

Habicht-Mauche, Judith A.
1993　*The Pottery from Arroyo Hondo Pueblo, New Mexico*. Arroyo Hondo Archaeological Series No. 8. School of American Research Press, Santa Fe.

Hack, John T.
1942　*The Changing Physical Environment of the Hopi Indians of Arizona*. Papers of the Peabody Museum of American Archaeology and Ethnography Vol. 35, No. 1. Harvard University, Cambridge.
1945　Recent Geology of the Tsegi Canyon. In *Archaeological Studies in Northeast Arizona*, by R. L. Beals, G. W. Brainerd, and W. Smith, pp. 151–158. University of California Publications in American Archaeology and Ethnology Vol. 44, No. 1. University of California Press, Berkeley.

Hage, Per, and Frank Harary
1983　*Structural Models in Anthropology*. Cambridge University Press, Cambridge.

Hagenbuckle, Kristen
2001　Ritual and the Individual: An Analysis of Cibicue Painted Corrugated Pottery from Grasshopper Pueblo, Arizona. Unpublished Master's thesis, Department of Anthropology, University of Arizona, Tucson.

Hale, Kenneth
1958　Internal Diversity in Uto-Aztecan, I. *International Journal of American Linguistics* 24:101–107.
1962　Jemez and Kiowa Correspondences in Reference to Kiowa-Tanoan. *International Journal of American Linguistics* 28:1–5.
1964　The Sub-grouping of Uto-Aztecan Languages: Lexical Evidence for Sonoran. *Proceedings of the 35th International Congress of Americanists* 2:511–517. Mexico.
1967　Toward a Reconstruction of Kiowa-Tanoan Phonology. *International Journal of American Linguistics* 33(2):112–120.

Hale, Kenneth, and David Harris
1979　Historical Linguistics and Archae-ology. In *Southwest*, edited by Albert Ortiz, pp. 170–77. Handbook of North American Indians, Vol. 9, William C. Sturtevant, general editor, Smithsonian Institution, Washington, D.C.

Hall, Stephen A.
1977　Late Quaternary Sedimentation and Paleoecologic History of Chaco Canyon, New Mexico. *Geological Society of America Bulletin* 88:1593–1618.
1985　Erosion of Zuni Indian Reservation Lands. Plaintiff's Exhibit 3,000. Expert testimony submitted to the United States Claims Court as evidence in the case *Zuni Indian Tribe v. United States*, Docket 327-81L.
1988　Rebuttal Report: Erosion of Zuni Indian Reservation Lands. Plaintiff's Exhibit 3,000. Expert testimony submitted to the United States Claims Court as evidence in the case *Zuni Indian Tribe v. United States*, Dockets 327-81L and 224-81L.
1990　Channel Trenching and Climatic Change in the Southern U.S. Great Plains. *Geology* 18:342–345.

Hally, David J.
1993　The Territorial Size of Mississippian Chiefdoms. In *Archaeology of Eastern North America: Papers in Honor of Stephen Williams*, edited by James B. Stoltman, pp. 143–168. Archaeological Report No. 25. Mississippi Department of Archives and History, Jackson.
2006　The Nature of Mississippian Regional Systems. In *Light on the Path: The Anthropology and History of the Southeastern Indians*, edited by Thomas J. Pluckham and Robbie Ethridge. University of Alabama Press, Tuscaloosa.

Hally, David J., and Hypatia Kelly
1998　The Nature of Mississippian Towns in Georgia: The King Site Example. In *Mississippian Towns and Sacred Spaces, Searching for an Architectural Grammar*, edited by R. Barry Lewis and Charles Stout, pp. 49–63. University of Alabama Press, Tuscaloosa.

Hammack, Laurens C.
1966　*Diablo Highway Salvage Archaeology*. Laboratory of Anthropology Notes No. 41. Museum of New Mexico, Santa Fe.

Hammel, E. A.
1980　Household Structure in Fourteenth Century Macedonia. *Journal of Family History* 5:242–273.
1984　On the *** of Studying Household Form and Function. In *Households: Comparative and Historical Studies of the Domestic Group*, edited by Robert McC. Netting, Richard R. Wilk, and Eric J. Arnould, pp. 29–43. University of California Press, Berkeley.

Hammond, George P., and Agapito Rey
1928　*Obregon's History of 16th Century Exploration in Western America*. Wetzel Publishing, Los Angeles.
1940　*Narratives of the Coronado Expedition, 1540–1542*. University of New Mexico Press, Albuquerque.
1953　*Don Juan de Oñate: Colonizer of New Mexico*. Coronado Cuarto Centennial Publications Vols. 5 and 6. University of New Mexico Press, Albuquerque.
1966　*The Rediscovery of New Mexico, 1580–1594*. University of New Mexico Press, Albuquerque.

Hamp, Eric
1975　On Zuni-Penutian Consonants. *International Journal of American Linguistics* 41(4):310–312.

Handy, Edward L.
1918　Zuni Tales. *Journal of American Folklore* 31:451–471.

Hansen, Eric
1994　Early Archaic Diet at Old Man Cave: A Perspective on Archaic Subsistence in Southeastern Utah. Unpublished Master's thesis, Department of Anthropology, Northern Arizona University, Flagstaff.

Harbottle, Garman, and Phil C. Weigand
1992　Turquoise in Pre-Columbian America. *Scientific American* (February):78–85.

Harbottle, Garman, Phil C. Weigand, and Michael S. Foster
1994　Archaeological Turquoise from Pueblo Grande and Comparison with the Turquoise Database. In *Material Culture*, edited by Michael S. Foster, pp. 369–89. The Pueblo Grande Project, Vol. 4. Soil Systems Publications in Archaeology No. 20. Soil Systems, Inc., Phoenix.

Hard, Robert J.
1990　Agricultural Dependence in the Mountain Mogollon. In *Perspectives on Southwestern Prehistory*, edited by Paul E. Minnis and Charles L. Redman, pp. 135–149. Westview Press, Boulder.

Hard, Robert J., and John R. Roney
1999a　A Massive Terraced Village Complex in Chihuahua, Mexico Dated to 3000 Years Before Present. *Science* 279:1661–1664.
1999b　Cerro Juanaqueña. *Archaeology Southwest* 13(1):4–5.

2005 The Transition to Farming on the Río Casas Grandes and in the Southern Jornada Mogollon Region. In *The Late Archaic across the Borderlands*, edited by Bradley Vierra, pp. 141–186. University of Texas Press, Austin.

Hardesty, Donald L., and Don D. Fowler

2001 Archaeology and Environmental Change. In *New Directions in Anthropology and Environment, Intersections*, edited by Carole L. Crumley, pp. 72–89. AltaMira Press, Walnut Creek, California.

Hargrave, Lyndon L.

1931a Excavations at Kin Tiel and Kokopnyama. In *Recently Dated Pueblo Ruins in Arizona*, edited by Emil W. Haury and Lyndon L. Hargrave, pp. 80–120. Smithsonian Miscellaneous Collections Vol. 82, No. 11. Smithsonian Institution, Washington, D.C.

1931b The Influence of Economic Geography upon the Rise and Fall of the Pueblo Culture in Arizona. *Museum of Northern Arizona, Museum Notes* 4(6):1–4.

1934 Archaeological Investigations in the Tsegi Canyons of Northeastern Arizona in 1934. *Museum of Northern Arizona, Museum Notes* 7(7):25–28.

1935 The Jeddito Valley and the First Pueblo Towns in Arizona to Be Visited by Europeans. *Museum Notes* 8(4):17–23.

1970 *Mexican Macaws: Comparative Osteology and Survey of Remains from the Southwest*. Anthropological Papers of the University of Arizona No. 20. University of Arizona Press, Tucson.

Harrington, J. A., Jr., R. Cerveny, and R. Balling Jr.

1992 Impact of the Southern Oscillation on the North American Southwest Monsoon. *Physical Geography* 13:318–330.

Harrington, John P.

1909 Notes on the Piro Language. *American Anthropologist* 11:563–594.

1916 The Ethnogeography of the Tewa Indians. *Twenty-ninth Annual Report of the Bureau of American Ethnology for the Years 1907–1908*, pp. 29–636. Washington, D.C.

Harrington, M. R.

1929 Ruins and Legends of Zuni Land. *Masterkey* 3(1):5–17.

Hart, E. Richard

1995a *Zuni and the Courts: A Struggle for Sovereign Land Rights*. University Press of Kansas, Lawrence.

1995b Zuni and the Grand Canyon: A Glen Canyon Environmental Studies Report. Zuni GCES Ethnohistorical Report. Institute of the North American West, Seattle.

1995c Protection of *Kolhu/wala:wa* ("Zuni Heaven"): Litigation and Legislation. In *Zuni and the Courts*, edited by E. Richard Hart, pp. 199–207. University Press of Kansas, Lawrence.

Hassan, Fekri

1981 *Demographic Archaeology*. Academic Press, New York.

Haury, Emil W.

1934 The Canyon Creek Ruin and the Cliff Dwellings of the Sierra Ancha. Medallion Papers No. 14. Gila Pueblo, Globe, Arizona.

1936a *The Mogollon Culture of Southwestern New Mexico*. Medallion Papers No. 20. Gila Pueblo, Globe, Arizona.

1936b *Some Southwestern Pottery Types, Series IV*. Medallion Papers No. 19. Gila Pueblo, Globe, Arizona.

1937a Shell. In *Excavations at Snaketown: Material Culture*, by Harold S. Gladwin, Emil W. Haury, E. B. Sayles, and Nora Gladwin, pp. 135–153. Medallion Papers No. 25. Gila Pueblo, Globe, Arizona.

1937b Stone Palettes and Ornaments. In *Excavations at Snaketown: Material Culture*, by Harold S. Gladwin, Emil W. Haury, E. B. Sayles, and Nora Gladwin, pp. 121–134. Medallion Papers No. 25. Gila Pueblo, Globe, Arizona.

1945a *The Excavations of Los Muertos and Neighboring Ruins in the Salt River Valley, Southern Arizona*. Papers of the Peabody Museum of American Archaeology and Ethnology Vol. 24, No. 1. Harvard University, Cambridge.

1945b The Problem of Contacts between the Southwestern United States and Mexico. *Southwestern Journal of Anthropology* 1(1):55–74.

1950 *The Stratigraphy and Archaeology of Ventana Cave*. University of Arizona Press, Tucson.

1957 An Alluvial Site on the San Carlos Indian Reservation, Arizona. *American Antiquity* 23:2–27.

1958 Evidence at Point of Pines for a Prehistoric Migration from Northern Arizona. In *Migrations in New World Culture History*, edited by Raymond H. Thompson, pp. 1–8. Social Science Bulletin No. 27. University of Arizona, Tucson.

1962 The Greater American Southwest. In *Courses toward Urban Life: Archaeological Considerations of Some Cultural Alternates*, edited by Robert J. Braidwood and Gordon R. Willey, pp. 106–131. Viking Fund Publications in Anthropology No. 32. Wenner-Gren Foundation, New York.

1975 *The Stratigraphy and Archaeology of Ventana Cave*. University of Arizona Press, Tucson.

1976 *The Hohokam: Desert Farmers and Craftsmen*. University of Arizona Press, Tucson.

1985a *Mogollon Culture in the Forestdale Valley, East-Central Arizona*. University of Arizona Press, Tucson.

1985b Excavations in the Forestdale Valley, East-Central Arizona. In *Mogollon Culture in the Forestdale Valley, East-Central Arizona*, by Emil W. Haury, pp. 135–279. University of Arizona Press, Tucson.

1986a Thoughts after Sixty Years as a Southwestern Archaeologist. In *Emil W. Haury's Prehistory of the American Southwest*, edited by J. Jefferson Reid and David E. Doyel, pp. 435–464. University of Arizona Press, Tucson.

1986b Recent Thoughts of the Mogollon. *Kiva* 53:195–196.

1986c Roosevelt 9:6, a Hohokam Site of the Colonial Period. In *Emil W. Haury's Prehistory of the American Southwest*, edited by J. Jefferson Reid and David E. Doyel, pp. 211–294. University of Arizona Press, Tucson.

1989 *Point of Pines, Arizona: A History of the University of Arizona Archaeological Field School*. Anthropological Papers of the University of Arizona No. 50. University of Arizona Press, Tucson.

Haury, Emil W. (editor)

1954 Southwest Issue. *American Anthropologist* 56:529–731.

Haury, Emil W., Ernest Antevs, and John Lance

1953 Artifacts with Mammoth Remains, Naco, Arizona. *American Antiquity* 19:1–24.

Haury, Emil W., and Carol A. Gifford

1959 A Thirteenth Century Strongbox. *Kiva* 24(4):1–11.

Haury, Emil W., and Lyndon L. Hargrave

1931 *Recently Dated Pueblo Ruins in Arizona*. Smithsonian Miscellaneous Collections Vol. 82, No. 11. Smithsonian Institution, Washington, D.C.

Haury, Emil W., and Julian Hayden

1975 Preface 1975. In *The Stratigraphy and Archaeology of Ventana Cave*, pp. v–vi. University of Arizona Press, Tucson.

Haury, Emil W., and Lisa W. Huckell (editors)
1993   A Cotton Cache from the Pinaleño Mountains, Arizona. *Kiva* 59:95–145.

Haury, Emil W., Robert L. Rands, Albert C. Spaulding, Walter W. Taylor, Raymond H. Thompson, Robert Wauchope, and Marian E. White
1956   An Archaeological Approach to the Study of Cultural Stability. In *Seminars in Archaeology: 1955*, edited by Robert Wauchope. Memoirs of the Society for American Archaeology. *American Antiquity* 22, No. 2, Pt. 2:33–57.

Haury, Emil W., E. B. Sayles, and William W. Wasley
1959   The Lehner Mammoth Site, Southeastern Arizona. *American Antiquity* 25:2–30.

Hawley, Florence
1936   Manual of Prehistoric Pottery Types. *University of New Mexico Bulletin, Anthropological Series* Vol. 1, No. 4.
1950   Big Kivas, Little Kivas, and Moiety Houses in Historical Reconstruction. *Southwestern Journal of Anthropology* 6:286–302.

Hayden, Julian D.
1972   Hohokam Petroglyphs of the Sierra Pinacate, Sonora and the Hohokam Shell Expeditions. *Kiva* 37:74–83.

Hayes, Alden C.
1981   *Excavation of Mound 7, Gran Quivira National Monument, New Mexico.* Publications in Archaeology No. 16. USDI National Park Service, Washington, D.C.

Haynes, C. Vance, Jr.
1968   Geochronology of Late Quaternary Alluvium. In *Means of Correlation of Quaternary Successions*, edited by Roger B. Morrison and Herbert E. Wright Jr., pp. 591–631. Proceedings of the VII Congress of the International Association of Quaternary Research Vol. 8. University of Utah Press, Salt Lake City.
1970   Geochronology of Man-Mammoth Sites and Their Bearing on the Origin of the Llano Complex. In *Pleistocene and Recent Environments of the Central Great Plains*, edited by Wakefield Dort Jr. and J. Knox Jones Jr., pp. 77–92. Department of Geology, Special Publication 3, University of Kansas, Lawrence.
1987   Clovis Origins Update. *Kiva* 52:83–93.

1991   Geoarchaeological and Paleohydrological Evidence for a Clovis-Age Drought in North America and Its Bearing on Extinction. *Quaternary Research* 35:438–450.
1993   Clovis-Folsom Geochronology and Climatic Change. In *Kostenki to Clovis: Upper Paleolithic–Paleo-Indian Adaptations*, edited by Olga Soffer and N. D. Praslov, pp. 219–236. Plenum, New York.

Haynes, C. Vance, Jr., and E. T. Hemmings
1968   Mammoth-Bone Shaft Wrench from Murray Springs, Arizona. *Science* 159:186–187.

Haynes, C. Vance, Jr., and Bruce B. Huckell
1985   *Geological and Archaeological Investigations along Airport Wash in the Southern Tucson Basin.* Technical Report No. 85-4. Institute for American Research, Tucson.

Haynes, Gary
2002   *The Early Settlement of North America: The Clovis Era.* Cambridge University Press, New York.

Hays, Kelley Ann
1992   *Anasazi Ceramics as Text and Tool: Toward a Theory of Ceramic Design "Messaging."* PhD dissertation, Department of Anthropology, University of Arizona, Tucson. University Microfilms, Ann Arbor.
1993   Ceramics from the Coronado Project. In *The Coronado Project: Anasazi Settlements Overlooking the Puerco Valley, Arizona.* Vol. 2, edited by Richard V. N. Ahlstrom, Marianne Marek, and David H. Greenwald, pp. 11–64. SWCA Anthropological Research Paper No. 3. Tucson.
1994   Kachina Depictions on Prehistoric Pottery. In *Kachinas in the Pueblo World*, edited by Polly Schaafsma, pp. 47–62. University of New Mexico Press, Albuquerque. Reprinted University of Utah Press, 2000.

Hays-Gilpin, Kelley Ann, Ann Cordy Deegan, and Elizabeth Ann Morris
1998   *Prehistoric Sandals from Northeastern Arizona: The Earl H. Morris and Ann Axtell Morris Research.* Anthropological Papers of the University of Arizona No. 62. University of Arizona Press, Tucson.

Hays-Gilpin, Kelley A., and Jane H. Hill
1999   The Flower World in Material Culture: An Iconographic Complex in the Southwest and Mesoamerica. *Journal of Anthropological Research* 55:1–37.

Hays-Gilpin, Kelley Ann, and Eric van Hartesveldt (editors)
1998   *Prehistoric Ceramics of the Puerco Valley: The 1995 Chambers-Sanders Trust Lands Ceramic Conference.* Museum of Northern Arizona Ceramic Series No. 7. Flagstaff.

Hegmon, Michelle
1992   Archaeological Research on Style. *Annual Review of Anthropology* 21:517–536.
1995   *The Social Dynamics of Pottery Style in the Early Puebloan Southwest.* Crow Canyon Archaeological Center, Occasional Paper No. 5. Cortez.
1998   Technology, Style, and Social Practice. In *The Archaeology of Social Boundaries*, edited by Miriam T. Stark, pp. 264–279. Smithsonian Institution Press, Washington, D.C.

Hegmon, Michelle, Margaret C. Nelson, Roger Anyon, Darrell Creel, Steven A. LeBlanc, and Harry J. Shafer
1999   Scale and Time-Space Systematics in the Post–AD 1100 Mimbres Region of the North American Southwest. *Kiva* 65:143–166.

Hegmon, Michelle, Margaret C. Nelson, and Susan Ruth
1998   Abandonment, Reorganization, and Social Change: Analysis of Pottery and Architecture from the Mimbres Region of the American Southwest. *American Anthropologist* 100:148–162.

Heidke, James M.
1999   Cienega Phase Incipient Plain Ware from Southeastern Arizona. *Kiva* 64:311–338.

Heidke, James M., and Judith A. Habicht-Mauche
1999   The First Occurrences and Early Distribution of Pottery in the North American Southwest. *Revista de Arqueología Americana* 14:65–99.

Heizer, Robert F., and Adan E. Treganza
1944   *Mines and Quarries of the Indians of California.* Reprint from *California Journal of Mines and Geology, Report XL of the State Mineralogist* (July):291–359. California State Printing Office, State of California Department of Natural Resources, Division of Mines, Sacramento, California.

Henige, David
1998   *Numbers from Nowhere: The American Indian Contact Population Debate.* University of Oklahoma Press, Norman.

Herder, Johann
1966 [1800]   *Outlines of a Philosophy of the*

History of Man. Bergman Publishers, New York.

Herhahn, Cynthia L., and J. Brett Hill
1998 Modeling Agricultural Production Strategies in the Northern Rio Grande Valley, New Mexico. *Human Ecology* 26(3):469–487.

Herr, Sarah A.
2001 *Beyond Chaco: Great Kiva Communities on the Mogollon Rim Frontier*. Anthropological Papers of the University of Arizona No. 66. University of Arizona Press, Tucson.

Herr, Sarah A., and Jeffery J. Clark
1997 Patterns in the Pathways: Early Historic Migration. *Kiva* 62:365–389.

Hevly, Richard H.
1988 Prehistoric Vegetation and Paleoclimates on the Colorado Plateaus. In *The Anasazi in a Changing Environment*, edited by George J. Gumerman, pp. 92–118. Cambridge University Press, Cambridge.

Hewett, Edgar L.
1906 *Antiquities of the Jemez Plateau, New Mexico*. Bulletin No. 32, Bureau of American Ethnology, Smithsonian Institution, Washington, D.C.
1993 *Ancient Communities in the American Desert*. Archaeological Society of New Mexico Monograph Series 1. Santa Fe. Originally published in French 1908.

Hewett, Edgar L., Junius Henderson, and Wilfred W. Robbins
1913 *The Physiography of the Rio Grande Valley, New Mexico, in Relation to Pueblo Culture*. Bulletin No. 54, Bureau of American Ethnology, Smithsonian Institution, Washington, D.C.

Hibben, Frank C.
1938 A Cache of Wooden Bows from the Mogollon Mountains. *American Antiquity* 4:36–38.
1975 *Kiva Art of the Anasazi at Pottery Mound*. KC Publications, Las Vegas, Nevada.

Hickerson, Harold
1962 *The Southwestern Chippewa, an Ethnohistorical Study*. American Anthropological Association Memoir No. 92.
1965 The Virginia Deer and Intertribal Buffer Zones in the Upper Mississippi Valley. In *Man, Culture, and Animals: The Role of Animals in Human Ecological Adjustments*, edited by Anthony Leeds and Andrew P. Vayda, pp. 43–65. AAAS Monograph.

Higgins, R. W., K. C. Mo, and Y. Yao
1998 Interannual Variability in the U.S.
Summer Precipitation Regime with Emphasis on the Southwestern Monsoon. *Journal of Climate* 5:2582–2606.

Hill, Carol W.
1989 Who Is What? A Preliminary Enquiry into Cultural and Physical Identity. In *Archaeological Approaches to Cultural Identity*, edited by Stephen J. Shennan, pp. 233–241. Unwin Hyman, London.

Hill, David V.
1998 Petrographic Analysis for Ceramics from the Ormand Site. In *The Ormand Village: Final Report on the 1965–1966 Excavation*, by L. T. Wallace, pp. 287–291. Archaeology Notes No. 229. Museum of New Mexico Office of Archaeological Studies, Santa Fe.

Hill, J. Brett
2000 Decision Making at the Margins: Settlement Trends, Temporal Scale, and Ecology in the Wadi at Hasa, West-Central Jordan. *Journal of Anthropological Archaeology* 19:221–241.

Hill, J. Brett, Jeffery J. Clark, William H. Doelle, and Patrick D. Lyons
2004 Prehistoric Demography in the Southwest: Migration, Coalescence, and Hohokam Population Decline. *American Antiquity* 69:689–716.

Hill, Jane H.
1996 The Prehistoric Differentiation of Uto-Aztecan Languages and the Lexicon of Early Southwestern Agriculture. Paper presented at the 61st Annual Meeting of the Society for American Archaeology, New Orleans.
2001 Proto-Uto-Aztecan: A Community of Cultivators in Central Mexico? *American Anthropologist* 103:913–934.
2002 Toward a Linguistic Prehistory of the Southwest: "Azteco-Tanoan" and the Arrival of Maize Cultivation. *Journal of Anthropological Research* 58:457–475.
2008 Northern Uto-Aztecan and Kiowa-Tanoan: Evidence for Contact between the Protolanguages? *International Journal of American Linguistics*, in press.

Hill, Jane, and Kelley A. Hays-Gilpin
1999 The Flower World in Material Culture: An Iconographic Complex in the Southwest and Mesoamerica. *Journal of Anthropological Research* 55:1037.

Hill, Jonathan D.
1996 Introduction: Ethnogenesis in the Americas, 1492–1992. In *History, Power and Identity: Ethnogenesis in the Americas, 1492–1992*, edited by Jonathan D. Hill, pp. 1–19. University of Iowa Press, Iowa City.

Hillier, Bill, and Julienne Hanson
1984 *The Social Logic of Space*. Cambridge University Press, Cambridge.

Hinsley, Curtis M., and Lea S. McChesney
1984 Anthropology as Cultural Exchange: The Shared Vision of Mary Hemenway and Frank Cushing. Paper presented at the joint meetings of the American Ethnological Society and the Southwestern Anthropological Association.

Hinsley, Curtis M., and David R. Wilcox (editors)
1995 A Hemenway Portfolio. *Journal of the Southwest* 37:517–744.
1996 *The Southwest in the American Imagination: The Writings of Sylvester Baxter, 1881–1889*. University of Arizona Press, Tucson.
2002 *The Lost Itinerary of Frank Hamilton Cushing*. University of Arizona Press, Tucson.

Hirschboeck, Katherine K.
1985 *Hydroclimatology of Flow Events in the Gila River Basin, Central and Southern Arizona*. PhD dissertation, Department of Geosciences, University of Arizona. University Microfilms, Ann Arbor.
1987 Hydroclimatically Defined Mixed Distributions in Partial Duration Flood Series. In *High Frequency Modeling*, edited by V. P. Singh, pp. 199–212. Reidel, Dordrecht.

Hodder, Ian
1979 Economic and Social Stress and Material Culture Patterning. *American Antiquity* 44:446–454.
1982a *Symbols in Action: Ethnoarchaeological Studies of Material Culture*. Cambridge University Press, Cambridge.
1982b Toward a Contextual Approach to Prehistoric Exchange. In *Contexts for Prehistoric Exchange*, edited by Jonathon E. Ericson and Timothy K. Earl, pp. 199–212. Academic Press, New York.

Hodge, Frederick Webb
1910 Shipapulima. In *Handbook of American Indians North of Mexico*, Pt. 2, edited by Frederick Webb Hodge, p. 551. Bulletin No. 30, Bureau of American Ethnology, Smithsonian Institution, Washington, D.C.
1921 *Turquoise Work of Hawikuh, New Mexico*. Leaflets of the Museum of the American Indian No. 2. Hyde Foundation, New York.

1923   Circular Kivas near Hawikuh. *Contributions of the Museum of the American Indian* 7(1):1–37.

1937   *History of Hawikuh, New Mexico: One of the So-Called Cities of Cíbola.* Museum of the American Indian, Heye Foundation, Los Angeles.

1955   Frederick Webb Hodge, Ethnologist, a Tape-recorded Interview (conducted by Corinne Gilb). Bound manuscript on file, Southwest Museum, Los Angeles.

Hoffecker, John F., W. Roger Powers, and Ted Goebel

1993   The Colonization of Beringia and the Peopling of the New World. *Science* 259:46–53.

Hogan, Patrick

1980   The Analysis of Human Coprolites from Cowboy Cave. In *Cowboy Cave,* edited by Jesse Jennings, pp. 201–211. University of Utah Anthropological Papers No. 104. University of Utah Press, Salt Lake City.

1985   Prehistoric Settlement Patterns in West-Central New Mexico: The Fence Lake Coal Lease Surveys. Prepared for the Salt River Project. UNM Proposal No. 185-211, New Mexico State Permit No. 83-017, Office of Contract Archeology, University of New Mexico, Albuquerque.

Holleran, Michael

1998   *Boston's "Changeful Times," Origins of Preservation and Planning in America.* Johns Hopkins University Press, Baltimore.

Holmes, Barbara E., and Andrew P. Fowler

1980   *The Alternate Dams Survey: An Archaeological Sample Survey and Evaluation of the Burned Timber and Coalmine Dams, Zuni Indian Reservation, McKinley County, New Mexico.* Zuni Archaeology Program, Zuni, New Mexico.

1985   *Mitigation of Adverse Effects to Cultural Resources to be Impacted by the Construction of the Oak Wash Dam on the Zuni Pueblo Watershed Project.* Zuni Archaeology Program Report No. 224a. Zuni, New Mexico.

Homburg, Jeffrey A.

2000   *Anthropogenic Influences on American Indian Agricultural Soils of the Southwestern United States.* PhD dissertation, Department of Soil Sciences, Iowa State University, Ames. University Microfilms, Ann Arbor.

Hopi Dictionary Project

1998   *Hopi Dictionary/Hopìikwa Lavàytutuveni.* University of Arizona Press, Tucson.

Hopi Tribe

2003   Kuwawata. Official Web Site of the Hopi Tribe. Electronic document, http://www.hopi.nsn.us, accessed October 1, 2001.

Hopkins, Nicholas A.

1965   Great Basin Prehistory and Uto-Aztecan. *American Antiquity* 31(1):48–60.

Hosler, Dorothy

1988a   Ancient West Mexican Metallurgy: South and Central American Origins and West Mexican Transformations. *American Anthropologist* 90:832–855.

1988b   Ancient West Mexico Metallurgy: A Technological Chronology. *Journal of Field Archaeology* 15:191–217.

Hough, Walter

1903   *Archaeological Field Work in Northeastern Arizona: The Museum-Gates Expedition of 1901.* Report of the U.S. National Museum, 1901. Smithsonian Institution, Washington, D.C.

1906   Sacred Springs in the Southwest. *Records of the Past* 5:164–169.

1907   *Antiquities of the Upper Gila and Salt River Valleys in Arizona and New Mexico.* Bulletin No. 35, Bureau of American Ethnology, Smithsonian Institution, Washington, D.C.

1914   *Culture of the Ancient Pueblos of the Upper Gila River Region, New Mexico and Arizona.* United States National Museum Bulletin 87. Washington, D.C.

Howard, Ann Valdo

1983   The Organization of Interregional Shell Production and Exchange within Southwestern Arizona. Unpublished Master's thesis, Department of Anthropology, Arizona State University, Tempe.

1985   A Reconstruction of Hohokam Interregional Shell Production and Exchange within Southwestern Arizona. In *Proceedings of the 1983 Hohokam Symposium,* edited by Alfred E. Dittert Jr. and Donald E. Dove, pp. 459–472. Occasional Paper No. 2. Phoenix Chapter, Arizona Archaeological Society, Phoenix.

Howard, E. B.

1932   Caves along the Slopes of the Guadalupe Mountains. *Bulletin of the Texas Archaeological and Paleontological Society* 4:7–19. Abilene.

1935   Evidence of Early Man in North America. *Museum Journal* 24(2–3):53–171. University Museum, University of Pennsylvania, Philadelphia.

Howell, Todd L.

1994a   The Decision-Making Structure of Protohistoric Zuni Society. In *Exploring Social, Political and Economic Organization in the Zuni Region,* edited by Todd L. Howell and Tammy Stone, pp. 61–90. Anthropological Research Papers No. 46. Arizona State University, Tempe.

1994b   *Leadership at the Ancestral Zuni Village of Hawikku.* PhD dissertation, Department of Anthropology, Arizona State University, Tempe. University Microfilms, Ann Arbor.

1995   Tracking Zuni Gender and Leadership Roles across the Contact Period. *Journal of Anthropological Research* 51:25–147.

2001   Foundations of Political Power in Ancestral Zuni Society. In *Ancient Burial Practices in the American Southwest: Archaeology, Physical Anthropology and Native American Perspectives,* edited by Douglas R. Mitchell and Judy L. Brunson-Hadley, pp. 149–166. University of New Mexico Press, Albuquerque.

Howell, Todd L., and Keith W. Kintigh

1996   Archaeological Identification of Kin Groups Using Mortuary and Biological Data: An Example from the American Southwest. *American Antiquity* 61:537–554.

Hoyt, Douglas, and Kenneth Schatten

1997   *The Role of the Sun in Climate Change.* Oxford University Press, Oxford.

Hrdlièka, Aleš

1925   The Origin and Antiquity of the American Indian. *Smithsonian Institution Annual Report for 1923,* pp. 481–494.

Huckell, Bruce B.

1984a   The Paleo-Indian and Archaic Occupations of the Tucson Basin: An Overview. *Kiva* 49:133–145.

1984b   *The Archaic Occupation of the Rosemont Area, Santa Rita Mountains, Southeastern Arizona.* Arizona State Museum Archaeological Series Vol. 147, No. 1. Arizona State Museum, Cultural Resource Management Division, Tucson.

1990   *Late Preceramic Farmer-Foragers in Southeastern Arizona: A Cultural and Ecological Consideration of the Spread of Agriculture into the Arid Southwestern*

United States. PhD dissertation, Department of Anthropology, University of Arizona, Tucson. University Microfilms, Ann Arbor.

1995 *Of Marshes and Maize: Preceramic Agricultural Settlements in the Cienega Valley, Southeastern Arizona.* Anthropological Papers of the University of Arizona No. 59. University of Arizona Press, Tucson.

1996 The Archaic Prehistory of the North American Southwest. *Journal of World Prehistory* 10:305–373.

2001 The First 10,000 Years in the Southwest. Paper presented at the 100th Annual Meeting of the American Anthropological Association, Washington, D.C.

2005 The First 10,000 Years in the Southwest. In *Southwest Archaeology in the Twentieth Century*, edited by Linda S. Cordell and Don D. Fowler, pp. 142–156. University of Utah Press, Salt Lake City.

Huckell, Bruce B., and Lisa Huckell

1984 Excavations at Milagro, a Late Archaic Site in the Eastern Tucson Basin. Report on file, Arizona State Museum, Tucson.

Huckell, Bruce B., Lisa Huckell, and Suzanne K. Fish

1995 *Investigations at Milagro, a Late Preceramic Site in the Eastern Tucson Basin.* Technical Report No. 94-5. Center for Desert Archaeology, Tucson, Arizona.

Huckell, Bruce, Lisa W. Huckell, and M. Steven Shackley

1999 McEuen Cave. *Archaeology Southwest* 13(1):12.

Huckell, Lisa W.

1976 Analysis of the Shell Remains from the Rabid Ruin, Arizona. Unpublished manuscript on file, Arizona State Museum Archives, University of Arizona, Tucson.

2000 Paleoethnobotany. In *A Highway through Time: Archaeological Investigations along NM 90*, Vol. 1, edited by Christopher A. Turnbow, pp. 509–564. TRC Inc., Technical Series No. 2000-3. New Mexico Highway and Transportation Department, Albuquerque.

Huddleston, Lee E.

1967 *Origins of American Indians: European Concepts, 1492–1729.* University of Texas Press, Austin.

Hudson, Charles

2002 Introduction. In *The Transformation of the Southeastern Indians, 1540–1760*, edited by Robbie Ethridge and Charles Hudson, pp. xi–xxxix. University Press of Mississippi, Jackson.

Hudson, Luanne Brandenburg

1978 *A Quantitative Analysis of Prehistoric Exchange in the Southwest United States.* PhD dissertation, Department of Anthropology, University of California, Los Angeles. University Microfilms, Ann Arbor.

Hunter-Anderson, Rosalind L.

1978 *An Archaeological Survey of the Yellowhouse Dam Area, Zuni Indian Reservation, New Mexico.* Office of Contract Archeology, University of New Mexico. Albuquerque.

1979 Observations on the Changing Role of Small Structural Sites in the Northern Rio Grande. In *Adaptive Change in the Northern Rio Grande Valley*, edited by Jan V. Biella and Richard C. Chapman, pp. 177–186. Archeological Investigations in Cochiti Reservoir, Vol. 4. Office of Contract Archeology, University of New Mexico, Albuquerque.

Huntington, Ellsworth

1914 *The Climatic Factor as Illustrated in Arid America.* Carnegie Institution of Washington, Washington, D.C.

1915 *Civilization and Climate.* Yale University Press, New Haven.

1924 *The Character of Race as Influenced by Physical Environment, Natural Selection and Historical Development.* C. Scribner's Sons, New York.

Huntley, Deborah L.

2004 *Interaction, Boundaries, and Identities: A Multiscalar Approach to the Organizational Scale of Pueblo IV Zuni Society.* PhD dissertation, Department of Anthropology, Arizona State University, Tempe. University Microfilms, Ann Arbor.

Huntley, Deborah L., and Keith W. Kintigh

2004 Archaeological Patterning and Organizational Scale of Late Prehistoric Settlement Clusters in the Zuni Region of New Mexico. In *The Protohistoric Pueblo World, AD 1275–1600*, edited by E. Charles Adams and Andrew I. Duff, pp. 62–64. University of Arizona Press, Tucson.

Hutt, Sherry

2004 Cultural Property Law Theory: A Comparative Assessment of Contemporary Thought. In *Legal Perspectives on Cultural Resources*, edited by Jennifer R. Richman and Marion P. Forsyth, pp. 2–16. AltaMira Press, Walnut Creek, California.

Hyland, David C.

1997 *Perishable Industries from the Jornada Basin, South-Central New Mexico.* PhD dissertation, University of Pittsburgh, Pittsburgh. University Microfilms, Ann Arbor.

Hyland, D. C., and J. M. Adovasio

2000 The Mexican Connection: A Study of Sociotechnical Change in Perishable Manufacture and Food Production in Prehistoric New Mexico. In *Beyond Cloth and Cordage: Archaeological Textile Research in the Americas*, edited by Penelope B. Drooker and Laurie D. Webster, pp. 141–159. University of Utah Press, Salt Lake City.

Iltis, Hugh H.

1983 From Teosinte to Maize: The Catastrophic Sexual Transformation. *Science* 222:886–894.

1987 Maize Evolution and Agricultural Origins. In *Grass, Systematics and Evolution*, edited by Thomas R. Soderstrom, Khidir W. Hilu, Christopher S. Campbell, and Mary E. Barkworth, pp. 195–213. Smithsonian Institution Press, Washington, D.C.

2000 Homeotic Sexual Translocations and the Origin of Maize (*Zea mays*, Poaceae): A New Look at an Old Problem. *Economic Botany* 54:7–42.

Ingram, M. J., G. Farmer, and T. M. L. Wigley

1981 Past Climates and Their Impact on Man: A Review. In *Climate and History: Studies in Past Climates and Their Impact on Man*, edited by T. M. L. Wigley, M. J. Ingram, and G. Farmer, pp. 3–50. Cambridge University Press, Cambridge.

Irwin-Williams, Cynthia

1967a Picosa: The Elementary Southwestern Culture. *American Antiquity* 32:441–457.

1967b Prehistoric Cultural and Linguistic Patterns in the Southwest since 5000 BC. Paper presented at the 32nd Annual Meeting of the Society for American Archaeology, Ann Arbor, Michigan.

1968 Archaic Culture History in the Southwestern United States. In *Early Man in Western North America: Symposium of the Society for American Archaeology*, edited by Cynthia Irwin-Williams, pp. 48–54. Eastern New Mexico Contributions in Anthropology 1(4).

1973   *The Oshara Tradition: Origins of Anasazi Culture.* Contributions in Anthropology Vol. 5, No. 1. Eastern New Mexico University, Portales.

1979   Post-Pleistocene Archaeology, 7000–2000 BC. In *Southwest*, edited by Alfonso Ortiz, pp. 31–42. Handbook of North American Indians, Vol. 9, William C. Sturtevant, general editor, Smithsonian Institution, Washington, D.C.

1994   The Archaic of the Southwestern United States: Changing Goals and Research Strategies in the Last Twenty-Five Years 1964–1989. In *Archaic Hunter-Gatherer Archaeology in the American Southwest*, edited by Bradley J. Vierra, pp. 566–670. Contributions in Anthropology Vol. 13, No. 1. Eastern New Mexico University, Portales.

Irwin-Williams, Cynthia (editor)

1968   *Archaic Prehistory in the Western United States: Symposium of the Society for American Archaeology.* Eastern New Mexico Contributions in Anthropology Vol. 1, No. 3. Santa Fe.

Irwin-Williams, Cynthia, and C. Vance Haynes Jr.

1970   Climatic Change and Early Population Dynamics in Southwestern United States. *Quaternary Research* 1:59–71.

Jacoby, Gordon C.

1987   Dendrochronological Investigation of the Zuni Indian Reservation. Defendant's Exhibit 14,000. Expert testimony submitted to the United States Claims Court as evidence in the case *Zuni Indian Tribe v. United States*, Docket 327-81L.

James, Steven R.

1995   Hunting and Fishing Patterns at Prehistoric Sites along the Salt River: The Archaeofaunal Analysis. In *Paleobotanical and Osteological Analyses*, edited by Mark D. Elson and Jeffery J. Clark, pp. 85–168. The Roosevelt Community Development Study, Vol. 3. Anthropological Papers No. 14. Center for Desert Archaeology, Tucson, Arizona.

Jemez Pueblo

2003   History of the Pueblo of Jemez. Electronic document, http://www .jemezpueblo.org, accessed August 15, 2003.

Jenkins, Richard

1996   *Social Identity.* Routledge, London.

Jennings, Jesse D.

1956   The American Southwest: A Problem in Cultural Isolation. *Society for American Archaeology Memoir* 11:59–127.

1964   The Desert West. In *Prehistoric Man in the New World*, edited by Jesse D. Jennings and E. Norbeck, pp. 149–174. University of Chicago Press, Chicago.

1980   *Cowboy Cave.* University of Utah Anthropological Papers No. 104. University of Utah Press, Salt Lake City.

Jennings, Jesse, A. R. Schroedl, and R. N. Holmer

1980   *Sudden Shelter.* University of Utah Anthropological Papers No. 103. University of Utah Press, Salt Lake City.

Jernigan, E. Wesley

1978   *Jewelry of the Prehistoric Southwest.* School of American Research Southwest Indian Arts Series. School of American Research, Santa Fe, and University of New Mexico Press, Albuquerque.

Jett, Stephen C., and Peter B. Moyle

1986   The Exotic Origins of Fishes Depicted on Prehistoric Mimbres Pottery from New Mexico. *American Antiquity* 51:688–720.

Jewett, Roberta A.

1989   Distance, Integration, and Complexity: The Spatial Organization of Pan-regional Settlement Clusters in the American Southwest. In *The Sociopolitical Structure of Prehistoric Southwestern Societies*, edited by Steadman Upham, Kent G. Lightfoot, and Roberta A. Jewett, pp. 363–388. Westview Press, Boulder.

Johnson, Alfred E.

1965   Turkey Creek Site: Excavations 1958–1960. Manuscript on file, Arizona State Museum, Archives #A-0855.

Johnson, Irmgard Weitlander

1971   Basketry and Textiles. In *Archaeology of Northern Mesoamerica, Part 1*, edited by Gordon F. Ekholm and Ignacio Bermal, pp. 297–321. Handbook of Middle American Indians, Vol. 10, Robert Wauchope, general editor. University of Texas Press, Austin.

Jones, Bruce A.

1994   Assessing the Nature of Aboriginal Nonriverine Occupation in the Lechuguilla Desert, Southwestern Arizona. In *Recent Research along the Lower Colorado River*, edited by Joseph A. Ezzo, pp. 127–147. Statistical Research Technical Series No. 51. Statistical Research, Inc., Tucson, Arizona.

Jones, Siân

1997   *The Archaeology of Ethnicity: Constructing Identities in the Past and the Present.* Routledge, New York.

Jones, Terry L., Gary M. Brown, L. Mark Raab, Janet L. McVickar, W. Geoffrey Spaulding, Douglas J. Kennett, Andrew York, and Phillip L. Walker

1999   Environmental Imperatives Reconsidered: Demographic Crises in Western North America during the Medieval Climatic Anomaly. *Current Anthropology* 40:137–170.

Judd, Neil M.

1926   *Archeological Observations North of the Rio Colorado.* Bulletin No. 82, Bureau of American Ethnology, Smithsonian Institution, Washington, D.C.

1954   *The Material Culture of Pueblo Bonito.* Smithsonian Miscellaneous Collections Vol. 124. Smithsonian Institution, Washington, D.C.

Judge, W. James

1973   *Paleo-Indian Occupation of the Central Rio Grande Valley in New Mexico.* University of New Mexico Press, Albuquerque.

1979   The Development of a Complex Cultural Ecosystem in the Chaco Basin, New Mexico. In *Proceedings of the First Conference on Scientific Research in the National Parks, Vol. I*, edited by R. M. Linn, pp. 901–905. USDI National Park Service, Transaction and Proceedings Series 5. Washington, D.C.

1982   The Paleo-Indian and Basketmaker Periods: An Overview and Some Research Problems. In *The San Juan Tomorrow*, edited by Fred Plog and W. Wait, pp. 5–57. USDI National Park Service, Southwest Region, Santa Fe.

1989   Chaco Canyon–San Juan Basin. In *Dynamics of Southwestern Prehistory*, edited by Linda Cordell and George Gumerman, pp. 209–262. Smithsonian Institution, Washington, D.C.

Kabotie, Fred

1982   *Designs from the Ancient Mimbreños with a Hopi Interpretation.* Northland Press, Flagstaff.

Kaldahl, Eric J., and Jeffrey S. Dean

1999   Climate, Vegetation, and Dendrochronology. In *Living on the Edge of the Rim: Excavations and Analysis of the Silver Creek Archaeological Research Project 1993–1998*, edited by Barbara J. Mills, Sarah A. Herr, and Scott Van Keuren, pp. 11–29. Arizona State Museum Archaeological Series 192. University of Arizona, Tucson.

Kaldahl, Eric J., Scott Van Keuren, and Barbara J. Mills
2004 Migration, Factionalism, and the Trajectories of Pueblo IV Period Clusters in the Mogollon Rim Region. In *The Protohistoric Pueblo World, AD 1275–1600*, edited by E. Charles Adams and Andrew I. Duff, pp. 85–94. University of Arizona Press, Tucson.

Kamp, Kathryn A., and Norman Yoffee
1980 Ethnicity in Ancient Western Asia during the Early Second Millennium BC: Archaeological Assessments and Ethnoarchaeological Prospectives. *Bulletin of the American Schools of Oriental Research* 237:85–103.

Kantner, John, and Nancy M. Mahoney (editors)
2000 *Great House Communities across the Chacoan Landscape*. Anthropological Papers of the University of Arizona No. 64. University of Arizona Press, Tucson.

Karlstrom, Thor N. V.
1988 Alluvial Chronology and Hydrologic Change of Black Mesa and Nearby Regions. In *The Anasazi in a Changing Environment*, edited by George J. Gumerman, pp. 45–91. Cambridge University Press, Cambridge.

Kayser, David W.
1972a *Whiskey Creek Project: Archaeological Highway Salvage along State Highway 32 in Apache Creek Valley, Catron County, New Mexico*. Laboratory of Anthropology Notes No. 57. Museum of New Mexico, Santa Fe.
1972b *Armijo Springs Project: Archaeological Salvage in the Harris Creek Valley Area of the Gallo Mountains*. Laboratory of Anthropology Notes No. 56. Museum of New Mexico, Santa Fe.
1972c *Gallita Springs Project: Archaeological Exploration and Salvage in the Gallo Mountains, Apache National Forest, Catron County, New Mexico*. Laboratory of Anthropology Notes No. 69. Museum of New Mexico, Santa Fe.
1975 *The Mesa Top Mogollon: A Report on the Excavations at Gallita Springs, Gallo Mountains, Gila National Forest, Catron County, New Mexico*. Laboratory of Anthropology Notes No. 113. Museum of New Mexico, Santa Fe.

Kayser, David W., and Charles Carroll
1988 *Report of the Final Field Season—San Augustine Coal Area*. Archaeological Investigations in West-Central New Mexico, Bureau of Land Management Cultural Resource Series Monograph 5. Santa Fe.

Kean, William L.
1965 Marine Mollusks and Aboriginal Trade in the Southwest. *Plateau* 38(1):17–31.

Kearns, Timothy M., and Janet L. McVickar
1996 Time, Place, and Society: Project Synthesis. Pipeline Archaeology 1990–1993: The El Paso Natural Gas North System Expansion Project, New Mexico and Arizona, Vol. 13. Draft submitted to Western Cultural Resource Management, Inc., Farmington, New Mexico.

Keeley, Lawrence H.
1995 Protoagricultural Practices among Hunter-Gatherers: A Cross-Cultural Survey. In *Last Hunters—First Farmers, New Perspectives on the Prehistoric Transition to Agriculture*, edited by T. Douglas Price and Anne Birgitte Gebauer, pp. 243–272. School of American Research Press, Santa Fe.

Keen, A. Myra
1971 *Sea Shells of Tropical West America; Marine Mollusks from Baja California to Peru*. 2nd ed. Stanford University Press, Stanford.

Kelley, J. Charles, and Ellen Abbott Kelley
1975 An Alternative Hypothesis for the Explanation of Anasazi Culture History. In *Collected Papers in Honor of Florence Hawley Ellis*, edited by Theodore R. Frisbie, pp. 178–223. Papers of the Archaeological Society of New Mexico. Archaeological Society of New Mexico, Santa Fe, New Mexico.

Kelley, Jane H.
1984 *The Archaeology of the Sierra Blanca Region of Southeastern New Mexico*. Anthropological Papers No. 74. University of Michigan, Ann Arbor.

Kelly, Dorothea S.
1937 McEuen Cave Report. Unpublished draft report. Folder A-164, Arizona State Museum Archives, Tucson.

Kelly, Robert L.
1995 *The Foraging Spectrum: Diversity in Hunter-Gatherer Lifeways*. Smithsonian Institution Press, Washington, D.C.

Kendrick, James W.
2000 Cibolan Basketmaker II Economy: Implications for Early Agriculture on the Colorado Plateau. Paper presented at the Annual Meeting of the Society for American Archaeology, Philadelphia.

Kent, Kate Peck
1957 The Cultivation and Weaving of Cotton in the Prehistoric Southwestern United States. *Transactions of the American Philosophical Society*, n.s. 47(3): 455–732. Philadelphia.
1983 *Prehistoric Textiles of the Southwest*. School of American Research Press, Santa Fe.

Kent, Susan
1990 Segmentation, Architecture, and Space. In *Domestic Architecture and the Use of Space*, edited by Susan Kent, pp. 127–152. Cambridge University Press, Cambridge.

Kerr, Richard
1999 El Niño Grew Strong as Cultures Were Born. *Science* 283:467–468.

Kessell, John L., and Rick Hendricks (editors)
1992 *By Force of Arms: The Journals of Don Diego de Vargas, 1691–1693*. University of New Mexico Press, Albuquerque.

Kidder, Alfred V.
1916 The Pottery of Casas Grandes District, Chihuahua. In *The Holmes Anniversary Volume: Anthropological Essays*, pp. 253–268. Privately printed, Washington, D.C.
1924 *An Introduction to the Study of Southwestern Archaeology, with a Preliminary Account of the Excavations at Pecos*. Papers of the Phillips Academy Southwestern Expedition 1. Yale University Press, New Haven.
1927 Southwestern Archeological Conference. *Science* 68:489–491.
1932 *The Artifacts of Pecos*. Papers of the Phillips Academy Southwestern Expedition 6. Yale University Press, New Haven.
1936 Speculations on New World Prehistory. In *Essays in Anthropology: Presented to A. L. Kroeber in Celebration of His Sixtieth Birthday, June 11, 1936*, edited by Robert H. Lowie, pp. 143–151. University of California Press, Berkeley.
1957 Unpublished Memoirs, 3 vols. Harvard University, Peabody Museum Archives, Cambridge.
1958 *Pecos, New Mexico: Archaeological Notes*. Papers of the Robert S. Peabody Foundation for Archaeology No. 5. Andover, Massachusetts.
1962 *An Introduction to the Study of Southwestern Archaeology*. Yale University Press, New Haven. Originally published 1924.

Kidder, Alfred Vincent, Harriet S. Cosgrove, and C. Burton Cosgrove

1949 The Pendleton Ruin, Hidalgo County, New Mexico. Carnegie Institution of Washington Publication 585. *Contributions to American Anthropology and History* 50:107–152.

Kidder, Alfred V., and Samuel J. Guernsey

1919 *Archaeological Explorations in Northeastern Arizona.* Bulletin No. 65, Bureau of American Ethnology, Smithsonian Institution, Washington, D.C.

Kidwell, Clara Sue

1999 Every Last Dishcloth: The Prodigious Collecting of George Gustav Heye. In *Collecting Native America, 1870–1960,* edited by Shepard Krech III and Barbara A. Hail, pp. 232–258. Smithsonian Institution Press, Washington, D.C.

Kiladis, George N., and Henry F. Diaz

1989 Global Climatic Anomalies Associated with Extremes in the Southern Oscillation. *Journal of Climate* 2:1069–1090.

King, Mary Elizabeth

1974 Medio Period Perishable Artifacts. In *Bone-Economy-Burials,* by Charles C. Di Peso, John B. Rinaldo, and Gloria J. Fenner, pp. 76–119. Casas Grandes: A Fallen Trading Center of the Gran Chichimeca, Vol. 8. Amerind Foundation Series No. 9. Amerind Foundation, Inc., Dragoon, and Northland Press, Flagstaff.

King, Thomas F.

2003 *Places That Count: Traditional Cultural Properties in Cultural Resources Management.* AltaMira Press, Walnut Creek, California.

Kintigh, Keith W.

1980 *Archaeological Clearance Investigation of the Miller Canyon and Southeastern Boundary Fencing Projects, Zuni Indian Reservation, New Mexico.* Zuni Archaeology Program, Pueblo of Zuni, New Mexico.

1982 An Outline for a Chronology of Zuni Ruins, Revisited: Sixty-five Years of Repeated Analysis and Collection. In *The Research Potential of Anthropological Museum Collections,* edited by Anne-Marie Cantwell, James B. Griffin, and Nan A. Rothschild. Annals of the New York Academy of Sciences 376:467–487.

1985 *Settlement, Subsistence, and Society in Late Zuni Prehistory.* Anthropological Papers of the University of Arizona No. 44. University of Arizona Press, Tucson.

1994 Chaco, Communal Architecture, and Cibolan Aggregation. In *The Ancient Southwestern Community,* edited by Wirt H. Wills and Robert D. Leonard, pp. 131–140. University of New Mexico Press, Albuquerque.

1996 The Cibola Region in the Post-Chacoan Era. In *The Prehistoric Pueblo World, AD 1150–1350,* edited by Michael A. Adler, pp. 131–144. University of Arizona Press, Tucson.

2000 Leadership Strategies in Protohistoric Zuni Towns. In *Alternative Leadership Strategies in the Prehispanic Southwest,* edited by Barbara J. Mills, pp. 95–116. University of Arizona Press, Tucson.

2003 Coming to Terms with the Chaco World. *Kiva* 69:93–116.

Kintigh, Keith W., and Andrew I. Duff

1993 The Changing Face of Community: Patterns from the Zuni River Drainage. Paper presented at the 58th Annual Meeting of the Society for American Archaeology, St. Louis.

Kintigh, Keith W., Donna M. Glowacki, and Deborah L. Huntley

2004 Long-Term Settlement History and the Emergence of Towns in the Zuni Area. *American Antiquity* 69:432–456.

Kintigh, Keith W., Todd L. Howell, and Andrew I. L. Duff

1996 Post-Chacoan Social Integration at the Hinkson Site, New Mexico. *Kiva* 61:257–274.

Kirch, Patrick V.

1994 *The Wet and the Dry: Irrigation and Agricultural Intensification in Polynesia.* University of Chicago Press, Chicago.

Kirch, Patrick V., and Marshall D. Sahlins

1992 *Anahulu: The Anthropology of History in the Kingdom of Hawaii.* Vol. 2. University of Chicago Press, Chicago.

Kirchoff, Paul

1954 Gatherers and Farmers in the Greater Southwest: A Problem in Classification. *American Anthropologist* 56:529–550.

Kissell, Mary Lois

1916 *Basketry of the Papago and Pima Indians.* Anthropological Papers Vol. 17, Pt. 4. American Museum of Natural History, New York.

Koepping, K. L.

1983 *Adolph Bastian and the Psychic Unity of Mankind.* University of Queensland Press, St. Lucia, Australia.

Kohler, Timothy A., Matthew W. Van Pelt, and Lorene Y. L. Yap

2000 Reciprocity and Its Limits: Considerations for a Study of the Prehispanic Pueblo World. In *Alternative Leadership Strategies in the Prehispanic Southwest,* edited by Barbara J. Mills, pp. 180–206. University of Arizona Press, Tucson.

Kowalewski, Stephen A.

2001 Coalescent Societies. Paper presented at the Southeastern Archaeological Conference, Chattanooga, Tennessee.

2003a Scale and the Explanation of Demographic Change: 3,500 Years in the Valley of Oaxaca. *American Anthropologist* 105:313–325.

2003b Intensification under Duress. Paper presented at the 68th Annual Meeting of the Society for American Archaeology, Milwaukee.

2004 The New Past: From Region to Macroregion. *Social Evolution & History* 3(1):81–105.

2006 Coalescent Societies. In *Light on the Path: Essays in the Anthropology and History of the Southeastern Indians,* edited by Thomas J. Pluckhahn and Robbie Ethridge. University of Alabama Press, Tuscaloosa.

Kozuch, Laura

2002 *Olivella* Beads from Spiro and the Plains. *American Antiquity* 67:697–709.

Kramer, Carol

1977 Pots and People. In *Mountains and Lowlands: Essays in the Archaeology of Greater Mesopotamia,* edited by L. D. Levine and T. C. Young Jr., pp. 91–112. Undena, Malibu.

Krantz, Grover S.

1977 *The Populating of Western North America.* Society for California Archaeology Occasional Papers in Method and Theory in California No. 1. Chico.

Kremenetski, C. V., L. D. Sulershitsky, and R. Hantemirov

1998 Holocene History of the Northern Range Limits of Some Trees and Shrubs in Russia. *Arctic and Alpine Research* 30:317–333.

Krieger, Alex D.

1953 New World Culture History: Anglo-America. In *Anthropology Today, an Encyclopedic Inventory,* assembled by A. L. Kroeber, pp. 238–264. University of Chicago Press, Chicago.

Kroeber, Alfred L.

1916 *Zuni Potsherds.* Anthropological Papers Vol. 18, Pt. 1, pp. 1–37. American Museum of Natural History, New York.

1917 *Zuni Kin and Clan.* Anthropological Papers Vol. 18, Pt. 2, pp. 39–204. American Museum of Natural History, New York.

Kroskrity, Paul W.

1993 *Language, History, and Identity: Ethnolinguistic Studies of the Arizona Tewa.* University of Arizona Press, Tucson.

1998 Arizona Tewa Kiva Speech as a Manifestation of a Dominant Language Ideology. In *Language Ideologies: Practice and Theory,* edited by Bambi B. Schieffelin, Kathryn A. Woolard, and Paul W. Kroskrity, pp. 103–122. Oxford Studies in Anthropological Linguistics No. 16. Oxford University Press, Oxford.

Ladd, Edmund J.

1979a Zuni Social and Political Organization. In *Southwest,* edited by Alfonso Ortiz, pp. 482–491. Handbook of North American Indians, Vol. 9, William C. Sturtevant, general editor, Smithsonian Institution, Washington, D.C.

1979b Zuni Economy. In *Southwest,* edited by Alfonso Ortiz, pp. 492–498. Handbook of North American Indians, Vol. 9, William G. Sturtevant, general editor, Smithsonian Institution, Washington, D.C.

1983 Pueblo Use of High Altitude Areas: Emphasis on the A:shiwi. In *High Altitude Adaptations in the Southwest,* edited by Joseph C. Winter, pp. 168–188. Cultural Resources Management Report 2. USDA Forest Service, Southwestern Region, Albuquerque.

1995 Achieving True Interpretation. In *Zuni and the Courts,* edited by E. Richard Hart, pp. 231–234. University Press of Kansas, Lawrence.

2001 Avifaunal Usage among the Zuni. In *Southwest Birds of Sacrifice,* by Charmion R. McKusick, pp. 11–13. Arizona Archaeologist No. 31. Arizona Archaeological Society, Phoenix.

LaMarche, Valmore C., Jr.

1973 Holocene Climatic Variations Inferred from Treeline Fluctuations in the White Mountains, California. *Quaternary Research* 3:632–660.

LaMarche, Valmore C., Jr., and Katherine K. Hirschboeck

1984 Frost Rings in Trees as Records of Major Volcanic Eruptions. *Nature* 307:121–126.

LaMarche, Valmore C., Jr., and H. A. Mooney

1967 Altithermal Timberline Advance in Western United States. *Nature* 213:908–982.

Lamb, Hubert H.

1995 *Climate, History, and the Modern World.* 2nd ed. Routledge, London.

Lamb, Sydney M.

1958 Linguistic Prehistory in the Great Basin. *International Journal of American Linguistics* 24:95–100.

1964 The Classification of the Uto-Aztecan Languages: A Historical Survey. In *Studies in California Linguistics,* edited by William Bright, pp. 106–125. University of California Publications in Linguistics 34. Berkeley.

Lambert, Marjorie F., and J. Richard Ambler

1961 *A Survey and Excavation of Caves in Hidalgo County, New Mexico.* School of American Research Monograph 25, Santa Fe.

Lancaster, James

1984 Groundstone Artifacts. In *The Galaz Ruin: A Prehistoric Mimbres Village in Southwestern New Mexico,* edited by Roger Anyon and Steven A. LeBlanc, pp. 247–262. University of New Mexico Press, Albuquerque.

Lang, Richard W.

1982 Transformation in White Ware Pottery of the Northern Rio Grande. In *Southwestern Ceramics: A Comparative Review: A School of American Research Advanced Seminar,* edited by Albert H. Schroeder, pp. 152–200. Arizona Archaeologist No. 15. Arizona Archaeological Society, Phoenix.

Lang, Richard W., and Arthur H. Harris

1984 *The Faunal Remains from Arroyo Hondo Pueblo, New Mexico: A Study in Short-Term Subsistence Change.* Arroyo Hondo Archaeological Series Vol. 5. School of American Research Press, Santa Fe.

Lawrence, Denise L., and Setha M. Low

1990 The Built Environment and Spatial Form. *Annual Review of Anthropology* 19:453–505.

Leach, E. R.

1954 *Political Systems of Highland Burma.* Beacon Press, Boston.

LeBlanc, Steven A.

1975 Micro-seriation: A Method for Fine Chronological Differentiation. *American Antiquity* 40:22–38.

1976 Temporal and Ceramic Relationships between Some Late PIII Sites in the Zuni Area. *Plateau* 48:75–84.

1978 Settlement Patterns in the El Morro Valley, New Mexico. In *Investigations of the Southwestern Anthropological Research Group,* edited by Robert Euler and George Gumerman, pp. 45–52. Museum of Northern Arizona, Flagstaff.

1982a Temporal Change in Mogollon Ceramics. In *Southwestern Ceramics: A Comparative Review,* edited by Albert H. Schroeder, pp. 106–127. Arizona Archaeologist No. 15. Arizona Archaeological Society, Phoenix.

1982b The Advent of Pottery in the Southwest. In *Southwestern Ceramics: A Comparative Review,* edited by Albert H. Shroeder, pp. 27–51. Arizona Archaeologist No. 15. Arizona Archeological Society, Phoenix.

1983 *The Mimbres People: Ancient Pueblo Painters of the American Southwest.* Thames and Hudson, New York.

1986 Development of Archaeological Thought on the Mimbres Mogollon. In *Emil W. Haury's Prehistory of the American Southwest,* edited by J. Jefferson Reid and David E. Doyel, pp. 297–304. University of Arizona Press, Tucson.

1989 Cibola. In *Dynamics of Southwest Prehistory,* edited by Linda S. Cordell and George J. Gumerman, pp. 337–370. Smithsonian Institution Press, Washington, D.C.

1999 *Prehistoric Warfare in the American Southwest.* University of Utah Press, Salt Lake City.

2001 Warfare and Aggregation in the El Morro Valley, New Mexico. In *Deadly Landscapes: Case Studies in Prehistoric Southwestern Warfare,* edited by Glen E. Rice and Steven A. LeBlanc, pp. 19–50. University of Utah Press, Salt Lake City.

LeBlanc, Steven A., and Michael W. Whalen

1980 An Archaeological Synthesis of South-Central and Southwestern New Mexico. Submitted to the U.S. Bureau of Land Management, Albuquerque.

Lechtman, Heather

1977 Style in Technology—Some Early Thoughts. In *Material Culture: Styles, Organization, and Dynamics of Technology,* edited by Heather Lechtman and

Robert Merrill, pp. 3–20. West Publishing, New York.

Lehmer, D. J.
1948 *The Jornada Branch of the Mogollon.* University of Arizona Bulletin Vol. 19, No. 2 (Social Science Bulletin No. 17). Tucson.

Leighton, Dorothea C., and John Adair
1966 *People of the Middle Place: A Study of the Zuni Indians.* Human Relations Area Files Press, New Haven.

Lekson, Stephen H.
1986 The Mimbres Region. In *Mogollon Variability*, edited by Charlotte Benson and Steadman Upham, pp. 141–146. University Museum Occasional Papers 15, New Mexico State University, Las Cruces.
1988 The Idea of the Kiva in Anasazi Archaeology. *Kiva* 53:213–234.
1990a *Mimbres Archaeology of the Upper Gila, New Mexico.* Anthropological Papers of the University of Arizona No. 53. University of Arizona Press, Tucson.
1990b Ceramic Analysis. In *Archaeological Studies along the Arizona Interconnection Project Transmission Corridor: Synthetic Survey Report*, prepared by Andrew Fowler, pp. 90–107. Zuni Archaeology Program Report No. 293, Research Series No. 5. Pueblo of Zuni, New Mexico.
1991 Settlement Patterns and the Chaco Region. In *Chaco & Hohokam: Prehistoric Regional Systems in the American Southwest*, edited by Patricia L. Crown and W. James Judge, pp. 31–56. School of American Research, Santa Fe.
1992 Salado of the East. In *Proceedings of the Second Salado Conference, Globe, Arizona, 1992*, edited by Richard C. Lange and Stephen Germick, pp. 17–22. Arizona Archaeological Society Occasional Papers. Phoenix.
1996 Southwestern New Mexico and Southeastern Arizona, AD 900–1300. In *The Prehistoric Pueblo World, AD 1150–1350*, edited by Michael A. Adler, pp. 170–176. University of Arizona Press, Tucson.
1999 *The Chaco Meridian: Centers of Political Power in the Ancient Southwest.* AltaMira Press, Walnut Creek, California.
2000 Salado in Chihuahua. In *Salado*, edited by Jeffrey S. Dean, pp. 275–295. Amerind Foundation New World Study Series No. 4. University of New Mexico Press, Albuquerque.

2005 Complexity. In *Southwest Archaeology in the Twentieth Century*, edited by Linda S. Cordell and Don D. Fowler, pp. 157–173. University of Utah Press, Salt Lake City.

Lemonnier, Pierre
1986 The Study of Material Culture Today: Towards an Anthropology of Technical Systems. *Journal of Anthropological Archaeology* 5:147–186.
1993 Introduction. In *Technical Choices: Transformations in Material Cultures since the Neolithic*, edited by Pierre Lemonnier, pp. 1–35. Routledge, New York.

Leonard, Robert D.
1989 Resource Specialization, Population Growth, and Agricultural Production in the American Southwest. *American Antiquity* 54:491–503.

Leonard, Robert D., and George T. Jones
1987 Elements of an Inclusive Model for Archaeology. *Journal of Anthropological Archaeology* 6:199–219.

Leonard, Robert D., and Heidi E. Reed
1993 Population Aggregation in the Prehistoric American Southwest: A Selectionist Model. *American Antiquity* 58:648–661.

Lévi-Strauss, Claude
1966 *The Savage Mind.* University of Chicago Press, Chicago.
1967 *Structural Anthropology*, translated by Claire Jacobson and Brooke Grundfest Schoepf. Anchor Books, Garden City, New York.
1978 *Myth and Meaning.* Routledge, London.

Lewis, R. Berry, and Charles Stout
1998 The Design of Mississippian Towns. In *Mississippian Towns and Sacred Spaces: Searching for an Architectural Grammar*, edited by R. Barry Lewis and Charles Stout, pp. 64–92. University of Alabama Press, Tuscaloosa.

Lewis-Williams, J. David, and Thomas A. Dowson
1988 The Signs of the Times: Entoptic Phenomena and Upper Paleolithic Art. *Current Anthropology* 29:201–245.

Lightfoot, Dale R.
1993 The Landscape Context of Anasazi Pebble-Mulched Fields in the Galisteo Basin, Northern New Mexico. *Geoarchaeology* 8:349–370.

Lightfoot, Kent G.
1984 *The Duncan Project: A Study of the Occupation Duration and Settlement*

of an Early Mogollon Pithouse Village. Anthropological Field Studies No. 11. Office of Cultural Resource Management, Department of Anthropology, Arizona State University, Tempe.

Lindsay, Alexander Johnston, Jr.
1987 Anasazi Population Movements to Southern Arizona. *American Archaeology* 6(3):190–198.

Lindsay, Alexander Johnston, Jr., Richard Ambler, Mary Anne Stein, and Philip M. Hobler
1968 *Survey and Excavations North and East of Navajo Mountain, Utah, 1959–1962.* Museum of Northern Arizona Bulletin No. 45. Glen Canyon Series No. 8. Northern Arizona Society of Science and Art, Inc., Flagstaff.

Lindstrom, S.
1990 Submerged Tree Stumps as Indicators of Mid-Holocene Aridity in the Lake Tahoe Region. *Journal of California and Great Basin Anthropology* 12:146–157.

Linse, Angela R.
1999 *Settlement Change Documentation and Analysis: A Case Study from the Mogollon Region of the American Southwest (New Mexico).* PhD dissertation. Department of Anthropology, University of Washington, Seattle. University Microfilms, Ann Arbor.

Linton, Ralph
1924 The Significance of Certain Traits in North American Maize Culture. *American Anthropologist* 26:345–349.

Lipe, William D.
1995 The Depopulation of the Northern San Juan: Conditions in the Turbulent 1200s. *Journal of Anthropological Archaeology* 14:143–169.

Lipe, William D., Mark D. Varien, and Richard H. Wilshusen (editors)
1999 *Colorado Prehistory: A Context for the Southern Colorado River Basin.* Colorado Council of Professional Archaeologists, Denver.

Lister, Robert H.
1958 *Archaeological Excavations in the Northern Sierra Madre Occidental, Chihuahua and Sonora, Mexico.* University of Colorado Studies, Series in Anthropology 7. University of Colorado Press, Boulder.
1961 Twenty-five Years of Archaeology in the Greater Southwest. *American Antiquity* 27:39–45.

Lister, Robert H., and Florence C. Lister
1978 *Anasazi Pottery: The Earl H. Morris Pottery Collection.* Maxwell Museum of

Anthropology and the University of New Mexico Press, Albuquerque.

Loendorf, Chris

1997   Burial Practices at the School House Point Mesa Sites. In *The Archaeology of Schoolhouse Point Mesa, Roosevelt Platform Mound Study: Report on the Schoolhouse Point Mesa Sites, Schoolhouse Management Group, Pinto Creek Complex*, by Owen Lindauer, pp. 549–629. Roosevelt Monograph Series 8, Anthropological Field Studies 37. Office of Cultural Resource Management, Department of Anthropology, Arizona State University, Tempe.

Long, Austin, B. F. Benz, Douglas J. Donahue, A. J. T. Jull, and L. J. Toolin

1989   First Direct AMS Dates on Early Maize from Tehuacán, Mexico. *Radiocarbon* 31(3):1035–1040.

Longacre, William A.

1970   *Archaeology as Anthropology: A Case Study*. Anthropological Papers of the University of Arizona No. 17. University of Arizona Press, Tucson.

Lough, J. M.

1992   An Index of the Southern Oscillation Reconstructed from Western North American Tree-Ring Chronologies. In *El Niño: Historical and Paleoclimatic Aspects of the Southern Oscillation*, edited by Henry F. Diaz and Vera Markgraf, pp. 215–226. Cambridge University Press, Cambridge.

Love, David W.

1980   Quaternary Geology of Chaco Canyon, Northwestern New Mexico. Unpublished PhD dissertation, Department of Geology, University of New Mexico, Albuquerque.

Love, David W., and Sean D. Connell

2005   Late Neogene Drainage Developments on the Southeastern Colorado Plateau, New Mexico. In *New Mexico's Ice Ages*, edited by Spencer G. Lucas, Gary S. Morgan, and Kate E. Zeigler, pp. 151–170. New Mexico Museum of Natural History and Science Bulletin No. 28. Albuquerque.

Lovis, William A., Keith W. Kintigh, Vincas P. Steponaitus, and Lynne Goldstein

2004   Archaeological Perspectives on NAGPRA: Underlying Principles. In *Legal Perspectives on Cultural Resources*, edited by Jennifer R. Richman and Marion P. Forsyth. AltaMira Press, Walnut Creek, California.

Lowenthal, David

1996   *Possessed by the Past: The Heritage Crusade and the Spoils of History*. Free Press, New York.

Lyneis, Margaret M.

1992   *The Main Ridge Community at Lost City: Virgin Anasazi Architecture, Ceramics, and Burials*. University of Utah Anthropological Papers No. 117. University of Utah Press, Salt Lake City.

Lyons, Patrick D.

2003   *Ancestral Hopi Migrations*. Anthropological Papers of the University of Arizona No. 68. University of Arizona Press, Tucson.

Mabry, Jonathan B.

1998   Conclusion. In *Archaeological Investigations of Early Village Sites in the Middle Santa Cruz Valley: Analyses and Synthesis*, edited by Jonathan B. Mabry, pp. 757–792. Anthropological Papers No. 19. Center for Desert Archaeology, Tucson.

1999   Las Capas and Early Irrigation Farming. *Archaeology Southwest* 13(1):14.

2002   The Role of Irrigation Agriculture and the Transition to Sedentism. In *Traditions, Transitions, and Technologies: Themes in Southwestern Archaeology*, edited by Sarah H. Schlanger, pp. 178–199. University Press of Colorado, Boulder.

Mabry, Jonathan B. (editor)

2007   *Las Capas: Early Irrigation and Sedentism in a Southwestern Floodplain*. Anthropological Papers No. 28. Center for Desert Archaeology, Tucson, draft.

MacNeish, Richard S. (editor)

1993   *Preliminary Investigations of the Archaic in the Region of Las Cruces, New Mexico*. Historic and Natural Resources Report No. 9. Cultural Resources Management Program, Fort Bliss, Texas.

MacNeish, Richard S., Antoinette Nelken-Terner, and Irmgard W. Johnson

1967   *Nonceramic Artifacts*. The Prehistory of the Tehuacan Valley, Vol. 2. University of Texas Press, Austin, for the Robert S. Peabody Foundation, Philips Academy, Andover, Massachusetts.

Maddox, R., M. Douglas, and K. Howard

1995   Large-Scale Patterns Associated with Severe Summertime Thunderstorms over Central Arizona. *Weather Forecasting* 10:763–778.

Madsen, David B., and David Rhode (editors)

1994   *Across the West: Human Population Movement and the Expansion of the Numa*. University of Utah Press, Salt Lake City.

Magers, Pamela C.

1986   Weaving at Antelope House. In *Archeological Investigations at Antelope House*, edited by Don P. Morris, pp. 224–276. USDI National Park Service, Washington, D.C.

Magne, M., and R. G. Matson

1982   Identification of "Salish" and "Athapaskan" Side-Notched Projectile Points from the Interior Plateau of British Columbia. In *Approaches to Algonquian Archaeology*, edited by M. Hanna and B. Kooyman, pp. 57–79. Archaeological Association, University of Calgary, Calgary.

1987   Projectile Point and Lithic Assemblage: Ethnicity in Interior British Columbia. In *Ethnicity and Culture*, edited by R. Auger, M. F. Glass, S. MacEachern, and P. H. McCarney, pp. 227–242. Archaeological Association, University of Calgary, Calgary.

Mahoney, Nancy M.

2000   Redefining the Scale of Chacoan Communities. In *Great House Communities across the Chacoan Landscape*, edited by John Kantner and Nancy M. Mahoney, pp. 17–27. Anthropological Papers of the University of Arizona No. 64. University of Arizona Press, Tucson.

Mahoney, Nancy M., Andrew I. Duff, and Keith W. Kintigh

1995   The Role of Chacoan Outliers in Local Organization. Paper presented at the 60th Annual Meeting of the Society for American Archaeology, Minneapolis.

Maker, H. J., H. E. Bullock Jr., and J. U. Anderson

1974   *Soil Associations and Land Classification for Irrigation, McKinley County*. New Mexico State University Agricultural Experiment Station Research Report 262. Las Cruces, New Mexico.

Malinowski, Bronislaw

1926   *Myth in Primitive Psychology*. Kegan Paul, London.

Malotki, Ekkehart

1991   Language as a Key to Cultural Understanding—New Interpretations of Central Hopi Concepts. *Baessler-Archiv* n.s. 39:43–75.

2000   *Kokopelli: The Making of an Icon*. University of Nebraska Press, Lincoln.

Manaster Ramer, Alexis

1996   Tonkawa and Zuni: Two Test Cases for the Greenberg Classification. *International Journal of American Linguistics 62(3):264–288.

Mandryk, Carole
1992   Paleoecology as Contextual Archaeology: Human Viability of the Late Quaternary Ice-Free Corridor, Alberta. PhD dissertation, Department of Anthropology, University of Alberta, Edmonton. University Microfilms, Ann Arbor.

Mandryk, Carole, H. Josenhans, D. W. Fedje, and Rolf Mathewes
2001   Late Quaternary Paleoenvironments of Northwestern North America: Implications for Inland versus Coastal Migration Routes. Quaternary Science Reviews 20:301–314.

Manglesdorf, Paul C.
1974   Corn: Its Origin, Evolution and Improvement. Harvard University Press, Cambridge.

Marmaduke, William S.
1978   Prehistoric Culture in Trans-Pecos Texas: An Ecological Explanation. PhD dissertation, University of Texas, Austin. University Microfilms, Ann Arbor.

Marmaduke, William S., and Richard J. Martynec (editors)
1993   Shelltown and the Hind Site: A Study of Two Hohokam Craftsman Communities in Southwestern Arizona. Northland Research, Inc., Flagstaff, Arizona.

Marquardt, William H.
1974   A Temporal Perspective on Late Prehistoric Societies in the Eastern Cibola Area: Factor Analytic Approaches to Short-Term Chronological Investigation. PhD dissertation, Washington University, St. Louis, Missouri. University Microfilms, Ann Arbor.
1978   Advances in Archaeological Seriation. In Advances in Archaeological Method and Theory 1, edited by Michael B. Schiffer, pp. 266–314. Academic Press, New York.

Marshack, Alexander
1991   The Roots of Civilization: The Cognitive Beginnings of Man's First Art, Symbol and Notation, rev. ed. Moyer Bell, Mt. Kisco, New York.

Marshall, John T.
2001   Appendix J: Hohokam Regional Ballcourt Data. In Project Background and Feature Descriptions, edited by Douglas B. Craig, pp. 571–586. Grewe Archaeological Research Project, Vol. 1. Anthropological Papers No. 99-1. Northland Research, Flagstaff.

Marshall, Michael P.
1989   Archaeological Investigations in the Rio Medio District of the Rio Grande Valley, New Mexico. Historic Preservation Division, Santa Fe.
1991   Ceramic Analysis. In The Prehistoric Cebolla Canyon Community: An Archaeological Class III Inventory of 320 Acres of BLM Land at the Mouth of Cebolla Canyon, by F. E. Wozniak and M. P. Marshall, pp. 6-1–6-42. Office of Contract Archeology, University of New Mexico, Albuquerque.

Marshall, Michael P., and Henry J. Walt
1984   Rio Abajo: Prehistory and History of a Rio Grande Province. Historic Preservation Division, New Mexico Historic Preservation Program, Santa Fe.

Martin, D. L., A. H. Goodman, G. J. Armelagos, and A. L. Magennis
1991   Black Mesa Anasazi Health: Reconstructing Life from Patterns of Death and Disease. Center for Archaeological Investigations, Occasional Paper No. 14. Southern Illinois University, Carbondale.

Martin, John
1972   On the Estimation of the Sizes of Local Groups in a Hunting-Gathering Environment. American Anthropologist 75:1448–1468.

Martin, Paul Schultz
1963   The Last 10,000 Years: A Fossil Pollen Record of the American Southwest. University of Arizona Press, Tucson.
1967   Pleistocene Overkill. In Pleistocene Extinctions: The Search for a Cause, edited by Paul S. Martin and Henry E. Wright Jr., pp. 75–120. Yale University Press, New Haven.

Martin, Paul Schultz, and R. G. Klein (editors)
1984   Quaternary Extinctions: A Prehistoric Revolution. University of Arizona Press, Tucson.

Martin, Paul Sidney
1936   Lowry Ruin in Southwest Colorado. Anthropological Series Vol. 23, No. 1. Field Museum of Natural History, Chicago.
1939   Modified Basket Maker Sites, Ackmen-Lowry Area, Southwestern Colorado, 1938. Anthropological Series Vol. 23, No. 3. Field Museum of Natural History, Chicago.
1940   The SU Site: Excavations at a Mogollon Village, Western New Mexico, 1939. Anthropological Series Vol. 32, No. 2, Publication 526. Field Museum of Natural History, Chicago.
1943   The SU Site: Excavations at a Mogollon Village, Western New Mexico, Sec-
ond Season, 1941. Anthropological Series Vol. 32, No. 2, Publication 526. Field Museum of Natural History, Chicago.
1959a   Foreword. In Foote Canyon Pueblo, Eastern Arizona, by John B. Rinaldo, pp. 149–150. Fieldiana: Anthropology Vol. 49, No. 2. Chicago Natural History Museum, Chicago.
1959b   Digging into History. Popular Series, Anthropology No. 38. Chicago Natural History Museum, Chicago.
1960   Preface. In Table Rock Pueblo, Arizona, by Paul S. Martin and John B. Rinaldo, pp. 131–133. Fieldiana: Anthropology Vol. 51, No. 2. Chicago Natural History Museum, Chicago.
1961   Preface. In Mineral Creek Site and Hooper Ranch Pueblo, Eastern Arizona, by Paul S. Martin, John B. Rinaldo, and William A. Longacre, pp. 3–7. Fieldiana: Anthropology Vol. 52. Chicago Natural History Museum, Chicago.
1971   The Revolution in Archaeology. American Antiquity 36:1–8.
1972   Conjectures Concerning the Social Organization of the Mogollon Indians. In Contemporary Archaeology, edited by Mark Leone, pp. 52–61. Southern Illinois Press, Carbondale.
1979   Prehistory: Mogollon. In Southwest, edited by Alfonso Ortiz, pp. 61–74. Handbook of North American Indians, Vol. 9, William C. Sturtevant, general editor, Smithsonian Institution, Washington, D.C.

Martin, Paul Sidney, William A. Longacre, and James N. Hill
1967   Chapters in the Prehistory of Eastern Arizona, III. Fieldiana: Anthropology Vol. 57. Field Museum of Natural History, Chicago.

Martin, Paul Sidney, and Fred Plog
1973   The Archaeology of Arizona: A Study of the Southwest Region. Doubleday Natural History Press, Garden City, New Jersey.

Martin, Paul Sidney, and John B. Rinaldo
1940   The SU Site: Excavations at a Mogollon Village, Western New Mexico, 1939. Anthropological Series Vol. 32, No. 1. Field Museum of Natural History, Chicago.
1947   The SU Site: Excavations at a Mogollon Village, Western New Mexico, Third Season, 1946. Anthropological Series Vol. 32, No. 2. Field Museum of Natural History, Chicago.
1950a   Sites of the Reserve Phase, Pine Lawn

Valley, Western New Mexico. Fieldiana: Anthropology Vol. 38, No. 3. Chicago Natural History Museum, Chicago.

1950b *Turkey Foot Ridge Site: A Mogollon Village, Pine Lawn Valley, Western New Mexico.* Fieldiana: Anthropology Vol. 38, No. 2. Chicago Natural History Museum, Chicago.

1951 The Southwestern Co-tradition. *Southwestern Journal of Anthropology* 7:215–229.

1960 *Table Rock Pueblo, Arizona.* Fieldiana: Anthropology Vol. 51, No. 2. Chicago Natural History Museum, Chicago.

Martin, Paul Sidney, John B. Rinaldo, and Ernst Antevs

1949 *Cochise and Mogollon Sites: Pine Lawn Valley, Western New Mexico.* Fieldiana: Anthropology Vol. 38, No. 1. Chicago Natural History Museum, Chicago.

Martin, Paul Sidney, John B. Rinaldo, and Eloise R. Baxter

1957 *Late Mogollon Communities: Four Sites of the Tularosa Phase, Western New Mexico.* Fieldiana: Anthropology Vol. 49, No. 1. Chicago Natural History Museum, Chicago.

Martin, Paul Sidney, John B. Rinaldo, and E. Bluhm

1954 *Caves of the Reserve Area.* Fieldiana: Anthropology Vol. 42. Chicago Natural History Museum, Chicago.

Martin, Paul Sidney, John B. Rinaldo, Elaine A. Bluhm, and Hugh C. Cutler

1956 *Higgins Flat Pueblo, Western New Mexico.* Fieldiana: Anthropology Vol. 45. Chicago Natural History Museum, Chicago.

Martin, Paul Sidney, John B. Rinaldo, Elaine A. Bluhm, Hugh C. Cutler, and Roger Grange, Jr.

1952 *Mogollon Cultural Continuity and Change: The Stratigraphic Analysis of Tularosa and Cordova Caves.* Fieldiana: Anthropology Vol. 40. Chicago Natural History Museum, Chicago.

Martin, Paul Sidney, John B. Rinaldo, and William A. Longacre

1961 *Mineral Creek Site and Hooper Ranch Pueblo, Eastern Arizona.* Fieldiana: Anthropology Vol. 52. Chicago Natural History Museum, Chicago.

Martin, Paul Sidney, John B. Rinaldo, William A. Longacre, Constance Cronin, Leslie G. Freeman Jr., and James Schoenwetter

1962 *Chapters in the Prehistory of Eastern Arizona I.* Fieldiana: Anthropology Vol. 53. Chicago Natural History Museum, Chicago.

Martin, Paul Sidney, John B. Rinaldo, William A. Longacre, Leslie G. Freeman Jr., James A. Brown, Richard H. Hevly, and Maurice E. Cooley

1964 *Chapters in the Prehistory of Eastern Arizona, II.* Fieldiana: Anthropology Vol. 55. Chicago Natural History Museum, Chicago.

Martin, Paul Sidney, and Elizabeth S. Willis

1940 *Anasazi Painted Pottery in the Field Museum of Natural History.* Anthropology Memoirs Vol. 5. Field Museum of Natural History, Chicago.

Martin, Steve L.

1999 Virgin Anasazi Diet as Demonstrated through the Analysis of Stable Carbon and Nitrogen Isotopes. *Kiva* 64:495–514.

Martinez del Río, Pablo

1953 A Preliminary Report on the Mortuary Cave of Candelaria, Coahuila, Mexico. *Bulletin of the Texas Archeological Society* 24:208–256.

Mason, Otis T.

1904 Aboriginal American Basketry: Studies in a Textile Art without Machinery. *Report of the U.S. National Museum for 1902*, pp. 171–548. Smithsonian Institution, Washington, D.C.

Mason, Owen K., Peter M. Bowers, and David M. Hopkins

2001 The Early Holocene Milankovitch Thermal Maximum and Humans: Adverse Conditions for the Denali Complex of Eastern Beringia. *Quaternary Science Reviews* 20:525–548.

Mathien, Frances J.

1993a Exchange Systems and Social Stratification among the Chaco Anasazi. In *The American Southwest and Mesoamerica: Systems of Prehistoric Exchange*, edited by Jonathon E. Ericson and Timothy G. Baugh, pp. 65–94. Plenum Publishing Corporation, New York.

1993b Ornaments and Minerals from 29SJ 629. In *Artifactual and Biological Analyses*, edited by Thomas C. Windes, pp. 269–316. The Spadefoot Toad Site: Investigations at 29SJ 629, Chaco Canyon, New Mexico, Vol. 2. Reports of the Chaco Center No. 12, Branch of Cultural Research, Division of Anthropology. USDI National Park Service, Santa Fe.

1997 Ornaments of the Chaco Anasazi. In *Ceramics, Lithics, and Ornaments of Chaco Canyon: Analyses of Artifacts from the Chaco Project 1971–1978*, edited by Frances Joan Mathien, pp. 1119–1220. Publications in Archaeology 18G, Chaco Canyon Studies. USDI National Park Service, Santa Fe.

2001 The Organization of Turquoise Production and Consumption by the Prehistoric Chacoans. *American Antiquity* 66:103–118.

Mathien, Frances J. (editor)

1985 *Environment and Subsistence of Chaco Canyon, New Mexico.* Publications in Archaeology 18E, Chaco Canyon Studies. USDI National Park Service, Albuquerque.

1991 *Excavations at 29SJ 633: The Eleventh Hour Site, Chaco Canyon, New Mexico.* Reports of the Chaco Center No. 10. Branch of Cultural Research, USDI National Park Service, Santa Fe.

Mathien, Frances J., and Randall H. McGuire (editors)

1986 *Ripples in the Chichimec Sea: New Considerations of Southwestern-Mesoamerican Interactions.* Southern Illinois University Press, Carbondale.

Matson, R. G.

1971 *Adaptation and Environment in the Cerbat Mountains, Arizona.* PhD dissertation, Department of Anthropology, University of California, Davis. University Microfilms, Ann Arbor.

1974 The Determination of Archaeological Structure: An Example from the Cerbat Mountains, Arizona. *Plateau* 47(1):26–40.

1991 *The Origins of Southwestern Agriculture.* University of Arizona Press, Tucson.

1999 The Spread of Maize to the Colorado Plateau. *Archaeology Southwest* 13(1):10–11.

2002 The Spread of Maize Agriculture into the U.S. Southwest. In *Examining the Farming/Language Dispersal Hypothesis*, edited by Peter Bellwood and Colin Renfrew, pp. 341–356. McDonald Institute for Archaeological Research, Cambridge.

2005 Many Perspectives but a Consistent Pattern: Comments on Contributions. In *The Late Archaic across the Borderlands*, edited by Bradley J. Vierra, pp. 279–299. University of Texas Press, Austin.

Matson, R. G., and B. Chisholm

1991 Basketmaker II Subsistence: Carbon Isotopes and Other Dietary Indicators from Cedar Mesa, Utah. *American Antiquity* 56:444–459.

Matson, R. G., and Gary Coupland
1995 *The Prehistory of the Northwest Coast.* Academic Press, San Diego.

Matson, R. G., W. D. Lipe, and W. Haase
1988 Adaptational Continuities and Occupational Discontinuities: The Cedar Mesa Anasazi. *Journal of Field Archaeology* 15:245–264.

Matson, R. G., and P. R. Magne
2007 *Athapaskan Migrations: The Archaeology of Eagle Lake, British Columbia.* University of Arizona Press, Tucson.

Mauldin, Raymond P.
1991 Agricultural Intensification in the Mogollon Highlands. In *Mogollon V*, edited by Patrick H. Beckett, pp. 62–74. COAS Publishing and Research, Las Cruces, New Mexico.

Mauss, Marcel
1954 *The Gift: Forms and Functions of Exchange in Archaic Societies.* Free Press, Glencoe, Illinois.

Maxwell, Timothy D., and Rafael Cruz Antillon
2003 Loma de Moctezuma: At the Edge of the Casas Grandes World. *Archaeology Southwest* 17(2):7.

Mayr, Ernst
1942 *Systematics and the Origin of Species.* Columbia University Press, New York.

McBride, Pamela
1991 Results of Macroscopic Botanical Analysis, Feature 12, Mogollon Village. In The Mogollon Village Archaeological Project, 1989, edited by Patricia A. Gilman, Raymond P. Mauldin, and Valli S. Powell, p. 68. Manuscript submitted to USDA, Gila National Forest, Silver City, New Mexico.
2001 Archaeobotanical Remains. In *Households and Farms in Early Zuni Prehistory: Settlement, Subsistence, and the Archaeology of Y Unit Draw—Archaeological Investigations at Eighteen Sites along New Mexico State Highway 602*, prepared by Jonathan E. Damp, James Kendrick, Donovan Quam, Jeffrey Waseta, and Jerome Zunie, pp. 639–664. New Mexico State Highway and Transportation Department Technical Series 2001-3/ZCRE Research Series No. 11. Zuni, New Mexico.

McBrinn, Maxine
2002 *Social Identity and Risk Sharing among Mobile Hunters and Gatherers of the Archaic Southwest.* PhD dissertation, Department of Anthropology, University of Colorado, Boulder. University Microfilms, Ann Arbor.
2005 *Social Identities among Archaic Mobile Hunters and Gatherers in the American Southwest.* Arizona State Museum Archaeological Series 197. University of Arizona Press, Tucson.

McBroom, Patricia
1999 In Remote Cave, Archaeologists Discover Earliest Sign Yet of Maize Agriculture in North America. Electronic document, http://www.berkeley.edu/news/berkeleyan/1999/kernel.html, accessed 1999. University of California, Berkeley.

McCartney, Peter H.
1995 Shell Artifacts from the Bass Point Mound, U:8:23/177. In *Where the Rivers Converge, Roosevelt Platform Mound Study: Report on the Rock Island Complex*, by Owen Lindauer, pp. 351–357. Roosevelt Monograph Series 4, Anthropological Field Studies 33. Office of Cultural Resource Management, Department of Anthropology, Arizona State University, Tempe.

McCreery, Patricia, and Ekkehart Malotki
1994 *Tapamveni: The Rock Art Galleries of Petrified Forest and Beyond.* Petrified Forest Museum Association, Petrified Forest, Arizona.

McDonald, Allison Meg
1992 *Indian Hill Rockshelter and Aboriginal Cultural Adaptation in Anza-Borrego Desert State Park, Southeastern California.* PhD dissertation, Department of Anthropology, University of California, Riverside. University Microfilms, Ann Arbor.

McGimsey, Charles R., III
1980 *Mariana Mesa: Seven Prehistoric Settlements in West-Central New Mexico.* Papers of the Peabody Museum of Archaeology and Ethnology Vol. 72. Harvard University, Cambridge.

McGregor, John C.
1943 Burial of an Early American Magician. *Proceedings of the American Philosophical Society* 86(2):270–298.

McGuire, Randall H.
1993 The Structure and Organization of Hohokam Exchange. In *The American Southwest and Mesoamerica: Systems of Prehistoric Exchange*, edited by Jonathon E. Ericson and Timothy G. Baugh, pp. 95–119. Plenum Press, New York.

McGuire, Randall H., and Ann Valdo Howard
1987 The Structure and Organization of Hohokam Shell Exchange. *Kiva* 52:113–146.

McGuire, Randall H., and Dean J. Saitta
1996 Although They Have Petty Captains, They Obey Them Badly: The Dialectics of Prehispanic Western Pueblo Social Organization. *American Antiquity* 61:197–216.

McGuire, Randall H., and Michael B. Schiffer
1983 A Theory of Architectural Design. *Journal of Anthropological Archaeology* 2:277–303.

McGuire, Randall H., and Elisa Villalpando
1989 Prehistory and the Making of History in Sonora. In *Archaeological and Historical Perspectives on the Spanish Borderlands West*, edited by David Hurst Thomas, pp. 159–178. Columbian Consequences, Vol. 1. Smithsonian Institution Press, Washington, D.C.

McGuire, Thomas
1983 Hualapai. In *Southwest*, edited by Alfonso Ortiz, pp. 25–38. Handbook of North American Indians, Vol. 10, William C. Sturtevant, general editor, Smithsonian Institution, Washington, D.C.

McIntosh, S. K., and R. J. McIntosh
1984 The Early City in West Africa: Towards an Understanding. *African Archaeological Review* 2:73–98.

McKenna, Peter
1998 *Pia Mesa Timber Sale, Zuni Pueblo Management Summary.* Bureau of Indian Affairs, Albuquerque.

McKusick, Charmion Randolph
1974 The Casas Grandes Avian Report. In *Bone-Economy-Burials*, by Charles C. Di Peso, John B. Rinaldo, and Gloria J. Fenner, pp. 273–284. Casas Grandes, a Fallen Trading Center of the Gran Chichimeca, Vol. 8. Amerind Foundation Series No. 9. Amerind Foundation, Inc., Dragoon, and Northland Press, Flagstaff.
1976 Avifauna. In *The Hohokam: Desert Farmers & Craftsmen, Excavations at Snaketown, 1964–1965*, by Emil W. Haury, pp. 374–377. University of Arizona Press, Tucson.
1986 The Avian Remains. In *Archaeological Investigations at Antelope House*, edited by Don P. Morris, pp. 142–158. USDI National Park Service, Washington, D.C.
1996 An Analysis of Miscellaneous Faunal Materials from the Wind Mountain

Locus and Analyses of Ridout Locus Faunal Materials. In *Mimbres Mogollon Archaeology: Charles C. Di Peso's Excavations at Wind Mountain*, by Anne I. Woosley and Allan J. McIntyre, pp. 407–439. Amerind Foundation, Inc., Dragoon, Arizona.

2001 *Southwest Birds of Sacrifice*. Arizona Archaeologist No. 31. Arizona Archaeological Society, Phoenix.

McKusick, Charmion R., and Jon Nathan Young

1997 *The Gila Pueblo Salado*. Salado Chapter, Arizona Archaeological Society, Globe.

McLaughlin, Robert H.

2004 NAGPRA, Dialogue, and the Politics of Historical Authority. In *Legal Perspectives on Cultural Resources*, edited by Jennifer R. Richman and Marion P. Forsyth. AltaMira Press, Walnut Creek, California.

McVickar, Janet L.

1991 Holocene Vegetation Change at Cowboy Cave, Southeastern Utah, and Its Effect upon Human Subsistence. Unpublished Master's thesis, Northern Arizona University, Flagstaff.

Meggers, Betty J.

1994 Archaeological Evidence for the Impact of Mega–El Niño Events on Amazonia during the Past Two Millennia. *Climate Change* 28:328–329.

Mehringer, Peter J., Jr.

1977 Great Basin Late Quaternary Environments and Chronology. In *Models and Great Basin Prehistory: A Symposium*, edited by Don D. Fowler, pp. 113–167. Desert Research Institute Publications in the Social Sciences 12.

1985 Late Quaternary Pollen Records from the Interior Pacific Northwest and Northern Great Basin of the United States. In *Pollen Records of Late Quaternary North American Sediments*, edited by Vaughn M. Bryant Jr. and Richard G. Holloway, pp. 167–190. American Association of Stratigraphic Palynologists, Dallas.

Mehringer, Peter J., Jr., and P. E. Wigand

1990 Composition of Late Holocene Environments from Woodrat Middens and Pollen: Diamond Craters, Oregon. In *Packrat Middens: The Last 40,000 Years of Biotic Change*, edited by Julio L. Betancourt, Thomas R. Van Devender, and Paul S. Martin, pp. 294–325. University of Arizona Press, Tucson.

Meko, David M.

1992 Spectral Properties of Tree-Ring Data in the U.S. Southwest as Related to El Niño/Southern Oscillation. In *El Niño: Historical and Paleoclimatic Aspects of the Southern Oscillation*, edited by Henry F. Diaz and Vera Markgraf, pp. 227–241. Cambridge University Press, Cambridge.

Mellars, Paul A.

1998 Neanderthals, Modern Humans and the Archaeological Evidence for Language. In *The Origin and Diversification of Language*, edited by Nina G. Jablonski and Leslie C. Aiello, pp. 89–116. Memoirs of the California Academy of Sciences No. 24. San Francisco.

Meltzer, David J.

1993 *Search for the First Americans*. Smithsonian Books, Washington, D.C.

2003 Who, When, from Where, How and How Often? Pleistocene Peopling of the Americas. Plenary paper presented at the 16th INQUA Congress, Reno.

Meltzer, David J., Donald K. Grayson, Gerardo Ardila, Alex W. Barker, Dena F. Dincauze, C. Vance Haynes, Francisco Mena, Lautaro Núñez, and Dennis J. Stanford

1997 On the Pleistocene Antiquity of Monte Verde, Southern Chile. *American Antiquity* 62:659–663.

Meltzer, David J., Lawrence C. Todd, and Vance T. Holliday

2002 The Folsom (Paleoindian) Type Site: Past Investigations, Current Studies. *American Antiquity* 67:5–36.

Mera, H. P.

1934 *A Survey of the Biscuit Ware Area in Northern New Mexico*. Laboratory of Anthropology Technical Series Bulletin No. 6. Santa Fe.

1935 *Ceramic Clues to the Prehistory of North Central New Mexico*. Laboratory of Anthropology Technical Series Bulletin 8. Santa Fe.

1938 *Reconnaissance and Excavation in Southeastern New Mexico*. Memoirs of the American Anthropological Association 51. Menasha, Wisconsin.

1940 *Population Changes in the Rio Grande Glaze-Paint Area*. Laboratory of Anthropology Technical Series Bulletin No. 9. Santa Fe.

1943 *An Outline of Ceramic Development in Southern and Southeastern New Mexico*. Laboratory of Anthropology Technical Series Bulletin No. 11. Santa Fe.

Merrill, William L., Edmund J. Ladd, and T. J. Ferguson

1993 The Return of the Ahayu:da: Lessons for Repatriation from Zuni Pueblo and the Smithsonian Institution. *Current Anthropology* 34:523–567.

Meshorer, Hank

1995 The Sacred Trail to Zuni Heaven: A Study in the Law of Prescriptive Easements. In *Zuni and the Courts*, edited by E. Richard Hart, pp. 208–219. University Press of Kansas, Lawrence.

Michaelsen, Joel

1989 Long-Period Fluctuations in El Niño Amplitude and Frequency Reconstructed from Tree-Rings. In *Aspects of Climate Variability in the Pacific and the Western Americas*, edited by Daniel H. Peterson, pp. 69–74. Geophysical Monograph 55, American Geophysical Union. Washington, D.C.

Miksa, Elizabeth, and James M. Heidke

1995 Drawing a Line in the Sands: Developing Compositional Models of Sand Temper Resource Procurement Zones for Archaeological Provenance Studies. In *Ceramic Chronology, Technology, and Economics*, edited by James M. Heidke and Miriam T. Stark, pp. 133–204. The Roosevelt Community Development Study, Vol. 2. Anthropological Papers No. 14. Center for Desert Archaeology, Tucson, Arizona.

Miksicek, Charles H., and Patricia L. Fall

1996 Wind Mountain Macrobotanical Plant Remains. In *Mimbres Mogollon Archaeology: Charles C. Di Peso's Excavations at Wind Mountain*, edited by Anne I. Woosley and Allan J. McIntyre, pp. 295–306. Amerind Foundation, Inc., Dragoon, Arizona.

Miller, Wick R.

1965 *Acoma Grammar and Texts*. University of California Publications in Linguistics Vol. 40. University of California Press, Berkeley.

1967 *Uto-Aztecan Cognate Sets*. University of California Publications in Linguistics Vol. 48. University of California Press, Berkeley.

1983 Uto-Aztecan Languages. In *Southwest*, edited by Alfonso Ortiz, pp. 113–124. Handbook of North American Indians, Vol. 10, William C. Sturtevant, general editor, Smithsonian Institution, Washington, D.C.

1984 The Classification of the Uto-Aztecan Languages Based on Lexical Evidence. *International Journal of American Linguistics* 50:1–24.

Miller, Wick R., and Irvine Davis
1963   Proto-Keresan Phonology. *International Journal of American Linguistics* 29(4):310–330.

Mills, Barbara J.
1980   *Zuni Rock Art Survey: A Review of Archaeological Site Records, Dating, and Bibliographic References.* Zuni Archaeology Program, Pueblo of Zuni, New Mexico.
1987a   Ceramic Analysis. In *Archaeological Investigations at Eight Small Sites in West-Central New Mexico*, edited by Patrick Hogan with contributions by Glenna Dean, Janette M. Elyea, Elizabeth M. Garrett, Linda Mick-O'Hara, and Barbara J. Mills, pp. 83–143. Office of Contract Archeology, University of New Mexico, Albuquerque.
1987b   Ceramic Production and Distribution Patterns. In *Archaeological Investigations at Eight Small Sites in West-Central New Mexico*, edited by Patrick Hogan with contributions by Glenna Dean, Janette M. Elyea, Elizabeth M. Garrett, Linda Mick-O'Hara, and Barbara J. Mills, pp. 145–154. Office of Contract Archeology, University of New Mexico, Albuquerque.
1995   The Organization of Zuni Ceramic Production. In *Ceramic Production in the American Southwest*, edited by Barbara J. Mills and Patricia L. Crown, pp. 200–230. University of Arizona Press, Tucson.
1998   Migration and Pueblo IV Community Reorganization in the Silver Creek Area, East-Central Arizona. In *Migration and Community Reorganization: The Pueblo IV Period in the American Southwest*, edited by Katherine A. Spielmann, pp. 65–80. Arizona State University Anthropological Research Papers 51, Tempe.
1999a   Ceramics and the Social Contexts of Food Consumption in the Northern Southwest. In *Pottery and People: A Dynamic Interaction*, edited by James Skibo and Gary Feinman, pp. 99–114. University of Utah Press, Salt Lake City.
1999b   Ceramic Ware and Type Systematics. In *Living on the Edge of the Rim: Excavations and Analysis of the Silver Creek Archaeological Research Project 1993–1998*, edited by Barbara J. Mills, Sarah A. Herr, and Scott Van Keuren, pp. 243–268. Arizona State Museum Archaeological Series 192. University of Arizona, Tucson.
2000   Gender, Craft Production, and Inequality. In *Women and Men in the Prehispanic Southwest: Labor, Power, and Prestige*, edited by Patricia L. Crown, pp. 301–344. School of American Research Press, Santa Fe.
2002a   Zuni Middle Village Ceramics, Report to the Pueblo of Zuni. Manuscript on file, Department of Anthropology, University of Arizona, and Zuni Cultural Resource Enterprise, Pueblo of Zuni, New Mexico.
2002b   Acts of Resistance: Zuni Ceramics, Social Identity, and the Pueblo Revolt. In *Archaeologies of the Pueblo Revolt: Identity, Meaning, and Renewal in the Pueblo World*, edited by Robert W. Preucel, pp. 85–98. University of New Mexico Press, Albuquerque.
2007   Performing the Feast: Visual Display and Suprahousehold Commensalism in the Puebloan Southwest. *American Antiquity* 72(2).

Mills, Barbara J., and T. J. Ferguson
1980   Processes of Architectural Change: Examples from the Historic Zuni Farming Villages. Paper presented at the meetings of the New Mexico Archaeological Council and the Society for American Archaeology. Manuscript on file, Museum of Northern Arizona Library, Flagstaff.
1998   Preservation and Research of Sacred Sites by the Zuni Indian Tribe of New Mexico. *Human Organization* 57(1):30–42.

Mills, Barbara J., and Sarah A. Herr
1999   Chronology of the Mogollon Rim Region. In *Living on the Edge of the Rim: Excavations and Analysis of the Silver Creek Archaeological Research Project, 1993–1998*, edited by Barbara J. Mills, Sarah A. Herr, and Scott Van Keuren, pp. 269–293. Arizona State Museum Archaeological Series No. 192. University of Arizona, Tucson.

Mills, Barbara J., Sarah A. Herr, and Scott Van Keuren (editors)
1999   *Living on the Edge of the Rim: Excavations and Analysis of the Silver Creek Archaeological Research Project, 1993–1998.* Arizona State Museum Archaeological Series No. 192. University of Arizona, Tucson.

Mills, Jack P., and Vera M. Mills
1975   *The Meredith Ranch Site: VIV Ruin.* Privately printed by J. and V. Mills, Elfrida, Arizona.

Mindeleff, Victor
1891   A Study of Pueblo Architecture in Tusayan and Cibola. In *Eighth Annual Report of the Bureau of American Ethnology for the Years 1886–1887*, pp. 13–653. U.S. Government Printing Office, Washington, D.C.

Minnis, Paul E.
1984   Macroplant Remains. In *The Galaz Ruin: A Prehistoric Mimbres Village in Southwestern New Mexico*, edited by Roger Anyon and Steven A. LeBlanc, pp. 193–200. Maxwell Museum of Anthropology and University of New Mexico Press, Albuquerque.
1985   *Social Adaptation to Food Stress: A Prehistoric Southwestern Example.* Prehistoric Archaeology and Ecology. University of Chicago Press, Chicago.

Minnis, Paul E., and Charles L. Redman (editors)
1990   *Perspectives on Southwestern Prehistory.* Westview Press, Boulder.

Minnis, Paul E., Michael E. Whalen, Jane H. Kelley, and Joe D. Stewart
1993   Prehistoric Macaw Breeding in the North American Southwest. *American Antiquity* 58:270–276.

Mitchell, Douglas R.
1991   An Investigation of Two Classic Period Hohokam Cemeteries. *North American Archaeologist* 12(2):109–127.

Mitchell, Douglas R. (editor)
1994   *An Analysis of Classic Period Mortuary Patterns.* The Pueblo Grande Project, Vol. 7. Soil Systems Publications in Archaeology No. 20. Soil Systems, Inc., Phoenix.

Moreno, Teresa K.
2000   Accelerator Mass Spectrometry Dates from McEuen Cave. *Kiva* 65:341–360.

Morgan, Lewis Henry
1877   *Ancient Society, or, Researches in the Lines of Human Progress from Savagery through Barbarism to Civilization.* Henry Holt & Company, New York.
1881   *Houses and House Life of the American Aborigines.* Contributions to North American Ethnology 4.

Morris, Earl H.
1939   *Archaeological Studies in the La Plata District, Southwestern Colorado and Northwestern New Mexico.* Carnegie Institution, Washington, D.C.

Morris, Earl, and Robert F. Burgh
1941   *Anasazi Basketry: Basket Maker II through Pueblo III.* Carnegie Institution of Washington Publication 533. Washington, D.C.
1954   *Basket Maker II Sites near Durango, Colorado.* Carnegie Institution of

Washington Publication 604. Washington, D.C.

Morris, Elizabeth Ann
n.d. High Altitude Sites in the Mogollon Rim Area of Arizona and New Mexico. Manuscript on file at Zuni Heritage and Historic Preservation Office, Zuni, New Mexico.
1980 *Basketmaker Caves in the Prayer Rock District, Northeastern Arizona.* Anthropological Papers of the University of Arizona No. 35. University of Arizona Press, Tucson.
1982 High Altitude Sites in the Mogollon Rim Area of Arizona and New Mexico. In *Mogollon Archaeology: Proceedings of the 1980 Mogollon Conference,* edited by Patrick H. Beckett and Kira Silverbird, pp. 41–53. Acoma Books, Ramona, California.

Moulard, Barbara L.
1984 *Within the Underworld Sky: Mimbres Ceramic Art in Context.* Twelvetrees Press, Pasadena, California.

Mowrer, Kathy
2003 Basketmaker II Mortuary Practices: Social Differentiation and Regional Variation. Unpublished Master's thesis, Department of Anthropology, Northern Arizona University, Flagstaff.

Munford, Barbara A., Christopher C. Giuliano, Carolyn L. Daniel, and Jeanne A. Schutt
1994 LA 50548: The Cuchillo Site. In *On the Periphery of the Mimbres Mogollon: The Cuchillo Negro Project,* Vol. 1, edited by Jeanne A. Schutt, Richard C. Chapman, and June-el Piper, pp. 57–180. Office of Contract Archaeology, University of New Mexico, Albuquerque.

Muro, Mark
1998 Not Just Another Roadside Attraction. *American Archaeology* 2(4):10–16.

Naroll, Raoul
1962 Floor Area and Settlement Population. *American Antiquity* 27:587–588.

Nash, Stephen E., and Jeffrey S. Dean
2005 Paleoenvironmental Reconstructions and Archaeology: Uniting the Social and Natural Sciences in the American Southwest and Beyond. In *Southwest Archaeology in the Twentieth Century,* edited by Linda S. Cordell and Don D. Fowler, pp. 125–141. University of Utah Press, Salt Lake City.

Nason, James D.
2001 Traditional Property and Modern Laws: The Need for Native American Community Intellectual Property Rights Legislation. *Stanford Law and Policy Review* 12(2):255–266.

National Cyclopaedia
1904 Stevenson, James. In *The National Cyclopaedia of American Biography,* Vol. 12, pp. 556–557. James T. White, New York.

NOAA (National Oceanic and Atmospheric Administration)
1999 Web Site on El Niño and La Niña. Electronic document, http://www.websites.noaa.gov/guide/sciences/atmo/elnino.html, accessed June 24, 2003.

Navajo Nation
2003 Official Web Site of the Navajo Nation. Electronic document, http://www.navajo.org, accessed August 15, 2003.

Neely, James A.
1974 *The Prehistoric Lunt and Stove Canyon Sites, Point of Pines, Arizona.* PhD dissertation, Department of Anthropology, University of Arizona, Tucson. University Microfilms, Ann Arbor.

Neilson, Ronald P.
1987 On the Interface between Current Ecological Studies and the Paleobotany of the Pinyon-Juniper Woodlands. *Proceedings—Pinyon-Juniper Conference: Reno, NV, January 13–16, 1986,* compiled by Richard L. Everett, pp. 93–98. Intermountain Research Station, USDA Forest Service, Ogden, Utah.

Neitzel, Jill E.
1989 Regional Exchange Networks in the American Southwest: A Comparative Analysis of Long-Distance Trade. In *The Sociopolitical Structure of Prehistoric Southwestern Societies,* edited by Steadman Upham, Kent G. Lightfoot, and Roberta A. Jewett, pp. 149–195. Westview Press, Boulder.

Neitzel, Jill (editor)
1999 *Great Towns and Regional Polities.* University of New Mexico Press, Albuquerque.

Nelson, Ben A., and Steven LeBlanc
1986 *Short-Term Sedentism in the America Southwest: The Mimbres Valley Salado.* The Maxwell Museum of Anthropology and the University of New Mexico Press, Albuquerque.

Nelson, Margaret C.
1999 *Mimbres in the Twelfth Century: Abandonment, Continuity, and Reorganization.* University of Arizona Press, Tucson.

Nelson, Nels C.
1914 *Pueblo Ruins of the Galisteo Basin, New Mexico.* Anthropological Papers Vol. 15, Pt. 1. American Museum of Natural History, New York.

Nelson, Richard S.
1981 *The Role of the Puchteca System in Hohokam Exchange.* PhD dissertation, Department of Anthropology, New York University. University Microfilms, Ann Arbor.
1991 *Hohokam Marine Shell Exchange and Artifacts.* Arizona State Museum Archaeological Series No. 179. Arizona State Museum, University of Arizona, Tucson.

Nesbitt, Paul H.
1931 *The Ancient Mimbreños Based on Investigations at the Mattocks Ruin, Mimbres Valley, New Mexico.* Logan Museum Bulletin No. 4. Beloit College, Beloit, Wisconsin.
1938 *Starkweather Ruin: A Mogollon-Pueblo Site in the Upper Gila Area of New Mexico, and Affiliative Aspects of the Mogollon Culture.* Publications in Anthropology Bulletin No. 6. Logan Museum, Beloit College, Beloit, Wisconsin.

Netting, Robert McC.
1993 *Smallholders, Householders: Farm Families and the Ecology of Intensive, Sustainable Agriculture.* Stanford University Press, Stanford.

Neuzil, Anna
2001 Ceramics and Social Dynamics: Technological Style and Corrugated Ceramics during the Pueblo III to Pueblo IV Transition, Silver Creek, Arizona. Unpublished Master's thesis, Department of Anthropology, University of Arizona, Tucson.

Newcomb, Joanne M.
1999 Silver Creek Settlement Patterns and Paleodemography. In *Living on the Edge of the Rim: Excavations and Analysis of the Silver Creek Archaeological Project, 1993–1998,* edited by Barbara J. Mills, Sarah A. Herr, and Scott Van Keuren. Arizona State Museum Archaeological Series 192. University of Arizona Press, Tucson.

Newman, Stanley
1944 *Yokuts Language of California.* Viking Fund Publications in Anthropology No. 6.
1958 Zuni Dictionary. Publication of the Indiana University Research Center in Anthropology, Folklore, and Linguistics 6. *International Journal of Ameri-*

can Linguistics Vol. 24, No. 1, Pt. 2. Bloomington.

1964 Comparison of Zuni and California Penutian. *International Journal of American Linguistics* 30(1):1–13.

1965 *Zuni Grammar.* University of New Mexico Publications in Anthropology No. 14. University of New Mexico Press, Albuquerque.

Nials, Fred L.

1983 Physical Characteristics of Chacoan Roads. In *Chaco Roads Project Phase I,* edited by C. Kincaid, pp. 6-1–6-50. Bureau of Land Management, New Mexico State Office, Albuquerque.

1991a Geology and Geomorphology of the Middle Rio Puerco Valley. In *Anasazi Puebloan Adaptation in Response to Climatic Stress: Prehistory of the Middle Rio Puerco Valley,* edited by Cynthia Irwin-Williams and Larry L. Baker, pp. 33–57. Eastern New Mexico University, Portales.

1991b Landform-Environment Classification, Rio Puerco Valley Project. In *Anasazi Puebloan Adaptation in Response to Climatic Stress: Prehistory of the Middle Rio Puerco Valley,* edited by Cynthia Irwin-Williams and Larry L. Baker, pp. 411–423. Eastern New Mexico University, Portales.

1999 *Geomorphic Systems and Stratigraphy in Internally Drained Watersheds of the Northern Great Basin: Implications for Archaeological Studies.* Sundance Archaeological Research Fund Technical Paper 5.

Nials, Fred L., E. E. Deeds, M. E. Mosley, S. G. Pozoroski, T. G. Pozoroski, and R. Feldman

1979a El Niño: The Catastrophic Flooding of Coastal Peru, Part I. *Field Museum of Natural History Bulletin* 50(7):4–14.

1979b El Niño: The Catastrophic Flooding of Coastal Peru, Part II. *Field Museum of Natural History Bulletin* 50(8):4–10.

Nials, Fred L., David A. Gregory, and Donald A. Graybill

1989 Salt River Streamflow and Hohokam Irrigation Systems. In *Environment and Subsistence,* by D. A. Graybill, D. A. Gregory, F. L. Nials, S. K. Fish, R. E. Gasser, and C. H. Miksicek, pp. 59–78. The 1982–1984 Excavations at Las Colinas, Vol. 5. Archaeological Series No. 162. Arizona State Museum, University of Arizona, Tucson.

Nials, Fred L., John R. Stein, and John R. Roney

1987 *Chacoan Roads in the Southern Periphery: Results of Phase II of the Bureau of Land Management Chaco Roads Project.* Cultural Resource Series 1. USDI Bureau of Land Management.

Nichols, Johanna

1990 Linguistic Diversity and the First Settlement of the New World. *Language* 66:475–521.

1992 *Linguistic Diversity in Space and Time.* University of Chicago Press, Chicago.

1998 The Origin and Dispersal of Languages: Linguistic Evidence. In *The Origin and Diversification of Language,* edited by Nina G. Jablonski and Leslie C. Aiello, pp. 127–170. Memoirs of the California Academy of Sciences No. 24. San Francisco.

Nichols, Lynn

1993 Keres Laryngeal Accent. In *Proceedings of the Twenty-third Western Conference on Linguistics,* Vol. 6, edited by Sharon Hargus, Gerald R. McMenamin, and Vida Samiian, pp. 311–321. California State University at Fresno, Department of Linguistics, Fresno.

1997 DP and Polysynthesis. In *Proceedings of the North East Linguistic Society 27,* edited by K. Kusumoto, pp. 305–320.

1999 Manuscript Proposal for a Zuni Reference Grammar. Harvard University, Cambridge.

2000 Rethinking Switch Reference. *Proceedings of the West Coast Conference on Formal Linguistics 18,* Special session in honor of Kenneth L. Hale.

2001 On the Absence of Non-factive Complementation in Certain Languages. *Proceedings of the North East Linguistic Society 31,* pp. 359–387.

North, Chris D., Louise Senior, and Michael S. Foster

2003 *An Archaeological Survey and Ethnohistoric Study of the Verde Wild and Scenic River Corridor.* SWCA Cultural Resources Report No. 02-415. Phoenix.

Nott, Josiah C., and George R. Gliddon

1854 *Types of Mankind: or, Ethnological Researches Based upon the Ancient Monuments, Paintings, Sculptures, and Crania of Races, and upon Their Natural, Geographical, Philological and Biblical History,* 6th ed. J. B. Lippincott, Grambo and Company, Philadelphia.

Nusbaum, Aileen B.

1926 *The Seven Cities of Cibola.* G. P. Putnam's Sons, New York.

Nusbaum, Jesse L.

1922 *A Basket-Maker Cave in Kane County, Utah.* Indian Notes and Monographs 29. Museum of the American Indian, Heye Foundation, New York.

Olsen, John W.

1990 *Vertebrate Faunal Remains from Grasshopper Pueblo, Arizona.* Anthropological Papers No. 83. Museum of Anthropology, University of Michigan, Ann Arbor.

Olsen, Sandra L., and John W. Olsen

1996 An Analysis of Faunal Remains at Wind Mountain. In *Mimbres Mogollon Archaeology: Charles C. Di Peso's Excavations at Wind Mountain,* edited by Anne I. Woosley and Allan J. McIntyre, pp. 389–406. Amerind Foundation, Inc., Dragoon, Arizona.

Olson, Alan P.

1960 The Dry Prong Site. *American Antiquity* 26:185–204.

Olson, Alan P. (compiler)

1961 Third Southwestern Ceramic Conference: Seminar on Brownware and Mogollon Brown Ware. Manuscript on file, Museum of Northern Arizona, Flagstaff.

Olszewski, Deborah I., Glenn P. Darrington, and Sharon K. Bauer

1996 *Across the Growler Valley from the Granite to the Growler Mountains: Cultural Resources Sample Survey of the South Tactical Range, Barry M. Goldwater Air Force Range, Southwestern Arizona.* Dames and Moore Intermountain Cultural Resource Services Research Paper No. 26. Dames and Moore, Phoenix.

O'Neale, Lila M.

1948 *Textiles of Pre-Columbian Chihuahua.* Contributions to American Anthropology and History 45. Carnegie Institution of Washington Publication 574. Washington, D.C.

O'Neil, Floyd

1995 The Trail to Kolhu/wala:wa. Report prepared for *United States v. Platt.* In *Zuni and the Courts CD-ROM,* compiled by E. Richard Hart. University Press of Kansas, Lawrence. Original date of report 1987.

Pachak, Joe

1994 *Blue Mountain Shadows* 13:16–21. San Juan Historical Commission. Moab, Utah.

Pailes, Richard A.

1972 *An Archaeological Reconnaissance of Southern Sonora and Reconsideration of the Rio Sonora Culture.* PhD dissertation, Southern Illinois University, Carbondale. University Microfilms, Ann Arbor.

Palmer, Wayne C.

1965 Meteorological Drought. *United States Weather Bureau Research Paper* 45. U.S. Department of Commerce, Washington, D.C.

Parezo, Nancy J.

1993 Matilda Coxe Stevenson: Pioneer Ethnologist. In *Hidden Scholars: Women Anthropologists and the Native American Southwest*, edited by Nancy J. Parezo, pp. 38–62. University of New Mexico Press, Albuquerque.

Parry, William, F. E. Smiley, and Galen Burgett

1994 The Archaic Occupation of Black Mesa, Arizona. In *Archaic Hunter-Gatherer Archaeology in the American Southwest*, edited by Bradley J. Vierra, pp. 185–230. Contributions in Anthropology Vol. 13, No. 1. Eastern New Mexico University, Portales.

Parsons, Elsie Clews

1917 Notes on Zuni. *Memoirs of the American Anthropological Association* 4(3–4):151–327.

1918a War God Shrines of Laguna and Zuni. *American Anthropologist* 20:381–405.

1918b Pueblo-Indian Folk-tales, Probably of Spanish Provenience. *Journal of American Folk-Lore* 31:216–255.

1923 The Origin Myth of Zuni. *Journal of American Folk-Lore* 36:135–162.

1930 Zuni Tales. *Journal of American Folk-Lore* 43:1–58.

1933 *Hopi and Zuni Ceremonialism.* Memoirs of the American Anthropological Association 39. Menasha, Wisconsin.

1936 Early Relations between Hopi and Keres. *American Anthropologist* 38:554–560.

1939 *Pueblo Indian Religion.* 2 vols. University of Chicago Press, Chicago.

Pasternak, B.

1972 *Kinship and Community in Two Chinese Villages.* Stanford University Press, Stanford.

Pearsall, Deborah M.

1995 Domestication and Agriculture in the New World Tropics. In *Last Hunters, First Farmers*, edited by T. Douglas Price and Anne Brigitte Gebauer, pp. 157–192. School of American Research, Santa Fe.

Peckham, Stewart

1957 The Switchback Site: A Stratified Ruin near Reserve, New Mexico. In *Highway Salvage Archaeology*, Vol. 3, edited by Stewart Peckham, pp. 10–38. New Mexico State Highway Department and the Museum of New Mexico, Santa Fe.

1963 Highway Salvage Archaeology No. 17, the Luna Junction Site: An Early Pit House in the Pine Lawn Valley, New Mexico. In *Highway Salvage Archaeology*, Vol. 4, edited by Stewart Peckham, pp. 41–55. New Mexico State Highway Department and the Museum of New Mexico, Santa Fe.

Pennington, Campbell W.

1963 *The Tarahumar of Mexico: Their Environment and Material Culture.* University of Utah Press, Salt Lake City.

1969 *The Tepehuan of Chihuahua: Their Material Culture.* University of Utah Press, Salt Lake City.

Pepper, George H.

1909 The Exploration of a Burial-Room in Pueblo Bonito, New Mexico. In *Anthropological Essays: Putnam Anniversary Volume*, pp. 196–252. G. E. Steckert and Company, New York.

1920 *Pueblo Bonito.* Anthropological Papers Vol. 27. American Museum of Natural History, New York.

Petersen, Kenneth L.

1988 *Climate and the Dolores River Anasazi.* University of Utah Anthropological Papers No. 113. University of Utah Press, Salt Lake City.

1994 A Warm and Wet Little Climatic Optimum and a Cold and Dry Little Ice Age in the Southern Rocky Mountains. *Climatic Change* 26:243–269.

Petersen, N. (editor)

1976 *Tribes and Boundaries in Australia.* Australian Institute for Aboriginal Studies, Canberra.

Philander, S. George

1985 El Niño and La Niña. *Journal of Atmospheric Science* 42:2652–2662.

1990 *El Niño, La Niña, and the Southern Oscillation.* Academic Press, San Diego.

Phillips, David A., Jr.

2000 The Chaco Meridian: A Skeptical Analysis. Poster presented at the 65th Annual Meeting of the Society for American Archaeology, Philadelphia. On file at http://www.unm.edu/dap, accessed September 16, 2003.

Phillips, Philip, and Gordon R. Willey

1953 Method and Theory in American Archaeology. An Operational Basis for Cultural-Historical Integration. *American Anthropologist* 55:615–633.

Pierce, Christopher

1999 *Explaining Corrugated Pottery in the American Southwest: An Evolutionary Approach.* PhD dissertation, Department of Anthropology, University of Washington, Seattle. University Microfilms, Ann Arbor.

Pierce, Linda J.

2001 Faunal Remains. In *Homol'ovi III, a Pueblo Hamlet in the middle Little Colorado River Valley*, edited by E. Charles Adams, pp. 273–283. Arizona State Museum Archaeological Series 193, University of Arizona, Tucson.

Pilles, Peter J., Jr.

1975 Petroglyphs of the Little Colorado River Valley, Arizona. *American Indian Rock Art* 1(1):1–26, edited by S. Groves. San Juan County Museum Association, Farmington, New Mexico.

1996 The Pueblo III Period along the Mogollon Rim: The Honanki, Elden, and Turkey Hill Phases of the Sinagua. In *The Prehistoric Pueblo World, AD 1150–1350*, edited by Michael A. Adler, pp. 59–72. University of Arizona Press, Tucson.

Pippen, Lonnie C.

1987 *Prehistory and Paleoecology of Guadalupe Ruin, New Mexico.* University of Utah Anthropological Papers No. 112. University of Utah Press, Salt Lake City.

Pitkin, Harvey, and William Shipley

1958 Comparative Survey of California Penutian. *International Journal of American Linguistics* 24:174–188.

Plog, Fred T.

1983 Political and Economic Alliances on the Colorado Plateaus, AD 400–1450. In *Advances in World Archaeology*, Vol. 2, edited by Fred Wendorf and Angela E. Close, pp. 289–330. Academic Press, New York.

1984 Exchange, Tribes, and Alliances: The Northern Southwest. *American Archaeology* 4(3):217–223.

Plog, Fred, George J. Gumerman, Robert C. Euler, Jeffrey S. Dean, Richard H. Hevly, and Thor N. V. Karlstrom

1988 Anasazi Adaptive Strategies: The Model, Predictions, and Results. In *The Anasazi in a Changing Environment*, edited by George J. Gumerman, pp. 230–296. Cambridge University Press, Cambridge.

Plog, Stephen

1990 Sociopolitical Implications of Stylistic Variation in the American South-west. In *The Uses of Style in Archaeology*, edited by Margaret W. Conkey and Christine A. Hastorf, pp. 61–72. Cambridge University Press, Cambridge.

Pogue, Joseph E.
1974 *The Turquoise: A Study of Its History, Mineralogy, Geology, Ethnology, Archeology, Mythology, Folklore, and Technology.* Memoirs of the National Academy of Sciences Vol. 12, Pt. 2. Originally published 1915. Rio Grande Press, Glorieta, New Mexico.

Poliakov, L.
1974 *The Aryan Myth: A History of Racist and Nationalist Ideas in Europe.* Basic Books, New York.

Pollock, Susan
1983 Style and Information: An Analysis of Susiana Ceramics. *Journal of Anthropological Archaeology* 2:354–390.

Polyani, Karl
1968 The Economy as Instituted Process. In *Primitive, Archaic and Modern Economies: Essays of Karl Polyani*, edited by George Dalton, pp. 139–174. Doubleday & Company, Garden City, New York.

Potter, James M.
1997 *Communal Ritual, Feasting, and Social Differentiation in Late Prehistoric Zuni Communities.* PhD dissertation, Arizona State University, Tempe. University Microfilms, Ann Arbor.
2000 Pots, Parties, and Politics: Communal Feasting in the American Southwest. *American Antiquity* 65:471–492.

Potter, James M., and Elizabeth M. Perry
2000 Ritual as a Power Resource in the American Southwest. In *Alternative Leadership Strategies in the Prehispanic Southwest*, edited by Barbara J. Mills, pp. 6–78. University of Arizona Press, Tucson.

Powell, Susan J.
1977 Changing Subsistence Patterns as Reflected in Faunal Remains from the Mimbres River Area, New Mexico. Unpublished Master's thesis, Department of Anthropology, University of California, Los Angeles.

Powers, Robert P., and Janet D. Orcutt (editors)
1999 *The Bandelier Archeological Survey, Volumes 1–2.* Intermountain Cultural Resources Management Professional Paper No. 57. USDI National Park Service, Santa Fe.

Preucel, Robert W.
2005 Ethnicity and Southwestern Ar-chaeology. In *Southwest Archaeology in the Twentieth Century*, edited by Linda S. Cordell and Don D. Fowler, pp. 174–193. University of Utah Press, Salt Lake City.

Preucel, Robert W., Loa P. Traxler, and Michael V. Wilcox
2002 "Now the God of the Spanish Is Dead": Ethnogenesis and Community Formation in the Aftermath of the Pueblo Revolt of 1680. In *Traditions, Transitions and Technologies: Themes in Southwestern Archaeology*, edited by Sarah H. Schlanger, pp. 71–93. University Press of Colorado, Boulder.

Putnam, Frederic Ward
1901 A Problem in American Anthropology. In *Annual Report of the Board of Regents of the Smithsonian Institution for the Year Ending June 30, 1899*, pp. 473–486. U.S. Government Printing Office, Washington, D.C.

Quam, Alvina (translator)
1972 *The Zunis: Self-Portrayals.* University of New Mexico Press, Albuquerque.

Quinn, William H.
1992 A Study of Southern Oscillation-Related Climatic Activity for AD 622–1990 Incorporating Nile River Flood Data. In *El Niño: Historical and Paleoclimatic Aspects of the Southern Oscillation*, edited by Henry F. Diaz and Vera Markgraf, pp. 119–149. Cambridge University Press, Cambridge.

Quinn, William H., and W. V. Burt
1970 Prediction of Abnormally Heavy Precipitation over the Equatorial Pacific Dry Zone. *Journal of Applied Meteorology* 9:20–28.
1972 Use of the Southern Oscillation in Weather Prediction. *Journal of Applied Meteorology* 5:616–628.

Quinn, William H., and V. T. Neal
1992 The Historical Record of El Niño Events. In *Climate since AD 1500*, edited by Raymond S. Bradley and Philip D. Jones, pp. 623–648. Routledge, London.

Quinn, William H., Victor T. Neal, and Santiago E. Antunez de Mayolo
1987 El Niño Occurrences over the Past Four and a Half Centuries. *Journal of Geophysical Research* 92(C13):14449–14461.

Quinn, William H., D. O. Zopf, K. S. Short, and R. T. W. Kuoyang
1978 Historical Trends and Statistics of the Southern Oscillation. *Fisheries Bulletin* 76:663–678.

Rankin, Adrianne G.
1995 *Archaeological Survey at Organ Pipe Cactus National Monument, Southwestern Arizona: 1989–1991.* Western Archeological and Conservation Center. USDI National Park Service, Tucson.

Rapaport, Amos
1969 *House Form and Culture.* Prentice-Hall, Englewood Cliffs, New Jersey.
1990 Systems of Activities and Their Settings. In *Domestic Architecture and the Use of Space*, edited by Susan Kent, pp. 9–20. Cambridge University Press, Cambridge.

Rathje, William L.
1971 The Origin and Development of Lowland Classic Maya Civilization. *American Antiquity* 36:275–285.

Rathje, William L., and Jeremy A. Sabloff
1975 Theoretical Background: General Models and Questions. In *A Study of Changing Pre-Columbian Commercial Systems: The 1972–1973 Seasons at Cozumel, Mexico*, edited by Jeremy A. Sabloff and William L. Rathje, pp. 6–20. Peabody Museum Monographs No. 3, Harvard University, Cambridge.

Rea, Amadeo M.
1981 Avian Remains from Las Colinas. In *The 1968 Excavations at Mound 8, Las Colinas Ruins Group, Phoenix, Arizona*, edited and assembled by Laurens C. Hammack and Alan P. Sullivan, pp. 297–302. Arizona State Museum Archaeological Series No. 154, University of Arizona, Tucson.
1983 *Once upon a River: Bird Life and Habitat Changes on the Middle Gila.* University of Arizona Press, Tucson.

Reagan, Albert B.
1928 The Small House and Semi-pueblo Ruins of the Painted (and Shiny Painted) Ware Series in the Cornfields-Hopi Volcanic Buttes' Field, in Navajo Country, Arizona. *El Palacio* 25(14–17):232–247.
1929 Continued Archaeological Studies in the Navajo Country, Arizona. *Transactions of the Kansas Academy of Science* 31:142–279.

Redmond, K. T., and R. W. Koch
1991 Surface Climate and Streamflow Variability in the Western United States and Their Relationship to Large Scale Circulation Indices. *Water Resources Research* 27:2381–2399.

Reed, Erik K.
1941 Notes on Zuni Ceramic History. Manuscript on file, Museum of Northern Arizona Library, Flagstaff.

1946 The Distinctive Features and Distribution of the San Juan Anasazi Culture. *Southwestern Journal of Anthropology* 2:295–305.

1948 The Western Pueblo Archaeological Complex. *El Palacio* 55(1):9–15.

1949 Sources of Upper Rio Grande Pueblo Culture and Population. *El Palacio* 56(6):163–184.

1950 Eastern-Central Arizona Archaeology in Relation to the Western Pueblos. *Southwestern Journal of Anthropology* 6:120–138.

1955 Painted Pottery and Zuni History. *Southwestern Journal of Anthropology* 11(2):178–193.

Reed, Lori Stephens, C. Dean Wilson, and Kelley A. Hays-Gilpin

2000 From Brown to Gray: The Origins of Ceramic Technology in the Northern Southwest. In *Foundations of Anasazi Culture: The Basketmaker–Pueblo Transition*, edited by Paul F. Reed, pp. 203–229. University of Utah Press, Salt Lake City.

Reff, Daniel T.

1994 Contextualizing Missionary Discourse: The Benavides Memorials of 1630 and 1634. *Journal of Anthropological Research* 50:51–67.

Reid, J. Jefferson

1984 What Is Black-on-white and Vague All Over? In *Regional Analysis of Prehistoric Ceramic Variation: Contemporary Studies of the Cibola Whitewares*, edited by Alan P. Sullivan and Jeffrey L. Hantman, pp. 135–152. Arizona State University Anthropological Research Papers No. 31. Tempe.

Reid, J. Jefferson, Barbara Klie Montgomery, and Maria Nieves Zedeño

1995 Refinements in Dating Late Cibola White Ware. *Kiva* 61:31–44.

Reid, J. Jefferson, and Stephanie M. Whittlesey

1997 *The Archaeology of Ancient Arizona*. University of Arizona Press, Tucson.

1999 *Grasshopper Pueblo: A Story of Archaeology and Ancient Life*. University of Arizona Press, Tucson.

Renfrew, Colin

1975 Trade as Action at a Distance: Questions of Integration and Communication. In *Ancient Civilization and Trade*, edited by Jeremy A. Sabloff and C. C. Lamberg-Karlovsky, pp. 3–60. School of American Research Advanced Seminar Series, University of New Mexico Press, Albuquerque.

1977 Alternative Models for Exchange and Spatial Distribution. In *Exchange Systems in Prehistory*, edited by Timothy Earle and Jonathon E. Ericson, pp. 71–90. Academic Press, New York.

1986 Introduction: Peer Polity Interaction and Socio-political Change. In *Peer Polity Interaction and Sociopolitical Change*, edited by Colin Renfrew and John F. Cherry, pp. 1–18. New Directions in Archaeology, Cambridge University Press, Cambridge.

1987a *Archaeology and Language: The Puzzle of Indo-European Origins*. Jonathan Cape, London.

1987b *Archaeology and Linguistics*. Cambridge University Press, Cambridge.

1989 Models of Change in Language and Archaeology. *Transactions of the Philosophical Society* 87(2):103–155.

1992a World Languages and Human Dispersals: A Minimalist View. In *Transition to Modernity: Essays on Power, Wealth and Belief*, edited by John A. Hall and I. C. Garvie, pp. 11–68. Cambridge University Press, Cambridge.

1992b Archaeology, Genetics and Linguistic Diversity. *Man* 27:445–478.

1996 Language Families and the Spread of Farming. In *The Origins and Spread of Agriculture and Pastoralism in Eurasia*, edited by David R. Harris, pp. 70–92. UCL Press, London.

1998a The Origins of World Linguistic Diversity: An Archaeological Perspective. In *The Origin and Diversification of Language*, edited by Nina G. Jablonski and Leslie C. Aiello, pp. 171–192. Memoirs of the California Academy of Sciences No. 24. San Francisco.

1998b The Origin and Dispersal of Languages: Linguistic Evidence. In *The Origin and Diversification of Language*, edited by Nina G. Jablonski and Leslie C. Aiello, pp. 127–170. Memoirs of the California Academy of Sciences No. 24. San Francisco.

2001 Production and Consumption in a Sacred Economy: The Material Correlates of High Devotional Expression at Chaco Canyon. *American Antiquity* 66:14–25.

2002 "The Emerging Synthesis": The Archaeogenetics of Farming/Language Dispersals and Other Spread Zones. In *Examining the Farming/Language Dispersal Hypothesis*, edited by Peter Bellwood and Colin Renfrew, pp. 3–16. McDonald Institute for Archaeological Research, Cambridge University.

Renfrew, Colin (editor)

2000 *America Past, America Present: Genes and Languages in the Americas and Beyond*. McDonald Institute for Archaeological Research, Cambridge University.

Renfrew, Colin, and Katie Boyle (editors)

2000 *Archaeogenetics: DNA and the Population Prehistory of Europe*. McDonald Institute for Archaeological Research, Cambridge University.

Renfrew, Colin, and John F. Cherry

1986 *Peer Polity Interaction and Sociopolitical Change*. Cambridge University Press, Cambridge.

Renfrew, Colin, April McMahon, and Larry Trask

2000 *Time Depth in Historical Linguistics*. McDonald Institute for Archaeological Research, Cambridge University.

Renfrew, Colin, and Daniel Nettle (editors)

1999 *Nostratic: Examining a Linguistic Macrofamily*. McDonald Institute for Archaeological Research, Cambridge University.

Rice, Glen E.

1990 Variability in the Development of Classic Period Elites. In *A Design for Salado Research*, edited by Glen E. Rice, pp. 65–78. Roosevelt Monograph Series No. 1, Anthropological Field Studies No. 22. Office of Cultural Resource Management, Arizona State University, Tempe.

Rice, Glen E., and Steven A. LeBlanc (editors)

2001 *Deadly Landscapes: Case Studies in Prehistoric Southwestern Warfare*. University of Utah Press, Salt Lake City.

Rice, Glen E., Arleyn W. Simon, and Christopher Loendorf

1998 Production and Exchange of Economic Goods. In *A Synthesis of Tonto Basin Prehistory: The Roosevelt Archaeology Studies, 1989 to 1998*, edited by Glen E. Rice, pp. 105–130. Roosevelt Monograph Series 12, Anthropological Field Studies 41. Arizona State University, Tempe.

Riley, Carroll L.

1981 Puaray and Coronado's Tiguex. In *Collected Papers in Honor of Erik Kellerman Reed*, edited by Albert H. Schroeder, pp. 197–213. Papers of the New Mexico Archaeological Society No. 6, Albuquerque.

1982 *The Frontier People: The Greater Southwest in the Protohistoric Period*. University of New Mexico Press, Albuquerque.

1985   Spanish Contact and the Collapse of the Sonoran Statelets. In *The Archaeology of West and Northwest Mesoamerica*, edited by Michael S. Foster and Phil C. Weigand, pp. 419–430. Westview Press, Boulder.

1987   *The Frontier People: The Greater Southwest in the Protohistoric Period*. Revised and expanded ed. University of New Mexico Press, Albuquerque.

1990   The Sonoran Statelets Revisited. In *Clues to the Past: Papers in Honor of William M. Sundt*, edited by Meliha S. Duran and David T. Kirkpatrick, pp. 229–235. Archaeological Society of New Mexico No. 16, Albuquerque.

1995   *Rio del Norte: People of the Upper Rio Grande from Earliest Times to the Pueblo Revolt*. University of Utah Press, Salt Lake City.

Rinaldo, John B.

1941   Conjectures on the Independent Development of the Mogollon Culture. *American Antiquity* 7:5–19.

1959   *Foote Canyon Pueblo, Eastern Arizona*. Fieldiana: Anthropology Vol. 49, No. 2. Chicago Natural History Museum, Chicago.

1962   Some Convergences and Continuities. In *Chapters in the Prehistory of Eastern Arizona I*, edited by Paul Sidney Martin, John B. Rinaldo, William A. Longacre, Constance Cronin, Leslie G. Freeman Jr., and James Schoenwetter, pp. 64–74. Fieldiana: Anthropology Vol. 53. Chicago Natural History Museum, Chicago.

1964   Notes on the Origin of Historic Zuni Culture. *Kiva* 29:86–98.

Rinaldo, John B., and Elaine A. Bluhm

1956   *Late Mogollon Pottery Types of the Reserve Area*. Fieldiana: Anthropology Vol. 36, No. 7. Chicago Natural History Museum, Chicago.

Rinaldo, John, and Jane Darrow

1943   Artifacts. In *The SU Site: Excavations at a Mogollon Village, Western New Mexico: Second Season, 1941*, edited by Paul S. Martin, pp. 171–235. Anthropology Series 32, No. 2. Field Museum of Natural History, Chicago.

Roberts, Frank H. H., Jr.

1929a   *Shabik'eshchee Village: A Late Basketmaker Site in the Chaco Canyon, New Mexico*. Bulletin No. 92, Bureau of American Ethnology, Smithsonian Institution, Washington, D.C.

1929b   *Recent Archeological Developments in the Vicinity of El Paso, Texas*. Smithsonian Miscellaneous Collections Vol. 81, No. 7. Washington, D.C.

1931   *The Ruins at Kiatuthlanna, Eastern Arizona*. Bulletin No. 100, Bureau of American Ethnology, Smithsonian Institution, Washington, D.C.

1932   *The Village of the Great Kivas on the Zuni Reservation, New Mexico*. Bulletin No. 111, Bureau of American Ethnology, Smithsonian Institution, Washington, D.C.

1935   A Survey of Southwestern Archaeology. *American Anthropologist* 37:1–35.

1937   Archaeology in the Southwest. *American Antiquity* 3:3–33.

1939a   *Archaeological Remains in the Whitewater District, Eastern Arizona, Part 1, House Types*. Bulletin No. 121, Bureau of American Ethnology, Smithsonian Institution, Washington, D.C.

1939b   The Development of the Unit-Type Dwelling. In *So Live the Works of Men: Seventieth Anniversary Volume Honoring Edgar Lee Hewett*, edited by Donald D. Brand and Fred E. Harvey. University of New Mexico Press, Albuquerque.

1940a   *Archeological Remains in the Whitewater District, Eastern Arizona, Part II: Artifacts and Burials*. Bulletin No. 126, Bureau of American Ethnology, Smithsonian Institution, Washington, D.C.

1940b   Developments in the Problem of the Paleo-Indian. In *Essays in Historical Anthropology of North America*. Smithsonian Miscellaneous Collections 100:51–116.

Roberts, John M.

1961   The Zuni. In *Variations in Value Orientations*, edited by Florence R. Kluckhohn and Fred Strodtbeck, pp. 285–316. Row, Peterson, and Company, Evanston, Illinois.

Robinson, William J.

1958   A New Type of Ceremonial Pottery Killing at Point of Pines. *Kiva* 23(3):12–16.

Rodbell, Donald, Geoffrey O. Seltzer, David M. Anderson, Mark B. Abbott, David B. Enfield, and Jeremy H. Newman

1999   A 15,000-Year Record of El Niño–Driven Alluviation in Southwestern Ecuador. *Science* 283:516–520.

Roediger, Virginia M.

1941   *Ceremonial Costumes of the Pueblo Indians: Their Evolution, Fabrication, and Significance in the Prayer Drama*. University of California Press, Berkeley.

Rogers, Edward S.

1962   *The Round Lake Ojibwa*. Occasional Paper 5. Art and Archaeology Division, Royal Ontario Museum, Toronto.

Rohn, Arthur H.

1965   Postulation of Socio-economic Groups from Archaeological Evidence. In *Contributions of the Wetherill Mesa Archaeological Project*, assembled by Douglas Osborne, pp. 65–69. Memoirs of the Society for American Archaeology No. 19, 31(2, Pt. 2).

Romney, A. Kimball

1957   The Genetic Model and Uto-Aztecan Time Perspective. *Davidson Journal of Anthropology* 3(2):35–41.

Rood, D.

1973   Swadesh's Keres-Caddo Comparison. *International Journal of American Linguistics* 39:189–190.

Rose, Martin R.

1987   Present and Past Climate of the Zuni Region. Plaintiff's Exhibit 5,000. Expert testimony submitted to the United States Claims Court as evidence in the case *Zuni Indian Tribe v. United States*, Docket 327-81L.

1989   Rebuttal Report: Present and Past Climate of the Zuni Region. Plaintiff's Exhibit 5,000. Expert testimony submitted to the United States Claims Court as evidence in the case *Zuni Indian Tribe v. United States*, Dockets 327-81L and 224-81L.

Rose, Martin R., William J. Robinson, and Jeffrey S. Dean

1982   Dendroclimatic Reconstruction for the Southeastern Colorado Plateau. Manuscript on file, Laboratory of Tree-Ring Research, University of Arizona, Tucson.

Rosen, Lawrence

1997   The Right to Be Different: Indigenous People and the Quest for a Unified Theory. *Yale Law Journal* 107:227–259.

Rosenthal, E. Jane, Douglas R. Brown, Marc Severson, and John B. Clonts

1978   *The Quijotoa Valley Project*. Cultural Resource Management Division, Western Archeological Center. USDI National Park Service, Tucson.

Rouse, Irving

1958   The Inference of Migrations from Anthropological Evidence. In *Migrations in New World Culture History*, edited by Raymond H. Thompson, pp. 63–68. Social Bulletin No. 27. University of Arizona Press, Tucson.

Rowe, Robert A.

1997a Ground Stone and Small Stone Artifacts. In *Turquoise Traders of the Silver Bells: Settlement, Subsistence, and Exchange on the Periphery of the Northern Tucson Basin*, edited by Laurie V. Slawson, pp. 309–338. Archaeological Series No. 2, Aztlan Archaeology, Inc., Tucson.

1997b The Trade Routes—the Lifeblood of the Silver Bells. In *Turquoise Traders of the Silver Bells: Settlement, Subsistence, and Exchange on the Periphery of the Northern Tucson Basin*, edited by Laurie V. Slawson, pp. 362–375. Archaeological Series No. 2, Aztlan Archaeology, Inc., Tucson.

Roys, Lawrence

1936 Lowry Ruin as an Introduction to the Study of Southwestern Masonry. In *Lowry Ruin in Southwestern Colorado*, by Paul S. Martin, pp. 115–142. Anthropological Series of the Field Museum of Natural History Vol. 13, No. 1. Chicago.

Ruble, Ellen

1996 Macaws in the Southwest. Unpublished Master's thesis, Department of Anthropology, Northern Arizona University, Flagstaff.

Ruhlen, Merritt

1991 The Amerind Phylum and the Prehistory of the New World. In *Sprung from Some Common Source: Investigations into the Prehistory of Languages*, edited by Sydney M. Lamb and E. Douglas Mitchell, pp. 328–350. Stanford University Press, Stanford.

1994 Amerind T'A?NA 'child, sibling.' In *On the Origin of Languages: Studies in Linguistic Taxonomy*, edited by Merritt Rhulen, pp. 183–206. Stanford University Press, Stanford.

Ruppé, Patricia A., and Harold Drollinger

1990 Environmental Setting, Culture History, and Previous Investigations. In *Archaeological Testing along New Mexico State Highway 53 from the Nutria Road to the Pinehill Road, McKinley and Cibola Counties, New Mexico*, pp. 12–21. Prepared by R. Vercruysse and H. Drollinger. Zuni Archaeology Program, Project No. ZAP-019-86, Report No. 264.

Ruppé, Reynold J., Jr.

1966 The Archaeological Survey: A

Defense. *American Antiquity* 31:313–333.

1990 *The Acoma Culture Province.* Garland Publishing, New York. Originally PhD dissertation, Harvard University, 1953.

Russell, Stephen M., and Gale Monson

1998 *The Birds of Sonora.* University of Arizona Press, Tucson.

Sackett, James R.

1973 Style, Function, and Artifact Variability in Paleolithic Assemblages. In *The Explanation of Culture Change*, edited by Colin Renfrew, pp. 317–325. Duckworth, London.

1977 The Meaning of Style in Archaeology: A General Model. *American Antiquity* 42:369–380.

1982 Approaches to Style in Lithic Archaeology. *Journal of Anthropological Archaeology* 1:59–112.

1985 Style and Ethnicity in the Kalahari: A Reply to Wiessner. *American Antiquity* 50:154–159.

1986 Isochrestism and Style: A Clarification. *Journal of Anthropological Archaeology* 5:266–277.

1990 Style and Ethnicity in Archaeology: The Case for Isochrestism. In *The Uses of Style in Archaeology*, edited by Margaret W. Conkey and Christine A. Hastorf, pp. 32–43. Cambridge University Press, Cambridge.

Saitta, Dean J.

1987 *Economic Integration and Social Development in Zuni Prehistory.* PhD dissertation, University of Massachusetts, Amherst. University Microfilms, Ann Arbor.

1991 Room Use and Community Organization at the Pettit Site, West Central New Mexico. *Kiva* 56:383–409.

1994 The Political Economy and Ideology of Early Population Aggregation in Togeye Canyon, AD 1150–1250. In *Exploring Social, Political, and Economic Organization in the Zuni Region*, edited by Todd L. Howell and Tammy Stone, pp. 47–60. Arizona State University Anthropological Research Papers No. 46. Arizona State University, Tempe.

Salzer, Matthew W.

2000a *Dendroclimatology in the San Francisco Peaks Region of Northern Arizona, USA.* PhD dissertation, University of Arizona, Tucson. University Microfilms, Ann Arbor.

2000b Temperature Variability and the

Northern Anasazi: Possible Implications for Regional Abandonment. *Kiva* 65:295–318.

Salzer, Matthew W., and Kurt F. Kipfmueller

2005 Reconstructed Temperature and Precipitation on a Millennial Timescale from Tree-Rings in the Southern Colorado Plateau, U.S.A. *Climatic Change* 70:465–487.

Sapir, Edward

1929 Central and North American Languages. In *Encyclopaedia Britannica*, 14th ed., Vol. 5, pp. 138–141. London: Encyclopaedia Britannica Company.

1949 Time Perspective in Aboriginal American Culture: A Study in Method. In *Selected Writings in Language, Culture and Personality*, edited by D. G. Mandelbaum, pp. 389–462. University of California Press, Berkeley. Originally published 1916.

Sauer, Carl O.

1934 *The Distribution of Aboriginal Tribes and Languages in Northwestern Mexico.* Ibero-Americana No. 3. Berkeley.

1935 *Aboriginal Population of Northwestern Mexico.* Ibero-Americana No. 10. Berkeley.

1954 Comments on P. Kirchoff, Gatherers and Farmers in the Greater Southwest. *American Anthropologist* 56:553–556.

Saxton, Dean, Lucille Saxton, and Suzanne Enos

1983 *Papago–English / English–Papago Dictionary.* University of Arizona Press, Tucson.

Sayles, E. B.

1945 *The San Simon Branch, Excavations at Cave Creek and in the San Simon Valley I: Material Culture.* Medallion Papers 34. Gila Pueblo, Globe, Arizona.

Scarre, Christopher, and Brian M. Fagan

1997 *Ancient Civilizations.* Longman, New York.

Schaafsma, Curtis F.

2002 *Apaches de Navajo: Seventeenth-Century Navajos in the Chama Valley of New Mexico.* University of Utah Press, Salt Lake City.

Schaafsma, Curtis F., and Carroll L. Riley

1999 The Casas Grandes World: Analysis and Conclusion. In *The Casas Grandes World*, edited by Curtis F. Schaafsma and Carroll L. Riley, pp. 237–249. University of Utah, Salt Lake City.

Schaafsma, Curtis F., and Carroll L. Riley (editors)

1999 *The Casas Grandes World*. University of Utah Press, Salt Lake City.

Schaafsma, Polly

1963 *Rock Art in the Navajo Reservoir District*. Papers in Anthropology 7, Museum of New Mexico Press, Santa Fe.

1971 Field Notes, New Mexico Rock Art Survey, State Planning Office. Records on file at the Laboratory of Anthropology, Santa Fe.

1975 *Rock Art in New Mexico*. Published for the Cultural Properties Review Committee in cooperation with the State Planning Office. University of New Mexico Press, Albuquerque.

1980 *Indian Rock Art of the Southwest*. School of American Research, Santa Fe, and University of New Mexico Press, Albuquerque.

1992 *Rock Art in New Mexico*. 2nd ed. Museum of New Mexico Press, Santa Fe.

1994 Trance and Transformation in the Canyons: Shamanism and Early Rock Art on the Colorado Plateau. In *Shamanism and Rock Art in North America*, edited by Solveig A. Turpin, pp. 45–72. Special Publications 1. Rock Art Foundation, Inc., San Antonio.

1996 The Prehistoric Kachina Cult and Its Origins as Suggested by Southwestern Rock Art. In *Kachinas in the Pueblo World*, edited by Polly Schaafsma, pp. 63–80. University of New Mexico Press, Albuquerque.

1998 The Paquime Rock Art Style, Chihuahua, Mexico. In *Rock Art of the Chihuahua Desert Borderlands*, edited by Sheron Smith-Savage and Robert J. Mallouf, pp. 33–44. Center for Big Bend Studies: Occasional Paper No. 3. Sul Ross State University and Texas Parks and Wildlife Department, Alpine.

1999 Tlalocs, Kachinas, Sacred Bundles, and Related Symbolism in the Southwest and Mesoamerica. In *The Casas Grandes World*, edited by Curtis F. Schaafsma and Carroll L. Riley, pp. 164–192. University of Utah Press, Salt Lake City.

2000 *Warrior, Shield and Star: Imagery and Ideology of Pueblo Warfare*. Western Edge Press, Santa Fe.

2005 The Pottery Mound Murals and Rock Art: The Broader Iconographic Context. Paper presented at the 70th Annual Meeting of the Society for American Archaeology, Salt Lake City.

2006 Emblems of Power: Visual Symbols as a Means of Social Identity and the Role of Rock Art in the Chaco System. In *Southwestern Interludes: Papers in Honor of Charlotte J. and Theodore R. Frisbie*, edited by Regge N. Wiseman, Thomas C. O'Laughlin, and Cordelia T. Snow, pp. 147–166. Archaeological Society of New Mexico No. 32, Albuquerque.

Schaafsma, Polly, and Curtis F. Schaafsma

1974 Evidence for the Origins of the Pueblo Kachina Cult as Suggested by Southwestern Rock Art. *American Antiquity* 39:535–545.

Schaafsma, Polly, and M. Jane Young

1983 Early Masks and Faces in Southwestern Rock Art. In *Papers in Honor of Charlie Steen*, edited by Nancy Fox, pp. 11–33. Archaeological Society of New Mexico Papers No. 9, Albuquerque.

Schachner, Gregson

1998 Big Towns, Little Roomblocks: The Impact of Migration on the El Morro Valley, AD 1200–1325. Department of Anthropology, Arizona State University, Tempe.

2006 The Decline of Zuni Glaze Ware Production in the Tumultuous Fifteenth Century. In *The Social Life of Pots: Glaze Wares and Cultural Dynamics in the Southwest, AD 1250–1680*, edited by Judith A. Habicht-Mauche, Suzanne L. Eckert, and Deborah L. Huntley, pp. 124–141. University of Arizona Press, Tucson.

Schlanger, Sarah H. (editor)

2002 *Traditions, Transitions, and Technologies: Themes in Southwestern Archaeology*. University Press of Colorado, Boulder.

Schneider, Alan L.

2004 Kennewick Man: The Three-Million-Dollar Skeleton. In *Legal Perspectives on Cultural Resources*, edited by Jennifer R. Richman and Marion P. Forsyth, pp. 202–215. AltaMira Press, Walnut Creek, California.

Schoenwetter, James, and Frank W. Eddy

1964 *Alluvial and Palynological Reconstruction of Environments, Navajo Reservoir District*. Museum of New Mexico Papers in Anthropology No. 13. Museum of New Mexico Press, Santa Fe.

Schroeder, Albert H.

1957 The Hakataya Cultural Tradition. *American Antiquity* 23:176–178.

1960 *The Hohokam, Sinagua and Hakataya*. Archives in Archaeology No. 5. Society for American Archaeology, Madison, Wisconsin.

1961 *The Archaeological Excavations at Willow Beach, Arizona, 1950*. University of Utah Anthropological Papers No. 50. University of Utah Press, Salt Lake City.

Schroeder, Albert H. (assembler)

1983 *The Pratt Cave Studies*. Artifact Vol. 21, Nos. 1–4. El Paso Archaeological Society, El Paso.

Schroedl, Alan R., and Nancy J. Coulam

1994 Cowboy Cave Revisited. *Utah Archaeology 1994* 7:1–34.

Schroedl, Gerald F.

1998 Mississippian Towns in the Eastern Tennessee Valley. In *Mississippian Towns and Sacred Spaces: Searching for an Architectural Grammar*, edited by R. Barry Lewis and Charles Stout, pp. 64–92. University of Alabama Press, Tuscaloosa.

Schurr, Mark R., and David A. Gregory

2002 Fluoride Dating of Faunal Materials by Ion-Selective Electrode: High Resolution Relative Dating at an Early Agricultural Period Site in the Tucson Basin. *American Antiquity* 67:281–299.

Schutt, Jeanne A., Richard C. Chapman, and June-el Piper

1994 *On the Periphery of the Mimbres Mogollon: The Cuchillo Negro Archaeological Project*, Vol. 1. Office of Contract Archaeology, University of New Mexico, Albuquerque.

Scott, Catherine J.

1983 The Evolution of Mimbres Pottery. In *Mimbres Pottery: Ancient Art of the American Southwest*, by J. J. Brody, Catherine J. Scott, and Steven A. LeBlanc, pp. 39–67. Hudson Hills Press, New York.

Seltzer, Carl C.

1944 *Racial Prehistory in the Southwest and the Hawikuh Zunis*. Papers of the Peabody Museum of American Archaeology and Ethnology Vol. 23, No. 1. Harvard University, Cambridge.

Setzler, Frank M.

1935 A Prehistoric Cave Culture in Southwestern Texas. *American Anthropologist*, n.s. 37(1):104–110.

Shafer, Harry J.

1995 Architecture and Symbolism in Transitional Pueblo Development in the Mimbres Valley, SW New Mexico. *Journal of Field Archaeology* 22:23–47.

Shapiro, Barbara J.
2000 *A Culture of Fact: England, 1550–1720.* Cornell University Press, Ithaca.
Shaul, David L.
1980a A Preliminary Analysis of the Pueblo Culture Area as a Linguistic Area. Manuscript on file, Department of Anthropology, University of Arizona, Tucson.
1980b Ergativity in Zuni. Manuscript on file, Department of Anthropology, University of Arizona, Tucson.
1980c The Location of the Proto-Keresan Speech Community. Manuscript on file, Department of Anthropology, University of Arizona, Tucson.
1980d Class Handout for Indians of the Southwest, ANTH 414a. Manuscript on file, Department of Anthropology, University of Arizona, Tucson.
1982 Glottalized Consonants in Zuni. *International Journal of American Linguistics* 48(1):83–85.
1985 Azteco-Tanoan *-1/r-. *International Journal of American Linguistics* 51:584–586.
Shaul, David Leedom, and Jane H. Hill
1998 Tepimans, Yumans, and Other Hohokam. *American Antiquity* 63:375–396.
Shelley, Steven D.
2001 Osteological Description and Observations on the Macaw Skeletal Remains. In *El Macayo, a Prehistoric Settlement in the Upper Santa Cruz River Valley,* edited by William L. Deaver and Carla R. Van West, pp. 123–128. Technical Series 74. Statistical Research, Inc., Tucson.
Shennan, Stephen J.
1989 Introduction: Archaeological Approaches to Cultural Identity. In *Archaeological Approaches to Cultural Identity,* edited by Stephen J. Shennan, pp. 1–32. Unwin Hyman, London.
2000 Population, Culture History, and the Dynamics of Culture Change. *Current Anthropology* 41:811–835.
Shepard, Anna O.
1942 *Rio Grande Glaze Paint Ware: A Study Illustrating the Place of Ceramic Technological Analysis in Archaeological Research.* Carnegie Institution of Washington Publication 528, pp. 129–260. Washington, D.C.
1953 Notes on Color and Paste Composition. In *Archaeological Studies in the Petrified Forest National Monument,* edited by Fred Wendorf, pp. 177–193.

Museum of Northern Arizona Bulletin 27. Flagstaff.
Sheppard, Paul R., Andrew C. Comrie, Gregory D. Packin, Kurt Angersbach, and Malcolm K. Hughes
1999 *The Climate of the Southwest: The Climate Assessment Project for the Southwest (CLIMAS),* Report Series: CL1-99. University of Arizona, Tucson.
Sherratt, Andrew
1990 Genesis of Megaliths: Monumentality, Ethnicity, and Social Complexity in *The Neolithic North-West Europe. World Archaeology* 22:147–167.
Simpson, Ruth De Ette
1950 Tracking the Hohokam. *Masterkey* 24(4):126–128.
Skibo, James M., and Eric Blinman
1999 Exploring the Origins of Pottery in the Colorado Plateau. In *Pottery and People: A Dynamic Interaction,* edited by James M. Skibo and Gary M. Feinman, pp. 171–183. University of Utah Press, Salt Lake City.
Skibo, James M., Eugene B. McCluney, and William H. Walker
2002 *The Joyce Wells Site: On the Frontier of the Casas Grandes World.* University of Utah Press, Salt Lake City.
Slawson, Laurie V. (editor)
1997 *Turquoise Traders of the Silver Bells: Settlement, Subsistence, and Exchange on the Periphery of the Northern Tucson Basin.* Archaeological Series No. 2. Aztlan Archaeology, Inc., Tucson.
Slifer, Dennis, and James Duffield
1994 *Kokopelli: Flute Player Images in Rock Art.* Ancient City Press, Santa Fe.
Sliva, R. Jane
1999 Cienega Points and Late Archaic Period Chronology in the Southern Southwest. *Kiva* 64:339–368.
Smalley, John, and Michael Blake
2003 Sweet Beginning: Stalk Sugar and the Domestication of Maize. *Current Anthropology* 44:675–703.
Smith, Anthony D.
1987 *The Ethnic Origins of Nations.* Basil Blackwell, Oxford.
Smith, Susan
2001 Palynology. In *Households and Farms in Early Zuni Prehistory: Settlement, Subsistence, and the Archaeology of Y Unit Draw—Archaeological Investigations at Eighteen Sites along New Mexico State Highway 602,* prepared by Jonathan E. Damp, James Kendrick, Donovan Quam, Jeffrey Waseta, and Jerome Zunie, pp. 629–638. New Mexico State Highway and Transpor-

tation Department Technical Series 2001-3/ZCRE Research Series No. 11. Zuni, New Mexico.
Smith, Walter
1986 *The Effects of Eastern North Pacific Tropical Cyclones on the Southwestern United States.* NOAA Technical Memorandum, NWS WR-197. Salt Lake City.
Smith, Watson
1952 *Kiva Mural Decorations at Awatovi and Kawaika-a, with a Survey of Other Wall Painting in the Pueblo Southwest.* Papers of the Peabody Museum of American Archaeology and Ethnology Vol. 37. Harvard University, Cambridge.
1971 *Painted Ceramics of the Western Mound at Awatovi.* Papers of the Peabody Museum of Archaeology and Ethnology No. 38. Harvard University, Cambridge.
1973 *The Williams Site: A Frontier Mogollon Village in West-Central New Mexico.* Papers of the Peabody Museum of Archaeology and Ethnology Vol. 39, No. 2. Harvard University, Cambridge.
Smith, Watson, Richard B. Woodbury, and Natalie F. S. Woodbury
1966 *The Excavation of Hawikuh by Frederick Webb Hodge: Report of the Hendricks-Hodge Expedition, 1917–1923.* Contributions No. 20. Museum of the American Indian, Heye Foundation. New York.
Snead, James
2001 *Ruins and Rivals: The Making of Southwestern Archaeology.* University of Arizona Press, Tucson.
Snodgrass, O. T.
1975 *Realistic Art and Times of the Mimbres Indians.* O. T. Snodgrass, El Paso.
Snow, David H.
1976 *Archeological Excavations at Pueblo del Encierro, LA70, Cochiti Dam Salvage Project, New Mexico, Final Report: 1964–1965 Field Seasons, A–K.* Heritage Conservation and Recreation Service, Denver.
Speth, John D.
1988 Do We Need Concepts Like "Mogollon," "Anasazi," and "Hohokam" Today? A Cultural Anthropological Perspective. *Kiva* 53:201–204.
2004 *Life on the Periphery: Economic Change in Late Prehistoric Southeastern New Mexico.* Museum of Anthropology Memoirs No. 5. University of Michigan, Ann Arbor.
Spicer, Edmund
1962 *Cycles of Conquest.* University of Arizona Press, Tucson.

Spielmann, Katherine A.

1982 Inter-societal Food Acquisition among Egalitarian Societies: An Ecological Study of Plains/Pueblo Interaction in the American Southwest. Department of Anthropology, University of Michigan, Ann Arbor.

1983 Late Prehistoric Exchange between the Southwest and Southern Plains. *Plains Anthropologist* 28:257–272.

1994 Clustered Confederacies: Sociopolitical Organization in the Protohistoric Rio Grande. In *The Ancient Southwestern Community*, edited by Wirt H. Wills and Robert D. Leonard, pp. 45–54. University of New Mexico Press, Albuquerque.

Spielmann, Katherine A. (editor)

1998 *Migration and Community Reorganization: The Pueblo IV Period in the American Southwest*. Arizona State University Anthropological Research Papers 51, Tempe.

Spier, Leslie

1917 *An Outline for a Chronology of Zuni Ruins*. Anthropological Papers Vol. 17, Pt. 3, pp. 207–331. American Museum of Natural History, New York.

1918 *Notes on Some Little Colorado Ruins*. Anthropological Papers Vol. 17, Pt. 4, pp. 333–362. American Museum of Natural History, New York.

1919 *Ruins in the White Mountains, Arizona*. Anthropological Papers Vol. 17, Pt. 5, pp. 363–387. American Museum of Natural History, New York.

1924 Zuni Weaving Technique. *American Anthropologist* 26:64–85.

Squier, E. G.

1848 New Mexico and California. *American Review, Devoted to Politics and Literature* 11(5):503–528.

Stahle, David W., Edward R. Cook, Malcolm K. Cleaveland, Matthew D. Therrell, David M. Meko, Henri D. Grissino-Mayer, Emma Watson, and Brian H. Luckman

2000 Tree-Ring Data Document 16th Century Megadrought over North America. *Eos, Transactions of the American Geophysical Union* 81(12):121, 125.

Stanislawski, Michael B.

1963 *Wupatki Pueblo: A Study in Cultural Fusion and Change in Sinagua and Hopi Prehistory*. PhD dissertation, Department of Anthropology, University of Arizona, Tucson. University Microfilms, Ann Arbor.

Stark, Miriam T.

1995 The Early Ceramic Horizon and Tonto Basin Prehistory. In *Ceramic Chronology, Technology, and Economics*, edited by James M. Heidke and Miriam T. Stark, pp. 249–271. The Roosevelt Community Development Study, Vol. 2. Anthropological Papers No. 14. Center for Desert Archaeology, Tucson.

Stark, Miriam T. (editor)

1998 *The Archaeology of Social Boundaries*. Smithsonian Institution Press, Washington, D.C.

Stark, Miriam T., Mark D. Elson, and Jeffery J. Clark

1998 Social Boundaries and Technical Choices in Tonto Basin Prehistory. In *The Archaeology of Social Boundaries*, edited by Miriam T. Stark, pp. 208–231. Smithsonian Institution Press, Washington, D.C.

Stark, Miriam T., and James M. Heidke

1995 Early Classic Period Variability in Utilitarian Ceramic Production and Distribution. In *Ceramic Chronology, Technology, and Economics*, edited by James M. Heidke and Miriam T. Stark, pp. 363–394. The Roosevelt Community Development Study, Vol. 2. Anthropological Papers No. 14. Center for Desert Archaeology, Tucson.

Steen, Charlie R., Lloyd M. Pierson, Vorsila L. Bohrer, and Kate Peck Kent

1962 *Archeological Studies at Tonto National Monument, Arizona*. Southwestern Monuments Association Technical Series 2. Globe, Arizona.

Stein, John R., and Stephen H. Lekson

1992 Anasazi Ritual Landscapes. In *Anasazi Regional Organization and the Chaco System*, edited by David E. Doyel, pp. 87–100. Maxwell Museum of Anthropology Papers 5. University of New Mexico, Albuquerque.

Stephen, Alexander M.

1929 Hopi Tales. *Journal of American Folk-Lore* 42:2–72.

1936 *Hopi Journal of Alexander M. Stephen*, edited by Elsie Clews Parsons. 2 vols. Columbia University Contributions to Anthropology 23. New York.

Stephenson, Christine, Suzanne DeRosa, Cathey Evans, and Charles A. Hoffman

1997 Near Bigelow Crossing: A Survey of Rock Art. Manuscript in the possession of the author.

Sterner, Judy

1989 Who Is Signalling Whom? Ceramic Style, Ethnicity and Taphonomy among the Sirak Bulahay. *Antiquity* 63:451–459.

Stevenson, James

1883 Illustrated Catalogue of the Collections Obtained from the Indians of New Mexico and Arizona in 1879. *Second Annual Report of the Bureau of American Ethnology for the Years 1880–1881*, pp. 307–422. Smithsonian Institution, Washington, D.C.

Stevenson, Matilda Coxe

1904 The Zuñi Indians: Their Mythology, Esoteric Fraternities, and Ceremonies. *Twenty-third Annual Report of the Bureau of American Ethnology for the Years 1901–1902*, pp. 1–608. Smithsonian Institution, Washington, D.C.

1915 Ethnobotany of the Zuni Indians. *Thirtieth Annual Report of the Bureau of American Ethnology for the Years 1908–1909*, pp. 31–102. Smithsonian Institution, Washington, D.C.

Steward, Julian H.

1936 The Economic and Social Basis of Primitive Bands. In *Essays in Anthropology Presented to A. L. Kroeber*, edited by Robert H. Lowie, pp. 331–345. University of California Press, Berkeley.

1937 Ecological Aspects of Southwestern Society. *Anthropos* 32:87–104.

1955 *Theory of Culture Change*. University of Illinois Press, Urbana.

Stewart, Joe D., Jonathan C. Driver, and Jane H. Kelley

1991 The Capitan North Project: Chronology. In *Mogollon V*, edited by Patrick H. Beckett and Regge N. Wiseman, pp. 177–190. COAS Publishing and Research, Las Cruces, New Mexico.

Stine, S.

1990 Late Holocene Fluctuations of Mono Lake, Eastern California. *Palaeogeography, Palaeoclimatology, Palaeoecology* 78:333–381.

Stinson, Susan L.

1996 Roosevelt Red Ware and the Organization of Ceramic Production in the Silver Creek Area. Unpublished Master's thesis, Department of Anthropology, University of Arizona, Tucson.

Stokes, M. A.

1980 The Dendrochronology of Fire History. In *Proceedings of the Fire History Workshop*, edited by M. A. Stokes and J. H. Dieterich, pp. 1–3. General Technical Report, RM-81. USDA Forest Service, Rocky Mountain Forest and Range Experiment Station, Fort Collins, Colorado.

Stokes, Robert J., and Barbara J. Roth

1999 Mobility, Sedentism, and Settlement Patterns in Transition: The Late Pithouse Period in the Sapillo Valley, New Mexico. *Journal of Field Archaeology* 26:423–434.

Stone, Tammy

1992   *The Process of Aggregation in the American Southwest: A Case Study from Zuni.* PhD dissertation, Department of Anthropology, Arizona State University, Tempe. University Microfilms, Ann Arbor.

1994   The Process of Aggregation in the Zuni Region: Reasons and Implications. In *Exploring Social, Political, and Economic Organization in the Zuni Region*, edited by Todd L. Howell and Tammy Stone, pp. 9–23. Arizona State University Anthropological Research Papers No. 46. Tempe.

1995   Miscellaneous Artifacts. In *Archaeological Investigations at Nine Sites on the Rio Verde–Blue Ridge No. 2 Land Exchange, Cave Creek Ranger District, Tonto National Forest, Maricopa County, Arizona*, edited by Robert I. Birnie, Tammy Stone, and Deirdre J. Hungerford, pp. 253–261. Technical Report No. 93-9. Soil Systems, Inc., Phoenix.

Stone, Tammy, and Michael S. Foster

1994   Miscellaneous Artifacts. In *Material Culture*, edited by Michael S. Foster, pp. 203–262. The Pueblo Grande Project, Vol. 4. Soil Systems Publications in Archaeology No. 20. Soil Systems, Inc., Phoenix.

Strauss, Lawrence

2000   Solutrean Settlement of North America? A Review of Reality. *American Antiquity* 65(2):219–226.

Stuart, David E., and Rory P. Gauthier

1981   *Prehistoric New Mexico: Background for Survey.* T. W. Merlan, contributor and editor. Historic Preservation Bureau, Santa Fe.

Stubbs, Stanley A., and William S. Stallings Jr.

1953   *The Excavation of Pindi Pueblo, New Mexico.* Monographs of the School of American Research and Laboratory of Anthropology No. 18. Santa Fe.

Stuiver, M., and T. F. Brazunias

1988   The Solar Component of the Atmospheric ^{14}C Record. In *Secular Solar and Geomagnetic Variations in the Last 10,000 Years*, edited by F. R. Stephenson and A. W. Wolfendale, pp. 245–266. Kluwer, Dordrecht.

Stuiver, M., T. F. Brazunias, B. Becker, and B. Kromer

1991   Climatic, Solar, Oceanic and Geo-magnetic Influences on Late-Glacial and Holocene Atmospheric ^{14}C/^{12}C Change. *Quaternary Research* 35:1–24.

Stuiver, M., P. J. Reimer, E. Bard, J. W. Beck, G. S. Burr, K. A. Hughen, B. Kromer, G. McCormac, J. van der Plicht, and M. Spurk

1998   INTCAL98 Radiocarbon Age Calibration, 24000–0 ca B.P. *Radiocarbon* 40:1041–1083.

Sullivan, Alan P.

1978   Inference and Evidence in Archaeology: A Discussion of the Conceptual Problems. In *Advances in Archaeological Method and Theory*, edited by Michael B. Schiffer, pp. 183–222. Academic Press, New York.

1982   Mogollon Agrarian Ecology. *Kiva* 48:1–15.

Sullivan, Alan P., and Jeffrey L. Hantman (editors)

1984   *Regional Analysis of Prehistoric Ceramic Variation: Contemporary Studies of the Cibola Whitewares.* Arizona State University Anthropological Research Papers No. 31. Tempe.

Sulman, F. G.

1982   *Short and Long-Term Changes in Climate.* CRC Press, Boca Raton.

Sundt, William H.

1972   Ceramics. In *Prieta Vista: A Small Pueblo III Ruin in North-Central New Mexico*, by Richard A. Bice and William H. Sundt, pp. 98–181. Albuquerque Archaeological Society, Albuquerque.

1987   Pottery of Central New Mexico and Its Role as Key to Both Time and Space. In *Secrets of a City: Papers on Albuquerque Area Archaeology in Honor of Richard A. Bice*, edited by Anne V. Poore and J. Montgomery, pp. 116–147. Archaeological Society of New Mexico 13. Albuquerque and Santa Fe.

Swadesh, Morris

1971   *The Origin and Diversification of Language*, edited by Joel Sherzer. Aldine-Atherton, Chicago.

Swetnam, Thomas W., and Julio L. Betancourt

1992   Temporal Patterns of El Niño/Southern Oscillation Wildfire Teleconnections in the Southwestern United States. In *El Niño: Historical and Paleoclimatic Aspects of the Southern Oscillation*, edited by Henry F. Diaz and Vera Markgraf, pp. 259–270. Cambridge University Press, Cambridge.

Sykes, Bryan

1999   *The Human Inheritance.* Oxford University Press, New York.

2001   *The Seven Daughters of Eve.* Bantam Press, New York.

Szuter, Christine R.

1984   Paleoenvironment and Species Richness along the Salt-Gila Aqueduct. In *Environment and Subsistence*, edited by Lynn S. Teague and Patricia L. Crown, pp. 81–93. Hohokam Archaeology along the Salt-Gila Aqueduct Central Arizona Project, Vol. 7. Archaeological Series No. 150. Arizona State Museum, University of Arizona, Tucson.

Tainter, Joseph A.

1982   Symbolism, Interaction, and Cultural Boundaries: The Anasazi-Mogollon Transition Zone in West-Central New Mexico. In *Mogollon Archaeology: Proceedings of the 1980 Mogollon Conference*, edited by Patrick H. Beckett, pp. 3–9. Acoma Books, Ramona.

Tainter, Joseph A., and David A. Gillio

1980   *Cultural Resource Overview, Mt. Taylor Area, New Mexico.* USDA Forest Service, Southwestern Regional Office, Albuquerque, and USDI Bureau of Land Management, New Mexico State Office, Santa Fe.

Tainter, Joseph A., and Fred Plog

1994   Strong and Weak Patterning in Southwestern Prehistory: The Formation of Puebloan Archaeology. In *Themes in Southwest Prehistory*, edited by George J. Gumerman, pp. 165–181. School of American Research, Santa Fe.

Taos Pueblo

2003   Taos Pueblo: A Thousand Years of Tradition. Electronic document, http://www.taospueblo.com, accessed August 15, 2003.

Taube, Karl

2001   The Breath of Life: The Symbolism of Wind in Mesoamerica and the American Southwest. In *The Road to Aztlan: Art from a Mythic Homeland*, edited by Virginia M. Fields and Victor Zamudio-Taylor, pp. 102–123. Los Angeles County Museum of Art, Los Angeles.

Taylor, Walter W.

1954   Southwestern Archaeology, Its History and Theory. *American Anthropologist* 56:561–575.

1961   Archaeology and Language in Western North America. *American Antiquity* 27(1):71–81.

Teague, George A.

1981   The Nonflaked Stone Artifacts from

Las Colinas. In *The 1968 Excavations at Mound 8, Las Colinas Ruins Group, Phoenix, Arizona*, edited and assembled by Laurens C. Hammack and Alan P. Sullivan, pp. 201–247. Arizona State Museum Archaeological Series No. 154. Arizona State Museum, University of Arizona, Tucson.

Teague, Lynn S.

1992a Textiles and Identity in the Prehistoric Southwest. In *Textiles in Daily Life: Proceedings of the Third Biennial Symposium of the Textile Society of America, 1992*, pp. 51–59. Textile Society of America, Inc., Earleville, Maryland.

1992b Textiles in Late Prehistory. In *Proceedings of the Second Salado Conference, Globe, Arizona, 1992*, edited by Richard C. Lange and Stephen Germick, pp. 304–311. Arizona Archaeological Society Occasional Papers. Phoenix.

1993 Prehistory and the Traditions of the O'odham and Hopi. *Kiva* 58:435–454.

1996 Textiles from the Upper Ruin. In *Archeological Investigations at the Upper Ruin, Tonto National Monument, Part 1, Salvage Excavations at the Upper Ruin, AZ U:8:48 (ASM)—1995*, edited by G. Fox, pp. 157–176. Publications in Archeology Vol. 70. Western Regional Archeological and Conservation Center, USDI National Park Service, Tucson.

1998 *Textiles in Southwestern Prehistory*. University of New Mexico Press, Albuquerque.

1999 Prehistoric Textile Production in East Central Arizona: Evidence and Implications. Paper presented at the Annual Meeting of the Society for American Archaeology, Chicago.

2000 Revealing Clothes: Textiles of the Upper Ruin, Tonto National Monument. In *Beyond Cloth and Cordage: Archaeological Textile Research in the Americas*, edited by Penelope Ballard Drooker and Laurie D. Webster, pp. 161–177. University of Utah Press, Salt Lake City.

Tedlock, Dennis

1983 *The Spoken Word and the Work of Interpretation*. University of Pennsylvania Press, Philadelphia.

Tedlock, Dennis (translator)

1972 *Finding the Center: Narrative Poetry of the Zuni Indians*. Dial Press, New York.

Teiwes, Helga

1996 *Hopi Basket Weaving: Artistry in Natural Fibers*. University of Arizona Press, Tucson.

ten Kate, H. F. C.

1917 A Zuni Folktale. *Journal of American Folklore* 30:496–499.

Thomason, Sarah G.

2001 *Language Contact: An Introduction*. Georgetown University Press, Washington, D.C.

Thompson, Raymond H. (editor)

1958 *Migrations in New World Culture History*. University of Arizona Bulletin No. 27. University of Arizona Press, Tucson.

Thompson, Raymond H., and William A. Longacre

1966 The University of Arizona Archaeological Field School at Grasshopper, East Central Arizona. *Kiva* 31:255–276.

Thompson, Robert S.

1984 *Late Pleistocene and Holocene Environments in the Great Basin*. PhD dissertation, Department of Geosciences, University of Arizona, Tucson. University Microfilms, Ann Arbor.

Thompson, Robert S., Katherine H. Anderson, and Laura E. Strickland

2003 Paleoenvironmental Change in Western North America during the Pleistocene–Holocene Transition. Paper presented at the 16th INQUA Congress, Reno.

Time-Life Books

1992 *Mound Builders and Cliff Dwellers*. Lost Civilizations. Time-Life Books, Alexandria, Virginia.

Tinsley, B. A., and G. W. Deen

1991 Apparent Tropospheric Response to MeV-GeV Particle Flux Variations: A Connection via Electrofreezing of Supercooled Water in High Level Clouds? *Journal of Geophysical Research* 96(D12):22283–22296.

Toll, H. Wolcott

1985 *Pottery Production, Public Architecture, and the Chaco System*. PhD dissertation, Department of Anthropology, University of Colorado, Boulder. University Microfilms, Ann Arbor.

2001 Making and Breaking Pots in the Chaco World. *American Antiquity* 66:56–78.

Toll, H. Wolcott, and Peter J. McKenna

1997 Chaco Ceramics. In *Ceramics, Lithics, and Ornaments of Chaco Canyon: Analyses of Artifacts from the Chaco Project 1971–1978*, edited by Frances Joan Mathien, pp. 17–530. Publica-

tions in Archeology 18G, Chaco Canyon Studies. USDI National Park Service, Santa Fe.

Toll, H. Wolcott, Dean C. Wilson, and Eric Blinman

1992 Chaco in the Context of Ceramic Regional Systems. In *Anasazi Regional Organization and the Chaco System*, edited by David E. Doyel, pp. 147–157. Anthropological Papers No. 5. Maxwell Museum of Anthropology, University of New Mexico, Albuquerque.

Toll, Mollie S.

1993 Botanical Indicators of Early Life in Chaco Canyon: Flotation Samples and Other Plant Materials from Basketmaker and Early Pueblo Occupations. Manuscript on file, USDI National Park Service, Santa Fe.

Toll, Mollie S., and A. C. Cully

1983 Archaic Subsistence in the Four Corners Area: Evidence for a Hypothetical Seasonal Round. In *Economy and Interaction along the Lower Chaco River*, edited by Patrick Hogan and Joseph C. Winter, pp. 385–392. Office of Contract Archaeology, University of New Mexico, Albuquerque.

Torroni, A., Y.-S. Chen, O. Semino, A. S. Santachiara-Benerecceretti, C. R. Scott, M. T. Lott, M. Winter, and D. C. Wallace

1994 Mitochondrial DNA and Y-chromosome Polymorphisms in Four Native American Populations from Southern Mexico. *American Journal of Human Genetics* 54:303–318.

Torroni, A., T. G. Schurr, M. F. Cabell, M. D. Brown, J. V. Neel, M. Larsen, D. G. Smith, C. M. Vullo, and D. C. Wallace

1993 Asian Affinities and Continental Radiation of the Four Founding Native American mtDNAs. *American Journal of Human Genetics* 53:563–590.

Toulouse, Joseph H.

1960 *Excavations at Pueblo Pardo, Central New Mexico*. Museum of New Mexico Papers in Anthropology No. 2. Museum of New Mexico Press, Albuquerque.

Tower, Donald B.

1945 *The Use of Marine Mollusca and Their Value in Reconstructing Prehistoric Trade Routes in the American Southwest*. Papers of the Excavators' Club Vol. 2, No. 3. Excavators' Club, Cambridge.

Towner, Ronald H. (editor)

1996 *The Archaeology of Navajo Origins*. University of Utah Press, Salt Lake City.

Towner, Ronald H., Alex V. Benitez, and Keith B. Knoblock
1998 Lithic Artifacts. In *Material Culture and Physical Anthropology*, edited by Stephanie M. Whittlesey and Barbara K. Montgomery, pp. 95–146. Vanishing River: Landscapes and Lives of the Lower Verde Valley: The Lower Verde Archaeology Project, Vol. 3 (CD-ROM). Statistical Research, Inc., Tucson.

Trager, George L.
1967 The Tanoan Settlement of the Rio Grande Area: A Possible Chronology. In *Studies in Southwestern Ethnolinguistics: Meaning and History in the Languages of the American Southwest*, edited by Dell H. Hymes and William E. Biddle, pp. 335–350. Mouton, The Hague.

Trenberth, Kevin
1991 General Characteristics of El Niño–Southern Oscillation. In *Teleconnections Linking Worldwide Climate Anomalies*, edited by Michael Glantz, Richard Katz, and Neville Nichols, pp. 13–42. Cambridge University Press, Cambridge.

Trenberth, Kevin E., and T. J. Hoar
1997 El Niño and Climate Change. *Geophysical Research Letter* 24:3057–3060.

Triadan, Daniella
1997 *Ceramic Commodities and Common Containers: Production and Distribution of White Mountain Red Ware in the Grasshopper Region, Arizona.* Anthropological Papers of the University of Arizona No. 61. University of Arizona Press, Tucson.

Trigger, Bruce G.
1989 *A History of Archaeological Thought.* Cambridge University Press, Cambridge.
2003 *Artifacts & Ideas: Essays in Archaeology.* Transaction Publishers, New Brunswick.

Trinkaus, Kathryn Mauer, and Wendy Ashmore (editors)
1987 *Polities and Partitions: Human Boundaries and the Growth of Complex Societies.* Anthropological Research Paper No. 37. Arizona State University, Tempe.

Tsosie, Rebecca
1999 Privileging Claims to the Past: Ancient Human Remains and Contemporary Cultural Values. *Arizona State Law Journal* 31(2):583–677.
2002 Reclaiming Native Stories: An Essay on Cultural Appropriation and Cultural Rights. *Arizona State Law Journal* 34(1):299–358.

Tuan, Yi-Fu
1966 New Mexican Gullies: A Critical Review and Some Recent Observations. *Annals of the Association of American Geographers* 56:573–597.

Tuggle, Harold David
1970 *Prehistoric Community Relationships in East Central Arizona.* PhD dissertation, University of Arizona, Tucson. University Microfilms, Ann Arbor.

Tuggle, H. David, and J. Jefferson Reid
2001 Conflict and Defense in the Grasshopper Region of East-Central Arizona. In *Deadly Landscapes: Case Studies in Prehistoric Southwestern Warfare*, edited by Glen E. Rice and Steven A. LeBlanc, pp. 85–108. University of Utah Press, Salt Lake City.

Turnbow, Christopher A. (editor)
2000 *A Highway through Time: Archaeological Investigations along NM 90,* Vols. 1 and 2. TRC Inc., Technical Series No. 2000-3. New Mexico Highway and Transportation Department, Albuquerque.

Turnbow, Christopher A., and Grant D. Smith
2000 The Wood Canyon Site (LA 99631; USFS No. AR 03-06-07-00589). In *A Highway through Time: Archaeological Investigations along NM 90*, Vol. 1, edited by Christopher A. Turnbow, pp. 91–173. TRC Inc., Technical Series No. 2000-3. New Mexico Highway and Transportation Department, Albuquerque.

Turner, Christy G., II
1993 Southwest Indian Teeth. *National Geographic Research & Exploration* 9(1):32–53.

Upham, Steadman
1982 *Polities and Power.* Academic Press, New York.

Upham, Steadman, Patricia L. Crown, and Stephen Plog
1994 Alliance Formation and Cultural Identity in the American Southwest. In *Themes in Southwestern Prehistory*, edited by George J. Gumerman, pp. 183–210. School of American Research, Santa Fe.

Urban, Sharon F.
1991 Shell. In *Homol'ovi II: Archaeology of an Ancestral Hopi Village, Arizona*, edited by E. Charles Adams and Kelley Ann Hays, pp. 112–115. Anthropological Papers of the University of Arizona No. 55. University of Arizona Press, Tucson.

Urton, Gary
1990 *The History of a Myth: Pacariqtambo and the Origin of the Inkas.* University of Texas Press, Austin.

USDA Forest Service
1996 *Prehistoric Cultural Affiliations of Southwestern Indian Tribes.* USDA Forest Service, Southwestern Region, Albuquerque.

Van Keuren, Scott
2001 *Ceramic Style and the Reorganization of Pueblo Communities in East-Central Arizona, AD 1275–1400.* PhD dissertation, Department of Anthropology, University of Arizona, Tucson. University Microfilms, Ann Arbor.

van Loon, H., and R. A. Madden
1981 The Southern Oscillation, Part I: Global Associations with Pressure and Temperature in the Northern Winter. *Monthly Weather Review* 109:1150–1162.

Van Ness, Margaret
1986 Desha Complex Macrobotanical Fecal Remains: An Archaic Diet in the American Southwest. Unpublished Master's thesis, Department of Anthropology, Northern Arizona University, Flagstaff.

Vansina, Jan
1965 *Oral Tradition: A Study in Historical Methodology.* Routledge & Kegan Paul, London.
1978 *The Children of Woot: A History of the Kuba Peoples.* University of Wisconsin Press, Madison.

Van Valkenburgh, Sallie
1954 Material Culture. In *Montezuma Castle Archeology, Part I: Excavations*, by Earl Jackson and Sallie Pierce Van Valkenburgh, pp. 28–46. Southwestern Monuments Association Technical Series Vol. 3, No. 1. Globe.

Van West, Carla R.
1990 *Modeling Prehistoric Climatic and Agricultural Production in Southwestern Colorado: A GIS Approach.* PhD dissertation, Department of Anthropology, Washington State University, Pullman. University Microfilms, Ann Arbor.
1994 Reconstructing Paleoenvironment in the middle Little Colorado River Area and Modeling Human Responses. In *River, Rain, or Ruin: Intermittent Prehistoric Land Use along the middle Little Colorado River*, by C. R. Van West, pp. 213–238. Statistical Research, Inc., Tucson.

1996 Modeling Prehistoric Agricultural Strategies and Human Settlement in the middle Little Colorado River Valley. In *River of Change: Prehistory of the middle Little Colorado River Valley, Arizona*, edited by E. Charles Adams, pp. 15–35. Arizona State Museum Archaeological Series 185. University of Arizona, Tucson.

Van West, Carla R., and Jeffrey S. Dean

2000 Environmental Characteristics of the AD 900–1300 Period in the Central Mesa Verde Region. *Kiva* 66:19–44.

Van West, Carla R., and Edgar K. Huber

1995 *Data Recovery Plan for Archaeological Investigations in the Fence Lake Transportation Corridor—Arizona*. Statistical Research Technical Series No. 56, Vol. 1. Tucson.

Van West, Carla R., and Edgar K. Huber (editors)

2005 *Fence Lake Project: Archaeological Data Recovery in the New Mexico Transportation Corridor and First Five-Year Permit Area, Fence Lake Coal Mine Project, Catron County, New Mexico*. Technical Series 84. Statistical Research Inc., Tucson. CD.

Vargas, Victoria D.

1995 *Copper Bell Trade Patterns in the Prehispanic US Southwest and Northwest Mexico*. Archaeological Series No. 187. Arizona State Museum, Tucson.

Varien, Mark D.

1987 *Survey, Testing, and Excavation along New Mexico State Highway 53, between the Black Rock Cutoff Road and the Nutria Road, Zuni Indian Reservation, McKinley County, New Mexico*. Zuni Archaeology Program Report No. 232. Zuni, New Mexico.

1990 *Excavations at Three Prehistoric Sites along Pia Mesa Road, Zuni Indian Reservation, McKinley County, New Mexico*. Zuni Archaeology Program Report No. 233, Research Series No. 4. Zuni, New Mexico.

1999 *Sedentism and Mobility in a Social Landscape: Mesa Verde and Beyond*. University of Arizona Press, Tucson.

Varien, Mark D., William D. Lipe, Michael A. Adler, Ian M. Thompson, and Bruce Bradley

1996 Southwestern Colorado and Southeastern Utah Settlement Patterns, AD 1100 to 1300. In *The Prehistoric Pueblo World, AD 1150–1350*, edited by Michael A. Adler, pp. 86–113. University of Arizona Press, Tucson.

Vayda, Andrew P. (editor)

1969 *Environment and Cultural Behavior*. Natural History Press, New York.

Vehik, Susan C.

2002 Conflict, Trade, and Political Development on the Southern Plains. *American Antiquity* 67:65–88.

Venn, Tamsin

1984 Shell Artifacts. In *The Faunal Remains from Arroyo Hondo Pueblo, New Mexico: A Study in Short-Term Subsistence Change*, by Richard W. Lang and Arthur H. Harris, pp. 226–253. Arroyo Hondo Archaeological Series Vol. 5. School of American Research Press, Santa Fe.

Vierra, Bradley J.

1994 Archaic Hunter-Gatherer Mobility Strategies in Northwestern New Mexico. In *Archaic Hunter-Gatherer Archaeology in the American Southwest*, edited by Bradley J. Vierra, pp. 121–154. Contributions in Anthropology Vol. 13, No. 1. Eastern New Mexico University, Portales.

Vierra, Bradley J., and Clara Gaultieri (editors)

1992 *Current Research on the Late Prehistory and Early History of New Mexico*. Special Publication No. 1, New Mexico Archaeological Council, Albuquerque.

Vivian, R. Gwinn

1965 An Archaeological Survey of the Lower Gila River, Arizona. *Kiva* 30:95–146.

1990 *The Chacoan Prehistory of the San Juan Basin*. New World Archaeological Record Series. Academic Press, New York.

1991 Chacoan Subsistence. In *Chaco and Hohokam: Prehistoric Regional Systems in the American Southwest*, edited by Patricia L. Crown and W. James Judge, pp. 57–76. School of American Research Press, Santa Fe.

Vivian, R. Gwinn, Dulce N. Dodgen, and Gayle H. Hartmann

1978 *Wooden Ritual Artifacts from Chaco Canyon, New Mexico: The Chetro Ketl Collection*. Anthropological Papers of the University of Arizona No. 32. University of Arizona Press, Tucson.

Voegelin, Carl F., and Florence Voegelin

1957 *Hopi Domains: A Lexical Approach to the Problem of Selection*. Indiana University Publications in Anthropology and Linguistics Memoir 14. Supplement to *International Journal of American Linguistics* 23(2). Waverly Press, Baltimore.

Vokes, Arthur W.

1984 The Shell Assemblage of the Salt-Gila Aqueduct Project Sites. In *Material Culture*, edited by Lynn S. Teague and Patricia L. Crown, pp. 465–574. Hohokam Archaeology along the Salt-Gila Aqueduct Central Arizona Project, Vol. 8. Archaeological Series No. 150. Cultural Resource Management Division, Arizona State Museum, University of Arizona, Tucson.

1986 Shell Assemblage. In *Material Culture*, edited by David A. Gregory and Carol H. Heathington, pp. 319–384. The 1982–1984 Excavations at Las Colinas, Vol. 4. Archaeological Series No. 162. Arizona State Museum, University of Arizona, Tucson.

1987 Shell Artifacts. In *The Archaeology of the San Xavier Bridge Site (AZ BB:13:14) Tucson Basin, Southern Arizona*, edited by John C. Ravesloot, pp. 251–269. Arizona State Museum Archaeological Series 171. University of Arizona, Tucson.

1991 Shell. In *Descriptive Report*, compiled by R. B. Niely and J. E. Kisselburg, pp. 12.1–12.18. The Riverine Hohokam of the Salt and Verde River Confluence Region: The Water Users Project, Mesa Ranger District, Tonto National Forest, Maricopa County, Arizona, Vol. 2. Cultural Resources Report No. 47. Archaeological Consulting Services, Tempe, Arizona.

1994 Shell Analysis. In *Prehistoric Rural Settlements in the Tonto Basin*, edited by Richard Ciolek-Torrello, Steven D. Shelley, and Su Benaron, pp. 551–558. The Roosevelt Rural Sites Study, Vol. 2. Technical Series No. 28. Statistical Research, Inc., Tucson.

1995 The Shell Assemblage. In *Stone and Shell Artifacts*, edited by Mark D. Elson and Jeffery J. Clark, pp. 151–212. The Roosevelt Community Development Study, Vol. 1. Anthropological Papers No. 14. Center for Desert Archaeology, Tucson.

1998 Shell Artifacts. *Archaeological Investigations of Early Village Sites in the Middle Santa Cruz Valley: Analyses and Synthesis*, Pt. 1, edited by Jonathan B. Mabry, pp. 437–470. Anthropological Papers No. 19. Center for Desert Archaeology, Tucson.

2001a Shell Artifacts. In *Excavations in the Santa Cruz River Floodplain: The Early Agricultural Period Component at*

Los Pozos, edited by David A. Gregory, pp. 135–152. Anthropological Papers No. 21. Center for Desert Archaeology, Tucson.

2001b The Stone and Clay Jewelry Assemblage. In *Tonto Creek Archaeological Project: Life and Death along Tonto Creek*, edited by Jeffery J. Clark and Penny Dufoe Minturn, pp. 421–457. Anthropological Papers No. 24. Center for Desert Archaeology, Tucson.

Wade, Edwin S., and Lea S. McChesney
1980 *America's Great Lost Expedition: The Thomas Keam Collection of Hopi Pottery from the Second Hemenway Expedition, 1890–1894*. Heard Museum, Phoenix.

Wallace, D. C., and A. Torroni
1992 American Indian Prehistory as Written in the Mitochondrial DNA: A Review. *Human Biology* 64:403–416.

Wallace, Henry D.
1994 An Iconographic Perspective on the Sequence of Culture Change in Central and Southern Arizona. Paper presented at the 4th Southwest Symposium, Tempe.

Wallace, Henry D., William H. Doelle, and James M. Heidke
1995 Hohokam Origins. *Kiva* 60:575–618.

Wallace, Laurel T.
1998 Site Description. In *The Ormand Village: Final Report on the 1965–1966 Excavation*, edited by L. T. Wallace, pp. 15–194. Archaeology Notes No. 229. Museum of New Mexico Office of Archaeological Studies, Santa Fe.

Wallerstein, Emmanuel
1973 The Two Modes of Ethnic Consciousness: Soviet Central Asia in Transition? In *The Nationality Question in Soviet Central Asia*, edited by E. Allworth, pp. 168–169. Praeger, New York.

Walt, Henry
1978 An Effigy Cache from the Cliff Valley, New Mexico. Unpublished Master's thesis, Department of Art History, University of New Mexico, Albuquerque.

Ward, R.
1999 Languages and Genes in the Americas. In *The Human Inheritance*, edited by B. Sykes, pp. 135–158. Oxford University Press, Oxford.

Warren, A. Helene
1970a *Centers of Manufacture and Trade of Rio Grande Glazes: A Preliminary Report*. Laboratory of Anthropology Notes No. 54. Museum of New Mexico, Santa Fe.

1970b *A Petrographic Study of the Pottery of Gran Quivira*. Laboratory of Anthropology Notes No. 94. Museum of New Mexico, Santa Fe.

1970c Tonque: One Pueblo's Glaze Pottery Industry. *El Palacio* 76(2):36–42.

1973 *New Dimensions in the Study of Prehistoric Pottery: A Preliminary Report Relating to the Excavations at Cochiti Dam, 1964–1966*. Laboratory of Anthropology Notes No. 90. Museum of New Mexico, Santa Fe.

Warren, A. Helene, and Frances Joan Mathien
1985 Prehistoric and Historic Turquoise Mining in the Cerrillos District: Time and Place. In *Southwestern Culture History: Collected Papers in Honor of Albert H. Schroeder*, edited by Charles H. Lange, pp. 93–127. Papers of the Archaeological Society of New Mexico 10. Archaeological Society of New Mexico, Santa Fe.

Warren, Claude N.
1967 The San Dieguito Complex: A Review and a Hypothesis. *American Antiquity* 32:168–185.

1984 The Desert Region. In *California Archaeology*, edited by M. Moratto, pp. 339–430. Academic Press, Inc., Orlando.

Warren, Claude, and D. L. True
1961 The San Dieguito Complex and Its Place in California Prehistory. In *University of California Archaeology Survey Annual Report 1960–1961*, pp. 246–338. Department of Anthropology, University of California, Los Angeles.

Washburn, Dorothy Koster
1977 *A Symmetry Analysis of Upper Gila Area Ceramic Design*. Papers of the Peabody Museum of Archaeology and Ethnology Vol. 68. Harvard University, Cambridge.

Washburn, Dorothy K., and Laurie D. Webster
2006 Symmetry and Color Perspectives on Basketmaker Cultural Identities: Evidence from Designs on Coiled Baskets and Ceramics. *Kiva* 71(3):235–264.

Wasley, William W.
1959 *Cultural Implications of Style Trends in Southwestern Prehistoric Pottery: Basketmaker III to Pueblo II in West Central New Mexico*. PhD dissertation, University of Arizona, Tucson. University Microfilms, Ann Arbor.

1962 A Ceremonial Cave on Bonita Creek, Arizona. *American Antiquity* 27:380–394.

Wasley, William W., and Alfred E. Johnson
1965 *Salvage Archaeology in Painted Rocks Reservoir, Western Arizona*. Anthropological Papers of the University of Arizona No. 9. University of Arizona Press, Tucson.

Waters, Jennifer A.
2005 Vertebrate Faunal Remains and Hunting Patterns during the Early Agricultural Period in Southern Arizona. In *Subsistence and Resource Use Strategies of Early Agricultural Communities in Southern Arizona*, edited by Michael W. Diehl, pp. 91–112. Anthropological Papers No. 34. Center for Desert Archaeology, Tucson.

Waters, M. R.
1985 *The Geoarchaeology of Whitewater Draw, Arizona*. Anthropological Papers of the University of Arizona No. 45. University of Arizona Press, Tucson.

Waterworth, Robert M. R.
1994 Ceramic Artifacts. In *Archaeological Data Recovery Excavations at the Sanders Great House and Six Other Sites along US Highway 191 South of Sanders, Apache County, Arizona*, Vol. 2, prepared by Thomas F. Fletcher, pp. 275–328. Zuni Archaeology Program Report No. 471, Research Series No. 9. Pueblo of Zuni, New Mexico.

Watkins, Joe
2000 *Indigenous Archaeology: American Indian Values and Scientific Practice*. AltaMira Press, Walnut Creek, California.

Watson, Patty Jo, and M. Fotiadis
1990 The Razor's Edge: Symbolic-Structuralist Archeology and the Expansion of Archeological Inference. *American Anthropologist* 92:613–629.

Watson, Patty Jo, Steven A. LeBlanc, and Charles Redman
1980 Aspects of Zuni Prehistory: Preliminary Report on Excavations and Survey in the El Morro Valley of New Mexico. *Journal of Field Archaeology* 7:201–218.

Wauchope, Robert (editor)
1956 *Seminars in Archaeology: 1955*. Memoirs of the Society for American Archaeology. *American Antiquity* 22(2), pt. 2.

Webb, Robert H., and Julio L. Betancourt
1990 The Spatial and Temporal Distribution of Radiocarbon Ages from Packrat

Middens. In *Packrat Middens: The Last 40,000 Years of Biotic Change*, edited by J. L. Betancourt, T. R. Van Devender, and P. S. Martin, pp. 85–102. University of Arizona Press, Tucson.

1992 *Climatic Variability and Flood Frequency of the Santa Cruz River, Pima County, Arizona*. U.S. Geological Survey Water Supply Paper 2379.

Webster, Laurie D.

n.d. An Initial Assessment of Perishable Relationships among Chaco, Salmon, and Aztec. Manuscript submitted for the volume *Chaco's Northern Prodigies: Salmon, Aztec, and the Ascendancy of the Middle San Juan Region after AD 1100*, edited by Paul F. Reed. University of Utah Press, Salt Lake City (under review).

1997 *Effects of European Contact on Textile Production and Exchange in the North American Southwest: A Pueblo Case Study*. PhD dissertation, Department of Anthropology, University of Arizona, Tucson. University Microfilms, Ann Arbor.

1999 Evidence of Affiliation: Relationships of Historic Hopi and Prehistoric Salado Textiles and Basketry. In *Hoopoq' Yaqam Niqw Wukoskyavi (Those Who Went to the Northeast and Tonto Basin)*, by T. J. Ferguson and Micah Lomaomvaya, pp. 261–300. Hopi Cultural Preservation Office, Kiqötsmovi, Arizona.

2000 The Economics of Pueblo Textile Production and Exchange in Colonial New Mexico. In *Beyond Cloth and Cordage: Archaeological Textile Research in the Americas*, edited by Penelope Ballard Drooker and Laurie D. Webster, pp. 179–204. University of Utah Press, Salt Lake City.

2001 Collections Notes on Basketry from Point of Pines Pueblo in the Arizona State Museum. Notes in possession of the author.

2003 Relationships of Hopi and Hohokam Textiles and Basketry. In *Yep Hisat Hoopoq'yaqam Yeesiwa (Hopi Ancestors Were Once Here): Hopi-Hohokam Cultural Affiliation Study*, edited by T. J. Ferguson, pp. 165–209. Hopi Cultural Preservation Office, Kiqötsmovi, Arizona.

2004 Textiles and Basketry from the Zuni Middle Village. Draft report submitted to Zuni Cultural Resource Enterprise. Pueblo of Zuni, New Mexico.

2006 Worked Fiber Artifacts from Salmon Pueblo. In *Archaeobotanical Research and Other Analytical Studies*, Vol. 3 of *Thirty-five Years of Archaeological Research at Salmon Ruins, New Mexico*, edited by Paul F. Reed, pp. 893–1012. Center for Desert Archaeology, Tucson, and Salmon Ruins Museum, Bloomfield, New Mexico.

Webster, Laurie D., and Kelley A. Hays-Gilpin

1994 New Trails for Old Shoes: Sandals, Textiles, and Baskets in Basketmaker Culture. *Kiva* 60:313–327.

Webster, Laurie D., and Micah Loma'omvaya

2004 Textiles, Baskets, and Hopi Cultural Identity. In *Identity, Feasting, and the Archaeology of the Greater Southwest: Proceedings of the 2002 Southwest Symposium*, edited by Barbara J. Mills, pp. 74–92. University Press of Colorado, Boulder.

Webster, Peter, and Timothy Palmer

1997 The Past and Future of El Niño. *Nature* 390:562.

Weigand, Phil C.

1968 The Mines and Mining Techniques of the Chalchihuites Culture. *American Antiquity* 33:45–61.

1994 Observations on Ancient Mining within the Northwestern Regions of the Mesoamerican Civilization, with Emphasis on Turquoise. In *In Quest of Mineral Wealth, Aboriginal and Colonial Mining and Metallurgy in Spanish America*, edited by Alan K. Craig and Robert C. West, pp. 21–35. Geoscience and Man Vol. 33. Louisiana State University, Baton Rouge.

Weigand, Phil C., and Garman Harbottle

1993 The Role of Turquoise in the Ancient Mesoamerican Trade Structure. In *The American Southwest and Mesoamerica: Systems of Prehistoric Exchange*, edited by Jonathon E. Ericson and Timothy G. Baugh, pp. 159–177. Plenum Press, New York.

Weigand, Phil C., Garman Harbottle, and Edward V. Sayre

1977 Turquoise Sources and Source Analysis: Mesoamerica and the Southwestern U.S.A. In *Exchange Systems in Prehistory*, edited by Timothy K. Earle and Jonathon E. Ericson, pp. 15–34. Academic Press, New York.

Welch, John R., and Daniela Triadan

1991 The Canyon Creek Turquoise Mine, Arizona. *Kiva* 56:145–164.

Wells, L. E.

1987 An Alluvial Record of El Niño Events from Northern Coastal Peru. *Journal of Geophysical Research* 92(C13):14463–14470.

Wells, Stephen G.

1987 A Quantitative Analysis of Arroyo Development and Geomorphic Processes in the Zuni River Drainage Basin, West-Central New Mexico. Defendant's Exhibit 12,000. Expert testimony submitted to the United States Claims Court as evidence in the case *Zuni Indian Tribe v. United States*, Dockets 327-81L and 224-81L.

Wells, Susan J.

1989 *Petrified Forest National Park Boundary Survey, 1988: The Final Season*. Publications in Anthropology No. 51. Western Archeological and Conservation Center, Tucson.

Weltfish, Gene

1932 *Preliminary Classification of Prehistoric Southwestern Basketry*. Smithsonian Miscellaneous Collections Vol. 87, No. 7. Washington, D.C.

Wendorf, Fred

1953 *Archaeological Studies in the Petrified Forest National Monument*. Museum of Northern Arizona Bulletin 27. Northern Arizona Society of Science and Art, Inc., Flagstaff.

1954 A Reconstruction of Northern Rio Grande Prehistory. *American Anthropologist* 56:200–227.

Wendorf, Fred (editor)

1961 *Paleoecology of the Llano Estacado*. Museum of New Mexico Press, Santa Fe.

Wendorf, Fred, and J. Hester (editors)

1975 *Late Pleistocene Environments of the Southern High Plains*. Fort Burgwin Publication No. 9. Taos.

Wendorf, Fred A., and Erik K. Reed

1955 An Alternative Construction of Northern Rio Grande Prehistory. *El Palacio* 62:131–173.

Whalen, Michael E.

1994 *Turquoise Ridge and Late Prehistoric Residential Mobility in the Desert Mogollon Region*. University of Utah Anthropological Papers No. 118. University of Utah Press, Salt Lake City.

Whalen, Michael E., and Paul E. Minnis

2001 *Casas Grandes and Its Hinterland: Prehistoric Regional Organization in Northwest Mexico*. University of Arizona Press, Tucson.

2003 The Local and the Distant in the Origin of Casas Grandes, Chihuahua,

Mexico. *American Antiquity* 68:314–332.

Whalen, Norman

1971 *Cochise Culture Sites in the Central San Pedro Drainage, Arizona*. PhD dissertation, University of Arizona, Tucson. University Microfilms, Ann Arbor.

1973 Agriculture and the Cochise. *Kiva* 39:89–96.

1975 Cochise Site Distributions in the San Pedro Valley. *Kiva* 40:203–211.

Wheat, Joe Ben

1954 *Crooked Ridge Village (AZ W:10:15)*. Social Science Bulletin No. 24. University of Arizona, Tucson.

1955 *Mogollon Culture prior to AD 1000*. Memoirs of the Society for American Archaeology 10. Society for American Archaeology, Salt Lake City.

2003 *Blanket Weaving in the Southwest*, edited by Ann Lane Hedlund. University of Arizona Press, Tucson.

Wheeler, S. M.

1973 *The Archaeology of Etna Cave, Lincoln County, Nevada*. Annotated reprint of the 1942 edition, edited by Don D. Fowler. Desert Research Institute Publications in the Social Sciences 7. Reno.

White, Leslie A.

1943 *New Material from Acoma*. Bulletin No. 136, Anthropological Papers No. 32. Bureau of American Ethnology, Smithsonian Institution, Washington, D.C.

1962 *The Pueblo of Sia, New Mexico*. Bulletin No. 184, Bureau of American Ethnology, Smithsonian Institution, Washington, D.C.

Whiteford, Andrew H.

1988 *Southwestern Indian Baskets: Their History and Their Makers*. School of American Research Press, Santa Fe.

Whiteley, Peter M.

2002a Archaeology and Oral Tradition: The Scientific Importance of Dialogue. *American Antiquity* 67:405–416.

2002b Re-imagining Awat'ovi. In *Archaeologies of the Pueblo Revolt*, edited by Robert W. Preucel, pp. 147–166. University of New Mexico Press, Albuquerque.

Whitley, David S.

1994 Shamanism, Natural Modeling and the Rock Art of Far Western North American Hunter-Gatherers. In *Shamanism and Rock Art in North America*, edited by S. A. Turpin, pp. 1–44. Special Publication 1, Rock Art Foundation, Inc., San Antonio.

Whittlesey, Stephanie M.

1982 Vessel Thinning Techniques and Ethnic Identification. In *Ceramic Studies*, edited by J. Jefferson Reid, pp. 18–21. Cholla Project Archaeology, Vol. 5. Arizona State Museum Archaeological Series No. 161. University of Arizona, Tucson.

Whorf, Benjamin Lee, and George L. Trager

1937 The Relationship of Uto-Aztecan and Tanoan. *American Anthropologist* 39:609–624.

Wichmann, Soren

1999 On the Relationship between Uto-Aztecan and MixeZoquean. *Kansas Working Papers in Linguistics* 24(2):101–113.

Wiens, Ruth W.

1994 The Early Archaic in Northwestern New Mexico: A Re-evaluation Based on Data from Gallegos Mesa. In *Archaic Hunter-Gatherer Archaeology in the American Southwest*, edited by Bradley J. Vierra, pp. 62–75. Contributions in Anthropology Vol. 13, No. 1. Eastern New Mexico University, Portales.

Wiessner, Polly

1983 Style and Social Information in Kalahari San Projectile Points. *American Antiquity* 48:253–276.

1984 Reconsidering the Behavioral Basis for Style: A Case Study among the Kalahari San. *Journal of Anthropological Archaeology* 3:190–234.

1985 Style or Isochrestic Variation? A Reply to Sackett. *American Antiquity* 50:160–166.

1990 Is There a Unity to Style? In *The Uses of Style in Archaeology*, edited by M. W. Conkey and C. A. Hastorf, pp. 105–112. Cambridge University Press, Cambridge.

Wiessner, Polly, and Akii Tumu

1998 *Historical Vines: Enga Networks of Exchange, Ritual, and Warfare in Papua New Guinea*. Smithsonian Institution Press, Washington, D.C.

Wiget, Andrew O.

1980 Sayatasha's Night Chant: A Literary Textual Analysis of a Zuni Ritual Poem. *American Indian Culture and Research Journal* 4:99–140.

Wilcox, David R.

1975 A Strategy for Perceiving Social Groups in Puebloan Sites. In *Chapters in the Prehistory of Eastern Arizona*, Vol. 4, by Paul S. Martin, Ezra B. W. Zubrow, Daniel C. Bowman, David A. Gregory, John A. Hanson, Michael B.

Schiffer, and David R. Wilcox, pp. 120–159. Fieldiana: Anthropology Vol. 65. Field Museum of Natural History, Chicago.

1976 How the Pueblos Came to Be as They Are: The Problem Today. Manuscript on file, Arizona State Museum Archives, University of Arizona, Tucson.

1978 The Theoretical Implications of Fieldhouses. In *Limited Activity and Occupation Sites: A Collection of Conference Papers*, edited by Albert E. Ward, pp. 25–34. Occasional Papers of the Center for Anthropological Studies No. 1. Albuquerque.

1979 The Hohokam Regional System. In *An Archaeological Test of Sites in the Gila Butte-Santan Region*, by Glen Rice, David R. Wilcox, Kevin Rafferty, and James Schoenwetter, pp. 77–116. Arizona State University Anthropological Research Papers No. 18. Tempe.

1980 The Current Status of the Hohokam Concept. In *Current Issues in Hohokam Prehistory: Proceedings of a Conference*, edited by David Doyel and Fred Plog, pp. 236–242. Arizona State University Anthropological Research Papers No. 23. Tempe.

1981 Changing Perspectives on the Protohistoric Pueblos, AD 1450–1700. In *The Protohistoric Period in the North American Southwest, AD 1450–1700*, edited by David R. Wilcox and W. Bruce Masse, pp. 378–409. Arizona State University Anthropological Research Papers No. 24. Tempe.

1984 Multi-ethnic Division of Labor in the Protohistoric Southwest. In *Collected Papers in Honor of Harry L. Hadlock*, edited by Nancy L. Fox, pp. 141–156. Papers of the Archaeological Society of New Mexico No. 9. Albuquerque.

1986a The Tepiman Connection: A Model of Mesoamerican-Southwestern Interaction. In *Ripples in the Chichimec Sea: New Considerations of Southwestern-Mesoamerican Interactions*, edited by Frances Joan Mathien and Randall H. McGuire, pp. 135–153. Southern Illinois University Press, Carbondale.

1986b A Historical Analysis of the Problem of Southwestern-Mesoamerican Connections. In *Ripples in the Chichimec Sea: New Considerations of Southwestern-Mesoamerican Interactions*, edited by Frances Joan Mathien and Randall H. McGuire, pp. 9–44. Southern Illinois University Press, Carbondale.

1987 *Frank Midvale's Investigation of the Site of La Ciudad*. Arizona State University Anthropological Field Studies No. 19. Tempe.

1988a Rethinking the Mogollon Concept. *Kiva* 53:205–209.

1988b The Regional Context of the Brady Wash and Picacho Area Sites. In *Hohokam Settlement along the Slopes of the Picacho Mountains, Synthesis and Conclusions, Tucson Aqueduct Project*, edited by Richard Ciolek-Torrello and David R. Wilcox, pp. 244–267. MNA Research Paper Vol. 6, No. 35. Flagstaff.

1991a Hohokam Religion: An Archaeologist's Perspective. In *The Hohokam, Ancient People of the Desert*, edited by David G. Noble, pp. 47–59. School of American Research Press, Santa Fe.

1991b Changing Context of Pueblo Adaptations, AD 1250–1600. In *Farmers, Hunters and Colonists: Interaction between the Southwest and the Southern Plains*, edited by Katherine A. Spielmann, pp. 128–154. University of Arizona Press, Tucson.

1991c Hohokam Social Complexity. In *Chaco and Hohokam: Prehistoric Regional Systems in the American Southwest*, edited by Patricia L. Crown and W. James Judge, pp. 251–275. School of American Research Advanced Seminar Series, School of American Research Press, Santa Fe.

1991d The Mesoamerican Ballgame in the American Southwest. In *The Mesoamerican Ballgame*, edited by Vernon Scarborough and David R. Wilcox, pp. 101–125. University of Arizona Press, Tucson.

1992 Discussion of the Pueblo Research. In *Current Research on the Late Prehistory and Early History of New Mexico*, edited by Brad Vierra and Clara Gaultieri, pp. 101–107. Special Publication No. 1, New Mexico Archaeological Council, Albuquerque.

1993 The Evolution of the Chacoan Polity. In *The Chimney Rock Archaeological Symposium*, edited by J. McCoy Melville and Gary Matlock, pp. 76–90. General Technical Report No. RM-227, USDA Forest Service, Fort Collins.

1995a A Processual Model of Charles C. Di Peso's Babocomari Site and Related Systems. In *The Gran Chichimeca: Essays on the Archaeology and Ethnohis-tory of Northern Mesoamerica*, edited by Jonathan E. Reyman, pp. 281–319. Avebury, London.

1995b Review of *Ancient Southwestern Communities*, edited by W. H. Wills and Robert Leonard. *American Antiquity* 60:567–568.

1996a The Diversity of Regional and Macroregional Systems in the American Southwest. In *Debating Complexity: Proceedings of the 26th Annual Chacmool Conference*, edited by Daniel A. Meyer, Peter C. Dawson, and Donald T. Hanna, pp. 375–390. Archaeological Association of the University of Calgary, Calgary.

1996b Pueblo III People and Polity in Relational Context. In *The Prehistoric Pueblo World, AD 1150–1350*, edited by Michael A. Adler, pp. 241–254. University of Arizona Press, Tucson.

1999a A Peregrine View of Macroregional Systems in the North American Southwest, AD 750–1250. In *Great Towns and Regional Polities*, edited by Jill E. Neitzel, pp. 115–142. New World Studies Series No. 3. Amerind Foundation, Inc., Dragoon, Arizona, and University of New Mexico Press, Albuquerque.

1999b A Preliminary Graph-Theoretic Analysis of Access Relationships at Casas Grandes, Chihuahua. In *The Casas Grandes World*, edited by Curtis Schaafsma and Carroll Riley, pp. 93–104. University of Utah Press, Salt Lake City.

2002 The Wupatki Nexus: Chaco-Hohokam-Chumash Connectivity, AD 1150–1225. In *The Archaeology of Contact: Processes and Consequences. Proceedings of the Twenty-Fifth Annual Conference of the Archaeological Association of the University of Calgary*, edited by Kurtis Lesick, Barbara Kulle, Christine Cluney, and Meaghan Peuramaki-Brown, pp. 218–234. Archaeological Association of the University of Calgary, Calgary.

2003a Creating Field Anthropology: Why Remembering Matters. In *Curators, Collections, and Change: A History of Field Museum Anthropology 1893–2001*, edited by Stephen E. Nash and Gary M. Feinman. Fieldiana: Anthropology n.s. No. 36. Field Museum of Natural History, Chicago.

2003b Restoring Authenticity: Judging Frank Hamilton Cushing's Veracity. In *Philadelphia and the Development of Americanist Archaeology*, edited by Don D. Fowler and David R. Wilcox, pp. 88–112. University of Alabama Press, Tuscaloosa.

2003c Appendix: Turquoise Encrusted Toads and Raptorial Birds in the North American Southwest. In *Philadelphia and the Development of Americanist Archaeology*, edited by Don D. Fowler and David R. Wilcox, pp. 189–193. University of Alabama Press, Tuscaloosa.

2004 Looking for Middle Ground: Archaeology on the Colorado Plateau Today. In *The Colorado Plateau: Cultural, Biological, and Physical Research*, edited by Charles van Riper III and Kenneth Coly, pp. 11–18. University of Arizona Press, Tucson.

2005a *Big Picture Archaeology*. Special issue, *Plateau* 2(1).

2005b Big Issues, New Synthesis. *Plateau* 2(1):8–21.

2005c Things Chaco: A Peregrine Perspective. *Plateau* 2(1):38–51.

2005d Perry Mesa and Its World. *Plateau* 2(1):24–35.

Wilcox, David R., and Don D. Fowler

2002 The Beginnings of Anthropological Archaeology in the North American Southwest: From Thomas Jefferson to the Pecos Conference. *Journal of the Southwest* 44:121–234.

Wilcox, David R., David A. Gregory, J. Brett Hill, and Gary Funkhouser

2006 The Changing Contexts of Warfare in the North American Southwest, AD 1200–1700. In *Southwestern Interludes: Papers in Honor of Charlotte J. and Theodore R. Frisbie*, edited by Regge N. Wiseman, Thomas C. O'Laughlin, and Cordelia T. Snow, pp. 203–232. Archaeological Society of New Mexico Papers No. 32.

Wilcox, David R., Donald Keller, and David Ortiz

2000 Long-Distance Exchange, Warfare, and the Indian Peak Ruin, Walnut Creek, Arizona. In *Archaeology in West-Central Arizona: Proceedings of the 1996 Arizona Archaeological Council Prescott Conference*, edited by Thomas N. Motsinger, Douglas R. Mitchell, and James M. McKie, pp. 119–144. Sharlot Hall Museum Press, Prescott.

Wilcox, David R., and W. Bruce Masse (editors)

1981 *The Protohistoric Period in the North American Southwest, AD 1450–1700*. Anthropological Research Papers

No. 24. Arizona State University, Tempe.

Wilcox, David R., Thomas R. McGuire, and Charles Sternberg
1981 *Snaketown Revisited*. Arizona State Museum Archaeological Series No. 155. University of Arizona, Tucson.

Wilcox, David R., Gerald Robertson Jr., and J. Scott Wood
1999 Perry Mesa, a 14th Century Gated Community in Central Arizona. *Plateau Journal* (Summer):44–61.
2001a Antecedents to Perry Mesa: Early Pueblo III Defensive Refuge Systems in West Central Arizona. In *Deadly Landscapes: Case Studies in Prehistoric Southwestern Warfare*, edited by Glen E. Rice and Steven A. LeBlanc, pp. 109–140. University of Utah Press, Salt Lake City.
2001b Organized for War: The Perry Mesa Settlement System and Its Central Arizona Neighbors. In *Deadly Landscapes: Case Studies in Prehistoric Southwestern Warfare*, edited by Glen E. Rice and Steven A. LeBlanc, pp. 141–194. University of Utah Press, Salt Lake City.

Wilcox, David R., and Charles Sternberg
1983 *Hohokam Ballcourts and Their Interpretation*. Archaeological Series No. 160. Arizona State Museum, University of Arizona, Tucson.

Wilcox, David R., Judith Rowe Taylor, Joseph Vogel, and J. Scott Wood
2007 Delineating Hilltop Settlement Systems in West-Central Arizona, AD 1100–1400. In *Trincheras Sites in Time, Space, and Society*, edited by Suzanne K. Fish, Paul R. Fish, and M. Elisa Villalpando. University of Arizona Press, Tucson.

Wilk, Richard R.
1991 *Household Ecology: Economic Change and Domestic Life among the Kekchi Maya in Belize*. University of Arizona Press, Tucson.

Wilk, Richard R., and Robert McC. Netting
1984 Households: Changing Forms and Functions. In *Households: Comparative and Historic Studies of the Domestic Group*, edited by R. McC. Netting, R. R. Wilk, and E. J. Arnould, pp. 1–28. University of California Press, Berkeley.

Willey, Gordon R.
1966 *Introduction to American Archaeology*. Prentice-Hall Anthropology Series. Englewood Cliffs, New Jersey.

Willey, Gordon R., Charles C. Di Peso, William A. Ritchie, Irving Rouse, John H. Rowe, and Donald W. Lathrap
1956 An Archaeological Classification of Culture Contact Situations. In *Seminars in Archaeology: 1955*, edited by Robert Wauchope. Memoirs of the Society for American Archaeology. *American Antiquity* 22(2), pt. 2:3–30.

Willey, Gordon R., and Phillip Phillips
1958 *Method and Theory in American Archaeology*. University of Chicago Press, Chicago.

Williams, Brackette F.
1992 Of Straightening Combs, Sodium Hydroxide, and Potassium Hydroxide in Archaeological and Cultural-Anthropological Analyses of Ethnogenesis. *American Antiquity* 57:608–612.

Williams, George C.
1966 *Adaptation and Natural Selection: A Critique of Some Current Evolutionary Thought*. Princeton University Press, Princeton.

Wills, Wirt Henry III
1985 *Early Agriculture in the Mogollon Highlands of New Mexico*. PhD dissertation, University of Michigan, Ann Arbor. University Microfilms, Ann Arbor.
1988a *Early Prehistoric Agriculture in the American Southwest*. School of American Research Press, Santa Fe.
1988b Early Agriculture and Sedentism in the American Southwest: Evidence and Interpretations. *Journal of World Prehistory* 2:445–488.
1995 Archaic Foraging and the Beginning of Food Production in the American Southwest. In *Last Hunters, First Farmers*, edited by T. Douglas Price and Anne Birgitte Gebauer, pp. 215–241. School of American Research Press, Santa Fe.
1996 The Transition from the Preceramic to Ceramic Period in the Mogollon Highlands of Western New Mexico. *Journal of Field Archaeology* 23:335–359.

Wills, Wirt H., and Bruce Huckell
1994 Economic Implications of Changing Land-Use Patterns in the Late Archaic. In *Themes in Southwest Prehistory*, edited by G. J. Gumerman, pp. 33–52. School of American Research, Santa Fe.

Wills, W. H., and Robert D. Leonard (editors)
1994 *The Ancient Southwestern Community: Models and Methods for the Study of Prehistoric Social Organization*. University of New Mexico Press, Albuquerque.

Wilson, C. Dean
1994 Implications of Ceramic Resource Surveys in the Northern Mogollon Country. In *Mogollon VII: The Collected Papers of the 1992 Mogollon Conference Held in Las Cruces, New Mexico*, edited by Patrick Beckett. COAS Publishing and Research, Las Cruces.
1998a Ormand Ceramic Analysis Part I: Methodology and Categories. In *The Ormand Village: Final Report on the 1965–1966 Excavation*, by L. T. Wallace, pp. 195–252. Archaeology Notes No. 229. Museum of New Mexico Office of Archaeological Studies, Santa Fe.
1998b Ormand Ceramic Analysis Part II: Ceramic Trends from the Ormand Village. In *The Ormand Village: Final Report on the 1965–1966 Excavation*, by L. T. Wallace, pp. 253–286. Archaeology Notes No. 229. Museum of New Mexico Office of Archaeological Studies, Santa Fe.
1999a Implications of Dating Reevaluations of Reserve Black-on-white Pottery. In *Sixty Years of Mogollon Archaeology*, edited by Stephanie M. Whittlesey, pp. 197–201. SRI Press, Tucson.
1999b Ceramic Trends at Luna Project Sites. In *Ceramics, Miscellaneous Artifacts, Bioarchaeology, Bone Tools, and Faunal Analysis*, edited by Y. R. Oales and D. A. Zamora, pp. 139–172. Archaeology of the Mogollon Highlands Settlement Systems and Adaptations, Vol. 4. Archaeology Notes No. 232. Museum of New Mexico Office of Archaeological Studies, Santa Fe.

Wilson, C. Dean, and Eric Blinman
1994 Early Anasazi Ceramics and the Basketmaker Transition. In *Proceedings of the Anasazi Symposium 1991*, compiled by A. Hutchinson and J. E. Smith, pp. 199–211. Mesa Verde Museum Association, Inc., Mesa Verde National Park, Mesa Verde, Colorado.

Wilson, C. Dean, Eric Blinman, James M. Skibo, and Michael B. Schiffer
1996 Designing Southwestern Pottery: A Technological and Experimental Approach. In *Interpreting Southwestern Diversity: Underlying Principles and Overarching Patterns*, edited by Paul R.

Fish and J. Jefferson Reid, pp. 249–256. Anthropological Research Papers No. 48. Arizona State University, Tempe.

Wilson, John P., Robert H. Leslie, and A. Helene Warren
1983   Tabira: Outpost on the East. In *Collected Papers in Honor of Charlie R. Steen, Jr.*, edited by Nancy L. Fox, pp. 87–158. Papers of the Archaeological Society of New Mexico No. 8. Archaeological Society of New Mexico, Albuquerque.

Windes, Thomas C.
1984   A View of the Cibola Whiteware from Chaco Canyon. In *Regional Analysis of Prehistoric Ceramic Variation: Contemporary Studies of the Cibola Whitewares*, edited by Alan P. Sullivan and Jeffrey L. Hantman, pp. 94–119. Arizona State University Anthropological Research Papers No. 31. Tempe.
1985   Chaco-McElmo Black-on-white from Chaco Canyon with an Emphasis on the Pueblo del Arroyo Collection. In *Prehistory and History in the Southwest: Collected Papers in Honor of Alden C. Hayes*, edited by Nancy L. Fox, pp. 19–42. Papers of the Archaeological Society of New Mexico No. 11. Archaeological Society of New Mexico, Albuquerque.
2001   Blue Notes: The Chacoan Turquoise Industry in the San Juan Basin. In *Anasazi Regional Organization and the Chaco System*, edited by David E. Doyel, pp. 159–168. Maxwell Museum of Anthropology Anthropological Papers No. 5. University of New Mexico, Albuquerque.

Winkler, James, and Emma Lou Davis
1961   Wetherill Mesa Project: Archaeological Survey in Socorro and McKinley Counties, New Mexico. Site Records and Field Journal. Manuscript on file, ARMS, Laboratory of Anthropology, Museum of New Mexico, Santa Fe.

Winship, George P.
1896   The Coronado Expedition, 1540–1542. *Fourteenth Annual Report of the Bureau of Ethnology for 1892–93*, Pt. 1, pp. 329–637. Smithsonian Institution, Washington, D.C.

Winslow, Anastasia P.
1996   Sacred Standards: Honoring the Establishment Clause in Protecting Native American Sacred Sites. *Arizona Law Review* 38:1291–1343.

Winter, Joseph C., and Patrick F. Hogan
1986   Plant Husbandry in the Great Basin and Adjacent Northern Colorado Plateau. In *Anthropology of the Desert West: Essays in Honor of Jesse D. Jennings*, edited by Carol J. Condie and Don D. Fowler, pp. 117–144. University of Utah Anthropological Papers No. 110. University of Utah Press, Salt Lake City.

Wiseman, Regge N.
1977   *The Blackrock Project: Archaeological Investigations on the Zuni Indian Reservation, McKinley County, New Mexico.* Archaeological Research Paper 3. Museum of New Mexico Division of Anthropology, Santa Fe.

Wissler, Clark
1917   The New Archaeology. *American Museum Journal* 17:100–101.

Withers, Allison G.
1946   Copper in the Prehistoric Southwest. Unpublished Master's thesis, Department of Anthropology, University of Arizona, Tucson.

Wittfogel, Karl
1957   *Oriental Despotism.* Yale University Press, New Haven.

Wittfogel, Karl A., and Esther S. Goldfrank
1943   Some Aspects of Pueblo Mythology and Society. *Journal of American Folklore* 56(210):17–30.

Wobst, H. Martin
1974   Boundary Conditions for Paleolithic Social Systems. *American Antiquity* 39:47–78.
1977   Stylistic Behavior and Information Exchange. In *Papers for the Director: Research Essays in Honor of James B. Griffin*, edited by C. E. Cleland, pp. 317–342. Anthropological Papers No. 61. Museum of Anthropology, University of Michigan, Ann Arbor.

Wolf, Eric R.
1984   Culture: Panacea or Problem? *American Antiquity* 49:393–400.
1999   *Envisioning Power: Ideologies of Dominance and Crisis.* University of California Press, Berkeley.

Wood, J. Scott
1987   *Checklist of Pottery Types for the Tonto National Forest: An Introduction to the Archeological Ceramics of Central Arizona.* Arizona Archaeologist No. 21. Phoenix.

Woodbury, Richard B.
1954   Columbia University Archaeological Fieldwork, 1952–1953. *Southwestern Lore* 19:11.
1956   The Antecedents of Zuni Culture. *Transactions of the New York Academy of Sciences* series 2, 18(6):557–563.
1979   Zuni Prehistory and History to 1850. In *Southwest*, edited by Alfonso Ortiz, pp. 467–473. Handbook of North American Indians, Vol. 9, William C. Sturtevant, general editor, Smithsonian Institution, Washington, D.C.
1993   *Sixty Years of Southwestern Archaeology: A History of the Pecos Conference.* University of New Mexico Press, Albuquerque.

Woodbury, Richard B., and Nathalie F. S. Woodbury
1966   Appendix II: Decorated Pottery of the Zuni Area. In *The Excavation of Hawikuh by Frederick Webb Hodge: Report of the Hendricks-Hodge Expedition, 1917–1923*, edited by Watson Smith, Richard B. Woodbury, and Nathalie F. S. Woodbury, pp. 302–336. Contributions from the Museum of the American Indian, Heye Foundation Vol. 20. New York.

Woodson, M. Kyle
1995   The Goat Hill Site: A western Anasazi Pueblo in the Safford Valley of Southeastern Arizona. Unpublished Master's thesis, Department of Anthropology, University of Texas, Austin.
1999   Migrations in Late Anasazi Prehistory: The Evidence from the Goat Hill Site. *Kiva* 65:63–84.

Woosley, Anne I., and Allan J. McIntyre
1996   *Mimbres Mogollon Archaeology: Charles C. Di Peso's Excavations at Wind Mountain.* Archaeology Series No. 10. Amerind Foundation, Inc., Dragoon, Arizona, and University of New Mexico Press, Albuquerque.

Wormington, H. M., and George Agogino
1994   Cynthia Irwin-Williams: 1936–1990. *American Antiquity* 59:667–671.

Wright, Barton
1985   *Kachinas of the Zuni: Original Paintings by Duane Dishta.* Northland Press, Flagstaff.

Wright, P. B.
1977   *The Southern Oscillation—Patterns and Mechanisms of the Teleconnections and the Persistence.* Hawaii Institute of Geophysics, MIG-77-13. University of Hawaii, Honolulu.

Wylie, Alison
2002   *Thinking from Things: Essays in the Philosophy of Archaeology.* University of California Press, Berkeley.

Wylie, Henry G.
1974 Promontory Pegs as Elements of Great Basin Subsistence Technology. *Tebiwa* 16(2):46–67. Journal of the Idaho State University Museum, Pocatello.

Wyrtki, K.
1973 Teleconnections in the Equatorial Pacific. *Science* 180:66–68.
1975 El Niño—the Dynamic Response of the Equatorial Pacific Ocean to Atmospheric Forcing. *Journal of Physical Oceanography* 5:572–584.

Wyrtki, K., E. Stroup, W. Patzert, R. Williams, and W. Quinn
1976 Predicting and Observing El Niño. *Science* 191:343–346.

Yarnal, Brent, and George Kiladis
1985 Tropical Teleconnections Associated with El Niño/Southern Oscillation (ENSO) Events. *Progress in Physical Geography* 9:541–544.

Yesner, David R., and Sergei Slobodin
2003 Chronology and Paleoecology of Human Colonization of Beringia. Paper presented at the 16th INQUA Congress, Reno.

Yoder, Donna, and Jane Kolber
2001 The Anasazi Rock Art of Chaco Canyon: A Preliminary Report of the Findings. Paper presented at the 28th Annual American Rock Art Research Association Conference, Pendleton, Oregon.

Yoffee, Norman
2001 The Chaco "Rituality" Revisited. In *Chaco Society and Polity: Papers from the 1999 Conference*, edited by Linda S. Cordell, W. James Judge, and June-el Piper, pp. 63–78. Special Publication 4. New Mexico Archaeological Council, Albuquerque.

Yoffee, Norman, and Jeffery J. Clark (editors)
1993 *Early Stages in the Evolution of Mesopotamian Civilization.* University of Arizona Press, Tucson.

Young, M. Jane
1979–1981 Zuni Rock Art Survey Site Records and Panel Reports. Records on file, Laboratory of Anthropology, Santa Fe, and Pueblo of Zuni, New Mexico.
1987 Toward an Understanding of "Place" for Southwestern Indians. *New Mexico Folklore Record* 16:1–13.
1988 *Signs from the Ancestors: Zuni Cultural Symbolism and Perceptions in Rock Art.* University of New Mexico Press, Albuquerque.

Zedeño, Maria Nieves
1994 *Sourcing Prehistoric Ceramics at Chodistaas Pueblo, Arizona: The Circulation of People and Pots in the Grasshopper Region.* Anthropological Papers of the University of Arizona No. 58. University of Arizona Press, Tucson.

Zier, Christian J.
1976 *Excavations near Zuni, New Mexico: 1973.* MNA Research Paper 2. Museum of Northern Arizona, Flagstaff.

Ziff, Bruce, and Pratima V. Rao (editors)
1997 *Borrowed Power: Essays on Cultural Appropriation.* Rutgers University Press, New Brunswick.

Zingg, Robert M.
1940 *Report on Archaeology of Southern Chihuahua.* Contributions of the University of Denver: Center of Latin American Studies 1. Denver.

Zuni Heritage and Historic Preservation Office and Institute of the North American West (compilers)
1995 *CD-ROM of the Zuni Land Claim,* distributed by University Press of Kansas, Lawrence.

Zunie, Jerome
1996 *A Cultural Resource Survey of the Twin Buttes to Crestview Road Improvement, McKinley County, New Mexico.* Zuni Cultural Resource Enterprise Report No. 496. Pueblo of Zuni, New Mexico.

Zvelebil, Marek
1996 The Agricultural Frontier and the Transition to Farming in the Circum-Baltic Region. In *The Origins and Spread of Agriculture and Pastoralism in Eurasia,* edited by David R. Harris, pp. 323–345. UCL Press, London.

Zvelebil, Marek, and Kamil V. Zvelebil
1988 Agricultural Transition and Indo-European Dispersals. *Antiquity* 62:574–583.

About the Contributors

Jeffery J. Clark received his PhD from the University of Arizona in 1997 and is currently a preservation archaeologist at the Center for Desert Archaeology, Tucson. During the 1980s and early 1990s Clark worked extensively in Southwest Asia, supervising excavations in Israel, Syria, and Iraq. Since that time he has focused on southern and central Arizona, directing excavations in the Tonto Basin, Safford Basin, and San Pedro Valley. His research interests include migration, cultural affiliation, and architectural analyses.

Jonathan E. Damp is an archaeologist with the Zuni Cultural Resource Enterprise. Most recently, his research interests have focused on Early Agricultural period occupations and irrigation systems along the Zuni River and its tributaries. He has lived in Zuni since 1995.

Jeffrey S. Dean is Agnese and Emil W. Haury Professor of Archaeological Dendrochronology at the Laboratory of Tree-Ring Research, professor of anthropology, and curator of archaeology (Arizona State Museum) at the University of Arizona, Tucson. His long-term research interests include dendroarchaeology, archaeological chronometry, paleoenvironmental reconstruction, human–environment interaction, and the archaeology of the American Southwest.

Michael W. Diehl is currently a research director at Desert Archaeology, Inc., in Tucson. His major research interests include paleobotany, human subsistence and social organization, behavioral ecology, and human-induced ecological

change in Arizona and New Mexico from the fourth millennium BC to the present.

T. J. Ferguson owns Anthropological Research, LLC, a research company in Tucson, Arizona, where he is also Professor of Practice in the Department of Anthropology at the University of Arizona. His thirty years of research into Zuni archaeology, traditional history, and cultural landscapes have resulted in the publication of three books, including *A Zuni Atlas* (1985, with E. Richard Hart), *Historic Zuni Architecture and Society, an Archaeological Application of Space Syntax* (1996), and *History Is in the Land* (2006, with Chip Colwell-Chanthaphonh).

Don D. Fowler is Mamie Kleberg Distinguished Professor of Historic Preservation and Anthropology, Emeritus, at the University of Nevada, Reno. His long career has included archaeological research in the American Southwest and the Great Basin. He has written extensively on the history of American anthropology and the history of western exploration. He is a past president of the Society for American Archaeology and a recipient of the society's Lifetime Achievement Award (2003).

David A. Gregory received his MA from the University of Arizona in 1972 and is currently a preservation archaeologist at the Center for Desert Archaeology, Tucson. He has worked in the American Southwest for over 35 years, with primary geographic foci on the Hohokam and Mogollon culture areas and theoretical emphasis on studies of settlement patterns and settlement systems. Most re-

cently, his research interests have been focused on the Early Agricultural period in the American Southwest, including the complex issues associated with the arrival and spread of maize.

J. Brett Hill received his PhD from Arizona State University in 2002 and is currently a preservation archaeologist at the Center for Desert Archaeology and visiting assistant professor at Hendrix College, Conway, Arkansas. He has participated in research projects in the American Southwest, the Near East, and in Europe, and his current research interests focus on human ecology in desert environments since the transition to agricultural economies. He is involved with multiple ongoing projects in Arizona and Jordan using large archaeological databases and GIS to study demography and human impacts on ancient environments at regional scales.

Jane H. Hill is Regents' Professor of Anthropology and Linguistics at the University of Arizona. She is a specialist in Native American languages, with emphasis on the Uto-Aztecan language family. Her broad research interests include language contact and multilingualism in the American Southwest and Mexico and the way that popular ideas about these phenomena shape the uses of language in communities in those regions, especially in the development of white racist culture. Hill has served as president of the Society for Linguistic Anthropology and president of the American Anthropological Association. She is a fellow of the American Association for the Advancement of Science, a member of the American Academy of Arts and Sciences, and a recipient of the Viking Fund Medal in Anthropology (2004). She is the author of over 100 books and articles.

Cynthia Irwin-Williams (1936–1990) was born in Denver, Colorado, and began her archaeological career as a volunteer for Marie Wormington at the Denver Natural History Museum. She received her PhD from Harvard in 1963 and later spent many years as professor of anthropology at Eastern New Mexico University. In 1985 she moved to Reno, Nevada, and became director of the Center for Quaternary Studies at the Desert Research Institute. During her too-short career she made fundamental and original contributions to Paleoindian, Archaic, early agricultural, and Chacoan studies in the American Far West and Mexico. She was president of the Society for American Archaeology from 1977 to 1979.

Keith W. Kintigh is professor of anthropology at Arizona State University. His archaeological research has focused on the political and social organization of ancestral Pueblo societies in the Cibola area of west-central New Mexico and east-central Arizona. More recently, he has become involved in collaborative research on understanding coupled socioecological systems. He also has published on a variety of topics concerning quantitative and formal methods in archaeology. Kintigh is a past president of the Society for American Archaeology and known for his work on national law and policy regarding the repatriation of Native American human remains and cultural items.

Stephen A. Kowalewski is professor of anthropology at the University of Georgia. His long-term research interests include regional analysis, human ecology, population history, and political economy. He has carried out archaeological surveys in Georgia and in Oaxaca, Mexico, where he and collaborators have recorded thousands of archaeological sites and studied the transformations from Neolithic village societies to urbanism and the state. Recently he has focused on the connections between regional cultural systems and the formation of macroregional scale systems, one of the major themes of this book.

R. G. Matson is professor emeritus of anthropology (since 2004) at the University of British Columbia in Vancouver. His field research has included work in California, the Great Basin, the American Southwest, and, more recently, the Northwest Coast. His long-term research interests include settlement patterns, ecology, quantitative methods, and large-scale archaeological processes and have resulted in publication of *The Glenrose Cannery Site* (1976), *The Origins of Southwestern Agriculture* (1991), *The Prehistory of the Northwest Coast* (1995, with Gary Coupland), *Emerging from the Mist* (2003, edited with Gary Coupland and Quentin Mackie) and *Athapaskan Migrations: The Archaeology of Eagle Lake, British Columbia* (2007, with P. R. Magne). He is a recipient of the Canadian Archaeological Association's Smith-Winterberg Award for contributions to Canadian Archaeology (2005).

Barbara J. Mills received her PhD from the University of New Mexico and is currently professor of anthropology at the University of Arizona, curator of archaeology (at the ArizonaStateMuseum), and affiliated faculty in the American Indian Studies Program. She has conducted fieldwork in Mesoamerica and the American Southwest, with a special focus on Ancestral Pueblo archaeology on the Colorado Plateau. She worked for the Zuni Tribe as an archaeologist for five years and, more recently, directed the University of Arizona Archaeological Field School as part of the Silver Creek Archaeological Research Project (1993–2004).Her long-term research interests include ceramic analysis, precontact and historic Pueblo pottery, identity, migration, ritual and materiality, colonialism, gender, and heritage preservation.

Fred L. Nials is a geomorphologist specializing in the geomorphology and stratigraphy of archaeological sites, particularly in the American Southwest. He has investigated numerous archaeological sites in western and southern North America, western South America, and the Mediterranean. His interests are currently focused on the geomorphology and geoarchaeology of streams in arid and semiarid lands, the arrival and development of agriculture in the American Southwest, and prehistoric irrigation technologies.

Polly Schaafsma is a research associate at the Museum of Indian Arts and Culture in Santa Fe, New Mexico.She pioneered rock art research in the Southwest, beginning in 1961.Her current interests and research projects are focused on cosmology, religion, and cultural landscapes in the American Southwest as expressed in rock art and other media. Her publications include *Indian Rock Art of the Southwest* (1980), *Rock Art in New Mexico* (1992),*Kachinas in the Pueblo World* (1994, editor),and *Warrior, Shield, and Star: Imagery and Ideology of Pueblo Warfare* (2000).

Arthur W. Vokes received his MA from the University of Arizona, with emphases in southwestern anthropology and museum collections management, and is currently curator of the Archaeological Repository at the Arizona State Museum, University of Arizona. He has been involved in archaeological research in the American Southwest for more than 35 years, with particular emphasis on the analysis and interpretation of shell and stone artifacts. He has published reports on more than 100 shell assemblages, including material from Yucatán and throughout the American Southwest, with emphasis on those from southern Arizona.

Laurie Webster is an independent scholar and textile consultant in Tucson, Arizona, and a visiting scholar in the Department of Anthropology at the University of Arizona. Her research interests focus on textiles and other perishable material culture traditions of the American Southwest. Her recent studies include postcontact changes in Pueblo weaving, an analysis of the ritual costuming depicted in murals at Pottery Mound, and a study of the perishable traditions of Salmon Pueblo. At present she is engaged in a study of the textiles and basketry from Aztec Ruin and Pueblo Bonito.

David R. Wilcox is currently a senior research anthropologist at the Museum of Northern Arizona, Flagstaff. Since 1969 he has worked on a wide variety of issues in southwestern archaeology. His long-term research program examines the history of American anthropology to 1927; the archaeology of the greater Flagstaff area, including a survey of hilltop sites in west-central Arizona; and macroregional syntheses of southwestern archaeology, the main focus of the present volume.

C. Dean Wilson is currently a staff archaeologist at the Office of Archaeological Studies of the Museum of New Mexico, where he also serves as director of the ceramic lab. He has been involved in fieldwork and analysis in the Southwest since 1977 and has conducted research on ceramics from the Four Corners Anasazi, western Anasazi, Fremont, Mogollon, Salado, Jornada Mogollon, Numic, Navajo, and Rio Grande Pueblo traditions. Much of his research has been concerned with the examination of various influences on Southwest pottery traditions and technologies, including raw material distributions, cultural identity, settlement patterns, and exchange networks.

M. Jane Young recently retired from her position as professor of American studies and Regents' Lecturer for the College of Arts and Sciences at the University of New Mexico. Her research interests include material culture and folk art, ritual and festival in the Southwest, and gender studies. She has conducted extensive fieldwork among the Zuni Indians of New Mexico and is an expert on the rock art of the area. More recently, her fieldwork has focused on sociocultural changes in family and community relationships among the potters of Mata Ortiz (in northern Chihuahua). Her research on Zuni rock art culminated in publication of *Signs from the Ancestors: Zuni Cultural Symbolism and Perceptions in Rock Art* (1988). She has also co-edited a collection of articles entitled *Feminist Theory and the Study of Folklore* (1993) and an anthology that serves as an introduction to Southwest studies, *The Multicultural Southwest: A Reader* (2001).

Index